Critical acclaim for
Programming Windows

"The classic book on Windows programming, of course, is Charles Petzold's PROGRAMMING WINDOWS. If you don't already have a copy, you need one."

Windows Tech Journal

"The serious programmer's guide . . . has been and continues to be Charles Petzold's PROGRAMMING WINDOWS. If you want to program Windows applications and haven't read this book, you need to do so."

IEEE Micro

"There are just three books that I regard as crucial texts for serious Windows programming: First, of course, is the classic PROGRAMMING WINDOWS by Charles Petzold."

INFOWORLD

"As you are building your library of the best Windows books, you want to make sure you include the classic—Petzold's best-selling PROGRAMMING WINDOWS. . . .

PC Techniques

"This remains the classic Windows programming guide."

Programmer's Journal

"Just take it as a given—if you're going to program for Windows, buy this book. It will pay for itself in a matter of hours."

Computer Language

"Broad in scope and omitting little, this book is a must for anyone serious about Windows."

Byte Magazine

PROGRAMMING
WINDOWS®
Fifth Edition

Charles Petzold

Microsoft·Press

PUBLISHED BY
Microsoft Press
A Division of Microsoft Corporation
One Microsoft Way
Redmond, Washington 98052-6399

Library of Congress Cataloging-in-Publication Data
Petzold, Charles, 1953–
    Programming Windows / Charles Petzold. -- 5th ed.
      p.   cm.
    Rev. ed. of: Programming Windows 95.
    Includes index.
    ISBN 1-57231-995-X
    1. Microsoft Windows (Computer file)   2. Operating systems
(Computers)   I. Petzold, Charles, 1953–. Programming Windows 95.
II. Title.
QA76.76.O63P533   1998
005.265--dc21   98-42529
                                                CIP

Printed and bound in the United States of America.

2 3 4 5 6 7 8 9 WCWC 4 3 2 1 0 9

Distributed in Canada by ITP Nelson, a division of Thomson Canada Limited.

A CIP catalogue record for this book is available from the British Library.

Microsoft Press books are available through booksellers and distributors worldwide. For further information about international editions, contact your local Microsoft Corporation office or contact Microsoft Press International directly at fax (425) 936-7329. Visit our Web site at mspress.microsoft.com.

Acquisitions Editor: Ben Ryan
Project Editor: Devon Musgrave
Technical Editor: Dail Magee, Jr.

Contents at a Glance

Contents

Section II   More Graphics

CONTENTS

Section III   Advanced Topics

Chapter 19 The Multiple-Document Interface   1173

Chapter 20 Multitasking and Multithreading   1197

Author's Note

Visit my web site at *www.cpetzold.com* for updated information regarding this book, including possible bug reports and new code listings. You can address mail regarding problems in this book to *charles@cpetzold.com*. Although I'll also try to answer any easy questions you may have, I can't make any promises. I'm usually pretty busy, and my cat refuses to learn the Windows API.

I'd like to thank everyone at Microsoft Press for another great job in putting together this book. I think this "10th Anniversary Edition" of *Programming Windows* is the best edition yet. Many other people at Microsoft (including some of the early developers of Microsoft Windows) also helped out when I was writing the earlier editions, and these fine people are listed in those editions.

Thanks also to my family and friends, and in particular those more recent friends (you know who you are!) whose support has made this book possible. To you this book is dedicated.

Charles Petzold
October 5, 1998

Section I

The Basics

Chapter 1

Getting Started

This book shows you how to write programs that run under Microsoft Windows 98, Microsoft Windows NT 4.0, and Windows NT 5.0. These programs are written in the C programming language and use the native Windows application programming interfaces (APIs). As I'll discuss later in this chapter, this is not the only way to write programs that run under Windows. However, it is important to understand the Windows APIs regardless of what you eventually use to write your code.

As you probably know, Windows 98 is the latest incarnation of the graphical operating system that has become the de facto standard for IBM-compatible personal computers built around 32-bit Intel microprocessors such as the 486 and Pentium. Windows NT is the industrial-strength version of Windows that runs on PC compatibles as well as some RISC (reduced instruction set computing) workstations.

There are three prerequisites for using this book. First, you should be familiar with Windows 98 from a user's perspective. You cannot hope to write applications for Windows without understanding its user interface. For this reason, I suggest that you do your program development (as well as other work) on a Windows-based machine using Windows applications.

Second, you should know C. If you don't know C, Windows programming is probably not a good place to start. I recommend that you learn C in a character-mode environment such as that offered under the Windows 98 MS-DOS Command Prompt window. Windows programming sometimes involves aspects of C that don't show up much in character-mode programming; in those cases, I'll devote some discussion to them. But for the most part, you should have a good working familiarity with the language, particularly with C structures and pointers. Some knowledge of the standard C run-time library is helpful but not required.

Third, you should have installed on your machine a 32-bit C compiler and development environment suitable for doing Windows programming. In this book, I'll be assuming that you're using Microsoft Visual C++ 6.0, which can be purchased separately or as a part of the Visual Studio 6.0 package.

That's it. I'm not going to assume that you have any experience at all programming for a graphical user interface such as Windows.

THE WINDOWS ENVIRONMENT

Windows hardly needs an introduction. Yet it's easy to forget the sea change that Windows brought to office and home desktop computing. Windows had a bumpy ride in its early years and was hardly destined to conquer the desktop market.

A History of Windows

Soon after the introduction of the IBM PC in the fall of 1981, it became evident that the predominant operating system for the PC (and compatibles) would be MS-DOS, which originally stood for Microsoft Disk Operating System. MS-DOS was a minimal operating system. For the user, MS-DOS provided a command-line interface to commands such as DIR and TYPE and loaded application programs into memory for execution. For the application programmer, MS-DOS offered little more than a set of function calls for doing file input/output (I/O). For other tasks—in particular, writing text and sometimes graphics to the video display—applications accessed the hardware of the PC directly.

Due to memory and hardware constraints, sophisticated graphical environments were slow in coming to small computers. Apple Computer offered an alternative to character-mode environments when it released its ill-fated Lisa in January 1983, and then set a standard for graphical environments with the Macintosh in January 1984. Despite the Mac's declining market share, it is still considered the standard against which other graphical environments are measured. All graphical environments, including the Macintosh and Windows, are indebted to the pioneering work done at the Xerox Palo Alto Research Center (PARC) beginning in the mid-1970s.

Windows was announced by Microsoft Corporation in November 1983 (post-Lisa but pre-Macintosh) and was released two years later in November 1985. Over the next two years, Microsoft Windows 1.0 was followed by several updates to support the international market and to provide drivers for additional video displays and printers.

Windows 2.0 was released in November 1987. This version incorporated several changes to the user interface. The most significant of these changes involved the use of overlapping windows rather than the "tiled" windows found in Windows 1.0. Windows 2.0 also included enhancements to the keyboard and mouse interface, particularly for menus and dialog boxes.

Up until this time, Windows required only an Intel 8086 or 8088 microprocessor running in "real mode" to access 1 megabyte (MB) of memory. Windows/386 (released shortly after Windows 2.0) used the "virtual 86" mode of the Intel 386 microprocessor to window and multitask many DOS programs that directly accessed hardware. For symmetry, Windows 2.1 was renamed Windows/286.

Windows 3.0 was introduced on May 22, 1990. The earlier Windows/286 and Windows/386 versions were merged into one product with this release. The big change in Windows 3.0 was the support of the 16-bit protected-mode operation of Intel's 286, 386, and 486 microprocessors. This gave Windows and Windows applications access to up to 16 megabytes of memory. The Windows "shell" programs for running programs and maintaining files were completely revamped. Windows 3.0 was the first version of Windows to gain a foothold in the home and the office.

Any history of Windows must also include a mention of OS/2, an alternative to DOS and Windows that was originally developed by Microsoft in collaboration with IBM. OS/2 1.0 (character-mode only) ran on the Intel 286 (or later) microprocessors and was released in late 1987. The graphical Presentation Manager (PM) came about with OS/2 1.1 in October 1988. PM was originally supposed to be a protected-mode version of Windows, but the graphical API was changed to such a degree that it proved difficult for software manufacturers to support both platforms.

By September 1990, conflicts between IBM and Microsoft reached a peak and required that the two companies go their separate ways. IBM took over OS/2 and Microsoft made it clear that Windows was the center of their strategy for operating systems. While OS/2 still has some fervent admirers, it has not nearly approached the popularity of Windows.

Microsoft Windows version 3.1 was released in April 1992. Several significant features included the TrueType font technology (which brought scalable outline fonts to Windows), multimedia (sound and music), Object Linking and Embedding (OLE), and standardized common dialog boxes. Windows 3.1 ran *only* in protected mode and required a 286 or 386 processor with at least 1 MB of memory.

Windows NT, introduced in July 1993, was the first version of Windows to support the 32-bit mode of the Intel 386, 486, and Pentium microprocessors. Programs that run under Windows NT have access to a 32-bit flat address space and use a 32-bit instruction set. (I'll have more to say about address spaces a little later in this chapter.) Windows NT was also designed to be portable to non-Intel processors, and it runs on several RISC-based workstations.

Windows 95 was introduced in August 1995. Like Windows NT, Windows 95 also supported the 32-bit programming mode of the Intel 386 and later microprocessors. Although it lacked some of the features of Windows NT, such as high security and portability to RISC machines, Windows 95 had the advantage of requiring fewer hardware resources.

Windows 98 was released in June 1998 and has a number of enhancements, including performance improvements, better hardware support, and a closer integration with the Internet and the World Wide Web.

Aspects of Windows

Both Windows 98 and Windows NT are 32-bit preemptive multitasking and multithreading graphical operating systems. Windows possesses a graphical user interface (GUI), sometimes also called a "visual interface" or "graphical windowing environment." The concepts behind the GUI date from the mid-1970s with the work done at the Xerox PARC for machines such as the Alto and the Star and for environments such as SmallTalk. This work was later brought into the mainstream and popularized by Apple Computer and Microsoft. Although somewhat controversial for a while, it is now quite obvious that the GUI is (in the words of Microsoft's Charles Simonyi) the single most important "grand consensus" of the personal-computer industry.

All GUIs make use of graphics on a bitmapped video display. Graphics provides better utilization of screen real estate, a visually rich environment for conveying information, and the possibility of a WYSIWYG (what you see is what you get) video display of graphics and formatted text prepared for a printed document.

In earlier days, the video display was used solely to echo text that the user typed using the keyboard. In a graphical user interface, the video display itself becomes a source of user input. The video display shows various graphical objects in the form of icons and input devices such as buttons and scroll bars. Using the keyboard (or, more directly, a pointing device such as a mouse), the user can directly manipulate these objects on the screen. Graphics objects can be dragged, buttons can be pushed, and scroll bars can be scrolled.

The interaction between the user and a program thus becomes more intimate. Rather than the one-way cycle of information from the keyboard to the program to the video display, the user directly interacts with the objects on the display.

Users no longer expect to spend long periods of time learning how to use the computer or mastering a new program. Windows helps because all applications have the same fundamental look and feel. The program occupies a window—usually a rectangular area on the screen. Each window is identified by a caption bar. Most program functions are initiated through the program's menus. A user can view the display of information too large to fit on a single screen by using scroll bars. Some menu items invoke dialog boxes, into which the user enters additional information. One dialog box in particular, that used to open a file, can be found in almost every large Windows program. This dialog box looks the same (or nearly the same) in all of these Windows programs, and it is almost always invoked from the same menu option.

Once you know how to use one Windows program, you're in a good position to easily learn another. The menus and dialog boxes allow a user to experiment with a new program and explore its features. Most Windows programs have both a keyboard interface and a mouse interface. Although most functions of Windows programs can be controlled through the keyboard, using the mouse is often easier for many chores.

From the programmer's perspective, the consistent user interface results from using the routines built into Windows for constructing menus and dialog boxes. All menus have the same keyboard and mouse interface because Windows—rather than the application program—handles this job.

To facilitate the use of multiple programs, and the exchange of information among them, Windows supports multitasking. Several Windows programs can be displayed and running at the same time. Each program occupies a window on the screen. The user can move the windows around on the screen, change their sizes, switch between different programs, and transfer data from one program to another. Because these windows look something like papers on a desktop (in the days before the desk became dominated by the computer itself, of course), Windows is sometimes said to use a "desktop metaphor" for the display of multiple programs.

Earlier versions of Windows used a system of multitasking called "nonpreemptive." This meant that Windows did not use the system timer to slice processing time between the various programs running under the system. The programs themselves had to voluntarily give up control so that other programs could run. Under Windows NT and Windows 98, multitasking is preemptive and programs themselves can split into multiple threads of execution that seem to run concurrently.

An operating system cannot implement multitasking without doing something about memory management. As new programs are started up and old ones terminate, memory can become fragmented. The system must be able to consolidate free memory space. This requires the system to move blocks of code and data in memory.

Even Windows 1.0, running on an 8088 microprocessor, was able to perform this type of memory management. Under real-mode restrictions, this ability can only be regarded as an astonishing feat of software engineering. In Windows 1.0, the 640-kilobyte (KB) memory limit of the PC's architecture was effectively stretched without requiring any additional memory. But Microsoft didn't stop there: Windows 2.0 gave the Windows applications access to expanded memory (EMS), and Windows 3.0 ran in protected mode to give Windows applications access to up to 16 MB of extended memory. Windows NT and Windows 98 blow away these old limits by being full-fledged 32-bit operating systems with flat memory space.

Programs running in Windows can share routines that are located in other files called "dynamic-link libraries." Windows includes a mechanism to link the program with the routines in the dynamic-link libraries at run time. Windows itself is basically a set of dynamic-link libraries.

Windows is a graphical interface, and Windows programs can make full use of graphics and formatted text on both the video display and the printer. A graphical interface not only is more attractive in appearance but also can impart a high level of information to the user.

Programs written for Windows do not directly access the hardware of graphics display devices such as the screen and printer. Instead, Windows includes a graphics programming language (called the Graphics Device Interface, or GDI) that allows the easy display of graphics and formatted text. Windows virtualizes display hardware. A program written for Windows will run with any video board or any printer for which a Windows device driver is available. The program does not need to determine what type of device is attached to the system.

Putting a device-independent graphics interface on the IBM PC was not an easy job for the developers of Windows. The PC design was based on the principle of open architecture. Third-party hardware manufacturers were encouraged to develop peripherals for the PC and have done so in great number. Although several standards have emerged, conventional MS-DOS programs for the PC had to individually support many different hardware configurations. It was fairly common for an MS-DOS word-processing program to be sold with one or two disks of small files, each one supporting a particular printer. Windows programs do not require these drivers because the support is part of Windows.

Dynamic Linking

Central to the workings of Windows is a concept known as "dynamic linking." Windows provides a wealth of function calls that an application can take advantage of, mostly to implement its user interface and display text and graphics on the video display. These functions are implemented in dynamic-link libraries, or DLLs. These are files with the extension .DLL or sometimes .EXE, and they are mostly located in the \WINDOWS\SYSTEM subdirectory under Windows 98 and the \WINNT\SYSTEM and \WINNT\SYSTEM32 subdirectories under Windows NT.

In the early days, the great bulk of Windows was implemented in just three dynamic-link libraries. These represented the three main subsystems of Windows, which were referred to as Kernel, User, and GDI. While the number of subsystems has proliferated in recent versions of Windows, most function calls that a typical Windows program makes will still fall in one of these three modules. Kernel (which is currently implemented by the 16-bit KRNL386.EXE and the 32-bit KERNEL32.DLL) handles all the stuff that an operating system kernel traditionally handles—memory management, file I/O, and tasking. User (implemented in the 16-bit USER.EXE and the 32-bit USER32.DLL) refers to the user interface, and implements all the windowing logic. GDI (implemented in the 16-bit GDI.EXE and the 32-bit GDI32.DLL) is the Graphics Device Interface, which allows a program to display text and graphics on the screen and printer.

Windows 98 supports several thousand function calls that applications can use. Each function has a descriptive name, such as *CreateWindow*. This function (as you might guess) creates a window for your program. All the Windows functions that an application may use are declared in header files.

In your Windows program, you use the Windows function calls in generally the same way you use C library functions such as *strlen*. The primary difference is that the machine code for C library functions is linked into your program code, whereas the code for Windows functions is located outside of your program in the DLLs.

When you run a Windows program, it interfaces to Windows through a process called "dynamic linking." A Windows .EXE file contains references to the various dynamic-link libraries it uses and the functions therein. When a Windows program is loaded into memory, the calls in the program are resolved to point to the entries of the DLL functions, which are also loaded into memory if not already there.

When you link a Windows program to produce an executable file, you must link with special "import libraries" provided with your programming environment. These import libraries contain the dynamic-link library names and reference information for all the Windows function calls. The linker uses this information to construct the table in the .EXE file that Windows uses to resolve calls to Windows functions when loading the program.

WINDOWS PROGRAMMING OPTIONS

To illustrate the various techniques of Windows programming, this book has lots of sample programs. These programs are written in C and use the native Windows APIs. I think of this approach as "classical" Windows programming. It is how we wrote programs for Windows 1.0 in 1985, and it remains a valid way of programming for Windows today.

APIs and Memory Models

To a programmer, an operating system is defined by its API. An API encompasses all the function calls that an application program can make of an operating system, as well as definitions of associated data types and structures. In Windows, the API also implies a particular program architecture that we'll explore in the chapters ahead.

Generally, the Windows API has remained quite consistent since Windows 1.0. A Windows programmer with experience in Windows 98 would find the source code for a Windows 1.0 program very familiar. One way the API has changed has been in enhancements. Windows 1.0 supported fewer than 450 function calls; today there are thousands.

The biggest change in the Windows API and its syntax came about during the switch from a 16-bit architecture to a 32-bit architecture. Versions 1.0 through 3.1 of Windows used the so-called segmented memory mode of the 16-bit Intel 8086, 8088, and 286 microprocessors, a mode that was also supported for compatibility purposes in the 32-bit Intel microprocessors beginning with the 386. The microprocessor register size in this mode was 16 bits, and hence the C *int* data type was also 16 bits wide. In the segmented memory model, memory addresses were formed from two components—a 16-bit *segment* pointer and a 16-bit *offset* pointer. From the programmer's perspective, this was quite messy and involved differentiating between *long,* or *far,* pointers (which involved both a segment address and an offset address) and *short,* or *near,* pointers (which involved an offset address with an assumed segment address).

Beginning in Windows NT and Windows 95, Windows supported a 32-bit flat memory model using the 32-bit modes of the Intel 386, 486, and Pentium processors. The C *int* data type was promoted to a 32-bit value. Programs written for 32-bit versions of Windows use simple 32-bit pointer values that address a flat linear address space.

The API for the 16-bit versions of Windows (Windows 1.0 through Windows 3.1) is now known as Win16. The API for the 32-bit versions of Windows (Windows 95, Windows 98, and all versions of Windows NT) is now known as Win32. Many function calls remained the same in the transition from Win16 to Win32, but some needed to be enhanced. For example, graphics coordinate points changed from 16-bit values in Win16 to 32-bit values in Win32. Also, some Win16 function calls returned a two-dimensional coordinate point packed in a 32-bit integer. This was not possible in Win32, so new function calls were added that worked in a different way.

All 32-bit versions of Windows support both the Win16 API to ensure compatibility with old applications and the Win32 API to run new applications. Interestingly enough, this works differently in Windows NT than in Windows 95 and Windows 98. In Windows NT, Win16 function calls go through a translation layer and are converted to Win32 function calls that are then processed by the operating system. In Windows 95 and Windows 98, the process is opposite that: Win32 function calls go through a translation layer and are converted to Win16 function calls to be processed by the operating system.

At one time, there were two other Windows API sets (at least in name). Win32s ("s" for "subset") was an API that allowed programmers to write 32-bit applications that ran under Windows 3.1. This API supported only 32-bit versions of functions already supported by Win16. Also, the Windows 95 API was once called Win32c ("c" for "compatibility"), but this term has been abandoned.

At this time, Windows NT and Windows 98 are both considered to support the Win32 API. However, each operating system supports some features not supported by the other. Still, because the overlap is considerable, it's possible to write programs that run under both systems. Also, it's widely assumed that the two products will be merged at some time in the future.

Language Options

Using C and the native APIs is not the only way to write programs for Windows 98. However, this approach offers you the best performance, the most power, and the greatest versatility in exploiting the features of Windows. Executables are relatively small and don't require external libraries to run (except for the Windows DLLs themselves, of course). Most importantly, becoming familiar with the API provides you with a deeper understanding of Windows internals, regardless of how you eventually write applications for Windows.

Although I think that learning classical Windows programming is important for any Windows programmer, I don't necessarily recommend using C and the API for every Windows application. Many programmers—particularly those doing in-house corporate programming or those who do recreational programming at home—enjoy the ease of development environments such as Microsoft Visual Basic or Borland Delphi (which incorporates an object-oriented dialect of Pascal). These environments allow a programmer to focus on the user interface of an application and associate code with user interface objects. To learn Visual Basic, you might want to consult some other Microsoft Press books, such as *Learn Visual Basic Now* (1996), by Michael Halvorson.

Among professional programmers—particularly those who write commercial applications—Microsoft Visual C++ with the Microsoft Foundation Class Library (MFC) has been a popular alternative in recent years. MFC encapsulates many of the messier aspects of Windows programming in a collection of C++ classes. Jeff Prosise's *Programming Windows with MFC, Second Edition* (Microsoft Press, 1999) provides tutorials on MFC.

Most recently, the popularity of the Internet and the World Wide Web has given a big boost to Sun Microsystems' Java, the processor-independent language inspired by C++ and incorporating a toolkit for writing graphical applications that will run on several operating system platforms. A good Microsoft Press book on Microsoft J++, Microsoft's Java development tool, is *Programming Visual J++ 6.0* (1999), by Stephen R. Davis.

Obviously, there's hardly any one right way to write applications for Windows. More than anything else, the nature of the application itself should probably dictate the tools. But learning the Windows API gives you vital insights into the workings of Windows that are essential regardless of what you end up using to actually do the coding. Windows is a complex system; putting a programming layer on top of the API doesn't eliminate the complexity—it merely hides it. Sooner or later that complexity is going to jump out and bite you in the leg. Knowing the API gives you a better chance at recovery.

Any software layer on top of the native Windows API necessarily restricts you to a subset of full functionality. You might find, for example, that Visual Basic is ideal for your application except that it doesn't allow you to do one or two essential chores. In that case, you'll have to use native API calls. The API defines the universe in which we as Windows programmers exist. No approach can be more powerful or versatile than using this API directly.

MFC is particularly problematic. While it simplifies some jobs immensely (such as OLE), I often find myself wrestling with other features (such as the Document/View architecture) to get them to work as I want. MFC has not been the Windows programming panacea that many hoped for, and few people would characterize it as a model of good object-oriented design. MFC programmers benefit greatly from understanding what's going on in class definitions they use, and find themselves frequently consulting MFC source code. Understanding that source code is one of the benefits of learning the Windows API.

The Programming Environment

In this book, I'll be assuming that you're running Microsoft Visual C++ 6.0, which comes in Standard, Professional, and Enterprise editions. The less-expensive Standard edition is fine for doing the programs in this book. Visual C++ is also part of Visual Studio 6.0.

The Microsoft Visual C++ package includes more than the C compiler and other files and tools necessary to compile and link Windows programs. It also includes the Visual C++ Developer Studio, an environment in which you can edit your source code; interactively create resources such as icons and dialog boxes; and edit, compile, run, and debug your programs.

If you're running Visual C++ 5.0, you might need to get updated header files and import libraries for Windows 98 and Windows NT 5.0. These are available at Microsoft's web site. Go to *http://www.microsoft.com/msdn/*, and choose Downloads and then Platform SDK ("software development kit"). You'll be able to download and install the updated files in directories of your choice. To direct the Microsoft Developer Studio to look in these directories, choose Options from the Tools menu and then pick the Directories tab.

The *msdn* portion of the Microsoft URL above stands for Microsoft Developer Network. This is a program that provides developers with frequently updated CD-ROMs containing much of what they need to be on the cutting edge of Windows development. You'll probably want to investigate subscribing to MSDN and avoid frequent downloading from Microsoft's web site.

API Documentation

This book is not a substitute for the official formal documentation of the Windows API. That documentation is no longer published in printed form; it is available only via CD-ROM or the Internet.

When you install Visual C++ 6.0, you'll get an online help system that includes API documentation. You can get updates to that documentation by subscribing to MSDN or by using Microsoft's Web-based online help system. Start by linking to *http://www.microsoft.com/ msdn/*, and select MSDN Library Online.

In Visual C++ 6.0, select the Contents item from the Help menu to invoke the MSDN window. The API documentation is organized in a tree-structured hierarchy. Find the section labeled Platform SDK. All the documentation I'll be citing in this book is from this section. I'll show the location of documentation using the nested levels starting with Platform SDK separated by slashes. (I know the Platform SDK looks like a small obscure part of the total wealth of MSDN knowledge, but I assure you that it's the essential core of Windows programming.) For example, for documentation on how to use the mouse in your Windows programs, you can consult */Platform SDK/User Interface Services/User Input/Mouse Input*.

I mentioned before that much of Windows is divided into the Kernel, User, and GDI subsystems. The kernel interfaces are in */Platform SDK/Windows Base Services*, the user interface functions are in */Platform SDK/User Interface Services*, and GDI is documented in */Platform SDK/Graphics and Multimedia Services/GDI*.

YOUR FIRST WINDOWS PROGRAM

Now it's time to do some coding. Let's begin by looking at a very short Windows program and, for comparison, a short character-mode program. These will help us get oriented in using the development environment and going through the mechanics of creating and compiling a program.

A Character-Mode Model

A favorite book among programmers is *The C Programming Language* (Prentice Hall, 1978 and 1988) by Brian W. Kernighan and Dennis M. Ritchie, affectionately referred to as K&R. Chapter 1 of this book begins with a C program that displays the words "hello, world."

Here's the program as it appeared on page 6 of the first edition of *The C Programming Language*:

```
main ()
{
    printf ("hello, world\n") ;
}
```

Yes, once upon a time C programmers used C run-time library functions such as *printf* without declaring them first. But this is the '90s, and we like to give our compilers a fighting chance to flag errors in our code. Here's the revised code from the second edition of K&R:

```
#include <stdio.h>

main ()
{
    printf ("hello, world\n") ;
}
```

This program still isn't really as small as it seems. It will certainly compile and run just fine, but many programmers these days would prefer to explicitly indicate the return value of the *main* function, in which case ANSI C dictates that the function actually returns a value:

```
#include <stdio.h>

int main ()
{
    printf ("hello, world\n") ;

    return 0 ;
}
```

We could make this even longer by including the arguments to *main*, but let's leave it at that—with an *include* statement, the program entry point, a call to a run-time library function, and a *return* statement.

The Windows Equivalent

The Windows equivalent to the "hello, world" program has exactly the same components as the character-mode version. It has an *include* statement, a program entry point, a function call, and a return statement. Here's the program:

```
/*-------------------------------------------------------------
   HelloMsg.c -- Displays "Hello, Windows 98!" in a message box
                 (c) Charles Petzold, 1998
   -------------------------------------------------------------*/

#include <windows.h>

int WINAPI WinMain (HINSTANCE hInstance, HINSTANCE hPrevInstance,
                    PSTR szCmdLine, int iCmdShow)
{
     MessageBox (NULL, TEXT ("Hello, Windows 98!"), TEXT ("HelloMsg"), 0) ;

     return 0 ;
}
```

Before I begin dissecting this program, let's go through the mechanics of creating a program in the Visual C++ Developer Studio.

To begin, select New from the File menu. In the New dialog box, pick the Projects tab. Select Win32 Application. In the Location field, select a subdirectory. In the Project Name field, type the name of the project, which in this case is HelloMsg. This will be a subdirectory of the directory indicated in the Location field. The Create New Workspace button should be checked. The Platforms section should indicate Win32. Choose OK.

A dialog box labeled Win32 Application - Step 1 Of 1 will appear. Indicate that you want to create an Empty Project, and press the Finish button.

Select New from the File menu again. In the New dialog box, pick the Files tab. Select C++ Source File. The Add To Project box should be checked, and HelloMsg should be indicated. Type HelloMsg.c in the File Name field. Choose OK.

Now you can type in the HELLOMSG.C file shown above. Or you can select the Insert menu and the File As Text option to copy the contents of HELLOMSG.C from the file on this book's companion CD-ROM.

Structurally, HELLOMSG.C is identical to the K&R "hello, world" program. The header file STDIO.H has been replaced with WINDOWS.H, the entry point *main* has been replaced with *WinMain*, and the C run-time library function *printf* has been replaced with the Windows API function *MessageBox*. However, there is much in the program that is new, including several strange-looking uppercase identifiers.

Let's start at the top.

The Header Files

HELLOMSG.C begins with a preprocessor directive that you'll find at the top of virtually every Windows program written in C:

```
#include <windows.h>
```

WINDOWS.H is a master include file that includes other Windows header files, some of which also include other header files. The most important and most basic of these header files are:

■ *WINDEF.H*   Basic type definitions.

■ *WINNT.H*   Type definitions for Unicode support.

■ *WINBASE.H*   Kernel functions.

■ *WINUSER.H*   User interface functions.

■ *WINGDI.H*   Graphics device interface functions.

These header files define all the Windows data types, function calls, data structures, and constant identifiers. They are an important part of Windows documentation. You might find it convenient to use the Find In Files option from the Edit menu in the Visual C++ Developer Studio to search through these header files. You can also open the header files in the Developer Studio and examine them directly.

Program Entry Point

Just as the entry point to a C program is the function *main*, the entry point to a Windows program is *WinMain*, which always appears like this:

```
int WINAPI WinMain (HINSTANCE hInstance, HINSTANCE hPrevInstance,
                    PSTR szCmdLine, int iCmdShow)
```

This entry point is documented in */Platform SDK/User Interface Services/Windowing/Windows/Window Reference/Window Functions*. It is declared in WINBASE.H like so (line breaks and all):

```
int
WINAPI
WinMain(
    HINSTANCE hInstance,
    HINSTANCE hPrevInstance,
    LPSTR lpCmdLine,
    int nShowCmd
    );
```

You'll notice I've made a couple of minor changes in HELLOMSG.C. The third parameter is defined as an LPSTR in WINBASE.H, and I've made it a PSTR. These two data types are both defined in WINNT.H as pointers to character strings. The LP prefix stands for "long pointer" and is an artifact of 16-bit Windows.

I've also changed two of the parameter names from the *WinMain* declaration; many Windows programs use a system called "Hungarian notation" for naming variables. This system involves prefacing the variable name with a short prefix that indicates the variable's data type. I'll discuss this concept more in Chapter 3. For now, just keep in mind that the prefix *i* stands for *int* and *sz* stands for "string terminated with a zero."

The *WinMain* function is declared as returning an *int*. The WINAPI identifier is defined in WINDEF.H with the statement:

```
#define WINAPI __stdcall
```

This statement specifies a calling convention that involves how machine code is generated to place function call arguments on the stack. Most Windows function calls are declared as WINAPI.

The first parameter to *WinMain* is something called an "instance handle." In Windows programming, a handle is simply a number that an application uses to identify something. In this case, the handle uniquely identifies the program. It is required as an argument to some other Windows function calls. In early versions of Windows, when you ran the same program concurrently more than once, you created *multiple instances* of that program. All instances of the same application shared code and read-only memory (usually resources such as menu and dialog box templates). A program could determine if other instances of itself were running by checking the *hPrevInstance* parameter. It could then skip certain chores and move some data from the previous instance into its own data area.

In the 32-bit versions of Windows, this concept has been abandoned. The second parameter to *WinMain* is always NULL (defined as 0).

The third parameter to *WinMain* is the command line used to run the program. Some Windows applications use this to load a file into memory when the program is started. The fourth parameter to *WinMain* indicates how the program should be initially displayed—either normally or maximized to fill the window, or minimized to be displayed in the task list bar. We'll see how this parameter is used in Chapter 3.

The *MessageBox* Function

The *MessageBox* function is designed to display short messages. The little window that *MessageBox* displays is actually considered to be a dialog box, although not one with a lot of versatility.

The first argument to *MessageBox* is normally a window handle. We'll see what this means in Chapter 3. The second argument is the text string that appears in the body of the message box, and the third argument is the text string that appears in the caption bar of the message box. In HELLMSG.C, each of these text strings is enclosed in a TEXT macro.

You don't normally have to enclose all character strings in the TEXT macro, but it's a good idea if you want to be ready to convert your programs to the Unicode character set. I'll discuss this in much more detail in Chapter 2.

The fourth argument to *MessageBox* can be a combination of constants beginning with the prefix MB_ that are defined in WINUSER.H. You can pick one constant from the first set to indicate what buttons you wish to appear in the dialog box:

```
#define MB_OK                   0x00000000L
#define MB_OKCANCEL             0x00000001L
#define MB_ABORTRETRYIGNORE     0x00000002L
#define MB_YESNOCANCEL          0x00000003L
#define MB_YESNO                0x00000004L
#define MB_RETRYCANCEL          0x00000005L
```

When you set the fourth argument to 0 in HELLOMSG, only the OK button appears. You can use the C OR (|) operator to combine one of the constants shown above with a constant that indicates which of the buttons is the default:

```
#define MB_DEFBUTTON1           0x00000000L
#define MB_DEFBUTTON2           0x00000100L
#define MB_DEFBUTTON3           0x00000200L
#define MB_DEFBUTTON4           0x00000300L
```

You can also use a constant that indicates the appearance of an icon in the message box:

```
#define MB_ICONHAND             0x00000010L
#define MB_ICONQUESTION         0x00000020L
#define MB_ICONEXCLAMATION      0x00000030L
#define MB_ICONASTERISK         0x00000040L
```

Some of these icons have alternate names:

```
#define MB_ICONWARNING          MB_ICONEXCLAMATION
#define MB_ICONERROR            MB_ICONHAND
#define MB_ICONINFORMATION      MB_ICONASTERISK
#define MB_ICONSTOP             MB_ICONHAND
```

There are a few other MB_ constants, but you can consult the header file yourself or the documentation in */Platform SDK/User Interface Services/Windowing/Dialog Boxes/Dialog Box Reference/Dialog Box Functions*.

In this program, the *MessageBox* function returns the value 1, but it's more proper to say that it returns IDOK, which is defined in WINUSER.H as equaling 1. Depending on the other buttons present in the message box, the *MessageBox* function can also return IDYES, IDNO, IDCANCEL, IDABORT, IDRETRY, or IDIGNORE.

Is this little Windows program really the equivalent of the K&R "hello, world" program? Well, you might think not because the *MessageBox* function doesn't really have all the potential formatting power of the *printf* function in "hello, world." But we'll see in the next chapter how to write a version of *MessageBox* that does *printf*-like formatting.

Compile, Link, and Run

When you're ready to compile HELLOMSG, you can select Build Hellomsg.exe from the Build menu, or press F7, or select the Build icon from the Build toolbar. (The appearance of this icon is shown in the Build menu. If the Build toolbar is not currently displayed, you can choose Customize from the Tools menu and select the Toolbars tab. Pick Build or Build MiniBar.)

Alternatively, you can select Execute Hellomsg.exe from the Build menu, or press Ctrl+F5, or click the Execute Program icon (which looks like a red exclamation point) from the Build toolbar. You'll get a message box asking you if you want to build the program.

As normal, during the compile stage, the compiler generates an .OBJ (object) file from the C source code file. During the link stage, the linker combines the .OBJ file with .LIB (library) files to create the .EXE (executable) file. You can see a list of these library files by selecting Settings from the Project tab and clicking the Link tab. In particular, you'll notice KERNEL32.LIB, USER32.LIB, and GDI32.LIB. These are "import libraries" for the three major Windows subsystems. They contain the dynamic-link library names and reference information that is bound into the .EXE file. Windows uses this information to resolve calls from the program to functions in the KERNEL32.DLL, USER32.DLL, and GDI32.DLL dynamic-link libraries.

In the Visual C++ Developer Studio, you can compile and link the program in different configurations. By default, these are called Debug and Release. The executable files are stored in subdirectories of these names. In the Debug configuration, information is added to the .EXE file that assists in debugging the program and in tracing through the program source code.

If you prefer working on the command line, the companion CD-ROM contains .MAK (make) files for all the sample programs. (You can tell the Developer Studio to generate make files by choosing Options from the Tools menu and selecting the Build tab. There's a check box to check.) You'll need to run VCVARS32.BAT located in the BIN subdirectory of the Developer Studio to set environment variables. To execute the make file from the command line, change to the HELLOMSG directory and execute:

```
NMAKE /f HelloMsg.mak CFG="HelloMsg - Win32 Debug"
```

or

```
NMAKE /f HelloMsg.mak CFG="HelloMsg - Win32 Release"
```

You can then run the .EXE file from the command line by typing:

```
DEBUG\HELLOMSG
```

or

```
RELEASE\HELLOMSG
```

I have made one change to the default Debug configuration in the project files on the companion CD-ROM for this book. In the Project Settings dialog box, after selecting the C/C++ tab, in the Preprocessor Definitions field I have defined the identifier UNICODE. I'll have much more to say about this in the next chapter.

An Introduction to Unicode

In the first chapter, I promised to elaborate on any aspects of C that you might not have encountered in conventional character-mode programming but that play a part in Microsoft Windows. The subject of wide-character sets and Unicode almost certainly qualifies in that respect.

Very simply, Unicode is an extension of ASCII character encoding. Rather than the 7 bits used to represent each character in strict ASCII, or the 8 bits per character that have become common on computers, Unicode uses a full 16 bits for character encoding. This allows Unicode to represent all the letters, ideographs, and other symbols used in all the written languages of the world that are likely to be used in computer communication. Unicode is intended initially to supplement ASCII and, with any luck, eventually replace it. Considering that ASCII is one of the most dominant standards in computing, this is certainly a tall order.

Unicode impacts every part of the computer industry, but perhaps most profoundly operating systems and programming languages. In this respect, we are almost halfway there. Windows NT supports Unicode from the ground up. (Unfortunately, Windows 98 includes only a small amount of Unicode support.) The C programming language as formalized by ANSI inherently supports Unicode through its support of wide characters, which I'll discuss in detail below.

Of course, as usual, we as programmers are confronted with much of the dirty work. I've tried to ease the load by making all of the programs in this book "Unicode-ready." What this means exactly will become more apparent as I discuss Unicode in this chapter.

A BRIEF HISTORY OF CHARACTER SETS

It is uncertain when human beings began speaking, but writing seems to be about six thousand years old. Early writing was pictographic in nature. Alphabets—in which individual letters correspond to spoken sounds—came about just three thousand years ago. Although the various written languages of the world served fine for some time, several nineteenth-century inventors saw a need for something more. When Samuel F. B. Morse developed the telegraph between 1838 and 1854, he also devised a code to use with it. Each letter in the alphabet corresponded to a series of short and long pulses (dots and dashes). There was no distinction between uppercase and lowercase letters, but numbers and punctuation marks had their own codes.

Morse code was not the first instance of written language being represented by something other than drawn or printed glyphs. Between 1821 and 1824, the young Louis Braille was inspired by a military system for writing and reading messages at night to develop a code for embossing raised dots into paper for reading by the blind. Braille is essentially a 6-bit code that encodes letters, common letter combinations, common words, and punctuation. A special escape code indicates that the following letter code is to be interpreted as uppercase. A special shift code allows subsequent letter codes to be interpreted as numbers.

Telex codes, including Baudot (named after a French engineer who died in 1903) and a code known as CCITT #2 (standardized in 1931), were 5-bit codes that included letter shifts and figure shifts.

American Standards

Early computer character codes evolved from the coding used on Hollerith ("do not fold, spindle, or mutilate") cards, invented by Herman Hollerith and first used in the 1890 United States census. A 6-bit character code known as BCDIC ("Binary-Coded Decimal Interchange Code") based on Hollerith coding was progressively extended to the 8-bit EBCDIC in the 1960s and remains the standard on IBM mainframes but nowhere else.

The American Standard Code for Information Interchange (ASCII) had its origins in the late 1950s and was finalized in 1967. During the development of ASCII, there was considerable debate over whether the code should be 6, 7, or 8 bits wide. Reliability considerations seemed to mandate that no shift character be used, so ASCII couldn't be a 6-bit code. Cost ruled out the 8-bit version. (Bits were very expensive back then.) The final code had 26 lowercase letters, 26 uppercase letters, 10 digits, 32 symbols, 33 control codes, and a space, for a total of 128 codes. ASCII is currently documented in ANSI X3.4-1986, "Coded Character Sets—7-Bit American National Standard Code for Information Interchange (7-Bit ASCII)," published by the American National Standards Institute. Figure 2-1 shows ASCII (for the zillionth time), very similar to how it appears in the ANSI document.

	0-	1-	2-	3-	4-	5-	6-	7-
-0	NUL	DLE	SP	0	@	P	`	p
-1	SOH	DC1	!	1	A	Q	a	q
-2	STX	DC2	"	2	B	R	b	r
-3	ETX	DC3	#	3	C	S	c	s
-4	EOT	DC4	$	4	D	T	d	t
-5	ENQ	NAK	%	5	E	U	e	u
-6	ACK	SYN	&	6	F	V	f	v
-7	BEL	ETB	'	7	G	W	g	w
-8	BS	CAN	(	8	H	X	h	x
-9	HT	EM	)	9	I	Y	I	y
-A	LF	SUB	*	:	J	Z	j	z
-B	VT	ESC	+	;	K	[	k	{
-C	FF	FS	,	<	L	\	l		
-D	CR	GS	-	=	M	]	m	}
-E	SO	RS	.	>	N	^	n	~
-F	SI	US	/	?	O	_	o	DEL

Figure 2-1. *The ASCII character set.*

There are a lot of good things you can say about ASCII. The 26 letter codes are contiguous, for example. (This is not the case with EBCDIC.) Uppercase letters can be converted to lowercase and back by flipping one bit. The codes for the 10 digits are easily derived from the value of the digits. (In BCDIC, the code for the character "0" followed the code for the character "9"!)

Best of all, ASCII is a very dependable standard. No other standard is as prevalent or as ingrained in our keyboards, video displays, system hardware, printers, font files, operating systems, and the Internet.

The World Beyond

The big problem with ASCII is indicated by the first word of the acronym. ASCII is truly an *American* standard, and it isn't even good enough for other countries where English is spoken. Where is the British pound symbol (£), for instance?

English uses the Latin (or Roman) alphabet. Among written languages that use the Latin alphabet, English is unusual in that very few words require letters with accent marks (or "diacritics"). Even for those English words where diacritics are traditionally proper, such as coöperate or résumé, the spellings without diacritics are perfectly acceptable.

But north and south of the United States and across the Atlantic are many countries and languages where diacritics are much more common. These accent marks originally aided in adopting the Latin alphabet to the differences in spoken sounds among these languages. Journey farther east or south of Western Europe, and you'll encounter languages that don't use the Latin alphabet at all, such as Greek, Hebrew, Arabic, and Russian (which uses the Cyrillic alphabet). And if you travel even farther east, you'll discover the ideographic Han characters of Chinese, which were also adopted in Japan and Korea.

The history of ASCII since 1967 is mostly a history of attempts to overcome its limitations and make it more applicable to languages other than American English. In 1967, for example, the International Standards Organization (ISO) recommended a variant of ASCII with codes 0x40, 0x5B, 0x5C, 0x5D, 0x7B, 0x7C, and 0x7D "reserved for national use" and codes 0x5E, 0x60, and 0x7E labeled as "may be used for other graphical symbols when it is necessary to have 8, 9, or 10 positions for national use." This is obviously not the best solution to internationalization because there's no guarantee of consistency. But it indicates how desperate people were to successfully code symbols necessary to various languages.

Extending ASCII

By the time the early small computers were being developed, the 8-bit byte had been firmly established. Thus, if a byte were used to store characters, 128 additional characters could be invented to supplement ASCII. When the original IBM PC was introduced in 1981, the video adapters included a ROM-based character set of 256 characters, which in itself was to become an important part of the IBM standard.

The original IBM extended character set included some accented characters and a lowercase Greek alphabet (useful for mathematics notation), as well as some block-drawing and line-drawing characters. Additional characters were also assigned to the code positions of the ASCII control characters, because the bulk of these control characters were not required.

This IBM extended character set was burned into countless ROMs on video boards and in printers, and it was used by numerous applications to decorate their character-mode displays. However, this character set did not include enough accented letters for all Western European languages that used the Latin alphabet, and it was not quite appropriate for Windows. Windows didn't need line-drawing characters because it had an entire graphics system.

In Windows 1.0 (released in November 1985), Microsoft didn't entirely abandon the IBM extended character set, but it was relegated to secondary importance. The native Windows character set was called the "ANSI character set" because it was based on a draft ANSI and ISO standard, which eventually became ANSI/ISO 8859-1-1987, "American National Standard for Information Processing—8-Bit Single-Byte Coded Graphic Character Sets—Part 1: Latin Alphabet No 1." This is also known more simply as "Latin 1."

The original version of the ANSI character set as printed in the Windows 1.0 *Programmer's Reference* is shown in Figure 2-2.

	0-	1-	2-	3-	4-	5-	6-	7-	8-	9-	A-	B-	C-	D-	E-	F-
-0	□	□		0	@	P	`	p	□	□		°	À	Ð	à	ð
-1	□	□	!	1	A	Q	a	q	□	□	¡	±	Á	Ñ	á	ñ
-2	□	□	"	2	B	R	b	r	□	□	¢	²	Â	Ò	â	ò
-3	□	□	#	3	C	S	c	s	□	□	£	³	Ã	Ó	ã	ó
-4	□	□	$	4	D	T	d	t	□	□	¤	´	Ä	Ô	ä	ô
-5	□	□	%	5	E	U	e	u	□	□	¥	µ	Å	Õ	å	õ
-6	□	□	&	6	F	V	f	v	□	□	¦	¶	Æ	Ö	æ	ö
-7	□	□	'	7	G	W	g	w	□	□	§	·	Ç	□	ç	□
-8	□	□	(	8	H	X	h	x	□	□	¨	¸	È	Ø	è	ø
-9	□	□	)	9	I	Y	i	y	□	□	©	¹	É	Ù	é	ù
-A	□	□	*	:	J	Z	j	z	□	□	ª	º	Ê	Ú	ê	ú
-B	□	□	+	;	K	[	k	{	□	□	«	»	Ë	Û	ë	û
-C	□	□	,	<	L	\	l	|	□	□	¬	¼	Ì	Ü	ì	ü
-D	□	□	-	=	M	]	m	}	□	□	-	½	Í	Ý	í	ý
-E	□	□	.	>	N	^	n	~	□	□	®	¾	Î	Þ	î	þ
-F	□	□	/	?	O	_	o	DEL	□	□	¯	¿	Ï	ß	ï	ÿ

Figure 2-2. *The Windows ANSI character set (based on ANSI/ISO 8859-1).*

The hollow rectangles indicate codes for which characters are not defined. This is close to how ANSI/ISO 8859-1 was ultimately defined. ANSI/ISO 8859-1 shows only graphic characters, not control characters, so it does not define the DEL. In addition, code 0xA0 is defined as a nonbreaking space (which means that it's a space that shouldn't be used to break a line when formatting), and code 0xAD is a soft hyphen (which means that it shouldn't be displayed unless it's used to break a word at the end of a line). Also, ANSI/ISO 8859-1 defines codes 0xD7 as a multiplication sign (×) and 0xF7 as a division sign (÷). Some fonts in Windows also define some of the characters from 0x80 through 0x9F, but these are not part of the ANSI/ISO 8859-1 standard.

MS-DOS 3.3 (released in April 1987) introduced the concept of code pages to IBM PC users, a concept that was also carried over to Windows. A code page defines a mapping of character codes to characters. The original IBM character set became known as code page 437, or "MS-DOS Latin US." Code page 850 is "MS-DOS Latin 1," which replaces some of the line-drawing characters with additional accented letters (but which is *not* the Latin 1 ISO/ANSI standard shown in Figure 2-2 above). Other code pages were defined for other languages. The lower 128 codes are always the same; the higher 128 codes depend on the language for which the code page is defined.

Under MS-DOS, if a user sets the PC's keyboard, video display, and printer to a specific code page and then creates, edits, and prints documents on the PC, all will be well. Everything's consistent. However, if the user attempts to exchange documents with another user using a different code page or to change the code page on the machine, problems will result. Character codes are associated with the wrong characters. Applications can save code page information with documents in an attempt to reduce problems, but this strategy involves some work in converting between code pages.

Although code pages originally provided only additional characters of the Latin alphabet beyond the unaccented characters, eventually code pages were devised where the higher 128 characters contained complete non-Latin alphabets, such as Hebrew, Greek, and Cyrillic. Such variety makes code page mix-ups potentially worse, of course; it's one thing if a few accented letters appear incorrect and quite another if an entire text is an incomprehensible jumble.

Code pages proliferated beyond all reason. Just to keep everyone on their toes, the MS-DOS code page 855 for Cyrillic is not the same as either the Windows code page 1251 for Cyrillic or the Macintosh code page 10007 for Cyrillic. Code pages in each environment are modifications of the standard character set for the environment. IBM OS/2 also supports a variety of EBCDIC code pages.

But wait. It gets worse.

Double-Byte Character Sets

So far we've been looking at character sets of 256 characters. But the ideographic symbols of Chinese, Japanese, and Korean number about 21,000. How can these languages be accommodated while still maintaining some kind of compatibility with ASCII?

The solution (if that's the right word for it) is the double-byte character set (DBCS). A DBCS starts off with 256 codes, just like ASCII. Like any well-behaved code page, the first 128 of these codes are ASCII. However, some of the codes in the higher 128 are always followed by a second byte. The two bytes together (called a lead byte and a trail byte) define a single character, usually a complex ideograph.

Although Chinese, Japanese, and Korean share many of the same ideographs, obviously the languages are different and often the same ideograph in the three different languages will represent three different things. Windows supports four different double-byte character sets: code page 932 (Japanese), 936 (Simplified Chinese), 949 (Korean), and 950 (Traditional Chinese). DBCS is supported in only the versions of Windows that are manufactured for these countries.

The problem with a double-byte character set is not that characters are represented by 2 bytes. The problem is that some characters (in particular, the ASCII characters) are represented by 1 byte. This creates odd programming problems. For example, the number of characters in a character string cannot be determined by the byte size of the string. The string has to be parsed to determine its length, and each byte has to be examined to see if it's the lead byte of a 2-byte character. If you have a pointer to a character somewhere in the middle of a DBCS string, what is the address of the *previous* character in the string? The customary solution is to parse the string starting at the beginning up to the pointer!

Unicode to the Rescue

The basic problem we have here is that the world's written languages simply cannot be represented by 256 8-bit codes. The previous solutions involving code pages and DBCS have proven insufficient and awkward. What's the *real* solution?

As programmers, we have experience with problems of this sort. If there are too many things to be represented by 8-bit values, we try wider values, perhaps 16-bit values. (Duh.) And that's the ridiculously simple concept behind Unicode. Rather than the confusion of multiple 256-character code mappings or double-byte character sets that have some 1-byte codes and some 2-byte codes, Unicode is a uniform 16-bit system, thus allowing the representation of 65,536 characters. This is sufficient for all the characters and ideographs in all the written languages of the world, including a bunch of math, symbol, and dingbat collections.

Understanding the difference between Unicode and DBCS is essential. Unicode is said to use (particularly in the context of the C programming language) "wide characters." *Each character in Unicode is 16 bits wide rather than 8 bits wide.* Eight-bit values have no meaning in Unicode. In contrast, in a double-byte character set we're still dealing with 8-bit values. Some bytes define characters by themselves, and some bytes indicate that another byte is necessary to completely define a character.

Whereas working with DBCS strings is quite messy, working with Unicode text is much like working with regular text. You'll probably be pleased to learn that the first 128 Unicode characters (16-bit codes 0x0000 through 0x007F) are ASCII, while the second 128 Unicode characters (codex 0x0080 through 0x00FF) are the ISO 8859-1 extensions to ASCII. Various blocks of characters within Unicode are similarly based on existing standards. This is to ease conversion. The Greek alphabet uses codes 0x0370 through 0x03FF, Cyrillic uses codes 0x0400 through 0x04FF, Armenian uses codes 0x0530 through 0x058F, and Hebrew uses codes 0x0590 through 0x05FF. The ideographs of Chinese, Japanese, and Korean (referred to collectively as CJK) occupy codes 0x3000 through 0x9FFF.

The best thing about Unicode is that there's only one character set. There's simply no ambiguity. Unicode came about through the cooperation of virtually every important company in the personal computer industry and is code-for-code identical with the ISO 10646-1 standard. The essential reference for Unicode is *The Unicode Standard, Version 2.0* (Addison-Wesley, 1996), an extraordinary book that reveals the richness and diversity of the world's written languages in a way that few other documents have. In addition, the book provides the rationale and details behind the development of Unicode.

Are there any drawbacks to Unicode? Sure. Unicode character strings occupy twice as much memory as ASCII strings. (File compression helps a lot to reduce the disk space differential, however.) But perhaps the worst drawback is that Unicode remains relatively unused just yet. As programmers, we have our work cut out for us.

WIDE CHARACTERS AND C

To a C programmer, the whole idea of 16-bit characters can certainly provoke uneasy chills. That a *char* is the same width as a byte is one of the very few certainties of this life. Few programmers are aware that ANSI/ISO 9899-1990, the "American National Standard for Programming Languages—C" (also known as "ANSI C") supports character sets that require more than one byte per character through a concept called "wide characters." These wide characters coexist nicely with normal and familiar characters.

ANSI C also supports multibyte character sets, such as those supported by the Chinese, Japanese, and Korean versions of Windows. However, these multibyte character sets are treated as strings of single-byte values in which some characters alter the meaning of successive characters. Multibyte character sets mostly impact the C run-time library functions. In contrast, wide characters are uniformly wider than normal characters and involve some compiler issues.

Wide characters aren't necessarily Unicode. Unicode is one possible wide-character encoding. However, because the focus in this book is Windows rather than an abstract implementation of C, I will tend to speak of wide characters and Unicode synonymously.

The *char* Data Type

Presumably, we are all quite familiar with defining and storing characters and character strings in our C programs by using the *char* data type. But to facilitate an understanding of how C handles wide characters, let's first review normal character definition as it might appear in a Win32 program.

The following statement defines and initializes a variable containing a single character:

```
char c = 'A' ;
```

The variable *c* requires 1 byte of storage and will be initialized with the hexadecimal value 0x41, which is the ASCII code for the letter A.

You can define a pointer to a character string like so:

```
char * p ;
```

Because Windows is a 32-bit operating system, the pointer variable *p* requires 4 bytes of storage. You can also initialize a pointer to a character string:

```
char * p = "Hello!" ;
```

The variable *p* still requires 4 bytes of storage as before. The character string is stored in static memory and uses 7 bytes of storage—the 6 bytes of the string in addition to a terminating 0.

You can also define an array of characters, like this:

```
char a[10] ;
```

In this case, the compiler reserves 10 bytes of storage for the array. The expression *sizeof (a)* will return 10. If the array is global (that is, defined outside any function), you can initialize an array of characters by using a statement like so:

```
char a[] = "Hello!" ;
```

If you define this array as a local variable to a function, it must be defined as a *static* variable, as follows:

```
static char a[] = "Hello!" ;
```

In either case, the string is stored in static program memory with a 0 appended at the end, thus requiring 7 bytes of storage.

Wider Characters

Nothing about Unicode or wide characters alters the meaning of the *char* data type in C. The *char* continues to indicate 1 byte of storage, and *sizeof (char)* continues to return 1. In theory, a byte in C can be greater than 8 bits, but for most of us, a byte (and hence a *char*) is 8 bits wide.

Wide characters in C are based on the *wchar_t* data type, which is defined in several header files, including WCHAR.H, like so:

```
typedef unsigned short wchar_t ;
```

Thus, the *wchar_t* data type is the same as an unsigned short integer: 16 bits wide.

To define a variable containing a single wide character, use the following statement:

```
wchar_t c = 'A' ;
```

The variable *c* is the two-byte value 0x0041, which is the Unicode representation of the letter A. (However, because Intel microprocessors store multibyte values with the least-significant bytes first, the bytes are actually stored in memory in the sequence 0x41, 0x00. Keep this in mind if you examine memory storage of Unicode text.)

You can also define an initialized pointer to a wide-character string:

```
wchar_t * p = L"Hello!" ;
```

Notice the capital L (for long) immediately preceding the first quotation mark. This indicates to the compiler that the string is to be stored with wide characters—that is, with every character occupying 2 bytes. The pointer variable *p* requires 4 bytes of storage, as usual, but the character string requires 14 bytes—2 bytes for each character with 2 bytes of zeros at the end.

Similarly, you can define an array of wide characters this way:

```
static wchar_t a[] = L"Hello!" ;
```

The string again requires 14 bytes of storage, and *sizeof (a)* will return 14. You can index the *a* array to get at the individual characters. The value *a[1]* is the wide character 'e', or 0x0065.

Although it looks more like a typo than anything else, that L preceding the first quotation mark is very important, and there must not be space between the two symbols. Only with that L will the compiler know you want the string to be stored with 2 bytes per character. Later on, when we look at wide-character strings in places other than variable definitions, you'll encounter the L preceding the first quotation mark again. Fortunately, the C compiler will often give you a warning or error message if you forget to include the L.

You can also use the L prefix in front of single character literals, as shown here, to indicate that they should be interpreted as wide characters.

```
wchar_t c = L'A' ;
```

But it's usually not necessary. The C compiler will zero-extend the character anyway.

Wide-Character Library Functions

We all know how to find the length of a string. For example, if we have defined a pointer to a character string like so:

```
char * pc = "Hello!" ;
```

we can call

```
iLength = strlen (pc) ;
```

The variable *iLength* will be set equal to 6, the number of characters in the string.

Excellent! Now let's try defining a pointer to a string of wide characters:

```
wchar_t * pw = L"Hello!" ;
```

And now we call *strlen* again:

```
iLength = strlen (pw) ;
```

Now the troubles begin. First, the C compiler gives you a warning message, probably something along the lines of

```
'function' : incompatible types - from 'unsigned short *' to 'const char *'
```

It's telling you that the *strlen* function is declared as accepting a pointer to a *char*, and it's getting a pointer to an *unsigned short*. You can still compile and run the program, but you'll find that *iLength* is set to 1. What happened?

The 6 characters of the character string "Hello!" have the 16-bit values:

```
0x0048 0x0065 0x006C 0x006C 0x006F 0x0021
```

which are stored in memory by Intel processors like so:

```
48 00 65 00 6C 00 6C 00 6F 00 21 00
```

The *strlen* function, assuming that it's attempting to find the length of a string of characters, counts the first byte as a character but then assumes that the second byte is a zero byte denoting the end of the string.

This little exercise clearly illustrates the differences between the C language itself and the run-time library functions. The compiler interprets the string L"Hello!" as a collection of 16-bit short integers and stores them in the *wchar_t* array. The compiler also handles any array indexing and the *sizeof* operator, so these work properly. But run-time library functions such as *strlen* are added during link time. These functions expect strings that comprise single-byte characters. When they are confronted with wide-character strings, they don't perform as we'd like.

Oh, great, you say. Now every C library function has to be rewritten to accept wide characters. Well, not *every* C library function. Only the ones that have string arguments. And *you* don't have to rewrite them. It's already been done.

The wide-character version of the *strlen* function is called *wcslen* ("wide-character string length"), and it's declared both in STRING.H (where the declaration for *strlen* resides) and WCHAR.H. The *strlen* function is declared like this:

```
size_t __cdecl strlen (const char *) ;
```

and the *wcslen* function looks like this:

```
size_t __cdecl wcslen (const wchar_t *) ;
```

So now we know that when we need to find out the length of a wide-character string we can call

```
iLength = wcslen (pw) ;
```

The function returns 6, the number of characters in the string. Keep in mind that the character length of a string does not change when you move to wide characters—only the byte length changes.

All your favorite C run-time library functions that take string arguments have wide-character versions. For example, *wprintf* is the wide-character version of *printf*. These functions are declared both in WCHAR.H and in the header file where the normal function is declared.

Maintaining a Single Source

There are, of course, certain disadvantages to using Unicode. First and foremost is that every string in your program will occupy twice as much space. In addition, you'll observe that the functions in the wide-character run-time library are larger than the usual functions. For this reason, you might want to create two versions of your program—one with ASCII strings and the other with Unicode strings. The best solution would be to maintain a single source code file that you could compile for either ASCII or Unicode.

That's a bit of a problem, though, because the run-time library functions have different names, you're defining characters differently, and then there's that nuisance of preceding the string literals with an L.

One answer is to use the TCHAR.H header file included with Microsoft Visual C++. This header file is not part of the ANSI C standard, so every function and macro definition defined therein is preceded by an underscore. TCHAR.H provides a set of alternative names for the normal run-time library functions requiring string parameters (for example, _tprintf and _tcslen). These are sometimes referred to as "generic" function names because they can refer to either the Unicode or non-Unicode versions of the functions.

If an identifier named _UNICODE is defined and the TCHAR.H header file is included in your program, _tcslen is defined to be wcslen:

```
#define _tcslen wcslen
```

If UNICODE isn't defined, _tcslen is defined to be strlen:

```
#define _tcslen strlen
```

And so on. TCHAR.H also solves the problem of the two character data types with a new data type named TCHAR. If the _UNICODE identifier is defined, TCHAR is wchar_t:

```
typedef wchar_t TCHAR ;
```

Otherwise, TCHAR is simply a char:

```
typedef char TCHAR ;
```

Now it's time to address that sticky L problem with the string literals. If the _UNICODE identifier is defined, a macro called __T is defined like this:

```
#define __T(x) L##x
```

This is fairly obscure syntax, but it's in the ANSI C standard for the C preprocessor. That pair of number signs is called a "token paste," and it causes the letter L to be appended to the macro parameter. Thus, if the macro parameter is "Hello!", then L##x is L"Hello!".

If the _UNICODE identifier is not defined, the __T macro is simply defined in the following way:

```
#define __T(x) x
```

Regardless, two other macros are defined to be the same as __T:

```
#define _T(x) __T(x)
#define _TEXT(x) __T(x)
```

Which one you use for your Win32 console programs depends on how concise or verbose you'd like to be. Basically, you must define your string literals inside the _T or _TEXT macro in the following way:

```
_TEXT ("Hello!")
```

Doing so causes the string to be interpreted as composed of wide characters if the _UNICODE identifier is defined and as 8-bit characters if not.

WIDE CHARACTERS AND WINDOWS

Windows NT supports Unicode from the ground up. What this means is that Windows NT internally uses character strings composed of 16-bit characters. Since much of the rest of the world doesn't use 16-bit character strings yet, Windows NT must often convert character strings on the way into the operating system or on the way out. Windows NT can run programs written for ASCII, for Unicode, or for a mix of ASCII and Unicode. That is, Windows NT supports different API function calls that accept 8-bit or 16-bit character strings. (We'll see how this works shortly.)

Windows 98 has much less support of Unicode than Windows NT does. Only a few Windows 98 function calls support wide-character strings. (These functions are listed in Microsoft Knowledge Base article Q125671; they include *MessageBox*.) If you're going to distribute only one .EXE file that must run under both Windows NT and Windows 98, it shouldn't use Unicode or else it won't run under Windows 98; in particular, the program shouldn't call the Unicode versions of the Windows function calls. However, so that you can be in a better position to distribute a Unicode version of your program sometime in the future, you should probably attempt to have a single source that can be compiled for either ASCII or Unicode. That's how all the programs in the book are written.

Windows Header File Types

As you saw in the first chapter, a Windows program includes the header file WINDOWS.H. This file includes a number of other header files, including WINDEF.H, which has many of the basic type definitions used in Windows and which itself includes WINNT.H. WINNT.H handles the basic Unicode support.

WINNT.H begins by including the C header file CTYPE.H, which is one of many C header files that have a definition of *wchar_t*. WINNT.H defines new data types named CHAR and WCHAR:

```
typedef char CHAR ;
typedef wchar_t WCHAR ; // wc
```

CHAR and WCHAR are the data types recommended for your use in a Windows program when you need to define an 8-bit character or a 16-bit character. That comment following the WCHAR definition is a suggestion for Hungarian notation: a variable based on the WCHAR data type can be preceded with the letters *wc* to indicate a wide character.

The WINNT.H header file goes on to define six data types you can use as pointers to 8-bit character strings and four data types you can use as pointers to *const* 8-bit character strings. I've condensed the actual header file statements a bit to show the data types here:

```
typedef CHAR * PCHAR, * LPCH, * PCH, * NPSTR, * LPSTR, * PSTR ;
typedef CONST CHAR * LPCCH, * PCCH, * LPCSTR, * PCSTR ;
```

The N and L prefixes stand for "near" and "long" and refer to the two different sizes of pointers in 16-bit Windows. There is no differentiation between near and long pointers in Win32.

Similarly, WINNT.H defines six data types you can use as pointers to 16-bit character strings and four data types you can use as pointers to *const* 16-bit character strings:

```
typedef WCHAR * PWCHAR, * LPWCH, * PWCH, * NWPSTR, * LPWSTR, * PWSTR ;
typedef CONST WCHAR * LPCWCH, * PCWCH, * LPCWSTR, * PCWSTR ;
```

So far, we have the data types CHAR (which is an 8-bit *char*) and WCHAR (which is a 16-bit *wchar_t*) and pointers to CHAR and WCHAR. As in TCHAR.H, WINNT.H defines TCHAR to be the generic character type. If the identifier UNICODE (*without* the underscore) is defined, TCHAR and pointers to TCHAR are defined based on WCHAR and pointers to WCHAR; if the identifier UNICODE is not defined, TCHAR and pointers to TCHAR are defined based on *char* and pointers to *char*:

```
#ifdef  UNICODE
typedef WCHAR TCHAR, * PTCHAR ;
typedef LPWSTR LPTCH, PTCH, PTSTR, LPTSTR ;
typedef LPCWSTR LPCTSTR ;
#else
typedef char TCHAR, * PTCHAR ;
typedef LPSTR LPTCH, PTCH, PTSTR, LPTSTR ;
typedef LPCSTR LPCTSTR ;
#endif
```

Both the WINNT.H and WCHAR.H header files are protected against redefinition of the TCHAR data type if it's already been defined by one or the other of these header files. However, whenever you're using other header files in your program, you should include WINDOWS.H before all others.

The WINNT.H header file also defines a macro that appends the L to the first quotation mark of a character string. If the UNICODE identifier is defined, a macro called __TEXT is defined as follows:

```
#define __TEXT(quote) L##quote
```

If the identifier UNICODE is not defined, the __TEXT macro is defined like so:

```
#define __TEXT(quote) quote
```

Regardless, the TEXT macro is defined like this:

```
#define TEXT(quote) __TEXT(quote)
```

This is very similar to the way the _TEXT macro is defined in TCHAR.H, except that you need not bother with the underscore. I'll be using the TEXT version of this macro throughout this book.

These definitions let you mix ASCII and Unicode characters strings in the same program or write a single program that can be compiled for either ASCII or Unicode. If you want to explicitly define 8-bit character variables and strings, use CHAR, PCHAR (or one of the others), and strings with quotation marks. For explicit 16-bit character variables and strings, use WCHAR, PWCHAR, and append an L before quotation marks. For variables and characters strings that will be 8 bit or 16 bit depending on the definition of the UNICODE identifier, use TCHAR, PTCHAR, and the TEXT macro.

The Windows Function Calls

In the 16-bit versions of Windows beginning with Windows 1.0 and ending with Windows 3.1, the *MessageBox* function was located in the dynamic-link library USER.EXE. In the WINDOWS.H header files included in the Windows 3.1 Software Development Kit, the *MessageBox* function was defined like so:

```
int WINAPI MessageBox (HWND, LPCSTR, LPCSTR, UINT) ;
```

Notice that the second and third arguments to the function are pointers to constant character strings. When a Win16 program was compiled and linked, Windows left the call to *MessageBox* unresolved. A table in the program's .EXE file allowed Windows to dynamically link the call from the program to the *MessageBox* function located in the USER library.

The 32-bit versions of Windows (that is, all versions of Windows NT, as well as Windows 95 and Windows 98) include USER.EXE for 16-bit compatibility but also have a dynamic-link library named USER32.DLL that contains entry points for the 32-bit versions of the user interface functions, including the 32-bit version of *MessageBox*.

But here's the key to Windows support of Unicode: In USER32.DLL, there is no entry point for a 32-bit function named *MessageBox*. Instead, there are two entry points, one named *MessageBoxA* (the ASCII version) and the other named *MessageBoxW* (the wide-character version). Every Win32 function that requires a character string argument has two entry points in the operating system! Fortunately, you usually don't have to worry about this. You can simply use *MessageBox* in your programs. As in the TCHAR header file, the various Windows header files perform the necessary tricks.

Here's how *MessageBoxA* is defined in WINUSER.H. This is quite similar to the earlier definition of *MessageBox*:

```
WINUSERAPI int WINAPI MessageBoxA (HWND hWnd, LPCSTR lpText,
                                   LPCSTR lpCaption, UINT uType) ;
```

And here's *MessageBoxW*:

```
WINUSERAPI int WINAPI MessageBoxW (HWND hWnd, LPCWSTR lpText,
                                   LPCWSTR lpCaption, UINT uType) ;
```

Notice that the second and third parameters to the *MessageBoxW* function are pointers to wide-character strings.

You can use the *MessageBoxA* and *MessageBoxW* functions explicitly in your Windows programs if you need to mix and match ASCII and wide-character function calls. But most programmers will continue to use *MessageBox*, which will be the same as *MessageBoxA* or *MessageBoxW* depending on whether UNICODE is defined. Here's the rather trivial code in WINUSER.H that does the trick:

```
#ifdef UNICODE
#define MessageBox   MessageBoxW
#else
#define MessageBox   MessageBoxA
#endif
```

Thus, all the *MessageBox* function calls that appear in your program will actually be *MessageBoxW* functions if the UNICODE identifier is defined and *MessageBoxA* functions if it's not defined.

When you run the program, Windows links the various function calls in your program to the entry points in the various Windows dynamic-link libraries. With just a few exceptions, however, the Unicode versions of the Windows functions are not implemented in Windows 98. The functions have entry points, but they usually return an error code. It is up to an application to take note of this error return and do something reasonable.

Windows' String Functions

As I noted earlier, Microsoft C includes wide-character and generic versions of all C runtime library functions that require character string arguments. However, Windows duplicates some of these. For example, here is a collection of string functions defined in Windows that calculate string lengths, copy strings, concatenate strings, and compare strings:

```
ILength = lstrlen (pString) ;
pString = lstrcpy (pString1, pString2) ;
pString = lstrcpyn (pString1, pString2, iCount) ;
pString = lstrcat (pString1, pString2) ;
iComp = lstrcmp (pString1, pString2) ;
iComp = lstrcmpi (pString1, pString2) ;
```

These work much the same as their C library equivalents. They accept wide-character strings if the UNICODE identifier is defined and regular strings if not. The wide-character version of the *lstrlenW* function is implemented in Windows 98.

Using *printf* in Windows

Programmers who have a background in character-mode, command-line C programming are often excessively fond of the *printf* function. It's no surprise that *printf* shows up in the Kernighan and Ritchie "hello, world" program even though a simpler alternative (such as *puts*) could have been used. Everyone knows that enhancements to "hello, world" will need the formatted text output of *printf* eventually, so we might as well start using it at the outset.

The bad news is that you can't use *printf* in a Windows program. Although you can use most of the C run-time library in Windows programs—indeed, many programmers prefer to use the C memory management and file I/O functions over the Windows equivalents—Windows has no concept of standard input and standard output. You can use *fprintf* in a Windows program, but not *printf*.

The good news is that you can still display text by using *sprintf* and other functions in the *sprintf* family. These functions work just like *printf*, except that they write the formatted output to a character string buffer that you provide as the function's first argument. You can then do what you want with this character string (such as pass it to *MessageBox*).

If you've never had occasion to use *sprintf* (as I didn't when I first began programming for Windows), here's a brief rundown. Recall that the *printf* function is declared like so:

```
int printf (const char * szFormat, ...) ;
```

The first argument is a formatting string that is followed by a variable number of arguments of various types corresponding to the codes in the formatting string.

The *sprintf* function is defined like this:

```
int sprintf (char * szBuffer, const char * szFormat, ...) ;
```

The first argument is a character buffer; this is followed by the formatting string. Rather than writing the formatted result in standard output, *sprintf* stores it in *szBuffer*. The function returns the length of the string. In character-mode programming,

```
printf ("The sum of %i and %i is %i", 5, 3, 5+3) ;
```

is functionally equivalent to

```
char szBuffer [100] ;
sprintf (szBuffer, "The sum of %i and %i is %i", 5, 3, 5+3) ;
puts (szBuffer) ;
```

In Windows, you can use *MessageBox* rather than *puts* to display the results.

Almost everyone has experience with *printf* going awry and possibly crashing a program when the formatting string is not properly in sync with the variables to be formatted. With *sprintf*, you still have to worry about that and you also have a new worry: the character buffer you define must be large enough for the result. A Microsoft-specific function named *_snprintf* solves this problem by introducing another argument that indicates the size of the buffer in characters.

A variation of *sprintf* is *vsprintf*, which has only three arguments. The *vsprintf* function is used to implement a function of your own that must perform *printf*-like formatting of a variable number of arguments. The first two arguments to *vsprintf* are the same as *sprintf:* the character buffer for storing the result and the formatting string. The third argument is a pointer to an array of arguments to be formatted. In practice, this pointer actually references variables that have been stored on the stack in preparation for a function call. The *va_list*, *va_start*, and *va_end* macros (defined in STDARG.H) help in working with this stack pointer. The SCRNSIZE program at the end of this chapter demonstrates how to use these macros. The *sprintf* function can be written in terms of *vsprintf* like so:

```
int sprintf (char * szBuffer, const char * szFormat, ...)
{
    int     iReturn ;
    va_list pArgs ;

    va_start (pArgs, szFormat) ;
    iReturn = vsprintf (szBuffer, szFormat, pArgs) ;
    va_end (pArgs) ;

    return iReturn ;
}
```

The *va_start* macro sets *pArg* to point to the variable on the stack right above the *szFormat* argument on the stack.

So many early Windows programs used *sprintf* and *vsprintf* that Microsoft eventually added two similar functions to the Windows API. The Windows *wsprintf* and *wvsprintf* functions are functionally equivalent to *sprintf* and *vsprintf*, except that they don't handle floating-point formatting.

Of course, with the introduction of wide characters, the *sprintf* functions blossomed in number, creating a thoroughly confusing jumble of function names. Here's a chart that shows all the *sprintf* functions supported by Microsoft's C run-time library and by Windows.

	ASCII	*Wide-Character*	*Generic*
Variable Number of Arguments			
Standard Version	*sprintf*	*swprintf*	*_stprintf*
Max-Length Version	*_snprintf*	*_snwprintf*	*_sntprintf*
Windows Version	*wsprintfA*	*wsprintfW*	*wsprintf*
Pointer to Array of Arguments			
Standard Version	*vsprintf*	*vswprintf*	*_vstprintf*
Max-Length Version	*_vsnprintf*	*_vsnwprintf*	*_vsntprintf*
Windows Version	*wvsprintfA*	*wvsprintfW*	*wvsprintf*

In the wide-character versions of the *sprintf* functions, the string buffer is defined as a wide-character string. In the wide-character versions of all these functions, the formatting string must be a wide-character string. However, it's up to you to make sure that any other strings you pass to these functions are also composed of wide characters.

A Formatting Message Box

The SCRNSIZE program shown in Figure 2-3 shows how to implement a *MessageBoxPrintf* function that takes a variable number of arguments and formats them like *printf*.

SCRNSIZE.C

```
/*-------------------------------------------------------
   SCRNSIZE.C -- Displays screen size in a message box
                 (c) Charles Petzold, 1998
   -------------------------------------------------------*/

#include <windows.h>
#include <tchar.h>
#include <stdio.h>

int CDECL MessageBoxPrintf (TCHAR * szCaption, TCHAR * szFormat, ...)
{
     TCHAR    szBuffer [1024] ;
     va_list pArgList ;

          // The va_start macro (defined in STDARG.H) is usually equivalent to:
          // pArgList = (char *) &szFormat + sizeof (szFormat) ;

     va_start (pArgList, szFormat) ;

          // The last argument to wvsprintf points to the arguments

     _vsntprintf (szBuffer, sizeof (szBuffer) / sizeof (TCHAR),
                  szFormat, pArgList) ;

          // The va_end macro just zeroes out pArgList for no good reason

     va_end (pArgList) ;

     return MessageBox (NULL, szBuffer, szCaption, 0) ;
}
```

Figure 2-3. *The SCRNSIZE program.*

(continued)

Figure 2-3. *continued*

```
int WINAPI WinMain (HINSTANCE hInstance, HINSTANCE hPrevInstance,
                    PSTR szCmdLine, int iCmdShow)
{
    int cxScreen, cyScreen ;

    cxScreen = GetSystemMetrics (SM_CXSCREEN) ;
    cyScreen = GetSystemMetrics (SM_CYSCREEN) ;

    MessageBoxPrintf (TEXT ("ScrnSize"),
                      TEXT ("The screen is %i pixels wide by %i pixels high."),
                      cxScreen, cyScreen) ;
    return 0 ;
}
```

The program displays the width and height of the video display in pixels by using information obtained from the *GetSystemMetrics* function. *GetSystemMetrics* is a useful function for obtaining information about the sizes of various objects in Windows. Indeed, in Chapter 4 I'll use the *GetSystemMetrics* function to show you how to display and scroll multiple lines of text in a Windows window.

Internationalization and This Book

Preparing your Windows programs for an international market involves more than using Unicode. Internationalization is beyond the scope of this book but is covered extensively in *Developing International Software for Windows 95 and Windows NT* by Nadine Kano (Microsoft Press, 1995).

This book will restrict itself to showing programs that can be compiled either with or without the UNICODE identifier defined. This involves using TCHAR for all character and string definitions, using the TEXT macro for string literals, and taking care not to confuse bytes and characters. For example, notice the *_vsntprintf* call in SCRNSIZE. The second argument is the size of the buffer in characters. Typically, you'd use *sizeof (szBuffer)*. But if the buffer has wide characters, that's not the size of the buffer in characters but the size of the buffer in bytes. You must divide it by *sizeof (TCHAR)*.

Normally in the Visual C++ Developer Studio, you can compile a program in two different configurations: Debug and Release. For convenience, for the sample programs in this book, I have modified the Debug configuration so that the UNICODE identifier is defined. In those programs that use C run-time functions that require string arguments, the _UNICODE identifier is also defined in the Debug configuration. (To see where this is done, choose Settings from the Project menu and click the C/C++ tab.) In this way, the programs can be easily recompiled and linked for testing.

All of the programs in this book—whether compiled for Unicode or not—run under Windows NT. With a few exceptions, the Unicode-compiled programs in this book will *not* run under Windows 98 but the non-Unicode versions will. The programs in this chapter and the first chapter are two of the few exceptions. *MessageBoxW* is one of the few wide-character Windows functions supported under Windows 98. If you replace *_vsntprintf* in SCRNSIZE.C with the Windows function *wprintf* (you'll also have to eliminate the second argument to the function), the Unicode version of SCRNSIZE.C will not run under Windows 98 because Windows 98 does not implement *wprintfW*.

As we'll see later in this book (particularly in Chapter 6, which covers using the keyboard), it is not easy writing a Windows program that can handle the double-byte character sets of the Far Eastern versions of Windows. This book does not show you how, and for that reason some of the non-Unicode versions of the programs in this book do not run properly under the Far Eastern versions of Windows. This is one reason why Unicode is so important to the future of programming. Unicode allows programs to more easily cross national borders.

Chapter 3

Windows and Messages

In the first two chapters, the sample programs used the *MessageBox* function to deliver text output to the user. The *MessageBox* function creates a "window." In Windows, the word "window" has a precise meaning. A window is a rectangular area on the screen that receives user input and displays output in the form of text and graphics.

The *MessageBox* function creates a window, but it is a special-purpose window of limited flexibility. The message box window has a title bar with a close button, an optional icon, one or more lines of text, and up to four buttons. However, the icons and buttons must be chosen from a small collection that Windows provides for you.

The *MessageBox* function is certainly useful, but we're not going to get very far with it. We can't display graphics in a message box, and we can't add a menu to a message box. For that we need to create our own windows, and now is the time.

A WINDOW OF ONE'S OWN

Creating a window is as easy as calling the *CreateWindow* function.

Well, not really. Although the function to create a window is indeed named *CreateWindow* and you can find documentation for this function at */Platform SDK/User Interface Services/Windowing/Windows/Window Reference/Window Functions*, you'll discover that the first argument to *CreateWindow* is something called a "window class name" and that a window class is connected to something called a "window procedure." Perhaps before we try calling *CreateWindow*, a little background information might prove helpful.

An Architectural Overview

When programming for Windows, you're really engaged in a type of object-oriented programming. This is most evident in the object you'll be working with most in Windows, the object that gives Windows its name, the object that will soon seem to take on anthropomorphic characteristics, the object that might even show up in your dreams: the object known as the "window."

The most obvious windows adorning your desktop are application windows. These windows contain a title bar that shows the program's name, a menu, and perhaps a toolbar and a scroll bar. Another type of window is the dialog box, which may or may not have a title bar.

Less obvious are the various push buttons, radio buttons, check boxes, list boxes, scroll bars, and text-entry fields that adorn the surfaces of dialog boxes. Each of these little visual objects is a window. More specifically, these are called "child windows" or "control windows" or "child window controls."

The user sees these windows as objects on the screen and interacts directly with them using the keyboard or the mouse. Interestingly enough, the programmer's perspective is analogous to the user's perspective. The window receives the user input in the form of "messages" to the window. A window also uses messages to communicate with other windows. Getting a good feel for messages is an important part of learning how to write programs for Windows.

Here's an example of Windows messages: As you know, most Windows programs have sizeable application windows. That is, you can grab the window's border with the mouse and change the window's size. Often the program will respond to this change in size by altering the contents of its window. You might guess (and you would be correct) that Windows itself rather than the application is handling all the messy code involved with letting the user resize the window. Yet the application "knows" that the window has been resized because it can change the format of what it displays.

How does the application know that the user has changed the window's size? For programmers accustomed to only conventional character-mode programming, there is no mechanism for the operating system to convey information of this sort to the user. It turns out that the answer to this question is central to understanding the architecture of Windows. When a user resizes a window, Windows sends a message to the program indicating the new window size. The program can then adjust the contents of its window to reflect the new size.

"Windows sends a message to the program." I hope you didn't read that statement without blinking. What on earth could it mean? We're talking about program code here, not a telegraph system. How can an operating system send a message to a program?

When I say that "Windows sends a message to the program" I mean that Windows calls a function within the program—a function that you write and which is an essential part of your program's code. The parameters to this function describe the particular message that is being sent by Windows and received by your program. This function in your program is known as the "window procedure."

You are undoubtedly accustomed to the idea of a program making calls to the operating system. This is how a program opens a disk file, for example. What you may not be accustomed to is the idea of an operating system making calls to a program. Yet this is fundamental to Windows' architecture.

Every window that a program creates has an associated window procedure. This window procedure is a function that could be either in the program itself or in a dynamic-link library. Windows sends a message to a window by calling the window procedure. The window procedure does some processing based on the message and then returns control to Windows.

More precisely, a window is always created based on a "window class." The window class identifies the window procedure that processes messages to the window. The use of a window class allows multiple windows to be based on the same window class and hence use the same window procedure. For example, all buttons in all Windows programs are based on the same window class. This window class is associated with a window procedure located in a Windows dynamic-link library that processes messages to all the button windows.

In object-oriented programming, an object is a combination of code and data. A window is an object. The code is the window procedure. The data is information retained by the window procedure and information retained by Windows for each window and window class that exists in the system.

A window procedure processes messages to the window. Very often these messages inform a window of user input from the keyboard or the mouse. For example, this is how a push-button window knows that it's being "clicked." Other messages tell a window when it is being resized or when the surface of the window needs to be redrawn.

When a Windows program begins execution, Windows creates a "message queue" for the program. This message queue stores messages to all the windows a program might create. A Windows application includes a short chunk of code called the "message loop" to retrieve these messages from the queue and dispatch them to the appropriate window procedure. Other messages are sent directly to the window procedure without being placed in the message queue.

If your eyes are beginning to glaze over with this excessively abstract description of the Windows architecture, maybe it will help to see how the window, the window class, the window procedure, the message queue, the message loop, and the window messages all fit together in the context of a real program.

The HELLOWIN Program

Creating a window first requires registering a window class, and that requires a window procedure to process messages to the window. This involves a bit of overhead that appears in almost every Windows program. The HELLOWIN program, shown in Figure 3-1, is a simple program showing mostly that overhead.

HELLOWIN.C

```c
/*------------------------------------------------------------
   HELLOWIN.C -- Displays "Hello, Windows 98!" in client area
                 (c) Charles Petzold, 1998
  ------------------------------------------------------------*/

#include <windows.h>

LRESULT CALLBACK WndProc (HWND, UINT, WPARAM, LPARAM) ;

int WINAPI WinMain (HINSTANCE hInstance, HINSTANCE hPrevInstance,
                    PSTR szCmdLine, int iCmdShow)
{
    static TCHAR szAppName[] = TEXT ("HelloWin") ;
    HWND        hwnd ;
    MSG         msg ;
    WNDCLASS    wndclass ;

    wndclass.style         = CS_HREDRAW | CS_VREDRAW ;
    wndclass.lpfnWndProc   = WndProc ;
    wndclass.cbClsExtra    = 0 ;
    wndclass.cbWndExtra    = 0 ;
    wndclass.hInstance     = hInstance ;
    wndclass.hIcon         = LoadIcon (NULL, IDI_APPLICATION) ;
    wndclass.hCursor       = LoadCursor (NULL, IDC_ARROW) ;
    wndclass.hbrBackground = (HBRUSH) GetStockObject (WHITE_BRUSH) ;
    wndclass.lpszMenuName  = NULL ;
    wndclass.lpszClassName = szAppName ;

    if (!RegisterClass (&wndclass))
    {
        MessageBox (NULL, TEXT ("This program requires Windows NT!"),
                    szAppName, MB_ICONERROR) ;
        return 0 ;
    }
```

Figure 3-1. *The HELLOWIN program.*

```
      hwnd = CreateWindow (szAppName,                    // window class name
                           TEXT ("The Hello Program"),  // window caption
                           WS_OVERLAPPEDWINDOW,          // window style
                           CW_USEDEFAULT,                // initial x position
                           CW_USEDEFAULT,                // initial y position
                           CW_USEDEFAULT,                // initial x size
                           CW_USEDEFAULT,                // initial y size
                           NULL,                         // parent window handle
                           NULL,                         // window menu handle
                           hInstance,                    // program instance handle
                           NULL) ;                       // creation parameters

     ShowWindow (hwnd, iCmdShow) ;
     UpdateWindow (hwnd) ;

     while (GetMessage (&msg, NULL, 0, 0))
     {
          TranslateMessage (&msg) ;
          DispatchMessage (&msg) ;
     }
     return msg.wParam ;
}

LRESULT CALLBACK WndProc (HWND hwnd, UINT message, WPARAM wParam, LPARAM lParam)
{
     HDC         hdc ;
     PAINTSTRUCT ps ;
     RECT        rect ;

     switch (message)
     {
     case WM_CREATE:
          PlaySound (TEXT ("hellowin.wav"), NULL, SND_FILENAME | SND_ASYNC) ;
          return 0 ;

     case WM_PAINT:
          hdc = BeginPaint (hwnd, &ps) ;

          GetClientRect (hwnd, &rect) ;

          DrawText (hdc, TEXT ("Hello, Windows 98!"), -1, &rect,
                    DT_SINGLELINE | DT_CENTER | DT_VCENTER) ;
```

(continued)

Figure 3-1. *continued*

```
        EndPaint (hwnd, &ps) ;
        return 0 ;

    case WM_DESTROY:
        PostQuitMessage (0) ;
        return 0 ;
    }
    return DefWindowProc (hwnd, message, wParam, lParam) ;
}
```

This program creates a normal application window, as shown in Figure 3-2, and displays, "Hello, Windows 98!" in the center of that window. If you have a sound board installed, you will also hear me saying the same thing.

Figure 3-2. *The HELLOWIN window.*

A couple of warnings: If you use Microsoft Visual C++ to create a new project for this program, you need to make an addition to the object libraries the linker uses. Select the Settings option from the Project menu, and pick the Link tab. Select General from the Category list box, and add WINMM.LIB ("Windows multimedia") to the Object/Library Modules text box. You need to do this because HELLOWIN makes use of a multimedia function call, and the multimedia object library isn't included in a default project. Otherwise you'll get an error message from the linker indicating that the *PlaySound* function is unresolved.

HELLOWIN accesses a file named HELLOWIN.WAV, which is on the companion CD-ROM in the HELLOWIN directory. When you execute HELLOWIN.EXE, the default directory must be HELLOWIN. This is the case when you execute the program within Visual C++, even though the executable will be in the RELEASE or DEBUG subdirectory of HELLOWIN.

Thinking Globally

Most of HELLOWIN.C is overhead found in virtually every Windows program. Nobody really memorizes all the syntax to write this overhead; generally, Windows programmers begin a new program by copying an existing program and making appropriate changes to it. You're free to use the programs on the companion CD-ROM in this manner.

I mentioned above that HELLOWIN displays the text string in the center of its window. That's not precisely true. The text is actually displayed in the center of the program's "client area," which in Figure 3-2 is the large white area within the title bar and the sizing border. This distinction will be important to us; the client area is that area of the window in which a program is free to draw and deliver visual output to the user.

When you think about it, this program has an amazing amount of functionality in its 80-odd lines of code. You can grab the title bar with the mouse and move the window around the screen. You can grab the sizing borders and resize the window. When the window changes size, the program automatically repositions the text string in the center of its client area. You can click the maximize button and zoom HELLOWIN to fill the screen. You can click the minimize button and clear it from the screen. You can invoke all these options from the system menu (the small icon at the far left of the title bar). You can also close the window to terminate the program by selecting the Close option from the system menu, by clicking the close button at the far right of the title bar, or by double-clicking the system menu icon.

We'll be examining this program in detail for much of the remainder of the chapter. First, however, let's take a more global look.

HELLOWIN.C has a *WinMain* function like the sample programs in the first two chapters, but it also has a second function named *WndProc*. This is the window procedure. (In conversation among Windows programmers, it's called the "win prock.") Notice that there's no code in HELLOWIN.C that calls *WndProc*. However, there is a reference to *WndProc* in *WinMain*, which is why the function is declared near the top of the program.

The Windows Function Calls

HELLOWIN makes calls to no fewer than 18 Windows functions. In the order they occur, these functions (with a brief description) are:

- *LoadIcon*   Loads an icon for use by a program.

- *LoadCursor*   Loads a mouse cursor for use by a program.

- *GetStockObject*   Obtains a graphic object, in this case a brush used for painting the window's background.

- *RegisterClass*   Registers a window class for the program's window.

- *MessageBox* Displays a message box.

- *CreateWindow* Creates a window based on a window class.

- *ShowWindow* Shows the window on the screen.

- *UpdateWindow* Directs the window to paint itself.

- *GetMessage* Obtains a message from the message queue.

- *TranslateMessage* Translates some keyboard messages.

- *DispatchMessage* Sends a message to a window procedure.

- *PlaySound* Plays a sound file.

- *BeginPaint* Initiates the beginning of window painting.

- *GetClientRect* Obtains the dimensions of the window's client area.

- *DrawText* Displays a text string.

- *EndPaint* Ends window painting.

- *PostQuitMessage* Inserts a "quit" message into the message queue.

- *DefWindowProc* Performs default processing of messages.

These functions are described in the Platform SDK documentation, and they are declared in various header files, mostly in WINUSER.H.

Uppercase Identifiers

You'll notice the use of quite a few uppercase identifiers in HELLOWIN.C. These identifiers are defined in the Windows header files. Several of these identifiers contain a two-letter or three-letter prefix followed by an underscore:

CS_HREDRAW	DT_VCENTER	SND_FILENAME
CS_VREDRAW	IDC_ARROW	WM_CREATE
CW_USEDEFAULT	IDI_APPLICATION	WM_DESTROY
DT_CENTER	MB_ICONERROR	WM_PAINT
DT_SINGLELINE	SND_ASYNC	WS_OVERLAPPEDWINDOW

These are simply numeric constants. The prefix indicates a general category to which the constant belongs, as indicated in this table:

Prefix	Constant
CS	Class style option
CW	Create window option
DT	Draw text option

Prefix	Constant
IDI	ID number for an icon
IDC	ID number for a cursor
MB	Message box options
SND	Sound option
WM	Window message
WS	Window style

You almost never need to remember numeric constants when programming for Windows. Virtually every numeric constant has an identifier defined in the header files.

New Data Types

Some other identifiers used in HELLOWIN.C are new data types, also defined in the Windows header files using either *typedef* or *#define* statements. This was originally done to ease the transition of Windows programs from the original 16-bit system to future operating systems that would be based on 32-bit technology. This didn't quite work as smoothly and transparently as everyone thought at the time, but the concept was fundamentally sound.

Sometimes these new data types are just convenient abbreviations. For example, the UINT data type used for the second parameter to *WndProc* is simply an *unsigned int*, which in Windows 98 is a 32-bit value. The PSTR data type used for the third parameter to *WinMain* is a pointer to a nonwide character string, that is, a *char *.*

Others are less obvious. For example, the third and fourth parameters to *WndProc* are defined as WPARAM and LPARAM, respectively. The origin of these names requires a bit of history. When Windows was a 16-bit system, the third parameter to *WndProc* was defined as a WORD, which was a 16-bit *unsigned short* integer, and the fourth parameter was defined as a LONG, which was a 32-bit signed *long* integer. That's the reason for the "W" and "L" prefixes on the word "PARAM." In the 32-bit versions of Windows, however, WPARAM is defined as a UINT and LPARAM is defined as a LONG (which is still the C *long* data type), so both parameters to the window procedure are 32-bit values. This may be a little confusing because the WORD data type is still defined as a 16-bit *unsigned short* integer in Windows 98, so the "W" prefix to "PARAM" creates somewhat of a misnomer.

The *WndProc* function returns a value of type LRESULT. That's simply defined as a LONG. The *WinMain* function is given a type of WINAPI (as is every Windows function call defined in the header files), and the *WndProc* function is given a type of CALLBACK. Both these identifiers are defined as *__stdcall*, which refers to a special calling sequence for function calls that occur between Windows itself and your application.

HELLOWIN also uses four data structures (which I'll discuss later in this chapter) defined in the Windows header files. These data structures are shown in the table beginning the next page.

Structure	Meaning
MSG	Message structure
WNDCLASS	Window class structure
PAINTSTRUCT	Paint structure
RECT	Rectangle structure

The first two data structures are used in *WinMain* to define two structures named *msg* and *wndclass*. The second two are used in *WndProc* to define two structures named *ps* and *rect*.

Getting a Handle on Handles

Finally, there are three uppercase identifiers for various types of "handles":

Identifier	Meaning
HINSTANCE	Handle to an "instance"—the program itself
HWND	Handle to a window
HDC	Handle to a device context

Handles are used quite frequently in Windows. Before the chapter is over, you will also encounter HICON (a handle to an icon), HCURSOR (a handle to a mouse cursor), and HBRUSH (a handle to a graphics brush).

A handle is simply a number (usually 32 bits in size) that refers to an object. The handles in Windows are similar to file handles used in conventional C or MS-DOS programming. A program almost always obtains a handle by calling a Windows function. The program uses the handle in other Windows functions to refer to the object. The actual value of the handle is unimportant to your program, but the Windows module that gives your program the handle knows how to use it to reference the object.

Hungarian Notation

You might also notice that some of the variables in HELLOWIN.C have peculiar-looking names. One example is *szCmdLine*, passed as a parameter to *WinMain*.

Many Windows programmers use a variable-naming convention known as "Hungarian Notation," in honor of the legendary Microsoft programmer Charles Simonyi. Very simply, the variable name begins with a lowercase letter or letters that denote the data type of the variable. For example, the *sz* prefix in *szCmdLine* stands for "string terminated by zero." The *h* prefix in *hInstance* and *hPrevInstance* stands for "handle;" the *i* prefix in *iCmdShow* stands for "integer." The last two parameters to *WndProc* also use Hungarian notation, although, as I explained before, *wParam* should more properly be named *uiParam* (*ui* for "unsigned integer"). But because these two parameters are defined using the data types WPARAM and LPARAM, I've chosen to retain their traditional names.

When naming structure variables, you can use the structure name (or an abbreviation of the structure name) in lowercase either as a prefix to the variable name or as the entire variable name. For example, in the *WinMain* function in HELLOWIN.C, the *msg* variable is a structure of the MSG type; *wndclass* is a structure of the WNDCLASS type. In the *WndProc* function, *ps* is a PAINTSTRUCT structure and *rect* is a RECT structure.

Hungarian notation helps you avoid errors in your code before they turn into bugs. Because the name of a variable describes both the use of a variable and its data type, you are much less likely to make coding errors involving mismatched data types.

The variable name prefixes I'll generally be using in this book are shown in the following table.

Prefix	*Data Type*
c	char or WCHAR or TCHAR
by	BYTE (unsigned char)
n	short
i	int
x, y	int used as x-coordinate or y-coordinate
cx, cy	int used as x or y length; c stands for "count"
b or *f*	BOOL (int); f stands for "flag"
w	WORD (unsigned short)
l	LONG (long)
dw	DWORD (unsigned long)
fn	function
s	string
sz	string terminated by 0 character
h	handle
p	pointer

Registering the Window Class

A window is always created based on a window class. The window class identifies the window procedure that processes messages to the window.

More than one window can be created based on a single window class. For example, all button windows—including push buttons, check boxes, and radio buttons—are created based on the same window class. The window class defines the window procedure and some other characteristics of the windows that are created based on that class. When you create a window, you define additional characteristics of the window that are unique to that window.

Before you create an application window, you must register a window class by calling *RegisterClass*. This function requires a single parameter, which is a pointer to a structure of type WNDCLASS. This structure includes two fields that are pointers to character strings, so the structure is defined two different ways in the WINUSER.H header file. First, there's the ASCII version, WNDCLASSA:

```
typedef struct tagWNDCLASSA
{
        UINT        style ;
        WNDPROC     lpfnWndProc ;
        int         cbClsExtra ;
        int         cbWndExtra ;
        HINSTANCE   hInstance ;
        HICON       hIcon ;
        HCURSOR     hCursor ;
        HBRUSH      hbrBackground ;
        LPCSTR      lpszMenuName ;
        LPCSTR      lpszClassName ;
}
WNDCLASSA, * PWNDCLASSA, NEAR * NPWNDCLASSA, FAR * LPWNDCLASSA ;
```

Notice some uses of Hungarian notation here: The *lpfn* prefix means "long pointer to a function." (Recall that in the Win32 API there is no distinction between long pointers and near pointers. This is a remnant of 16-bit Windows.) The *cb* prefix stands for "count of bytes" and is often used for a variable that denotes a byte size. The *h* prefix is a handle, and the *hbr* prefix means "handle to a brush." The *lpsz* prefix is a "long pointer to a string terminated with a zero."

The Unicode version of the structure is defined like so:

```
typedef struct tagWNDCLASSW
{
        UINT        style ;
        WNDPROC     lpfnWndProc ;
        int         cbClsExtra ;
        int         cbWndExtra ;
        HINSTANCE   hInstance ;
        HICON       hIcon ;
        HCURSOR     hCursor ;
        HBRUSH      hbrBackground ;
        LPCWSTR     lpszMenuName ;
        LPCWSTR     lpszClassName ;
}
WNDCLASSW, * PWNDCLASSW, NEAR * NPWNDCLASSW, FAR * LPWNDCLASSW ;
```

The only difference is that the last two fields are defined as pointers to constant wide-character strings rather than pointers to constant ASCII character strings.

After WINUSER.H defines the WNDCLASSA and WNDCLASSW structures (and pointers to the structures), the header file defines WNDCLASS and pointers to WNDCLASS (some included for backward compatibility) based on the definition of the UNICODE identifier:

```
#ifdef UNICODE
typedef WNDCLASSW WNDCLASS ;
typedef PWNDCLASSW PWNDCLASS ;
typedef NPWNDCLASSW NPWNDCLASS ;
typedef LPWNDCLASSW LPWNDCLASS ;
#else
typedef WNDCLASSA WNDCLASS ;
typedef PWNDCLASSA PWNDCLASS ;
typedef NPWNDCLASSA NPWNDCLASS ;
typedef LPWNDCLASSA LPWNDCLASS ;
#endif
```

When I show subsequent structures in this book, I'll just show the functionally equivalent definition of the structure, which for WNDCLASS is this:

```
typedef struct
{
     UINT        style ;
     WNDPROC     lpfnWndProc ;
     int         cbClsExtra ;
     int         cbWndExtra ;
     HINSTANCE   hInstance ;
     HICON       hIcon ;
     HCURSOR     hCursor ;
     HBRUSH      hbrBackground ;
     LPCTSTR     lpszMenuName ;
     LPCTSTR     lpszClassName ;
}
WNDCLASS, * PWNDCLASS ;
```

I'll also go easy on the various pointer definitions. There's no reason for you to clutter up your code with variable types beginning with LP and NP.

In *WinMain*, you define a structure of type WNDCLASS, generally like this:

```
WNDCLASS wndclass ;
```

You then initialize the 10 fields of the structure and call *RegisterClass*.

The two most important fields in the WNDCLASS structure are the second and the last. The second field (*lpfnWndProc*) is the address of a window procedure used for all windows based on this class. In HELLOWIN.C, this window procedure is *WndProc*. The last field is the text name of the window class. This can be whatever you want. In programs that create only one window, the window class name is commonly set to the name of the program.

The other fields describe some characteristics of the window class, as described below. Let's take a look at each field of the WNDCLASS structure in order.

The statement

```
wndclass.style = CS_HREDRAW | CS_VREDRAW ;
```

combines two 32-bit "class style" identifiers with a C bitwise OR operator. The WINUSER.H header files defines a whole collection of identifiers with the CS prefix:

```
#define CS_VREDRAW          0x0001
#define CS_HREDRAW          0x0002
#define CS_KEYCVTWINDOW     0x0004
#define CS_DBLCLKS          0x0008
#define CS_OWNDC            0x0020
#define CS_CLASSDC          0x0040
#define CS_PARENTDC         0x0080
#define CS_NOKEYCVT         0x0100
#define CS_NOCLOSE          0x0200
#define CS_SAVEBITS         0x0800
#define CS_BYTEALIGNCLIENT  0x1000
#define CS_BYTEALIGNWINDOW  0x2000
#define CS_GLOBALCLASS      0x4000
#define CS_IME              0x00010000
```

Identifiers defined in this way are often called "bit flags" because each identifier sets a single bit in a composite value. Only a few of these class styles are commonly used. The two identifiers used in HELLOWIN indicate that all windows created based on this class are to be completely repainted whenever the horizontal window size (CS_HREDRAW) or the vertical window size (CS_VREDRAW) changes. If you resize HELLOWIN's window, you'll see that the text string is redrawn to be in the new center of the window. These two identifiers ensure that this happens. We'll see shortly how the window procedure is notified of this change in window size.

The second field of the WNDCLASS structure is initialized by the statement:

```
wndclass.lpfnWndProc = WndProc ;
```

This sets the window procedure for this window class to *WndProc*, which is the second function in HELLOWIN.C. This window procedure will process all messages to all windows created based on this window class. In C, when you use a function name in a statement like this, you're really referring to a pointer to a function.

The next two fields are used to reserve some extra space in the class structure and the window structure that Windows maintains internally:

```
wndclass.cbClsExtra = 0 ;
wndclass.cbWndExtra = 0 ;
```

A program can use this extra space for its own purposes. HELLOWIN does not use this feature, so 0 is specified. Otherwise, as the Hungarian notation indicates, the field would be set to a "count of bytes." (I'll use the *cbWndExtra* field in the CHECKER3 program shown in Chapter 7.)

The next field is simply the instance handle of the program (which is one of the parameters to *WinMain*):

```
wndclass.hInstance = hInstance ;
```

The statement

```
wndclass.hIcon = LoadIcon (NULL, IDI_APPLICATION) ;
```

sets an icon for all windows created based on this window class. The icon is a small bitmap picture that represents the program to the user. When the program is running, the icon appears in the Windows taskbar and at the left side of the program window's title bar. Later in this book, you'll learn how to create customized icons for your Windows programs. Right now, we'll take an easy approach and use a predefined icon.

To obtain a handle to a predefined icon, you call *LoadIcon* with the first argument set to NULL. When you're loading your own customized icons that are stored in your program's .EXE file on disk, this argument would be set to *hInstance*, the instance handle of the program. The second argument identifies the icon. For the predefined icons, this argument is an identifier beginning with the prefix IDI ("ID for an icon") defined in WIN-USER.H. The IDI_APPLICATION icon is simply a little picture of a window. The *LoadIcon* function returns a handle to this icon. We don't really care about the actual value of the handle. It's simply used to set the value of the *hIcon* field. This field is defined in the WNDCLASS structure to be of type HICON, which stands for "handle to an icon."

The statement

```
wndclass.hCursor = LoadCursor (NULL, IDC_ARROW) ;
```

is similar to the previous statement. The *LoadCursor* function loads a predefined mouse cursor known as IDC_ARROW and returns a handle to the cursor. This handle is assigned to the *hCursor* field of the WNDCLASS structure. When the mouse cursor appears over the client area of a window that is created based on this class, the cursor becomes a small arrow.

The next field specifies the background color of the client area of windows created based on this class. The *hbr* prefix of the *hbrBackground* field name stands for "handle to a brush." A brush is a graphics term that refers to a colored pattern of pixels used to fill an area. Windows has several standard, or "stock," brushes. The *GetStockObject* call shown here returns a handle to a white brush:

```
wndclass.hbrBackground = GetStockObject (WHITE_BRUSH) ;
```

This means that the background of the client area of the window will be solid white, which is a common choice.

The next field specifies the window class menu. HELLOWIN has no application menu, so the field is set to NULL:

```
wndclass.lpszMenuName = NULL ;
```

Finally the class must be given a name. For a small program, this can be simply the name of the program, which is the "HelloWin" string stored in the *szAppName* variable.

```
wndclass.lpszClassName = szAppName ;
```

This string is composed of either ASCII characters or Unicode characters depending on whether the UNICODE identifier has been defined.

When all 10 fields of the structure have been initialized, HELLOWIN registers the window class by calling *RegisterClass*. The only argument to the function is a pointer to the WNDCLASS structure. Actually, there's a *RegisterClassA* function that takes a pointer to the WNDCLASSA structure, and a *RegisterClassW* function that takes a pointer to the WNDCLASSW structure. Which function the program uses to register the window class determines whether messages sent to the window will contain ASCII text or Unicode text.

Now here's a problem: If you have compiled the program with the UNICODE identifier defined, your program will call *RegisterClassW*. That's fine if you're running the program on Microsoft Windows NT. But if you're running the program on Windows 98, the *RegisterClassW* function is not really implemented. There's an entry point for the function, but it just returns a zero from the function call, indicating an error. This is a good opportunity for a Unicode program running under Windows 98 to inform the user of the problem and terminate. Here's the way most of the programs in this book will handle the *RegisterClass* function call:

```
if (!RegisterClass (&wndclass))
{
     MessageBox (NULL, TEXT ("This program requires Windows NT!"),
               szAppName, MB_ICONERROR) ;
     return 0 ;
}
```

The *MessageBoxW* function works properly because it is one of the few Unicode functions implemented in Windows 98.

This code fragment assumes, of course, that *RegisterClass* is not failing for some other reason, such as a NULL *lpfnWndProc* field of the WNDCLASS structure. The *GetLastError* function helps you determine the cause of the error in cases like this. *GetLastError* is a general-purpose function in Windows to get extended error information when a function call fails. The documentation of the various functions will indicate whether you can use *GetLastError* to obtain this information. In the case of calling *RegisterClassW* in Windows 98, *GetLastError* returns 120. You can look in WINERROR.H to see that the value 120 corresponds to the identifier ERROR_CALL_NOT_IMPLEMENTED. You can also look up the error in *Platform SDK/Windows Base Services/Debugging and Error Handling/Error Codes/System Errors - Numerical Order*.

Some Windows programmers like to check the return value of every function call for errors. This certainly makes some sense, and here's why: I'm sure you're familiar with the rule that you always, always check for an error when you're allocating memory. Well, many

Windows functions need to allocate some memory. For example, *RegisterClass* needs to allocate memory to store information about the window class. So you should be checking the function regardless. On the other hand, if *RegisterClass* fails because it can't allocate the memory it needs, Windows has probably already ground to a halt.

I do a minimum of error checking in the sample programs in this book. This is not because I don't think error checking is a good idea, but because it would distract from what the programs are supposed to illustrate.

Finally, a historical note: In some sample Windows programs, you might see the following code in *WinMain*:

```
if (!hPrevInstance)
{
    wndclass.cbStyle = CS_HREDRAW | CS_VREDRAW ;

        [other wndclass initialization]

    RegisterClass (&wndclass) ;
}
```

This comes under the category of "old habits die hard." In 16-bit versions of Windows, if you started up a new instance of a program that was already running, the *hPrevInstance* parameter to *WinMain* would be the instance handle of the previous instance. To save memory, two or more instances were allowed to share the same window class. Thus, the window class was registered only if *hPrevInstance* was NULL, indicating that no other instances of the program were running.

In 32-bit versions of Windows, *hPrevInstance* is always NULL. This code will still work properly, but it's not necessary to check *hPrevInstance*.

Creating the Window

The window class defines general characteristics of a window, thus allowing the same window class to be used for creating many different windows. When you go ahead and create a window by calling *CreateWindow*, you specify more detailed information about the window.

Programmers new to Windows are sometimes confused about the distinction between the window class and the window and why all the characteristics of a window can't be specified in one shot. Actually, dividing the information in this way is quite convenient. For example, all push-button windows are created based on the same window class. The window procedure associated with this window class is located inside Windows itself, and it is responsible for processing keyboard and mouse input to the push button and defining the button's visual appearance on the screen. All push buttons work the same way in this respect. But not all push buttons are the same. They almost certainly have different sizes, different locations on the screen, and different text strings. These latter characteristics are part of the window definition rather than the window class definition.

While the information passed to the *RegisterClass* function is specified in a data structure, the information passed to the *CreateWindow* function is specified as separate arguments to the function. Here's the *CreateWindow* call in HELLOWIN.C, complete with comments identifying the fields:

```
hwnd = CreateWindow (szAppName,                    // window class name
                     TEXT ("The Hello Program"),   // window caption
                     WS_OVERLAPPEDWINDOW,          // window style
                     CW_USEDEFAULT,                // initial x position
                     CW_USEDEFAULT,                // initial y position
                     CW_USEDEFAULT,                // initial x size
                     CW_USEDEFAULT,                // initial y size
                     NULL,                         // parent window handle
                     NULL,                         // window menu handle
                     hInstance,                    // program instance handle
                     NULL) ;                       // creation parameters
```

At this point I won't bother to mention that there are actually a *CreateWindowA* function and a *CreateWindowW* function, which treat the first two parameters to the function as ASCII or Unicode, respectively.

The argument marked "window class name" is *szAppName*, which contains the string "HelloWin"—the name of the window class the program just registered. This is how the window we're creating is associated with a window class.

The window created by this program is a normal overlapped window. It will have a title bar; a system menu button to the left of the title bar; a thick window-sizing border; and minimize, maximize, and close buttons to the right of the title bar. That's a standard style for windows, and it has the name WS_OVERLAPPEDWINDOW, which appears as the "window style" parameter in *CreateWindow*. If you look in WINUSER.H, you'll find that this style is a combination of several bit flags:

```
#define WS_OVERLAPPEDWINDOW (WS_OVERLAPPED   | \
                             WS_CAPTION      | \
                             WS_SYSMENU      | \
                             WS_THICKFRAME   | \
                             WS_MINIMIZEBOX  | \
                             WS_MAXIMIZEBOX)
```

The "window caption" is the text that will appear in the title bar of the window.

The arguments marked "initial x position" and "initial y position" specify the initial position of the upper left corner of the window relative to the upper left corner of the screen. By using the identifier CW_USEDEFAULT for these parameters, we are indicating that we want Windows to use the default position for an overlapped window. (CW_USEDEFAULT is defined as 0x80000000.) By default, Windows positions successive newly created windows at stepped horizontal and vertical offsets from the upper left corner of the display. Similarly, the "initial x size" and "initial y size" arguments specify the initial width and height of the window. The CW_USEDEFAULT identifier again indicates that we want Windows to use a default size for the window.

The argument marked "parent window handle" is set to NULL when creating a "top-level" window, such as an application window. Normally, when a parent-child relationship exists between two windows, the child window always appears on the surface of its parent. An application window appears on the surface of the desktop window, but you don't need to find out the desktop window's handle to call *CreateWindow*.

The "window menu handle" is also set to NULL because the window has no menu. The "program instance handle" is set to the instance handle passed to the program as a parameter of *WinMain*. Finally, a "creation parameters" pointer is set to NULL. You could use this parameter to point to some data that you might later want to reference in your program.

The *CreateWindow* call returns a handle to the created window. This handle is saved in the variable *hwnd*, which is defined to be of type HWND ("handle to a window"). Every window in Windows has a handle. Your program uses the handle to refer to the window. Many Windows functions require *hwnd* as an argument so that Windows knows which window the function applies to. If a program creates many windows, each has a different handle. The handle to a window is one of the most important handles that a Windows program (pardon the expression) handles.

Displaying the Window

After the *CreateWindow* call returns, the window has been created internally in Windows. What this means basically is that Windows has allocated a block of memory to hold all the information about the window that you specified in the *CreateWindow* call, plus some other information, all of which Windows can find later based on the window handle.

However, the window does not yet appear on the video display. Two more calls are needed. The first is

```
ShowWindow (hwnd, iCmdShow) ;
```

The first argument is the handle to the window just created by *CreateWindow*. The second argument is the *iCmdShow* value passed as a parameter to *WinMain*. This determines how the window is to be initially displayed on the screen, whether it's normal, minimized, or maximized. The user probably selected a preference when adding the program to the Start menu. The value you receive from *WinMain* and pass to *ShowWindow* is SW_SHOWNORMAL if the window is displayed normally, SW_SHOWMAXIMIZED if the window is to be maximized, and SW_SHOWMINNOACTIVE if the window is just to be displayed in the taskbar.

The *ShowWindow* function puts the window on the display. If the second argument to *ShowWindow* is SW_SHOWNORMAL, the client area of the window is erased with the background brush specified in the window class. The function call

```
UpdateWindow (hwnd) ;
```

then causes the client area to be painted. It accomplishes this by sending the window procedure (that is, the *WndProc* function in HELLOWIN.C) a WM_PAINT message. We'll soon examine how *WndProc* deals with this message.

The Message Loop

After the *UpdateWindow* call, the window is fully visible on the video display. The program must now make itself ready to read keyboard and mouse input from the user. Windows maintains a "message queue" for each Windows program currently running under Windows. When an input event occurs, Windows translates the event into a "message" that it places in the program's message queue.

A program retrieves these messages from the message queue by executing a block of code known as the "message loop":

```
while (GetMessage (&msg, NULL, 0, 0))
{
     TranslateMessage (&msg) ;
     DispatchMessage (&msg) ;
}
```

The *msg* variable is a structure of type MSG, which is defined in the WINUSER.H header file like this:

```
typedef struct tagMSG
{
     HWND    hwnd ;
     UINT    message ;
     WPARAM  wParam ;
     LPARAM  lParam ;
     DWORD   time ;
     POINT   pt ;
}
MSG, * PMSG ;
```

The POINT data type is yet another structure, defined in the WINDEF.H header file like this:

```
typedef struct tagPOINT
{
     LONG  x ;
     LONG  y ;
}
POINT, * PPOINT;
```

The *GetMessage* call that begins the message loop retrieves a message from the message queue:

```
GetMessage (&msg, NULL, 0, 0)
```

This call passes to Windows a pointer to a MSG structure named *msg*. The second, third, and fourth arguments are set to NULL or 0 to indicate that the program wants all messages for all windows created by the program. Windows fills in the fields of the message structure with the next message from the message queue. The fields of this structure are:

- *hwnd*   The handle to the window which the message is directed to. In the HELLOWIN program, this is the same as the *hwnd* value returned from *Create-Window*, because that's the only window the program has.

- *message*   The message identifier. This is a number that identifies the message. For each message, there is a corresponding identifier defined in the Windows header files (most of them in WINUSER.H) that begins with the identifier WM ("window message"). For example, if you position the mouse pointer over HELLOWIN's client area and press the left mouse button, Windows will put a message in the message queue with a *message* field equal to WM_LBUTTON-DOWN, which is the value 0x0201.

- *wParam*   A 32-bit "message parameter," the meaning and value of which depend on the particular message.

- *lParam*   Another 32-bit message parameter dependent on the message.

- *time*   The time the message was placed in the message queue.

- *pt*   The mouse coordinates at the time the message was placed in the message queue.

If the *message* field of the message retrieved from the message queue is anything except WM_QUIT (which equals 0x0012), *GetMessage* returns a nonzero value. A WM_QUIT message causes *GetMessage* to return 0.

The statement:

```
TranslateMessage (&msg) ;
```

passes the *msg* structure back to Windows for some keyboard translation. (I'll discuss this more in Chapter 6.) The statement

```
DispatchMessage (&msg) ;
```

again passes the *msg* structure back to Windows. Windows then sends the message to the appropriate window procedure for processing. What this means is that Windows calls the window procedure. In HELLOWIN, the window procedure is *WndProc*. After *WndProc* processes the message, it returns control to Windows, which is still servicing the *DispatchMessage* call. When Windows returns to HELLOWIN following the *DispatchMessage* call, the message loop continues with the next *GetMessage* call.

The Window Procedure

All that I've described so far is really just overhead. The window class has been registered, the window has been created, the window has been displayed on the screen, and the program has entered a message loop to retrieve messages from the message queue.

The real action occurs in the window procedure. The window procedure determines what the window displays in its client area and how the window responds to user input.

In HELLOWIN, the window procedure is the function named *WndProc*. A window procedure can have any name (as long as it doesn't conflict with some other name, of course). A Windows program can contain more than one window procedure. A window procedure is always associated with a particular window class that you register by calling *RegisterClass*. The *CreateWindow* function creates a window based on a particular window class. More than one window can be created based on the same window class.

A window procedure is always defined like this:

```
LRESULT CALLBACK WndProc (HWND hwnd, UINT message, WPARAM wParam, LPARAM lParam)
```

The four parameters to the window procedure are identical to the first four fields of the MSG structure. The first parameter is *hwnd*, the handle to the window receiving the message. This is the same handle returned from the *CreateWindow* function. For a program like HELLOWIN, which creates only one window, this is the only window handle the program knows about. If a program creates multiple windows based on the same window class (and hence the same window procedure), *hwnd* identifies the particular window receiving the message.

The second parameter is the same as the *message* field in the MSG structure. It's a number that identifies the message. The last two parameters are 32-bit message parameters that provide more information about the message. What these parameters contain is specific to each type of message. Sometimes a message parameter is two 16-bit values stuck together, and sometimes a message parameter is a pointer to a text string or to a data structure.

Programs generally don't call window procedures directly. The window procedure is almost always called from Windows itself. A program can indirectly call its own window procedure by calling a function named *SendMessage*, which we'll examine in later chapters.

Processing the Messages

Every message that a window procedure receives is identified by a number, which is the *message* parameter to the window procedure. The Windows header file WINUSER.H defines identifiers beginning with the prefix WM ("window message") for each type of message.

Generally, Windows programmers use a *switch* and *case* construction to determine what message the window procedure is receiving and how to process it accordingly. When a window procedure processes a message, it should return 0 from the window procedure. All messages that a window procedure chooses not to process must be passed to a Windows function named *DefWindowProc*. The value returned from *DefWindowProc* must be returned from the window procedure.

In HELLOWIN, *WndProc* chooses to process only three messages: WM_CREATE, WM_PAINT, and WM_DESTROY. The window procedure is structured like this:

```
switch (iMsg)
{
case WM_CREATE :
     [process WM_CREATE message]
     return 0 ;

case WM_PAINT :
     [process WM_PAINT message]
     return 0 ;

case WM_DESTROY :
     [process WM_DESTROY message]
     return 0 ;
}
return DefWindowProc (hwnd, iMsg, wParam, lParam) ;
```

It is important to call *DefWindowProc* for default processing of all messages that your window procedure does not process. Otherwise behavior regarded as normal, such as being able to terminate the program, will not work.

Playing a Sound File

The very first message that a window procedure receives—and the first that HELLOWIN's *WndProc* chooses to process—is WM_CREATE. *WndProc* receives this message while Windows is processing the *CreateWindow* function in *WinMain*. That is, when HELLOWIN calls *CreateWindow*, Windows does what it has to do and, in the process, Windows calls *WndProc* with the first argument set to the window handle and the second argument set to WM_CREATE (the value 1). *WndProc* processes the WM_CREATE message and returns controls back to Windows. Windows can then return to HELLOWIN from the *CreateWindow* call to continue further progress in *WinMain*.

Often a window procedure performs one-time window initialization during WM_CREATE processing. HELLOWIN chooses to process this message by playing a waveform sound file named HELLOWIN.WAV. It does this using the simple *PlaySound* function, which is described in */Platform SDK/Graphics and Multimedia Services/Multimedia Audio/ Waveform Audio* and documented in */Platform SDK/Graphics and Multimedia Services/ Multimedia Reference/Multimedia Functions*.

The first argument to *PlaySound* is the name of a waveform file. (It could also be a sound alias name defined in the Sounds section of the Control Panel or a program resource.)

The second argument is used only if the sound file is a resource. The third argument specifies a couple of options. In this case, I've indicated that the first argument is a filename and that the sound is to be played asynchronously—that is, the *PlaySound* function call is to return as soon as the sound file starts playing without waiting for it to complete. That way the program can continue with its initialization.

WndProc concludes WM_CREATE processing by returning 0 from the window procedure.

The WM_PAINT Message

The second message that *WndProc* processes is WM_PAINT. This message is extremely important in Windows programming. It informs a program when part or all of the window's client area is "invalid" and must be "updated," which means that it must be redrawn or "painted."

How does a client area become invalid? When the window is first created, the entire client area is invalid because the program has not yet drawn anything on the window. The first WM_PAINT message (which normally occurs when the program calls *UpdateWindow* in *WinMain*) directs the window procedure to draw something on the client area.

When you resize HELLOWIN's window, the client area becomes invalid. You'll recall that the *style* field of HELLOWIN's *wndclass* structure was set to the flags CS_HREDRAW and CS_VREDRAW. This directs Windows to invalidate the whole window when the size changes. The window procedure then receives a WM_PAINT message.

When you minimize HELLOWIN and then restore the window again to its previous size, Windows does not save the contents of the client area. Under a graphical environment, this would be too much data to retain. Instead, Windows invalidates the window. The window procedure receives a WM_PAINT message and itself restores the contents of its window.

When you move windows around the screen so that they overlap, Windows does not save the area of a window covered by another window. When that area of the window is later uncovered, it is flagged as invalid. The window procedure receives a WM_PAINT message to repaint the contents of the window.

WM_PAINT processing almost always begins with a call to *BeginPaint*:

```
hdc = BeginPaint (hwnd, &ps) ;
```

and ends with a call to *EndPaint*:

```
EndPaint (hwnd, &ps) ;
```

In both cases, the first argument is a handle to the program's window, and the second argument is a pointer to a structure of type PAINTSTRUCT. The PAINTSTRUCT structure contains some information that a window procedure can use for painting the client area. I'll discuss the fields of this structure in the next chapter; for now, we'll just use it in the *BeginPaint* and *EndPaint* functions.

During the *BeginPaint* call, Windows erases the background of the client area if it hasn't been erased already. It erases the background using the brush specified in the *hbrBackground* field of the WNDCLASS structure used to register the window class. In the case of HELLOWIN, this is a stock white brush, which means that Windows erases the background of the window by coloring it white. The *BeginPaint* call validates the entire client area and returns a "handle to a device context." A device context refers to a physical output device (such as a video display) and its device driver. You need the device context handle to display text and graphics in the client area of a window. Using the device context handle returned from *BeginPaint*, you cannot draw outside the client area, even if you try. *EndPaint* releases the device context handle so that it is no longer valid.

If a window procedure does not process WM_PAINT messages (which is very rare), they must be passed on to *DefWindowProc*. *DefWindowProc* simply calls *BeginPaint* and *EndPaint* in succession so that the client area is validated.

After *WndProc* calls *BeginPaint*, it calls *GetClientRect*:

```
GetClientRect (hwnd, &rect) ;
```

The first argument is the handle to the program's window. The second argument is a pointer to a rectangle structure of type RECT. This structure has four LONG fields named *left*, *top*, *right*, and *bottom*. The *GetClientRect* function sets these four fields to the dimensions of the client area of the window. The *left* and *top* fields are always set to 0. Thus, the *right* and *bottom* fields represent the width and height of the client area in pixels.

WndProc doesn't do anything with this RECT structure except pass a pointer to it as the fourth argument to *DrawText*:

```
DrawText (hdc, TEXT ("Hello, Windows 98!"), -1, &rect,
          DT_SINGLELINE | DT_CENTER | DT_VCENTER) ;
```

DrawText, as the name implies, draws text. Because this function draws something, the first argument is a handle to the device context returned from *BeginPaint*. The second argument is the text to draw, and the third argument is set to −1 to indicate that the text string is terminated with a zero character.

The last argument to *DrawText* is a series of bit flags defined in WINUSER.H. (Although *DrawText* seems to be a GDI function call because it displays output, it's actually considered part of the User module because it's a fairly high-level drawing function. The function is documented in */Platform SDK/Graphics and Multimedia Services/GDI/Fonts and Text.*) The flags indicate that the text should be displayed as a single line centered horizontally and vertically within the rectangle specified by the fourth argument. This function call thus causes the string "Hello, Windows 98!" to be displayed centered in the client area.

Whenever the client area becomes invalid (as it does when you change the size of the window), *WndProc* receives a new WM_PAINT message. *WndProc* obtains the updated window size by calling *GetClientRect* and again displays the text in the next center of the window.

The WM_DESTROY Message

The WM_DESTROY message is another important message. This message indicates that Windows is in the process of destroying a window based on a command from the user. The message is a result of the user clicking on the Close button or selecting Close from the program's system menu. (Later in this chapter, I'll discuss in more detail how the WM_DESTROY message gets generated.)

HELLOWIN responds to the WM_DESTROY message in a standard way by calling

```
PostQuitMessage (0) ;
```

This function inserts a WM_QUIT message in the program's message queue. I mentioned earlier that *GetMessage* returns nonzero for any message other than WM_QUIT that it retrieves from the message queue. When *GetMessage* retrieves a WM_QUIT message, *GetMessage* returns 0. This causes *WinMain* to drop out of the message loop. The program then executes the following statement:

```
return msg.wParam ;
```

The *wParam* field of the structure is the value passed to the *PostQuitMessage* function (generally 0). The return statement exits from *WinMain* and terminates the program.

THE WINDOWS PROGRAMMING HURDLES

Even with my explanation of HELLOWIN, the structure and workings of the program are probably still quite mysterious. In a short C program written for a character-mode environment, the entire program might be contained in the *main* function. In HELLOWIN, *WinMain* contains only program overhead necessary to register the window class, create the window, and retrieve and dispatch messages from the message queue.

All the real action of the program occurs in the window procedure. In HELLOWIN, this action is not much—*WndProc* simply plays a sound file and displays a text string in its window. But in later chapters, you'll find that almost everything a Windows program does is in response to a message to a window procedure. This is one of the major conceptual hurdles you must leap to begin writing Windows programs.

Don't Call Me, I'll Call You

Programmers are well acquainted with the idea of calling on the operating system to do something. For example, C programmers use the *fopen* function to open a file. The *fopen* function is implemented with a call to the operating system to open a file. No problem.

But Windows is different. Although Windows has a couple thousand function calls, Windows also makes calls to *your* program, specifically to the window procedure we have called *WndProc*. The window procedure is associated with a window class that the program registers by calling *RegisterClass*. A window that is created based on this window class uses this window procedure for processing all messages to the window. Windows sends a message to the window by calling the window procedure.

Windows calls *WndProc* when a window is first created. Windows calls *WndProc* when the window is eventually destroyed. Windows calls *WndProc* when the window has been resized or moved or minimized. Windows calls *WndProc* when a user clicks on the window with the mouse. Windows calls *WndProc* when characters are typed from the keyboard. Windows calls *WndProc* when an item has been selected from a menu. Windows calls *WndProc* when a scroll bar is manipulated or clicked with the mouse. Windows calls *WndProc* to tell it when it must repaint its client area.

All these calls to *WndProc* are in the form of messages. In most Windows programs, the bulk of the program is dedicated to handling these messages. The messages that Windows can send to a program are generally identified with names that begin with the letters WM and are defined in the WINUSER.H header file.

Actually, the idea of a routine within a program that is called from outside the program is not unheard of in character-mode programming. The *signal* function in C can trap a Ctrl-C break or other interrupts from the operating system. Old programs written for MS-DOS often trapped hardware interrupts.

But in Windows this concept is extended to cover everything. Everything that happens to a window is relayed to the window procedure in the form of a message. The window procedure then responds to this message in some way or passes the message to *DefWindowProc* for default processing.

The *wParam* and *lParam* parameters to the window procedure are not used in HELLOWIN except as parameters to *DefWindowProc*. These parameters give the window procedure additional information about the message. The meaning of the parameters is message-dependent.

Let's look at an example. Whenever the client area of a window changes in size, Windows calls that window's window procedure. The *hwnd* parameter to the window procedure is the handle of the window changing in size. (Remember that one window procedure could be handling messages for multiple windows that were created based on the same window class. The *hwnd* parameter lets the window procedure know which window is receiving the message.) The *message* parameter is WM_SIZE. The *wParam* parameter for a WM_SIZE message is the value SIZE_RESTORED, SIZE_MINIMIZED, SIZE_MAXIMIZED, SIZE_MAXSHOW, or SIZE_MAXHIDE (defined in the WINUSER.H header file as the numbers 0 through 4). That is, the *wParam* parameter indicates whether the window is being changed to a nonminimized or nonmaximized size, being minimized, being maximized, or being hidden.

The *lParam* parameter contains the new size of the window. The new width (a 16-bit value) and the new height (a 16-bit value) are stuck together in the 32-bit *lParam*. The WINDEF.H header file defines some handy macros that help you extract these two values from *lParam*. We'll do this in the next chapter.

Sometimes messages generate other messages as a result of *DefWindowProc* processing. For example, suppose you run HELLOWIN and you eventually click the Close button, or suppose you select Close from the system menu using either the keyboard or the mouse. *DefWindowProc* processes this keyboard or mouse input. When it detects that you have selected the Close option, it sends a WM_SYSCOMMAND message to the window procedure. *WndProc* passes this message to *DefWindowProc*. *DefWindowProc* responds by sending a WM_CLOSE message to the window procedure. *WndProc* again passes this message to *DefWindowProc*. *DefWindowProc* responds to the WM_CLOSE message by calling *DestroyWindow*. *DestroyWindow* causes Windows to send a WM_DESTROY message to the window procedure. *WndProc* finally responds to this message by calling *PostQuitMessage* to put a WM_QUIT message in the message queue. This message causes the message loop in *WinMain* to terminate and the program to end.

Queued and Nonqueued Messages

I've talked about Windows sending messages to a window, which means that Windows calls the window procedure. But a Windows program also has a message loop that retrieves messages from a message queue by calling *GetMessage* and dispatches these messages to the window procedure by calling *DispatchMessage*.

So, does a Windows program poll for messages (much like a character-mode program polling for keyboard input) and then route these messages to some location? Or does it receive messages directly from outside the program? Well, both.

Messages can be either "queued" or "nonqueued." The queued messages are those that are placed in a program's message queue by Windows. In the program's message loop, the messages are retrieved and dispatched to the window procedure. The nonqueued messages are the results of calls by Windows directly to the window procedure. It is said that queued messages are "posted" to a message queue and that nonqueued messages are "sent" to the window procedure. In any case, the window procedure gets all the messages— both queued and nonqueued—for the window. The window procedure is "message central" for the window.

The queued messages are primarily those that result from user input in the form of keystrokes (such as the WM_KEYDOWN and WM_KEYUP messages), characters that result from keystrokes (WM_CHAR), mouse movement (WM_MOUSEMOVE), and mouse-button clicks (WM_LBUTTONDOWN). Queued messages also include the timer message (WM_TIMER), the repaint message (WM_PAINT), and the quit message (WM_QUIT).

The nonqueued messages are everything else. Nonqueued messages often result from calling certain Windows functions. For example, when *WinMain* calls *CreateWindow*, Windows creates the window and in the process sends the window procedure a WM_CREATE message. When *WinMain* calls *ShowWindow*, Windows sends the window procedure WM_SIZE and WM_SHOWWINDOW messages. When *WinMain* calls *UpdateWindow*,

Windows sends the window procedure a WM_PAINT message. Queued messages signaling keyboard or mouse input can also result in nonqueued messages. For example, when you select a menu item with the keyboard or mouse, the keyboard or mouse message is queued but the eventual WM_COMMAND message indicating that a menu item has been selected is nonqueued.

This process is obviously complex, but fortunately most of the complexity is Windows' problem rather than our program's. From the perspective of the window procedure, these messages come through in an orderly and synchronized manner. The window procedure can do something with these messages or ignore them.

When I say that messages come through in an orderly and synchronized manner, I mean first that messages are not like hardware interrupts. While processing one message in a window procedure, the program will not be suddenly interrupted by another message.

Although Windows programs can have multiple threads of execution, each thread's message queue handles messages for only the windows whose window procedures are executed in that thread. In other words, the message loop and the window procedure do not run concurrently. When a message loop retrieves a message from its message queue and calls *DispatchMessage* to send the message off to the window procedure, *DispatchMessage* does not return until the window procedure has returned control back to Windows.

However, the window procedure could call a function that sends the window procedure another message, in which case the window procedure must finish processing the second message before the function call returns, at which time the window procedure proceeds with the original message. For example, when a window procedure calls *UpdateWindow*, Windows calls the window procedure with a WM_PAINT message. When the window procedure finishes processing the WM_PAINT message, the *UpdateWindow* call will return controls back to the window procedure.

This means that window procedures must be reentrant. In most cases, this doesn't cause problems, but you should be aware of it. For example, suppose you set a static variable in the window procedure while processing a message and then you call a Windows function. Upon return from that function, can you be assured that the variable is still the same? Not necessarily—not if the particular Windows function you call generated another message and the window procedure changes the variable while processing that second message. This is one of the reasons why certain forms of compiler optimization must be turned off when compiling Windows programs.

In many cases, the window procedure must retain information it obtains in one message and use it while processing another message. This information must be saved in variables defined as *static* in the window procedure, or saved in global variables.

Of course, you'll get a much better feel for all of this in later chapters as the window procedures are expanded to process more messages.

Get In and Out Fast

Windows 98 and Windows NT are preemptive multitasking environments. This means that as one program is doing a lengthy job, Windows can allow the user to switch control to another program. This is a good thing, and it is one advantage of the current versions of Windows over the older 16-bit versions.

However, because of the way that Windows is structured, this preemptive multitasking does not always work the way you might like. For example, suppose your program spends a minute or two processing a particular message. Yes, the user can switch to another program. But the user cannot do anything with *your* program. The user cannot move your program's window, resize it, minimize it, close it, nothing. That's because your window procedure is busy doing a lengthy job. Oh, it may not seem like the window procedure performs its own moving and sizing operations, but it does. That's part of the job of *DefWindowProc*, which must be considered as part of your window procedure.

If your program needs to perform lengthy jobs while processing particular messages, there are ways to do so politely that I'll describe in Chapter 20. Even with preemptive multitasking, it's not a good idea to leave your window sitting inert on the screen. It annoys users. It annoys users just as much as bugs, nonstandard behavior, and incomplete help files. Give the user a break, and return quickly from all messages.

Chapter 4

An Exercise in Text Output

In the previous chapter, we explored the workings of a simple Windows 98 program that displayed a single line of text in the center of its window or, more precisely, the center of its client area. As we learned, the client area is that part of the total application window that is not taken up by the title bar, the window-sizing border, and, optionally, the menu bar, tool bars, status bar, and scroll bars. In short, the client area is the part of the window on which a program is free to draw and deliver visual information to the user.

You can do almost anything you want with your program's client area—anything, that is, except assume that it will be a particular size or that the size will remain constant while your program is running. If you are not accustomed to writing programs for a graphical windowing environment, these stipulations may come as a bit of a shock. You can't think in terms of a fixed number of 80-character lines. Your program must share the video display with other Windows programs. The Windows user controls how the programs' windows are arranged on the screen. Although it is possible for a programmer to create a window of a fixed size (which might be appropriate for calculators or similar utilities), users are usually able to size application windows. Your program must accept the size it's given and do something reasonable with it.

This works both ways. Just as your program may find itself with a client area barely large enough in which to say "Hello," it may also someday be run on a big-screen, high-resolution video system and discover a client area large enough for two entire pages of text and plenty of closet space besides. Dealing intelligently with both eventualities is an important part of Windows programming.

In this chapter, we will learn how a program displays something on the surface of its client area with more sophistication than that illustrated in the last chapter. When a program displays text or graphics in its client area, it is often said to be "painting" its client area. This chapter is about learning to paint.

Although Windows has extensive Graphics Device Interface (GDI) functions for displaying graphics, in this chapter I'll stick to displaying simple lines of text. I'll also ignore the various font faces and font sizes that Windows makes available and use only Windows' default "system font." This may seem limiting, but it really isn't. The problems we will encounter and solve in this chapter apply to all Windows programming. When you display a combination of text and graphics, the character dimensions of Windows' default font often determine the dimensions of the graphics.

Although this chapter is ostensibly about learning how to paint, it's really about learning the basics of device-independent programming. Windows programs can assume little about the size of their client areas or even the size of text characters. Instead, they must use the facilities that Windows provides to obtain information about the environment in which the program runs.

PAINTING AND REPAINTING

In character-mode environments, programs can generally write to any part of the video display. What the program puts on the display will stay there and not mysteriously disappear. The program can then discard the information needed to re-create the screen display.

In Windows, you can draw text and graphics only in the client area of your window, and you cannot be assured that what you put will remain there until your program specifically writes over it. For instance, the user may move another program's window on the screen so that it partially covers your application's window. Windows will not attempt to save the area of your window that the other program covers. When the program is moved away, Windows will request that your program repaint this portion of your client area.

Windows is a message-driven system. Windows informs applications of various events by posting messages in the application's message queue or sending messages to the appropriate window procedure. Windows informs a window procedure that part of the window's client area needs painting by posting a WM_PAINT message.

The WM_PAINT Message

Most Windows programs call the function *UpdateWindow* during initialization in *WinMain* shortly before entering the message loop. Windows takes this opportunity to send the window procedure its first WM_PAINT message. This message informs the window procedure that the client area must be painted. Thereafter, that window procedure should be ready at almost any time to process additional WM_PAINT messages and even to repaint the entire client area of the window if necessary. A window procedure receives a WM_PAINT message whenever one of the following events occurs:

- A previously hidden area of the window is brought into view when a user moves a window or uncovers a window.

- The user resizes the window (if the window class style has the CS_HREDRAW and CW_VREDRAW bits set).

- The program uses the *ScrollWindow* or *ScrollDC* function to scroll part of its client area.

- The program uses the *InvalidateRect* or *InvalidateRgn* function to explicitly generate a WM_PAINT message.

In some cases when part of the client area is temporarily written over, Windows attempts to save an area of the display and restore it later. This is not always successful. Windows may sometimes post a WM_PAINT message when:

- Windows removes a dialog box or message box that was overlaying part of the window.

- A menu is pulled down and then released.

- A tool tip is displayed.

In a few cases, Windows always saves the area of the display it overwrites and then restores it. This is the case whenever:

- The mouse cursor is moved across the client area.

- An icon is dragged across the client area.

Dealing with WM_PAINT message requires that you alter the way you think about how you write to the video display. Your program should be structured so that it accumulates all the information necessary to paint the client area but paints only "on demand"— when Windows sends the window procedure a WM_PAINT message. If your program needs to update its client area at some other time, it can force Windows to generate this WM_PAINT message. This may seem a roundabout method of displaying something on the screen, but the structure of your program will benefit from it.

Valid and Invalid Rectangles

Although a window procedure should be prepared to update the entire client area whenever it receives a WM_PAINT message, it often needs to update only a smaller area, most often a rectangular area within the client area. This is most obvious when a dialog box overlies part of the client area. Repainting is required only for the rectangular area uncovered when the dialog box is removed.

That area is known as an "invalid region" or "update region." The presence of an invalid region in a client area is what prompts Windows to place a WM_PAINT message in the application's message queue. Your window procedure receives a WM_PAINT message only if part of your client area is invalid.

Windows internally maintains a "paint information structure" for each window. This structure contains, among other information, the coordinates of the smallest rectangle that encompasses the invalid region. This is known as the "invalid rectangle." If another region of the client area becomes invalid before the window procedure processes a pending WM_PAINT message, Windows calculates a new invalid region (and a new invalid rectangle) that encompasses both areas and stores this updated information in the paint information structure. Windows does not place multiple WM_PAINT messages in the message queue.

A window procedure can invalidate a rectangle in its own client area by calling *InvalidateRect*. If the message queue already contains a WM_PAINT message, Windows calculates a new invalid rectangle. Otherwise, it places a WM_PAINT message in the message queue. A window procedure can obtain the coordinates of the invalid rectangle when it receives a WM_PAINT message (as we'll see later in this chapter). It can also obtain these coordinates at any other time by calling *GetUpdateRect*.

After the window procedure calls *BeginPaint* during the WM_PAINT message, the entire client area is validated. A program can also validate any rectangular area within the client area by calling the *ValidateRect* function. If this call has the effect of validating the entire invalid area, then any WM_PAINT message currently in the queue is removed.

AN INTRODUCTION TO GDI

To paint the client area of your window, you use Windows' Graphics Device Interface (GDI) functions. Windows provides several GDI functions for writing text strings to the client area of the window. We've already encountered the *DrawText* function in the last chapter, but the most commonly used text output function is undoubtedly *TextOut*. This function has the following format:

```
TextOut (hdc, x, y, psText, iLength) ;
```

TextOut writes a character string to the client area of the window. The *psText* argument is a pointer to the character string, and *iLength* is the length of the string in characters. The *x* and *y* arguments define the starting position of the character string in the client area. (More details soon on how these work.) The *hdc* argument is a "handle to a device context," and it is an important part of GDI. Virtually every GDI function requires this handle as the first argument to the function.

The Device Context

A handle, you'll recall, is simply a number that Windows uses for internal reference to an object. You obtain the handle from Windows and then use the handle in other functions. The device context handle is your window's passport to the GDI functions. With that device context handle you are free to paint your client area and make it as beautiful or as ugly as you like.

The device context (also called simply the "DC") is really just a data structure maintained internally by GDI. A device context is associated with a particular display device, such as a video display or a printer. For a video display, a device context is usually associated with a particular window on the display.

Some of the values in the device context are graphics "attributes." These attributes define some particulars of how GDI drawing functions work. With *TextOut*, for instance, the attributes of the device context determine the color of the text, the color of the text background, how the x-coordinate and y-coordinate in the *TextOut* function are mapped to the client area of the window, and what font Windows uses when displaying the text.

When a program needs to paint, it must first obtain a handle to a device context. When you obtain this handle, Windows fills the internal device context structure with default attribute values. As you'll see in later chapters, you can change these defaults by calling various GDI functions. Other GDI functions let you obtain the current values of these attributes. Then, of course, there are still other GDI functions that let you actually paint the client area of the window.

After a program has finished painting its client area, it should release the device context handle. When a program releases the handle, the handle is no longer valid and must not be used. The program should obtain the handle and release the handle during the processing of a single message. Except for a device context created with a call to *CreateDC* (a function I won't discuss in this chapter), you should not keep a device context handle around from one message to another.

Windows applications generally use two methods for getting a device context handle in preparation for painting the screen.

Getting a Device Context Handle: Method One

You use this method when you process WM_PAINT messages. Two functions are involved: *BeginPaint* and *EndPaint*. These two functions require the handle to the window, which is passed to the window procedure as an argument, and the address of a structure variable of type PAINTSTRUCT, which is defined in the WINUSER.H header file. Windows programmers usually name this structure variable *ps* and define it within the window procedure like so:

```
PAINTSTRUCT ps ;
```

While processing a WM_PAINT message, the window procedure first calls *BeginPaint*. The *BeginPaint* function generally causes the background of the invalid region to be erased in preparation for painting. The function also fills in the fields of the *ps* structure. The value returned from *BeginPaint* is the device context handle. This is commonly saved in a variable named *hdc*. You define this variable in your window procedure like so:

```
HDC hdc ;
```

The HDC data type is defined as a 32-bit unsigned integer. The program may then use GDI functions, such as *TextOut*, that require the handle to the device context. A call to *EndPaint* releases the device context handle.

Typically, processing of the WM_PAINT message looks like this:

```
case WM_PAINT:
    hdc = BeginPaint (hwnd, &ps) ;
        [use GDI functions]
    EndPaint (hwnd, &ps) ;
    return 0 ;
```

The window procedure must call *BeginPaint* and *EndPaint* as a pair while processing the WM_PAINT message. If a window procedure does not process WM_PAINT messages, it must pass the WM_PAINT message to *DefWindowProc*, which is the default window procedure located in Windows. *DefWindowProc* processes WM_PAINT messages with the following code:

```
case WM_PAINT:
    BeginPaint (hwnd, &ps) ;
    EndPaint (hwnd, &ps) ;
    return 0 ;
```

The sequence of *BeginPaint* and *EndPaint* calls with nothing in between validates the previously invalid region.

But don't do this:

```
case WM_PAINT:
    return 0 ;    // WRONG !!!
```

Windows places a WM_PAINT message in the message queue because part of the client area is invalid. Unless you call *BeginPaint* and *EndPaint* (or *ValidateRect*), Windows will not validate that area. Instead, Windows will send you another WM_PAINT message, and another, and another, and another....

The Paint Information Structure

Earlier I mentioned a "paint information structure" that Windows maintains for each window. That's what PAINTSTRUCT is. The structure is defined as follows:

```
typedef struct tagPAINTSTRUCT
{
     HDC        hdc ;
     BOOL       fErase ;
     RECT       rcPaint ;
     BOOL       fRestore ;
     BOOL       fIncUpdate ;
     BYTE       rgbReserved[32] ;
} PAINTSTRUCT ;
```

Windows fills in the fields of this structure when your program calls *BeginPaint*. Your program can use only the first three fields. The others are used internally by Windows. The *hdc* field is the handle to the device context. In a redundancy typical of Windows, the value returned from *BeginPaint* is also this device context handle. In most cases, *fErase* will be flagged FALSE (0), meaning that Windows has already erased the background of the invalid rectangle. This happens earlier in the *BeginPaint* function. (If you want to do some customized background erasing in your window procedure, you can process the WM_ERASEBKGND message.) Windows erases the background using the brush specified in the *hbrBackground* field of the WNDCLASS structure that you use when registering the window class during *WinMain* initialization. Many Windows programs specify a white brush for the window background. This is indicated when the program sets up the fields of the window class structure with a statement like this:

```
wndclass.hbrBackground = (HBRUSH) GetStockObject (WHITE_BRUSH) ;
```

However, if your program invalidates a rectangle of the client area by calling *InvalidateRect*, the last argument of the function specifies whether you want the background erased. If this argument is FALSE (that is, 0), Windows will not erase the background and the *fErase* field of the PAINTSTRUCT structure will be TRUE (nonzero) after you call *BeginPaint*.

The *rcPaint* field of the PAINTSTRUCT structure is a structure of type RECT. As you learned in Chapter 3, the RECT structure defines a rectangle with four fields named *left*, *top*, *right*, and *bottom*. The *rcPaint* field in the PAINTSTRUCT structure defines the boundaries of the invalid rectangle, as shown in Figure 4-1 on the next page. The values are in units of pixels relative to the upper left corner of the client area. The invalid rectangle is the area that you should repaint.

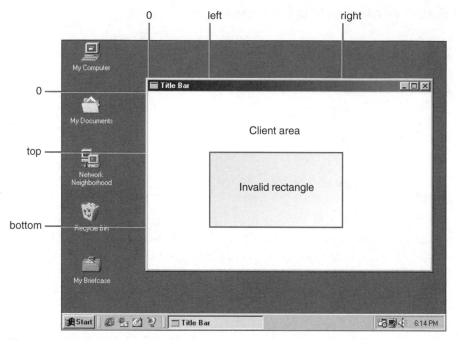

Figure 4-1. *The boundaries of the invalid rectangle.*

The *rcPaint* rectangle in PAINTSTRUCT is not only the invalid rectangle; it is also a "clipping" rectangle. This means that Windows restricts painting to within the clipping rectangle. More precisely, if the invalid region is not rectangular, Windows restricts painting to within that region.

To paint outside the update rectangle while processing WM_PAINT messages, you can make this call:

```
InvalidateRect (hwnd, NULL, TRUE) ;
```

before calling *BeginPaint*. This invalidates the entire client area and causes *BeginPaint* to erase the background. A FALSE value in the last argument will not erase the background. Whatever was there will stay.

It is usually most convenient for a Windows program to simply repaint the entire client area whenever it receives a WM_PAINT message, regardless of the *rcPaint* structure. For example, if part of the display output in the client area includes a circle but only part of the circle falls within the invalid rectangle, it makes little sense to draw only the invalid part of the circle. Draw the whole circle. When you use the device context handle returned from *BeginPaint*, Windows will not paint outside the *rcPaint* rectangle anyway.

In the HELLOWIN program in Chapter 2, we didn't care about invalid rectangles when processing the WM_PAINT message. If the area where the text was displayed happened to be within the invalid rectangle, *DrawText* restored it. If not, then at some point during processing of the *DrawText* call Windows determined it didn't need to write anything on the display. But this determination takes time. A programmer concerned about performance and speed (and that includes all of us, I hope) will want to use the invalid rectangle during processing of the WM_PAINT message to avoid unnecessary GDI calls. This is particularly important if painting requires accessing disk files such as bitmaps.

Getting a Device Context Handle: Method Two

Although it is best to structure your program so that you can update the entire client area during the WM_PAINT message, you may also find it useful to paint part of the client area while processing messages other than WM_PAINT. Or you may need a device context handle for other purposes, such as obtaining information about the device context.

To get a handle to the device context of the client area of the window, you call *GetDC* to obtain the handle and *ReleaseDC* after you're done with it:

```
hdc = GetDC (hwnd) ;
[use GDI functions]
ReleaseDC (hwnd, hdc) ;
```

Like *BeginPaint* and *EndPaint*, the *GetDC* and *ReleaseDC* functions should be called in pairs. When you call *GetDC* while processing a message, you should call *ReleaseDC* before you exit the window procedure. Do not call *GetDC* in one message and *ReleaseDC* in another.

Unlike the device context handle returned from *BeginPaint*, the device context handle returned from *GetDC* has a clipping rectangle equal to the entire client area. You can paint on any part of the client area, not merely on the invalid rectangle (if indeed there is an invalid rectangle). Unlike *BeginPaint*, *GetDC* does not validate any invalid regions. If you need to validate the entire client area, you can call

```
ValidateRect (hwnd, NULL) ;
```

Generally, you'll use the *GetDC* and *ReleaseDC* calls in response to keyboard messages (such as in a word processing program) or mouse messages (such as in a drawing program). This allows the program to draw on the client area in prompt reaction to the user's keyboard or mouse input without deliberately invalidating part of the client area to generate WM_PAINT messages. However, even if you paint during messages other than WM_PAINT, your program must still accumulate enough information to be able to update the display whenever you do receive a WM_PAINT message.

A function similar to *GetDC* is *GetWindowDC*. While *GetDC* returns a device context handle for writing on the client area of the window, *GetWindowDC* returns a device context handle that lets you write on the entire window. For example, your program can use the device context handle returned from *GetWindowDC* to write on the window's title bar. However, your program would also have to process WM_NCPAINT ("nonclient paint") messages as well.

TextOut: The Details

TextOut is the most common GDI function for displaying text. Its syntax is

```
TextOut (hdc, x, y, psText, iLength) ;
```

Let's examine this function in more detail.

The first argument is the handle to the device context—either the *hdc* value returned from *GetDC* or the *hdc* value returned from *BeginPaint* during processing of a WM_PAINT message.

The attributes of the device context control the characteristics of this displayed text. For instance, one attribute of the device context specifies the text color. The default color (we discover with some degree of comfort) is black. The default device context also defines a text background color, and this is white. When a program writes text to the display, Windows uses this background color to fill in the rectangular space surrounding each character, called the "character box."

The text background color is not the same background you set when defining the window class. The background in the window class is a brush—which is a pattern that may or may not be a pure color—that Windows uses to erase the client area. It is not part of the device context structure. When defining the window class structure, most Windows applications use WHITE_BRUSH so that the default text background color in the default device context is the same color as the brush Windows uses to erase the background of the client area.

The *psText* argument is a pointer to a character string, and *iLength* is the number of characters in the string. If *psText* points to a Unicode character string, then the number of bytes in the string is double the *iLength* value. The string should not contain any ASCII control characters such as carriage returns, linefeeds, tabs, or backspaces. Windows displays these control characters as boxes or solid blocks. *TextOut* does not recognize a zero byte (or for Unicode, a zero short integer) as denoting the end of a string. The function uses the *iLength* argument to determine the string's length.

The *x* and *y* arguments to *TextOut* define the starting point of the character string within the client area. The *x* value is the horizontal position; the *y* value is the vertical position. The upper left corner of the first character is positioned at the coordinate point (*x*, *y*). In the default device context, the origin (that is, the point where *x* and *y* both equal 0) is the upper left corner of the client area. If you use zero values for *x* and *y* in *TextOut*, the character string starts flush against the upper left corner of the client area.

When you read the documentation of a GDI drawing function such as *TextOut*, you'll find that the coordinates passed to the function are usually documented as "logical coordinates." What this means exactly we'll examine in more detail in Chapter 5. For now, be aware that Windows has a variety of "mapping modes" that govern how the logical coordinates specified in GDI drawing functions are translated to the physical pixel coordinates of the display. The mapping mode is defined in the device context. The default mapping mode is called MM_TEXT (using the identifier defined in the WINGDI.H header file). Under the MM_TEXT mapping mode, logical units are the same as physical units, which are pixels, relative to the upper left corner of the client area. Values of x increase as you move to the right in the client area, and values of y increase as you move down in the client area. (See Figure 4-2.) The MM_TEXT coordinate system is identical to the coordinate system that Windows uses to define the invalid rectangle in the PAINTSTRUCT structure. (Things are not quite as convenient with the other mapping modes, however.)

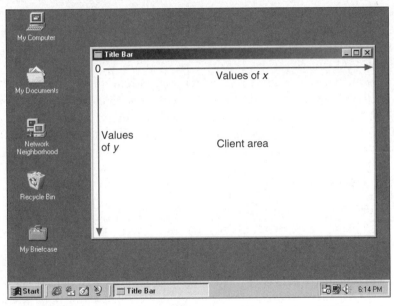

Figure 4-2. *The x-coordinate and y-coordinate in the MM_TEXT mapping mode.*

The device context also defines a clipping region. As you've seen, the default clipping region is the entire client area for a device context handle obtained from *GetDC* and the invalid region for the device context handle obtained from *BeginPaint*. When you call *TextOut*, Windows will not display any part of the character string that lies outside the clipping region. If a character is partly within the clipping region, Windows displays only the portion of the character inside the region. Writing outside the client area of your window isn't easy to do, so don't worry about doing it inadvertently.

The System Font

The device context also defines the font that Windows uses when you call *TextOut* to display text. The default is a font called the "system font" or (using the identifier in the WINGDI.H header file) SYSTEM_FONT. The system font is the font that Windows uses by default for text strings in title bars, menus, and dialog boxes.

In the early days of Windows, the system font was a fixed-pitch font, which means that all the characters had the same width, much like a typewriter. However, beginning with Windows 3.0, the system font became a variable-pitch font, which means that different characters have different widths. A "W" is wider than an "i", for example. It has been well established by studies in reading that text printed with variable-pitch fonts is more readable than fixed-pitch font texts. It seems to have something to do with the letters being closer together, allowing the eyes and mind to more clearly see entire words rather than individual letters. As you might imagine, the change from fixed-pitch fonts to variable-pitch fonts broke a lot of early Windows code and required that programmers learn some new techniques for working with text.

The system font is a "raster font," which means that the characters are defined as blocks of pixels. (In Chapter 17, we'll work with TrueType fonts, which are defined by scalable outlines.) To a certain extent, the size of the characters in the system font is based on the size of the video display. The system font is designed to allow at least 25 lines of 80-character text to fit on the screen.

The Size of a Character

To display multiple lines of text by using the *TextOut* function, you need to know the dimensions of characters in the font. You can space successive lines of text based on the height of the characters, and you can space columns of text across the client area based on the average width of the characters.

What is the height and average width of characters in the system font? Well, I'm not going to tell you. Or rather, I *can't* tell you. Or rather, I could tell you, but I might be wrong. The problem is that it all depends on the pixel size of the video display. Windows requires a minimum display size of 640 by 480, but many users prefer 800 by 600 or 1024 by 768. In addition, for these larger display sizes, Windows allows the user to select different sized system fonts.

Just as a program can determine information about the sizes (or "metrics") of user interface items by calling the *GetSystemMetrics* function, a program can determine font sizes by calling *GetTextMetrics*. *GetTextMetrics* requires a handle to a device context because it returns information about the font currently selected in the device context. Windows copies the various values of text metrics into a structure of type TEXTMETRIC defined in WINGDI.H. The TEXTMETRIC structure has 20 fields, but we're interested in only the first seven:

```
typedef struct tagTEXTMETRIC
{
     LONG tmHeight ;
     LONG tmAscent ;
     LONG tmDescent ;
     LONG tmInternalLeading ;
     LONG tmExternalLeading ;
     LONG tmAveCharWidth ;
     LONG tmMaxCharWidth ;
          [other structure fields]
}
TEXTMETRIC, * PTEXTMETRIC ;
```

The values of these fields are in units that depend on the mapping mode currently selected for the device context. In the default device context, this mapping mode is MM_TEXT, so the dimensions are in units of pixels.

To use the *GetTextMetrics* function, you first need to define a structure variable, commonly called *tm*:

```
TEXTMETRIC tm ;
```

When you need to determine the text metrics, you get a handle to a device context and call *GetTextMetrics*:

```
hdc = GetDC (hwnd) ;
GetTextMetrics (hdc, &tm) ;
ReleaseDC (hwnd, hdc) ;
```

You can then examine the values in the text metric structure and probably save a few of them for future use.

Text Metrics: The Details

The TEXTMETRIC structure provides various types of information about the font currently selected in the device context. However, the vertical size of a font is defined by only five fields of the structure, four of which are shown in Figure 4-3 on the following page.

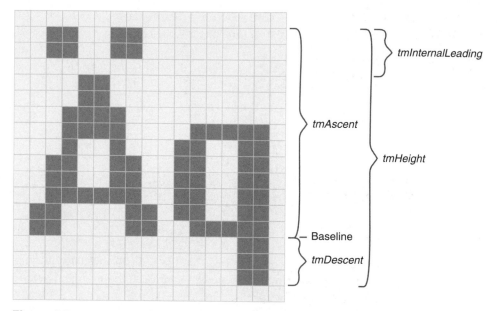

Figure 4-3. *Four values defining vertical character sizes in a font.*

The most important value is *tmHeight*, which is the sum of *tmAscent* and *tmDescent*. These two values represent the maximum vertical extents of characters in the font above and below the baseline. The term "leading" refers to space that a printer inserts between lines of text. In the TEXTMETRIC structure, internal leading is included in *tmAscent* (and thus in *tmHeight*) and is often the space in which accent marks appear. The *tmInternalLeading* field could be set to 0, in which case accented letters are made a little shorter so that the accent marks fit within the ascent of the character.

The TEXTMETRIC structure also includes a field named *tmExternalLeading*, which is not included in the *tmHeight* value. This is an amount of space that the designer of the font suggests be added between successive rows of displayed text. You can accept or reject the font designer's suggestion for including external leading when spacing lines of text. In the system fonts that I've encountered recently, *tmExternalLeading* has been zero, which is why I didn't include it in Figure 4-3. (Despite my vow not to tell you the dimensions of a system font, Figure 4-3 is accurate for the system font that Windows uses by default for a 640 by 480 display.)

The TEXTMETRIC structure contains two fields that describe character widths: the *tmAveCharWidth* field is a weighted average of lowercase characters, and *tmMaxCharWidth* is the width of the widest character in the font. For a fixed-pitch font, these values are the same. (For the font illustrated in Figure 4-3, these values are 7 and 14, respectively.)

The sample programs in this chapter will require another character width—the average width of uppercase letters. You can calculate this fairly accurately as 150% of *tmAveCharWidth*.

It's important to realize that the dimensions of a system font are dependent on the pixel size of the video display on which Windows runs and, in some cases, on the system font size the user has selected. Windows provides a device-independent graphics interface, but you have to help. Don't write your Windows programs so that they guess at character dimensions. Don't hard-code any values. Use the *GetTextMetrics* function to obtain this information.

Formatting Text

Because the dimensions of the system font do not change during a Windows session, you need to call *GetTextMetrics* only once when your program executes. A good place to make this call is while processing the WM_CREATE message in the window procedure. The WM_CREATE message is the first message the window procedure receives. Windows calls your window procedure with a WM_CREATE message when you call *CreateWindow* in *WinMain*.

Suppose you're writing a Windows program that displays several lines of text running down the client area. You'll want to obtain values for the character width and height. Within the window procedure you can define two variables to save the average character width (*cxChar*) and the total character height (*cyChar*):

```
static int cxChar, cyChar ;
```

The prefix *c* added to the variables names stands for "count," and in this case means a count of (or number of) pixels. In combination with *x* or *y*, the prefix refers to a width or height. These variables are defined as *static* because they must be valid when the window procedure processes other messages, such as WM_PAINT. Or you can define the variables globally outside of any function.

Here's the WM_CREATE code to obtain the width and height of characters in the system font:

```
case WM_CREATE:
     hdc = GetDC (hwnd) ;

     GetTextMetrics (hdc, &tm) ;
     cxChar = tm.tmAveCharWidth ;
     cyChar = tm.tmHeight + tm.tmExternalLeading ;

     ReleaseDC (hwnd, hdc) ;
     return 0 ;
```

Notice that I've included the *tmExternalLeading* field in the calculation of *cyChar*. Even though this field is 0 in the system fonts I've seen lately, it should be included if it's ever nonzero because it makes for more readable line spacing. Each successive line of text is displayed *cyChar* pixels further down the window.

You'll often find it necessary to display formatted numbers as well as simple character strings. As I discussed in Chapter 2, you can't use the traditional tool for this job (the beloved *printf* function), but you can use *sprintf* and the Windows version of *sprintf*, *wsprintf*. These functions work just like *printf* except that they put the formatted string into a character string. You can then use *TextOut* to write the string to the display. Very conveniently, the value returned from *sprintf* and *wsprintf* is the length of the string. You can pass that value to *TextOut* as the *iLength* argument. This code shows a typical *wsprintf* and *TextOut* combination:

```
int    iLength ;
TCHAR szBuffer [40] ;
[ other program lines ]
iLength = wsprintf (szBuffer, TEXT ("The sum of %i and %i is %i"),
                    iA, iB, iA + iB) ;
TextOut (hdc, x, y, szBuffer, iLength) ;
```

For something as simple as this, you could dispense with the *iLength* definition and combine the two statements into one:

```
TextOut (hdc, x, y, szBuffer,
       wsprintf (szBuffer, TEXT ("The sum of %i and %i is %i"),
                    iA, iB, iA + iB)) ;
```

It ain't pretty, but it works.

Putting It All Together

Now we seem to have everything we need to write a simple program that displays multiple lines of text on the screen. We know how to get a handle to a device context during the WM_PAINT message, how to use the *TextOut* function, and how to space text based on the size of a single character. The only thing left for us to do is to display something interesting.

In the previous chapter, we took a little peek at the interesting information available from the Windows *GetSystemMetrics* function. The function returns information about the size of various graphical items in Windows, such as icons, cursors, title bars, and scroll bars. These sizes vary with the display adapter and driver. *GetSystemMetrics* is an important function for achieving device-independent graphical output in your program.

The function requires a single argument called an "index." The index is one of 75 integer identifiers defined in the Windows header files. (The number of identifiers has increased with each release of Windows; the programmer's documentation in Windows 1.0 listed only 26 of them.) *GetSystemMetrics* returns an integer, usually the size of the item specified in the argument.

Let's write a program that displays some of the information available from the *GetSystemMetrics* calls in a simple one-line-per-item format. Working with this information is easier if we create a header file that defines an array of structures containing both the Windows header-file identifiers for the *GetSystemMetrics* index and the text we want to display for each value returned from the call. This header file is called SYSMETS.H and is shown in Figure 4-4.

SYSMETS.H

```
/*-------------------------------------------------
   SYSMETS.H -- System metrics display structure
  -------------------------------------------------*/

#define NUMLINES ((int) (sizeof sysmetrics / sizeof sysmetrics [0]))

struct
{
    int      iIndex ;
    TCHAR * szLabel ;
    TCHAR * szDesc ;
}
sysmetrics [] =
[
    SM_CXSCREEN,            TEXT ("SM_CXSCREEN"),
                           TEXT ("Screen width in pixels"),
    SM_CYSCREEN,            TEXT ("SM_CYSCREEN"),
                           TEXT ("Screen height in pixels"),
    SM_CXVSCROLL,           TEXT ("SM_CXVSCROLL"),
                           TEXT ("Vertical scroll width"),
    SM_CYHSCROLL,           TEXT ("SM_CYHSCROLL"),
                           TEXT ("Horizontal scroll height"),
    SM_CYCAPTION,           TEXT ("SM_CYCAPTION"),
                           TEXT ("Caption bar height"),
    SM_CXBORDER,            TEXT ("SM_CXBORDER"),
                           TEXT ("Window border width"),
    SM_CYBORDER,            TEXT ("SM_CYBORDER"),
                           TEXT ("Window border height"),
    SM_CXFIXEDFRAME,        TEXT ("SM_CXFIXEDFRAME"),
                           TEXT ("Dialog window frame width"),
    SM_CYFIXEDFRAME,        TEXT ("SM_CYFIXEDFRAME"),
                           TEXT ("Dialog window frame height"),
    SM_CYVTHUMB,            TEXT ("SM_CYVTHUMB"),
                           TEXT ("Vertical scroll thumb height"),
    SM_CXHTHUMB,            TEXT ("SM_CXHTHUMB"),
                           TEXT ("Horizontal scroll thumb width"),
```

Figure 4-4. *The SYSMETS.H file.* *(continued)*

Figure 4-4. *continued*

```
SM_CXICON,              TEXT ("SM_CXICON"),
                        TEXT ("Icon width"),
SM_CYICON,              TEXT ("SM_CYICON"),
                        TEXT ("Icon height"),
SM_CXCURSOR,            TEXT ("SM_CXCURSOR"),
                        TEXT ("Cursor width"),
SM_CYCURSOR,            TEXT ("SM_CYCURSOR"),
                        TEXT ("Cursor height"),
SM_CYMENU,              TEXT ("SM_CYMENU"),
                        TEXT ("Menu bar height"),
SM_CXFULLSCREEN,        TEXT ("SM_CXFULLSCREEN"),
                        TEXT ("Full screen client area width"),
SM_CYFULLSCREEN,        TEXT ("SM_CYFULLSCREEN"),
                        TEXT ("Full screen client area height"),
SM_CYKANJIWINDOW,       TEXT ("SM_CYKANJIWINDOW"),
                        TEXT ("Kanji window height"),
SM_MOUSEPRESENT,        TEXT ("SM_MOUSEPRESENT"),
                        TEXT ("Mouse present flag"),
SM_CYVSCROLL,           TEXT ("SM_CYVSCROLL"),
                        TEXT ("Vertical scroll arrow height"),
SM_CXHSCROLL,           TEXT ("SM_CXHSCROLL"),
                        TEXT ("Horizontal scroll arrow width"),
SM_DEBUG,               TEXT ("SM_DEBUG"),
                        TEXT ("Debug version flag"),
SM_SWAPBUTTON,          TEXT ("SM_SWAPBUTTON"),
                        TEXT ("Mouse buttons swapped flag"),
SM_CXMIN,               TEXT ("SM_CXMIN"),
                        TEXT ("Minimum window width"),
SM_CYMIN,               TEXT ("SM_CYMIN"),
                        TEXT ("Minimum window height"),
SM_CXSIZE,              TEXT ("SM_CXSIZE"),
                        TEXT ("Min/Max/Close button width"),
SM_CYSIZE,              TEXT ("SM_CYSIZE"),
                        TEXT ("Min/Max/Close button height"),
SM_CXSIZEFRAME,         TEXT ("SM_CXSIZEFRAME"),
                        TEXT ("Window sizing frame width"),
SM_CYSIZEFRAME,         TEXT ("SM_CYSIZEFRAME"),
                        TEXT ("Window sizing frame height"),
SM_CXMINTRACK,          TEXT ("SM_CXMINTRACK"),
                        TEXT ("Minimum window tracking width"),
SM_CYMINTRACK,          TEXT ("SM_CYMINTRACK"),
                        TEXT ("Minimum window tracking height"),
SM_CXDOUBLECLK,         TEXT ("SM_CXDOUBLECLK"),
                        TEXT ("Double click x tolerance"),
SM_CYDOUBLECLK,         TEXT ("SM_CYDOUBLECLK"),
                        TEXT ("Double click y tolerance"),
```

```
SM_CXICONSPACING,       TEXT ("SM_CXICONSPACING"),
                        TEXT ("Horizontal icon spacing"),
SM_CYICONSPACING,       TEXT ("SM_CYICONSPACING"),
                        TEXT ("Vertical icon spacing"),
SM_MENUDROPALIGNMENT,   TEXT ("SM_MENUDROPALIGNMENT"),
                        TEXT ("Left or right menu drop"),
SM_PENWINDOWS,          TEXT ("SM_PENWINDOWS"),
                        TEXT ("Pen extensions installed"),
SM_DBCSENABLED,         TEXT ("SM_DBCSENABLED"),
                        TEXT ("Double-Byte Char Set enabled"),
SM_CMOUSEBUTTONS,       TEXT ("SM_CMOUSEBUTTONS"),
                        TEXT ("Number of mouse buttons"),
SM_SECURE,              TEXT ("SM_SECURE"),
                        TEXT ("Security present flag"),
SM_CXEDGE,              TEXT ("SM_CXEDGE"),
                        TEXT ("3-D border width"),
SM_CYEDGE,              TEXT ("SM_CYEDGE"),
                        TEXT ("3-D border height"),
SM_CXMINSPACING,        TEXT ("SM_CXMINSPACING"),
                        TEXT ("Minimized window spacing width"),
SM_CYMINSPACING,        TEXT ("SM_CYMINSPACING"),
                        TEXT ("Minimized window spacing height"),
SM_CXSMICON,            TEXT ("SM_CXSMICON"),
                        TEXT ("Small icon width"),
SM_CYSMICON,            TEXT ("SM_CYSMICON"),
                        TEXT ("Small icon height"),
SM_CYSMCAPTION,         TEXT ("SM_CYSMCAPTION"),
                        TEXT ("Small caption height"),
SM_CXSMSIZE,            TEXT ("SM_CXSMSIZE"),
                        TEXT ("Small caption button width"),
SM_CYSMSIZE,            TEXT ("SM_CYSMSIZE"),
                        TEXT ("Small caption button height"),
SM_CXMENUSIZE,          TEXT ("SM_CXMENUSIZE"),
                        TEXT ("Menu bar button width"),
SM_CYMENUSIZE,          TEXT ("SM_CYMENUSIZE"),
                        TEXT ("Menu bar button height"),
SM_ARRANGE,             TEXT ("SM_ARRANGE"),
                        TEXT ("How minimized windows arranged"),
SM_CXMINIMIZED,         TEXT ("SM_CXMINIMIZED"),
                        TEXT ("Minimized window width"),
SM_CYMINIMIZED,         TEXT ("SM_CYMINIMIZED"),
                        TEXT ("Minimized window height"),
SM_CXMAXTRACK,          TEXT ("SM_CXMAXTRACK"),
                        TEXT ("Maximum draggable width"),
SM_CYMAXTRACK,          TEXT ("SM_CYMAXTRACK"),
                        TEXT ("Maximum draggable height"),
```

(continued)

Figure 4-4. *continued*

```
        SM_CXMAXIMIZED,         TEXT ("SM_CXMAXIMIZED"),
                                TEXT ("Width of maximized window"),
        SM_CYMAXIMIZED,         TEXT ("SM_CYMAXIMIZED"),
                                TEXT ("Height of maximized window"),
        SM_NETWORK,             TEXT ("SM_NETWORK"),
                                TEXT ("Network present flag"),
        SM_CLEANBOOT,           TEXT ("SM_CLEANBOOT"),
                                TEXT ("How system was booted"),
        SM_CXDRAG,              TEXT ("SM_CXDRAG"),
                                TEXT ("Avoid drag x tolerance"),
        SM_CYDRAG,              TEXT ("SM_CYDRAG"),
                                TEXT ("Avoid drag y tolerance"),
        SM_SHOWSOUNDS,          TEXT ("SM_SHOWSOUNDS"),
                                TEXT ("Present sounds visually"),
        SM_CXMENUCHECK,         TEXT ("SM_CXMENUCHECK"),
                                TEXT ("Menu check-mark width"),
        SM_CYMENUCHECK,         TEXT ("SM_CYMENUCHECK"),
                                TEXT ("Menu check-mark height"),
        SM_SLOWMACHINE,         TEXT ("SM_SLOWMACHINE"),
                                TEXT ("Slow processor flag"),
        SM_MIDEASTENABLED,      TEXT ("SM_MIDEASTENABLED"),
                                TEXT ("Hebrew and Arabic enabled flag"),
        SM_MOUSEWHEELPRESENT,   TEXT ("SM_MOUSEWHEELPRESENT"),
                                TEXT ("Mouse wheel present flag"),
        SM_XVIRTUALSCREEN,      TEXT ("SM_XVIRTUALSCREEN"),
                                TEXT ("Virtual screen x origin"),
        SM_YVIRTUALSCREEN,      TEXT ("SM_YVIRTUALSCREEN"),
                                TEXT ("Virtual screen y origin"),
        SM_CXVIRTUALSCREEN,     TEXT ("SM_CXVIRTUALSCREEN"),
                                TEXT ("Virtual screen width"),
        SM_CYVIRTUALSCREEN,     TEXT ("SM_CYVIRTUALSCREEN"),
                                TEXT ("Virtual screen height"),
        SM_CMONITORS,           TEXT ("SM_CMONITORS"),
                                TEXT ("Number of monitors"),
        SM_SAMEDISPLAYFORMAT,   TEXT ("SM_SAMEDISPLAYFORMAT"),
                                TEXT ("Same color format flag")
} ;
```

The program that displays this information is called SYSMETS1. The SYSMETS1.C source code file is shown in Figure 4-5. Most of the code should look familiar by now. The code in *WinMain* is virtually identical to that in HELLOWIN, and much of the code in *WndProc* has already been discussed.

SYSMETS1.C

```
/*------------------------------------------------------
   SYSMETS1.C -- System Metrics Display Program No. 1
                 (c) Charles Petzold, 1998
   ------------------------------------------------------*/

#include <windows.h>
#include "sysmets.h"

LRESULT CALLBACK WndProc (HWND, UINT, WPARAM, LPARAM) ;

int WINAPI WinMain (HINSTANCE hInstance, HINSTANCE hPrevInstance,
                    PSTR szCmdLine, int iCmdShow)
{
     static TCHAR szAppName[] = TEXT ("SysMets1") ;
     HWND         hwnd ;
     MSG          msg ;
     WNDCLASS     wndclass ;

     wndclass.style         = CS_HREDRAW | CS_VREDRAW ;
     wndclass.lpfnWndProc   = WndProc ;
     wndclass.cbClsExtra    = 0 ;
     wndclass.cbWndExtra    = 0 ;
     wndclass.hInstance     = hInstance ;
     wndclass.hIcon         = LoadIcon (NULL, IDI_APPLICATION) ;
     wndclass.hCursor       = LoadCursor (NULL, IDC_ARROW) ;
     wndclass.hbrBackground = (HBRUSH) GetStockObject (WHITE_BRUSH) ;
     wndclass.lpszMenuName  = NULL ;
     wndclass.lpszClassName = szAppName ;

     if (!RegisterClass (&wndclass))
     {
          MessageBox (NULL, TEXT ("This program requires Windows NT!"),
                      szAppName, MB_ICONERROR) ;
          return 0 ;
     }

     hwnd = CreateWindow (szAppName, TEXT ("Get System Metrics No. 1"),
                          WS_OVERLAPPEDWINDOW,
                          CW_USEDEFAULT, CW_USEDEFAULT,
                          CW_USEDEFAULT, CW_USEDEFAULT,
                          NULL, NULL, hInstance, NULL) ;

     ShowWindow (hwnd, iCmdShow) ;
     UpdateWindow (hwnd) ;
```

Figure 4-5. *SYSMETS1.C.*   *(continued)*

Figure 4-5. *continued*

```
    while (GetMessage (&msg, NULL, 0, 0))
         {
         TranslateMessage (&msg) ;
         DispatchMessage (&msg) ;
         }
    return msg.wParam ;
    }

LRESULT CALLBACK WndProc (HWND hwnd, UINT message, WPARAM wParam, LPARAM lParam)
{
    static int   cxChar, cxCaps, cyChar ;
    HDC          hdc ;
    int          i ;
    PAINTSTRUCT  ps ;
    TCHAR        szBuffer [10] ;
    TEXTMETRIC   tm ;

    switch (message)
    {
    case WM_CREATE:
         hdc = GetDC (hwnd) ;

         GetTextMetrics (hdc, &tm) ;
         cxChar = tm.tmAveCharWidth ;
         cxCaps = (tm.tmPitchAndFamily & 1 ? 3 : 2) * cxChar / 2 ;
         cyChar = tm.tmHeight + tm.tmExternalLeading ;

         ReleaseDC (hwnd, hdc) ;
         return 0 ;

    case WM_PAINT :
         hdc = BeginPaint (hwnd, &ps) ;

         for (i = 0 ; i < NUMLINES ; i++)
         {
              TextOut (hdc, 0, cyChar * i,
                       sysmetrics[i].szLabel,
                       lstrlen (sysmetrics[i].szLabel)) ;

              TextOut (hdc, 22 * cxCaps, cyChar * i,
                       sysmetrics[i].szDesc,
                       lstrlen (sysmetrics[i].szDesc)) ;

              SetTextAlign (hdc, TA_RIGHT | TA_TOP) ;
```

```
                    TextOut (hdc, 22 * cxCaps + 40 * cxChar, cyChar * i, szBuffer,
                           wsprintf (szBuffer, TEXT ("%5d"),
                                   GetSystemMetrics (sysmetrics[i].iIndex))) ;

                    SetTextAlign (hdc, TA_LEFT | TA_TOP) ;
               }
          EndPaint (hwnd, &ps) ;
          return 0 ;

     case WM_DESTROY :
          PostQuitMessage (0) ;
          return 0 ;
     }
     return DefWindowProc (hwnd, message, wParam, lParam) ;
}
```

Figure 4-6 shows SYSMETS1 running on a standard VGA. As you can see from the first two lines in the program's client area, the screen width is 640 pixels and the screen height is 480 pixels. These two values, as well as many of the other values shown by the program, may be different for different types of video displays.

	Get System Metrics No. 1			_ □ ×
SM_CXSCREEN	Screen width in pixels	640		
SM_CYSCREEN	Screen height in pixels	480		
SM_CXVSCROLL	Vertical scroll width	16		
SM_CYHSCROLL	Horizontal scroll height	16		
SM_CYCAPTION	Caption bar height	19		
SM_CXBORDER	Window border width	1		
SM_CYBORDER	Window border height	1		
SM_CXFIXEDFRAME	Dialog window frame width	3		
SM_CYFIXEDFRAME	Dialog window frame height	3		
SM_CYVTHUMB	Vertical scroll thumb height	16		
SM_CXHTHUMB	Horizontal scroll thumb width	16		
SM_CXICON	Icon width	32		
SM_CYICON	Icon height	32		
SM_CXCURSOR	Cursor width	32		
SM_CYCURSOR	Cursor height	32		
SM_CYMENU	Menu bar height	19		
SM_CXFULLSCREEN	Full screen client area width	640		
SM_CYFULLSCREEN	Full screen client area height	433		
SM_CYKANJIWINDOW	Kanji window height	0		
SM_MOUSEPRESENT	Mouse present flag	1		
SM_CYVSCROLL	Vertical scroll arrow height	16		
SM_CXHSCROLL	Horizontal scroll arrow width	16		
SM_DEBUG	Debug version flag	0		
SM_SWAPBUTTON	Mouse buttons swapped flag	0		
SM_CXMIN	Minimum window width	112		
SM_CYMIN	Minimum window height	27		

Figure 4-6. *The SYSMETS1 display.*

The SYSMETS1.C Window Procedure

The *WndProc* window procedure in the SYSMETS1.C program processes three messages: WM_CREATE, WM_PAINT, and WM_DESTROY. The WM_DESTROY message is processed in the same way as the HELLOWIN program in Chapter 3.

The WM_CREATE message is the first message the window procedure receives. Windows generates the message when the *CreateWindow* function creates the window. During the WM_CREATE message, SYSMETS1 obtains a device context for the window by calling *GetDC* and gets the text metrics for the default system font by calling *GetTextMetrics*. SYSMETS1 saves the average character width in *cxChar* and the total height of the characters (including external leading) in *cyChar*.

SYSMETS1 also saves an average width of uppercase letters in the static variable *cxCaps*. For a fixed-pitch font, *cxCaps* would equal *cxChar*. For a variable-width font, *cxCaps* is set to 150 percent of *cxChar*. The low bit of the *tmPitchAndFamily* field in the TEXTMETRIC structure is 1 for a variable-width font and 0 for a fixed-pitch font. SYSMETS1 uses this bit to calculate *cxCaps* from *cxChar*:

```
cxCaps = (tm.tmPitchAndFamily & 1 ? 3 : 2) * cxChar / 2 ;
```

SYSMETS1 does all window painting during the WM_PAINT message. As normal, the window procedure first obtains a handle to the device context by calling *BeginPaint*. A *for* statement loops through all the lines of the *sysmetrics* structure defined in SYSMETS.H. The three columns of text are displayed with three *TextOut* function calls. In each case, the third argument to *TextOut* (that is, the *y* starting position) is set to

```
cyChar * i
```

This argument indicates the pixel position of the top of the character string relative to the top of the client area.

The first *TextOut* statement displays the uppercase identifiers in the first of the three columns. The second argument to *TextOut* is 0 to begin the text at the left edge of the client area. The text is obtained from the *szLabel* field of the *sysmetrics* structure. I use the Windows function *lstrlen* to calculate the length of the string, which is required as the last argument to *TextOut*.

The second *TextOut* statement displays the description of the system metrics value. These descriptions are stored in the *szDesc* field of the *sysmetrics* structure. In this case, the second argument to *TextOut* is set to

```
22 * cxCaps
```

The longest uppercase identifier displayed in the first column is 20 characters, so the second column must begin at least 20 × *cxCaps* to the right of the beginning of the first column of text. I use 22 to add a little extra space between the columns.

The third *TextOut* statement displays the numeric values obtained from the *GetSystemMetrics* function. The variable-width font makes formatting a column of right-justified numbers a little tricky. Fortunately, in all variable-width fonts used today, the digits from 0 through 9 all have the same width. Otherwise, displaying columns of numbers would be monstrous. However, the width of the digits is greater than the width of a space. Numbers can be one or more digits wide, so different numbers can begin at different horizontal positions.

Wouldn't it be easier if we could display a column of right-justified numbers by specifying the horizontal pixel position where the number ends rather than begins? This is what the *SetTextAlign* function lets us do (among other things). After SYSMETS1 calls

```
SetTextAlign (hdc, TA_RIGHT | TA_TOP) ;
```

Windows will interpret the coordinates passed to subsequent *TextOut* functions as specifying the top-right corner of the text string rather than the top-left corner.

The *TextOut* function to display the column of numbers has its second argument set to

```
22 * cxCaps + 40 * cxChar
```

The 40 × *cxChar* value accommodates the width of the second column and the width of the third column. Following the *TextOut* function, another call to *SetTextAlign* sets things back to normal for the next time through the loop.

Not Enough Room

One nasty little problem exists with the SYSMETS1 program: Unless you have a gigantic, big-screen, high-resolution video adapter, you can't see many of the lines in the system metrics lists. If you make the window narrower, you can't even see the values.

SYSMETS1 is not aware of this problem. Otherwise we might have included a message box that said, "Sorry!" It's not aware of the problem because the program doesn't even know how large its client area is. It begins displaying the text at the top of the window and relies on Windows to clip everything that drifts beyond the bottom of the client area.

Clearly, this is not desirable. Our first job in solving this problem is to determine how much of the program's output can actually fit within the client area.

The Size of the Client Area

If you experiment with existing Windows applications, you'll find that window sizes can vary widely. If a window is maximized, the client area occupies nearly the entire video display. The dimensions of a maximized client area are, in fact, available from the *GetSystemMetrics* call by using arguments of SM_CXFULLSCREEN and SM_CYFULL-SCREEN (assuming that the window has only a title bar and no menu). The minimum size of a window can be quite small—sometimes almost nonexistent—virtually eliminating the client area.

In the last chapter, we used the *GetClientRect* function for determining the dimensions of the client area. There's nothing really wrong with this function, but it's a bit inefficient to call it every time you need to use this information. A much better method for determining the size of a window's client is to process the WM_SIZE message within your window procedure. Windows sends a WM_SIZE message to a window procedure whenever the size of the window changes. The *lParam* variable passed to the window procedure contains the width of the client area in the low word and the height in the high word. To save these dimensions, you'll want to define two static variables in your window procedure:

```
static int cxClient, cyClient ;
```

Like *cxChar* and *cyChar*, these variables are defined as static because they are set while processing one message and used while processing another message. You handle the WM_SIZE method like so:

```
case WM_SIZE:
    cxClient = LOWORD (lParam) ;
    cyClient = HIWORD (lParam) ;
    return 0 ;
```

You'll see code like this in virtually every Windows program. LOWORD and HIWORD are macros that are defined in the Windows header file WINDEF.H. If you're curious, the definitions of these macros look like this:

```
#define LOWORD(l) ((WORD)(l))
#define HIWORD(l) ((WORD)(((DWORD)(l) >> 16) & 0xFFFF))
```

The two macros return WORD values—that is, 16-bit unsigned short integers that range from 0 through 0xFFFF. Typically you'll store these values in 32-bit signed integers. That doesn't involve any conversion problems and makes the values easier to use in any calculations you may later need.

In many Windows programs, a WM_SIZE message will eventually be followed by a WM_PAINT message. How do we know this? Because when we define the window class we specify the class style as

```
CS_HREDRAW | CS_VREDRAW
```

This class style tells Windows to force a repaint if either the horizontal or vertical size changes.

You can calculate the number of full lines of text displayable within the client area with the formula:

```
cyClient / cyChar
```

This can be 0 if the height of the client area is too small to display a full character. Similarly, the approximate number of lowercase characters you can display horizontally within the client area is equal to

```
cxClient / cxChar
```

If you determine *cxChar* and *cyChar* during the WM_CREATE message, don't worry about dividing by 0 in these calculations. Your window procedure receives a WM_CREATE message when *WinMain* calls *CreateWindow*. The first WM_SIZE message comes a little later, when *WinMain* calls *ShowWindow*, at which point *cxChar* and *cyChar* have already been assigned positive nonzero values.

Knowing the size of the window's client area is the first step in providing a way for the user to move the text within the client area if the client area is not large enough to hold everything. If you're familiar with other Windows-based applications that have similar requirements, you probably know what we need: this is a job for those wonderful inventions known as scroll bars.

SCROLL BARS

Scroll bars are one of the best features of a graphical user interface. They are easy to use and provide excellent visual feedback. You can use scroll bars whenever you need to display anything—text, graphics, a spreadsheet, database records, pictures, Web pages—that requires more space than is available in the window's client area.

Scroll bars are positioned either vertically (for up and down movement) or horizontally (for left and right movement). You can click with the mouse the arrows at each end of a scroll bar or the area between the arrows. A "scroll box" (or "thumb") travels the length of the scroll bar to indicate the approximate location of the material shown on the display in relation to the entire document. You can also drag the thumb with the mouse to move to a particular location. Figure 4-7 on the following page shows the recommended use of a vertical scroll bar for text.

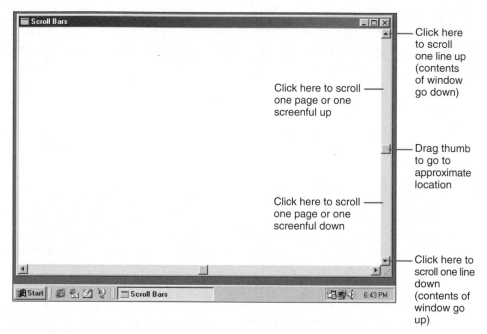

Figure 4-7. *The vertical scroll bar.*

Programmers sometimes have problems with scrolling terminology because their perspective is different from the user's. A user who scrolls down wants to bring a lower part of the document into view; however, the program actually moves the document up in relation to the display window. The Window documentation and the header file identifiers are based on the user's perspective: scroll up means moving toward the beginning of the document; scroll down means moving toward the end.

It is easy to include a horizontal or vertical scroll bar in your application window. All you need do is include the window style (WS) identifier WS_VSCROLL (vertical scroll) or WS_HSCROLL (horizontal scroll) or both in the third argument to *CreateWindow*. The scroll bars specified in the *CreateWindow* function are always placed against the right side or bottom of the window and extend the full length or width of the client area. The client area does not include the space occupied by the scroll bar. The width of the vertical scroll bar and the height of the horizontal scroll bar are constant for a particular video driver and display resolution. If you need these values, you can obtain them (as you may have observed) from the *GetSystemMetrics* calls.

Windows takes care of processing all mouse messages to the scroll bars. However, scroll bars do not have an automatic keyboard interface. If you want the cursor keys to duplicate some of the functionality of the scroll bars, you must explicitly provide logic for that (as we'll do when we make another version of the SYSMETS program in the next chapter).

Scroll Bar Range and Position

Every scroll bar has an associated "range" and "position." The scroll bar range is a pair of integers representing a minimum and maximum value associated with the scroll bar. The position is the location of the thumb within the range. When the thumb is at the top (or left) of the scroll bar, the position of the thumb is the minimum value of the range. At the bottom (or right) of the scroll bar, the thumb position is the maximum value of the range.

By default, the range of a scroll bar is 0 (top or left) through 100 (bottom or right), but it's easy to change the range to something that is more convenient for the program:

```
SetScrollRange (hwnd, iBar, iMin, iMax, bRedraw) ;
```

The *iBar* argument is either SB_VERT or SB_HORZ, *iMin* and *iMax* are the new minimum and maximum positions of the range, and you set *bRedraw* to TRUE if you want Windows to redraw the scroll bar based on the new range. (If you will be calling other functions that affect the appearance of the scroll bar after you call *SetScrollRange*, you'll probably want to set *bRedraw* to FALSE to avoid excessive redrawing.)

The thumb position is always a discrete integral value. For instance, a scroll bar with a range of 0 through 4 has five thumb positions, as shown in Figure 4-8.

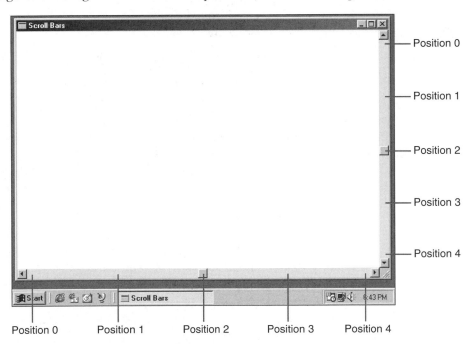

Figure 4-8. *Scroll bars with five thumb positions.*

You can use *SetScrollPos* to set a new thumb position within the scroll bar range:

```
SetScrollPos (hwnd, iBar, iPos, bRedraw) ;
```

The *iPos* argument is the new position and must be within the range of *iMin* and *iMax*. Windows provides similar functions (*GetScrollRange* and *GetScrollPos*) to obtain the current range and position of a scroll bar.

When you use scroll bars within your program, you share responsibility with Windows for maintaining the scroll bars and updating the position of the scroll bar thumb. These are Windows' responsibilities for scroll bars:

■ Handle all processing of mouse messages to the scroll bar.

■ Provide a reverse-video "flash" when the user clicks the scroll bar.

■ Move the thumb as the user drags the thumb within the scroll bar.

■ Send scroll bar messages to the window procedure of the window containing the scroll bar.

These are the responsibilities of your program:

■ Initialize the range and position of the scroll bar.

■ Process the scroll bar messages to the window procedure.

■ Update the position of the scroll bar thumb.

■ Change the contents of the client area in response to a change in the scroll bar.

Like almost everything in life, this will make a lot more sense when we start looking at some code.

Scroll Bar Messages

Windows sends the window procedure WM_VSCROLL (vertical scroll) and WM_HSCROLL (horizontal scroll) messages when the scroll bar is clicked with the mouse or the thumb is dragged. Each mouse action on the scroll bar generates at least two messages, one when the mouse button is pressed and another when it is released.

Like all messages, WM_VSCROLL and WM_HSCROLL are accompanied by the *wParam* and *lParam* message parameters. For messages from scroll bars created as part of your window, you can ignore *lParam*; that's used only for scroll bars created as child windows, usually within dialog boxes.

The *wParam* message parameter is divided into a low word and a high word. The low word of *wParam* is a number that indicates what the mouse is doing to the scroll bar.

This number is referred to as a "notification code." Notification codes have values defined by identifiers that begin with SB, which stands for "scroll bar." Here's how the notification codes are defined in WINUSER.H:

```
#define SB_LINEUP             0
#define SB_LINELEFT           0
#define SB_LINEDOWN           1
#define SB_LINERIGHT          1
#define SB_PAGEUP             2
#define SB_PAGELEFT           2
#define SB_PAGEDOWN           3
#define SB_PAGERIGHT          3
#define SB_THUMBPOSITION      4
#define SB_THUMBTRACK         5
#define SB_TOP                6
#define SB_LEFT               6
#define SB_BOTTOM             7
#define SB_RIGHT              7
#define SB_ENDSCROLL          8
```

You use the identifiers containing the words LEFT and RIGHT for horizontal scroll bars, and the identifiers with UP, DOWN, TOP, and BOTTOM with vertical scroll bars. The notification codes associated with clicking the mouse on various areas of the scroll bar are shown in Figure 4-9.

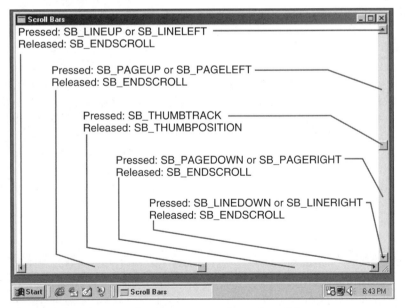

Figure 4-9. *Identifiers for the* wParam *values of scroll bar messages.*

If you hold down the mouse button on the various parts of the scroll bar, your program can receive multiple scroll bar messages. When the mouse button is released, you'll get a message with a notification code of SB_ENDSCROLL. You can generally ignore messages with the SB_ENDSCROLL notification code. Windows will not change the position of the scroll bar thumb. Your application does that by calling *SetScrollPos*.

When you position the mouse cursor over the scroll bar thumb and press the mouse button, you can move the thumb. This generates scroll bar messages with notification codes of SB_THUMBTRACK and SB_THUMBPOSITION. When the low word of *wParam* is SB_THUMBTRACK, the high word of *wParam* is the current position of the scroll bar thumb as the user is dragging it. This position is within the minimum and maximum values of the scroll bar range. When the low word of *wParam* is SB_THUMBPOSITION, the high word of *wParam* is the final position of the scroll bar thumb when the user released the mouse button. For other scroll bar actions, the high word of *wParam* should be ignored.

To provide feedback to the user, Windows will move the scroll bar thumb when you drag it with the mouse as your program is receiving SB_THUMBTRACK messages. However, unless you process SB_THUMBTRACK or SB_THUMBPOSITION messages by calling *SetScrollPos*, the thumb will snap back to its original position when the user releases the mouse button.

A program can process either the SB_THUMBTRACK or SB_THUMBPOSITION messages, but doesn't usually process both. If you process SB_THUMBTRACK messages, you'll move the contents of your client area as the user is dragging the thumb. If instead you process SB_THUMBPOSITION messages, you'll move the contents of the client area only when the user *stops* dragging the thumb. It's preferable (but more difficult) to process SB_THUMBTRACK messages; for some types of data your program may have a hard time keeping up with the messages.

As you'll note, the WINUSER.H header files includes notification codes of SB_TOP, SB_BOTTOM, SB_LEFT, and SB_RIGHT, indicating that the scroll bar has been moved to its minimum or maximum position. However, you will never receive these notification codes for a scroll bar created as part of your application window.

Although it's not common, using 32-bit values for the scroll bar range is perfectly valid. However, the high word of *wParam*, which is only a 16-bit value, cannot properly indicate the position for SB_THUMBTRACK and SB_THUMBPOSITION actions. In this case, you need to use the function *GetScrollInfo* (described later in this chapter) to get this information.

Scrolling SYSMETS

Enough explanation. It's time to put this stuff into practice. Let's start simply. We'll begin with vertical scrolling because that's what we desperately need. The horizontal scrolling can wait. SYSMET2 is shown in Figure 4-10. This program is probably the simplest implementation of a scroll bar you'll want in an application.

SYSMETS2.C

```
/*-------------------------------------------------------
   SYSMETS2.C -- System Metrics Display Program No. 2
                 (c) Charles Petzold, 1998
   -------------------------------------------------------*/

#include <windows.h>
#include "sysmets.h"

LRESULT CALLBACK WndProc (HWND, UINT, WPARAM, LPARAM) ;

int WINAPI WinMain (HINSTANCE hInstance, HINSTANCE hPrevInstance,
                    PSTR szCmdLine, int iCmdShow)
{
     static TCHAR szAppName[] = TEXT ("SysMets2") ;
     HWND         hwnd ;
     MSG          msg ;
     WNDCLASS     wndclass ;

     wndclass.style         = CS_HREDRAW | CS_VREDRAW ;
     wndclass.lpfnWndProc   = WndProc ;
     wndclass.cbClsExtra    = 0 ;
     wndclass.cbWndExtra    = 0 ;
     wndclass.hInstance     = hInstance ;
     wndclass.hIcon         = LoadIcon (NULL, IDI_APPLICATION) ;
     wndclass.hCursor       = LoadCursor (NULL, IDC_ARROW) ;
     wndclass.hbrBackground = (HBRUSH) GetStockObject (WHITE_BRUSH) ;
     wndclass.lpszMenuName  = NULL ;
     wndclass.lpszClassName = szAppName ;

     if (!RegisterClass (&wndclass))
     {
          MessageBox (NULL, TEXT ("This program requires Windows NT!"),
                      szAppName, MB_ICONERROR) ;
          return 0 ;
     }

     hwnd = CreateWindow (szAppName, TEXT ("Get System Metrics No. 2"),
                          WS_OVERLAPPEDWINDOW | WS_VSCROLL,
                          CW_USEDEFAULT, CW_USEDEFAULT,
                          CW_USEDEFAULT, CW_USEDEFAULT,
                          NULL, NULL, hInstance, NULL) ;
```

Figure 4-10. *The SYSMETS2 program.*   *(continued)*

Figure 4-10. *continued*

```
     ShowWindow (hwnd, iCmdShow) ;
     UpdateWindow (hwnd) ;

     while (GetMessage (&msg, NULL, 0, 0))
     {
          TranslateMessage (&msg) ;
          DispatchMessage (&msg) ;
     }
     return msg.wParam ;
}

LRESULT CALLBACK WndProc (HWND hwnd, UINT message, WPARAM wParam, LPARAM lParam)
{
     static int  cxChar, cxCaps, cyChar, cyClient, iVscrollPos ;
     HDC         hdc ;
     int         i, y ;
     PAINTSTRUCT ps ;
     TCHAR       szBuffer[10] ;
     TEXTMETRIC  tm ;

     switch (message)
     {
     case WM_CREATE:
          hdc = GetDC (hwnd) ;

          GetTextMetrics (hdc, &tm) ;
          cxChar = tm.tmAveCharWidth ;
          cxCaps = (tm.tmPitchAndFamily & 1 ? 3 : 2) * cxChar / 2 ;
          cyChar = tm.tmHeight + tm.tmExternalLeading ;

          ReleaseDC (hwnd, hdc) ;

          SetScrollRange (hwnd, SB_VERT, 0, NUMLINES - 1, FALSE) ;
          SetScrollPos   (hwnd, SB_VERT, iVscrollPos, TRUE) ;
          return 0 ;

     case WM_SIZE:
          cyClient = HIWORD (lParam) ;
          return 0 ;

     case WM_VSCROLL:
          switch (LOWORD (wParam))
          {
          case SB_LINEUP:
               iVscrollPos -= 1 ;
               break ;
```

```
        case SB_LINEDOWN:
             iVscrollPos += 1 ;
             break ;

        case SB_PAGEUP:
             iVscrollPos -= cyClient / cyChar ;
             break ;

        case SB_PAGEDOWN:
             iVscrollPos += cyClient / cyChar ;
             break ;

        case SB_THUMBPOSITION:
             iVscrollPos = HIWORD (wParam) ;
             break ;

        default :
             break ;
        }

        iVscrollPos = max (0, min (iVscrollPos, NUMLINES - 1)) ;

        if (iVscrollPos != GetScrollPos (hwnd, SB_VERT))
        {
             SetScrollPos (hwnd, SB_VERT, iVscrollPos, TRUE) ;
             InvalidateRect (hwnd, NULL, TRUE) ;
        }
        return 0 ;

   case WM_PAINT:
        hdc = BeginPaint (hwnd, &ps) ;

        for (i = 0 ; i < NUMLINES ; i++)
        {
             y = cyChar * (i - iVscrollPos) ;

             TextOut (hdc, 0, y,
                      sysmetrics[i].szLabel,
                      lstrlen (sysmetrics[i].szLabel)) ;

             TextOut (hdc, 22 * cxCaps, y,
                      sysmetrics[i].szDesc,
                      lstrlen (sysmetrics[i].szDesc)) ;

             SetTextAlign (hdc, TA_RIGHT | TA_TOP) ;
```

(continued)

Figure 4-10. *continued*

```
                TextOut (hdc, 22 * cxCaps + 40 * cxChar, y, szBuffer,
                        wsprintf (szBuffer, TEXT ("%5d"),
                                GetSystemMetrics (sysmetrics[i].iIndex))) ;

             SetTextAlign (hdc, TA_LEFT | TA_TOP) ;
          }
          EndPaint (hwnd, &ps) ;
          return 0 ;

     case WM_DESTROY:
          PostQuitMessage (0) ;
          return 0 ;
     }
     return DefWindowProc (hwnd, message, wParam, lParam) ;
}
```

The new *CreateWindow* call adds a vertical scroll bar to the window by including the WS_VSCROLL window style in the third argument:

```
WS_OVERLAPPEDWINDOW | WS_VSCROLL
```

WM_CREATE message processing in the *WndProc* window procedure has two additional lines to set the range and initial position of the vertical scroll bar:

```
SetScrollRange (hwnd, SB_VERT, 0, NUMLINES - 1, FALSE) ;
SetScrollPos (hwnd, SB_VERT, iVscrollPos, TRUE) ;
```

The *sysmetrics* structure array has NUMLINES lines of text, so the scroll bar range is set to 0 through NUMLINES − 1. Each position of the scroll bar corresponds to a line of text displayed at the top of the client area. If the scroll bar thumb is at position 0, the first line will be positioned at the top of the client area. For positions greater than zero, other lines appear at the top. When the position is NUMLINES − 1, the last line of text appears at the top of the client area.

To help with processing of the WM_VSCROLL messages, a static variable named *iVscrollPos* is defined within the window procedure. This variable is the current position of the scroll bar thumb. For SB_LINEUP and SB_LINEDOWN, all we need to do is adjust the scroll position by 1. For SB_PAGEUP and SB_PAGEDOWN, we want to move the text by the context of one screen, or *cyClient* divided by *cyChar*. For SB_THUMBPOSITION, the new thumb position is the high word of *wParam*. The SB_ENDSCROLL and SB_THUMB-TRACK messages are ignored.

After the program calculates a new value of *iVscrollPos* based on the type of WM_VSCROLL message it receives, it makes sure that it is still between the minimum and maximum range value of the scroll bar by using the *min* and *max* macros. The program then compares the value of *iVscrollPos* with the previous position, which is obtained by calling *GetScrollPos*. If the scroll position has changed, it is updated by calling *SetScrollPos*, and the entire window is invalidated by a call to *InvalidateRect*.

The *InvalidateRect* function generates a WM_PAINT message. When the original SYSMETS1 program processed WM_PAINT messages, the *y*-coordinate of each line was calculated as

```
cyChar * i
```

In SYSMETS2, the formula is

```
cyChar * (i - iVscrollPos)
```

The loop still displays NUMLINES lines of text, but for nonzero values of *iVscrollPos* this value is negative. The program is actually displaying the early lines of text above and outside the client area. Windows, of course, doesn't allow these lines to appear on the screen, so everything looks all nice and neat.

I told you we'd start simply. This is rather wasteful and inefficient code. We'll fix it shortly, but first consider how we update the client area after a WM_VSCROLL message.

Structuring Your Program for Painting

The window procedure in SYSMETS2 does not directly repaint the client area after processing a scroll bar message. Instead, it calls *InvalidateRect* to invalidate the client area. This causes Windows to place a WM_PAINT message in the message queue.

It is best to structure your Windows programs so that you do all your client-area painting in response to a WM_PAINT message. Because your program should be able to repaint the entire client area of the window at any time on receipt of a WM_PAINT message, painting in response to other messages will probably involve code that duplicates the functionality of your WM_PAINT logic.

At first, you may rebel at this dictum because it seems such a roundabout way of doing things. In the early days of Windows, programmers found this concept difficult to master because it was so different from character-mode PC programming. And, as I mentioned earlier, there are frequently times when your program will respond to some keyboard or mouse logic by drawing something immediately. This is done for both convenience and efficiency. But in many cases it's simply unnecessary. After you master the discipline of accumulating all the information you need to paint in response to a WM_PAINT message, you'll be pleased with the results.

As SYSMETS2 demonstrates, a program will often determine that it must repaint a particular area of the display while processing a message other than WM_PAINT. This is where *InvalidateRect* comes in handy. You can use it to invalidate specific rectangles of the client area or the entire client area.

Simply marking areas of the window as invalid to generate WM_PAINT messages might not be entirely satisfactory in some applications. After you make an *InvalidateRect* call, Windows places a WM_PAINT message in the message queue and the window procedure eventually processes it. However, Windows treats WM_PAINT messages as low priority, so if a lot of other activity is occurring in the system, it may be awhile before your window procedure receives the WM_PAINT message. Everyone has seen blank, white "holes" in Windows after a dialog box is removed and the program is still waiting to refresh its window.

If you prefer to update the invalid area immediately, you can call *UpdateWindow* after you call *InvalidateRect*:

```
UpdateWindow (hwnd) ;
```

UpdateWindow causes the window procedure to be called immediately with a WM_PAINT message if any part of the client area is invalid. (*UpdateWindow* will not call the window procedure if the entire client area is valid.) In this case, the WM_PAINT message bypasses the message queue. The window procedure is called directly from Windows. When the window procedure has finished repainting, it exits and the *UpdateWindow* function returns control to the code that called it.

You'll note that *UpdateWindow* is the same function used in *WinMain* to generate the first WM_PAINT message. When a window is first created, the entire client area is invalid. *UpdateWindow* directs the window procedure to paint it.

BUILDING A BETTER SCROLL

SYSMETS2 works well, but it's too inefficient a model to be imitated in other programs. Soon I'll present a new version that corrects its deficiencies. Most interesting, perhaps, is that this new version will not use any of the four scroll bar functions discussed so far. Instead, it will use new functions unique to the Win32 API.

The Scroll Bar Information Functions

The scroll bar documentation (in */Platform SDK/User Interface Services/Controls/Scroll Bars*) indicates that the *SetScrollRange*, *SetScrollPos*, *GetScrollRange*, and *GetScrollPos* functions are "obsolete." This is not entirely accurate. While these functions have been around since Windows 1.0, they were upgraded to handle 32-bit arguments in the Win32 API. They are still perfectly functional and are likely to remain functional. Moreover, they are simple enough not to overwhelm a newcomer to Windows programming at the outset, which is why I continue to use them in this book.

The two scroll bar functions introduced in the Win32 API are called *SetScrollInfo* and *GetScrollInfo*. These functions do everything the earlier functions do and add two new important features.

The first feature involves the size of the scroll bar thumb. As you may have noticed, the size of the thumb was constant in the SYSMETS2 program. However, in some Windows applications you may have used, the size of the thumb is proportional to the amount of the document displayed in the window. This displayed amount is known as the "page size." In arithmetic terms,

$$\frac{Thumb\ size}{Scroll\ length} \approx \frac{Page\ size}{Range} \approx \frac{Amount\ of\ document\ displayed}{Total\ size\ of\ document}$$

You can use *SetScrollInfo* to set the page size (and hence the size of the thumb), as we'll see in the SYSMETS3 program coming up shortly.

The *GetScrollInfo* function adds a second important feature, or rather it corrects a deficiency in the current API. Suppose you want to use a range that is 65,536 or more units. Back in the days of 16-bit Windows, this was not possible. In Win32, of course, the functions are defined as accepting 32-bit arguments, and indeed they do. (Keep in mind that if you do use a range this large, the number of actual physical positions of the thumb is still limited by the pixel size of the scroll bar.) However, when you get a WM_VSCROLL or WM_HSCROLL message with a notification code of SB_THUMBTRACK or SB_THUMB-POSITION, only 16 bits are provided to indicate the current position of the thumb. The *GetScrollInfo* function lets you obtain the actual 32-bit value.

The syntax of the *SetScrollInfo* and *GetScrollInfo* functions is

```
SetScrollInfo (hwnd, iBar, &si, bRedraw) ;
GetScrollInfo (hwnd, iBar, &si) ;
```

The *iBar* argument is either SB_VERT or SB_HORZ, as in the other scroll bar functions. As with those functions also, it can be SB_CTL for a scroll bar control. The last argument for *SetScrollInfo* can be TRUE or FALSE to indicate if you want Windows to redraw the scroll bar taking into account the new information.

The third argument to both functions is a SCROLLINFO structure, which is defined like so:

```
typedef struct tagSCROLLINFO
{
     UINT cbSize ;       // set to sizeof (SCROLLINFO)
     UINT fMask ;        // values to set or get
     int  nMin ;         // minimum range value
     int  nMax ;         // maximum range value
     UINT nPage ;        // page size
     int  nPos ;         // current position
     int  nTrackPos ;    // current tracking position
}
SCROLLINFO, * PSCROLLINFO ;
```

In your program, you can define a structure of type SCROLLINFO like this:

```
SCROLLINFO si ;
```

Before calling *SetScrollInfo* or *GetScrollInfo*, you must set the *cbSize* field to the size of the structure:

```
si.cbSize = sizeof (si) ;
```

or

```
si.cbSize = sizeof (SCROLLINFO) ;
```

As you get acquainted with Windows, you'll find several other structures that have a first field like this one to indicate the size of the structure. This field allows for a future version of Windows to expand the structure and add new features while still being compatible with previously compiled programs.

You set the *fMask* field to one or more flags beginning with the SIF prefix. You can combine these flags with the C bitwise OR function (|).

When you use the SIF_RANGE flag with the *SetScrollInfo* function, you must set the *nMin* and *nMax* fields to the desired scroll bar range. When you use the SIF_RANGE flag with the *GetScrollInfo* function, the *nMin* and *nMax* fields will be set to the current range on return from the function.

The SIF_POS flag is similar. When used with the *SetScrollInfo* function, you must set the *nPos* field of the structure to the desired position. You use the SIF_POS flag with *GetScrollInfo* to obtain the current position.

The SIF_PAGE flag lets you set and obtain the page size. You set *nPage* to the desired page size with the *SetScrollInfo* function. *GetScrollInfo* with the SIF_PAGE flag lets you obtain the current page size. Don't use this flag if you don't want a proportional scroll bar thumb.

You use the SIF_TRACKPOS flag only with *GetScrollInfo* while processing a WM_VSCROLL or WM_HSCROLL message with a notification code of SB_THUMBTRACK or SB_THUMBPOSITION. On return from the function, the *nTrackPos* field of the SCROLL-INFO structure will indicate the current 32-bit thumb position.

You use the SIF_DISABLENOSCROLL flag only with the *SetScrollInfo* function. If this flag is specified and the new scroll bar arguments would normally render the scroll bar invisible, this scroll renders the scroll bar disabled instead. (I'll explain this more shortly.)

The SIF_ALL flag is a combination of SIF_RANGE, SIF_POS, SIF_PAGE, and SIF_TRACKPOS. This is handy when setting the scroll bar arguments during a WM_SIZE message. (The SIF_TRACKPOS flag is ignored when specified in a *SetScrollInfo* function.) It's also handy when processing a scroll bar message.

How Low Can You Scroll?

In SYSMETS2, the scrolling range is set to a minimum of 0 and a maximum of NUMLINES − 1. When the scroll bar position is 0, the first line of information is at the top of the client area; when the scroll bar position is NUMLINES − 1, the last line is at the top of the client area and no other lines are visible.

You could say that SYSMETS2 scrolls too far. It really only needs to scroll far enough so that the last line of information appears at the *bottom* of the client area rather than at the top. We could make some changes to SYSMETS2 to accomplish this. Rather than set the scroll bar range when we process the WM_CREATE message, we could wait until we receive the WM_SIZE message:

```
iVscrollMax = max (0, NUMLINES - cyClient / cyChar) ;
SetScrollRange (hwnd, SB_VERT, 0, iVscrollMax, TRUE) ;
```

Suppose NUMLINES equals 75, and suppose for a particular window size that *cyClient* divided by *cyChar* equals 50. In other words, we have 75 lines of information but only 50 can fit in the client area at any time. Using the two lines of code shown above, the range is set to a minimum of 0 and a maximum of 25. When the scroll bar position equals 0, the program displays lines 0 through 49. When the scroll bar position equals 1, the program displays lines 1 through 50; and when the scroll bar position equals 25 (the maximum), the program displays lines 25 through 74. Obviously we'd have to make changes to other parts of the program, but this is entirely doable.

One nice feature of the new scroll bar functions is that when you use a scroll bar page size, much of this logic is done for you. Using the SCROLLINFO structure and *SetScrollInfo*, you'd have code that looked something like this:

```
si.cbSize = sizeof (SCROLLINFO) ;
si.cbMask = SIF_RANGE | SIF_PAGE ;
si.nMin   = 0 ;
si.nMax   = NUMLINES - 1 ;
si.nPage  = cyClient / cyChar ;
SetScrollInfo (hwnd, SB_VERT, &si, TRUE) ;
```

When you do this, Windows limits the maximum scroll bar position not to *si.nMax* but to *si.nMax − si.nPage* + 1. Let's make the same assumptions as earlier: NUMLINES equals 75 (so *si.nMax* equals 74), and *si.nPage* equals 50. This means that the maximum scroll bar position is limited to 74 − 50 + 1, or 25. This is exactly what we want.

What happens when the page size is as large as the scroll bar range? That is, in this example, what if *nPage* is 75 or above? Windows conveniently hides the scroll bar because it's no longer needed. If you don't want the scroll bar to be hidden, use SIF_DISABLE-NOSCROLL when calling *SetScrollInfo* and Windows will merely disable the scroll bar rather than hide it.

The New SYSMETS

SYSMETS3—our final version of the SYSMETS program in this chapter—is shown in Figure 4-11, beginning on the following page. This version uses the *SetScrollInfo* and *GetScrollInfo* functions, adds a horizontal scroll bar for left and right scrolling, and repaints the client area more efficiently.

SYSMETS3.C

```
/*-------------------------------------------------------
   SYSMETS3.C -- System Metrics Display Program No. 3
                 (c) Charles Petzold, 1998
   -------------------------------------------------------*/

#include <windows.h>
#include "sysmets.h"

LRESULT CALLBACK WndProc (HWND, UINT, WPARAM, LPARAM) ;

int WINAPI WinMain (HINSTANCE hInstance, HINSTANCE hPrevInstance,
                    PSTR szCmdLine, int iCmdShow)
{
     static TCHAR szAppName[] = TEXT ("SysMets3") ;
     HWND         hwnd ;
     MSG          msg ;
     WNDCLASS     wndclass ;

     wndclass.style         = CS_HREDRAW | CS_VREDRAW ;
     wndclass.lpfnWndProc   = WndProc ;
     wndclass.cbClsExtra    = 0 ;
     wndclass.cbWndExtra    = 0 ;
     wndclass.hInstance     = hInstance ;
     wndclass.hIcon         = LoadIcon (NULL, IDI_APPLICATION) ;
     wndclass.hCursor       = LoadCursor (NULL, IDC_ARROW) ;
     wndclass.hbrBackground = (HBRUSH) GetStockObject (WHITE_BRUSH) ;
     wndclass.lpszMenuName  = NULL ;
     wndclass.lpszClassName = szAppName ;

     if (!RegisterClass (&wndclass))
     {
          MessageBox (NULL, TEXT ("Program requires Windows NT!"),
                      szAppName, MB_ICONERROR) ;
          return 0 ;
     }

     hwnd = CreateWindow (szAppName, TEXT ("Get System Metrics No. 3"),
                          WS_OVERLAPPEDWINDOW | WS_VSCROLL | WS_HSCROLL,
                          CW_USEDEFAULT, CW_USEDEFAULT,
                          CW_USEDEFAULT, CW_USEDEFAULT,
                          NULL, NULL, hInstance, NULL) ;
```

Figure 4-11. *The SYSMETS3 program.*

```
      ShowWindow (hwnd, iCmdShow) ;
      UpdateWindow (hwnd) ;

      while (GetMessage (&msg, NULL, 0, 0))
      {
           TranslateMessage (&msg) ;
           DispatchMessage (&msg) ;
      }
      return msg.wParam ;
}

LRESULT CALLBACK WndProc (HWND hwnd, UINT message, WPARAM wParam, LPARAM lParam)
{
      static int  cxChar, cxCaps, cyChar, cxClient, cyClient, iMaxWidth ;
      HDC         hdc ;
      int         i, x, y, iVertPos, iHorzPos, iPaintBeg, iPaintEnd ;
      PAINTSTRUCT ps ;
      SCROLLINFO  si ;
      TCHAR       szBuffer[10] ;
      TEXTMETRIC  tm ;

      switch (message)
      {
      case WM_CREATE:
           hdc = GetDC (hwnd) ;

           GetTextMetrics (hdc, &tm) ;
           cxChar = tm.tmAveCharWidth ;
           cxCaps = (tm.tmPitchAndFamily & 1 ? 3 : 2) * cxChar / 2 ;
           cyChar = tm.tmHeight + tm.tmExternalLeading ;

           ReleaseDC (hwnd, hdc) ;

                // Save the width of the three columns

           iMaxWidth = 40 * cxChar + 22 * cxCaps ;
           return 0 ;

      case WM_SIZE:
           cxClient = LOWORD (lParam) ;
           cyClient = HIWORD (lParam) ;

                // Set vertical scroll bar range and page size

           si.cbSize = sizeof (si) ;
           si.fMask  = SIF_RANGE | SIF_PAGE ;
```

(continued)

Figure 4-11. *continued*

```
            si.nMin   = 0 ;
            si.nMax   = NUMLINES - 1 ;
            si.nPage  = cyClient / cyChar ;
            SetScrollInfo (hwnd, SB_VERT, &si, TRUE) ;

                  // Set horizontal scroll bar range and page size

            si.cbSize = sizeof (si) ;
            si.fMask  = SIF_RANGE | SIF_PAGE ;
            si.nMin   = 0 ;
            si.nMax   = 2 + iMaxWidth / cxChar ;
            si.nPage  = cxClient / cxChar ;
            SetScrollInfo (hwnd, SB_HORZ, &si, TRUE) ;
            return 0 ;

     case WM_VSCROLL:
                  // Get all the vertical scroll bar information

            si.cbSize = sizeof (si) ;
            si.fMask  = SIF_ALL ;
            GetScrollInfo (hwnd, SB_VERT, &si) ;

                  // Save the position for comparison later on

            iVertPos = si.nPos ;

            switch (LOWORD (wParam))
            {
            case SB_TOP:
                 si.nPos = si.nMin ;
                 break ;

            case SB_BOTTOM:
                 si.nPos = si.nMax ;
                 break ;

            case SB_LINEUP:
                 si.nPos -= 1 ;
                 break ;

            case SB_LINEDOWN:
                 si.nPos += 1 ;
                 break ;

            case SB_PAGEUP:
                 si.nPos -= si.nPage ;
                 break ;
```

```
          case SB_PAGEDOWN:
               si.nPos += si.nPage ;
               break ;

          case SB_THUMBTRACK:
               si.nPos = si.nTrackPos ;
               break ;

          default:
               break ;
          }
               // Set the position and then retrieve it.  Due to adjustments
               //   by Windows it may not be the same as the value set.

          si.fMask = SIF_POS ;
          SetScrollInfo (hwnd, SB_VERT, &si, TRUE) ;
          GetScrollInfo (hwnd, SB_VERT, &si) ;

               // If the position has changed, scroll the window and update it

          if (si.nPos != iVertPos)
          {
               ScrollWindow (hwnd, 0, cyChar * (iVertPos - si.nPos),
                              NULL, NULL) ;
               UpdateWindow (hwnd) ;
          }
          return 0 ;

     case WM_HSCROLL:
               // Get all the vertical scroll bar information

          si.cbSize = sizeof (si) ;
          si.fMask  = SIF_ALL ;

               // Save the position for comparison later on

          GetScrollInfo (hwnd, SB_HORZ, &si) ;
          iHorzPos = si.nPos ;

          switch (LOWORD (wParam))
          {
          case SB_LINELEFT:
               si.nPos -= 1 ;
               break ;

          case SB_LINERIGHT:
```

(continued)

Figure 4-11. *continued*

```
            si.nPos += 1 ;
            break ;

        case SB_PAGELEFT:
            si.nPos -= si.nPage ;
            break ;

        case SB_PAGERIGHT:
            si.nPos += si.nPage ;
            break ;

        case SB_THUMBPOSITION:
            si.nPos = si.nTrackPos ;
            break ;

        default :
            break ;
        }
            // Set the position and then retrieve it.  Due to adjustments
            //   by Windows it may not be the same as the value set.

        si.fMask = SIF_POS ;
        SetScrollInfo (hwnd, SB_HORZ, &si, TRUE) ;
        GetScrollInfo (hwnd, SB_HORZ, &si) ;

            // If the position has changed, scroll the window

        if (si.nPos != iHorzPos)
        {
            ScrollWindow (hwnd, cxChar * (iHorzPos - si.nPos), 0,
                        NULL, NULL) ;
        }
        return 0 ;

case WM_PAINT :
    hdc = BeginPaint (hwnd, &ps) ;

        // Get vertical scroll bar position

    si.cbSize = sizeof (si) ;
    si.fMask  = SIF_POS ;
    GetScrollInfo (hwnd, SB_VERT, &si) ;
    iVertPos = si.nPos ;

        // Get horizontal scroll bar position
```

```
            GetScrollInfo (hwnd, SB_HORZ, &si) ;
            iHorzPos = si.nPos ;

                 // Find painting limits

            iPaintBeg = max (0, iVertPos + ps.rcPaint.top / cyChar) ;
            iPaintEnd = min (NUMLINES - 1,
                             iVertPos + ps.rcPaint.bottom / cyChar) ;

            for (i = iPaintBeg ; i <= iPaintEnd ; i++)
            {
                 x = cxChar * (1 - iHorzPos) ;
                 y = cyChar * (i - iVertPos) ;

                 TextOut (hdc, x, y,
                          sysmetrics[i].szLabel,
                          lstrlen (sysmetrics[i].szLabel)) ;

                 TextOut (hdc, x + 22 * cxCaps, y,
                          sysmetrics[i].szDesc,
                          lstrlen (sysmetrics[i].szDesc)) ;

                 SetTextAlign (hdc, TA_RIGHT | TA_TOP) ;

                 TextOut (hdc, x + 22 * cxCaps + 40 * cxChar, y, szBuffer,
                          wsprintf (szBuffer, TEXT ("%5d"),
                               GetSystemMetrics (sysmetrics[i].iIndex))) ;

                 SetTextAlign (hdc, TA_LEFT | TA_TOP) ;
            }

            EndPaint (hwnd, &ps) ;
            return 0 ;

       case WM_DESTROY :
            PostQuitMessage (0) ;
            return 0 ;
       }
       return DefWindowProc (hwnd, message, wParam, lParam) ;
}
```

This version of the program relies on Windows to maintain the scroll bar information and do a lot of the bounds checking. At the beginning of WM_VSCROLL and WM_HSCROLL processing, it obtains all the scroll bar information, adjusts the position based on the notification code, and then sets the position by calling *SetScrollInfo*. The program then calls *GetScrollInfo*. If the position was out of range in the *SetScrollInfo* call, the position is corrected by Windows and the correct value is returned in the *GetScrollInfo* call.

SYSMETS3 uses the *ScrollWindow* function to scroll information in the window's client area rather than repaint it. Although the function is rather complex (and has been superseded in recent versions of Windows by the even more complex *ScrollWindowEx*), SYSMETS3 uses it in a fairly simple way. The second argument to the function gives an amount to scroll the client area horizontally in pixels, and the third argument is an amount to scroll the client area vertically.

The last two arguments to *ScrollWindow* are set to NULL. This indicates that the entire client area is to be scrolled. Windows automatically invalidates the rectangle in the client area "uncovered" by the scrolling operation. This generates a WM_PAINT message. *InvalidateRect* is no longer needed. Note that *ScrollWindow* is *not* a GDI function because it does not require a handle to a device context. It is one of the few non-GDI Windows functions that changes the appearance of the client area of a window. Rather peculiarly but conveniently, it is documented along with the scroll bar functions.

The WM_HSCROLL processing traps the SB_THUMBPOSITION notification code and ignores SB_THUMBTRACK. Thus, if the user drags the thumb on the horizontal scroll bar, the program will not scroll the contents of the window horizontally until the user releases the mouse button.

The WM_VSCROLL strategy is different: here, the program traps SB_THUMBTRACK messages and ignores SB_THUMBPOSITION. Thus, the program scrolls its contents vertically in direct response to the user dragging the thumb on the vertical scroll bar. This is considered preferable, but watch out: It is well known that when users find out a program scrolls in direct response to dragging the scroll bar thumb, they will frenetically jerk the thumb back and forth trying to bring the program to its knees. Fortunately, today's fast PCs are much more likely to survive this torture test. But try your code out on a slow machine, and perhaps think about using the SB_SLOWMACHINE argument to *GetSystemMetrics* for alternative processing for slow machines.

One way to speed up WM_PAINT processing is illustrated by SYSMETS3: The WM_PAINT code determines which lines are within the invalid rectangle and rewrites only those lines. The code is more complex, of course, but it is faster.

But I Don't Like to Use the Mouse

In the early days of Windows, a significant number of users didn't care for using the mouse, and indeed, Windows itself (and many Windows programs) did not require a mouse. Although mouseless PCs have now generally gone the way of monochrome displays and dot-matrix printers, it is still recommended that you write programs that duplicate mouse operations with the keyboard. This is particularly true for something as fundamental as scroll bars, because our keyboards have a whole array of cursor movement keys that should offer alternatives to the mouse.

In the next chapter, you'll learn how to use the keyboard and how to add a keyboard interface to this program. You'll notice that SYSMETS3 seems to process WM_VSCROLL messages when the notification code equals SB_TOP and SB_BOTTOM. I mentioned earlier that a window procedure doesn't receive these messages for scroll bars, so right now this is superfluous code. When we come back to this program in the next chapter, you'll see the reason for including those operations.

Chapter 5

Basic Drawing

The subsystem of Microsoft Windows responsible for displaying graphics on video displays and printers is known as the Graphics Device Interface (GDI). As you might imagine, GDI is an extremely important part of Windows. Not only do the applications you write for Windows use GDI for the display of visual information, but Windows itself uses GDI for the visual display of user interface items such as menus, scroll bars, icons, and mouse cursors.

Unfortunately, a comprehensive discussion of GDI would require an entire book, and this is not that book. Instead, in this chapter I want to provide you with the basics of drawing lines and filled areas. This is enough GDI to get you through the next few chapters. In later chapters, we'll look at GDI support of bitmaps, metafiles, and formatted text.

THE STRUCTURE OF GDI

From the programmer's perspective, GDI consists of several hundred function calls and some associated data types, macros, and structures. But before we begin looking at some of these functions in detail, let's step back and get a feel for the overall structure of GDI.

The GDI Philosophy

Graphics in Windows 98 and Microsoft Windows NT is handled primarily by functions exported from the dynamic-link library GDI32.DLL. In Windows 98, this GDI32.DLL makes use of the 16-bit GDI.EXE dynamic-link library for the actual implementation of many of the functions. In Windows NT, GDI.EXE is used only for 16-bit programs.

These dynamic-link libraries call routines in device drivers for the video display and any printers you may have set up. The video driver accesses the hardware of the video display, and the printer driver converts GDI commands into codes or commands that the various printers understand. Obviously, different video display adapters and printers require different device drivers.

A wide variety of display devices can be attached to PC compatibles. One of the primary goals of GDI is to support device-independent graphics. Windows programs should be able to run without problems on any graphics output device that Windows supports. GDI accomplishes this goal by providing facilities to insulate your programs from the particular characteristics of different output devices.

The world of graphics output devices is divided into two broad groups: raster devices and vector devices. Most PC output devices are raster devices, which means that they represent images as a rectangular pattern of dots. This category includes video display adapters, dot-matrix printers, and laser printers. Vector devices, which draw images using lines, are generally limited these days to plotters.

Much of traditional computer graphics programming (the type you'll find in older books) is based solely on vectors. This means that a program using a vector graphics system is a level of abstraction away from the hardware. The output device uses pixels for a graphics representation, but the program doesn't talk to the interface in terms of pixels. While you can certainly use the Windows GDI as a high-level vector drawing system, you can also use it for relatively low-level pixel manipulation.

In this respect, Windows GDI is to traditional graphics interface languages what C is to other programming languages. C is well known for its high degree of portability among different operating systems and environments. Yet C is also well known for allowing a programmer to perform low-level system functions that are often impossible in other high-level languages. Just as C is sometimes thought of as a "high-level assembly language," you can think of GDI as a high-level interface to the hardware of the graphics device.

As you've seen, by default Windows uses a coordinate system based on pixels. Most traditional graphics languages use a "virtual" coordinate system with horizontal and vertical axes that range (for instance) from 0 to 32,767. Although some graphics languages don't let you use pixel coordinates, Windows GDI lets you use either system (as well as additional coordinate systems based on physical measurements). You can use a virtual coordinate system and keep your program distanced from the hardware, or you can use the device coordinate system and snuggle right up to the hardware.

Some programmers think that when you're working in terms of pixels, you've abandoned device independence. We've already seen in the last chapter that this is not necessarily the case. The trick is to use the pixels in a device-independent manner. This requires that the graphics interface language provide facilities for a program to determine the hardware characteristics of the device and make appropriate adjustments. For example, in the SYSMETS programs we used the pixel size of a standard system font character to space text on the screen. This approach allowed the programs to adjust to different display adapters with different resolutions, text sizes, and aspect ratios. You'll see other methods in this chapter for determining display sizes.

In the early days, many users ran Windows with a monochrome display. Even in more recent years, laptop users were restricted to gray shades. For this reason, GDI was constructed so that you can write a program without worrying much about color—that is, Windows can convert colors to gray shades. Even today, video displays used with Windows 98 have different color capabilities (16 color, 256 color, "high color," and "true color"). Although ink-jet printers have brought low-cost hard-copy color to the masses, many users still prefer their black-only laser printers for high-quality output. It is possible to use these devices blindly, but your program can also determine how many colors are available on the particular display device and take best advantage of the hardware.

Of course, just as you can write C programs that have subtle portability problems when they run on other computers, you can also inadvertently let device dependencies creep into your Windows programs. That's part of the price of not being fully insulated from the hardware. You should also be aware of the limitations of Windows GDI. Although you can certainly move graphics objects around the display, GDI is generally a static display system with only limited animation support. If you need to write sophisticated animations for games, you should explore Microsoft DirectX, which provides the support you'll need.

The GDI Function Calls

The several hundred function calls that comprise GDI can be classified in several broad groups:

- *Functions that get (or create) and release (or destroy) a device context* As we saw in earlier chapters, you need a handle to a device context in order to draw. The *BeginPaint* and *EndPaint* functions (although technically a part of the USER module rather than the GDI module) let you do this during the WM_PAINT message, and *GetDC* and *ReleaseDC* functions let you do this during other messages. We'll examine some other functions regarding device contexts shortly.

- *Functions that obtain information about the device context* In the SYSMETS programs in Chapter 4, we used the *GetTextMetrics* function to obtain information about the dimensions of the font currently selected in the device context. Later in this chapter, we'll look at the DEVCAPS1 program, which obtains other, more general, device context information.

- *Functions that draw something* Obviously, once all the preliminaries are out of the way, this is the really important stuff. In the last chapter, we used the *TextOut* function to display some text in the client area of the window. As we'll see, other GDI functions let us draw lines and filled areas. In Chapters 14 and 15, we'll also see how to draw bit-mapped images.

- *Functions that set and get attributes of the device context* An "attribute" of the device context determines various details regarding how the drawing functions work. For example, you can use *SetTextColor* to specify the color of any text you draw using *TextOut* or other text output functions. In the SYSMETS programs in Chapter 4, we used *SetTextAlign* to tell GDI that the starting position of the text string in the *TextOut* function should be the right side of the string rather than the left, which is the default. All attributes of the device context have default values that are set when the device context is obtained. For all *Set* functions, there are *Get* functions that let you obtain the current device context attributes.

■   *Functions that work with GDI "objects"*   Here's where GDI gets a bit messy. First an example: By default, any lines you draw using GDI are solid and of a standard width. You may wish to draw thicker lines or use lines composed of a series of dots or dashes. The line width and this line style are *not* attributes of the device context. Instead, they are characteristics of a "logical pen." You can think of a pen as a collection of bundled attributes. You create a logical pen by specifying these characteristics in the *CreatePen*, *CreatePenIndirect*, or *ExtCreatePen* function. Although these functions are considered to be part of GDI, unlike most GDI functions they do *not* require a handle to a device context. The functions return a handle to a logical pen. To use this pen, you "select" the pen handle into the device context. The current pen selected in the device context is considered an attribute of the device context. From then on, whatever lines you draw use this pen. Later on, you deselect the pen object from the device context and destroy the object. Destroying the pen is necessary because the pen definition occupies allocated memory space. Besides pens, you also use GDI objects for creating brushes that fill enclosed areas, for fonts, for bitmaps, and for other aspects of GDI.

The GDI Primitives

The types of graphics you display on the screen or the printer can themselves be divided into several categories, which are called "primitives." These are:

■   *Lines and curves*   Lines are the foundation of any vector graphics drawing system. GDI supports straight lines, rectangles, ellipses (including that subset of ellipses known as circles), "arcs" that are partial curves on the circumference of an ellipse, and Bezier splines, all of which I'll discuss in this chapter. If you need to draw a different type of curve, you can draw it as a polyline, which is a series of very short lines that define a curve. GDI draws lines using the current pen selected in the device context.

■   *Filled areas*   Whenever a series of lines or curves encloses an area, you can cause that area to be filled with the current GDI brush object. This brush can be a solid color, a pattern (which can be a series of horizontal, vertical, or diagonal hatch marks), or a bitmapped image that is repeated vertically or horizontally within the area.

■ *Bitmaps*   A bitmap is a rectangular array of bits that correspond to the pixels of a display device. The bitmap is the fundamental tool of raster graphics. Bitmaps are generally used for displaying complex (often real-world) images on the video display or printer. Bitmaps are also used for displaying small images that must be drawn very quickly, such as icons, mouse cursors, and buttons that appear in application toolbars. GDI supports two types of bitmaps—the old (although still quite useful) "device-dependent" bitmap, which is a GDI object, and the newer (as of Windows 3.0) "device-independent" bitmap (or DIB), which can be stored in disk files. I'll discuss bitmaps in Chapters 14 and 15.

■ *Text*   Text is not quite as mathematical as other aspects of computer graphics; instead it is bound to hundreds of years of traditional typography, which many typographers and other observers appreciate as an art. For this reason, text is often the most complex part of any computer graphics system, but it is also (assuming literacy remains the norm) the most important. Data structures used for defining GDI font objects and for obtaining font information are among the largest in Windows. Beginning with Windows 3.1, GDI began supporting True-Type fonts, which are based on filled outlines that can be manipulated with other GDI functions. Windows 98 continues to support the older bitmap-based fonts for compatibility and small memory requirements. I'll discuss fonts in Chapter 17.

Other Stuff

Other aspects of GDI are not so easily classifiable. These are:

■ *Mapping modes and transforms*   Although by default you draw in units of pixels, you are not limited to doing that. The GDI mapping modes allow you to draw in units of inches (or rather, fractions of inches), millimeters, or anything you want. In addition, Windows NT supports a traditional "world transform" expressed as a 3-by-3 matrix. This allows for skewing and rotation of graphics objects. The world transform is not supported under Windows 98.

■ *Metafiles*   A metafile is a collection of GDI commands stored in a binary form. Metafiles are used primarily to transfer representations of vector graphic drawings through the clipboard. I'll discuss metafiles in Chapter 18.

■ *Regions*   A region is a complex area of any shape and is generally defined as a Boolean combination of simpler regions. More complex regions can be stored internally in GDI as a series of scan lines derived from the original definition of the region. You can use regions for outlining, filling, and clipping.

■   *Paths*   A path is a collection of straight lines and curves stored internally in GDI. Paths can be used for drawing, filling, and clipping. Paths can also be converted to regions.

■   *Clipping*   Drawing can be restricted to a particular section of the client area. This is known as clipping. The clipping area can be rectangular or non-rectangular, generally specified as a region or a path.

■   *Palettes*   The use of a customized palette is generally restricted to displays that show 256 colors. Windows reserves only 20 of these colors for use by the system. You can alter the other 236 colors to accurately display the colors of real-world images stored in bitmaps. I'll discuss palettes in Chapter 16.

■   *Printing*   Although this chapter is restricted to the video display, almost everything you learn here can be applied to printing. I discuss printing in Chapter 13.

THE DEVICE CONTEXT

Before we begin drawing, let's examine the device context with more rigor than we did in Chapter 4.

When you want to draw on a graphics output device such as the screen or printer, you must first obtain a handle to a device context (or DC). In giving your program this handle, Windows is giving you permission to use the device. You then include the handle as an argument to the GDI functions to identify to Windows the device on which you wish to draw.

The device context contains many "attributes" that determine how the GDI functions work on the device. These attributes allow GDI functions to have just a few arguments, such as starting coordinates. The GDI functions do not need arguments for everything else that Windows needs to display the object on the device. For example, when you call *TextOut*, you need specify in the function only the device context handle, the starting coordinates, the text, and the length of the text. You don't need to specify the font, the color of the text, the color of the background behind the text, or the intercharacter spacing. These are all attributes that are part of the device context. When you want to change one of these attributes, you call a function that does so. Subsequent *TextOut* calls to that device context use the new attribute.

Getting a Device Context Handle

Windows provides several methods for obtaining a device context handle. If you obtain a video display device context handle while processing a message, you should release it before exiting the window procedure. After you release the handle, it is no longer valid. For a printer device context handle, the rules are not as strict. Again, we'll look at printing in Chapter 13.

The most common method for obtaining a device context handle and then releasing it involves using the *BeginPaint* and *EndPaint* calls when processing the WM_PAINT message:

```
hdc = BeginPaint (hwnd, &ps) ;
[other program lines]
EndPaint (hwnd, &ps) ;
```

The variable *ps* is a structure of type PAINTSTRUCT. The *hdc* field of this structure is the same handle to the device context that *BeginPaint* returns. The PAINTSTRUCT structure also contains a RECT (rectangle) structure named *rcPaint* that defines a rectangle encompassing the invalid region of the window's client area. With the device context handle obtained from *BeginPaint* you can draw only within this region. The *BeginPaint* call also validates this region.

Windows programs can also obtain a handle to a device context while processing messages other than WM_PAINT:

```
hdc = GetDC (hwnd) ;
[other program lines]
ReleaseDC (hwnd, hdc) ;
```

This device context applies to the client area of the window whose handle is *hwnd*. The primary difference between the use of these calls and the use of the *BeginPaint* and *EndPaint* combination is that you can draw on your entire client area with the handle returned from *GetDC*. However, *GetDC* and *ReleaseDC* don't validate any possibly invalid regions of the client area.

A Windows program can also obtain a handle to a device context that applies to the entire window and not only to the window's client area:

```
hdc = GetWindowDC (hwnd) ;
[other program lines]
ReleaseDC (hwnd, hdc) ;
```

This device context includes the window title bar, menu, scroll bars, and frame in addition to the client area. Applications programs rarely use the *GetWindowDC* function. If you want to experiment with it, you should also trap the WM_NCPAINT ("nonclient paint") message, which is the message Windows uses to draw on the nonclient areas of the window.

The *BeginPaint*, *GetDC*, and *GetWindowDC* calls obtain a device context associated with a particular window on the video display. A much more general function for obtaining a handle to a device context is *CreateDC*:

```
hdc = CreateDC (pszDriver, pszDevice, pszOutput, pData) ;
[other program lines]
DeleteDC (hdc) ;
```

For example, you can obtain a device context handle for the entire display by calling

```
hdc = CreateDC (TEXT ("DISPLAY"), NULL, NULL, NULL) ;
```

Writing outside your window is generally impolite, but it's convenient for some unusual applications. (Although this fact is not documented, you can also retrieve a device context for the entire screen by calling *GetDC* with a NULL argument.) In Chapter 13, we'll use the *CreateDC* function to obtain a handle to a printer device context.

Sometimes you need only to obtain some information about a device context and not do any drawing. In these cases, you can obtain a handle to an "information context" by using *CreateIC*. The arguments are the same as for the *CreateDC* function. For example,

```
hdc = CreateIC (TEXT ("DISPLAY"), NULL, NULL, NULL) ;
```

You can't write to the device by using this information context handle.

When working with bitmaps, it can sometimes be useful to obtain a "memory device context":

```
hdcMem = CreateCompatibleDC (hdc) ;
[other program lines]
DeleteDC (hdcMem) ;
```

You can select a bitmap into the memory device context and use GDI functions to draw on the bitmap. I'll discuss these techniques in Chapter 14.

I mentioned earlier that a metafile is a collection of GDI function calls encoded in binary form. You can create a metafile by obtaining a metafile device context:

```
hdcMeta = CreateMetaFile (pszFilename) ;
[other program lines]
hmf = CloseMetaFile (hdcMeta) ;
```

During the time the metafile device context is valid, any GDI calls you make using *hdcMeta* are not displayed but become part of the metafile. When you call *CloseMetaFile*, the device context handle becomes invalid. The function returns a handle to the metafile (*hmf*). I'll discuss metafiles in Chapter 18.

Getting Device Context Information

A device context usually refers to a physical display device such as a video display or a printer. Often, you need to obtain information about this device, including the size of the display, in terms of both pixels and physical dimensions, and its color capabilities. You can get this information by calling the *GetDeviceCap* ("get device capabilities") function:

```
iValue = GetDeviceCaps (hdc, iIndex) ;
```

The *iIndex* argument is one of 29 identifiers defined in the WINGDI.H header file. For example, the *iIndex* value of HORZRES causes *GetDeviceCaps* to return the width of the device in pixels; a VERTRES argument returns the height of the device in pixels. If *hdc* is a handle to a screen device context, that's the same information you can get from *GetSystemMetrics*. If *hdc* is a handle to a printer device context, *GetDeviceCaps* returns the height and width of the printer display area in pixels.

You can also use *GetDeviceCaps* to determine the device's capabilities of processing various types of graphics. This is usually not important for dealing with the video display, but it becomes more important with working with printers. For example, most pen plotters can't draw bitmapped images and *GetDeviceCaps* can tell you that.

The DEVCAPS1 Program

The DEVCAPS1 program, shown in Figure 5-1, displays some (but not all) of the information available from the *GetDeviceCaps* function using a device context for the video display. In Chapter 13, I'll present a second, expanded version of this program, called DEVCAPS2, that gets information for the printer.

DEVCAPS1.C

```
/*-----------------------------------------------------------
   DEVCAPS1.C -- Device Capabilities Display Program No. 1
                 (c) Charles Petzold, 1998
   -----------------------------------------------------------*/

#include <windows.h>

#define NUMLINES ((int) (sizeof devcaps / sizeof devcaps [0]))

struct
{
    int     iIndex ;
    TCHAR * szLabel ;
    TCHAR * szDesc ;
}
devcaps [] =
{
    HORZSIZE,       TEXT ("HORZSIZE"),      TEXT ("Width in millimeters:"),
    VERTSIZE,       TEXT ("VERTSIZE"),      TEXT ("Height in millimeters:"),
    HORZRES,        TEXT ("HORZRES"),       TEXT ("Width in pixels:"),
    VERTRES,        TEXT ("VERTRES"),       TEXT ("Height in raster lines:"),
    BITSPIXEL,      TEXT ("BITSPIXEL"),     TEXT ("Color bits per pixel:"),
    PLANES,         TEXT ("PLANES"),        TEXT ("Number of color planes:"),
    NUMBRUSHES,     TEXT ("NUMBRUSHES"),    TEXT ("Number of device brushes:"),
    NUMPENS,        TEXT ("NUMPENS"),       TEXT ("Number of device pens:"),
    NUMMARKERS,     TEXT ("NUMMARKERS"),    TEXT ("Number of device markers:"),
    NUMFONTS,       TEXT ("NUMFONTS"),      TEXT ("Number of device fonts:"),
    NUMCOLORS,      TEXT ("NUMCOLORS"),     TEXT ("Number of device colors:"),
    PDEVICESIZE,    TEXT ("PDEVICESIZE"),   TEXT ("Size of device structure:"),
    ASPECTX,        TEXT ("ASPECTX"),       TEXT ("Relative width of pixel:"),
    ASPECTY,        TEXT ("ASPECTY"),       TEXT ("Relative height of pixel:"),
```

Figure 5-1. *The DEVCAPS1 program.*   *(continued)*

Figure 5-1. *continued*

```
      ASPECTXY,          TEXT ("ASPECTXY"),       TEXT ("Relative diagonal of pixel:"),
      LOGPIXELSX,        TEXT ("LOGPIXELSX"),      TEXT ("Horizontal dots per inch:"),
      LOGPIXELSY,        TEXT ("LOGPIXELSY"),      TEXT ("Vertical dots per inch:"),
      SIZEPALETTE,       TEXT ("SIZEPALETTE"),     TEXT ("Number of palette entries:"),
      NUMRESERVED,       TEXT ("NUMRESERVED"),     TEXT ("Reserved palette entries:"),
      COLORRES,          TEXT ("COLORRES"),        TEXT ("Actual color resolution:")
} ;

LRESULT CALLBACK WndProc (HWND, UINT, WPARAM, LPARAM) ;

int WINAPI WinMain (HINSTANCE hInstance, HINSTANCE hPrevInstance,
                    PSTR szCmdLine, int iCmdShow)
{
     static TCHAR szAppName[] = TEXT ("DevCaps1") ;
     HWND          hwnd ;
     MSG           msg ;
     WNDCLASS      wndclass ;

     wndclass.style         = CS_HREDRAW | CS_VREDRAW ;
     wndclass.lpfnWndProc   = WndProc ;
     wndclass.cbClsExtra    = 0 ;
     wndclass.cbWndExtra    = 0 ;
     wndclass.hInstance     = hInstance ;
     wndclass.hIcon         = LoadIcon (NULL, IDI_APPLICATION) ;
     wndclass.hCursor       = LoadCursor (NULL, IDC_ARROW) ;
     wndclass.hbrBackground = (HBRUSH) GetStockObject (WHITE_BRUSH) ;
     wndclass.lpszMenuName  = NULL ;
     wndclass.lpszClassName = szAppName ;

     if (!RegisterClass (&wndclass))
     {
          MessageBox (NULL, TEXT ("This program requires Windows NT!"),
                      szAppName, MB_ICONERROR) ;
          return 0 ;
     }

     hwnd = CreateWindow (szAppName, TEXT ("Device Capabilities"),
                          WS_OVERLAPPEDWINDOW,
                          CW_USEDEFAULT, CW_USEDEFAULT,
                          CW_USEDEFAULT, CW_USEDEFAULT,
                          NULL, NULL, hInstance, NULL) ;

     ShowWindow (hwnd, iCmdShow) ;
     UpdateWindow (hwnd) ;
```

```
    while (GetMessage (&msg, NULL, 0, 0))
    {
         TranslateMessage (&msg) ;
         DispatchMessage (&msg) ;
    }
    return msg.wParam ;
}

LRESULT CALLBACK WndProc (HWND hwnd, UINT message, WPARAM wParam, LPARAM lParam)
{
    static int  cxChar, cxCaps, cyChar ;
    TCHAR       szBuffer[10] ;
    HDC         hdc ;
    int         i ;
    PAINTSTRUCT ps ;
    TEXTMETRIC  tm ;

    switch (message)
    {
    case WM_CREATE:
         hdc = GetDC (hwnd) ;

         GetTextMetrics (hdc, &tm) ;
         cxChar = tm.tmAveCharWidth ;
         cxCaps = (tm.tmPitchAndFamily & 1 ? 3 : 2) * cxChar / 2 ;
         cyChar = tm.tmHeight + tm.tmExternalLeading ;

         ReleaseDC (hwnd, hdc) ;
         return 0 ;

    case WM_PAINT:
         hdc = BeginPaint (hwnd, &ps) ;

         for (i = 0 ; i < NUMLINES ; i++)
         {
              TextOut (hdc, 0, cyChar * i,
                       devcaps[i].szLabel,
                       lstrlen (devcaps[i].szLabel)) ;

              TextOut (hdc, 14 * cxCaps, cyChar * i,
                       devcaps[i].szDesc,
                       lstrlen (devcaps[i].szDesc)) ;

              SetTextAlign (hdc, TA_RIGHT | TA_TOP) ;
```

(continued)

Figure 5-1. *continued*

```
            TextOut (hdc, 14 * cxCaps + 35 * cxChar, cyChar * i, szBuffer,
                    wsprintf (szBuffer, TEXT ("%5d"),
                        GetDeviceCaps (hdc, devcaps[i].iIndex))) ;

            SetTextAlign (hdc, TA_LEFT | TA_TOP) ;
        }

        EndPaint (hwnd, &ps) ;
        return 0 ;

    case WM_DESTROY:
        PostQuitMessage (0) ;
        return 0 ;
    }
    return DefWindowProc (hwnd, message, wParam, lParam) ;
}
```

As you can see, this program is quite similar to the SYSMETS1 program shown in Chapter 4. To keep the code short, I didn't include scroll bars because I knew the information would fit on one screen. The results for a 256-color, 640-by-480 VGA are shown in Figure 5-2.

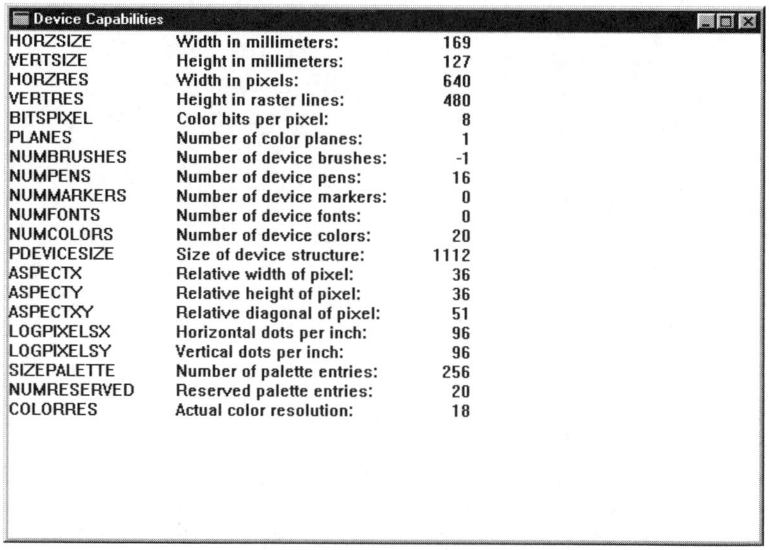

Figure 5-2. *The DEVCAPS1 display for a 256-color, 640-by-480 VGA.*

The Size of the Device

Suppose you want to draw a square with sides that are 1 inch in length. To do this, either you (the programmer) or Windows (the operating system) would need to know how many pixels corresponded to 1 inch on the video display. The *GetDeviceCaps* function helps you obtain information regarding the physical size of the output device, be it the video display or printer.

Video displays and printers are two very different devices. But perhaps the least obvious difference is how the word "resolution" is used in connection with the device. With printers, we often indicate a resolution in dots per inch. For example, most laser printers have a resolution of 300 or 600 dots per inch. However, the resolution of a video display is given as the total number of pixels horizontally and vertically, for example, 1024 by 768. Most people couldn't tell you the total number of pixels their printers display horizontally and vertically on a sheet of paper or the number of pixels per inch on their video displays.

In this book I'm going to use the word "resolution" in the strict sense of a number of pixels per metrical unit, generally an inch. I'll use the phrase "pixel size" or "pixel dimension" to indicate the total number of pixels that the device displays horizontally or vertically. The "metrical size" or "metrical dimension" is the size of the display area of the device in inches or millimeters. (For a printer page, this is not the whole size of the paper but only the printable area.) Dividing the pixel size by the metrical size gives you a resolution.

Most video displays used with Windows these days have screens that are 33 percent wider than they are high. This represents an aspect ratio of 1.33:1 or (as it's more commonly written) 4:3. Historically, this aspect ratio goes way back to when Thomas Edison was making movies. It remained the standard aspect ratio for motion pictures until various types of widescreen projection started to be used beginning in 1953. Television sets also have an aspect ratio of 4:3.

However, your Windows applications should not assume that the video display has a 4:3 aspect ratio. People who do mostly word processing sometimes prefer a video display that resembles the height and width of a sheet of paper. The most common alternative to a 4:3 display is a 3:4 display—essentially a standard display turned on its side.

If the horizontal resolution of a device equals the vertical resolution, the device is said to have "square pixels." Nowadays all video displays in common use with Windows have square pixels, but this was not always the case. (Nor should your applications assume that the video display always has square pixels.) When Windows was first introduced, the standard video adapter boards were the IBM Color Graphics Adapter (CGA), which had a pixel dimension area of 640 by 200 pixels; the Enhanced Graphics Adapter (EGA), which had a pixel dimension of 640 by 350 pixels; and the Hercules Graphics Card, which had a pixel dimension of 720 by 348 pixels. All these video boards used a display that had a 4:3 aspect ratio, but the number of pixels horizontally and vertically was not in the ratio 4:3.

It's quite easy for a user running Windows to determine the pixel dimensions of a video display. Run the Display applet in Control Panel, and select the Settings tab. In the area labeled Screen Area, you'll probably see one of these pixel dimensions:

■ 640 by 480 pixels

■ 800 by 600 pixels

■ 1024 by 768 pixels

■ 1280 by 1024 pixels

■ 1600 by 1200 pixels

All of these are in the ratio 4:3. (Well, all except the 1280 by 1024 pixel size. This should probably be considered an annoying anomaly rather than anything more significant. As we'll see, all these pixel dimensions when combined with a 4:3 monitor are considered to yield square pixels.)

A Windows application can obtain the pixel dimensions of the display from *GetSystemMetrics* with the SM_CXSCREEN and SM_CYSCREEN arguments. As you'll note from the DEVCAPS1 program, a program can obtain the same values from *GetDeviceCaps* with the HORZRES ("horizontal resolution") and VERTRES arguments. This is a use of the word "resolution" that means the pixel size rather than the pixels per metrical unit.

That's the simple part of the device size. Now the confusion begins.

The first two device capabilities, HORZSIZE and VERTSIZE, are documented as "Width, in millimeters, of the physical screen" and "Height, in millimeters, of the physical screen" (in */Platform SDK/Graphics and Multimedia Services/GDI/Device Contexts/Device Context Reference/Device Context Functions/GetDeviceCaps*). These seem like straightforward definitions until one begins to think through their implications. For example, given the nature of the interface between video display adapters and monitors, how can Windows really know the monitor size? And what if you have a laptop (in which the video driver conceivably *could* know the exact physical dimensions of the screen) and you attach an external monitor to it? And what if you attach a video projector to your PC?

In the 16-bit versions of Windows (and in Windows NT), Windows uses a "standard" display size for the HORZSIZE and VERTSIZE values. Beginning with Windows 95, however, the HORZSIZE and VERTSIZE values are derived from the HORZRES, VERTRES, LOGPIXELSX, and LOGPIXELSY values. Here's how it works.

When you use the Display applet of the Control Panel to select a pixel size of the display, you can also select a size of your system font. The reason for this option is that the font used for the 640 by 480 display may be too small to read when you go up to 1024 by 768 or beyond. Instead, you'll want a larger system font. These system font sizes are referred to on the Settings tab of the Display applet as Small Fonts and Large Fonts.

In traditional typography, the size of the characters in a font is indicated by a "point size." A point is approximately 1/72 inch and in computer typography is often assumed to be exactly 1/72 inch.

In theory, the point size of a font is the distance from the top of the tallest character in the font to the bottom of descenders in characters such as j, p, q, and y, excluding accent marks. For example, in a 10-point font this distance would be 10/72 inch. In terms of the TEXTMETRIC structure, the point size of the font is equivalent to the *tmHeight* field minus the *tmInternalLeading* field, as shown in Figure 5-3. (This figure is the same as Figure 4-3 in the last chapter.)

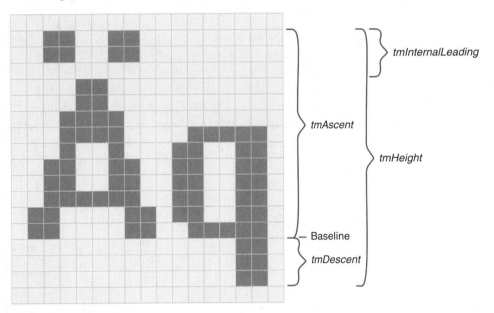

Figure 5-3. *The small font and the TEXTMETRIC fields.*

In real-life typography, the point size of a font is not so precisely related to the actual size of the font characters. The designer of the font might make the actual characters a bit larger or smaller than the point size would indicate. After all, font design is an art rather than a science.

The *tmHeight* field of the TEXTMETRIC structure indicates how successive lines of text should be spaced on the screen or printer. This can also be measured in points. For example, a 12-point line spacing indicates the baselines of successive lines of text should be 12/72 (or 1/6) inch apart. You don't want to use 10-point line spacing for a 10-point font because the successive lines of text could actually touch each other.

This book is printed with a 10-point font and 13-point line spacing. A 10-point font is considered comfortable for reading. Anything much smaller than 10 points would be difficult to read for long periods of time.

The Windows system font—regardless of whether it is the "small font" or the "large font" and regardless of what video pixel dimension you've selected—is assumed to be a 10-point font with a 12-point line spacing. I know this sounds odd. Why call the system fonts "small font" and "large font" if they're both 10-point fonts?

Here's the key: *When you select the small font or the large font in the Display applet of the Control Panel, you are actually selecting an assumed video display resolution in dots per inch.* When you select the small font, you are saying that you want Windows to assume that the video display resolution is 96 dots per inch. When you select the large font, you want Windows to assume that the video display resolution is 120 dots per inch.

Look at Figure 5-3 again. That's the small font, which is based on a display resolution of 96 dots per inch. I said it's a 10-point font. Ten points is 10/72 inch, which if you multiply by 96 dots per inch yields a result of (approximately) 13 pixels. That's *tmHeight* minus *tmInternalLeading*. The line spacing is 12 points, or 12/72 inch, which multiplied by 96 dots per inch yields 16 pixels. That's *tmHeight*.

Figure 5-4 shows the large font. This is based on a resolution of 120 dots per inch. Again, it's a 10-point font, and 10/72 times 120 dots per inch equals 16 pixels (if you round down), which is *tmHeight* minus *tmInternalLeading*. The 12-point line spacing is equivalent to 20 pixels, which is *tmHeight*. (As in Chapter 4, let me emphasize again that I'm showing you actual metrics so that you can understand how this works. Do not code these numbers in your programs.)

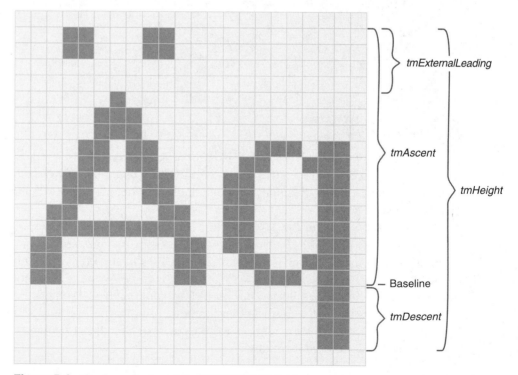

Figure 5-4. *The large font and the FONTMETRIC fields.*

Within a Windows program you can use the *GetDeviceCaps* function to obtain the assumed resolution in dots per inch that the user selected in the Display applet of the Control Panel. To get these values—which in theory could be different if the video display doesn't have square pixels—you use the indices LOGPIXELSX and LOGPIXELSY. The name LOGPIXELS stands for "logical pixels," which basically means "not the *actual* resolution in pixels per inch."

The device capabilities that you obtain from *GetDeviceCaps* with the HORZSIZE and VERTSIZE indices are documented (as I indicated earlier) as "Width, in millimeters, of the physical screen" and "Height, in millimeters, of the physical screen." These should be documented as a "logical width" and a "logical height," because the values are derived from the HORZRES, VERTRES, LOGPIXELSX, and LOGPIXELSY values. The formulas are

$$Horizontal\ Size\ (mm) = 25.4 \times \frac{Horizontal\ Resolution\ (pixels)}{Logical\ Pixels\ X\ (dots\ per\ inch)}$$

$$Vertical\ Size\ (mm) = 25.4 \times \frac{Vertical\ Resolution\ (pixels)}{Logical\ Pixels\ Y\ (dots\ per\ inch)}$$

The 25.4 constant is necessary to convert from inches to millimeters.

This may seem backward and illogical. After all, your video display has a size in millimeters that you can actually measure with a ruler (at least approximately). But Windows 98 doesn't care about that size. Instead it calculates a display size in millimeters based on the pixel size of the display the user selects and also the resolution the user selects for sizing the system font. Change the pixel size of your display and according to *GetDeviceCaps* the metrical size changes. How much sense does that make?

It makes more sense than you might suspect. Let's suppose you have a 17-inch monitor. The actual display size will probably be about 12 inches by 9 inches. Suppose you were running Windows with the minimum required pixel dimensions of 640 by 480. This means that the actual resolution is 53 dots per inch. A 10-point font—perfectly readable on paper—on the screen would be only 7 pixels in height from the top of the A to the bottom of the q. Such a font would be ugly and just about unreadable. (Ask people who ran Windows on the old Color Graphics Adapter.)

Now hook up a video projector to your PC. Let's say the projected video display is a 4 feet wide and 3 feet high. That same 640 by 480 pixel dimension now implies a resolution of about 13 dots per inch. It would be ridiculous to try displaying a 10-point font under such conditions.

A 10-point font should be readable on the video display because it is surely readable when printed. The 10-point font thus becomes an important frame of reference. When a Windows application is guaranteed that a 10-point screen font is of average size, it can then display smaller (but still readable) text using an 8-point font and larger text using fonts of point sizes greater than 10. Thus, it makes sense that the video resolution (in dots per inch) be implied by the pixel size of that 10-point font.

In Windows NT, however, an older approach is used in defining the HORZSIZE and VERTSIZE values. This approach is consistent with 16-bit versions of Windows. The HORZRES and VERTRES values still indicate the number of pixels horizontally and vertically (of course), and LOGPIXELSX and LOGPIXELSY are still related to the font that you choose when setting the video resolution in the Display applet of the Control Panel. As with Windows 98, typical values of LOGPIXELSX and LOGPIXELSY are 96 and 120 dots per inch, depending on whether you select a small font or large font.

The difference in Windows NT is that the HORZSIZE and VERTSIZE values are fixed to indicate a standard monitor size. For common adapters, the values of HORZSIZE and VERTSIZE you'll obtain are 320 and 240 millimeters, respectively. These values are the same regardless of what pixel dimension you choose. Therefore, these values are *inconsistent* with the values you obtain from *GetDeviceCaps* with the HORZRES, VERTRES, LOGPIXELSX, and LOGPIXELSY indices. However, you can always calculate HORZSIZE and VERTSIZE values like those you'd obtain under Windows 98 by using the formulas shown earlier.

What if your program needs the actual physical dimensions of the video display? Probably the best solution is to actually request them of the user with a dialog box.

Finally, three other values from *GetDeviceCaps* are related to the video dimensions. The ASPECTX, ASPECTY, and ASPECTXY values are the *relative* width, height, and diagonal size of each pixel, rounded to the nearest integer. For square pixels, the ASPECTX and ASPECTY values will be the same. Regardless, the ASPECTXY value equals the square root of the sum of the squares of the ASPECTX and ASPECTY values, as you'll recall from Pythogoras.

Finding Out About Color

A video display capable of displaying only black pixels and white pixels requires only one bit of memory per pixel. Color displays require multiple bits per pixels. The more bits, the more colors; or more specifically, the number of unique simultaneous colors is equal to 2 to the number of bits per pixel.

A "full color" video display resolution has 24 bits per pixel—8 bits for red, 8 bits for green, and 8 bits for blue. Red, green, and blue are known as the "additive primaries." Mixes of these three primary colors can create many other colors, as you can verify by peering at your color video display through a magnifying glass.

A "high color" display resolution has 16 bits per pixel, generally 5 bits for red, 6 bits for green, and 5 bits for blue. More bits are used for the green primary because the human eye is more sensitive to variations in green than to the other two primaries.

A video adapter that displays 256 colors requires 8 bits per pixel. However, these 8-bit values are generally indices into a palette table that defines the actual colors. I'll discuss this more in Chapter 16.

Finally, a video board that displays 16 colors requires 4 bits per pixel. These 16 colors are generally fixed as dark and light versions of red, green, blue, cyan, magenta, yellow, two shades of gray, black, and white. These 16 colors date back to the old IBM CGA.

Only in some odd programming jobs is it necessary to know how memory is organized on the video adapter board, but *GetDeviceCaps* will help you determine that. Video memory can be organized either with consecutive color bits for each pixel or with each color bit in a separate plane of memory. This call returns the number of color planes:

```
iPlanes = GetDeviceCaps (hdc, PLANES) ;
```

and this call returns the number of color bits per pixel:

```
iBitsPixel = GetDeviceCaps (hdc, BITSPIXEL) ;
```

One of these calls will return a value of 1. The number of colors that can be simultaneously rendered on the video adapter can be calculated by the formula

```
iColors = 1 << (iPlanes * iBitsPixel) ;
```

This value may or may not be the same as the number of colors obtainable with the NUMCOLORS argument:

```
iColors = GetDeviceCaps (hdc, NUMCOLORS) ;
```

I mentioned that 256-color video adapters use color palettes. In that case, *GetDeviceCaps* with the NUMCOLORS index returns the number of colors reserved by Windows, which will be 20. The remaining 236 colors can be set by a Windows program using the palette manager. For high-color and full-color display resolutions, *GetDeviceCaps* with the NUM-COLORS index often returns −1, making it a generally unreliable function for determining this information. Instead, use the *iColors* formula shown earlier that uses the PLANES and BITSPIXEL values.

In most GDI function calls, you use a COLORREF value (which is simply a 32-bit unsigned long integer) to refer to a particular color. The COLORREF value specifies a color in terms of red, green, and blue intensities and is often called an "RGB color." The 32 bits of the COLORREF value are set as shown in Figure 5-5 on the following page.

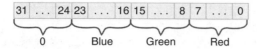

Figure 5-5. *The 32-bit COLORREF value.*

Notice that the most-significant 8 bits are zero, and that each primary is specified as an 8-bit value. In theory, a COLORREF value can refer to 2^{24} or about 16 million colors.

The Windows header file WINGDI.H provides several macros for working with RGB color values. The *RGB* macro takes three arguments representing red, green, and blue values and combines them into an unsigned long:

```
#define RGB(r,g,b) ((COLORREF)(((BYTE)(r) | \
                   ((WORD)((BYTE)(g)) << 8)) | \
                   (((DWORD)(BYTE)(b)) << 16)))
```

Notice that the order of the three arguments is red, green, and blue. Thus, the value

```
RGB (255, 255, 0)
```

is 0x0000FFFF or yellow—the combination of red and green. When all three arguments are set to 0, the color is black; when all the arguments are set to 255, the color is white. The *GetRValue*, *GetGValue*, and *GetBValue* macros extract the primary color values from a COLORREF value. These macros are sometimes handy when you're using a Windows function that returns RGB color values to your program.

On 16-color or 256-color video adapters, Windows can use "dithering" to simulate more colors than the device can display. Dithering involves a small pattern that combines pixels of different colors. You can determine the closest pure nondithered color of a particular color value by calling *GetNearestColor*:

```
crPureColor = GetNearestColor (hdc, crColor) ;
```

The Device Context Attributes

As I noted above, Windows uses the device context to store "attributes" that govern how the GDI functions operate on the display. For instance, when you display some text using the *TextOut* function, you don't have to specify the color of the text or the font. Windows uses the device context to obtain this information.

When a program obtains a handle to a device context, Windows sets all the attributes to default values. (However, see the next section for how to override this behavior.) The following table shows many of the device context attributes supported under Windows 98, along with the default values and the functions to change or obtain their values.

Device Context Attribute	Default	Function(s) to Change	Function to Obtain
Mapping Mode	MM_TEXT	*SetMapMode*	*GetMapMode*
Window Origin	(0, 0)	*SetWindowOrgEx* *OffsetWindowOrgEx*	*GetWindowOrgEx*
Viewport Origin	(0, 0)	*SetViewportOrgEx* *OffsetViewportOrgEx*	*GetViewportOrgEx*
Window Extents	(1, 1)	*SetWindowExtEx* *SetMapMode* *ScaleWindowExtEx*	*GetWindowExtEx*
Viewport Extents	(1, 1)	*SetViewportExtEx* *SetMapMode* *ScaleViewportExtEx*	*GetViewportExtEx*
Pen	BLACK_PEN	*SelectObject*	*SelectObject*
Brush	WHITE_BRUSH	*SelectObject*	*SelectObject*
Font	SYSTEM_FONT	*SelectObject*	*SelectObject*
Bitmap	None	*SelectObject*	*SelectObject*
Current Position	(0, 0)	*MoveToEx* *LineTo* *PolylineTo* *PolyBezierTo*	*GetCurrentPositionEx*
Background Mode	OPAQUE	*SetBkMode*	*GetBkMode*
Background Color	White	*SetBkColor*	*GetBkColor*
Text Color	Black	*SetTextColor*	*GetTextColor*
Drawing Mode	R2_COPYPEN	*SetROP2*	*GetROP2*
Stretching Mode	BLACKONWHITE	*SetStretchBltMode*	*GetStretchBltMode*
Polygon Fill Mode	ALTERNATE	*SetPolyFillMode*	*GetPolyFillMode*
Intercharacter Spacing	0	*SetTextCharacterExtra*	*GetTextCharacterExtra*
Brush Origin	(0, 0)	*SetBrushOrgEx*	*GetBrushOrgEx*
Clipping Region	None	*SelectObject* *SelectClipRgn* *IntersectClipRgn* *OffsetClipRgn* *ExcludeClipRect* *SelectClipPath*	*GetClipBox*

Saving Device Contexts

Normally when you call *GetDC* or *BeginPaint*, Windows gives you a device context with default values for all the attributes. Any changes you make to the attributes are lost when the device context is released with the *ReleaseDC* or *EndPaint* call. If your program needs to use nondefault device context attributes, you'll have to initialize the device context every time you obtain a new device context handle:

```
case WM_PAINT:
    hdc = BeginPaint (hwnd, &ps) ;
    [initialize device context attributes]
    [paint client area of window]
    EndPaint (hwnd, &ps) ;
    return 0 ;
```

Although this approach is generally satisfactory, you might prefer that changes you make to the attributes be saved when you release the device context so that they will be in effect the next time you call *GetDC* or *BeginPaint*. You can accomplish this by including the CS_OWNDC flag as part of the window class style when you register the window class:

```
wndclass.style = CS_HREDRAW | CS_VREDRAW | CS_OWNDC ;
```

Now each window that you create based on this window class will have its own private device context that continues to exist when the window is destroyed. When you use the CS_OWNDC style, you need to initialize the device context attributes only once, perhaps while processing the WM_CREATE message:

```
case WM_CREATE:
    hdc = GetDC (hwnd) ;
    [initialize device context attributes]
    ReleaseDC (hwnd, hdc) ;
```

The attributes continue to be valid until you change them.

The CS_OWNDC style affects only the device contexts retrieved from *GetDC* and *BeginPaint* and not device contexts obtained from the other functions (such as *GetWindowDC*). Employing CS_OWNDC was once discouraged because it required some memory overhead; nowadays it can improve performance in some graphics-intensive Windows NT applications. Even if you use CS_OWNDC, you should still release the device context handle before exiting the window procedure.

In some cases you might want to change certain device context attributes, do some painting using the changed attributes, and then revert to the original device context. To simplify this process, you save the state of a device context by calling

```
idSaved = SaveDC (hdc) ;
```

Now you can change some attributes. When you want to return to the device context as it existed before the *SaveDC* call, you use

```
RestoreDC (hdc, idSaved) ;
```

You can call *SaveDC* any number of times before you call *RestoreDC*.

Most programmers use *SaveDC* and *RestoreDC* in a different manner, however, much like PUSH and POP instructions in assembly language. When you call *SaveDC*, you don't need to save the return value:

```
SaveDC (hdc) ;
```

You can then change some attributes and call *SaveDC* again. To restore the device context to a saved state, call

```
RestoreDC (hdc, -1) ;
```

This restores the device context to the state saved by the most recent *SaveDC* function.

DRAWING DOTS AND LINES

In the first chapter, I discussed how the Windows Graphics Device Interface makes use of device drivers for the graphics output devices attached to your computer. In theory, all that a graphics device driver needs for drawing is a *SetPixel* function and a *GetPixel* function. Everything else could be handled with higher-level routines implemented in the GDI module. Drawing a line, for instance, simply requires that GDI call the *SetPixel* routine numerous times, adjusting the x- and y-coordinates appropriately.

In reality, you can indeed do almost any drawing you need with only *SetPixel* and *GetPixel* functions. You can also design a neat and well-structured graphics programming system on top of these functions. The only problem is performance. A function that is several calls away from each *SetPixel* function will be painfully slow. It is much more efficient for a graphics system to do line drawing and other complex graphics operations at the level of the device driver, which can have its own optimized code to perform the operations. Moreover, some video adapter boards contain graphics coprocessors that allow the video hardware itself to draw the figures.

Setting Pixels

Even though the Windows GPI includes *SetPixel* and *GetPixel* functions, they are not commonly used. In this book, the only use of the *SetPixel* function is in the CONNECT program in Chapter 7, and the only use of *GetPixel* is in the WHATCLR program in Chapter 8. Still, they provide a convenient place to begin examining graphics.

The *SetPixel* function sets the pixel at a specified x- and y-coordinate to a particular color:

```
SetPixel (hdc, x, y, crColor) ;
```

As in any drawing function, the first argument is a handle to a device context. The second and third arguments indicate the coordinate position. Mostly you'll obtain a device context for the client area of your window, and *x* and *y* will be relative to the upper left corner of that client area. The final argument is of type COLORREF to specify the color. If the color you specify in the function cannot be realized on the video display, the function sets the pixel to the nearest pure nondithered color and returns that value from the function.

The *GetPixel* function returns the color of the pixel at the specified coordinate position:

```
crColor = GetPixel (hdc, x, y) ;
```

Straight Lines

Windows can draw straight lines, elliptical lines (curved lines on the circumference of an ellipse), and Bezier splines. Windows 98 supports seven functions that draw lines:

- *LineTo*   Draws a straight line.
- *Polyline and PolylineTo*   Draw a series of connected straight lines.
- *PolyPolyline*   Draws multiple polylines.
- *Arc*   Draws elliptical lines.
- *PolyBezier and PolyBezierTo*   Draw Bezier splines.

In addition, Windows NT supports three more line-drawing functions:

- *ArcTo and AngleArc*   Draw elliptical lines.
- *PolyDraw*   Draws a series of connected straight lines and Bezier splines.

These three functions are not supported under Windows 98.

Later in this chapter I'll also be discussing some functions that draw lines but that also fill the enclosed area within the figure they draw. These functions are

- *Rectangle*   Draws a rectangle.
- *Ellipse*   Draws an ellipse.
- *RoundRect*   Draws a rectangle with rounded corners.
- *Pie*   Draws a part of an ellipse that looks like a pie slice.
- *Chord*   Draws part of an ellipse formed by a chord.

Five attributes of the device context affect the appearance of lines that you draw using these functions: current pen position (for *LineTo*, *PolylineTo*, *PolyBezierTo*, and *ArcTo* only), pen, background mode, background color, and drawing mode.

To draw a straight line, you must call two functions. The first function specifies the point at which the line begins, and the second function specifies the end point of the line:

```
MoveToEx (hdc, xBeg, yBeg, NULL) ;
LineTo (hdc, xEnd, yEnd) ;
```

MoveToEx doesn't actually draw anything; instead, it sets the attribute of the device context known as the "current position." The *LineTo* function then draws a straight line from the current position to the point specified in the *LineTo* function. The current position is simply a starting point for several other GDI functions. In the default device context, the current position is initially set to the point (0, 0). If you call *LineTo* without first setting the current position, it draws a line starting at the upper left corner of the client area.

A brief historical note: In the 16-bit versions of Windows, the function to set the current position was *MoveTo*. This function had just three arguments—the device context handle and x- and y-coordinates. The function returned the previous current position packed as two 16-bit values in a 32-bit unsigned long. However, in the 32-bit versions of Windows, coordinates are 32-bit values. Because the 32-bit versions of C do not define a 64-bit integral data type, this change meant that *MoveTo* could no longer indicate the previous current position in its return value. Although the return value from *MoveTo* was almost never used in real-life programming, a new function was required, and this was *MoveToEx*.

The last argument to *MoveToEx* is a pointer to a POINT structure. On return from the function, the *x* and *y* fields of the POINT structure will indicate the previous current position. If you don't need this information (which is almost always the case), you can simply set the last argument to NULL as in the example shown above.

And now the caveat: Although coordinate values in Windows 98 appear to be 32-bit values, only the lower 16 bits are used. Coordinate values are effectively restricted to −32,768 to 32,767. In Windows NT, the full 32-bit values are used.

If you ever need the current position, you can obtain it by calling

```
GetCurrentPositionEx (hdc, &pt) ;
```

where *pt* is a POINT structure.

The following code draws a grid in the client area of a window, spacing the lines 100 pixels apart starting from the upper left corner. The variable *hwnd* is assumed to be a handle to the window, *hdc* is a handle to the device context, and *x* and *y* are integers:

```
GetClientRect (hwnd, &rect) ;
for (x = 0 ; x < rect.right ; x+= 100)
{
     MoveToEx (hdc, x, 0, NULL) ;
     LineTo (hdc, x, rect.bottom) ;
}
```

(continued)

145

```
for (y = 0 ; y < rect.bottom ; y += 100)
{
     MoveToEx (hdc, 0, y, NULL) ;
     LineTo (hdc, rect.right, y) ;
}
```

Although it seems like a nuisance to be forced to use two functions to draw a single line, the current position comes in handy when you want to draw a series of connected lines. For instance, you might want to define an array of 5 points (10 values) that define the outline of a rectangle:

```
POINT apt[5] = { 100, 100, 200, 100, 200, 200, 100, 200, 100, 100 } ;
```

Notice that the last point is the same as the first. Now you need only use *MoveToEx* for the first point and *LineTo* for the successive points:

```
MoveToEx (hdc, apt[0].x, apt[0].y, NULL) ;

for (i = 1 ; i < 5 ; i++)
     LineTo (hdc, apt[i].x, apt[i].y) ;
```

Because *LineTo* draws from the current position up to (but not including) the point in the *LineTo* function, no coordinate gets written twice by this code. While overwriting points is not a problem with a video display, it might not look good on a plotter or with some drawing modes that I'll discuss later in this chapter.

When you have an array of points that you want connected with lines, you can draw the lines more easily using the *Polyline* function. This statement draws the same rectangle as in the code shown above:

```
Polyline (hdc, apt, 5) ;
```

The last argument is the number of points. We could also have represented this value by *sizeof (apt) / sizeof (POINT)*. *Polyline* has the same effect on drawing as an initial *MoveToEx* followed by multiple *LineTo* functions. However, *Polyline* doesn't use or change the current position. *PolylineTo* is a little different. This function uses the current position for the starting point and sets the current position to the end of the last line drawn. The code below draws the same rectangle as that last shown above:

```
MoveToEx (hdc, apt[0].x, apt[0].y, NULL) ;
PolylineTo (hdc, apt + 1, 4) ;
```

Although you can use *Polyline* and *PolylineTo* to draw just a few lines, the functions are most useful when you need to draw a complex curve. You do this by using hundreds or even thousands of very short lines. If they're short enough and there are enough of them, together they'll look like a curve. For example, suppose you need to draw a sine wave. The SINEWAVE program in Figure 5-6 shows how to do it.

SINEWAVE.C

```c
/*-------------------------------------------
   SINEWAVE.C -- Sine Wave Using Polyline
                 (c) Charles Petzold, 1998
  -------------------------------------------*/

#include <windows.h>
#include <math.h>

#define NUM    1000
#define TWOPI  (2 * 3.14159)

LRESULT CALLBACK WndProc (HWND, UINT, WPARAM, LPARAM) ;

int WINAPI WinMain (HINSTANCE hInstance, HINSTANCE hPrevInstance,
                    PSTR szCmdLine, int iCmdShow)
{
     static TCHAR szAppName[] = TEXT ("SineWave") ;
     HWND         hwnd ;
     MSG          msg ;
     WNDCLASS     wndclass ;

     wndclass.style         = CS_HREDRAW | CS_VREDRAW ;
     wndclass.lpfnWndProc   = WndProc ;
     wndclass.cbClsExtra    = 0 ;
     wndclass.cbWndExtra    = 0 ;
     wndclass.hInstance     = hInstance ;
     wndclass.hIcon         = LoadIcon (NULL, IDI_APPLICATION) ;
     wndclass.hCursor       = LoadCursor (NULL, IDC_ARROW) ;
     wndclass.hbrBackground = (HBRUSH) GetStockObject (WHITE_BRUSH) ;
     wndclass.lpszMenuName  = NULL ;
     wndclass.lpszClassName = szAppName ;

     if (!RegisterClass (&wndclass))
     {
          MessageBox (NULL, TEXT ("Program requires Windows NT!"),
                      szAppName, MB_ICONERROR) ;
          return 0 ;
     }

     hwnd = CreateWindow (szAppName, TEXT ("Sine Wave Using Polyline"),
                          WS_OVERLAPPEDWINDOW,
                          CW_USEDEFAULT, CW_USEDEFAULT,
                          CW_USEDEFAULT, CW_USEDEFAULT,
                          NULL, NULL, hInstance, NULL) ;
```

Figure 5-6. *The SINEWAVE program.*   *(continued)*

Figure 5-6. *continued*

```
     ShowWindow (hwnd, iCmdShow) ;
     UpdateWindow (hwnd) ;

     while (GetMessage (&msg, NULL, 0, 0))
     {
          TranslateMessage (&msg) ;
          DispatchMessage (&msg) ;
     }
     return msg.wParam ;
}

LRESULT CALLBACK WndProc (HWND hwnd, UINT message, WPARAM wParam, LPARAM lParam)
{
     static int  cxClient, cyClient ;
     HDC         hdc ;
     int         i ;
     PAINTSTRUCT ps ;
     POINT       apt [NUM] ;

     switch (message)
     {
     case WM_SIZE:
          cxClient = LOWORD (lParam) ;
          cyClient = HIWORD (lParam) ;
          return 0 ;

     case WM_PAINT:
          hdc = BeginPaint (hwnd, &ps) ;

          MoveToEx (hdc, 0,         cyClient / 2, NULL) ;
          LineTo   (hdc, cxClient, cyClient / 2) ;

          for (i = 0 ; i < NUM ; i++)
          {
               apt[i].x = i * cxClient / NUM ;
               apt[i].y = (int) (cyClient / 2 * (1 - sin (TWOPI * i / NUM))) ;
          }

          Polyline (hdc, apt, NUM) ;
          return 0 ;

     case WM_DESTROY:
          PostQuitMessage (0) ;
          return 0 ;
     }
     return DefWindowProc (hwnd, message, wParam, lParam) ;
}
```

The program has an array of 1000 POINT structures. As the *for* loop is incremented from 0 through 999, the *x* fields of the POINT structure are set to incrementally increasing values from 0 to *cxClient*. The program sets the *y* fields of the POINT structure to sine curve values for one cycle and enlarged to fill the client area. The whole curve is drawn using a single *Polyline* call. Because the *Polyline* function is implemented at the device driver level, it is faster than calling *LineTo* 1000 times. The results are shown in Figure 5-7.

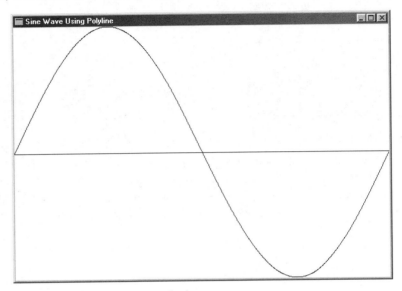

Figure 5-7. *The SINEWAVE display.*

The Bounding Box Functions

I next want to discuss the *Arc* function, which draws an elliptical curve. However, the *Arc* function does not make much sense without first discussing the *Ellipse* function, and the *Ellipse* function doesn't make much sense without first discussing the *Rectangle* function, and if I discuss *Ellipse* and *Rectangle*, I might as well discuss *RoundRect*, *Chord*, and *Pie*.

The problem is that the *Rectangle, Ellipse, RoundRect, Chord*, and *Pie* functions are not strictly line-drawing functions. Yes, the functions draw lines, but they also fill an enclosed area with the current area-filling brush. This brush is solid white by default, so it may not be obvious that these functions do more than draw lines when you first begin experimenting with them. The functions really belong in the later section "Drawing Filled Areas," but I'll discuss them here regardless.

The functions I've listed above are all similar in that they are built up from a rectangular "bounding box." You define the coordinates of a box that encloses the object—the bounding box—and Windows draws the object within this box.

The simplest of these functions draws a rectangle:

```
Rectangle (hdc, xLeft, yTop, xRight, yBottom) ;
```

The point (*xLeft*, *yTop*) is the upper left corner of the rectangle, and (*xRight*, *yBottom*) is the lower right corner. A figure drawn using the *Rectangle* function is shown in Figure 5-8. The sides of the rectangle are always parallel to the horizontal and vertical sides of the display.

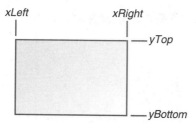

Figure 5-8. *A figure drawn using the* Rectangle *function.*

Programmers who have experience with graphics programming are often familiar with "off-by-one" errors. Some graphics programming systems draw a figure to encompass the right and bottom coordinates, and some draw figures up to (but not including) the right and bottom coordinates. Windows uses the latter approach, but there's an easier way to think about it.

Consider the function call

```
Rectangle (hdc, 1, 1, 5, 4) ;
```

I mentioned above that Windows draws the figure within a "bounding box." You can think of the display as a grid where each pixel is within a grid cell. The imaginary bounding box is drawn on the grid, and the rectangle is then drawn within this bounding box. Here's how the figure would be drawn:

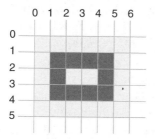

The area separating the rectangle from the top and left of the client area is 1 pixel wide.

As I mentioned earlier, *Rectangle* is not strictly just a line-drawing function. GDI also fills the enclosed area. However, because by default the area is filled with white, it might not be immediately obvious that GDI is filling the area.

Once you know how to draw a rectangle, you also know how to draw an ellipse, because it uses the same arguments:

```
Ellipse (hdc, xLeft, yTop, xRight, yBottom) ;
```

A figure drawn using the *Ellipse* function is shown (with the imaginary bounding box) in Figure 5-9.

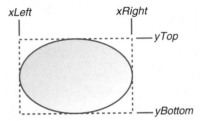

Figure 5-9. *A figure drawn using the* Ellipse *function.*

The function to draw rectangles with rounded corners uses the same bounding box as the *Rectangle* and *Ellipse* functions but includes two more arguments:

```
RoundRect (hdc, xLeft, yTop, xRight, yBottom,
          xCornerEllipse, yCornerEllipse) ;
```

A figure drawn using this function is shown in Figure 5-10.

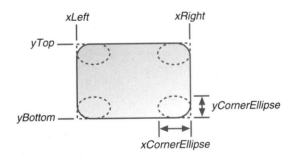

Figure 5-10. *A figure drawn using the* RoundRect *function.*

Windows uses a small ellipse to draw the rounded corners. The width of this ellipse is *xCornerEllipse*, and the height is *yCornerEllipse*. Imagine Windows splitting this small ellipse into four quadrants and using one quadrant for each of the four corners. The rounding of the corners is more pronounced for larger values of *xCornerEllipse* and *yCornerEllipse*. If *xCornerEllipse* is equal to the difference between *xLeft* and *xRight*, and *yCornerEllipse* is equal to the difference between *yTop* and *yBottom*, then the *RoundRect* function will draw an ellipse.

The rounded rectangle in Figure 5-10 was drawn using corner ellipse dimensions calculated with the formulas on the following page.

```
xCornerEllipse = (xRight - xLeft) / 4 ;
yCornerEllipse = (yBottom- yTop) / 4 ;
```

This is an easy approach, but the results admittedly don't look quite right because the rounding of the corners is more pronounced along the larger rectangle dimension. To correct this problem, you'll probably want to make *xCornerEllipse* equal to *yCornerEllipse* in real dimensions.

The *Arc*, *Chord*, and *Pie* functions all take identical arguments:

```
Arc   (hdc, xLeft, yTop, xRight, yBottom, xStart, yStart, xEnd, yEnd) ;
Chord (hdc, xLeft, yTop, xRight, yBottom, xStart, yStart, xEnd, yEnd) ;
Pie   (hdc, xLeft, yTop, xRight, yBottom, xStart, yStart, xEnd, yEnd) ;
```

A line drawn using the *Arc* function is shown in Figure 5-11; figures drawn using the *Chord* and *Pie* functions are shown in Figures 5-12 and 5-13. Windows uses an imaginary line to connect (*xStart*, *yStart*) with the center of the ellipse. At the point at which that line intersects the ellipse, Windows begins drawing an arc in a counterclockwise direction around the circumference of the ellipse. Windows also uses an imaginary line to connect (*xEnd*, *yEnd*) with the center of the ellipse. At the point at which that line intersects the ellipse, Windows stops drawing the arc.

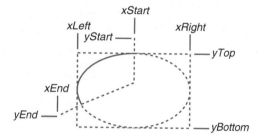

Figure 5-11. *A line drawn using the* Arc *function.*

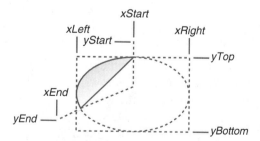

Figure 5-12. *A figure drawn using the* Chord *function.*

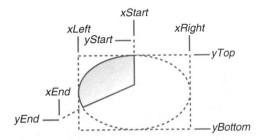

Figure 5-13. *A figure drawn using the* Pie *function.*

For the *Arc* function, Windows is now finished, because the arc is an elliptical line rather than a filled area. For the *Chord* function, Windows connects the endpoints of the arc. For the *Pie* function, Windows connects each endpoint of the arc with the center of the ellipse. The interiors of the chord and pie-wedge figures are filled with the current brush.

You may wonder about this use of starting and ending positions in the *Arc*, *Chord*, and *Pie* functions. Why not simply specify starting and ending points on the circumference of the ellipse? Well, you can, but you would have to figure out what those points are. Windows' method gets the job done without requiring such precision.

The LINEDEMO program shown in Figure 5-14 draws a rectangle, an ellipse, a rectangle with rounded corners, and two lines, but not in that order. The program demonstrates that these functions that define closed areas do indeed fill them, because the lines are hidden behind the ellipse. The results are shown in Figure 5-15.

LINEDEMO.C

```
/*-------------------------------------------------------
   LINEDEMO.C -- Line-Drawing Demonstration Program
                  (c) Charles Petzold, 1998
   -------------------------------------------------*/

#include <windows.h>

LRESULT CALLBACK WndProc (HWND, UINT, WPARAM, LPARAM) ;

int WINAPI WinMain (HINSTANCE hInstance, HINSTANCE hPrevInstance,
                    PSTR szCmdLine, int iCmdShow)
{
     static TCHAR szAppName[] = TEXT ("LineDemo") ;
     HWND         hwnd ;
     MSG          msg ;
     WNDCLASS     wndclass ;

     wndclass.style         = CS_HREDRAW | CS_VREDRAW ;
     wndclass.lpfnWndProc   = WndProc ;
```

Figure 5-14. *The LINEDEMO program.*

(continued)

Figure 5-14. *continued*

```
        wndclass.cbClsExtra    = 0 ;
        wndclass.cbWndExtra    = 0 ;
        wndclass.hInstance     = hInstance ;
        wndclass.hIcon         = LoadIcon (NULL, IDI_APPLICATION) ;
        wndclass.hCursor       = LoadCursor (NULL, IDC_ARROW) ;
        wndclass.hbrBackground = (HBRUSH) GetStockObject (WHITE_BRUSH) ;
        wndclass.lpszMenuName  = NULL ;
        wndclass.lpszClassName = szAppName ;

        if (!RegisterClass (&wndclass))
        {
             MessageBox (NULL, TEXT ("Program requires Windows NT!"),
                         szAppName, MB_ICONERROR) ;
             return 0 ;
        }

        hwnd = CreateWindow (szAppName, TEXT ("Line Demonstration"),
                             WS_OVERLAPPEDWINDOW,
                             CW_USEDEFAULT, CW_USEDEFAULT,
                             CW_USEDEFAULT, CW_USEDEFAULT,
                             NULL, NULL, hInstance, NULL) ;

        ShowWindow (hwnd, iCmdShow) ;
        UpdateWindow (hwnd) ;

        while (GetMessage (&msg, NULL, 0, 0))
        {
             TranslateMessage (&msg) ;
             DispatchMessage (&msg) ;
        }
        return msg.wParam ;
}

LRESULT CALLBACK WndProc (HWND hwnd, UINT message, WPARAM wParam, LPARAM lParam)
{
        static int  cxClient, cyClient ;
        HDC         hdc ;
        PAINTSTRUCT ps ;

        switch (message)
        {
        case WM_SIZE:
             cxClient = LOWORD (lParam) ;
             cyClient = HIWORD (lParam) ;
             return 0 ;

        case WM_PAINT:
```

```
        hdc = BeginPaint (hwnd, &ps) ;

        Rectangle (hdc,      cxClient / 8,      cyClient / 8,
                   7 * cxClient / 8, 7 * cyClient / 8) ;

        MoveToEx (hdc,        0,         0, NULL) ;
        LineTo    (hdc, cxClient, cyClient) ;

        MoveToEx (hdc,        0, cyClient, NULL) ;
        LineTo    (hdc, cxClient,         0) ;

        Ellipse   (hdc,      cxClient / 8,      cyClient / 8,
                   7 * cxClient / 8, 7 * cyClient / 8) ;

        RoundRect (hdc,      cxClient / 4,      cyClient / 4,
                   3 * cxClient / 4, 3 * cyClient / 4,
                       cxClient / 4,      cyClient / 4) ;

        EndPaint (hwnd, &ps) ;
        return 0 ;

    case WM_DESTROY:
        PostQuitMessage (0) ;
        return 0 ;
    }
    return DefWindowProc (hwnd, message, wParam, lParam) ;
}
```

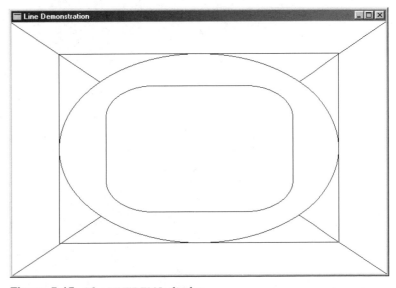

Figure 5-15. *The LINEDEMO display.*

Bezier Splines

The word "spline" once referred to a piece of flexible wood, rubber, or metal used to draw curves on a piece of paper. For example, if you had some disparate graph points, and you wanted to draw a curve between them (either for interpolation or extrapolation), you'd first mark the points on a piece of graph paper. You'd then anchor a spline to the points and use a pencil to draw the curve along the spline as it bent around the points.

Nowadays, of course, splines are mathematical formulas. They come in many different flavors, but the Bezier spline has become the most popular for computer graphics programming. It is a fairly recent addition to the arsenal of graphics tools available on the operating system level, and it comes from an unlikely source: In the 1960s, the Renault automobile company was switching over from a manual design of car bodies (which involved clay) to a computer-based design. Mathematical tools were required, and Pierre Bezier came up with a set of formulas that proved to be useful for this job.

Since then, the two-dimensional form of the Bezier spline has shown itself to be the most useful curve (after the straight line and ellipse) for computer graphics. In PostScript, the Bezier spline is used for *all* curves—even elliptical lines are approximated from Beziers. Bezier curves are also used to define the character outlines of PostScript fonts. (TrueType uses a simpler and faster form of spline.)

A single two-dimensional Bezier spline is defined by four points—two end points and two control points. The ends of the curve are anchored at the two end points. The control points act as "magnets" to pull the curve away from the straight line between the two end points. This is best illustrated by an interactive program, called BEZIER, which is shown in Figure 5-16.

BEZIER.C

```
/*-----------------------------------------
   BEZIER.C -- Bezier Splines Demo
               (c) Charles Petzold, 1998
   -----------------------------------------*/

#include <windows.h>

LRESULT CALLBACK WndProc (HWND, UINT, WPARAM, LPARAM) ;

int WINAPI WinMain (HINSTANCE hInstance, HINSTANCE hPrevInstance,
                    PSTR szCmdLine, int iCmdShow)
{
     static TCHAR szAppName[] = TEXT ("Bezier") ;
     HWND         hwnd ;
     MSG          msg ;
     WNDCLASS     wndclass ;
```

Figure 5-16. *The BEZIER program.*

```
        wndclass.style         = CS_HREDRAW | CS_VREDRAW ;
        wndclass.lpfnWndProc   = WndProc ;
        wndclass.cbClsExtra    = 0 ;
        wndclass.cbWndExtra    = 0 ;
        wndclass.hInstance     = hInstance ;
        wndclass.hIcon         = LoadIcon (NULL, IDI_APPLICATION) ;
        wndclass.hCursor       = LoadCursor (NULL, IDC_ARROW) ;
        wndclass.hbrBackground = (HBRUSH) GetStockObject (WHITE_BRUSH) ;
        wndclass.lpszMenuName  = NULL ;
        wndclass.lpszClassName = szAppName ;

        if (!RegisterClass (&wndclass))
        {
                MessageBox (NULL, TEXT ("Program requires Windows NT!"),
                            szAppName, MB_ICONERROR) ;
                return 0 ;
        }

        hwnd = CreateWindow (szAppName, TEXT ("Bezier Splines"),
                             WS_OVERLAPPEDWINDOW,
                             CW_USEDEFAULT, CW_USEDEFAULT,
                             CW_USEDEFAULT, CW_USEDEFAULT,
                             NULL, NULL, hInstance, NULL) ;

        ShowWindow (hwnd, iCmdShow) ;
        UpdateWindow (hwnd) ;

        while (GetMessage (&msg, NULL, 0, 0))
        {
                TranslateMessage (&msg) ;
                DispatchMessage (&msg) ;
        }
        return msg.wParam ;
}

void DrawBezier (HDC hdc, POINT apt[])
{
        PolyBezier (hdc, apt, 4) ;

        MoveToEx (hdc, apt[0].x, apt[0].y, NULL) ;
        LineTo   (hdc, apt[1].x, apt[1].y) ;

        MoveToEx (hdc, apt[2].x, apt[2].y, NULL) ;
        LineTo   (hdc, apt[3].x, apt[3].y) ;
}
```

(continued)

Figure 5-16. *continued*

```
LRESULT CALLBACK WndProc (HWND hwnd, UINT message, WPARAM wParam, LPARAM lParam)
{
    static POINT apt[4] ;
    HDC        hdc ;
    int        cxClient, cyClient ;
    PAINTSTRUCT ps ;

    switch (message)
    {
    case WM_SIZE:
        cxClient = LOWORD (lParam) ;
        cyClient = HIWORD (lParam) ;

        apt[0].x = cxClient / 4 ;
        apt[0].y = cyClient / 2 ;

        apt[1].x = cxClient / 2 ;
        apt[1].y = cyClient / 4 ;

        apt[2].x =     cxClient / 2 ;
        apt[2].y = 3 * cyClient / 4 ;

        apt[3].x = 3 * cxClient / 4 ;
        apt[3].y =     cyClient / 2 ;

        return 0 ;

    case WM_LBUTTONDOWN:
    case WM_RBUTTONDOWN:
    case WM_MOUSEMOVE:
        if (wParam & MK_LBUTTON || wParam & MK_RBUTTON)
        {
            hdc = GetDC (hwnd) ;

            SelectObject (hdc, GetStockObject (WHITE_PEN)) ;
            DrawBezier (hdc, apt) ;

            if (wParam & MK_LBUTTON)
            {
                apt[1].x = LOWORD (lParam) ;
                apt[1].y = HIWORD (lParam) ;
            }
```

```
                    if (wParam & MK_RBUTTON)
                    {
                         apt[2].x = LOWORD (lParam) ;
                         apt[2].y = HIWORD (lParam) ;
                    }

                    SelectObject (hdc, GetStockObject (BLACK_PEN)) ;
                    DrawBezier (hdc, apt) ;
                    ReleaseDC (hwnd, hdc) ;
               }
          return 0 ;

     case WM_PAINT:
          InvalidateRect (hwnd, NULL, TRUE) ;

          hdc = BeginPaint (hwnd, &ps) ;

          DrawBezier (hdc, apt) ;

          EndPaint (hwnd, &ps) ;
          return 0 ;

     case WM_DESTROY:
          PostQuitMessage (0) ;
          return 0 ;
     }
     return DefWindowProc (hwnd, message, wParam, lParam) ;
}
```

Because this program uses some mouse processing logic that we won't learn about until Chapter 7, I won't discuss its inner workings (which might be obvious nonetheless). Instead, you can use the program to experiment with manipulating Bezier splines. In this program, the two end points are set to be halfway down the client area, and ¼ and ¾ of the way across the client area. The two control points are manipulable, the first by pressing the left mouse button and moving the mouse, the second by pressing the right mouse button and moving the mouse. Figure 5-17 on the following page shows a typical display.

Aside from the Bezier spline itself, the program also draws a straight line from the first control point to the first end point (also called the begin point) at the left, and from the second control point to the end point at the right.

Bezier splines are considered to be useful for computer-assisted design work because of several characteristics. First, with a little practice, you can usually manipulate the curve into something close to a desired shape.

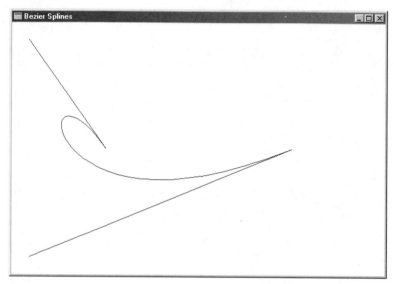

Figure 5-17. *The BEZIER display.*

Second, the Bezier spline is very well controlled. In some splines, the curve does not pass through any of the points that define the curve. The Bezier spline is always anchored at the two end points. (This is one of the assumptions that is used to derive the Bezier formulas.) Also, some forms of splines have singularities where the curve veers off into infinity. In computer-based design work, this is rarely desired. The Bezier curve never does this; indeed, it is always bounded by a four-sided polygon (called a "convex hull") that is formed by connecting the end points and control points.

Third, another characteristic of the Bezier spline involves the relationship between the end points and the control points. The curve is always tangential to and in the same direction as a straight line draw from the begin point to the first control point. (This is visually illustrated by the Bezier program.) Also, the curve is always tangential to and in the same direction as a straight line drawn from the second control point to the end point. These are two other assumptions used to derive the Bezier formulas.

Fourth, the Bezier spline is often aesthetically pleasing. I know this is a subjective criterion, but I'm not the only person who thinks so.

Prior to the 32-bit versions of Windows, you'd have to create your own Bezier splines using the *Polyline* function. You would also need knowledge of the following parametric equations for the Bezier spline. The begin point is (x_0, y_0), and the end point is (x_3, y_3). The two control points are (x_1, y_1) and (x_2, y_2). The curve is drawn for values of t ranging from 0 to 1:

$$x(t) = (1 - t)^3 x_0 + 3t (1 - t)^2 x_1 + 3t^2 (1 - t) x_2 + t^3 x_3$$
$$y(t) = (1 - t)^3 y_0 + 3t (1 - t)^2 y_1 + 3t^2 (1 - t) y_2 + t^3 y_3$$

You don't need to know these formulas in Windows 98. To draw one or more connected Bezier splines, you simply call

```
PolyBezier (hdc, apt, iCount) ;
```

or

```
PolyBezierTo (hdc, apt, iCount) ;
```

In both cases, *apt* is an array of POINT structures. With *PolyBezier*, the first four points indicate (in this order) the begin point, first control point, second control point, and end point of the first Bezier curve. Each subsequent Bezier requires only three more points because the begin point of the second Bezier curve is the same as the end point of the first Bezier curve, and so on. The *iCount* argument is always one plus three times the number of connected curves you're drawing.

The *PolyBezierTo* function uses the current position for the first begin point. The first and each subsequent Bezier spline requires only three points. When the function returns, the current position is set to the last end point.

One note: when you draw a series of connected Bezier splines, the point of connection will be smooth only if the second control point of the first Bezier, the end point of the first Bezier (which is also the begin point of the second Bezier), and the first control point of the second Bezier are colinear; that is, they lie on the same straight line.

Using Stock Pens

When you call any of the line-drawing functions that I've discussed in this section, Windows uses the "pen" currently selected in the device context to draw the line. The pen determines the line's color, its width, and its style, which can be solid, dotted, or dashed. The pen in the default device context is called BLACK_PEN. This pen draws a solid black line with a width of one pixel. BLACK_PEN is one of three "stock pens" that Windows provides. The other two are WHITE_PEN and NULL_PEN. NULL_PEN is a pen that doesn't draw. You can also create your own customized pens.

In your Windows programs, you refer to pens by using a handle. The Windows header file WINDEF.H defines the type HPEN, a handle to a pen. You can define a variable (for instance, *hPen*) using this type definition:

```
HPEN hPen ;
```

You obtain the handle to one of the stock pens by a call to *GetStockObject*. For instance, suppose you want to use the stock pen called WHITE_PEN. You get the pen handle like this:

```
hPen = GetStockObject (WHITE_PEN) ;
```

Now you must "select" that pen into the device context:

```
SelectObject (hdc, hPen) ;
```

Now the white pen is the current pen. After this call, any lines you draw will use WHITE_PEN until you select another pen into the device context or release the device context handle.

Rather than explicitly defining an *hPen* variable, you can instead combine the *GetStockObject* and *SelectObject* calls in one statement:

```
SelectObject (hdc, GetStockObject (WHITE_PEN)) ;
```

If you then want to return to using BLACK_PEN, you can get the handle to that stock object and select it into the device context in one statement:

```
SelectObject (hdc, GetStockObject (BLACK_PEN)) ;
```

SelectObject returns the handle to the pen that had been previously selected into the device context. If you start off with a fresh device context and call

```
hPen = SelectObject (hdc, GetStockobject (WHITE_PEN)) ;
```

the current pen in the device context will be WHITE_PEN and the variable *hPen* will be the handle to BLACK_PEN. You can then select BLACK_PEN into the device context by calling

```
SelectObject (hdc, hPen) ;
```

Creating, Selecting, and Deleting Pens

Although the pens defined as stock objects are certainly convenient, you are limited to only a solid black pen, a solid white pen, or no pen at all. If you want to get fancier than that, you must create your own pens.

Here's the general procedure: You create a "logical pen," which is merely a description of a pen, using the function *CreatePen* or *CreatePenIndirect*. These functions return a handle to the logical pen. You select the pen into the device context by calling *SelectObject*. You can then draw lines with this new pen. Only one pen can be selected into the device context at any time. After you release the device context (or after you select another pen into the device context) you can delete the logical pen you've created by calling *DeleteObject*. When you do so, the handle to the pen is no longer valid.

A logical pen is a "GDI object," one of six GDI objects a program can create. The other five are brushes, bitmaps, regions, fonts, and palettes. Except for palettes, all of these objects are selected into the device context using *SelectObject*.

Three rules govern the use of GDI objects such as pens:

■ You should eventually delete all GDI objects that you create.

■ Don't delete GDI objects while they are selected in a valid device context.

■ Don't delete stock objects.

These are not unreasonable rules, but they can be a little tricky sometimes. We'll run through some examples to get the hang of how the rules work.

The general syntax for the *CreatePen* function looks like this:

```
hPen = CreatePen (iPenStyle, iWidth, crColor) ;
```

The *iPenStyle* argument determines whether the pen draws a solid line or a line made up of dots or dashes. The argument can be one of the following identifiers defined in WIN-GDI.H. Figure 5-18 shows the kind of line that each style produces.

PS_SOLID ─────────────
PS_DASH ─ ─ ─ ─ ─
PS_DOT ···············
PS_DASHDOT ─·─·─·─·─
PS_DASHDOTDOT ─··─··─··─
PS_NULL
PS_INSIDEFRAME ─────────────

Figure 5-18. *The seven pen styles.*

For the PS_SOLID, PS_NULL, and PS_INSIDEFRAME styles, the *iWidth* argument is the width of the pen. An *iWidth* value of 0 directs Windows to use one pixel for the pen width. The stock pens are 1 pixel wide. If you specify a dotted or dashed pen style with a physical width greater than 1, Windows will use a solid pen instead.

The *crColor* argument to *CreatePen* is a COLORREF value specifying the color of the pen. For all the pen styles except PS_INSIDEFRAME, when you select the pen into the device context, Windows converts the color to the nearest pure color that the device can render. The PS_INSIDEFRAME is the only pen style that can use a dithered color, and then only when the width is greater than 1.

The PS_INSIDEFRAME style has another peculiarity when used with functions that define a filled area. For all pen styles except PS_INSIDEFRAME, if the pen used to draw the outline is greater than 1 pixel wide, then the pen is centered on the border so that part of the line can be outside the bounding box. For the PS_INSIDEFRAME pen style, the entire line is drawn inside the bounding box.

You can also create a pen by setting up a structure of type LOGPEN ("logical pen") and calling *CreatePenIndirect*. If your program uses a lot of different pens that you initialize in your source code, this method is probably more efficient.

To use *CreatePenIndirect*, first you define a structure of type LOGPEN:

```
LOGPEN logpen ;
```

This structure has three members: *lopnStyle* (an unsigned integer or UINT) is the pen style, *lopnWidth* (a POINT structure) is the pen width in logical units, and *lopnColor* (COLORREF) is the pen color. Windows uses only the *x* field of the *lopnWidth* structure to set the pen width; it ignores the *y* field.

You create the pen by passing the address of the structure to *CreatePenIndirect*:

```
hPen = CreatePenIndirect (&logpen) ;
```

Note that the *CreatePen* and *CreatePenIndirect* functions do not require a handle to a device context. These functions create logical pens that have no connection with a device context until you call *SelectObject*. You can use the same logical pen for several different devices, such as the screen and a printer.

Here's one method for creating, selecting, and deleting pens. Suppose your program uses three pens—a black pen of width 1, a red pen of width 3, and a black dotted pen. You can first define static variables for storing the handles to these pens:

```
static HPEN hPen1, hPen2, hPen3 ;
```

During processing of WM_CREATE, you can create the three pens:

```
hPen1 = CreatePen (PS_SOLID, 1, 0) ;
hPen2 = CreatePen (PS_SOLID, 3, RGB (255, 0, 0)) ;
hPen3 = CreatePen (PS_DOT, 0, 0) ;
```

During processing of WM_PAINT (or any other time you have a valid handle to a device context), you can select one of these pens into the device context and draw with it:

```
SelectObject (hdc, hPen2) ;
[ line-drawing functions ]
SelectObject (hdc, hPen1) ;
[ line-drawing functions ]
```

During processing of WM_DESTROY, you can delete the three pens you created:

```
DeleteObject (hPen1) ;
DeleteObject (hPen2) ;
DeleteObject (hPen3) ;
```

This is the most straightforward method of creating selecting, and deleting pens, but obviously your program must know what pens will be needed. You might instead want to create the pens during each WM_PAINT message and delete them after you call *EndPaint*. (You can delete them before calling *EndPaint*, but you have to be careful not to delete the pen currently selected in the device context.)

You might want to create pens on the fly and combine the *CreatePen* and *SelectObject* calls in the same statement:

```
SelectObject (hdc, CreatePen (PS_DASH, 0, RGB (255, 0, 0))) ;
```

Now when you draw lines, you'll be using a red dashed pen. When you're finished drawing the red dashed lines, you can delete the pen. Whoops! How can you delete the pen when you haven't saved the pen handle? Recall that *SelectObject* returns the handle to the pen previously selected in the device context. This means that you can delete the pen by selecting the stock BLACK_PEN into the device context and deleting the value returned from *SelectObject*:

```
DeleteObject (SelectObject (hdc, GetStockObject (BLACK_PEN))) ;
```

Here's another method. When you select a pen into a newly created device context, save the handle to the pen that *SelectObject* returns:

```
hPen = SelectObject (hdc, CreatePen (PS_DASH, 0, RGB (255, 0, 0))) ;
```

What is *hPen*? If this is the first *SelectObject* call you've made since obtaining the device context, *hPen* is a handle to the BLACK_PEN stock object. You can now select that pen into the device context and delete the pen you create (the handle returned from this second *SelectObject* call) in one statement:

```
DeleteObject (SelectObject (hdc, hPen)) ;
```

If you have a handle to a pen, you can obtain the values of the LOGPEN structure fields by calling *GetObject*:

```
GetObject (hPen, sizeof (LOGPEN), (LPVOID) &logpen) ;
```

If you need the pen handle currently selected in the device context, call

```
hPen = GetCurrentObject (hdc, OBJ_PEN) ;
```

I'll discuss another pen creation function, *ExtCreatePen*, in Chapter 17.

Filling in the Gaps

The use of dotted and dashed pens raises the question: what happens to the gaps between the dots and dashes? Well, what do you want to happen?

The coloring of the gaps depends on two attributes of the device context—the background mode and the background color. The default background mode is OPAQUE, which means that Windows fills in the gaps with the background color, which by default is white. This is consistent with the WHITE_BRUSH that many programs use in the window class for erasing the background of the window.

You can change the background color that Windows uses to fill in the gaps by calling

```
SetBkColor (hdc, crColor) ;
```

As with the *crColor* argument used for the pen color, Windows converts this background color to a pure color. You can obtain the current background color defined in the device context by calling *GetBkColor*.

You can also prevent Windows from filling in the gaps by changing the background mode to TRANSPARENT:

```
SetBkMode (hdc, TRANSPARENT) ;
```

Windows will then ignore the background color and not fill in the gaps. You can obtain the current background mode (either TRANSPARENT or OPAQUE) by calling *GetBkMode*.

Drawing Modes

The appearance of lines drawn on the display is also affected by the drawing mode defined in the device context. Imagine drawing a line that has a color based not only on the color of the pen but also on the color of the display area where the line is drawn. Imagine a way in which you could use the same pen to draw a black line on a white surface and a white line on a black surface without knowing what color the surface is. Could such a facility be useful to you? It's made possible by the drawing mode.

When Windows uses a pen to draw a line, it actually performs a bitwise Boolean operation between the pixels of the pen and the pixels of the destination display surface, where the pixels determine the color of the pen and display surface. Performing a bitwise Boolean operation with pixels is called a "raster operation," or "ROP." Because drawing a line involves only two pixel patterns (the pen and the destination), the Boolean operation is called a "binary raster operation," or "ROP2." Windows defines 16 ROP2 codes that indicate how Windows combines the pen pixels and the destination pixels. In the default device context, the drawing mode is defined as R2_COPYPEN, meaning that Windows simply copies the pixels of the pen to the destination, which is how we normally think about pens. There are 15 other ROP2 codes.

Where do these 16 different ROP2 codes come from? For illustrative purposes, let's assume a monochrome system that uses 1 bit per pixel. The destination color (the color of the window's client area) can be either black (which we'll represent by a 0 pixel) or white (represented by a 1 pixel). The pen also can be either black or white. There are four combinations of using a black or white pen to draw on a black or white destination: a white pen on a white destination, a white pen on a black destination, a black pen on a white destination, and a black pen on a black destination.

What is the color of the destination after you draw with the pen? One possibility is that the line is always drawn as black regardless of the pen color or the destination color. This drawing mode is indicated by the ROP2 code R2_BLACK. Another possibility is that the line is drawn as black except when both the pen and destination are black, in which case the line is drawn as white. Although this might be a little strange, Windows has a name for it. The drawing mode is called R2_NOTMERGEPEN. Windows performs a bitwise OR operation on the destination pixels and the pen pixels and then inverts the result.

The table on the facing page shows all 16 ROP2 drawing modes. The table indicates how the pen (P) and destination (D) colors are combined for the result. The column labeled "Boolean Operation" uses C notation to show how the destination pixels and pen pixels are combined.

| Pen (P): | 1 | 1 | 0 | 0 | Boolean | |
Destination (D):	1	0	1	0	Operation	Drawing Mode
Results:	0	0	0	0	0	R2_BLACK
	0	0	0	1	~(P ¦ D)	R2_NOTMERGEPEN
	0	0	1	0	~P & D	R2_MASKNOTPEN
	0	0	1	1	~P	R2_NOTCOPYPEN
	0	1	0	0	P & ~D	R2_MASKPENNOT
	0	1	0	1	~D	R2_NOT
	0	1	1	0	P ∧ D	R2_XORPEN
	0	1	1	1	~(P & D)	R2_NOTMASKPEN
	1	0	0	0	P & D	R2_MASKPEN
	1	0	0	1	~(P ∧ D)	R2_NOTXORPEN
	1	0	1	0	D	R2_NOP
	1	0	1	1	~P ¦ D	R2_MERGENOTPEN
	1	1	0	0	P	R2_COPYPEN (default)
	1	1	0	1	P ¦ ~D	R2_MERGEPENNOT
	1	1	1	0	P ¦ D	R2_MERGEPEN
	1	1	1	1	1	R2_WHITE

You can set a new drawing mode for the device context by calling

```
SetROP2 (hdc, iDrawMode) ;
```

The *iDrawMode* argument is one of the values listed in the "Drawing Mode" column of the table. You can obtain the current drawing mode by using the function:

```
iDrawMode = GetROP2 (hdc) ;
```

The device context default is R2_COPYPEN, which simply transfers the pen color to the destination. The R2_NOTCOPYPEN mode draws white if the pen color is black and black if the pen color is white. The R2_BLACK mode always draws black, regardless of the color of the pen or the background. Likewise, the R2_WHITE mode always draws white. The R2_NOP mode is a "no operation." It leaves the destination unchanged.

We've been examining the drawing mode in the context of a monochrome system. Most systems are color, however. On color systems Windows performs the bitwise operation of the drawing mode for each color bit of the pen and destination pixels and again uses the 16 ROP2 codes described in the previous table. The R2_NOT drawing mode always inverts the destination color to determine the color of the line, regardless of the color of the pen. For example, a line drawn on a cyan destination will appear as magenta. The R2_NOT mode always results in a visible pen except if the pen is drawn on a medium gray background. I'll demonstrate the use of the R2_NOT drawing mode in the BLOKOUT programs in Chapter 7.

Drawing Filled Areas

The next step up from drawing lines is filling enclosed areas. Windows' seven functions for drawing filled areas with borders are listed in the table below.

Function	Figure
Rectangle	Rectangle with square corners
Ellipse	Ellipse
RoundRect	Rectangle with rounded corners
Chord	Arc on the circumference of an ellipse with endpoints connected by a chord
Pie	Pie wedge defined by the circumference of an ellipse
Polygon	Multisided figure
PolyPolygon	Multiple multisided figures

Windows draws the outline of the figure with the current pen selected in the device context. The current background mode, background color, and drawing mode are all used for this outline, just as if Windows were drawing a line. Everything we learned about lines also applies to the borders around these figures.

The figure is filled with the current brush selected in the device context. By default, this is the stock object called WHITE_BRUSH, which means that the interior will be drawn as white. Windows defines six stock brushes: WHITE_BRUSH, LTGRAY_BRUSH, GRAY_BRUSH, DKGRAY_BRUSH, BLACK_BRUSH, and NULL_BRUSH (or HOLLOW_BRUSH). You can select one of the stock brushes into the device context the same way you select a stock pen. Windows defines HBRUSH to be a handle to a brush, so you can first define a variable for the brush handle:

```
HBRUSH hBrush ;
```

You can get the handle to the GRAY_BRUSH by calling *GetStockObject*:

```
hBrush = GetStockObject (GRAY_BRUSH) ;
```

You can select it into the device context by calling *SelectObject*:

```
SelectObject (hdc, hBrush) ;
```

Now when you draw one of the figures listed above, the interior will be gray.

To draw a figure without a border, select the NULL_PEN into the device context:

```
SelectObject (hdc, GetStockObject (NULL_PEN)) ;
```

If you want to draw the outline of the figure without filling in the interior, select the NULL_BRUSH into the device context:

```
SelectObject (hdc, GetStockobject (NULL_BRUSH) ;
```

You can also create customized brushes just as you can create customized pens. We'll cover that topic shortly.

The *Polygon* Function and the Polygon-Filling Mode

I've already discussed the first five area-filling functions. *Polygon* is the sixth function for drawing a bordered and filled figure. The function call is similar to the *Polyline* function:

```
Polygon (hdc, apt, iCount) ;
```

The *apt* argument is an array of POINT structures, and *iCount* is the number of points. If the last point in this array is different from the first point, Windows adds another line that connects the last point with the first point. (This does not happen with the *Polyline* function.) The *PolyPolygon* function looks like this:

```
PolyPolygon (hdc, apt, aiCounts, iPolyCount) ;
```

The function draws multiple polygons. The number of polygons it draws is given as the last argument. For each polygon, the *aiCounts* array gives the number of points in the polygon. The *apt* array has all the points for all the polygons. Aside from the return value, *PolyPolygon* is functionally equivalent to the following code:

```
for (i = 0, iAccum = 0 ; i < iPolyCount ; i++)
{
     Polygon (hdc, apt + iAccum, aiCounts[i]) ;
     iAccum += aiCounts[i] ;
}
```

For both *Polygon* and *PolyPolygon*, Windows fills the bounded area with the current brush defined in the device context. How the interior is filled depends on the polygon-filling mode, which you can set using the *SetPolyFillMode* function:

```
SetPolyFillMode (hdc, iMode) ;
```

By default, the polygon-filling mode is ALTERNATE, but you can set it to WINDING. The difference between the two modes is shown in Figure 5-19 on the following page.

Figure 5-19. *Figures drawn with the two polygon-filling modes: ALTERNATE (left) and WINDING (right).*

At first, the difference between alternate and winding modes seems rather simple. For alternate mode, you can imagine a line drawn from a point in an enclosed area to infinity. The enclosed area is filled only if that imaginary line crosses an odd number of boundary lines. This is why the points of the star are filled but the center is not.

The example of the five-pointed star makes winding mode seem simpler than it actually is. When you're drawing a single polygon, in most cases winding mode will cause all enclosed areas to be filled. But there are exceptions.

To determine whether an enclosed area is filled in winding mode, you again imagine a line drawn from a point in that area to infinity. If the imaginary line crosses an odd number of boundary lines, the area is filled, just as in alternate mode. If the imaginary line crosses an even number of boundary lines, the area can either be filled or not filled. The area is filled if the number of boundary lines going in one direction (relative to the imaginary line) is not equal to the number of boundary lines going in the other direction.

For example, consider the object shown in Figure 5-20. The arrows on the lines indicate the direction in which the lines are drawn. Both winding mode and alternate mode will fill the three enclosed L-shaped areas numbered 1 through 3. The two smaller interior areas, numbered 4 and 5, will not be filled in alternate mode. But in winding mode, area number 5 is filled because you must cross two lines going in the same direction to get from the inside of that area to the outside of the figure. Area number 4 is not filled. You must again cross two lines, but the two lines go in opposite directions.

If you doubt that Windows is clever enough to do this, the ALTWIND program in Figure 5-21 demonstrates that it is.

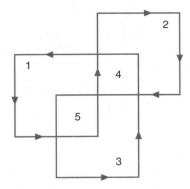

Figure 5-20. *A figure in which winding mode does not fill all interior areas.*

ALTWIND.C

```
/*------------------------------------------------
   ALTWIND.C -- Alternate and Winding Fill Modes
              (c) Charles Petzold, 1998
   ------------------------------------------------*/

#include <windows.h>

LRESULT CALLBACK WndProc (HWND, UINT, WPARAM, LPARAM) ;

int WINAPI WinMain (HINSTANCE hInstance, HINSTANCE hPrevInstance,
                    PSTR szCmdLine, int iCmdShow)
{
     static TCHAR szAppName[] = TEXT ("AltWind") ;
     HWND         hwnd ;
     MSG          msg ;
     WNDCLASS     wndclass ;

     wndclass.style         = CS_HREDRAW | CS_VREDRAW ;
     wndclass.lpfnWndProc   = WndProc ;
     wndclass.cbClsExtra    = 0 ;
     wndclass.cbWndExtra    = 0 ;
     wndclass.hInstance     = hInstance ;
     wndclass.hIcon         = LoadIcon (NULL, IDI_APPLICATION) ;
     wndclass.hCursor       = LoadCursor (NULL, IDC_ARROW) ;
     wndclass.hbrBackground = (HBRUSH) GetStockObject (WHITE_BRUSH) ;
     wndclass.lpszMenuName  = NULL ;
     wndclass.lpszClassName = szAppName ;

     if (!RegisterClass (&wndclass))
     {
```

Figure 5-21. *The ALTWIND program.*   *(continued)*

171

Figure 5-21. *continued*

```
        MessageBox (NULL, TEXT ("Program requires Windows NT!"),
                    szAppName, MB_ICONERROR) ;
        return 0 ;
    }

    hwnd = CreateWindow (szAppName, TEXT ("Alternate and Winding Fill Modes"),
                        WS_OVERLAPPEDWINDOW,
                        CW_USEDEFAULT, CW_USEDEFAULT,
                        CW_USEDEFAULT, CW_USEDEFAULT,
                        NULL, NULL, hInstance, NULL) ;

    ShowWindow (hwnd, iCmdShow) ;
    UpdateWindow (hwnd) ;

    while (GetMessage (&msg, NULL, 0, 0))
    {
        TranslateMessage (&msg) ;
        DispatchMessage (&msg) ;
    }
    return msg.wParam ;
}

LRESULT CALLBACK WndProc (HWND hwnd, UINT message, WPARAM wParam, LPARAM lParam)
{
    static POINT aptFigure [10] = { 10,70, 50,70, 50,10, 90,10, 90,50,
                                    30,50, 30,90, 70,90, 70,30, 10,30 };
    static int   cxClient, cyClient ;
    HDC          hdc ;
    int          i ;
    PAINTSTRUCT  ps ;
    POINT        apt[10] ;

    switch (message)
    {
    case WM_SIZE:
        cxClient = LOWORD (lParam) ;
        cyClient = HIWORD (lParam) ;
        return 0 ;

    case WM_PAINT:
        hdc = BeginPaint (hwnd, &ps) ;

        SelectObject (hdc, GetStockObject (GRAY_BRUSH)) ;

        for (i = 0 ; i < 10 ; i++)
        {
            apt[i].x = cxClient * aptFigure[i].x / 200 ;
```

```
            apt[i].y = cyClient * aptFigure[i].y / 100 ;
        }

        SetPolyFillMode (hdc, ALTERNATE) ;
        Polygon (hdc, apt, 10) ;

        for (i = 0 ; i < 10 ; i++)
        {
            apt[i].x += cxClient / 2 ;
        }

        SetPolyFillMode (hdc, WINDING) ;
        Polygon (hdc, apt, 10) ;

        EndPaint (hwnd, &ps) ;
        return 0 ;

    case WM_DESTROY:
        PostQuitMessage (0) ;
        return 0 ;
    }
    return DefWindowProc (hwnd, message, wParam, lParam) ;
}
```

The coordinates of the figure—scaled to an arbitrary 100-unit-by-100-unit area—are stored in the *aptFigure* array. These coordinates are scaled based on the width and height of the client area. The program displays the figure twice, once using the ALTERNATE filling mode and then using WINDING. The results are shown in Figure 5-22.

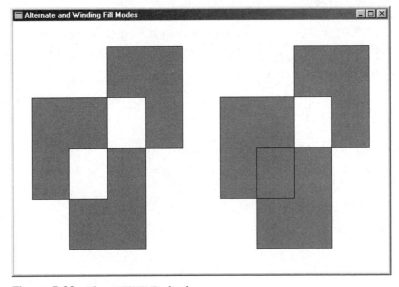

Figure 5-22. *The ALTWIND display.*

Brushing the Interior

The interiors of the *Rectangle*, *RoundRect*, *Ellipse*, *Chord*, *Pie*, *Polygon*, and *PolyPolygon* figures are filled with the current brush (sometimes also called a "pattern") selected in the device context. A brush is a small 8-pixel-by-8-pixel bitmap that is repeated horizontally and vertically to fill the area.

When Windows uses dithering to display more colors than are normally available on a display, it actually uses a brush for the color. On a monochrome system, Windows can use dithering of black and white pixels to create 64 different shades of gray. More precisely, Windows can create 64 different monochrome brushes. For pure black, all bits in the 8-by-8 bitmap are 0. One bit out of the 64 is made 1 (that is, white) for the first gray shade, two bits are white for the second gray shade, and so on, until all bits in the 8-by-8 bitmap are 1 for pure white. With a 16-color or 256-color video system, dithered colors are also brushes and Windows can display a much wider range of color than would normally be available.

Windows has five functions that let you create logical brushes. You select the brush into the device context with *SelectObject*. Like logical pens, logical brushes are GDI objects. Any brush that you create must be deleted, but it must not be deleted while it is selected in a device context.

Here's the first function to create a logical brush:

```
hBrush = CreateSolidBrush (crColor) ;
```

The word *Solid* in this function doesn't really mean that the brush is a pure color. When you select the brush into the device context, Windows may create a dithered bitmap and use that for the brush.

You can also create a brush with "hatch marks" made up of horizontal, vertical, or diagonal lines. Brushes of this style are most commonly used for coloring the interiors of bar graphs and when drawing to plotters. The function for creating a hatch brush is

```
hBrush = CreateHatchBrush (iHatchStyle, crColor) ;
```

The *iHatchStyle* argument describes the appearance of the hatch marks. Figure 5-23 shows the six available hatch style constants and what they look like.

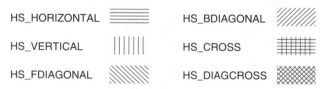

Figure 5-23. *The six hatch brush styles.*

The *crColor* argument to *CreateHatchBrush* specifies the color of the hatch lines. When you select the brush into a device context, Windows converts this color to the nearest pure color available on the display. The area between the hatch lines is colored based on the current background mode and the background color. If the background mode is OPAQUE, the background color (which is also converted to a pure color) is used to fill in the spaces between the lines. If the background mode is TRANSPARENT, Windows draws the hatch lines without filling in the area between them.

You can also create your own brushes based on bitmaps using *CreatePatternBrush* and *CreateDIBPatternBrushPt*.

The fifth function for creating a logical brush encompasses the other four functions:

```
hBrush = CreateBrushIndirect (&logbrush) ;
```

The *logbrush* variable is a structure of type LOGBRUSH ("logical brush"). The three fields of this structure are shown below. The value of the *lbStyle* field determines how Windows interprets the other two fields:

lbStyle (UINT)	*lbColor (COLORREF)*	*lbHatch (LONG)*
BS_SOLID	Color of brush	Ignored
BS_HOLLOW	Ignored	Ignored
BS_HATCHED	Color of hatches	Hatch brush style
BS_PATTERN	Ignored	Handle to bitmap
BS_DIBPATTERNPT	Ignored	Pointer to DIB

Earlier we used *SelectObject* to select a logical pen into a device context, *DeleteObject* to delete a logical pen, and *GetObject* to get information about a logical pen. You can use these same three functions with brushes. Once you have a handle to a brush, you can select the brush into a device context using *SelectObject*:

```
SelectObject (hdc, hBrush) ;
```

You can later delete a created brush with the *DeleteObject* function:

```
DeleteObject (hBrush) ;
```

Do not delete a brush that is currently selected in a device context.

If you need to obtain information about a brush, you can call *GetObject*,

```
GetObject (hBrush, sizeof (LOGBRUSH), (LPVOID) &logbrush) ;
```

where *logbrush* is a structure of type LOGBRUSH.

THE GDI MAPPING MODE

Up until now, all the sample programs have been drawing in units of pixels relative to the upper left corner of the client area. This is the default, but it's not your only choice. One device context attribute that affects virtually all the drawing you do on the client area is the "mapping mode." Four other device context attributes—the window origin, the viewport origin, the window extents, and the viewport extents—are closely related to the mapping mode attribute.

Most of the GDI drawing functions require coordinate values or sizes. For instance, this is the *TextOut* function:

```
TextOut (hdc, x, y, psText, iLength) ;
```

The *x* and *y* arguments indicate the starting position of the text. The *x* argument is the position on the horizontal axis, and the *y* argument is the position on the vertical axis. Often the notation (*x,y*) is used to indicate this point.

In *TextOut*, as in virtually all GDI functions, these coordinate values are "logical units." Windows must translate the logical units into "device units," or pixels. This translation is governed by the mapping mode, the window and viewport origins, and the window and viewport extents. The mapping mode also implies an orientation of the *x*-axis and the *y*-axis; that is, it determines whether values of *x* increase as you move toward the left or right side of the display and whether values of *y* increase as you move up or down the display.

Windows defines eight mapping modes. These are listed in the following table using the identifiers defined in WINGDI.H.

| Mapping Mode | Logical Unit | *Increasing Value* | |
		x-axis	y-axis
MM_TEXT	Pixel	Right	Down
MM_LOMETRIC	0.1 mm	Right	Up
MM_HIMETRIC	0.01 mm	Right	Up
MM_LOENGLISH	0.01 in.	Right	Up
MM_HIENGLISH	0.001 in.	Right	Up
MM_TWIPS	1/1440 in.	Right	Up
MM_ISOTROPIC	Arbitrary ($x = y$)	Selectable	Selectable
MM_ANISOTROPIC	Arbitrary ($x != y$)	Selectable	Selectable

The words METRIC and ENGLISH refer to popular systems of measurement; LO and HI are "low" and "high" and refer to precision. "Twip" is a fabricated word meaning "twentieth of a point." I mentioned earlier that a point is a unit of measurement in typography that is approximately 1/72 inch but that is often assumed in graphics programming to be exactly 1/72 inch. A "twip" is 1/20 point and hence 1/1440 inch. "Isotropic" and "anisotropic" are actually real words, meaning "identical in all directions" and "not isotropic," respectively.

You can set the mapping mode by using

```
SetMapMode (hdc, iMapMode) ;
```

where *iMapMode* is one of the eight mapping mode identifiers. You can obtain the current mapping mode by calling

```
iMapMode = GetMapMode (hdc) ;
```

The default mapping mode is MM_TEXT. In this mapping mode, logical units are the same as physical units, which allows us (or, depending on your perspective, forces us) to work directly in units of pixels. In a *TextOut* call that looks like this:

```
TextOut (hdc, 8, 16, TEXT ("Hello"), 5) ;
```

the text begins 8 pixels from the left of the client area and 16 pixels from the top.

If the mapping mode is set to MM_LOENGLISH like so,

```
SetMapMode (hdc, MM_LOENGLISH) ;
```

logical units are in terms of hundredths of an inch. Now the *TextOut* call might look like this:

```
TextOut (hdc, 50, -100, TEXT ("Hello"), 5) ;
```

The text begins 0.5 inch from the left and 1 inch from the top of the client area. (The reason for the negative sign in front of the y-coordinate will soon become clear when I discuss the mapping modes in more detail.) Other mapping modes allow programs to specify coordinates in terms of millimeters, a point size, or an arbitrarily scaled axis.

If you feel comfortable working in units of pixels, you don't need to use any mapping modes except the default MM_TEXT mode. If you need to display an image in inch or millimeter dimensions, you can obtain the information you need from *GetDeviceCaps* and do your own scaling. The other mapping modes are simply a convenient way to avoid doing your own scaling.

Although the coordinates you specify in GDI functions are 32-bit values, only Windows NT can handle all 32 bits. In Windows 98, coordinates are limited to 16 bits and thus may range only from −32,768 to 32,767. Some Windows functions that use coordinates for the starting point and ending point of a rectangle also require that the width and height of the rectangle be 32,767 or less.

Device Coordinates and Logical Coordinates

You may ask: if I use the MM_LOENGLISH mapping mode, will I start getting WM_SIZE messages in terms of hundredths of an inch? Absolutely not. Windows continues to use device coordinates for all messages (such as WM_MOVE, WM_SIZE, and WM_MOUSE-MOVE), for all non-GDI functions, and even for some GDI functions. Think of it this way: the mapping mode is an attribute of the device context, so the only time the mapping mode comes into play is when you use GDI functions that require a handle to the device context as one of the arguments. *GetSystemMetrics* is not a GDI function, so it will continue to return sizes in device units, which are pixels. And although *GetDeviceCaps* is a GDI function that requires a handle to a device context, Windows continues to return device units for the HORZRES and VERTRES indexes, because one of the purposes of this function is to provide a program with the size of the device in pixels.

However, the values in the TEXTMETRIC structure that you obtain from the *GetTextMetrics* call are in terms of logical units. If the mapping mode is MM_LOENGLISH at the time the call is made, *GetTextMetrics* provides character widths and heights in terms of hundredths of an inch. To make things easy on yourself, when you call *GetTextMetrics* for information about the height and width of characters, the mapping mode should be set to the same mapping mode that you'll be using when you draw text based on these sizes.

The Device Coordinate Systems

Windows maps logical coordinates that are specified in GDI functions to device coordinates. Before we discuss the logical coordinate system used with the various mapping modes, let's examine the different device coordinate systems that Windows defines for the video display. Although we have been working mostly within the client area of our window, Windows uses two other device coordinate systems at various times. In all device coordinate systems, units are expressed in terms of pixels. Values on the horizontal x-axis increase from left to right, and values on the vertical y-axis increase from top to bottom.

When we use the entire screen, we are working in terms of "screen coordinates." The upper left corner of the screen is the point (0, 0). Screen coordinates are used in the WM_MOVE message (for nonchild windows) and in the following Windows functions: *CreateWindow* and *MoveWindow* (for nonchild windows), *GetMessagePos*, *GetCursorPos*, *SetCursorPos*, *GetWindowRect*, and *WindowFromPoint*. (This is not a complete list.) These are generally either functions that don't have a window associated with them (such as the two cursor functions) or functions that must move or find a window based on a screen point. If you use *CreateDC* with a "DISPLAY" argument to obtain a device context for the entire screen, logical coordinates in GDI calls will be mapped to screen coordinates by default.

"Whole-window coordinates" refer to a program's entire application window, including the title bar, menu, scroll bars, and border. For a common application window, the point (0, 0) is the upper left corner of the sizing border. Whole-window coordinates are rare in Windows, but if you obtain a device context from *GetWindowDC*, logical coordinates in GDI functions will be mapped to whole-window coordinates by default.

The third device coordinate system—the one we've been working with the most—uses "client area coordinates." The point (0, 0) is the upper left corner of the client area. When you obtain a device context using *GetDC* or *BeginPaint*, logical coordinates in GDI functions will be translated to client-area coordinates by default.

You can convert client-area coordinates to screen coordinates and vice versa using the functions *ClientToScreen* and *ScreenToClient*. You can also obtain the position and size of the whole window in terms of screen coordinates using the *GetWindowRect* functions. These three functions provide enough information to translate from any one device coordinate system to the other.

The Viewport and the Window

The mapping mode defines how Windows maps logical coordinates that are specified in GDI functions to device coordinates, where the particular device coordinate system depends on the function you use to obtain the device context. To continue this discussion of the mapping mode, we need some additional terminology. The mapping mode is said to define the mapping of the "window" (logical coordinates) to the "viewport" (device coordinates).

The use of these two terms is unfortunate. In other graphics interface systems, the viewport often implies a clipping region. And in Windows, the term "window" has a very specific meaning to describe the area that a program occupies on the screen. We'll have to put aside our preconceptions of these terms during this discussion.

The viewport is specified in terms of device coordinates (pixels). Most often the viewport is the same as the client area, but it can also refer to whole-window coordinates or screen coordinates if you've obtained a device context from *GetWindowDC* or *CreateDC*. The point (0, 0) is the upper left corner of the client area (or the whole window or the screen). Values of *x* increase to the right, and values of *y* increase going down.

The window is specified in terms of logical coordinates, which might be pixels, millimeters, inches, or any other unit you want. You specify logical window coordinates in the GDI drawing functions.

But in a very real sense, the viewport and the window are just mathematical constructs. For all mapping modes, Windows translates window (logical) coordinates to viewport (device) coordinates by the use of two formulas,

$$xViewport = (xWindow - xWinOrg) \times \frac{xViewExt}{xWinExt} + xViewOrg$$

$$yViewport = (yWindow - yWinOrg) \times \frac{yViewExt}{yWinExt} + yViewOrg$$

where (*xWindow*, *yWindow*) is a logical point to be translated and (*xViewport*, *yViewport*) is the translated point in device coordinates, most likely client-area coordinates.

These formulas use two points that specify an "origin" of the window and the viewport. The point (*xWinOrg*, *yWinOrg*) is the window origin in logical coordinates; the point (*xViewOrg*, *yViewOrg*) is the viewport origin in device coordinates. By default, these two points are set to (0, 0), but you can change them. The formulas imply that the logical point (*xWinOrg*, *yWinOrg*) is always mapped to the device point (*xViewOrg*, *yViewOrg*). If the window and viewport origins are left at their default (0, 0) values, the formulas simplify to

$$xViewport = xWindow \times \frac{xViewExt}{xWinExt}$$

$$yViewport = yWindow \times \frac{yViewExt}{yWinExt}$$

The formulas also include two points that specify "extents": the point ($xWinExt$, $yWinExt$) is the window extent in logical coordinates; ($xViewExt$, $yViewExt$) is the viewport extent in device coordinates. In most mapping modes, the extents are implied by the mapping mode and cannot be changed. Each extent means nothing by itself, but the ratio of the viewport extent to the window extent is a scaling factor for converting logical units to device units.

For example, when you set the MM_LOENGLISH mapping mode, Windows sets $xViewExt$ to be a certain number of pixels and $xWinExt$ to be the length in hundredths of an inch occupied by $xViewExt$ pixels. The ratio gives you pixels per hundredths of an inch. The scaling factors are expressed as ratios of integers rather than floating point values for performance reasons.

The extents can be negative. This implies that values on the logical x-axis don't necessarily have to increase to the right and that values on the logical y-axis don't necessarily have to increase going down.

Windows can also translate from viewport (device) coordinates to window (logical) coordinates:

$$xWindow = (xViewport - xViewOrg) \times \frac{xWinExt}{xViewExt} + xWinOrg$$

$$yWindow = (yViewport - yViewOrg) \times \frac{yWinExt}{yViewExt} + yWinOrg$$

Windows provides two functions that let you convert between device points to logical points in a program. The following function converts device points to logical points:

```
DPtoLP (hdc, pPoints, iNumber) ;
```

The variable *pPoints* is a pointer to an array of POINT structures, and *iNumber* is the number of points to be converted. For example, you'll find this function useful for converting the size of the client area obtained from *GetClientRect* (which is always in terms of device units) to logical coordinates:

```
GetClientRect (hwnd, &rect) ;
DPtoLP (hdc, (PPOINT) &rect, 2) ;
```

This function converts logical points to device points:

```
LPtoDP (hdc, pPoints, iNumber) ;
```

Working with MM_TEXT

For the MM_TEXT mapping mode, the default origins and extents are shown below.

Window origin:	(0, 0)	Can be changed
Viewport origin:	(0, 0)	Can be changed
Window extent:	(1, 1)	Cannot be changed
Viewport extent:	(1, 1)	Cannot be changed

The ratio of the viewport extent to the window extent is 1, so no scaling is performed between logical coordinates and device coordinates. The formulas to convert from window coordinates to viewport coordinates shown earlier reduce to these:

$$xViewport = xWindow - xWinOrg + xViewOrg$$
$$yViewport = yWindow - yWinOrg + yViewOrg$$

This is a "text" mapping mode not because it is most suitable for text but because of the orientation of the axes. In most languages, text is read from left to right and top to bottom, and MM_TEXT defines values on the axes to increase the same way:

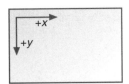

Windows provides the functions *SetViewportOrgEx* and *SetWindowOrgEx* for changing the viewport and window origins. These functions have the effect of shifting the axes so that the logical point (0, 0) no longer refers to the upper left corner. Generally, you'll use either *SetViewportOrgEx* or *SetWindowOrgEx* but not both.

Here's how the functions work: If you change the viewport origin to (*xViewOrg, yViewOrg*), the logical point (0, 0) will be mapped to the device point (*xViewOrg, yViewOrg*). If you change the window origin to (*xWinOrg, yWinOrg*), the logical point (*xWinOrg, yWinOrg*) will be mapped to the device point (0, 0), which is the upper left corner. Regardless of any changes you make to the window and viewport origins, the device point (0, 0) is always the upper left corner of the client area.

For instance, suppose your client area is *cxClient* pixels wide and *cyClient* pixels high. If you want to define the logical point (0, 0) to be the center of the client area, you can do so by calling

```
SetViewportOrgEx (hdc, cxClient / 2, cyClient / 2, NULL) ;
```

The arguments to *SetViewportOrgEx* are always in terms of device units. The logical point (0, 0) will now be mapped to the device point (*cxClient / 2, cyClient / 2*). Now you can use your client area as if it had the coordinate system shown at the top of the following page.

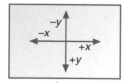

The logical *x*-axis ranges from −*cxClient/2* to +*cxClient/2*, and the logical *y*-axis ranges from −*cyClient/2* to +*cyClient/2*. The lower right corner of the client area is the logical point (*cxClient/2*, *cyClient/2*). If you want to display text starting at the upper left corner of the client area, which is the device point (0, 0), you need to use negative coordinates:

```
TextOut (hdc, -cxClient / 2, -cyClient / 2, "Hello", 5) ;
```

You can achieve the same result with *SetWindowOrgEx* as you did when you used *SetViewportOrgEx*:

```
SetWindowOrgEx (hdc, -cxClient / 2, -cyClient / 2, NULL) ;
```

The arguments to *SetWindowOrgEx* are always in terms of logical units. After this call, the logical point (−*cxClient / 2*, −*cyClient / 2*) is mapped to the device point (0, 0), the upper left corner of the client area.

What you probably don't want to do (unless you know what's going to happen) is to use both function calls together:

```
SetViewportOrgEx (hdc, cxClient / 2, cyClient / 2, NULL) ;
SetWindowOrgEx (hdc, -cxClient / 2, -cyClient / 2, NULL) ;
```

This means that the logical point (−*cxClient/2*, −*cyClient/2*) is mapped to the device point (*cxClient/2*, *cyClient/2*), giving you a coordinate system that looks like this:

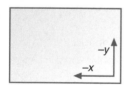

You can obtain the current viewport and window origins from these functions:

```
GetViewportOrgEx (hdc, &pt) ;
GetWindowOrgEx (hdc, &pt) ;
```

where *pt* is a POINT structure. The values returned from *GetViewportOrgEx* are in device coordinates; the values returned from *GetWindowOrgEx* are in logical coordinates.

You might want to change the viewport or window origin to shift display output within the client area of your window—for instance, in response to scroll bar input from the user. For example, in the SYSMETS2 program in Chapter 4, we used the *iVscrollPos* value (the current position of the vertical scroll bar) to adjust the y-coordinates of the display output:

```
case WM_PAINT:
     hdc = BeginPaint (hwnd, &ps) ;

     for (i = 0 ; i < NUMLINES ; i++)
     {
          y = cyChar * (i - iVscrollPos) ;
          [display text]
     }
     EndPaint (hwnd, &ps) ;
     return 0 ;
```

We can achieve the same result using *SetWindowOrgEx*:

```
case WM_PAINT:
     hdc = BeginPaint (hwnd, &ps) ;

     SetWindowOrgEx (hdc, 0, cyChar * iVscrollPos) ;

     for (i = 0 ; i < NUMLINES ; i++)
     {
          y = cyChar * i ;
          [display text]
     }
     EndPaint (hwnd, &ps) ;
     return 0 ;
```

Now the calculation of the y-coordinate for the *TextOut* functions doesn't require the *iVscrollPos* value. This means that you can put the text output calls in a separate function and not have to pass the *iVscrollPos* value to the function, because the display is adjusted by changing the window origin.

If you have some experience working with rectangular (or Cartesian) coordinate systems, moving the logical point (0, 0) to the center of the client area as we did earlier may have seemed a reasonable action. However, there's a slight problem with the MM_TEXT mapping mode. Usually a Cartesian coordinate system defines values on the y-axis as increasing as you move up the axis, whereas MM_TEXT defines the values to increase as you move down the axis. In this sense, MM_TEXT is an oddity, and the next five mapping modes do it correctly.

The Metric Mapping Modes

Windows includes five mapping modes that express logical coordinates in physical measurements. Because logical coordinates on the x-axis and y-axis are mapped to identical physical units, these mapping modes help you to draw round circles and square squares, even on a device that does not feature square pixels.

The five metric mapping modes are arranged below in order of lowest precision to highest precision. The two columns at the right show the size of the logical units in terms of inches (in.) and millimeters (mm.) for comparison.

Mapping Mode	*Logical Unit*	*Inch*	*Millimeter*
MM_LOENGLISH	0.01 in.	0.01	0.254
MM_LOMETRIC	0.1 mm.	0.00394	0.1
MM_HIENGLISH	0.001 in.	0.001	0.0254
MM_TWIPS	1/1400 in.	0.000694	0.0176
MM_HIMETRIC	0.01 mm.	0.000394	0.01

The default window and viewport origins and extents are

Window origin:	(0, 0)	Can be changed
Viewport origin:	(0, 0)	Can be changed
Window extent:	(?, ?)	Cannot be changed
Viewport extent:	(?, ?)	Cannot be changed

The question marks indicate that the window and viewport extents depend on the mapping mode and the resolution of the device. As I mentioned earlier, the extents aren't important by themselves but take on meaning when expressed as ratios. Here are the translation formulas again:

$$xViewport = (xWindow - xWinOrg) \times \frac{xViewExt}{xWinExt} + xViewOrg$$

$$yViewport = (yWindow - yWinOrg) \times \frac{yViewExt}{yWinExt} + yViewOrg$$

For MM_LOENGLISH, for example, Windows calculates the extents to be the following:

$$\frac{xViewExt}{xWinExt} = \textit{number of horizontal pixels in 0.01 in.}$$

$$\frac{-yViewExt}{yWinExt} = \textit{negative number of vertical pixels in 0.01 in.}$$

Windows uses information available from *GetDeviceCaps* to set these extents. This is somewhat different in Windows 98 and Windows NT.

First, here's how it works in Windows 98: Suppose you have used the Display applet of the Control Panel to select a 96 dpi system font. *GetDeviceCaps* will return a value of

96 for both the LOGPIXELSX and LOGPIXELSY indexes. Windows uses these values for the viewport extents and sets the viewport and window extents as shown in the following table.

Mapping Mode	Viewport Extents (x, y)	Window Extents (x, y)
MM_LOMETRIC	(96, 96)	(254, –254)
MM_HIMETRIC	(96, 96)	(2540, –2540)
MM_LOENGLISH	(96, 96)	(100, –100)
MM_HIENGLISH	(96, 96)	(1000, –1000)
MM_TWIPS	(96, 96)	(1440, –1440)

Thus, for MM_LOENGLISH, the ratio 96 divided by 100 is the number of pixels in 0.01 inches. For MM_LOMETRIC, the ratio 96 divided by 254 is the number of pixels in 0.1 millimeters.

Windows NT uses a different approach to set the viewport and window extents (an approach actually consistent with earlier 16-bit versions of Windows). The viewport extents are based on the pixel dimensions of the screen. This is information obtained from *GetDeviceCaps* using the HORZRES and VERTRES indexes. The window extents are based on the assumed size of the display, which *GetDeviceCaps* returns when you use the HORZSIZE and VERTSIZE indexes. As I mentioned earlier, these values are commonly 320 and 240 millimeters. If you've set the pixel dimensions of your display to 1024 by 768, here are the values of the viewport and window extents that Windows NT reports.

Mapping Mode	Viewport Extents (x, y)	Window Extents (x, y)
MM_LOMETRIC	(1024, –768)	(3200, 2400)
MM_HIMETRIC	(1024, –768)	(32000, 24000)
MM_LOENGLISH	(1024, –768)	(1260, 945)
MM_HIENGLISH	(1024, –768)	(12598, 9449)
MM_TWIPS	(1024, –768)	(18142, 13606)

These window extents represent the number of logical units encompassing the full width and height of the display. A 320-millimeters wide screen is also 1260 MM_LOENGLISH units or 12.6 inches (320 divided by 25.4 millimeters per inch).

Those negative signs in front of the *y* extents change the orientation of the axis. For these five mapping modes, *y* values increase as you move up the device. However, notice that the default window and viewport origins are both (0, 0). This has an interesting implication. When you first change to one of these five mapping modes, the coordinate system looks like the graph at the top of the following page.

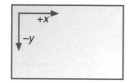

The only way you can display anything in the client area is to use negative values of *y*. For instance, this code,

```
SetMapMode (hdc, MM_LOENGLISH) ;
TextOut (hdc, 100, -100, "Hello", 5) ;
```

displays the text one inch from the top and left edges of the client area.

To preserve your sanity, you'll probably want to avoid this. One solution is to set the logical (0, 0) point to the lower left corner of the client area. Assuming that *cyClient* is the height of the client area in pixels, you can do this by calling *SetViewportOrgEx*:

```
SetViewportOrgEx (hdc, 0, cyClient, NULL) ;
```

Now the coordinate system looks like this:

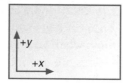

This is the upper right quadrant of a rectangular coordinate system.

Alternatively, you can set the logical (0, 0) point to the center of the client area:

```
SetViewportOrgEx (hdc, cxClient / 2, cyClient / 2, NULL) ;
```

The coordinate system looks like this:

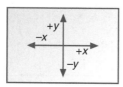

Now we have a real four-quadrant Cartesian coordinate system with equal logical units on the *x*-axis and *y*-axis in terms of inches, millimeters, or twips.

You can also use the *SetWindowOrgEx* function to change the logical (0, 0) point, but the task is a little more difficult because the arguments to *SetWindowOrgEx* have to be in logical coordinates. You would first need to convert (*cxClient*, *cyClient*) to a logical coordinate using the *DPtoLP* function. Assuming that the variable *pt* is a structure of type POINT, this code changes the logical (0, 0) point to the center of the client area:

```
pt.x = cxClient ;
pt.y = cyClient ;
DptoLP (hdc, &pt, 1) ;
SetWindowOrgEx (hdc, -pt.x / 2, -pt.y / 2, NULL) ;
```

The "Roll Your Own" Mapping Modes

The two remaining mapping modes are named MM_ISOTROPIC and MM_ANISOTROPIC. These are the only two mapping modes for which Windows lets you change the viewport and window extents, which means that you can change the scaling factor that Windows uses to translate logical and device coordinates. The word *isotropic* means "equal in all directions"; *anisotropic* is the opposite—"not equal." Like the metric mapping modes shown earlier, MM_ISOTROPIC uses equally scaled axes. Logical units on the *x*-axis have the same physical dimensions as logical units on the *y*-axis. This helps when you need to create images that retain the correct aspect ratio regardless of the aspect ratio of the display device.

The difference between MM_ISOTROPIC and the metric mapping modes is that with MM_ISOTROPIC you can control the physical size of the logical unit. If you want, you can adjust the size of the logical unit based on the client area. This lets you draw images that are always contained within the client area, shrinking and expanding appropriately. The two clock programs in Chapter 8 have isotropic images. As you size the window, the clocks are resized appropriately.

A Windows program can handle the resizing of an image entirely through adjusting the window and viewport extents. The program can then use the same logical units in the drawing functions regardless of the size of the window.

Sometimes MM_TEXT and the metric mapping modes are called "fully constrained" mapping modes. This means that you cannot change the window and viewport extents and the way Windows scales logical coordinates to device coordinates. MM_ISOTROPIC is a "partly constrained" mapping mode. Windows allows you to change the window and viewport extents, but it adjusts them so that *x* and *y* logical units represent the same physical dimensions. The MM_ANISOTROPIC mapping mode is "unconstrained." You can change the window and viewport extents, and Windows doesn't adjust the values.

The MM_ISOTROPIC Mapping Mode

The MM_ISOTROPIC mapping mode is ideal for using arbitrarily scaled axes while preserving equal logical units on the two axes. Rectangles with equal logical widths and heights are displayed as squares, and ellipses with equal logical widths and heights are displayed as circles.

When you first set the mapping mode to MM_ISOTROPIC, Windows uses the same window and viewport extents that it uses with MM_LOMETRIC. (Don't rely on this fact, however.) The difference is that you can now change the extents to suit your preferences by calling *SetWindowExtEx* and *SetViewportExtEx*. Windows will then adjust the extents so that the logical units on both axes represent equal physical distances.

Generally, you'll use arguments to *SetWindowExtEx* with the desired logical size of the logical windows, and arguments to *SetViewportExtEx* with the actual height and width of the client area. When Windows adjusts these extents, it has to fit the logical window within the physical viewport, which can result in a section of the client area falling outside the logical window. You should call *SetWindowExtEx* before you call *SetViewportExtEx* to make the most efficient use of space in the client area.

For example, suppose you want a traditional one-quadrant virtual coordinate system where (0, 0) is at the lower left corner of the client area and the logical width and height ranges from 0 to 32,767. You want the *x* and *y* units to have the same physical dimensions. Here's what you need to do:

```
SetMapMode (hdc, MM_ISOTROPIC) ;
SetWindowExtEx (hdc, 32767, 32767, NULL) ;
SetViewportExtEx (hdc, cxClient, -cyClient, NULL) ;
SetViewportOrgEx (hdc, 0, cyClient, NULL) ;
```

If you then obtain the window and viewport extents using *GetWindowExtEx* and *GetViewportExtEx*, you'll find that they are not the values you specified. Windows has adjusted the extents based on the aspect ratio of the display device so that logical units on the two axes represent the same physical dimensions.

If the client area is wider than it is high (in physical dimensions), Windows adjusts the *x* extents so that the logical window is narrower than the client-area viewport. The logical window will be positioned at the left of the client area:

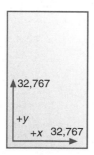

Windows 98 will actually not allow you to display anything in the right side of the client area because it is limited to 16-bit signed coordinates. Windows NT uses a full 32-bits for coordinates, and you would be able to display something over in the right side.

If the client area is higher than it is wide (in physical dimensions), Windows adjust the *y* extents. The logical window will be positioned at the bottom of the client area:

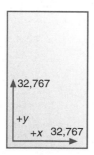

Windows 98 will not allow you to display anything at the top of the client area.

If you prefer that the logical window always be positioned at the left and top of the client area, you can change the code to the following:

```
SetMapMode (MM_ISOTROPIC) ;
SetWindowExtEx (hdc, 32767, 32767, NULL) ;
SetViewportExtEx (hdc, cxClient, -cyClient, NULL) ;
SetWindowOrgEx (hdc, 0, 32767, NULL) ;
```

In the *SetWindowOrgEx* call, we're saying that we want the logical point (0, 32767) to be mapped to the device point (0, 0). Now, if the client area is higher than it is wide, the coordinates are arranged like this:

For a clock program, you might want to use a four-quadrant Cartesian coordinate system with arbitrarily scaled axes in four directions in which the logical point (0, 0) is in the center of the client area. If you want each axis to range from 0 to 1000 (for instance), you use this code:

```
SetMapMode (hdc, MM_ISOTROPIC) ;
SetWindowExtEx (hdc, 1000, 1000, NULL) ;
SetViewportExtEx (hdc, cxClient / 2, -cyClient / 2, NULL) ;
SetViewportOrgEx (hdc, cxClient / 2, cyClient / 2, NULL) ;
```

The logical coordinates look like this if the client area is wider than it is high:

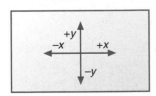

The logical coordinates are also centered if the client area is higher than it is wide, as shown on the following page.

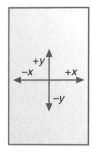

Keep in mind that no clipping is implied in window or viewport extents. When calling GDI functions, you are still free to use logical *x* and *y* values less than −1000 and greater than +1000. Depending on the shape of the client area, these points might or might not be visible.

With the MM_ISOTROPIC mapping mode, you can make logical units larger than pixels. For instance, suppose you want a mapping mode with the point (0, 0) at the upper left corner of the display and values of *y* increasing as you move down (like MM_TEXT) but with logical coordinates in sixteenths of an inch. Here's one way to do it:

```
SetMapMode (hdc, MM_ISOTROPIC) ;
SetWindowExtEx (hdc, 16, 16, NULL) ;
SetViewportExtEx (hdc, GetDeviceCaps (hdc, LOGPIXELSX),
                       GetDeviceCaps (hdc, LOGPIXELSY), NULL) ;
```

The arguments to the *SetWindowExtEx* function indicate the number of logical units in one inch. The arguments to the *SetViewportExtEx* function indicate the number of physical units (pixels) in one inch.

However, this approach would *not* be consistent with the metric mapping modes in Windows NT. These mapping modes use the pixel size and metric size of the display. To be consistent with the metric mapping modes, you can use this code:

```
SetMapMode (hdc, MM_ISOTROPIC) ;
SetWindowExtEx (hdc, 160 * GetDeviceCaps (hdc, HORZSIZE) / 254,
                     160 * GetDeviceCaps (hdc, VERTSIZE) / 254, NULL) ;
SetViewportExtEx (hdc, GetDeviceCaps (hdc, HORZRES),
                       GetDeviceCaps (hdc, VERTRES), NULL) ;
```

In this code, the viewport extents are set to the pixel dimensions of the entire screen. The window extents are set to the assumed dimension of the screen in units of sixteenths of an inch. *GetDeviceCaps* with the HORZRES and VERTRES indexes return the dimensions of the device in millimeters. If we were working with floating-point numbers, we would convert the millimeters to inches by dividing by 25.4 and then convert inches to sixteenths of an inch by multiplying by 16. However, because we're working with integers, we must multiply by 160 and divide by 254.

Of course, such a coordinate system makes logical units much larger than physical units. Everything you draw on the device will have coordinate values that map to an increment of 1/16 inch. You cannot draw two horizontal lines that are 1/32 inch apart because that would require a fractional logical coordinate.

MM_ANISOTROPIC: Stretching the Image to Fit

When you set the viewport and window extents in the MM_ISOTROPIC mapping mode, Windows adjusts the values so that logical units on the two axes have the same physical dimensions. In the MM_ANISOTROPIC mapping mode, Windows makes no adjustments to the values you set. This means that MM_ANISOTROPIC does not necessarily maintain the correct aspect ratio.

One way you can use MM_ANISOTROPIC is to have arbitrary coordinates for the client area, as we did with MM_ISOTROPIC. This code sets the point (0, 0) at the lower left corner of the client area with the x and y axes ranging from 0 to 32,767:

```
SetMapMode (hdc, MM_ANISOTROPIC) ;
SetWindowExtEx (hdc, 32767, 32767, NULL) ;
SetViewportExtEx (hdc, cxClient, -cyClient, NULL) ;
SetViewportOrgEx (hdc, 0, cyClient, NULL) ;
```

With MM_ISOTROPIC, similar code caused part of the client area to be beyond the range of the axes. With MM_ANISOTROPIC, the upper right corner of the client area is always the point (32767, 32767), regardless of its dimensions. If the client area is not square, logical x and y units will have different physical dimensions.

In the previous section on the MM_ISOTROPIC mapping mode, I discussed how you might draw a round clock in the client area where the x and y axes ranged from −1000 to 1000. You can do something similar with MM_ANISOTROPIC:

```
SetMapMode (hdc, MM_ANISOTROPIC) ;
SetWindowExtEx (hdc, 1000, 1000, NULL) ;
SetViewportExtEx (hdc, cxClient / 2, -cyClient / 2, NULL) ;
SetViewportOrgEx (hdc, cxClient / 2, cyClient / 2, NULL) ;
```

The difference with MM_ANISOTROPIC is that in general the clock would be drawn as an ellipse rather than a circle.

Another way to use MM_ANISOTROPIC is to set x and y units to fixed but unequal values. For instance, if you have a program that displays only text, you may want to set coarse coordinates based on the height and width of a single character:

```
SetMapMode (hdc, MM_ANISOTROPIC) ;
SetWindowExtEx (hdc, 1, 1, NULL) ;
SetViewportExtEx (hdc, cxChar, cyChar, NULL) ;
```

Of course, I've assumed that *cxChar* and *cyChar* are the width and height of characters in that font. Now you can specify coordinates in terms of character rows and columns. For instance, the following statement displays text three characters from the left and two character rows from the top of the client area:

```
TextOut (hdc, 3, 2, TEXT ("Hello"), 5) ;
```

This might be more appropriate if you're using a fixed-point font, as in the upcoming WHATSIZE program.

When you first set the MM_ANISOTROPIC mapping mode, it always inherits the extents of the previously set mapping mode. This can be very convenient. One way of thinking about MM_ANISTROPIC is that it "unlocks" the extents; that is, it allows you to change the extents of an otherwise fully-constrained mapping mode. For instance, suppose you want to use the MM_LOENGLISH mapping mode because you want logical units to be 0.01 inch. But you don't want the values along the *y*-axis to increase as you move up the screen—you prefer the MM_TEXT orientation, where *y* values increase moving down. Here's the code:

```
SIZE size ;
[other program lines]
SetMapMode (hdc, MM_LOENGLISH) ;
SetMapMode (hdc, MM_ANISOTROPIC) ;
GetViewportExtEx (hdc, &size) ;
SetViewportExtEx (hdc, size.cx, -size.cy, NULL) ;
```

We first set the mapping mode to MM_LOENGLISH. Then we liberate the extents by setting the mapping mode to MM_ANISOTROPIC. The *GetViewportExtEx* function obtains the viewport extents in a SIZE structure. Then we call *SetViewportExtEx* with the extents, except that the *y* extent is made negative.

The WHATSIZE Program

A little Windows history: The first how-to-program-for-Windows article appeared in the December 1986 issue of *Microsoft Systems Journal*. The sample program in that article was called WSZ ("what size"), and it displayed the size of a client area in pixels, inches, and millimeters. A simplified version of that program is WHATSIZE, shown in Figure 5-24. The program shows the dimensions of the window's client area in terms of the five metric mapping modes.

WHATSIZE.C

```
/*-------------------------------------------
   WHATSIZE.C -- What Size is the Window?
                 (c) Charles Petzold, 1998
   -------------------------------------------*/
```

Figure 5-24. *The WHATSIZE program.*

```
#include <windows.h>

LRESULT CALLBACK WndProc (HWND, UINT, WPARAM, LPARAM) ;

int WINAPI WinMain (HINSTANCE hInstance, HINSTANCE hPrevInstance,
                    PSTR szCmdLine, int iCmdShow)
{
    static TCHAR szAppName[] = TEXT ("WhatSize") ;
    HWND          hwnd ;
    MSG           msg ;
    WNDCLASS      wndclass ;

    wndclass.style         = CS_HREDRAW | CS_VREDRAW;
    wndclass.lpfnWndProc   = WndProc ;
    wndclass.cbClsExtra    = 0 ;
    wndclass.cbWndExtra    = 0 ;
    wndclass.hInstance     = hInstance ;
    wndclass.hIcon         = LoadIcon (NULL, IDI_APPLICATION) ;
    wndclass.hCursor       = LoadCursor (NULL, IDC_ARROW) ;
    wndclass.hbrBackground = (HBRUSH) GetStockObject (WHITE_BRUSH) ;
    wndclass.lpszMenuName  = NULL ;
    wndclass.lpszClassName = szAppName ;

    if (!RegisterClass (&wndclass))
    {
        MessageBox (NULL, TEXT ("This program requires Windows NT!"),
                    szAppName, MB_ICONERROR) ;
        return 0 ;
    }

    hwnd = CreateWindow (szAppName, TEXT ("What Size is the Window?"),
                         WS_OVERLAPPEDWINDOW,
                         CW_USEDEFAULT, CW_USEDEFAULT,
                         CW_USEDEFAULT, CW_USEDEFAULT,
                         NULL, NULL, hInstance, NULL) ;

    ShowWindow (hwnd, iCmdShow) ;
    UpdateWindow (hwnd) ;

    while (GetMessage (&msg, NULL, 0, 0))
    {
        TranslateMessage (&msg) ;
        DispatchMessage (&msg) ;
    }
    return msg.wParam ;
}
```

(continued)

Figure 5-24. *continued*

```
void Show (HWND hwnd, HDC hdc, int xText, int yText, int iMapMode,
           TCHAR * szMapMode)
{
     TCHAR szBuffer [60] ;
     RECT  rect ;

     SaveDC (hdc) ;

     SetMapMode (hdc, iMapMode) ;
     GetClientRect (hwnd, &rect) ;
     DPtoLP (hdc, (PPOINT) &rect, 2) ;

     RestoreDC (hdc, -1) ;

     TextOut (hdc, xText, yText, szBuffer,
              wsprintf (szBuffer, TEXT ("%-20s %7d %7d %7d %7d"), szMapMode,
              rect.left, rect.right, rect.top, rect.bottom)) ;
}

LRESULT CALLBACK WndProc (HWND hwnd, UINT message, WPARAM wParam, LPARAM lParam)
{
     static TCHAR szHeading [] =
          TEXT ("Mapping Mode             Left     Right      Top   Bottom") ;
     static TCHAR szUndLine [] =
          TEXT ("------------           ----    -----      ---   ------") ;
     static int   cxChar, cyChar ;
     HDC          hdc ;
     PAINTSTRUCT  ps ;
     TEXTMETRIC   tm ;

     switch (message)
     {
     case WM_CREATE:
          hdc = GetDC (hwnd) ;
          SelectObject (hdc, GetStockObject (SYSTEM_FIXED_FONT)) ;

          GetTextMetrics (hdc, &tm) ;
          cxChar = tm.tmAveCharWidth ;
          cyChar = tm.tmHeight + tm.tmExternalLeading ;

          ReleaseDC (hwnd, hdc) ;
          return 0 ;

     case WM_PAINT:
          hdc = BeginPaint (hwnd, &ps) ;
          SelectObject (hdc, GetStockObject (SYSTEM_FIXED_FONT)) ;
```

```
        SetMapMode (hdc, MM_ANISOTROPIC) ;
        SetWindowExtEx (hdc, 1, 1, NULL) ;
        SetViewportExtEx (hdc, cxChar, cyChar, NULL) ;

        TextOut (hdc, 1, 1, szHeading, lstrlen (szHeading)) ;
        TextOut (hdc, 1, 2, szUndLine, lstrlen (szUndLine)) ;

        Show (hwnd, hdc, 1, 3, MM_TEXT,      TEXT ("TEXT (pixels)")) ;
        Show (hwnd, hdc, 1, 4, MM_LOMETRIC,  TEXT ("LOMETRIC (.1 mm)")) ;
        Show (hwnd, hdc, 1, 5, MM_HIMETRIC,  TEXT ("HIMETRIC (.01 mm)")) ;
        Show (hwnd, hdc, 1, 6, MM_LOENGLISH, TEXT ("LOENGLISH (.01 in)")) ;
        Show (hwnd, hdc, 1, 7, MM_HIENGLISH, TEXT ("HIENGLISH (.001 in)")) ;
        Show (hwnd, hdc, 1, 8, MM_TWIPS,     TEXT ("TWIPS (1/1440 in)")) ;

        EndPaint (hwnd, &ps) ;
        return 0 ;

  case WM_DESTROY:
        PostQuitMessage (0) ;
        return 0 ;
  }
  return DefWindowProc (hwnd, message, wParam, lParam) ;
}
```

For ease in displaying the information using the *TextOut* function, WHATSIZE uses a fixed-pitch font. Switching to a fixed-pitch font (which was the default prior to Windows 3.0) involves this simple statement:

```
SelectObject (hdc, GetStockObject (SYSTEM_FIXED_FONT)) ;
```

These are the same two functions used for selecting stock pens and brushes. WHATSIZE also uses the MM_ANISTROPIC mapping mode with logical units set to character dimensions, as shown earlier.

When WHATSIZE needs to obtain the size of the client area for one of the six mapping modes, it saves the current device context, sets a new mapping mode, obtains the client-area coordinates, converts them to logical coordinates, and then restores the original mapping mode before displaying the information. This code is in WHATSIZE's *Show* function:

```
SaveDC (hdc) ;
SetMapMode (hdc, iMapMode) ;
GetClientRect (hwnd, &rect) ;
DptoLP (hdc, (PPOINT) &rect, 2) ;
RestoreDC (hdc, -1) ;
```

Figure 5-25 on the following page shows a typical display from WHATSIZE.

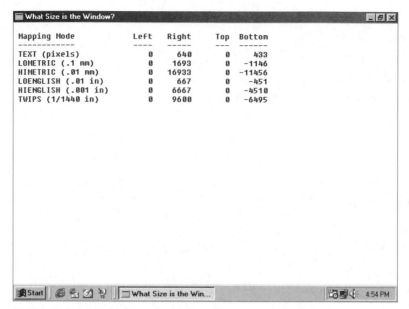

Figure 5-25. *A typical WHATSIZE display.*

RECTANGLES, REGIONS, AND CLIPPING

Windows includes several additional drawing functions that work with RECT (rectangle) structures and regions. A region is an area of the screen that is a combination of rectangles, polygons, and ellipses.

Working with Rectangles

These three drawing functions require a pointer to a rectangle structure:

```
FillRect (hdc, &rect, hBrush) ;
FrameRect (hdc, &rect, hBrush) ;
InvertRect (hdc, &rect) ;
```

In these functions, the *rect* parameter is a structure of type RECT with four fields: *left*, *top*, *right*, and *bottom*. The coordinates in this structure are treated as logical coordinates.

FillRect fills the rectangle (up to but not including the right and bottom coordinates) with the specified brush. This function doesn't require that you first select the brush into the device context.

FrameRect uses the brush to draw a rectangular frame, but it does not fill in the rectangle. Using a brush to draw a frame may seem a little strange, because with the functions that you've seen so far (such as *Rectangle*) the border is drawn with the current pen.

FrameRect allows you to draw a rectangular frame that isn't necessarily a pure color. This frame is one logical unit wide. If logical units are larger than device units, the frame will be 2 or more pixels wide.

InvertRect inverts all the pixels in the rectangle, turning ones to zeros and zeros to ones. This function turns a white area to black, a black area to white, and a green area to magenta.

Windows also includes nine functions that allow you to manipulate RECT structures easily and cleanly. For instance, to set the four fields of a RECT structure to particular values, you would conventionally use code that looks like this:

```
rect.left   = xLeft ;
rect.top    = xTop ;
rect.right  = xRight ;
rect.bottom = xBottom ;
```

By calling the *SetRect* function, however, you can achieve the same result with a single line:

```
SetRect (&rect, xLeft, yTop, xRight, yBottom) ;
```

The other eight functions can also come in handy when you want to do one of the following:

■ Move a rectangle a number of units along the *x* and *y* axes:

```
OffsetRect (&rect, x, y) ;
```

■ Increase or decrease the size of a rectangle:

```
InflateRect (&rect, x, y) ;
```

■ Set the fields of a rectangle equal to 0:

```
SetRectEmpty (&rect) ;
```

■ Copy one rectangle to another:

```
CopyRect (&DestRect, &SrcRect) ;
```

■ Obtain the intersection of two rectangles:

```
IntersectRect (&DestRect, &SrcRect1, &SrcRect2) ;
```

■ Obtain the union of two rectangles:

```
UnionRect (&DestRect, &SrcRect1, &SrcRect2) ;
```

■ Determine whether a rectangle is empty:

```
bEmpty = IsRectEmpty (&rect) ;
```

■ Determine whether a point is in a rectangle:

```
bInRect = PtInRect (&rect, point) ;
```

In most cases, the equivalent code for these functions is simple. For example, you can duplicate the *CopyRect* function call with a field-by-field structure copy, accomplished by the statement

```
DestRect = SrcRect ;
```

Random Rectangles

A fun program in any graphics system is one that runs "forever," simply drawing a hypnotic series of images with random sizes and colors— for example, rectangles of a random size and color. You can create such a program in Windows, but it's not quite as easy as it first seems. I hope you realize that you can't simply put a *while(TRUE)* loop in the WM_PAINT message. Sure, it will work, but the program will effectively prevent itself from processing other messages. The program cannot be exited or minimized.

One acceptable alternative is setting a Windows timer to send WM_TIMER messages to your window function. (I'll discuss the timer in Chapter 8.) For each WM_TIMER message, you obtain a device context with *GetDC*, draw a random rectangle, and then release the device context with *ReleaseDC*. But that takes some of the fun out of the program, because the program can't draw the random rectangles as quickly as possible. It must wait for each WM_TIMER message, and that's based on the resolution of the system clock.

There must be plenty of "dead time" in Windows—time during which all the message queues are empty and Windows is just sitting around waiting for keyboard or mouse input. Couldn't we somehow get control during that dead time and draw the rectangles, relinquishing control only when a message is added to a program's message queue? That's one of the purposes of the *PeekMessage* function. Here's one example of a *PeekMessage* call:

```
PeekMessage (&msg, NULL, 0, 0, PM_REMOVE) ;
```

The first four parameters (a pointer to a MSG structure, a window handle, and two values indicating a message range) are identical to those of *GetMessage*. Setting the second, third, and fourth parameters to NULL or 0 indicates that we want *PeekMessage* to return all messages for all windows in the program. The last parameter to *PeekMessage* is set to PM_REMOVE if the message is to be removed from the message queue. You can set it to PM_NOREMOVE if the message isn't to be removed. This is why *PeekMessage* is a "peek" rather than a "get"—it allows a program to check the next message in the program's queue without actually removing it.

GetMessage doesn't return control to a program unless it retrieves a message from the program's message queue. But *PeekMessage* always returns right away regardless whether a message is present or not. When there's a message in the program's message queue, the return value of *PeekMessage* is TRUE (nonzero) and the message can be processed as normal. When there is no message in the queue, *PeekMessage* returns FALSE (0).

This allows us to replace the normal message loop, which looks like this:

```
while (GetMessage (&msg, NULL, 0, 0))
{
     TranslateMessage (&msg) ;
     DispatchMessage (&msg) ;
}
return msg.wParam ;
```

with an alternative message loop like this:

```
while (TRUE)
{
     if (PeekMessage (&msg, NULL, 0, 0, PM_REMOVE))
     {
          if (msg.message == WM_QUIT)
               break ;

          TranslateMessage (&msg) ;
          DispatchMessage (&msg) ;
     }
     else
     {
          [other program lines to do some work]
     }
}
return msg.wParam ;
```

Notice that the WM_QUIT message is explicitly checked. You don't have to do this in a normal message loop, because the return value of *GetMessage* is FALSE (0) when it retrieves a WM_QUIT message. But *PeekMessage* uses its return value to indicate whether a message was retrieved, so the check of WM_QUIT is required.

If the return value of *PeekMessage* is TRUE, the message is processed normally. If the value is FALSE, the program can do some work (such as displaying yet another random rectangle) before returning control to Windows.

(Although the Windows documentation notes that you can't use *PeekMessage* to remove WM_PAINT messages from the message queue, this isn't really a problem. After all, *GetMessage* doesn't remove WM_PAINT messages from the queue either. The only way to remove a WM_PAINT message from the queue is to validate the invalid regions of the window's client area, which you can do with *ValidateRect*, *ValidateRgn*, or a *BeginPaint* and *EndPaint* pair. If you process a WM_PAINT message normally after retrieving it from the queue with *PeekMessage*, you'll have no problems. What you can't do is use code like this to empty your message queue of all messages:

```
while (PeekMessage (&msg, NULL, 0, 0, PM_REMOVE)) ;
```

This statement removes and discards all messages from your message queue except WM_PAINT. If a WM_PAINT message is in the queue, you'll be stuck inside the while loop forever.)

PeekMessage was much more important in earlier versions of Windows than it is in Windows 98. This is because the 16-bit versions of Windows employed nonpreemptive multitasking (which I'll discuss in Chapter 20). The Windows Terminal program used a *PeekMessage* loop to check for incoming data from a communications port. The Print Manager program used this technique for printing, and Windows applications that printed also generally used a *PeekMessage* loop. With the preemptive multitasking of Windows 98, programs can create multiple threads of execution, as we'll see in Chapter 20.

Armed only with the *PeekMessage* function, however, we can write a program that relentlessly displays random rectangles. The program, called RANDRECT, is shown in Figure 5-26.

RANDRECT.C

```
/*------------------------------------------
   RANDRECT.C -- Displays Random Rectangles
                 (c) Charles Petzold, 1998
   ------------------------------------------*/

#include <windows.h>
#include <stdlib.h>              // for the rand function

LRESULT CALLBACK WndProc (HWND, UINT, WPARAM, LPARAM) ;
void DrawRectangle (HWND) ;

int cxClient, cyClient ;

int WINAPI WinMain (HINSTANCE hInstance, HINSTANCE hPrevInstance,
                    PSTR szCmdLine, int iCmdShow)
{
    static TCHAR szAppName[] = TEXT ("RandRect") ;
    HWND         hwnd ;
    MSG          msg ;
    WNDCLASS     wndclass ;

    wndclass.style         = CS_HREDRAW | CS_VREDRAW ;
    wndclass.lpfnWndProc   = WndProc ;
    wndclass.cbClsExtra    = 0 ;
    wndclass.cbWndExtra    = 0 ;
    wndclass.hInstance     = hInstance ;
    wndclass.hIcon         = LoadIcon (NULL, IDI_APPLICATION) ;
    wndclass.hCursor       = LoadCursor (NULL, IDC_ARROW) ;
    wndclass.hbrBackground = (HBRUSH) GetStockObject (WHITE_BRUSH) ;
    wndclass.lpszMenuName  = NULL ;
    wndclass.lpszClassName = szAppName ;
```

Figure 5-26. *The RANDRECT program.*

```
     if (!RegisterClass (&wndclass))
     {
          MessageBox (NULL, TEXT ("This program requires Windows NT!"),
                    szAppName, MB_ICONERROR) ;
          return 0 ;
     }

     hwnd = CreateWindow (szAppName, TEXT ("Random Rectangles"),
                         WS_OVERLAPPEDWINDOW,
                         CW_USEDEFAULT, CW_USEDEFAULT,
                         CW_USEDEFAULT, CW_USEDEFAULT,
                         NULL, NULL, hInstance, NULL) ;

     ShowWindow (hwnd, iCmdShow) ;
     UpdateWindow (hwnd) ;

     while (TRUE)
     {
          if (PeekMessage (&msg, NULL, 0, 0, PM_REMOVE))
          {
               if (msg.message == WM_QUIT)
                    break ;
               TranslateMessage (&msg) ;
               DispatchMessage (&msg) ;
          }
          else
               DrawRectangle (hwnd) ;
     }
     return msg.wParam ;
}

LRESULT CALLBACK WndProc (HWND hwnd, UINT iMsg, WPARAM wParam, LPARAM lParam)
{
     switch (iMsg)
     {
     case WM_SIZE:
          cxClient = LOWORD (lParam) ;
          cyClient = HIWORD (lParam) ;
          return 0 ;

     case WM_DESTROY:
          PostQuitMessage (0) ;
          return 0 ;
     }
     return DefWindowProc (hwnd, iMsg, wParam, lParam) ;
}
```

(continued)

Figure 5-26. *continued*

```
void DrawRectangle (HWND hwnd)
{
    HBRUSH hBrush ;
    HDC    hdc ;
    RECT   rect ;

    if (cxClient == 0 || cyClient == 0)
         return ;

    SetRect (&rect, rand () % cxClient, rand () % cyClient,
                   rand () % cxClient, rand () % cyClient) ;

    hBrush = CreateSolidBrush (
                 RGB (rand () % 256, rand () % 256, rand () % 256)) ;
    hdc = GetDC (hwnd) ;

    FillRect (hdc, &rect, hBrush) ;
    ReleaseDC (hwnd, hdc) ;
    DeleteObject (hBrush) ;
}
```

This program actually runs so fast on today's speedy machines that it no longer looks like a series of random rectangles! The program uses the *SetRect* and *FillRect* function I discussed above, basing rectangle coordinates and solid brush colors on random values obtained from the C *rand* function. I'll show another version of this program using multiple threads of execution in Chapter 20.

Creating and Painting Regions

A region is a description of an area of the display that is a combination of rectangles, polygons, and ellipses. You can use regions for drawing or for clipping. You use a region for clipping (that is, restricting drawing to a specific part of your client area) by selecting the region into the device context. Like pens and brushes, regions are GDI objects. You should delete any regions that you create by calling *DeleteObject*.

When you create a region, Windows returns a handle to the region of type HRGN. The simplest type of region describes a rectangle. You can create a rectangular region in one of two ways:

```
hRgn = CreateRectRgn (xLeft, yTop, xRight, yBottom) ;
```

or

```
hRgn = CreateRectRgnIndirect (&rect) ;
```

You can also create elliptical regions using

```
hRgn = CreateEllipticRgn (xLeft, yTop, xRight, yBottom) ;
```

or

```
hRgn = CreateEllipticRgnIndirect (&rect) ;
```

The *CreateRoundRectRgn* creates a rectangular region with rounded corners.

Creating a polygonal region is similar to using the *Polygon* function:

```
hRgn = CreatePolygonRgn (&point, iCount, iPolyFillMode) ;
```

The point parameter is an array of structures of type POINT, *iCount* is the number of points, and *iPolyFillMode* is either ALTERNATE or WINDING. You can also create multiple polygonal regions using *CreatePolyPolygonRgn*.

So what, you say? What makes these regions so special? Here's the function that unleashes the power of regions:

```
iRgnType = CombineRgn (hDestRgn, hSrcRgn1, hSrcRgn2, iCombine) ;
```

This function combines two source regions (*hSrcRgn1* and *hSrcRgn2*) and causes the destination region handle (*hDestRgn*) to refer to that combined region. All three region handles must be valid, but the region previously described by *hDestRgn* is destroyed. (When you use this function, you might want to make *hDestRgn* refer initially to a small rectangular region.)

The *iCombine* parameter describes how the *hSrcRgn1* and *hSrcRgn2* regions are to be combined:

iCombine Value	New Region
RGN_AND	Overlapping area of the two source regions
RGN_OR	All of the two source regions
RGN_XOR	All of the two source regions, excluding the overlapping area
RGN_DIFF	All of *hSrcRgn1* not in *hSrcRgn2*
RGN_COPY	All of *hSrcRgn1* (ignores *hSrcRgn2*)

The *iRgnType* value returned from *CombineRgn* is one of the following: NULLREGION, indicating an empty region; SIMPLEREGION, indicating a simple rectangle, ellipse, or polygon; COMPLEXREGION, indicating a combination of rectangles, ellipses, or polygons; and ERROR, meaning that an error has occurred.

Once you have a handle to a region, you can use it with four drawing functions:

```
FillRgn (hdc, hRgn, hBrush) ;
FrameRgn (hdc, hRgn, hBrush, xFrame, yFrame) ;
InvertRgn (hdc, hRgn) ;
PaintRgn (hdc, hRgn) ;
```

The *FillRgn*, *FrameRgn*, and *InvertRgn* functions are similar to the *FillRect*, *FrameRect*, and *InvertRect* functions. The *xFrame* and *yFrame* parameters to *FrameRgn* are the logical width and height of the frame to be painted around the region. The *PaintRgn* function fills in the region with the brush currently selected in the device context. All these functions assume the region is defined in logical coordinates.

When you're finished with a region, you can delete it using the same function that deletes other GDI objects:

```
DeleteObject (hRgn) ;
```

Clipping with Rectangles and Regions

Regions can also play a role in clipping. The *InvalidateRect* function invalidates a rectangular area of the display and generates a WM_PAINT message. For example, you can use the *InvalidateRect* function to erase the client area and generate a WM_PAINT message:

```
InvalidateRect (hwnd, NULL, TRUE) ;
```

You can obtain the coordinates of the invalid rectangle by calling *GetUpdateRect*, and you can validate a rectangle of the client area using the *ValidateRect* function. When you receive a WM_PAINT message, the coordinates of the invalid rectangle are available from the PAINTSTRUCT structure that is filled in by the *BeginPaint* function. This invalid rectangle also defines a "clipping region." You cannot paint outside the clipping region.

Windows has two functions similar to *InvalidateRect* and *ValidateRect* that work with regions rather than rectangles:

```
InvalidateRgn (hwnd, hRgn, bErase) ;
```

and

```
ValidateRgn (hwnd, hRgn) ;
```

When you receive a WM_PAINT message as a result of an invalid region, the clipping region will not necessarily be rectangular in shape.

You can create a clipping region of your own by selecting a region into the device context using either

```
SelectObject (hdc, hRgn) ;
```

or

```
SelectClipRgn (hdc, hRgn) ;
```

A clipping region is assumed to be measured in device coordinates.

GDI makes a copy of the clipping region, so you can delete the region object after you select it in the device context. Windows also includes several functions to manipulate this clipping region, such as *ExcludeClipRect* to exclude a rectangle from the clipping region, *IntersectClipRect* to create a new clipping region that is the intersection of the previous clipping region and a rectangle, and *OffsetClipRgn* to move a clipping region to another part of the client area.

The CLOVER Program

The CLOVER program forms a region out of four ellipses, selects this region into the device context, and then draws a series of lines emanating from the center of the window's client area. The lines appear only in the area defined by the region. The resulting display is shown in Figure 5-28 on page 208.

To draw this graphic by conventional methods, you would have to calculate the end point of each line based on formulas involving the circumference of an ellipse. By using a complex clipping region, you can draw the lines and let Windows determine the end points. The CLOVER program is shown in Figure 5-27.

CLOVER.C

```
/*-----------------------------------------------------
   CLOVER.C -- Clover Drawing Program Using Regions
               (c) Charles Petzold, 1998
   -----------------------------------------------------*/

#include <windows.h>
#include <math.h>

#define TWO_PI (2.0 * 3.14159)

LRESULT CALLBACK WndProc (HWND, UINT, WPARAM, LPARAM) ;

int WINAPI WinMain (HINSTANCE hInstance, HINSTANCE hPrevInstance,
                    PSTR szCmdLine, int iCmdShow)
{
     static TCHAR szAppName[] = TEXT ("Clover") ;
     HWND         hwnd ;
     MSG          msg ;
     WNDCLASS     wndclass ;

     wndclass.style         = CS_HREDRAW | CS_VREDRAW ;
     wndclass.lpfnWndProc   = WndProc ;
     wndclass.cbClsExtra    = 0 ;
     wndclass.cbWndExtra    = 0 ;
     wndclass.hInstance     = hInstance ;
     wndclass.hIcon         = LoadIcon (NULL, IDI_APPLICATION) ;
     wndclass.hCursor       = LoadCursor (NULL, IDC_ARROW) ;
```

Figure 5-27. *The CLOVER program.*   *(continued)*

Figure 5-27. *continued*

```
    wndclass.hbrBackground = (HBRUSH) GetStockObject (WHITE_BRUSH) ;
    wndclass.lpszMenuName  = NULL ;
    wndclass.lpszClassName = szAppName ;

    if (!RegisterClass (&wndclass))
    {
         MessageBox (NULL, TEXT ("This program requires Windows NT!"),
                     szAppName, MB_ICONERROR) ;
         return 0 ;
    }

    hwnd = CreateWindow (szAppName, TEXT ("Draw a Clover"),
                         WS_OVERLAPPEDWINDOW,
                         CW_USEDEFAULT, CW_USEDEFAULT,
                         CW_USEDEFAULT, CW_USEDEFAULT,
                         NULL, NULL, hInstance, NULL) ;

    ShowWindow (hwnd, iCmdShow) ;
    UpdateWindow (hwnd) ;

    while (GetMessage (&msg, NULL, 0, 0))
    {
         TranslateMessage (&msg) ;
         DispatchMessage (&msg) ;
    }
    return msg.wParam ;
}

LRESULT CALLBACK WndProc (HWND hwnd, UINT iMsg, WPARAM wParam, LPARAM lParam)
{
    static HRGN hRgnClip ;
    static int  cxClient, cyClient ;
    double      fAngle, fRadius ;
    HCURSOR     hCursor ;
    HDC         hdc ;
    HRGN        hRgnTemp[6] ;
    int         i ;
    PAINTSTRUCT ps ;

    switch (iMsg)
    {
    case WM_SIZE:
         cxClient = LOWORD (lParam) ;
         cyClient = HIWORD (lParam) ;
```

```
        hCursor = SetCursor (LoadCursor (NULL, IDC_WAIT)) ;
        ShowCursor (TRUE) ;

        if (hRgnClip)
            DeleteObject (hRgnClip) ;

        hRgnTemp[0] = CreateEllipticRgn (0, cyClient / 3,
                                    cxClient / 2, 2 * cyClient / 3) ;
        hRgnTemp[1] = CreateEllipticRgn (cxClient / 2, cyClient / 3,
                                    cxClient, 2 * cyClient / 3) ;
        hRgnTemp[2] = CreateEllipticRgn (cxClient / 3, 0,
                                    2 * cxClient / 3, cyClient / 2) ;
        hRgnTemp[3] = CreateEllipticRgn (cxClient / 3, cyClient / 2,
                                    2 * cxClient / 3, cyClient) ;
        hRgnTemp[4] = CreateRectRgn (0, 0, 1, 1) ;
        hRgnTemp[5] = CreateRectRgn (0, 0, 1, 1) ;
        hRgnClip    = CreateRectRgn (0, 0, 1, 1) ;

        CombineRgn (hRgnTemp[4], hRgnTemp[0], hRgnTemp[1], RGN_OR) ;
        CombineRgn (hRgnTemp[5], hRgnTemp[2], hRgnTemp[3], RGN_OR) ;
        CombineRgn (hRgnClip,    hRgnTemp[4], hRgnTemp[5], RGN_XOR) ;

        for (i = 0 ; i < 6 ; i++)
            DeleteObject (hRgnTemp[i]) ;

        SetCursor (hCursor) ;
        ShowCursor (FALSE) ;
        return 0 ;

case WM_PAINT:
        hdc = BeginPaint (hwnd, &ps) ;

        SetViewportOrgEx (hdc, cxClient / 2, cyClient / 2, NULL) ;
        SelectClipRgn (hdc, hRgnClip) ;

        fRadius = _hypot (cxClient / 2.0, cyClient / 2.0) ;

        for (fAngle = 0.0 ; fAngle < TWO_PI ; fAngle += TWO_PI / 360)
        {
            MoveToEx (hdc, 0, 0, NULL) ;
            LineTo (hdc, (int) ( fRadius * cos (fAngle) + 0.5),
                        (int) (-fRadius * sin (fAngle) + 0.5)) ;
        }
        EndPaint (hwnd, &ps) ;
        return 0 ;
```

(continued)

Figure 5-27. *continued*

```
    case WM_DESTROY:
        DeleteObject (hRgnClip) ;
        PostQuitMessage (0) ;
        return 0 ;
    }
    return DefWindowProc (hwnd, iMsg, wParam, lParam) ;
}
```

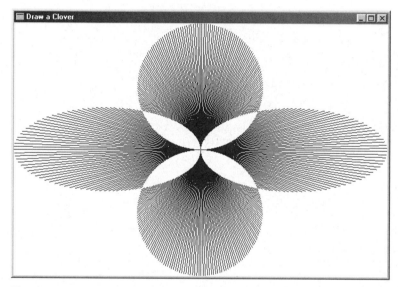

Figure 5-28. *The CLOVER display, drawn using a complex clipping region.*

Because regions always use device coordinates, the CLOVER program has to re-create the region every time it receives a WM_SIZE message. Years ago, the machines that ran Windows took several seconds to redraw this figure. Today's fast machines draw it nearly instantaneously.

CLOVER begins by creating four elliptical regions that are stored as the first four elements of the *hRgnTemp* array. Then the program creates three "dummy" regions:

```
hRgnTemp [4] = CreateRectRgn (0, 0, 1, 1) ;
hRgnTemp [5] = CreateRectRgn (0, 0, 1, 1) ;
hRgnClip     = CreateRectRgn (0, 0, 1, 1) ;
```

The two elliptical regions at the left and right of the client area are combined:

```
CombineRgn (hRgnTemp [4], hRgnTemp [0], hRgnTemp [1], RGN_OR) ;
```

Similarly, the two elliptical regions at the top and bottom of the client area are combined:

```
CombineRgn (hRgnTemp [5], hRgnTemp [2], hRgnTemp [3], RGN_OR) ;
```

Finally these two combined regions are in turn combined into *hRgnClip*:

```
CombineRgn (hRgnClip, hRgnTemp [4], hRgnTemp [5], RGN_XOR) ;
```

The RGN_XOR identifier is used to exclude overlapping areas from the resultant region. Finally the six temporary regions are deleted:

```
for (i = 0 ; i < 6 ; i++)
    DeleteObject (hRgnTemp [i]) ;
```

The WM_PAINT processing is simple, considering the results. The viewport origin is set to the center of the client area (to make the line drawing easier), and the region created during the WM_SIZE message is selected as the device context's clipping region:

```
SetViewportOrg (hdc, xClient / 2, yClient / 2) ;
SelectClipRgn (hdc, hRgnClip) ;
```

Now all that's left is drawing the lines—360 of them, spaced 1 degree apart. The length of each line is the variable *fRadius*, which is the distance from the center to the corner of the client area:

```
fRadius = hypot (xClient / 2.0, yClient / 2.0) ;

for (fAngle = 0.0 ; fAngle < TWO_PI ; fAngle += TWO_PI / 360)
{
    MoveToEx (hdc, 0, 0, NULL) ;
    LineTo (hdc, (int) ( fRadius * cos (fAngle) + 0.5),
                 (int) (-fRadius * sin (fAngle) + 0.5)) ;
}
```

During processing of WM_DESTROY, the region is deleted:

```
DeleteObject (hRgnClip) ;
```

This is not the end of graphics programming in this book. Chapter 13 looks at printing, Chapters 14 and 15 at bitmaps, Chapter 17 at text and fonts, and Chapter 18 at metafiles.

Chapter 6

The Keyboard

The keyboard and the mouse are the two standard sources of user input in Microsoft Windows 98, often complementing each other with some overlap. The mouse is, of course, much more utilized in today's applications than those of a decade ago. We are even accustomed to using the mouse almost exclusively in some applications, such as games, drawing programs, music programs, and Web browsers. Yet while we could probably make do without the mouse, removing the keyboard from the average PC would be disastrous.

Compared with the other components of the personal computer, the keyboard has a positively ancient ancestry beginning with the first Remington typewriter in 1874. Early computer programmers used keyboards to punch holes in Hollerith cards and later used keyboards on dumb terminals to communicate directly with large mainframe computers. The PC has been expanded somewhat to include function keys, cursor positioning keys, and (usually) a separate numeric keypad, but the principles of typing are basically the same.

KEYBOARD BASICS

You've probably already surmised how a Windows program gets keyboard input: Keyboard input is delivered to your program's window procedures in the form of messages. Indeed, when first learning about messages, the keyboard is an obvious example of the type of information that messages might deliver to applications.

There are eight different messages that Windows uses to indicate various keyboard events. This may seem like a lot, but (as we'll see) your program can safely ignore at least half of them. Also, in most cases, the keyboard information encoded in these messages is probably more than your program needs. Part of the job of handling the keyboard is knowing which messages are important and which are not.

Ignoring the Keyboard

Although the keyboard is often the primary source of user input in Windows programs, your program does not need to act on every keyboard message it receives. Windows handles many keyboard functions itself.

For instance, you can usually ignore keystrokes that pertain to system functions. These keystrokes generally involve the Alt key. You do not need to monitor these actual keystrokes because Windows notifies a program of the *effect* of the keystrokes. (A program can monitor the keystrokes itself if it wants to, however.) The keystrokes that invoke a program's menu come through a window's window procedure, but they are usually passed on to *DefWindowProc* for default processing. Eventually, the window procedure gets a message indicating that a menu item has been selected. This is generally all the window procedure needs to know. (Menus are covered in Chapter 10.)

Many Windows programs use keyboard accelerators to invoke common menu items. The accelerators usually involve the Ctrl key in combination with a function key or a letter key (for example, Ctrl-S to save a file). These keyboard accelerators are defined in a program's resource script along with a program's menu, as we'll see in Chapter 10. Windows translates these keyboard accelerators into menu command messages. You don't have to do the translation yourself.

Dialog boxes also have a keyboard interface, but programs usually do not need to monitor the keyboard when a dialog box is active. The keyboard interface is handled by Windows, and Windows sends messages to your program about the effects of the keystrokes. Dialog boxes can contain edit controls for text input. These are generally small boxes in which the user types a character string. Windows handles all the edit control logic and gives your program the final contents of the edit control when the user is done. See Chapter 11 for more on dialog boxes.

Edit controls don't have to be limited to a single line, and they don't have to be located only in dialog boxes. A multiline edit control in your program's main window can function as a rudimentary text editor. (This is shown in the POPPAD programs in Chapters 9, 10, 11, and 13.) And Windows even has a fancier rich-text edit control that lets you edit and display formatted text. (See */Platform SDK/User Interface Services/Controls/Rich Edit Controls*.)

You'll also find that when structuring your Windows programs, you can use child window controls to process keyboard and mouse input to deliver a higher level of information back to the parent window. Accumulate enough of these controls and you'll never have to be bothered with processing keyboard messages at all.

Who's Got the Focus?

Like all personal computer hardware, the keyboard must be shared by all applications running under Windows. Some applications might have more than one window, and the keyboard must be shared by all the windows within the application.

As you'll recall, the MSG structure that a program uses to retrieve messages from the message queue includes a *hwnd* field. This field indicates the handle of the window that is to receive the message. The *DispatchMessage* function in the message loop sends that message to the window procedure associated with the window for which the message is intended. When a key on the keyboard is pressed, only one window procedure receives a keyboard message, and this message includes a handle to the window that is to receive the message.

The window that receives a particular keyboard event is the window that has the input focus. The concept of input focus is closely related to the concept of the active window. The window with the input focus is either the active window or a descendant window of the active window—that is, a child of the active window, or a child of a child of the active window, and so forth.

The active window is usually easy to identify. It is always a top-level window—that is, its parent window handle is NULL. If the active window has a title bar, Windows highlights the title bar. If the active window has a dialog frame (a form most commonly seen in dialog boxes) instead of a title bar, Windows highlights the frame. If the active window is currently minimized, Windows highlights its entry in the task bar by showing it as a depressed button.

If the active window has child windows, the window with the input focus can be either the active window or one of its descendants. The most common child windows are controls such as push buttons, radio buttons, check boxes, scroll bars, edit boxes, and list boxes that appear in dialog boxes. Child windows are never themselves active windows. A child window can have the input focus only if it is a descendent of the active window. Child window controls indicate that they have the input focus generally by displaying a flashing caret or a dotted line.

Sometimes no window has the input focus. This is the case if all your programs have been minimized. Windows continues to send keyboard messages to the active window, but these messages are in a different form from keyboard messages sent to active windows that are not minimized.

A window procedure can determine when its window has the input focus by trapping WM_SETFOCUS and WM_KILLFOCUS messages. WM_SETFOCUS indicates that the window is receiving the input focus, and WM_KILLFOCUS signals that the window is losing the input focus. I'll have more to say about these messages later in this chapter.

Queues and Synchronization

As the user presses and releases keys on the keyboard, Windows and the keyboard device driver translate the hardware scan codes into formatted messages. However, these messages are not placed in an application's message queue right away. Instead, Windows stores these messages in something called the *system message queue*. The system message queue is a single message queue maintained by Windows specifically for the preliminary storage of user input from the keyboard and the mouse. Windows will take the next message from the system message queue and place it in an application's message queue only when a Windows application has finished processing a previous user input message.

The reasons for this two-step process—storing messages first in the system message queue and then passing them to the application message queue—involves synchronization. As we just learned, the window that is supposed to receive keyboard input is the window with the input focus. A user can be typing faster than an application can handle the keystrokes, and a particular keystroke might have the effect of switching focus from one window to another. Subsequent keystrokes should then go to another window. But they won't if the subsequent keystrokes have already been addressed with a destination window and placed in an application message queue.

Keystrokes and Characters

The messages that an application receives from Windows about keyboard events distinguish between keystrokes and characters. This is in accordance with the two ways you can view the keyboard.

First, you can think of the keyboard as a collection of keys. The keyboard has only one key labeled "A." Pressing that key is a keystroke. Releasing that key is also considered a keystroke. But the keyboard is also an input device that generates displayable characters or control characters. The "A" key can generate several different characters depending on the status of the Ctrl, Shift, and Caps Lock keys. Normally, the character is a lowercase "a." If the Shift key is down or Caps Lock is toggled on, the character is an uppercase "A." If Ctrl is down, the character is a Ctrl-A (which has meaning in ASCII but in Windows is probably a keyboard accelerator if anything). On some keyboards, the "A" keystroke might be preceded by a dead-character key or by Shift, Ctrl, or Alt in various combinations. The combinations could generate a lowercase or uppercase letter with an accent mark, such as à, á, â, ã, Ä, or Å.

For keystroke combinations that result in displayable characters, Windows sends a program both keystroke messages and character messages. Some keys do not generate characters. These include the shift keys, the function keys, the cursor movement keys, and special keys such as Insert and Delete. For these keys, Windows generates only keystroke messages.

KEYSTROKE MESSAGES

When you press a key, Windows places either a WM_KEYDOWN or WM_SYSKEYDOWN message in the message queue of the window with the input focus. When you release a key, Windows places either a WM_KEYUP or WM_SYSKEYUP message in the message queue.

	Key Pressed	*Key Released*
Nonsystem Keystroke:	WM_KEYDOWN	WM_KEYUP
System Keystroke:	WM_SYSKEYDOWN	WM_SYSKEYUP

Usually the up and down messages occur in pairs. However, if you hold down a key so that the typematic (autorepeat) action takes over, Windows sends the window procedure a series of WM_KEYDOWN (or WM_SYSKEYDOWN) messages and a single WM_KEYUP (or WM_SYSKEYUP) message when the key is finally released. Like all queued messages, keystroke messages are time-stamped. You can retrieve the relative time a key was pressed or released by calling *GetMessageTime*.

System and Nonsystem Keystrokes

The "SYS" in WM_SYSKEYDOWN and WM_SYSKEYUP stands for "system" and refers to keystrokes that are more important to Windows than to Windows applications. The WM_SYSKEYDOWN and WM_SYSKEYUP messages are usually generated for keys typed in combination with the Alt key. These keystrokes invoke options on the program's menu or system menu, or they are used for system functions such as switching the active window (Alt-Tab or Alt-Esc) or for system menu accelerators (Alt in combination with a function key such as Alt-F4 to close an application). Programs usually ignore the WM_SYSKEYUP and WM_SYSKEYDOWN messages and pass them to *DefWindowProc*. Because Windows takes care of all the Alt-key logic, you really have no need to trap these messages. Your window procedure will eventually receive other messages concerning the result of these keystrokes (such as a menu selection). If you want to include code in your window procedure to trap the system keystroke messages (as we will do in the KEYVIEW1 and KEYVIEW2 programs shown later in this chapter), pass the messages to *DefWindowProc* after you process them so that Windows can still use them for their intended purposes.

But think about this for a moment. Almost everything that affects your program's window passes through your window procedure first. Windows does something with the message only if you pass the message to *DefWindowProc*. For instance, if you add the lines

```
case WM_SYSKEYDOWN:
case WM_SYSKEYUP:
case WM_SYSCHAR:
    return 0 ;
```

to a window procedure, you effectively disable all Alt-key operations when your program's main window has the input focus. (I'll discuss the WM_SYSCHAR message later in this chapter.) This includes Alt-Tab, Alt-Esc, and menu operations. Although I doubt you would want to do this, I trust you sense the power inherent in the window procedure.

The WM_KEYDOWN and WM_KEYUP messages are usually generated for keys that are pressed and released without the Alt key. Your program can use or discard these keystroke messages. Windows doesn't care about them.

For all four keystroke messages, *wParam* is a virtual key code that identifies the key being pressed or released and *lParam* contains other data pertaining to the keystroke.

Virtual Key Codes

The virtual key code is stored in the *wParam* parameter of the WM_KEYDOWN, WM_KEYUP, WM_SYSKEYDOWN, and WM_SYSKEYUP messages. This code identifies the key being pressed or released.

Ah, that ubiquitous word "virtual." Don't you love it? It's supposed to refer to something that exists in the mind rather than in the real world, but only veteran programmers of DOS assembly language applications might figure out why the key codes so essential to Windows keyboard processing are considered virtual rather than real.

To old-time programmers, the *real* keyboard codes are generated by the hardware of the physical keyboard. These are referred to in the Windows documentation as *scan codes*. On IBM compatibles, a scan code of 16 is the Q key, 17 is the W key, 18 is E, 19 is R, 20 is T, 21 is Y, and so on. You get the idea—the scan codes are based on the physical layout of the keyboard. The developers of Windows considered these scan codes too device-dependent. They thus attempted to treat the keyboard in a device-independent manner by defining the so-called virtual key codes. Some of these virtual key codes cannot be generated on IBM compatibles but may be found on other manufacturer's keyboards, or perhaps on keyboards of the future.

The virtual key codes you use most often have names beginning with VK_ defined in the WINUSER.H header file. The tables below show these names along with the numeric values (in both decimal and hexadecimal) and the IBM-compatible keyboard key that corresponds to the virtual key. The tables also indicate whether these keys are required for Windows to run properly. The tables show the virtual key codes in numeric order.

Three of the first four virtual key codes refer to mouse buttons:

Decimal	Hex	WINUSER.H Identifier	Required?	IBM-Compatible Keyboard
1	01	VK_LBUTTON		Mouse Left Button
2	02	VK_RBUTTON		Mouse Right Button
3	03	VK_CANCEL	✓	Ctrl-Break
4	04	VK_MBUTTON		Mouse Middle Button

You will never get these mouse button codes in the keyboard messages. They are found in mouse messages, as we'll see in the next chapter. The VK_CANCEL code is the only virtual key code that involves pressing two keys at once (Ctrl-Break). Windows applications generally do not use this key.

Several of the following keys—Backspace, Tab, Enter, Escape, and Spacebar—are commonly used by Windows programs. However, Windows programs generally use character messages (rather than keystroke messages) to process these keys.

Decimal	Hex	WINUSER.H Identifier	Required?	IBM-Compatible Keyboard
8	08	VK_BACK	✓	Backspace
9	09	VK_TAB	✓	Tab
12	0C	VK_CLEAR		Numeric keyboard 5 with Num Lock OFF
13	0D	VK_RETURN	✓	Enter (either one)
16	10	VK_SHIFT	✓	Shift (either one)
17	11	VK_CONTROL	✓	Ctrl (either one)
18	12	VK_MENU	✓	Alt (either one)
19	13	VK_PAUSE		Pause
20	14	VK_CAPITAL	✓	Caps Lock
27	1B	VK_ESCAPE	✓	Esc
32	20	VK_SPACE	✓	Spacebar

Also, Windows programs usually do not need to monitor the status of the Shift, Ctrl, or Alt keys.

The first eight codes listed in the following table are perhaps the most commonly used virtual key codes along with VK_INSERT and VK_DELETE:

Decimal	Hex	WINUSER.H Identifier	Required?	IBM-Compatible Keyboard
33	21	VK_PRIOR	✓	Page Up
34	22	VK_NEXT	✓	Page Down
35	23	VK_END	✓	End
36	24	VK_HOME	✓	Home
37	25	VK_LEFT	✓	Left Arrow
38	26	VK_UP	✓	Up Arrow
39	27	VK_RIGHT	✓	Right Arrow
40	28	VK_DOWN	✓	Down Arrow

(continued)

continued

Decimal	Hex	WINUSER.H Identifier	Required?	IBM-Compatible Keyboard
41	29	VK_SELECT		
42	2A	VK_PRINT		
43	2B	VK_EXECUTE		
44	2C	VK_SNAPSHOT		Print Screen
45	2D	VK_INSERT	✓	Insert
46	2E	VK_DELETE	✓	Delete
47	2F	VK_HELP		

Notice that many of the names (such as VK_PRIOR and VK_NEXT) are unfortunately quite different from the labels on the keys and also not consistent with the identifiers used in scroll bars. The Print Screen key is largely ignored by Windows applications. Windows itself responds to the key by storing a bitmap copy of the video display into the clipboard. VK_SELECT, VK_PRINT, VK_EXECUTE, and VK_HELP might be found on a hypothetical keyboard that few of us have ever seen.

Windows also includes virtual key codes for the letter keys and number keys on the main keyboard. (The number pad is handled separately.)

Decimal	Hex	WINUSER.H Identifier	Required?	IBM-Compatible Keyboard
48–57	30–39	None	✓	0 through 9 on main keyboard
65–90	41–5A	None	✓	A through Z

Notice that the virtual key codes are the ASCII codes for the numbers and letters. Windows programs almost never use these virtual key codes; instead, the programs rely on character messages for ASCII characters.

The following keys are generated from the Microsoft Natural Keyboard and compatibles:

Decimal	Hex	WINUSER.H Identifier	Required?	Microsoft Natural Keyboard
91	5B	VK_LWIN		Left Windows key
92	5C	VK_RWIN		Right Windows key
93	5D	VK_APPS		Applications key

The VK_LWIN and VK_RWIN keys are handled by Windows to open the Start menu or (in older versions) to launch the Task Manager. Together, they can log on or off Windows (in Microsoft Windows NT only), or log on or off a network (in Windows for Workgroups). Applications can process the application key by displaying help information or shortcuts.

The following codes are for the keys on the numeric keypad (if present):

Decimal	*Hex*	*WINUSER.H Identifier*	*Required?*	*IBM-Compatible Keyboard*
96–105	60–69	VK_NUMPAD0 through VK_NUMPAD9		Numeric keypad 0 through 9 with Num Lock ON
106	6A	VK_MULTIPLY		Numeric keypad *
107	6B	VK_ADD		Numeric keypad +
108	6C	VK_SEPARATOR		
109	6D	VK_SUBTRACT		Numeric keypad −
110	6E	VK_DECIMAL		Numeric keypad .
111	6F	VK_DIVIDE		Numeric keypad /

Finally, although most keyboards have 12 function keys, Windows requires only 10 but has numeric identifiers for 24. Again, programs generally use the function keys as keyboard accelerators so they usually don't process the keystrokes in this table:

Decimal	*Hex*	*WINUSER.H Identifier*	*Required?*	*IBM-Compatible Keyboard*
112–121	70–79	VK_F1 through VK_F10	✓	Function keys F1 through F10
122–135	7A–87	VK_F11 through VK_F24		Function keys F11 through F24
144	90	VK_NUMLOCK		Num Lock
145	91	VK_SCROLL		Scroll Lock

Some other virtual key codes are defined, but they are reserved for keys specific to nonstandard keyboards or for keys most commonly found on mainframe terminals. Check */Platform SDK/User Interface Services/User Input/Virtual-Key Codes* for a complete list.

The *lParam* Information

In the four keystroke messages (WM_KEYDOWN, WM_KEYUP, WM_SYSKEYDOWN, and WM_SYSKEYUP), the *wParam* message parameter contains the virtual key code as described above, and the *lParam* message parameter contains other information useful in understanding the keystroke. The 32 bits of *lParam* are divided into six fields as shown in Figure 6-1.

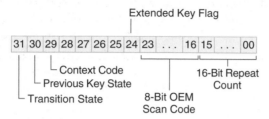

Figure 6-1. *The six keystroke-message fields of the* lParam *variable.*

Repeat Count

The repeat count is the number of keystrokes represented by the message. In most cases, this will be set to 1. However, if a key is held down and your window procedure is not fast enough to process key-down messages at the typematic rate (which you can set in the Keyboard applet in the Control Panel), Windows combines several WM_KEYDOWN or WM_SYSKEYDOWN messages into a single message and increases the Repeat Count field accordingly. The Repeat Count is always 1 for a WM_KEYUP or WM_SYSKEYUP message.

Because a Repeat Count greater than 1 indicates that typematic keystrokes are occurring faster than your program can process them, you may want to ignore the Repeat Count when processing the keyboard messages. Almost everyone has had the experience of "overscrolling" a word-processing document or spreadsheet because extra keystrokes have accumulated. If your program ignores the Repeat Count in cases where your program spends some time processing each keystroke, you can eliminate this problem. However, in other cases you will want to use the Repeat Count. You may want to try using the programs both ways and see which feels the most natural.

OEM Scan Code

The OEM Scan Code is the code generated by the hardware of the keyboard. This is familiar to middle-aged assembly language programmers as the value obtained from the ROM BIOS services of PC compatibles. (OEM refers to the Original Equipment Manufacturer of the PC and in this context is synonymous with "IBM Standard.") We don't need this stuff anymore. Windows programs can almost always ignore the OEM Scan Code except when dependent on the physical layout of the keyboard, such as the KBMIDI program in Chapter 22.

Extended Key Flag

The Extended Key Flag is 1 if the keystroke results from one of the additional keys on the IBM enhanced keyboard. (The enhanced keyboard has 101 or 102 keys. Function keys are across the top. Cursor movement keys are separate from the numeric keypad, but the numeric keypad also duplicates the cursor movement keys.) This flag is set to 1 for the Alt and Ctrl keys at the right of the keyboard, the cursor movement keys (including Insert and Delete) that are not part of the numeric keypad, the slash (/) and Enter keys on the numeric keypad, and the Num Lock key. Windows programs generally ignore the Extended Key Flag.

Context Code

The Context Code is 1 if the Alt key is depressed during the keystroke. This bit will always be 1 for the WM_SYSKEYUP and WM_SYSKEYDOWN messages and 0 for the WM_KEYUP and WM_KEYDOWN messages, with two exceptions:

- If the active window is minimized, it does not have the input focus. All keystrokes generate WM_SYSKEYUP and WM_SYSKEYDOWN messages. If the Alt key is not pressed, the Context Code field is set to 0. Windows uses WM_SYSKEYUP and WM_SYSKEYDOWN messages so that a minimized active window doesn't process these keystrokes.

- On some foreign-language keyboards, certain characters are generated by combining Shift, Ctrl, or Alt with another key. In these cases, the Context Code is set to 1 but the messages are not system keystroke messages.

Previous Key State

The Previous Key State is 0 if the key was previously up and 1 if the key was previously down. It is always set to 1 for a WM_KEYUP or WM_SYSKEYUP message, but it can be 0 or 1 for a WM_KEYDOWN or WM_SYSKEYDOWN message. A 1 indicates second and subsequent messages that are the result of typematic repeats.

Transition State

The Transition State is 0 if the key is being pressed and 1 if the key is being released. The field is set to 0 for a WM_KEYDOWN or WM_SYSKEYDOWN message and to 1 for a WM_KEYUP or WM_SYSKEYUP message.

Shift States

When you process a keystroke message, you may need to know whether any of the shift keys (Shift, Ctrl, and Alt) or toggle keys (Caps Lock, Num Lock, and Scroll Lock) are pressed. You can obtain this information by calling the *GetKeyState* function. For instance:

```
iState = GetKeyState (VK_SHIFT) ;
```

The *iState* variable will be negative (that is, the high bit is set) if the Shift key is down. The value returned from

```
iState = GetKeyState (VK_CAPITAL) ;
```

has the low bit set if the Caps Lock key is toggled on. This bit will agree with the little light on the keyboard.

Generally, you'll use *GetKeyState* with the virtual key codes VK_SHIFT, VK_CONTROL, and VK_MENU (which you'll recall indicates the Alt key). You can also use the following identifiers with *GetKeyState* to determine if the left or right Shift, Ctrl, or Alt keys are pressed: VK_LSHIFT, VK_RSHIFT, VK_LCONTROL, VK_RCONTROL, VK_LMENU, VK_RMENU. These identifiers are used *only* with *GetKeyState* and *GetAsyncKeyState* (described below).

You can also obtain the state of the mouse buttons using the virtual key codes VK_LBUTTON, VK_RBUTTON, and VK_MBUTTON. However, most Windows programs that need to monitor a combination of mouse buttons and keystrokes usually do it the other way around—by checking keystrokes when they receive a mouse message. In fact, shift-state information is conveniently included in the mouse messages, as we'll see in the next chapter.

Be careful with *GetKeyState*. It is not a real-time keyboard status check. Rather, it reflects the keyboard status up to and including the current message being processed. For the most part, this is exactly what you want. If you need to determine if the user typed Shift-Tab, you can call *GetKeyState* with the VK_SHIFT parameter while processing the WM_KEYDOWN message for the Tab key. If the return value of *GetKeyState* is negative, you know that the Shift key was pressed *before* the Tab key. And it doesn't matter if the Shift key has already been released by the time you get around to processing the Tab key. You know that the Shift key was down when Tab was pressed.

GetKeyState does not let you retrieve keyboard information independent of normal keyboard messages. For instance, you may feel a need to hold up processing in your window procedure until the user presses the F1 function key:

```
while (GetKeyState (VK_F1) >= 0) ;    // WRONG !!!
```

Don't do it! This is guaranteed to hang your program (unless, of course, the WM_KEYDOWN message for F1 was retrieved from the message queue before you executed the statement). If you really need to know the current real-time state of a key, you can use *GetAsyncKeyState*.

Using Keystroke Messages

A Windows program gets information about each and every keystroke that occurs while the program is running. This is certainly helpful. However, most Windows programs ignore all but a few keystroke messages. The WM_SYSKEYDOWN and WM_SYSKEYUP messages are for Windows system functions, and you don't need to look at them. If you process WM_KEYDOWN messages, you can usually also ignore WM_KEYUP messages.

Windows programs generally use WM_KEYDOWN messages for keystrokes that do not generate characters. Although you may think that it's possible to use keystroke messages in combination with shift-state information to translate keystroke messages into characters, don't do it. You'll have problems with non-English keyboards. For example, if you get a WM_KEYDOWN message with *wParam* equal to 0x33, you know the user pressed the 3 key. So far, so good. If you use *GetKeyState* and find out that the Shift key is down, you might assume that the user is typing a pound sign (#). Not necessarily. A British user is typing another type of pound sign, the one that looks like this: £.

The WM_KEYDOWN messages are most useful for the cursor movement keys, the function keys, Insert, and Delete. However, Insert, Delete, and the function keys often appear as menu accelerators. Because Windows translates menu accelerators into menu command messages, you don't have to process the keystrokes themselves.

It was common for pre-Windows applications for MS-DOS to use the function keys extensively in combination with the Shift, Ctrl, and Alt keys. You can do something similar in your Windows programs (indeed, Microsoft Word uses the function keys extensively as command short cuts), but it's not really recommended. If you want to use the function keys, they should duplicate menu commands. One objective in Windows is to provide a user interface that doesn't require memorization or consultation of complex command charts.

So, it comes down to this: Most of the time, you will process WM_KEYDOWN messages only for cursor movement keys, and sometimes for Insert and Delete. When you use these keys, you can check the Shift-key and Ctrl-key states through *GetKeyState*. Windows programs often use the Shift key in combination with the cursor keys to extend a selection in (for instance) a word-processing document. The Ctrl key is often used to alter the meaning of the cursor key. For example, Ctrl in combination with the Right Arrow key might mean to move the cursor one word to the right.

One of the best ways to determine how to use the keyboard in your application is to examine how the keyboard is used in existing popular Windows programs. If you don't like those definitions, you arc frcc to do something different. But keep in mind that doing so might be detrimental to a user's ability to learn your program quickly.

Enhancing SYSMETS for the Keyboard

The three versions of the SYSMETS program in Chapter 4 were written without any knowledge of the keyboard. We were able to scroll the text only by using the mouse on the scroll bars. Now that we know how to process keystroke messages, let's add a keyboard interface to the program. This is obviously a job for cursor movement keys. We'll use most of these keys (Home, End, Page Up, Page Down, Up Arrow, and Down Arrow) for vertical scrolling. The Left Arrow and Right Arrow keys can take care of the less important horizontal scrolling.

One obvious way to create a keyboard interface is to add some WM_KEYDOWN logic to the window procedure that parallels and essentially duplicates all the WM_VSCROLL and WM_HSCROLL logic. However, this is unwise, because if we ever wanted to change the scroll bar logic we'd have to make the same changes in WM_KEYDOWN.

Wouldn't it be better to simply translate each of these WM_KEYDOWN messages into an equivalent WM_VSCROLL or WM_HSCROLL message? Then we could perhaps fool *WndProc* into thinking that it's getting a scroll bar message, perhaps by sending a phony message to the window procedure.

Windows lets you do this. The function is named *SendMessage*, and it takes the same parameters as those passed to the window procedure:

```
SendMessage (hwnd, message, wParam, lParam) ;
```

When you call *SendMessage*, Windows calls the window procedure whose window handle is *hwnd*, passing to it these four function arguments. When the window procedure has completed processing the message, Windows returns control to the next statement following the *SendMessage* call. The window procedure you send the message to could be the same window procedure, another window procedure in the same program, or even a window procedure in another application.

Here's how we might use *SendMessage* for processing WM_KEYDOWN codes in the SYSMETS program:

```
case WM_KEYDOWN:
    switch (wParam)
    {
    case VK_HOME:
        SendMessage (hwnd, WM_VSCROLL, SB_TOP, 0) ;
        break ;

    case VK_END:
        SendMessage (hwnd, WM_VSCROLL, SB_BOTTOM, 0) ;
        break ;

    case VK_PRIOR:
        SendMessage (hwnd, WM_VSCROLL, SB_PAGEUP, 0) ;
        break ;
```

And so forth. You get the general idea. Our goal was to add a keyboard interface to the scroll bars, and that's exactly what we've done. We've made the cursor movement keys duplicate scroll bar logic by actually sending the window procedure a scroll bar message. Now you can see why I included SB_TOP and SB_BOTTOM processing for WM_VSCROLL messages in the SYSMETS3 program. It wasn't used then, but it's used now for processing the Home and End keys. The SYSMETS4 program, shown in Figure 6-2, incorporates these changes. You'll also need the SYSMETS.H file from Chapter 4 to compile this program.

SYSMETS4.C

```
/*----------------------------------------------------------
   SYSMETS4.C -- System Metrics Display Program No. 4
                 (c) Charles Petzold, 1998
   ----------------------------------------------------------*/

#include <windows.h>
#include "sysmets.h"
```

Figure 6-2. *The SYSMETS4 program.*

```
LRESULT CALLBACK WndProc (HWND, UINT, WPARAM, LPARAM) ;

int WINAPI WinMain (HINSTANCE hInstance, HINSTANCE hPrevInstance,
                    PSTR szCmdLine, int iCmdShow)
{
     static TCHAR szAppName[] = TEXT ("SysMets4") ;
     HWND         hwnd ;
     MSG          msg ;
     WNDCLASS     wndclass ;

     wndclass.style         = CS_HREDRAW | CS_VREDRAW ;
     wndclass.lpfnWndProc   = WndProc ;
     wndclass.cbClsExtra    = 0 ;
     wndclass.cbWndExtra    = 0 ;
     wndclass.hInstance     = hInstance ;
     wndclass.hIcon         = LoadIcon (NULL, IDI_APPLICATION) ;
     wndclass.hCursor       = LoadCursor (NULL, IDC_ARROW) ;
     wndclass.hbrBackground = (HBRUSH) GetStockObject (WHITE_BRUSH) ;
     wndclass.lpszMenuName  = NULL ;
     wndclass.lpszClassName = szAppName ;

     if (!RegisterClass (&wndclass))
     {
          MessageBox (NULL, TEXT ("Program requires Windows NT!"),
                      szAppName, MB_ICONERROR) ;
          return 0 ;
     }

     hwnd = CreateWindow (szAppName, TEXT ("Get System Metrics No. 4"),
                          WS_OVERLAPPEDWINDOW | WS_VSCROLL | WS_HSCROLL,
                          CW_USEDEFAULT, CW_USEDEFAULT,
                          CW_USEDEFAULT, CW_USEDEFAULT,
                          NULL, NULL, hInstance, NULL) ;

     ShowWindow (hwnd, iCmdShow) ;
     UpdateWindow (hwnd) ;

     while (GetMessage (&msg, NULL, 0, 0))
     {
          TranslateMessage (&msg) ;
          DispatchMessage (&msg) ;
     }
     return msg.wParam ;
}
```

(continued)

Figure 6-2. *continued*

```
LRESULT CALLBACK WndProc (HWND hwnd, UINT message, WPARAM wParam, LPARAM lParam)
{
     static int   cxChar, cxCaps, cyChar, cxClient, cyClient, iMaxWidth ;
     HDC          hdc ;
     int          i, x, y, iVertPos, iHorzPos, iPaintBeg, iPaintEnd ;
     PAINTSTRUCT  ps ;
     SCROLLINFO   si ;
     TCHAR        szBuffer[10] ;
     TEXTMETRIC   tm ;

     switch (message)
     {
     case WM_CREATE:
          hdc = GetDC (hwnd) ;

          GetTextMetrics (hdc, &tm) ;
          cxChar = tm.tmAveCharWidth ;
          cxCaps = (tm.tmPitchAndFamily & 1 ? 3 : 2) * cxChar / 2 ;
          cyChar = tm.tmHeight + tm.tmExternalLeading ;

          ReleaseDC (hwnd, hdc) ;

               // Save the width of the three columns

          iMaxWidth = 40 * cxChar + 22 * cxCaps ;
          return 0 ;

     case WM_SIZE:
          cxClient = LOWORD (lParam) ;
          cyClient = HIWORD (lParam) ;

               // Set vertical scroll bar range and page size

          si.cbSize = sizeof (si) ;
          si.fMask  = SIF_RANGE | SIF_PAGE ;
          si.nMin   = 0 ;
          si.nMax   = NUMLINES - 1 ;
          si.nPage  = cyClient / cyChar ;
          SetScrollInfo (hwnd, SB_VERT, &si, TRUE) ;

               // Set horizontal scroll bar range and page size

          si.cbSize = sizeof (si) ;
          si.fMask  = SIF_RANGE | SIF_PAGE ;
          si.nMin   = 0 ;
          si.nMax   = 2 + iMaxWidth / cxChar ;
          si.nPage  = cxClient / cxChar ;
```

```
        SetScrollInfo (hwnd, SB_HORZ, &si, TRUE) ;
        return 0 ;

case WM_VSCROLL:
        // Get all the vertical scroll bar information

        si.cbSize = sizeof (si) ;
        si.fMask  = SIF_ALL ;
        GetScrollInfo (hwnd, SB_VERT, &si) ;

        // Save the position for comparison later on

        iVertPos = si.nPos ;

        switch (LOWORD (wParam))
        {
        case SB_TOP:
             si.nPos = si.nMin ;
             break ;

        case SB_BOTTOM:
             si.nPos = si.nMax ;
             break ;

        case SB_LINEUP:
             si.nPos -= 1 ;
             break ;

        case SB_LINEDOWN:
             si.nPos += 1 ;
             break ;

        case SB_PAGEUP:
             si.nPos -= si.nPage ;
             break ;

        case SB_PAGEDOWN:
             si.nPos += si.nPage ;
             break ;

        case SB_THUMBTRACK:
             si.nPos = si.nTrackPos ;
             break ;

        default:
             break ;
        }
```

(continued)

Figure 6-2. *continued*

```
          // Set the position and then retrieve it.  Due to adjustments
          //   by Windows it might not be the same as the value set.

     si.fMask = SIF_POS ;
     SetScrollInfo (hwnd, SB_VERT, &si, TRUE) ;
     GetScrollInfo (hwnd, SB_VERT, &si) ;

          // If the position has changed, scroll the window and update it

     if (si.nPos != iVertPos)
     {
          ScrollWindow (hwnd, 0, cyChar * (iVertPos - si.nPos),
                              NULL, NULL) ;
          UpdateWindow (hwnd) ;
     }
     return 0 ;

case WM_HSCROLL:
          // Get all the vertical scroll bar information

     si.cbSize = sizeof (si) ;
     si.fMask  = SIF_ALL ;

          // Save the position for comparison later on

     GetScrollInfo (hwnd, SB_HORZ, &si) ;
     iHorzPos = si.nPos ;

     switch (LOWORD (wParam))
     {
     case SB_LINELEFT:
          si.nPos -= 1 ;
          break ;

     case SB_LINERIGHT:
          si.nPos += 1 ;
          break ;

     case SB_PAGELEFT:
          si.nPos -= si.nPage ;
          break ;

     case SB_PAGERIGHT:
          si.nPos += si.nPage ;
          break ;
```

```
        case SB_THUMBPOSITION:
             si.nPos = si.nTrackPos ;
             break ;

        default:
             break ;
        }
             // Set the position and then retrieve it.  Due to adjustments
             //   by Windows it might not be the same as the value set.

        si.fMask = SIF_POS ;
        SetScrollInfo (hwnd, SB_HORZ, &si, TRUE) ;
        GetScrollInfo (hwnd, SB_HORZ, &si) ;

             // If the position has changed, scroll the window

        if (si.nPos != iHorzPos)
        {
             ScrollWindow (hwnd, cxChar * (iHorzPos - si.nPos), 0,
                           NULL, NULL) ;
        }
        return 0 ;

case WM_KEYDOWN:
        switch (wParam)
        {
        case VK_HOME:
             SendMessage (hwnd, WM_VSCROLL, SB_TOP, 0) ;
             break ;

        case VK_END:
             SendMessage (hwnd, WM_VSCROLL, SB_BOTTOM, 0) ;
             break ;

        case VK_PRIOR:
             SendMessage (hwnd, WM_VSCROLL, SB_PAGEUP, 0) ;
             break ;

        case VK_NEXT:
             SendMessage (hwnd, WM_VSCROLL, SB_PAGEDOWN, 0) ;
             break ;

        case VK_UP:
             SendMessage (hwnd, WM_VSCROLL, SB_LINEUP, 0) ;
             break ;
```

(continued)

Figure 6-2. *continued*

```
            case VK_DOWN:
                 SendMessage (hwnd, WM_VSCROLL, SB_LINEDOWN, 0) ;
                 break ;

            case VK_LEFT:
                 SendMessage (hwnd, WM_HSCROLL, SB_PAGEUP, 0) ;
                 break ;

            case VK_RIGHT:
                 SendMessage (hwnd, WM_HSCROLL, SB_PAGEDOWN, 0) ;
                 break ;
            }
            return 0 ;

       case WM_PAINT:
            hdc = BeginPaint (hwnd, &ps) ;

                 // Get vertical scroll bar position

            si.cbSize = sizeof (si) ;
            si.fMask  = SIF_POS ;
            GetScrollInfo (hwnd, SB_VERT, &si) ;
            iVertPos = si.nPos ;

                 // Get horizontal scroll bar position

            GetScrollInfo (hwnd, SB_HORZ, &si) ;
            iHorzPos = si.nPos ;

                 // Find painting limits

            iPaintBeg = max (0, iVertPos + ps.rcPaint.top / cyChar) ;
            iPaintEnd = min (NUMLINES - 1,
                             iVertPos + ps.rcPaint.bottom / cyChar) ;

            for (i = iPaintBeg ; i <= iPaintEnd ; i++)
            {
                 x = cxChar * (1 - iHorzPos) ;
                 y = cyChar * (i - iVertPos) ;

                 TextOut (hdc, x, y,
                          sysmetrics[i].szLabel,
                          lstrlen (sysmetrics[i].szLabel)) ;

                 TextOut (hdc, x + 22 * cxCaps, y,
                          sysmetrics[i].szDesc,
                          lstrlen (sysmetrics[i].szDesc)) ;
```

```
            SetTextAlign (hdc, TA_RIGHT | TA_TOP) ;

            TextOut (hdc, x + 22 * cxCaps + 40 * cxChar, y, szBuffer,
                     wsprintf (szBuffer, TEXT ("%5d"),
                         GetSystemMetrics (sysmetrics[i].iIndex))) ;

            SetTextAlign (hdc, TA_LEFT | TA_TOP) ;
      }

      EndPaint (hwnd, &ps) ;
      return 0 ;

 case WM_DESTROY:
      PostQuitMessage (0) ;
      return 0 ;
      }
    return DefWindowProc (hwnd, message, wParam, lParam) ;
}
```

CHARACTER MESSAGES

Earlier in this chapter, I discussed the idea of translating keystroke messages into character messages by taking shift-state information into account. I warned you that shift-state information is not enough: you also need to know about country-dependent keyboard configurations. For this reason, you should not attempt to translate keystroke messages into character codes yourself. Instead, Windows does it for you. You've seen this code before:

```
while (GetMessage (&msg, NULL, 0, 0))
{
    TranslateMessage (&msg) ;
    DispatchMessage (&msg) ;
}
```

This is a typical message loop that appears in *WinMain*. The *GetMessage* function fills in the *msg* structure fields with the next message from the queue. *DispatchMessage* calls the appropriate window procedure with this message.

Between these two functions is *TranslateMessage*, which takes on the responsibility of translating keystroke messages to character messages. If the keystroke message is WM_KEYDOWN or WM_SYSKEYDOWN, and if the keystroke in combination with the shift state produces a character, *TranslateMessage* places a character message in the message queue. This character message will be the next message that *GetMessage* retrieves from the queue after the keystroke message.

The Four Character Messages

There are four character messages:

	Characters	*Dead Characters*
Nonsystem Characters:	WM_CHAR	WM_DEADCHAR
System Characters:	WM_SYSCHAR	WM_SYSDEADCHAR

The WM_CHAR and WM_DEADCHAR messages are derived from WM_KEYDOWN messages. The WM_SYSCHAR and WM_SYSDEADCHAR messages are derived from WM_SYSKEY-DOWN messages. (I'll discuss what a dead character is shortly.)

Here's the good news: In most cases, your Windows program can process the WM_CHAR message while ignoring the other three character messages. The *lParam* parameter that accompanies the four character messages is the same as the *lParam* parameter for the keystroke message that generated the character code message. However, the *wParam* parameter is not a virtual key code. Instead, it is an ANSI or Unicode character code.

These character messages are the first messages we've encountered that deliver text to the window procedure. They're not the only ones. Other messages are accompanied by entire zero-terminated text strings. How does the window procedure know whether this character data is 8-bit ANSI or 16-bit Unicode? It's simple: Any window procedure associated with a window class that you register with *RegisterClassA* (the ANSI version of *RegisterClass*) gets messages that contain ANSI character codes. Messages to window procedures that were registered with *RegisterClassW* (the wide-character version of *RegisterClass*) come with Unicode character codes. If your program registers its window class using *RegisterClass*, that's really *RegisterClassW* if the UNICODE identifier was defined and *RegisterClassA* otherwise.

Unless you're explicitly doing mixed coding of ANSI and Unicode functions and window procedures, the character code delivered with the WM_CHAR message (and the three other character messages) is

```
(TCHAR) wParam
```

The same window procedure might be used with two window classes, one registered with *RegisterClassA* and the other registered with *RegisterClassW*. This means that the window procedure might get some messages with ANSI character codes and some messages with Unicode character codes. If your window procedure needs help to sort things out, it can call

```
fUnicode = IsWindowUnicode (hwnd) ;
```

The *fUnicode* variable will be TRUE if the window procedure for *hwnd* gets Unicode messages, which means the window is based on a window class that was registered with *RegisterClassW*.

Message Ordering

Because the character messages are generated by the *TranslateMessage* function from WM_KEYDOWN and WM_SYSKEYDOWN messages, the character messages are delivered to your window procedure sandwiched between keystroke messages. For instance, if Caps Lock is not toggled on and you press and release the A key, the window procedure receives the following three messages:

Message	Key or Code
WM_KEYDOWN	Virtual key code for 'A' (0x41)
WM_CHAR	Character code for 'a' (0x61)
WM_KEYUP	Virtual key code for 'A' (0x41)

If you type an uppercase A by pressing the Shift key, pressing the A key, releasing the A key, and then releasing the Shift key, the window procedure receives five messages:

Message	Key or Code
WM_KEYDOWN	Virtual key code VK_SHIFT (0x10)
WM_KEYDOWN	Virtual key code for 'A' (0x41)
WM_CHAR	Character code for 'A' (0x41)
WM_KEYUP	Virtual key code for 'A' (0x41)
WM_KEYUP	Virtual key code VK_SHIFT (0x10)

The Shift key by itself does not generate a character message.

If you hold down the A key so that the typematic action generates keystrokes, you'll get a character message for each WM_KEYDOWN message:

Message	Key or Code
WM_KEYDOWN	Virtual key code for 'A' (0x41)
WM_CHAR	Character code for 'a' (0x61)
WM_KEYDOWN	Virtual key code for 'A' (0x41)
WM_CHAR	Character code for 'a' (0x61)
WM_KEYDOWN	Virtual key code for 'A' (0x41)
WM_CHAR	Character code for 'a' (0x61)
WM_KEYDOWN	Virtual key code for 'A' (0x41)
WM_CHAR	Character code for 'a' (0x61)
WM_KEYUP	Virtual key code for 'A' (0x41)

If some of the WM_KEYDOWN messages have a Repeat Count greater than 1, the corresponding WM_CHAR message will have the same Repeat Count.

The Ctrl Key in combination with a letter key generates ASCII control characters from 0x01 (Ctrl-A) through 0x1A (Ctrl-Z). Several of these control codes are also generated by the keys shown in the following table:

Key	Character Code	Duplicated by	ANSI C Escape
Backspace	0x08	Ctrl-H	\b
Tab	0x09	Ctrl-I	\t
Ctrl-Enter	0x0A	Ctrl-J	\n
Enter	0x0D	Ctrl-M	\r
Esc	0x1B	Ctrl-[	

The rightmost column shows the escape code defined in ANSI C to represent the character codes for these keys.

Windows programs sometimes use the Ctrl key in combination with letter keys for menu accelerators (which I'll discuss in Chapter 10). In this case, the letter keys are not translated into character messages.

Control Character Processing

The basic rule for processing keystroke and character messages is this: If you need to read keyboard character input in your window, you process the WM_CHAR message. If you need to read the cursor keys, function keys, Delete, Insert, Shift, Ctrl, and Alt, you process the WM_KEYDOWN message.

But what about the Tab key? Or Enter or Backspace or Escape? Traditionally, these keys generate ASCII control characters, as shown in the preceding table. But in Windows they also generate virtual key codes. Should these keys be processed during WM_CHAR processing or WM_KEYDOWN processing?

After a decade of considering this issue (and looking back over Windows code I've written over the years), I seem to prefer treating the Tab, Enter, Backspace, and Escape keys as control characters rather than as virtual keys. My WM_CHAR processing often looks something like this:

```
case WM_CHAR:
    [other program lines]
    switch (wParam)
    {
    case '\b':            // backspace
        [other program line
        break ;
```

```
case '\t':            // tab
    [other program lines]
    break ;

case '\n':            // linefeed
    [other program lines]
    break ;

case '\r':            // carriage return
    [other program lines]
    break ;

default:              // character codes
    [other program lines]
    break ;
}
return 0 ;
```

Dead-Character Messages

Windows programs can usually ignore WM_DEADCHAR and WM_SYSDEADCHAR messages, but you should definitely know what dead characters are and how they work.

On some non-U.S. English keyboards, certain keys are defined to add a diacritic to a letter. These are called "dead keys" because they don't generate characters by themselves. For instance, when a German keyboard is installed, the key that is in the same position as the +/= key on a U.S. keyboard is a dead key for the grave accent (`) when shifted and the acute accent (´) when unshifted.

When a user presses this dead key, your window procedure receives a WM_DEAD-CHAR message with *wParam* equal to ASCII or Unicode code for the diacritic by itself. When the user then presses a letter key that can be written with this diacritic (for instance, the A key), the window procedure receives a WM_CHAR message where *wParam* is the ANSI code for the letter 'a' with the diacritic.

Thus, your program does not have to process the WM_DEADCHAR message because the WM_CHAR message gives the program all the information it needs. The Windows logic even has built-in error handling: If the dead key is followed by a letter that can't take a diacritic (such as 's'), the window procedure receives two WM_CHAR messages in a row—the first with *wParam* equal to the ASCII code for the diacritic by itself (the same *wParam* value delivered with the WM_DEADCHAR message) and the second with *wParam* equal to the ASCII code for the letter 's'.

Of course, the best way to get a feel for this is to see it in action. You need to load a foreign keyboard that uses dead keys, such as the German keyboard that I described earlier. You do this in the Control Panel by selecting Keyboard and then the Language tab. Then you need an application that shows you the details of every keyboard message a program can receive. That's the KEYVIEW1 program coming up next.

KEYBOARD MESSAGES AND CHARACTER SETS

The remaining sample programs in this chapter have flaws. They will not always run correctly under all versions of Windows. Their flaws are not something I deliberately introduced into the code; indeed, you might never notice them. These problems—I hesitate to call them "bugs"—reveal themselves only when switching among certain different keyboard languages and layouts, and when running the programs under Far Eastern versions of Windows that use multibyte character sets.

However, the programs *will* work much better when compiled for Unicode and run under Windows NT. This is the promise I made in Chapter 2, and it demonstrates why Unicode is so important in simplifying the work involved in internationalization.

The KEYVIEW1 Program

The first step in understanding keyboard internationalization issues is to examine the contents of the keyboard and character messages that Windows delivers to your window procedure. The KEYVIEW1 program shown in Figure 6-3 will help. This program displays in its client area all the information that Windows sends the window procedure for the eight different keyboard messages.

KEYVIEW1.C

```
/*-----------------------------------------------------------
   KEYVIEW1.C -- Displays Keyboard and Character Messages
                 (c) Charles Petzold, 1998
   -----------------------------------------------------------*/

#include <windows.h>

LRESULT CALLBACK WndProc (HWND, UINT, WPARAM, LPARAM) ;

int WINAPI WinMain (HINSTANCE hInstance, HINSTANCE hPrevInstance,
                    PSTR szCmdLine, int iCmdShow)
{
     static TCHAR szAppName[] = TEXT ("KeyView1") ;
     HWND         hwnd ;
     MSG          msg ;
     WNDCLASS     wndclass ;

     wndclass.style         = CS_HREDRAW | CS_VREDRAW ;
     wndclass.lpfnWndProc   = WndProc ;
     wndclass.cbClsExtra    = 0 ;
     wndclass.cbWndExtra    = 0 ;
     wndclass.hInstance     = hInstance ;
```

Figure 6-3. *The KEYVIEW1 program.*

```
      wndclass.hIcon         = LoadIcon (NULL, IDI_APPLICATION) ;
      wndclass.hCursor       = LoadCursor (NULL, IDC_ARROW) ;
      wndclass.hbrBackground = (HBRUSH) GetStockObject (WHITE_BRUSH) ;
      wndclass.lpszMenuName  = NULL ;
      wndclass.lpszClassName = szAppName ;

      if (!RegisterClass (&wndclass))
      {
           MessageBox (NULL, TEXT ("This program requires Windows NT!"),
                       szAppName, MB_ICONERROR) ;
           return 0 ;
      }

      hwnd = CreateWindow (szAppName, TEXT ("Keyboard Message Viewer #1"),
                           WS_OVERLAPPEDWINDOW,
                           CW_USEDEFAULT, CW_USEDEFAULT,
                           CW_USEDEFAULT, CW_USEDEFAULT,
                           NULL, NULL, hInstance, NULL) ;

      ShowWindow (hwnd, iCmdShow) ;
      UpdateWindow (hwnd) ;

      while (GetMessage (&msg, NULL, 0, 0))
      {
           TranslateMessage (&msg) ;
           DispatchMessage (&msg) ;
      }
      return msg.wParam ;
}

LRESULT CALLBACK WndProc (HWND hwnd, UINT message, WPARAM wParam, LPARAM lParam)
{
      static int    cxClientMax, cyClientMax, cxClient, cyClient, cxChar, cyChar ;
      static int    cLinesMax, cLines ;
      static PMSG   pmsg ;
      static RECT   rectScroll ;
      static TCHAR szTop[] = TEXT ("Message        Key       Char      ")
                             TEXT ("Repeat Scan Ext ALT Prev Tran") ;
      static TCHAR szUnd[] = TEXT ("_____        ___       ____      ")
                             TEXT ("_____ ____ ___ ___ ____ ____") ;

      static TCHAR * szFormat[2] = {

              TEXT ("%-13s %3d %-15s%c%6u  %4d %3s %3s %4s %4s"),
              TEXT ("%-13s          0x%04X%1s%c  %6u  %4d %3s %3s %4s %4s") } ;
```

(continued)

Figure 6-3. *continued*

```
static TCHAR * szYes  = TEXT ("Yes") ;
static TCHAR * szNo   = TEXT ("No") ;
static TCHAR * szDown = TEXT ("Down") ;
static TCHAR * szUp   = TEXT ("Up") ;

static TCHAR * szMessage [] = {
                    TEXT ("WM_KEYDOWN"),    TEXT ("WM_KEYUP"),
                    TEXT ("WM_CHAR"),       TEXT ("WM_DEADCHAR"),
                    TEXT ("WM_SYSKEYDOWN"), TEXT ("WM_SYSKEYUP"),
                    TEXT ("WM_SYSCHAR"),    TEXT ("WM_SYSDEADCHAR") } ;
HDC          hdc ;
int          i, iType ;
PAINTSTRUCT  ps ;
TCHAR        szBuffer[128], szKeyName [32] ;
TEXTMETRIC   tm ;

switch (message)
{
case WM_CREATE:
case WM_DISPLAYCHANGE:

        // Get maximum size of client area

    cxClientMax = GetSystemMetrics (SM_CXMAXIMIZED) ;
    cyClientMax = GetSystemMetrics (SM_CYMAXIMIZED) ;

        // Get character size for fixed-pitch font

    hdc = GetDC (hwnd) ;

    SelectObject (hdc, GetStockObject (SYSTEM_FIXED_FONT)) ;
    GetTextMetrics (hdc, &tm) ;
    cxChar = tm.tmAveCharWidth ;
    cyChar = tm.tmHeight ;

    ReleaseDC (hwnd, hdc) ;

        // Allocate memory for display lines

    if (pmsg)
        free (pmsg) ;

    cLinesMax = cyClientMax / cyChar ;
    pmsg = malloc (cLinesMax * sizeof (MSG)) ;
    cLines = 0 ;
                            // fall through
```

```
case WM_SIZE:
     if (message == WM_SIZE)
     {
          cxClient = LOWORD (lParam) ;
          cyClient = HIWORD (lParam) ;
     }
          // Calculate scrolling rectangle

     rectScroll.left   = 0 ;
     rectScroll.right  = cxClient ;
     rectScroll.top    = cyChar ;
     rectScroll.bottom = cyChar * (cyClient / cyChar) ;

     InvalidateRect (hwnd, NULL, TRUE) ;
     return 0 ;

case WM_KEYDOWN:
case WM_KEYUP:
case WM_CHAR:
case WM_DEADCHAR:
case WM_SYSKEYDOWN:
case WM_SYSKEYUP:
case WM_SYSCHAR:
case WM_SYSDEADCHAR:

          // Rearrange storage array

     for (i = cLinesMax - 1 ; i > 0 ; i--)
     {
          pmsg[i] = pmsg[i - 1] ;
     }
          // Store new message

     pmsg[0].hwnd = hwnd ;
     pmsg[0].message = message ;
     pmsg[0].wParam = wParam ;
     pmsg[0].lParam = lParam ;

     cLines = min (cLines + 1, cLinesMax) ;

          // Scroll up the display

     ScrollWindow (hwnd, 0, -cyChar, &rectScroll, &rectScroll) ;

     break ;          // i.e., call DefWindowProc so Sys messages work
```

(continued)

Figure 6-3. *continued*

```
        case WM_PAINT:
             hdc = BeginPaint (hwnd, &ps) ;

             SelectObject (hdc, GetStockObject (SYSTEM_FIXED_FONT)) ;
             SetBkMode (hdc, TRANSPARENT) ;
             TextOut (hdc, 0, 0, szTop, lstrlen (szTop)) ;
             TextOut (hdc, 0, 0, szUnd, lstrlen (szUnd)) ;

             for (i = 0 ; i < min (cLines, cyClient / cyChar - 1) ; i++)
             {
                  iType = pmsg[i].message == WM_CHAR ||
                          pmsg[i].message == WM_SYSCHAR ||
                          pmsg[i].message == WM_DEADCHAR ||
                          pmsg[i].message == WM_SYSDEADCHAR ;

                  GetKeyNameText (pmsg[i].lParam, szKeyName,
                               sizeof (szKeyName) / sizeof (TCHAR)) ;

                  TextOut (hdc, 0, (cyClient / cyChar - 1 - i) * cyChar, szBuffer,
                        wsprintf (szBuffer, szFormat [iType],
                             szMessage [pmsg[i].message - WM_KEYFIRST],
                             pmsg[i].wParam,
                             (PTSTR) (iType ? TEXT (" ") : szKeyName),
                             (TCHAR) (iType ? pmsg[i].wParam : ' '),
                             LOWORD (pmsg[i].lParam),
                             HIWORD (pmsg[i].lParam) & 0xFF,
                             0x01000000 & pmsg[i].lParam ? szYes  : szNo,
                             0x20000000 & pmsg[i].lParam ? szYes  : szNo,
                             0x40000000 & pmsg[i].lParam ? szDown : szUp,
                             0x80000000 & pmsg[i].lParam ? szUp   : szDown)) ;
             }
             EndPaint (hwnd, &ps) ;
             return 0 ;

        case WM_DESTROY:
             PostQuitMessage (0) ;
             return 0 ;
        }
        return DefWindowProc (hwnd, message, wParam, lParam) ;
}
```

KEYVIEW1 displays the contents of each keystroke and character message that it receives in its window procedure. It saves the messages in an array of MSG structures. The size of the array is based on the size of the maximized window size and the fixed-pitch system font. If the user resizes the video display while the program is running (in which case KEYVIEW1 gets a WM_DISPLAYCHANGE message), the array is reallocated. KEYVIEW1 uses the standard C *malloc* function to allocate memory for this array.

Figure 6-4 shows the KEYVIEW1 display after the word "Windows" has been typed. The first column shows the keyboard message. The second column shows the virtual key code for keystroke messages followed by the name of the key. This is obtained by using the *GetKeyNameText* function. The third column (labeled "Char") shows the hexadecimal character code for character messages followed by the character itself. The remaining six columns display the status of the six fields in the *lParam* message parameter.

```
Keyboard Message Viewer #1                              _ □ ×

Message          Key         Char       Repeat Scan Ext ALT Prev Tran

WM_KEYDOWN       16 Right Shift              1   54  No  No   Up Down
WM_KEYDOWN       87 W                        1   17  No  No   Up Down
WM_CHAR                      0x0057 W        1   17  No  No   Up Down
WM_KEYUP         87 W                        1   17  No  No Down   Up
WM_KEYUP         16 Right Shift              1   54  No  No Down   Up
WM_KEYDOWN       73 I                        1   23  No  No   Up Down
WM_CHAR                      0x0069 i        1   23  No  No   Up Down
WM_KEYUP         73 I                        1   23  No  No Down   Up
WM_KEYDOWN       78 N                        1   49  No  No   Up Down
WM_CHAR                      0x006E n        1   49  No  No   Up Down
WM_KEYUP         78 N                        1   49  No  No Down   Up
WM_KEYDOWN       68 D                        1   32  No  No   Up Down
WM_CHAR                      0x0064 d        1   32  No  No   Up Down
WM_KEYUP         68 D                        1   32  No  No Down   Up
WM_KEYDOWN       79 O                        1   24  No  No   Up Down
WM_CHAR                      0x006F o        1   24  No  No   Up Down
WM_KEYUP         79 O                        1   24  No  No Down   Up
WM_KEYDOWN       87 W                        1   17  No  No   Up Down
WM_CHAR                      0x0077 w        1   17  No  No   Up Down
WM_KEYUP         87 W                        1   17  No  No Down   Up
WM_KEYDOWN       83 S                        1   31  No  No   Up Down
WM_CHAR                      0x0073 s        1   31  No  No   Up Down
WM_KEYUP         83 S                        1   31  No  No Down   Up
```

Figure 6-4. *The KEYVIEW1 display.*

To ease the columnar display of this information, KEYVIEW1 uses a fixed-pitch font. As discussed in the last chapter, this requires calls to *GetStockObject* and *SelectObject*:

```
SelectObject (hdc, GetStockObject (SYSTEM_FIXED_FONT)) ;
```

KEYVIEW1 draws a header at the top of the client area identifying the nine columns. The text in this column is underlined. Although it's possible to create an underlined font, I took a different approach here. I defined two character string variables named *szTop* (which has the text) and *szUnd* (which has the underlining) and displayed both of them at the same position at the top of the window during the WM_PAINT message. Normally, Windows displays text in an "opaque" mode, meaning that Windows erases the character background area while displaying a character. This would cause the second character string (*szUnd*) to erase the first (*szTop*). To prevent this, switch the device context into the "transparent" mode:

```
SetBkMode (hdc, TRANSPARENT) ;
```

This method of underlining is possible only when using a fixed-pitch font. Otherwise, the underline character wouldn't necessarily be the same width as the character the underline is to appear under.

The Foreign-Language Keyboard Problem

If you're running the American English version of Windows, you can install different keyboard layouts and pretend that you're typing in a foreign language. You install foreign language keyboard layouts in the Keyboard applet in the Control Panel. Select the Language tab, and click Add. To see how dead keys work, you might want to install the German keyboard. I'll also be discussing the Russian and Greek keyboard layouts, so you might want to install those as well. If the Russian and Greek keyboard layouts are not available in the list that the Keyboard applet displays, you might need to install multilanguage support. Select the Add/Remove Programs applet from the Control Panel, and choose the Windows Setup tab. Make sure the Multilanguage Support box is checked. In any case, you'll need to have your original Windows CD-ROM handy for these changes.

After you install other keyboard layouts, you'll see a blue box with a two-letter code in the tray at the right side of the task bar. It'll be "EN" if the default is English. When you click on this icon, you get a list of all the installed keyboard layouts. You can change the keyboard for the currently active program by clicking on the one you want. This change affects only the currently active program.

Now we're ready to experiment. Compile the KEYVIEW1 program *without* the UNICODE identifier defined. (On this book's companion disc, the non-Unicode version of KEYVIEW1 is located in the RELEASE subdirectory.) Run the program under the American English version of Windows, and type the letters "abcde." The WM_CHAR messages are exactly what you expect: the ASCII character codes 0x61, 0x62, 0x63, 0x64, and 0x65 and the characters a, b, c, d, and e.

Now, while still running KEYVIEW1, select the German keyboard layout. Press the = key and then a vowel (a, e, i, o, or u). The = key generates a WM_DEADCHAR message, and the vowel generates a WM_CHAR message with (respectively) the character codes 0xE1, 0xE9, 0xED, 0xF3, 0xFA, and the characters á, é, í, ó, and ú. This is how dead keys work.

Now select the Greek keyboard layout. Type "abcde" and what do you get? You get WM_CHAR messages with the character codes 0xE1, 0xE2, 0xF8, 0xE4, 0xE5, and the characters á, â, ø, ä, and å. Something doesn't seem to be right here. Shouldn't you be getting letters in the Greek alphabet?

Now switch to the Russian keyboard and again type "abcde." Now you get WM_CHAR messages with the character codes 0xF4, 0xE8, 0xF1, 0xE2, and 0xF3, and the characters ô, è, ñ, â, and ó. Again, something is wrong. You should be getting letters in the Cyrillic alphabet.

The problem is this: you have switched the keyboard to generate different character codes, but you haven't informed GDI of this switch so that GDI can interpret these character codes by displaying the proper symbols.

If you're very brave, and you have a spare PC to play with, and if you have a Professional or Universal Subscription to Microsoft Developer Network (MSDN), you might want to install (for example) the Greek version of Windows. You can also install the same four keyboard layouts (English, Greek, German, and Russian). Now run KEYLOOK1. Switch to the English keyboard layout, and type "abcde". You get the ASCII character codes 0x61, 0x62, 0x63, 0x64, and 0x65 and the characters a, b, c, d, and e. (And you can breathe a sigh of relief that ASCII still works, even in Greece.)

Under this Greek version of Windows, switch to the Greek keyboard layout and type "abcde." You get WM_CHAR messages with the character codes 0xE1, 0xE2, 0xF8, 0xE4, and 0xE5. These are the same character codes you got under the English version of Windows with the Greek keyboard layout installed. But now the displayed characters are α, β, ψ, δ, and ε. These are indeed the lowercase Greek letters alpha, beta, psi, delta, and epsilon. (What happened to gamma? Well, if you were using the Greek version of Windows for real, you'd probably be using a keyboard with Greek letters on the keycaps. The key corresponding to the English c happens to be a psi. The gamma is generated by the key corresponding to the English g. You can see the complete Greek keyboard layout on page 587 of Nadine Kano's *Developing International Software for Windows 95 and Windows NT*.

Still running KEYVIEW1 under the Greek version of Windows, switch to the German keyboard layout. Type the = key followed by a, then e, then i, then o, and then u. You get WM_CHAR messages with the character codes 0xE1, 0xE9, 0xED, 0xF3, and 0xFA. These are the same character codes as under the English version of Windows with the German keyboard installed. However, the displayed characters are α, ι, ν, σ, and ï, not the correct á, é, í, ó, and ú.

Now switch to the Russian keyboard and type "abcde." You get the character codes 0xF4, 0xE8, 0xF1, 0xE2, and 0xF3, which are the same as under the English version of Windows with the Russian keyboard installed. However, the displayed characters are τ, θ, ρ, β, and σ, not letters in the Cyrillic alphabet.

You can also install the Russian version of Windows. As you may have guessed by now, the English and Russian keyboard layouts will work, but not the German or Greek.

Now, if you're really, really brave, you can install the Japanese version of Windows and run KEYVIEW1. If you type at your American keyboard, you can enter English text and everything will seem to work fine. However, if you switch to the German, Greek, or Russian keyboard layouts and try any of the exercises described above, you'll see the characters displayed as dots. If you type capital letters—either accented German letters, Greek letters, or Russian letters—you'll see the characters rendered as katakana, which is the Japanese alphabet generally used to spell words from other languages. You may have fun typing katakana, but it's not German, Greek, or Russian.

The Far East versions of Windows include a utility called the Input Method Editor (IME) that appears as a floating toolbar. This utility lets you use the normal keyboard for entering ideographs, which are the complex characters used in Chinese, Japanese, and Korean. Basically, you type combinations of letters and the composed symbols appear in another floating window. You then press Enter and the resultant character codes are sent to the active window (that is, KEYVIEW1). KEYVIEW1 responds with almost total nonsense—the WM_CHAR messages have character codes above 128, but the characters are meaningless. (Nadine Kano's book has much more information on using the IME.)

So, we've seen a couple examples of KEYLOOK1 displaying incorrect characters—when running the English version of Windows with the Russian or Greek keyboard layouts installed, when running the Greek version of Windows with the Russian or German keyboard layouts installed, and when running the Russian version of Windows with the German, Russian, or Greek keyboards installed. We've also seen errors when entering characters from the Input Method Editor in the Japanese version of Windows.

Character Sets and Fonts

The problem with KEYLOOK1 is a font problem. The font that it's using to display characters on the screen is inconsistent with the character codes it's receiving from the keyboard. So, let's take a look at some fonts.

As I'll discuss in more detail in Chapter 17, Windows supports three types of fonts—bitmap fonts, vector fonts, and (beginning in Windows 3.1) TrueType fonts.

The vector fonts are virtually obsolete. The characters in these fonts were composed of simple lines, but these lines did not define filled areas. The vector fonts had the benefit of being scalable to any size, but the characters often looked anemic.

TrueType fonts are outline fonts with characters defined by filled areas. TrueType fonts are scalable; indeed the character definitions contain "hints" for avoiding rounding problems that could result in unsightly or unreadable text. It is with TrueType that Windows achieves a true WYSIWYG ("what you see is what you get") display of text on the video display that accurately matches printer output.

In bitmap fonts, each character is defined by an array of bits that correspond to the pixels of the video display. Bitmaps fonts can be scalable to larger sizes, but they look jagged as a result. Bitmap fonts are often tweaked by their designers to be more easily readable on the video display. Thus, Windows uses bitmap fonts for the text that appears in title bars, menus, buttons, and dialog boxes.

The bitmap font that you get in a default device context is known as the system font. You can obtain a handle to this font by calling the *GetStockObject* function with the identifier SYSTEM_FONT. The KEYVIEW1 program elects to use a fixed-pitch version of the system font, denoted by SYSTEM_FIXED_FONT. Another alternative in the *GetStockObject* function is OEM_FIXED_FONT.

These three fonts have typeface names of (respectively) System, FixedSys, and Terminal. A program can use the typeface name to refer to the font in a *CreateFont* or *Create-*

FontIndirect function call. These three fonts are stored in two sets of three files in the FONTS subdirectory of the Windows directory. The particular set of files that Windows uses depends on whether you've elected to display "Small Fonts" or "Large Fonts" in the Display applet of the Control Panel (that is, whether you want Windows to assume that the video display has a 96 dpi resolution or a 120 dpi resolution). This is all summarized in the following table:

GetStockObject Identifier	*Typeface Name*	*Small Font File*	*Large Font File*
SYSTEM_FONT	System	VGASYS.FON	8514SYS.FON
SYSTEM_FIXED_FONT	FixedSys	VGAFIX.FON	8514FIX.FON
OEM_FIXED_FONT	Terminal	VGAOEM.FON	8514OEM.FON

In the file names, "VGA" refers to the Video Graphics Array, the video adapter that IBM introduced in 1987. It was IBM's first PC video adapter to have a pixel display size of 640 by 480. If you select Small Fonts from the Display applet in the Control Panel (meaning that you want Windows to assume that the video display has a resolution of 96 dpi), Windows uses the filenames beginning with "VGA" for these three fonts. If you select Large Fonts (meaning that you want a resolution of 120 dpi), Windows uses the filenames beginning with "8514." The 8514 was another video adapter that IBM introduced in 1987, and it had a maximum display size of 1024 by 768.

Windows does not want you to see these files. The files have the system and hidden file attributes set, and if you use the Windows Explorer to view the contents of your FONTS subdirectory, you won't see them at all, even if you've elected to view system and hidden files. Use the Find option from the Tools menu to search for files with a specification of *.FON. From there, you can double-click the filename to see what the font characters look like.

For many standard controls and user interface items, Windows doesn't use the System font. Instead, it uses a font with the typeface name MS Sans Serif. (MS stands for Microsoft.) This is also a bitmap font. The file (named SSERIFE.FON) contains fonts based on a 96-dpi video display, with point sizes of 8, 10, 12, 14, 18, and 24. You can get this font by using the DEFAULT_GUI_FONT identifier in *GetStockObject*. The point size Windows uses will be based on the display resolution you've selected in the Display applet of the Control Panel.

So far, I've mentioned four of the identifiers you can use with *GetStockObject* to obtain a font for use in a device context. There are three others: ANSI_FIXED_FONT, ANSI_VAR_FONT, and DEVICE_DEFAULT_FONT. To begin approaching the problem of the keyboard and character displays, let's take a look at all the stock fonts in Windows. The program that displays the fonts is named STOKFONT and is shown in Figure 6-5 beginning on the following page.

STOKFONT.C

```
/*-------------------------------------------
   STOKFONT.C -- Stock Font Objects
                 (c) Charles Petzold, 1998
   -------------------------------------------*/

#include <windows.h>

LRESULT CALLBACK WndProc (HWND, UINT, WPARAM, LPARAM) ;

int WINAPI WinMain (HINSTANCE hInstance, HINSTANCE hPrevInstance,
                    PSTR szCmdLine, int iCmdShow)
{
     static TCHAR szAppName[] = TEXT ("StokFont") ;
     HWND         hwnd ;
     MSG          msg ;
     WNDCLASS     wndclass ;

     wndclass.style         = CS_HREDRAW | CS_VREDRAW ;
     wndclass.lpfnWndProc   = WndProc ;
     wndclass.cbClsExtra    = 0 ;
     wndclass.cbWndExtra    = 0 ;
     wndclass.hInstance     = hInstance ;
     wndclass.hIcon         = LoadIcon (NULL, IDI_APPLICATION) ;
     wndclass.hCursor       = LoadCursor (NULL, IDC_ARROW) ;
     wndclass.hbrBackground = (HBRUSH) GetStockObject (WHITE_BRUSH) ;
     wndclass.lpszMenuName  = NULL ;
     wndclass.lpszClassName = szAppName ;

     if (!RegisterClass (&wndclass))
     {
          MessageBox (NULL, TEXT ("Program requires Windows NT!"),
                      szAppName, MB_ICONERROR) ;
          return 0 ;
     }

     hwnd = CreateWindow (szAppName, TEXT ("Stock Fonts"),
                          WS_OVERLAPPEDWINDOW | WS_VSCROLL,
                          CW_USEDEFAULT, CW_USEDEFAULT,
                          CW_USEDEFAULT, CW_USEDEFAULT,
                          NULL, NULL, hInstance, NULL) ;

     ShowWindow (hwnd, iCmdShow) ;
     UpdateWindow (hwnd) ;
```

Figure 6-5. *The STOKFONT program.*

```
     while (GetMessage (&msg, NULL, 0, 0))
     {
          TranslateMessage (&msg) ;
          DispatchMessage (&msg) ;
     }
     return msg.wParam ;
}

LRESULT CALLBACK WndProc (HWND hwnd, UINT message, WPARAM wParam, LPARAM lParam)
{
     static struct
     {
          int     idStockFont ;
          TCHAR * szStockFont ;
     }
     stockfont [] = { OEM_FIXED_FONT,      "OEM_FIXED_FONT",
                      ANSI_FIXED_FONT,     "ANSI_FIXED_FONT",
                      ANSI_VAR_FONT,       "ANSI_VAR_FONT",
                      SYSTEM_FONT,         "SYSTEM_FONT",
                      DEVICE_DEFAULT_FONT, "DEVICE_DEFAULT_FONT",
                      SYSTEM_FIXED_FONT,   "SYSTEM_FIXED_FONT",
                      DEFAULT_GUI_FONT,    "DEFAULT_GUI_FONT" } ;

     static int  iFont, cFonts = sizeof stockfont / sizeof stockfont[0] ;
     HDC         hdc ;
     int         i, x, y, cxGrid, cyGrid ;
     PAINTSTRUCT ps ;
     TCHAR       szFaceName [LF_FACESIZE], szBuffer [LF_FACESIZE + 64] ;
     TEXTMETRIC  tm ;

     switch (message)
     {
     case WM_CREATE:
          SetScrollRange (hwnd, SB_VERT, 0, cFonts - 1, TRUE) ;
          return 0 ;

     case WM_DISPLAYCHANGE:
          InvalidateRect (hwnd, NULL, TRUE) ;
          return 0 ;

     case WM_VSCROLL:
          switch (LOWORD (wParam))
          {
          case SB_TOP:              iFont = 0 ;                 break ;
          case SB_BOTTOM:           iFont = cFonts - 1 ;        break ;
          case SB_LINEUP:
```

(continued)

Figure 6-5. *continued*

```
        case SB_PAGEUP:           iFont -= 1 ;                  break ;
        case SB_LINEDOWN:
        case SB_PAGEDOWN:         iFont += 1 ;                  break ;
        case SB_THUMBPOSITION:    iFont = HIWORD (wParam) ;     break ;
        }
        iFont = max (0, min (cFonts - 1, iFont)) ;
        SetScrollPos (hwnd, SB_VERT, iFont, TRUE) ;
        InvalidateRect (hwnd, NULL, TRUE) ;
        return 0 ;

case WM_KEYDOWN:
        switch (wParam)
        {
        case VK_HOME: SendMessage (hwnd, WM_VSCROLL, SB_TOP, 0) ;        break ;
        case VK_END:  SendMessage (hwnd, WM_VSCROLL, SB_BOTTOM, 0) ;     break ;
        case VK_PRIOR:
        case VK_LEFT:
        case VK_UP:   SendMessage (hwnd, WM_VSCROLL, SB_LINEUP, 0) ;     break ;
        case VK_NEXT:
        case VK_RIGHT:
        case VK_DOWN: SendMessage (hwnd, WM_VSCROLL, SB_PAGEDOWN, 0) ; break ;
        }
        return 0 ;

case WM_PAINT:
        hdc = BeginPaint (hwnd, &ps) ;

        SelectObject (hdc, GetStockObject (stockfont[iFont].idStockFont)) ;
        GetTextFace (hdc, LF_FACESIZE, szFaceName) ;
        GetTextMetrics (hdc, &tm) ;
        cxGrid = max (3 * tm.tmAveCharWidth, 2 * tm.tmMaxCharWidth) ;
        cyGrid = tm.tmHeight + 3 ;

        TextOut (hdc, 0, 0, szBuffer,
            wsprintf (szBuffer, TEXT (" %s: Face Name = %s, CharSet = %i"),
                    stockfont[iFont].szStockFont,
                    szFaceName, tm.tmCharSet)) ;

        SetTextAlign (hdc, TA_TOP | TA_CENTER) ;

            // vertical and horizontal lines
```

```
        for (i = 0 ; i < 17 ; i++)
        {
              MoveToEx (hdc, (i + 2) * cxGrid,  2 * cyGrid, NULL) ;
              LineTo   (hdc, (i + 2) * cxGrid, 19 * cyGrid) ;

              MoveToEx (hdc,       cxGrid, (i + 3) * cyGrid, NULL) ;
              LineTo   (hdc, 18 * cxGrid, (i + 3) * cyGrid) ;
        }
              // vertical and horizontal headings

        for (i = 0 ; i < 16 ; i++)
        {
              TextOut (hdc, (2 * i + 5) * cxGrid / 2, 2 * cyGrid + 2, szBuffer,
                    wsprintf (szBuffer, TEXT ("%X-"), i)) ;

              TextOut (hdc, 3 * cxGrid / 2, (i + 3) * cyGrid + 2, szBuffer,
                    wsprintf (szBuffer, TEXT ("-%X"), i)) ;
        }
              // characters

        for (y = 0 ; y < 16 ; y++)
        for (x = 0 ; x < 16 ; x++)
        {
              TextOut (hdc, (2 * x + 5) * cxGrid / 2,
                                (y + 3) * cyGrid + 2, szBuffer,
                    wsprintf (szBuffer, TEXT ("%c"), 16 * x + y)) ;
        }

        EndPaint (hwnd, &ps) ;
        return 0 ;

    case WM_DESTROY:
        PostQuitMessage (0) ;
        return 0 ;
    }
    return DefWindowProc (hwnd, message, wParam, lParam) ;
}
```

This program is fairly simple. It uses the scroll bar and cursor movement keys to let you select one of the seven stock fonts to display. The program displays the 256 characters of the font in a grid. The headings at the top and left of the grid show the hexadecimal values of the character codes.

At the top of the client area, STOKFONT shows the identifier it uses to select the font using the *GetStockObject* function. It also displays the typeface name of the font obtained from the *GetTextFace* function and the *tmCharSet* field of the TEXTMETRIC structure. This "character set identifier" turns out to be crucial in understanding how Windows deals with foreign-language versions of Windows.

If you run STOKFONT under the American English version of Windows, the first screen you'll see shows you the font obtained by using the OEM_FIXED_FONT identifier with the *GetStockObject* function. This is shown in Figure 6-6.

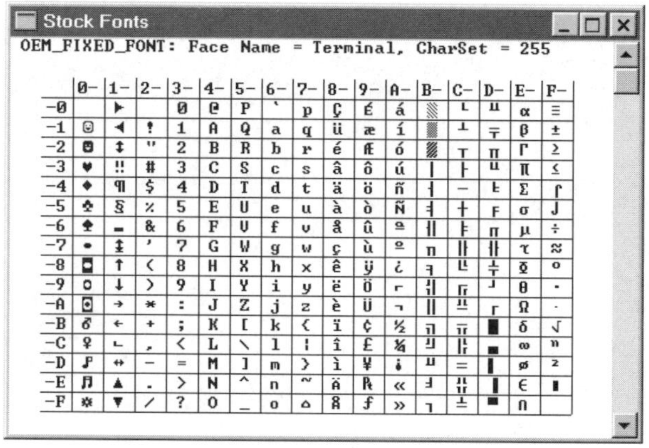

Figure 6-6. *The OEM_FIXED_FONT in the U.S. version of Windows.*

In this character set (as in all the others in this chapter), you'll see some ASCII. But remember that ASCII is a 7-bit code that defines displayable characters for codes 0x20 through 0x7E. By the time IBM developed the original IBM PC the 8-bit byte had been firmly established, so a full 8 bits could be used for character codes. IBM decided to extend the ASCII character set with a bunch of line- and block-drawing characters, accented letters, Greek letters, math symbols, and some miscellany. Many character-mode MS-DOS programs used the line-drawing characters in their on-screen displays, and many MS-DOS programs used some of the extended characters in their files.

This particular character set posed a problem for the original developers of Windows. On the one hand, the line- and block-drawing characters are not needed in Windows because Windows has a complete graphics programming language. The 48 codes used for these characters could better be used for additional accented letters required by many Western European languages. On the other hand, the IBM character set was definitely a standard that couldn't be ignored completely.

So, the original developers of Windows decided to support the IBM character set but to relegate it to secondary importance—mostly for old MS-DOS applications that ran in a window and for Windows programs that needed to use files created by MS-DOS applications. Windows applications do not use the IBM character set, and over the years it has faded in importance. Still, however, if you need it you can use it. In this context, "OEM" means "IBM."

(Be aware that foreign-language versions of Windows do not necessarily support the same OEM character set as the American English version does. Other countries had their own MS-DOS character sets. That's a whole subject in itself, but not one for this book.)

Because the IBM character set was deemed inappropriate for Windows, a different extended character set was selected. This is called the "ANSI character set," referring to the American National Standards Institute, but it's actually an ISO (International Standards Organization) standard, namely standard 8859. It's also known as Latin 1, Western European, or code page 1252. Figure 6-7 shows one version of the ANSI character set—the system font in the American English version of Windows.

Stock Fonts

SYSTEM_FONT: Face Name = System, CharSet = 0

	0-	1-	2-	3-	4-	5-	6-	7-	8-	9-	A-	B-	C-	D-	E-	F-
-0	▮	▮		0	@	P	`	p	▮	▮		°	À	Ð	à	ð
-1	▮	▮	!	1	A	Q	a	q	▮	'	¡	±	Á	Ñ	á	ñ
-2	▮	▮	"	2	B	R	b	r	,	'	¢	²	Â	Ò	â	ò
-3	▮	▮	#	3	C	S	c	s	ƒ	"	£	³	Ã	Ó	ã	ó
-4	▮	▮	$	4	D	T	d	t	„	"	¤	´	Ä	Ô	ä	ô
-5	▮	▮	%	5	E	U	e	u	…	•	¥	µ	Å	Õ	å	õ
-6	▮	▮	&	6	F	V	f	v	†	–	¦	¶	Æ	Ö	æ	ö
-7	▮	▮	'	7	G	W	g	w	‡	—	§	·	Ç	×	ç	÷
-8	▮	▮	(	8	H	X	h	x	ˆ	˜	¨	¸	È	Ø	è	ø
-9	▮	▮	)	9	I	Y	i	y	‰	™	©	¹	É	Ù	é	ù
-A	▮	▮	*	:	J	Z	j	z	Š	š	ª	º	Ê	Ú	ê	ú
-B	▮	▮	+	;	K	[	k	{	‹	›	«	»	Ë	Û	ë	û
-C	▮	▮	,	<	L	\	l	|	Œ	œ	¬	¼	Ì	Ü	ì	ü
-D	▮	▮	-	=	M	]	m	}	▮	▮		½	Í	Ý	í	ý
-E	▮	▮	.	>	N	^	n	~	▮	▮	®	¾	Î	Þ	î	þ
-F	▮	▮	/	?	O	_	o	▮	▮	Ÿ		¿	Ï	ß	ï	ÿ

Figure 6-7. *The SYSTEM_FONT in the U.S. version of Windows.*

The thick vertical bars indicate codes for which characters are not defined. Notice that codes 0x20 through 0x7E are once again ASCII. Also, the ASCII control characters (0x00 through 0x1F, and 0x7F) are not associated with displayable characters. This is as it should be.

The codes 0xC0 through 0xFF make the ANSI character set important to foreign-language versions of Windows. These codes provide 64 characters commonly found in Western European languages. The character 0xA0, which looks like a space, is actually defined as a nonbreaking space, such as the space in "WW II."

I say this is "one version" of the ANSI character set because of the presence of the characters for codes 0x80 through 0x9F. The fixed-pitch system font includes only two of these characters, as shown in Figure 6-8.

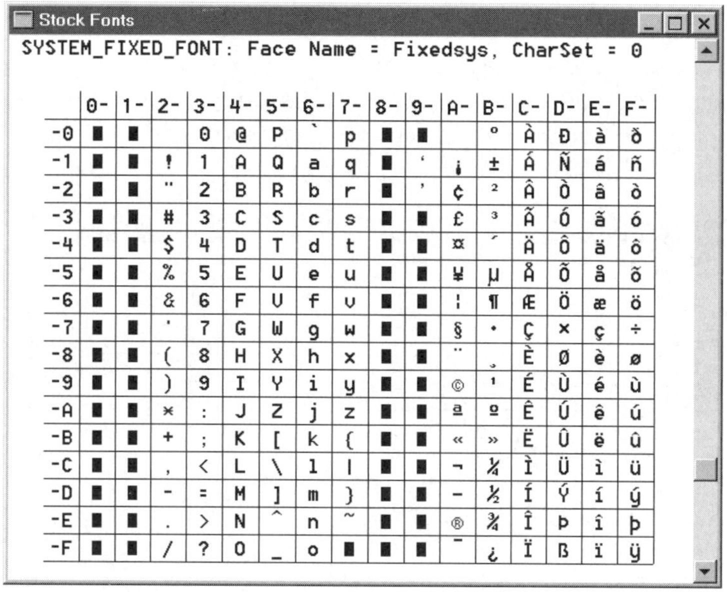

Figure 6-8. *The SYSTEM_FIXED_FONT in the U.S. version of Windows.*

In Unicode, codes 0x0000 through 0x007F are the same as ASCII, codes 0x0080 through 0x009F duplicate control characters 0x0000 through 0x001F, and codes 0x00A0 through 0x00FF are the same as the ANSI character set used in Windows.

If you run the German version of Windows, you'll get the same ANSI character sets when you call *GetStockObject* with the SYSTEM_FONT or SYSTEM_FIXED_FONT identifiers. This is true of other Western European versions of Windows as well. The ANSI character set was designed to have all the characters that are required in these languages.

However, when you run the Greek version of Windows, the default character set is *not* the same. Instead, the SYSTEM_FONT is that shown in Figure 6-9.

Stock Fonts

SYSTEM_FONT: Face Name = System, CharSet = 161

	0-	1-	2-	3-	4-	5-	6-	7-	8-	9-	A-	B-	C-	D-	E-	F-
-0	I	I		0	@	P	`	p	I	I		°	Ϊ	Π	ϋ	π
-1	I	I	!	1	A	Q	a	q	I	΄	¨	±	Α	Ρ	α	ρ
-2	I	I	"	2	B	R	b	r	I	΄	Ά	²	Β	•	β	s
-3	I	I	#	3	C	S	c	s	I	I	£	³	Γ	Σ	γ	σ
-4	I	I	$	4	D	T	d	t	I	I	¤	΄	Δ	Τ	δ	τ
-5	I	I	%	5	E	U	e	u	I	I	¥	μ	Ε	Υ	ε	υ
-6	I	I	&	6	F	V	f	v	I	I	¦	¶	Ζ	Φ	ζ	φ
-7	I	I	'	7	G	W	g	w	I	I	§	·	Η	Χ	η	χ
-8	I	I	(	8	H	X	h	x	I	I	¨	Έ	Θ	Ψ	θ	ψ
-9	I	I	)	9	I	Y	i	y	I	I	©	Ή	Ι	Ω	ι	ω
-A	I	I	*	:	J	Z	j	z	I	I	ª	Ί	Κ	Ϊ	κ	ϊ
-B	I	I	+	;	K	[	k	{	I	I	«	»	Λ	Ϋ	ñ	ü
-C	I	I	,	<	L	\	l	|	I	I	¬	Ό	Μ	ά	μ	ό
-D	I	I	-	=	M	]	m	}	I	I	-	½	Ν	έ	ν	ú
-E	I	I	.	>	N	^	n	~	I	I	®	Ύ	Ξ	ή	ξ	ώ
-F	I	I	/	?	O	_	o	I	I	I	―	Ώ	Ο	ί	o	•

Figure 6-9. *The SYSTEM_FONT in the Greek version of Windows.*

The SYSTEM_FIXED_FONT has the same characters. Notice the codes from 0xC0 through 0xFF. These codes contain uppercase and lowercase letters from the Greek alphabet. When you're running the Russian version of Windows, the default character set is shown in Figure 6-10.

Stock Fonts

SYSTEM_FONT: Face Name = System, CharSet = 204

	0-	1-	2-	3-	4-	5-	6-	7-	8-	9-	A-	B-	C-	D-	E-	F-
-0	Ђ	Ђ		0	@	P	`	p	Ђ	ђ		°	А	Р	а	р
-1	Ђ	Ђ	!	1	A	Q	a	q	ѓ	'	ў	±	Б	С	б	с
-2	Ђ	Ђ	"	2	B	R	b	r	,	'	ў	I	В	Т	в	т
-3	Ђ	Ђ	#	3	C	S	c	s	ѓ	"	¤	і	Г	У	г	у
-4	Ђ	Ђ	$	4	D	T	d	t	„	"	¤	ґ	Д	Ф	д	ф
-5	Ђ	Ђ	%	5	E	U	e	u	…	•	Ґ	μ	Е	Х	е	х
-6	Ђ	Ђ	&	6	F	V	f	v	†	-	¦	¶	Ж	Ц	ж	ц
-7	Ђ	Ђ	'	7	G	W	g	w	‡	—	§	·	З	Ч	з	ч
-8	Ђ	Ђ	(	8	H	X	h	x	I	™	Ё	ё	И	Ш	и	ш
-9	Ђ	Ђ	)	9	I	Y	i	y	‰	™	©	№	Й	Щ	й	щ
-A	Ђ	Ђ	*	:	J	Z	j	z	љ	љ	Є	є	К	Ъ	к	ъ
-B	Ђ	Ђ	+	;	K	[	k	{	‹	›	«	»	Л	Ы	л	ы
-C	Ђ	Ђ	,	<	L	\	l	|	њ	њ	¬	ј	М	Ь	м	ь
-D	Ђ	Ђ	-	=	M	]	m	}	Ќ	ќ	-	S	Н	Э	н	э
-E	Ђ	Ђ	.	>	N	^	n	~	Ћ	ћ	®	s	О	Ю	о	ю
-F	Ђ	Ђ	/	?	O	_	o	I	Џ	џ	Ї	ї	П	Я	п	я

Figure 6-10. *The SYSTEM_FONT in the Russian version of Windows.*

Again, notice that uppercase and lowercase letters of the Cyrillic alphabet occupy codes 0xC0 and 0xFF.

Figure 6-11 on the following page shows the SYSTEM_FONT from the Japanese version of Windows. The characters from 0xA5 through 0xDF are all part of the katakana alphabet.

Stock Fonts

SYSTEM_FONT: Face Name = System, CharSet = 128

	0-	1-	2-	3-	4-	5-	6-	7-	8-	9-	A-	B-	C-	D-	E-	F-
-0	■	■		0	@	P	`	p	■	■	■	−	タ	ミ	■	■
-1	■	■	!	1	A	Q	a	q	■	■	。	ア	チ	ム	■	■
-2	■	■	"	2	B	R	b	r	■	■	「	イ	ツ	メ	■	■
-3	■	■	#	3	C	S	c	s	■	■	」	ウ	テ	モ	■	■
-4	■	■	$	4	D	T	d	t	■	■	、	エ	ト	ヤ	■	■
-5	■	■	%	5	E	U	e	u	■	■	・	オ	ナ	ユ	■	■
-6	■	■	&	6	F	V	f	v	■	■	ヲ	カ	ニ	ヨ	■	■
-7	■	■	'	7	G	W	g	w	■	■	ァ	キ	ヌ	ラ	■	■
-8	■	■	(	8	H	X	h	x	■	■	ィ	ク	ネ	リ	■	■
-9	■	■	)	9	I	Y	i	y	■	■	ゥ	ケ	ノ	ル	■	■
-A	■	■	*	:	J	Z	j	z	■	■	ェ	コ	ハ	レ	■	■
-B	■	■	+	;	K	[	k	{	■	■	ォ	サ	ヒ	ロ	■	■
-C	■	■	,	<	L	¥	l	|	■	■	ャ	シ	フ	ワ	■	■
-D	■	■	−	=	M	]	m	}	■	■	ュ	ス	ヘ	ン	■	■
-E	■	■	.	>	N	^	n	~	■	■	ョ	セ	ホ	゛	■	■
-F	■	■	/	?	O	_	o		■	■	ッ	ソ	マ	゜	■	■

Figure 6-11. *The SYSTEM_FONT in the Japanese version of Windows.*

The Japanese system font shown in Figure 6-11 is different from those shown previously because it is actually a double-byte character set (DBCS) called Shift-JIS. (JIS stands for Japanese Industrial Standard.) Most of the character codes from 0x81 through 0x9F and from 0xE0 through 0xFF are really just the first byte of a 2-byte code. The second byte is usually in the range 0x40 through 0xFC. (See Appendix G in Nadine Kano's book for a complete table of these codes.)

So now we can see where the problem is in KEYVIEW1: If you have the Greek keyboard layout installed and you type "abcde," *regardless of the version of Windows you're running,* Windows generates WM_CHAR messages with the character codes 0xE1, 0xE2, 0xF8, 0xE4, and 0xE5. But these character codes will correspond to the characters α, β, ψ, δ, and ε only if you're running the Greek version of Windows with the Greek system font.

If you have the Russian keyboard layout installed and you type "abcde," *regardless of the version of Windows you're running,* Windows generates WM_CHAR messages with the character codes 0xF4, 0xE8, 0xF1, 0xE2, and 0xF3. But these character codes will correspond to the characters ф, и, с, в, and у only if you're running the Russian version of Windows or another language that uses the Cyrillic alphabet, and you're using the Cyrillic system font.

If you have the German keyboard layout installed and you type the = key (or the key in that same position) followed by the a, e, i, o, or u key, *regardless of the version of Windows you're running,* Windows generates WM_CHAR messages with the character codes 0xE1, 0xE9, 0xED, 0xF3, and 0xFA. Only if you're running a Western European or American version of Windows, which means that you have the Western European system font, will these character codes correspond to the characters á, é, í, ó, or ú.

If you have the American English keyboard layout installed, you can type anything on your keyboard and Windows will generate WM_CHAR messages with character codes that correctly match to the proper characters.

What About Unicode?

I claimed in Chapter 2 that Unicode support in Windows NT helps out in writing programs for an international market. Let's try compiling KEYVIEW1 with the UNICODE identifier defined and running it under various versions of Windows NT. (On this book's companion disc, the Unicode version of KEYVIEW1 is located in the DEBUG directory.)

If the UNICODE identifier is defined when the program is compiled, the "KeyView1" window class is registered with the *RegisterClassW* rather than the *RegisterClassA* function. This means that any message delivered to *WndProc* that has character or text data will use 16-bit characters rather than 8-bit characters. In particular, the WM_CHAR message will deliver a 16-bit character code rather than an 8-bit character code.

Run the Unicode version of KEYVIEW1 under the American English version of Windows NT. I'll assume you've installed at least the other three keyboard layouts we've been experimenting with—that is, German, Greek, and Russian.

With the American English version of Windows NT and either the English or German keyboard layout installed, the Unicode version of KEYVIEW1 will appear to work the same as the non-Unicode version. It will receive the same character codes (all of which will be 0xFF or lower in value) and display the same correct characters. This is because the first 256 characters of Unicode are the same as the ANSI character set used in Windows.

Now switch to the Greek keyboard layout, and type "abcde." The WM_CHAR messages will have the Unicode character codes 0x03B1, 0x03B2, 0x03C8, 0x03B4, and 0x03B5. Note that for the first time we're seeing character codes with values higher than 0xFF. These Unicode character codes correspond to the Greek letters α, β, ψ, δ, and ϵ. However, all five characters are displayed as solid blocks! This is because the SYSTEM_FIXED_FONT only has 256 characters.

Now switch to the Russian keyboard layout, and type "abcde." KEYVIEW1 displays WM_CHAR messages with the Unicode character codes 0x0444, 0x0438, 0x0441, 0x0432, and 0x0443, corresponding to the Cyrillic characters ф, и, с, в, and у. Once again, however, all five characters are displayed as solid blocks.

In short, where the non-Unicode version of KEYVIEW1 displayed incorrect characters, the Unicode version of KEYVIEW1 displays solid blocks, indicating that the current font does not have that particular character. I hesitate to say that the Unicode version of KEYVIEW1 represents an "improvement" over the non-Unicode version, but it does. The non-Unicode version displays characters that are not correct. The Unicode version does not.

The differences between the Unicode and non-Unicode versions of KEYVIEW1 are mostly in two areas.

First, the WM_CHAR message is accompanied by a 16-bit character code rather than an 8-bit character code. The 8-bit character code in the non-Unicode version of KEYVIEW1 could have different meanings depending what keyboard layout is active. A code of 0xE1 could mean á if it came from the German keyboard, α if it came from the Greek keyboard, and б if it came from the Russian keyboard. In the Unicode version of the program, the 16-bit character code is totally unambiguous. The á character is 0x00E1, the α character is 0x03B1, and the б character is 0x0431.

Second, the Unicode *TextOutW* function displays characters based on 16-bit character codes rather than on the 8-bit character codes of the non-Unicode *TextOutA* function. Because these 16-bit character codes are totally unambiguous, GDI can determine whether the font currently selected in the device context is capable of displaying each character.

Running the Unicode version of KEYVIEW1 under the American version of Windows NT is somewhat deceptive, because it appears as if GDI is simply displaying character codes in the range 0x0000 through 0x00FF and not those above 0x00FF. That is, it appears as if there's a simple one-to-one mapping between the character codes and the 256 characters of the system font.

However, if you install the Greek or Russian versions of Windows NT, you'll discover that this is not the case. For example, if you install the Greek version of Windows NT, the American English, German, Greek, and Russian keyboards will generate the same Unicode character codes as the American version of Windows NT. However, the Greek version of Windows NT will not display German-accented characters or Russian characters because these characters are not in the Greek system font. Similarly, the Russian version of Windows NT will not display the German-accented characters or Greek characters because these characters are not in the Russian system font.

Where the Unicode version of KEYVIEW1 makes the most dramatic difference is under the Japanese version of Windows NT. You enter Japanese characters from the IME and they display correctly. The only problem is formatting: because the Japanese characters are often visually complex, they are displayed twice as wide as other characters.

TrueType and Big Fonts

The bitmap fonts that we've been using (with the exception of the fonts in the Japanese version of Windows) contain a maximum of 256 characters. This is to be expected, because the format of the bitmap font file goes back to the early days of Windows when character codes were assumed to be mere 8-bit values. That's why when we use the SYSTEM_FONT or the SYSTEM_FIXED_FONT, there are always some characters from some languages that we can't display properly. (The Japanese system font is a bit different because it's a double-byte character set; most of the characters are actually stored in TrueType Collection files with a filename extension of .TCC.)

TrueType fonts can contain more than 256 characters. Not all TrueType fonts have more than 256 characters, but the ones shipped with Windows 98 and Windows NT do. Or rather, they do if you've installed multilanguage support. In the Add/Remove Programs applet of the Control Panel, click the Windows Setup tab and make sure Multilanguage

Support is checked. This multilanguage support involves five character sets: Baltic, Central European, Cyrillic, Greek, and Turkish. The Baltic character set is used for Estonian, Latvian, and Lithuanian. The Central European character set is used for Albanian, Czech, Croatian, Hungarian, Polish, Romanian, Slovak, and Slovenian. The Cyrillic character set is used for Bulgarian, Belarusian, Russian, Serbian, and Ukrainian.

The TrueType fonts shipped with Windows 98 support those five character sets, plus the Western European (ANSI) character set that is used for virtually all other languages except those in the Far East (Chinese, Japanese, and Korean). TrueType fonts that support multiple character sets are sometimes referred to as "big fonts." The word "big" in this context does not refer to the size of the characters, but to their quantity.

You can take advantage of big fonts even in a non-Unicode program, which means that you can use big fonts to display characters in several different alphabets. However, you need to go beyond the *GetStockObject* function in obtaining a font to select into a device context.

The functions *CreateFont* and *CreateFontIndirect* create a logical font, similar to the way *CreatePen* creates a logical pen and *CreateBrush* creates a logical brush. *CreateFont* has 14 arguments that describe the font you want to create. *CreateFontIndirect* has one argument, but that argument is a pointer to a LOGFONT structure, which has 14 fields that correspond to the arguments of the *CreateFont* function. I'll discuss these functions in more detail in Chapter 17. For now, we'll look at the *CreateFont* function, but we'll focus on only a couple arguments. All the other arguments can be set to zero.

If you need a fixed-pitch font (as we've been using for the KEYVIEW1 program), set the thirteenth argument to *CreateFont* to FIXED_PITCH. If you need a font of a nondefault character set (as we will be needing), set the ninth argument to *CreateFont* to something called the "character set ID." This character set ID will be one of the following values defined in WINGDI.H. I've added comments that indicate the code pages associated with these character sets:

```
#define ANSI_CHARSET            0       // 1252 Latin 1 (ANSI)
#define DEFAULT_CHARSET         1
#define SYMBOL_CHARSET          2
#define MAC_CHARSET             77
#define SHIFTJIS_CHARSET        128     // 932 (DBCS, Japanese)
#define HANGEUL_CHARSET         129     // 949 (DBCS, Korean)
#define HANGUL_CHARSET          129     // "                   "
#define JOHAB_CHARSET           130     // 1361 (DBCS, Korean)
#define GB2312_CHARSET          134     // 936 (DBCS, Simplified Chinese)
#define CHINESEBIG5_CHARSET     136     // 950 (DBCS, Traditional Chinese)
#define GREEK_CHARSET           161     // 1253 Greek
#define TURKISH_CHARSET         162     // 1254 Latin 5 (Turkish)
#define VIETNAMESE_CHARSET      163     // 1258 Vietnamese
#define HEBREW_CHARSET          177     // 1255 Hebrew
#define ARABIC_CHARSET          178     // 1256 Arabic
```

(continued)

```
#define BALTIC_CHARSET              186      // 1257 Baltic Rim
#define RUSSIAN_CHARSET             204      // 1251 Cyrillic (Slavic)
#define THAI_CHARSET                222      // 874 Thai
#define EASTEUROPE_CHARSET          238      // 1250 Latin 2 (Central Europe)
#define OEM_CHARSET                 255      // Depends on country
```

Why does Windows have two different numbers—a character set ID and a code page ID—to refer to the same character sets? It's just one of the confusing quirks in Windows. Notice that the character set ID requires only 1 byte of storage, which is the size of the character set field in the LOGFONT structure. (Back in the Windows 1.0 days, memory and storage space were limited and every byte counted.) Notice that many different MS-DOS code pages are used in other countries, but only one character set ID—OEM_CHARSET— is used to refer to the MS-DOS character set.

You'll also notice that these character set values agree with the "CharSet" value shown on the top line of the STOKFONT program. In the American English version of Windows, we saw stock fonts that had character set IDs of 0 (ANSI_CHARSET) and 255 (OEM_CHAR-SET). We saw 161 (GREEK_CHARSET) in the Greek version of Windows, 204 (RUSSIAN_ CHARSET) in the Russian version, and 128 (SHIFTJIS_CHARSET) in the Japanese version.

In the code above, DBCS stands for double-byte character set, which is used in the Far East versions of Windows. Other versions of Windows do not support DBCS fonts, so you can't use those character set IDs.

CreateFont returns an HFONT value—a handle to a logical font. You can select this font into a device context using *SelectObject*. You must eventually delete every logical font you create by calling *DeleteObject*.

The other part of the big font solution is the WM_INPUTLANGCHANGE message. Whenever you change the keyboard layout using the popup menu in the desktop tray, Windows sends your window procedure the WM_INPUTLANGCHANGE message. The *wParam* message parameter is the character set ID of the new keyboard layout.

The KEYVIEW2 program shown in Figure 6-12 implements logic to change the font whenever the keyboard layout changes.

KEYVIEW2.C

```
/*-----------------------------------------------------------
   KEYVIEW2.C -- Displays Keyboard and Character Messages
                 (c) Charles Petzold, 1998
   -----------------------------------------------------------*/

#include <windows.h>

LRESULT CALLBACK WndProc (HWND, UINT, WPARAM, LPARAM) ;
```

Figure 6-12. *The KEYVIEW2 program.*

```
int WINAPI WinMain (HINSTANCE hInstance, HINSTANCE hPrevInstance,
                    PSTR szCmdLine, int iCmdShow)
{
     static TCHAR szAppName[] = TEXT ("KeyView2") ;
     HWND         hwnd ;
     MSG          msg ;
     WNDCLASS     wndclass ;

     wndclass.style         = CS_HREDRAW | CS_VREDRAW ;
     wndclass.lpfnWndProc   = WndProc ;
     wndclass.cbClsExtra    = 0 ;
     wndclass.cbWndExtra    = 0 ;
     wndclass.hInstance     = hInstance ;
     wndclass.hIcon         = LoadIcon (NULL, IDI_APPLICATION) ;
     wndclass.hCursor       = LoadCursor (NULL, IDC_ARROW) ;
     wndclass.hbrBackground = (HBRUSH) GetStockObject (WHITE_BRUSH) ;
     wndclass.lpszMenuName  = NULL ;
     wndclass.lpszClassName = szAppName ;

     if (!RegisterClass (&wndclass))
     {
          MessageBox (NULL, TEXT ("This program requires Windows NT!"),
                      szAppName, MB_ICONERROR) ;
          return 0 ;
     }

     hwnd = CreateWindow (szAppName, TEXT ("Keyboard Message Viewer #2"),
                          WS_OVERLAPPEDWINDOW,
                          CW_USEDEFAULT, CW_USEDEFAULT,
                          CW_USEDEFAULT, CW_USEDEFAULT,
                          NULL, NULL, hInstance, NULL) ;

     ShowWindow (hwnd, iCmdShow) ;
     UpdateWindow (hwnd) ;

     while (GetMessage (&msg, NULL, 0, 0))
     {
          TranslateMessage (&msg) ;
          DispatchMessage (&msg) ;
     }
     return msg.wParam ;
}

LRESULT CALLBACK WndProc (HWND hwnd, UINT message, WPARAM wParam, LPARAM lParam)
```

(continued)

Figure 6-12. *continued*

```
{
    static DWORD dwCharSet = DEFAULT_CHARSET ;
    static int   cxClientMax, cyClientMax, cxClient, cyClient, cxChar, cyChar ;
    static int   cLinesMax, cLines ;
    static PMSG  pmsg ;
    static RECT  rectScroll ;
    static TCHAR szTop[] = TEXT ("Message           Key        Char      ")
                           TEXT ("Repeat Scan Ext ALT Prev Tran") ;
    static TCHAR szUnd[] = TEXT ("_____           ___        ____      ")
                           TEXT ("_____ ____ ___ ___ ____ ____") ;

    static TCHAR * szFormat[2] = {

            TEXT ("%-13s %3d %-15s%c%6u %4d %3s %3s %4s %4s"),
            TEXT ("%-13s          0x%04X%1s%c %6u %4d %3s %3s %4s %4s") } ;

    static TCHAR * szYes  = TEXT ("Yes") ;
    static TCHAR * szNo   = TEXT ("No") ;
    static TCHAR * szDown = TEXT ("Down") ;
    static TCHAR * szUp   = TEXT ("Up") ;

    static TCHAR * szMessage [] = {
                    TEXT ("WM_KEYDOWN"),    TEXT ("WM_KEYUP"),
                    TEXT ("WM_CHAR"),       TEXT ("WM_DEADCHAR"),
                    TEXT ("WM_SYSKEYDOWN"), TEXT ("WM_SYSKEYUP"),
                    TEXT ("WM_SYSCHAR"),    TEXT ("WM_SYSDEADCHAR") } ;
    HDC         hdc ;
    int         i, iType ;
    PAINTSTRUCT ps ;
    TCHAR       szBuffer[128], szKeyName [32] ;
    TEXTMETRIC  tm ;

    switch (message)
    {
    case WM_INPUTLANGCHANGE:
        dwCharSet = wParam ;
                                    // fall through
    case WM_CREATE:
    case WM_DISPLAYCHANGE:

            // Get maximum size of client area

        cxClientMax = GetSystemMetrics (SM_CXMAXIMIZED) ;
        cyClientMax = GetSystemMetrics (SM_CYMAXIMIZED) ;

            // Get character size for fixed-pitch font
```

```
        hdc = GetDC (hwnd) ;

        SelectObject (hdc, CreateFont (0, 0, 0, 0, 0, 0, 0, 0,
                            dwCharSet, 0, 0, 0, FIXED_PITCH, NULL)) ;

        GetTextMetrics (hdc, &tm) ;
        cxChar = tm.tmAveCharWidth ;
        cyChar = tm.tmHeight ;

        DeleteObject (SelectObject (hdc, GetStockObject (SYSTEM_FONT))) ;
        ReleaseDC (hwnd, hdc) ;

            // Allocate memory for display lines

        if (pmsg)
            free (pmsg) ;

        cLinesMax = cyClientMax / cyChar ;
        pmsg = malloc (cLinesMax * sizeof (MSG)) ;
        cLines = 0 ;
                                // fall through
case WM_SIZE:
        if (message == WM_SIZE)
        {
            cxClient = LOWORD (lParam) ;
            cyClient = HIWORD (lParam) ;
        }
            // Calculate scrolling rectangle

        rectScroll.left   = 0 ;
        rectScroll.right  = cxClient ;
        rectScroll.top    = cyChar ;
        rectScroll.bottom = cyChar * (cyClient / cyChar) ;

        InvalidateRect (hwnd, NULL, TRUE) ;

        if (message == WM_INPUTLANGCHANGE)
            return TRUE ;

        return 0 ;

case WM_KEYDOWN:
case WM_KEYUP:
case WM_CHAR:
case WM_DEADCHAR:
case WM_SYSKEYDOWN:
```

(continued)

Figure 6-12. *continued*

```
case WM_SYSKEYUP:
case WM_SYSCHAR:
case WM_SYSDEADCHAR:

          // Rearrange storage array

     for (i = cLinesMax - 1 ; i > 0 ; i--)
     {
          pmsg[i] = pmsg[i - 1] ;
     }
          // Store new message

     pmsg[0].hwnd = hwnd ;
     pmsg[0].message = message ;
     pmsg[0].wParam = wParam ;
     pmsg[0].lParam = lParam ;

     cLines = min (cLines + 1, cLinesMax) ;

          // Scroll up the display

     ScrollWindow (hwnd, 0, -cyChar, &rectScroll, &rectScroll) ;

     break ;          // ie, call DefWindowProc so Sys messages work

case WM_PAINT:
     hdc = BeginPaint (hwnd, &ps) ;

     SelectObject (hdc, CreateFont (0, 0, 0, 0, 0, 0, 0, 0,
                              dwCharSet, 0, 0, 0, FIXED_PITCH, NULL)) ;

     SetBkMode (hdc, TRANSPARENT) ;
     TextOut (hdc, 0, 0, szTop, lstrlen (szTop)) ;
     TextOut (hdc, 0, 0, szUnd, lstrlen (szUnd)) ;

     for (i = 0 ; i < min (cLines, cyClient / cyChar - 1) ; i++)
     {
          iType = pmsg[i].message == WM_CHAR ||
                  pmsg[i].message == WM_SYSCHAR ||
                  pmsg[i].message == WM_DEADCHAR ||
                  pmsg[i].message == WM_SYSDEADCHAR ;

          GetKeyNameText (pmsg[i].lParam, szKeyName,
                     sizeof (szKeyName) / sizeof (TCHAR)) ;

          TextOut (hdc, 0, (cyClient / cyChar - 1 - i) * cyChar, szBuffer,
                 wsprintf (szBuffer, szFormat [iType],
```

```
                                   szMessage [pmsg[i].message -
WM_KEYFIRST],

                                   pmsg[i].wParam,
                                   (PTSTR) (iType ? TEXT (" ") : szKeyName),
                                   (TCHAR) (iType ? pmsg[i].wParam : ' '),
                                   LOWORD (pmsg[i].lParam),
                                   HIWORD (pmsg[i].lParam) & 0xFF,
                                   0x01000000 & pmsg[i].lParam ? szYes  : szNo,
                                   0x20000000 & pmsg[i].lParam ? szYes  : szNo,
                                   0x40000000 & pmsg[i].lParam ? szDown : szUp,
                                   0x80000000 & pmsg[i].lParam ? szUp   : szDown)) ;
          }
          DeleteObject (SelectObject (hdc, GetStockObject (SYSTEM_FONT))) ;
          EndPaint (hwnd, &ps) ;
          return 0 ;

     case WM_DESTROY:
          PostQuitMessage (0) ;
          return 0 ;
     }
     return DefWindowProc (hwnd, message, wParam, lParam) ;
}
```

Notice that KEYVIEW2 clears the screen and reallocates its storage space whenever the keyboard input language changes. There are two reasons for this: First, because KEYVIEW2 isn't being specific about the font it wants, the size of the font characters can change when the input language changes. The program needs to recalculate some variables based on the new character size. Second, KEYVIEW2 doesn't retain the character set ID in effect at the time it receives each character message. Thus, if the keyboard input language changed and KEYVIEW2 needed to redraw its client area, all the characters would be displayed with the new font.

I'll discuss fonts and character sets more in Chapter 17. If you'd like to research internationalization issues more, you can find documentation at */Platform SDK/Windows Base Services/International Features*, but much essential information is also located in */Platform SDK/Windows Base Services/General Library/String Manipulation*.

THE CARET (NOT THE CURSOR)

When you type text into a program, generally a little underline, vertical bar, or box shows you where the next character you type will appear on the screen. You may know this as a "cursor," but you'll have to get out of that habit when programming for Windows. In Windows, it's called the "caret." The word "cursor" is reserved for the little bitmap image that represents the mouse position.

The Caret Functions

There are five essential caret functions:

- *CreateCaret* Creates a caret associated with a window.

- *SetCaretPos* Sets the position of the caret within the window.

- *ShowCaret* Shows the caret.

- *HideCaret* Hides the caret.

- *DestroyCaret* Destroys the caret.

There are also functions to get the current caret position (*GetCaretPos*) and to get and set the caret blink time (*GetCaretBlinkTime* and *SetCaretBlinkTime*).

In Windows, the caret is customarily a horizontal line or box that is the size of a character, or a vertical line that is the height of a character. The vertical line caret is recommended when you use a proportional font such as the Windows default system font. Because the characters in a proportional font are not of a fixed size, the horizontal line or box can't be set to the size of a character.

If you need a caret in your program, you should not simply create it during the WM_CREATE message of your window procedure and destroy it during the WM_DESTROY message. The reason this is not advised is that a message queue can support only one caret. Thus, if your program has more than one window, the windows must effectively share the same caret.

This is not as restrictive as it sounds. When you think about it, the display of a caret in a window makes sense only when the window has the input focus. Indeed, the existence of a blinking caret is one of the visual cues that allows a user to recognize that he or she may type text into a program. Since only one window has the input focus at any time, it doesn't make sense for multiple windows to have carets blinking all at the same time.

A program can determine if it has the input focus by processing the WM_SETFOCUS and WM_KILLFOCUS messages. As the names imply, a window procedure receives a WM_SETFOCUS message when it receives the input focus and a WM_KILLFOCUS message when it loses the input focus. These messages occur in pairs: A window procedure will always receive a WM_SETFOCUS message before it receives a WM_KILLFOCUS message, and it always receives an equal number of WM_SETFOCUS and WM_KILLFOCUS messages over the course of the window's lifetime.

The main rule for using the caret is simple: a window procedure calls *CreateCaret* during the WM_SETFOCUS message and *DestroyWindow* during the WM_KILLFOCUS message.

There are a few other rules: The caret is created hidden. After calling *CreateCaret*, the window procedure must call *ShowCaret* for the caret to be visible. In addition, the window procedure must hide the caret by calling *HideCaret* whenever it draws something on its window during a message other than WM_PAINT. After it finishes drawing on the window, the program calls *ShowCaret* to display the caret again. The effect of *HideCaret* is additive: if you call *HideCaret* several times without calling *ShowCaret*, you must call *ShowCaret* the same number of times before the caret becomes visible again.

The TYPER Program

The TYPER program shown in Figure 6-13 brings together much of what we've learned in this chapter. You can think of TYPER as an extremely rudimentary text editor. You can type in the window, move the cursor (I mean caret) around with the cursor movement keys (or are they caret movement keys?), and erase the contents of the window by pressing Escape. The contents of the window are also erased when you resize the window or change the keyboard input language. There's no scrolling, no search and replace, no way to save files, no spelling checker, and no anthropomorphous paper clip, but it's a start.

TYPER.C

```
/*------------------------------------------
   TYPER.C -- Typing Program
              (c) Charles Petzold, 1998
   ------------------------------------------*/

#include <windows.h>

#define BUFFER(x,y) *(pBuffer + y * cxBuffer + x)

LRESULT CALLBACK WndProc (HWND, UINT, WPARAM, LPARAM) ;

int WINAPI WinMain (HINSTANCE hInstance, HINSTANCE hPrevInstance,
                    PSTR szCmdLine, int iCmdShow)
{
    static TCHAR szAppName[] = TEXT ("Typer") ;
    HWND         hwnd ;
    MSG          msg ;
    WNDCLASS     wndclass ;

    wndclass.style         = CS_HREDRAW | CS_VREDRAW ;
    wndclass.lpfnWndProc   = WndProc ;
    wndclass.cbClsExtra    = 0 ;
    wndclass.cbWndExtra    = 0 ;
    wndclass.hInstance     = hInstance ;
    wndclass.hIcon         = LoadIcon (NULL, IDI_APPLICATION) ;
    wndclass.hCursor       = LoadCursor (NULL, IDC_ARROW) ;
    wndclass.hbrBackground = (HBRUSH) GetStockObject (WHITE_BRUSH) ;
    wndclass.lpszMenuName  = NULL ;
    wndclass.lpszClassName = szAppName ;
```

Figure 6-13. *The TYPER program.*

(continued)

Figure 6-13. *continued*

```
    if (!RegisterClass (&wndclass))
    {
         MessageBox (NULL, TEXT ("This program requires Windows NT!"),
                     szAppName, MB_ICONERROR) ;
         return 0 ;
    }

    hwnd = CreateWindow (szAppName, TEXT ("Typing Program"),
                         WS_OVERLAPPEDWINDOW,
                         CW_USEDEFAULT, CW_USEDEFAULT,
                         CW_USEDEFAULT, CW_USEDEFAULT,
                         NULL, NULL, hInstance, NULL) ;

    ShowWindow (hwnd, iCmdShow) ;
    UpdateWindow (hwnd) ;

    while (GetMessage (&msg, NULL, 0, 0))
    {
         TranslateMessage (&msg) ;
         DispatchMessage (&msg) ;
    }
    return msg.wParam ;
}

LRESULT CALLBACK WndProc (HWND hwnd, UINT message, WPARAM wParam, LPARAM lParam)
{
    static DWORD   dwCharSet = DEFAULT_CHARSET ;
    static int     cxChar, cyChar, cxClient, cyClient, cxBuffer, cyBuffer,
                   xCaret, yCaret ;
    static TCHAR * pBuffer = NULL ;
    HDC            hdc ;
    int            x, y, i ;
    PAINTSTRUCT    ps ;
    TEXTMETRIC     tm ;

    switch (message)
    {
    case WM_INPUTLANGCHANGE:
         dwCharSet = wParam ;
                                         // fall through
    case WM_CREATE:
         hdc = GetDC (hwnd) ;
         SelectObject (hdc, CreateFont (0, 0, 0, 0, 0, 0, 0, 0,
                              dwCharSet, 0, 0, 0, FIXED_PITCH, NULL)) ;
```

```
        GetTextMetrics (hdc, &tm) ;
        cxChar = tm.tmAveCharWidth ;
        cyChar = tm.tmHeight ;

        DeleteObject (SelectObject (hdc, GetStockObject (SYSTEM_FONT))) ;
        ReleaseDC (hwnd, hdc) ;
                                        // fall through
case WM_SIZE:
             // obtain window size in pixels

        if (message == WM_SIZE)
        {
             cxClient = LOWORD (lParam) ;
             cyClient = HIWORD (lParam) ;
        }
             // calculate window size in characters

        cxBuffer = max (1, cxClient / cxChar) ;
        cyBuffer = max (1, cyClient / cyChar) ;

             // allocate memory for buffer and clear it

        if (pBuffer != NULL)
             free (pBuffer) ;

        pBuffer = (TCHAR *) malloc (cxBuffer * cyBuffer * sizeof (TCHAR)) ;

        for (y = 0 ; y < cyBuffer ; y++)
             for (x = 0 ; x < cxBuffer ; x++)
                  BUFFER(x,y) = ' ' ;

             // set caret to upper left corner

        xCaret = 0 ;
        yCaret = 0 ;

        if (hwnd == GetFocus ())
             SetCaretPos (xCaret * cxChar, yCaret * cyChar) ;

        InvalidateRect (hwnd, NULL, TRUE) ;
        return 0 ;

case WM_SETFOCUS:
             // create and show the caret
```

(continued)

Figure 6-13. *continued*

```
        CreateCaret (hwnd, NULL, cxChar, cyChar) ;
        SetCaretPos (xCaret * cxChar, yCaret * cyChar) ;
        ShowCaret (hwnd) ;
        return 0 ;

case WM_KILLFOCUS:
            // hide and destroy the caret

        HideCaret (hwnd) ;
        DestroyCaret () ;
        return 0 ;

case WM_KEYDOWN:
        switch (wParam)
        {
        case VK_HOME:
            xCaret = 0 ;
            break ;

        case VK_END:
            xCaret = cxBuffer - 1 ;
            break ;

        case VK_PRIOR:
            yCaret = 0 ;
            break ;

        case VK_NEXT:
            yCaret = cyBuffer - 1 ;
            break ;

        case VK_LEFT:
            xCaret = max (xCaret - 1, 0) ;
            break ;

        case VK_RIGHT:
            xCaret = min (xCaret + 1, cxBuffer - 1) ;
            break ;

        case VK_UP:
            yCaret = max (yCaret - 1, 0) ;
            break ;

        case VK_DOWN:
            yCaret = min (yCaret + 1, cyBuffer - 1) ;
            break ;
```

```
      case VK_DELETE:
           for (x = xCaret ; x < cxBuffer - 1 ; x++)
                BUFFER (x, yCaret) = BUFFER (x + 1, yCaret) ;

           BUFFER (cxBuffer - 1, yCaret) = ' ' ;

           HideCaret (hwnd) ;
           hdc = GetDC (hwnd) ;

           SelectObject (hdc, CreateFont (0, 0, 0, 0, 0, 0, 0, 0,
                                dwCharSet, 0, 0, 0, FIXED_PITCH, NULL)) ;

           TextOut (hdc, xCaret * cxChar, yCaret * cyChar,
                    & BUFFER (xCaret, yCaret),
                    cxBuffer - xCaret) ;

           DeleteObject (SelectObject (hdc, GetStockObject (SYSTEM_FONT))) ;
           ReleaseDC (hwnd, hdc) ;
           ShowCaret (hwnd) ;
           break ;
      }
      SetCaretPos (xCaret * cxChar, yCaret * cyChar) ;
      return 0 ;

case WM_CHAR:
      for (i = 0 ; i < (int) LOWORD (lParam) ; i++)
      {
           switch (wParam)
           {
           case '\b':                       // backspace
                if (xCaret > 0)
                {
                     xCaret-- ;
                     SendMessage (hwnd, WM_KEYDOWN, VK_DELETE, 1) ;
                }
                break ;

           case '\t':                       // tab
                do
                {
                     SendMessage (hwnd, WM_CHAR, ' ', 1) ;
                }
                while (xCaret % 8 != 0) ;
                break ;
```

(continued)

Figure 6-13. *continued*

```
            case '\n':                      // line feed
                if (++yCaret == cyBuffer)
                    yCaret = 0 ;
                break ;

            case '\r':                      // carriage return
                xCaret = 0 ;

                if (++yCaret == cyBuffer)
                    yCaret = 0 ;
                break ;

            case '\x1B':                     // escape
                for (y = 0 ; y < cyBuffer ; y++)
                    for (x = 0 ; x < cxBuffer ; x++)
                        BUFFER (x, y) = ' ' ;

                xCaret = 0 ;
                yCaret = 0 ;

                InvalidateRect (hwnd, NULL, FALSE) ;
                break ;

            default:                         // character codes
                BUFFER (xCaret, yCaret) = (TCHAR) wParam ;

                HideCaret (hwnd) ;
                hdc = GetDC (hwnd) ;

                SelectObject (hdc, CreateFont (0, 0, 0, 0, 0, 0, 0, 0,
                            dwCharSet, 0, 0, 0, FIXED_PITCH, NULL)) ;

                TextOut (hdc, xCaret * cxChar, yCaret * cyChar,
                        & BUFFER (xCaret, yCaret), 1) ;

                DeleteObject (
                    SelectObject (hdc, GetStockObject (SYSTEM_FONT))) ;
                ReleaseDC (hwnd, hdc) ;
                ShowCaret (hwnd) ;

                if (++xCaret == cxBuffer)
                {
                    xCaret = 0 ;
```

```
                       if (++yCaret == cyBuffer)
                            yCaret = 0 ;
                  }
             break ;
        }
   }

   SetCaretPos (xCaret * cxChar, yCaret * cyChar) ;
   return 0 ;

case WM_PAINT:
   hdc = BeginPaint (hwnd, &ps) ;

   SelectObject (hdc, CreateFont (0, 0, 0, 0, 0, 0, 0, 0,
                          dwCharSet, 0, 0, 0, FIXED_PITCH, NULL)) ;

   for (y = 0 ; y < cyBuffer ; y++)
        TextOut (hdc, 0, y * cyChar, & BUFFER(0,y), cxBuffer) ;

   DeleteObject (SelectObject (hdc, GetStockObject (SYSTEM_FONT))) ;
   EndPaint (hwnd, &ps) ;
   return 0 ;

case WM_DESTROY:
   PostQuitMessage (0) ;
   return 0 ;
}
return DefWindowProc (hwnd, message, wParam, lParam) ;
}
```

To keep things reasonably simple, TYPER uses a fixed-pitch font. Writing a text editor for a proportional font is, as you might imagine, much more difficult. The program obtains a device context in several places: during the WM_CREATE message, the WM_KEYDOWN message, the WM_CHAR message, and the WM_PAINT message. Each time, calls to *GetStockObject* and *SelectObject* select a fixed-pitch font with the current character set.

During the WM_SIZE message, TYPER calculates the character width and height of the window and saves these values in the variables *cxBuffer* and *cyBuffer*. It then uses *malloc* to allocate a buffer to hold all the characters that can be typed in the window. Notice that the size of this buffer in bytes is the product of *cxBuffer*, *cyBuffer*, and *sizeof (TCHAR)*, which can be 1 or 2 depending on whether the program is compiled for 8-bit character processing or Unicode.

The *xCaret* and *yCaret* variables store the character position of the caret. During the WM_SETFOCUS message, TYPER calls *CreateCaret* to create a caret that is the width and height of a character. It then calls *SetCaretPos* to set the caret position and *ShowCaret* to make the caret visible. During the WM_KILLFOCUS message, TYPER calls *HideCaret* and *DestroyCaret*.

The WM_KEYDOWN processing mostly involves the cursor movement keys. Home and End send the caret to the beginning and end of a line, and Page Up and Page Down send the caret to the top and bottom of the window. The arrow keys work as you would expect. For the Delete key, TYPER must move everything remaining in the buffer from the next caret position to the end of the line and then display a blank space at the end of the line.

The WM_CHAR processing handles the Backspace, Tab, Linefeed (Ctrl-Enter), Enter, Escape, and character keys. Notice that I've used Repeat Count in *lParam* when processing the WM_CHAR message (under the assumption that every character the user types is important) but not during the WM_KEYDOWN message (to prevent inadvertent over-scrolling). The Backspace and Tab processing is simplified somewhat by the use of the *SendMessage* function. Backspace is emulated by the Delete logic, and Tab is emulated by a series of spaces.

As I mentioned earlier, a program should hide the caret when drawing on the window during messages other than WM_PAINT. TYPER does this when processing the WM_ KEYDOWN message for the Delete key and the WM_CHAR message for character keys. In both these cases, TYPER alters the contents of the buffer and then draws the new character or characters on the window.

Although TYPER uses the same logic as KEYVIEW2 to switch between character sets as the user switches keyboard layouts, it does not work quite right for Far Eastern versions of Windows. TYPER does not make any allowance for the double-width characters. This raises issues that are better covered in Chapter 17, which explores fonts and text output in more detail.

Chapter 7

The Mouse

The mouse is a pointing device with one or more buttons. Despite much experimentation with other alternative input devices such as touch screens and light pens, the mouse reigns supreme. Together with variations such as trackballs, which are common on laptop computers, the mouse is the only alternative input device to achieve a massive—virtually universal—penetration in the PC market.

This was not always the case. Indeed, the early developers of Microsoft Windows felt that they shouldn't require users to buy a mouse in order to use the product. So they made the mouse an optional accessory and provided a keyboard interface to all operations in Windows and the "applets" distributed with Windows. (For example, check out the help information for the Windows Calculator to see how each button is obsessively assigned a keyboard equivalent.) Third-party software developers were also encouraged to duplicate mouse functions with a keyboard interface in their applications. The early editions of this book attempted to further disseminate this philosophy.

In theory, Windows now requires a mouse. At least that's what the box says. However, you can unplug your mouse and Windows will boot up fine (aside from a message box informing you that a mouse is not attached). Trying to use Windows without the mouse is akin to playing the piano with your toes (at least initially), but you can definitely do it. For that reason, I still like the idea of providing keyboard equivalents for mouse actions. Touch typists in particular prefer keeping their hands on the keyboard, and I suppose everyone has had the experience of "losing" a mouse on a cluttered desk or having a mouse too clogged up with mouse gunk to work well. The keyboard equivalents usually don't cost much in terms of thought or effort, and they can deliver more functionality to users who prefer them.

Just as the keyboard is usually identified with entering and manipulating text data, the mouse is identified with drawing and manipulating graphical objects. Indeed, most of the sample programs in this chapter draw some graphics, putting to use what we learned in Chapter 5.

MOUSE BASICS

Windows 98 can support a one-button, two-button, or three-button mouse, or it can use a joystick or light pen to mimic a mouse. In the early days, Windows applications avoided the use of the second or third buttons in deference to users who had a one-button mouse. However, the two-button mouse has become the de facto standard, so the traditional reticence to use the second button is no longer justified. Indeed, the second button is now the standard for invoking a "context menu," which is a menu that appears in a window outside the normal menu bar, or for special dragging operations. (Dragging will be explained shortly.) However, programs should not rely upon the presence of a two-button mouse.

In theory, you can determine if a mouse is present by using our old friend the *GetSystemMetrics* function:

```
fMouse = GetSystemMetrics (SM_MOUSEPRESENT) ;
```

The value of *fMouse* will be TRUE (nonzero) if a mouse is installed and 0 if a mouse is not installed. However, in Windows 98 this function always returns TRUE whether a mouse is attached or not. In Microsoft Windows NT, it works correctly.

To determine the number of buttons on the installed mouse, use

```
cButtons = GetSystemMetrics (SM_CMOUSEBUTTONS) ;
```

This function should also return 0 if a mouse is not installed. However, under Windows 98 the function returns 2 if a mouse is not installed.

Left-handed users can switch the mouse buttons using the Windows Control Panel. Although an application can determine whether this has been done by calling *GetSystemMetrics* with the SM_SWAPBUTTON parameter, this is not usually necessary. The button triggered by the index finger is considered to be the left button, even if it's physically on the right side of the mouse. However, in a training program, you might want to draw a mouse on the screen, and in that case, you might want to know if the mouse buttons have been swapped.

You can set other mouse parameters in the Control Panel, such as the double-click speed. From a Windows application you can set or obtain this information using the *SystemParametersInfo* function.

Some Quick Definitions

When the Windows user moves the mouse, Windows moves a small bitmapped picture on the display. This is called the "mouse cursor." The mouse cursor has a single-pixel "hot spot" that points to a precise location on the display. When I refer to the position of the mouse cursor on the screen, I really mean the position of the hot spot.

Windows supports several predefined mouse cursors that programs can use. The most common is the slanted arrow named IDC_ARROW (using the identifier defined in WINUSER.H).

The hot spot is the tip of the arrow. The IDC_CROSS cursor (used in the BLOKOUT programs shown later in this chapter) has a hot spot in the center of a crosshair pattern. The IDC_WAIT cursor is an hourglass generally used by programs to indicate they are busy. Programmers can also design their own cursors. You'll learn how in Chapter 10. The default cursor for a particular window is specified when defining the window class structure, for instance:

```
wndclass.hCursor = LoadCursor (NULL, IDC_ARROW) ;
```

The following terms describe the actions you take with mouse buttons:

- *Clicking* Pressing and releasing a mouse button.

- *Double-clicking* Pressing and releasing a mouse button twice in quick succession.

- *Dragging* Moving the mouse while holding down a button.

On a three-button mouse, the buttons are called the left button, the middle button, and the right button. Mouse-related identifiers defined in the Windows header files use the abbreviations LBUTTON, MBUTTON, and RBUTTON. A two-button mouse has only a left button and a right button. The single button on a one-button mouse is a left button.

The Plural of Mouse Is...

And now, to demonstrate my bravery, I will confront one of the most perplexing issues in the field of alternative input devices: what is the plural of "mouse"?

Although everyone knows that multiple rodents are called mice, no one seems to have a definitive answer for what we call multiple input devices. Neither "mice" nor "mouses" sounds quite right. My customary reference—the third edition of the *American Heritage Dictionary of the English Language*—says that either is acceptable (with "mice" preferred), while the third edition of the *Microsoft Press Computer Dictionary* avoids the issue entirely.

The book *Wired Style: Principles of English Usage in the Digital Age* (HardWired, 1996) by the editors of *Wired* magazine indicates that "mouses" is preferred to avoid confusion with rodents. Doug Engelbart, who invented the mouse in 1964, is of no help at all in resolving this issue. I once asked him about the plural of mouse and so did the editors of *Wired*. He says he doesn't know.

Finally, with an air of high authority, the *Microsoft Manual of Style for Technical Publications* instructs us to "Avoid using the plural *mice*; if you need to refer to more than one mouse, use *mouse devices*." This may sound like a cop-out, but it's really quite sensible advice when neither plural sounds right. Indeed, most sentences that might require a plural for "mouse" can be recast to avoid it. For example, rather than saying "People use mice almost as much as keyboards," try "People use the mouse almost as much as the keyboard."

CLIENT-AREA MOUSE MESSAGES

In the previous chapter, you saw how Windows sends keyboard messages only to the window that has the input focus. Mouse messages are different: a window procedure receives mouse messages whenever the mouse passes over the window or is clicked within the window, even if the window is not active or does not have the input focus. Windows defines 21 messages for the mouse. However, 11 of these messages do not relate to the client area. These are called "nonclient-area messages," and Windows applications usually ignore them.

When the mouse is moved over the client area of a window, the window procedure receives the message WM_MOUSEMOVE. When a mouse button is pressed or released within the client area of a window, the window procedure receives the messages in this table:

Button	Pressed	Released	Pressed (Second Click)
Left	WM_LBUTTONDOWN	WM_LBUTTONUP	WM_LBUTTONDBLCLK
Middle	WM_MBUTTONDOWN	WM_MBUTTONUP	WM_MBUTTONDBLCLK
Right	WM_RBUTTONDOWN	WM_RBUTTONUP	WM_RBUTTONDBLCLK

Your window procedure receives MBUTTON messages only for a three-button mouse and RBUTTON messages only for a two-button mouse. The window procedure receives DBLCLK (double-click) messages only if the window class has been defined to receive them (as described on page 283 in the section titled "Mouse Double-Clicks").

For all these messages, the value of *lParam* contains the position of the mouse. The low word is the *x*-coordinate, and the high word is the *y*-coordinate relative to the upper left corner of the client area of the window. You can extract these values using the LOWORD and HIWORD macros:

```
x = LOWORD (1Param) ;
y = HIWORD (1Param) ;
```

The value of *wParam* indicates the state of the mouse buttons and the Shift and Ctrl keys. You can test *wParam* using these bit masks defined in the WINUSER.H header file. The MK prefix stands for "mouse key."

MK_LBUTTON	Left button is down
MK_MBUTTON	Middle button is down
MK_RBUTTON	Right button is down
MK_SHIFT	Shift key is down
MK_CONTROL	Ctrl key is down

For example, if you receive a WM_LBUTTONDOWN message, and if the value

```
wparam & MK_SHIFT
```

is TRUE (nonzero), you know that the Shift key was down when the left button was pressed.

As you move the mouse over the client area of a window, Windows does not generate a WM_MOUSEMOVE message for every possible pixel position of the mouse. The number of WM_MOUSEMOVE messages your program receives depends on the mouse hardware and on the speed at which your window procedure can process the mouse movement messages. In other words, Windows does not fill up a message queue with unprocessed WM_MOUSEMOVE messages. You'll get a good idea of the rate of WM_MOUSEMOVE messages when you experiment with the CONNECT program described below.

If you click the left mouse button in the client area of an inactive window, Windows changes the active window to the window that is being clicked and then passes the WM_LBUTTONDOWN message to the window procedure. When your window procedure gets a WM_LBUTTONDOWN message, your program can safely assume the window is active. However, your window procedure can receive a WM_LBUTTONUP message without first receiving a WM_LBUTTONDOWN message. This can happen if the mouse button is pressed in one window, moved to your window, and released. Similarly, the window procedure can receive a WM_LBUTTONDOWN without a corresponding WM_LBUTTONUP message if the mouse button is released while positioned over another window.

There are two exceptions to these rules:

- A window procedure can "capture the mouse" and continue to receive mouse messages even when the mouse is outside the window's client area. You'll learn how to capture the mouse later in this chapter.

- If a system modal message box or a system modal dialog box is on the display, no other program can receive mouse messages. System modal message boxes and dialog boxes prohibit switching to another window while the box is active. An example of a system modal message box is the one that appears when you shut down your Windows session.

Simple Mouse Processing: An Example

The CONNECT program, shown in Figure 7-1, does some simple mouse processing to let you get a good feel for how Windows sends mouse messages to your program.

CONNECT.C

```
/*------------------------------------------------
   CONNECT.C -- Connect-the-Dots Mouse Demo Program
                (c) Charles Petzold, 1998
   ------------------------------------------------*/

#include <windows.h>

#define MAXPOINTS 1000
```

Figure 7-1. *The CONNECT program.*

(continued)

Figure 7-1. *continued*

```
LRESULT CALLBACK WndProc (HWND, UINT, WPARAM, LPARAM) ;

int WINAPI WinMain (HINSTANCE hInstance, HINSTANCE hPrevInstance,
                    PSTR szCmdLine, int iCmdShow)
{
     static TCHAR szAppName[] = TEXT ("Connect") ;
     HWND         hwnd ;
     MSG          msg ;
     WNDCLASS     wndclass ;

     wndclass.style         = CS_HREDRAW | CS_VREDRAW ;
     wndclass.lpfnWndProc   = WndProc ;
     wndclass.cbClsExtra    = 0 ;
     wndclass.cbWndExtra    = 0 ;
     wndclass.hInstance     = hInstance ;
     wndclass.hIcon         = LoadIcon (NULL, IDI_APPLICATION) ;
     wndclass.hCursor       = LoadCursor (NULL, IDC_ARROW) ;
     wndclass.hbrBackground = (HBRUSH) GetStockObject (WHITE_BRUSH) ;
     wndclass.lpszMenuName  = NULL ;
     wndclass.lpszClassName = szAppName ;

     if (!RegisterClass (&wndclass))
     {
          MessageBox (NULL, TEXT ("Program requires Windows NT!"),
                      szAppName, MB_ICONERROR) ;
          return 0 ;
     }

     hwnd = CreateWindow (szAppName, TEXT ("Connect-the-Points Mouse Demo"),
                          WS_OVERLAPPEDWINDOW,
                          CW_USEDEFAULT, CW_USEDEFAULT,
                          CW_USEDEFAULT, CW_USEDEFAULT,
                          NULL, NULL, hInstance, NULL) ;

     ShowWindow (hwnd, iCmdShow) ;
     UpdateWindow (hwnd) ;

     while (GetMessage (&msg, NULL, 0, 0))
     {
          TranslateMessage (&msg) ;
          DispatchMessage (&msg) ;
     }

return msg.wParam ;
}

LRESULT CALLBACK WndProc (HWND hwnd, UINT message, WPARAM wParam, LPARAM lParam)
```

```
{
     static POINT  pt[MAXPOINTS] ;
     static int    iCount ;
     HDC           hdc ;
     int           i, j ;
     PAINTSTRUCT   ps ;

     switch (message)
     {
     case WM_LBUTTONDOWN:
          iCount = 0 ;
          InvalidateRect (hwnd, NULL, TRUE) ;
          return 0 ;

     case WM_MOUSEMOVE:
          if (wParam & MK_LBUTTON && iCount < 1000)
          {
               pt[iCount  ].x = LOWORD (lParam) ;
               pt[iCount++].y = HIWORD (lParam) ;

               hdc = GetDC (hwnd) ;
               SetPixel (hdc, LOWORD (lParam), HIWORD (lParam), 0) ;
               ReleaseDC (hwnd, hdc) ;
          }
          return 0 ;

     case WM_LBUTTONUP:
          InvalidateRect (hwnd, NULL, FALSE) ;
          return 0 ;

     case WM_PAINT:
          hdc = BeginPaint (hwnd, &ps) ;

          SetCursor (LoadCursor (NULL, IDC_WAIT)) ;
          ShowCursor (TRUE) ;

          for (i = 0 ; i < iCount - 1 ; i++)
               for (j = i + 1 ; j < iCount ; j++)
               {
                    MoveToEx (hdc, pt[i].x, pt[i].y, NULL) ;
                    LineTo   (hdc, pt[j].x, pt[j].y) ;
               }

          ShowCursor (FALSE) ;
          SetCursor (LoadCursor (NULL, IDC_ARROW)) ;
```

(continued)

Figure 7-1. *continued*

```
        EndPaint (hwnd, &ps) ;
        return 0 ;

    case WM_DESTROY:
        PostQuitMessage (0) ;
        return 0 ;
    }
    return DefWindowProc (hwnd, message, wParam, lParam) ;
}
```

CONNECT processes three mouse messages:

- *WM_LBUTTONDOWN* CONNECT clears the client area.

- *WM_MOUSEMOVE* If the left button is down, CONNECT draws a black dot on the client area at the mouse position and saves the coordinates.

- *WM_LBUTTONUP* CONNECT connects every dot shown in the client area to every other dot. Sometimes this results in a pretty design, sometimes in a dense blob. (See Figure 7-2.)

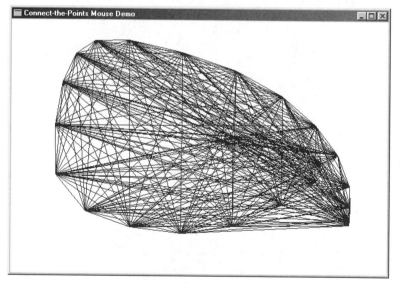

Figure 7-2. *The CONNECT display.*

To use CONNECT, bring the mouse cursor into the client area, press the left button, move the mouse around a little, and then release the left button. CONNECT works best for a curved pattern of a few dots, which you can draw by moving the mouse quickly while the left button is depressed.

CONNECT uses three GDI function calls that I discussed in Chapter 5: *SetPixel* draws a black pixel for each WM_MOUSEMOVE message when the left mouse button is depressed. (On high-resolution displays, these pixels might be nearly invisible.) Drawing the lines requires *MoveToEx* and *LineTo*.

If you move the mouse cursor out of the client area before releasing the button, CONNECT does not connect the dots because it doesn't receive the WM_LBUTTONUP message. If you move the mouse back into the client area and press the left button again, CONNECT clears the client area. If you want to continue a design after releasing the button outside the client area, press the left button again while the mouse is outside the client area and then move the mouse back inside.

CONNECT stores a maximum of 1000 points. If the number of points is P, the number of lines CONNECT draws is equal to $P \times (P - 1) / 2$. With 1000 points, this involves almost 500,000 lines, which might take a minute or so to draw, depending on your hardware. Because Windows 98 is a preemptive multitasking environment, you can switch to other programs at this time. However, you can't do anything else with the CONNECT program (such as move it or change the size) while the program is busy. In Chapter 20, we'll examine methods for dealing with problems such as this.

Because CONNECT might take some time to draw the lines, it switches to an hourglass cursor and then back again while processing the WM_PAINT message. This requires two calls to the *SetCursor* function using two stock cursors. CONNECT also calls *ShowCursor* twice, once with a TRUE parameter and the second time with a FALSE parameter. I'll discuss these calls in more detail later in this chapter, in the section "Emulating the Mouse with the Keyboard."

Sometimes the word "tracking" is used to refer to the way that programs process mouse movement. Tracking does not mean, however, that your program sits in a loop in its window procedure while attempting to follow the mouse's movements on the display. The window procedure instead processes each mouse message as it comes and then quickly returns control to Windows.

Processing Shift Keys

When CONNECT receives a WM_MOUSEMOVE message, it performs a bitwise AND operation on the value of *wParam* and MK_LBUTTON to determine if the left button is depressed. You can also use *wParam* to determine the state of the Shift keys. For instance, if processing must be dependent on the status of the Shift and Ctrl keys, you might use logic that looks like this:

```
if (wParam & MK_SHIFT)
{
     if (wParam & MK_CONTROL)
     {
          [Shift and Ctrl keys are down]
     }
     else
     {
          [Shift key is down]
     }
{
else
{
     if (wParam & MK_CONTROL]
     {
          [Ctrl key is down]
     }
     else
     {
          [neither Shift nor Ctrl key is down]
     }
}
```

If you want to use both the left and right mouse buttons in your program, and if you also want to accommodate those users with a one-button mouse, you can write your code so that Shift in combination with the left button is equivalent to the right button. In that case, your mouse button-click processing might look something like this:

```
case WM_LBUTTONDOWN:
     if (!(wParam & MK_SHIFT))
     {
          [left button logic]
          return 0 ;
     }
                    // Fall through
case WM_RBUTTONDOWN:
     [right button logic]
     return 0 ;
```

The Window function *GetKeyState* (described in Chapter 6) can also return the status of the mouse buttons or shift keys using the virtual key codes VK_LBUTTON, VK_RBUTTON, VK_MBUTTON, VK_SHIFT, and VK_CONTROL. The button or key is down if the value returned from *GetKeyState* is negative. Because *GetKeyState* returns mouse or key states as of the message currently being processed, the status information is properly synchronized with the messages. Just as you cannot use *GetKeyState* for a key that has yet to be pressed, you cannot use it for a mouse button that has yet to be pressed. Don't do this:

```
while (GetKeyState (VK_LBUTTON) >= 0) ;  // WRONG !!!
```

The *GetKeyState* function will report that the left button is depressed only if the button is already depressed when you process the message during which you call *GetKeyState*.

Mouse Double-Clicks

A mouse double-click is two clicks in quick succession. To qualify as a double-click, the two clicks must occur in close physical proximity of one another (by default, about an area as wide as an average system font character and half as high) and within a specific interval of time called the "double-click speed." You can change that time interval in the Control Panel.

If you want your window procedure to receive double-click mouse messages, you must include the identifier CS_DBLCLKS when initializing the style field in the window class structure before calling *RegisterClass*:

```
wndclass.style = CS_HREDRAW | CS_VREDRAW | CS_DBLCLKS ;
```

If you do *not* include CS_DBLCLKS in the window style and the user clicks the left mouse button twice in quick succession, your window procedure receives these messages:

WM_LBUTTONDOWN
WM_LBUTTONUP
WM_LBUTTONDOWN
WM_LBUTTONUP

The window procedure might also receive other messages between these button messages. If you want to implement your own double-click logic, you can use the Windows function *GetMessageTime* to obtain the relative times of the WM_LBUTTONDOWN messages. This function is discussed in more detail in Chapter 8.

If you include CS_DBLCLKS in your window class style, the window procedure receives these messages for a double-click:

WM_LBUTTONDOWN
WM_LBUTTONUP
WM_LBUTTONDBLCLK
WM_LBUTTONUP

The WM_LBUTTONDBLCLK message simply replaces the second WM_LBUTTONDOWN message.

Double-click messages are much easier to process if the first click of a double-click performs the same action as a single click. The second click (the WM_LBUTTONDBLCLK message) then does something in addition to the first click. For example, look at how the mouse works with the file lists in Windows Explorer. A single click selects the file.

Windows Explorer highlights the file with a reverse-video bar. A double-click performs two actions: the first click selects the file, just as a single click does; the second click directs Windows Explorer to open the file. That's fairly easy logic. Mouse-handling logic could get more complex if the first click of a double-click did not perform the same action as a single click.

NONCLIENT-AREA MOUSE MESSAGES

The 10 mouse messages discussed so far occur when the mouse is moved or clicked within the client area of a window. If the mouse is outside a window's client area but within the window, Windows sends the window procedure a "nonclient-area" mouse message. The nonclient area of a window includes the title bar, the menu, and the window scroll bars.

You do not usually need to process nonclient-area mouse messages. Instead, you simply pass them on to *DefWindowProc* so that Windows can perform system functions. In this respect, the nonclient-area mouse messages are similar to the system keyboard messages WM_SYSKEYDOWN, WM_SYSKEYUP, and WM_SYSCHAR.

The nonclient-area mouse messages parallel almost exactly the client-area mouse messages. The message identifiers include the letters "NC" to indicate "nonclient." If the mouse is moved within a nonclient area of a window, the window procedure receives the message WM_NCMOUSEMOVE. The mouse buttons generate these messages:

Button	*Pressed*	*Released*	*Pressed (Second Click)*
Left	WM_NCLBUTTONDOWN	WM_NCLBUTTONUP	WM_NCLBUTTONDBLCLK
Middle	WM_NCMBUTTONDOWN	WM_NCMBUTTONUP	WM_NCMBUTTONDBLCLK
Right	WM_NCRBUTTONDOWN	WM_NCRBUTTONUP	WM_NCRBUTTONDBLCLK

The *wParam* and *lParam* parameters for nonclient-area mouse messages are somewhat different from those for client-area mouse messages. The *wParam* parameter indicates the nonclient area where the mouse was moved or clicked. It is set to one of the identifiers beginning with HT (standing for "hit-test") that are defined in the WINUSER.H.

The *lParam* parameter contains an *x*-coordinate in the low word and a *y*-coordinate in the high word. However, these are screen coordinates, not client-area coordinates as they are for client-area mouse messages. For screen coordinates, the upper-left corner of the display area has *x* and *y* values of 0. Values of *x* increase as you move to the right, and values of *y* increase as you move down the screen. (See Figure 7-3.)

You can convert screen coordinates to client-area coordinates and vice versa with these two Windows functions:

```
ScreenToClient (hwnd, &pt) ;
ClientToScreen (hwnd, &pt) ;
```

where *pt* is a POINT structure. These two functions convert the values stored in the structure without preserving the old values. Note that if a screen-coordinate point is above or to the left of the window's client area, the *x* or *y* value of the client-area coordinate could be negative.

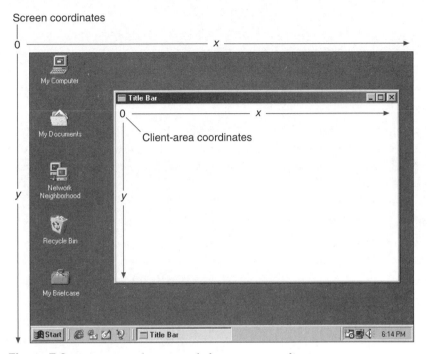

Figure 7-3. *Screen coordinates and client-area coordinates.*

The Hit-Test Message

If you've been keeping count, you know that so far we've covered 20 of the 21 mouse messages. The last message is WM_NCHITTEST, which stands for "nonclient hit test." This message precedes all other client-area and nonclient-area mouse messages. The *lParam* parameter contains the *x* and *y* screen coordinates of the mouse position. The *wParam* parameter is not used.

Windows applications generally pass this message to *DefWindowProc*. Windows then uses the WM_NCHITTEST message to generate all other mouse messages based on the position of the mouse. For nonclient-area mouse messages, the value returned from *DefWindowProc* when processing WM_NCHITTEST becomes the *wParam* parameter in the mouse message. This value can be any of the *wParam* values that accompany the nonclient-area mouse messages plus the following:

HTCLIENT	Client area
HTNOWHERE	Not on any window
HTTRANSPARENT	A window covered by another window
HTERROR	Causes *DefWindowProc* to produce a beep

If *DefWindowProc* returns HTCLIENT after it processes a WM_NCHITTEST message, Windows converts the screen coordinates to client-area coordinates and generates a client-area mouse message.

If you remember how we disabled all system keyboard functions by trapping the WM_SYSKEYDOWN message, you may wonder if you can do something similar by trapping mouse messages. Sure! If you include the lines

```
case WM_NCHITTEST:
    return (LRESULT) HTNOWHERE ;
```

in your window procedure, you will effectively disable all client-area and nonclient-area mouse messages to your window. The mouse buttons will simply not work while the mouse is anywhere within your window, including the system menu icon, the sizing buttons, and the close button.

Messages Beget Messages

Windows uses the WM_NCHITTEST message to generate all other mouse messages. The idea of messages giving birth to other messages is common in Windows. Let's take an example. As you may know, if you double-click the system menu icon of a Windows program, the window will be terminated. The double-click generates a series of WM_NCHITTEST messages. Because the mouse is positioned over the system menu icon, *DefWindowProc* returns a value of HTSYSMENU and Windows puts a WM_NCLBUTTONDBLCLK message in the message queue with *wParam* equal to HTSYSMENU.

The window procedure usually passes that mouse message to *DefWindowProc*. When *DefWindowProc* receives the WM_NCLBUTTONDBLCLK message with *wParam* equal to HTSYSMENU, it puts a WM_SYSCOMMAND message with *wParam* equal to SC_CLOSE in the message queue. (This WM_SYSCOMMAND message is also generated when a user selects Close from the system menu.) Again the window procedure usually passes that message to *DefWindowProc*. *DefWindowProc* processes the message by sending a WM_CLOSE message to the window procedure.

If the program wants to require confirmation from a user before terminating, the window procedure can trap WM_CLOSE. Otherwise, *DefWindowProc* processes WM_CLOSE by calling the *DestroyWindow* function. Among other chores, *DestroyWindow* sends a WM_DESTROY message to the window procedure. Normally, a window procedure processes WM_DESTROY with the code

```
case WM_DESTROY:
    PostQuitMessage (0) ;
    return 0 ;
```

The *PostQuitMessage* causes Windows to place a WM_QUIT message in the message queue. This message never reaches the window procedure because it causes *GetMessage* to return 0, which terminates the message loop and the program.

HIT-TESTING IN YOUR PROGRAMS

Earlier I discussed how Windows Explorer responds to mouse clicks and double-clicks. Obviously, the program (or more precisely the list view control that Windows Explorer uses) must first determine exactly which file or directory the user is pointing at with the mouse.

This is called "hit-testing." Just as *DefWindowProc* must do some hit-testing when processing WM_NCHITTEST messages, a window procedure often must do hit-testing of its own within the client area. In general, hit-testing involves calculations using the *x* and *y* coordinates passed to your window procedure in the *lParam* parameter of the mouse message.

A Hypothetical Example

Here's an example. Suppose your program needs to display several columns of alphabetically sorted files. Normally, you would use the list view control because it does all the hit-testing work for you. But let's suppose you can't use it for some reason. You need to do it yourself. Let's assume that the filenames are stored in a sorted array of pointers to character strings named *szFileNames*.

Let's also assume that the file list starts at the top of the client area, which is *cxClient* pixels wide and *cyClient* pixels high. The columns are *cxColWidth* pixels wide; the characters are *cyChar* pixels high. The number of files you can fit in each column is

```
iNumInCol = cyClient / cyChar ;
```

When your program receives a mouse click message, you can obtain the *cxMouse* and *cyMouse* coordinates from *lParam*. You then calculate which column of filenames the user is pointing at by using this formula:

```
iColumn = cxMouse / cxColWidth ;
```

The position of the filename in relation to the top of the column is

```
iFromTop = cyMouse / cyChar ;
```

Now you can calculate an index to the *szFileNames* array.

```
iIndex = iColumn * iNumInCol + iFromTop ;
```

If *iIndex* exceeds the number of files in the array, the user is clicking on a blank area of the display.

In many cases, hit-testing is more complex than this example suggests. When you display a graphical image containing many parts, you must determine the coordinates for each item you display. In hit-testing calculations, you must go backward from the coordinates to the object. This can become quite messy in a word-processing program that uses variable font sizes, because you must work backward to find the character position with the string.

A Sample Program

The CHECKER1 program, shown in Figure 7-4, demonstrates some simple hit-testing. The program divides the client area into a 5-by-5 array of 25 rectangles. If you click the mouse on one of the rectangles, the rectangle is filled with an X. If you click there again, the X is removed.

CHECKER1.C

```c
/*-------------------------------------------------
   CHECKER1.C -- Mouse Hit-Test Demo Program No. 1
                 (c) Charles Petzold, 1998
  -------------------------------------------------*/

#include <windows.h>

#define DIVISIONS 5

LRESULT CALLBACK WndProc (HWND, UINT, WPARAM, LPARAM) ;

int WINAPI WinMain (HINSTANCE hInstance, HINSTANCE hPrevInstance,
                    PSTR  szCmdLine, int iCmdShow)
{
     static TCHAR szAppName[] = TEXT ("Checker1") ;
     HWND         hwnd ;
     MSG          msg ;
     WNDCLASS     wndclass ;

     wndclass.style         = CS_HREDRAW | CS_VREDRAW ;
     wndclass.lpfnWndProc   = WndProc ;
     wndclass.cbClsExtra    = 0 ;
     wndclass.cbWndExtra    = 0 ;
     wndclass.hInstance     = hInstance ;
     wndclass.hIcon         = LoadIcon (NULL, IDI_APPLICATION) ;
     wndclass.hCursor       = LoadCursor (NULL, IDC_ARROW) ;
     wndclass.hbrBackground = (HBRUSH) GetStockObject (WHITE_BRUSH) ;
     wndclass.lpszMenuName  = NULL ;
     wndclass.lpszClassName = szAppName ;

     if (!RegisterClass (&wndclass))
     {
          MessageBox (NULL, TEXT ("Program requires Windows NT!"),
                      szAppName, MB_ICONERROR) ;
          return 0 ;
     }
```

Figure 7-4. *The CHECKER1 program.*

```
      hwnd = CreateWindow (szAppName, TEXT ("Checker1 Mouse Hit-Test Demo"),
                          WS_OVERLAPPEDWINDOW,
                          CW_USEDEFAULT, CW_USEDEFAULT,
                          CW_USEDEFAULT, CW_USEDEFAULT,
                          NULL, NULL, hInstance, NULL) ;

      ShowWindow (hwnd, iCmdShow) ;
      UpdateWindow (hwnd) ;

      while (GetMessage (&msg, NULL, 0, 0))
      {
           TranslateMessage (&msg) ;
           DispatchMessage (&msg) ;
      }
      return msg.wParam ;
}

LRESULT CALLBACK WndProc (HWND hwnd, UINT message, WPARAM wParam, LPARAMlParam)
{
      static BOOL fState[DIVISIONS][DIVISIONS] ;
      static int  cxBlock, cyBlock ;
      HDC         hdc ;
      int         x, y ;
      PAINTSTRUCT ps ;
      RECT        rect ;

      switch (message)
      {
      case WM_SIZE :
           cxBlock = LOWORD (lParam) / DIVISIONS ;
           cyBlock = HIWORD (lParam) / DIVISIONS ;
           return 0 ;

      case WM_LBUTTONDOWN :
           x = LOWORD (lParam) / cxBlock ;
           y = HIWORD (lParam) / cyBlock ;

           if (x < DIVISIONS && y < DIVISIONS)
           {
                fState [x][y] ^= 1 ;

                rect.left   = x * cxBlock ;
                rect.top    = y * cyBlock ;
```

(continued)

Figure 7-4. *continued*

```
            rect.right  = (x + 1) * cxBlock ;
            rect.bottom = (y + 1) * cyBlock ;

            InvalidateRect (hwnd, &rect, FALSE) ;
      }
      else
            MessageBeep (0) ;
      return 0 ;

  case WM_PAINT :
      hdc = BeginPaint (hwnd, &ps) ;

      for (x = 0 ; x < DIVISIONS ; x++)
      for (y = 0 ; y < DIVISIONS ; y++)
      {
            Rectangle (hdc, x * cxBlock, y * cyBlock,
                       (x + 1) * cxBlock, (y + 1) * cyBlock) ;

            if (fState [x][y])
            {
                  MoveToEx (hdc,  x    * cxBlock, y    * cyBlock, NULL) ;
                  LineTo   (hdc, (x+1) * cxBlock, (y+1) * cyBlock) ;
                  MoveToEx (hdc,  x    * cxBlock, (y+1) * cyBlock, NULL) ;
                  LineTo   (hdc, (x+1) * cxBlock,  y    * cyBlock) ;
            }
      }
      EndPaint (hwnd, &ps) ;
      return 0 ;

  case WM_DESTROY :
      PostQuitMessage (0) ;
      return 0 ;
  }
  return DefWindowProc (hwnd, message, wParam, lParam) ;
}
```

Figure 7-5 shows the CHECKER1 display. All 25 rectangles drawn by the program have the same width and the same height. These width and height values are stored in *cxBlock* and *cyBlock*, which are recalculated whenever the size of the client area changes. The WM_LBUTTONDOWN logic uses the mouse coordinates to determine which rectangle has been clicked. It flags the current state of the rectangle in the array *fState* and invalidates the rectangle to generate a WM_PAINT message.

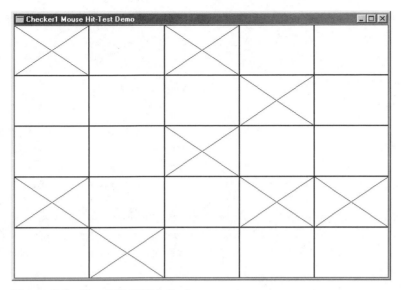

Figure 7-5. *The CHECKER1 display.*

If the width or height of the client area is not evenly divisible by five, a small strip of client area at the left or bottom will not be covered by a rectangle. For error processing, CHECKER1 responds to a mouse click in this area by calling *MessageBeep*.

When CHECKER1 receives a WM_PAINT message, it repaints the entire client area by drawing rectangles using the GDI *Rectangle* function. If the *fState* value is set, CHECKER1 draws two lines using the *MoveToEx* and *LineTo* functions. During WM_PAINT processing, CHECKER1 does not check whether each rectangular area lies within the invalid rectangle, but it could. One method for checking validity involves building a RECT structure for each rectangular block within the loop (using the same formulas as in the WM_LBUTTONDOWN logic) and checking whether that rectangle intersects the invalid rectangle (available as *ps.rcPaint*) by using the function *IntersectRect*.

Emulating the Mouse with the Keyboard

To use CHECKER1, you need to use the mouse. We'll be adding a keyboard interface to the program shortly, as we did for the SYSMETS program in Chapter 6. However, adding a keyboard interface to a program that uses the mouse cursor for pointing purposes requires that we also must worry about displaying and moving the mouse cursor.

Even if a mouse device is not installed, Windows can still display a mouse cursor. Windows maintains something called a "display count" for this cursor. If a mouse is installed, the display count is initially 0; if not, the display count is initially −1. The mouse cursor is displayed only if the display count is non-negative. You can increment the display count by calling

```
ShowCursor (TRUE) ;
```

and decrement it by calling

```
ShowCursor (FALSE) ;
```

You do not need to determine if a mouse is installed before using *ShowCursor*. If you want to display the mouse cursor regardless of the presence of the mouse, simply increment the display count by calling *ShowCursor*. After you increment the display count once, decrementing it will hide the cursor if no mouse is installed but leave it displayed if a mouse is present.

Windows maintains a current mouse cursor position even if a mouse is not installed. If a mouse is not installed and you display the mouse cursor, it might appear in any part of the display and will remain in that position until you explicitly move it. You can obtain the cursor position by calling

```
GetCursorPos (&pt) ;
```

where *pt* is a POINT structure. The function fills in the POINT fields with the *x* and *y* coordinates of the mouse. You can set the cursor position by using

```
SetCursorPos (x, y) ;
```

In both cases, the *x* and *y* values are screen coordinates, not client-area coordinates. (This should be evident because the functions do not require a *hwnd* parameter.) As noted earlier, you can convert screen coordinates to client-area coordinates and vice versa by calling *ScreenToClient* and *ClientToScreen*.

If you call *GetCursorPos* while processing a mouse message and you convert to client-area coordinates, these coordinates might be slightly different from those encoded in the *lParam* parameter of the mouse message. The coordinates returned from *GetCursorPos* indicate the current position of the mouse. The coordinates in *lParam* are the coordinates of the mouse at the time the message was generated.

You'll probably want to write keyboard logic that moves the mouse cursor with the keyboard arrow keys and that simulates the mouse button with the Spacebar or Enter key. What you *don't* want to do is move the mouse cursor one pixel per keystroke. That forces a user to hold down an arrow key for too long a time to move it.

If you need to implement a keyboard interface to the mouse cursor but still maintain the ability to position the cursor at precise pixel locations, you can process keystroke messages in such as way that when you hold down an arrow key the mouse cursor starts moving slowly but then speeds up. You'll recall that the *lParam* parameter in WM_KEYDOWN messages indicates whether the keystroke messages are the result of typematic action. This is an excellent application of that information.

Add a Keyboard Interface to CHECKER

The CHECKER2 program, shown in Figure 7-6, is the same as CHECKER1, except that it includes a keyboard interface. You can use the Left, Right, Up, and Down arrow keys to move the cursor among the 25 rectangles. The Home key sends the cursor to the upper left rectangle; the End key drops it down to the lower right rectangle. Both the Spacebar and Enter keys toggle the X mark.

CHECKER2.C

```
/*-------------------------------------------------
   CHECKER2.C -- Mouse Hit-Test Demo Program No. 2
                 (c) Charles Petzold, 1998
   -------------------------------------------------*/

#include <windows.h>

#define DIVISIONS 5

LRESULT CALLBACK WndProc (HWND, UINT, WPARAM, LPARAM) ;

int WINAPI WinMain (HINSTANCE hInstance, HINSTANCE hPrevInstance,
                    PSTR szCmdLine, int iCmdShow)
{
     static TCHAR szAppName[] = TEXT ("Checker2") ;
     HWND          hwnd ;
     MSG           msg ;
     WNDCLASS      wndclass ;

     wndclass.style         = CS_HREDRAW | CS_VREDRAW ;
     wndclass.lpfnWndProc   = WndProc ;
     wndclass.cbClsExtra    = 0 ;
     wndclass.cbWndExtra    = 0 ;
     wndclass.hInstance     = hInstance ;
     wndclass.hIcon         = LoadIcon (NULL, IDI_APPLICATION) ;
     wndclass.hCursor       = LoadCursor (NULL, IDC_ARROW) ;
     wndclass.hbrBackground = (HBRUSH) GetStockObject (WHITE_BRUSH) ;
     wndclass.lpszMenuName  = NULL ;
     wndclass.lpszClassName = szAppName ;

     if (!RegisterClass (&wndclass))
     {
          MessageBox (NULL, TEXT ("Program requires Windows NT!"),
                      szAppName, MB_ICONERROR) ;
          return 0 ;
     }
```

Figure 7-6. *The CHECKER2 program.*

(continued)

Figure 7-6. *continued*

```
        hwnd = CreateWindow (szAppName, TEXT ("Checker2 Mouse Hit-Test Demo"),
                        WS_OVERLAPPEDWINDOW,
                        CW_USEDEFAULT, CW_USEDEFAULT,
                        CW_USEDEFAULT, CW_USEDEFAULT,
                        NULL, NULL, hInstance, NULL) ;

        ShowWindow (hwnd, iCmdShow) ;
        UpdateWindow (hwnd) ;

        while (GetMessage (&msg, NULL, 0, 0))
        {
             TranslateMessage (&msg) ;
             DispatchMessage (&msg) ;
        }
        return msg.wParam ;
}

LRESULT CALLBACK WndProc (HWND hwnd, UINT message, WPARAM wParam, LPARAM lParam)
{
        static BOOL fState[DIVISIONS][DIVISIONS] ;
        static int  cxBlock, cyBlock ;
        HDC         hdc ;
        int         x, y ;
        PAINTSTRUCT ps ;
        POINT       point ;
        RECT        rect ;

        switch (message)
        {
        case WM_SIZE :
             cxBlock = LOWORD (lParam) / DIVISIONS ;
             cyBlock = HIWORD (lParam) / DIVISIONS ;
             return 0 ;

        case WM_SETFOCUS :
             ShowCursor (TRUE) ;
             return 0 ;

        case WM_KILLFOCUS :
             ShowCursor (FALSE) ;
             return 0 ;

        case WM_KEYDOWN :
             GetCursorPos (&point) ;
             ScreenToClient (hwnd, &point) ;
```

```
     x = max (0, min (DIVISIONS - 1, point.x / cxBlock)) ;
     y = max (0, min (DIVISIONS - 1, point.y / cyBlock)) ;

     switch (wParam)
     {
     case VK_UP :
          y-- ;
          break ;

     case VK_DOWN :
          y++ ;
          break ;

     case VK_LEFT :
          x-- ;
          break ;

     case VK_RIGHT :
          x++ ;
          break ;

     case VK_HOME :
          x = y = 0 ;
          break ;

     case VK_END :
          x = y = DIVISIONS - 1 ;
          break ;

     case VK_RETURN :
     case VK_SPACE :
          SendMessage (hwnd, WM_LBUTTONDOWN, MK_LBUTTON,
                      MAKELONG (x * cxBlock, y * cyBlock)) ;
          break ;
     }
     x = (x + DIVISIONS) % DIVISIONS ;
     y = (y + DIVISIONS) % DIVISIONS ;

     point.x = x * cxBlock + cxBlock / 2 ;
     point.y = y * cyBlock + cyBlock / 2 ;

     ClientToScreen (hwnd, &point) ;
     SetCursorPos (point.x, point.y) ;
     return 0 ;
```

(continued)

Figure 7-6. *continued*

```
     case WM_LBUTTONDOWN :
          x = LOWORD (lParam) / cxBlock ;
          y = HIWORD (lParam) / cyBlock ;

          if (x < DIVISIONS && y < DIVISIONS)
          {
               fState[x][y] ^= 1 ;

               rect.left   = x * cxBlock ;
               rect.top    = y * cyBlock ;
               rect.right  = (x + 1) * cxBlock ;
               rect.bottom = (y + 1) * cyBlock ;

               InvalidateRect (hwnd, &rect, FALSE) ;
          }
          else
               MessageBeep (0) ;
          return 0 ;

     case WM_PAINT :
          hdc = BeginPaint (hwnd, &ps) ;

          for (x = 0 ; x < DIVISIONS ; x++)
          for (y = 0 ; y < DIVISIONS ; y++)
          {
               Rectangle (hdc, x * cxBlock, y * cyBlock,
                          (x + 1) * cxBlock, (y + 1) * cyBlock) ;

               if (fState [x][y])
               {
                    MoveToEx (hdc, x   *cxBlock, y   *cyBlock, NULL) ;
                    LineTo   (hdc, (x+1)*cxBlock, (y+1)*cyBlock) ;
                    MoveToEx (hdc, x   *cxBlock, (y+1)*cyBlock, NULL) ;
                    LineTo   (hdc, (x+1)*cxBlock, y   *cyBlock) ;
               }
          }
          EndPaint (hwnd, &ps) ;
          return 0 ;

     case WM_DESTROY :
          PostQuitMessage (0) ;
          return 0 ;
     }
     return DefWindowProc (hwnd, message, wParam, lParam) ;
}
```

The WM_KEYDOWN logic in CHECKER2 determines the position of the cursor using *GetCursorPos*, converts the screen coordinates to client-area coordinates using *ScreenToClient*, and divides the coordinates by the width and height of the rectangular block. This produces *x* and *y* values that indicate the position of the rectangle in the 5-by-5 array. The mouse cursor might or might not be in the client area when a key is pressed, so *x* and *y* must be passed through the *min* and *max* macros to ensure that they range from 0 through 4.

For arrow keys, CHECKER2 increments or decrements *x* and *y* appropriately. If the key is the Enter key or the Spacebar, CHECKER2 uses *SendMessage* to send a WM_LBUTTONDOWN message to itself. This technique is similar to the method used in the SYSMETS program in Chapter 6 to add a keyboard interface to the window scroll bar. The WM_KEYDOWN logic finishes by calculating client-area coordinates that point to the center of the rectangle, converting to screen coordinates using *ClientToScreen*, and setting the cursor position using *SetCursorPos*.

Using Child Windows for Hit-Testing

Some programs (for example, the Windows Paint program) divide the client area into several smaller logical areas. The Paint program has an area at the left for its icon-based tool menu and an area at the bottom for the color menu. When Paint hit-tests these two areas, it must take into account the location of the smaller area within the entire client area before determining the actual item being selected by the user.

Or maybe not. In reality, Paint simplifies both the drawing and hit-testing of these smaller areas through the use of "child windows." The child windows divide the entire client area into several smaller rectangular regions. Each child window has its own window handle, window procedure, and client area. Each child window procedure receives mouse messages that apply only to its own window. The *lParam* parameter in the mouse message contains coordinates relative to the upper left corner of the client area of the child window, not relative to the client area of the "parent" window (which is Paint's main application window).

Child windows used in this way can help you structure and modularize your programs. If the child windows use different window classes, each child window can have its own window procedure. The different window classes can also define different background colors and different default cursors. In Chapter 9, we'll look at "child window controls," which are predefined windows that take the form of scroll bars, buttons, and edit boxes. Right now, let's see how we can use child windows in the CHECKER program.

Child Windows in CHECKER

Figure 7-7, beginning on the following page, shows CHECKER3. This version of the program creates 25 child windows to process mouse clicks. It does not have a keyboard interface, but one could be added as I'll demonstrate in CHECKER4 later in this chapter.

CHECKER3.C

```
/*-----------------------------------------------------
   CHECKER3.C -- Mouse Hit-Test Demo Program No. 3
                 (c) Charles Petzold, 1998
   -----------------------------------------------------*/

#include <windows.h>

#define DIVISIONS 5

LRESULT CALLBACK WndProc    (HWND, UINT, WPARAM, LPARAM) ;
LRESULT CALLBACK ChildWndProc (HWND, UINT, WPARAM, LPARAM) ;

TCHAR szChildClass[] = TEXT ("Checker3_Child") ;

int WINAPI WinMain (HINSTANCE hInstance, HINSTANCE hPrevInstance,
                    PSTR szCmdLine, int iCmdShow)
{
     static TCHAR szAppName[] = TEXT ("Checker3") ;
     HWND          hwnd ;
     MSG           msg ;
     WNDCLASS      wndclass ;

     wndclass.style          = CS_HREDRAW | CS_VREDRAW ;
     wndclass.lpfnWndProc    = WndProc ;
     wndclass.cbClsExtra     = 0 ;
     wndclass.cbWndExtra     = 0 ;
     wndclass.hInstance      = hInstance ;
     wndclass.hIcon          = LoadIcon (NULL, IDI_APPLICATION) ;
     wndclass.hCursor        = LoadCursor (NULL, IDC_ARROW) ;
     wndclass.hbrBackground  = (HBRUSH) GetStockObject (WHITE_BRUSH) ;
     wndclass.lpszMenuName   = NULL ;
     wndclass.lpszClassName  = szAppName ;

     if (!RegisterClass (&wndclass))
     {
          MessageBox (NULL, TEXT ("Program requires Windows NT!"),
                      szAppName, MB_ICONERROR) ;
          return 0 ;
     }

     wndclass.lpfnWndProc    = ChildWndProc ;
     wndclass.cbWndExtra     = sizeof (long) ;
```

Figure 7-7. *The CHECKER3 program.*

```
        wndclass.hIcon        = NULL ;
        wndclass.lpszClassName = szChildClass ;

        RegisterClass (&wndclass) ;

        hwnd = CreateWindow (szAppName, TEXT ("Checker3 Mouse Hit-Test Demo"),
                            WS_OVERLAPPEDWINDOW,
                            CW_USEDEFAULT, CW_USEDEFAULT,
                            CW_USEDEFAULT, CW_USEDEFAULT,
                            NULL, NULL, hInstance, NULL) ;

        ShowWindow (hwnd, iCmdShow) ;
        UpdateWindow (hwnd) ;

        while (GetMessage (&msg, NULL, 0, 0))
        {
            TranslateMessage (&msg) ;
            DispatchMessage (&msg) ;
        }
        return msg.wParam ;
}

LRESULT CALLBACK WndProc (HWND hwnd, UINT message, WPARAM wParam, LPARAM lParam)
{
        static HWND hwndChild[DIVISIONS][DIVISIONS] ;
        int         cxBlock, cyBlock, x, y ;

        switch (message)
        {
        case WM_CREATE :
            for (x = 0 ; x < DIVISIONS ; x++)
                for (y = 0 ; y < DIVISIONS ; y++)
                    hwndChild[x][y] = CreateWindow (szChildClass, NULL,
                            WS_CHILDWINDOW | WS_VISIBLE,
                            0, 0, 0, 0,
                            hwnd, (HMENU) (y << 8 | x),
                            (HINSTANCE) GetWindowLong (hwnd, GWL_HINSTANCE),
                            NULL) ;
            return 0 ;

        case WM_SIZE :
            cxBlock = LOWORD (lParam) / DIVISIONS ;
            cyBlock = HIWORD (lParam) / DIVISIONS ;
```

(continued)

Figure 7-7. *continued*

```
            for (x = 0 ; x < DIVISIONS ; x++)
                for (y = 0 ; y < DIVISIONS ; y++)
                    MoveWindow (hwndChild[x][y],
                                    x * cxBlock, y * cyBlock,
                                    cxBlock, cyBlock, TRUE) ;
            return 0 ;

    case WM_LBUTTONDOWN :
            MessageBeep (0) ;
            return 0 ;

    case WM_DESTROY :
            PostQuitMessage (0) ;
            return 0 ;
    }
    return DefWindowProc (hwnd, message, wParam, lParam) ;
}

LRESULT CALLBACK ChildWndProc (HWND hwnd, UINT message,
                                WPARAM wParam, LPARAM lParam)
{
    HDC         hdc ;
    PAINTSTRUCT ps ;
    RECT        rect ;

    switch (message)
    {
    case WM_CREATE :
            SetWindowLong (hwnd, 0, 0) ;        // on/off flag
            return 0 ;

    case WM_LBUTTONDOWN :
            SetWindowLong (hwnd, 0, 1 ^ GetWindowLong (hwnd, 0)) ;
            InvalidateRect (hwnd, NULL, FALSE) ;
            return 0 ;

    case WM_PAINT :
            hdc = BeginPaint (hwnd, &ps) ;

            GetClientRect (hwnd, &rect) ;
            Rectangle (hdc, 0, 0, rect.right, rect.bottom) ;

            if (GetWindowLong (hwnd, 0))
            {
                MoveToEx (hdc, 0,            0, NULL) ;
```

```
            LineTo   (hdc, rect.right, rect.bottom) ;
            MoveToEx (hdc, 0,          rect.bottom, NULL) ;
            LineTo   (hdc, rect.right, 0) ;
        }

     EndPaint (hwnd, &ps) ;
     return 0 ;
  }
  return DefWindowProc (hwnd, message, wParam, lParam) ;
}
```

CHECKER3 has two window procedures named *WndProc* and *ChildWndProc*. *WndProc* is still the window procedure for the main (or parent) window. *ChildWndProc* is the window procedure for the 25 child windows. Both window procedures must be defined as CALLBACK functions.

Because a window procedure is associated with a particular window class structure that you register with Windows by calling the *RegisterClass* function, CHECKER3 requires two window classes. The first window class is for the main window and has the name "Checker3". The second window class is given the name "Checker3_Child". You don't have to choose quite so reasonable names as these, though.

CHECKER3 registers both window classes in the *WinMain* function. After registering the normal window class, CHECKER3 simply reuses most of the fields in the *wndclass* structure for registering the Checker3_Child class. Four fields, however, are set to different values for the child window class:

■ The *lpfnWndProc* field is set to *ChildWndProc*, the window procedure for the child window class.

■ The *cbWndExtra* field is set to 4 bytes or, more precisely, *sizeof (long)*. This field tells Windows to reserve 4 bytes of extra space in an internal structure that Windows maintains for each window based on this window class. You can use this space to store information that might be different for each window.

■ The *hIcon* field is set to NULL because child windows such as the ones in CHECKER3 do not require icons.

■ The *pszClassName* field is set to "Checker3_Child", the name of the class.

The *CreateWindow* call in *WinMain* creates the main window based on the Checker3 class. This is normal. However, when *WndProc* receives a WM_CREATE message, it calls *CreateWindow* 25 times to create 25 child windows based on the Checker3_Child class. The table on the following page provides a comparison of the arguments to the *CreateWindow* call in *WinMain* and the *CreateWindow* call in *WndProc* that creates the 25 child windows.

Argument	Main Window	Child Window
window class	"Checker3"	"Checker3_Child"
window caption	"Checker3…"	NULL
window style	WS_OVERLAPPEDWINDOW	WS_CHILDWINDOW | WS_VISIBLE
horizontal position	CW_USEDEFAULT	0
vertical position	CW_USEDEFAULT	0
width	CW_USEDEFAULT	0
height	CW_USEDEFAULT	0
parent window handle	NULL	hwnd
menu handle/ child ID	NULL	(HMENU) (y << 8 | x)
instance handle	hInstance	(HINSTANCE) GetWindowLong (hwnd, GWL_HINSTANCE)
extra parameters	NULL	NULL

Normally, the position and size parameters are required for child window, but in CHECKER3 the child windows are positioned and sized later in *WndProc*. The parent window handle is NULL for the main window because it is the parent. The parent window handle is required when using the *CreateWindow* call to create a child window.

The main window doesn't have a menu, so that parameter is NULL. For child windows, the same parameter is called a "child ID" or a "child windows ID." This is a number that uniquely identifies the child window. The child ID becomes much more important when working with child window controls in dialog boxes, as we'll see in Chapter 11. For CHECKER3, I've simply set the child ID to a number that is a composite of the x and y positions that each child window occupies in the 5-by-5 array within the main window.

The *CreateWindow* function requires an instance handle. Within *WinMain*, the instance handle is easily available because it is a parameter to *WinMain*. When the child window is created, CHECKER3 must use *GetWindowLong* to extract the *hInstance* value from the structure that Windows maintains for the window. (Rather than use *GetWindowLong*, I could have saved the value of *hInstance* in a global variable and used it directly.)

Each child window has a different window handle that is stored in the *hwndChild* array. When *WndProc* receives a WM_SIZE message, it calls *MoveWindow* for each of the 25 child windows. The parameters to *MoveWindow* indicate the upper left corner of the child window relative to the parent window client-area coordinates, the width and height of the child window, and whether the child window needs repainting.

Now let's take a look at *ChildWndProc*. This window procedure processes messages for all 25 child windows. The *hwnd* parameter to *ChildWndProc* is the handle to the child window receiving the message. When *ChildWndProc* processes a WM_CREATE message (which will happen 25 times because there are 25 child windows), it uses *SetWindowWord* to store a 0 in the extra area reserved within the window structure. (Recall that we reserved this space by using the *cbWndExtra* field when defining the window class.) *ChildWndProc* uses this value to store the current state (X or no X) of the rectangle. When the child window is clicked, the WM_LBUTTONDOWN logic simply flips the value of this integer (from 0 to 1 or from 1 to 0) and invalidates the entire child window. This area is the rectangle being clicked. The WM_PAINT processing is trivial because the size of the rectangle it draws is the same size as its client area.

Because the C source code file and the .EXE file of CHECKER3 are larger than those for CHECKER1 (to say nothing of my explanation of the programs), I will not try to convince you that CHECKER3 is "simpler" than CHECKER1. But note that we no longer have to do any mouse hit-testing! If a child window in CHECKER3 gets a WM_LBUTTONDOWN message the window has been hit, and that's all it needs to know.

Child Windows and the Keyboard

Adding a keyboard interface to CHECKER3 seems the logical last step in the CHECKER series. But in doing this, a different approach might be appropriate. In CHECKER2, the position of the mouse cursor indicated which square would get a check mark when the Spacebar was pressed. When we're dealing with child windows, we can take a cue from the functioning of dialog boxes. In dialog boxes, a child window indicates that it has the input focus (and hence will be toggled by the keyboard) with a flashing caret or a dotted rectangle.

We're not going to reproduce all the dialog box logic that exists internally in Windows; we're just going to get a rough idea of how you can emulate dialog boxes in an application. When exploring how to do this, one thing you'll discover is that the parent window and the child windows should probably share processing of keyboard messages. The child window should toggle the check mark when the Spacebar or Enter key is pressed. The parent window should move the input focus among the child windows when the cursor keys are pressed. The logic is complicated somewhat by the fact that when you click on a child window, the parent window rather than the child window gets the input focus.

CHECKER4.C is shown in Figure 7-8.

CHECKER4.C

```
/*-----------------------------------------------------
   CHECKER4.C -- Mouse Hit-Test Demo Program No. 4
                 (c) Charles Petzold, 1998
   -----------------------------------------------------*/

#include <windows.h>
```

Figure 7-8. *The CHECKER4 program.*   *(continued)*

Figure 7-8. *continued*

```
#define DIVISIONS 5

LRESULT CALLBACK WndProc    (HWND, UINT, WPARAM, LPARAM) ;
LRESULT CALLBACK ChildWndProc (HWND, UINT, WPARAM, LPARAM) ;

int   idFocus = 0 ;
TCHAR szChildClass[] = TEXT ("Checker4_Child") ;

int WINAPI WinMain (HINSTANCE hInstance, HINSTANCE hPrevInstance,
                    PSTR szCmdLine, int iCmdShow)
{
    static TCHAR szAppName[] = TEXT ("Checker4") ;
    HWND         hwnd ;
    MSG          msg ;
    WNDCLASS     wndclass ;

    wndclass.style         = CS_HREDRAW | CS_VREDRAW ;
    wndclass.lpfnWndProc   = WndProc ;
    wndclass.cbClsExtra    = 0 ;
    wndclass.cbWndExtra    = 0 ;
    wndclass.hInstance     = hInstance ;
    wndclass.hIcon         = LoadIcon (NULL, IDI_APPLICATION) ;
    wndclass.hCursor       = LoadCursor (NULL, IDC_ARROW) ;
    wndclass.hbrBackground = (HBRUSH) GetStockObject (WHITE_BRUSH) ;
    wndclass.lpszMenuName  = NULL ;
    wndclass.lpszClassName = szAppName ;

    if (!RegisterClass (&wndclass))
    {
        MessageBox (NULL, TEXT ("Program requires Windows NT!"),
                    szAppName, MB_ICONERROR) ;
        return 0 ;
    }

    wndclass.lpfnWndProc   = ChildWndProc ;
    wndclass.cbWndExtra    = sizeof (long) ;
    wndclass.hIcon         = NULL ;
    wndclass.lpszClassName = szChildClass ;

    RegisterClass (&wndclass) ;

    hwnd = CreateWindow (szAppName, TEXT ("Checker4 Mouse Hit-Test Demo"),
                        WS_OVERLAPPEDWINDOW,
                        CW_USEDEFAULT, CW_USEDEFAULT,
                        CW_USEDEFAULT, CW_USEDEFAULT,
                        NULL, NULL, hInstance, NULL) ;
```

```
    ShowWindow (hwnd, iCmdShow) ;
    UpdateWindow (hwnd) ;

    while (GetMessage (&msg, NULL, 0, 0))
    {
        TranslateMessage (&msg) ;
        DispatchMessage (&msg) ;
    }
    return msg.wParam ;
}

LRESULT CALLBACK WndProc (HWND hwnd, UINT message, WPARAM wParam, LPARAM lParam)
{
    static HWND hwndChild[DIVISIONS][DIVISIONS] ;
    int         cxBlock, cyBlock, x, y ;

    switch (message)
    {
    case WM_CREATE :
        for (x = 0 ; x < DIVISIONS ; x++)
            for (y = 0 ; y < DIVISIONS ; y++)
                hwndChild[x][y] = CreateWindow (szChildClass, NULL,
                            WS_CHILDWINDOW | WS_VISIBLE,
                            0, 0, 0, 0,
                            hwnd, (HMENU) (y << 8 | x),
                            (HINSTANCE) GetWindowLong (hwnd, GWL_HINSTANCE),
                            NULL) ;
        return 0 ;

    case WM_SIZE :
        cxBlock = LOWORD (lParam) / DIVISIONS ;
        cyBlock = HIWORD (lParam) / DIVISIONS ;

        for (x = 0 ; x < DIVISIONS ; x++)
            for (y = 0 ; y < DIVISIONS ; y++)
                MoveWindow (hwndChild[x][y],
                            x * cxBlock, y * cyBlock,
                            cxBlock, cyBlock, TRUE) ;
        return 0 ;

    case WM_LBUTTONDOWN :
        MessageBeep (0) ;
        return 0 ;

        // On set-focus message, set focus to child window
```

(continued)

Figure 7-8. *continued*

```
        case WM_SETFOCUS:
              SetFocus (GetDlgItem (hwnd, idFocus)) ;
              return 0 ;

              // On key-down message, possibly change the focus window

        case WM_KEYDOWN:
              x = idFocus & 0xFF ;
              y = idFocus >> 8 ;

              switch (wParam)
              {
              case VK_UP:     y-- ;                        break ;
              case VK_DOWN:   y++ ;                        break ;
              case VK_LEFT:   x-- ;                        break ;
              case VK_RIGHT:  x++ ;                        break ;
              case VK_HOME:   x = y = 0 ;                  break ;
              case VK_END:    x = y = DIVISIONS - 1 ;      break ;
              default:        return 0 ;
              }

              x = (x + DIVISIONS) % DIVISIONS ;
              y = (y + DIVISIONS) % DIVISIONS ;

              idFocus = y << 8 | x ;

              SetFocus (GetDlgItem (hwnd, idFocus)) ;
              return 0 ;

        case WM_DESTROY :
              PostQuitMessage (0) ;
              return 0 ;
        }
      return DefWindowProc (hwnd, message, wParam, lParam) ;
}

LRESULT CALLBACK ChildWndProc (HWND hwnd, UINT message,
                               WPARAM wParam, LPARAM lParam)
{
      HDC         hdc ;
      PAINTSTRUCT ps ;
      RECT        rect ;

      switch (message)
      {
```

```
case WM_CREATE :
     SetWindowLong (hwnd, 0, 0) ;          // on/off flag
     return 0 ;

case WM_KEYDOWN:
          // Send most key presses to the parent window

     if (wParam != VK_RETURN && wParam != VK_SPACE)
     {
          SendMessage (GetParent (hwnd), message, wParam, lParam) ;
          return 0 ;
     }
          // For Return and Space, fall through to toggle the square

case WM_LBUTTONDOWN :
     SetWindowLong (hwnd, 0, 1 ^ GetWindowLong (hwnd, 0)) ;
     SetFocus (hwnd) ;
     InvalidateRect (hwnd, NULL, FALSE) ;
     return 0 ;

          // For focus messages, invalidate the window for repaint

case WM_SETFOCUS:
     idFocus = GetWindowLong (hwnd, GWL_ID) ;

          // Fall through

case WM_KILLFOCUS:
     InvalidateRect (hwnd, NULL, TRUE) ;
     return 0 ;

case WM_PAINT :
     hdc = BeginPaint (hwnd, &ps) ;

     GetClientRect (hwnd, &rect) ;
     Rectangle (hdc, 0, 0, rect.right, rect.bottom) ;

          // Draw the "x" mark

     if (GetWindowLong (hwnd, 0))
     {
          MoveToEx (hdc, 0,          0, NULL) ;
          LineTo   (hdc, rect.right, rect.bottom) ;
          MoveToEx (hdc, 0,          rect.bottom, NULL) ;
          LineTo   (hdc, rect.right, 0) ;
     }
```

(continued)

Figure 7-8. *continued*

```
                // Draw the "focus" rectangle

        if (hwnd == GetFocus ())
        {
                rect.left   += rect.right / 10 ;
                rect.right  -= rect.left ;
                rect.top    += rect.bottom / 10 ;
                rect.bottom -= rect.top ;

                SelectObject (hdc, GetStockObject (NULL_BRUSH)) ;
                SelectObject (hdc, CreatePen (PS_DASH, 0, 0)) ;
                Rectangle (hdc, rect.left, rect.top, rect.right, rect.bottom) ;
                DeleteObject (SelectObject (hdc, GetStockObject (BLACK_PEN))) ;
        }

        EndPaint (hwnd, &ps) ;
        return 0 ;
    }
    return DefWindowProc (hwnd, message, wParam, lParam) ;
}
```

You'll recall that each child window has a unique "child window ID" number defined when the window is created by the *CreateWindow* call. In CHECKER3, this ID number is a combination of the *x* and *y* positions of the rectangle. A program can obtain a child window ID for a particular child window by calling:

```
idChild = GetWindowLong (hwndChild, GWL_ID) ;
```

This function does the same:

```
idChild = GetDlgCtrlID (hwndChild) ;
```

As the function name suggests, it's primarily used with dialog boxes and control windows. It's also possible to obtain the handle of a child window if you know the handle of the parent window and the child window ID:

```
hwndChild = GetDlgItem (hwndParent, idChild) ;
```

In CHECKER4, the global variable *idFocus* is used to save the child ID number of the window that currently has the input focus. I mentioned earlier that child windows don't automatically get the input focus when you click on them with the mouse. Thus, the parent window in CHECKER4 processes the WM_SETFOCUS message by calling

```
SetFocus (GetDlgItem (hwnd, idFocus)) ;
```

thus setting the input focus to one of the child windows.

ChildWndProc processes both WM_SETFOCUS and WM_KILLFOCUS messages. For WM_SETFOCUS, it saves the child window ID receiving the input focus in the global variable *idFocus*. For both messages, the window is invalidated, generating a WM_PAINT message. If the WM_PAINT message is drawing the child window with the input focus, it draws a rectangle with a PS_DASH pen style to indicate that the window has the input focus.

ChildWndProc also processes WM_KEYDOWN messages. For anything but the Spacebar and Return keys, the WM_KEYDOWN message is sent to the parent window. Otherwise, the window procedure does the same thing as a WM_LBUTTONDOWN message.

Processing the cursor movement keys is delegated to the parent window. In a manner similar to CHECKER2, this program obtains the *x* and *y* coordinates of the child window with the input focus and changes them based on the particular cursor key being pressed. The input focus is then set to the new child window with a call to *SetFocus*.

CAPTURING THE MOUSE

A window procedure normally receives mouse messages only when the mouse cursor is positioned over the client or nonclient area of the window. A program might need to receive mouse messages when the mouse is outside the window. If so, the program can "capture" the mouse. Don't worry: it won't bite.

Blocking Out a Rectangle

To examine why capturing the mouse might be necessary, let's look at the BLOKOUT1 program shown in Figure 7-9. This program may seem functional, but it has a nasty flaw.

BLOKOUT1.C

```
/*-------------------------------------------
   BLOKOUT1.C -- Mouse Button Demo Program
                 (c) Charles Petzold, 1998
   -------------------------------------------*/

#include <windows.h>

LRESULT CALLBACK WndProc (HWND, UINT, WPARAM, LPARAM) ;

int WINAPI WinMain (HINSTANCE hInstance, HINSTANCE hPrevInstance,
                    PSTR szCmdLine, int iCmdShow)
{
     static TCHAR szAppName[] = TEXT ("BlokOut1") ;
     HWND         hwnd ;
     MSG          msg ;
     WNDCLASS     wndclass ;

     wndclass.style         = CS_HREDRAW | CS_VREDRAW ;
     wndclass.lpfnWndProc   = WndProc ;
     wndclass.cbClsExtra    = 0 ;
```

Figure 7-9. *The BLOKOUT1 program.*

(continued)

Figure 7-9. *continued*

```
        wndclass.cbWndExtra     = 0 ;
        wndclass.hInstance      = hInstance ;
        wndclass.hIcon          = LoadIcon (NULL, IDI_APPLICATION) ;
        wndclass.hCursor        = LoadCursor (NULL, IDC_ARROW) ;
        wndclass.hbrBackground  = (HBRUSH) GetStockObject (WHITE_BRUSH) ;
        wndclass.lpszMenuName   = NULL ;
        wndclass.lpszClassName  = szAppName ;

        if (!RegisterClass (&wndclass))
        {
             MessageBox (NULL, TEXT ("Program requires Windows NT!"),
                         szAppName, MB_ICONERROR) ;
             return 0 ;
        }

        hwnd = CreateWindow (szAppName, TEXT ("Mouse Button Demo"),
                             WS_OVERLAPPEDWINDOW,
                             CW_USEDEFAULT, CW_USEDEFAULT,
                             CW_USEDEFAULT, CW_USEDEFAULT,
                             NULL, NULL, hInstance, NULL) ;

        ShowWindow (hwnd, iCmdShow) ;
        UpdateWindow (hwnd) ;

        while (GetMessage (&msg, NULL, 0, 0))
        {
             TranslateMessage (&msg) ;
             DispatchMessage (&msg) ;
        }
        return msg.wParam ;
}

void DrawBoxOutline (HWND hwnd, POINT ptBeg, POINT ptEnd)
{
        HDC hdc ;

        hdc = GetDC (hwnd) ;

        SetROP2 (hdc, R2_NOT) ;
        SelectObject (hdc, GetStockObject (NULL_BRUSH)) ;
        Rectangle (hdc, ptBeg.x, ptBeg.y, ptEnd.x, ptEnd.y) ;

        ReleaseDC (hwnd, hdc) ;
}
```

```
LRESULT CALLBACK WndProc (HWND hwnd, UINT message, WPARAM wParam, LPARAM lParam)
{
     static BOOL  fBlocking, fValidBox ;
     static POINT ptBeg, ptEnd, ptBoxBeg, ptBoxEnd ;
     HDC          hdc ;
     PAINTSTRUCT  ps ;

     switch (message)
     {
     case WM_LBUTTONDOWN :
          ptBeg.x = ptEnd.x = LOWORD (lParam) ;
          ptBeg.y = ptEnd.y = HIWORD (lParam) ;

          DrawBoxOutline (hwnd, ptBeg, ptEnd) ;

          SetCursor (LoadCursor (NULL, IDC_CROSS)) ;

          fBlocking = TRUE ;
          return 0 ;

     case WM_MOUSEMOVE :
          if (fBlocking)
          {
               SetCursor (LoadCursor (NULL, IDC_CROSS)) ;

               DrawBoxOutline (hwnd, ptBeg, ptEnd) ;

               ptEnd.x = LOWORD (lParam) ;
               ptEnd.y = HIWORD (lParam) ;

               DrawBoxOutline (hwnd, ptBeg, ptEnd) ;
          }
          return 0 ;

     case WM_LBUTTONUP :
          if (fBlocking)
          {
               DrawBoxOutline (hwnd, ptBeg, ptEnd) ;

               ptBoxBeg   = ptBeg ;
               ptBoxEnd.x = LOWORD (lParam) ;
               ptBoxEnd.y = HIWORD (lParam) ;

               SetCursor (LoadCursor (NULL, IDC_ARROW)) ;
```

(continued)

311

Figure 7-9. *continued*

```
            fBlocking = FALSE ;
            fValidBox  = TRUE ;

            InvalidateRect (hwnd, NULL, TRUE) ;
       }
       return 0 ;

  case WM_CHAR :
       if (fBlocking & wParam == '\x1B')          // i.e., Escape
       {
            DrawBoxOutline (hwnd, ptBeg, ptEnd) ;

            SetCursor (LoadCursor (NULL, IDC_ARROW)) ;

            fBlocking = FALSE ;
       }
       return 0 ;

  case WM_PAINT :
       hdc = BeginPaint (hwnd, &ps) ;

       if (fValidBox)
       {
            SelectObject (hdc, GetStockObject (BLACK_BRUSH)) ;
            Rectangle (hdc, ptBoxBeg.x, ptBoxBeg.y,
                 ptBoxEnd.x, ptBoxEnd.y) ;
       }

       if (fBlocking)
       {
            SetROP2 (hdc, R2_NOT) ;
            SelectObject (hdc, GetStockObject (NULL_BRUSH)) ;
            Rectangle (hdc, ptBeg.x, ptBeg.y, ptEnd.x, ptEnd.y) ;
       }

       EndPaint (hwnd, &ps) ;
       return 0 ;

  case WM_DESTROY :
       PostQuitMessage (0) ;
       return 0 ;
  }
  return DefWindowProc (hwnd, message, wParam, lParam) ;
}
```

This program demonstrates a little something that might be implemented in a Windows drawing program. You begin by depressing the left mouse button to indicate one corner of a rectangle. You then drag the mouse. The program draws an outlined rectangle with the opposite corner at the current mouse position. When you release the mouse, the program fills in the rectangle. Figure 7-10 shows one rectangle already drawn and another in progress.

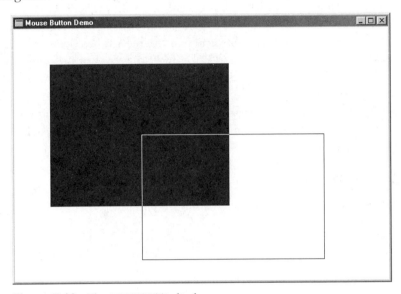

Figure 7-10. *The BLOKOUT1 display.*

So, what's the problem?

Try this: Press the left mouse button within BLOKOUT1's client area and then move the cursor outside the window. The program stops receiving WM_MOUSEMOVE messages. Now release the button. BLOKOUT1 doesn't get that WM_BUTTONUP message because the cursor is outside the client area. Move the cursor back within BLOKOUT1's client area. The window procedure still thinks the button is pressed.

This is not good. The program doesn't know what's going on.

The Capture Solution

BLOKOUT1 shows some common program functionality, but the code is obviously flawed. This is the type of problem for which mouse capturing was invented. If the user is dragging the mouse, it should be no big deal if the cursor drifts out of the window for a moment. The program should still be in control of the mouse.

Capturing the mouse is easier than baiting a mousetrap. You need only call

```
SetCapture (hwnd) ;
```

After this function call Windows sends all mouse messages to the window procedure for the window whose handle is *hwnd*. The mouse messages always come through as client-area messages, even when the mouse is in a nonclient area of the window. The *lParam* parameter still indicates the position of the mouse in client-area coordinates. These *x* and *y* coordinates, however, can be negative if the mouse is to the left of or above the client area. When you want to release the mouse, call

```
ReleaseCapture () ;
```

which will returns things to normal.

In the 32-bit versions of Windows, mouse capturing is a bit more restrictive than it was in earlier versions of Windows. Specifically, if the mouse has been captured, and if a mouse button is not currently down, and if the mouse cursor passes over another window, the window underneath the cursor will receive the mouse messages rather than the window that captured the mouse. This is necessary to prevent one program from messing up the whole system by capturing the mouse and not releasing it.

To avoid problems, your program should capture the mouse only when the button is depressed in your client area. You should release the capture when the button is released.

The BLOKOUT2 Program

The BLOKOUT2 program that demonstrates mouse capturing is shown in Figure 7-11.

BLOKOUT2.C

```
/*-------------------------------------------------------
    BLOKOUT2.C -- Mouse Button & Capture Demo Program
                  (c) Charles Petzold, 1998
   -------------------------------------------------------*/

#include <windows.h>

LRESULT CALLBACK WndProc (HWND, UINT, WPARAM, LPARAM) ;

int WINAPI WinMain (HINSTANCE hInstance, HINSTANCE hPrevInstance,
                    PSTR szCmdLine, int iCmdShow)
{
    static TCHAR szAppName[] = TEXT ("BlokOut2") ;
    HWND        hwnd ;
    MSG         msg ;
    WNDCLASS    wndclass ;

    wndclass.style         = CS_HREDRAW | CS_VREDRAW ;
    wndclass.lpfnWndProc   = WndProc ;
    wndclass.cbClsExtra    = 0 ;
    wndclass.cbWndExtra    = 0 ;
    wndclass.hInstance     = hInstance ;
```

Figure 7-11. *The BLOKOUT2 program.*

```
        wndclass.hIcon         = LoadIcon (NULL, IDI_APPLICATION) ;
        wndclass.hCursor       = LoadCursor (NULL, IDC_ARROW) ;
        wndclass.hbrBackground = (HBRUSH) GetStockObject (WHITE_BRUSH) ;
        wndclass.lpszMenuName  = NULL ;
        wndclass.lpszClassName = szAppName ;

        if (!RegisterClass (&wndclass))
        {
             MessageBox (NULL, TEXT ("Program requires Windows NT!"),
                         szAppName, MB_ICONERROR) ;
             return 0 ;
        }

        hwnd = CreateWindow (szAppName, TEXT ("Mouse Button & Capture Demo"),
                             WS_OVERLAPPEDWINDOW,
                             CW_USEDEFAULT, CW_USEDEFAULT,
                             CW_USEDEFAULT, CW_USEDEFAULT,
                             NULL, NULL, hInstance, NULL) ;

        ShowWindow (hwnd, iCmdShow) ;
        UpdateWindow (hwnd) ;

        while (GetMessage (&msg, NULL, 0, 0))
        {
             TranslateMessage (&msg) ;
             DispatchMessage (&msg) ;
        }
        return msg.wParam ;
}

void DrawBoxOutline (HWND hwnd, POINT ptBeg, POINT ptEnd)
{
     HDC hdc ;

     hdc = GetDC (hwnd) ;

     SetROP2 (hdc, R2_NOT) ;
     SelectObject (hdc, GetStockObject (NULL_BRUSH)) ;
     Rectangle (hdc, ptBeg.x, ptBeg.y, ptEnd.x, ptEnd.y) ;

     ReleaseDC (hwnd, hdc) ;
}

LRESULT CALLBACK WndProc (HWND hwnd, UINT message, WPARAM wParam, LPARAM lParam)
{
     static BOOL  fBlocking, fValidBox ;
     static POINT ptBeg, ptEnd, ptBoxBeg, ptBoxEnd ;
```

(continued)

Figure 7-11. *continued*

```
HDC          hdc ;
PAINTSTRUCT  ps ;

switch (message)
{
case WM_LBUTTONDOWN :
     ptBeg.x = ptEnd.x = LOWORD (lParam) ;
     ptBeg.y = ptEnd.y = HIWORD (lParam) ;

     DrawBoxOutline (hwnd, ptBeg, ptEnd) ;

     SetCapture (hwnd) ;
     SetCursor (LoadCursor (NULL, IDC_CROSS)) ;

     fBlocking = TRUE ;
     return 0 ;

case WM_MOUSEMOVE :
     if (fBlocking)
     {
          SetCursor (LoadCursor (NULL, IDC_CROSS)) ;

          DrawBoxOutline (hwnd, ptBeg, ptEnd) ;

          ptEnd.x = LOWORD (lParam) ;
          ptEnd.y = HIWORD (lParam) ;

          DrawBoxOutline (hwnd, ptBeg, ptEnd) ;
     }
     return 0 ;

case WM_LBUTTONUP :
     if (fBlocking)
     {
          DrawBoxOutline (hwnd, ptBeg, ptEnd) ;

          ptBoxBeg   = ptBeg ;
          ptBoxEnd.x = LOWORD (lParam) ;
          ptBoxEnd.y = HIWORD (lParam) ;

          ReleaseCapture () ;
          SetCursor (LoadCursor (NULL, IDC_ARROW)) ;

          fBlocking = FALSE ;
          fValidBox = TRUE ;

          InvalidateRect (hwnd, NULL, TRUE) ;
     }
```

```
          return 0 ;

     case WM_CHAR :
          if (fBlocking & wParam == '\x1B')          // i.e., Escape
          {
               DrawBoxOutline (hwnd, ptBeg, ptEnd) ;
               ReleaseCapture () ;
               SetCursor (LoadCursor (NULL, IDC_ARROW)) ;

               fBlocking = FALSE ;
          }
          return 0 ;

     case WM_PAINT :
          hdc = BeginPaint (hwnd, &ps) ;

          if (fValidBox)
          {
               SelectObject (hdc, GetStockObject (BLACK_BRUSH)) ;
               Rectangle (hdc, ptBoxBeg.x, ptBoxBeg.y,
                    ptBoxEnd.x, ptBoxEnd.y) ;
          }

          if (fBlocking)
          {
               SetROP2 (hdc, R2_NOT) ;
               SelectObject (hdc, GetStockObject (NULL_BRUSH)) ;
               Rectangle (hdc, ptBeg.x, ptBeg.y, ptEnd.x, ptEnd.y) ;
          }

          EndPaint (hwnd, &ps) ;
          return 0 ;

     case WM_DESTROY :
          PostQuitMessage (0) ;
          return 0 ;
     }
     return DefWindowProc (hwnd, message, wParam, lParam) ;
}
```

BLOKOUT2 is the same as BLOKOUT1, except with three new lines of code: a call to *SetCapture* during the WM_LBUTTONDOWN message and calls to *ReleaseCapture* during the WM_LBUTTONDOWN and WM_CHAR messages. And check this out: Make the window smaller than the screen size, begin blocking out a rectangle within the client area, and then move the mouse cursor outside the client and to the right or bottom, and finally release the mouse button. The program will have the coordinates of the entire rectangle. Just enlarge the window to see it.

Capturing the mouse isn't something suited only for oddball applications. You should do it anytime you need to track WM_MOUSEMOVE messages after a mouse button has been depressed in your client area until the mouse button is released. Your program will be simpler, and the user's expectations will have been met.

The Mouse Wheel

"Build a better mousetrap and the world will beat a path to your door," my mother told me, unknowingly paraphrasing Emerson. Of course, nowadays it might make more sense to build a better *mouse*.

The Microsoft IntelliMouse features an enhancement to the traditional mouse in the form of a little wheel between the two buttons. You can press down on this wheel, in which case it functions as a middle mouse button, or you can turn it with your index finger. This generates a special message named WM_MOUSEWHEEL. Programs that use the mouse wheel respond to this message by scrolling or zooming a document. It sounds like an unnecessary gimmick at first, but I must confess I got accustomed very quickly to using the mouse wheel for scrolling through Microsoft Word and Microsoft Internet Explorer. I won't attempt to discuss all the ways the mouse wheel can be used. Instead, I'll show how you can add mouse wheel logic to an existing program that scrolls data within its client area, a program such as SYSMETS4. The final SYSMETS program is shown in Figure 7-12.

SYSMETS.C

```
/*-------------------------------------------------------
   SYSMETS.C -- Final System Metrics Display Program
                (c) Charles Petzold, 1998
   -----------------------------------------------------*/

#include <windows.h>
#include "sysmets.h"

LRESULT CALLBACK WndProc (HWND, UINT, WPARAM, LPARAM) ;

int WINAPI WinMain (HINSTANCE hInstance, HINSTANCE hPrevInstance,
                    PSTR szCmdLine, int iCmdShow)
{
     static TCHAR szAppName[] = TEXT ("SysMets") ;
     HWND        hwnd ;
     MSG         msg ;
     WNDCLASS    wndclass ;
```

Figure 7-12. *The SYSMETS program.*

```
    wndclass.style         = CS_HREDRAW | CS_VREDRAW ;
    wndclass.lpfnWndProc   = WndProc ;
    wndclass.cbClsExtra    = 0 ;
    wndclass.cbWndExtra    = 0 ;
    wndclass.hInstance     = hInstance ;
    wndclass.hIcon         = LoadIcon (NULL, IDI_APPLICATION) ;
    wndclass.hCursor       = LoadCursor (NULL, IDC_ARROW) ;
    wndclass.hbrBackground = (HBRUSH) GetStockObject (WHITE_BRUSH) ;
    wndclass.lpszMenuName  = NULL ;
    wndclass.lpszClassName = szAppName ;

    if (!RegisterClass (&wndclass))
    {
         MessageBox (NULL, TEXT ("Program requires Windows NT!"),
                     szAppName, MB_ICONERROR) ;
         return 0 ;
    }

    hwnd = CreateWindow (szAppName, TEXT ("Get System Metrics"),
                         WS_OVERLAPPEDWINDOW | WS_VSCROLL | WS_HSCROLL,
                         CW_USEDEFAULT, CW_USEDEFAULT,
                         CW_USEDEFAULT, CW_USEDEFAULT,
                         NULL, NULL, hInstance, NULL) ;

    ShowWindow (hwnd, iCmdShow) ;
    UpdateWindow (hwnd) ;

    while (GetMessage (&msg, NULL, 0, 0))
    {
         TranslateMessage (&msg) ;
         DispatchMessage (&msg) ;
    }
    return msg.wParam ;
}

LRESULT CALLBACK WndProc (HWND hwnd, UINT message, WPARAM wParam, LPARAM lParam)
{
    static int  cxChar, cxCaps, cyChar, cxClient, cyClient, iMaxWidth ;
    static int  iDeltaPerLine, iAccumDelta ;    // for mouse wheel logic
    HDC         hdc ;
    int         i, x, y, iVertPos, iHorzPos, iPaintBeg, iPaintEnd ;
    PAINTSTRUCT ps ;
    SCROLLINFO  si ;
    TCHAR       szBuffer[10] ;
    TEXTMETRIC  tm ;
    ULONG       ulScrollLines ;                 // for mouse wheel logic
```

(continued)

Figure 7-12. *continued*

```
switch (message)
{
case WM_CREATE:
     hdc = GetDC (hwnd) ;

     GetTextMetrics (hdc, &tm) ;
     cxChar = tm.tmAveCharWidth ;
     cxCaps = (tm.tmPitchAndFamily & 1 ? 3 : 2) * cxChar / 2 ;
     cyChar = tm.tmHeight + tm.tmExternalLeading ;

     ReleaseDC (hwnd, hdc) ;

         // Save the width of the three columns

     iMaxWidth = 40 * cxChar + 22 * cxCaps ;

         // Fall through for mouse wheel information

case WM_SETTINGCHANGE:
     SystemParametersInfo (SPI_GETWHEELSCROLLLINES, 0, &ulScrollLines, 0) ;

         // ulScrollLines usually equals 3 or 0 (for no scrolling)
         // WHEEL_DELTA equals 120, so iDeltaPerLine will be 40

     if (ulScrollLines)
         iDeltaPerLine = WHEEL_DELTA / ulScrollLines ;
     else
         iDeltaPerLine = 0 ;

     return 0 ;

case WM_SIZE:
     cxClient = LOWORD (lParam) ;
     cyClient = HIWORD (lParam) ;

         // Set vertical scroll bar range and page size

     si.cbSize = sizeof (si) ;
     si.fMask  = SIF_RANGE | SIF_PAGE ;
     si.nMin   = 0 ;
     si.nMax   = NUMLINES - 1 ;
     si.nPage  = cyClient / cyChar ;
     SetScrollInfo (hwnd, SB_VERT, &si, TRUE) ;

         // Set horizontal scroll bar range and page size

     si.cbSize = sizeof (si) ;
```

```
            si.fMask  = SIF_RANGE | SIF_PAGE ;
            si.nMin   = 0 ;
            si.nMax   = 2 + iMaxWidth / cxChar ;
            si.nPage  = cxClient / cxChar ;
            SetScrollInfo (hwnd, SB_HORZ, &si, TRUE) ;
            return 0 ;

     case WM_VSCROLL:
                 // Get all the vertical scroll bar information

            si.cbSize = sizeof (si) ;
            si.fMask  = SIF_ALL ;
            GetScrollInfo (hwnd, SB_VERT, &si) ;

                 // Save the position for comparison later on

            iVertPos = si.nPos ;

            switch (LOWORD (wParam))
            {
            case SB_TOP:
                 si.nPos = si.nMin ;
                 break ;

            case SB_BOTTOM:
                 si.nPos = si.nMax ;
                 break ;

            case SB_LINEUP:
                 si.nPos -= 1 ;
                 break ;

            case SB_LINEDOWN:
                 si.nPos += 1 ;
                 break ;

            case SB_PAGEUP:
                 si.nPos -= si.nPage ;
                 break ;

            case SB_PAGEDOWN:
                 si.nPos += si.nPage ;
                 break ;

            case SB_THUMBTRACK:
                 si.nPos = si.nTrackPos ;
                 break ;
```

(continued)

Figure 7-12. *continued*

```
              default:
                   break ;
              }
                   // Set the position and then retrieve it.  Due to adjustments
                   //    by Windows it may not be the same as the value set.

              si.fMask = SIF_POS ;
              SetScrollInfo (hwnd, SB_VERT, &si, TRUE) ;
              GetScrollInfo (hwnd, SB_VERT, &si) ;

                   // If the position has changed, scroll the window and update it

              if (si.nPos != iVertPos)
              {
                   ScrollWindow (hwnd, 0, cyChar * (iVertPos - si.nPos),
                                        NULL, NULL) ;
                   UpdateWindow (hwnd) ;
              }
              return 0 ;

         case WM_HSCROLL:
                   // Get all the vertical scroll bar information

              si.cbSize = sizeof (si) ;
              si.fMask  = SIF_ALL ;

                   // Save the position for comparison later on

              GetScrollInfo (hwnd, SB_HORZ, &si) ;
              iHorzPos = si.nPos ;

              switch (LOWORD (wParam))
              {
              case SB_LINELEFT:
                   si.nPos -= 1 ;
                   break ;

              case SB_LINERIGHT:
                   si.nPos += 1 ;
                   break ;

              case SB_PAGELEFT:
                   si.nPos -= si.nPage ;
                   break ;
```

```
     case SB_PAGERIGHT:
          si.nPos += si.nPage ;
          break ;

     case SB_THUMBPOSITION:
          si.nPos = si.nTrackPos ;
          break ;

     default:
          break ;
     }
          // Set the position and then retrieve it.  Due to adjustments
          //   by Windows it may not be the same as the value set.

     si.fMask = SIF_POS ;
     SetScrollInfo (hwnd, SB_HORZ, &si, TRUE) ;
     GetScrollInfo (hwnd, SB_HORZ, &si) ;

          // If the position has changed, scroll the window

     if (si.nPos != iHorzPos)
     {
          ScrollWindow (hwnd, cxChar * (iHorzPos - si.nPos), 0,
                         NULL, NULL) ;
     }
     return 0 ;

case WM_KEYDOWN :
     switch (wParam)
     {
     case VK_HOME :
          SendMessage (hwnd, WM_VSCROLL, SB_TOP, 0) ;
          break ;

     case VK_END :
          SendMessage (hwnd, WM_VSCROLL, SB_BOTTOM, 0) ;
          break ;

     case VK_PRIOR :
          SendMessage (hwnd, WM_VSCROLL, SB_PAGEUP, 0) ;
          break ;

     case VK_NEXT :
          SendMessage (hwnd, WM_VSCROLL, SB_PAGEDOWN, 0) ;
          break ;
```

(continued)

Figure 7-12. *continued*

```
            case VK_UP :
                 SendMessage (hwnd, WM_VSCROLL, SB_LINEUP, 0) ;
                 break ;

            case VK_DOWN :
                 SendMessage (hwnd, WM_VSCROLL, SB_LINEDOWN, 0) ;
                 break ;

            case VK_LEFT :
                 SendMessage (hwnd, WM_HSCROLL, SB_PAGEUP, 0) ;
                 break ;

            case VK_RIGHT :
                 SendMessage (hwnd, WM_HSCROLL, SB_PAGEDOWN, 0) ;
                 break ;
            }
            return 0 ;

     case WM_MOUSEWHEEL:
            if (iDeltaPerLine == 0)
                 break ;

            iAccumDelta += (short) HIWORD (wParam) ;       // 120 or -120

            while (iAccumDelta >= iDeltaPerLine)
            {
                 SendMessage (hwnd, WM_VSCROLL, SB_LINEUP, 0) ;
                 iAccumDelta -= iDeltaPerLine ;
            }

            while (iAccumDelta <= -iDeltaPerLine)
            {
                 SendMessage (hwnd, WM_VSCROLL, SB_LINEDOWN, 0) ;
                 iAccumDelta += iDeltaPerLine ;
            }

            return 0 ;

     case WM_PAINT :
            hdc = BeginPaint (hwnd, &ps) ;

                 // Get vertical scroll bar position

            si.cbSize = sizeof (si) ;
            si.fMask  = SIF_POS ;
```

```
        GetScrollInfo (hwnd, SB_VERT, &si) ;
        iVertPos = si.nPos ;

             // Get horizontal scroll bar position

        GetScrollInfo (hwnd, SB_HORZ, &si) ;
        iHorzPos = si.nPos ;

             // Find painting limits

        iPaintBeg = max (0, iVertPos + ps.rcPaint.top / cyChar) ;
        iPaintEnd = min (NUMLINES - 1,
                         iVertPos + ps.rcPaint.bottom / cyChar) ;

        for (i = iPaintBeg ; i <= iPaintEnd ; i++)
        {
             x = cxChar * (1 - iHorzPos) ;
             y = cyChar * (i - iVertPos) ;

             TextOut (hdc, x, y,
                      sysmetrics[i].szLabel,
                      lstrlen (sysmetrics[i].szLabel)) ;

             TextOut (hdc, x + 22 * cxCaps, y,
                      sysmetrics[i].szDesc,
                      lstrlen (sysmetrics[i].szDesc)) ;

             SetTextAlign (hdc, TA_RIGHT | TA_TOP) ;

             TextOut (hdc, x + 22 * cxCaps + 40 * cxChar, y, szBuffer,
                      wsprintf (szBuffer, TEXT ("%5d"),
                          GetSystemMetrics (sysmetrics[i].iIndex))) ;

             SetTextAlign (hdc, TA_LEFT | TA_TOP) ;
        }

        EndPaint (hwnd, &ps) ;
        return 0 ;

   case WM_DESTROY :
        PostQuitMessage (0) ;
        return 0 ;
   }
   return DefWindowProc (hwnd, message, wParam, lParam) ;
}
```

Rotating the wheel causes Windows to generate WM_MOUSEWHEEL messages to the window with the input focus (*not* the window underneath the mouse cursor). As usual, *lParam* contains the position of the mouse; however, the coordinates are relative to the upper left corner of the screen rather than the client area. Also as usual, the low word of *wParam* contains a series of flags indicating the state of the mouse buttons and the Shift and Ctrl keys.

The new information is in the high word of *wParam*. This is a "delta" value that is currently likely to be either 120 or −120, depending on whether the wheel is rotated forward (that is, toward the front of the mouse, the end with the buttons and cable) or backward. The values of 120 or −120 indicate that the document is to be scrolled three lines up or down, respectively. The idea here is that future versions of the mouse wheel can have a finer gradation than the current mouse and would generate WM_MOUSEWHEEL messages with delta values of (for example) 40 and −40. These values would cause the document to be scrolled just one line up or down.

To keep the program generalized, SYSMETS calls *SystemParametersInfo* with the SPI_GETWHEELSCROLLLINES during the WM_CREATE and WM_SETTINGCHANGE messages. This value indicates how many lines to scroll for a delta value of WHEEL_DELTA, which is defined in WINUSER.H. WHEEL_DELTA equals 120 and by default *SystemParametersInfo* returns 3, so the delta value associated with scrolling one line is 40. SYSMETS stores this value in *iDeltaPerLine*.

During the WM_MOUSEWHEEL messages, SYSMETS adds the delta value to the static variable *iAccumDelta*. Then, if *iAccumDelta* is greater than or equal to *iDeltaPerLine* (or less than or equal to −*iDeltaPerLine*), SYSMETS generates WM_VSCROLL messages using SB_LINEUP or SB_LINEDOWN values. For each WM_VSCROLL message, *iAccumDelta* is decreased (or increased) by *iDeltaPerLine*. This code allows for delta values that are greater than, less than, or equal to the delta value required to scroll one line.

STILL TO COME

The only other outstanding mouse issue is the creation of customized mouse cursors. I'll cover this subject in Chapter 10 along with an introduction to other Windows resources.

Chapter 8

The Timer

The Microsoft Windows timer is an input device that periodically notifies an application when a specified interval of time has elapsed. Your program tells Windows the interval, in effect saying, for example, "Give me a nudge every 10 seconds." Windows then sends your program recurrent WM_TIMER messages to signal the intervals.

At first, the Windows timer might seem a less important input device than the keyboard and mouse, and certainly it is for many applications. But the timer is more useful than you may think, and not only for programs that display time, such as the Windows clock that appears in the taskbar and the two clock programs in this chapter. Here are some other uses for the Windows timer, some perhaps not so obvious:

- *Multitasking* Although Windows 98 is a preemptive multitasking environment, sometimes it is more efficient for a program to return control to Windows as quickly as possible after processing a message. If a program must do a large amount of processing, it can divide the job into smaller pieces and process each piece upon receipt of a WM_TIMER message. (I'll have more to say on this subject in Chapter 20.)

- *Maintaining an updated status report* A program can use the timer to display "real-time" updates of continuously changing information, such as a display of system resources or the progress of a certain task.

- *Implementing an "autosave" feature* The timer can prompt a Windows program to save a user's work to disk whenever a specified period of time has elapsed.

- *Terminating "demo" versions of programs* Some demonstration versions of programs are designed to terminate, say, 30 minutes after they begin. The timer can signal such applications when the time is up.

■ *Pacing movement* Graphical objects in a game or successive displays in a computer-assisted instruction program might need to proceed at a set rate. Using the timer eliminates the inconsistencies that might result from variations in microprocessor speed.

■ *Multimedia* Programs that play CD audio, sound, or music often let the audio data play in the background. A program can use the timer to periodically determine how much of the audio has played and to coordinate on-screen visual information.

Another way to think of the timer is as a guarantee that a program can regain control sometime in the future after exiting the window procedure. Usually a program can't know when the next message is coming.

TIMER BASICS

You can allocate a timer for your Windows program by calling the *SetTimer* function. *SetTimer* includes an unsigned integer argument specifying a time-out interval that can range (in theory) from 1 msec (millisecond) to 4,294,967,295 msec, which is nearly 50 days. The value indicates the rate at which Windows sends your program WM_TIMER messages. For instance, an interval of 1000 msec causes Windows to send your program a WM_TIMER message every second.

When your program is done using the timer, it calls the *KillTimer* function to stop the timer messages. You can program a "one-shot" timer by calling *KillTimer* during the processing of the WM_TIMER message. The *KillTimer* call purges the message queue of any pending WM_TIMER messages. Your program will never receive a stray WM_TIMER message following a *KillTimer* call.

The System and the Timer

The Windows timer is a relatively simple extension of the timer logic built into the PC's hardware and the ROM BIOS. Back in the pre-Windows days of MS-DOS programming, an application could implement a clock or a timer by trapping a BIOS interrupt called the "timer tick." This interrupt occurred every 54.925 msec, or about 18.2 times per second. This is the original 4.772720 MHz microprocessor clock of the original IBM PC divided by 2^{18}.

Windows applications do not trap BIOS interrupts. Instead, Windows itself handles the hardware interrupts so that applications don't have to. For every timer that is currently set, Windows maintains a counter value that it decrements on every hardware timer tick. When this counter reaches 0, Windows places a WM_TIMER message in the appropriate application's message queue and resets the counter to its original value.

Because a Windows application receives WM_TIMER messages through the normal message queue, you never have to worry about your program being "interrupted" by a sudden WM_TIMER message while doing other processing. In this way, the timer is similar to the keyboard and mouse: the driver handles the asynchronous hardware interrupt events, and Windows translates these events into orderly, structured, serialized messages.

In Windows 98, the timer has the same 55-msec resolution as the underlying PC timer. In Microsoft Windows NT, the resolution of the timer is about 10 msec.

A Windows application cannot receive WM_TIMER messages at a rate faster than this resolution—about 18.2 times per second under Windows 98 and about 100 times per second under Windows NT. Windows rounds down the time-out interval you specify in the *SetTimer* call to an integral multiple of clock ticks. For instance, a 1000-msec interval divided by 54.925 msec is 18.207 clock ticks, which is rounded down to 18 clock ticks, which is really a 989-msec interval. For intervals shorter than 55 msec, each clock tick generates a single WM_TIMER message.

Timer Messages Are Not Asynchronous

Because the timer is based on a hardware timer interrupt, programmers sometimes get led astray in thinking that their programs might get interrupted asynchronously to process WM_TIMER messages.

However, the WM_TIMER messages are not asynchronous. The WM_TIMER messages are placed in the normal message queue and ordered with all the other messages. Therefore, if you specify 1000 msec in the *SetTimer* call, your program is not guaranteed to receive a WM_TIMER message every second or even (as I mentioned earlier) every 989 msec. If your application is busy for more than a second, it will not get any WM_TIMER messages during that time. You can demonstrate this to yourself using the programs shown in this chapter. In fact, Windows handles WM_TIMER messages much like WM_PAINT messages. Both these messages are low priority, and the program will receive them only if the message queue has no other messages.

The WM_TIMER messages are similar to WM_PAINT messages in another respect. Windows does not keep loading up the message queue with multiple WM_TIMER messages. Instead, Windows combines multiple WM_TIMER messages in the message queue into a single message. Therefore, the application won't get a bunch of them at once, although it might get two WM_TIMER messages in quick succession. An application cannot determine the number of "missing" WM_TIMER messages that result from this process.

Thus, a clock program cannot keep time by counting the WM_TIMER messages it receives. The WM_TIMER messages can only inform the application that the time is due to be updated. Later in this chapter, we'll write two clock applications that update themselves every second, and we'll see precisely how this is accomplished.

For convenience, I'll be talking about the timer in terms of "getting a WM_TIMER message every second." But keep in mind that these messages are not precise clock tick interrupts.

USING THE TIMER: THREE METHODS

If you need a timer for the entire duration of your program, you'll probably call *SetTimer* from the *WinMain* function or while processing the WM_CREATE message, and *KillTimer* on exiting *WinMain* or in response to a WM_DESTROY message. You can use a timer in one of three ways, depending on the arguments to the *SetTimer* call.

Method One

This method, the easiest, causes Windows to send WM_TIMER messages to the normal window procedure of the application. The *SetTimer* call looks like this:

```
SetTimer (hwnd, 1, uiMsecInterval, NULL) ;
```

The first argument is a handle to the window whose window procedure will receive the WM_TIMER messages. The second argument is the timer ID, which should be a nonzero number. I have arbitrarily set it to 1 in this example. The third argument is a 32-bit unsigned integer that specifies an interval in milliseconds. A value of 60,000 will deliver a WM_TIMER message once a minute.

You can stop the WM_TIMER messages at any time (even while processing a WM_TIMER message) by calling

```
KillTimer (hwnd, 1) ;
```

The second argument is the same timer ID used in the *SetTimer* call. It's considered good form to kill any active timers in response to a WM_DESTROY message before your program terminates.

When your window procedure receives a WM_TIMER message, *wParam* is equal to the timer ID (which in the above case is simply 1) and *lParam* is 0. If you need to set more than one timer, use a different timer ID for each. The value of *wParam* will differentiate the WM_TIMER message passed to your window procedure. To make your program more readable, you may want to use *#define* statements for the different timer IDs:

```
#define TIMER_SEC 1
#define TIMER_MIN 2
```

You can then set the two timers with two *SetTimer* calls:

```
SetTimer (hwnd, TIMER_SEC, 1000, NULL) ;
SetTimer (hwnd, TIMER_MIN, 60000, NULL) ;
```

The WM_TIMER logic might look something like this:

```
case WM_TIMER:
     switch (wParam)
     {
     case TIMER_SEC:
          [once-per-second processing]
          break ;
     case TIMER_MIN:
          [once-per-minute processing]
          break ;
     }
return 0 ;
```

If you want to set an existing timer to a different elapsed time, you can simply call *SetTimer* again with a different time value. You may want to do this in a clock program if it has an option to show or not show seconds. You'd simply change the timer interval to between 1000 msec and 60,000 msec.

Figure 8-1 shows a simple program that uses the timer. This program, named BEEPER1, sets a timer for 1-second intervals. When it receives a WM_TIMER message, it alternates coloring the client area blue and red and it beeps by calling the function *MessageBeep*. (Although *MessageBeep* is often used as a companion to *MessageBox*, it's really an all-purpose beep function. In PCs equipped with sound boards, you can use the various MB_ICON parameters normally used with *MessageBox* as parameters to *MessageBeep* to make different sounds as selected by the user in the Control Panel Sounds applet.)

BEEPER1 sets the timer while processing the WM_CREATE message in the window procedure. During the WM_TIMER message, BEEPER1 calls *MessageBeep*, inverts the value of *bFlipFlop*, and invalidates the window to generate a WM_PAINT message. During the WM_PAINT message, BEEPER1 obtains a RECT structure for the size of the window by calling *GetClientRect* and colors the window by calling *FillRect*.

BEEPER1.C

```
/*--------------------------------------------
   BEEPER1.C  -- Timer Demo Program No. 1
                 (c) Charles Petzold, 1998
   --------------------------------------------*/

#include <windows.h>

#define ID_TIMER    1

LRESULT CALLBACK WndProc (HWND, UINT, WPARAM, LPARAM) ;
```

Figure 8-1. *The BEEPER1 program.*   *(continued)*

Figure 8-1. *continued*

```
int WINAPI WinMain (HINSTANCE hInstance, HINSTANCE hPrevInstance,
                    PSTR szCmdLine, int iCmdShow)
{
     static TCHAR szAppName[] = TEXT ("Beeper1") ;
     HWND         hwnd ;
     MSG          msg ;
     WNDCLASS     wndclass ;

     wndclass.style         = CS_HREDRAW | CS_VREDRAW ;
     wndclass.lpfnWndProc   = WndProc ;
     wndclass.cbClsExtra    = 0 ;
     wndclass.cbWndExtra    = 0 ;
     wndclass.hInstance     = hInstance ;
     wndclass.hIcon         = LoadIcon (NULL, IDI_APPLICATION) ;
     wndclass.hCursor       = LoadCursor (NULL, IDC_ARROW) ;
     wndclass.hbrBackground = (HBRUSH) GetStockObject (WHITE_BRUSH) ;
     wndclass.lpszMenuName  = NULL ;
     wndclass.lpszClassName = szAppName ;

     if (!RegisterClass (&wndclass))
     {
          MessageBox (NULL, TEXT ("Program requires Windows NT!"),
                      szAppName, MB_ICONERROR) ;
          return 0 ;
     }

     hwnd = CreateWindow (szAppName, TEXT ("Beeper1 Timer Demo"),
                          WS_OVERLAPPEDWINDOW,
                          CW_USEDEFAULT, CW_USEDEFAULT,
                          CW_USEDEFAULT, CW_USEDEFAULT,
                          NULL, NULL, hInstance, NULL) ;

     ShowWindow (hwnd, iCmdShow) ;
     UpdateWindow (hwnd) ;

     while (GetMessage (&msg, NULL, 0, 0))
     {
          TranslateMessage (&msg) ;
          DispatchMessage (&msg) ;
     }
     return msg.wParam ;
}

LRESULT CALLBACK WndProc (HWND hwnd, UINT message, WPARAM wParam, LPARAM lParam)
{
```

```
        static BOOL fFlipFlop = FALSE ;
        HBRUSH      hBrush ;
        HDC         hdc ;
        PAINTSTRUCT ps ;
        RECT        rc ;

        switch (message)
        {
        case WM_CREATE:
             SetTimer (hwnd, ID_TIMER, 1000, NULL) ;
             return 0 ;

        case WM_TIMER :
             MessageBeep (-1) ;
             fFlipFlop = !fFlipFlop ;
             InvalidateRect (hwnd, NULL, FALSE) ;
             return 0 ;

        case WM_PAINT :
             hdc = BeginPaint (hwnd, &ps) ;

             GetClientRect (hwnd, &rc) ;
             hBrush = CreateSolidBrush (fFlipFlop ? RGB(255,0,0) : RGB(0,0,255)) ;
             FillRect (hdc, &rc, hBrush) ;

             EndPaint (hwnd, &ps) ;
             DeleteObject (hBrush) ;
             return 0 ;

        case WM_DESTROY :
             KillTimer (hwnd, ID_TIMER) ;
             PostQuitMessage (0) ;
             return 0 ;
        }
        return DefWindowProc (hwnd, message, wParam, lParam) ;
}
```

Because BEEPER1 audibly indicates every WM_TIMER message it receives, you can get a good idea of the erratic nature of WM_TIMER messages by loading BEEPER1 and performing some other actions within Windows.

Here's a revealing experiment: First invoke the Display applet from the Control Panel, and select the Effects tab. Make sure the "Show window contents while dragging" button is *unchecked*. Now try moving or resizing the BEEPER1 window. This causes the program to enter a "modal message loop." Windows prevents anything from interfering with the move or resize operation by trapping all messages through a message loop inside Windows rather than the message loop in your program. Most messages to a program's window that come through this loop are simply discarded, which is why BEEPER1 stops beeping. When you complete the move or resize, you'll notice that BEEPER1 doesn't get all the WM_TIMER messages it has missed, although the first two messages might be less than a second apart.

When the "Show window contents while dragging" button is checked, the modal message loop within Windows attempts to pass on to your window procedure some of the messages it would otherwise have missed. This sometimes works nicely, and sometimes it doesn't.

Method Two

The first method for setting the timer causes WM_TIMER messages to be sent to the normal window procedure. With this second method, you can direct Windows to send the timer messages to another function within your program.

The function that receives these timer messages is termed a "call-back" function. This is a function in your program that is called from Windows. You tell Windows the address of this function, and Windows later calls the function. This should sound familiar, because a program's window procedure is really just a type of call-back function. You tell Windows the address of the window procedure when registering the window class, and then Windows calls the function when sending messages to the program.

SetTimer is not the only Windows function that uses a call-back. The *CreateDialog* and *DialogBox* functions (discussed in Chapter 11) use call-back functions to process messages in a dialog box; several Windows functions (*EnumChildWindow*, *EnumFonts*, *EnumObjects*, *EnumProps*, and *EnumWindow*) pass enumerated information to call-back functions; and several less commonly used functions (*GrayString*, *LineDDA*, and *SetWindowHookEx*) also require call-back functions.

Like a window procedure, a call-back function must be defined as CALLBACK because it is called by Windows from outside the code space of the program. The parameters to the call-back function and the value returned from the call-back function depend on the purpose of the function. In the case of the call-back function associated with the timer, the parameters are actually the same as the parameters to a window procedure although they are defined differently. However, the timer call-back function does not return a value to Windows.

Let's name the call-back function *TimerProc*. (You can choose any name that doesn't conflict with something else.) This function will process only WM_TIMER messages:

```
VOID CALLBACK TimerProc (HWND hwnd, UINT message, UINT iTimerID, DWORD dwTime)
{
     [process WM_TIMER messages]
}
```

The *hwnd* parameter to *TimerProc* is the handle to the window specified when you call *SetTimer*. Windows will send only WM_TIMER messages to *TimerProc*, so the *message* parameter will always equal WM_TIMER. The *iTimerID* value is the timer ID, and *dwTimer* is a value compatible with the return value from the *GetTickCount* function. This is the number of milliseconds that has elapsed since Windows was started.

As we saw in BEEPER1, the first method for setting a timer requires a *SetTimer* call that looks like this:

```
SetTimer (hwnd, iTimerID, iMsecInterval, NULL) ;
```

When you use a call-back function to process WM_TIMER messages, the fourth argument to *SetTimer* is instead the address of the call-back function, like so:

```
SetTimer (hwnd, iTimerID, iMsecInterval, TimerProc) ;
```

Let's look at some sample code so that you can see how this stuff fits together. The BEEPER2 program, shown in Figure 8-2, is functionally the same as BEEPER1, except that Windows sends the timer messages to *TimerProc* rather than to *WndProc*. Notice that *TimerProc* is declared at the top of the program along with *WndProc*.

BEEPER2.C

```
/*------------------------------------------
   BEEPER2.C -- Timer Demo Program No. 2
                (c) Charles Petzold, 1998
   ------------------------------------------*/

#include <windows.h>

#define ID_TIMER    1

LRESULT CALLBACK WndProc    (HWND, UINT, WPARAM, LPARAM) ;
VOID    CALLBACK TimerProc (HWND, UINT, UINT,   DWORD ) ;

int WINAPI WinMain (HINSTANCE hInstance, HINSTANCE hPrevInstance,
                    PSTR szCmdLine, int iCmdShow)
{
     static char szAppName[] = "Beeper2" ;
     HWND        hwnd ;
     MSG         msg ;
     WNDCLASS    wndclass ;

     wndclass.style         = CS_HREDRAW | CS_VREDRAW ;
     wndclass.lpfnWndProc   = WndProc ;
```

Figure 8-2. *The BEEPER2 program.* (continued)

Figure 8-2. *continued*

```
        wndclass.cbClsExtra    = 0 ;
        wndclass.cbWndExtra    = 0 ;
        wndclass.hInstance     = hInstance ;
        wndclass.hIcon         = LoadIcon (NULL, IDI_APPLICATION) ;
        wndclass.hCursor       = LoadCursor (NULL, IDC_ARROW) ;
        wndclass.hbrBackground = (HBRUSH) GetStockObject (WHITE_BRUSH) ;
        wndclass.lpszMenuName  = NULL ;
        wndclass.lpszClassName = szAppName ;

        if (!RegisterClass (&wndclass))
        {
             MessageBox (NULL, TEXT ("Program requires Windows NT!"),
                         szAppName, MB_ICONERROR) ;
             return 0 ;
        }

        hwnd = CreateWindow (szAppName, "Beeper2 Timer Demo",
                             WS_OVERLAPPEDWINDOW,
                             CW_USEDEFAULT, CW_USEDEFAULT,
                             CW_USEDEFAULT, CW_USEDEFAULT,
                             NULL, NULL, hInstance, NULL) ;

        ShowWindow (hwnd, iCmdShow) ;
        UpdateWindow (hwnd) ;

        while (GetMessage (&msg, NULL, 0, 0))
        {
             TranslateMessage (&msg) ;
             DispatchMessage (&msg) ;
        }
        return msg.wParam ;
}

LRESULT CALLBACK WndProc (HWND hwnd, UINT message, WPARAM wParam, LPARAM lParam)
{
     switch (message)
     {
     case WM_CREATE:
          SetTimer (hwnd, ID_TIMER, 1000, TimerProc) ;
          return 0 ;

     case WM_DESTROY:
          KillTimer (hwnd, ID_TIMER) ;
          PostQuitMessage (0) ;
          return 0 ;
     }
```

```
    return DefWindowProc (hwnd, message, wParam, lParam) ;
}

VOID CALLBACK TimerProc (HWND hwnd, UINT message, UINT iTimerID, DWORD dwTime)
{
    static BOOL fFlipFlop = FALSE ;
    HBRUSH      hBrush ;
    HDC         hdc ;
    RECT        rc ;

    MessageBeep (-1) ;
    fFlipFlop = !fFlipFlop ;

    GetClientRect (hwnd, &rc) ;

    hdc = GetDC (hwnd) ;
    hBrush = CreateSolidBrush (fFlipFlop ? RGB(255,0,0) : RGB(0,0,255)) ;

    FillRect (hdc, &rc, hBrush) ;
    ReleaseDC (hwnd, hdc) ;
    DeleteObject (hBrush) ;
}
```

Method Three

The third method of setting the timer is similar to the second method, except that the *hwnd* parameter to *SetTimer* is set to NULL and the second parameter (normally the timer ID) is ignored. Instead, the function returns a timer ID:

```
iTimerID = SetTimer (NULL, 0, wMsecInterval, TimerProc) ;
```

The *iTimerID* returned from *SetTimer* will be 0 in the rare event that no timer is available.

The first parameter to *KillTimer* (usually the window handle) must also be NULL. The timer ID must be the value returned from *SetTimer*:

```
KillTimer (NULL, iTimerID) ;
```

The *hwnd* parameter passed to the *TimerProc* timer function will also be NULL. This method for setting a timer is rarely used. It might come in handy if you do a lot of *SetTimer* calls at different times in your program and don't want to keep track of which timer IDs you've already used.

Now that you know how to use the Windows timer, you're ready for a couple of useful timer applications.

USING THE TIMER FOR A CLOCK

A clock is the most obvious application for the timer, so let's look at two of them, one digital and one analog.

Building a Digital Clock

The DIGCLOCK program, shown in Figure 8-3, displays the current time using a simulated LED-like 7-segment display.

DIGCLOCK.C

```
/*------------------------------------------
   DIGCLOCK.C -- Digital Clock
                 (c) Charles Petzold, 1998
   ------------------------------------------*/

#include <windows.h>

#define ID_TIMER    1

LRESULT CALLBACK WndProc (HWND, UINT, WPARAM, LPARAM) ;

int WINAPI WinMain (HINSTANCE hInstance, HINSTANCE hPrevInstance,
                    PSTR szCmdLine, int iCmdShow)
{
     static TCHAR szAppName[] = TEXT ("DigClock") ;
     HWND          hwnd ;
     MSG           msg ;
     WNDCLASS      wndclass ;

     wndclass.style         = CS_HREDRAW | CS_VREDRAW ;
     wndclass.lpfnWndProc   = WndProc ;
     wndclass.cbClsExtra    = 0 ;
     wndclass.cbWndExtra    = 0 ;
     wndclass.hInstance     = hInstance ;
     wndclass.hIcon         = LoadIcon (NULL, IDI_APPLICATION) ;
     wndclass.hCursor       = LoadCursor (NULL, IDC_ARROW) ;
     wndclass.hbrBackground = (HBRUSH) GetStockObject (WHITE_BRUSH) ;
     wndclass.lpszMenuName  = NULL ;
     wndclass.lpszClassName = szAppName ;

     if (!RegisterClass (&wndclass))
     {
```

Figure 8-3. *The DIGCLOCK program.*

```
               MessageBox (NULL, TEXT ("Program requires Windows NT!"),
                           szAppName, MB_ICONERROR) ;
               return 0 ;
          }

     hwnd = CreateWindow (szAppName, TEXT ("Digital Clock"),
                          WS_OVERLAPPEDWINDOW,
                          CW_USEDEFAULT, CW_USEDEFAULT,
                          CW_USEDEFAULT, CW_USEDEFAULT,
                          NULL, NULL, hInstance, NULL) ;

     ShowWindow (hwnd, iCmdShow) ;
     UpdateWindow (hwnd) ;

     while (GetMessage (&msg, NULL, 0, 0))
          {
          TranslateMessage (&msg) ;
          DispatchMessage (&msg) ;
          }
     return msg.wParam ;
     }

void DisplayDigit (HDC hdc, int iNumber)
{
     static BOOL  fSevenSegment [10][7] = {
                          1, 1, 1, 0, 1, 1, 1,      // 0
                          0, 0, 1, 0, 0, 1, 0,      // 1
                          1, 0, 1, 1, 1, 0, 1,      // 2
                          1, 0, 1, 1, 0, 1, 1,      // 3
                          0, 1, 1, 1, 0, 1, 0,      // 4
                          1, 1, 0, 1, 0, 1, 1,      // 5
                          1, 1, 0, 1, 1, 1, 1,      // 6
                          1, 0, 1, 0, 0, 1, 0,      // 7
                          1, 1, 1, 1, 1, 1, 1,      // 8
                          1, 1, 1, 1, 0, 1, 1 } ;   // 9
     static POINT ptSegment [7][6] = {
                          7,  6,  11,  2,  31,  2,  35,  6,  31, 10,  11, 10,
                          6,  7,  10, 11,  10, 31,   6, 35,   2, 31,   2, 11,
                         36,  7,  40, 11,  40, 31,  36, 35,  32, 31,  32, 11,
                          7, 36,  11, 32,  31, 32,  35, 36,  31, 40,  11, 40,
                          6, 37,  10, 41,  10, 61,   6, 65,   2, 61,   2, 41,
                         36, 37,  40, 41,  40, 61,  36, 65,  32, 61,  32, 41,
                          7, 66,  11, 62,  31, 62,  35, 66,  31, 70,  11, 70 } ;
     int          iSeg ;
```

(continued)

339

Figure 8-3. *continued*

```
        for (iSeg = 0 ; iSeg < 7 ; iSeg++)
             if (fSevenSegment [iNumber][iSeg])
                  Polygon (hdc, ptSegment [iSeg], 6) ;
     }

void DisplayTwoDigits (HDC hdc, int iNumber, BOOL fSuppress)
     {
        if (!fSuppress || (iNumber / 10 != 0))
             DisplayDigit (hdc, iNumber / 10) ;

        OffsetWindowOrgEx (hdc, -42, 0, NULL) ;
        DisplayDigit (hdc, iNumber % 10) ;
        OffsetWindowOrgEx (hdc, -42, 0, NULL) ;
     }

void DisplayColon (HDC hdc)
     {
        POINT ptColon [2][4] = { 2,  21,  6,  17,  10, 21,  6, 25,
                                 2,  51,  6,  47,  10, 51,  6, 55 } ;

        Polygon (hdc, ptColon [0], 4) ;
        Polygon (hdc, ptColon [1], 4) ;

        OffsetWindowOrgEx (hdc, -12, 0, NULL) ;
     }

void DisplayTime (HDC hdc, BOOL f24Hour, BOOL fSuppress)
     {
        SYSTEMTIME st ;

        GetLocalTime (&st) ;

        if (f24Hour)
             DisplayTwoDigits (hdc, st.wHour, fSuppress) ;
        else
             DisplayTwoDigits (hdc, (st.wHour %= 12) ? st.wHour : 12, fSuppress) ;

        DisplayColon (hdc) ;
        DisplayTwoDigits (hdc, st.wMinute, FALSE) ;
        DisplayColon (hdc) ;
        DisplayTwoDigits (hdc, st.wSecond, FALSE) ;
     }
```

```
LRESULT CALLBACK WndProc (HWND hwnd, UINT message, WPARAM wParam, LPARAM lParam)
{
     static BOOL    f24Hour, fSuppress ;
     static HBRUSH  hBrushRed ;
     static int     cxClient, cyClient ;
     HDC            hdc ;
     PAINTSTRUCT    ps ;
     TCHAR          szBuffer [2] ;

     switch (message)
     {
     case WM_CREATE:
          hBrushRed = CreateSolidBrush (RGB (255, 0, 0)) ;
          SetTimer (hwnd, ID_TIMER, 1000, NULL) ;

                                                   // fall through

     case WM_SETTINGCHANGE:
          GetLocaleInfo (LOCALE_USER_DEFAULT, LOCALE_ITIME, szBuffer, 2) ;
          f24Hour = (szBuffer[0] == '1') ;

          GetLocaleInfo (LOCALE_USER_DEFAULT, LOCALE_ITLZERO, szBuffer, 2) ;
          fSuppress = (szBuffer[0] == '0') ;

          InvalidateRect (hwnd, NULL, TRUE) ;
          return 0 ;

     case WM_SIZE:
          cxClient = LOWORD (lParam) ;
          cyClient = HIWORD (lParam) ;
          return 0 ;

     case WM_TIMER:
          InvalidateRect (hwnd, NULL, TRUE) ;
          return 0 ;

     case WM_PAINT:
          hdc = BeginPaint (hwnd, &ps) ;

          SetMapMode (hdc, MM_ISOTROPIC) ;
          SetWindowExtEx (hdc, 276, 72, NULL) ;
          SetViewportExtEx (hdc, cxClient, cyClient, NULL) ;

          SetWindowOrgEx (hdc, 138, 36, NULL) ;
          SetViewportOrgEx (hdc, cxClient / 2, cyClient / 2, NULL) ;
```

(continued)

Figure 8-3. *continued*

```
        SelectObject (hdc, GetStockObject (NULL_PEN)) ;
        SelectObject (hdc, hBrushRed) ;

        DisplayTime (hdc, f24Hour, fSuppress) ;

        EndPaint (hwnd, &ps) ;
        return 0 ;

   case WM_DESTROY:
        KillTimer (hwnd, ID_TIMER) ;
        DeleteObject (hBrushRed) ;
        PostQuitMessage (0) ;
        return 0 ;
   }
   return DefWindowProc (hwnd, message, wParam, lParam) ;
}
```

The DIGCLOCK window is shown in Figure 8-4.

Figure 8-4. *The DIGCLOCK display.*

Although you can't see it in Figure 8-4, the clock numbers are red. DIGCLOCK's window procedure creates a red brush during the WM_CREATE message and destroys it during the WM_DESTROY message. The WM_CREATE message also provides DIGCLOCK with an opportunity to set a 1-second timer, which is stopped during the WM_DESTROY message. (I'll discuss the calls to *GetLocaleInfo* shortly.)

Upon receipt of a WM_TIMER message, DIGCLOCK's window procedure simply invalidates the entire window with a call to *InvalidateRect*. Aesthetically, this is not the best approach because it means that the entire window will be erased and redrawn every second, sometimes causing flickering in the display. A better solution is to invalidate only those parts of the window that need updating based on the current time. The logic to do this is rather messy, however.

Invalidating the window during the WM_TIMER message forces all the program's real activity into WM_PAINT. DIGCLOCK begins the WM_PAINT message by setting the mapping mode to MM_ISOTROPIC. Thus, DIGCLOCK will use arbitrarily scaled axes that are equal in the horizontal and vertical directions. These axes (set by a call to *SetWindowExtEx*) are 276 units horizontally by 72 units vertically. Of course, these axes seem *quite* arbitrary, but they are based on the size and spacing of the clock numbers.

DIGCLOCK sets the window origin to the point (138, 36), which is the center of the window extents, and the viewport origin to (*cxClient / 2*, *cyClient / 2*). This means that the clock display will be centered in DIGCLOCK's client area but that DIGCLOCK can use axes with an origin of (0, 0) at the upper-left corner of the display.

The WM_PAINT processing then sets the current brush to the red brush created earlier and the current pen to the NULL_PEN and calls the function in DIGCLOCK named *DisplayTime*.

Getting the Current Time

The *DisplayTime* function begins by calling the Windows function *GetLocalTime*, which takes as a single argument the SYSTEMTIME structure, defined in WINBASE.H like so:

```
typedef struct _SYSTEMTIME
{
    WORD wYear ;
    WORD wMonth ;
    WORD wDayOfWeek ;
    WORD wDay ;
    WORD wHour ;
    WORD wMinute ;
    WORD wSecond ;
    WORD wMilliseconds ;
}
SYSTEMTIME, * PSYSTEMTIME ;
```

As is obvious, the SYSTEMTIME structure encodes the date as well as the time. The month is 1-based (that is, January is 1), and the day of the week is 0-based (Sunday is 0). The *wDay* field is the current day of the month, which is also 1-based.

The SYSTEMTIME structure is used primarily with the *GetLocalTime* and *GetSystem-Time* functions. The *GetSystemTime* function reports the current Coordinated Universal Time (UTC), which is roughly the same as Greenwich mean time—the date and time at

Greenwich, England. The *GetLocalTime* function reports the local time, based on the time zone of the location of the computer. The accuracy of these values is entirely dependent on the diligence of the user in keeping the time accurate and in indicating the correct time zone. You can check the time zone set on your machine by double-clicking the time display in the task bar. A program to set your PC's clock from an accurate, exact time source on the Internet is shown in Chapter 23.

Windows also has *SetLocalTime* and *SetSystemTime* functions, as well as some other useful time-related functions that are discussed in */Platform SDK/Windows Base Services/ General Library/Time*.

Displaying Digits and Colons

DIGCLOCK might be somewhat simplified if it used a font that simulated a 7-segment display. Instead, it has to do all the work itself using the *Polygon* function.

The *DisplayDigit* function in DIGCLOCK defines two arrays. The *fSevenSegment* array has 7 BOOL values for each of the 10 decimal digits from 0 through 9. These values indicate which of the segments are illuminated (a 1 value) and which are not (a 0 value). In this array, the 7 segments are ordered from top to bottom and from left to right. Each of the 7 segments is a 6-sided polygon. The *ptSegment* array is an array of POINT structures indicating the graphical coordinates of each point in each of the 7 segments. Each digit is then drawn by this code:

```
for (iSeg = 0 ; iSeg < 7 ; iSeg++)
    if (fSevenSegment [iNumber][iSeg])
        Polygon (hdc, ptSegment [iSeg], 6) ;
```

Similarly (but more simply), the *DisplayColon* function draws the colons that separate the hour and minutes, and the minutes and seconds. The digits are 42 units wide and the colons are 12 units wide, so with 6 digits and 2 colons, the total width is 276 units, which is the size used in the *SetWindowExtEx* call.

Upon entry to the *DisplayTime* function, the origin is at the upper left corner of the position of the leftmost digit. *DisplayTime* calls *DisplayTwoDigits*, which calls *DisplayDigit* twice, and after each time calls *OffsetWindowOrgEx* to move the window origin 42 units to the right. Similarly, the *DisplayColon* function moves the window origin 12 units to the right after drawing the colon. In this way, the functions can use the same coordinates for the digits and colons, regardless of where the object is to appear within the window.

The only other tricky aspects of this code involve displaying the time in a 12-hour or 24-hour format and suppressing the leftmost hours digit if it's 0.

Going International

Although displaying the time as DIGCLOCK does is fairly foolproof, for any more complex displays of the date or time you should rely upon Windows' international support. The easiest way to format a date or time is to use the *GetDateFormat* and *GetTimeFormat* functions. These functions are documented in */Platform SDK/Windows Base Services/ General Library/String Manipulation/String Manipulation Reference/String Manipulation Functions*, but they are discussed in */Platform SDK/Windows Base Services/International Features/National Language Support*. These functions accept SYSTEMTIME structures and format the date and time based on options the user has chosen in the Regional Settings applet of the Control Panel.

DIGCLOCK can't use the *GetDateFormat* function because it knows how to display only digits and colons. However, DIGCLOCK should respect the user's preferences for displaying the time in a 12-hour or 24-hour format, and for suppressing (or not suppressing) the leading hours digit. You can obtain this information from the *GetLocaleInfo* function. Although *GetLocaleInfo* is documented in */Platform SDK/Windows Base Services/ General Library/String Manipulation/String Manipulation Reference/String Manipulation Functions*, the identifiers you use with this function are documented in */Platform SDK/ Windows Base Services/International Features/National Language Support/National Language Support Constants*.

DIGCLOCK initially calls *GetLocaleInfo* twice while processing the WM_CREATE message—the first time with the LOCALE_ITIME identifier (to determine whether the 12-hour or 24-hour format is to be used) and then with the LOCALE_ITLZERO identifier (to suppress a leading zero on the hour display). The *GetLocaleInfo* function returns all information in strings, but in most cases it's fairly easy to convert this to integer data if necessary. DIGCLOCK stores the settings in two static variables and passes them to the *DisplayTime* function.

If the user changes any system setting, the WM_SETTINGCHANGE message is broadcast to all applications. DIGCLOCK processes this message by calling *GetLocaleInfo* again. In this way, you can experiment with different settings by using the Regional Settings applet of the Control Panel.

In theory, DIGCLOCK should probably also call *GetLocaleInfo* with the LOCALE_STIME identifier. This returns the character that the user has selected for separating the hours, minutes, and seconds parts of the time. Because DIGCLOCK is set up to display only colons, this is what the user will get even if something else is preferred. To indicate whether the time is A.M. or P.M., an application can use *GetLocaleInfo* with the LOCALE_S1159 and LOCALE_S2359 identifiers. These identifiers let the program obtain strings that are appropriate for the user's country and language.

We could also have DIGCLOCK process WM_TIMECHANGE messages, which notifies applications of changes to the system date or time. Because DIGCLOCK is updated every second by WM_TIMER messages, this is unnecessary. Processing WM_TIMECHANGE messages would make more sense for a clock that was updated every minute.

Building an Analog Clock

An analog clock program needn't concern itself with internationalization, but the complexity of the graphics more than make up for that simplification. To get it right, you'll need to know some trigonometry. The CLOCK program is shown in Figure 8-5.

CLOCK.C

```
/*----------------------------------------
   CLOCK.C -- Analog Clock Program
              (c) Charles Petzold, 1998
   ---------------------------------------*/

#include <windows.h>
#include <math.h>

#define ID_TIMER    1
#define TWOPI       (2 * 3.14159)

LRESULT CALLBACK WndProc (HWND, UINT, WPARAM, LPARAM) ;

int WINAPI WinMain (HINSTANCE hInstance, HINSTANCE hPrevInstance,
                    PSTR szCmdLine, int iCmdShow)
{
    static TCHAR szAppName[] = TEXT ("Clock") ;
    HWND         hwnd;
    MSG          msg;
    WNDCLASS     wndclass ;

    wndclass.style         = CS_HREDRAW | CS_VREDRAW ;
    wndclass.lpfnWndProc   = WndProc ;
    wndclass.cbClsExtra    = 0 ;
    wndclass.cbWndExtra    = 0 ;
    wndclass.hInstance     = hInstance ;
    wndclass.hIcon         = NULL ;
    wndclass.hCursor       = LoadCursor (NULL, IDC_ARROW) ;
    wndclass.hbrBackground = (HBRUSH) GetStockObject (WHITE_BRUSH) ;
    wndclass.lpszMenuName  = NULL ;
    wndclass.lpszClassName = szAppName ;

    if (!RegisterClass (&wndclass))
    {
        MessageBox (NULL, TEXT ("Program requires Windows NT!"),
                    szAppName, MB_ICONERROR) ;
        return 0 ;
    }
```

Figure 8-5. *The CLOCK program.*

```
        hwnd = CreateWindow (szAppName, TEXT ("Analog Clock"),
                            WS_OVERLAPPEDWINDOW,
                            CW_USEDEFAULT, CW_USEDEFAULT,
                            CW_USEDEFAULT, CW_USEDEFAULT,
                            NULL, NULL, hInstance, NULL) ;

        ShowWindow (hwnd, iCmdShow) ;
        UpdateWindow (hwnd) ;

        while (GetMessage (&msg, NULL, 0, 0))
        {
             TranslateMessage (&msg) ;
             DispatchMessage (&msg) ;
        }
        return msg.wParam ;
}

void SetIsotropic (HDC hdc, int cxClient, int cyClient)
{
     SetMapMode (hdc, MM_ISOTROPIC) ;
     SetWindowExtEx (hdc, 1000, 1000, NULL) ;
     SetViewportExtEx (hdc, cxClient / 2, -cyClient / 2, NULL) ;
     SetViewportOrgEx (hdc, cxClient / 2,  cyClient / 2, NULL) ;
}

void RotatePoint (POINT pt[], int iNum, int iAngle)
{
     int   i ;
     POINT ptTemp ;

     for (i = 0 ; i < iNum ; i++)
     {
         ptTemp.x = (int) (pt[i].x * cos (TWOPI * iAngle / 360) +
             pt[i].y * sin (TWOPI * iAngle / 360)) ;

         ptTemp.y = (int) (pt[i].y * cos (TWOPI * iAngle / 360) -
             pt[i].x * sin (TWOPI * iAngle / 360)) ;

         pt[i] = ptTemp ;
     }
}

void DrawClock (HDC hdc)
{
     int    iAngle ;
     POINT pt[3] ;
```

(continued)

Figure 8-5. *continued*

```
     for (iAngle = 0 ; iAngle < 360 ; iAngle += 6)
     {
          pt[0].x =   0 ;
          pt[0].y = 900 ;

          RotatePoint (pt, 1, iAngle) ;

          pt[2].x = pt[2].y = iAngle % 5 ? 33 : 100 ;

          pt[0].x -= pt[2].x / 2 ;
          pt[0].y -= pt[2].y / 2 ;

          pt[1].x  = pt[0].x + pt[2].x ;
          pt[1].y  = pt[0].y + pt[2].y ;

          SelectObject (hdc, GetStockObject (BLACK_BRUSH)) ;

          Ellipse (hdc, pt[0].x, pt[0].y, pt[1].x, pt[1].y) ;
     }
}

void DrawHands (HDC hdc, SYSTEMTIME * pst, BOOL fChange)
{
     static POINT pt[3][5] = { 0, -150, 100, 0, 0, 600, -100, 0, 0, -150,
                               0, -200,  50, 0, 0, 800,  -50, 0, 0, -200,
                               0,    0,   0, 0, 0,   0,    0, 0, 0,  800 } ;
     int          i, iAngle[3] ;
     POINT        ptTemp[3][5] ;

     iAngle[0] = (pst->wHour * 30) % 360 + pst->wMinute / 2 ;
     iAngle[1] =  pst->wMinute  * 6 ;
     iAngle[2] =  pst->wSecond  * 6 ;

     memcpy (ptTemp, pt, sizeof (pt)) ;

     for (i = fChange ? 0 : 2 ; i < 3 ; i++)
     {
          RotatePoint (ptTemp[i], 5, iAngle[i]) ;

          Polyline (hdc, ptTemp[i], 5) ;
     }
}

LRESULT CALLBACK WndProc (HWND hwnd, UINT message, WPARAM wParam, LPARAM lParam)
{
```

```
    static int         cxClient, cyClient ;
    static SYSTEMTIME  stPrevious ;
    BOOL               fChange ;
    HDC                hdc ;
    PAINTSTRUCT        ps ;
    SYSTEMTIME         st ;

    switch (message)
    {
    case WM_CREATE :
         SetTimer (hwnd, ID_TIMER, 1000, NULL) ;
         GetLocalTime (&st) ;
         stPrevious = st ;
         return 0 ;

    case WM_SIZE :
         cxClient = LOWORD (lParam) ;
         cyClient = HIWORD (lParam) ;
         return 0 ;

    case WM_TIMER :
         GetLocalTime (&st) ;

         fChange = st.wHour   != stPrevious.wHour ||
                   st.wMinute != stPrevious.wMinute ;

         hdc = GetDC (hwnd) ;

         SetIsotropic (hdc, cxClient, cyClient) ;

         SelectObject (hdc, GetStockObject (WHITE_PEN)) ;
         DrawHands (hdc, &stPrevious, fChange) ;

         SelectObject (hdc, GetStockObject (BLACK_PEN)) ;
         DrawHands (hdc, &st, TRUE) ;

         ReleaseDC (hwnd, hdc) ;

         stPrevious = st ;
         return 0 ;

    case WM_PAINT :
         hdc = BeginPaint (hwnd, &ps) ;

         SetIsotropic (hdc, cxClient, cyClient) ;
```

(continued)

349

Figure 8-5. *continued*

```
        DrawClock       (hdc) ;
        DrawHands       (hdc, &stPrevious, TRUE) ;

        EndPaint (hwnd, &ps) ;
        return 0 ;

    case WM_DESTROY :
        KillTimer (hwnd, ID_TIMER) ;
        PostQuitMessage (0) ;
        return 0 ;
    }
    return DefWindowProc (hwnd, message, wParam, lParam) ;
}
```

The CLOCK screen display is shown in Figure 8-6.

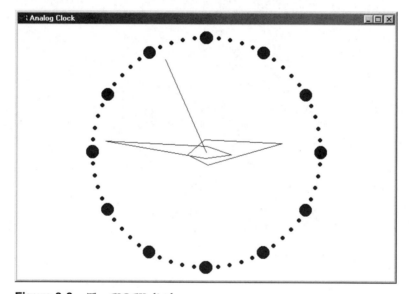

Figure 8-6. *The CLOCK display.*

The isotropic mapping mode is once again ideal for such an application, and setting it is the responsibility of the *SetIsotropic* function in CLOCK.C. After calling *SetMapMode*, the function sets the window extents to 1000 and the viewport extents to half the width of the client area and the negative of half the height of the client area. The viewport origin is set to the center of the client area. As I discussed in Chapter 5, this creates a Cartesian coordinate system with the point (0,0) in the center of the client area and extending 1000 units in all directions.

The *RotatePoint* function is where the trigonometry comes into play. The three parameters to the function are an array of one or more points, the number of points in that array, and the angle of rotation in degrees. The function rotates the points clockwise (as is appropriate for a clock) around the origin. For example, if the point passed to the function is (0,100)—that is, the position of 12:00—and the angle is 90 degrees, the point is converted to (100,0)—which is 3:00. It does this using these formulas:

$$x' = x * cos(a) + y * sin(a)$$

$$y' = y * cos(a) - x * sin(a)$$

The *RotatePoint* function is useful for drawing both the dots of the clock face and the clock hands, as we'll see shortly.

The *DrawClock* function draws the 60 clock face dots starting with the one at the top (12:00 high). Each of them is 900 units from the origin, so the first is located at the point (0, 900) and each subsequent one is 6 additional clockwise degrees from the vertical. Twelve of the dots are 100 units in diameter; the rest are 33 units. The dots are drawn using the *Ellipse* function.

The *DrawHands* function draws the hour, minute, and second hands of the clock. The coordinates defining the outlines of the hands (as they appear when pointing straight up) are stored in an array of POINT structures. Depending upon the time, these coordinates are rotated using the *RotatePoint* function and are displayed with the Windows *Polyline* function. Notice that the hour and minute hands are displayed only if the *bChange* parameter to *DrawHands* is TRUE. When the program updates the clock hands, in most cases the hour and minute hands will not need to be redrawn.

Now let's turn our attention to the window procedure. During the WM_CREATE message, the window procedure obtains the current time and also stores it in the variable named *dtPrevious*. This variable will later be used to determine whether the hour or minute has changed from the previous update.

The first time the clock is drawn is during the first WM_PAINT message. That's just a matter of calling the *SetIsotropic*, *DrawClock*, and *DrawHands* functions, the latter with the *bChange* parameter set to TRUE.

During the WM_TIMER message, *WndProc* first obtains the new time and determines if the hour and minute hands need to be redrawn. If so, all the hands are drawn with a white pen using the previous time, effectively erasing them. Otherwise, only the second hand is erased using the white pen. Then, all the hands are drawn with a black pen.

USING THE TIMER FOR A STATUS REPORT

The final program in this chapter is something I alluded to in Chapter 5. It's the only good use I've found for the *GetPixel* function.

WHATCLR (shown in Figure 8-7) displays the RGB color of the pixel currently under the hot point of the mouse cursor.

WHATCLR.C

```
/*----------------------------------------------
   WHATCLR.C -- Displays Color Under Cursor
                (c) Charles Petzold, 1998
   ----------------------------------------------*/

#include <windows.h>

#define ID_TIMER     1

void FindWindowSize (int *, int *) ;
LRESULT CALLBACK WndProc (HWND, UINT, WPARAM, LPARAM) ;

int WINAPI WinMain (HINSTANCE hInstance, HINSTANCE hPrevInstance,
                    PSTR szCmdLine, int iCmdShow)
{
     static TCHAR szAppName[] = TEXT ("WhatClr") ;
     HWND         hwnd ;
     int          cxWindow, cyWindow ;
     MSG          msg ;
     WNDCLASS     wndclass ;

     wndclass.style         = CS_HREDRAW | CS_VREDRAW ;
     wndclass.lpfnWndProc   = WndProc ;
     wndclass.cbClsExtra    = 0 ;
     wndclass.cbWndExtra    = 0 ;
     wndclass.hInstance     = hInstance ;
     wndclass.hIcon         = LoadIcon (NULL, IDI_APPLICATION) ;
     wndclass.hCursor       = LoadCursor (NULL, IDC_ARROW) ;
     wndclass.hbrBackground = (HBRUSH) GetStockObject (WHITE_BRUSH) ;
     wndclass.lpszMenuName  = NULL ;
     wndclass.lpszClassName = szAppName ;

     if (!RegisterClass (&wndclass))
     {
          MessageBox (NULL, TEXT ("This program requires Windows NT!"),
                      szAppName, MB_ICONERROR) ;
          return 0 ;
     }

     FindWindowSize (&cxWindow, &cyWindow) ;

     hwnd = CreateWindow (szAppName, TEXT ("What Color"),
                          WS_OVERLAPPED | WS_CAPTION | WS_SYSMENU | WS_BORDER,
```

Figure 8-7. *The WHATCLR program.*

```
                         CW_USEDEFAULT, CW_USEDEFAULT,
                         cxWindow, cyWindow,
                         NULL, NULL, hInstance, NULL) ;

     ShowWindow (hwnd, iCmdShow) ;
     UpdateWindow (hwnd) ;

     while (GetMessage (&msg, NULL, 0, 0))
     {
          TranslateMessage (&msg) ;
          DispatchMessage (&msg) ;
     }
     return msg.wParam ;
}

void FindWindowSize (int * pcxWindow, int * pcyWindow)
{
     HDC          hdcScreen ;
     TEXTMETRIC tm ;

     hdcScreen = CreateIC (TEXT ("DISPLAY"), NULL, NULL, NULL) ;
     GetTextMetrics (hdcScreen, &tm) ;
     DeleteDC (hdcScreen) ;

     * pcxWindow = 2 * GetSystemMetrics (SM_CXBORDER) +
                       12 * tm.tmAveCharWidth ;

     * pcyWindow = 2 * GetSystemMetrics (SM_CYBORDER) +
                       GetSystemMetrics (SM_CYCAPTION) +
                       2 * tm.tmHeight ;
}

LRESULT CALLBACK WndProc (HWND hwnd, UINT message, WPARAM wParam, LPARAM lParam)
{
     static COLORREF cr, crLast ;
     static HDC      hdcScreen ;
     HDC             hdc ;
     PAINTSTRUCT     ps ;
     POINT           pt ;
     RECT            rc ;
     TCHAR           szBuffer [16] ;

     switch (message)
     {
     case WM_CREATE:
          hdcScreen = CreateDC (TEXT ("DISPLAY"), NULL, NULL, NULL) ;
```

(continued)

353

Figure 8-7. *continued*

```
          SetTimer (hwnd, ID_TIMER, 100, NULL) ;
          return 0 ;

     case WM_TIMER:
          GetCursorPos (&pt) ;
          cr = GetPixel (hdcScreen, pt.x, pt.y) ;

          SetPixel (hdcScreen, pt.x, pt.y, 0) ;

          if (cr != crLast)
          {
               crLast = cr ;
               InvalidateRect (hwnd, NULL, FALSE) ;
          }
          return 0 ;

     case WM_PAINT:
          hdc = BeginPaint (hwnd, &ps) ;

          GetClientRect (hwnd, &rc) ;

          wsprintf (szBuffer, TEXT ("  %02X %02X %02X  "),
                    GetRValue (cr), GetGValue (cr), GetBValue (cr)) ;

          DrawText (hdc, szBuffer, -1, &rc,
                    DT_SINGLELINE | DT_CENTER | DT_VCENTER) ;

          EndPaint (hwnd, &ps) ;
          return 0 ;

     case WM_DESTROY:
          DeleteDC (hdcScreen) ;
          KillTimer (hwnd, ID_TIMER) ;
          PostQuitMessage (0) ;
          return 0 ;
     }
     return DefWindowProc (hwnd, message, wParam, lParam) ;
}
```

WHATCLR does a little something different while still in *WinMain*. Because WHATCLR's window need only be large enough to display a hexadecimal RGB value, it creates a nonsizeable window using the WS_BORDER window style in the *CreateWindow* function. To calculate the size of the window, WHATCLR obtains an information device context for the video display by calling *CreateIC* and then calls *GetSystemMetrics*. The calculated width and height values of the window are passed to *CreateWindow*.

WHATCLR's window procedure creates a device context for the whole video display by calling *CreateDC* during the WM_CREATE message. This device context is maintained for the lifetime of the program. During the WM_TIMER message, the program obtains the pixel color at the current mouse cursor position. The RGB color is displayed during WM_PAINT.

You may be wondering whether that device context handle obtained from the *CreateDC* function will let you *display* something on any part of the screen rather than just obtain a pixel color. The answer is Yes. It's generally considered impolite for one application to draw on another, but it could come in useful in some odd circumstances.

Chapter 9

Child Window Controls

Recall from Chapter 7 the programs in the CHECKER series. These programs display a grid of rectangles. When you click the mouse in a rectangle, the program draws an X. When you click again, the X disappears. Although the CHECKER1 and CHECKER2 versions of this program use only one main window, the CHECKER3 version uses a child window for each rectangle. The rectangles are maintained by a separate window procedure named *ChildProc*.

If we wanted to, we could add a facility to *ChildProc* to send a message to its parent window procedure (*WndProc*) whenever a rectangle is checked or unchecked. Here's how: The child window procedure can determine the window handle of its parent by calling *GetParent*,

```
hwndParent = GetParent (hwnd) ;
```

where *hwnd* is the window handle of the child window. It can then send a message to the parent window procedure:

```
SendMessage (hwndParent, message, wParam, lParam) ;
```

What would *message* be set to? Well, anything you want, really, as long as the numeric value is set to WM_USER or above. These numbers represent a range of messages that do not conflict with the predefined WM_ messages. Perhaps for this message the child window could set *wParam* to its child window ID. The *lParam* could then be set to a 1 if the child window were being checked and a 0 if it were being unchecked. That's one possibility.

This in effect creates a "child window control." The child window processes mouse and keyboard messages and notifies the parent window when the child window's state has changed. In this way, the child window becomes a high-level input device for the parent window. It encapsulates a specific functionality with regard to its graphical appearance on the screen, its response to user input, and its method of notifying another window when an important input event has occurred.

Although you can create your own child window controls, you can also take advantage of several predefined window classes (and window procedures) that your program can use to create standard child window controls that you've undoubtedly seen in other Windows programs. These controls take the form of buttons, check boxes, edit boxes, list boxes, combo boxes, text strings, and scroll bars. For instance, if you want to put a button labeled "Recalculate" in a corner of your spreadsheet program, you can create it with a single *CreateWindow* call. You don't have to worry about the mouse logic or button painting logic or making the button flash when it's clicked. That's all done in Windows. All you have to do is trap WM_COMMAND messages—that's how the button informs your window procedure when it has been triggered. Is it really that simple? Well, almost.

Child window controls are used most often in dialog boxes. As you'll see in Chapter 11, the position and size of the child window controls are defined in a dialog box template contained in the program's resource script. However, you can also use predefined child window controls on the surface of a normal window's client area. You create each child window with a *CreateWindow* call and adjust the position and size of the child windows with calls to *MoveWindow*. The parent window procedure sends messages to the child window controls, and the child window controls send messages back to the parent window procedure.

As we've been doing since Chapter 3, to create your normal application window you first define a window class and register it with Windows using *RegisterClass*. You then create the window based on that class using *CreateWindow*. When you use one of the predefined controls, however, you do *not* register a window class for the child window. The class already exists within Windows and has a predefined name. You simply use the name as the window class parameter in *CreateWindow*. The window style parameter to *CreateWindow* defines more precisely the appearance and functionality of the child window control. Windows contains the window procedures that process messages to the child windows based on these classes.

Using child window controls directly on the surface of your window involves tasks of a lower level than are required for using child window controls in dialog boxes, where the dialog box manager adds a layer of insulation between your program and the controls themselves. In particular, you'll discover that the child window controls you create on the surface of your window have no built-in facility to move the input focus from one control to another using the Tab or cursor movement keys. A child window control can obtain the input focus, but once it does it won't freely relinquish the input focus back to the parent window. This is a problem we'll struggle with throughout this chapter.

The Windows programming documentation discusses child window controls in two places: First, the simple standard controls that you've seen in countless dialog boxes are described in */Platform SDK/User Interface Services/Controls*. These are buttons (including check boxes and radio buttons), static controls (such as text labels), edit boxes (which let you enter and edit lines or multiple lines of text), scroll bars, list boxes, and combo boxes. With the exception of the combo box, these controls have been around since Windows 1.0. This section of the Windows documentation also includes the rich edit control, which is similar to the edit box but allows editing formatted text with different fonts and such, and application desktop toolbars.

There is also a collection of more esoteric and specialized controls that are perversely referred to as "common controls." These are described in */Platform SDK/User Interface Services/Shell and Common Controls/Common Controls*. I won't be discussing the common controls in this chapter, but they'll appear in various programs throughout the rest of the book. This section of the Windows documentation is a good place to look if you see something in a Windows application that could be useful to your own application.

THE BUTTON CLASS

We'll begin our exploration of the button window class with a program named BTNLOOK ("button look"), which is shown in Figure 9-1. BTNLOOK creates 10 child window button controls, one for each of the 10 standard styles of buttons.

BTNLOOK.C

```
/*-------------------------------------------
   BTNLOOK.C -- Button Look Program
                (c) Charles Petzold, 1998
   -------------------------------------------*/

#include <windows.h>

struct
{
    int     iStyle ;
    TCHAR * szText ;
}
button[] =
{
    BS_PUSHBUTTON,      TEXT ("PUSHBUTTON"),
    BS_DEFPUSHBUTTON,   TEXT ("DEFPUSHBUTTON"),
    BS_CHECKBOX,        TEXT ("CHECKBOX"),
    BS_AUTOCHECKBOX,    TEXT ("AUTOCHECKBOX"),
```

Figure 9-1. *The BTNLOOK program.*

(continued)

Figure 9-1. *continued*

```
      BS_RADIOBUTTON,      TEXT ("RADIOBUTTON"),
      BS_3STATE,           TEXT ("3STATE"),
      BS_AUTO3STATE,       TEXT ("AUTO3STATE"),
      BS_GROUPBOX,         TEXT ("GROUPBOX"),
      BS_AUTORADIOBUTTON,  TEXT ("AUTORADIO"),
      BS_OWNERDRAW,        TEXT ("OWNERDRAW")
} ;

#define NUM (sizeof button / sizeof button[0])

LRESULT CALLBACK WndProc (HWND, UINT, WPARAM, LPARAM) ;

int WINAPI WinMain (HINSTANCE hInstance, HINSTANCE hPrevInstance,
                    PSTR szCmdLine, int iCmdShow)
{
      static TCHAR szAppName[] = TEXT ("BtnLook") ;
      HWND         hwnd ;
      MSG          msg ;
      WNDCLASS     wndclass ;

      wndclass.style         = CS_HREDRAW | CS_VREDRAW ;
      wndclass.lpfnWndProc   = WndProc ;
      wndclass.cbClsExtra    = 0 ;
      wndclass.cbWndExtra    = 0 ;
      wndclass.hInstance     = hInstance ;
      wndclass.hIcon         = LoadIcon (NULL, IDI_APPLICATION) ;
      wndclass.hCursor       = LoadCursor (NULL, IDC_ARROW) ;
      wndclass.hbrBackground = (HBRUSH) GetStockObject (WHITE_BRUSH) ;
      wndclass.lpszMenuName  = NULL ;
      wndclass.lpszClassName = szAppName ;

      if (!RegisterClass (&wndclass))
      {
            MessageBox (NULL, TEXT ("This program requires Windows NT!"),
                        szAppName, MB_ICONERROR) ;
            return 0 ;
      }

      hwnd = CreateWindow (szAppName, TEXT ("Button Look"),
                           WS_OVERLAPPEDWINDOW,
                           CW_USEDEFAULT, CW_USEDEFAULT,
                           CW_USEDEFAULT, CW_USEDEFAULT,
                           NULL, NULL, hInstance, NULL) ;

      ShowWindow (hwnd, iCmdShow) ;
```

```
      UpdateWindow (hwnd) ;

      while (GetMessage (&msg, NULL, 0, 0))
      {
   TranslateMessage (&msg) ;
         DispatchMessage (&msg) ;
      }
      return msg.wParam ;
}

LRESULT CALLBACK WndProc (HWND hwnd, UINT message, WPARAM wParam, LPARAM lParam)
{
      static HWND   hwndButton[NUM] ;
      static RECT   rect ;
      static TCHAR szTop[]    = TEXT ("message          wParam        lParam"),
                   szUnd[]    = TEXT ("_____        _____       _____"),
                   szFormat[] = TEXT ("%-16s%04X-%04X   %04X-%04X"),
                   szBuffer[50] ;
      static int   cxChar, cyChar ;
      HDC          hdc ;
      PAINTSTRUCT  ps ;
      int          i ;

      switch (message)
      {
      case WM_CREATE :
           cxChar = LOWORD (GetDialogBaseUnits ()) ;
           cyChar = HIWORD (GetDialogBaseUnits ()) ;

           for (i = 0 ; i < NUM ; i++)
                hwndButton[i] = CreateWindow ( TEXT("button"),
                                 button[i].szText,
                                 WS_CHILD | WS_VISIBLE | button[i].iStyle,
                                 cxChar, cyChar * (1 + 2 * i),
                                 20 * cxChar, 7 * cyChar / 4,
                                 hwnd, (HMENU) i,
                                 ((LPCREATESTRUCT) lParam)->hInstance, NULL) ;

           return 0 ;

      case WM_SIZE :
           rect.left   = 24 * cxChar ;
           rect.top    =  2 * cyChar ;
           rect.right  = LOWORD (lParam) ;
           rect.bottom = HIWORD (lParam) ;
           return 0 ;
```

(continued)

Figure 9-1. *continued*

```
     case WM_PAINT :
          InvalidateRect (hwnd, &rect, TRUE) ;

          hdc = BeginPaint (hwnd, &ps) ;
          SelectObject (hdc, GetStockObject (SYSTEM_FIXED_FONT)) ;
          SetBkMode (hdc, TRANSPARENT) ;

          TextOut (hdc, 24 * cxChar, cyChar, szTop, lstrlen (szTop)) ;
          TextOut (hdc, 24 * cxChar, cyChar, szUnd, lstrlen (szUnd)) ;

          EndPaint (hwnd, &ps) ;
          return 0 ;

     case WM_DRAWITEM :
     case WM_COMMAND :
          ScrollWindow (hwnd, 0, -cyChar, &rect, &rect) ;

          hdc = GetDC (hwnd) ;
          SelectObject (hdc, GetStockObject (SYSTEM_FIXED_FONT)) ;

          TextOut (hdc, 24 * cxChar, cyChar * (rect.bottom / cyChar - 1),
                   szBuffer,
                   wsprintf (szBuffer, szFormat,
                        message == WM_DRAWITEM ? TEXT ("WM_DRAWITEM") :
                                                 TEXT ("WM_COMMAND"),
                        HIWORD (wParam), LOWORD (wParam),
                        HIWORD (lParam), LOWORD (lParam))) ;

          ReleaseDC (hwnd, hdc) ;
          ValidateRect (hwnd, &rect) ;
          break ;

     case WM_DESTROY :
          PostQuitMessage (0) ;
          return 0 ;
     }
     return DefWindowProc (hwnd, message, wParam, lParam) ;
}
```

As you click on each button, the button sends a WM_COMMAND message to the parent window procedure, which is the familiar *WndProc*. BTNLOOK's *WndProc* displays the *wParam* and *lParam* parameters of this message in the right half of the client area, as shown in Figure 9-2.

The button with the style BS_OWNERDRAW is displayed on this window only with a background shading because this is a style of button that the program is responsible for drawing. The button indicates it needs drawing by WM_DRAWITEM messages containing an *lParam* message parameter that is a pointer to a structure of type DRAWITEMSTRUCT. These messages are also displayed in BTNLOOK. I'll discuss owner-draw buttons in more detail later in this chapter.

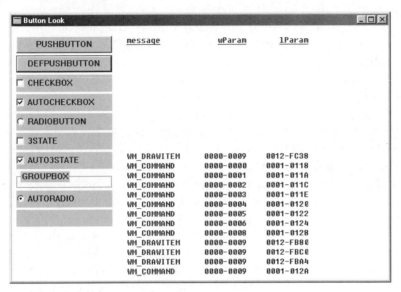

Figure 9-2. *The BTNLOOK display.*

Creating the Child Windows

BTNLOOK defines a structure called *button* that contains button window styles and descriptive text strings for each of the 10 types of buttons. The button window styles all begin with the letters BS, which stand for "button style." The 10 button child windows are created in a *for* loop during WM_CREATE message processing in *WndProc*. The *CreateWindow* call uses the following parameters:

Class name	TEXT ("button")
Window text	button[i].szText
Window style	WS_CHILD | WS_VISIBLE | button[i].iStyle
x position	cxChar
y position	cyChar * (1 + 2 * i)
Width	20 * xChar
Height	7 * yChar / 4
Parent window	hwnd
Child window ID	(HMENU) i
Instance handle	((LPCREATESTRUCT) lParam) -> hInstance
Extra parameters	NULL

The class name parameter is the predefined name. The window style uses WS_CHILD, WS_VISIBLE, and one of the 10 button styles (BS_PUSHBUTTON, BS_DEFPUSHBUTTON, and so forth) that are defined in the button structure. The window text parameter (which for a normal window is the text that appears in the caption bar) is text that will be displayed with each button. I've simply used text that identifies the button style.

The *x* position and *y* position parameters indicate the placement of the upper left corner of the child window relative to the upper left corner of the parent window's client area. The width and height parameters specify the width and height of each child window. Notice that I'm using a function named *GetDialogBaseUnits* to obtain the width and height of the characters in the default font. This is the function that dialog boxes use to obtain text dimensions. The function returns a 32-bit value comprising a width in the low word and a height in the high word. While *GetDialogBaseUnits* returns roughly the same values as can be obtained from the *GetTextMetrics* function, it's somewhat easier to use and will ensure more consistency with controls in dialog boxes.

The child window ID parameter should be unique for each child window. This ID helps your window procedure identify the child window when processing WM_COMMAND messages from it. Notice that the child window ID is passed in the *CreateWindow* parameter normally used to specify the program's menu, so it must be cast to an HMENU.

The instance handle parameter of the *CreateWindow* call looks a little strange, but we're taking advantage of the fact that during a WM_CREATE message *lParam* is actually a pointer to a structure of type CREATESTRUCT ("creation structure") that has a member *hInstance*. So we cast *lParam* into a pointer to a CREATESTRUCT structure and get *hInstance* out.

(Some Windows programs use a global variable named *hInst* to give window procedures access to the instance handle available in *WinMain*. In *WinMain*, you need to simply set

```
hInst = hInstance ;
```

before creating the main window. In the CHECKER3 program in Chapter 7, we used *GetWindowLong* to obtain this instance handle:

```
GetWindowLong (hwnd, GWL_HINSTANCE)
```

Any of these methods is fine.)

After the *CreateWindow* call, we needn't do anything more with these child windows. The button window procedure within Windows maintains the buttons for us and handles all repainting jobs. (The exception is the button with the BS_OWNERDRAW style; as I'll discuss later, this button style requires the program to draw the button.) At the program's termination, Windows destroys these child windows when the parent window is destroyed.

The Child Talks to Its Parent

When you run BTNLOOK, you see the different button types displayed on the left side of the client area. As I mentioned earlier, when you click a button with the mouse, the child window control sends a WM_COMMAND message to its parent window. BTNLOOK traps the WM_COMMAND message and displays the values of *wParam* and *lParam*. Here's what they mean:

LOWORD (wParam)	Child window ID
HIWORD (wParam)	Notification code
lParam	Child window handle

If you're converting programs written for the 16-bit versions of Windows, be aware that these message parameters have been altered to accommodate 32-bit handles.

The child window ID is the value passed to *CreateWindow* when the child window is created. In BTNLOOK, these IDs are 0 through 9 for the 10 buttons displayed in the client area. The child window handle is the value that Windows returns from the *CreateWindow* call.

The notification code indicates in more detail what the message means. The possible values of button notification codes are defined in the Windows header files:

Button Notification Code Identifier	*Value*
BN_CLICKED	0
BN_PAINT	1
BN_HILITE or BN_PUSHED	2
BN_UNHILITE or BN_UNPUSHED	3
BN_DISABLE	4
BN_DOUBLECLICKED or BN_DBLCLK	5
BN_SETFOCUS	6
BN_KILLFOCUS	7

In reality, you'll never see most of these button values. The notification codes 1 through 4 are for an obsolete button style called BS_USERBUTTON. (It's been replaced with BS_OWNERDRAW and a different notification mechanism.) The notification codes 6 and 7 are sent only if the button style includes the flag BS_NOTIFY. The notification code 5 is sent only for BS_RADIOBUTTON, BS_AUTORADIOBUTTON, and BS_OWNERDRAW buttons, or for other buttons if the button style includes BS_NOTIFY.

You'll notice that when you click a button with the mouse, a dashed line surrounds the text of the button. This indicates that the button has the input focus. All keyboard input now goes to the child window button control rather than to the main window. However, when the button control has the input focus, it ignores all keystrokes except the Spacebar, which now has the same effect as a mouse click.

The Parent Talks to Its Child

Although BTNLOOK does not demonstrate this fact, a window procedure can also send messages to the child window control. These messages include many of the window messages beginning with the prefix WM. In addition, eight button-specific messages are defined in WINUSER.H; each begins with the letters BM, which stand for "button message." These button messages are shown in the following table:

Button Message	Value
BM_GETCHECK	0x00F0
BM_SETCHECK	0x00F1
BM_GETSTATE	0x00F2
BM_SETSTATE	0x00F3
BM_SETSTYLE	0x00F4
BM_CLICK	0x00F5
BM_GETIMAGE	0x00F6
BM_SETIMAGE	0x00F7

The BM_GETCHECK and BM_SETCHECK messages are sent by a parent window to a child window control to get and set the check mark of check boxes and radio buttons. The BM_GETSTATE and BM_SETSTATE messages refer to the normal, or pushed, state of a window when you click it with the mouse or press it with the Spacebar. We'll see how these messages work when we look at each type of button. The BM_SETSTYLE message lets you change the button style after the button is created.

Each child window has a window handle and an ID that is unique among its siblings. Knowing one of these items allows you to get the other. If you know the window handle of the child, you can obtain the ID using

```
id = GetWindowLong (hwndChild, GWL_ID) ;
```

This function (along with *SetWindowLong*) was used in the CHECKER3 program in Chapter 7 to maintain data in a special area reserved when the window class was registered. The area accessed with the GWL_ID identifier is reserved by Windows when the child window is created. You can also use

```
id = GetDlgCtrlID (hwndChild) ;
```

Even though the "Dlg" part of the function name refers to a dialog box, this is really a general-purpose function.

Knowing the ID and the parent window handle, you can get the child window handle:

```
hwndChild = GetDlgItem (hwndParent, id) ;
```

Push Buttons

The first two buttons shown in BTNLOOK are "push" buttons. A push button is a rectangle enclosing text specified in the window text parameter of the *CreateWindow* call. The rectangle takes up the full height and width of the dimensions given in the *CreateWindow* or *MoveWindow* call. The text is centered within the rectangle.

Push-button controls are used mostly to trigger an immediate action without retaining any type of on/off indication. The two types of push-button controls have window styles called BS_PUSHBUTTON and BS_DEFPUSHBUTTON. The "DEF" in BS_DEFPUSHBUTTON stands for "default." When used to design dialog boxes, BS_PUSHBUTTON controls and BS_DEFPUSHBUTTON controls function differently from one another. When used as child window controls, however, the two types of push buttons function the same way, although BS_DEFPUSHBUTTON has a heavier outline.

A push button looks best when its height is 7/4 times the height of a text character, which is what BTNLOOK uses. The push button's width must accommodate at least the width of the text, plus two additional characters.

When the mouse cursor is inside the push button, pressing the mouse button causes the button to repaint itself using 3D-style shading to appear as if it's been depressed. Releasing the mouse button restores the original appearance and sends a WM_COMMAND message to the parent window with the notification code BN_CLICKED. As with the other button types, when a push button has the input focus, a dashed line surrounds the text and pressing and releasing the Spacebar has the same effect as pressing and releasing the mouse button.

You can simulate a push-button flash by sending the window a BM_SETSTATE message. This causes the button to be depressed:

```
SendMessage (hwndButton, BM_SETSTATE, 1, 0) ;
```

This call causes the button to return to normal:

```
SendMessage (hwndButton, BM_SETSTATE, 0, 0) ;
```

The *hwndButton* window handle is the value returned from the *CreateWindow* call.

You can also send a BM_GETSTATE message to a push button. The child window control returns the current state of the button: TRUE if the button is depressed and FALSE if it isn't depressed. Most applications do not require this information, however. And because push buttons do not retain any on/off information, the BM_SETCHECK and BM_GETCHECK messages are not used.

Check Boxes

A check box is a square box with text; the text usually appears to the right of the check box. (If you include the BS_LEFTTEXT style when creating the button, the text appears to the left; you'll probably want to combine this style with BS_RIGHT to right-justify the text.) Check boxes are usually incorporated in an application to allow a user to select options. The check box commonly functions as a toggle switch: clicking the box once causes a check mark to appear; clicking again toggles the check mark off.

The two most common styles for a check box are BS_CHECKBOX and BS_AUTO-CHECKBOX. When you use the BS_CHECKBOX style, you must set the check mark yourself by sending the control a BM_SETCHECK message. The *wParam* parameter is set to 1 to create a check mark and to 0 to remove it. You can obtain the current check state of the box by sending the control a BM_GETCHECK message. You might use code like this to toggle the X mark when processing a WM_COMMAND message from the control:

```
SendMessage ((HWND) lParam, BM_SETCHECK, (WPARAM)
        !SendMessage ((HWND) lParam, BM_GETCHECK, 0, 0), 0) ;
```

Notice the ! operator in front of the second *SendMessage* call. The *lParam* value is the child window handle that is passed to your window procedure in the WM_COMMAND message. When you later need to know the state of the button, send it another BM_GETCHECK message. Or you can retain the current check state in a static variable in your window procedure. You can also initialize a BS_CHECKBOX check box with a check mark by sending it a BM_SETCHECK message:

```
SendMessage (hwndButton, BM_SETCHECK, 1, 0) ;
```

For the BS_AUTOCHECKBOX style, the button control itself toggles the check mark on and off. Your window procedure can ignore WM_COMMAND messages. When you need the current state of the button, send the control a BM_GETCHECK message:

```
iCheck = (int) SendMessage (hwndButton, BM_GETCHECK, 0, 0) ;
```

The value of iCheck is TRUE or nonzero if the button is checked and FALSE or 0 if not.

The other two check box styles are BS_3STATE and BS_AUTO3STATE. As their names indicate, these styles can display a third state as well—a gray color within the check box—which occurs when you send the control a WM_SETCHECK message with *wParam* equal to 2. The gray color indicates to the user that the selection is indeterminate or irrelevant.

The check box is aligned with the rectangle's left edge and is centered within the top and bottom dimensions of the rectangle that were specified during the *CreateWindow* call. Clicking anywhere within the rectangle causes a WM_COMMAND message to be sent to the parent. The minimum height for a check box is one character height. The minimum width is the number of characters in the text, plus two.

Radio Buttons

A radio button is named after the row of buttons that were once quite common on car radios. Each button on a car radio is set for a different radio station, and only one button can be pressed at a time. In dialog boxes, groups of radio buttons are conventionally used to indicate mutually exclusive options. Unlike check boxes, radio buttons do not work as toggles—that is, when you click a radio button a second time, its state remains unchanged.

The radio button looks very much like a check box except that it contains a little circle rather than a box. A heavy dot within the circle indicates that the radio button has been checked. The radio button has the window style BS_RADIOBUTTON or BS_ AUTORADIOBUTTON, but the latter is used only in dialog boxes.

When you receive a WM_COMMAND message from a radio button, you should display its check by sending it a BM_SETCHECK message with *wParam* equal to 1:

```
SendMessage (hwndButton, BM_SETCHECK, 1, 0) ;
```

For all other radio buttons in the same group, you can turn off the checks by sending them BM_SETCHECK messages with *wParam* equal to 0:

```
SendMessage (hwndButton, BM_SETCHECK, 0, 0) ;
```

Group Boxes

The group box, which has the BS_GROUPBOX style, is an oddity in the button class. It neither processes mouse or keyboard input nor sends WM_COMMAND messages to its parent. The group box is a rectangular outline with its window text at the top. Group boxes are often used to enclose other button controls.

Changing the Button Text

You can change the text in a button (or in any other window) by calling *SetWindowText*:

```
SetWindowText (hwnd, pszString) ;
```

where *hwnd* is a handle to the window whose text is being changed and *pszString* is a pointer to a null-terminated string. For a normal window, this text is the text of the caption bar. For a button control, it's the text displayed with the button.

You can also obtain the current text of a window:

```
iLength = GetWindowText (hwnd, pszBuffer, iMaxLength) ;
```

The *iMaxLength* parameter specifies the maximum number of characters to copy into the buffer pointed to by *pszBuffer*. The function returns the string length copied. You can prepare your program for a particular text length by first calling

```
iLength = GetWindowTextLength (hwnd) ;
```

Visible and Enabled Buttons

To receive mouse and keyboard input, a child window must be both visible (displayed) and enabled. When a child window is visible but not enabled, Windows displays the text in gray rather than black.

If you don't include WS_VISIBLE in the window class when creating the child window, the child window will not be displayed until you make a call to *ShowWindow*:

ShowWindow (hwndChild, SW_SHOWNORMAL) ;

But if you include WS_VISIBLE in the window class, you don't need to call *ShowWindow*. However, you can hide the child window by this call to *ShowWindow*:

ShowWindow (hwndChild, SW_HIDE) ;

You can determine if a child window is visible by a call to

IsWindowVisible (hwndChild) ;

You can also enable and disable a child window. By default, a window is enabled. You can disable it by calling

EnableWindow (hwndChild, FALSE) ;

For button controls, this call has the effect of graying the button text string. The button no longer responds to mouse or keyboard input. This is the best method for indicating that a button option is currently unavailable.

You can reenable a child window by calling

EnableWindow (hwndChild, TRUE) ;

You can determine whether a child window is enabled by calling

IsWindowEnabled (hwndChild) ;

Buttons and Input Focus

As I noted earlier in this chapter, push buttons, check boxes, radio buttons, and owner-draw buttons receive the input focus when they are clicked with the mouse. The control indicates it has the input focus with a dashed line that surrounds the text. When the child window control gets the input focus, the parent window loses it; all keyboard input then goes to the control rather than to the parent window. However, the child window control responds only to the Spacebar, which now functions like the mouse. This situation presents an obvious problem: your program has lost control of keyboard processing. Let's see what we can do about it.

As I discussed in Chapter 6, when Windows switches the input focus from one window (such as a parent) to another (such as a child window control), it first sends a

WM_KILLFOCUS message to the window losing the input focus. The *wParam* parameter is the handle of the window that is to receive the input focus. Windows then sends a WM_SETFOCUS message to the window receiving the input focus, with *wParam* specifying the handle of the window losing the input focus. (In both cases, *wParam* might be NULL, which indicates that no window has or is receiving the input focus.)

A parent window can prevent a child window control from getting the input focus by processing WM_KILLFOCUS messages. Assume that the array *hwndChild* contains the window handles of all child windows. (These were saved in the array during the *CreateWindow* calls that created the windows.) NUM is the number of child windows.

```
case WM_KILLFOCUS :
    for (i = 0 ; i < NUM ; i++)
        if (hwndChild [i] == (HWND) wParam)
        {
            SetFocus (hwnd) ;
            break ;
        }
    return 0 ;
```

In this code, when the parent window detects that it's losing the input focus to one of its child window controls, it calls *SetFocus* to restore the input focus to itself.

Here's a simpler (but less obvious) way of doing it:

```
case WM_KILLFOCUS :
    if (hwnd == GetParent ((HWND) wParam))
        SetFocus (hwnd) ;
    return 0 ;
```

Both these methods have a shortcoming, however: they prevent the button from responding to the Spacebar, because the button never gets the input focus. A better approach would be to let the button get the input focus but also to include the facility for the user to move from button to button using the Tab key. At first this sounds impossible, but I'll show you how to accomplish it with a technique called "window subclassing" in the COLORS1 program shown later in this chapter.

CONTROLS AND COLORS

As you can see in Figure 9-2, the display of many of the buttons doesn't look quite right. The push buttons are fine, but the others are drawn with a rectangular gray background that simply shouldn't be there. This is because the buttons are designed to be displayed in dialog boxes, and in Windows 98 dialog boxes have a gray surface. Our window has a white surface because that's how we defined it in the WNDCLASS structure:

```
wndclass.hbrBackground = (HBRUSH) GetStockObject (WHITE_BRUSH) ;
```

We've been doing this because we often display text to the client area, and GDI uses the text color and background color defined in the default device context. These are always black and white. To make these buttons look a little better, we must either change the color of the client area to agree with the background color of the buttons or somehow change the button background color to be white.

The first step to solving this problem is understanding Windows' use of "system colors."

System Colors

Windows maintains 29 system colors for painting various parts of the display. You can obtain and set these colors using *GetSysColor* and *SetSysColors*. Identifiers defined in the windows header files specify the system color. Setting a system color with *SetSysColors* changes it only for the current Windows session.

You can change some (but not all) system colors using the Display section of the Windows Control Panel. The selected colors are stored in the Registry in Microsoft Windows NT and in the WIN.INI file in Microsoft Windows 98. The Registry and WIN.INI file use keywords for the 29 system colors (different from the *GetSysColor* and *SetSysColors* identifiers), followed by red, green, and blue values that can range from 0 to 255. The following table shows how the 29 system colors are identified applying the constants used for *GetSysColor* and *SetSysColors* and also the WIN.INI keywords. The table is arranged sequentially by the values of the COLOR_ constants, beginning with 0 and ending with 28.

GetSysColor *and* SetSysColors	*Registry Key or WIN.INI Identifer*	*Default RGB Value*
COLOR_SCROLLBAR	Scrollbar	C0-C0-C0
COLOR_BACKGROUND	Background	00-80-80
COLOR_ACTIVECAPTION	ActiveTitle	00-00-80
COLOR_INACTIVECAPTION	InactiveTitle	80-80-80
COLOR_MENU	Menu	C0-C0-C0
COLOR_WINDOW	Window	FF-FF-FF
COLOR_WINDOWFRAME	WindowFrame	00-00-00
COLOR_MENUTEXT	MenuText	C0-C0-C0
COLOR_WINDOWTEXT	WindowText	00-00-00
COLOR_CAPTIONTEXT	TitleText	FF-FF-FF
COLOR_ACTIVEBORDER	ActiveBorder	C0-C0-C0
COLOR_INACTIVEBORDER	InactiveBorder	C0-C0-C0
COLOR_APPWORKSPACE	AppWorkspace	80-80-80
COLOR_HIGHLIGHT	Highlight	00-00-80

GetSysColor *and* SetSysColors	Registry Key or WIN.INI Identifer	Default RGB Value
COLOR_HIGHLIGHTTEXT	HighlightText	FF-FF-FF
COLOR_BTNFACE	ButtonFace	C0-C0-C0
COLOR_BTNSHADOW	ButtonShadow	80-80-80
COLOR_GRAYTEXT	GrayText	80-80-80
COLOR_BTNTEXT	ButtonText	00-00-00
COLOR_INACTIVECAPTIONTEXT	InactiveTitleText	C0-C0-C0
COLOR_BTNHIGHLIGHT	ButtonHighlight	FF-FF-FF
COLOR_3DDKSHADOW	ButtonDkShadow	00-00-00
COLOR_3DLIGHT	ButtonLight	C0-C0-C0
COLOR_INFOTEXT	InfoText	00-00-00
COLOR_INFOBK	InfoWindow	FF-FF-FF
[no identifier; use value 25]	ButtonAlternateFace	B8-B4-B8
COLOR_HOTLIGHT	HotTrackingColor	00-00-FF
COLOR_GRADIENTACTIVECAPTION	GradientActiveTitle	00-00-80
COLOR_GRADIENTINACTIVECAPTION	GradientInactiveTitle	80-80-80

Default values for these 29 colors are provided by the display driver, and they might be a little different on different machines.

Now for the bad news: Although many of these colors seem self-explanatory (for example, COLOR_BACKGROUND is the color of the desktop area behind all the windows), the use of system colors in recent versions of Windows has become quite chaotic. Back in the old days, Windows was visually much simpler than it is today. Indeed, prior to Windows 3.0, only the first 13 system colors shown above were defined. With the increased use of more visually complex controls using three-dimensional appearances, more system colors were needed.

The Button Colors

This problem is particularly evident for buttons, each of which requires multiple colors. COLOR_BTNFACE is used for the main surface color of the push buttons and the background color of the others. (This is also the system color used for dialog boxes and message boxes.) COLOR_BTNSHADOW is used for suggesting a shadow at the right and bottom sides of the push buttons and the insides of the checkbox squares and radio button circles. For push buttons, COLOR_BTNTEXT is used for the text color; for the others it's COLOR_WINDOWTEXT. Several other system colors are also used for various parts of the button designs.

So if we want to display buttons on the surface of our client area, one way to avoid the color clash is to yield to these system colors. To begin, you use COLOR_BTNFACE for the background of your client area when defining the window class:

```
wndclass.hbrBackground = (HBRUSH) (COLOR_BTNFACE + 1) ;
```

You can try this in the BTNLOOK program. Windows understands that when the value of *hbrBackground* in the WNDCLASS structure is this low in value, it actually refers to a system color rather than an actual handle. Windows requires that you add 1 when you use these identifiers and are specifying them in the *hbrBackground* field of the WNDCLASS structure, but doing so has no profound purpose other than to prevent the value from being NULL. If the system color happens to be changed while your program is running, the surface of your client area will be invalidated and Windows will use the new COLOR_BTNFACE value. But now we've caused another problem. When you display text using *TextOut*, Windows uses values defined in the device context for the text background color (which erases the background behind the text) and the text color. The default values are white (background) and black (text), regardless of either the system colors or the *hbrBackground* field of the window class structure. So you need to use *SetTextColor* and *SetBkColor* to change your text and text background colors to the system colors. You do this after you obtain the handle to a device context:

```
SetBkColor (hdc, GetSysColor (COLOR_BTNFACE)) ;
SetTextColor (hdc, GetSysColor (COLOR_WINDOWTEXT)) ;
```

Now the client-area background, text background, and text color are all consistent with the button colors. However, if the user changes the system colors while your program is running, you'll want to change the text background color and text color. You can do this using the following code:

```
case WM_SYSCOLORCHANGE:
     InvalidateRect (hwnd, NULL, TRUE) ;
     break ;
```

The WM_CTLCOLORBTN Message

We've seen how we can adjust our client area color and text color to the background colors of the buttons. Can we adjust the colors of the buttons to the colors we prefer in our program? Well, in theory, yes, but in practice, no. What you probably don't want to do is use *SetSysColors* to change the appearance of the buttons. This will affect all programs currently running under Windows; it's something users would not appreciate very much.

A better approach (again, in theory) is to process the WM_CTLCOLORBTN message. This is a message that button controls send to the parent window procedure when the child window is about to paint its client area. The parent window can use this opportunity to alter the colors that the child window procedure will use for painting. (In 16-bit versions of Windows, a message named WM_CTLCOLOR was used for all controls. This has been replaced with separate messages for each type of standard control.)

When the parent window procedure receives a WM_CTLCOLORBTN message, the *wParam* message parameter is the handle to the button's device context and *lParam* is the button's window handle. When the parent window procedure gets this message, the button control has already obtained its device context. When processing a WM_CTLCOLORBTN message in your window procedure, you:

■ Optionally set a text color using *SetTextColor*

■ Optionally set a text background color using *SetBkColor*

■ Return a brush handle to the child window

In theory, the child window uses the brush for coloring a background. It is your responsibility to destroy the brush when it is no longer needed.

Here's the problem with WM_CTLCOLORBTN: Only the push buttons and owner-draw buttons send WM_CTLCOLORBTN to their parent windows, and only owner-draw buttons respond to the parent window processing of the message using the brush for coloring the background. This is fairly useless because the parent window is responsible for drawing owner-draw buttons anyway.

Later on in this chapter, we'll examine cases in which messages similar to WM_CTLCOLORBTN but applying to other types of controls are more useful.

Owner-Draw Buttons

If you want to have total control over the visual appearance of a button but don't want to bother with keyboard and mouse logic, you can create a button with the BS_OWNERDRAW style. This is demonstrated in the OWNDRAW program shown in Figure 9-3.

OWNDRAW.C

```
/*-------------------------------------------
   OWNDRAW.C -- Owner-Draw Button Demo Program
                (c) Charles Petzold, 1996
   ---------------------------------------*/

#include <windows.h>

#define ID_SMALLER     1
#define ID_LARGER      2
```

Figure 9-3. *The OWNDRAW program.*

(continued)

Figure 9-3. *continued*

```
#define BTN_WIDTH        (8 * cxChar)
#define BTN_HEIGHT       (4 * cyChar)

LRESULT CALLBACK WndProc (HWND, UINT, WPARAM, LPARAM) ;

HINSTANCE hInst ;
int WINAPI WinMain (HINSTANCE hInstance, HINSTANCE hPrevInstance,
                    PSTR szCmdLine, int iCmdShow)
{
     static TCHAR szAppName[] = TEXT ("OwnDraw") ;
     MSG         msg ;
     HWND        hwnd ;
     WNDCLASS    wndclass ;

     hInst = hInstance ;

     wndclass.style         = CS_HREDRAW | CS_VREDRAW ;
     wndclass.lpfnWndProc   = WndProc ;
     wndclass.cbClsExtra    = 0 ;
     wndclass.cbWndExtra    = 0 ;
     wndclass.hInstance     = hInstance ;
     wndclass.hIcon         = LoadIcon (NULL, IDI_APPLICATION) ;
     wndclass.hCursor       = LoadCursor (NULL, IDC_ARROW) ;
     wndclass.hbrBackground = (HBRUSH) GetStockObject (WHITE_BRUSH) ;
     wndclass.lpszMenuName  = szAppName ;
     wndclass.lpszClassName = szAppName ;

     if (!RegisterClass (&wndclass))
     {
          MessageBox (NULL, TEXT ("This program requires Windows NT!"),
                      szAppName, MB_ICONERROR) ;
          return 0 ;
     }

     hwnd = CreateWindow (szAppName, TEXT ("Owner-Draw Button Demo"),
                          WS_OVERLAPPEDWINDOW,
                          CW_USEDEFAULT, CW_USEDEFAULT,
                          CW_USEDEFAULT, CW_USEDEFAULT,
                          NULL, NULL, hInstance, NULL) ;

     ShowWindow (hwnd, iCmdShow) ;
     UpdateWindow (hwnd) ;

     while (GetMessage (&msg, NULL, 0, 0))
```

```
        {
             TranslateMessage (&msg) ;
             DispatchMessage (&msg) ;
        }
        return msg.wParam ;
}

void Triangle (HDC hdc, POINT pt[])
{
        SelectObject (hdc, GetStockObject (BLACK_BRUSH)) ;
        Polygon (hdc, pt, 3) ;
        SelectObject (hdc, GetStockObject (WHITE_BRUSH)) ;
}

LRESULT CALLBACK WndProc (HWND hwnd, UINT message, WPARAM wParam, LPARAM lParam)
{
        static HWND       hwndSmaller, hwndLarger ;
        static int        cxClient, cyClient, cxChar, cyChar ;
        int               cx, cy ;
        LPDRAWITEMSTRUCT  pdis ;
        POINT             pt[3] ;
        RECT              rc ;

        switch (message)
        {
        case WM_CREATE :
             cxChar = LOWORD (GetDialogBaseUnits ()) ;
             cyChar = HIWORD (GetDialogBaseUnits ()) ;

                    // Create the owner-draw pushbuttons

             hwndSmaller = CreateWindow (TEXT ("button"), TEXT (""),
                                         WS_CHILD | WS_VISIBLE | BS_OWNERDRAW,
                                         0, 0, BTN_WIDTH, BTN_HEIGHT,
                                         hwnd, (HMENU) ID_SMALLER, hInst, NULL) ;

             hwndLarger  = CreateWindow (TEXT ("button"), TEXT (""),
                                         WS_CHILD | WS_VISIBLE | BS_OWNERDRAW,
                                         0, 0, BTN_WIDTH, BTN_HEIGHT,
                                         hwnd, (HMENU) ID_LARGER, hInst, NULL) ;

             return 0 ;

        case WM_SIZE :
             cxClient = LOWORD (lParam) ;
             cyClient = HIWORD (lParam) ;
```

(continued)

Figure 9-3. *continued*

```
            // Move the buttons to the new center

        MoveWindow (hwndSmaller, cxClient / 2 - 3 * BTN_WIDTH  / 2,
                                 cyClient / 2 -     BTN_HEIGHT / 2,
                    BTN_WIDTH, BTN_HEIGHT, TRUE) ;
        MoveWindow (hwndLarger,  cxClient / 2 +     BTN_WIDTH  / 2,
                                 cyClient / 2 -     BTN_HEIGHT / 2,
                    BTN_WIDTH, BTN_HEIGHT, TRUE) ;
        return 0 ;

    case WM_COMMAND :
        GetWindowRect (hwnd, &rc) ;

            // Make the window 10% smaller or larger

        switch (wParam)
        {
        case ID_SMALLER :
            rc.left   += cxClient / 20 ;
            rc.right  -= cxClient / 20 ;
            rc.top    += cyClient / 20 ;
            rc.bottom -= cyClient / 20 ;
            break ;

        case ID_LARGER :
            rc.left   -= cxClient / 20 ;
            rc.right  += cxClient / 20 ;
            rc.top    -= cyClient / 20 ;
            rc.bottom += cyClient / 20 ;
            break ;
        }

        MoveWindow (hwnd, rc.left, rc.top, rc.right  - rc.left,
                          rc.bottom - rc.top, TRUE) ;
        return 0 ;

    case WM_DRAWITEM :
        pdis = (LPDRAWITEMSTRUCT) lParam ;

            // Fill area with white and frame it black

        FillRect (pdis->hDC, &pdis->rcItem,
                  (HBRUSH) GetStockObject (WHITE_BRUSH)) ;

        FrameRect (pdis->hDC, &pdis->rcItem,
                   (HBRUSH) GetStockObject (BLACK_BRUSH)) ;
```

```
        // Draw inward and outward black triangles
cx = pdis->rcItem.right  - pdis->rcItem.left ;
cy = pdis->rcItem.bottom - pdis->rcItem.top  ;

switch (pdis->CtlID)
{
case ID_SMALLER :
     pt[0].x = 3 * cx / 8 ;  pt[0].y = 1 * cy / 8 ;
     pt[1].x = 5 * cx / 8 ;  pt[1].y = 1 * cy / 8 ;
     pt[2].x = 4 * cx / 8 ;  pt[2].y = 3 * cy / 8 ;

     Triangle (pdis->hDC, pt) ;

     pt[0].x = 7 * cx / 8 ;  pt[0].y = 3 * cy / 8 ;
     pt[1].x = 7 * cx / 8 ;  pt[1].y = 5 * cy / 8 ;
     pt[2].x = 5 * cx / 8 ;  pt[2].y = 4 * cy / 8 ;

     Triangle (pdis->hDC, pt) ;

     pt[0].x = 5 * cx / 8 ;  pt[0].y = 7 * cy / 8 ;
     pt[1].x = 3 * cx / 8 ;  pt[1].y = 7 * cy / 8 ;
     pt[2].x = 4 * cx / 8 ;  pt[2].y = 5 * cy / 8 ;

     Triangle (pdis->hDC, pt) ;

     pt[0].x = 1 * cx / 8 ;  pt[0].y = 5 * cy / 8 ;
     pt[1].x = 1 * cx / 8 ;  pt[1].y = 3 * cy / 8 ;
     pt[2].x = 3 * cx / 8 ;  pt[2].y = 4 * cy / 8 ;

     Triangle (pdis->hDC, pt) ;
     break ;

case ID_LARGER :
     pt[0].x = 5 * cx / 8 ;  pt[0].y = 3 * cy / 8 ;
     pt[1].x = 3 * cx / 8 ;  pt[1].y = 3 * cy / 8 ;
     pt[2].x = 4 * cx / 8 ;  pt[2].y = 1 * cy / 8 ;

     Triangle (pdis->hDC, pt) ;

     pt[0].x = 5 * cx / 8 ;  pt[0].y = 5 * cy / 8 ;
     pt[1].x = 5 * cx / 8 ;  pt[1].y = 3 * cy / 8 ;
     pt[2].x = 7 * cx / 8 ;  pt[2].y = 4 * cy / 8 ;

     Triangle (pdis->hDC, pt) ;
     pt[0].x = 3 * cx / 8 ;  pt[0].y = 5 * cy / 8 ;
     pt[1].x = 5 * cx / 8 ;  pt[1].y = 5 * cy / 8 ;
```

(continued)

Figure 9-3. *continued*

```
                    pt[2].x = 4 * cx / 8 ;   pt[2].y = 7 * cy / 8 ;

                Triangle (pdis->hDC, pt) ;
                pt[0].x = 3 * cx / 8 ;   pt[0].y = 3 * cy / 8 ;
                pt[1].x = 3 * cx / 8 ;   pt[1].y = 5 * cy / 8 ;
                pt[2].x = 1 * cx / 8 ;   pt[2].y = 4 * cy / 8 ;

                Triangle (pdis->hDC, pt) ;
                break ;
            }

                // Invert the rectangle if the button is selected

        if (pdis->itemState & ODS_SELECTED)
                InvertRect (pdis->hDC, &pdis->rcItem) ;

                // Draw a focus rectangle if the button has the focus

        if (pdis->itemState & ODS_FOCUS)
        {
                pdis->rcItem.left   += cx / 16 ;
                pdis->rcItem.top    += cy / 16 ;
                pdis->rcItem.right  -= cx / 16 ;
                pdis->rcItem.bottom -= cy / 16 ;

                DrawFocusRect (pdis->hDC, &pdis->rcItem) ;
        }
        return 0 ;

    case WM_DESTROY :
        PostQuitMessage (0) ;
        return 0 ;
    }
    return DefWindowProc (hwnd, message, wParam, lParam) ;
}
```

This program contains two buttons in the center of its client area, as shown in Figure 9-4. The button on the left has four triangles pointing to the center of the button. Clicking the button decreases the size of the window by 10 percent. The button on the right has four triangles pointing outward, and clicking this button increases the window size by 10 percent.

If you need to display only an icon or a bitmap in the button, you can use the BS_ICON or BS_BITMAP style and set the bitmap using the BM_SETIMAGE message. The BS_OWNERDRAW button style, however, allows complete freedom in drawing the button.

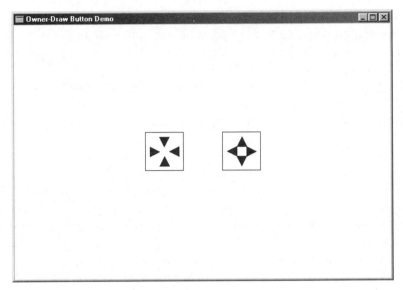

Figure 9-4. *The OWNDRAW display.*

During the WM_CREATE message, OWNDRAW creates two buttons with the BS_ OWNERDRAW style; the buttons are given a width of eight times the system font and four times the system font height. (When using predefined bitmaps to draw buttons, it's useful to know that these dimensions create buttons that are 64 by 64 pixels on a VGA.) The buttons are not yet positioned. During the WM_SIZE message, OWNDRAW positions the buttons in the center of the client area by calling *MoveWindow*.

Clicking on the buttons causes them to generate WM_COMMAND messages. To process the WM_COMMAND message, OWNDRAW calls *GetWindowRect* to store the position and size of the entire window (not only the client area) in a RECT (rectangle) structure. This position is relative to the screen. OWNDRAW then adjusts the fields of this rectangle structure depending on whether the left or right button was clicked. Then the program repositions and resizes the window by calling *MoveWindow*. This generates another WM_SIZE message, and the buttons are repositioned in the center of the client area.

If this were all the program did, it would be entirely functional but the buttons would not be visible. A button created with the BS_OWNERDRAW style sends its parent window a WM_DRAWITEM message whenever the button needs to be repainted. This occurs when the button is first created, when it is pressed or released, when it gains or loses the input focus, and whenever else it needs repainting.

During the WM_DRAWITEM message, the *lParam* message parameter is a pointer to a structure of type DRAWITEMSTRUCT. The OWNDRAW program stores this pointer in a variable named *pdis*. This structure contains the information necessary for a program to draw the button. (The same structure is also used for owner-draw list boxes and menu items.) The structure fields important for working with buttons are *hDC* (the device context for the button), *rcItem* (a RECT structure providing the size of the button), *CtlID* (the control window ID), and *itemState* (which indicates whether the button is pushed or has the input focus).

OWNDRAW begins WM_DRAWITEM processing by calling *FillRect* to erase the surface of the button with a white brush and *FrameRect* to draw a black frame around the button. Then OWNDRAW draws four black-filled triangles on the button by calling *Polygon*. That's the normal case.

If the button is currently being pressed, a bit of the *itemState* field of the DRAWITEMSTRUCT will be set. You can test this bit using the ODS_SELECTED constant. If the bit is set, OWNDRAW inverts the colors of the button by calling *InvertRect*. If the button has the input focus, the ODS_FOCUS bit of the *itemState* field will be set. In this case, OWNDRAW draws a dotted rectangle just inside the periphery of the button by calling *DrawFocusRect*.

A word of warning when using owner-draw buttons: Windows obtains a device context for you and includes it as a field of the DRAWITEMSTRUCT structure. Leave the device context in the same state you found it. Any GDI objects selected into the device context must be unselected. Also, be careful not to draw outside the rectangle defining the boundaries of the button.

THE STATIC CLASS

You create static child window controls by using "static" as the window class in the *CreateWindow* function. These are fairly benign child windows. They do not accept mouse or keyboard input, and they do not send WM_COMMAND messages back to the parent window.

When you move or click the mouse over a static child window, the child window traps the WM_NCHITTEST message and returns a value of HTTRANSPARENT to Windows. This causes Windows to send the same WM_NCHITTEST message to the underlying window, which is usually the parent. The parent usually passes the message to *DefWindowProc*, where it is converted to a client-area mouse message.

The first six static window styles simply draw a rectangle or a frame in the client area of the child window. The "RECT" static styles (left column below) are filled-in rectangles; the three "FRAME" styles (right column) are rectangular outlines that are not filled in.

SS_BLACKRECT	SS_BLACKFRAME
SS_GRAYRECT	SS_GRAYFRAME
SS_WHITERECT	SS_WHITEFRAME

"BLACK," "GRAY," and "WHITE" do not mean the colors are black, gray, and white. Rather, the colors are based on system colors, as shown here:

Static Control	System Color
BLACK	COLOR_3DDKSHADOW
GRAY	COLOR_BTNSHADOW
WHITE	COLOR_BTNHIGHLIGHT

The window text field of the *CreateWindow* call is ignored for these styles. The upper left corner of the rectangle begins at the *x* position and *y* position coordinates relative to the parent window. You can also use the SS_ETCHEDHORZ, SS_ETCHEDVERT, or SS_ETCHEDFRAME styles to create a shadowed-looking frame with the white and gray colors.

The static class also includes three text styles: SS_LEFT, SS_RIGHT, and SS_CENTER. These create left-justified, right-justified, and centered text. The text is given in the window text parameter of the *CreateWindow* call, and it can be changed later using *SetWindowText*. When the window procedure for static controls displays this text, it uses the *DrawText* function with DT_WORDBREAK, DT_NOCLIP, and DT_EXPANDTABS parameters. The text is wordwrapped within the rectangle of the child window.

The background of these three text-style child windows is normally COLOR_BTNFACE, and the text itself is COLOR_WINDOWTEXT. You can intercept WM_CTLCOLOR-STATIC messages to change the text color by calling *SetTextColor* and the background color by calling *SetBkColor* and by returning the handle to the background brush. This will be demonstrated in the COLORS1 program shortly.

Finally, the static class also includes the window styles SS_ICON and SS_USERITEM. However, these styles have no meaning when they are used as child window controls. We'll look at them again when we discuss dialog boxes.

THE SCROLL BAR CLASS

When the subject of scroll bars first came up in Chapter 4, I discussed some of the differences between "window scroll bars" and "scroll bar controls." The SYSMETS programs use window scroll bars, which appear at the right and bottom of the window. You add window scroll bars to a window by including the identifier WS_VSCROLL or WS_HSCROLL or both in the window style when creating the window. Now we're ready to make some scroll bar controls, which are child windows that can appear anywhere in the client area of the parent window. You create child window scroll bar controls by using the predefined window class "scrollbar" and one of the two scroll bar styles SBS_VERT and SBS_HORZ.

Unlike the button controls (and the edit and list box controls to be discussed later), scroll bar controls do not send WM_COMMAND messages to the parent window. Instead, they send WM_VSCROLL and WM_HSCROLL messages, just like window scroll bars. When processing the scroll bar messages, you can differentiate between window scroll bars and scroll bar controls by the *lParam* parameter. It will be 0 for window scroll bars and the scroll bar window handle for scroll bar controls. The high and low words of the *wParam* parameter have the same meaning for window scroll bars and scroll bar controls.

Although window scroll bars have a fixed width, Windows uses the full rectangle dimensions given in the *CreateWindow* call (or later in the *MoveWindow* call) to size the scroll bar controls. You can make long, thin scroll bar controls or short, pudgy scroll bar controls.

If you want to create scroll bar controls that have the same dimensions as window scroll bars, you can use *GetSystemMetrics* to obtain the height of a horizontal scroll bar:

```
GetSystemMetrics (SM_CYHSCROLL) ;
```

or the width of a vertical scroll bar:

```
GetSystemMetrics (SM_CXVSCROLL) ;
```

The scroll bar window style identifiers SBS_LEFTALIGN, SBS_RIGHTALIGN, SBS_TOP ALIGN, and SBS_BOTTOMALIGN are documented to give standard dimensions to scroll bars. However, these styles work only for scroll bars in dialog boxes.

You can set the range and position of a scroll bar control with the same calls used for window scroll bars:

```
SetScrollRange (hwndScroll, SB_CTL, iMin, iMax, bRedraw) ;
SetScrollPos (hwndScroll, SB_CTL, iPos, bRedraw) ;
SetScrollInfo (hwndScroll, SB_CTL, &si, bRedraw) ;
```

The difference is that window scroll bars use a handle to the main window as the first parameter and SB_VERT or SB_HORZ as the second parameter.

Amazingly enough, the system color named COLOR_SCROLLBAR is no longer used for scroll bars. The end buttons and thumb are based on COLOR_BTNFACE, COLOR_BTNHILIGHT, COLOR_BTNSHADOW, COLOR_BTNTEXT (for the little arrows), COLOR_DKSHADOW, and COLOR_BTNLIGHT. The large area between the two end buttons is based on a combination of COLOR_BTNFACE and COLOR_BTNHIGHLIGHT.

If you trap WM_CTLCOLORSCROLLBAR messages, you can return a brush from the message to override the color used for this area. Let's do it.

The COLORS1 Program

To see some uses of scroll bars and static child windows—and also to explore color in more depth—we'll use the COLORS1 program, shown in Figure 9-5. COLORS1 displays three scroll bars in the left half of the client area labeled "Red," "Green," and "Blue." As you scroll the scroll bars, the right half of the client area changes to the composite color indicated by the mix of the three primary colors. The numeric values of the three primary colors are displayed under the three scroll bars.

COLORS1.C

```
/*-------------------------------------------
   COLORS1.C -- Colors Using Scroll Bars
                (c) Charles Petzold, 1998
   -------------------------------------------*/

#include <windows.h>

LRESULT CALLBACK WndProc    (HWND, UINT, WPARAM, LPARAM) ;
LRESULT CALLBACK ScrollProc (HWND, UINT, WPARAM, LPARAM) ;

int     idFocus ;
WNDPROC OldScroll[3] ;

int WINAPI WinMain (HINSTANCE hInstance, HINSTANCE hPrevInstance,
                    PSTR szCmdLine, int iCmdShow)
{
    static TCHAR szAppName[] = TEXT ("Colors1") ;
    HWND         hwnd ;
    MSG          msg ;
    WNDCLASS     wndclass ;

    wndclass.style         = CS_HREDRAW | CS_VREDRAW ;
    wndclass.lpfnWndProc   = WndProc ;
    wndclass.cbClsExtra    = 0 ;
    wndclass.cbWndExtra    = 0 ;
    wndclass.hInstance     = hInstance ;
    wndclass.hIcon         = LoadIcon (NULL, IDI_APPLICATION) ;
    wndclass.hCursor       = LoadCursor (NULL, IDC_ARROW) ;
    wndclass.hbrBackground = CreateSolidBrush (0) ;
    wndclass.lpszMenuName  = NULL ;
    wndclass.lpszClassName = szAppName ;

    if (!RegisterClass (&wndclass))
    {
        MessageBox (NULL, TEXT ("This program requires Windows NT!"),
                    szAppName, MB_ICONERROR) ;
        return 0 ;
    }
```

Figure 9-5. *The COLORS1 program.*   *(continued)*

Figure 9-5. *continued*

```
    hwnd = CreateWindow (szAppName, TEXT ("Color Scroll"),
                        WS_OVERLAPPEDWINDOW,
                        CW_USEDEFAULT, CW_USEDEFAULT,
                        CW_USEDEFAULT, CW_USEDEFAULT,
                        NULL, NULL, hInstance, NULL) ;

    ShowWindow (hwnd, iCmdShow) ;
    UpdateWindow (hwnd) ;

    while (GetMessage (&msg, NULL, 0, 0))
    {
        TranslateMessage (&msg) ;
        DispatchMessage  (&msg) ;
    }
    return msg.wParam ;
}

LRESULT CALLBACK WndProc (HWND hwnd, UINT message, WPARAM wParam, LPARAM lParam)
{
    static COLORREF crPrim[3] = { RGB (255, 0, 0), RGB (0, 255, 0),
                                  RGB (0, 0, 255) } ;
    static HBRUSH   hBrush[3], hBrushStatic ;
    static HWND     hwndScroll[3], hwndLabel[3], hwndValue[3], hwndRect ;
    static int      color[3], cyChar ;
    static RECT     rcColor ;
    static TCHAR *  szColorLabel[] = { TEXT ("Red"), TEXT ("Green"),
                                       TEXT ("Blue") } ;

    HINSTANCE       hInstance ;
    int             i, cxClient, cyClient ;
    TCHAR           szBuffer[10] ;

    switch (message)
    {
    case WM_CREATE :
        hInstance = (HINSTANCE) GetWindowLong (hwnd, GWL_HINSTANCE) ;

            // Create the white-rectangle window against which the
            // scroll bars will be positioned. The child window ID is 9.

        hwndRect = CreateWindow (TEXT ("static"), NULL,
                                 WS_CHILD | WS_VISIBLE | SS_WHITERECT,
                                 0, 0, 0, 0,
                                 hwnd, (HMENU) 9, hInstance, NULL) ;

        for (i = 0 ; i < 3 ; i++)
        {
```

```
                // The three scroll bars have IDs 0, 1, and 2, with
                // scroll bar ranges from 0 through 255.

           hwndScroll[i] = CreateWindow (TEXT ("scrollbar"), NULL,
                                WS_CHILD | WS_VISIBLE |
                                WS_TABSTOP | SBS_VERT,
                                0, 0, 0, 0,
                                hwnd, (HMENU) i, hInstance, NULL) ;

           SetScrollRange (hwndScroll[i], SB_CTL, 0, 255, FALSE) ;
           SetScrollPos   (hwndScroll[i], SB_CTL, 0, FALSE) ;

                // The three color-name labels have IDs 3, 4, and 5,
                // and text strings "Red", "Green", and "Blue".

           hwndLabel [i] = CreateWindow (TEXT ("static"), szColorLabel[i],
                                WS_CHILD | WS_VISIBLE | SS_CENTER,
                                0, 0, 0, 0,
                                hwnd, (HMENU) (i + 3),
                                hInstance, NULL) ;

                // The three color-value text fields have IDs 6, 7,
                // and 8, and initial text strings of "0".

           hwndValue [i] = CreateWindow (TEXT ("static"), TEXT ("0"),
                                WS_CHILD | WS_VISIBLE | SS_CENTER,
                                0, 0, 0, 0,
                                hwnd, (HMENU) (i + 6),
                                hInstance, NULL) ;

           OldScroll[i] = (WNDPROC) SetWindowLong (hwndScroll[i],
                                GWL_WNDPROC, (LONG) ScrollProc) ;

           hBrush[i] = CreateSolidBrush (crPrim[i]) ;
      }

      hBrushStatic = CreateSolidBrush (
                        GetSysColor (COLOR_BTNHIGHLIGHT)) ;

      cyChar = HIWORD (GetDialogBaseUnits ()) ;
      return 0 ;

case WM_SIZE :
      cxClient = LOWORD (lParam) ;
      cyClient = HIWORD (lParam) ;
```

(continued)

Figure 9-5. *continued*

```
      SetRect (&rcColor, cxClient / 2, 0, cxClient, cyClient) ;

      MoveWindow (hwndRect, 0, 0, cxClient / 2, cyClient, TRUE) ;

      for (i = 0 ; i < 3 ; i++)
      {
           MoveWindow (hwndScroll[i],
                     (2 * i + 1) * cxClient / 14, 2 * cyChar,
                     cxClient / 14, cyClient - 4 * cyChar, TRUE) ;

           MoveWindow (hwndLabel[i],
                     (4 * i + 1) * cxClient / 28, cyChar / 2,
                     cxClient / 7, cyChar, TRUE) ;

           MoveWindow (hwndValue[i],
                     (4 * i + 1) * cxClient / 28,
                     cyClient - 3 * cyChar / 2,
                     cxClient / 7, cyChar, TRUE) ;
      }
      SetFocus (hwnd) ;
      return 0 ;

case WM_SETFOCUS :
      SetFocus (hwndScroll[idFocus]) ;
      return 0 ;

case WM_VSCROLL :
      i = GetWindowLong ((HWND) lParam, GWL_ID) ;

      switch (LOWORD (wParam))
      {
      case SB_PAGEDOWN :
           color[i] += 15 ;
                                        // fall through
      case SB_LINEDOWN :
           color[i] = min (255, color[i] + 1) ;
           break ;

      case SB_PAGEUP :
           color[i] -= 15 ;
                                        // fall through
      case SB_LINEUP :
           color[i] = max (0, color[i] - 1) ;
           break ;
```

```
        case SB_TOP :
            color[i] = 0 ;
            break ;

        case SB_BOTTOM :
            color[i] = 255 ;
            break ;

        case SB_THUMBPOSITION :
        case SB_THUMBTRACK :
            color[i] = HIWORD (wParam) ;
            break ;

        default :
            break ;
        }
        SetScrollPos (hwndScroll[i], SB_CTL, color[i], TRUE) ;
        wsprintf (szBuffer, TEXT ("%i"), color[i]) ;
        SetWindowText (hwndValue[i], szBuffer) ;

        DeleteObject ((HBRUSH)
            SetClassLong (hwnd, GCL_HBRBACKGROUND, (LONG)
                CreateSolidBrush (RGB (color[0], color[1], color[2])))) ;

        InvalidateRect (hwnd, &rcColor, TRUE) ;
        return 0 ;

case WM_CTLCOLORSCROLLBAR :
        i = GetWindowLong ((HWND) lParam, GWL_ID) ;
        return (LRESULT) hBrush[i] ;

case WM_CTLCOLORSTATIC :
        i = GetWindowLong ((HWND) lParam, GWL_ID) ;

        if (i >= 3 && i <= 8)     // static text controls
        {
            SetTextColor ((HDC) wParam, crPrim[i % 3]) ;
            SetBkColor ((HDC) wParam, GetSysColor (COLOR_BTNHIGHLIGHT));
            return (LRESULT) hBrushStatic ;
        }
        break ;

case WM_SYSCOLORCHANGE :
        DeleteObject (hBrushStatic) ;
        hBrushStatic = CreateSolidBrush (GetSysColor (COLOR_BTNHIGHLIGHT)) ;
        return 0 ;
```

(continued)

Figure 9-5. *continued*

```
    case WM_DESTROY :
        DeleteObject ((HBRUSH)
            SetClassLong (hwnd, GCL_HBRBACKGROUND, (LONG)
                GetStockObject (WHITE_BRUSH))) ;

        for (i = 0 ; i < 3 ; i++)
            DeleteObject (hBrush[i]) ;

        DeleteObject (hBrushStatic) ;
        PostQuitMessage (0) ;
        return 0 ;
    }
    return DefWindowProc (hwnd, message, wParam, lParam) ;
}

LRESULT CALLBACK ScrollProc (HWND hwnd, UINT message,
                             WPARAM wParam, LPARAM lParam)
{
    int id = GetWindowLong (hwnd, GWL_ID) ;

    switch (message)
    {
    case WM_KEYDOWN :
        if (wParam == VK_TAB)
            SetFocus (GetDlgItem (GetParent (hwnd),
                (id + (GetKeyState (VK_SHIFT) < 0 ? 2 : 1)) % 3)) ;
        break ;

    case WM_SETFOCUS :
        idFocus = id ;
        break ;
    }
    return CallWindowProc (OldScroll[id], hwnd, message, wParam, lParam) ;
}
```

COLORS1 puts its children to work. The program uses 10 child window controls: 3 scroll bars, 6 windows of static text, and 1 static rectangle. COLORS1 traps WM_CTL-COLORSCROLLBAR messages to color the interior sections of the three scroll bars red, green, and blue and traps WM_CTLCOLORSTATIC messages to color the static text.

You can scroll the scroll bars using either the mouse or the keyboard. You can use COLORS1 as a development tool in experimenting with color and choosing attractive (or, if you prefer, ugly) colors for your own Windows programs. The COLORS1 display is shown in Figure 9-6, unfortunately reduced to gray shades for the printed page.

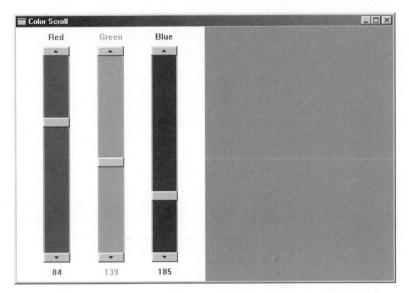

Figure 9-6. *The COLORS1 display.*

COLORS1 doesn't process WM_PAINT messages. Virtually all of the work in COLORS1 is done by the child windows.

The color shown in the right half of the client area is actually the window's background color. A static child window with style SS_WHITERECT blocks out the left half of the client area. The three scroll bars are child window controls with the style SBS_VERT. These scroll bars are positioned on top of the SS_WHITERECT child. Six more static child windows of style SS_CENTER (centered text) provide the labels and the color values. COLORS1 creates its normal overlapped window and the 10 child windows within the *WinMain* function using *CreateWindow*. The SS_WHITERECT and SS_CENTER static windows use the window class "static"; the three scroll bars use the window class "scrollbar."

The x position, y position, width, and height parameters of the *CreateWindow* calls are initially set to 0 because the position and sizing depend on the size of the client area, which is not yet known. COLORS1's window procedure resizes all 10 child windows using *MoveWindow* when it receives a WM_SIZE message. So whenever you resize the COLORS1 window, the size of the scroll bars changes proportionally.

When the *WndProc* window procedure receives a WM_VSCROLL message, the high word of the *lParam* parameter is the handle to the child window. We can use *GetWindowWord* to get the window ID number:

```
i = GetWindowLong ((HWND) lParam, GWL_ID) ;
```

For the three scroll bars, we have conveniently set the ID numbers to 0, 1, and 2, so *WndProc* can tell which scroll bar is generating the message.

Because the handles to the child windows were saved in arrays when the windows were created, *WndProc* can process the scroll bar message and set the new value of the appropriate scroll bar using the *SetScrollPos* call:

```
SetScrollPos (hwndScroll[i], SB_CTL, color[i], TRUE) ;
```

WndProc also changes the text of the child window at the bottom of the scroll bar:

```
wsprintf (szBuffer, TEXT ("%i"), color[I]) ;
SetWindowText (hwndValue[i], szBuffer) ;
```

The Automatic Keyboard Interface

Scroll bar controls can also process keystrokes, but only if they have the input focus. The following table shows how keyboard cursor keys translate into scroll bar messages:

Cursor Key	*Scroll Bar Message* wParam *Value*
Home	SB_TOP
End	SB_BOTTOM
Page Up	SB_PAGEUP
Page Down	SB_PAGEDOWN
Left or Up	SB_LINEUP
Right or Down	SB_LINEDOWN

In fact, the SB_TOP and SB_BOTTOM scroll bar messages can be generated only by using the keyboard. If you want a scroll bar control to obtain the input focus when the scroll bar is clicked with the mouse, you must include the WS_TABSTOP identifier in the window class parameter of the *CreateWindow* call. When a scroll bar has the input focus, a blinking gray block is displayed on the scroll bar thumb.

To provide a full keyboard interface to the scroll bars, however, more work is necessary. First the *WndProc* window procedure must specifically give a scroll bar the input focus. It does this by processing the WM_SETFOCUS message, which the parent window receives when it obtains the input focus. *WndProc* simply sets the input focus to one of the scroll bars:

```
SetFocus (hwndScroll[idFocus]) ;
```

where *idFocus* is a global variable.

But you also need some way to get from one scroll bar to another by using the keyboard, preferably by using the Tab key. This is more difficult, because once a scroll bar has the input focus it processes all keystrokes. But the scroll bar cares only about the cursor keys; it ignores the Tab key. The way out of this dilemma lies in a technique called "window subclassing." We'll use it to add a facility to COLORS1 to jump from one scroll bar to another using the Tab key.

Window Subclassing

The window procedure for the scroll bar controls is somewhere inside Windows. However, you can obtain the address of this window procedure by a call to *GetWindowLong* using the GWL_WNDPROC identifier as a parameter. Moreover, you can set a new window procedure for the scroll bars by calling *SetWindowLong*. This technique, which is called "window subclassing," is very powerful. It lets you hook into existing window procedures, process some messages within your own program, and pass all other messages to the old window procedure.

The window procedure that does preliminary scroll bar message processing in COLORS1 is named *ScrollProc*; it is toward the end of the COLORS1.C listing. Because *ScrollProc* is a function within COLORS1 that is called by Windows, it must be defined as a CALLBACK.

For each of the three scroll bars, COLORS1 uses *SetWindowLong* to set the address of the new scroll bar window procedure and also obtain the address of the existing scroll bar window procedure:

```
OldScroll[i] = (WNDPROC) SetWindowLong (hwndScroll[i], GWL_WNDPROC,
                                        (LONG) ScrollProc)) ;
```

Now the function *ScrollProc* gets all messages that Windows sends to the scroll bar window procedure for the three scroll bars in COLORS1 (but not, of course, for scroll bars in other programs). The *ScrollProc* window procedure simply changes the input focus to the next (or previous) scroll bar when it receives a Tab or Shift-Tab keystroke. It calls the old scroll bar window procedure using *CallWindowProc*.

Coloring the Background

When COLORS1 defines its window class, it gives the background of its client area a solid black brush:

```
wndclass.hbrBackground = CreateSolidBrush (0) ;
```

When you change the settings of COLORS1's scroll bars, the program must create a new brush and put the new brush handle in the window class structure. Just as we were able to get and set the scroll bar window procedure using *GetWindowLong* and *SetWindowLong*, we can get and set the handle to this brush using *GetClassWord* and *SetClassWord*.

You can create the new brush and insert the handle in the window class structure and then delete the old brush:

```
DeleteObject ((HBRUSH)
    SetClassLong (hwnd, GCL_HBRBACKGROUND, (LONG)
        CreateSolidBrush (RGB (color[0], color[1], color[2])))) ;
```

The next time Windows recolors the background of the window, Windows will use this new brush. To force Windows to erase the background, we invalidate the right half of the client area:

```
InvalidateRect (hwnd, &rcColor, TRUE) ;
```

The TRUE (nonzero) value as the third parameter indicates that we want the background erased before repainting.

InvalidateRect causes Windows to put a WM_PAINT message in the message queue of the window procedure. Because WM_PAINT messages are low priority, this message will not be processed immediately if you are still moving the scroll bar with the mouse or the cursor keys. Alternatively, if you want the window to be updated immediately after the color is changed, you can add the statement

```
UpdateWindow (hwnd) ;
```

after the *InvalidateRect* call. But this might slow down keyboard and mouse processing.

COLORS1's *WndProc* function doesn't process the WM_PAINT message but passes it to *DefWindowProc*. Windows' default processing of WM_PAINT messages simply involves calling *BeginPaint* and *EndPaint* to validate the window. Because we specified in the *InvalidateRect* call that the background should be erased, the *BeginPaint* call causes Windows to generate a WM_ERASEBKGND (erase background) message. *WndProc* ignores this message also. Windows processes it by erasing the background of the client area using the brush specified in the window class.

It's always a good idea to clean up before termination, so during processing of the WM_DESTROY message, *DeleteObject* is called once more:

```
DeleteObject ((HBRUSH)
    SetClassLong (hwnd, GCL_HBRBACKGROUND,
        (LONG) GetStockObject (WHITE_BRUSH))) ;
```

Coloring the Scroll Bars and Static Text

In COLORS1, the interiors of the three scroll bars and the text in the six text fields are colored red, green, and blue. The coloring of the scroll bars is accomplished by processing WM_CTLCOLORSCROLLBAR messages.

In *WndProc* we define a static array of three handles to brushes:

```
static HBRUSH hBrush [3] ;
```

During processing of WM_CREATE, we create the three brushes:

```
for (I = 0 ; I < 3 ; I++)
    hBrush[0] = CreateSolidBrush (crPrim [I]) ;
```

where the *crPrim* array contains the RGB values of the three primary colors. During the WM_CTLCOLORSCROLLBAR processing, the window procedure returns one of these three brushes:

```
case WM_CTLCOLORSCROLLBAR:
     i = GetWindowLong ((HWND) lParam, GWL_ID) ;
     return (LRESULT) hBrush [i] ;
```

These brushes must be destroyed during processing of the WM_DESTROY message:

```
for (i = 0 ; i < 3 ; i++)
     DeleteObject (hBrush [i])) ;
```

The text in the static text fields is colored similarly by processing the WM_CTLCOLOR-STATIC message and calling *SetTextColor*. The text background is set using *SetBkColor* with the system color COLOR_BTNHIGHLIGHT. This causes the text background to be the same color as the static rectangle control behind the scrollbars and text displays. For static text controls, this text background color applies only to the rectangle behind each character in the string and not to the entire width of the control window. To accomplish this, the window procedure must also return a handle to a brush of the COLOR_BTNHIGHLIGHT color. This brush is named *hBrushStatic*; it is created during the WM_CREATE message and destroyed during the WM_DESTROY message.

By creating a brush based on the COLOR_BTNHIGHLIGHT color during the WM_CREATE message and using it through the duration of the program, we've exposed ourselves to a little problem. If the COLOR_BTNHIGHLIGHT color is changed while the program is running, the color of the static rectangle will change and the text background color will change but the whole background of the text window controls will remain the old COLOR_BTNHIGHLIGHT color.

To fix this problem, COLORS1 also processes the WM_SYSCOLORCHANGE message by simply recreating *hBrushStatic* using the new color.

THE EDIT CLASS

The edit class is in some ways the simplest predefined window class and in other ways the most complex. When you create a child window using the class name "edit," you define a rectangle based on the *x* position, *y* position, width, and height parameters of the *CreateWindow* call. This rectangle contains editable text. When the child window control has the input focus, you can type text, move the cursor, select portions of text using either the mouse or the Shift key and a cursor key, delete selected text to the clipboard by pressing Ctrl-X, copy text by pressing Ctrl-C, and insert text from the clipboard by pressing Ctrl-V.

One of the simplest uses of edit controls is for single-line entry fields. But edit controls are not limited to single lines, as I'll demonstrate in the POPPAD1 program shown in Figure 9-7. As we encounter various other topics in this book, the POPPAD program will be enhanced to use menus, dialog boxes (to load and save files), and printing. The final version will be a simple but complete text editor with surprisingly little overhead required in our code.

POPPAD1.C

```
/*-------------------------------------------
   POPPAD1.C -- Popup Editor using child window edit box
                (c) Charles Petzold, 1998
   -------------------------------------------*/

#include <windows.h>

#define ID_EDIT      1

LRESULT CALLBACK WndProc (HWND, UINT, WPARAM, LPARAM);

TCHAR szAppName[] = TEXT ("PopPad1") ;

int WINAPI WinMain (HINSTANCE hInstance, HINSTANCE hPrevInstance,
                    PSTR szCmdLine, int iCmdShow)
{
     HWND      hwnd ;
     MSG       msg ;
     WNDCLASS wndclass ;

     wndclass.style         = CS_HREDRAW | CS_VREDRAW ;
     wndclass.lpfnWndProc   = WndProc ;
     wndclass.cbClsExtra    = 0 ;
     wndclass.cbWndExtra    = 0 ;
     wndclass.hInstance     = hInstance ;
     wndclass.hIcon         = LoadIcon (NULL, IDI_APPLICATION) ;
     wndclass.hCursor       = LoadCursor (NULL, IDC_ARROW) ;
     wndclass.hbrBackground = (HBRUSH) GetStockObject (WHITE_BRUSH) ;
     wndclass.lpszMenuName  = NULL ;
     wndclass.lpszClassName = szAppName ;

     if (!RegisterClass (&wndclass))
     {
          MessageBox (NULL, TEXT ("This program requires Windows NT!"),
                      szAppName, MB_ICONERROR) ;
          return 0 ;
     }

     hwnd = CreateWindow (szAppName, szAppName,
                          WS_OVERLAPPEDWINDOW,
                          CW_USEDEFAULT, CW_USEDEFAULT,
                          CW_USEDEFAULT, CW_USEDEFAULT,
                          NULL, NULL, hInstance, NULL) ;
```

Figure 9-7. *The POPPAD1 program.*

```
        ShowWindow (hwnd, iCmdShow) ;
        UpdateWindow (hwnd) ;

        while (GetMessage (&msg, NULL, 0, 0))
        {
             TranslateMessage (&msg) ;
             DispatchMessage (&msg) ;
        }
        return msg.wParam ;
}

LRESULT CALLBACK WndProc (HWND hwnd, UINT message, WPARAM wParam, LPARAM lParam)
{
        static HWND hwndEdit ;

        switch (message)
        {
        case WM_CREATE :
             hwndEdit = CreateWindow (TEXT ("edit"), NULL,
                             WS_CHILD | WS_VISIBLE | WS_HSCROLL | WS_VSCROLL |
                                  WS_BORDER | ES_LEFT | ES_MULTILINE |
                                  ES_AUTOHSCROLL | ES_AUTOVSCROLL,
                             0, 0, 0, 0, hwnd, (HMENU) ID_EDIT,
                             ((LPCREATESTRUCT) lParam) -> hInstance, NULL) ;
             return 0 ;

        case WM_SETFOCUS :
             SetFocus (hwndEdit) ;
             return 0 ;

        case WM_SIZE :
             MoveWindow (hwndEdit, 0, 0, LOWORD (lParam), HIWORD (lParam), TRUE) ;
             return 0 ;

        case WM_COMMAND :
             if (LOWORD (wParam) == ID_EDIT)
                  if (HIWORD (wParam) == EN_ERRSPACE ||
                          HIWORD (wParam) == EN_MAXTEXT)
                      MessageBox (hwnd, TEXT ("Edit control out of space."),
                                  szAppName, MB_OK | MB_ICONSTOP) ;
             return 0 ;

        case WM_DESTROY :
             PostQuitMessage (0) ;
             return 0 ;
        }
        return DefWindowProc (hwnd, message, wParam, lParam) ;
}
```

POPPAD1 is a multiline editor (without any file I/O just yet) in less than 100 lines of C. (One drawback, however, is that the predefined multiline edit control is limited to 30,000 characters of text.) As you can see, POPPAD1 itself doesn't do very much. The predefined edit control is doing quite a lot. In this form, the program lets you explore what edit controls can do without any help from a program.

The Edit Class Styles

As noted earlier, you create an edit control using "edit" as the window class in the *CreateWindow* call. The window style is WS_CHILD, plus several options. As in static child window controls, the text in edit controls can be left-justified, right-justified, or centered. You specify this formatting with the window styles ES_LEFT, ES_RIGHT, and ES_CENTER.

By default, an edit control has a single line. You can create a multiline edit control with the window style ES_MULTILINE. For a single-line edit control, you can normally enter text only to the end of the edit control rectangle. To create an edit control that automatically scrolls horizontally, you use the style ES_AUTOHSCROLL. For a multiline edit control, text wordwraps unless you use the ES_AUTOHSCROLL style, in which case you must press the Enter key to start a new line. You can also include vertical scrolling in a multiline edit control by using the style ES_AUTOVSCROLL.

When you include these scrolling styles in multiline edit controls, you might also want to add scroll bars to the edit control. You do so by using the same window style identifiers as for nonchild windows: WS_HSCROLL and WS_VSCROLL. By default, an edit control does not have a border. You can add one by using the style WS_BORDER.

When you select text in an edit control, Windows displays it in reverse video. When the edit control loses the input focus, however, the selected text is no longer highlighted. If you want the selection to be highlighted even when the edit control does not have the input focus, you can use the style ES_NOHIDESEL.

When POPPAD1 creates its edit control, the style is given in the *CreateWindow* call:

```
WS_CHILD | WS_VISIBLE | WS_HSCROLL | WS_VSCROLL |
    WS_BORDER | ES_LEFT | ES_MULTILINE |
    ES_AUTOHSCROLL | ES_AUTOVSCROLL
```

In POPPAD1, the dimensions of the edit control are later defined by a call to *MoveWindow* when *WndProc* receives a WM_SIZE message. The size of the edit control is simply set to the size of the main window:

```
MoveWindow (hwndEdit, 0, 0, LOWORD (lParam),
                        HIWORD (lParam), TRUE) ;
```

For a single-line edit control, the height of the control must accommodate the height of a character. If the edit control has a border (as most do), use 1.5 times the height of a character (including external leading).

Edit Control Notification

Edit controls send WM_COMMAND messages to the parent window procedure. The meanings of the *wParam* and *lParam* variables are the same as for button controls:

LOWORD (*wParam*)	Child window ID
HIWORD (*wParam*)	Notification code
lParam	Child window handle

The notification codes are shown below:

EN_SETFOCUS	*Edit control has gained the input focus.*
EN_KILLFOCUS	*Edit control has lost the input focus.*
EN_CHANGE	*Edit control's contents will change.*
EN_UPDATE	*Edit control's contents have changed.*
EN_ERRSPACE	*Edit control has run out of space.*
EN_MAXTEXT	*Edit control has run out of space on insertion.*
EN_HSCROLL	*Edit control's horizontal scroll bar has been clicked.*
EN_VSCROLL	*Edit control's vertical scroll bar has been clicked.*

POPPAD1 traps only EN_ERRSPACE and EN_MAXTEXT notification codes and displays a message box in response.

Using the Edit Controls

If you use several single-line edit controls on the surface of your main window, you'll need to use window subclassing to move the input focus from one control to another. You can accomplish this much as COLORS1 does, by intercepting Tab and Shift-Tab keystrokes. (Another example of window subclassing is shown later in this chapter in the HEAD program.) How you handle the Enter key is up to you. You can use it the same way as the Tab key or as a signal to your program that all the edit fields are ready.

If you want to insert text into an edit field, you can do so by using *SetWindowText*. Getting text out of an edit control involves *GetWindowTextLength* and *GetWindowText*. We'll see examples of these facilities in our later revisions to the POPPAD program.

Messages to an Edit Control

I won't cover all the messages you can send to an edit control using *SendMessage* because there are quite a few of them, and several will be used in the later POPPAD revisions. Here's a broad overview.

These messages let you cut, copy, or clear the current selection. A user selects the text to be acted upon by using the mouse or the Shift key and a cursor key, thereby highlighting the selected text in the edit control:

```
SendMessage (hwndEdit, WM_CUT, 0, 0) ;
SendMessage (hwndEdit, WM_COPY, 0, 0) ;
SendMessage (hwndEdit, WM_CLEAR, 0, 0) ;
```

WM_CUT removes the current selection from the edit control and sends it to the clipboard. WM_COPY copies the selection to the clipboard but leaves it intact in the edit control. WM_CLEAR deletes the selection from the edit control without passing it to the clipboard.

You can also insert clipboard text into the edit control at the cursor position:

```
SendMessage (hwndEdit, WM_PASTE, 0, 0) ;
```

You can obtain the starting and ending positions of the current selection:

```
SendMessage (hwndEdit, EM_GETSEL, (WPARAM) &iStart,
                                  (LPARAM) &iEnd) ;
```

The ending position is actually the position of the last selected character plus 1.

You can select text:

```
SendMessage (hwndEdit, EM_SETSEL, iStart, iEnd) ;
```

You can also replace a current selection with other text:

```
SendMessage (hwndEdit, EM_REPLACESEL, 0, (LPARAM) szString) ;
```

For multiline edit controls, you can obtain the number of lines:

```
iCount = SendMessage (hwndEdit, EM_GETLINECOUNT, 0, 0) ;
```

For any particular line, you can obtain an offset from the beginning of the edit buffer text:

```
iOffset = SendMessage (hwndEdit, EM_LINEINDEX, iLine, 0) ;
```

Lines are numbered starting at 0. An *iLine* value of -1 returns the offset of the line containing the cursor. You obtain the length of the line from

```
iLength = SendMessage (hwndEdit, EM_LINELENGTH, iLine, 0) ;
```

and copy the line itself into a buffer using

```
iLength = SendMessage (hwndEdit, EM_GETLINE, iLine, (LPARAM) szBuffer) ;
```

THE LISTBOX CLASS

The final predefined child window control I'll discuss in this chapter is the list box. A list box is a collection of text strings displayed as a scrollable columnar list within a rectangle. A program can add or remove strings in the list by sending messages to the list box window procedure. The list box control sends WM_COMMAND messages to its parent window when an item in the list is selected. The parent window can then determine which item has been selected.

A list box can be either single selection or multiple selection. The latter allows the user to select more than one item from the list box. When a list box has the input focus, it displays a dashed line surrounding an item in the list box. This cursor does not indicate the selected item in the list box. The selected item is indicated by highlighting, which displays the item in reverse video.

In a single-selection list box, the user can select the item that the cursor is positioned on by pressing the Spacebar. The arrow keys move both the cursor and the current selection and can scroll the contents of the list box. The Page Up and Page Down keys also scroll the list box by moving the cursor but not the selection. Pressing a letter key moves the cursor and the selection to the first (or next) item that begins with that letter. An item can also be selected by clicking or double-clicking the mouse on the item.

In a multiple-selection list box, the Spacebar toggles the selection state of the item where the cursor is positioned. (If the item is already selected, it is deselected.) The arrow keys deselect all previously selected items and move the cursor and selection, just as in single-selection list boxes. However, the Ctrl key and the arrow keys can move the cursor without moving the selection. The Shift key and arrow keys can extend a selection.

Clicking or double-clicking an item in a multiple-selection list box deselects all previously selected items and selects the clicked item. However, clicking an item while pressing the Shift key toggles the selection state of the item without changing the selection state of any other item.

List Box Styles

You create a list box child window control with *CreateWindow* using "listbox" as the window class and WS_CHILD as the window style. However, this default list box style does not send WM_COMMAND messages to its parent, meaning that a program would have to interrogate the list box (via messages to the list box controls) regarding the selection of items within the list box. Therefore, list box controls almost always include the list box style identifier LBS_NOTIFY, which allows the parent window to receive WM_COMMAND messages from the list box. If you want the list box control to sort the items in the list box, you can also use LBS_SORT, another common style.

By default, list boxes are single selection. Multiple-selection list boxes are relatively rare. If you want to create one, you use the style LBS_MULTIPLESEL. Normally, a list box updates itself when a new item is added to the scroll box list. You can prevent this by including the style LBS_NOREDRAW. You will probably not want to use this style, however. Instead, you can temporarily prevent the repainting of a list box control by using the WM_SETREDRAW message that I'll describe a little later.

By default, the list box window procedure displays only the list of items without any border around it. You can add a border with the window style identifier WS_BORDER. And to add a vertical scroll bar for scrolling through the list with the mouse, you use the window style identifier WS_VSCROLL.

The Windows header files define a list box style called LBS_STANDARD that includes the most commonly used styles. It is defined as

```
(LBS_NOTIFY ¦ LBS_SORT ¦ WS_VSCROLL ¦ WS_BORDER)
```

You can also use the WS_SIZEBOX and WS_CAPTION identifiers, but these will allow the user to resize the list box and to move it around its parent's client area.

The width of a list box should accommodate the width of the longest string plus the width of the scroll bar. You can get the width of the vertical scroll bar using

```
GetSystemMetrics (SM_CXVSCROLL) ;
```

You can calculate the height of the list box by multiplying the height of a character by the number of items you want to appear in view.

Putting Strings in the List Box

After you've created the list box, the next step is to put text strings in it. You do this by sending messages to the list box window procedure using the *SendMessage* call. The text strings are generally referenced by an index number that starts at 0 for the topmost item. In the examples that follow, *hwndList* is the handle to the child window list box control, and *iIndex* is the index value. In cases where you pass a text string in the *SendMessage* call, the *lParam* parameter is a pointer to a null-terminated string.

In most of these examples, the *SendMessage* call can return LB_ERRSPACE (defined as −2) if the window procedure runs out of available memory space to store the contents of the list box. *SendMessage* returns LB_ERR (−1) if an error occurs for other reasons and LB_OKAY (0) if the operation is successful. You can test *SendMessage* for a nonzero value to detect either of the two errors.

If you use the LBS_SORT style (or if you are placing strings in the list box in the order that you want them to appear), the easiest way to fill up a list box is with the LB_ADDSTRING message:

```
SendMessage (hwndList, LB_ADDSTRING, 0, (LPARAM) szString) ;
```

If you do not use LBS_SORT, you can insert strings into your list box by specifying an index value with LB_INSERTSTRING:

```
SendMessage (hwndList, LB_INSERTSTRING, iIndex, (LPARAM) szString) ;
```

For instance, if *iIndex* is equal to 4, *szString* becomes the new string with an index value of 4—the fifth string from the top because counting starts at 0. Any strings below this point are pushed down. An *iIndex* value of −1 adds the string to the bottom. You can use LB_INSERTSTRING with list boxes that have the LBS_SORT style, but the list box contents will not be re-sorted. (You can also insert strings into a list box using the LB_DIR message, a topic I discuss in detail toward the end of this chapter.)

You can delete a string from the list box by specifying the index value with the LB_DELETESTRING message:

```
SendMessage (hwndList, LB_DELETESTRING, iIndex, 0) ;
```

You can clear out the list box by using LB_RESETCONTENT:

```
SendMessage (hwndList, LB_RESETCONTENT, 0, 0) ;
```

The list box window procedure updates the display when an item is added to or deleted from the list box. If you have a number of strings to add or delete, you may want to temporarily inhibit this action by turning off the control's redraw flag:

```
SendMessage (hwndList, WM_SETREDRAW, FALSE, 0) ;
```

After you've finished, you can turn the redraw flag back on:

```
SendMessage (hwndList, WM_SETREDRAW, TRUE, 0) ;
```

A list box created with the LBS_NOREDRAW style begins with the redraw flag turned off.

Selecting and Extracting Entries

The *SendMessage* calls that carry out the tasks shown below usually return a value. If an error occurs, this value is set to LB_ERR (defined as -1).

After you've put some items into a list box, you can find out how many items are in the list box:

```
iCount = SendMessage (hwndList, LB_GETCOUNT, 0, 0) ;
```

Some of the other calls are different for single-selection and multiple-selection list boxes. Let's first look at single-selection list boxes.

Normally, you'll let a user select from a list box. But if you want to highlight a default selection, you can use

```
SendMessage (hwndList, LB_SETCURSEL, iIndex, 0) ;
```

Setting *iParam* to -1 in this call deselects all items.

You can also select an item based on its initial characters:

```
iIndex = SendMessage (hwndList, LB_SELECTSTRING, iIndex,
                      (LPARAM) szSearchString) ;
```

The *iIndex* given as the *iParam* parameter to the *SendMessage* call is the index following which the search begins for an item with initial characters that match *szSearchString*. An *iIndex* value of −1 starts the search from the top. *SendMessage* returns the index of the selected item, or LB_ERR if no initial characters match *szSearchString*.

When you get a WM_COMMAND message from the list box (or at any other time), you can determine the index of the current selection using LB_GETCURSEL:

```
iIndex = SendMessage (hwndList, LB_GETCURSEL, 0, 0) ;
```

The *iIndex* value returned from the call is LB_ERR if no item is selected.

You can determine the length of any string in the list box:

```
iLength = SendMessage (hwndList, LB_GETTEXTLEN, iIndex, 0) ;
```

and copy the item into the text buffer:

```
iLength = SendMessage (hwndList, LB_GETTEXT, iIndex,
                 (LPARAM) szBuffer) ;
```

In both cases, the *iLength* value returned from the call is the length of the string. The *szBuffer* array must be large enough for the length of the string and a terminating NULL. You may want to use LB_GETTEXTLEN to first allocate some memory to hold the string.

For a multiple-selection list box, you cannot use LB_SETCURSEL, LB_GETCURSEL, or LB_SELECTSTRING. Instead, you use LB_SETSEL to set the selection state of a particular item without affecting other items that might also be selected:

```
SendMessage (hwndList, LB_SETSEL, wParam, iIndex) ;
```

The *wParam* parameter is nonzero to select and highlight the item and 0 to deselect it. If the *lParam* parameter is −1, all items are either selected or deselected. You can also determine the selection state of a particular item using

```
iSelect = SendMessage (hwndList, LB_GETSEL, iIndex, 0) ;
```

where *iSelect* is set to nonzero if the item indexed by *iIndex* is selected and 0 if it is not.

Receiving Messages from List Boxes

When a user clicks on a list box with the mouse, the list box receives the input focus. A parent window can give the input focus to a list box control by using

```
SetFocus (hwndList) ;
```

When a list box has the input focus, the cursor movement keys, letter keys, and Spacebar can also be used to select items from the list box.

A list box control sends WM_COMMAND messages to its parent. The meanings of the *wParam* and *lParam* variables are the same as for the button and edit controls:

LOWORD (*wParam*)	Child window ID
HIWORD (*wParam*)	Notification code
lParam	Child window handle

The notification codes and their values are as follows:

LBN_ERRSPACE	−2
LBN_SELCHANGE	1
LBN_DBLCLK	2
LBN_SELCANCEL	3
LBN_SETFOCUS	4
LBN_KILLFOCUS	5

The list box control sends the parent window LBN_SELCHANGE and LBN_DBLCLK codes only if the list box window style includes LBS_NOTIFY.

The LBN_ERRSPACE code indicates that the list box control has run out of space. The LBN_SELCHANGE code indicates that the current selection has changed; these messages occur as the user moves the highlight through the list box, toggles the selection state with the Spacebar, or clicks an item with the mouse. The LBN_DBLCLK code indicates that a list box item has been double-clicked with the mouse. (The notification code values for LBN_SELCHANGE and LBN_DBLCLK refer to the number of mouse clicks.)

Depending on your application, you may want to use either LBN_SELCHANGE or LBN_DBLCLK messages or both. Your program will get many LBN_SELCHANGE messages, but LBN_DBLCLK messages occur only when the user double-clicks with the mouse. If your program uses double-clicks, you'll need to provide a keyboard interface that duplicates LBN_DBLCLK.

A Simple List Box Application

Now that you know how to create a list box, fill it with text items, receive messages from the list box, and extract strings, it's time to program an application. The ENVIRON program, shown in Figure 9-8, uses a list box in its client area to display the name of your current operating system environment variables (such as PATH and WINDIR). As you select an environment variable, the environment string is displayed across the top of the client area.

ENVIRON.C

```
/*------------------------------------------------
   ENVIRON.C -- Environment List Box
                (c) Charles Petzold, 1998
  ------------------------------------------*/

#include <windows.h>
```

Figure 9-8. *The ENVIRON program.* *(continued)*

Figure 9-8. *continued*

```
#define ID_LIST     1
#define ID_TEXT     2

LRESULT CALLBACK WndProc (HWND, UINT, WPARAM, LPARAM) ;

int WINAPI WinMain (HINSTANCE hInstance, HINSTANCE hPrevInstance,
                    PSTR szCmdLine, int iCmdShow)
{
     static TCHAR szAppName[] = TEXT ("Environ") ;
     HWND          hwnd ;
     MSG           msg ;
     WNDCLASS      wndclass ;

     wndclass.style         = CS_HREDRAW | CS_VREDRAW ;
     wndclass.lpfnWndProc   = WndProc ;
     wndclass.cbClsExtra    = 0 ;
     wndclass.cbWndExtra    = 0 ;
     wndclass.hInstance     = hInstance ;
     wndclass.hIcon         = LoadIcon (NULL, IDI_APPLICATION) ;
     wndclass.hCursor       = LoadCursor (NULL, IDC_ARROW) ;
     wndclass.hbrBackground = (HBRUSH) (COLOR_WINDOW + 1) ;
     wndclass.lpszMenuName  = NULL ;
     wndclass.lpszClassName = szAppName ;

     if (!RegisterClass (&wndclass))
     {
         MessageBox (NULL, TEXT ("This program requires Windows NT!"),
                     szAppName, MB_ICONERROR) ;
         return 0 ;
     }

     hwnd = CreateWindow (szAppName, TEXT ("Environment List Box"),
                     WS_OVERLAPPEDWINDOW,
                     CW_USEDEFAULT, CW_USEDEFAULT,
                     CW_USEDEFAULT, CW_USEDEFAULT,
                     NULL, NULL, hInstance, NULL) ;

     ShowWindow (hwnd, iCmdShow) ;
     UpdateWindow (hwnd) ;

     while (GetMessage (&msg, NULL, 0, 0))
     {
         TranslateMessage (&msg) ;
         DispatchMessage (&msg) ;
     }
```

```
        return msg.wParam ;
}

void FillListBox (HWND hwndList)
{
    int      iLength ;
    TCHAR * pVarBlock, * pVarBeg, * pVarEnd, * pVarName ;

    pVarBlock = GetEnvironmentStrings () ;  // Get pointer to environment block

    while (*pVarBlock)
    {
        if (*pVarBlock != '=')   // Skip variable names beginning with '='
        {
            pVarBeg = pVarBlock ;               // Beginning of variable name
            while (*pVarBlock++ != '=') ;       // Scan until '='
            pVarEnd = pVarBlock - 1 ;           // Points to '=' sign
            iLength = pVarEnd - pVarBeg ;       // Length of variable name

                // Allocate memory for the variable name and terminating
                // zero. Copy the variable name and append a zero.

            pVarName = calloc (iLength + 1, sizeof (TCHAR)) ;
            CopyMemory (pVarName, pVarBeg, iLength * sizeof (TCHAR)) ;
            pVarName[iLength] = '\0' ;

                // Put the variable name in the list box and free memory.
            SendMessage (hwndList, LB_ADDSTRING, 0, (LPARAM) pVarName) ;
            free (pVarName) ;
        }
        while (*pVarBlock++ != '\0') ;          // Scan until terminating zero
    }
    FreeEnvironmentStrings (pVarBlock) ;
}

LRESULT CALLBACK WndProc (HWND hwnd, UINT message, WPARAM wParam, LPARAM lParam)
{
    static HWND  hwndList, hwndText ;
    int          iIndex, iLength, cxChar, cyChar ;
    TCHAR        * pVarName, * pVarValue ;

    switch (message)
    {
    case WM_CREATE :
        cxChar = LOWORD (GetDialogBaseUnits ()) ;
        cyChar = HIWORD (GetDialogBaseUnits ()) ;
```

(continued)

Figure 9-8. *continued*

```
                // Create listbox and static text windows.

        hwndList = CreateWindow (TEXT ("listbox"), NULL,
                        WS_CHILD | WS_VISIBLE | LBS_STANDARD,
                        cxChar, cyChar * 3,
                        cxChar * 16 + GetSystemMetrics (SM_CXVSCROLL),
                        cyChar * 5,
                        hwnd, (HMENU) ID_LIST,
                        (HINSTANCE) GetWindowLong (hwnd, GWL_HINSTANCE),
                        NULL) ;

        hwndText = CreateWindow (TEXT ("static"), NULL,
                        WS_CHILD | WS_VISIBLE | SS_LEFT,
                        cxChar, cyChar,
                        GetSystemMetrics (SM_CXSCREEN), cyChar,
                        hwnd, (HMENU) ID_TEXT,
                        (HINSTANCE) GetWindowLong (hwnd, GWL_HINSTANCE),
                        NULL) ;

        FillListBox (hwndList) ;
        return 0 ;

    case WM_SETFOCUS :
        SetFocus (hwndList) ;
        return 0 ;
    case WM_COMMAND :
        if (LOWORD (wParam) == ID_LIST && HIWORD (wParam) == LBN_SELCHANGE)
        {
                // Get current selection.

            iIndex  = SendMessage (hwndList, LB_GETCURSEL, 0, 0) ;
            iLength = SendMessage (hwndList, LB_GETTEXTLEN, iIndex, 0) + 1 ;
            pVarName = calloc (iLength, sizeof (TCHAR)) ;
            SendMessage (hwndList, LB_GETTEXT, iIndex, (LPARAM) pVarName) ;

                // Get environment string.

            iLength = GetEnvironmentVariable (pVarName, NULL, 0) ;
            pVarValue = calloc (iLength, sizeof (TCHAR)) ;
            GetEnvironmentVariable (pVarName, pVarValue, iLength) ;

                // Show it in window.

            SetWindowText (hwndText, pVarValue) ;
            free (pVarName) ;
```

```
            free (pVarValue) ;
        }
        return 0 ;

    case WM_DESTROY :
        PostQuitMessage (0) ;
        return 0 ;
    }
    return DefWindowProc (hwnd, message, wParam, lParam) ;
}
```

ENVIRON creates two child windows: a list box with the style LBS_STANDARD and a static window with the style SS_LEFT (left-justified text). ENVIRON uses the *Get-EnvironmentStrings* function to obtain a pointer to a memory block containing all the environment variable names and values. ENVIRON parses through this block in its *FillList-Box* function, using the message LB_ADDSTRING to direct the list box window procedure to place each string in the list box.

When you run ENVIRON, you can select an environment variable using the mouse or the keyboard. Each time you change the selection, the list box sends a WM_COMMAND message to the parent window, which is *WndProc*. When *WndProc* receives a WM_COMMAND message, it checks to see whether the low word of *wParam* is ID_LIST (the child ID of the list box) and whether the high word of *wParam* (the notification code) is equal to LBN_SELCHANGE. If so, it obtains the index of the selection using the LB_GET-CURSEL message and the text itself—the environment variable name—using LB_GETTEXT. The ENVIRON program uses the C function *GetEnvironmentVariable* to obtain the environment string corresponding to that variable and *SetWindowText* to pass this string to the static child window control, which displays the text.

Listing Files

I've been saving the best for last: LB_DIR, the most powerful list box message. This function call fills the list box with a file directory list, optionally including subdirectories and valid disk drives:

```
SendMessage (hwndList, LB_DIR, iAttr, (LPARAM) szFileSpec) ;
```

Using file attribute codes

The *iAttr* parameter is a file attribute code. The least significant byte is a file attribute code that can be a combination of the values in the following table.

iAttr	Value	Attribute
DDL_READWRITE	0x0000	Normal file
DDL_READONLY	0x0001	Read-only file
DDL_HIDDEN	0x0002	Hidden file
DDL_SYSTEM	0x0004	System file
DDL_DIRECTORY	0x0010	Subdirectory
DDL_ARCHIVE	0x0020	File with archive bit set

The next highest byte provides some additional control over the items desired:

iAttr	Value	Option
DDL_DRIVES	0x4000	Include drive letters
DDL_EXCLUSIVE	0x8000	Exclusive search only

The DDL prefix stands for "dialog directory list."

When the *iAttr* value of the LB_DIR message is DDL_READWRITE, the list box lists normal files, read-only files, and files with the archive bit set. When the value is DDL_DIRECTORY, the list includes child subdirectories in addition to these files with the directory names in square brackets. A value of DDL_DRIVES | DDL_DIRECTORY expands the list to include all valid drives where the drive letters are shown between dashes.

Setting the topmost bit of *iAttr* lists the files with the indicated flag while excluding normal files. For a Windows file backup program, for instance, you might want to list only files that have been modified since the last backup. Such files have their archive bits set, so you would use DDL_EXCLUSIVE | DDL_ARCHIVE.

Ordering file lists

The *lParam* parameter is a pointer to a file specification string such as "*.*". This file specification does not affect the subdirectories that the list box includes.

You'll want to use the LBS_SORT message for list boxes with file lists. The list box will first list files satisfying the file specification and then (optionally) list subdirectory names. The first subdirectory listing will take this form:

[..]

This "double-dot" subdirectory entry lets the user back up one level toward the root directory. (The entry will not appear if you're listing files in the root directory.) Finally, the specific subdirectory names are listed in this form:

[SUBDIR]

These are followed (also optionally) by a list of valid disk drives in the form

[-A-]

A *head* for Windows

A well-known UNIX utility named *head* displays the beginning lines of a file. Let's use a list box to write a similar program for Windows. HEAD, shown in Figure 9-9, lists all files and child subdirectories in the list box. It allows you to choose a file to display by double-clicking on the filename with the mouse or by pressing the Enter key when the filename is selected. You can also change the subdirectory using either of these methods. The program displays up to 8 KB of the beginning of the file in the right side of the client area of HEAD's window.

HEAD.C

```
/*----------------------------------------
   HEAD.C -- Displays beginning (head) of file
            (c) Charles Petzold, 1998
   ----------------------------------------*/

#include <windows.h>

#define ID_LIST    1
#define ID_TEXT    2

#define MAXREAD    8192
#define DIRATTR    (DDL_READWRITE | DDL_READONLY | DDL_HIDDEN | DDL_SYSTEM | \
                    DDL_DIRECTORY | DDL_ARCHIVE  | DDL_DRIVES)
#define DTFLAGS    (DT_WORDBREAK | DT_EXPANDTABS | DT_NOCLIP | DT_NOPREFIX)
LRESULT CALLBACK WndProc  (HWND, UINT, WPARAM, LPARAM) ;
LRESULT CALLBACK ListProc (HWND, UINT, WPARAM, LPARAM) ;

WNDPROC OldList ;

int WINAPI WinMain (HINSTANCE hInstance, HINSTANCE hPrevInstance,
                    PSTR szCmdLine, int iCmdShow)
{
    static TCHAR szAppName[] = TEXT ("head") ;
    HWND        hwnd ;
    MSG         msg ;
    WNDCLASS    wndclass ;

    wndclass.style          = CS_HREDRAW | CS_VREDRAW ;
    wndclass.lpfnWndProc    = WndProc ;
```

Figure 9-9. *The HEAD program.*   *(continued)*

Figure 9-9. *continued*

```
    wndclass.cbClsExtra    = 0 ;
    wndclass.cbWndExtra    = 0 ;
    wndclass.hInstance     = hInstance ;
    wndclass.hIcon         = LoadIcon (NULL, IDI_APPLICATION) ;
    wndclass.hCursor       = LoadCursor (NULL, IDC_ARROW) ;
    wndclass.hbrBackground = (HBRUSH) (COLOR_BTNFACE + 1) ;
    wndclass.lpszMenuName  = NULL ;
    wndclass.lpszClassName = szAppName ;

    if (!RegisterClass (&wndclass))
    {
        MessageBox (NULL, TEXT ("This program requires Windows NT!"),
                    szAppName, MB_ICONERROR) ;
        return 0 ;
    }

    hwnd = CreateWindow (szAppName, TEXT ("head"),
                        WS_OVERLAPPEDWINDOW | WS_CLIPCHILDREN,
                        CW_USEDEFAULT, CW_USEDEFAULT,
                        CW_USEDEFAULT, CW_USEDEFAULT,
                        NULL, NULL, hInstance, NULL) ;

    ShowWindow (hwnd, iCmdShow) ;
    UpdateWindow (hwnd) ;

    while (GetMessage (&msg, NULL, 0, 0))
    {
        TranslateMessage (&msg) ;
        DispatchMessage (&msg) ;
    }
    return msg.wParam ;
}

LRESULT CALLBACK WndProc (HWND hwnd, UINT message, WPARAM wParam, LPARAM lParam)
{
    static BOOL     bValidFile ;
    static BYTE     buffer[MAXREAD] ;
    static HWND     hwndList, hwndText ;
    static RECT     rect ;
    static TCHAR    szFile[MAX_PATH + 1] ;
    HANDLE          hFile ;
    HDC             hdc ;
    int             i, cxChar, cyChar ;
    PAINTSTRUCT     ps ;
    TCHAR           szBuffer[MAX_PATH + 1] ;
```

```
         switch (message)
         {
         case WM_CREATE :
              cxChar = LOWORD (GetDialogBaseUnits ()) ;
              cyChar = HIWORD (GetDialogBaseUnits ()) ;

              rect.left = 20 * cxChar ;
              rect.top  =  3 * cyChar ;

              hwndList = CreateWindow (TEXT ("listbox"), NULL,
                            WS_CHILDWINDOW | WS_VISIBLE | LBS_STANDARD,
                            cxChar, cyChar * 3,
                            cxChar * 13 + GetSystemMetrics (SM_CXVSCROLL),
                            cyChar * 10,
                            hwnd, (HMENU) ID_LIST,
                            (HINSTANCE) GetWindowLong (hwnd, GWL_HINSTANCE),
                            NULL) ;

              GetCurrentDirectory (MAX_PATH + 1, szBuffer) ;

              hwndText = CreateWindow (TEXT ("static"), szBuffer,
                            WS_CHILDWINDOW | WS_VISIBLE | SS_LEFT,
                            cxChar, cyChar, cxChar * MAX_PATH, cyChar,
                            hwnd, (HMENU) ID_TEXT,
                            (HINSTANCE) GetWindowLong (hwnd, GWL_HINSTANCE),
                            NULL) ;

              OldList = (WNDPROC) SetWindowLong (hwndList, GWL_WNDPROC,
                                                (LPARAM) ListProc) ;

              SendMessage (hwndList, LB_DIR, DIRATTR, (LPARAM) TEXT ("*.*")) ;
              return 0 ;

         case WM_SIZE :
              rect.right  = LOWORD (lParam) ;
              rect.bottom = HIWORD (lParam) ;
              return 0 ;

         case WM_SETFOCUS :
              SetFocus (hwndList) ;
              return 0 ;

         case WM_COMMAND :
              if (LOWORD (wParam) == ID_LIST && HIWORD (wParam) == LBN_DBLCLK)
              {
```

(continued)

Figure 9-9. *continued*

```
          if (LB_ERR == (i = SendMessage (hwndList, LB_GETCURSEL, 0, 0)))
               break ;

          SendMessage (hwndList, LB_GETTEXT, i, (LPARAM) szBuffer) ;

          if (INVALID_HANDLE_VALUE != (hFile = CreateFile (szBuffer,
                    GENERIC_READ, FILE_SHARE_READ, NULL,
                    OPEN_EXISTING, 0, NULL)))

          {
               CloseHandle (hFile) ;
               bValidFile = TRUE ;
               lstrcpy (szFile, szBuffer) ;
               GetCurrentDirectory (MAX_PATH + 1, szBuffer) ;

               if (szBuffer [lstrlen (szBuffer) - 1] != '\\')
                    lstrcat (szBuffer, TEXT ("\\")) ;
               SetWindowText (hwndText, lstrcat (szBuffer, szFile)) ;
          }
          else
          {
               bValidFile = FALSE ;
               szBuffer [lstrlen (szBuffer) - 1] = '\0' ;

                    // If setting the directory doesn't work, maybe it's
                    // a drive change, so try that.

               if (!SetCurrentDirectory (szBuffer + 1))
               {
                    szBuffer [3] = ':' ;
                    szBuffer [4] = '\0' ;
                    SetCurrentDirectory (szBuffer + 2) ;
               }

                    // Get the new directory name and fill the list box.

               GetCurrentDirectory (MAX_PATH + 1, szBuffer) ;
               SetWindowText (hwndText, szBuffer) ;
               SendMessage (hwndList, LB_RESETCONTENT, 0, 0) ;
               SendMessage (hwndList, LB_DIR, DIRATTR,
                                   (LPARAM) TEXT ("*.*")) ;
          }
          InvalidateRect (hwnd, NULL, TRUE) ;
     }
     return 0 ;
```

```
     case WM_PAINT :
          if (!bValidFile)
               break ;

          if (INVALID_HANDLE_VALUE == (hFile = CreateFile (szFile,
                    GENERIC_READ, FILE_SHARE_READ, NULL, OPEN_EXISTING, 0, NULL)))
          {
               bValidFile = FALSE ;
               break ;
          }

          ReadFile (hFile, buffer, MAXREAD, &i, NULL) ;
          CloseHandle (hFile) ;

               // i now equals the number of bytes in buffer.
               // Commence getting a device context for displaying text.

          hdc = BeginPaint (hwnd, &ps) ;
          SelectObject (hdc, GetStockObject (SYSTEM_FIXED_FONT)) ;
          SetTextColor (hdc, GetSysColor (COLOR_BTNTEXT)) ;
          SetBkColor   (hdc, GetSysColor (COLOR_BTNFACE)) ;

               // Assume the file is ASCII

          DrawTextA (hdc, buffer, i, &rect, DTFLAGS) ;

          EndPaint (hwnd, &ps) ;
          return 0 ;

     case WM_DESTROY :
          PostQuitMessage (0) ;
          return 0 ;
     }
     return DefWindowProc (hwnd, message, wParam, lParam) ;
}

LRESULT CALLBACK ListProc (HWND hwnd, UINT message,
                      WPARAM wParam, LPARAM lParam)
{
     if (message == WM_KEYDOWN && wParam == VK_RETURN)
          SendMessage (GetParent (hwnd), WM_COMMAND,
                    MAKELONG (1, LBN_DBLCLK), (LPARAM) hwnd) ;

     return CallWindowProc (OldList, hwnd, message, wParam, lParam) ;
}
```

In ENVIRON, when we selected an environment variable—either with a mouse click or with the keyboard—the program displayed an environment string. If we used this select-display approach in HEAD, however, the program would be too slow because it would continually need to open and close files as you moved the selection through the list box. Instead, HEAD requires that the file or subdirectory be double-clicked. This presents a bit of a problem because list box controls have no automatic keyboard interface that corresponds to a mouse double-click. As we know, we should provide keyboard interfaces when possible.

The solution? Window subclassing, of course. The list box subclass function in HEAD is named *ListProc*. It simply looks for a WM_KEYDOWN message with *wParam* equal to VK_RETURN and sends a WM_COMMAND message with an LBN_DBLCLK notification code back to the parent. The WM_COMMAND processing in *WndProc* uses the Windows function *CreateFile* to check for the selection from the list. If *CreateFile* returns an error, the selection is not a file, so it's probably a subdirectory. HEAD then uses *SetCurrentDirectory* to change the subdirectory. If *SetCurrentDirectory* doesn't work, the program assumes the user has selected a drive letter. Changing drives also requires a call to *SetCurrentDirectory*, except the preliminary dash needs to be avoided and a colon needs to be added. It sends an LB_RESETCONTENT message to the list box to clear out the contents and an LB_DIR message to fill the list box with files from the new subdirectory.

The WM_PAINT message processing in *WndProc* opens the file using the Windows *CreateFile* function. This returns a handle to the file that can be passed to the Windows functions *ReadFile* and *CloseHandle*.

And now, for the first time in this chapter, we encounter an issue involving Unicode. In a perfect world, perhaps, text files would be recognized by the operating system so that *ReadFile* could convert an ASCII file into Unicode text, or a Unicode file into ASCII text. But this is not the case. *ReadFile* just reads the bytes of the file without any conversion. This means that *DrawTextA* (in an executable compiled without the UNICODE identifier defined) would interpret the text as ASCII and *DrawTextW* (in the Unicode version) would assume the text is Unicode.

So what the program should really be doing is trying to figure out whether the file has ASCII text or Unicode text and then calling *DrawTextA* or *DrawTextW* appropriately. Instead, HEAD takes a much simpler approach and uses *DrawTextA* regardless.

Chapter 10

Menus and Other Resources

Most Microsoft Windows programs include a customized icon that Windows displays in the upper left corner of the title bar of the application window. Windows also displays the program's icon when the program is listed in the Start menu, shown in the taskbar at the bottom of the screen, listed in the Windows Explorer, or shown as a shortcut on the desktop. Some programs—most notably graphical drawing tools such as Windows Paint—use customized mouse cursors to represent different operations of the program. Many Windows programs use menus and dialog boxes. Along with scroll bars, menus and dialog boxes are the bread and butter of the Windows user interface.

Icons, cursors, menus, and dialog boxes are all related. They are all types of Windows "resources." Resources are data and they are often stored in a program's .EXE file, but they do not reside in the executable program's data area. In other words, the resources are not immediately addressable by variables in the program's code. Instead, Windows provides functions that explicitly or implicitly load a program's resources into memory so that they can be used. We've already encountered two of these functions. They are *LoadIcon* and *LoadCursor*, and they have appeared in the sample programs in the assignment statements that define a program's window class structure. So far, these functions have loaded a binary icon or cursor image from within Windows and returned a handle to that icon or cursor. In this chapter, we'll begin by creating our own customized icons that are loaded from the program's own .EXE file.

This book covers these resources:

- Icons
- Cursors
- Character strings
- Custom resources
- Menus
- Keyboard accelerators
- Dialog boxes
- Bitmaps

The first six resources in the list are discussed in this chapter. Dialog boxes are covered in Chapter 11 and bitmaps in Chapter 14.

ICONS, CURSORS, STRINGS, AND CUSTOM RESOURCES

One of the benefits of using resources is that many components of a program can be bound into the program's .EXE file. Without the concept of resources, a binary file such as an icon image would probably have to reside in a separate file that the .EXE would read into memory to use. Or the icon would have to be defined in the program as an array of bytes (which might make it tough to visualize the actual icon image). As a resource, the icon is stored in a separate editable file on the developer's computer but is bound into the .EXE file during the build process.

Adding an Icon to a Program

Adding resources to a program involves using some additional features of Visual C++ Developer Studio. In the case of icons, you use the Image Editor (also called the Graphics Editor) to draw a picture of your icon. This image is stored in an icon file with an extension .ICO. Developer Studio also generates a resource script (that is, a file with the extension .RC, sometimes also called a resource definition file) that lists all the program's resources and a header file (RESOURCE.H) that lets your program reference the resources.

So that you can see how these new files fit together, let's begin by creating a new project, called ICONDEMO. As usual, in Developer Studio you pick New from the File menu, select the Projects tab, and choose Win32 Application. In the Project Name field, type ICONDEMO and click OK. At this point, Developer Studio creates five files that it uses to maintain the workspace and the project. These include the text files ICONDEMO.DSW, ICONDEMO.DSP, and ICONDEMO.MAK (assuming you've selected "Export makefile when saving project file" from the Build tab of the Options dialog box displayed when you select Options from the Tools menu).

Now let's create a C source code file as usual. Select New from the File menu, select the Files tab, and click C++ Source File. In the File Name field, type ICONDEMO.C and click OK. At this point, Developer Studio has created an empty ICONDEMO.C file. Type in the program shown in Figure 10-1, or pick the Insert menu and then the File As Text option to copy in the source code from this book's companion CD-ROM.

ICONDEMO.C

```
/*------------------------------------------------
   ICONDEMO.C -- Icon Demonstration Program
                 (c) Charles Petzold, 1998
  ------------------------------------------------*/

#include <windows.h>
#include "resource.h"

LRESULT CALLBACK WndProc (HWND, UINT, WPARAM, LPARAM) ;

int WINAPI WinMain (HINSTANCE hInstance, HINSTANCE hPrevInstance,
                    PSTR szCmdLine, int iCmdShow)
{
     TCHAR     szAppName[] = TEXT ("IconDemo") ;
     HWND      hwnd ;
     MSG       msg ;
     WNDCLASS wndclass ;

     wndclass.style         = CS_HREDRAW | CS_VREDRAW ;
     wndclass.lpfnWndProc   = WndProc ;
     wndclass.cbClsExtra    = 0 ;
     wndclass.cbWndExtra    = 0 ;
     wndclass.hInstance     = hInstance ;
     wndclass.hIcon         = LoadIcon (hInstance, MAKEINTRESOURCE (IDI_ICON)) ;
     wndclass.hCursor       = LoadCursor (NULL, IDC_ARROW) ;
     wndclass.hbrBackground = GetStockObject (WHITE_BRUSH) ;
     wndclass.lpszMenuName  = NULL ;
     wndclass.lpszClassName = szAppName ;
```

Figure 10-1. *The ICONDEMO program.* *(continued)*

Figure 10-1. *continued*

```
      if (!RegisterClass (&wndclass))
      {
            MessageBox (NULL, TEXT ("This program requires Windows NT!"),
                       szAppName, MB_ICONERROR) ;
            return 0 ;
      }

      hwnd = CreateWindow (szAppName, TEXT ("Icon Demo"),
                           WS_OVERLAPPEDWINDOW,
                           CW_USEDEFAULT, CW_USEDEFAULT,
                           CW_USEDEFAULT, CW_USEDEFAULT,
                           NULL, NULL, hInstance, NULL) ;

      ShowWindow (hwnd, iCmdShow) ;
      UpdateWindow (hwnd) ;

      while (GetMessage (&msg, NULL, 0, 0))
      {
            TranslateMessage (&msg) ;
            DispatchMessage (&msg) ;
      }
      return msg.wParam ;
}

LRESULT CALLBACK WndProc (HWND hwnd, UINT message, WPARAM wParam, LPARAM lParam)
{
      static HICON hIcon ;
      static int   cxIcon, cyIcon, cxClient, cyClient ;
      HDC          hdc ;
      HINSTANCE    hInstance ;
      PAINTSTRUCT  ps ;
      int          x, y ;

      switch (message)
      {
      case WM_CREATE :
            hInstance = ((LPCREATESTRUCT) lParam)->hInstance ;
            hIcon = LoadIcon (hInstance, MAKEINTRESOURCE (IDI_ICON)) ;
            cxIcon = GetSystemMetrics (SM_CXICON) ;
            cyIcon = GetSystemMetrics (SM_CYICON) ;
            return 0 ;

      case WM_SIZE :
            cxClient = LOWORD (lParam) ;
            cyClient = HIWORD (lParam) ;
            return 0 ;
```

```
    case WM_PAINT :
        hdc = BeginPaint (hwnd, &ps) ;

        for (y = 0 ; y < cyClient ; y += cyIcon)
            for (x = 0 ; x < cxClient ; x += cxIcon)
                DrawIcon (hdc, x, y, hIcon) ;

            EndPaint (hwnd, &ps) ;
            return 0 ;

    case WM_DESTROY :
        PostQuitMessage (0) ;
        return 0 ;
    }
    return DefWindowProc (hwnd, message, wParam, lParam) ;
}
```

If you try compiling this program, you'll get an error because the RESOURCE.H file referenced at the top of the program does not yet exist. However, you do not create this RESOURCE.H file directly. Instead, you let Developer Studio create it for you.

You do this by adding a resource script to the project. Select New from the File menu, select the Files tab, click Resource Script, and type ICONDEMO in the File Name field. Click OK. At this time, Developer Studio creates two new text files: ICONDEMO.RC, the resource script, and RESOURCE.H, a header file that will allow the C source code file and the resource script to refer to the same defined identifiers. Don't try to edit these two files directly; let Developer Studio maintain them for you. If you want to take a look at the resource script and RESOURCE.H without any interference from Developer Studio, try loading them into Notepad. Don't change them there unless you really know what you're doing. Also, keep in mind that Developer Studio will save new versions of these files only when you explicitly direct it to or when it rebuilds the project.

The resource script is a text file. It contains text representations of those resources that can be expressed in text, such as menus and dialog boxes. The resource script also contains references to binary files that contain nontext resources, such as icons and customized mouse cursors.

Now that RESOURCE.H exists, you can try compiling ICONDEMO again. Now you get an error message indicating that IDI_ICON is not defined. This identifier occurs first in the statement

```
wndclass.hIcon = LoadIcon (hInstance, MAKEINTRESOURCE (IDI_ICON)) ;
```

That statement in ICONDEMO has replaced this statement found in previous programs in this book:

```
wndclass.hIcon = LoadIcon (NULL, IDI_APPLICATION) ;
```

It makes sense that we're changing this statement because we've been using a standard icon for our applications and our goal here is to use a customized icon.

So let's create an icon. In the File View window of Developer Studio, you'll see two files listed now—ICONDEMO.C and ICONDEMO.RC. When you click ICONDEMO.C, you can edit the source code. When you click ICONDEMO.RC, you can add resources to that file or edit an existing resource. To add an icon, select Resource from the Insert menu. Click the resource you want to add, which is Icon, and then click the New button.

You are now presented with a blank 32-pixel-by-32-pixel icon that is ready to be colored. You'll see a floating toolbar with a collection of painting tools and a bunch of available colors. Be aware that the color toolbar includes two options that are not exactly colors. These are sometimes referred to as "screen" and "inverse screen." When a pixel is colored with "screen," it is actually transparent. Whatever surface the icon is displayed against will show through. This allows you to create icons that appear to be nonrectangular.

Before you get too far, double-click the area surrounding the icon. You'll get an Icon Properties dialog box that allows you to change the ID of the icon and its filename. Developer Studio will probably have set the ID to IDI_ICON1. Change that to IDI_ICON since that's how ICONDEMO refers to the icon. (The IDI prefix stands for "id for an icon.") Also, change the filename to ICONDEMO.ICO.

For now, I want you to select a distinctive color (such as red) and draw a large B (standing for "big") on this icon. It doesn't have to be as neat as Figure 10-2.

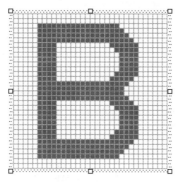

Figure 10-2. *The standard (32×32) ICONDEMO file as displayed in Developer Studio.*

The program should now compile and run fine. Developer Studio has put a line in the ICONDEMO.RC resource script that equates the icon file (ICONDEMO.ICO) with an identifier (IDI_ICON). The RESOURCE.H header file contains a definition of the IDI_ICON identifier. (We'll take a look at this in more detail shortly.)

Developer Studio compiles resources by using the resource compiler RC.EXE. The text resource script is converted into a binary form, which is a file with the extension .RES. This compiled resource file is then specified along with .OBJ and .LIB files in the LINK step. This is how the resources are added to the final .EXE file.

When you run ICONDEMO, the program's icon is displayed in the upper left corner of the title bar and in the taskbar. If you add the program to the Start Menu, or if you add a shortcut on your desktop, you'll see the icon there as well.

ICONDEMO also displays the icon in its client area, repeated horizontally and vertically. Using the statement

```
hIcon = LoadIcon (hInstance, MAKEINTRESOURCE (IDI_ICON)) ;
```

the program obtains a handle to the icon. Using the statements

```
cxIcon = GetSystemMetrics (SM_CXICON) ;
cyIcon = GetSystemMetrics (SM_CYICON) ;
```

it obtains the size of the icon. The program can then display the icon with multiple calls to

```
DrawIcon (hdc, x, y, hIcon) ;
```

where *x* and *y* are the coordinates of where the upper left corner of the displayed icon is positioned.

With most video display adapters in current use, *GetSystemMetrics* with the SM_CXICON and SM_CYICON indices will report that the size of an icon is 32 by 32 pixels. This is the size of the icon that we created in the Developer Studio. It is also the size of the icon as it appears on the desktop and the size of the icon displayed in the client area of the ICONDEMO program. It is *not*, however, the size of the icon displayed in the program's title bar or in the taskbar. That smaller icon size can be obtained from *GetSystemMetrics* with the SM_CXSMSIZE and SM_CYSMSIZE indices. (The first "SM" means "system metrics"; the embedded "SM" means "small.") For most display adapters in current use, the small icon size is 16 by 16 pixels.

This can be a problem. When Windows reduces a 32-by-32 icon to a 16-by-16 size, it must eliminate every other row and column of pixels. For some complex icon images, this might cause distortions. For this reason, you should probably create special 16-by-16 icons for images where shrinkage is undesirable. Above the icon image in Developer Studio is a combo box labeled Device. To the right of that is a button. Pushing the button invokes a New Icon Image dialog box. Select Small (16x16). Now you can draw another icon. For now, use an S (for "small") as shown in Figure 10-3.

Figure 10-3. *The small (16×16) ICONDEMO file as displayed in Developer Studio.*

There's nothing else you need to do in the program. The second icon image is stored in the same ICONDEMO.ICO file and referenced with the same INI_ICON identifier. Windows will now automatically use the smaller icon when it's more appropriate, such as in the title bar and the taskbar. Windows uses the large image when displaying a shortcut on the desktop and when the program calls *DrawIcon* to adorn its client area.

Now that we've mastered the practical stuff, let's take a closer look at what's going on under the hood.

Getting a Handle on Icons

If you take a look ICONDEMO.RC and RESOURCE.H, you'll see a bunch of stuff that Developer Studio generates to help it maintain the files. However, when the resource script is compiled, only a few lines are important. These critical excerpts from the ICONDEMO.RC and RESOURCE.H files are shown in Figure 10-4.

ICONDEMO.RC (excerpts)

```
//Microsoft Developer Studio generated resource script.

#include "resource.h"
#include "afxres.h"

/////////////////////////////////////////////////////////////////////////////
// Icon

IDI_ICON                ICON    DISCARDABLE     "icondemo.ico"
```

RESOURCE.H (excerpts)

```
// Microsoft Developer Studio generated include file.
// Used by IconDemo.rc

#define IDI_ICON                        101
```

Figure 10-4. *Excerpts from the ICONDEMO.RC and RESOURCE.H files.*

Figure 10-4 shows ICONDEMO.RC and RESOURCE.H files that look much like they would look if you were creating them manually in a normal text editor, just as Windows programmers did in the old days way back in the 1980s. The only real difference is the presence of AFXRES.H, which is a header file that includes many common identifiers used by Developer Studio when creating machine-generated MFC projects. I will not make use of AFXRES.H in this book.

This line in ICONDEMO.RC,

```
IDI_ICON ICON DISCARDABLE "icondemo.ico"
```

is a resource script ICON statement. The icon has a numeric identifier of IDI_ICON, which equals 101. The DISCARDABLE keyword that Developer Studio adds indicates that Windows can discard the icon from memory, if necessary, to obtain some additional space. The icon can always be reloaded later by Windows without any special action by the program. The DISCARDABLE attribute is the default and doesn't need to be specified. Developer Studio puts the filename in quotes just in case the name or a directory path contains spaces.

When the resource compiler stores the compiled resource in ICONDEMO.RES and the linker adds the resource to ICONDEMO.EXE, the resource is identified by just a resource type, which is RT_ICON, and an identifier, which is IDI_ICON or 101. A program can obtain a handle to this icon by calling the *LoadIcon* function:

```
hIcon = LoadIcon (hInstance, MAKEINTRESOURCE (IDI_ICON)) ;
```

Notice that ICONDEMO calls this function in two places—once when defining the window class and again in the window procedure to obtain a handle to the icon for drawing. *LoadIcon* returns a value of type HICON, a handle to an icon.

The first argument to *LoadIcon* is the instance handle that indicates what file the resource comes from. Using *hInstance* means it comes from the program's own .EXE file. The second argument to *LoadIcon* is actually defined as a pointer to a character string. As we'll see shortly, you can identify resources by character strings instead of numeric identifiers. The macro MAKEINTRESOURCE ("make an integer into a resource string") makes a pointer out of the number like so:

```
#define MAKEINTRESOURCE(i)  (LPTSTR) ((DWORD) ((WORD) (i)))
```

The *LoadIcon* function knows that if the high word of the second argument is 0, then the low word is a numeric identifier for the icon. The icon identifier must be a 16-bit value.

Sample programs presented earlier in this book use predefined icons:

```
LoadIcon (NULL, IDI_APPLICATION) ;
```

Windows knows that this is a predefined icon because the *hInstance* parameter is set to NULL. And IDI_APPLICATION happens also to be defined in WINUSER.H in terms of MAKEINTRESOURCE:

```
#define IDI_APPLICATION MAKEINTRESOURCE(32512)
```

The second argument to *LoadIcon* raises an intriguing question: can the icon identifier be a character string? Yes, and here's how: In the Developer Studio list of files for the ICONDEMO project, select IDONDEMO.RC. You'll see a tree structure beginning at the top with IconDemo Resources, then the resource type Icon, and then the icon IDI_ICON.

If you right-click the icon identifier and select Properties from the menu, you can change the ID. In fact, you can change it to a string by enclosing a name in quotation marks. This is the method I prefer for specifying the names of resources and that I will use in general for the rest of this book.

I prefer using text names for icons (and some other resources) because the name can be the name of the program. For example, suppose the program is named MYPROG. If you use the Icon Properties dialog box to specify the ID of the icon as "MyProg" (with quotation marks), the resource script would contain the following statement:

```
MYPROG ICON DISCARDABLE myprog.ico
```

However, there will be no *#define* statement in RESOURCE.H that will indicate MYPROG as a numeric identifier. The resource script will instead assume that MYPROG is a *string* identifier.

In your C program, you use the *LoadIcon* function to obtain a handle to the icon. Recall that you already probably have a string variable indicating the name of the program:

```
static TCHAR szAppName [] = TEXT ("MyProg") ;
```

This means that the program can load the icon using the statement

```
hIcon = LoadIcon (hInstance, szAppName) ;
```

which looks a whole lot cleaner than the MAKEINTRESOURCE macro.

But if you really prefer numbers to names, you can use them instead of identifiers or strings. In the Icon Properties dialog, enter a number in the ID field. The resource script will have an ICON statement that looks something like this:

```
125 ICON DISCARDABLE myprog.ico
```

You can reference the icon using one of two methods. The obvious one is this:

```
hIcon = LoadIcon (hInstance, MAKEINTRESOURCE (125)) ;
```

The obscure method is this:

```
hIcon = LoadIcon (hInstance, TEXT ("#125")) ;
```

Windows recognizes the initial # character as prefacing a number in ASCII form.

Using Icons in Your Program

Although Windows uses icons in several ways to denote a program, many Windows programs specify an icon only when defining the window class with the WNDCLASS structure and *RegisterClass*. As we've seen, this works well, particularly when the icon file contains both standard and small image sizes. Windows will choose the best image size in the icon file whenever it needs to display the icon image.

There is an enhanced version of *RegisterClass* named *RegisterClassEx* that uses a structure named WNDCLASSEX. WNDCLASSEX has two additional fields: *cbSize* and *hIconSm*. The *cbSize* field indicates the size of the WNDCLASSEX structure, and *hIconSm* is supposed to be set to the icon handle of the small icon. Thus, in the WNDCLASSEX structure you set two icon handles associated with two icon files—one for a standard icon and one for the small icon.

Is this necessary? Well, no. As we've seen, Windows already extracts the correctly sized icon images from a single icon file. And *RegisterClassEx* seems to have lost the intelligence of *RegisterClass*. If the *hIconSm* field references an icon file that contains multiple images, only the first image will be used. This might be a standard size icon that is then reduced in size. *RegisterClassEx* seems to have been designed for using multiple icon images, each of which contains only one icon size. Because we can now include multiple icon sizes in the same file, my advice is to use WNDCLASS and *RegisterClass*.

If you later want to dynamically change the program's icon while the program is running, you can do so using *SetClassLong*. For example, if you have a second icon file associated with the identifier IDI_ALTICON, you can switch to that icon using the statement

```
SetClassLong (hwnd, GCL_HICON,
    LoadIcon (hInstance, MAKEINTRESOURCE (IDI_ALTICON))) ;
```

If you don't want to save the handle to your program's icon but instead use the *DrawIcon* function to display it someplace, you can obtain the handle by using *GetClassLong*. For example:

```
DrawIcon (hdc, x, y, GetClassLong (hwnd, GCL_HICON)) ;
```

At some places in the Windows documentation, *LoadIcon* is said to be "obsolete" and *LoadImage* is recommended instead. (*LoadIcon* is documented in */Platform SDK/User Interface Services/Resources/Icons*, and *LoadImage* in */Platform SDK/User Interface Services/Resources/Resources*.) *LoadImage* is certainly more flexible, but it hasn't replaced the simplicity of *LoadIcon* just yet. You'll notice that *LoadIcon* is called twice in ICONDEMO for the same icon. This presents no problem and doesn't involve extra memory being used. *LoadIcon* is one of the few functions that obtain a handle but do not require the handle to be destroyed. There actually *is* a *DestroyIcon* function, but it is used in conjunction with the *CreateIcon*, *CreateIconIndirect*, and *CreateIconFromResource* functions. These functions allow your program to dynamically create an icon image algorithmically.

Using Customized Cursors

Using customized mouse cursors in your program is similar to using customized icons, except that most programmers seem to find the cursors that Windows supplies to be quite adequate. Customized cursors are generally monochrome with a dimension of 32 by 32 pixels. You create a cursor in the Developer Studio in the same way as an icon (that is, select Resource from the Insert menu, and pick Cursor), but don't forget to define the hotspot.

You can set a customized cursor in your class definition with a statement such as

```
wndclass.hCursor = LoadCursor (hInstance, MAKEINTRESOURCE (IDC_CURSOR)) ;
```

or, if the cursor is defined with a text name,

```
wndclass.hCursor = LoadCursor (hInstance, szCursor) ;
```

Whenever the mouse is positioned over a window created based on this class, the customized cursor associated with IDC_CURSOR or *szCursor* will be displayed.

If you use child windows, you may want the cursor to appear differently, depending on the child window below the cursor. If your program defines the window class for these child windows, you can use different cursors for each class by appropriately setting the *hCursor* field in each window class. And if you use predefined child window controls, you can alter the *hCursor* field of the window class by using

```
SetClassLong (hwndChild, GCL_HCURSOR,
              LoadCursor (hInstance, TEXT ("childcursor")) ;
```

If you separate your client area into smaller logical areas without using child windows, you can use *SetCursor* to change the mouse cursor:

```
SetCursor (hCursor) ;
```

You should call *SetCursor* during processing of the WM_MOUSEMOVE message. Otherwise, Windows uses the cursor specified in the window class to redraw the cursor when it is moved. The documentation indicates that *SetCursor* is fast if the cursor doesn't have to be changed.

Character String Resources

Having a resource for character strings may seem odd at first. Certainly we haven't had any problems using regular old character strings defined as variables right in our source code.

Character string resources are primarily for easing the translation of your program to other languages. As you'll discover later in this chapter and in the next chapter, menus and dialog boxes are also part of the resource script. If you use character string resources rather than putting strings directly into your source code, all the text that your program uses will be in one file—the resource script. If the text in this resource script is translated into another language, all you need to do to create a foreign-language version of your program is relink the program. This method is much safer than messing around with your source code. (However, aside from the next sample program, I will not be using string tables for any other programs in this book. The reason is that string tables tend to make code look more obscure and complicated rather than clarifying it.)

You create a string table by selecting Resource from the Insert menu and then selecting String Table. The strings will be shown in a list at the right of the screen. Select a string by double-clicking it. For each string, you specify an identifier and the string itself.

In the resource script, the strings show up in a multiline statement that looks something like this:

```
STRINGTABLE DISCARDABLE
BEGIN
     IDS_STRING1, "character string 1"
     IDS_STRING2, "character string 2"
     [other string definitions]
END
```

If you were programming for Windows back in the old days and creating this string table manually in a text editor (which you might correctly guess was easier than creating the string table in Developer Studio), you could substitute left and right curly brackets for the BEGIN and END statements.

The resource script can have multiple string tables, but each ID must uniquely identify only a single string. Each string can be only one line long with a maximum of 4097 characters. Use \t and \n for tabs and ends of lines. These control characters are recognized by the *DrawText* and *MessageBox* functions.

Your program can use the *LoadString* call to copy a string resource into a buffer in the program's data segment:

```
LoadString (hInstance, id, szBuffer, iMaxLength) ;
```

The *id* argument refers to the ID number that precedes each string in the resource script; *szBuffer* is a pointer to a character array that receives the character string; and *iMaxLength* is the maximum number of characters to transfer into the *szBuffer*. The function returns the number of characters in the string.

The string ID numbers that precede each string are generally macro identifiers defined in a header file. Many Windows programmers use the prefix IDS_ to denote an ID number for a string. Sometimes a filename or other information must be embedded in the string when the string is displayed. In this case, you can put C formatting characters in the string and use it as a formatting string in *wsprintf*.

All resource text—including the text in the string table—is stored in the .RES compiled resource file and in the final .EXE file in Unicode format. The *LoadStringW* function loads the Unicode text directly. The *LoadStringA* function (the only function available under Windows 98) performs a conversion of the text from Unicode to the local code page.

Let's look at an example of a function that uses three character strings to display three error messages in a message box. As you can see at the top of the following page, the RESOURCE.H header file contains three identifiers for these messages.

```
#define IDS_FILENOTFOUND 1
#define IDS_FILETOOBIG   2
#define IDS_FILEREADONLY 3
```

The resource script has this string table:

```
STRINGTABLE
BEGIN
     IDS_FILENOTFOUND,    "File %s not found."
     IDS_FILETOOBIG,      "File %s too large to edit."
     IDS_FILEREADONLY,    "File %s is read-only."
END
```

The C source code file also includes this header file and defines a function to display a message box. (I'll also assume that *szAppName* is a global variable that contains the program name.)

```
OkMessage (HWND hwnd, int iErrorNumber, TCHAR *szFileName)
{
     TCHAR szFormat [40] ;
     TCHAR szBuffer [60] ;

     LoadString (hInst, iErrorNumber, szFormat, 40) ;
     wsprintf (szBuffer, szFormat, szFilename) ;

     return MessageBox (hwnd, szBuffer, szAppName,
                        MB_OK | MB_ICONEXCLAMATION) ;
}
```

To display a message box containing the "file not found" message, the program calls

```
OkMessage (hwnd, IDS_FILENOTFOUND, szFileName) ;
```

Custom Resources

Windows also defines a "custom resource," also called the "user-defined resource" (where the user is *you*, the programmer, rather than the lucky person who gets to use your program). The custom resource is convenient for attaching miscellaneous data to your .EXE file and obtaining access to that data within the program. The data can be in absolutely any format you want. The Windows functions that a program uses to access the custom resource cause Windows to load the data into memory and return a pointer to it. You can do whatever you want with that data. You'll probably find this to be a more convenient way to store and access miscellaneous private data than storing it in external files and accessing it with file input functions.

For instance, suppose you have a file called BINDATA.BIN that contains a bunch of data that your program needs for display purposes. This file can be in any format you choose. If you have a MYPROG.RC resource script in your MYPROG project, you can create a custom resource in Developer Studio by selecting Resource from the Insert menu and pressing the Custom button. Type in a type name by which the resource is to be known: for example, BINTYPE. Developer Studio will then make up a resource name (in this case, IDR_BINTYPE1) and display a window that lets you enter binary data. But you don't need to do that. Click the IDR_BINTYPE1 name with the right mouse button, and select Properties. Then you can enter a filename: for example, BINDATA.BIN.

The resource script will then contain a statement like this:

```
IDR_BINTYPE1 BINTYPE BINDATA.BIN
```

This statement looks just like the ICON statement in ICONDEMO, except that the resource type BINTYPE is something we've just made up. As with icons, you can use text names rather than numeric identifiers for the resource name.

When you compile and link the program, the entire BINDATA.BIN file will be bound into the MYPROG.EXE file.

During program initialization (for example, while processing the WM_CREATE message), you can obtain a handle to this resource:

```
hResource = LoadResource (hInstance,
        FindResource (hInstance, TEXT ("BINTYPE"),
                MAKEINTRESOURCE (IDR_BINTYPE1))) ;
```

The variable *hResource* is defined with type HGLOBAL, which is a handle to a memory block. Despite its name, *LoadResource* does not actually load the resource into memory. The *LoadResource* and *FindResource* functions used together like this are essentially equivalent to the *LoadIcon* and *LoadCursor* functions. In fact, *LoadIcon* and *LoadCursor* use the *LoadResource* and *FindResource* functions.

When you need access to the text, call *LockResource*:

```
pData = LockResource (hResource) ;
```

LockResource loads the resource into memory (if it has not already been loaded) and returns a pointer to it. When you're finished with the resource, you can free it from memory:

```
FreeResource (hResource) ;
```

The resource will also be freed when your program terminates, even if you don't call *FreeResource*.

Let's look at a sample program that uses three resources—an icon, a string table, and a custom resource. The POEPOEM program, shown in Figure 10-5 beginning on the following page, displays the text of Edgar Allan Poe's "Annabel Lee" in its client area. The custom resource is the file POEPOEM.TXT, which contains the text of the poem. The text file is terminated with a backslash (\).

POEPOEM.C

```
/*-----------------------------------------------
   POEPOEM.C -- Demonstrates Custom Resource
               (c) Charles Petzold, 1998
   -----------------------------------------------*/

#include <windows.h>
#include "resource.h"

LRESULT CALLBACK WndProc (HWND, UINT, WPARAM, LPARAM) ;

HINSTANCE hInst ;

int WINAPI WinMain (HINSTANCE hInstance, HINSTANCE hPrevInstance,
                    PSTR szCmdLine, int iCmdShow)
{
    TCHAR      szAppName [16], szCaption [64], szErrMsg [64] ;
    HWND       hwnd ;
    MSG        msg ;
    WNDCLASS wndclass ;

    LoadString (hInstance, IDS_APPNAME, szAppName,
                          sizeof (szAppName) / sizeof (TCHAR)) ;

    LoadString (hInstance, IDS_CAPTION, szCaption,
                          sizeof (szCaption) / sizeof (TCHAR)) ;

    wndclass.style         = CS_HREDRAW | CS_VREDRAW ;
    wndclass.lpfnWndProc   = WndProc ;
    wndclass.cbClsExtra    = 0 ;
    wndclass.cbWndExtra    = 0 ;
    wndclass.hInstance     = hInstance ;
    wndclass.hIcon         = LoadIcon (hInstance, szAppName) ;
    wndclass.hCursor       = LoadCursor (NULL, IDC_ARROW) ;
    wndclass.hbrBackground = (HBRUSH) GetStockObject (WHITE_BRUSH) ;
    wndclass.lpszMenuName  = NULL ;
    wndclass.lpszClassName = szAppName ;

    if (!RegisterClass (&wndclass))
    {
        LoadStringA (hInstance, IDS_APPNAME, (char *) szAppName,
                                sizeof (szAppName)) ;

        LoadStringA (hInstance, IDS_ERRMSG, (char *) szErrMsg,
                                sizeof (szErrMsg)) ;
```

Figure 10-5. *The POEPOEM program, including an icon and a user defined resource.*

```
            MessageBoxA (NULL, (char *) szErrMsg,
                             (char *) szAppName, MB_ICONERROR) ;
            return 0 ;
     }

     hwnd = CreateWindow (szAppName, szCaption,
                          WS_OVERLAPPEDWINDOW | WS_CLIPCHILDREN,
                          CW_USEDEFAULT, CW_USEDEFAULT,
                          CW_USEDEFAULT, CW_USEDEFAULT,
                          NULL, NULL, hInstance, NULL) ;

     ShowWindow (hwnd, iCmdShow) ;
     UpdateWindow (hwnd) ;

     while (GetMessage (&msg, NULL, 0, 0))
     {
          TranslateMessage (&msg) ;
          DispatchMessage (&msg) ;
     }
     return msg.wParam ;
}

LRESULT CALLBACK WndProc (HWND hwnd, UINT message, WPARAM wParam, LPARAM lParam)
{
     static char   * pText ;
     static HGLOBAL hResource ;
     static HWND    hScroll ;
     static int     iPosition, cxChar, cyChar, cyClient, iNumLines, xScroll ;
     HDC            hdc ;
     PAINTSTRUCT    ps ;
     RECT           rect ;
     TEXTMETRIC     tm ;

     switch (message)
     {
     case WM_CREATE :
          hdc = GetDC (hwnd) ;
          GetTextMetrics (hdc, &tm) ;
          cxChar = tm.tmAveCharWidth ;
          cyChar = tm.tmHeight + tm.tmExternalLeading ;
          ReleaseDC (hwnd, hdc) ;

          xScroll = GetSystemMetrics (SM_CXVSCROLL) ;
```

(continued)

Figure 10-5. *continued*

```
            hScroll = CreateWindow (TEXT ("scrollbar"), NULL,
                              WS_CHILD | WS_VISIBLE | SBS_VERT,
                              0, 0, 0, 0,
                              hwnd, (HMENU) 1, hInst, NULL) ;

            hResource = LoadResource (hInst,
                      FindResource (hInst, TEXT ("AnnabelLee"),
                                        TEXT ("TEXT"))) ;

            pText = (char *) LockResource (hResource) ;
            iNumLines = 0 ;

            while (*pText != '\\' && *pText != '\0')
            {
                if (*pText == '\n')
                      iNumLines ++ ;
                pText = AnsiNext (pText) ;
            }
            *pText = '\0' ;

            SetScrollRange (hScroll, SB_CTL, 0, iNumLines, FALSE) ;
            SetScrollPos   (hScroll, SB_CTL, 0, FALSE) ;
            return 0 ;

      case WM_SIZE :
            MoveWindow (hScroll, LOWORD (lParam) - xScroll, 0,
                      xScroll, cyClient = HIWORD (lParam), TRUE) ;
            SetFocus (hwnd) ;
            return 0 ;

      case WM_SETFOCUS :
            SetFocus (hScroll) ;
            return 0 ;

      case WM_VSCROLL :
            switch (wParam)
            {
            case SB_TOP :
                iPosition = 0 ;
                break ;
            case SB_BOTTOM :
                iPosition = iNumLines ;
                break ;
            case SB_LINEUP :
                iPosition -= 1 ;
                break ;
```

```
          case SB_LINEDOWN :
               iPosition += 1 ;
               break ;
          case SB_PAGEUP :
               iPosition -= cyClient / cyChar ;
               break ;
          case SB_PAGEDOWN :
               iPosition += cyClient / cyChar ;
               break ;
          case SB_THUMBPOSITION :
               iPosition = LOWORD (lParam) ;
               break ;
          }
          iPosition = max (0, min (iPosition, iNumLines)) ;

          if (iPosition != GetScrollPos (hScroll, SB_CTL))
          {
               SetScrollPos (hScroll, SB_CTL, iPosition, TRUE) ;
               InvalidateRect (hwnd, NULL, TRUE) ;
          }
          return 0 ;

     case WM_PAINT :
          hdc = BeginPaint (hwnd, &ps) ;

          pText = (char *) LockResource (hResource) ;

          GetClientRect (hwnd, &rect) ;
          rect.left += cxChar ;
          rect.top  += cyChar * (1 - iPosition) ;
          DrawTextA (hdc, pText, -1, &rect, DT_EXTERNALLEADING) ;

          EndPaint (hwnd, &ps) ;
          return 0 ;

     case WM_DESTROY :
          FreeResource (hResource) ;
          PostQuitMessage (0) ;
          return 0 ;
     }
     return DefWindowProc (hwnd, message, wParam, lParam) ;
}
```

(continued)

Figure 10-5. *continued*

POEPOEM.RC (excerpts)

```
//Microsoft Developer Studio generated resource script.

#include "resource.h"
#include "afxres.h"


/////////////////////////////////////////////////////////////////////////////
// TEXT

ANNABELLEE              TEXT    DISCARDABLE     "poepoem.txt"


/////////////////////////////////////////////////////////////////////////////
// Icon

POEPOEM                 ICON    DISCARDABLE     "poepoem.ico"


/////////////////////////////////////////////////////////////////////////////
// String Table

STRINGTABLE DISCARDABLE
BEGIN
    IDS_APPNAME             "PoePoem"
    IDS_CAPTION             """Annabel Lee"" by Edgar Allan Poe"
    IDS_ERRMSG              "This program requires Windows NT!"
END
```

RESOURCE.H (excerpts)

```
// Microsoft Developer Studio generated include file.
// Used by PoePoem.rc

#define IDS_APPNAME                     1
#define IDS_CAPTION                     2
#define IDS_ERRMSG                      3
```

POEPOEM.TXT

```
It was many and many a year ago,
   In a kingdom by the sea,
That a maiden there lived whom you may know
   By the name of Annabel Lee;
```

```
And this maiden she lived with no other thought
    Than to love and be loved by me.

I was a child and she was a child
    In this kingdom by the sea,
But we loved with a love that was more than love --
    I and my Annabel Lee --
With a love that the winged seraphs of Heaven
    Coveted her and me.

And this was the reason that, long ago,
    In this kingdom by the sea,
A wind blew out of a cloud, chilling
    My beautiful Annabel Lee;
So that her highborn kinsmen came
    And bore her away from me,
To shut her up in a sepulchre
    In this kingdom by the sea.

The angels, not half so happy in Heaven,
    Went envying her and me --
Yes! that was the reason (as all men know,
    In this kingdom by the sea)
That the wind came out of the cloud by night,
    Chilling and killing my Annabel Lee.

But our love it was stronger by far than the love
    Of those who were older than we --
    Of many far wiser than we --
And neither the angels in Heaven above
    Nor the demons down under the sea
Can ever dissever my soul from the soul
    Of the beautiful Annabel Lee:

For the moon never beams, without bringing me dreams
    Of the beautiful Annabel Lee;
And the stars never rise, but I feel the bright eyes
    Of the beautiful Annabel Lee:
And so, all the night-tide, I lie down by the side
Of my darling -- my darling -- my life and my bride,
    In her sepulchre there by the sea --
    In her tomb by the sounding sea.

                        [May, 1849]

\
```

(continued)

Figure 10-5. *continued*

POEPOEM.ICO

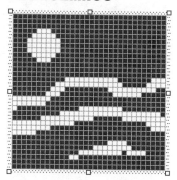

In the POEPOEM.RC resource script, the user-defined resource is given the type TEXT and the text name "AnnabelLee":

```
ANNABELLEE  TEXT  POEPOEM.TXT
```

During WM_CREATE processing in *WndProc*, a handle to the resource is obtained using *FindResource* and *LoadResource*. The resource is locked using *LockResource*, and a small routine replaces the backslash (\) at the end of the file with a 0. This is for the benefit of the *DrawText* function used later during the WM_PAINT message.

Note the use of a child window scroll bar control rather than a window scroll bar. The child window scroll bar control has an automatic keyboard interface, so no WM_KEYDOWN processing is required in POEPOEM.

POEPOEM also uses three character strings, the IDs of which are defined in the RESOURCE.H header file. At the outset of the program, the IDS_APPNAME and IDS_CAPTION strings are loaded into memory using *LoadString*:

```
LoadString (hInstance, IDS_APPNAME, szAppName, sizeof (szAppName) /
                                          sizeof (TCHAR)) ;

LoadString (hInstance, IDS_CAPTION, szCaption, sizeof (szCaption) /
                                          sizeof (TCHAR)) ;
```

Notice that these two calls precede *RegisterClass*. If you run the Unicode version of POEPOEM under Windows 98, these two function calls will fail. Despite the fact that *LoadStringA* is more complex than *LoadStringW* (because *LoadStringA* must convert the resource string from Unicode to ANSI, while *LoadStringW* just loads it directly), *LoadStringW* is *not* one of the few string functions that is supported under Windows 98. This means that when the *RegisterClassW* function fails under Windows 98, the *MessageBoxW* function (which *is* supported in Windows 98) cannot use strings loaded into the program using *LoadStringW*. For this reason, the program loads the IDS_APPNAME and IDS_ERRMSG strings using *LoadStringA* and then displays the customary message box using *MessageBoxA*:

```
if (!RegisterClass (&wndclass))
{
     LoadStringA (hInstance, IDS_APPNAME, (char *) szAppName,
                           sizeof (szAppName)) ;

     LoadStringA (hInstance, IDS_ERRMSG, (char *) szErrMsg,
                           sizeof (szErrMsg)) ;

     MessageBoxA (NULL, (char *) szErrMsg,
                        (char *) szAppName, MB_ICONERROR) ;
     return 0 ;
}
```

Notice the casting of the TCHAR string variables into *char* pointers.

With all character strings used in POEPOEM defined as resources, the program is now easier for translators to convert to a foreign-language version. Of course, they'd also have to translate the text of "Annabel Lee"—which would be, I suspect, a more difficult task.

MENUS

Do you remember the Monty Python skit about the cheese shop? Here's how it goes: A guy comes into a cheese shop and wants a particular type of cheese. The shop doesn't have it. So he asks for another type of cheese, and another, and another, and another (eventually totaling about 40 types, most of which are quite obscure), and still the answer is "No, no, no, no, no." Ultimately, there's a shooting involved.

This whole unfortunate incident could have been avoided through the use of menus. A menu is a list of available options. A menu tells a hungry patron what the kitchen can serve up and—for a Windows program—tells the user what operations an application is capable of performing.

A menu is probably the most important part of the consistent user interface that Windows programs offer, and adding a menu to your program is a relatively easy part of Windows programming. You define the menu in Developer Studio. Each selectable menu item is given a unique ID number. You specify the name of the menu in the window class structure. When the user chooses a menu item, Windows sends your program a WM_COMMAND message containing that ID.

After discussing menus, I'll conclude this chapter with a section on keyboard accelerators, which are key combinations that are used primarily to duplicate menu functions.

Menu Concepts

A window's menu bar is displayed immediately below the caption bar. This menu bar is sometimes called a program's "main menu" or the "top-level menu." Items listed in the top-level menu usually invoke drop-down menus, which are also called "popup menus" or "submenus." You can also define multiple nestings of popups: that is, an item on a popup menu can invoke another popup menu. Sometimes items in popup menus invoke a dialog box for more information. (Dialog boxes are covered in the next chapter.) Most parent windows have, to the far left of the caption bar, a display of the program's small icon. This icon invokes the system menu, which is really another popup menu.

Menu items in popups can be "checked," which means that Windows draws a small check mark to the left of the menu text. The use of check marks lets the user choose different program options from the menu. These options can be mutually exclusive, but they don't have to be. Top-level menu items cannot be checked.

Menu items in the top-level menu or in popup menus can be "enabled," "disabled," or "grayed." The words "active" and "inactive" are sometimes used synonymously with "enabled" and "disabled." Menu items flagged as enabled or disabled look the same to the user, but a grayed menu item is displayed in gray text.

From the perspective of the user, enabled, disabled, and grayed menu items can all be "selected" (highlighted). That is, the user can click the mouse on a disabled menu item, or move the reverse-video cursor bar to a disabled menu item, or trigger the menu item by using the item's key letter. However, from the perspective of your program, enabled, disabled, and grayed menu items function differently. Windows sends your program a WM_COMMAND message only for enabled menu items. You use disabled and grayed menu items for options that are not currently valid. If you want to let the user know the option is not valid, make it grayed.

Menu Structure

When you create or change menus in a program, it's useful to think of the top-level menu and each popup menu as being separate menus. The top-level menu has a menu handle, each popup menu within a top-level menu has its own menu handle, and the system menu (which is also a popup) has a menu handle.

Each item in a menu is defined by three characteristics. The first characteristic is what appears in the menu. This is either a text string or a bitmap. The second characteristic is either an ID number that Windows sends to your program in a WM_COMMAND message or the handle to a popup menu that Windows displays when the user chooses that menu item. The third characteristic describes the attribute of the menu item, including whether the item is disabled, grayed, or checked.

Defining the Menu

To use Developer Studio to add a menu to your program's resource script, select Resource from the Insert menu and pick Menu. (But you probably figured that out already.) You can then interactively define your menu. Each item in the menu has an associated Menu Item Properties dialog box that indicates the item's text string. If the Pop-up box is checked, the item invokes a popup menu and no ID is associated with the item. If the Pop-up box is not checked, the item generates a WM_COMMAND message with a specified ID. These two types of menu items will appear in the resource script as POPUP and MENUITEM statements, respectively.

When you type the text for an item in a menu, you can type an ampersand (&) to indicate that the following character is to be underlined when Windows displays the menu. Such an underlined character is the character Windows searches for when you select a menu item using the Alt key. If you don't include an ampersand in the text, no underline will appear, and Windows will instead use the first letter of the menu item's text for Alt-key searches.

If you select the Grayed option in the Menu Items Properties dialog box, the menu item is inactive, its text is grayed, and the item does not generate a WM_COMMAND message. If you select the Inactive option, the menu item is inactive and does not generate a WM_COMMAND message but its text is displayed normally. The Checked option places a check mark next to a menu item. The Separator option causes a horizontal separator bar to be drawn on popup menus.

For items in popup menus, you can use the columnar tab character \t in the character string. Text following the \t is placed in a new column spaced far enough to the right to accommodate the longest text string in the first column of the popup. We'll see how this works when we look at keyboard accelerators toward the end of this chapter. A \a in the character string right-justifies the text that follows it.

The ID values you specify are the numbers that Windows sends to the window procedure in menu messages. The ID values should be unique within a menu. By convention, I use identifiers beginning with the letters IDM ("ID for a Menu").

Referencing the Menu in Your Program

Most Windows applications have only one menu in the resource script. You can give the menu a text name that is the same as the name of the program. Programmers often use the name of the program as the name of the menu so that the same character string can be used for the window class, the name of the program's icon, and the name of the menu. The program then makes reference to this menu in the definition of the window class:

```
wndclass.lpszMenuName = szAppName ;
```

Although specifying the menu in the window class is the most common way to reference a menu resource, that's not the only way to do it. A Windows application can load a menu resource into memory with the *LoadMenu* function, which is similar to the *LoadIcon* and *LoadCursor* functions described earlier. *LoadMenu* returns a handle to the menu. If you use a name for the menu in the resource script, the statement looks like this:

```
hMenu = LoadMenu (hInstance, TEXT ("MyMenu")) ;
```

If you use a number, the *LoadMenu* call takes this form:

```
hMenu = LoadMenu (hInstance, MAKEINTRESOURCE (ID_MENU)) ;
```

You can then specify this menu handle as the ninth parameter to *CreateWindow*:

```
hwnd = CreateWindow (TEXT ("MyClass"), TEXT ("Window Caption"),
                     WS_OVERLAPPEDWINDOW,
                     CW_USEDEFAULT, CW_USEDEFAULT,
                     CW_USEDEFAULT, CW_USEDEFAULT,
                     NULL, hMenu, hInstance, NULL) ;
```

In this case, the menu specified in the *CreateWindow* call overrides any menu specified in the window class. You can think of the menu in the window class as being a default menu for the windows based on the window class if the ninth parameter to *CreateWindow* is NULL. Therefore, you can use different menus for several windows based on the same window class.

You can also have a NULL menu name in the window class and a NULL menu handle in the *CreateWindow* call and assign a menu to a window after the window has been created:

```
SetMenu (hwnd, hMenu) ;
```

This form lets you dynamically change a window's menu. We'll see an example of this in the NOPOPUPS program, shown later in this chapter.

Any menu that is attached to a window is destroyed when the window is destroyed. Any menus not attached to a window should be explicitly destroyed by calls to *DestroyMenu* before the program terminates.

Menus and Messages

Windows usually sends a window procedure several different messages when the user selects a menu item. In most cases, your program can ignore many of these messages and simply pass them to *DefWindowProc*. One such message is WM_INITMENU with the following parameters:

wParam: Handle to main menu
lParam: 0

The value of *wParam* is the handle to your main menu even if the user is selecting an item from the system menu. Windows programs generally ignore the WM_INITMENU message. Although the message exists to give you the opportunity to change the menu before an item is chosen, I suspect any changes to the top-level menu at this time would be disconcerting to the user.

Your program also receives WM_MENUSELECT messages. A program can receive many WM_MENUSELECT messages as the user moves the cursor or mouse among the menu items. This is helpful for implementing a status bar that contains a full text description of the menu option. The parameters that accompany WM_MENUSELECT are as follows:

LOWORD (*wParam*):	Selected item: Menu ID or popup menu index
HIWORD (*wParam*):	Selection flags
lParam:	Handle to menu containing selected item

WM_MENUSELECT is a menu-tracking message. The value of *wParam* tells you what item of the menu is currently selected (highlighted). The "selection flags" in the high word of *wParam* can be a combination of the following: MF_GRAYED, MF_DISABLED, MF_CHECKED, MF_BITMAP, MF_POPUP, MF_HELP, MF_SYSMENU, and MF_MOUSESELECT. You may want to use WM_MENUSELECT if you need to change something in the client area of your window based on the movement of the highlight among the menu items. Most programs pass this message to *DefWindowProc*.

When Windows is ready to display a popup menu, it sends the window procedure a WM_INITMENUPOPUP message with the following parameters:

wParam:	Popup menu handle
LOWORD (*lParam*):	Popup index
HIWORD (*lParam*):	1 for system menu, 0 otherwise

This message is important if you need to enable or disable items in a popup menu before it is displayed. For instance, suppose your program can copy text from the clipboard using the Paste command on a popup menu. When you receive a WM_INITMENUPOPUP message for that popup, you should determine whether the clipboard has text in it. If it doesn't, you should gray the Paste menu item. We'll see an example of this in the revised POPPAD program shown toward the end of this chapter.

The most important menu message is WM_COMMAND. This message indicates that the user has chosen an enabled menu item from your window's menu. You'll recall from Chapter 8 that WM_COMMAND messages also result from child window controls. If you happen to use the same ID codes for menus and child window controls, you can differentiate between them by examining the value of *lParam*, which will be 0 for a menu item.

	Menus	*Controls*
LOWORD (*wParam*):	Menu ID	Control ID
HIWORD (*wParam*):	0	Notification code
lParam:	0	Child window handle

The WM_SYSCOMMAND message is similar to the WM_COMMAND message except that WM_SYSCOMMAND signals that the user has chosen an enabled menu item from the system menu:

wParam:	Menu ID
lParam:	0

However, if the WM_SYSCOMMAND message is the result of a mouse click, LOWORD (*lParam*) and HIWORD (*lParam*) will contain the *x* and *y* screen coordinates of the mouse cursor's location.

For WM_SYSCOMMAND, the menu ID indicates which item on the system menu has been chosen. For the predefined system menu items, the bottom four bits should be masked out by ANDing with 0xFFF0. The resultant value will be one of the following: SC_SIZE, SC_MOVE, SC_MINIMIZE, SC_MAXIMIZE, SC_NEXTWINDOW, SC_PREVWINDOW, SC_CLOSE, SC_VSCROLL, SC_HSCROLL, SC_ARRANGE, SC_RESTORE, and SC_TASKLIST. In addition, *wParam* can be SC_MOUSEMENU or SC_KEYMENU.

If you add menu items to the system menu, the low word of *wParam* will be the menu ID that you define. To avoid conflicts with the predefined menu IDs, use values below 0xF000. It is important that you pass normal WM_SYSCOMMAND messages to *DefWindowProc*. If you do not, you'll effectively disable the normal system menu commands.

The final message we'll look at is WM_MENUCHAR, which isn't really a menu message at all. Windows sends this message to your window procedure in one of two circumstances: if the user presses Alt and a character key that does not correspond to a menu item, or, when a popup is displayed, if the user presses a character key that does not correspond to an item in the popup. The parameters that accompany the WM_MENUCHAR message are as follows:

LOWORD (*wParam*):	Character code (ASCII or Unicode)
HIWORD (*wParam*):	Selection code
lParam:	Handle to menu

The selection code is:

- *0* No popup is displayed.
- *MF_POPUP* Popup is displayed.
- *MF_SYSMENU* System menu popup is displayed.

Windows programs usually pass this message to *DefWindowProc*, which normally returns a 0 to Windows, which causes Windows to beep. We'll see a use for the WM_MENUCHAR message in the GRAFMENU program shown in Chapter 14.

A Sample Program

Let's look at a simple example. The MENUDEMO program, shown in Figure 10-6, has five items in the main menu—File, Edit, Background, Timer, and Help. Each of these items has a popup. MENUDEMO does the simplest and most common type of menu processing, which involves trapping WM_COMMAND messages and checking the low word of *wParam*.

MENUDEMO.C

```
/*-------------------------------------------
   MENUDEMO.C -- Menu Demonstration
                 (c) Charles Petzold, 1998
   -------------------------------------------*/

#include <windows.h>
#include "resource.h"

#define ID_TIMER 1

LRESULT CALLBACK WndProc (HWND, UINT, WPARAM, LPARAM) ;

TCHAR szAppName[] = TEXT ("MenuDemo") ;

int WINAPI WinMain (HINSTANCE hInstance, HINSTANCE hPrevInstance,
                    PSTR szCmdLine, int iCmdShow)
{
    HWND     hwnd ;
    MSG      msg ;
    WNDCLASS wndclass ;

    wndclass.style         = CS_HREDRAW | CS_VREDRAW ;
    wndclass.lpfnWndProc   = WndProc ;
    wndclass.cbClsExtra    = 0 ;
    wndclass.cbWndExtra    = 0 ;
    wndclass.hInstance     = hInstance ;
    wndclass.hIcon         = LoadIcon (NULL, IDI_APPLICATION) ;
    wndclass.hCursor       = LoadCursor (NULL, IDC_ARROW) ;
    wndclass.hbrBackground = (HBRUSH) GetStockObject (WHITE_BRUSH) ;
    wndclass.lpszMenuName  = szAppName ;
    wndclass.lpszClassName = szAppName ;
```

Figure 10-6. *The MENUDEMO program.*   *(continued)*

Figure 10-6. *continued*

```
    if (!RegisterClass (&wndclass))
    {
        MessageBox (NULL, TEXT ("This program requires Windows NT!"),
                    szAppName, MB_ICONERROR) ;
        return 0 ;
    }

    hwnd = CreateWindow (szAppName, TEXT ("Menu Demonstration"),
                        WS_OVERLAPPEDWINDOW,
                        CW_USEDEFAULT, CW_USEDEFAULT,
                        CW_USEDEFAULT, CW_USEDEFAULT,
                        NULL, NULL, hInstance, NULL) ;

    ShowWindow (hwnd, iCmdShow) ;
    UpdateWindow (hwnd) ;

    while (GetMessage (&msg, NULL, 0, 0))
    {
        TranslateMessage (&msg) ;
        DispatchMessage (&msg) ;
    }
    return msg.wParam ;
}

LRESULT CALLBACK WndProc (HWND hwnd, UINT message, WPARAM wParam, LPARAM lParam)
{
    static int idColor [5] = { WHITE_BRUSH,  LTGRAY_BRUSH, GRAY_BRUSH,
                               DKGRAY_BRUSH, BLACK_BRUSH } ;
    static int iSelection = IDM_BKGND_WHITE ;
    HMENU      hMenu ;

    switch (message)
    {
    case WM_COMMAND:
        hMenu = GetMenu (hwnd) ;

        switch (LOWORD (wParam))
        {
        case IDM_FILE_NEW:
        case IDM_FILE_OPEN:
        case IDM_FILE_SAVE:
        case IDM_FILE_SAVE_AS:
            MessageBeep (0) ;
            return 0 ;
```

```
case IDM_APP_EXIT:
     SendMessage (hwnd, WM_CLOSE, 0, 0) ;
     return 0 ;

case IDM_EDIT_UNDO:
case IDM_EDIT_CUT:
case IDM_EDIT_COPY:
case IDM_EDIT_PASTE:
case IDM_EDIT_CLEAR:
     MessageBeep (0) ;
     return 0 ;

case IDM_BKGND_WHITE:            // Note: Logic below
case IDM_BKGND_LTGRAY:           //   assumes that IDM_WHITE
case IDM_BKGND_GRAY:             //   through IDM_BLACK are
case IDM_BKGND_DKGRAY:           //   consecutive numbers in
case IDM_BKGND_BLACK:            //   the order shown here.

     CheckMenuItem (hMenu, iSelection, MF_UNCHECKED) ;
     iSelection = LOWORD (wParam) ;
     CheckMenuItem (hMenu, iSelection, MF_CHECKED) ;

     SetClassLong (hwnd, GCL_HBRBACKGROUND, (LONG)
          GetStockObject
                   (idColor [LOWORD (wParam) - IDM_BKGND_WHITE])) ;

     InvalidateRect (hwnd, NULL, TRUE) ;
     return 0 ;

case IDM_TIMER_START:
     if (SetTimer (hwnd, ID_TIMER, 1000, NULL))
     {
          EnableMenuItem (hMenu, IDM_TIMER_START, MF_GRAYED) ;
          EnableMenuItem (hMenu, IDM_TIMER_STOP,  MF_ENABLED) ;
     }
     return 0 ;

case IDM_TIMER_STOP:
     KillTimer (hwnd, ID_TIMER) ;
     EnableMenuItem (hMenu, IDM_TIMER_START, MF_ENABLED) ;
     EnableMenuItem (hMenu, IDM_TIMER_STOP,  MF_GRAYED) ;
     return 0 ;
```

(continued)

Figure 10-6. *continued*

```
        case IDM_APP_HELP:
            MessageBox (hwnd, TEXT ("Help not yet implemented!"),
                        szAppName, MB_ICONEXCLAMATION | MB_OK) ;
            return 0 ;

        case IDM_APP_ABOUT:
            MessageBox (hwnd, TEXT ("Menu Demonstration Program\n")
                              TEXT ("(c) Charles Petzold, 1998"),
                        szAppName, MB_ICONINFORMATION | MB_OK) ;
            return 0 ;
        }
        break ;

    case WM_TIMER:
        MessageBeep (0) ;
        return 0 ;

    case WM_DESTROY:
        PostQuitMessage (0) ;
        return 0 ;
    }
    return DefWindowProc (hwnd, message, wParam, lParam) ;
}
```

MENUDEMO.RC (excerpts)

```
//Microsoft Developer Studio generated resource script.

#include "resource.h"
#include "afxres.h"

/////////////////////////////////////////////////////////////////////////////
// Menu

MENUDEMO MENU DISCARDABLE
BEGIN
    POPUP "&File"
    BEGIN
        MENUITEM "&New",                        IDM_FILE_NEW
        MENUITEM "&Open",                       IDM_FILE_OPEN
        MENUITEM "&Save",                       IDM_FILE_SAVE
        MENUITEM "Save &As...",                 IDM_FILE_SAVE_AS
        MENUITEM SEPARATOR
        MENUITEM "E&xit",                       IDM_APP_EXIT
    END
```

```
    POPUP "&Edit"
    BEGIN
        MENUITEM "&Undo",                        IDM_EDIT_UNDO
        MENUITEM SEPARATOR
        MENUITEM "C&ut",                         IDM_EDIT_CUT
        MENUITEM "&Copy",                        IDM_EDIT_COPY
        MENUITEM "&Paste",                       IDM_EDIT_PASTE
        MENUITEM "De&lete",                      IDM_EDIT_CLEAR
    END
    POPUP "&Background"
    BEGIN
        MENUITEM "&White",                       IDM_BKGND_WHITE, CHECKED
        MENUITEM "&Light Gray",                  IDM_BKGND_LTGRAY
        MENUITEM "&Gray",                        IDM_BKGND_GRAY
        MENUITEM "&Dark Gray",                   IDM_BKGND_DKGRAY
        MENUITEM "&Black",                       IDM_BKGND_BLACK
    END
    POPUP "&Timer"
    BEGIN
        MENUITEM "&Start",                       IDM_TIMER_START
        MENUITEM "S&top",                        IDM_TIMER_STOP, GRAYED
    END
    POPUP "&Help"
    BEGIN
        MENUITEM "&Help...",                     IDM_APP_HELP
        MENUITEM "&About MenuDemo...",           IDM_APP_ABOUT
    END
END
```

RESOURCE.H (excerpts)

```
// Microsoft Developer Studio generated include file.
// Used by MenuDemo.rc

#define IDM_FILE_NEW              40001
#define IDM_FILE_OPEN             40002
#define IDM_FILE_SAVE             40003
#define IDM_FILE_SAVE_AS          40004
#define IDM_APP_EXIT              40005
#define IDM_EDIT_UNDO             40006
#define IDM_EDIT_CUT              40007
#define IDM_EDIT_COPY             40008
#define IDM_EDIT_PASTE            40009
#define IDM_EDIT_CLEAR            40010
```

(continued)

Figure 10-6. *continued*

```
#define IDM_BKGND_WHITE            40011
#define IDM_BKGND_LTGRAY           40012
#define IDM_BKGND_GRAY             40013
#define IDM_BKGND_DKGRAY           40014
#define IDM_BKGND_BLACK            40015
#define IDM_TIMER_START            40016
#define IDM_TIMER_STOP             40017
#define IDM_APP_HELP               40018
#define IDM_APP_ABOUT              40019
```

The MENUDEMO.RC resource script should give you hints on defining the menu. The menu has a text name of "MenuDemo." Most items have underlined letters, which means you must type an ampersand (&) before the letter. The MENUITEM SEPARATOR statement results from checking the Separator box in the Menu Item Properties dialog box. Notice that one item in the menu has the Checked option and another has the Grayed option. Also, the five items in the Background popup menu should be entered in the order shown to ensure that the identifiers are in numeric order; the program relies on this. All the menu item identifiers are defined in RESOURCE.H.

The MENUDEMO program simply beeps when it receives a WM_COMMAND message for most items in the File and Edit popups. The Background popup lists five stock brushes that MENUDEMO can use to color the background. In the MENUDEMO.RC resource script, the White menu item (with a menu ID of IDM_BKGND_WHITE) is flagged as CHECKED, which places a check mark next to the item. In MENUDEMO.C, the value of *iSelection* is initially set to IDM_BKGND_WHITE.

The five brushes on the Background popup menu are mutually exclusive. When MENUDEMO.C receives a WM_COMMAND message where *wParam* is one of these five items on the Background popup, it must remove the check mark from the previously chosen background color and add a check mark to the new background color. To do this, it first gets a handle to its menu:

```
hMenu = GetMenu (hwnd) ;
```

The *CheckMenuItem* function is used to uncheck the currently checked item:

```
CheckMenuItem (hMenu, iSelection, MF_UNCHECKED) ;
```

The *iSelection* value is set to the value of *wParam*, and the new background color is checked:

```
iSelection = wParam ;
CheckMenuItem (hMenu, iSelection, MF_CHECKED) ;
```

The background color in the window class is then replaced with the new background color, and the window client area is invalidated. Windows erases the window, using the new background color.

The Timer popup lists two options—Start and Stop. Initially, the Stop option is grayed (as indicated in the menu definition for the resource script). When you choose the Start option, MENUDEMO tries to start a timer and, if successful, grays the Start option and makes the Stop option active:

```
EnableMenuItem (hMenu, IDM_TIMER_START, MF_GRAYED) ;
EnableMenuItem (hMenu, IDM_TIMER_STOP,  MF_ENABLED) ;
```

On receipt of a WM_COMMAND message with *wParam* equal to IDM_TIMER_STOP, MENUDEMO kills the timer, activates the Start option, and grays the Stop option:

```
EnableMenuItem (hMenu, IDM_TIMER_START, MF_ENABLED) ;
EnableMenuItem (hMenu, IDM_TIMER_STOP,  MF_GRAYED) ;
```

Notice that it's impossible for MENUDEMO to receive a WM_COMMAND message with *wParam* equal to IDM_TIMER_START while the timer is going. Similarly, it's impossible to receive a WM_COMMAND with *wParam* equal to IDM_TIMER_STOP while the timer is not going.

When MENUDEMO receives a WM_COMMAND message with the *wParam* parameter equal to IDM_APP_ABOUT or IDM_APP_HELP, it displays a message box. (In the next chapter, we'll change this to a dialog box.)

When MENUDEMO receives a WM_COMMAND message with *wParam* equal to IDM_APP_EXIT, it sends itself a WM_CLOSE message. This is the same message that *DefWindowProc* sends the window procedure when it receives a WM_SYSCOMMAND message with *wParam* equal to SC_CLOSE. We'll examine this more in the POPPAD2 program shown near the end of this chapter.

Menu Etiquette

The format of the File and Edit popups in MENUDEMO is quite similar to those in other Windows programs. One of the objectives of Windows is to provide a user with a recognizable interface that does not require relearning basic concepts for each program. It certainly helps if the File and Edit menus look the same in every Windows program and use the same letters for selection in combination with the Alt key.

Beyond the File and Edit popups, the menus of most Windows programs will probably be different. When designing a menu, you should look at existing Windows programs and aim for some consistency. Of course, if you think these other programs are wrong and you know the right way to do it, nobody's going to stop you. Also keep in mind that revising a menu usually requires revising only the resource script and not your program code. You can move menu items around at a later time without many problems.

Although your program menu can have MENUITEM statements on the top level, these are not typical because they can be too easily chosen by mistake. If you do this, use an exclamation point after the text string to indicate that the menu item does not invoke a popup.

Defining a Menu the Hard Way

Defining a menu in a program's resource script is usually the easiest way to add a menu in your window, but it's not the only way. You can dispense with the resource script and create a menu entirely within your program by using two functions called *CreateMenu* and *AppendMenu*. After you finish defining the menu, you can pass the menu handle to *CreateWindow* or use *SetMenu* to set the window's menu.

Here's how it's done. *CreateMenu* simply returns a handle to a new menu:

```
hMenu = CreateMenu () ;
```

The menu is initially empty. *AppendMenu* inserts items into the menu. You must obtain a different menu handle for the top-level menu item and for each popup. The popups are constructed separately; the popup menu handles are then inserted into the top-level menu. The code shown in Figure 10-7 creates a menu in this fashion; in fact, it is the same menu that I used in the MENUDEMO program. For illustrative simplicity, the code uses ASCII character strings.

```
hMenu = CreateMenu () ;

hMenuPopup = CreateMenu () ;

AppendMenu (hMenuPopup, MF_STRING,    IDM_FILE_NEW,     "&New") ;
AppendMenu (hMenuPopup, MF_STRING,    IDM_FILE_OPEN,    "&Open...") ;
AppendMenu (hMenuPopup, MF_STRING,    IDM_FILE_SAVE,    "&Save") ;
AppendMenu (hMenuPopup, MF_STRING,    IDM_FILE_SAVE_AS, "Save &As...") ;
AppendMenu (hMenuPopup, MF_SEPARATOR, 0,                NULL) ;
AppendMenu (hMenuPopup, MF_STRING,    IDM_APP_EXIT,     "E&xit") ;

AppendMenu (hMenu, MF_POPUP, hMenuPopup, "&File") ;

hMenuPopup = CreateMenu () ;

AppendMenu (hMenuPopup, MF_STRING,    IDM_EDIT_UNDO,  "&Undo") ;
AppendMenu (hMenuPopup, MF_SEPARATOR, 0,              NULL) ;
AppendMenu (hMenuPopup, MF_STRING,    IDM_EDIT_CUT,   "Cu&t") ;
AppendMenu (hMenuPopup, MF_STRING,    IDM_EDIT_COPY,  "&Copy") ;
AppendMenu (hMenuPopup, MF_STRING,    IDM_EDIT_PASTE, "&Paste") ;
AppendMenu (hMenuPopup, MF_STRING,    IDM_EDIT_CLEAR, "De&lete") ;
```

Figure 10-7. *C code that creates the same menu as used in the MENUDEMO program but without requiring a resource script file.*

```
AppendMenu (hMenu, MF_POPUP, hMenuPopup, "&Edit") ;

hMenuPopup = CreateMenu () ;

AppendMenu (hMenuPopup, MF_STRING| MF_CHECKED, IDM_BKGND_WHITE,  "&White") ;
AppendMenu (hMenuPopup, MF_STRING,             IDM_BKGND_LTGRAY, "&Light Gray");
AppendMenu (hMenuPopup, MF_STRING,             IDM_BKGND_GRAY,   "&Gray") ;
AppendMenu (hMenuPopup, MF_STRING,             IDM_BKGND_DKGRAY, "&Dark Gray");
AppendMenu (hMenuPopup, MF_STRING,             IDM_BKGND_BLACK,  "&Black") ;

AppendMenu (hMenu, MF_POPUP, hMenuPopup, "&Background") ;

hMenuPopup = CreateMenu () ;

AppendMenu (hMenuPopup, MF_STRING,             IDM_TIMER_START, "&Start") ;
AppendMenu (hMenuPopup, MF_STRING | MF_GRAYED, IDM_TIMER_STOP,  "S&top") ;

AppendMenu (hMenu, MF_POPUP, hMenuPopup, "&Timer") ;

hMenuPopup = CreateMenu () ;

AppendMenu (hMenuPopup, MF_STRING, IDM_HELP_HELP,  "&Help") ;
AppendMenu (hMenuPopup, MF_STRING, IDM_APP_ABOUT,  "&About MenuDemo...") ;

AppendMenu (hMenu, MF_POPUP, hMenuPopup, "&Help") ;
```

I think you'll agree that the resource script menu template is easier and clearer. I'm not recommending that you define a menu in this way, only showing that it can be done. Certainly you could cut down on the code size substantially by using some arrays of structures containing all the menu item character strings, IDs, and flags. But if you do that, you might as well take advantage of the third method Windows provides for defining a menu. The *LoadMenuIndirect* function accepts a pointer to a structure of type MENUITEM-TEMPLATE and returns a handle to a menu. This function is used within Windows to construct a menu after loading the normal menu template from a resource script. If you're brave, you can try using it yourself.

Floating Popup Menus

You can also make use of menus without having a top-level menu bar. You can instead cause a popup menu to appear on top of any part of the screen. One approach is to invoke this popup menu in response to a click of the right mouse button. The POPMENU program in Figure 10-8 beginning on the following page shows how this is done.

POPMENU.C

```
/*-------------------------------------------
   POPMENU.C -- Popup Menu Demonstration
                (c) Charles Petzold, 1998
   -------------------------------------------*/

#include <windows.h>
#include "resource.h"

LRESULT CALLBACK WndProc (HWND, UINT, WPARAM, LPARAM) ;

HINSTANCE hInst ;
TCHAR     szAppName[] = TEXT ("PopMenu") ;

int WINAPI WinMain (HINSTANCE hInstance, HINSTANCE hPrevInstance,
                    PSTR szCmdLine, int iCmdShow)
{
    HWND      hwnd ;
    MSG       msg ;
    WNDCLASS wndclass ;

    wndclass.style         = CS_HREDRAW | CS_VREDRAW ;
    wndclass.lpfnWndProc   = WndProc ;
    wndclass.cbClsExtra    = 0 ;
    wndclass.cbWndExtra    = 0 ;
    wndclass.hInstance     = hInstance ;
    wndclass.hIcon         = LoadIcon (NULL, szAppName) ;
    wndclass.hCursor       = LoadCursor (NULL, IDC_ARROW) ;
    wndclass.hbrBackground = (HBRUSH) GetStockObject (WHITE_BRUSH) ;
    wndclass.lpszMenuName  = NULL ;
    wndclass.lpszClassName = szAppName ;

    if (!RegisterClass (&wndclass))
    {
        MessageBox (NULL, TEXT ("This program requires Windows NT!"),
                    szAppName, MB_ICONERROR) ;
        return 0 ;
    }

    hInst = hInstance ;

    hwnd = CreateWindow (szAppName, TEXT ("Popup Menu Demonstration"),
                         WS_OVERLAPPEDWINDOW,
                         CW_USEDEFAULT, CW_USEDEFAULT,
                         CW_USEDEFAULT, CW_USEDEFAULT,
                         NULL, NULL, hInstance, NULL) ;
```

Figure 10-8. *The POPMENU program.*

```
     ShowWindow (hwnd, iCmdShow) ;
     UpdateWindow (hwnd) ;

     while (GetMessage (&msg, NULL, 0, 0))
     {
          TranslateMessage (&msg) ;
          DispatchMessage (&msg) ;
     }
     return msg.wParam ;
}

LRESULT CALLBACK WndProc (HWND hwnd, UINT message, WPARAM wParam, LPARAM lParam)
{
     static HMENU hMenu ;
     static int   idColor [5] = { WHITE_BRUSH,  LTGRAY_BRUSH, GRAY_BRUSH,
                                   DKGRAY_BRUSH, BLACK_BRUSH } ;
     static int   iSelection = IDM_BKGND_WHITE ;
     POINT        point ;

     switch (message)
     {
     case WM_CREATE:
          hMenu = LoadMenu (hInst, szAppName) ;
          hMenu = GetSubMenu (hMenu, 0) ;
          return 0 ;

     case WM_RBUTTONUP:
          point.x = LOWORD (lParam) ;
          point.y = HIWORD (lParam) ;
          ClientToScreen (hwnd, &point) ;

          TrackPopupMenu (hMenu, TPM_RIGHTBUTTON, point.x, point.y,
                          0, hwnd, NULL) ;
          return 0 ;

     case WM_COMMAND:
          switch (LOWORD (wParam))
          {
          case IDM_FILE_NEW:
          case IDM_FILE_OPEN:
          case IDM_FILE_SAVE:
          case IDM_FILE_SAVE_AS:
          case IDM_EDIT_UNDO:
          case IDM_EDIT_CUT:
          case IDM_EDIT_COPY:
          case IDM_EDIT_PASTE:
```

(continued)

Figure 10-8. *continued*

```
            case IDM_EDIT_CLEAR:
                 MessageBeep (0) ;
                 return 0 ;

            case IDM_BKGND_WHITE:            // Note: Logic below
            case IDM_BKGND_LTGRAY:           //    assumes that IDM_WHITE
            case IDM_BKGND_GRAY:             //    through IDM_BLACK are
            case IDM_BKGND_DKGRAY:           //    consecutive numbers in
            case IDM_BKGND_BLACK:            //    the order shown here.

                 CheckMenuItem (hMenu, iSelection, MF_UNCHECKED) ;
                 iSelection = LOWORD (wParam) ;
                 CheckMenuItem (hMenu, iSelection, MF_CHECKED) ;

                 SetClassLong (hwnd, GCL_HBRBACKGROUND, (LONG)
                     GetStockObject
                         (idColor [LOWORD (wParam) - IDM_BKGND_WHITE])) ;

                 InvalidateRect (hwnd, NULL, TRUE) ;
                 return 0 ;

            case IDM_APP_ABOUT:
                 MessageBox (hwnd, TEXT ("Popup Menu Demonstration Program\n")
                                   TEXT ("(c) Charles Petzold, 1998"),
                             szAppName, MB_ICONINFORMATION | MB_OK) ;
                 return 0 ;

            case IDM_APP_EXIT:
                 SendMessage (hwnd, WM_CLOSE, 0, 0) ;
                 return 0 ;

            case IDM_APP_HELP:
                 MessageBox (hwnd, TEXT ("Help not yet implemented!"),
                             szAppName, MB_ICONEXCLAMATION | MB_OK) ;
                 return 0 ;
            }
            break ;

     case WM_DESTROY:
          PostQuitMessage (0) ;
          return 0 ;
     }
     return DefWindowProc (hwnd, message, wParam, lParam) ;
}
```

POPMENU.RC (excerpts)

```
//Microsoft Developer Studio generated resource script.

#include "resource.h"
#include "afxres.h"


/////////////////////////////////////////////////////////////////////////////
// Menu

POPMENU MENU DISCARDABLE
BEGIN
    POPUP "MyMenu"
    BEGIN
        POPUP "&File"
        BEGIN
            MENUITEM "&New",                        IDM_FILE_NEW
            MENUITEM "&Open",                       IDM_FILE_OPEN
            MENUITEM "&Save",                       IDM_FILE_SAVE
            MENUITEM "Save &As",                    IDM_FILE_SAVE_AS
            MENUITEM SEPARATOR
            MENUITEM "E&xit",                       IDM_APP_EXIT
        END
        POPUP "&Edit"
        BEGIN
            MENUITEM "&Undo",                       IDM_EDIT_UNDO
            MENUITEM SEPARATOR
            MENUITEM "Cu&t",                        IDM_EDIT_CUT
            MENUITEM "&Copy",                       IDM_EDIT_COPY
            MENUITEM "&Paste",                      IDM_EDIT_PASTE
            MENUITEM "De&lete",                     IDM_EDIT_CLEAR
        END
        POPUP "&Background"
        BEGIN
            MENUITEM "&White",                      IDM_BKGND_WHITE, CHECKED
            MENUITEM "&Light Gray",                 IDM_BKGND_LTGRAY
            MENUITEM "&Gray",                       IDM_BKGND_GRAY
            MENUITEM "&Dark Gray",                  IDM_BKGND_DKGRAY
            MENUITEM "&Black",                      IDM_BKGND_BLACK
        END
        POPUP "&Help"
        BEGIN
            MENUITEM "&Help...",                    IDM_APP_HELP
            MENUITEM "&About PopMenu...",           IDM_APP_ABOUT
        END
    END
END
```

(continued)

Figure 10-8. *continued*

RESOURCE.H (excerpts)

```
// Microsoft Developer Studio generated include file.
// Used by PopMenu.rc

#define IDM_FILE_NEW                   40001
#define IDM_FILE_OPEN                  40002
#define IDM_FILE_SAVE                  40003
#define IDM_FILE_SAVE_AS               40004
#define IDM_APP_EXIT                   40005
#define IDM_EDIT_UNDO                  40006
#define IDM_EDIT_CUT                   40007
#define IDM_EDIT_COPY                  40008
#define IDM_EDIT_PASTE                 40009
#define IDM_EDIT_CLEAR                 40010
#define IDM_BKGND_WHITE                40011
#define IDM_BKGND_LTGRAY               40012
#define IDM_BKGND_GRAY                 40013
#define IDM_BKGND_DKGRAY               40014
#define IDM_BKGND_BLACK                40015
#define IDM_APP_HELP                   40016
#define IDM_APP_ABOUT                  40017
```

The POPMENU.RC resource script defines a menu similar to the one in MENU-DEMO.RC. The difference is that the top-level menu contains only one item—a popup named "MyMenu" that invokes the File, Edit, Background, and Help options. These four options will be arranged on the popup menu in a vertical list rather than on the main menu in a horizontal list.

During the WM_CREATE message in *WndProc*, POPMENU obtains a handle to the first popup menu—that is, the popup with the text "MyMenu":

```
hMenu = LoadMenu (hInst, szAppName) ;
hMenu = GetSubMenu (hMenu, 0) ;
```

During the WM_RBUTTONUP message, POPMENU obtains the position of the mouse pointer, converts the position to screen coordinates, and passes the coordinates to *TrackPopupMenu*:

```
point.x = LOWORD (lParam) ;
point.y = HIWORD (lParam) ;
ClientToScreen (hwnd, &point) ;

TrackPopupMenu (hMenu, TPM_RIGHTBUTTON, point.x, point.y,
                0, hwnd, NULL) ;
```

Windows then displays the popup menu with the items File, Edit, Background, and Help. Selecting any of these options causes the nested popup menus to appear to the right. The menu functions the same as a normal menu.

If you want to use the same menu for the program's main menu and with the *TrackPopupMenu*, you'll have a bit of a problem because the function requires a popup menu handle. A workaround is provided in the Microsoft Knowledge Base article ID Q99806.

Using the System Menu

Parent windows created with a style that includes WS_SYSMENU have a system menu box at the left of the caption bar. If you like, you can modify this menu by adding your own menu commands. In the early days of Windows, programs commonly put the "About" menu item on the system menu. While modifying the system menu is not nearly as common these days, it remains a quick-and-dirty way to add a menu to a short program without defining it in the resource script. The only restriction is this: the ID numbers you use to add commands to the system menu must be lower than 0xF000. Otherwise, they will conflict with the IDs that Windows uses for the normal system menu commands. And keep in mind that when you process WM_SYSCOMMAND messages in your window procedure for these new menu items, you must pass the other WM_SYSCOMMAND messages to *DefWindowProc*. If you don't, you'll effectively disable all normal options on the system menu.

The program POORMENU ("Poor Person's Menu"), shown in Figure 10-9, adds a separator bar and three commands to the system menu. The last of these commands removes the additions.

POORMENU.C

```
/*---------------------------------------------
   POORMENU.C -- The Poor Person's Menu
                 (c) Charles Petzold, 1998
   ---------------------------------------------*/

#include <windows.h>

#define IDM_SYS_ABOUT    1
#define IDM_SYS_HELP     2
#define IDM_SYS_REMOVE   3

LRESULT CALLBACK WndProc (HWND, UINT, WPARAM, LPARAM) ;

static TCHAR szAppName[] = TEXT ("PoorMenu") ;
```

Figure 10-9. *The POORMENU program.*

(continued)

Figure 10-9. *continued*

```
int WINAPI WinMain (HINSTANCE hInstance, HINSTANCE hPrevInstance,
                    PSTR szCmdLine, int iCmdShow)
{
     HMENU    hMenu ;
     HWND     hwnd ;
     MSG      msg ;
     WNDCLASS wndclass ;

     wndclass.style         = CS_HREDRAW | CS_VREDRAW ;
     wndclass.lpfnWndProc   = WndProc ;
     wndclass.cbClsExtra    = 0 ;
     wndclass.cbWndExtra    = 0 ;
     wndclass.hInstance     = hInstance ;
     wndclass.hIcon         = LoadIcon (NULL, IDI_APPLICATION) ;
     wndclass.hCursor       = LoadCursor (NULL, IDC_ARROW) ;
     wndclass.hbrBackground = (HBRUSH) GetStockObject (WHITE_BRUSH) ;
     wndclass.lpszMenuName  = NULL ;
     wndclass.lpszClassName = szAppName ;

     if (!RegisterClass (&wndclass))
     {
          MessageBox (NULL, TEXT ("This program requires Windows NT!"),
                      szAppName, MB_ICONERROR) ;
          return 0 ;
     }

     hwnd = CreateWindow (szAppName, TEXT ("The Poor-Person's Menu"),
                          WS_OVERLAPPEDWINDOW,
                          CW_USEDEFAULT, CW_USEDEFAULT,
                          CW_USEDEFAULT, CW_USEDEFAULT,
                          NULL, NULL, hInstance, NULL) ;

     hMenu = GetSystemMenu (hwnd, FALSE) ;

     AppendMenu (hMenu, MF_SEPARATOR, 0,              NULL) ;
     AppendMenu (hMenu, MF_STRING, IDM_SYS_ABOUT,  TEXT ("About...")) ;
     AppendMenu (hMenu, MF_STRING, IDM_SYS_HELP,   TEXT ("Help...")) ;
     AppendMenu (hMenu, MF_STRING, IDM_SYS_REMOVE, TEXT ("Remove Additions")) ;

     ShowWindow (hwnd, iCmdShow) ;
     UpdateWindow (hwnd) ;

     while (GetMessage (&msg, NULL, 0, 0))
     {
          TranslateMessage (&msg) ;
```

```
            DispatchMessage (&msg) ;
     }
     return msg.wParam ;
}

LRESULT CALLBACK WndProc (HWND hwnd, UINT message, WPARAM wParam, LPARAM lParam)
{
     switch (message)
     {
     case WM_SYSCOMMAND:
          switch (LOWORD (wParam))
          {
          case IDM_SYS_ABOUT:
               MessageBox (hwnd, TEXT ("A Poor-Person's Menu Program\n")
                                 TEXT ("(c) Charles Petzold, 1998"),
                          szAppName, MB_OK | MB_ICONINFORMATION) ;
               return 0 ;

          case IDM_SYS_HELP:
               MessageBox (hwnd, TEXT ("Help not yet implemented!"),
                          szAppName, MB_OK | MB_ICONEXCLAMATION) ;
               return 0 ;

          case IDM_SYS_REMOVE:
               GetSystemMenu (hwnd, TRUE) ;
               return 0 ;
          }
          break ;

     case WM_DESTROY:
          PostQuitMessage (0) ;
          return 0 ;
     }
     return DefWindowProc (hwnd, message, wParam, lParam) ;
}
```

The three menu IDs are defined near the top of POORMENU.C:

```
#define IDM_ABOUT    1
#define IDM_HELP     2
#define IDM_REMOVE   3
```

After the program's window has been created, POORMENU obtains a handle to the system menu:

```
hMenu = GetSystemMenu (hwnd, FALSE) ;
```

When you first call *GetSystemMenu*, you should set the second parameter to FALSE in preparation for modifying the menu.

The menu is altered with four *AppendMenu* calls:

```
AppendMenu (hMenu, MF_SEPARATOR, 0,              NULL) ;
AppendMenu (hMenu, MF_STRING, IDM_SYS_ABOUT,  TEXT ("About...")) ;
AppendMenu (hMenu, MF_STRING, IDM_SYS_HELP,   TEXT ("Help...")) ;
AppendMenu (hMenu, MF_STRING, IDM_SYS_REMOVE, TEXT ("Remove Additions"));
```

The first *AppendMenu* call adds the separator bar. Choosing the Remove Additions menu item causes POORMENU to remove these additions, which it accomplishes simply by calling *GetSystemMenu* again with the second parameter set to TRUE:

```
GetSystemMenu (hwnd, TRUE) ;
```

The standard system menu has the options Restore, Move, Size, Minimize, Maximize, and Close. These generate WM_SYSCOMMAND messages with *wParam* equal to SC_RESTORE, SC_MOVE, SC_SIZE, SC_MINIMUM, SC_MAXIMUM, and SC_CLOSE. Although Windows programs do not normally do so, you can process these messages yourself rather than pass them on to *DefWindowProc*. You can also disable or remove some of these standard options from the system menu using methods described below. The Windows documentation also includes some standard additions to the system menu. These use the identifiers SC_NEXTWINDOW, SC_PREVWINDOW, SC_VSCROLL, SC_HSCROLL, and SC_ARRANGE. You might find it appropriate to add these commands to the system menu in some applications.

Changing the Menu

We've already seen how the *AppendMenu* function can be used to define a menu entirely within a program and to add menu items to the system menu. Prior to Windows 3.0, you would have been forced to use the *ChangeMenu* function for this job. *ChangeMenu* was so versatile that it was one of the most complex functions in all of Windows (at least at that time). Times have changed. Many other current functions are now more complex than *ChangeMenu* ever was, and *ChangeMenu* has been replaced with five newer functions:

- *AppendMenu*   Adds a new item to the end of a menu.

- *DeleteMenu*   Deletes an existing item from a menu and destroys the item.

- *InsertMenu*   Inserts a new item into a menu.

- *ModifyMenu*   Changes an existing menu item.

- *RemoveMenu*   Removes an existing item from a menu.

The difference between *DeleteMenu* and *RemoveMenu* is important if the item is a popup menu. *DeleteMenu* destroys the popup menu—but *RemoveMenu* does not.

Other Menu Commands

In this section, you'll find some more functions useful for working with menus.

When you change a top-level menu item, the change is not shown until Windows redraws the menu bar. You can force this redrawing by calling

```
DrawMenuBar (hwnd) ;
```

Notice that the argument to *DrawMenuBar* is a handle to the window rather than a handle to the menu.

You can obtain the handle to a popup menu using

```
hMenuPopup = GetSubMenu (hMenu, iPosition) ;
```

where *iPosition* is the index (starting at 0) of the popup within the top-level menu indicated by *hMenu*. You can then use the popup menu handle with other functions (such as *AppendMenu*).

You can obtain the current number of items in a top-level or popup menu by using

```
iCount = GetMenuItemCount (hMenu) ;
```

You can obtain the menu ID for an item in a popup menu from

```
id = GetMenuItemID (hMenuPopup, iPosition) ;
```

where *iPosition* is the position (starting at 0) of the item within the popup.

In MENUDEMO, you saw how to check or uncheck an item in a popup menu using

```
CheckMenuItem (hMenu, id, iCheck) ;
```

In MENUDEMO, *hMenu* was the handle to the top-level menu, *id* was the menu ID, and the value of *iCheck* was either MF_CHECKED or MF_UNCHECKED. If *hMenu* is a handle to a popup menu, the *id* parameter can be a positional index rather than a menu ID. If an index is more convenient, you include MF_BYPOSITION in the third argument:

```
CheckMenuItem (hMenu, iPosition, MF_CHECKED | MF_BYPOSITION) ;
```

The *EnableMenuItem* function works similarly to *CheckMenuItem*, except that the third argument is MF_ENABLED, MF_DISABLED, or MF_GRAYED. If you use *Enable-MenuItem* on a top-level menu item that has a popup, you must also use the MF_BYPOSITION identifier in the third parameter because the menu item has no menu ID. We'll see an example of *EnableMenuItem* in the POPPAD2 program shown later in this chapter. *HiliteMenuItem* is similar to *CheckMenuItem* and *EnableMenuItem* but uses MF_HILITE and MF_UNHILITE. This highlighting is the reverse video that Windows uses when you move among menu items. You do not normally need to use *HiliteMenuItem*.

What else do you need to do with your menu? Have you forgotten what character string you used in a menu? You can refresh your memory by calling

```
iCharCount = GetMenuString (hMenu, id, pString, iMaxCount, iFlag) ;
```

The *iFlag* is either MF_BYCOMMAND (where *id* is a menu ID) or MF_BYPOSITION (where *id* is a positional index). The function copies up to *iMaxCount* characters into *pString* and returns the number of characters copied.

Or perhaps you'd like to know what the current flags of a menu item are:

```
iFlags = GetMenuState (hMenu, id, iFlag) ;
```

Again, *iFlag* is either MF_BYCOMMAND or MF_BYPOSITION. The *iFlags* parameter is a combination of all the current flags. You can determine the current flags by testing against the MF_DISABLED, MF_GRAYED, MF_CHECKED, MF_MENUBREAK, MF_MENUBAR-BREAK, and MF_SEPARATOR identifiers.

Or maybe by this time you're a little fed up with menus. In that case, you'll be pleased to know that if you no longer need a menu in your program, you can destroy it:

```
DestroyMenu (hMenu) ;
```

This function invalidates the menu handle.

An Unorthodox Approach to Menus

Now let's step a little off the beaten path. Instead of having drop-down menus in your program, how about creating multiple top-level menus without any popups and switching between the top-level menus using the *SetMenu* call? Such a menu might remind old-timers of that character-mode classic, Lotus 1-2-3. The NOPOPUPS program, shown in Figure 10-10, demonstrates how to do it. This program includes File and Edit items similar to those that MENUDEMO uses but displays them as alternate top-level menus.

NOPOPUPS.C

```
/*--------------------------------------------------
   NOPOPUPS.C -- Demonstrates No-Popup Nested Menu
                 (c) Charles Petzold, 1998
   --------------------------------------------------*/

#include <windows.h>
#include "resource.h"

LRESULT CALLBACK WndProc (HWND, UINT, WPARAM, LPARAM) ;

int WINAPI WinMain (HINSTANCE hInstance, HINSTANCE hPrevInstance,
                    PSTR szCmdLine, int iCmdShow)
```

Figure 10-10. *The NOPOPUPS program.*

```
{
     static TCHAR szAppName[] = TEXT ("NoPopUps") ;
     HWND         hwnd ;
     MSG          msg ;
     WNDCLASS     wndclass ;

     wndclass.style         = CS_HREDRAW | CS_VREDRAW ;
     wndclass.lpfnWndProc   = WndProc ;
     wndclass.cbClsExtra    = 0 ;
     wndclass.cbWndExtra    = 0 ;
     wndclass.hInstance     = hInstance ;
     wndclass.hIcon         = LoadIcon (NULL, IDI_APPLICATION) ;
     wndclass.hCursor       = LoadCursor (NULL, IDC_ARROW) ;
     wndclass.hbrBackground = (HBRUSH) GetStockObject (WHITE_BRUSH) ;
     wndclass.lpszMenuName  = NULL ;
     wndclass.lpszClassName = szAppName ;

     if (!RegisterClass (&wndclass))
     {
          MessageBox (NULL, TEXT ("This program requires Windows NT!"),
                      szAppName, MB_ICONERROR) ;
          return 0 ;
     }

     hwnd = CreateWindow (szAppName,
                          TEXT ("No-Popup Nested Menu Demonstration"),
                          WS_OVERLAPPEDWINDOW,
                          CW_USEDEFAULT, CW_USEDEFAULT,
                          CW_USEDEFAULT, CW_USEDEFAULT,
                          NULL, NULL, hInstance, NULL) ;

     ShowWindow (hwnd, iCmdShow) ;
     UpdateWindow (hwnd) ;

     while (GetMessage (&msg, NULL, 0, 0))
     {
          TranslateMessage (&msg) ;
          DispatchMessage (&msg) ;
     }
     return msg.wParam ;
}

LRESULT CALLBACK WndProc (HWND hwnd, UINT message, WPARAM wParam, LPARAM lParam)
{
     static HMENU hMenuMain, hMenuEdit, hMenuFile ;
     HINSTANCE    hInstance ;
```

(continued)

Figure 10-10. *continued*

```
    switch (message)
    {
    case WM_CREATE:
         hInstance = (HINSTANCE) GetWindowLong (hwnd, GWL_HINSTANCE) ;

         hMenuMain = LoadMenu (hInstance, TEXT ("MenuMain")) ;
         hMenuFile = LoadMenu (hInstance, TEXT ("MenuFile")) ;
         hMenuEdit = LoadMenu (hInstance, TEXT ("MenuEdit")) ;

         SetMenu (hwnd, hMenuMain) ;
         return 0 ;

    case WM_COMMAND:
         switch (LOWORD (wParam))
         {
         case IDM_MAIN:
              SetMenu (hwnd, hMenuMain) ;
              return 0 ;

         case IDM_FILE:
              SetMenu (hwnd, hMenuFile) ;
              return 0 ;

         case IDM_EDIT:
              SetMenu (hwnd, hMenuEdit) ;
              return 0 ;

         case IDM_FILE_NEW:
         case IDM_FILE_OPEN:
         case IDM_FILE_SAVE:
         case IDM_FILE_SAVE_AS:
         case IDM_EDIT_UNDO:
         case IDM_EDIT_CUT:
         case IDM_EDIT_COPY:
         case IDM_EDIT_PASTE:
         case IDM_EDIT_CLEAR:
              MessageBeep (0) ;
              return 0 ;
         }
         break ;

    case WM_DESTROY:
         SetMenu (hwnd, hMenuMain) ;
         DestroyMenu (hMenuFile) ;
         DestroyMenu (hMenuEdit) ;
```

```
            PostQuitMessage (0) ;
            return 0 ;
        }
    return DefWindowProc (hwnd, message, wParam, lParam) ;
}
```

NOPOPUPS.RC (excerpts)

```
//Microsoft Developer Studio generated resource script.

#include "resource.h"
#include "afxres.h"


/////////////////////////////////////////////////////////////////////////////
// Menu

MENUMAIN MENU DISCARDABLE
BEGIN
    MENUITEM "MAIN:",                   0, INACTIVE
    MENUITEM "&File...",                IDM_FILE
    MENUITEM "&Edit...",                IDM_EDIT
END

MENUFILE MENU DISCARDABLE
BEGIN
    MENUITEM "FILE:",                   0, INACTIVE
    MENUITEM "&New",                    IDM_FILE_NEW
    MENUITEM "&Open...",                IDM_FILE_OPEN
    MENUITEM "&Save",                   IDM_FILE_SAVE
    MENUITEM "Save &As",                IDM_FILE_SAVE_AS
    MENUITEM "(&Main)",                 IDM_MAIN
END

MENUEDIT MENU DISCARDABLE
BEGIN
    MENUITEM "EDIT:",                   0, INACTIVE
    MENUITEM "&Undo",                   IDM_EDIT_UNDO
    MENUITEM "Cu&t",                    IDM_EDIT_CUT
    MENUITEM "&Copy",                   IDM_EDIT_COPY
    MENUITEM "&Paste",                  IDM_EDIT_PASTE
    MENUITEM "De&lete",                 IDM_EDIT_CLEAR
    MENUITEM "(&Main)",                 IDM_MAIN
END
```

(continued)

Figure 10-10. *continued*

RESOURCE.H (excerpts)

```
// Microsoft Developer Studio generated include file.
// Used by NoPopups.rc

#define IDM_FILE                40001
#define IDM_EDIT                40002
#define IDM_FILE_NEW            40003
#define IDM_FILE_OPEN           40004
#define IDM_FILE_SAVE           40005
#define IDM_FILE_SAVE_AS        40006
#define IDM_MAIN                40007
#define IDM_EDIT_UNDO           40008
#define IDM_EDIT_CUT            40009
#define IDM_EDIT_COPY           40010
#define IDM_EDIT_PASTE          40011
#define IDM_EDIT_CLEAR          40012
```

In Microsoft Developer Studio, you create three menus rather than one. You'll be selecting Resource from the Insert menu three times. Each menu has a different text name. When the window procedure processes the WM_CREATE message, Windows loads each menu resource into memory:

```
hMenuMain = LoadMenu (hInstance, TEXT ("MenuMain")) ;
hMenuFile = LoadMenu (hInstance, TEXT ("MenuFile")) ;
hMenuEdit = LoadMenu (hInstance, TEXT ("MenuEdit")) ;
```

Initially, the program displays the main menu:

```
SetMenu (hwnd, hMenuMain) ;
```

The main menu lists the three options using the character strings "MAIN:", "File...", and "Edit..." However, "MAIN:" is disabled, so it doesn't cause WM_COMMAND messages to be sent to the window procedure. The File and Edit menus begin "FILE:" and "EDIT:" to identify these as submenus. The last item in each menu is the character string "(Main)"; this option indicates a return to the main menu. Switching among these three menus is simple:

```
case WM_COMMAND :
     switch (wParam)
     {
     case IDM_MAIN :
          SetMenu (hwnd, hMenuMain) ;
          return 0 ;
```

```
case IDM_FILE :
     SetMenu (hwnd, hMenuFile) ;
     return 0 ;

case IDM_EDIT :
     SetMenu (hwnd, hMenuEdit) ;
     return 0 ;

[other program lines]
}
break ;
```

During the WM_DESTROY message, NOPOPUPS sets the program's menu to the Main menu and destroys the File and Edit menus with calls to *DestroyMenu*. The Main menu is destroyed automatically when the window is destroyed.

KEYBOARD ACCELERATORS

Keyboard accelerators are key combinations that generate WM_COMMAND (or, in some cases, WM_SYSCOMMAND) messages. Most often, programs use keyboard accelerators to duplicate the action of common menu options, but they can also perform nonmenu functions. For instance, some Windows programs have an Edit menu that includes a Delete or Clear option; these programs conventionally assign the Del key as a keyboard accelerator for this option. The user can choose the Delete option from the menu by pressing an Alt-key combination or can use the keyboard accelerator simply by pressing the Del key. When the window procedure receives a WM_COMMAND message, it does not have to determine whether the menu or the keyboard accelerator was used.

Why You Should Use Keyboard Accelerators

You might ask: Why should I use keyboard accelerators? Why can't I simply trap WM_KEYDOWN or WM_CHAR messages and duplicate the menu functions myself? What's the advantage? For a single-window application, you can certainly trap keyboard messages, but one simple advantage of using keyboard accelerators is that you don't need to duplicate the menu and keyboard accelerator logic.

For applications with multiple windows and multiple window procedures, keyboard accelerators become very important. As we've seen, Windows sends keyboard messages to the window procedure for the window that currently has the input focus. For keyboard accelerators, however, Windows sends the WM_COMMAND message to the window procedure whose handle is specified in the Windows function *TranslateAccelerator*. Generally, this will be your main window, the same window that has the menu, which means that the logic for acting upon keyboard accelerators does not have to be duplicated in every window procedure.

This advantage becomes particularly important if you use modeless dialog boxes (discussed in the next chapter) or child windows on your main window's client area. If a particular keyboard accelerator is defined to move among windows, only one window procedure has to include this logic. The child windows do not receive WM_COMMAND messages from the keyboard accelerators.

Some Rules on Assigning Accelerators

In theory, you can define a keyboard accelerator for almost any virtual key or character key in combination with the Shift key, Ctrl key, or Alt key. However, you should try to achieve some consistency with other applications and avoid interfering with Windows' use of the keyboard. You should avoid using Tab, Enter, Esc, and the Spacebar in keyboard accelerators because these are often used for system functions.

The most common use of keyboard accelerators is for items on the program's Edit menu. The recommended keyboard accelerators for these items changed between Windows 3.0 and Windows 3.1, so it's become common to support both the old and the new accelerators, as shown in the following table:

Function	Old Accelerator	New Accelerator
Undo	Alt+Backspace	Ctrl+Z
Cut	Shift+Del	Ctrl+X
Copy	Ctrl+Ins	Ctrl+C
Paste	Shift+Ins	Ctrl+V
Delete or Clear	Del	Del

Another common accelerator is the F1 function key to invoke help. Avoid use of the F4, F5, and F6 keys because these are often used for special functions in Multiple Document Interface (MDI) programs, which are discussed in Chapter 19.

The Accelerator Table

You can define an accelerator table in Developer Studio. For ease in loading the accelerator table in your program, give it the same text name as your program (and your menu and your icon).

Each accelerator has an ID and a keystroke combination that you define in the Accel Properties dialog box. If you've already defined your menu, the menu IDs will be available in the combo box, so you don't have to retype them.

Accelerators can be either virtual key codes or ASCII characters in combination with the Shift, Ctrl, or Alt keys. You can specify that an ASCII character is to be typed with the Ctrl key by typing a ^ before the letter. You can also pick virtual key codes from a combo box.

When you define keyboard accelerators for a menu item, you should include the key combination in the menu item text. The tab (\t) character separates the text from the accelerator so that the accelerators align in a second column. To notate accelerator keys in a menu, use the text Ctrl, Shift, or Alt followed by a plus sign and the key (for example, Shift+F6 or Ctrl+F6).

Loading the Accelerator Table

Within your program, you use the *LoadAccelerators* function to load the accelerator table into memory and obtain a handle to it. The *LoadAccelerators* statement is similar to the *LoadIcon*, *LoadCursor*, and *LoadMenu* statements.

First define a handle to an accelerator table as type HANDLE:

```
HANDLE hAccel ;
```

Then load the accelerator table:

```
hAccel = LoadAccelerators (hInstance, TEXT ("MyAccelerators")) ;
```

As with icons, cursors, and menus, you can use a number for the accelerator table name and then use that number in the *LoadAccelerators* statement with the MAKEINTRESOURCE macro or enclosed in quotation marks and preceded by a # character.

Translating the Keystrokes

We will now tamper with three lines of code that are common to all the Windows programs we've created so far in this book. The code is the standard message loop:

```
while (GetMessage (&msg, NULL, 0, 0))
{
     TranslateMessage (&msg) ;
     DispatchMessage (&msg) ;
}
```

Here's how we change it to use the keyboard accelerator table:

```
while (GetMessage (&msg, NULL, 0, 0))
{
     if (!TranslateAccelerator (hwnd, hAccel, &msg))
     {
          TranslateMessage (&msg) ;
          DispatchMessage (&msg) ;
     }
}
```

The *TranslateAccelerator* function determines whether the message stored in the *msg* message structure is a keyboard message. If it is, the function searches for a match in the accelerator table whose handle is *hAccel*. If it finds a match, it calls the window procedure for the window whose handle is *hwnd*. If the keyboard accelerator ID corresponds to a menu item in the system menu, the message is WM_SYSCOMMAND. Otherwise, the message is WM_COMMAND.

When *TranslateAccelerator* returns, the return value is nonzero if the message has been translated (and already sent to the window procedure) and 0 if not. If *Translate-Accelerator* returns a nonzero value, you should not call *TranslateMessage* and *Dispatch-Message* but rather should loop back to the *GetMessage* call.

The *hwnd* parameter in *TranslateMessage* looks a little out of place because it's not required in the other three functions in the message loop. Moreover, the message structure itself (the structure variable *msg*) has a member named *hwnd*, which is also a handle to a window.

Here's why the function is a little different: The fields of the *msg* structure are filled in by the *GetMessage* call. When the second parameter of *GetMessage* is NULL, the function retrieves messages for all windows belonging to the application. When *GetMessage* returns, the *hwnd* member of the *msg* structure is the window handle of the window that will get the message. However, when *TranslateAccelerator* translates a keyboard message into a WM_COMMAND or WM_SYSCOMMAND message, it replaces the *msg.hwnd* window handle with the *hwnd* window handle specified as the first parameter to the function. That is how Windows sends all keyboard accelerator messages to the same window procedure even if another window in the application currently has the input focus. *TranslateAccelerator* does not translate keyboard messages when a modal dialog box or message box has the input focus, because messages for these windows do not come through the program's message loop.

In some cases in which another window in your program (such as a modeless dialog box) has the input focus, you may not want keyboard accelerators to be translated. You'll see how to handle this situation in the next chapter.

Receiving the Accelerator Messages

When a keyboard accelerator corresponds to a menu item in the system menu, *Translate-Accelerator* sends the window procedure a WM_SYSCOMMAND message. Otherwise, *TranslateAccelerator* sends the window procedure a WM_COMMAND message. The following table shows the types of WM_COMMAND messages you can receive for keyboard accelerators, menu commands, and child window controls:

	Accelerator	*Menu*	*Control*
LOWORD (*wParam*)	Accelerator ID	Menu ID	Control ID
HIWORD (*wParam*)	1	0	Notification code
lParam	0	0	Child window handle

If the keyboard accelerator corresponds to a menu item, the window procedure also receives WM_INITMENU, WM_INITMENUPOPUP, and WM_MENUSELECT messages, just as if the menu option had been chosen. Programs usually enable and disable items in a popup menu when processing WM_INITMENUPOPUP, so you still have that facility when using keyboard accelerators. If the keyboard accelerator corresponds to a disabled or grayed menu item, *TranslateAccelerator* does not send the window procedure a WM_COMMAND or WM_SYSCOMMAND message.

If the active window is minimized, *TranslateAccelerator* sends the window procedure WM_SYSCOMMAND messages—but not WM_COMMAND messages—for keyboard accelerators that correspond to enabled system menu items. *TranslateAccelerator* also sends that window procedure WM_COMMAND messages for accelerators that do not correspond to any menu items.

POPPAD with a Menu and Accelerators

In Chapter 9, we created a program called POPPAD1 that uses a child window edit control to implement a rudimentary notepad. In this chapter, we'll add File and Edit menus and call it POPPAD2. The Edit items will all be functional; we'll finish the File functions in Chapter 11 and the Print function in Chapter 13. POPPAD2 is shown in Figure 10-11.

POPPAD2.C

```
/*-------------------------------------------------------
   POPPAD2.C -- Popup Editor Version 2 (includes menu)
                (c) Charles Petzold, 1998
   -------------------------------------------------------*/

#include <windows.h>
#include "resource.h"

#define ID_EDIT     1

LRESULT CALLBACK WndProc (HWND, UINT, WPARAM, LPARAM);

TCHAR szAppName[] = TEXT ("PopPad2") ;

int WINAPI WinMain (HINSTANCE hInstance, HINSTANCE hPrevInstance,
                    PSTR szCmdLine, int iCmdShow)
{
    HACCEL   hAccel ;
    HWND     hwnd ;
    MSG      msg ;
    WNDCLASS wndclass ;
```

Figure 10-11. *The POPPAD2 program.* (continued)

Figure 10-11. *continued*

```
        wndclass.style         = CS_HREDRAW | CS_VREDRAW ;
        wndclass.lpfnWndProc    = WndProc ;
        wndclass.cbClsExtra     = 0 ;
        wndclass.cbWndExtra     = 0 ;
        wndclass.hInstance      = hInstance ;
        wndclass.hIcon          = LoadIcon (hInstance, szAppName) ;
        wndclass.hCursor        = LoadCursor (NULL, IDC_ARROW) ;
        wndclass.hbrBackground  = (HBRUSH) GetStockObject (WHITE_BRUSH) ;
        wndclass.lpszMenuName   = szAppName ;
        wndclass.lpszClassName  = szAppName ;

        if (!RegisterClass (&wndclass))
        {
             MessageBox (NULL, TEXT ("This program requires Windows NT!"),
                         szAppName, MB_ICONERROR) ;
             return 0 ;
        }

        hwnd = CreateWindow (szAppName, szAppName,
                             WS_OVERLAPPEDWINDOW,
                             GetSystemMetrics (SM_CXSCREEN) / 4,
                             GetSystemMetrics (SM_CYSCREEN) / 4,
                             GetSystemMetrics (SM_CXSCREEN) / 2,
                             GetSystemMetrics (SM_CYSCREEN) / 2,
                             NULL, NULL, hInstance, NULL) ;

        ShowWindow (hwnd, iCmdShow) ;
        UpdateWindow (hwnd) ;

        hAccel = LoadAccelerators (hInstance, szAppName) ;

        while (GetMessage (&msg, NULL, 0, 0))
        {
             if (!TranslateAccelerator (hwnd, hAccel, &msg))
             {
                  TranslateMessage (&msg) ;
                  DispatchMessage (&msg) ;
             }
        }
        return msg.wParam ;
}

AskConfirmation (HWND hwnd)
{
        return MessageBox (hwnd, TEXT ("Really want to close PopPad2?"),
                           szAppName, MB_YESNO | MB_ICONQUESTION) ;
}
```

```
LRESULT CALLBACK WndProc (HWND hwnd, UINT message, WPARAM wParam, LPARAM lParam)
{
     static HWND hwndEdit ;
     int        iSelect, iEnable ;

     switch (message)
     {
     case WM_CREATE:
          hwndEdit = CreateWindow (TEXT ("edit"), NULL,
                              WS_CHILD | WS_VISIBLE | WS_HSCROLL | WS_VSCROLL |
                              WS_BORDER | ES_LEFT | ES_MULTILINE |
                              ES_AUTOHSCROLL | ES_AUTOVSCROLL,
                              0, 0, 0, 0, hwnd, (HMENU) ID_EDIT,
                              ((LPCREATESTRUCT) lParam)->hInstance, NULL) ;

          return 0 ;

     case WM_SETFOCUS:
          SetFocus (hwndEdit) ;
          return 0 ;

     case WM_SIZE:
          MoveWindow (hwndEdit, 0, 0, LOWORD (lParam), HIWORD (lParam), TRUE) ;
          return 0 ;

     case WM_INITMENUPOPUP:
          if (lParam == 1)
          {
               EnableMenuItem ((HMENU) wParam, IDM_EDIT_UNDO,
                    SendMessage (hwndEdit, EM_CANUNDO, 0, 0) ?
                              MF_ENABLED : MF_GRAYED) ;

               EnableMenuItem ((HMENU) wParam, IDM_EDIT_PASTE,
                    IsClipboardFormatAvailable (CF_TEXT) ?
                              MF_ENABLED : MF_GRAYED) ;

               iSelect = SendMessage (hwndEdit, EM_GETSEL, 0, 0) ;

               if (HIWORD (iSelect) == LOWORD (iSelect))
                    iEnable = MF_GRAYED ;
               else
                    iEnable = MF_ENABLED ;

               EnableMenuItem ((HMENU) wParam, IDM_EDIT_CUT,   iEnable) ;
               EnableMenuItem ((HMENU) wParam, IDM_EDIT_COPY,  iEnable) ;
               EnableMenuItem ((HMENU) wParam, IDM_EDIT_CLEAR, iEnable) ;
               return 0 ;
          }
          break ;
```

(continued)

475

Figure 10-11. *continued*

```
        case WM_COMMAND:
             if (lParam)
             {
                  if (LOWORD (lParam) == ID_EDIT &&
                            (HIWORD (wParam) == EN_ERRSPACE ||
                             HIWORD (wParam) == EN_MAXTEXT))
                       MessageBox (hwnd, TEXT ("Edit control out of space."),
                                 szAppName, MB_OK | MB_ICONSTOP) ;
                  return 0 ;
             }
             else switch (LOWORD (wParam))
             {
             case IDM_FILE_NEW:
             case IDM_FILE_OPEN:
             case IDM_FILE_SAVE:
             case IDM_FILE_SAVE_AS:
             case IDM_FILE_PRINT:
                  MessageBeep (0) ;
                  return 0 ;

             case IDM_APP_EXIT:
                  SendMessage (hwnd, WM_CLOSE, 0, 0) ;
                  return 0 ;

             case IDM_EDIT_UNDO:
                  SendMessage (hwndEdit, WM_UNDO, 0, 0) ;
                  return 0 ;

             case IDM_EDIT_CUT:
                  SendMessage (hwndEdit, WM_CUT, 0, 0) ;
                  return 0 ;

             case IDM_EDIT_COPY:
                  SendMessage (hwndEdit, WM_COPY, 0, 0) ;
                  return 0 ;

             case IDM_EDIT_PASTE:
                  SendMessage (hwndEdit, WM_PASTE, 0, 0) ;
                  return 0 ;

             case IDM_EDIT_CLEAR:
                  SendMessage (hwndEdit, WM_CLEAR, 0, 0) ;
                  return 0 ;
```

```
            case IDM_EDIT_SELECT_ALL:
                 SendMessage (hwndEdit, EM_SETSEL, 0, -1) ;
                 return 0 ;

            case IDM_HELP_HELP:
                 MessageBox (hwnd, TEXT ("Help not yet implemented!"),
                             szAppName, MB_OK | MB_ICONEXCLAMATION) ;
                 return 0 ;

            case IDM_APP_ABOUT:
                 MessageBox (hwnd, TEXT ("POPPAD2 (c) Charles Petzold, 1998"),
                             szAppName, MB_OK | MB_ICONINFORMATION) ;
                 return 0 ;
            }
            break ;

       case WM_CLOSE:
            if (IDYES == AskConfirmation (hwnd))
                 DestroyWindow (hwnd) ;
            return 0 ;

       case WM_QUERYENDSESSION:
            if (IDYES == AskConfirmation (hwnd))
                 return 1 ;
            else
                 return 0 ;

       case WM_DESTROY:
            PostQuitMessage (0) ;
            return 0 ;
       }
       return DefWindowProc (hwnd, message, wParam, lParam) ;
}
```

POPPAD2.RC (excerpts)

```
//Microsoft Developer Studio generated resource script.

#include "resource.h"
#include "afxres.h"


/////////////////////////////////////////////////////////////////////////////
// Icon

POPPAD2                   ICON    DISCARDABLE     "poppad2.ico"
```

(continued)

Figure 10-11. *continued*

```
///////////////////////////////////////////////////////////////////////////
// Menu

POPPAD2 MENU DISCARDABLE
BEGIN
    POPUP "&File"
    BEGIN
        MENUITEM "&New",                        IDM_FILE_NEW
        MENUITEM "&Open...",                    IDM_FILE_OPEN
        MENUITEM "&Save",                       IDM_FILE_SAVE
        MENUITEM "Save &As...",                 IDM_FILE_SAVE_AS
        MENUITEM SEPARATOR
        MENUITEM "&Print",                      IDM_FILE_PRINT
        MENUITEM SEPARATOR
        MENUITEM "E&xit",                       IDM_APP_EXIT
    END
    POPUP "&Edit"
    BEGIN
        MENUITEM "&Undo\tCtrl+Z",               IDM_EDIT_UNDO
        MENUITEM SEPARATOR
        MENUITEM "Cu&t\tCtrl+X",                IDM_EDIT_CUT
        MENUITEM "&Copy\tCtrl+C",               IDM_EDIT_COPY
        MENUITEM "&Paste\tCtrl+V",              IDM_EDIT_PASTE
        MENUITEM "De&lete\tDel",                IDM_EDIT_CLEAR
        MENUITEM SEPARATOR
        MENUITEM "&Select All",                 IDM_EDIT_SELECT_ALL
    END
    POPUP "&Help"
    BEGIN
        MENUITEM "&Help...",                    IDM_HELP_HELP
        MENUITEM "&About PopPad2...",           IDM_APP_ABOUT
    END
END


///////////////////////////////////////////////////////////////////////////
// Accelerator

POPPAD2 ACCELERATORS DISCARDABLE
BEGIN
    VK_BACK,        IDM_EDIT_UNDO,      VIRTKEY, ALT, NOINVERT
    VK_DELETE,      IDM_EDIT_CLEAR,     VIRTKEY, NOINVERT
    VK_DELETE,      IDM_EDIT_CUT,       VIRTKEY, SHIFT, NOINVERT
    VK_F1,          IDM_HELP_HELP,      VIRTKEY, NOINVERT
    VK_INSERT,      IDM_EDIT_COPY,      VIRTKEY, CONTROL, NOINVERT
    VK_INSERT,      IDM_EDIT_PASTE,     VIRTKEY, SHIFT, NOINVERT
    "^C",           IDM_EDIT_COPY,      ASCII,   NOINVERT
```

```
    "^V",           IDM_EDIT_PASTE,        ASCII,  NOINVERT
    "^X",           IDM_EDIT_CUT,          ASCII,  NOINVERT
    "^Z",           IDM_EDIT_UNDO,         ASCII,  NOINVERT
END
```

RESOURCE.H (excerpts)

```
// Microsoft Developer Studio generated include file.
// Used by POPPAD2.RC

#define IDM_FILE_NEW                40001
#define IDM_FILE_OPEN               40002
#define IDM_FILE_SAVE               40003
#define IDM_FILE_SAVE_AS            40004
#define IDM_FILE_PRINT              40005
#define IDM_APP_EXIT                40006
#define IDM_EDIT_UNDO               40007
#define IDM_EDIT_CUT                40008
#define IDM_EDIT_COPY               40009
#define IDM_EDIT_PASTE              40010
#define IDM_EDIT_CLEAR              40011
#define IDM_EDIT_SELECT_ALL         40012
#define IDM_HELP_HELP               40013
#define IDM_APP_ABOUT               40014
```

POPPAD2.ICO

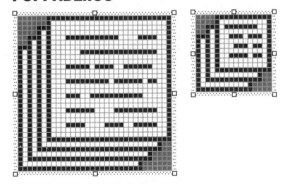

The POPPAD2.RC resource script file contains the menu and the accelerator table. You'll notice that the accelerators are all indicated within the character strings of the Edit popup menu following the tab (\t) character.

Enabling Menu Items

The major job in the window procedure now involves enabling and graying the options in the Edit menu, which is done when processing the WM_INITMENUPOPUP message. First the program checks to see if the Edit popup is about to be displayed. Because the position index of Edit in the menu (starting with File at 0) is 1, *lParam* equals 1 if the Edit popup is about to be displayed.

To determine whether the Undo option can be enabled, POPPAD2 sends an EM_CANUNDO message to the edit control. The *SendMessage* call returns nonzero if the edit control can perform an Undo action, in which case the option is enabled; otherwise, the option is grayed:

```
EnableMenuItem (wParam, IDM_UNDO,
    SendMessage (hwndEdit, EM_CANUNDO, 0, 0) ?
            MF_ENABLED : MF_GRAYED) ;
```

The Paste option should be enabled only if the clipboard currently contains text. We can determine this through the *IsClipboardFormatAvailable* call with the CF_TEXT identifier:

```
EnableMenuItem (wParam, IDM_PASTE,
    IsClipboardFormatAvailable (CF_TEXT) ? MF_ENABLED : MF_GRAYED) ;
```

The Cut, Copy, and Delete options should be enabled only if text in the edit control has been selected. Sending the edit control an EM_GETSEL message returns an integer containing this information:

```
iSelect = SendMessage (hwndEdit, EM_GETSEL, 0, 0) ;
```

The low word of *iSelect* is the position of the first selected character; the high word of *iSelect* is the position of the character following the selection. If these two words are equal, no text has been selected:

```
if (HIWORD (iSelect) == LOWORD (iSelect))
    iEnable = MF_GRAYED ;
else
    iEnable = MF_ENABLED ;
```

The value of *iEnable* is then used for the Cut, Copy, and Delete options:

```
EnableMenuItem (wParam, IDM_CUT,  iEnable) ;
EnableMenuItem (wParam, IDM_COPY, iEnable) ;
EnableMenuItem (wParam, IDM_DEL,  iEnable) ;
```

Processing the Menu Options

Of course, if we were not using a child window edit control for POPPAD2, we would now be faced with the problems involved with actually implementing the Undo, Cut, Copy, Paste, Clear, and Select All options from the Edit menu. But the edit control makes this process easy, because we merely send the edit control a message for each of these options:

```
case IDM_UNDO :
     SendMessage (hwndEdit, WM_UNDO, 0, 0) ;
     return 0 ;

case IDM_CUT :
     SendMessage (hwndEdit, WM_CUT, 0, 0) ;
     return 0 ;

case IDM_COPY :
     SendMessage (hwndEdit, WM_COPY, 0, 0) ;
     return 0 ;

case IDM_PASTE :
     SendMessage (hwndEdit, WM_PASTE, 0, 0) ;
     return 0 ;

case IDM_DEL :
     SendMessage (hwndEdit, WM_DEL, 0, 0) ;
     return 0 ;

case IDM_SELALL :
     SendMessage (hwndEdit, EM_SETSEL, 0, -1) ;
     return 0 ;
```

Notice that we could have simplified this even further by making the values of IDM_ UNDO, IDM_CUT, and so forth equal to the values of the corresponding window messages WM_UNDO, WM_CUT, and so forth.

The About option on the File popup invokes a simple message box:

```
case IDM_ABOUT :
     MessageBox (hwnd, TEXT ("POPPAD2 (c) Charles Petzold, 1998"),
                 szAppName, MB_OK ¦ MB_ICONINFORMATION) ;
     return 0 ;
```

In the next chapter, we'll make this a dialog box. A message box is also invoked when you select the Help option from this menu or when you press the F1 accelerator key.

The Exit option sends the window procedure a WM_CLOSE message:

```
case IDM_EXIT :
     SendMessage (hwnd, WM_CLOSE, 0, 0) ;
     return 0 ;
```

That is precisely what *DefWindowProc* does when it receives a WM_SYSCOMMAND message with *wParam* equal to SC_CLOSE.

In previous programs, we have not processed the WM_CLOSE messages in our window procedure but have simply passed them to *DefWindowProc*. *DefWindowProc* does something simple with WM_CLOSE: it calls the *DestroyWindow* function. Rather than send WM_CLOSE messages to *DefWindowProc*, however, POPPAD2 processes them. (This fact is not so important now, but it will become very important in Chapter 11 when POPPAD can actually edit files.)

```
case WM_CLOSE :
     if (IDYES == AskConfirmation (hwnd))
          DestroyWindow (hwnd) ;
     return 0 ;
```

AskConfirmation is a function in POPPAD2 that displays a message box asking for confirmation to close the program:

```
AskConfirmation (HWND hwnd)
{
     return MessageBox (hwnd, TEXT ("Really want to close Poppad2?"),
                     szAppName, MB_YESNO | MB_ICONQUESTION) ;
}
```

The message box (as well as the *AskConfirmation* function) returns IDYES if the Yes button is selected. Only then does POPPAD2 call *DestroyWindow*. Otherwise, the program is not terminated.

If you want confirmation before terminating a program, you must also process WM_QUERYENDSESSION messages. Windows begins sending every window procedure a WM_QUERYENDSESSION message when the user chooses to shut down Windows. If any window procedure returns 0 from this message, the Windows session is not terminated. Here's how we handle WM_QUERYENDSESSION:

```
case WM_QUERYENDSESSION :
     if (IDYES == AskConfirmation (hwnd))
          return 1 ;
     else
          return 0 ;
```

The WM_CLOSE and WM_QUERYENDSESSION messages are the only two messages you have to process if you want to ask for user confirmation before ending a program. That's why we made the Exit menu option in POPPAD2 send the window procedure a WM_CLOSE message—by doing so, we avoided asking for confirmation at yet a third point.

If you process WM_QUERYENDSESSION messages, you may also be interested in the WM_ENDSESSION message. Windows sends this message to every window procedure that has previously received a WM_QUERYENDSESSION message. The *wParam* parameter is 0 if the session fails to terminate because another program has returned 0 from WM_QUERYENDSESSION. The WM_ENDSESSION message essentially answers the question: I told Windows it was OK to terminate me, but did I really get terminated?

Although I've included the normal New, Open, Save, and Save As options in POPPAD2's File menu, they are currently nonfunctional. To process these commands, we need to use dialog boxes. And you're now ready to learn about them.

Chapter 11

Dialog Boxes

Dialog boxes are most often used for obtaining additional input from the user beyond what can be easily managed through a menu. The programmer indicates that a menu item invokes a dialog box by adding an ellipsis (...) to the menu item.

A dialog box generally takes the form of a popup window containing various child window controls. The size and placement of these controls are specified in a "dialog box template" in the program's resource script file. Although a programmer can define a dialog box template "manually," these days dialog boxes are usually interactively designed in the Visual C++ Developer Studio. Developer Studio then generates the dialog template.

When a program invokes a dialog box based on a template, Microsoft Windows 98 is responsible for creating the dialog box popup window and the child window controls, and for providing a window procedure to process dialog box messages, including all keyboard and mouse input. The code within Windows that does all this is sometimes referred to as the "dialog box manager."

Many of the messages that are processed by that dialog box window procedure located within Windows are also passed to a function within your own program, called a "dialog box procedure" or "dialog procedure." The dialog procedure is similar to a normal window procedure, but with some important differences. Generally, you will not be doing much within the dialog procedure beyond initializing the child window controls when the dialog box is created, processing messages from the child window controls, and ending the dialog box. Dialog procedures generally do not process WM_PAINT messages, nor do they directly process keyboard and mouse input.

The subject of dialog boxes would normally be a big one because it involves the use of child window controls. However, we have already explored child window controls in Chapter 9. When you use child window controls in dialog boxes, the Windows dialog box manager picks up many of the responsibilities that we assumed in Chapter 9. In particular, the problems we encountered with passing the input focus among the scroll bars in the COLORS1 program disappear when working with dialog boxes. Windows handles all the logic necessary to shift input focus among controls in a dialog box.

However, adding a dialog box to a program is a bit more involved than adding an icon or a menu. We'll begin with a simple dialog box to give you a feel for the interconnections between these various pieces.

MODAL DIALOG BOXES

Dialog boxes are either "modal" or "modeless." The modal dialog box is the most common. When your program displays a modal dialog box, the user cannot switch between the dialog box and another window in your program. The user must explicitly end the dialog box, usually by clicking a push button marked either OK or Cancel. The user can, however, switch to another program while the dialog box is still displayed. Some dialog boxes (called "system modal") do not allow even this. System modal dialog boxes must be ended before the user can do anything else in Windows.

Creating an "About" Dialog Box

Even if a Windows program requires no user input, it will often have a dialog box that is invoked by an About option on the menu. This dialog box displays the name and icon of the program, a copyright notice, a push button labeled OK, and perhaps some other information. (Perhaps a telephone number for technical support?) The first program we'll look at does nothing except display an About dialog box. The ABOUT1 program is shown in Figure 11-1.

ABOUT1.C

```
/*-----------------------------------------------
   ABOUT1.C -- About Box Demo Program No. 1
               (c) Charles Petzold, 1998
   -----------------------------------------------*/

#include <windows.h>
#include "resource.h"

LRESULT CALLBACK WndProc      (HWND, UINT, WPARAM, LPARAM) ;
BOOL    CALLBACK AboutDlgProc (HWND, UINT, WPARAM, LPARAM) ;

int WINAPI WinMain (HINSTANCE hInstance, HINSTANCE hPrevInstance,
                    PSTR szCmdLine, int iCmdShow)
```

Figure 11-1. *The ABOUT1 program.*

```
{
     static TCHAR szAppName[] = TEXT ("About1") ;
     MSG          msg ;
     HWND         hwnd ;
     WNDCLASS     wndclass ;

     wndclass.style         = CS_HREDRAW | CS_VREDRAW ;
     wndclass.lpfnWndProc   = WndProc ;
     wndclass.cbClsExtra    = 0 ;
     wndclass.cbWndExtra    = 0 ;
     wndclass.hInstance     = hInstance ;
     wndclass.hIcon         = LoadIcon (hInstance, szAppName) ;
     wndclass.hCursor       = LoadCursor (NULL, IDC_ARROW) ;
     wndclass.hbrBackground = (HBRUSH) GetStockObject (WHITE_BRUSH) ;
     wndclass.lpszMenuName  = szAppName ;
     wndclass.lpszClassName = szAppName ;

     if (!RegisterClass (&wndclass))
     {
          MessageBox (NULL, TEXT ("This program requires Windows NT!"),
                     szAppName, MB_ICONERROR) ;
          return 0 ;
     }

     hwnd = CreateWindow (szAppName, TEXT ("About Box Demo Program"),
                         WS_OVERLAPPEDWINDOW,
                         CW_USEDEFAULT, CW_USEDEFAULT,
                         CW_USEDEFAULT, CW_USEDEFAULT,
                         NULL, NULL, hInstance, NULL) ;

     ShowWindow (hwnd, iCmdShow) ;
     UpdateWindow (hwnd) ;

     while (GetMessage (&msg, NULL, 0, 0))
     {
          TranslateMessage (&msg) ;
          DispatchMessage (&msg) ;
     }
     return msg.wParam ;
}

LRESULT CALLBACK WndProc (HWND hwnd, UINT message, WPARAM wParam, LPARAM lParam)
{
     static HINSTANCE hInstance ;
```

(continued)

Figure 11-1. *continued*

```
     switch (message)
     {
     case WM_CREATE :
          hInstance = ((LPCREATESTRUCT) lParam)->hInstance ;
          return 0 ;

     case WM_COMMAND :
          switch (LOWORD (wParam))
          {
          case IDM_APP_ABOUT :
               DialogBox (hInstance, TEXT ("AboutBox"), hwnd, AboutDlgProc) ;
               break ;
          }
          return 0 ;

     case WM_DESTROY :
          PostQuitMessage (0) ;
          return 0 ;
     }
     return DefWindowProc (hwnd, message, wParam, lParam) ;
}

BOOL CALLBACK AboutDlgProc (HWND hDlg, UINT message,
                            WPARAM wParam, LPARAM lParam)
{
     switch (message)
     {
     case WM_INITDIALOG :
          return TRUE ;

     case WM_COMMAND :
          switch (LOWORD (wParam))
          {
          case IDOK :
          case IDCANCEL :
               EndDialog (hDlg, 0) ;
               return TRUE ;
          }
          break ;
     }
     return FALSE ;
}
```

ABOUT1.RC (excerpts)

```
//Microsoft Developer Studio generated resource script.

#include "resource.h"
#include "afxres.h"


/////////////////////////////////////////////////////////////////////////
// Dialog

ABOUTBOX DIALOG DISCARDABLE  32, 32, 180, 100
STYLE DS_MODALFRAME | WS_POPUP
FONT 8, "MS Sans Serif"
BEGIN
    DEFPUSHBUTTON   "OK",IDOK,66,80,50,14
    ICON            "ABOUT1",IDC_STATIC,7,7,21,20
    CTEXT           "About1",IDC_STATIC,40,12,100,8
    CTEXT           "About Box Demo Program",IDC_STATIC,7,40,166,8
    CTEXT           "(c) Charles Petzold, 1998",IDC_STATIC,7,52,166,8
END


/////////////////////////////////////////////////////////////////////////
// Menu

ABOUT1 MENU DISCARDABLE
BEGIN
    POPUP "&Help"
    BEGIN
        MENUITEM "&About About1...",            IDM_APP_ABOUT
    END
END


/////////////////////////////////////////////////////////////////////////
// Icon

ABOUT1                  ICON    DISCARDABLE     "About1.ico"
```

RESOURCE.H (excerpts)

```
// Microsoft Developer Studio generated include file.
// Used by About1.rc

#define IDM_APP_ABOUT           40001
#define IDC_STATIC              -1
```

(continued)

Figure 11-1. *continued*

ABOUT1.ICO

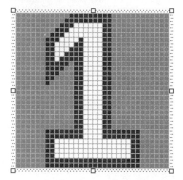

You create the icon and the menu in this program the same way as described in the last chapter. Both the icon and the menu have text ID names of "About1." The menu has one option, which generates a WM_COMMAND message with an ID of IDM_APP_ABOUT. This causes the program to display the dialog box shown in Figure 11-2.

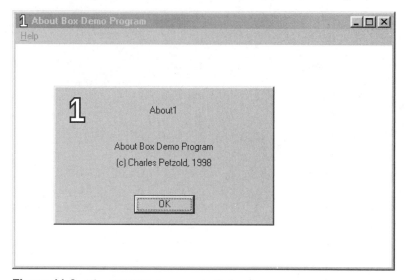

Figure 11-2. *The ABOUT1 program's dialog box.*

The Dialog Box and Its Template

To add a dialog box to an application in the Visual C++ Developer Studio, you begin by selecting Resource from the Insert menu and choosing Dialog Box. You are then presented with a dialog box with a title bar and caption ("Dialog") and OK and Cancel buttons. A Controls toolbar allows you to insert various controls in the dialog box.

Developer Studio gives the dialog box a standard ID of IDD_DIALOG1. You can right-click this name (or the dialog box itself) and select Properties from the menu. For this program, change the ID to "AboutBox" (with quotation marks). To be consistent with the dialog box I created, change the X Pos and Y Pos fields to 32. This is to indicate where the dialog box is displayed relative to the upper left corner of the client area of the program's window. (I'll discuss dialog box coordinates in more detail shortly.)

Now, still in the Properties dialog, select the Styles tab. Unclick the Title Bar check box because this dialog box does not have a title bar. Click the close button on the Properties dialog.

Now it's time to actually design the dialog box. We won't be needing the Cancel button, so click that button and press the Delete key on your keyboard. Click the OK button, and move it to the bottom of the dialog. At the bottom of the Developer Studio window will be a small bitmap on a toolbar that lets you center the control horizontally in the window. Press that button.

We want the program's icon to appear in the dialog box. To do so, press the Pictures button on the floating Controls toolbar. Move the mouse to the surface of the dialog box, press the left button, and drag a square. This is where the icon will appear. Press the right mouse button on this square, and select Properties from the menu. Leave the ID as IDC_STATIC. This identifier will be defined in RESOURCE.H as −1, which is used for all IDs that the C program does not refer to. Change the Type to Icon. You should be able to type the name of the program's icon in the Image field, or, if you've already created the icon, you can select the name ("About1") from the combo box.

For the three static text strings in the dialog box, select Static Text from the Controls toolbar and position the text in the dialog window. Right-click the control, and select Properties from the menu. You'll type the text you want to appear in the Caption field of the Properties box. Select the Styles tab to select Center from the Align Text field.

As you add these text strings, you may want to make the dialog box larger. Select it and drag the outline. You can also select and size controls. It's often easier to use the keyboard cursor movement keys for this. The arrow keys by themselves move the controls; the arrow keys with Shift depressed let you change the controls' sizes. The coordinates and sizes of the selected control are shown in the lower right corner of the Developer Studio window.

If you build the application and later look at the ABOUT1.RC resource script file, you'll see the dialog box template that Developer Studio generated. The dialog box that I designed has a template that looks like this:

```
ABOUTBOX DIALOG DISCARDABLE  32, 32, 180, 100
STYLE DS_MODALFRAME | WS_POPUP
FONT 8, "MS Sans Serif"
```

(continued)

```
BEGIN
    DEFPUSHBUTTON    "OK",IDOK,66,80,50,14
    ICON             "ABOUT1",IDC_STATIC,7,7,21,20
    CTEXT            "About1",IDC_STATIC,40,12,100,8
    CTEXT            "About Box Demo Program",IDC_STATIC,7,40,166,8
    CTEXT            "(c) Charles Petzold, 1998",IDC_STATIC,7,52,166,8
END
```

The first line gives the dialog box a name (in this case, ABOUTBOX). As is the case for other resources, you can use a number instead. The name is followed by the keywords DIALOG and DISCARDABLE, and four numbers. The first two numbers are the *x* and *y* co-ordinates of the upper left corner of the dialog box, relative to the client area of its parent when the dialog box is invoked by the program. The second two numbers are the width and height of the dialog box.

These coordinates and sizes are not in units of pixels. They are instead based on a special coordinate system used only for dialog box templates. The numbers are based on the size of the font used for the dialog box (in this case, an 8-point MS Sans Serif font): *x*-coordinates and width are expressed in units of 1/4 of an average character width; *y*-co-ordinates and height are expressed in units of 1/8 of the character height. Thus, for this particular dialog box, the upper left corner of the dialog box is 5 characters from the left edge of the main window's client area and 2-1/2 characters from the top edge. The dialog itself is 40 characters wide and 10 characters high.

This coordinate system allows you to use coordinates and sizes that will retain the general dimensions and look of the dialog box regardless of the resolution of the video display and the font you've selected. Because font characters are often approximately twice as high as they are wide, the dimensions on both the *x*-axis and the *y*-axis are nearly the same.

The STYLE statement in the template is similar to the style field of a *CreateWindow* call. WS_POPUP and DS_MODALFRAME are normally used for modal dialog boxes, but we'll explore some alternatives later on.

Within the BEGIN and END statements (or left and right brackets, if you'd prefer, when designing dialog box templates by hand), you define the child window controls that will appear in the dialog box. This dialog box uses three types of child window controls: DEFPUSHBUTTON (a default push button), ICON (an icon), and CTEXT (centered text). The format of these statements is

```
control-type "text" id, xPos, yPos, xWidth, yHeight, iStyle
```

The *iStyle* value at the end is optional; it specifies additional window styles using identi-fiers defined in the Windows header files.

These DEFPUSHBUTTON, ICON, and CTEXT identifiers are used in dialog boxes only. They are shorthand for a particular window class and window style. For example, CTEXT indicates that the class of the child window control is "static" and that the style is

```
WS_CHILD ¦ SS_CENTER ¦ WS_VISIBLE ¦ WS_GROUP
```

Although this is the first time we've encountered the WS_GROUP identifier, we used the WS_CHILD, SS_CENTER, and WS_VISIBLE window styles when creating static child window text controls in the COLORS1 program in Chapter 9.

For the icon, the text field is the name of the program's icon resource, which is also defined in the ABOUT1 resource script. For the push button, the text field is the text that appears inside the push button. This text is equivalent to the text specified as the second argument in a *CreateWindow* call when you create a child window control in a program.

The *id* field is a value that the child window uses to identify itself when sending messages (usually WM_COMMMAND messages) to its parent. The parent window of these child window controls is the dialog box window itself, which sends these messages to a window procedure in Windows. However, this window procedure also sends these messages to the dialog box procedure that you'll include in your program. The ID values are equivalent to the child window IDs used in the *CreateWindow* function when we created child windows in Chapter 9. Because the text and icon controls do not send messages back to the parent window, these values are set to IDC_STATIC, which is defined in RESOURCE.H as −1. The ID value for the push button is IDOK, which is defined in WINUSER.H as 1.

The next four numbers set the position of the child window control (relative to the upper left corner of the dialog box's client area) and the size. The position and size are expressed in units of 1/4 of the average width and 1/8 of the height of a font character. The width and height values are ignored for the ICON statement.

The DEFPUSHBUTTON statement in the dialog box template includes the window style WS_GROUP in addition to the window style implied by the DEFPUSHBUTTON keyword. I'll have more to say about WS_GROUP (and the related WS_TABSTOP style) when discussing the second version of this program, ABOUT2, a bit later.

The Dialog Box Procedure

The dialog box procedure within your program handles messages to the dialog box. Although it looks very much like a window procedure, it is not a true window procedure. The window procedure for the dialog box is within Windows. That window procedure calls your dialog box procedure with many of the messages that it receives. Here's the dialog box procedure for ABOUT1:

```
BOOL CALLBACK AboutDlgProc (HWND hDlg, UINT message,
                            WPARAM wParam, LPARAM lParam)
{
    switch (message)
    {
    case WM_INITDIALOG :
        return TRUE ;
```

(continued)

```
case WM_COMMAND :
     switch (LOWORD (wParam))
     {
     case IDOK :
     case IDCANCEL :
          EndDialog (hDlg, 0) ;
          return TRUE ;
     }
     break ;
}
return FALSE ;
}
```

The parameters to this function are the same as those for a normal window procedure; as with a window procedure, the dialog box procedure must be defined as a CALL-BACK function. Although I've used *hDlg* for the handle to the dialog box window, you can use *hwnd* instead if you like. Let's note first the differences between this function and a window procedure:

■ A window procedure returns an LRESULT; a dialog box procedure returns a BOOL, which is defined in the Windows header files as an *int*.

■ A window procedure calls *DefWindowProc* if it does not process a particular message; a dialog box procedure returns TRUE (nonzero) if it processes a message and FALSE (0) if it does not.

■ A dialog box procedure does not need to process WM_PAINT or WM_DESTROY messages. A dialog box procedure will not receive a WM_CREATE message; instead, the dialog box procedure performs initialization during the special WM_INITDIALOG message.

The WM_INITDIALOG message is the first message the dialog box procedure receives. This message is sent only to dialog box procedures. If the dialog box procedure returns TRUE, Windows sets the input focus to the first child window control in the dialog box that has a WS_TABSTOP style (which I'll explain in the discussion of ABOUT2). In this dialog box, the first child window control that has a WS_TABSTOP style is the push button. Alternatively, during the processing of WM_INITDIALOG, the dialog box procedure can use *SetFocus* to set the focus to one of the child window controls in the dialog box and then return FALSE.

The only other message this dialog box processes is WM_COMMAND. This is the message the push-button control sends to its parent window either when the button is clicked with the mouse or when the Spacebar is pressed while the button has the input focus. The ID of the control (which we set to IDOK in the dialog box template) is in the low word of *wParam*. For this message, the dialog box procedure calls *EndDialog*, which tells Windows to destroy the dialog box. For all other messages, the dialog box procedure returns FALSE to tell the dialog box window procedure within Windows that our dialog box procedure did not process the message.

The messages for a modal dialog box don't go through your program's message queue, so you needn't worry about the effect of keyboard accelerators within the dialog box.

Invoking the Dialog Box

During the processing of WM_CREATE in *WndProc*, ABOUT1 obtains the program's instance handle and stores it in a static variable:

```
hInstance = ((LPCREATESTRUCT) lParam)->hInstance ;
```

ABOUT1 checks for WM_COMMAND messages where the low word of *wParam* is equal to IDM_APP_ABOUT. When it gets one, the program calls *DialogBox*:

```
DialogBox (hInstance, TEXT ("AboutBox"), hwnd, AboutDlgProc) ;
```

This function requires the instance handle (saved during WM_CREATE), the name of the dialog box (as defined in the resource script), the parent of the dialog box (which is the program's main window), and the address of the dialog procedure. If you use a numeric identifier rather than a name for the dialog box template, you can convert it to a string using the MAKEINTRESOURCE macro.

Selecting About About1 from the menu displays the dialog box, as shown in Figure 11-2 on page 488. You can end this dialog box by clicking the OK button with the mouse, by pressing the Spacebar, or by pressing Enter. For any dialog box that contains a default push button, Windows sends a WM_COMMAND message to the dialog box, with the low word of *wParam* equal to the ID of the default push button when Enter or the Spacebar is pressed. That ID is IDOK. You can also end the dialog box by pressing Escape. In that case Windows sends a WM_COMMAND message with an ID equal to IDCANCEL.

The *DialogBox* function you call to display the dialog box will not return control to *WndProc* until the dialog box is ended. The value returned from *DialogBox* is the second parameter to the *EndDialog* function called within the dialog box procedure. (This value is not used in ABOUT1 but *is* used in ABOUT2.) *WndProc* can then return control to Windows.

Even when the dialog box is displayed, however, *WndProc* can continue to receive messages. In fact, you can send messages to *WndProc* from within the dialog box procedure. ABOUT1's main window is the parent of the dialog box popup window, so the *SendMessage* call in *AboutDlgProc* would start off like this:

```
SendMessage (GetParent (hDlg),  . . . ) ;
```

Variations on a Theme

Although the dialog editor and other resource editors in the the Visual C++ Developer Studio seemingly make it unnecessary to even look at resource scripts, it is still helpful to learn resource script syntax. Particularly for dialog templates, knowing the syntax allows you to have a better feel for the scope and limitations of dialog boxes. You may even want to create a dialog box template manually if there's something you need to do that can't be done otherwise (such as in the HEXCALC program later in this chapter). The resource compiler and resource script syntax is documented in *Platform SDK/Windows Programming Guidelines/ Platform SDK Tools/Compiling/Using the Resource Compiler.*

The window style of the dialog box is specified in the Properties dialog in the Developer Studio, which is translated into the STYLE line of the dialog box template. For ABOUT1, we used a style that is most common for modal dialog boxes:

```
STYLE WS_POPUP | DS_MODALFRAME
```

However, you can also experiment with other styles. Some dialog boxes have a caption bar that identifies the dialog's purpose and lets the user move the dialog box around the display using the mouse. This is the style WS_CAPTION. When you use WS_CAPTION, the *x* and *y* coordinates specified in the DIALOG statement are the coordinates of the dialog box's client area, relative to the upper left corner of the parent window's client area. The caption bar will be shown above the *y*-coordinate.

If you have a caption bar, you can put text in it using the CAPTION statement, following the STYLE statement, in the dialog box template:

```
CAPTION "Dialog Box Caption"
```

Or while processing the WM_INITDIALOG message in the dialog procedure, you can use

```
SetWindowText (hDlg, TEXT ("Dialog Box Caption")) ;
```

If you use the WS_CAPTION style, you can also add a system menu box with the WS_SYSMENU style. This style allows the user to select Move or Close from the system menu.

Selecting Resizing from the Border list box of the Properties dialog (equivalent to the style WS_THICKFRAME) allows the user to resize the dialog box, although this is unusual. If you don't mind being even more unusual, you can also try adding a maximize box to the dialog box style.

You can even add a menu to a dialog box. The dialog box template will include the statement

```
MENU menu-name
```

The argument is either the name or the number of a menu in the resource script. Menus are highly uncommon for modal dialog boxes. If you use one, be sure that all the ID numbers in the menu and the dialog box controls are unique, or if they're not, that they duplicate the same commands.

The FONT statement lets you set something other than the system font for use with dialog box text. This was once uncommon in dialog boxes but is now quite normal. Indeed, Developer Studio selects the 8-point MS Sans Serif font by default in any dialog box you create. A Windows program can achieve a unique look by shipping a special font with a program that is used solely by the program for dialog boxes and other text output.

Although the dialog box window procedure is normally within Windows, you can use one of your own window procedures to process dialog box messages. To do so, specify a window class name in the dialog box template:

```
CLASS "class-name"
```

There are some other considerations involved, but I'll demonstrate this approach in the HEXCALC program shown later in this chapter.

When you call *DialogBox*, specifying the name of a dialog box template, Windows has almost everything it needs to create a popup window by calling the normal *Create-Window* function. Windows obtains the coordinates and size of the window, the window style, the caption, and the menu from the dialog box template. Windows gets the instance handle and the parent window handle from the arguments to *DialogBox*. The only other piece of information it needs is a window class (assuming the dialog box template does not specify one). Windows registers a special window class for dialog boxes. The window procedure for this window class has access to the address of your dialog box procedure (which you provide in the *DialogBox* call), so it can keep your program informed of messages that this popup window receives. Of course, you can create and maintain your own dialog box by creating the popup window yourself. Using *DialogBox* is simply an easier approach.

You may want the benefit of using the Windows dialog manager, but you may not want to (or be able to) define the dialog template in a resource script. Perhaps you want the program to create a dialog box dynamically as it's running. The function to look at is *DialogBoxIndirect*, which uses data structures to define the template.

In the dialog box template in ABOUT1.RC, the shorthand notation CTEXT, ICON, and DEFPUSHBUTTON is used to define the three types of child window controls we want in the dialog box. There are several others that you can use. Each type implies a particular predefined window class and a window style. The following table shows the equivalent window class and window style for some common control types:

Control Type	*Window Class*	*Window Style*
PUSHBUTTON	button	BS_PUSHBUTTON ¦ WS_TABSTOP
DEFPUSHBUTTON	button	BS_DEFPUSHBUTTON ¦ WS_TABSTOP
CHECKBOX	button	BS_CHECKBOX ¦ WS_TABSTOP

(continued)

continued

Control Type	Window Class	Window Style
RADIOBUTTON	button	BS_RADIOBUTTON ¦ WS_TABSTOP
GROUPBOX	button	BS_GROUPBOX ¦ WS_TABSTOP
LTEXT	static	SS_LEFT ¦ WS_GROUP
CTEXT	static	SS_CENTER ¦ WS_GROUP
RTEXT	static	SS_RIGHT ¦ WS_GROUP
ICON	static	SS_ICON
EDITTEXT	edit	ES_LEFT ¦ WS_BORDER ¦ WS_TABSTOP
SCROLLBAR	scrollbar	SBS_HORZ
LISTBOX	listbox	LBS_NOTIFY ¦ WS_BORDER ¦ WS_VSCROLL
COMBOBOX	combobox	CBS_SIMPLE ¦ WS_TABSTOP

The resource compiler is the only program that understands this shorthand notation. In addition to the window styles shown above, each of these controls has the style

```
WS_CHILD ¦ WS_VISIBLE
```

For all these control types except EDITTEXT, SCROLLBAR, LISTBOX, and COMBO-BOX, the format of the control statement is

```
control-type "text", id, xPos, yPos, xWidth, yHeight, iStyle
```

For EDITTEXT, SCROLLBAR, LISTBOX, and COMBOBOX, the format is

```
control-type id, xPos, yPos, xWidth, yHeight, iStyle
```

which excludes the text field. In both statements, the *iStyle* parameter is optional.

In Chapter 9, I discussed rules for determining the width and height of predefined child window controls. You might want to refer back to that chapter for these rules, keeping in mind that sizes specified in dialog box templates are always in terms of 1/4 of the average character width and 1/8 of the character height.

The "style" field of the control statements is optional. It allows you to include other window style identifiers. For instance, if you wanted to create a check box consisting of text to the left of a square box, you could use

```
CHECKBOX "text", id, xPos, yPos, xWidth, yHeight, BS_LEFTTEXT
```

Notice that the control type EDITTEXT automatically has a border. If you want to create a child window edit control without a border, you can use

```
EDITTEXT id, xPos, yPos, xWidth, yHeight, NOT WS_BORDER
```

The resource compiler also recognizes a generalized control statement that looks like

```
CONTROL "text", id, "class", iStyle, xPos, yPos, xWidth, yHeight
```

This statement allows you to create any type of child window control by specifying the window class and the complete window style. For example, instead of using

```
PUSHBUTTON "OK", IDOK, 10, 20, 32, 14
```

you can use

```
CONTROL "OK", IDOK, "button", WS_CHILD | WS_VISIBLE |
        BS_PUSHBUTTON | WS_TABSTOP, 10, 20, 32, 14
```

When the resource script is compiled, these two statements are encoded identically in the .RES file and the .EXE file. In Developer Studio, you create a statement like this using the Custom Control option from the Controls toolbar. In the ABOUT3 program, shown in Figure 11-5 beginning on page 513, I show how you can use this to create a control whose window class is defined in your program.

When you use CONTROL statements in a dialog box template, you don't need to include the WS_CHILD and WS_VISIBLE styles. Windows includes these in the window style when creating the child windows. The format of the CONTROL statement also clarifies what the Windows dialog manager does when it creates a dialog box. First, as I described earlier, it creates a popup window whose parent is the window handle that was provided in the *DialogBox* function. Then, for each control in the dialog template, the dialog box manager creates a child window. The parent of each of these controls is the popup dialog box. The CONTROL statement shown above is translated into a *CreateWindow* call that looks like

```
hCtrl = CreateWindow (TEXT ("button"), TEXT ("OK"),
                WS_CHILD | WS_VISIBLE | WS_TABSTOP | BS_PUSHBUTTON,
                10 * cxChar / 4, 20 * cyChar / 8,
                32 * cxChar / 4, 14 * cyChar / 8,
                hDlg, IDOK, hInstance, NULL) ;
```

where *cxChar* and *cyChar* are the width and height of the dialog box font character in pixels. The *hDlg* parameter is returned from the *CreateWindow* call that creates the dialog box window. The *hInstance* parameter is obtained from the original *DialogBox* call.

A More Complex Dialog Box

The simple dialog box in ABOUT1 demonstrates the basics of getting a dialog box up and running; now let's try something a little more complex. The ABOUT2 program, shown in Figure 11-3 beginning on the following page, demonstrates how to manage controls (in this case, radio buttons) within a dialog box procedure and also how to paint on the client area of the dialog box.

ABOUT2.C

```
/*-------------------------------------------
   ABOUT2.C -- About Box Demo Program No. 2
              (c) Charles Petzold, 1998
   -------------------------------------------*/

#include <windows.h>
#include "resource.h"

LRESULT CALLBACK WndProc        (HWND, UINT, WPARAM, LPARAM) ;
BOOL    CALLBACK AboutDlgProc (HWND, UINT, WPARAM, LPARAM) ;

int iCurrentColor  = IDC_BLACK,
    iCurrentFigure = IDC_RECT ;

int WINAPI WinMain (HINSTANCE hInstance, HINSTANCE hPrevInstance,
                    PSTR szCmdLine, int iCmdShow)
{
    static TCHAR szAppName[] = TEXT ("About2") ;
    MSG          msg ;
    HWND         hwnd ;
    WNDCLASS     wndclass ;

    wndclass.style         = CS_HREDRAW | CS_VREDRAW ;
    wndclass.lpfnWndProc   = WndProc ;
    wndclass.cbClsExtra    = 0 ;
    wndclass.cbWndExtra    = 0 ;
    wndclass.hInstance     = hInstance ;
    wndclass.hIcon         = LoadIcon (hInstance, szAppName) ;
    wndclass.hCursor       = LoadCursor (NULL, IDC_ARROW) ;
    wndclass.hbrBackground = (HBRUSH) GetStockObject (WHITE_BRUSH) ;
    wndclass.lpszMenuName  = szAppName ;
    wndclass.lpszClassName = szAppName ;

    if (!RegisterClass (&wndclass))
    {
        MessageBox (NULL, TEXT ("This program requires Windows NT!"),
                    szAppName, MB_ICONERROR) ;
        return 0 ;
    }

    hwnd = CreateWindow (szAppName, TEXT ("About Box Demo Program"),
                         WS_OVERLAPPEDWINDOW,
                         CW_USEDEFAULT, CW_USEDEFAULT,
```

Figure 11-3. *The ABOUT2 program.*

```
                        CW_USEDEFAULT, CW_USEDEFAULT,
                        NULL, NULL, hInstance, NULL) ;

     ShowWindow (hwnd, iCmdShow) ;
     UpdateWindow (hwnd) ;

     while (GetMessage (&msg, NULL, 0, 0))
     {
          TranslateMessage (&msg) ;
          DispatchMessage (&msg) ;
     }
     return msg.wParam ;
}

void PaintWindow (HWND hwnd, int iColor, int iFigure)
{
     static COLORREF crColor[8] = { RGB (  0,   0, 0), RGB (  0,   0, 255),
                                    RGB (  0, 255, 0), RGB (  0, 255, 255),
                                    RGB (255,   0, 0), RGB (255,   0, 255),
                                    RGB (255, 255, 0), RGB (255, 255, 255) } ;

     HBRUSH          hBrush ;
     HDC             hdc ;
     RECT            rect ;

     hdc = GetDC (hwnd) ;
     GetClientRect (hwnd, &rect) ;
     hBrush = CreateSolidBrush (crColor[iColor - IDC_BLACK]) ;
     hBrush = (HBRUSH) SelectObject (hdc, hBrush) ;

     if (iFigure == IDC_RECT)
          Rectangle (hdc, rect.left, rect.top, rect.right, rect.bottom) ;
     else
          Ellipse   (hdc, rect.left, rect.top, rect.right, rect.bottom) ;

     DeleteObject (SelectObject (hdc, hBrush)) ;
     ReleaseDC (hwnd, hdc) ;
}

void PaintTheBlock (HWND hCtrl, int iColor, int iFigure)
{
     InvalidateRect (hCtrl, NULL, TRUE) ;
     UpdateWindow (hCtrl) ;
     PaintWindow (hCtrl, iColor, iFigure) ;
}
```

(continued)

Figure 11-3. *continued*

```
LRESULT CALLBACK WndProc (HWND hwnd, UINT message, WPARAM wParam, LPARAM lParam)
{
     static HINSTANCE hInstance ;
     PAINTSTRUCT      ps ;

     switch (message)
     {
     case WM_CREATE:
          hInstance = ((LPCREATESTRUCT) lParam)->hInstance ;
          return 0 ;

     case WM_COMMAND:
          switch (LOWORD (wParam))
          {
          case IDM_APP_ABOUT:
               if (DialogBox (hInstance, TEXT ("AboutBox"), hwnd, AboutDlgProc))
                    InvalidateRect (hwnd, NULL, TRUE) ;
               return 0 ;
          }
          break ;

     case WM_PAINT:
          BeginPaint (hwnd, &ps) ;
          EndPaint (hwnd, &ps) ;

          PaintWindow (hwnd, iCurrentColor, iCurrentFigure) ;
          return 0 ;

     case WM_DESTROY:
          PostQuitMessage (0) ;
          return 0 ;
     }
     return DefWindowProc (hwnd, message, wParam, lParam) ;
}

BOOL CALLBACK AboutDlgProc (HWND hDlg, UINT message,
                            WPARAM wParam, LPARAM lParam)
{
     static HWND hCtrlBlock ;
     static int  iColor, iFigure ;

     switch (message)
```

```
{
case WM_INITDIALOG:
      iColor  = iCurrentColor ;
      iFigure = iCurrentFigure ;

      CheckRadioButton (hDlg, IDC_BLACK, IDC_WHITE,   iColor) ;
      CheckRadioButton (hDlg, IDC_RECT,  IDC_ELLIPSE, iFigure) ;

      hCtrlBlock = GetDlgItem (hDlg, IDC_PAINT) ;

      SetFocus (GetDlgItem (hDlg, iColor)) ;
      return FALSE ;

case WM_COMMAND:
      switch (LOWORD (wParam))
      {
      case IDOK:
           iCurrentColor  = iColor ;
           iCurrentFigure = iFigure ;
           EndDialog (hDlg, TRUE) ;
           return TRUE ;

      case IDCANCEL:
           EndDialog (hDlg, FALSE) ;
           return TRUE ;

      case IDC_BLACK:
      case IDC_RED:
      case IDC_GREEN:
      case IDC_YELLOW:
      case IDC_BLUE:
      case IDC_MAGENTA:
      case IDC_CYAN:
      case IDC_WHITE:
           iColor = LOWORD (wParam) ;
           CheckRadioButton (hDlg, IDC_BLACK, IDC_WHITE, LOWORD (wParam)) ;
           PaintTheBlock (hCtrlBlock, iColor, iFigure) ;
           return TRUE ;

      case IDC_RECT:
      case IDC_ELLIPSE:
           iFigure = LOWORD (wParam) ;
           CheckRadioButton (hDlg, IDC_RECT, IDC_ELLIPSE, LOWORD (wParam)) ;
           PaintTheBlock (hCtrlBlock, iColor, iFigure) ;
           return TRUE ;
      }
```

(continued)

Figure 11-3. *continued*

```
        break ;

    case WM_PAINT:
        PaintTheBlock (hCtrlBlock, iColor, iFigure) ;
        break ;
    }
    return FALSE ;
}
```

ABOUT2.RC (excerpts)

```
//Microsoft Developer Studio generated resource script.

#include "resource.h"
#include "afxres.h"


/////////////////////////////////////////////////////////////////////////////
// Dialog

ABOUTBOX DIALOG DISCARDABLE  32, 32, 200, 234
STYLE DS_MODALFRAME | WS_POPUP | WS_CAPTION
FONT 8, "MS Sans Serif"
BEGIN
    ICON            "ABOUT2",IDC_STATIC,7,7,20,20
    CTEXT           "About2",IDC_STATIC,57,12,86,8
    CTEXT           "About Box Demo Program",IDC_STATIC,7,40,186,8
    LTEXT           "",IDC_PAINT,114,67,74,72
    GROUPBOX        "&Color",IDC_STATIC,7,60,84,143
    RADIOBUTTON     "&Black",IDC_BLACK,16,76,64,8,WS_GROUP | WS_TABSTOP
    RADIOBUTTON     "B&lue",IDC_BLUE,16,92,64,8
    RADIOBUTTON     "&Green",IDC_GREEN,16,108,64,8
    RADIOBUTTON     "Cya&n",IDC_CYAN,16,124,64,8
    RADIOBUTTON     "&Red",IDC_RED,16,140,64,8
    RADIOBUTTON     "&Magenta",IDC_MAGENTA,16,156,64,8
    RADIOBUTTON     "&Yellow",IDC_YELLOW,16,172,64,8
    RADIOBUTTON     "&White",IDC_WHITE,16,188,64,8
    GROUPBOX        "&Figure",IDC_STATIC,109,156,84,46,WS_GROUP
    RADIOBUTTON     "Rec&tangle",IDC_RECT,116,172,65,8,WS_GROUP | WS_TABSTOP
    RADIOBUTTON     "&Ellipse",IDC_ELLIPSE,116,188,64,8
    DEFPUSHBUTTON   "OK",IDOK,35,212,50,14,WS_GROUP
    PUSHBUTTON      "Cancel",IDCANCEL,113,212,50,14,WS_GROUP
END


/////////////////////////////////////////////////////////////////////////////
// Icon
```

```
ABOUT2                    ICON   DISCARDABLE    "About2.ico"

/////////////////////////////////////////////////////////////////////////
// Menu

ABOUT2 MENU DISCARDABLE
BEGIN
    POPUP "&Help"
    BEGIN
        MENUITEM "&About",                      IDM_APP_ABOUT
    END
END
```

RESOURCE.H (excerpts)

```
// Microsoft Developer Studio generated include file.
// Used by About2.rc

#define IDC_BLACK               1000
#define IDC_BLUE                1001
#define IDC_GREEN               1002
#define IDC_CYAN                1003
#define IDC_RED                 1004
#define IDC_MAGENTA             1005
#define IDC_YELLOW              1006
#define IDC_WHITE               1007
#define IDC_RECT                1008
#define IDC_ELLIPSE             1009
#define IDC_PAINT               1010
#define IDM_APP_ABOUT           40001
#define IDC_STATIC              -1
```

ABOUT2.ICO

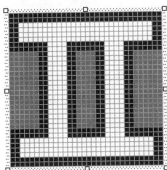

The About box in ABOUT2 has two groups of radio buttons. One group is used to select a color, and the other group is used to select either a rectangle or an ellipse. The rectangle or ellipse is shown in the dialog box with the interior colored with the current color selection. If you press the OK button, the dialog box is ended, and the program's window procedure draws the selected figure in its own client area. If you press Cancel, the client area of the main window remains the same. The dialog box is shown in Figure 11-4. Although the ABOUT2 dialog box uses the predefined identifiers IDOK and IDCANCEL for the two push buttons, each of the radio buttons has its own identifier beginning with the letters IDC ("ID for a control"). These identifiers are defined in RESOURCE.H.

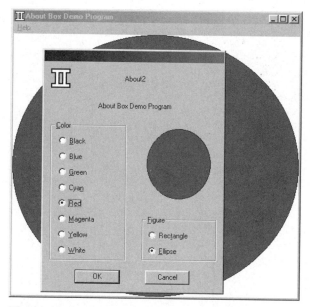

Figure 11-4. *The ABOUT2 program's dialog box.*

When you create the radio buttons in the ABOUT2 dialog box, create them in the order shown. This ensures that Developer Studio defines sequentially valued identifiers, which is assumed by the program. Also, uncheck the Auto option for each radio button. The Auto Radio Button requires less code but is initially more mysterious. Give them the identifiers shown above in ABOUT2.RC.

Check the Group option in the Properties dialog for the OK and Cancel buttons, and for the Figure group box, and for the first radio buttons (Black and Rectangle) in each group. Check the Tab Stop check box for these two radio buttons.

When you have all the controls in the dialog box approximately positioned and sized, choose the Tab Order option from the Layout menu. Click each control in the order shown in the ABOUT2.RC resource script.

Working with Dialog Box Controls

In Chapter 9, you discovered that most child window controls send WM_COMMAND messages to the parent window. (The exception is scroll bar controls.) You also saw that the parent window can alter child window controls (for instance, checking or unchecking radio buttons or check boxes) by sending messages to the controls. You can similarly alter controls in a dialog box procedure. If you have a series of radio buttons, for example, you can check and uncheck the buttons by sending them messages. However, Windows also provides several shortcuts when working with controls in dialog boxes. Let's look at the way in which the dialog box procedure and the child window controls communicate.

The dialog box template for ABOUT2 is shown in the ABOUT2.RC resource script in Figure 11-3. The GROUPBOX control is simply a frame with a title (either Color or Figure) that surrounds each of the two groups of radio buttons. The eight radio buttons in the first group are mutually exclusive, as are the two radio buttons in the second group.

When one of the radio buttons is clicked with the mouse (or when the Spacebar is pressed while the radio button has the input focus), the child window sends its parent a WM_COMMAND message with the low word of *wParam* set to the ID of the control. The high word of *wParam* is a notification code, and *lParam* is the window handle of the control. For a radio button, this notification code is always BN_CLICKED, which equals 0. The dialog box window procedure in Windows then passes this WM_COMMAND message to the dialog box procedure within ABOUT2.C. When the dialog box procedure receives a WM_COMMAND message for one of the radio buttons, it turns on the check mark for that button and turns off the check marks for all the other buttons in the group.

You might recall from Chapter 9 that checking and unchecking a button requires that you send the child window control a BM_CHECK message. To turn on a button check mark, you use

```
SendMessage (hwndCtrl, BM_SETCHECK, 1, 0) ;
```

To turn off the check mark, you use

```
SendMessage (hwndCtrl, BM_SETCHECK, 0, 0) ;
```

The *hwndCtrl* parameter is the window handle of the child window button control.

But this method presents a little problem in the dialog box procedure, because you don't know the window handles of all the radio buttons. You know only the one from which you're getting the message. Fortunately, Windows provides you with a function to obtain the window handle of a dialog box control using the dialog box window handle and the control ID:

```
hwndCtrl = GetDlgItem (hDlg, id) ;
```

(You can also obtain the ID value of a control from the window handle by using

```
id = GetWindowLong (hwndCtrl, GWL_ID) ;
```

but this is rarely necessary.)

You'll notice in the ABOUT2.H header file shown in Figure 11-3 that the ID values for the eight colors are sequential from IDC_BLACK to IDC_WHITE. This arrangement helps in processing the WM_COMMAND messages from the radio buttons. For a first attempt at checking and unchecking the radio buttons, you might try something like the following in the dialog box procedure:

```
static int iColor ;
[other program lines]
case WM_COMMAND:
     switch (LOWORD (wParam))
     {
     [other program lines]
     case IDC_BLACK:
     case IDC_RED:
     case IDC_GREEN:
     case IDC_YELLOW:
     case IDC_BLUE:
     case IDC_MAGENTA:
     case IDC_CYAN:
     case IDC_WHITE:
          iColor = LOWORD (wParam) ;

          for (i = IDC_BLACK, i <= IDC_WHITE, i++)
               SendMessage (GetDlgItem (hDlg, i),
                         BM_SETCHECK, i == LOWORD (wParam), 0) ;
          return TRUE ;
     [other program lines]
```

This approach works satisfactorily. You've saved the new color value in *iColor*, and you've also set up a loop that cycles through all the ID values for the eight colors. You obtain the window handle of each of these eight radio button controls and use *SendMessage* to send each handle a BM_SETCHECK message. The *wParam* value of this message is set to 1 only for the button that sent the WM_COMMAND message to the dialog box window procedure.

The first shortcut is the special dialog box procedure *SendDlgItemMessage*:

```
SendDlgItemMessage (hDlg, id, iMsg, wParam, lParam) ;
```

It is equivalent to

```
SendMessage (GetDlgItem (hDlg, id), id, wParam, lParam) ;
```

Now the loop would look like this:

```
for (i = IDC_BLACK, i <= IDC_WHITE, i++)
    SendDlgItemMessage (hDlg, i, BM_SETCHECK, i == LWORD (wParam), 0) ;
```

That's a little better. But the real breakthrough comes when you discover the *Check-RadioButton* function:

```
CheckRadioButton (hDlg, idFirst, idLast, idCheck) ;
```

This function turns off the check marks for all radio button controls with IDs from *idFirst* to *idLast* except for the radio button with an ID of *idCheck*, which is checked. The IDs must be sequential. Now we can get rid of the loop entirely and use:

```
CheckRadioButton (hDlg, IDC_BLACK, IDC_WHITE, LOWORD (wParam)) ;
```

That's how it's done in the dialog box procedure in ABOUT2.

A similar shortcut function is provided for working with check boxes. If you create a CHECKBOX dialog window control, you can turn the check mark on and off using the function

```
CheckDlgButton (hDlg, idCheckbox, iCheck) ;
```

If *iCheck* is set to 1, the button is checked; if it's set to 0, the button is unchecked. You can obtain the status of a check box in a dialog box by using

```
iCheck = IsDlgButtonChecked (hDlg, idCheckbox) ;
```

You can either retain the current status of the check mark as a static variable within the dialog box procedure or do something like this to toggle the button on a WM_COMMAND message:

```
CheckDlgButton (hDlg, idCheckbox,
    !IsDlgButtonChecked (hDlg, idCheckbox)) ;
```

If you define a BS_AUTOCHECKBOX control, you don't need to process the WM_COMMAND message at all. You can simply obtain the current status of the button by using *IsDlgButtonChecked* before terminating the dialog box. However, if you use the BS_AUTORADIOBUTTON style, *IsDlgButtonChecked* is not quite satisfactory because you'd need to call it for each radio button until the function returned TRUE. Instead, you'd still trap WM_COMMAND messages to keep track of which button gets pressed.

The OK and Cancel Buttons

ABOUT2 has two push buttons, labeled OK and Cancel. In the dialog box template in ABOUT2.RC, the OK button has an ID of IDOK (defined in WINUSER.H as 1) and the Cancel button has an ID of IDCANCEL (defined as 2). The OK button is the default:

```
DEFPUSHBUTTON   "OK",IDOK,35,212,50,14
PUSHBUTTON      "Cancel",IDCANCEL,113,212,50,14
```

This arrangement is normal for OK and Cancel buttons in dialog boxes; having the OK button as the default helps out with the keyboard interface. Here's how: Normally, you would end the dialog box by clicking one of these buttons with the mouse or pressing the Spacebar when the desired button has the input focus. However, the dialog box window procedure also generates a WM_COMMAND message when the user presses Enter, regardless of which control has the input focus. The LOWORD of *wParam* is set to the ID value of the default push button in the dialog box unless another push button has the input focus. In that case, the LOWORD of *wParam* is set to the ID of the push button with the input focus. If no push button in the dialog box is the default push button, Windows sends the dialog box procedure a WM_COMMAND message with the LOWORD of *wParam* equal to IDOK. If the user presses the Esc key or Ctrl-Break, Windows sends the dialog box procedure a WM_COMMAND message with the LOWORD of *wParam* equal to IDCANCEL. So you don't have to add separate keyboard logic to the dialog box procedure, because the keystrokes that normally terminate a dialog box are translated by Windows into WM_COMMAND messages for these two push buttons.

The *AboutDlgProc* function handles these two WM_COMMAND messages by calling *EndDialog*:

```
switch (LWORD (wParam))
{
case IDOK:
     iCurrentColor  = iColor ;
     iCurrentFigure = iFigure ;
     EndDialog (hDlg, TRUE) ;
     return TRUE ;

case IDCANCEL :
     EndDialog (hDlg, FALSE) ;
     return TRUE ;
```

ABOUT2's window procedure uses the global variables *iCurrentColor* and *iCurrentFigure* when drawing the rectangle or ellipse in the program's client area. *AboutDlgProc* uses the static local variables *iColor* and *iFigure* when drawing the figure within the dialog box.

Notice the different value in the second parameter of *EndDialog*. This is the value that is passed back as the return value from the original *DialogBox* function in *WndProc*:

```
case IDM_ABOUT:
     if (DialogBox (hInstance, TEXT ("AboutBox"), hwnd, AboutDlgProc))
          InvalidateRect (hwnd, NULL, TRUE) ;
     return 0 ;
```

If *DialogBox* returns TRUE (nonzero), meaning that the OK button was pressed, then the *WndProc* client area needs to be updated with the new figure and color. These were saved in the global variables *iCurrentColor* and *iCurrentFigure* by *AboutDlgProc* when it received a WM_COMMAND message with the low word of *wParam* equal to IDOK. If *DialogBox* returns FALSE, the main window continues to use the original settings of *iCurrentColor* and *iCurrentFigure*.

TRUE and FALSE are commonly used in *EndDialog* calls to signal to the main window procedure whether the user ended the dialog box with OK or Cancel. However, the argument to *EndDialog* is actually an *int*, and *DialogBox* returns an *int*, so it's possible to return more information in this way than simply TRUE or FALSE.

Avoiding Global Variables

The use of global variables in ABOUT2 may or may not be disturbing to you. Some programmers (myself included) prefer to keep the use of global variables to a bare minimum. The *iCurrentColor* and *iCurrentFigure* variables in ABOUT2 certainly seem to qualify as legitimate candidates for global definitions because they must be used in both the window procedure and the dialog procedure. However, a program that has many dialog boxes, each of which can alter the values of several variables, could easily have a confusing proliferation of global variables.

You might prefer to conceive of each dialog box within a program as being associated with a data structure containing all the variables that can be altered by the dialog box. You would define these structures in *typedef* statements. For example, in ABOUT2 you might define a structure associated with the About box like so:

```
typedef struct
{
    int iColor, iFigure ;
}
ABOUTBOX_DATA ;
```

In *WndProc*, you define and initialize a static variable based on this structure:

```
static ABOUTBOX_DATA ad = { IDC_BLACK, IDC_RECT } ;
```

Also in *WndProc*, replace all occurrences of *iCurrentColor* and *iCurrentFigure* with *ad.iColor* and *ad.iFigure*. When you invoke the dialog box, use *DialogBoxParam* rather than *DialogBox*. This function has a fifth argument that can be any 32-bit value you'd like. Generally, it is set to a pointer to a structure, in this case the ABOUTBOX_DATA structure in *WndProc*:

```
case IDM_ABOUT:
    if (DialogBoxParam (hInstance, TEXT ("AboutBox"),
                        hwnd, AboutDlgProc, &ad))
        InvalidateRect (hwnd, NULL, TRUE) ;
    return 0 ;
```

Here's the key: the last argument to *DialogBoxParam* is passed to the dialog procedure as *lParam* in the WM_INITDIALOG message.

The dialog procedure would have two static variables (a structure and a pointer to a structure) based on the ABOUTBOX_DATA structure:

```
static ABOUTBOX_DATA ad, * pad ;
```

In *AboutDlgProc* this definition replaces the definitions of *iColor* and *iFigure*. At the outset of the WM_INITDIALOG message, the dialog procedure sets the values of these two variables from *lParam*:

```
pad = (ABOUTBOX_DATA *) lParam ;
ad = * pad ;
```

In the first statement, *pad* is set to the *lParam* pointer. That is, *pad* actually points to the ABOUTBOX_DATA structure defined in *WndProc*. The second statement performs a field-by-field structure copy from the structure in *WndProc* to the local structure in *DlgProc*.

Now, throughout *AboutDlgProc*, replace *iFigure* and *iColor* with *ad.iColor* and *ad.iFigure* except in the code for when the user presses the OK button. In that case, copy the contents of the local structure back to the structure in *WndProc*:

```
case IDOK:
    * pad = ad ;
    EndDialog (hDlg, TRUE) ;
    return TRUE ;
```

Tab Stops and Groups

In Chapter 9, we used window subclassing to add a facility to COLORS1 that let us move from one scroll bar to another by pressing the Tab key. In a dialog box, window subclassing is unnecessary: Windows does all the logic for moving the input focus from one control to another. However, you have to help out by using the WS_TABSTOP and WS_GROUP window styles in the dialog box template. For all controls that you want to access using the Tab key, specify WS_TABSTOP in the window style.

If you refer back to the table beginning on page 495, you'll notice that many of the controls include WS_TABSTOP as a default, while others do not. Generally the controls that do not include the WS_TABSTOP style (particularly the static controls) should not get the input focus because they can't do anything with it. Unless you set the input focus to a specific control in a dialog box during processing of the WM_INITDIALOG message and return FALSE from the message, Windows sets the input focus to the first control in the dialog box that has the WS_TABSTOP style.

The second keyboard interface that Windows adds to a dialog box involves the cursor movement keys. This interface is of particular importance with radio buttons. After you use the Tab key to move to the currently checked radio button within a group, you need to use the cursor movement keys to change the input focus from that radio button to other radio buttons within the group. You accomplish this by using the WS_GROUP window style. For a particular series of controls in the dialog box template, Windows will use the cursor movement keys to shift the input focus from the first control that has the WS_GROUP style up to, but not including, the next control that has the WS_GROUP style. Windows will cycle from the last control in a dialog box to the first control, if necessary, to find the end of the group.

By default, the controls LTEXT, CTEXT, RTEXT, and ICON include the WS_GROUP style, which conveniently marks the end of a group. You often have to add WS_GROUP styles to other types of controls.

Look at the dialog box template in ABOUT2.RC. The four controls that have the WS_TABSTOP style are the first radio buttons of each group (explicitly included) and the two push buttons (by default). When you first invoke the dialog box, these are the four controls you can move among using the Tab key.

Within each group of radio buttons, you use the cursor movement keys to change the input focus and the check mark. For example, the first radio button (Black) in the Color group box and the Figure group box have the WS_GROUP style. This means that you can use the cursor movement keys to move the focus from the Black radio button up to, but not including, the Figure group box. Similarly, the first radio button (Rectangle) in the Figure group box and DEFPUSHBUTTON have the WS_GROUP style, so you can use the cursor movement keys to move between the two radio buttons in this group: Rectangle and Ellipse. Both push buttons get the WS_GROUP style to prevent the cursor movement keys from doing anything when the push buttons have the input focus.

When using ABOUT2, the dialog box manager in Windows performs some magic in the two groups of radio buttons. As expected, the cursor movement keys within a group of radio buttons shift the input focus and send a WM_COMMAND message to the dialog box procedure. But when you change the checked radio button within the group, Windows also assigns the newly checked radio button the WS_TABSTOP style. The next time you tab to that group, Windows will set the input focus to the checked radio button.

An ampersand (&) in the text field causes the letter that follows to be underlined and adds another keyboard interface. You can move the input focus to any of the radio buttons by pressing the underlined letter. By pressing C (for the Color group box) or F (for the Figure group box), you can move the input focus to the currently checked radio button in that group.

Although programmers normally let the dialog box manager take care of all this, Windows includes two functions that let you search for the next or previous tab stop or group item. These functions are

```
hwndCtrl = GetNextDlgTabItem (hDlg, hwndCtrl, bPrevious) ;
```

and

```
hwndCtrl = GetNextDlgGroupItem (hDlg, hwndCtrl, bPrevious) ;
```

If *bPrevious* is TRUE, the functions return the previous tab stop or group item; if FALSE, they return the next tab stop or group item.

Painting on the Dialog Box

ABOUT2 also does something relatively unusual: it paints on the dialog box. Let's see how this works. Within the dialog box template in ABOUT2.RC, a blank text control is defined with a position and size for the area we want to paint:

```
LTEXT  ""  IDC_PAINT, 114, 67, 72, 72
```

This area is 18 characters wide and 9 characters high. Because this control has no text, all that the window procedure for the "static" class does is erase the background when the child window control has to be repainted.

When the current color or figure selection changes or when the dialog box itself gets a WM_PAINT message, the dialog box procedure calls *PaintTheBlock*, which is a function in ABOUT2.C:

```
PaintTheBlock (hCtrlBlock, iColor, iFigure) ;
```

In *AboutDlgProc*, the window handle *hCtrlBlock* had been set during the processing of the WM_INITDIALOG message:

```
hCtrlBlock = GetDlgItem (hDlg, IDD_PAINT) ;
```

Here's the *PaintTheBlock* function:

```
void PaintTheBlock (HWND hCtrl, int iColor, int iFigure)
{
     InvalidateRect (hCtrl, NULL, TRUE) ;
     UpdateWindow (hCtrl) ;
     PaintWindow (hCtrl, iColor, iFigure) ;
}
```

This invalidates the child window control, generates a WM_PAINT message to the control window procedure, and then calls another function in ABOUT2 called *PaintWindow*.

The *PaintWindow* function obtains a device context handle for *hCtrl* and draws the selected figure, filling it with a colored brush based on the selected color. The size of the child window control is obtained from *GetClientRect*. Although the dialog box template defines the size of the control in terms of characters, *GetClientRect* obtains the dimensions in pixels. You can also use the function *MapDialogRect* to convert the character coordinates in the dialog box to pixel coordinates in the client area.

We're not really painting the dialog box's client area—we're actually painting the client area of the child window control. Whenever the dialog box gets a WM_PAINT message, the child window control is invalidated and then updated to make it believe that its client area is now valid. We then paint on top of it.

Using Other Functions with Dialog Boxes

Most functions that you can use with child windows you can also use with controls in a dialog box. For instance, if you're feeling devious, you can use *MoveWindow* to move the controls around the dialog box and force the user to chase them around with the mouse.

Sometimes you need to dynamically enable or disable certain controls in a dialog box, depending on the settings of other controls. This call,

```
EnableWindow (hwndCtrl, bEnable) ;
```

enables the control when *bEnable* is TRUE (nonzero) and disables it when *bEnable* is FALSE (0). When a control is disabled, it receives no keyboard or mouse input. Don't disable a control that has the input focus.

Defining Your Own Controls

Although Windows assumes much of the responsibility for maintaining the dialog box and child window controls, various methods let you slip some of your own code into this process. We've already seen a method that allows you to paint on the surface of a dialog box. You can also use window subclassing (discussed in Chapter 9) to alter the operation of child window controls.

You can also define your own child window controls and use them in a dialog box. For example, suppose you don't particularly care for the normal rectangular push buttons and would prefer to create elliptical push buttons. You can do this by registering a window class and using your own window procedure to process messages for your customized child window. You then specify this window class in Developer Studio in the Properties dialog box associated with a custom control. This translates into a CONTROL statement in the dialog box template. The ABOUT3 program, shown in Figure 11-5, does exactly that.

ABOUT3.C

```
/*------------------------------------------------
   ABOUT3.C -- About Box Demo Program No. 3
               (c) Charles Petzold, 1998
   ------------------------------------------*/

#include <windows.h>
#include "resource.h"
```

Figure 11-5. *The ABOUT3 program.*

(continued)

Figure 11-5. *continued*

```
LRESULT CALLBACK WndProc (HWND, UINT, WPARAM, LPARAM) ;
BOOL    CALLBACK AboutDlgProc (HWND, UINT, WPARAM, LPARAM) ;
LRESULT CALLBACK EllipPushWndProc (HWND, UINT, WPARAM, LPARAM) ;

int WINAPI WinMain (HINSTANCE hInstance, HINSTANCE hPrevInstance,
                    PSTR szCmdLine, int iCmdShow)
{
     static TCHAR szAppName[] = TEXT ("About3") ;
     MSG          msg ;
     HWND         hwnd ;
     WNDCLASS     wndclass ;

     wndclass.style         = CS_HREDRAW | CS_VREDRAW ;
     wndclass.lpfnWndProc   = WndProc ;
     wndclass.cbClsExtra    = 0 ;
     wndclass.cbWndExtra    = 0 ;
     wndclass.hInstance     = hInstance ;
     wndclass.hIcon         = LoadIcon (hInstance, szAppName) ;
     wndclass.hCursor       = LoadCursor (NULL, IDC_ARROW) ;
     wndclass.hbrBackground = (HBRUSH) GetStockObject (WHITE_BRUSH) ;
     wndclass.lpszMenuName  = szAppName ;
     wndclass.lpszClassName = szAppName ;

     if (!RegisterClass (&wndclass))
     {
          MessageBox (NULL, TEXT ("This program requires Windows NT!"),
                      szAppName, MB_ICONERROR) ;
          return 0 ;
     }

     wndclass.style         = CS_HREDRAW | CS_VREDRAW ;
     wndclass.lpfnWndProc   = EllipPushWndProc ;
     wndclass.cbClsExtra    = 0 ;
     wndclass.cbWndExtra    = 0 ;
     wndclass.hInstance     = hInstance ;
     wndclass.hIcon         = NULL ;
     wndclass.hCursor       = LoadCursor (NULL, IDC_ARROW) ;
     wndclass.hbrBackground = (HBRUSH) (COLOR_BTNFACE + 1) ;
     wndclass.lpszMenuName  = NULL ;
     wndclass.lpszClassName = TEXT ("EllipPush") ;

     RegisterClass (&wndclass) ;
```

```
        hwnd = CreateWindow (szAppName, TEXT ("About Box Demo Program"),
                             WS_OVERLAPPEDWINDOW,
                             CW_USEDEFAULT, CW_USEDEFAULT,
                             CW_USEDEFAULT, CW_USEDEFAULT,
                             NULL, NULL, hInstance, NULL) ;

        ShowWindow (hwnd, iCmdShow) ;
        UpdateWindow (hwnd) ;

        while (GetMessage (&msg, NULL, 0, 0))
        {
             TranslateMessage (&msg) ;
             DispatchMessage (&msg) ;
        }
        return msg.wParam ;
}

LRESULT CALLBACK WndProc (HWND hwnd, UINT message, WPARAM wParam, LPARAM lParam)
{
        static HINSTANCE hInstance ;

        switch (message)
        {
        case WM_CREATE :
             hInstance = ((LPCREATESTRUCT) lParam)->hInstance ;
             return 0 ;

        case WM_COMMAND :
             switch (LOWORD (wParam))
             {
             case IDM_APP_ABOUT :
                  DialogBox (hInstance, TEXT ("AboutBox"), hwnd, AboutDlgProc) ;
                  return 0 ;
             }
             break ;

        case WM_DESTROY :
             PostQuitMessage (0) ;
             return 0 ;
        }
        return DefWindowProc (hwnd, message, wParam, lParam) ;
}

BOOL CALLBACK AboutDlgProc (HWND hDlg, UINT message,
                            WPARAM wParam, LPARAM lParam)
```

(continued)

Figure 11-5. *continued*

```
{
    switch (message)
    {
    case WM_INITDIALOG :
        return TRUE ;

    case WM_COMMAND :
        switch (LOWORD (wParam))
        {
        case IDOK :
            EndDialog (hDlg, 0) ;
            return TRUE ;
        }
        break ;
    }
    return FALSE ;
}

LRESULT CALLBACK EllipPushWndProc (HWND hwnd, UINT message,
                                   WPARAM wParam, LPARAM lParam)
{
    TCHAR       szText[40] ;
    HBRUSH      hBrush ;
    HDC         hdc ;
    PAINTSTRUCT ps ;
    RECT        rect ;

    switch (message)
    {
    case WM_PAINT :
        GetClientRect (hwnd, &rect) ;
        GetWindowText (hwnd, szText, sizeof (szText)) ;

        hdc = BeginPaint (hwnd, &ps) ;

        hBrush = CreateSolidBrush (GetSysColor (COLOR_WINDOW)) ;
        hBrush = (HBRUSH) SelectObject (hdc, hBrush) ;
        SetBkColor (hdc, GetSysColor (COLOR_WINDOW)) ;
        SetTextColor (hdc, GetSysColor (COLOR_WINDOWTEXT)) ;

        Ellipse (hdc, rect.left, rect.top, rect.right, rect.bottom) ;
        DrawText (hdc, szText, -1, &rect,
                  DT_SINGLELINE | DT_CENTER | DT_VCENTER) ;
```

```
        DeleteObject (SelectObject (hdc, hBrush)) ;

        EndPaint (hwnd, &ps) ;
        return 0 ;

    case WM_KEYUP :
        if (wParam != VK_SPACE)
            break ;
                                        // fall through
    case WM_LBUTTONUP :
        SendMessage (GetParent (hwnd), WM_COMMAND,
            GetWindowLong (hwnd, GWL_ID), (LPARAM) hwnd) ;
        return 0 ;
    }
    return DefWindowProc (hwnd, message, wParam, lParam) ;
}
```

ABOUT3.RC (excerpts)

```
//Microsoft Developer Studio generated resource script.

#include "resource.h"
#include "afxres.h"

/////////////////////////////////////////////////////////////////////////
// Dialog

ABOUTBOX DIALOG DISCARDABLE  32, 32, 180, 100
STYLE DS_MODALFRAME | WS_POPUP
FONT 8, "MS Sans Serif"
BEGIN
    CONTROL         "OK",IDOK,"EllipPush",WS_GROUP | WS_TABSTOP,73,79,32,14
    ICON            "ABOUT3",IDC_STATIC,7,7,20,20
    CTEXT           "About3",IDC_STATIC,40,12,100,8
    CTEXT           "About Box Demo Program",IDC_STATIC,7,40,166,8
    CTEXT           "(c) Charles Petzold, 1998",IDC_STATIC,7,52,166,8
END


/////////////////////////////////////////////////////////////////////////
// Menu

ABOUT3 MENU DISCARDABLE
BEGIN
```

(continued)

Figure 11-5. *continued*

```
    POPUP "&Help"
    BEGIN
        MENUITEM "&About About3...",              IDM_APP_ABOUT
    END
END


///////////////////////////////////////////////////////////////////////////
// Icon

ABOUT3                  ICON    DISCARDABLE     "icon1.ico"
```

RESOURCE.H (excerpts)

```
// Microsoft Developer Studio generated include file.
// Used by About3.rc

#define IDM_APP_ABOUT                   40001
#define IDC_STATIC                      -1
```

ABOUT3.ICO

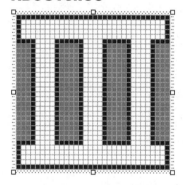

The window class we'll be registering is called EllipPush ("elliptical push button"). In the dialog editor in Developer Studio, delete both the Cancel and OK buttons. To add a control based on this window class, select Custom Control from the Controls toolbar. In the Properties dialog for this control, type EllipPush in the Class field. Rather than a DEF-PUSHBUTTON statement appearing in the dialog box template, you'll see a CONTROL statement that specifies this window class:

```
CONTROL "OK" IDOK, "EllipPush", TABGRP, 64, 60, 32, 14
```

The dialog box manager uses this window class in a *CreateWindow* call when creating the child window control in the dialog box.

The ABOUT3.C program registers the EllipPush window class in *WinMain*:

```
wndclass.style         = CS_HREDRAW | CS_VREDRAW ;
wndclass.lpfnWndProc   = EllipPushWndProc ;
wndclass.cbClsExtra    = 0 ;
wndclass.cbWndExtra    = 0 ;
wndclass.hInstance     = hInstance ;
wndclass.hIcon         = NULL ;
wndclass.hCursor       = LoadCursor (NULL, IDC_ARROW) ;
wndclass.hbrBackground = (HBRUSH) (COLOR_WINDOW + 1) ;
wndclass.lpszMenuName  = NULL ;
wndclass.lpszClassName = TEXT ("EllipPush") ;

RegisterClass (&wndclass) ;
```

The window class specifies that the window procedure is *EllipPushWndProc*, which is also in ABOUT3.C.

The *EllipPushWndProc* window procedure processes only three messages: WM_PAINT, WM_KEYUP, and WM_LBUTTONUP. During the WM_PAINT message, it obtains the size of its window from *GetClientRect* and obtains the text that appears in the push button from *GetWindowText*. It uses the Windows functions *Ellipse* and *DrawText* to draw the ellipse and the text.

The processing of the WM_KEYUP and WM_LBUTTONUP messages is simple:

```
case WM_KEYUP :
    if (wParam != VK_SPACE)
        break ;
                            // fall through
case WM_LBUTTONUP :
    SendMessage (GetParent (hwnd), WM_COMMAND,
        GetWindowLong (hwnd, GWL_ID), (LPARAM) hwnd) ;
    return 0 ;
```

The window procedure obtains the handle of its parent window (the dialog box) using *GetParent* and sends a WM_COMMAND message with *wParam* equal to the control's ID. The ID is obtained using *GetWindowLong*. The dialog box window procedure then passes this message on to the dialog box procedure within ABOUT3. The result is a customized push button, as shown in Figure 11-6 on the following page. You can use this same method to create other customized controls for dialog boxes.

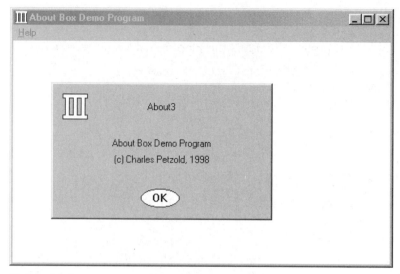

Figure 11-6. *A customized push button created by ABOUT3.*

Is that all there is to it? Well, not really. *EllipPushWndProc* is a bare-bones version of the logic generally involved in maintaining a child window control. For instance, the button doesn't flash like normal push buttons. To invert the colors on the interior of the push button, the window procedure would have to process WM_KEYDOWN (from the Spacebar) and WM_LBUTTONDOWN messages. The window procedure should also capture the mouse on a WM_LBUTTONDOWN message and release the mouse (and return the button's interior color to normal) if the mouse is moved outside the child window's client area while the button is still depressed. Only if the button is released while the mouse is captured should the child window send a WM_COMMAND message back to its parent.

EllipPushWndProc also does not process WM_ENABLE messages. As mentioned above, a dialog box procedure can disable a window by using the *EnableWindow* function. The child window would then display gray rather than black text to indicate that it has been disabled and cannot receive messages.

If the window procedure for a child window control needs to store data that are different for each created window, it can do so by using a positive value of *cbWndExtra* in the window class structure. This reserves space in the internal window structure that can be accessed by using *SetWindowLong* and *GetWindowLong*.

MODELESS DIALOG BOXES

At the beginning of this chapter, I explained that dialog boxes can be either "modal" or "modeless." So far we've been looking at modal dialog boxes, the more common of the two types. Modal dialog boxes (except system modal dialog boxes) allow the user to switch between the dialog box and other programs. However, the user cannot switch to another window in the program that initiated the dialog box until the modal dialog box is destroyed. Modeless dialog boxes allow the user to switch between the dialog box and the window that created it as well as between the dialog box and other programs. The modeless dialog box is thus more akin to the regular popup windows that your program might create.

Modeless dialog boxes are preferred when the user would find it convenient to keep the dialog box displayed for a while. For instance, word processors often use modeless dialog boxes for the text Find and Change dialogs. If the Find dialog box were modal, the user would have to choose Find from the menu, enter the string to be found, end the dialog box to return to the document, and then repeat the entire process to search for another occurrence of the same string. Allowing the user to switch between the document and the dialog box is much more convenient.

As you've seen, modal dialog boxes are created using *DialogBox*. The function returns a value only after the dialog box is destroyed. It returns the value specified in the second parameter of the *EndDialog* call that was used within the dialog box procedure to terminate the dialog box. Modeless dialog boxes are created using *CreateDialog*. This function takes the same parameters as *DialogBox*:

```
hDlgModeless = CreateDialog (hInstance, szTemplate,
                             hwndParent, DialogProc) ;
```

The difference is that the *CreateDialog* function returns immediately with the window handle of the dialog box. Normally, you store this window handle in a global variable.

Although the use of the names *DialogBox* with modal dialog boxes and *CreateDialog* with modeless dialog boxes may seem arbitrary, you can remember which is which by keeping in mind that modeless dialog boxes are similar to normal windows. *CreateDialog* should remind you of the *CreateWindow* function, which creates normal windows.

Differences Between Modal and Modeless Dialog Boxes

Working with modeless dialog boxes is similar to working with modal dialog boxes, but there are several important differences.

First, modeless dialog boxes usually include a caption bar and a system menu box. These are actually the default options when you create a dialog box in Developer Studio. The STYLE statement in the dialog box template for a modeless dialog box will look something like this:

```
STYLE WS_POPUP ¦ WS_CAPTION ¦ WS_SYSMENU ¦ WS_VISIBLE
```

The caption bar and system menu allow the user to move the modeless dialog box to another area of the display using either the mouse or the keyboard. You don't normally provide a caption bar and system menu with a modal dialog box, because the user can't do anything in the underlying window anyway.

The second big difference: Notice that the WS_VISIBLE style is included in our sample STYLE statement. In Developer Studio, select this option from the More Styles tab of the Dialog Properties dialog. If you omit WS_VISIBLE, you must call *ShowWindow* after the *CreateDialog* call:

```
hDlgModeless = CreateDialog (  . . .  ) ;
ShowWindow (hDlgModeless, SW_SHOW) ;
```

If you neither include WS_VISIBLE nor call *ShowWindow*, the modeless dialog box will not be displayed. Programmers who have mastered modal dialog boxes often overlook this peculiarity and thus experience difficulties when first trying to create a modeless dialog box.

The third difference: Unlike messages to modal dialog boxes and message boxes, messages to modeless dialog boxes come through your program's message queue. The message queue must be altered to pass these messages to the dialog box window procedure. Here's how you do it: When you use *CreateDialog* to create a modeless dialog box, you should save the dialog box handle returned from the call in a global variable (for instance, *hDlgModeless*). Change your message loop to look like

```
while (GetMessage (&msg, NULL, 0, 0))
{
    if (hDlgModeless == 0 || !IsDialogMessage (hDlgModeless, &msg))
    {
        TranslateMessage (&msg) ;
        DispatchMessage  (&msg) ;
    }
}
```

If the message is intended for the modeless dialog box, then *IsDialogMessage* sends it to the dialog box window procedure and returns TRUE (nonzero); otherwise, it returns FALSE (0). The *TranslateMessage* and *DispatchMessage* functions should be called only if *hDlgModeless* is 0 or if the message is not for the dialog box. If you use keyboard accelerators for your program's window, the message loop looks like this:

```
while (GetMessage (&msg, NULL, 0, 0))
{
    if (hDlgModeless == 0 || !IsDialogMessage (hDlgModeless, &msg))
    {
        if (!TranslateAccelerator (hwnd, hAccel, &msg))
        {
            TranslateMessage (&msg) ;
            DispatchMessage  (&msg) ;
        }
    }
}
```

Because global variables are initialized to 0, *hDlgModeless* will be 0 until the dialog box is created, thus ensuring that *IsDialogMessage* is not called with an invalid window handle. You must take the same precaution when you destroy the modeless dialog box, as explained below.

The *hDlgModeless* variable can also be used by other parts of the program as a test of the existence of the modeless dialog box. For example, other windows in the program can send messages to the dialog box while *hDlgModeless* is not equal to 0.

The final big difference: Use *DestroyWindow* rather than *EndDialog* to end a modeless dialog box. When you call *DestroyWindow*, set the *hDlgModeless* global variable to NULL.

The user customarily terminates a modeless dialog box by choosing Close from the system menu. Although the Close option is enabled, the dialog box window procedure within Windows does not process the WM_CLOSE message. You must do this yourself in the dialog box procedure:

```
case WM_CLOSE :
    DestroyWindow (hDlg) ;
    hDlgModeless = NULL ;
    break ;
```

Note the difference between these two window handles: the *hDlg* parameter to *Destroy-Window* is the parameter passed to the dialog box procedure; *hDlgModeless* is the global variable returned from *CreateDialog* that you test within the message loop.

You can also allow a user to close a modeless dialog box using push buttons. Use the same logic as for the WM_CLOSE message. Any information that the dialog box must "return" to the window that created it can be stored in global variables. If you'd prefer not using global variables, you can create the modeless dialog box by using *CreateDialogParam* and pass to it a structure pointer, as described earlier.

The New COLORS Program

The COLORS1 program described in Chapter 9 created nine child windows to display three scroll bars and six text items. At that time, the program was one of the more complex we had developed. Converting COLORS1 to use a modeless dialog box makes the program—and particularly its *WndProc* function—almost ridiculously simple. The revised COLORS2 program is shown in Figure 11-7.

COLORS2.C

```
/*---------------------------------------------------
   COLORS2.C -- Version using Modeless Dialog Box
                (c) Charles Petzold, 1998
   --------------------------------------------------*/
```

Figure 11-7. *The COLORS2 program.* *(continued)*

Figure 11-7. *continued*

```
#include <windows.h>

LRESULT CALLBACK WndProc     (HWND, UINT, WPARAM, LPARAM) ;
BOOL    CALLBACK ColorScrDlg (HWND, UINT, WPARAM, LPARAM) ;

HWND hDlgModeless ;

int WINAPI WinMain (HINSTANCE hInstance, HINSTANCE hPrevInstance,
                    PSTR szCmdLine, int iCmdShow)
{
     static TCHAR szAppName[] = TEXT ("Colors2") ;
     HWND        hwnd ;
     MSG         msg ;
     WNDCLASS    wndclass ;

     wndclass.style         = CS_HREDRAW | CS_VREDRAW ;
     wndclass.lpfnWndProc   = WndProc ;
     wndclass.cbClsExtra    = 0 ;
     wndclass.cbWndExtra    = 0 ;
     wndclass.hInstance     = hInstance ;
     wndclass.hIcon         = LoadIcon (NULL, IDI_APPLICATION) ;
     wndclass.hCursor       = LoadCursor (NULL, IDC_ARROW) ;
     wndclass.hbrBackground = CreateSolidBrush (0L) ;
     wndclass.lpszMenuName  = NULL ;
     wndclass.lpszClassName = szAppName ;

     if (!RegisterClass (&wndclass))
     {
          MessageBox (NULL, TEXT ("This program requires Windows NT!"),
                      szAppName, MB_ICONERROR) ;
          return 0 ;
     }

     hwnd = CreateWindow (szAppName, TEXT ("Color Scroll"),
                          WS_OVERLAPPEDWINDOW | WS_CLIPCHILDREN,
                          CW_USEDEFAULT, CW_USEDEFAULT,
                          CW_USEDEFAULT, CW_USEDEFAULT,
                          NULL, NULL, hInstance, NULL) ;

     ShowWindow (hwnd, iCmdShow) ;
     UpdateWindow (hwnd) ;

     hDlgModeless = CreateDialog (hInstance, TEXT ("ColorScrDlg"),
                                  hwnd, ColorScrDlg) ;
```

```
        while (GetMessage (&msg, NULL, 0, 0))
        {
                if (hDlgModeless == 0 || !IsDialogMessage (hDlgModeless, &msg))
                {
                        TranslateMessage (&msg) ;
                        DispatchMessage  (&msg) ;
                }
        }
        return msg.wParam ;
}

LRESULT CALLBACK WndProc (HWND hwnd, UINT message, WPARAM wParam, LPARAM lParam)
{
        switch (message)
        {
        case WM_DESTROY :
                DeleteObject ((HGDIOBJ) SetClassLong (hwnd, GCL_HBRBACKGROUND,
                                  (LONG) GetStockObject (WHITE_BRUSH))) ;
                PostQuitMessage (0) ;
                return 0 ;
        }
        return DefWindowProc (hwnd, message, wParam, lParam) ;
}

BOOL CALLBACK ColorScrDlg (HWND hDlg, UINT message,
                           WPARAM wParam, LPARAM lParam)
{
        static int iColor[3] ;
        HWND       hwndParent, hCtrl ;
        int        iCtrlID, iIndex ;

        switch (message)
        {
        case WM_INITDIALOG :
                for (iCtrlID = 10 ; iCtrlID < 13 ; iCtrlID++)
                {
                        hCtrl = GetDlgItem (hDlg, iCtrlID) ;
                        SetScrollRange (hCtrl, SB_CTL, 0, 255, FALSE) ;
                        SetScrollPos   (hCtrl, SB_CTL, 0, FALSE) ;
                }
                return TRUE ;

        case WM_VSCROLL :
                hCtrl   = (HWND) lParam ;
                iCtrlID = GetWindowLong (hCtrl, GWL_ID) ;
```

(continued)

Figure 11-7. *continued*

```
        iIndex  = iCtrlID - 10 ;
        hwndParent = GetParent (hDlg) ;

        switch (LOWORD (wParam))
        {
        case SB_PAGEDOWN :
            iColor[iIndex] += 15 ;          // fall through
        case SB_LINEDOWN :
            iColor[iIndex] = min (255, iColor[iIndex] + 1) ;
            break ;
        case SB_PAGEUP :
            iColor[iIndex] -= 15 ;          // fall through
        case SB_LINEUP :
            iColor[iIndex] = max (0, iColor[iIndex] - 1) ;
            break ;
        case SB_TOP :
            iColor[iIndex] = 0 ;
            break ;
        case SB_BOTTOM :
            iColor[iIndex] = 255 ;
            break ;
        case SB_THUMBPOSITION :
        case SB_THUMBTRACK :
            iColor[iIndex] = HIWORD (wParam) ;
            break ;
        default :
            return FALSE ;
        }
        SetScrollPos  (hCtrl, SB_CTL,     iColor[iIndex], TRUE) ;
        SetDlgItemInt (hDlg,  iCtrlID + 3, iColor[iIndex], FALSE) ;

        DeleteObject ((HGDIOBJ) SetClassLong (hwndParent, GCL_HBRBACKGROUND,
                        (LONG) CreateSolidBrush (
                            RGB (iColor[0], iColor[1], iColor[2])))) ;

        InvalidateRect (hwndParent, NULL, TRUE) ;
        return TRUE ;
    }
    return FALSE ;
}
```

COLORS2.RC (excerpts)

```
//Microsoft Developer Studio generated resource script.

#include "resource.h"
#include "afxres.h"


/////////////////////////////////////////////////////////////////////////////
// Dialog

COLORSCRDLG DIALOG DISCARDABLE  16, 16, 120, 141
STYLE DS_MODALFRAME | WS_POPUP | WS_VISIBLE | WS_CAPTION
CAPTION "Color Scroll Scrollbars"
FONT 8, "MS Sans Serif"
BEGIN
    CTEXT           "&Red",IDC_STATIC,8,8,24,8,NOT WS_GROUP
    SCROLLBAR       10,8,20,24,100,SBS_VERT | WS_TABSTOP
    CTEXT           "0",13,8,124,24,8,NOT WS_GROUP
    CTEXT           "&Green",IDC_STATIC,48,8,24,8,NOT WS_GROUP
    SCROLLBAR       11,48,20,24,100,SBS_VERT | WS_TABSTOP
    CTEXT           "0",14,48,124,24,8,NOT WS_GROUP
    CTEXT           "&Blue",IDC_STATIC,89,8,24,8,NOT WS_GROUP
    SCROLLBAR       12,89,20,24,100,SBS_VERT | WS_TABSTOP
    CTEXT           "0",15,89,124,24,8,NOT WS_GROUP
END
```

RESOURCE.H (excerpts)

```
// Microsoft Developer Studio generated include file.
// Used by Colors2.rc

#define IDC_STATIC                      -1
```

Although the original COLORS1 program displayed scroll bars that were based on the size of the window, the new version keeps them at a constant size within the modeless dialog box, as shown in Figure 11-8 on the following page.

When you create the dialog box template, use explicit ID numbers of 10, 11, and 12 for the three scroll bars, and 13, 14, and 15 for the three static text fields displaying the current values of the scroll bars. Give each scroll bar a Tab Stop style, but remove the Group style from all six static text fields.

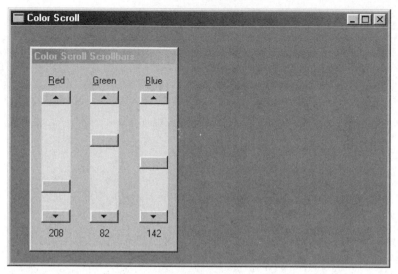

Figure 11-8. *The COLORS2 display.*

The modeless dialog box is created in COLORS2's *WinMain* function following the *ShowWindow* call for the program's main window. Note that the window style for the main window includes WS_CLIPCHILDREN, which allows the program to repaint the main window without erasing the dialog box.

The dialog box window handle returned from *CreateDialog* is stored in the global variable *hDlgModeless* and tested during the message loop, as described above. In this program, however, it isn't necessary to store the handle in a global variable or to test the value before calling *IsDialogMessage*. The message loop could have been written like this:

```
while (GetMessage (&msg, NULL, 0, 0))
{
     if (!IsDialogMessage (hDlgModeless, &msg))
     {
          TranslateMessage (&msg) ;
          DispatchMessage  (&msg) ;
     }
}
```

Because the dialog box is created before the program enters the message loop and is not destroyed until the program terminates, the value of *hDlgModeless* will always be valid. I included the logic in case you want to add some code to the dialog box window procedure to destroy the dialog box:

```
case WM_CLOSE :
     DestroyWindow (hDlg) ;
     hDlgModeless = NULL ;
     break ;
```

In the original COLORS1 program, *SetWindowText* set the values of the three numeric labels after converting the integers to text with *wsprintf*. The code looked like this:

```
wsprintf (szBuffer, TEXT ("%i"), color[i]) ;
SetWindowText (hwndValue[i], szBuffer) ;
```

The value of *i* was the ID number of the current scroll bar being processed, and *hwndValue* was an array containing the window handles of the three static text child windows for the numeric values of the colors.

The new version uses *SetDlgItemInt* to set each text field of each child window to a number:

```
SetDlgItemInt (hDlg, iCtrlID + 3, color [iCtrlID], FALSE) ;
```

Although *SetDlgItemInt* and its companion, *GetDlgItemInt*, are most often used with edit controls, they can also be used to set the text field of other controls, such as static text controls. The *iCtrlID* variable is the ID number of the scroll bar; adding 3 to the number converts it to the ID for the corresponding numeric label. The third argument is the color value. The fourth argument indicates whether the value in the third argument is to be treated as signed (if the fourth argument is TRUE) or unsigned (if the fourth argument is FALSE). For this program, however, the values range from 0 to 255, so the fourth argument has no effect.

In the process of converting COLORS1 to COLORS2, we passed more and more of the work to Windows. The earlier version called *CreateWindow* 10 times; the new version calls *CreateWindow* once and *CreateDialog* once. But if you think that we've reduced our *CreateWindow* calls to a minimum, get a load of this next program.

HEXCALC: Window or Dialog Box?

Perhaps the epitome of lazy programming is the HEXCALC program, shown in Figure 11-9, beginning on the following page. This program doesn't call *CreateWindow* at all, never processes WM_PAINT messages, never obtains a device context, and never processes mouse messages. Yet it manages to incorporate a 10-function hexadecimal calculator with a full keyboard and mouse interface in fewer than 150 lines of source code. The calculator is shown in Figure 11-10 on page 535.

HEXCALC.C

```
/*-------------------------------------------
   HEXCALC.C -- Hexadecimal Calculator
                (c) Charles Petzold, 1998
   -------------------------------------------*/

#include <windows.h>

LRESULT CALLBACK WndProc (HWND, UINT, WPARAM, LPARAM) ;

int WINAPI WinMain (HINSTANCE hInstance, HINSTANCE hPrevInstance,
                    PSTR szCmdLine, int iCmdShow)
{
    static TCHAR szAppName[] = TEXT ("HexCalc") ;
    HWND         hwnd ;
    MSG          msg ;
    WNDCLASS     wndclass ;

    wndclass.style         = CS_HREDRAW | CS_VREDRAW;
    wndclass.lpfnWndProc   = WndProc ;
    wndclass.cbClsExtra    = 0 ;
    wndclass.cbWndExtra    = DLGWINDOWEXTRA ;     // Note!
    wndclass.hInstance     = hInstance ;
    wndclass.hIcon         = LoadIcon (hInstance, szAppName) ;
    wndclass.hCursor       = LoadCursor (NULL, IDC_ARROW) ;
    wndclass.hbrBackground = (HBRUSH) (COLOR_BTNFACE + 1) ;
    wndclass.lpszMenuName  = NULL ;
    wndclass.lpszClassName = szAppName ;

    if (!RegisterClass (&wndclass))
    {
        MessageBox (NULL, TEXT ("This program requires Windows NT!"),
                    szAppName, MB_ICONERROR) ;
        return 0 ;
    }

    hwnd = CreateDialog (hInstance, szAppName, 0, NULL) ;

    ShowWindow (hwnd, iCmdShow) ;

    while (GetMessage (&msg, NULL, 0, 0))
    {
        TranslateMessage (&msg) ;
        DispatchMessage (&msg) ;
    }
```

Figure 11-9. *The HEXCALC program.*

```
     return msg.wParam ;
}

void ShowNumber (HWND hwnd, UINT iNumber)
{
     TCHAR szBuffer[20] ;

     wsprintf (szBuffer, TEXT ("%X"), iNumber) ;
     SetDlgItemText (hwnd, VK_ESCAPE, szBuffer) ;
}

DWORD CalcIt (UINT iFirstNum, int iOperation, UINT iNum)
{
     switch (iOperation)
     {
     case '=': return iNum ;
     case '+': return iFirstNum +  iNum ;
     case '-': return iFirstNum -  iNum ;
     case '*': return iFirstNum *  iNum ;
     case '&': return iFirstNum &  iNum ;
     case '|': return iFirstNum |  iNum ;
     case '^': return iFirstNum ^  iNum ;
     case '<': return iFirstNum << iNum ;
     case '>': return iFirstNum >> iNum ;
     case '/': return iNum ? iFirstNum / iNum: MAXDWORD ;
     case '%': return iNum ? iFirstNum % iNum: MAXDWORD ;
     default : return 0 ;
     }
}

LRESULT CALLBACK WndProc (HWND hwnd, UINT message, WPARAM wParam, LPARAM lParam)
{
     static BOOL  bNewNumber = TRUE ;
     static int   iOperation = '=' ;
     static UINT  iNumber, iFirstNum ;
     HWND         hButton ;

     switch (message)
     {
     case WM_KEYDOWN:                        // left arrow --> backspace
          if (wParam != VK_LEFT)
               break ;
          wParam = VK_BACK ;
                                             // fall through
```

(continued)

Figure 11-9. *continued*

```
        case WM_CHAR:
             if ((wParam = (WPARAM) CharUpper ((TCHAR *) wParam)) == VK_RETURN)
                 wParam = '=' ;

             if (hButton = GetDlgItem (hwnd, wParam))
             {
                 SendMessage (hButton, BM_SETSTATE, 1, 0) ;
                 Sleep (100) ;
                 SendMessage (hButton, BM_SETSTATE, 0, 0) ;
             }
             else
             {
                 MessageBeep (0) ;
                 break ;
             }
                                         // fall through
        case WM_COMMAND:
             SetFocus (hwnd) ;

             if (LOWORD (wParam) == VK_BACK)          // backspace
                 ShowNumber (hwnd, iNumber /= 16) ;

             else if (LOWORD (wParam) == VK_ESCAPE)   // escape
                 ShowNumber (hwnd, iNumber = 0) ;

             else if (isxdigit (LOWORD (wParam)))     // hex digit
             {
                 if (bNewNumber)
                 {
                     iFirstNum = iNumber ;
                     iNumber = 0 ;
                 }
                 bNewNumber = FALSE ;

                 if (iNumber <= MAXDWORD >> 4)
                     ShowNumber (hwnd, iNumber = 16 * iNumber + wParam -
                     (isdigit (wParam) ? '0': 'A' - 10)) ;
                 else
                     MessageBeep (0) ;
             }
             else                                     // operation
             {
                 if (!bNewNumber)
                     ShowNumber (hwnd, iNumber =
```

```
                          CalcIt (iFirstNum, iOperation, iNumber)) ;
               bNewNumber = TRUE ;
               iOperation = LOWORD (wParam) ;
          }
          return 0 ;

     case WM_DESTROY:
          PostQuitMessage (0) ;
          return 0 ;
     }
     return DefWindowProc (hwnd, message, wParam, lParam) ;
}
```

HEXCALC.RC (excerpts)

```
//Microsoft Developer Studio generated resource script.

#include "resource.h"
#include "afxres.h"


/////////////////////////////////////////////////////////////////////////////
// Icon

HEXCALC                 ICON     DISCARDABLE      "HexCalc.ico"

/////////////////////////////////////////////////////////////////////////////

#include "hexcalc.dlg"
```

HEXCALC.DLG

```
/*---------------------------
   HEXCALC.DLG dialog script
  ---------------------------*/

HexCalc DIALOG -1, -1, 102, 122
STYLE WS_OVERLAPPED | WS_CAPTION | WS_SYSMENU | WS_MINIMIZEBOX
CLASS "HexCalc"
CAPTION "Hex Calculator"
{
     PUSHBUTTON "D",        68,  8,  24, 14, 14
     PUSHBUTTON "A",        65,  8,  40, 14, 14
     PUSHBUTTON "7",        55,  8,  56, 14, 14
```

(continued)

Figure 11-9. *continued*

```
    PUSHBUTTON "4",      52,  8,  72, 14, 14
    PUSHBUTTON "1",      49,  8,  88, 14, 14
    PUSHBUTTON "0",      48,  8, 104, 14, 14
    PUSHBUTTON "0",      27, 26,   4, 50, 14
    PUSHBUTTON "E",      69, 26,  24, 14, 14
    PUSHBUTTON "B",      66, 26,  40, 14, 14
    PUSHBUTTON "8",      56, 26,  56, 14, 14
    PUSHBUTTON "5",      53, 26,  72, 14, 14
    PUSHBUTTON "2",      50, 26,  88, 14, 14
    PUSHBUTTON "Back",    8, 26, 104, 32, 14
    PUSHBUTTON "C",      67, 44,  40, 14, 14
    PUSHBUTTON "F",      70, 44,  24, 14, 14
    PUSHBUTTON "9",      57, 44,  56, 14, 14
    PUSHBUTTON "6",      54, 44,  72, 14, 14
    PUSHBUTTON "3",      51, 44,  88, 14, 14
    PUSHBUTTON "+",      43, 62,  24, 14, 14
    PUSHBUTTON "-",      45, 62,  40, 14, 14
    PUSHBUTTON "*",      42, 62,  56, 14, 14
    PUSHBUTTON "/",      47, 62,  72, 14, 14
    PUSHBUTTON "%",      37, 62,  88, 14, 14
    PUSHBUTTON "Equals", 61, 62, 104, 32, 14
    PUSHBUTTON "&&",     38, 80,  24, 14, 14
    PUSHBUTTON "|",     124, 80,  40, 14, 14
    PUSHBUTTON "^",      94, 80,  56, 14, 14
    PUSHBUTTON "<",      60, 80,  72, 14, 14
    PUSHBUTTON ">",      62, 80,  88, 14, 14
}
```

HEXCALC.ICO

Figure 11-10. *The HEXCALC display.*

HEXCALC is a normal infix notation calculator that uses C notation for the operations. It works with unsigned 32-bit integers and does addition, subtraction, multiplication, division, and remainders; bitwise AND, OR, and exclusive OR operations; and left and right bit shifts. Division by 0 causes the result to be set to FFFFFFFF.

You can use either the mouse or keyboard with HEXCALC. You begin by "clicking in" or typing the first number (up to eight hexadecimal digits), then the operation, and then the second number. You can then show the result by clicking the Equals button or by pressing either the Equals key or the Enter key. To correct your entries, use the Back button or the Backspace or Left Arrow key. Click the "display" box or press the Esc key to clear the current entry.

What's so strange about HEXCALC is that the window displayed on the screen seems to be a hybrid of a normal overlapped window and a modeless dialog box. On the one hand, all the messages to HEXCALC are processed in a function called *WndProc* that appears to be a normal window procedure. The function returns a long, it processes the WM_DESTROY message, and it calls *DefWindowProc* just like a normal window procedure. On the other hand, the window is created in *WinMain* with a call to *CreateDialog* that uses a dialog box template defined in HEXCALC.DLG. So is HEXCALC a normal overlapped window or a modeless dialog box?

The simple answer is that a dialog box *is* a window. Normally, Windows uses its own internal window procedure to process messages to a dialog box window. Windows then passes these messages to a dialog box procedure within the program that creates the dialog box. In HEXCALC we are forcing Windows to use the dialog box template to create a window, but we're processing messages to that window ourselves.

Unfortunately, there's something that the dialog box template needs that you can't add in the Dialog Editor in Developer Studio. For this reason, the dialog box template is contained in the HEXCALC.DLG file, which you might guess (correctly) was typed in manually. You can add a text file to any project by picking New from the File menu, picking the Files tab, and selecting Text File from the list of file types. A file such as this, containing additional resource definitions, needs to be included in the resource script. From the View menu, select Resource Includes. This displays a dialog box. In the Compile-time Directives edit field, type

```
#include "hexcalc.dlg"
```

This line will then be inserted into the HEXCALC.RC resource script, as shown above.

A close look at the dialog box template in the HEXCALC.DLG file will reveal how HEXCALC uses its own window procedure for the dialog box. The top of the dialog box template looks like

```
HexCalc DIALOG -1, -1, 102, 122
STYLE WS_OVERLAPPED | WS_CAPTION | WS_SYSMENU | WS_MINIMIZEBOX
CLASS "HexCalc"
CAPTION "Hex Calculator"
```

Notice the identifiers, such as WS_OVERLAPPED and WS_MINIMIZEBOX, which we might use to create a normal window by using a *CreateWindow* call. The CLASS statement is the crucial difference between this dialog box and the others we've created so far (and it is what the Dialog Editor in Developer Studio doesn't allow us to specify). When we omitted this statement in previous dialog box templates, Windows registered a window class for the dialog box and used its own window procedure to process the dialog box messages. The inclusion of a CLASS statement here tells Windows to send the messages elsewhere—specifically, to the window procedure specified in the HexCalc window class.

The HexCalc window class is registered in the *WinMain* function of HEXCALC, just like a window class for a normal window. However, note this very important difference: the *cbWndExtra* field of the WNDCLASS structure is set to DLGWINDOWEXTRA. This is essential for dialog procedures that you register yourself.

After registering the window class, *WinMain* calls *CreateDialog*:

```
hwnd = CreateDialog (hInstance, szAppName, 0, NULL) ;
```

The second argument (the string "HexCalc") is the name of the dialog box template. The third argument, which is normally the window handle of the parent window, is set to 0 because the window has no parent. The last argument, which is normally the address of the dialog procedure, isn't required because Windows won't be processing the messages and therefore can't send them to a dialog procedure.

This *CreateDialog* call, in conjunction with the dialog box template, is effectively translated by Windows into a *CreateWindow* call that does the equivalent of

```
hwnd = CreateWindow (TEXT ("HexCalc"), TEXT ("Hex Calculator"),
        WS_OVERLAPPED | WS_CAPTION | WS_SYSMENU | WS_MINIMIZEBOX,
        CW_USEDEFAULT, CW_USEDEFAULT,
        102 * 4 / cxChar, 122 * 8 / cyChar,
        NULL, NULL, hInstance, NULL) ;
```

where the *cxChar* and *cyChar* variables are the width and height of the dialog font character.

We reap an enormous benefit from letting Windows make this *CreateWindow* call: Windows will not stop at creating the one popup window but will also call *CreateWindow* for all 29 child window push-button controls defined in the dialog box template. All these controls send WM_COMMAND messages to the window procedure of the parent window, which is none other than *WndProc*. This is an excellent technique for creating a window that must contain a collection of child windows.

Here's another way HEXCALC's code size is kept down to a minimum: You'll notice that HEXCALC contains no header file normally required to define the identifiers for all the child window controls in the dialog box template. We can dispense with this file because the ID number for each of the push-button controls is set to the ASCII code of the text that appears in the control. This means that *WndProc* can treat WM_COMMAND messages and WM_CHAR messages in much the same way. In each case, the low word of *wParam* is the ASCII code of the button.

Of course, a little massaging of the keyboard messages is necessary. *WndProc* traps WM_KEYDOWN messages to translate the Left Arrow key to a Backspace key. During processing of WM_CHAR messages, *WndProc* converts the character code to uppercase and the Enter key to the ASCII code for the Equals key.

Calling *GetDlgItem* checks the validity of a WM_CHAR message. If the *GetDlgItem* function returns 0, the keyboard character is not one of the ID numbers defined in the dialog box template. If the character is one of the IDs, however, the appropriate button is flashed by sending it a couple of BM_SETSTATE messages:

```
if (hButton = GetDlgItem (hwnd, wParam))
{
    SendMessage (hButton, BM_SETSTATE, 1, 0) ;
    Sleep (100) ;
    SendMessage (hButton, BM_SETSTATE, 0, 0) ;
}
```

This adds a nice touch to HEXCALC's keyboard interface, and with a minimum of effort. The *Sleep* function suspends the program for 100 milliseconds. This prevents the buttons from being "clicked" so quickly that they aren't noticeable.

When *WndProc* processes WM_COMMAND messages, it always sets the input focus to the parent window:

```
case WM_COMMAND :
    SetFocus (hwnd) ;
```

Otherwise, the input focus would be shifted to one of the buttons whenever it was clicked with the mouse.

THE COMMON DIALOG BOXES

One of the primary goals of Windows when it was initially released was to promote a standardized user interface. For many common menu items, this happened fairly quickly. Almost every software manufacturer adopted the Alt-File-Open selection to open a file. However, the actual file-open dialog boxes were often quite dissimilar.

Beginning with Windows 3.1, a solution to this problem became available. This is an enhancement called the "common dialog box library." This library consists of several functions that invoke standard dialog boxes for opening and saving files, searching and replacing, choosing colors, choosing fonts (all of which I'll demonstrate in this chapter), and printing (which I'll demonstrate in Chapter 13).

To use these functions, you basically initialize the fields of a structure and pass a pointer to the structure to a function in the common dialog box library. The function creates and displays the dialog box. When the user makes the dialog box go away, the function you called returns control to your program and you obtain information from the structure you passed to it.

You'll need to include the COMMDLG.H header file in any C source code file that uses the common dialog box library. The common dialog boxes are documented in /Platform SDK/User Interface Services/User Input/Common Dialog Box Library.

POPPAD Revisited

When we added a menu to POPPAD in Chapter 10, several standard menu options were left unimplemented. We are now ready to add logic to POPPAD to open files, read them in, and save the edited files on disk. In the process, we'll also add font selection and search-and-replace logic to POPPAD.

The files that contribute to the POPPAD3 program are shown in Figure 11-11.

POPPAD.C

```
/*-----------------------------------------
   POPPAD.C -- Popup Editor
              (c) Charles Petzold, 1998
   -----------------------------------------*/

#include <windows.h>
#include <commdlg.h>
#include "resource.h"

#define EDITID   1
#define UNTITLED TEXT ("(untitled)")

LRESULT CALLBACK WndProc       (HWND, UINT, WPARAM, LPARAM) ;
BOOL    CALLBACK AboutDlgProc (HWND, UINT, WPARAM, LPARAM) ;

     // Functions in POPFILE.C

void PopFileInitialize (HWND) ;
BOOL PopFileOpenDlg    (HWND, PTSTR, PTSTR) ;
BOOL PopFileSaveDlg    (HWND, PTSTR, PTSTR) ;
BOOL PopFileRead       (HWND, PTSTR) ;
BOOL PopFileWrite      (HWND, PTSTR) ;

     // Functions in POPFIND.C

HWND PopFindFindDlg     (HWND) ;
HWND PopFindReplaceDlg  (HWND) ;
BOOL PopFindFindText    (HWND, int *, LPFINDREPLACE) ;
BOOL PopFindReplaceText (HWND, int *, LPFINDREPLACE) ;
BOOL PopFindNextText    (HWND, int *) ;
BOOL PopFindValidFind   (void) ;

     // Functions in POPFONT.C

void PopFontInitialize   (HWND) ;
BOOL PopFontChooseFont   (HWND) ;
void PopFontSetFont      (HWND) ;
void PopFontDeinitialize (void) ;
```

Figure 11-11. *The POPPAD3 program.* *(continued)*

Figure 11-11. *continued*

```
    // Functions in POPPRNT.C

BOOL PopPrntPrintFile (HINSTANCE, HWND, HWND, PTSTR) ;

    // Global variables

static HWND   hDlgModeless ;
static TCHAR  szAppName[] = TEXT ("PopPad") ;

int WINAPI WinMain (HINSTANCE hInstance, HINSTANCE hPrevInstance,
                    PSTR szCmdLine, int iCmdShow)
{
    MSG       msg ;
    HWND      hwnd ;
    HACCEL    hAccel ;
    WNDCLASS  wndclass ;

    wndclass.style         = CS_HREDRAW | CS_VREDRAW ;
    wndclass.lpfnWndProc   = WndProc ;
    wndclass.cbClsExtra    = 0 ;
    wndclass.cbWndExtra    = 0 ;
    wndclass.hInstance     = hInstance ;
    wndclass.hIcon         = LoadIcon (hInstance, szAppName) ;
    wndclass.hCursor       = LoadCursor (NULL, IDC_ARROW) ;
    wndclass.hbrBackground = (HBRUSH) GetStockObject (WHITE_BRUSH) ;
    wndclass.lpszMenuName  = szAppName ;
    wndclass.lpszClassName = szAppName ;

    if (!RegisterClass (&wndclass))
    {
        MessageBox (NULL, TEXT ("This program requires Windows NT!"),
                    szAppName, MB_ICONERROR) ;
        return 0 ;
    }

    hwnd = CreateWindow (szAppName, NULL,
                        WS_OVERLAPPEDWINDOW,
                        CW_USEDEFAULT, CW_USEDEFAULT,
                        CW_USEDEFAULT, CW_USEDEFAULT,
                        NULL, NULL, hInstance, szCmdLine) ;

    ShowWindow (hwnd, iCmdShow) ;
    UpdateWindow (hwnd) ;
```

```
    hAccel = LoadAccelerators (hInstance, szAppName) ;

    while (GetMessage (&msg, NULL, 0, 0))
    {
        if (hDlgModeless == NULL || !IsDialogMessage (hDlgModeless, &msg))
        {
            if (!TranslateAccelerator (hwnd, hAccel, &msg))
            {
                TranslateMessage (&msg) ;
                DispatchMessage (&msg) ;
            }
        }
    }
    return msg.wParam ;
}

void DoCaption (HWND hwnd, TCHAR * szTitleName)
{
    TCHAR szCaption[64 + MAX_PATH] ;

    wsprintf (szCaption, TEXT ("%s - %s"), szAppName,
              szTitleName[0] ? szTitleName : UNTITLED) ;

    SetWindowText (hwnd, szCaption) ;
}

void OkMessage (HWND hwnd, TCHAR * szMessage, TCHAR * szTitleName)
{
    TCHAR szBuffer[64 + MAX_PATH] ;

    wsprintf (szBuffer, szMessage, szTitleName[0] ? szTitleName : UNTITLED) ;

    MessageBox (hwnd, szBuffer, szAppName, MB_OK | MB_ICONEXCLAMATION) ;
}

short AskAboutSave (HWND hwnd, TCHAR * szTitleName)
{
    TCHAR szBuffer[64 + MAX_PATH] ;
    int   iReturn ;

    wsprintf (szBuffer, TEXT ("Save current changes in %s?"),
              szTitleName[0] ? szTitleName : UNTITLED) ;

    iReturn = MessageBox (hwnd, szBuffer, szAppName,
                          MB_YESNOCANCEL | MB_ICONQUESTION) ;
```

(continued)

Figure 11-11. *continued*

```
      if (iReturn == IDYES)
          if (!SendMessage (hwnd, WM_COMMAND, IDM_FILE_SAVE, 0))
              iReturn = IDCANCEL ;

      return iReturn ;
}

LRESULT CALLBACK WndProc (HWND hwnd, UINT message, WPARAM wParam, LPARAM lParam)
{
      static BOOL       bNeedSave = FALSE ;
      static HINSTANCE  hInst ;
      static HWND       hwndEdit ;
      static int        iOffset ;
      static TCHAR      szFileName[MAX_PATH], szTitleName[MAX_PATH] ;
      static UINT       messageFindReplace ;
      int               iSelBeg, iSelEnd, iEnable ;
      LPFINDREPLACE     pfr ;

      switch (message)
      {
      case WM_CREATE:
          hInst = ((LPCREATESTRUCT) lParam) -> hInstance ;

              // Create the edit control child window

          hwndEdit = CreateWindow (TEXT ("edit"), NULL,
                          WS_CHILD | WS_VISIBLE | WS_HSCROLL | WS_VSCROLL |
                          WS_BORDER | ES_LEFT | ES_MULTILINE |
                          ES_NOHIDESEL | ES_AUTOHSCROLL | ES_AUTOVSCROLL,
                          0, 0, 0, 0,
                          hwnd, (HMENU) EDITID, hInst, NULL) ;

          SendMessage (hwndEdit, EM_LIMITTEXT, 32000, 0L) ;

              // Initialize common dialog box stuff

          PopFileInitialize (hwnd) ;
          PopFontInitialize (hwndEdit) ;

          messageFindReplace = RegisterWindowMessage (FINDMSGSTRING) ;

          DoCaption (hwnd, szTitleName) ;
          return 0 ;
```

```
      case WM_SETFOCUS:
           SetFocus (hwndEdit) ;
           return 0 ;

      case WM_SIZE:
           MoveWindow (hwndEdit, 0, 0, LOWORD (lParam), HIWORD (lParam), TRUE) ;
           return 0 ;

      case WM_INITMENUPOPUP:
           switch (lParam)
           {
           case 1:               // Edit menu

                     // Enable Undo if edit control can do it

                EnableMenuItem ((HMENU) wParam, IDM_EDIT_UNDO,
                     SendMessage (hwndEdit, EM_CANUNDO, 0, 0L) ?
                                        MF_ENABLED : MF_GRAYED) ;

                     // Enable Paste if text is in the clipboard

                EnableMenuItem ((HMENU) wParam, IDM_EDIT_PASTE,
                     IsClipboardFormatAvailable (CF_TEXT) ?
                                        MF_ENABLED : MF_GRAYED) ;

                     // Enable Cut, Copy, and Del if text is selected

                SendMessage (hwndEdit, EM_GETSEL, (WPARAM) &iSelBeg,
                                        (LPARAM) &iSelEnd) ;

                iEnable = iSelBeg != iSelEnd ? MF_ENABLED : MF_GRAYED ;

                EnableMenuItem ((HMENU) wParam, IDM_EDIT_CUT,   iEnable) ;
                EnableMenuItem ((HMENU) wParam, IDM_EDIT_COPY,  iEnable) ;
                EnableMenuItem ((HMENU) wParam, IDM_EDIT_CLEAR, iEnable) ;
                break ;

           case 2:               // Search menu

                // Enable Find, Next, and Replace if modeless
                //    dialogs are not already active

                iEnable = hDlgModeless == NULL ?
                          MF_ENABLED : MF_GRAYED ;
```

(continued)

Figure 11-11. *continued*

```
                EnableMenuItem ((HMENU) wParam, IDM_SEARCH_FIND,    iEnable) ;
                EnableMenuItem ((HMENU) wParam, IDM_SEARCH_NEXT,    iEnable) ;
                EnableMenuItem ((HMENU) wParam, IDM_SEARCH_REPLACE, iEnable) ;
                break ;
          }
          return 0 ;

     case WM_COMMAND:
               // Messages from edit control

          if (lParam && LOWORD (wParam) == EDITID)
          {
               switch (HIWORD (wParam))
               {
               case EN_UPDATE :
                    bNeedSave = TRUE ;
                    return 0 ;

               case EN_ERRSPACE :
               case EN_MAXTEXT :
                    MessageBox (hwnd, TEXT ("Edit control out of space."),
                                szAppName, MB_OK | MB_ICONSTOP) ;
                    return 0 ;
               }
               break ;
          }

          switch (LOWORD (wParam))
          {
               // Messages from File menu

          case IDM_FILE_NEW:
               if (bNeedSave && IDCANCEL == AskAboutSave (hwnd, szTitleName))
                    return 0 ;

               SetWindowText (hwndEdit, TEXT ("\0")) ;
               szFileName[0]  = '\0' ;
               szTitleName[0] = '\0' ;
               DoCaption (hwnd, szTitleName) ;
               bNeedSave = FALSE ;
               return 0 ;

          case IDM_FILE_OPEN:
               if (bNeedSave && IDCANCEL == AskAboutSave (hwnd, szTitleName))
                    return 0 ;
```

```
            if (PopFileOpenDlg (hwnd, szFileName, szTitleName))
            {
                 if (!PopFileRead (hwndEdit, szFileName))
                 {
                      OkMessage (hwnd, TEXT ("Could not read file %s!"),
                                 szTitleName) ;
                      szFileName[0]  = '\0' ;
                      szTitleName[0] = '\0' ;
                 }
            }

            DoCaption (hwnd, szTitleName) ;
            bNeedSave = FALSE ;
            return 0 ;

       case IDM_FILE_SAVE:
            if (szFileName[0])
            {
                 if (PopFileWrite (hwndEdit, szFileName))
                 {
                      bNeedSave = FALSE ;
                      return 1 ;
                 }
                 else
                 {
                      OkMessage (hwnd, TEXT ("Could not write file %s"),
                                 szTitleName) ;
                      return 0 ;
                 }
            }
                              // fall through
       case IDM_FILE_SAVE_AS:
            if (PopFileSaveDlg (hwnd, szFileName, szTitleName))
            {
                 DoCaption (hwnd, szTitleName) ;

                 if (PopFileWrite (hwndEdit, szFileName))
                 {
                      bNeedSave = FALSE ;
                      return 1 ;
                 }
                 else
                 {
                      OkMessage (hwnd, TEXT ("Could not write file %s"),
                                 szTitleName) ;
```

(continued)

Figure 11-11. *continued*

```
                    return 0 ;
            }
    }
    return 0 ;

case IDM_FILE_PRINT:
    if (!PopPrntPrintFile (hInst, hwnd, hwndEdit, szTitleName))
        OkMessage (hwnd, TEXT ("Could not print file %s"),
                        szTitleName) ;
    return 0 ;

case IDM_APP_EXIT:
    SendMessage (hwnd, WM_CLOSE, 0, 0) ;
    return 0 ;

        // Messages from Edit menu

case IDM_EDIT_UNDO:
    SendMessage (hwndEdit, WM_UNDO, 0, 0) ;
    return 0 ;

case IDM_EDIT_CUT:
    SendMessage (hwndEdit, WM_CUT, 0, 0) ;
    return 0 ;

case IDM_EDIT_COPY:
    SendMessage (hwndEdit, WM_COPY, 0, 0) ;
    return 0 ;

case IDM_EDIT_PASTE:
    SendMessage (hwndEdit, WM_PASTE, 0, 0) ;
    return 0 ;

case IDM_EDIT_CLEAR:
    SendMessage (hwndEdit, WM_CLEAR, 0, 0) ;
    return 0 ;

case IDM_EDIT_SELECT_ALL:
    SendMessage (hwndEdit, EM_SETSEL, 0, -1) ;
    return 0 ;

        // Messages from Search menu
```

```
      case IDM_SEARCH_FIND:
           SendMessage (hwndEdit, EM_GETSEL, 0, (LPARAM) &iOffset) ;
           hDlgModeless = PopFindFindDlg (hwnd) ;
           return 0 ;

      case IDM_SEARCH_NEXT:
           SendMessage (hwndEdit, EM_GETSEL, 0, (LPARAM) &iOffset) ;

           if (PopFindValidFind ())
                PopFindNextText (hwndEdit, &iOffset) ;
           else
                hDlgModeless = PopFindFindDlg (hwnd) ;

           return 0 ;

      case IDM_SEARCH_REPLACE:
           SendMessage (hwndEdit, EM_GETSEL, 0, (LPARAM) &iOffset) ;
           hDlgModeless = PopFindReplaceDlg (hwnd) ;
           return 0 ;

      case IDM_FORMAT_FONT:
           if (PopFontChooseFont (hwnd))
                PopFontSetFont (hwndEdit) ;

           return 0 ;

                // Messages from Help menu

      case IDM_HELP:
           OkMessage (hwnd, TEXT ("Help not yet implemented!"),
                          TEXT ("\0")) ;
           return 0 ;

      case IDM_APP_ABOUT:
           DialogBox (hInst, TEXT ("AboutBox"), hwnd, AboutDlgProc) ;
           return 0 ;
      }
      break ;

case WM_CLOSE:
      if (!bNeedSave || IDCANCEL != AskAboutSave (hwnd, szTitleName))
           DestroyWindow (hwnd) ;

      return 0 ;
```

(continued)

Figure 11-11. *continued*

```
    case WM_QUERYENDSESSION :
         if (!bNeedSave || IDCANCEL != AskAboutSave (hwnd, szTitleName))
              return 1 ;

         return 0 ;

    case WM_DESTROY:
         PopFontDeinitialize () ;
         PostQuitMessage (0) ;
         return 0 ;

    default:
              // Process "Find-Replace" messages

         if (message == messageFindReplace)
         {
              pfr = (LPFINDREPLACE) lParam ;

              if (pfr->Flags & FR_DIALOGTERM)
                   hDlgModeless = NULL ;

              if (pfr->Flags & FR_FINDNEXT)
                   if (!PopFindFindText (hwndEdit, &iOffset, pfr))
                        OkMessage (hwnd, TEXT ("Text not found!"),
                                         TEXT ("\0")) ;

              if (pfr->Flags & FR_REPLACE || pfr->Flags & FR_REPLACEALL)
                   if (!PopFindReplaceText (hwndEdit, &iOffset, pfr))
                        OkMessage (hwnd, TEXT ("Text not found!"),
                                         TEXT ("\0")) ;

              if (pfr->Flags & FR_REPLACEALL)
                   while (PopFindReplaceText (hwndEdit, &iOffset, pfr)) ;

              return 0 ;
         }
         break ;
    }
    return DefWindowProc (hwnd, message, wParam, lParam) ;
}

BOOL CALLBACK AboutDlgProc (HWND hDlg, UINT message,
                            WPARAM wParam, LPARAM lParam)
```

```
{
     switch (message)
     {
     case WM_INITDIALOG:
          return TRUE ;

     case WM_COMMAND:
          switch (LOWORD (wParam))
          {
          case IDOK:
               EndDialog (hDlg, 0) ;
               return TRUE ;
          }
          break ;
     }
     return FALSE ;
}
```

POPFILE.C

```
/*-------------------------------------------
   POPFILE.C -- Popup Editor File Functions
  -------------------------------------------*/

#include <windows.h>
#include <commdlg.h>

static OPENFILENAME ofn ;

void PopFileInitialize (HWND hwnd)
{
     static TCHAR szFilter[] = TEXT ("Text Files (*.TXT)\0*.txt\0")  \
                               TEXT ("ASCII Files (*.ASC)\0*.asc\0") \
                               TEXT ("All Files (*.*)\0*.*\0\0") ;

     ofn.lStructSize       = sizeof (OPENFILENAME) ;
     ofn.hwndOwner         = hwnd ;
     ofn.hInstance         = NULL ;
     ofn.lpstrFilter       = szFilter ;
     ofn.lpstrCustomFilter = NULL ;
     ofn.nMaxCustFilter    = 0 ;
     ofn.nFilterIndex      = 0 ;
     ofn.lpstrFile         = NULL ;              // Set in Open and Close functions
```

(continued)

Figure 11-11. *continued*

```
    ofn.nMaxFile          = MAX_PATH ;
    ofn.lpstrFileTitle    = NULL ;              // Set in Open and Close functions
    ofn.nMaxFileTitle     = MAX_PATH ;
    ofn.lpstrInitialDir   = NULL ;
    ofn.lpstrTitle        = NULL ;
    ofn.Flags             = 0 ;                 // Set in Open and Close functions
    ofn.nFileOffset       = 0 ;
    ofn.nFileExtension    = 0 ;
    ofn.lpstrDefExt       = TEXT ("txt") ;
    ofn.lCustData         = 0L ;
    ofn.lpfnHook          = NULL ;
    ofn.lpTemplateName    = NULL ;
}

BOOL PopFileOpenDlg (HWND hwnd, PTSTR pstrFileName, PTSTR pstrTitleName)
{
    ofn.hwndOwner         = hwnd ;
    ofn.lpstrFile         = pstrFileName ;
    ofn.lpstrFileTitle    = pstrTitleName ;
    ofn.Flags             = OFN_HIDEREADONLY | OFN_CREATEPROMPT ;

    return GetOpenFileName (&ofn) ;
}

BOOL PopFileSaveDlg (HWND hwnd, PTSTR pstrFileName, PTSTR pstrTitleName)
{
    ofn.hwndOwner         = hwnd ;
    ofn.lpstrFile         = pstrFileName ;
    ofn.lpstrFileTitle    = pstrTitleName ;
    ofn.Flags             = OFN_OVERWRITEPROMPT ;

    return GetSaveFileName (&ofn) ;
}

BOOL PopFileRead (HWND hwndEdit, PTSTR pstrFileName)
{
    BYTE   bySwap ;
    DWORD  dwBytesRead ;
    HANDLE hFile ;
    int    i, iFileLength, iUniTest ;
    PBYTE  pBuffer, pText, pConv ;

        // Open the file.
```

```
    if (INVALID_HANDLE_VALUE ==
            (hFile = CreateFile (pstrFileName, GENERIC_READ, FILE_SHARE_READ,
                              NULL, OPEN_EXISTING, 0, NULL)))
        return FALSE ;

        // Get file size in bytes and allocate memory for read.
        // Add an extra two bytes for zero termination.

iFileLength = GetFileSize (hFile, NULL) ;
pBuffer = malloc (iFileLength + 2) ;

        // Read file and put terminating zeros at end.

ReadFile (hFile, pBuffer, iFileLength, &dwBytesRead, NULL) ;
CloseHandle (hFile) ;
pBuffer[iFileLength] = '\0' ;
pBuffer[iFileLength + 1] = '\0' ;

        // Test to see if the text is Unicode

iUniTest = IS_TEXT_UNICODE_SIGNATURE | IS_TEXT_UNICODE_REVERSE_SIGNATURE ;

if (IsTextUnicode (pBuffer, iFileLength, &iUniTest))
{
    pText = pBuffer + 2 ;
    iFileLength -= 2 ;

    if (iUniTest & IS_TEXT_UNICODE_REVERSE_SIGNATURE)
    {
        for (i = 0 ; i < iFileLength / 2 ; i++)
        {
            bySwap = ((BYTE *) pText) [2 * i] ;
            ((BYTE *) pText) [2 * i] = ((BYTE *) pText) [2 * i + 1] ;
            ((BYTE *) pText) [2 * i + 1] = bySwap ;
        }
    }

        // Allocate memory for possibly converted string

    pConv = malloc (iFileLength + 2) ;

        // If the edit control is not Unicode, convert Unicode text to
        // non-Unicode (i.e., in general, wide character).
```

(continued)

Figure 11-11. *continued*

```
#ifndef UNICODE
        WideCharToMultiByte (CP_ACP, 0, (PWSTR) pText, -1, pConv,
                             iFileLength + 2, NULL, NULL) ;

             // If the edit control is Unicode, just copy the string
#else
        lstrcpy ((PTSTR) pConv, (PTSTR) pText) ;
#endif

     }
     else      // the file is not Unicode
     {
        pText = pBuffer ;

             // Allocate memory for possibly converted string.

        pConv = malloc (2 * iFileLength + 2) ;

             // If the edit control is Unicode, convert ASCII text.

#ifdef UNICODE
        MultiByteToWideChar (CP_ACP, 0, pText, -1, (PTSTR) pConv,
                             iFileLength + 1) ;

             // If not, just copy buffer
#else
        lstrcpy ((PTSTR) pConv, (PTSTR) pText) ;
#endif
     }

     SetWindowText (hwndEdit, (PTSTR) pConv) ;
     free (pBuffer) ;
     free (pConv) ;

     return TRUE ;
}

BOOL PopFileWrite (HWND hwndEdit, PTSTR pstrFileName)
{
     DWORD  dwBytesWritten ;
     HANDLE hFile ;
     int    iLength ;
     PTSTR  pstrBuffer ;
     WORD   wByteOrderMark = 0xFEFF ;
```

```
          // Open the file, creating it if necessary

     if (INVALID_HANDLE_VALUE ==
              (hFile = CreateFile (pstrFileName, GENERIC_WRITE, 0,
                                 NULL, CREATE_ALWAYS, 0, NULL)))
          return FALSE ;

          // Get the number of characters in the edit control and allocate
          // memory for them.

     iLength = GetWindowTextLength (hwndEdit) ;
     pstrBuffer = (PTSTR) malloc ((iLength + 1) * sizeof (TCHAR)) ;

     if (!pstrBuffer)
     {
          CloseHandle (hFile) ;
          return FALSE ;
     }

          // If the edit control will return Unicode text, write the
          // byte order mark to the file.

#ifdef UNICODE
     WriteFile (hFile, &wByteOrderMark, 2, &dwBytesWritten, NULL) ;
#endif

          // Get the edit buffer and write that out to the file.

     GetWindowText (hwndEdit, pstrBuffer, iLength + 1) ;
     WriteFile (hFile, pstrBuffer, iLength * sizeof (TCHAR),
              &dwBytesWritten, NULL) ;

     if ((iLength * sizeof (TCHAR)) != (int) dwBytesWritten)
     {
          CloseHandle (hFile) ;
          free (pstrBuffer) ;
          return FALSE ;
     }

     CloseHandle (hFile) ;
     free (pstrBuffer) ;

     return TRUE ;
}
```

(continued)

Figure 11-11. *continued*

POPFIND.C

```
/*----------------------------------------------------------
   POPFIND.C -- Popup Editor Search and Replace Functions
   ----------------------------------------------------------*/

#include <windows.h>
#include <commdlg.h>
#include <tchar.h>                // for _tcsstr (strstr for Unicode & non-Unicode)

#define MAX_STRING_LEN   256

static TCHAR szFindText [MAX_STRING_LEN] ;
static TCHAR szReplText [MAX_STRING_LEN] ;

HWND PopFindFindDlg (HWND hwnd)
{
     static FINDREPLACE fr ;          // must be static for modeless dialog!!!

     fr.lStructSize       = sizeof (FINDREPLACE) ;
     fr.hwndOwner         = hwnd ;
     fr.hInstance         = NULL ;
     fr.Flags             = FR_HIDEUPDOWN | FR_HIDEMATCHCASE | FR_HIDEWHOLEWORD ;
     fr.lpstrFindWhat     = szFindText ;
     fr.lpstrReplaceWith  = NULL ;
     fr.wFindWhatLen      = MAX_STRING_LEN ;
     fr.wReplaceWithLen   = 0 ;
     fr.lCustData         = 0 ;
     fr.lpfnHook          = NULL ;
     fr.lpTemplateName    = NULL ;

     return FindText (&fr) ;
}

HWND PopFindReplaceDlg (HWND hwnd)
{
     static FINDREPLACE fr ;          // must be static for modeless dialog!!!

     fr.lStructSize       = sizeof (FINDREPLACE) ;
     fr.hwndOwner         = hwnd ;
     fr.hInstance         = NULL ;
     fr.Flags             = FR_HIDEUPDOWN | FR_HIDEMATCHCASE | FR_HIDEWHOLEWORD ;
     fr.lpstrFindWhat     = szFindText ;
     fr.lpstrReplaceWith  = szReplText ;
```

```
        fr.wFindWhatLen    = MAX_STRING_LEN ;
        fr.wReplaceWithLen = MAX_STRING_LEN ;
        fr.lCustData       = 0 ;
        fr.lpfnHook        = NULL ;
        fr.lpTemplateName  = NULL ;

        return ReplaceText (&fr) ;
}

BOOL PopFindFindText (HWND hwndEdit, int * piSearchOffset, LPFINDREPLACE pfr)
{
        int    iLength, iPos ;
        PTSTR  pstrDoc, pstrPos ;

            // Read in the edit document

        iLength = GetWindowTextLength (hwndEdit) ;

        if (NULL == (pstrDoc = (PTSTR) malloc ((iLength + 1) * sizeof (TCHAR))))
            return FALSE ;

        GetWindowText (hwndEdit, pstrDoc, iLength + 1) ;

            // Search the document for the find string

        pstrPos = _tcsstr (pstrDoc + * piSearchOffset, pfr->lpstrFindWhat) ;
        free (pstrDoc) ;

            // Return an error code if the string cannot be found

        if (pstrPos == NULL)
            return FALSE ;

            // Find the position in the document and the new start offset

        iPos = pstrPos - pstrDoc ;
        * piSearchOffset = iPos + lstrlen (pfr->lpstrFindWhat) ;

            // Select the found text

        SendMessage (hwndEdit, EM_SETSEL, iPos, * piSearchOffset) ;
        SendMessage (hwndEdit, EM_SCROLLCARET, 0, 0) ;

        return TRUE ;
}
```

(continued)

Figure 11-11. *continued*

```
BOOL PopFindNextText (HWND hwndEdit, int * piSearchOffset)
{
    FINDREPLACE fr ;

    fr.lpstrFindWhat = szFindText ;

    return PopFindFindText (hwndEdit, piSearchOffset, &fr) ;
}

BOOL PopFindReplaceText (HWND hwndEdit, int * piSearchOffset, LPFINDREPLACE pfr)
{
        // Find the text

    if (!PopFindFindText (hwndEdit, piSearchOffset, pfr))
        return FALSE ;

        // Replace it

    SendMessage (hwndEdit, EM_REPLACESEL, 0, (LPARAM) pfr->lpstrReplaceWith) ;

    return TRUE ;
}

BOOL PopFindValidFind (void)
{
    return * szFindText != '\0' ;
}
```

POPFONT.C

```
/*------------------------------------------------
   POPFONT.C -- Popup Editor Font Functions
   ------------------------------------------------*/

#include <windows.h>
#include <commdlg.h>

static LOGFONT logfont ;
static HFONT   hFont ;

BOOL PopFontChooseFont (HWND hwnd)
{
    CHOOSEFONT cf ;
```

```
    cf.lStructSize    = sizeof (CHOOSEFONT) ;
    cf.hwndOwner      = hwnd ;
    cf.hDC            = NULL ;
    cf.lpLogFont      = &logfont ;
    cf.iPointSize     = 0 ;
    cf.Flags          = CF_INITTOLOGFONTSTRUCT | CF_SCREENFONTS | CF_EFFECTS ;
    cf.rgbColors      = 0 ;
    cf.lCustData      = 0 ;
    cf.lpfnHook       = NULL ;
    cf.lpTemplateName = NULL ;
    cf.hInstance      = NULL ;
    cf.lpszStyle      = NULL ;
    cf.nFontType      = 0 ;                  // Returned from ChooseFont
    cf.nSizeMin       = 0 ;
    cf.nSizeMax       = 0 ;

    return ChooseFont (&cf) ;
}

void PopFontInitialize (HWND hwndEdit)
{
    GetObject (GetStockObject (SYSTEM_FONT), sizeof (LOGFONT),
            (PTSTR) &logfont) ;

    hFont = CreateFontIndirect (&logfont) ;
    SendMessage (hwndEdit, WM_SETFONT, (WPARAM) hFont, 0) ;
}

void PopFontSetFont (HWND hwndEdit)
{
    HFONT hFontNew ;
    RECT  rect ;

    hFontNew = CreateFontIndirect (&logfont) ;
    SendMessage (hwndEdit, WM_SETFONT, (WPARAM) hFontNew, 0) ;
    DeleteObject (hFont) ;
    hFont = hFontNew ;
    GetClientRect (hwndEdit, &rect) ;
    InvalidateRect (hwndEdit, &rect, TRUE) ;
}

void PopFontDeinitialize (void)
{
    DeleteObject (hFont) ;
}
```

(continued)

Figure 11-11. *continued*

POPPRNT0.C

```
/*-------------------------------------------------------------
   POPPRNT0.C -- Popup Editor Printing Functions (dummy version)
   -------------------------------------------------------------*/

#include <windows.h>

BOOL PopPrntPrintFile (HINSTANCE hInst, HWND hwnd, HWND hwndEdit,
                       PTSTR pstrTitleName)
{
     return FALSE ;
}
```

POPPAD.RC (excerpts)

```
//Microsoft Developer Studio generated resource script.

#include "resource.h"
#include "afxres.h"

/////////////////////////////////////////////////////////////////////////////
// Dialog

ABOUTBOX DIALOG DISCARDABLE  32, 32, 180, 100
STYLE DS_MODALFRAME | WS_POPUP
FONT 8, "MS Sans Serif"
BEGIN
    DEFPUSHBUTTON   "OK",IDOK,66,80,50,14
    ICON            "POPPAD",IDC_STATIC,7,7,20,20
    CTEXT           "PopPad",IDC_STATIC,40,12,100,8
    CTEXT           "Popup Editor for Windows",IDC_STATIC,7,40,166,8
    CTEXT           "(c) Charles Petzold, 1998",IDC_STATIC,7,52,166,8
END

PRINTDLGBOX DIALOG DISCARDABLE  32, 32, 186, 95
STYLE DS_MODALFRAME | WS_POPUP | WS_VISIBLE | WS_CAPTION | WS_SYSMENU
CAPTION "PopPad"
FONT 8, "MS Sans Serif"
BEGIN
    PUSHBUTTON      "Cancel",IDCANCEL,67,74,50,14
    CTEXT           "Sending",IDC_STATIC,8,8,172,8
    CTEXT           "",IDC_FILENAME,8,28,172,8
```

```
    CTEXT              "to print spooler.",IDC_STATIC,8,48,172,8
END


//////////////////////////////////////////////////////////////////////////
// Menu

POPPAD MENU DISCARDABLE
BEGIN
    POPUP "&File"
    BEGIN
        MENUITEM "&New\tCtrl+N",                IDM_FILE_NEW
        MENUITEM "&Open...\tCtrl+O",             IDM_FILE_OPEN
        MENUITEM "&Save\tCtrl+S",                IDM_FILE_SAVE
        MENUITEM "Save &As...",                  IDM_FILE_SAVE_AS
        MENUITEM SEPARATOR
        MENUITEM "&Print\tCtrl+P",               IDM_FILE_PRINT
        MENUITEM SEPARATOR
        MENUITEM "E&xit",                        IDM_APP_EXIT
    END
    POPUP "&Edit"
    BEGIN
        MENUITEM "&Undo\tCtrl+Z",                IDM_EDIT_UNDO
        MENUITEM SEPARATOR
        MENUITEM "Cu&t\tCtrl+X",                 IDM_EDIT_CUT
        MENUITEM "&Copy\tCtrl+C",                IDM_EDIT_COPY
        MENUITEM "&Paste\tCtrl+V",               IDM_EDIT_PASTE
        MENUITEM "De&lete\tDel",                 IDM_EDIT_CLEAR
        MENUITEM SEPARATOR
        MENUITEM "&Select All",                  IDM_EDIT_SELECT_ALL
    END
    POPUP "&Search"
    BEGIN
        MENUITEM "&Find...\tCtrl+F",             IDM_SEARCH_FIND
        MENUITEM "Find &Next\tF3",               IDM_SEARCH_NEXT
        MENUITEM "&Replace...\tCtrl+R",          IDM_SEARCH_REPLACE
    END
    POPUP "F&ormat"
    BEGIN
        MENUITEM "&Font...",                     IDM_FORMAT_FONT
    END
    POPUP "&Help"
    BEGIN
        MENUITEM "&Help",                        IDM_HELP
        MENUITEM "&About PopPad...",             IDM_APP_ABOUT
    END
END
```

(continued)

Figure 11-11. *continued*

```
//////////////////////////////////////////////////////////////////////////
// Accelerator

POPPAD ACCELERATORS DISCARDABLE
BEGIN
    VK_BACK,        IDM_EDIT_UNDO,          VIRTKEY, ALT, NOINVERT
    VK_DELETE,      IDM_EDIT_CLEAR,         VIRTKEY, NOINVERT
    VK_DELETE,      IDM_EDIT_CUT,           VIRTKEY, SHIFT, NOINVERT
    VK_F1,          IDM_HELP,               VIRTKEY, NOINVERT
    VK_F3,          IDM_SEARCH_NEXT,        VIRTKEY, NOINVERT
    VK_INSERT,      IDM_EDIT_COPY,          VIRTKEY, CONTROL, NOINVERT
    VK_INSERT,      IDM_EDIT_PASTE,         VIRTKEY, SHIFT, NOINVERT
    "^C",           IDM_EDIT_COPY,          ASCII,   NOINVERT
    "^F",           IDM_SEARCH_FIND,        ASCII,   NOINVERT
    "^N",           IDM_FILE_NEW,           ASCII,   NOINVERT
    "^O",           IDM_FILE_OPEN,          ASCII,   NOINVERT
    "^P",           IDM_FILE_PRINT,         ASCII,   NOINVERT
    "^R",           IDM_SEARCH_REPLACE,     ASCII,   NOINVERT
    "^S",           IDM_FILE_SAVE,          ASCII,   NOINVERT
    "^V",           IDM_EDIT_PASTE,         ASCII,   NOINVERT
    "^X",           IDM_EDIT_CUT,           ASCII,   NOINVERT
    "^Z",           IDM_EDIT_UNDO,          ASCII,   NOINVERT
END


//////////////////////////////////////////////////////////////////////////
// Icon

POPPAD                  ICON    DISCARDABLE     "poppad.ico"
```

RESOURCE.H (excerpts)

```
// Microsoft Developer Studio generated include file.
// Used by poppad.rc

#define IDC_FILENAME                1000
#define IDM_FILE_NEW                40001
#define IDM_FILE_OPEN               40002
#define IDM_FILE_SAVE               40003
#define IDM_FILE_SAVE_AS            40004
#define IDM_FILE_PRINT              40005
#define IDM_APP_EXIT                40006
#define IDM_EDIT_UNDO               40007
#define IDM_EDIT_CUT                40008
```

```
#define IDM_EDIT_COPY            40009
#define IDM_EDIT_PASTE           40010
#define IDM_EDIT_CLEAR           40011
#define IDM_EDIT_SELECT_ALL      40012
#define IDM_SEARCH_FIND          40013
#define IDM_SEARCH_NEXT          40014
#define IDM_SEARCH_REPLACE       40015
#define IDM_FORMAT_FONT          40016
#define IDM_HELP                 40017
#define IDM_APP_ABOUT            40018
```

POPPAD.ICO

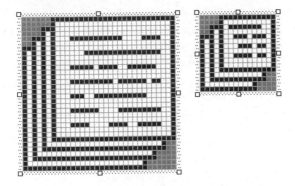

To avoid duplicating source code in Chapter 13, I've added printing to the menu in POPPAD.RC along with some other support.

POPPAD.C contains all the basic source code for the program. POPFILE.C has the code to invoke the File Open and File Save dialog boxes, and it also contains the file I/O routines. POPFIND.C contains the search-and-replace logic. POPFONT.C has the font selection logic. POPPRNT0.C doesn't do much: POPPRNT0.C will be replaced with POPPRNT.C in Chapter 13 to create the final POPPAD program.

Let's look at POPPAD.C first. POPPAD.C maintains two filename strings: The first, stored in *WndProc* using the name *szFileName*, is the fully qualified drive, path, and filename. The second, stored as *szTitleName*, is the filename by itself. This is used in the *DoCaption* function in POPPAD3 to display the filename in the title bar of the window and is used in the *OKMessage* and *AskAboutSave* functions to display message boxes to the user.

POPFILE.C contains several functions to display the File Open and File Save dialog boxes and to perform the actual file I/O. The dialog boxes are displayed using the functions *GetOpenFileName* and *GetSaveFileName*. Both of these functions use a structure of type OPENFILENAME, defined in COMMDLG.H. In POPFILE.C, a global variable named *ofn* is used for this structure. Most of the fields of *ofn* are initialized in the *PopFileInitialize* function, which POPPAD.C calls when processing the WM_CREATE message in *WndProc*.

It's convenient to make *ofn* a static global structure because *GetOpenFileName* and *GetSaveFileName* return some information to the structure that should be used in subsequent calls to these functions.

Although common dialog boxes have a lot of options—including setting your own dialog box template and hooking into the dialog box procedure—my use of the File Open and File Save dialog boxes in POPFILE.C is quite basic. The only fields of the OPENFILENAME structure that are set are *lStructSize* (the size of the structure), *hwndOwner* (the dialog box's owner), *lpstrFilter* (which I'll discuss shortly), *lpstrFile* and *nMaxFile* (a pointer to a buffer to receive the fully qualified filename and the size of that buffer), *lpstrFileTitle* and *nMaxFileTitle* (a buffer and its size for the filename by itself), *Flags* (which sets options for the dialog box), and *lpstrDefExt* (which is set to a text string containing the default filename extension if the user does not specify one when typing a filename in the dialog box).

When the user selects Open from the File menu, POPPAD3 calls POPFILE's *PopFileOpenDlg* function, passing to it the window handle, a pointer to the filename buffer, and a pointer to the file title buffer. *PopFileOpenDlg* sets the *hwndOwner*, *lpstrFile*, and *lpstrFileTitle* fields of the OPENFILENAME structure appropriately, sets *Flags* to OFN_CREATEPROMPT, and then calls *GetOpenFileName*, which displays the familiar dialog box shown in Figure 11-12.

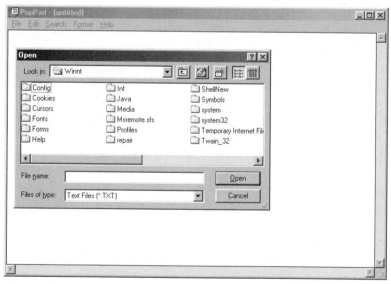

Figure 11-12. *The File Open dialog box.*

When the user ends this dialog box, the *GetOpenFileName* function returns. The OFN_CREATEPROMPT flag instructs *GetOpenFileName* to display a message box asking the user whether the file should be created if the selected file does not exist.

The combo box in the lower left corner lists the types of files that will be displayed in the file list. This is known as a "filter." The user can change the filter by selecting another file type from the combo box list. In the *PopFileInitialize* function in POPFILE.C, I define a filter in the variable *szFilter* (an array of character strings) for three types of files: text files with the extension .TXT, ASCII files with the extension .ASC, and all files. A pointer to the first string in this array is set to the *lpstrFilter* field of the OPENFILENAME structure.

If the user changes the filter when the dialog box is active, the *nFilterIndex* field of OPENFILENAME reflects the user's choice. Because the structure is stored as a static variable, the next time the dialog box is invoked the filter will be set to the selected file type.

The *PopFileSaveDlg* function in POPFILE.C is similar. It sets the Flags parameter to OFN_OVERWRITEPROMPT and calls *GetSaveFileName* to invoke the File Save dialog box. The OFN_OVERWRITEPROMPT flag causes a message box to be displayed asking the user whether a file should be overwritten if the selected file already exists.

Unicode File I/O

In many of the programs in this book, you may never notice a difference between the Unicode and non-Unicode versions. In the Unicode version of POPPAD3, for example, the edit control maintains Unicode text and all the common dialog boxes use Unicode text strings. When the program needs to do a search-and-replace, for example, the entire operation is done with Unicode strings with no conversion necessary.

However, POPPAD3 does file I/O, and that means that the program is not entirely self-enclosed. If the Unicode version of POPPAD3 obtains the contents of the edit buffer and writes it out to the disk, that file will be in Unicode. If the non-Unicode version of POPPAD3 reads that file and puts it into its edit buffer, the result will be garbage. The same goes for files saved by the non-Unicode version and read by the Unicode version.

The solution involves identification and conversion. First, in the *PopFileWrite* function in POPFILE.C, you'll see that the Unicode version of the program writes out the word 0xFEFF at the beginning of the file. This is defined as a byte order mark, indicating that the text file actually contains Unicode text.

Secondly, in the *PopFileRead* function, the program uses the *IsTextUnicode* functions to determine whether the file contains the byte order mark. The function even checks to see if the byte order mark is reversed, which means that a Unicode text file was created on a Macintosh or other machine that used the opposite byte order from Intel processors. In this case, every pair of bytes is reversed. If the file is Unicode but it's being read by the non-Unicode version of POPPAD3, then the text is converted by *WideCharToMultiChar*, which is really a wide-char-to-ANSI function (unless you're running a Far East version of Windows). Only then can the text be put into the edit buffer.

Similarly, if the file is a non-Unicode text file but the Unicode version of the program is running, the text must be converted using *MultiCharToWideChar*.

Changing the Font

We'll be looking at fonts in more detail in Chapter 17, but nothing quite beats the common dialog box functions for choosing fonts.

During the WM_CREATE message, POPPAD calls *PopFontInitialize* in POPFONT.C. This function obtains a LOGFONT structure based on the system font, creates a font from it, and sends a WM_SETFONT message to the edit control to set a new font. (Although the default edit control font is the system font, the *PopFontInitialize* function creates a new font for the edit control because eventually the font will be deleted and it wouldn't be wise to delete the stock system font.)

When POPPAD receives a WM_COMMAND message for the program's font option, it calls *PopFontChooseFont*. This function initializes a CHOOSEFONT structure and then calls *ChooseFont* to display the font selection dialog box. If the user presses the OK button, *ChooseFont* will return TRUE. POPPAD then calls *PopFontSetFont* to set the new font in the edit control. The old font is deleted.

Finally, during the WM_DESTROY message, POPPAD calls *PopFontDeinitialize* to delete the last font that *PopFontSetFont* created.

Search and Replace

The common dialog box library also includes two dialog boxes for the text search and replace functions. These two functions (*FindText* and *ReplaceText*) use a structure of type FINDREPLACE. The POPFIND.C file, shown in Figure 10-11, has two routines (*PopFindFindDlg* and *PopFindReplaceDlg*) to call these functions, and it also has a couple of functions to search through the text in the edit control and to replace text.

There are a few considerations with using the search and replace functions. First, the dialog boxes they invoke are modeless dialog boxes, which means you should alter your message loop to call *IsDialogMessage* when the dialog boxes are active. Second, the FINDREPLACE structure you pass to *FindText* and *ReplaceText* must be a static variable; because the dialog box is modal, the functions return after the dialog box is displayed rather than after it's destroyed. Nevertheless, the dialog box procedure must be able to continue to access the structure.

Third, while the *FindText* and *ReplaceText* dialogs are displayed, they communicate with the owner window through a special message. The message number can be obtained by calling the *RegisterWindowMessage* function with the FINDMSGSTRING parameter. This is done while processing the WM_CREATE message in *WndProc*, and the message number is stored in a static variable.

While processing the default message case, *WndProc* compares the message variable with the value returned from *RegisterWindowMessage*. The *lParam* message parameter is a pointer to the FINDREPLACE structure, and the Flags field indicates whether the user has used the dialog box to find text or replace text or whether the dialog box is terminating. POPPAD3 calls the *PopFindFindText* and *PopFindReplaceText* functions in POPFIND.C to perform the search and replace functions.

The One-Function-Call Windows Program

So far I've shown two programs that let you view selected colors: COLORS1 in Chapter 9 and COLORS2 in this chapter. Now it's time for COLORS3, a program that makes only one Windows function call. The COLORS3 source code is shown in Figure 11-13.

The one Windows function that COLORS3 calls is *ChooseColor*, another function in the common dialog box library. It displays the dialog box shown in Figure 11-14 on the following page. Color selection is similar to that in COLORS1 and COLORS2, but it's somewhat more interactive.

COLORS3.C

```
/*-----------------------------------------------
   COLORS3.C -- Version using Common Dialog Box
              (c) Charles Petzold, 1998
   -----------------------------------------------*/

#include <windows.h>
#include <commdlg.h>

int WINAPI WinMain (HINSTANCE hInstance, HINSTANCE hPrevInstance,
                    PSTR szCmdLine, int iCmdShow)
{
     static CHOOSECOLOR cc ;
     static COLORREF    crCustColors[16] ;

     cc.lStructSize    = sizeof (CHOOSECOLOR) ;
     cc.hwndOwner      = NULL ;
     cc.hInstance      = NULL ;
     cc.rgbResult      = RGB (0x80, 0x80, 0x80) ;
     cc.lpCustColors   = crCustColors ;
     cc.Flags          = CC_RGBINIT | CC_FULLOPEN ;
     cc.lCustData      = 0 ;
     cc.lpfnHook       = NULL ;
     cc.lpTemplateName = NULL ;

     return ChooseColor (&cc) ;
}
```

Figure 11-13. *The COLORS3 program.*

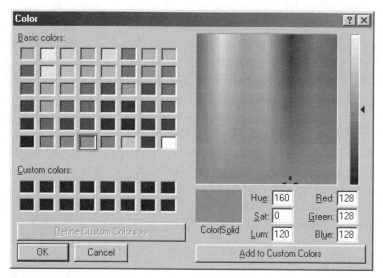

Figure 11-14. *The COLORS3 display.*

The *ChooseColor* function uses a structure of type CHOOSECOLOR and an array of 16 DWORDs to store custom colors that the user selects from the dialog box. The *rgbResult* field can be initialized to a color value that will be displayed if the CC_RGBINIT flag is set in the *Flags* field. When using the function normally, the *rgbResult* field will be set to the color that the user selects.

Notice that the *hwndOwner* field of the Color dialog box is set to NULL. When the *ChooseColor* function calls *DialogBox* to display the dialog box, the third parameter to *DialogBox* is also set to NULL. This is perfectly legitimate. It means that the dialog box is not owned by another window. The caption in the dialog box will appear in the Task List, and the dialog box will seem to function much like a normal window.

You can also use this technique with your own dialog boxes in your own programs. It's possible to make a Windows program that creates only a dialog box and does all processing within the dialog box procedure.

Chapter 12

The Clipboard

The Microsoft Windows clipboard allows data to be transferred from one program to another. It is a relatively simple mechanism that doesn't require much overhead in either the program that places data in the clipboard or the program that later gets access to it. Windows 98 and Microsoft Windows NT come with Clipboard Viewer programs that show the current contents of the clipboard.

Many programs that deal with documents or other data include an Edit menu with the options Cut, Copy, and Paste. When a user selects Cut or Copy, the program transfers data from the program to the clipboard. This data is in a particular format, usually text, a bitmap (a rectangular array of bits that correspond to the pixels of a display surface), or a metafile (a binary collection of drawing commands). When a user selects Paste from the menu, the program determines if the clipboard contains data in a format that the program can use and, if so, transfers data from the clipboard to the program.

Programs should not transfer data into or out of the clipboard without an explicit instruction from the user. For example, a user who performs a Cut or a Copy (or a Ctrl-X or Ctrl-C) operation in one program should be able to assume that the data will remain in the clipboard until the next Cut or Copy operation.

You may recall that an Edit menu was implemented in the later versions of the POPPAD programs shown in Chapters 10 and 11. However, that simply involved sending messages to the edit control. In most cases you don't have that convenience; you must instead call the clipboard transfer functions yourself.

This chapter will focus on transferring text to and from the clipboard. In later chapters, I'll show you how to use the clipboard with bitmaps (Chapters 14, 15, and 16) and metafiles (Chapter 18).

SIMPLE USE OF THE CLIPBOARD

We'll begin by looking at the code involved for transferring data to the clipboard (Cut and Copy) and getting access to clipboard data (Paste).

The Standard Clipboard Data Formats

Windows supports various predefined clipboard formats that have identifiers beginning with the prefix CF defined in WINUSER.H.

First, there are three types of text data that can be stored in the clipboard, and another related clipboard format:

- *CF_TEXT*   A NULL-terminated ANSI character-set character string containing a carriage return and a linefeed character at the end of each line. This is the simplest form of clipboard data. The data to be transferred to the clipboard is stored in a memory block and is transferred using the handle to the block. (I'll discuss this concept shortly.) The memory block becomes the property of the clipboard, and the program that creates the block should not continue to use it.

- *CF_OEMTEXT*   A memory block containing text data (similar to CF_TEXT) but using the OEM character set. Windows programs usually don't need to worry about this; it comes into play when using the clipboard in conjunction with MS-DOS programs running in a window.

- *CF_UNICODETEXT*   A memory block containing Unicode text. Like CF_TEXT, each line is terminated with a carriage return and linefeed character, and a NULL character (two zero bytes) indicates the end of the data. CF_UNICODETEXT is supported under Windows NT only.

- *CF_LOCALE*   A handle to a locale identifier indicating the locale associated with clipboard text.

There are two additional clipboard formats that are conceptually similar to the CF_TEXT format (that is, they are text-based), but they are not necessarily NULL-terminated, because the formats define the end of the data. These formats are rarely used these days:

- *CF_SYLK*   A memory block containing data in the Microsoft "Symbolic Link" format. This format is used for exchanging data between Microsoft's Multiplan, Chart, and Excel programs. It is an ASCII format with each line terminated with a carriage return and a linefeed.

- *CF_DIF*   A memory block containing data in the Data Interchange Format (DIF). This is a format devised by Software Arts for use in transferring data to the

VisiCalc spreadsheet program. This is also an ASCII format with lines terminated with carriage returns and linefeeds.

There are three clipboard formats used in conjunction with bitmaps, which are rectangular arrays of bits that correspond to the pixels of an output device. Bitmaps and these bitmap clipboard formats are discussed in more detail in Chapters 14 and 15:

- *CF_BITMAP*   A device-dependent bitmap. The bitmap is transferred to the clipboard using the bitmap handle. Again, a program should not continue to use this bitmap after giving it to the clipboard.

- *CF_DIB*   A memory block defining a device-independent bitmap, as described in Chapter 15. The memory block begins with a bitmap information structure followed by a possible color table and the bitmap bits.

- *CF_PALETTE*   A handle to a color palette. This is generally used in conjunction with CF_DIB for defining a color palette used by a device-dependent bitmap.

It is also possible to store bitmap data in the clipboard in the industry-standard TIFF format:

- *CF_TIFF*   A memory block containing data in the Tag Image File Format (TIFF). This is a format devised by Microsoft, Aldus Corporation, and Hewlett-Packard Company in conjunction with some hardware manufacturers. The format is available from the Hewlett-Packard Web site.

There are two metafile formats that I'll describe in more detail in Chapter 18. A metafile is a collection of drawing commands stored in a binary form:

- *CF_METAFILEPICT*   A "metafile picture" based on the old metafile support of Windows.

- *CF_ENHMETAFILE*   A handle to an enhanced metafile supported under the 32-bit versions of Windows.

And finally there are also a few other miscellaneous clipboard formats:

- *CF_PENDATA*   Used in conjunction with the pen extensions to Windows.

- *CF_WAVE*   A sound (waveform) file.

- *CF_RIFF*   Multimedia data in the Resource Interchange File Format.

- *CF_HDROP*   A list of files used in conjunction with drag-and-drop services.

Memory Allocation

When your program transfers something to the clipboard, it must allocate a memory block and essentially hand it over to the clipboard. When we've needed to allocate memory in earlier programs in this book, we've simply used the *malloc* function that is supported by the standard C run-time library. However, because the memory blocks stored by the clipboard must be shared among applications running under Windows, the *malloc* function is inadequate for this task.

Instead, we must dredge up memory allocation functions that were designed back in the dark ages of Windows, in the days when the operating system ran in a 16-bit real-mode memory architecture. These functions are still supported and you can still use them, but they are not often needed.

To allocate a memory block using the Windows API, you can call

```
hGlobal = GlobalAlloc (uiFlags, dwSize) ;
```

The function takes two parameters: a possible series of flags and a size in bytes of the allocated block. The function returns a handle of type HGLOBAL, called a "handle to a global memory block" or a "global handle." A NULL return value indicates that sufficient memory was not available for the allocation.

Although the two parameters to *GlobalAlloc* are defined a bit differently, they are both 32-bit unsigned integers. If you set the first parameter to zero, you effectively use the flag GMEM_FIXED. In this case, the global handle that *GlobalAlloc* returns is actually a pointer to the allocated memory block.

You can also use the flag GMEM_ZEROINIT if you'd like every byte in the memory block to be initially set to zero. The succinct GPTR flag combines the GMEM_FIXED and GMEM_ZEROINIT flags as defined in the Windows header files:

```
#define GPTR (GMEM_FIXED | GMEM_ZEROINIT)
```

There is also a reallocation function:

```
hGlobal = GlobalReAlloc (hGlobal, dwSize, uiFlags) ;
```

You can use the GMEM_ZEROINIT flag to zero out the new bytes if the memory block is being enlarged.

Here's the function to obtain the size of the memory block:

```
dwSize = GlobalSize (hGlobal) ;
```

and the function to free it:

```
GlobalFree (hGlobal) ;
```

In the early 16-bit versions of Windows, the GMEM_FIXED flag was strongly discouraged because Windows could not move the block in physical memory. In the 32-bit versions of Windows, the GMEM_FIXED flag is normal because it returns a virtual address and the operating system can move the block in physical memory by altering the page table. When programming for the 16-bit versions of Windows, using the flag GMEM_MOVEABLE in *GlobalAlloc* was instead recommended. (Note that most dictionaries prefer the spelling "movable" over "moveable," so that's how I'll spell the word otherwise.) There's also a shorthand identifier identified in the Windows header files to additionally zero out the movable memory:

```
#define GHND (GMEM_MOVEABLE | GMEM_ZEROINIT)
```

The GMEM_MOVEABLE flag allows Windows to move a memory block in virtual memory. This doesn't necessarily mean that the memory block will be moved in physical memory, but the address that the application uses to read and write to the block can change.

Although GMEM_MOVEABLE was the rule in 16-bit versions of Windows, it is generally less useful now. However, if your application frequently allocates, reallocates, and frees memory blocks of various sizes, the virtual address space of your application can become fragmented. Conceivably, you could run out of virtual memory addresses. If this is a potential problem, then you'll want to use movable memory, and here's how to do it.

First define a pointer (for example, to an *int* type) and a variable of type GLOBALHANDLE:

```
int * p ;
GLOBALHANDLE hGlobal ;
```

Then allocate the memory. For example:

```
hGlobal = GlobalAlloc (GHND, 1024) ;
```

As with any Windows handle, don't worry too much about what the number really means. Just store it. When you need to access that memory block, call

```
p = (int *) GlobalLock (hGlobal) ;
```

This translates the handle into a pointer. During the time that the block is locked, Windows will fix the address in virtual memory. It will not move. When you are finished accessing the block, call

```
GlobalUnlock (hGlobal) ;
```

This gives Windows the freedom to move the block in virtual memory. To be really compulsively correct about this process (and to experience the torments of early Windows programmers), you should lock and unlock the memory block in the course of a single message.

When you want to free the memory, call *GlobalFree* with the handle rather than the pointer. If you don't currently have access to the handle, use the function

```
hGlobal = GlobalHandle (p) ;
```

You can lock a memory block multiple times before unlocking it. Windows maintains a lock count, and each lock requires a corresponding unlock before the block is free to be moved. When Windows moves a block in virtual memory, it doesn't need to copy the bytes from one location to another—it needs only manipulate the page tables. In general, in the 32-bit versions of Windows the only real reason for allocating a movable block for your own program's use is to prevent fragmentation of virtual memory. When using the clipboard, you should also use movable memory.

When allocating memory for the clipboard, you should use the *GlobalAlloc* function with both the GMEM_MOVEABLE and the GMEM_SHARE flags. The GMEM_SHARE flag makes the block available to other Windows applications.

Transferring Text to the Clipboard

Let's assume that you want to transfer an ANSI character string to the clipboard. You have a pointer (called *pString*) to this string, and you want to transfer *iLength* characters that might or might not be NULL-terminated.

You must first use *GlobalAlloc* to allocate a memory block of sufficient size to hold the character string. Include room for a terminating NULL:

```
hGlobal = GlobalAlloc (GHND | GMEM_SHARE, iLength + 1) ;
```

The value of *hGlobal* will be NULL if the block could not be allocated. If the allocation is successful, lock the block to get a pointer to it:

```
pGlobal = GlobalLock (hGlobal) ;
```

Copy the character string into the global memory block:

```
for (i = 0 ; i < wLength ; i++)
    *pGlobal++ = *pString++ ;
```

You don't need to add the terminating NULL because the GHND flag for *GlobalAlloc* zeroes out the entire memory block during allocation. Unlock the block:

```
GlobalUnlock (hGlobal) ;
```

Now you have a global memory handle that references a memory block containing the NULL-terminated text. To get this into the clipboard, open the clipboard and empty it:

```
OpenClipboard (hwnd) ;
EmptyClipboard () ;
```

Give the clipboard the memory handle by using the CF_TEXT identifier, and close the clipboard:

```
SetClipboardData (CF_TEXT, hGlobal) ;
CloseClipboard () ;
```

You're done.

Here are some rules concerning this process:

- Call *OpenClipboard* and *CloseClipboard* while processing a single message. Don't leave the clipboard open any longer than necessary.

- Don't give the clipboard a locked memory handle.

- After you call *SetClipboardData*, don't continue to use the memory block. It no longer belongs to your program, and you should treat the handle as invalid. If you need to continue to access the data, make another copy of it or read it from the clipboard (as described in the next section). You can also continue to reference the block between the *SetClipboardData* call and the *CloseClipboard* call, but don't use the global handle you passed to the *SetClipboardData* function. This function also *returns* a global handle that you can use instead. Lock this handle to access the memory. Unlock the handle before you call *CloseClipboard*.

Getting Text from the Clipboard

Getting text from the clipboard is only a little more complex than transferring text to the clipboard. You must first determine whether the clipboard does in fact contain data in the CF_TEXT format. One of the easiest methods is to use the call

```
bAvailable = IsClipboardFormatAvailable (CF_TEXT) ;
```

This function returns TRUE (nonzero) if the clipboard contains CF_TEXT data. We used this function in the POPPAD2 program in Chapter 10 to determine whether the Paste item on the Edit menu should be enabled or grayed. *IsClipboardFormatAvailable* is one of the few clipboard functions that you can use without first opening the clipboard. However, if you later open the clipboard to get this text, you should also check again (using the same function or one of the other methods) to determine whether the CF_TEXT data is still in the clipboard.

To transfer the text out, first open the clipboard:

```
OpenClipboard (hwnd) ;
```

Obtain the handle to the global memory block referencing the text:

```
hGlobal = GetClipboardData (CF_TEXT) ;
```

This handle will be NULL if the clipboard doesn't contain data in the CF_TEXT format. This is another way to determine whether the clipboard contains text. If *GetClipboardData* returns NULL, close the clipboard without doing anything else.

The handle you receive from *GetClipboardData* doesn't belong to your program—it belongs to the clipboard. The handle is valid only between the *GetClipboardData* and *CloseClipboard* calls. You can't free that handle or alter the data it references. If you need to have continued access to the data, you should make a copy of the memory block.

Here's one method for copying the data into your program. Just allocate a pointer to a block of the same size as the clipboard data block:

```
pText = (char *) malloc (GlobalSize (hGlobal)) ;
```

Recall that *hGlobal* was the global handle obtained from the *GetClipboardData* call. Now lock the handle to get a pointer to the clipboard block:

```
pGlobal = GlobalLock (hGlobal) ;
```

Now just copy the data:

```
strcpy (pText, pGlobal) ;
```

Or you can use some simple C code:

```
while (*pText++ = *pGlobal++) ;
```

Unlock the block before closing the clipboard:

```
GlobalUnlock (hGlobal) ;
CloseClipboard () ;
```

Now you have a pointer called *pText* that references the program's own copy of the text.

Opening and Closing the Clipboard

Only one program can have the clipboard open at any time. The purpose of the *Open-Clipboard* call is to prevent the clipboard contents from changing while a program is using the clipboard. *OpenClipboard* returns a BOOL value indicating whether the clipboard was successfully opened. It will not be opened if another application failed to close it. If every program politely opens and then closes the clipboard as quickly as possible responding to a user command, you'll probably never run into the problem of being unable to open the clipboard.

In the world of impolite programs and preemptive multitasking, some problems could arise. Even if your program hasn't lost input focus between the time it put something into the clipboard and the time the user invokes a Paste option, don't assume that what you've put in there is still there. A background process *could* have accessed the clipboard during that time.

Watch out for a more subtle problem involving message boxes: If you can't allocate enough memory to copy something to the clipboard, then you might want to display a message box. If this message box isn't system modal, however, the user can switch to another application while the message box is displayed. You should either make the message box system modal or close the clipboard before you display the message box.

You can also run into problems if you leave the clipboard open while you display a dialog box. Edit fields in a dialog box use the clipboard for cutting and pasting text.

The Clipboard and Unicode

So far I've been discussing using the clipboard solely with ANSI (one byte per character) text. This is the format when you use the CF_TEXT identifier. You may be wondering about CF_OEMTEXT and CF_UNICODETEXT.

I have some good news: you only need to call *SetClipboardData* and *GetClipboardData* with your preferred text format and Windows will handle all text conversions in the clipboard. For example, under Windows NT if a program uses *SetClipboardData* with a CF_TEXT clipboard data type, programs can also call *GetClipboardData* using CF_OEMTEXT. Similarly, the clipboard can convert CF_OEMTEXT data to CF_TEXT.

Under Windows NT, conversions occur between CF_UNICODETEXT, CF_TEXT, and CF_OEMTEXT. A program should call *SetClipboardData* using whatever text format is most convenient for the program. Similarly, a program should call *GetClipboardData* using whatever text form is desired by the program. As you know, the programs shown in this book are written so that they can be compiled with and without the UNICODE identifier. If your programs are like that, you'll probably implement code that calls *SetClipboardData* and *GetClipboardData* using CF_UNICODETEXT if the UNICODE identifier is defined and CF_TEXT if it is not.

The CLIPTEXT program shown in Figure 12-1 demonstrates one way this can be done.

CLIPTEXT.C

```
/*-------------------------------------------
   CLIPTEXT.C -- The Clipboard and Text
                 (c) Charles Petzold, 1998
   -------------------------------------------*/

#include <windows.h>
#include "resource.h"

LRESULT CALLBACK WndProc (HWND, UINT, WPARAM, LPARAM) ;

#ifdef UNICODE

#define CF_TCHAR CF_UNICODETEXT
TCHAR szDefaultText[] = TEXT ("Default Text - Unicode Version") ;
TCHAR szCaption[]     = TEXT ("Clipboard Text Transfers - Unicode Version") ;
```

Figure 12-1. *The CLIPTEXT program.*　　　*(continued)*

Figure 12-1. *continued*

```
#else

#define CF_TCHAR CF_TEXT
TCHAR szDefaultText[] = TEXT ("Default Text - ANSI Version") ;
TCHAR szCaption[]     = TEXT ("Clipboard Text Transfers - ANSI Version") ;

#endif

int WINAPI WinMain (HINSTANCE hInstance, HINSTANCE hPrevInstance,
                    PSTR szCmdLine, int iCmdShow)
{
     static TCHAR szAppName[] = TEXT ("ClipText") ;
     HACCEL        hAccel ;
     HWND          hwnd ;
     MSG           msg ;
     WNDCLASS      wndclass ;

     wndclass.style         = CS_HREDRAW | CS_VREDRAW ;
     wndclass.lpfnWndProc   = WndProc ;
     wndclass.cbClsExtra    = 0 ;
     wndclass.cbWndExtra    = 0 ;
     wndclass.hInstance     = hInstance ;
     wndclass.hIcon         = LoadIcon (NULL, IDI_APPLICATION) ;
     wndclass.hCursor       = LoadCursor (NULL, IDC_ARROW) ;
     wndclass.hbrBackground = (HBRUSH) GetStockObject (WHITE_BRUSH) ;
     wndclass.lpszMenuName  = szAppName ;
     wndclass.lpszClassName = szAppName ;

     if (!RegisterClass (&wndclass))
     {
          MessageBox (NULL, TEXT ("This program requires Windows NT!"),
                      szAppName, MB_ICONERROR) ;
          return 0 ;
     }

     hwnd = CreateWindow (szAppName, szCaption,
                          WS_OVERLAPPEDWINDOW,
                          CW_USEDEFAULT, CW_USEDEFAULT,
                          CW_USEDEFAULT, CW_USEDEFAULT,
                          NULL, NULL, hInstance, NULL) ;

     ShowWindow (hwnd, iCmdShow) ;
     UpdateWindow (hwnd) ;

     hAccel = LoadAccelerators (hInstance, szAppName) ;

     while (GetMessage (&msg, NULL, 0, 0))
```

```
      {
         if (!TranslateAccelerator (hwnd, hAccel, &msg))
         {
              TranslateMessage (&msg) ;
              DispatchMessage (&msg) ;
         }
      }
      return msg.wParam ;
}

LRESULT CALLBACK WndProc (HWND hwnd, UINT message, WPARAM wParam, LPARAM lParam)
{
     static PTSTR pText ;
     BOOL         bEnable ;
     HGLOBAL      hGlobal ;
     HDC          hdc ;
     PTSTR        pGlobal ;
     PAINTSTRUCT  ps ;
     RECT         rect ;

     switch (message)
     {
     case WM_CREATE:
          SendMessage (hwnd, WM_COMMAND, IDM_EDIT_RESET, 0) ;
          return 0 ;

     case WM_INITMENUPOPUP:
          EnableMenuItem ((HMENU) wParam, IDM_EDIT_PASTE,
               IsClipboardFormatAvailable (CF_TCHAR) ? MF_ENABLED : MF_GRAYED) ;

          bEnable = pText ? MF_ENABLED : MF_GRAYED ;

          EnableMenuItem ((HMENU) wParam, IDM_EDIT_CUT,   bEnable) ;
          EnableMenuItem ((HMENU) wParam, IDM_EDIT_COPY,  bEnable) ;
          EnableMenuItem ((HMENU) wParam, IDM_EDIT_CLEAR, bEnable) ;
          break ;

     case WM_COMMAND:
          switch (LOWORD (wParam))
          {
          case IDM_EDIT_PASTE:
               OpenClipboard (hwnd) ;

               if (hGlobal = GetClipboardData (CF_TCHAR))
               {
                    pGlobal = GlobalLock (hGlobal) ;
```

(continued)

Figure 12-1. *continued*

```
                    if (pText)
                    {
                         free (pText) ;
                         pText = NULL ;
                    }
                    pText = malloc (GlobalSize (hGlobal)) ;
                    lstrcpy (pText, pGlobal) ;
                    InvalidateRect (hwnd, NULL, TRUE) ;
               }
               CloseClipboard () ;
               return 0 ;

     case IDM_EDIT_CUT:
     case IDM_EDIT_COPY:
          if (!pText)
               return 0 ;

          hGlobal = GlobalAlloc (GHND | GMEM_SHARE,
                              (lstrlen (pText) + 1) * sizeof (TCHAR)) ;
          pGlobal = GlobalLock (hGlobal) ;
          lstrcpy (pGlobal, pText) ;
          GlobalUnlock (hGlobal) ;

          OpenClipboard (hwnd) ;
          EmptyClipboard () ;
          SetClipboardData (CF_TCHAR, hGlobal) ;
          CloseClipboard () ;

          if (LOWORD (wParam) == IDM_EDIT_COPY)
               return 0 ;
                                        // fall through for IDM_EDIT_CUT
     case IDM_EDIT_CLEAR:
          if (pText)
          {
               free (pText) ;
               pText = NULL ;
          }
          InvalidateRect (hwnd, NULL, TRUE) ;
          return 0 ;

     case IDM_EDIT_RESET:
          if (pText)
          {
               free (pText) ;
               pText = NULL ;
          }
```

```
                pText = malloc ((lstrlen (szDefaultText) + 1) * sizeof (TCHAR)) ;
                lstrcpy (pText, szDefaultText) ;
                InvalidateRect (hwnd, NULL, TRUE) ;
                return 0 ;
          }
          break ;

     case WM_PAINT:
          hdc = BeginPaint (hwnd, &ps) ;

          GetClientRect (hwnd, &rect) ;

          if (pText != NULL)
                DrawText (hdc, pText, -1, &rect, DT_EXPANDTABS | DT_WORDBREAK) ;

          EndPaint (hwnd, &ps) ;
          return 0 ;

     case WM_DESTROY:
          if (pText)
                free (pText) ;

          PostQuitMessage (0) ;
          return 0 ;
     }
     return DefWindowProc (hwnd, message, wParam, lParam) ;
}
```

CLIPTEXT.RC (excerpts)

```
//Microsoft Developer Studio generated resource script.

#include "resource.h"
#include "afxres.h"

/////////////////////////////////////////////////////////////////////////////
// Menu

CLIPTEXT MENU DISCARDABLE
BEGIN
    POPUP "&Edit"
    BEGIN
        MENUITEM "Cu&t\tCtrl+X",                  IDM_EDIT_CUT
        MENUITEM "&Copy\tCtrl+C",                 IDM_EDIT_COPY
        MENUITEM "&Paste\tCtrl+V",                IDM_EDIT_PASTE
```

(continued)

Figure 12-1. *continued*

```
        MENUITEM "De&lete\tDel",                    IDM_EDIT_CLEAR
        MENUITEM SEPARATOR
        MENUITEM "&Reset",                          IDM_EDIT_RESET
    END
END


/////////////////////////////////////////////////////////////////////////////
// Accelerator

CLIPTEXT ACCELERATORS DISCARDABLE
BEGIN
    "C",            IDM_EDIT_COPY,          VIRTKEY, CONTROL, NOINVERT
    "V",            IDM_EDIT_PASTE,         VIRTKEY, CONTROL, NOINVERT
    VK_DELETE,      IDM_EDIT_CLEAR,         VIRTKEY, NOINVERT
    "X",            IDM_EDIT_CUT,           VIRTKEY, CONTROL, NOINVERT
END
```

RESOURCE.H (excerpts)

```
// Microsoft Developer Studio generated include file.
// Used by ClipText.rc

#define IDM_EDIT_CUT             40001
#define IDM_EDIT_COPY            40002
#define IDM_EDIT_PASTE           40003
#define IDM_EDIT_CLEAR           40004
#define IDM_EDIT_RESET           40005
```

The idea here is that you can run both the Unicode and ANSI versions of this program under Windows NT and see how the clipboard translates between the two character sets. Notice the *#ifdef* statement at the top of CLIPTEXT.C. If the UNICODE identifier is defined, then CF_TCHAR (a generic text clipboard format name I made up) is equal to CF_UNICODETEXT; if not, it's equal to CF_TEXT. The *IsClipboardFormatAvailable*, *GetClipboardData*, and *SetClipboardData* function calls later in the program all use this CF_TCHAR name to specify the data type.

At the outset of the program (and whenever you select the Reset option from the Edit menu), the static variable *pText* contains a pointer to the Unicode string "Default Text – Unicode version" in the Unicode version of the program and "Default Text – ANSI version" in the non-Unicode version. You can use the Cut or Copy command to transfer this text string to the clipboard, and you can use the Cut or Delete command to delete the string from the program. The Paste command copies any text contents of the clipboard to *pText*. The *pText* string is displayed on the program's client area during the WM_PAINT message.

If you first select the Copy command from the Unicode version of CLIPTEXT and then the Paste command from the non-Unicode version, you can see that the text has been converted from Unicode to ANSI. Similarly, if you do the opposite commands, the text is converted from ANSI to Unicode.

BEYOND SIMPLE CLIPBOARD USE

We've seen that transferring text from the clipboard requires four calls after the data has been prepared:

```
OpenClipboard (hwnd) ;
EmptyClipboard () ;
SetClipboardData (iFormat, hGlobal) ;
CloseClipboard () ;
```

Getting access to this data requires three calls:

```
OpenClipboard (hwnd) ;
hGlobal = GetClipboardData (iFormat) ;
[other program lines]
CloseClipboard () ;
```

You can make a copy of the clipboard data or use it in some other manner between the *GetClipboardData* and *CloseClipboard* calls. That approach may be all you'll need for most purposes, but you can also use the clipboard in more sophisticated ways.

Using Multiple Data Items

When you open the clipboard to put data into it, you must call *EmptyClipboard* to signal Windows to free or delete the contents of the clipboard. You can't add something to the existing contents of the clipboard. So, in this sense, the clipboard holds only one item at a time.

However, between the *EmptyClipboard* and the *CloseClipboard* calls, you can call *SetClipboardData* several times, each time using a different clipboard format. For instance, if you want to store a short string of text in the clipboard, you can write that text to a metafile and to a bitmap. In this way, you make that character string available not only to programs that can read text from the clipboard but also to programs that read bitmaps and metafiles from the clipboard. Of course, these programs won't be able to easily recognize that the metafile or bitmap actually contains a character string.

If you want to write several handles to the clipboard, you call *SetClipboardData* for each of them:

```
OpenClipboard (hwnd) ;
EmptyClipboard () ;
SetClipboardData (CF_TEXT, hGlobalText) ;
SetClipboardData (CF_BITMAP, hBitmap) ;
SetClipboardData (CF_METAFILEPICT, hGlobalMFP) ;
CloseClipboard () ;
```

While these three formats of data are in the clipboard, an *IsClipboardFormatAvailable* call with the CF_TEXT, CF_BITMAP, or CF_METAFILEPICT argument will return TRUE. A program can get access to these handles by calling

```
hGlobalText = GetClipboardData (CF_TEXT) ;
```

or

```
hBitmap = GetClipboardData (CF_BITMAP) ;
```

or

```
hGlobalMFP = GetClipboardData (CF_METAFILEPICT) ;
```

The next time a program calls *EmptyClipboard*, Windows will free or delete all three of the handles retained by the clipboard.

Don't use this technique to add different text formats, different bitmap formats, or different metafile formats to the clipboard. Use only one text format, one bitmap format, and one metafile format. As I mentioned, Windows will convert among CF_TEXT, CF_OEMTEXT, and CF_UNICODETEXT. It will also convert between CF_BITMAP and CF_DIB, and between CF_METAFILEPICT and CF_ENHMETAFILE.

A program can determine all the formats stored by the clipboard by first opening the clipboard and then calling *EnumClipboardFormats*. Start off by setting a variable *iFormat* to 0:

```
iFormat = 0 ;
OpenClipboard (hwnd) ;
```

Now make successive *EnumClipboardFormats* calls starting with the 0 value. The function will return a positive *iFormat* value for each format currently in the clipboard. When the function returns 0, you're done:

```
while (iFormat = EnumClipboardFormats (iFormat))
{
     [logic for each iFormat value]
}
CloseClipboard () ;
```

You can obtain the number of different formats currently in the clipboard by calling

```
iCount = CountClipboardFormats () ;
```

Delayed Rendering

When you put data into the clipboard, you generally make a copy of the data and give the clipboard a handle to a global memory block that contains the copy. For very large data items, this approach can waste memory. If the user never pastes that data into another program, it will continue to occupy memory space until it is replaced by something else.

You can avoid this problem by using a technique called "delayed rendering," in which your program doesn't actually supply the data until another program needs it. Rather than give Windows a handle to the data, you simply use a NULL in the *SetClipboardData* call:

```
OpenClipboard (hwnd) ;
EmptyClipboard () ;
SetClipboardData (iFormat, NULL) ;
CloseClipboard () ;
```

You can have multiple *SetClipboardData* calls using different values of *iFormat*. You can use NULL parameters with some of them and real handles with others.

That's simple enough, but now the process gets a little more complex. When another program calls *GetClipboardData*, Windows will check to see if the handle for that format is NULL. If it is, Windows will send a message to the "clipboard owner" (your program) asking for a real handle to the data. Your program must then supply this handle.

More specifically, the "clipboard owner" is the last window that put data into the clipboard. When a program calls *OpenClipboard*, Windows stores the window handle required by this function. This handle identifies the window that has the clipboard open. On receipt of an *EmptyClipboard* call, Windows establishes this window as the new clipboard owner.

A program that uses delayed rendering must process three messages in its window procedure: WM_RENDERFORMAT, WM_RENDERALLFORMATS, and WM_DESTROY-CLIPBOARD. Windows sends your window procedure a WM_RENDERFORMAT message when another program calls *GetClipboardData*. The value of *wParam* is the format requested. When you process the WM_RENDERFORMAT message, don't open and empty the clipboard. Simply create a global memory block for the format given by *wParam*, transfer the data to it, and call *SetClipboardData* with the correct format and the global handle. Obviously, you'll need to retain information in your program to construct this data properly when processing WM_RENDERFORMAT. When another program calls *EmptyClipboard*, Windows sends your program a WM_DESTROYCLIPBOARD message. This tells you that the information to construct the clipboard data is no longer needed. You are no longer the clipboard owner.

If your program terminates while it is still the clipboard owner, and the clipboard still contains NULL data handles that your program set with *SetClipboardData*, you'll receive a WM_RENDERALLFORMATS message. You should open the clipboard, empty it, put the data in global memory blocks, and call *SetClipboardData* for each format. Then close the clipboard. The WM_RENDERALLFORMATS message is one of the last messages your window procedure receives. It is followed by a WM_DESTROYCLIPBOARD message—because you've rendered all the data—and then the normal WM_DESTROY.

If your program can transfer only one format of data to the clipboard (text, for instance), you can combine the WM_RENDERALLFORMATS and WM_RENDERFORMAT processing. The code will look something like this:

```
case WM_RENDERALLFORMATS :
     OpenClipboard (hwnd) ;
     EmptyClipboard () ;
                                  // fall through
case WM_RENDERFORMAT :
     [put text into global memory block]
     SetClipboardData (CF_TEXT, hGlobal) ;

     if (message == WM_RENDERALLFORMATS)
          CloseClipboard () ;
     return 0 ;
```

If your program uses several clipboard formats, you'll want to process the WM_RENDERFORMAT message only for the format requested by *wParam*. You don't need to process the WM_DESTROYCLIPBOARD message unless it is burdensome for your program to retain the information necessary to construct the data.

Private Data Formats

So far we've dealt with only the standard clipboard formats defined by Windows. However, you may want to use the clipboard to store a "private data format." Many word processors use this technique to store text that contains font and formatting information.

At first, this concept may seem nonsensical. If the purpose of the clipboard is to transfer data between applications, why should the clipboard contain data that only one application understands? The answer is simple: The clipboard also exists to allow the transfer of data to and from itself (or perhaps between different instances of the same program), and these instances obviously understand the same private formats.

There are several ways to use private data formats. The easiest involves data that is ostensibly in one of the standard clipboard formats (that is, text, bitmap, or metafile) but that has meaning only to your program. In this case, you use one of the following *wFormat* values in your *SetClipboardData* and *GetClipboardData* calls: CF_DSPTEXT, CF_DSPBITMAP, CF_DSPMETAFILEPICT, or CF_DSPENHMETAFILE. (The letters DSP stand for "display.") These formats allow the Windows clipboard viewer to display the data as text, a bitmap, or a metafile. However, another program that calls *GetClipboardData* using the normal CF_TEXT, CF_BITMAP, CF_DIB, CF_METAFILEPICT, or CF_ENHMETAFILE format won't obtain this data.

If you use one of these formats to put data in the clipboard, you must also use the same format to get the data out. But how do you know if the data is from another instance of your program or from another program using one of these formats? Here's one way: You can first obtain the clipboard owner by calling

```
hwndClipOwner = GetClipboardOwner () ;
```

You can then get the name of the window class of this window handle:

```
TCHAR szClassName [32] ;
[other program lines]
GetClassName (hwndClipOwner, szClassName, 32) ;
```

If the class name is the same as your program's, then the data was put in the clipboard by another instance of your program.

The second way to use private formats involves the CF_OWNERDISPLAY flag. The global memory handle to *SetClipboardData* is NULL:

```
SetClipboardData (CF_OWNERDISPLAY, NULL) ;
```

This is the method that some word processors use to show formatted text in the client area of the clipboard viewer included with Windows. Obviously, the clipboard viewer doesn't know how to display this formatted text. When a word processor specifies the CF_OWNER-DISPLAY format, it is also taking responsibility for painting the clipboard viewer's client area.

Because the global memory handle is NULL, a program that calls *SetClipboardData* with the CF_OWNERDISPLAY format (the clipboard owner) must process the delayed rendering messages sent to the clipboard owner by Windows, as well as five additional messages. The following five messages are sent by the clipboard viewer to the clipboard owner:

■ *WM_ASKCBFORMATNAME*   The clipboard viewer sends this message to the clipboard owner to get a name for the format of the data. The *lParam* parameter is a pointer to a buffer, and *wParam* is the maximum number of characters for this buffer. The clipboard owner must copy the name of the clipboard format into this buffer.

■ *WM_SIZECLIPBOARD*   This message tells the clipboard owner that the size of the clipboard viewer's client area has changed. The *wParam* parameter is a handle to the clipboard viewer, and *lParam* is a pointer to a RECT structure containing the new size. If the RECT structure contains all zeros, the clipboard viewer is being destroyed or minimized. And, although the Windows clipboard viewer allows only one instance of itself to be running, other clipboard viewers can also send this message to the clipboard owner. Handling these multiple clipboard viewers isn't impossible for the clipboard owner (given that *wParam* identifies the particular viewer), but it isn't easy, either.

- *WM_PAINTCLIPBOARD*   This message tells the clipboard owner to update the clipboard viewer's client area. Again, *wParam* is a handle to the clipboard viewer's window. The *lParam* parameter is a global handle to a PAINTSTRUCT structure. The clipboard owner can lock the handle and obtain a handle to the clipboard viewer's device context from the *hdc* field of this structure.

- *WM_HSCROLLCLIPBOARD* and *WM_VSCROLLCLIPBOARD*   These messages inform the clipboard owner that a user has scrolled the clipboard viewer's scroll bars. The *wParam* parameter is a handle to the clipboard viewer's window, the low word of *lParam* is the scrolling request, and the high word of *lParam* is the thumb position if the low word is SB_THUMBPOSITION.

Handling these messages may look like more trouble than it's worth. However, the process does provide a benefit to the user: when copying text from a word processsor to the clipboard, the user will find it comforting to see the text still formatted in the clipboard viewer's client area.

The third way to use private clipboard data formats is to register your own clipboard format name. You supply a name for this format to Windows, and Windows gives your program a number to use as the format parameter in *SetClipboardData* and *GetClipboardData*. Programs that use this method generally also copy data to the clipboard in one of the standard formats. This approach allows the clipboard viewer to display data in its client area (without the hassles involved with CF_OWNERDISPLAY) and permits other programs to copy data from the clipboard.

As an example, let's assume we've written a vector-drawing program that copies data to the clipboard in a bitmap format, a metafile format, and its own registered clipboard format. The clipboard viewer will display the metafile or bitmap. Other programs that can read bitmaps or metafiles from the clipboard will obtain those formats. However, when the vector-drawing program itself needs to read data from the clipboard, it will copy the data in its own registered format because that format probably contains more information than the bitmap or metafile.

A program registers a new clipboard format by calling

```
iFormat = RegisterClipboardFormat (szFormatName) ;
```

The *iFormat* value is between 0xC000 and 0xFFFF. A clipboard viewer (or a program that obtains all the current clipboard formats by calling *EnumClipboardFormats*) can obtain the ASCII name of this format by calling

```
GetClipboardFormatName (iFormat, psBuffer, iMaxCount) ;
```

Windows copies up to *iMaxCount* characters into *psBuffer*.

Programmers who use this method for copying data to the clipboard might want to publicize the format name and the actual format of the data. If the program becomes popular, other programs can then copy data in this format from the clipboard.

BECOMING A CLIPBOARD VIEWER

A program that is notified of changes in the clipboard contents is called a "clipboard viewer." You get a clipboard viewer with Windows, but you can also write your own clipboard viewer program. Clipboard viewers are notified of changes to the clipboard through messages to the viewer's window procedure.

The Clipboard Viewer Chain

Any number of clipboard viewer applications can be running in Windows at the same time, and they can all be notified of changes to the clipboard. From Windows' perspective, however, there is only one clipboard viewer, which I'll call the "current clipboard viewer." Windows maintains only one window handle to identify the current clipboard viewer, and it sends messages only to that window when the contents of the clipboard change.

Clipboard viewer applications have the responsibility of participating in the "clipboard viewer chain" so that all running clipboard viewer programs receive the messages that Windows sends to the current clipboard viewer. When a program registers itself as a clipboard viewer, that program becomes the current clipboard viewer. Windows gives that program the window handle of the previous current clipboard viewer, and the program saves this handle. When the program receives a clipboard viewer message, it sends that message to the window procedure of the next program in the clipboard chain.

Clipboard Viewer Functions and Messages

A program can become part of the clipboard viewer chain by calling the *SetClipboardViewer* function. If the primary purpose of the program is to serve as a clipboard viewer, the program can call this function during processing of the WM_CREATE message. The function returns the window handle of the previous current clipboard viewer. The program should save that handle in a static variable:

```
static HWND hwndNextViewer ;
[other program lines]
case WM_CREATE :
    [other program lines]
    hwndNextViewer = SetClipboardViewer (hwnd) ;
```

If your program is the first program to become a clipboard viewer during the Windows session, then *hwndNextViewer* will be NULL.

Windows sends a WM_DRAWCLIPBOARD message to the current clipboard viewer (the most recent window to register itself as a clipboard viewer) whenever the contents of the clipboard change. Each program in the clipboard viewer chain should use *SendMessage* to pass this message to the next clipboard viewer. The last program in the clipboard viewer chain (the first window to register itself as a clipboard viewer) will have stored a NULL *hwndNextViewer* value. If *hwndNextViewer* is NULL, the program simply returns without sending the message to another program. (Don't confuse the WM_DRAWCLIPBOARD and WM_PAINTCLIPBOARD messages. The WM_PAINTCLIPBOARD message is sent by a clipboard viewer to programs that use the CF_OWNERDISPLAY clipboard format. The WM_DRAWCLIPBOARD message is sent by Windows to the current clipboard viewer.)

The easiest way to process the WM_DRAWCLIPBOARD message is to send the message to the next clipboard viewer (unless *hwndNextViewer* is NULL) and invalidate the client area of your window:

```
case WM_DRAWCLIPBOARD :
    if (hwndNextViewer)
        SendMessage (hwndNextViewer, message, wParam, lParam) ;

    InvalidateRect (hwnd, NULL, TRUE) ;
    return 0 ;
```

During processing of the WM_PAINT message, you can read the contents of the clipboard by using the normal *OpenClipboard*, *GetClipboardData*, and *CloseClipboard* calls.

When a program wants to remove itself from the clipboard viewer chain, it must call *ChangeClipboardChain*. This function requires the window handle of the program leaving the viewer chain and the window handle of the next clipboard viewer:

```
ChangeClipboardChain (hwnd, hwndNextViewer) ;
```

When a program calls *ChangeClipboardChain*, Windows sends a WM_CHANGECBCHAIN message to the current clipboard viewer. The *wParam* parameter is the handle of the window removing itself from the chain (that is, the first parameter to *ChangeClipboardChain*), and *lParam* is the window handle of the next clipboard viewer after the one removing itself from the chain (the second argument to *ChangeClipboardChain*).

When your program receives a WM_CHANGECBCHAIN message, you must therefore check to see if *wParam* is equal to the value of *hwndNextViewer* that you've saved. If it is, your program must set *hwndNextViewer* to *lParam*. This action ensures that any future WM_DRAWCLIPBOARD messages you get won't be sent to the window removing itself from the clipboard viewer chain. If *wParam* isn't equal to *hwndNextViewer* and *hwndNextViewer* isn't NULL, send the message to the next clipboard viewer:

```
case WM_CHANGECBCHAIN :
    if ((HWND) wParam == hwndNextViewer)
        hwndNextViewer = (HWND) lParam ;

    else if (hwndNextViewer)
        SendMessage (hwndNextViewer, message, wParam, lParam) ;
    return 0 ;
```

You shouldn't really need to include the *else if* statement, which checks *hwndNextViewer* for a non-NULL value. A NULL *hwndNextViewer* value would indicate that the program executing this code is the last viewer on the chain, in which case the message should never have gotten this far.

If your program is still in the clipboard viewer chain when it is about to terminate, you must remove it from the chain. You can do this during processing of the WM_DESTROY message by calling *ChangeClipboardChain*:

```
case WM_DESTROY :
    ChangeClipboardChain (hwnd, hwndNextViewer) ;
    PostQuitMessage (0) ;
    return 0 ;
```

Windows also has a function that allows a program to obtain the window handle of the first clipboard viewer:

```
hwndViewer = GetClipboardViewer () ;
```

This function isn't normally needed. The return value can be NULL if there is no current clipboard viewer.

Here's an example to illustrate how the clipboard viewer chain works. When Windows first starts up, the current clipboard viewer is NULL:

Current clipboard viewer:	NULL

A program with a window handle of *hwnd1* calls *SetClipboardViewer*. The function returns NULL, which becomes the *hwndNextViewer* value in this program:

Current clipboard viewer:	*hwnd1*
hwnd1's next viewer:	NULL

A second program, with a window handle of *hwnd2*, now calls *SetClipboardViewer* and gets back *hwnd1*:

Current clipboard viewer:	*hwnd2*
hwnd2's next viewer:	*hwnd1*
hwnd1's next viewer:	NULL

A third program (*hwnd3*) and then a fourth (*hwnd4*) also call *SetClipboardViewer* and get back *hwnd2* and *hwnd3*:

Current clipboard viewer:	*hwnd4*
hwnd4's next viewer:	*hwnd3*
hwnd3's next viewer:	*hwnd2*
hwnd2's next viewer:	*hwnd1*
hwnd1's next viewer:	NULL

When the contents of the clipboard change, Windows sends a WM_DRAWCLIPBOARD message to *hwnd4*, *hwnd4* sends the message to *hwnd3*, *hwnd3* sends it to *hwnd2*, *hwnd2* sends it to *hwnd1*, and *hwnd1* returns.

Now *hwnd2* decides to remove itself from the chain by calling

```
ChangeClipboardChain (hwnd2, hwnd1) ;
```

Windows sends *hwnd4* a WM_CHANGECBCHAIN message with *wParam* equal to *hwnd2* and *lParam* equal to *hwnd1*. Because *hwnd4*'s next viewer is *hwnd3*, *hwnd4* sends this message to *hwnd3*. Now *hwnd3* notes that *wParam* is equal to its next viewer (*hwnd2*), so it sets its next viewer equal to *lParam* (*hwnd1*) and returns. The mission is accomplished. The clipboard viewer chain now looks like this:

Current clipboard viewer:	*hwnd4*
hwnd4's next viewer:	*hwnd3*
hwnd3's next viewer:	*hwnd1*
hwnd1's next viewer:	NULL

A Simple Clipboard Viewer

Clipboard viewers don't have to be as sophisticated as the one supplied with Windows. A clipboard viewer can, for instance, display a single clipboard format. The CLIPVIEW program, shown in Figure 12-2, is a clipboard viewer that displays only the CF_TEXT format.

CLIPVIEW.C

```c
/*----------------------------------------
   CLIPVIEW.C -- Simple Clipboard Viewer
                 (c) Charles Petzold, 1998
  ----------------------------------------*/

#include <windows.h>

LRESULT CALLBACK WndProc (HWND, UINT, WPARAM, LPARAM) ;

int WINAPI WinMain (HINSTANCE hInstance, HINSTANCE hPrevInstance,
                    PSTR szCmdLine, int iCmdShow)
{
     static TCHAR szAppName[] = TEXT ("ClipView") ;
     HWND         hwnd ;
     MSG          msg ;
     WNDCLASS     wndclass ;

     wndclass.style         = CS_HREDRAW | CS_VREDRAW ;
     wndclass.lpfnWndProc   = WndProc ;
```

Figure 12-2. *The CLIPVIEW program.*

```
     wndclass.cbClsExtra    = 0 ;
     wndclass.cbWndExtra    = 0 ;
     wndclass.hInstance     = hInstance ;
     wndclass.hIcon         = LoadIcon (NULL, IDI_APPLICATION) ;
     wndclass.hCursor       = LoadCursor (NULL, IDC_ARROW) ;
     wndclass.hbrBackground = (HBRUSH) GetStockObject (WHITE_BRUSH) ;
     wndclass.lpszMenuName  = NULL ;
     wndclass.lpszClassName = szAppName ;

     if (!RegisterClass (&wndclass))
     {
          MessageBox (NULL, TEXT ("This program requires Windows NT!"),
                      szAppName, MB_ICONERROR) ;
          return 0 ;
     }

     hwnd = CreateWindow (szAppName,
                          TEXT ("Simple Clipboard Viewer (Text Only)"),
                          WS_OVERLAPPEDWINDOW,
                          CW_USEDEFAULT, CW_USEDEFAULT,
                          CW_USEDEFAULT, CW_USEDEFAULT,
                          NULL, NULL, hInstance, NULL) ;

     ShowWindow (hwnd, iCmdShow) ;
     UpdateWindow (hwnd) ;

     while (GetMessage (&msg, NULL, 0, 0))
     {
          TranslateMessage (&msg) ;
          DispatchMessage (&msg) ;
     }
     return msg.wParam ;
}

LRESULT CALLBACK WndProc (HWND hwnd, UINT message, WPARAM wParam, LPARAM lParam)
{
     static HWND hwndNextViewer ;
     HGLOBAL    hGlobal ;
     HDC        hdc ;
     PTSTR      pGlobal ;
     PAINTSTRUCT ps ;
     RECT       rect ;

     switch (message)
     {
```

(continued)

Figure 12-2. *continued*

```
    case WM_CREATE:
         hwndNextViewer = SetClipboardViewer (hwnd) ;
         return 0 ;

    case WM_CHANGECBCHAIN:
         if ((HWND) wParam == hwndNextViewer)
              hwndNextViewer = (HWND) lParam ;

         else if (hwndNextViewer)
              SendMessage (hwndNextViewer, message, wParam, lParam) ;

         return 0 ;

    case WM_DRAWCLIPBOARD:
         if (hwndNextViewer)
              SendMessage (hwndNextViewer, message, wParam, lParam) ;

         InvalidateRect (hwnd, NULL, TRUE) ;
         return 0 ;

    case WM_PAINT:
         hdc = BeginPaint (hwnd, &ps) ;
         GetClientRect (hwnd, &rect) ;
         OpenClipboard (hwnd) ;

#ifdef UNICODE
         hGlobal = GetClipboardData (CF_UNICODETEXT) ;
#else
         hGlobal = GetClipboardData (CF_TEXT) ;
#endif

         if (hGlobal != NULL)
         {
              pGlobal = (PTSTR) GlobalLock (hGlobal) ;
              DrawText (hdc, pGlobal, -1, &rect, DT_EXPANDTABS) ;
              GlobalUnlock (hGlobal) ;
         }

         CloseClipboard () ;
         EndPaint (hwnd, &ps) ;
         return 0 ;
```

```
    case WM_DESTROY:
        ChangeClipboardChain (hwnd, hwndNextViewer) ;
        PostQuitMessage (0) ;
        return 0 ;
    }
    return DefWindowProc (hwnd, message, wParam, lParam) ;
}
```

CLIPVIEW processes WM_CREATE, WM_CHANGECBCHAIN, WM_DRAWCLIPBOARD, and WM_DESTROY messages as discussed above. The WM_PAINT message simply opens the clipboard and uses *GetClipboardData* with a format of CF_TEXT. If the function returns a global memory handle, CLIPVIEW locks it and uses *DrawText* to display the text in its client area.

A clipboard viewer that handles data formats beyond the standard formats (as the one supplied with Windows does) has additional work to do, such as displaying the names of all the formats currently in the clipboard. You can do this by calling *EnumClipboardFormats* and obtaining the names of the nonstandard formats from *GetClipboardFormatName*. A clipboard viewer that uses the CF_OWNERDISPLAY format must send the following four messages to the clipboard owner to display the data:

WM_PAINTCLIPBOARD   WM_VSCROLLCLIPBOARD

WM_SIZECLIPBOARD   WM_HSCROLLCLIPBOARD

If you want to write such a clipboard viewer, you have to obtain the window handle of the clipboard owner using *GetClipboardOwner* and send that window these messages when you need to update the clipboard viewer's client area.

Section II

More Graphics

Chapter 13

Using the Printer

The concept of device independence may have seemed all well and good when we were using the video display for text and graphics. But how well does the concept hold up for printers?

In general, the news is good. From a Microsoft Windows program, you can print text and graphics on paper using the same GDI functions that we've been using for the video display. Many of the issues of device independence that we've explored earlier in this book—mostly related to the size and resolution of the display surface and its color capabilities—can be approached and resolved in the same way. Yet a printer is not simply a display that uses paper rather than a cathode-ray tube. There are some significant differences. For example, we have never had to consider the problem of a video display not being connected to the display adapter or the problem of the display "running out of screen," but it is common for a printer to be off line or to run out of paper.

Nor have we worried about the video display adapter being incapable of performing certain graphics operations. Either the display adapter can handle graphics or it can't. And if it can't, then it can't be used with Windows at all. But some printers can't print graphics (although they can still be used with Windows), and plotters can do vector graphics but have a real problem with bitmaps.

Here are some other issues to consider:

- Printers are slower than video displays. Although we have on occasion tried to tune our programs for best performance, we haven't worried much about the time required for the video display to be refreshed. But nobody wants to wait for a slow printer to finish printing before getting back to work.

■ Programs reuse the surface of the video display as they overwrite previous display output with new output. This can't be done on a printer. Instead, a printer must eject a completed page and go on to the next page.

■ On the video display, different applications are windowed. On a printer, output from different applications must be separated into distinct documents or *print jobs*.

To add printer support to the rest of GDI, Windows provides several functions that apply only to printers. These printer-specific functions—*StartDoc*, *EndDoc*, *StartPage*, and *EndPage*—are responsible for organizing the printer output into pages. A program continues to call the normal GDI function calls to display text and graphics on a page in the same way as they display on the screen.

Chapters 15, 17, and 18 have additional information on printing bitmaps, formatted text, and metafiles.

PRINTING FUNDAMENTALS

When you use a printer in Windows, you're initiating a complex interaction involving the GDI32 library module, the printer device driver library module (which has a .DRV extension), and the Windows print spooler, as well as some other modules that get into the act. Before we start programming for the printer, let's examine how this process works.

Printing and Spooling

When an application program wants to begin using a printer, it first obtains a handle to the printer device context using *CreateDC* or *PrintDlg*. This causes the printer device driver library module to be loaded into memory (if it's not present already) and to initialize itself. The program then calls the *StartDoc* function, which signals the beginning of a new document. The *StartDoc* function is handled by the GDI module. The GDI module calls the *Control* function in the printer device driver, telling the device driver to prepare for printing.

The call to *StartDoc* begins the process of printing a document; the process ends when the program calls *EndDoc*. These two calls act as bookends for the normal GDI functions that display text or graphics to the document pages. Each page is itself delimited by a call to *StartPage* to begin a page and *EndPage* to end the page.

For example, if a program wants to draw an ellipse on the page, it first calls *StartDoc* to begin the print job, then *StartPage* to signal a new page. It then calls *Ellipse*, just as it does when drawing an ellipse on the screen. The GDI module generally stores any GDI call the program makes to the printer device context in a disk-based metafile, which has a filename that begins with the characters ~EMF ("enhanced metafile") and has a .TMP extension. However, as I'll discuss shortly, it's possible for the printer driver to skip this step.

When the application program is finished with the GDI calls that define the first page, the program calls *EndPage*. Now the real work begins. The printer driver must translate the various drawing commands stored in the metafile into output for the printer. The printer output required to define a page of graphics can be very large, particularly if the printer has no high-level page-composition language. For example, a 600-dots-per-inch laser printer using $8^1/_2$-by-11-inch paper might require more than 4 megabytes of data to define just one page of graphics.

For this reason, printer drivers often implement a technique called "banding," which divides the page into rectangular bands. The GDI module obtains the dimensions of each band from the printer driver. It then sets a clipping region equal to this band and calls the printer device driver *Output* function for each of the drawing functions contained in the metafile. This process is called "playing the metafile into the device driver." The GDI module must play the entire metafile into the device driver for each band that the device driver defines on the page. After the process is completed, the metafile can be deleted.

For each band, the device driver translates these drawing functions into the output necessary to realize them on the printer. The format of this output will be specific to the printer. For dot-matrix printers, it will be a collection of control sequences, including graphics sequences. (For some assistance with constructing this output, the printer driver can call various "helper" routines also located in the GDI module.) For laser printers with a high-level page-composition language (such as PostScript), the printer output will be in that language.

The printer driver passes the printer output for each band to the GDI module, which then stores this printer output in another temporary file. This file begins with the characters ~SPL and has a .TMP extension. When the entire page is finished, the GDI module makes an interprocess call to the print spooler indicating that a new print job is ready. The application program then goes on to the next page. When the application is finished with all the pages it must print, it calls *EndDoc* to signal that the print job is completed. Figure 13-1 on the following page shows the interaction of the program, the GDI module, and the printer driver.

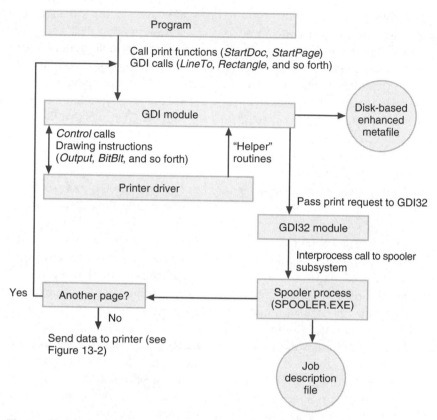

Figure 13-1. *The interaction of the application program, the GDI module, the printer driver, and the spooler.*

The Windows print spooler is actually a collection of several components:

Spooler Component	Description
Print Request Spooler	Routes a data stream to the print provider
Local Print Provider	Creates spool files destined for a local printer
Network Print Provider	Creates spool files destined for a network printer
Print Processor	Performs despooling, which is the conversion of spooled device-independent data into a form specific to the target printer
Port Monitor	Controls the port to which the printer is connected
Language Monitor	Controls printers capable of two-way communication to set device configuration and to monitor printer status

The spooler relieves application programs of some of the work involved with printing. Windows loads the print spooler at startup, so it is already active when a program begins printing. When the program prints a document, the GDI module creates the files that contain printer output. The print spooler's job is to send these files to the printer. It is notified of a new print job by the GDI module. It then begins reading the file and transferring it directly to the printer. To transfer the files, the spooler uses various communications functions for the parallel or serial port to which the printer is connected. When the spooler is done sending a file to a printer, it deletes the temporary file holding the output. This process is shown in Figure 13-2.

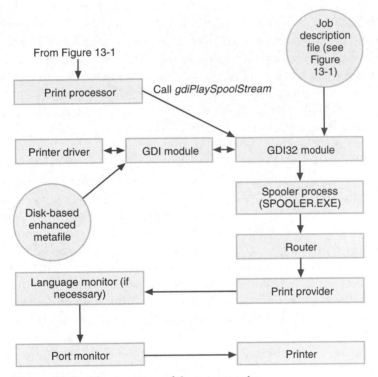

Figure 13-2. *The operation of the print spooler.*

Most of this process is transparent to the application program. From the perspective of the application, "printing" occurs only during the time required for the GDI module to save all the printer output in disk files. After that—or even before, if printing is handled by a second thread—the program is freed up to do other things. The actual printing of the document becomes the print spooler's responsibility rather than the program's. The user is responsible for pausing print jobs, changing their priority, or canceling them if necessary.

This arrangement allows programs to "print" faster than would be possible if they were printing in real time and had to wait for the printer to finish one page before proceeding to the next.

Although I've described how printing works in general, there are some variations on this theme. One variation is that the print spooler doesn't have to be present for Windows programs to use the printer. The user can usually turn off spooling for a printer from the printer's property sheet.

Why would a user want to bypass the Windows spooler? Well, perhaps the user has a hardware or software print spooler that works faster than the Windows spooler. Or perhaps the printer is on a network that has its own spooler. The general rule is that one spooler is faster than two. Removing the Windows spooler would speed up printing in these cases, because the printer output doesn't have to be stored on disk. It can go right out to the printer and be intercepted by the external hardware or software print spooler.

If the Windows spooler isn't active, the GDI module doesn't store the printer output from the device driver in a file. Instead, GDI itself sends the output directly to the parallel or serial printer port. Unlike the printing done by the spooler, the printing done by GDI has the potential of holding up the operation of application programs (particularly the program doing the printing) until the printing is completed.

Here's another variation: Normally, the GDI module stores all the functions necessary to define a page in a metafile and then plays this metafile into the printer driver once for each band defined by the driver. If the printer driver doesn't require banding, however, the metafile isn't created; GDI simply passes the drawing functions directly to the driver. In a further variation, it is also possible for an application to assume responsibility for dividing printer output into bands. This makes the printing code in the application program more complex, but it relieves the GDI module of creating the metafile. Once again, GDI simply passes the functions for each band to the printer driver.

Now perhaps you're starting to see how printing from a Windows program might involve a bit more overhead than that required for using the video display. Several problems can occur—particularly if the GDI module runs out of disk space while creating the metafile or the printer output files. Either you can get very involved in reporting these problems to the user and attempting to do something about them or you can remain relatively aloof.

For an application, the first step in printing is obtaining a printer device context.

The Printer Device Context

Just as you must obtain a handle to a device context before you paint on the video display, you must obtain a printer device context handle before printing. Once you have this handle (and have called *StartDoc* to announce your intention of creating a new document and *StartPage* to begin a page), you can use this printer device context handle the same way you use the video display device context handle—as the first parameter to the various GDI drawing functions.

Many applications use a standard print dialog box invoked by calling the *PrintDlg* function. (I'll show how to use this function later in this chapter.) *PrintDlg* gives the user the opportunity to change printers or specify other job characteristics before printing. It then gives the application a printer device context handle. This function can save an application some work. However, some applications (such as Notepad) prefer instead to just obtain a printer device context without displaying a dialog box. This task requires a job to *CreateDC*.

In Chapter 5, we discovered that we can get a handle to a device context for the entire video display by calling

```
hdc = CreateDC (TEXT ("DISPLAY"), NULL, NULL, NULL) ;
```

You obtain a printer device context handle using this same function. However, for a printer device context, the general syntax of *CreateDC* is

```
hdc = CreateDC (NULL, szDeviceName, NULL, pInitializationData) ;
```

The *pInitializationData* argument is generally also set to NULL. The *szDeviceName* argument points to a character string that tells Windows the name of the printer device. Before you can set the device name, you must find out what printers are available.

A system can have more than one printer attached to it. It may even have other programs, such as fax software, masquerading as printers. Regardless of the number of attached printers, only one can be considered the "current" or "default" printer. This is the most recent printer that the user has chosen. Some small Windows programs use only this printer for printing.

Methods for obtaining the default printer device context have changed over the years. Currently, the standard method involves using the *EnumPrinters* function. This function fills an array of structures that contain information about each attached printer. You even have a choice of several structures to use with this function, depending on the level of detail you want. These structures have names of PRINTER_INFO_x, where *x* is a number.

Unfortunately, which structure you use also depends on whether your program is running under Windows 98 or Microsoft Windows NT. Figure 13-3 shows a *GetPrinterDC* function that will work under either operating system.

GETPRNDC.C

```
/*-------------------------------------
   GETPRNDC.C -- GetPrinterDC function
 -------------------------------------*/

#include <windows.h>

HDC GetPrinterDC (void)
```

Figure 13-3. *The GETPRNDC.C file.*

(continued)

Figure 13-3. *continued*

```
{
    DWORD            dwNeeded, dwReturned ;
    HDC              hdc ;
    PRINTER_INFO_4 * pinfo4 ;
    PRINTER_INFO_5 * pinfo5 ;

    if (GetVersion () & 0x80000000)              // Windows 98
    {
        EnumPrinters (PRINTER_ENUM_DEFAULT, NULL, 5, NULL,
                    0, &dwNeeded, &dwReturned) ;

        pinfo5 = malloc (dwNeeded) ;

        EnumPrinters (PRINTER_ENUM_DEFAULT, NULL, 5, (PBYTE) pinfo5,
                    dwNeeded, &dwNeeded, &dwReturned) ;

        hdc = CreateDC (NULL, pinfo5->pPrinterName, NULL, NULL) ;

        free (pinfo5) ;
    }
    else                                         // Windows NT
    {
        EnumPrinters (PRINTER_ENUM_LOCAL, NULL, 4, NULL,
                    0, &dwNeeded, &dwReturned) ;

        pinfo4 = malloc (dwNeeded) ;

        EnumPrinters (PRINTER_ENUM_LOCAL, NULL, 4, (PBYTE) pinfo4,
                    dwNeeded, &dwNeeded, &dwReturned) ;

        hdc = CreateDC (NULL, pinfo4->pPrinterName, NULL, NULL) ;

        free (pinfo4) ;
    }
    return hdc ;
}
```

This function uses the *GetVersion* function to determine whether the program is running under Windows 98 or Windows NT. Regardless of which is running, the function calls *EnumPrinters* twice—once to obtain the size of a structure it needs, and again to actually fill the structure. Under Windows 98, the function uses the PRINTER_INFO_5 structure; under Windows NT, it uses the PRINTER_INFO_4 structure. These structures are specifically indicated in the *EnumPrinters* documentation (*/Platform SDK/Graphics and Multimedia Services/GDI/Printing and Print Spooler/Printing and Print Spooler Reference/ Printing and Print Spooler Functions/EnumPrinters*, right before the Examples section) as being "easy and extremely fast."

The Revised DEVCAPS Program

The original DEVCAPS1 program in Chapter 5 displayed basic information available from the *GetDeviceCaps* function for the video display. The new version, shown in Figure 13-4, shows more information for both the video display and all printers attached to the system.

DEVCAPS2.C

```
/*---------------------------------------------------------------
   DEVCAPS2.C -- Displays Device Capability Information (Version 2)
                 (c) Charles Petzold, 1998
  ---------------------------------------------------------------*/

#include <windows.h>
#include "resource.h"

LRESULT CALLBACK WndProc (HWND, UINT, WPARAM, LPARAM) ;
void DoBasicInfo     (HDC, HDC, int, int) ;
void DoOtherInfo     (HDC, HDC, int, int) ;
void DoBitCodedCaps  (HDC, HDC, int, int, int) ;

typedef struct
{
     int      iMask ;
     TCHAR * szDesc ;
}
BITS ;

#define IDM_DEVMODE      1000

int WINAPI WinMain (HINSTANCE hInstance, HINSTANCE hPrevInstance,
                    PSTR szCmdLine, int iCmdShow)
{
     static TCHAR szAppName[] = TEXT ("DevCaps2") ;
     HWND         hwnd ;
     MSG          msg ;
     WNDCLASS     wndclass ;

     wndclass.style         = CS_HREDRAW | CS_VREDRAW ;
     wndclass.lpfnWndProc   = WndProc ;
     wndclass.cbClsExtra    = 0 ;
     wndclass.cbWndExtra    = 0 ;
     wndclass.hInstance     = hInstance ;
     wndclass.hIcon         = LoadIcon (NULL, IDI_APPLICATION) ;
     wndclass.hCursor       = LoadCursor (NULL, IDC_ARROW) ;
     wndclass.hbrBackground = (HBRUSH) GetStockObject (WHITE_BRUSH) ;
```

Figure 13-4. *The DEVCAPS2 program.*   *(continued)*

605

Figure 13-4. *continued*

```
        wndclass.lpszMenuName  = szAppName ;
        wndclass.lpszClassName = szAppName ;

        if (!RegisterClass (&wndclass))
        {
             MessageBox (NULL, TEXT ("This program requires Windows NT!"),
                          szAppName, MB_ICONERROR) ;
             return 0 ;
        }

        hwnd = CreateWindow (szAppName, NULL,
                            WS_OVERLAPPEDWINDOW,
                            CW_USEDEFAULT, CW_USEDEFAULT,
                            CW_USEDEFAULT, CW_USEDEFAULT,
                            NULL, NULL, hInstance, NULL) ;

        ShowWindow (hwnd, iCmdShow) ;
        UpdateWindow (hwnd) ;

        while (GetMessage (&msg, NULL, 0, 0))
        {
             TranslateMessage (&msg) ;
             DispatchMessage (&msg) ;
        }
        return msg.wParam ;
}

LRESULT CALLBACK WndProc (HWND hwnd, UINT message, WPARAM wParam, LPARAM lParam)
{
        static TCHAR            szDevice[32], szWindowText[64] ;
        static int             cxChar, cyChar, nCurrentDevice = IDM_SCREEN,
                                            nCurrentInfo    = IDM_BASIC ;
        static DWORD           dwNeeded, dwReturned ;
        static PRINTER_INFO_4 * pinfo4 ;
        static PRINTER_INFO_5 * pinfo5 ;
        DWORD                  i ;
        HDC                    hdc, hdcInfo ;
        HMENU                  hMenu ;
        HANDLE                 hPrint ;
        PAINTSTRUCT            ps ;
        TEXTMETRIC             tm ;

        switch (message)
        {
        case WM_CREATE :
             hdc = GetDC (hwnd) ;
```

```
        SelectObject (hdc, GetStockObject (SYSTEM_FIXED_FONT)) ;
        GetTextMetrics (hdc, &tm) ;
        cxChar = tm.tmAveCharWidth ;
        cyChar = tm.tmHeight + tm.tmExternalLeading ;
        ReleaseDC (hwnd, hdc) ;
                                                // fall through
case WM_SETTINGCHANGE:
        hMenu = GetSubMenu (GetMenu (hwnd), 0) ;

        while (GetMenuItemCount (hMenu) > 1)
            DeleteMenu (hMenu, 1, MF_BYPOSITION) ;

            // Get a list of all local and remote printers
            //
            // First, find out how large an array we need; this
            //   call will fail, leaving the required size in dwNeeded
            //
            // Next, allocate space for the info array and fill it
            //
            // Put the printer names on the menu

        if (GetVersion () & 0x80000000)        // Windows 98
        {
            EnumPrinters (PRINTER_ENUM_LOCAL, NULL, 5, NULL,
                        0, &dwNeeded, &dwReturned) ;

            pinfo5 = malloc (dwNeeded) ;

            EnumPrinters (PRINTER_ENUM_LOCAL, NULL, 5, (PBYTE) pinfo5,
                        dwNeeded, &dwNeeded, &dwReturned) ;

            for (i = 0 ; i < dwReturned ; i++)
            {
                AppendMenu (hMenu, (i+1) % 16 ? 0 : MF_MENUBARBREAK, i + 1,
                        pinfo5[i].pPrinterName) ;
            }
            free (pinfo5) ;
        }
        else                                    // Windows NT
        {
            EnumPrinters (PRINTER_ENUM_LOCAL, NULL, 4, NULL,
                        0, &dwNeeded, &dwReturned) ;

            pinfo4 = malloc (dwNeeded) ;
```

(continued)

607

Figure 13-4. *continued*

```
        EnumPrinters (PRINTER_ENUM_LOCAL, NULL, 4, (PBYTE) pinfo4,
                    dwNeeded, &dwNeeded, &dwReturned) ;

        for (i = 0 ; i < dwReturned ; i++)
        {
            AppendMenu (hMenu, (i+1) % 16 ? 0 : MF_MENUBARBREAK, i + 1,
                        pinfo4[i].pPrinterName) ;
        }
        free (pinfo4) ;
    }

    AppendMenu (hMenu, MF_SEPARATOR, 0, NULL) ;
    AppendMenu (hMenu, 0, IDM_DEVMODE, TEXT ("Properties")) ;

    wParam = IDM_SCREEN ;
                                        // fall through
case WM_COMMAND :
    hMenu = GetMenu (hwnd) ;

    if (LOWORD (wParam) == IDM_SCREEN ||        // IDM_SCREEN & Printers
        LOWORD (wParam) < IDM_DEVMODE)
    {
        CheckMenuItem (hMenu, nCurrentDevice, MF_UNCHECKED) ;
        nCurrentDevice = LOWORD (wParam) ;
        CheckMenuItem (hMenu, nCurrentDevice, MF_CHECKED) ;
    }
    else if (LOWORD (wParam) == IDM_DEVMODE)    // Properties selection
    {
        GetMenuString (hMenu, nCurrentDevice, szDevice,
                    sizeof (szDevice) / sizeof (TCHAR), MF_BYCOMMAND);

        if (OpenPrinter (szDevice, &hPrint, NULL))
        {
            PrinterProperties (hwnd, hPrint) ;
            ClosePrinter (hPrint) ;
        }
    }
    else                                    // info menu items
    {
        CheckMenuItem (hMenu, nCurrentInfo, MF_UNCHECKED) ;
        nCurrentInfo = LOWORD (wParam) ;
        CheckMenuItem (hMenu, nCurrentInfo, MF_CHECKED) ;
    }
    InvalidateRect (hwnd, NULL, TRUE) ;
    return 0 ;
```

```
     case WM_INITMENUPOPUP :
          if (lParam == 0)
               EnableMenuItem (GetMenu (hwnd), IDM_DEVMODE,
                    nCurrentDevice == IDM_SCREEN ? MF_GRAYED : MF_ENABLED) ;
          return 0 ;

     case WM_PAINT :
          lstrcpy (szWindowText, TEXT ("Device Capabilities: ")) ;

          if (nCurrentDevice == IDM_SCREEN)
          {
               lstrcpy (szDevice, TEXT ("DISPLAY")) ;
               hdcInfo = CreateIC (szDevice, NULL, NULL, NULL) ;
          }
          else
          {
               hMenu = GetMenu (hwnd) ;
               GetMenuString (hMenu, nCurrentDevice, szDevice,
                              sizeof (szDevice), MF_BYCOMMAND) ;
               hdcInfo = CreateIC (NULL, szDevice, NULL, NULL) ;
          }

          lstrcat (szWindowText, szDevice) ;
          SetWindowText (hwnd, szWindowText) ;

          hdc = BeginPaint (hwnd, &ps) ;
          SelectObject (hdc, GetStockObject (SYSTEM_FIXED_FONT)) ;

          if (hdcInfo)
          {
               switch (nCurrentInfo)
               {
               case IDM_BASIC :
                    DoBasicInfo (hdc, hdcInfo, cxChar, cyChar) ;
                    break ;

               case IDM_OTHER :
                    DoOtherInfo (hdc, hdcInfo, cxChar, cyChar) ;
                    break ;

               case IDM_CURVE :
               case IDM_LINE :
               case IDM_POLY :
               case IDM_TEXT :
                    DoBitCodedCaps (hdc, hdcInfo, cxChar, cyChar,
                                    nCurrentInfo - IDM_CURVE) ;
```

(continued)

Figure 13-4. *continued*

```
                    break ;
            }
            DeleteDC (hdcInfo) ;
        }

        EndPaint (hwnd, &ps) ;
        return 0 ;

    case WM_DESTROY :
        PostQuitMessage (0) ;
        return 0 ;
    }
    return DefWindowProc (hwnd, message, wParam, lParam) ;
}

void DoBasicInfo (HDC hdc, HDC hdcInfo, int cxChar, int cyChar)
{
    static struct
    {
        int     nIndex ;
        TCHAR * szDesc ;
    }
    info[] =
    {
        HORZSIZE,       TEXT ("HORZSIZE         Width in millimeters:"),
        VERTSIZE,       TEXT ("VERTSIZE         Height in millimeters:"),
        HORZRES,        TEXT ("HORZRES          Width in pixels:"),
        VERTRES,        TEXT ("VERTRES          Height in raster lines:"),
        BITSPIXEL,      TEXT ("BITSPIXEL        Color bits per pixel:"),
        PLANES,         TEXT ("PLANES           Number of color planes:"),
        NUMBRUSHES,     TEXT ("NUMBRUSHES       Number of device brushes:"),
        NUMPENS,        TEXT ("NUMPENS          Number of device pens:"),
        NUMMARKERS,     TEXT ("NUMMARKERS       Number of device markers:"),
        NUMFONTS,       TEXT ("NUMFONTS         Number of device fonts:"),
        NUMCOLORS,      TEXT ("NUMCOLORS        Number of device colors:"),
        PDEVICESIZE,    TEXT ("PDEVICESIZE      Size of device structure:"),
        ASPECTX,        TEXT ("ASPECTX          Relative width of pixel:"),
        ASPECTY,        TEXT ("ASPECTY          Relative height of pixel:"),
        ASPECTXY,       TEXT ("ASPECTXY         Relative diagonal of pixel:"),
        LOGPIXELSX,     TEXT ("LOGPIXELSX       Horizontal dots per inch:"),
        LOGPIXELSY,     TEXT ("LOGPIXELSY       Vertical dots per inch:"),
        SIZEPALETTE,    TEXT ("SIZEPALETTE      Number of palette entries:"),
        NUMRESERVED,    TEXT ("NUMRESERVED      Reserved palette entries:"),
        COLORRES,       TEXT ("COLORRES         Actual color resolution:"),
        PHYSICALWIDTH,  TEXT ("PHYSICALWIDTH    Printer page pixel width:"),
        PHYSICALHEIGHT, TEXT ("PHYSICALHEIGHT   Printer page pixel height:"),
```

```
            PHYSICALOFFSETX, TEXT ("PHYSICALOFFSETX Printer page x offset:"),
            PHYSICALOFFSETY, TEXT ("PHYSICALOFFSETY Printer page y offset:")
      } ;
      int  i ;
      TCHAR szBuffer[80] ;

      for (i = 0 ; i < sizeof (info) / sizeof (info[0]) ; i++)
            TextOut (hdc, cxChar, (i + 1) * cyChar, szBuffer,
                  wsprintf (szBuffer, TEXT ("%-45s%8d"), info[i].szDesc,
                        GetDeviceCaps (hdcInfo, info[i].nIndex))) ;
}

void DoOtherInfo (HDC hdc, HDC hdcInfo, int cxChar, int cyChar)
{
      static BITS clip[] =
      {
            CP_RECTANGLE,     TEXT ("CP_RECTANGLE    Can Clip To Rectangle:")
      } ;

      static BITS raster[] =
      {
            RC_BITBLT,        TEXT ("RC_BITBLT        Capable of simple BitBlt:"),
            RC_BANDING,       TEXT ("RC_BANDING       Requires banding support:"),
            RC_SCALING,       TEXT ("RC_SCALING       Requires scaling support:"),
            RC_BITMAP64,      TEXT ("RC_BITMAP64      Supports bitmaps >64K:"),
            RC_GDI20_OUTPUT,  TEXT ("RC_GDI20_OUTPUT Has 2.0 output calls:"),
            RC_DI_BITMAP,     TEXT ("RC_DI_BITMAP     Supports DIB to memory:"),
            RC_PALETTE,       TEXT ("RC_PALETTE       Supports a palette:"),
            RC_DIBTODEV,      TEXT ("RC_DIBTODEV      Supports bitmap conversion:"),
            RC_BIGFONT,       TEXT ("RC_BIGFONT       Supports fonts >64K:"),
            RC_STRETCHBLT,    TEXT ("RC_STRETCHBLT    Supports StretchBlt:"),
            RC_FLOODFILL,     TEXT ("RC_FLOODFILL     Supports FloodFill:"),
            RC_STRETCHDIB,    TEXT ("RC_STRETCHDIB    Supports StretchDIBits:")
      } ;

      static TCHAR * szTech[] = { TEXT ("DT_PLOTTER (Vector plotter)"),
                                  TEXT ("DT_RASDISPLAY (Raster display)"),
                                  TEXT ("DT_RASPRINTER (Raster printer)"),
                                  TEXT ("DT_RASCAMERA (Raster camera)"),
                                  TEXT ("DT_CHARSTREAM (Character stream)"),
                                  TEXT ("DT_METAFILE (Metafile)"),
                                  TEXT ("DT_DISPFILE (Display file)") } ;
      int          i ;
      TCHAR        szBuffer[80] ;

      TextOut (hdc, cxChar, cyChar, szBuffer,
```

(continued)

Figure 13-4. *continued*

```
            wsprintf (szBuffer, TEXT ("%-24s%04XH"), TEXT ("DRIVERVERSION:"),
                GetDeviceCaps (hdcInfo, DRIVERVERSION))) ;

    TextOut (hdc, cxChar, 2 * cyChar, szBuffer,
        wsprintf (szBuffer, TEXT ("%-24s%-40s"), TEXT ("TECHNOLOGY:"),
            szTech[GetDeviceCaps (hdcInfo, TECHNOLOGY)])) ;

    TextOut (hdc, cxChar, 4 * cyChar, szBuffer,
        wsprintf (szBuffer, TEXT ("CLIPCAPS (Clipping capabilities)"))) ;

    for (i = 0 ; i < sizeof (clip) / sizeof (clip[0]) ; i++)
        TextOut (hdc, 9 * cxChar, (i + 6) * cyChar, szBuffer,
            wsprintf (szBuffer, TEXT ("%-45s %3s"), clip[i].szDesc,
                GetDeviceCaps (hdcInfo, CLIPCAPS) & clip[i].iMask ?
                    TEXT ("Yes") : TEXT ("No"))) ;

    TextOut (hdc, cxChar, 8 * cyChar, szBuffer,
        wsprintf (szBuffer, TEXT ("RASTERCAPS (Raster capabilities)"))) ;

    for (i = 0 ; i < sizeof (raster) / sizeof (raster[0]) ; i++)
        TextOut (hdc, 9 * cxChar, (i + 10) * cyChar, szBuffer,
            wsprintf (szBuffer, TEXT ("%-45s %3s"), raster[i].szDesc,
                GetDeviceCaps (hdcInfo, RASTERCAPS) & raster[i].iMask ?
                    TEXT ("Yes") : TEXT ("No"))) ;
}

void DoBitCodedCaps (HDC hdc, HDC hdcInfo, int cxChar, int cyChar, int iType)
{
    static BITS curves[] =
    {
        CC_CIRCLES,     TEXT ("CC_CIRCLES     Can do circles:"),
        CC_PIE,         TEXT ("CC_PIE         Can do pie wedges:"),
        CC_CHORD,       TEXT ("CC_CHORD       Can do chord arcs:"),
        CC_ELLIPSES,    TEXT ("CC_ELLIPSES    Can do ellipses:"),
        CC_WIDE,        TEXT ("CC_WIDE        Can do wide borders:"),
        CC_STYLED,      TEXT ("CC_STYLED      Can do styled borders:"),
        CC_WIDESTYLED,  TEXT ("CC_WIDESTYLED Can do wide and styled borders:"),
        CC_INTERIORS,   TEXT ("CC_INTERIORS   Can do interiors:")
    } ;

    static BITS lines[] =
    {
        LC_POLYLINE,    TEXT ("LC_POLYLINE    Can do polyline:"),
        LC_MARKER,      TEXT ("LC_MARKER      Can do markers:"),
        LC_POLYMARKER,  TEXT ("LC_POLYMARKER Can do polymarkers"),
```

```
        LC_WIDE,        TEXT ("LC_WIDE        Can do wide lines:"),
        LC_STYLED,      TEXT ("LC_STYLED      Can do styled lines:"),
        LC_WIDESTYLED,  TEXT ("LC_WIDESTYLED Can do wide and styled lines:"),
        LC_INTERIORS,   TEXT ("LC_INTERIORS  Can do interiors:")
} ;

static BITS poly[] =
{
        PC_POLYGON,
            TEXT ("PC_POLYGON     Can do alternate fill polygon:"),
        PC_RECTANGLE,   TEXT ("PC_RECTANGLE    Can do rectangle:"),
        PC_WINDPOLYGON,
            TEXT ("PC_WINDPOLYGON Can do winding number fill polygon:"),
        PC_SCANLINE,    TEXT ("PC_SCANLINE     Can do scanlines:"),
        PC_WIDE,        TEXT ("PC_WIDE         Can do wide borders:"),
        PC_STYLED,      TEXT ("PC_STYLED       Can do styled borders:"),
        PC_WIDESTYLED,
            TEXT ("PC_WIDESTYLED  Can do wide and styled borders:"),
        PC_INTERIORS,   TEXT ("PC_INTERIORS    Can do interiors:")
} ;

static BITS text[] =
{
        TC_OP_CHARACTER,
            TEXT ("TC_OP_CHARACTER Can do character output precision:"),
        TC_OP_STROKE,
            TEXT ("TC_OP_STROKE    Can do stroke output precision:"),
        TC_CP_STROKE,
            TEXT ("TC_CP_STROKE    Can do stroke clip precision:"),
        TC_CR_90,
            TEXT ("TC_CP_90        Can do 90 degree character rotation:"),
        TC_CR_ANY,
            TEXT ("TC_CR_ANY       Can do any character rotation:"),
        TC_SF_X_YINDEP,
            TEXT ("TC_SF_X_YINDEP Can do scaling independent of X and Y:"),
        TC_SA_DOUBLE,
            TEXT ("TC_SA_DOUBLE    Can do doubled character for scaling:"),
        TC_SA_INTEGER,
            TEXT ("TC_SA_INTEGER  Can do integer multiples for scaling:"),
        TC_SA_CONTIN,
            TEXT ("TC_SA_CONTIN   Can do any multiples for exact scaling:"),
        TC_EA_DOUBLE,
            TEXT ("TC_EA_DOUBLE   Can do double weight characters:"),
        TC_IA_ABLE,     TEXT ("TC_IA_ABLE      Can do italicizing:"),
        TC_UA_ABLE,     TEXT ("TC_UA_ABLE      Can do underlining:"),
        TC_SO_ABLE,     TEXT ("TC_SO_ABLE      Can do strikeouts:"),
```

(continued)

Figure 13-4. *continued*

```
        TC_RA_ABLE,        TEXT ("TC_RA_ABLE      Can do raster fonts:"),
        TC_VA_ABLE,        TEXT ("TC_VA_ABLE      Can do vector fonts:")
    } ;

    static struct
    {
        int     iIndex ;
        TCHAR * szTitle ;
        BITS    (*pbits)[] ;
        int     iSize ;
    }
    bitinfo[] =
    {
        CURVECAPS,   TEXT ("CURVCAPS (Curve Capabilities)"),
            (BITS (*)[]) curves, sizeof (curves) / sizeof (curves[0]),
        LINECAPS,    TEXT ("LINECAPS (Line Capabilities)"),
            (BITS (*)[]) lines, sizeof (lines) / sizeof (lines[0]),
        POLYGONALCAPS, TEXT ("POLYGONALCAPS (Polygonal Capabilities)"),
            (BITS (*)[]) poly, sizeof (poly) / sizeof (poly[0]),
        TEXTCAPS,    TEXT ("TEXTCAPS (Text Capabilities)"),
            (BITS (*)[]) text, sizeof (text) / sizeof (text[0])
    } ;

    static TCHAR szBuffer[80] ;
    BITS         (*pbits)[] = bitinfo[iType].pbits ;
    int          i, iDevCaps = GetDeviceCaps (hdcInfo, bitinfo[iType].iIndex) ;

    TextOut (hdc, cxChar, cyChar, bitinfo[iType].szTitle,
            lstrlen (bitinfo[iType].szTitle)) ;

    for (i = 0 ; i < bitinfo[iType].iSize ; i++)
        TextOut (hdc, cxChar, (i + 3) * cyChar, szBuffer,
            wsprintf (szBuffer, TEXT ("%-55s %3s"), (*pbits)[i].szDesc,
                iDevCaps & (*pbits)[i].iMask ? TEXT ("Yes") : TEXT ("No"))) ;
}
```

DEVCAPS2.RC (excerpts)

```
//Microsoft Developer Studio generated resource script.

#include "resource.h"
#include "afxres.h"


/////////////////////////////////////////////////////////////////////////////
// Menu
```

```
DEVCAPS2 MENU DISCARDABLE
BEGIN
    POPUP "&Device"
    BEGIN
        MENUITEM "&Screen",                     IDM_SCREEN, CHECKED
    END
    POPUP "&Capabilities"
    BEGIN
        MENUITEM "&Basic Information",          IDM_BASIC
        MENUITEM "&Other Information",          IDM_OTHER
        MENUITEM "&Curve Capabilities",         IDM_CURVE
        MENUITEM "&Line Capabilities",          IDM_LINE
        MENUITEM "&Polygonal Capabilities",     IDM_POLY
        MENUITEM "&Text Capabilities",          IDM_TEXT
    END
END
```

RESOURCE.H (excerpts)

```
// Microsoft Developer Studio generated include file.
// Used by DevCaps2.rc

#define IDM_SCREEN                      40001
#define IDM_BASIC                       40002
#define IDM_OTHER                       40003
#define IDM_CURVE                       40004
#define IDM_LINE                        40005
#define IDM_POLY                        40006
#define IDM_TEXT                        40007
```

Because DEVCAPS2 obtains only an information context for the printer, you can select printers from DEVCAPS's menu, even though they may have an output port of "none." If you want to compare the capabilities of different printers, you can first use the Printers folder to add various printer drivers.

The *PrinterProperties* Call

The Device menu of the DEVCAPS2 program includes an option called Properties. To use it, first select a printer from the Device menu and then select Properties. Up pops a dialog box. Where does the dialog box come from? It is invoked by the printer driver, and—at the very least—it requests that you make a choice of paper size. Most printer drivers also give you a choice of "portrait" or "landscape" mode. In portrait mode (often the default), the short side of the paper is the top; in landscape mode, the long side is the top. If you change this mode, the change is reflected in the information the DEVCAPS2 program obtains from the

GetDeviceCaps function: the horizontal size and resolution are switched with the vertical size and resolution. Properties dialog boxes for color plotters can be quite extensive, requesting the colors of the pens installed in the plotter and the type of paper (or transparencies) being used.

All printer drivers contain an exported function called *ExtDeviceMode* that invokes this dialog box and saves the information that the user enters. Some printer drivers store this information in their own section of the Registry, and some don't. Those that store the information have access to it during the next Windows session.

Windows programs that allow the user a choice of printers generally just call *PrintDlg*, which I'll show you how to use later in this chapter. This useful function takes care of all the work of communicating with the user and handles any changes the user requests in preparation for printing. *PrintDlg* also invokes the property sheet dialog when the user clicks the Properties button.

A program can also display a printer's properties dialog by directly calling the printer driver's *ExtDeviceMode* or *ExtDeveModePropSheet* functions. However, I don't recommend this. It's far better to invoke the dialog indirectly by calling *PrinterProperties*, as DEVCAPS2 does.

PrinterProperties requires a handle to a printer object, which you get by calling the *OpenPrinter* function. When the user cancels a property sheet dialog, *PrinterProperties* returns. You can then close the printer handle by calling *ClosePrinter*. Here's how DEVCAPS2 does it:

The program first obtains the name of the printer currently selected in the Device menu and saves it in a character array named *szDevice*:

```
GetMenuString (hMenu, nCurrentDevice, szDevice,
               sizeof (szDevice) / sizeof (TCHAR), MF_BYCOMMAND) ;
```

Then it obtains the handle of this device by using *OpenPrinter*. If the call is successful, the program next calls *PrinterProperties* to invoke the dialog box and then *ClosePrinter* to delete the device handle:

```
if (OpenPrinter (szDevice, &hPrint, NULL))
{
     PrinterProperties (hwnd, hPrint) ;
     ClosePrinter (hPrint) ;
}
```

Checking for *BitBlt* Capability

You can use the *GetDeviceCaps* function to obtain the size and resolution of the printable area of the page. (In most cases, this area won't be the same as the full size of the paper.) You can also obtain the relative pixel width and height, if you want to do your own scaling.

Much of the information regarding various capabilities of the printer is for the purpose of GDI rather than applications. Often when a printer can't do something itself, GDI will simulate it. However, there is one capability that some applications should check.

This is the printer characteristic obtained from the RC_BITBLT bit of the value returned from *GetDeviceCaps* with a parameter of RASTERCAPS ("raster capabilities"). This bit indicates whether the device is capable of bit-block transfers. Most dot-matrix, laser, and ink-jet printers are capable of bit-block transfers, but plotters are not. Devices that can't handle bit-block transfers do not support the following GDI functions: *CreateCompatibleDC*, *CreateCompatibleBitmap*, *PatBlt*, *BitBlt*, *StretchBlt*, *GrayString*, *DrawIcon*, *SetPixel*, *GetPixel*, *FloodFill*, *ExtFloodFill*, *FillRgn*, *FrameRgn*, *InvertRgn*, *PaintRgn*, *FillRect*, *FrameRect*, and *InvertRect*. This is the single most important distinction between using GDI calls on a video display and using them on a printer.

The Simplest Printing Program

We're now ready to print, and we're going to start as simply as possible. In fact, our first printing program does nothing but cause a printer form feed to eject the page. The FORMFEED program, shown in Figure 13-5, demonstrates the absolute minimum requirements for printing.

FORMFEED.C

```
/*------------------------------------------------
   FORMFEED.C -- Advances printer to next page
                 (c) Charles Petzold, 1998
   ------------------------------------------------*/

#include <windows.h>

HDC GetPrinterDC (void) ;

int WINAPI WinMain (HINSTANCE hInstance, HINSTANCE hPrevInstance,
                    LPSTR lpszCmdLine, int iCmdShow)
{
     static DOCINFO di = { sizeof (DOCINFO), TEXT ("FormFeed") } ;
     HDC             hdcPrint = GetPrinterDC () ;

     if (hdcPrint != NULL)
     {
          if (StartDoc (hdcPrint, &di) > 0)
               if (StartPage (hdcPrint) > 0 && EndPage (hdcPrint) > 0)
                    EndDoc (hdcPrint) ;

          DeleteDC (hdcPrint) ;
     }
     return 0 ;
}
```

Figure 13-5. *The FORMFEED program.*

This program also requires the GETPRNDC.C file shown previously in Figure 13-3.

Other than obtaining the printer device context (and later deleting it), the program calls only the four print functions discussed earlier in this chapter. FORMFEED first calls *StartDoc* to start a new document. The program tests the return value from the function and proceeds only if the value is positive:

```
if (StartDoc (hdcPrint, &di) > 0)
```

The second argument to *StartDoc* is a pointer to a DOCINFO structure. This structure contains the size of the structure in the first field and the text string "FormFeed" in the second. As the document prints or while it is waiting to print, this string appears in the Document Name column of the printer's job queue. Generally the identification string includes the name of the application doing the printing and the file being printed.

If *StartDoc* is successful (indicated by a positive return value), FORMFEED calls *StartPage*, followed immediately by a call to *EndPage*. This sequence advances the printer to a new page. Once again, the return values are tested:

```
if (StartPage (hdcPrint) > 0 && EndPage (hdcPrint) > 0)
```

Finally, if everything has proceeded without error to this point, the document is ended:

```
EndDoc (hdcPrint) ;
```

Note that the *EndDoc* function is called only if no printing errors have been reported. If one of the other print functions returns an error code, GDI has already aborted the document. If the printer is not currently printing, such an error code often results in the printer being reset. Simply testing the return values from the print functions is the easiest way to check for errors. If you want to report a particular error to the user, you must call *GetLastError* to determine the error.

If you've ever written a simple form-feed program for MS-DOS, you know that ASCII code 12 (Ctrl-L) activates a form feed for most printers. Why not simply open the printer port using the C library function *open* and then output an ASCII code 12 using *write*? Well, nothing prevents you from doing this. You first have to determine the parallel port or the serial port the printer is attached to. You then have to determine whether another program (the print spooler, for instance) is currently using the printer. (You don't want the form feed to be output in the middle of some other program's document, do you?) Finally, you have to determine if ASCII code 12 is a form-feed character for the connected printer. It's not universal, you know. In fact, the form-feed command in PostScript isn't a 12; it's the word *showpage*.

In short, don't even think about going around Windows; stick with the Windows functions for printing.

PRINTING GRAPHICS AND TEXT

Printing from a Windows program usually involves more overhead than shown in the FORMFEED program, as well as some GDI calls to actually print something. Let's write a program that prints one page of text and graphics. We'll start with the method shown in the FORMFEED program and then add some enhancements. We'll be looking at three versions of this program called PRINT1, PRINT2, and PRINT3. To avoid a lot of duplicated source code, each of these programs will use the GETPRNDC.C file shown earlier and functions contained in the PRINT.C file, which is shown in Figure 13-6.

PRINT.C

```
/*----------------------------------------------------------
   PRINT.C -- Common routines for Print1, Print2, and Print3
   ------------------------------------------------------------*/

#include <windows.h>

LRESULT CALLBACK WndProc (HWND, UINT, WPARAM, LPARAM) ;
BOOL PrintMyPage (HWND) ;

extern HINSTANCE hInst ;
extern TCHAR     szAppName[] ;
extern TCHAR     szCaption[] ;

int WINAPI WinMain (HINSTANCE hInstance, HINSTANCE hPrevInstance,
                    PSTR szCmdLine, int iCmdShow)
{
    HWND      hwnd ;
    MSG       msg ;
    WNDCLASS  wndclass ;

    wndclass.style         = CS_HREDRAW | CS_VREDRAW ;
    wndclass.lpfnWndProc   = WndProc ;
    wndclass.cbClsExtra    = 0 ;
    wndclass.cbWndExtra    = 0 ;
    wndclass.hInstance     = hInstance ;
    wndclass.hIcon         = LoadIcon (NULL, IDI_APPLICATION) ;
    wndclass.hCursor       = LoadCursor (NULL, IDC_ARROW) ;
    wndclass.hbrBackground = (HBRUSH) GetStockObject (WHITE_BRUSH) ;
    wndclass.lpszMenuName  = NULL ;
    wndclass.lpszClassName = szAppName ;

    if (!RegisterClass (&wndclass))
```

Figure 13-6. *The PRINT.C file used in the PRINT1, PRINT2, and PRINT3 programs.*   *(continued)*

Figure 13-6. *continued*

```
    {
        MessageBox (NULL, TEXT ("This program requires Windows NT!"),
                    szAppName, MB_ICONERROR) ;
        return 0 ;
    }

    hInst = hInstance ;

    hwnd = CreateWindow (szAppName, szCaption,
                        WS_OVERLAPPEDWINDOW,
                        CW_USEDEFAULT, CW_USEDEFAULT,
                        CW_USEDEFAULT, CW_USEDEFAULT,
                        NULL, NULL, hInstance, NULL) ;

    ShowWindow (hwnd, iCmdShow) ;
    UpdateWindow (hwnd) ;

    while (GetMessage (&msg, NULL, 0, 0))
    {
        TranslateMessage (&msg) ;
        DispatchMessage (&msg) ;
    }
    return msg.wParam ;
}

void PageGDICalls (HDC hdcPrn, int cxPage, int cyPage)
{
    static TCHAR szTextStr[] = TEXT ("Hello, Printer!") ;

    Rectangle (hdcPrn, 0, 0, cxPage, cyPage) ;

    MoveToEx (hdcPrn, 0, 0, NULL) ;
    LineTo   (hdcPrn, cxPage, cyPage) ;
    MoveToEx (hdcPrn, cxPage, 0, NULL) ;
    LineTo   (hdcPrn, 0, cyPage) ;

    SaveDC (hdcPrn) ;

    SetMapMode       (hdcPrn, MM_ISOTROPIC) ;
    SetWindowExtEx   (hdcPrn, 1000, 1000, NULL) ;
    SetViewportExtEx (hdcPrn, cxPage / 2, -cyPage / 2, NULL) ;
    SetViewportOrgEx (hdcPrn, cxPage / 2,  cyPage / 2, NULL) ;

    Ellipse (hdcPrn, -500, 500, 500, -500) ;

    SetTextAlign (hdcPrn, TA_BASELINE | TA_CENTER) ;
    TextOut (hdcPrn, 0, 0, szTextStr, lstrlen (szTextStr)) ;
```

```
     RestoreDC (hdcPrn, -1) ;
}

LRESULT CALLBACK WndProc (HWND hwnd, UINT message, WPARAM wParam, LPARAM lParam)
{
     static int    cxClient, cyClient ;
     HDC           hdc ;
     HMENU         hMenu ;
     PAINTSTRUCT   ps ;

     switch (message)
     {
     case WM_CREATE:
          hMenu = GetSystemMenu (hwnd, FALSE) ;
          AppendMenu (hMenu, MF_SEPARATOR, 0, NULL) ;
          AppendMenu (hMenu, 0, 1, TEXT ("&Print")) ;
          return 0 ;

     case WM_SIZE:
          cxClient = LOWORD (lParam) ;
          cyClient = HIWORD (lParam) ;
          return 0 ;

     case WM_SYSCOMMAND:
          if (wParam == 1)
          {
               if (!PrintMyPage (hwnd))
                    MessageBox (hwnd, TEXT ("Could not print page!"),
                                szAppName, MB_OK | MB_ICONEXCLAMATION) ;
               return 0 ;
          }
          break ;

     case WM_PAINT :
          hdc = BeginPaint (hwnd, &ps) ;

          PageGDICalls (hdc, cxClient, cyClient) ;

          EndPaint (hwnd, &ps) ;
          return 0 ;

     case WM_DESTROY :
          PostQuitMessage (0) ;
          return 0 ;
     }
     return DefWindowProc (hwnd, message, wParam, lParam) ;
}
```

PRINT.C contains the functions *WinMain* and *WndProc*, and also a function called *PageGDICalls*, which expects to receive a handle to the printer device context and two variables containing the width and height of the printer page. *PageGDICalls* draws a rectangle that encompasses the entire page, two lines between opposite corners of the page, an ellipse in the middle of the page (its diameter half the lesser of the printer height and width), and the text "Hello, Printer!" in the center of this ellipse.

During processing of the WM_CREATE message, *WndProc* adds a Print option to the system menu. Selecting this option causes a call to *PrintMyPage*, a function that we'll enhance over the course of the three versions of the program. *PrintMyPage* returns TRUE if it successfully prints the page and FALSE if it encounters an error during printing. If *PrintMyPage* returns FALSE, *WndProc* displays a message box to inform you of the error.

Bare-Bones Printing

PRINT1, the first version of the printing program, is shown in Figure 13-7. After compiling PRINT1, you can execute it and then select Print from the system menu. In quick succession, GDI saves the necessary printer output in a temporary file, and then the spooler sends it to the printer.

PRINT1.C

```
/*------------------------------------------
   PRINT1.C -- Bare Bones Printing
               (c) Charles Petzold, 1998
   ------------------------------------------*/

#include <windows.h>

HDC  GetPrinterDC (void) ;              // in GETPRNDC.C
void PageGDICalls (HDC, int, int) ;     // in PRINT.C

HINSTANCE hInst ;
TCHAR     szAppName[] = TEXT ("Print1") ;
TCHAR     szCaption[] = TEXT ("Print Program 1") ;

BOOL PrintMyPage (HWND hwnd)
{
     static DOCINFO di = { sizeof (DOCINFO), TEXT ("Print1: Printing") } ;
     BOOL          bSuccess = TRUE ;
     HDC           hdcPrn ;
     int           xPage, yPage ;

     if (NULL == (hdcPrn = GetPrinterDC ()))
          return FALSE ;
```

Figure 13-7. *The PRINT1 program.*

```
    xPage = GetDeviceCaps (hdcPrn, HORZRES) ;
    yPage = GetDeviceCaps (hdcPrn, VERTRES) ;

    if (StartDoc (hdcPrn, &di) > 0)
    {
        if (StartPage (hdcPrn) > 0)
        {
            PageGDICalls (hdcPrn, xPage, yPage) ;

            if (EndPage (hdcPrn) > 0)
                EndDoc (hdcPrn) ;
            else
                bSuccess = FALSE ;
        }
    }
    else
        bSuccess = FALSE ;

    DeleteDC (hdcPrn) ;
    return bSuccess ;
}
```

Let's look at the code in PRINT1.C. If *PrintMyPage* can't obtain a device context handle for the printer, it returns FALSE and *WndProc* displays the message box indicating an error. If the function succeeds in obtaining the device context handle, it then determines the horizontal and vertical size of the page in pixels by calling *GetDeviceCaps*:

```
xPage = GetDeviceCaps (hdcPrn, HORZRES) ;
yPage = GetDeviceCaps (hdcPrn, VERTRES) ;
```

This is not the full size of the paper but rather its printable area. After that call, the code in PRINT1's *PrintMyPage* function is structurally the same as the code in FORMFEED, except that PRINT1 calls *PageGDICalls* between the *StartPage* and *EndPage* calls. Only if the calls to *StartDoc*, *StartPage*, and *EndPage* are successful does PRINT1 call the *EndDoc* print function.

Canceling Printing with an Abort Procedure

For large documents, a program should provide the user with a convenient way to cancel a print job while the application is still printing. Perhaps the user intended to print only one page of a document but instead elected to print all 537 pages. That should be a mistake that is correctable before all 537 pages have printed.

Canceling a print job from within an application requires something called an "abort procedure." The abort procedure is a small exported function in your program. You give Windows the address of this function as an argument to the *SetAbortProc* function; GDI then calls the procedure repeatedly during printing, in essence asking, "Shall I continue printing?"

Let's look first at what's required to add an abort procedure to the printing logic and then examine some of the ramifications. The abort procedure is commonly called *AbortProc*, and it takes the following form:

```
BOOL CALLBACK AbortProc (HDC hdcPrn, int iCode)
{
     [other program lines]
}
```

Before printing, you must register the abort procedure by calling *SetAbortProc*:

```
SetAbortProc (hdcPrn, AbortProc) ;
```

You make this call before the *StartDoc* call. You don't need to "unset" the abort procedure after you finish printing.

While processing the *EndPage* call (that is, while playing the metafile into the device driver and creating the temporary printer output files), GDI frequently calls the abort procedure. The *hdcPrn* parameter is the printer device context handle. The *iCode* parameter is 0 if all is going well or is SP_OUTOFDISK if the GDI module has run out of disk space because of the temporary printer output files.

AbortProc must return TRUE (nonzero) if the print job is to be continued and returns FALSE (0) if the print job is to be aborted. The abort procedure can be as simple as this:

```
BOOL CALLBACK AbortProc (HDC hdcPrn, int iCode)
{
     MSG    msg ;

     while (PeekMessage (&msg, NULL, 0, 0, PM_REMOVE))
     {
          TranslateMessage (&msg) ;
          DispatchMessage (&msg) ;
     }
     return TRUE ;
}
```

This function may seem a little peculiar. In fact, it looks suspiciously like a message loop. What's a message loop doing here of all places? Well, it *is* a message loop. You'll note, however, that this message loop calls *PeekMessage* rather than *GetMessage*. I discussed *PeekMessage* in connection with the RANDRECT program at the end of Chapter 5. You'll recall that *PeekMessage* returns control to a program with a message from the program's message queue (just like *GetMessage*) but also returns control if there are no messages waiting in any program's message queue.

The message loop in the *AbortProc* function repeatedly calls *PeekMessage* while *PeekMessage* returns TRUE. This TRUE value means that *PeekMessage* has retrieved a message that can be sent to one of the program's window procedures using *Translate-*

Message and *DispatchMessage*. When there are no more messages in the program's message queue, the return value of *PeekMessage* is then FALSE, so *AbortProc* returns control to Windows.

How Windows Uses *AbortProc*

When a program is printing, the bulk of the work takes place during the call to *EndPage*. Before that call, the GDI module simply adds another record to the disk-based metafile every time the program calls a GDI drawing function. When GDI gets the *EndPage* call, it plays this metafile into the device driver once for each band the device driver defines on a page. GDI then stores in a file the printer output created by the printer driver. If the spooler isn't active, the GDI module itself must write this printer output to the printer.

During the call to *EndPage*, the GDI module calls the abort procedure you've set. Normally, the *iCode* parameter is 0, but if GDI has run out of disk space because of the presence of other temporary files that haven't been printed yet, the *iCode* parameter is SP_OUTOFDISK. (You wouldn't normally check this value, but you can if you want.) The abort procedure then goes into its *PeekMessage* loop to retrieve messages from the program's message queue.

If there are no messages in the program's message queue, *PeekMessage* returns FALSE. The abort procedure then drops out of its message loop and returns a TRUE value to the GDI module to indicate that printing should continue. The GDI module then continues to process the *EndPage* call.

The GDI module stops the print process if an error occurs, so the main purpose of the abort procedure is to allow the user to cancel printing. For that we also need a dialog box that displays a Cancel button. Let's take these two steps one at a time. First we'll add an abort procedure to create the PRINT2 program, and then we'll add a dialog with a Cancel button in PRINT3 to make the abort procedure useful.

Implementing an Abort Procedure

Let's quickly review the mechanics of the abort procedure. You define an abort procedure that looks like this:

```
BOOL CALLBACK AbortProc (HDC hdcPrn, int iCode)
{
    MSG  msg ;

    while (PeekMessage (&msg, NULL, 0, 0, PM_REMOVE))
    {
        TranslateMessage (&msg) ;
        DispatchMessage (&msg) ;
    }
    return TRUE ;
}
```

To print something, you give Windows a pointer to the abort procedure:

```
SetAbortProc (hdcPrn, AbortProc) ;
```

You make this call before the *StartDoc* call. And that's it.

Well, not quite. We've overlooked a problem with that *PeekMessage* loop in *Abort-Proc*—a big problem. *AbortProc* is called only while your program is in the midst of printing. Some very ugly things can happen if you retrieve a message in *AbortProc* and dispatch it to your own window procedure. A user could select Print from the menu again. But the program is already in the middle of the printing routine. A user could load a new file into the program while the program is trying to print the previous file. A user could even quit your program! If that happens, all your program's windows will be destroyed. You'll eventually return from the printing routine, but you'll have nowhere to go except to a window procedure that's no longer valid.

This stuff boggles the mind. And your program isn't prepared for it. For this reason, when you set an abort procedure, you should first disable your program's window so that it can't receive keyboard and mouse input. You do this with

```
EnableWindow (hwnd, FALSE) ;
```

This prevents keyboard and mouse input from getting into the message queue. The user therefore can't do anything with your program during the time it's printing. When printing is finished, you reenable the window for input:

```
EnableWindow (hwnd, TRUE) ;
```

So why, you ask, do we even bother with the *TranslateMessage* and *DispatchMessage* calls in *AbortProc* when no keyboard or mouse messages will get into the message queue in the first place? It's true that the *TranslateMessage* call isn't strictly needed (although it's almost always included). But we must use *DispatchMessage* in case a WM_PAINT message gets in the message queue. If WM_PAINT isn't processed properly with a *BeginPaint* and *EndPaint* pair in the window procedure, the message will remain in the queue and clog up the works, because *PeekMessage* will never return a FALSE.

When you disable your window during the time you're printing, your program remains inert on the display. But a user can switch to another program and do some work there, and the spooler can continue sending output files to the printer.

The PRINT2 program, shown in Figure 13-8, adds to PRINT1 an abort procedure and the necessary support—a call to the *AbortProc* function and two calls to *EnableWindow*, the first to disable the window and the second to reenable it.

PRINT2.C

```
/*-----------------------------------------------
   PRINT2.C -- Printing with Abort Procedure
               (c) Charles Petzold, 1998
   ------------------------------------------*/

#include <windows.h>

HDC  GetPrinterDC (void) ;                 // in GETPRNDC.C
void PageGDICalls (HDC, int, int) ;        // in PRINT.C

HINSTANCE hInst ;
TCHAR     szAppName[] = TEXT ("Print2") ;
TCHAR     szCaption[] = TEXT ("Print Program 2 (Abort Procedure)") ;

BOOL CALLBACK AbortProc (HDC hdcPrn, int iCode)
{
    MSG msg ;

    while (PeekMessage (&msg, NULL, 0, 0, PM_REMOVE))
    {
        TranslateMessage (&msg) ;
        DispatchMessage (&msg) ;
    }
    return TRUE ;
}

BOOL PrintMyPage (HWND hwnd)
{
    static DOCINFO di = { sizeof (DOCINFO), TEXT ("Print2: Printing") } ;
    BOOL           bSuccess = TRUE ;
    HDC            hdcPrn ;
    short          xPage, yPage ;

    if (NULL == (hdcPrn = GetPrinterDC ()))
        return FALSE ;

    xPage = GetDeviceCaps (hdcPrn, HORZRES) ;
    yPage = GetDeviceCaps (hdcPrn, VERTRES) ;

    EnableWindow (hwnd, FALSE) ;

    SetAbortProc (hdcPrn, AbortProc) ;

    if (StartDoc (hdcPrn, &di) > 0)
```

Figure 13-8. *The PRINT2 program.*

(continued)

Figure 13-8. *continued*

```
    {
        if (StartPage (hdcPrn) > 0)
        {
            PageGDICalls (hdcPrn, xPage, yPage) ;

            if (EndPage (hdcPrn) > 0)
                EndDoc (hdcPrn) ;
            else
                bSuccess = FALSE ;
        }
    }
    else
        bSuccess = FALSE ;

    EnableWindow (hwnd, TRUE) ;
    DeleteDC (hdcPrn) ;
    return bSuccess ;
}
```

Adding a Printing Dialog Box

PRINT2 is not entirely satisfactory. First, the program doesn't directly indicate when it is printing and when it is finished with printing. Only when you poke at the program with the mouse and find that it doesn't respond can you determine that it must still be processing the *PrintMyPage* routine. Nor does PRINT2 give the user the opportunity to cancel the print job while it is spooling.

You're probably aware that most Windows programs give users a chance to cancel a printing operation currently in progress. A small dialog box comes up on the screen; it contains some text and a push button labeled Cancel. The program displays this dialog box during the entire time that GDI is saving the printer output in a disk file or (if the spooler is disabled) while the printer is printing. This is a modeless dialog box, and you must supply the dialog procedure.

This dialog box is often called the "abort dialog box," and the dialog procedure is often called the "abort dialog procedure." To distinguish it more clearly from the "abort procedure," I'll call this dialog procedure the "printing dialog procedure." The abort procedure (with the name *AbortProc*) and the printing dialog procedure (which I'll name *PrintDlgProc*) are two separate exported functions. If you want to print in a professional, Windows-like manner, you must have both of these.

These two functions interact as follows. The *PeekMessage* loop in *AbortProc* must be modified to send messages for the modeless dialog box to the dialog box window procedure. *PrintDlgProc* must process WM_COMMAND messages to check the status of the Cancel button. If the Cancel button is pressed, it sets a global variable called *bUserAbort* to TRUE.

The value returned from *AbortProc* is the inverse of *bUserAbort*. You will recall that *AbortProc* returns TRUE to continue printing and FALSE to abort printing. In PRINT2 we always returned TRUE. Now we'll return FALSE if the user clicks the Cancel button in the printing dialog box. This logic is implemented in the PRINT3 program, shown in Figure 13-9.

PRINT3.C

```
/*-------------------------------------------
   PRINT3.C -- Printing with Dialog Box
               (c) Charles Petzold, 1998
   -------------------------------------------*/

#include <windows.h>

HDC  GetPrinterDC (void) ;                  // in GETPRNDC.C
void PageGDICalls (HDC, int, int) ;         // in PRINT.C

HINSTANCE hInst ;
TCHAR     szAppName[] = TEXT ("Print3") ;
TCHAR     szCaption[] = TEXT ("Print Program 3 (Dialog Box)") ;

BOOL bUserAbort ;
HWND hDlgPrint ;

BOOL CALLBACK PrintDlgProc (HWND hDlg, UINT message,
                            WPARAM wParam, LPARAM lParam)
{
     switch (message)
     {
     case WM_INITDIALOG:
          SetWindowText (hDlg, szAppName) ;
          EnableMenuItem (GetSystemMenu (hDlg, FALSE), SC_CLOSE, MF_GRAYED) ;
          return TRUE ;

     case WM_COMMAND:
          bUserAbort = TRUE ;
          EnableWindow (GetParent (hDlg), TRUE) ;
          DestroyWindow (hDlg) ;
          hDlgPrint = NULL ;
          return TRUE ;
     }
     return FALSE ;
}

BOOL CALLBACK AbortProc (HDC hdcPrn, int iCode)
```

Figure 13-9. *The PRINT3 program.* *(continued)*

Figure 13-9. *continued*

```
{
     MSG msg ;

     while (!bUserAbort && PeekMessage (&msg, NULL, 0, 0, PM_REMOVE))
     {
          if (!hDlgPrint || !IsDialogMessage (hDlgPrint, &msg))
          {
               TranslateMessage (&msg) ;
               DispatchMessage (&msg) ;
          }
     }
     return !bUserAbort ;
}

BOOL PrintMyPage (HWND hwnd)
{
     static DOCINFO di = { sizeof (DOCINFO), TEXT ("Print3: Printing") } ;
     BOOL           bSuccess = TRUE ;
     HDC            hdcPrn ;
     int            xPage, yPage ;

     if (NULL == (hdcPrn = GetPrinterDC ()))
          return FALSE ;

     xPage = GetDeviceCaps (hdcPrn, HORZRES) ;
     yPage = GetDeviceCaps (hdcPrn, VERTRES) ;

     EnableWindow (hwnd, FALSE) ;

     bUserAbort = FALSE ;
     hDlgPrint = CreateDialog (hInst, TEXT ("PrintDlgBox"),
                               hwnd, PrintDlgProc) ;

     SetAbortProc (hdcPrn, AbortProc) ;

     if (StartDoc (hdcPrn, &di) > 0)
     {
          if (StartPage (hdcPrn) > 0)
          {
               PageGDICalls (hdcPrn, xPage, yPage) ;

               if (EndPage (hdcPrn) > 0)
                    EndDoc (hdcPrn) ;
               else
                    bSuccess = FALSE ;
          }
     }
```

```
        else
            bSuccess = FALSE ;

        if (!bUserAbort)
        {
            EnableWindow (hwnd, TRUE) ;
            DestroyWindow (hDlgPrint) ;
        }

        DeleteDC (hdcPrn) ;

        return bSuccess && !bUserAbort ;
}
```

PRINT.RC (excerpts)

```
//Microsoft Developer Studio generated resource script.

#include "resource.h"
#include "afxres.h"


/////////////////////////////////////////////////////////////////////////////
// Dialog

PRINTDLGBOX DIALOG DISCARDABLE  20, 20, 186, 63
STYLE DS_MODALFRAME | WS_POPUP | WS_VISIBLE | WS_CAPTION | WS_SYSMENU
FONT 8, "MS Sans Serif"
BEGIN
    PUSHBUTTON      "Cancel",IDCANCEL,67,42,50,14
    CTEXT           "Cancel Printing",IDC_STATIC,7,21,172,8
END
```

If you experiment with PRINT3, you may want to temporarily disable print spooling. Otherwise, the Cancel button, which is visible only while the spooler collects data from PRINT3, might disappear too quickly for you to actually click on it. Don't be surprised if things don't come to an immediate halt when you click the Cancel button, especially on a slow printer. The printer has an internal buffer that must drain before the printer stops. Clicking Cancel merely tells GDI not to send any more data to the printer's buffer.

Two global variables are added to PRINT3: a BOOL called *bUserAbort* and a handle to the dialog box window called *hDlgPrint*. The *PrintMyPage* function initializes *bUserAbort* to FALSE, and as in PRINT2, the program's main window is disabled. The pointer to *AbortProc* is used in the *SetAbortProc* call, and the pointer to *PrintDlgProc* is used in a *CreateDialog* call. The window handle returned from *CreateDialog* is saved in *hDlgPrint*.

The message loop in *AbortProc* now looks like this:

```
while (!bUserAbort && PeekMessage (&msg, NULL, 0, 0, PM_REMOVE))
{
     if (!hDlgPrint || !IsDialogMessage (hDlgPrint, &msg))
     {
          TranslateMessage (&msg) ;
          DispatchMessage (&msg) ;
     }
}
return !bUserAbort ;
```

It calls *PeekMessage* only if *bUserAbort* is FALSE—that is, if the user hasn't yet aborted the printing operation. The *IsDialogMessage* function is required to send the message to the modeless dialog box. As is normal with modeless dialog boxes, the handle to the dialog box window is checked before this call is made. *AbortProc* returns the inverse of *bUserAbort*. Initially, *bUserAbort* is FALSE, so *AbortProc* returns TRUE, indicating that printing is to continue. But *bUserAbort* could be set to TRUE in the printing dialog procedure.

The *PrintDlgProc* function is fairly simple. While processing WM_INITDIALOG, the function sets the window caption to the name of the program and disables the Close option on the system menu. If the user clicks the Cancel button, *PrintDlgProc* receives a WM_COMMAND message:

```
case WM_COMMAND :
     bUserAbort = TRUE ;
     EnableWindow (GetParent (hDlg), TRUE) ;
     DestroyWindow (hDlg) ;
     hDlgPrint = NULL ;
     return TRUE ;
```

Setting *bUserAbort* to TRUE indicates that the user has decided to cancel the printing operation. The main window is enabled, and the dialog box is destroyed. (It is important that you perform these two actions in this order. Otherwise, some other program running under Windows will become the active program, and your program might disappear into the background.) As is normal, *hDlgPrint* is set to NULL to prevent *IsDialogMessage* from being called in the message loop.

The only time this dialog box receives messages is when *AbortProc* retrieves messages with *PeekMessage* and sends them to the dialog box window procedure with *IsDialogMessage*. The only time *AbortProc* is called is when the GDI module is processing the *EndPage* function. If GDI sees that the return value from *AbortProc* is FALSE, it returns control from the *EndPage* call back to *PrintMyPage*. It doesn't return an error code. At that point, *PrintMyPage* thinks that the page is complete and calls the *EndDoc* function. Nothing is printed, however, because the GDI module didn't finish processing the *EndPage* call.

Some cleanup remains. If the user didn't cancel the print job from the dialog box, then the dialog box is still displayed. *PrintMyPage* reenables its main window and destroys the dialog box:

```
if (!bUserAbort)
{
     EnableWindow (hwnd, TRUE) ;
     DestroyWindow (hDlgPrint) ;
}
```

Two variables tell you what happened: *bUserAbort* tells you whether the user aborted the print job, and *bSuccess* tells you whether an error occurred. You can do what you want with these variables. *PrintMyPage* simply performs a logical AND operation to return to *WndProc*:

```
return bSuccess && !bUserAbort ;
```

Adding Printing to POPPAD

Now we're ready to add a printing facility to the POPPAD series of programs and declare POPPAD finished. You'll need the various POPPAD files from Chapter 11, plus the POP-PRNT.C file in Figure 13-10.

POPPRNT.C

```
/*---------------------------------------------
   POPPRNT.C -- Popup Editor Printing Functions
   ---------------------------------------------*/

#include <windows.h>
#include <commdlg.h>
#include "resource.h"

BOOL bUserAbort ;
HWND hDlgPrint ;

BOOL CALLBACK PrintDlgProc (HWND hDlg, UINT msg, WPARAM wParam, LPARAM lParam)
{
     switch (msg)
     {
     case WM_INITDIALOG :
          EnableMenuItem (GetSystemMenu (hDlg, FALSE), SC_CLOSE, MF_GRAYED) ;
          return TRUE ;

     case WM_COMMAND :
          bUserAbort = TRUE ;
          EnableWindow (GetParent (hDlg), TRUE) ;
          DestroyWindow (hDlg) ;
```

Figure 13-10. *The POPPRNT.C file to add printing capability to POPPAD.*   *(continued)*

Figure 13-10. *continued*

```
            hDlgPrint = NULL ;
            return TRUE ;
      }
      return FALSE ;
}


BOOL CALLBACK AbortProc (HDC hPrinterDC, int iCode)
{
      MSG msg ;

      while (!bUserAbort && PeekMessage (&msg, NULL, 0, 0, PM_REMOVE))
      {
            if (!hDlgPrint || !IsDialogMessage (hDlgPrint, &msg))
            {
                  TranslateMessage (&msg) ;
                  DispatchMessage (&msg) ;
            }
      }
      return !bUserAbort ;
}


BOOL PopPrntPrintFile (HINSTANCE hInst, HWND hwnd, HWND hwndEdit,
                       PTSTR szTitleName)
{
      static DOCINFO  di = { sizeof (DOCINFO) } ;
      static PRINTDLG pd ;
      BOOL            bSuccess ;
      int             yChar, iCharsPerLine, iLinesPerPage, iTotalLines,
                      iTotalPages, iPage, iLine, iLineNum ;
      PTSTR           pstrBuffer ;
      TCHAR           szJobName [64 + MAX_PATH] ;
      TEXTMETRIC      tm ;
      WORD            iColCopy, iNoiColCopy ;

           // Invoke Print common dialog box

      pd.lStructSize       = sizeof (PRINTDLG) ;
      pd.hwndOwner         = hwnd ;
      pd.hDevMode          = NULL ;
      pd.hDevNames         = NULL ;
      pd.hDC               = NULL ;
      pd.Flags             = PD_ALLPAGES | PD_COLLATE |
                             PD_RETURNDC | PD_NOSELECTION ;
      pd.nFromPage         = 0 ;
      pd.nToPage           = 0 ;
      pd.nMinPage          = 0 ;
```

```
pd.nMaxPage            = 0 ;
pd.nCopies             = 1 ;
pd.hInstance           = NULL ;
pd.lCustData           = 0L ;
pd.lpfnPrintHook       = NULL ;
pd.lpfnSetupHook       = NULL ;
pd.lpPrintTemplateName = NULL ;
pd.lpSetupTemplateName = NULL ;
pd.hPrintTemplate      = NULL ;
pd.hSetupTemplate      = NULL ;

if (!PrintDlg (&pd))
    return TRUE ;

if (0 == (iTotalLines = SendMessage (hwndEdit, EM_GETLINECOUNT, 0, 0)))
    return TRUE ;

    // Calculate necessary metrics for file

GetTextMetrics (pd.hDC, &tm) ;
yChar = tm.tmHeight + tm.tmExternalLeading ;

iCharsPerLine = GetDeviceCaps (pd.hDC, HORZRES) / tm.tmAveCharWidth ;
iLinesPerPage = GetDeviceCaps (pd.hDC, VERTRES) / yChar ;
iTotalPages   = (iTotalLines + iLinesPerPage - 1) / iLinesPerPage ;

    // Allocate a buffer for each line of text

pstrBuffer = malloc (sizeof (TCHAR) * (iCharsPerLine + 1)) ;

    // Display the printing dialog box

EnableWindow (hwnd, FALSE) ;

bSuccess   = TRUE ;
bUserAbort = FALSE ;

hDlgPrint = CreateDialog (hInst, TEXT ("PrintDlgBox"),
                          hwnd, PrintDlgProc) ;

SetDlgItemText (hDlgPrint, IDC_FILENAME, szTitleName) ;
SetAbortProc (pd.hDC, AbortProc) ;

    // Start the document

GetWindowText (hwnd, szJobName, sizeof (szJobName)) ;
di.lpszDocName = szJobName ;
```

(continued)

Figure 13-10. *continued*

```
if (StartDoc (pd.hDC, &di) > 0)
{
        // Collation requires this loop and iNoiColCopy

     for (iColCopy = 0 ;
          iColCopy < ((WORD) pd.Flags & PD_COLLATE ? pd.nCopies : 1) ;
          iColCopy++)
     {
        for (iPage = 0 ; iPage < iTotalPages ; iPage++)
        {
           for (iNoiColCopy = 0 ;
                iNoiColCopy < (pd.Flags & PD_COLLATE ? 1 : pd.nCopies);
                iNoiColCopy++)
           {
                   // Start the page

                if (StartPage (pd.hDC) < 0)
                {
                     bSuccess = FALSE ;
                     break ;
                }

                   // For each page, print the lines

                for (iLine = 0 ; iLine < iLinesPerPage ; iLine++)
                {
                     iLineNum = iLinesPerPage * iPage + iLine ;

                     if (iLineNum > iTotalLines)
                          break ;

                     *(int *) pstrBuffer = iCharsPerLine ;

                     TextOut (pd.hDC, 0, yChar * iLine, pstrBuffer,
                             (int) SendMessage (hwndEdit, EM_GETLINE,
                             (WPARAM) iLineNum, (LPARAM) pstrBuffer));
                }

                if (EndPage (pd.hDC) < 0)
                {
                     bSuccess = FALSE ;
                     break ;
                }

                if (bUserAbort)
                     break ;
           }
```

```
                         if (!bSuccess || bUserAbort)
                              break ;
                    }

               if (!bSuccess || bUserAbort)
                    break ;
          }
     }
     else
          bSuccess = FALSE ;

     if (bSuccess)
          EndDoc (pd.hDC) ;

     if (!bUserAbort)
     {
          EnableWindow (hwnd, TRUE) ;
          DestroyWindow (hDlgPrint) ;
     }

     free (pstrBuffer) ;
     DeleteDC (pd.hDC) ;

     return bSuccess && !bUserAbort ;
}
```

In keeping with the philosophy of making POPPAD as simple as possible by taking advantage of high-level Windows features, the POPPRNT.C file demonstrates how to use the *PrintDlg* function. This function is included in the common dialog box library and uses a structure of type PRINTDLG.

Normally, a Print option is included on a program's File menu. When the user selects the Print option, a program can initialize the fields of the PRINTDLG structure and call *PrintDlg*.

PrintDlg displays a dialog box that allows the user to select a page range to print. Thus, this dialog box is particularly suitable for programs such as POPPAD that can print multipage documents. The dialog box also provides an edit field to specify the number of copies and a check-box labeled "Collate." Collation affects the page ordering of multiple copies. For example, if the document is three pages long and the user requests that three copies be printed, the program can print them in one of two orders. Collated copies are in the page order 1, 2, 3, 1, 2, 3, 1, 2, 3. Noncollated copies are in the order 1, 1, 1, 2, 2, 2, 3, 3, 3. It's up to your program to print the copies in the correct order.

The dialog box also allows the user to select a nondefault printer, and it includes a button labeled Properties that invokes a device mode dialog box. At the very least, this allows the user to select portrait or landscape mode.

On return from the *PrintDlg* function, fields of the PRINTDLG structure indicate the range of pages to print and whether multiple copies should be collated. The structure also provides the printer device context handle, ready to be used.

In POPPRNT.C, the *PopPrntPrintFile* function (which is called from POPPAD when the user selects the Print option from the File menu) calls *PrintDlg* and then proceeds to print the file. *PopPrntPrintFile* then performs some calculations to determine the number of characters it can fit on a line and the number of lines it can fit on a page. This process involves calls to *GetDeviceCaps* to determine the resolution of the page and to *GetTextMetrics* for the dimensions of a character.

The program obtains the total number of lines in the document (the variable *iTotalLines*) by sending an EM_GETLINECOUNT message to the edit control. A buffer for holding the contents of each line is allocated from local memory. For each line, the first word of this buffer is set to the number of characters in the line. Sending the edit control an EM_GETLINE message copies a line into the buffer; the line is then sent to the printer device context using *TextOut*. (POPPRNT.C is not smart enough to wrap lines that exceed the width of the printer page. We'll examine a technique for wrapping such lines in Chapter 17.)

Notice that the logic to print the document includes two *for* loops for the number of copies. The first uses a variable named *iColCopy* and takes effect when the user has specified collated copies; the second uses the *iNonColCopy* variable and takes effect for noncollated copies.

The program breaks from the *for* loop incrementing the page number if either *StartPage* or *EndPage* returns an error or if *bUserAbort* is TRUE. If the return value of the abort procedure is FALSE, *EndPage* doesn't return an error. For this reason, *bUserAbort* is tested explicitly before the next page is started. If no error is reported, the call to *EndDoc* is made:

```
if (!bError)
     EndDoc (hdcPrn) ;
```

You might want to experiment with POPPAD by printing a multipage file. You can monitor progress from the print job window. The file being printed first shows up in this window after GDI has finished processing the first *EndPage* call. At that time, the spooler starts sending the file to the printer. If you then cancel the print job from POPPAD, the spooler aborts the printing also—that's a result of returning FALSE from the abort procedure. Once the file appears in the print job window, you can also cancel the printing by selecting Cancel Printing from the Document menu. In that case, the *EndPage* call in progress in POPPAD returns an error.

Programmers new to Windows often become inordinately obsessed with the *AbortDoc* function. This function is rarely used in printing. As you can see in POPPAD, a user can cancel a print job at almost any time, either through POPPAD's printing dialog box or through the print job window. Neither requires that the program use the *AbortDoc* function. The only time that *AbortDoc* would be allowed in POPPAD is between the call to *StartDoc* and the first call to *EndPage*, but that code goes so quickly that *AbortDoc* isn't necessary.

Figure 13-11 shows the correct sequence of print function calls for printing a multipage document. The best place to check for a *bUserAbort* value of TRUE is after each call to *EndPage*. The *EndDoc* function is used only when the previous print functions have proceeded without error. In fact, once you get an error from any call to a print function, the show is over and you can go home.

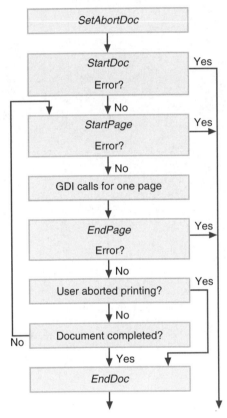

Figure 13-11. *The sequence of function calls for multipage printing.*

Chapter 14

Bitmaps and Bitblts

A bitmap is a two-dimensional rectangular array of bits that correspond to the pixels of an image. When real-world images are captured in bitmaps, the image is divided into a grid and the pixel is the sampling unit. The value of each pixel in the bitmap indicates the average color of the image within a unit of this grid. Monochrome bitmaps require only one bit per pixel; gray shade or color bitmaps require multiple bits per pixel.

Bitmaps represent one of two methods for storing pictorial information in a Windows program. The other form of stored pictorial information is the metafile, which I'll cover in Chapter 18. A metafile is a description of a picture rather than a digital representation of it.

As I'll discuss in more detail shortly, Microsoft Windows 3.0 introduced something called the device-independent bitmap (DIB). I'll discuss DIBs in the next chapter. This chapter covers the GDI bitmap object, which is the bitmap support implemented in Windows prior to the DIB. As the various sample programs in this chapter demonstrate, the pre-DIB bitmap support of Windows is still quite useful and valuable.

BITMAP BASICS

Both bitmaps and metafiles have their place in computer graphics. Bitmaps are often used for very complex images originating in the real world, such as digitized photographs or video captures. Metafiles are more suitable for human-generated or machine-generated images, such as architectural drawings. Both bitmaps and metafiles can exist in memory or be stored on a disk as files, and both can be transferred among Windows applications through the clipboard.

The difference between bitmaps and metafiles is the difference between raster graphics and vector graphics. Raster graphics treats output devices in terms of discrete pixels; vector graphics treats the output device as a Cartesian coordinate system upon which lines and filled objects can be drawn. Most graphics output devices these days are raster devices. These include video displays, dot-matrix printers, laser printers, and ink-jet printers. A pen plotter, however, is a vector output device.

Bitmaps have two major drawbacks. First, they are susceptible to problems involving device dependence. The most obvious device dependency is color. Displaying a color bitmap on a monochrome device is often unsatisfactory. Another problem is that a bitmap often implies a particular resolution and aspect ratio of an image. Although bitmaps can be stretched or compressed, this process generally involves duplicating or dropping rows or columns of pixels, and this can lead to distortion in the scaled image. A metafile can be scaled to almost any size without distortion.

The second major drawback of bitmaps is that they require a large amount of storage space. For instance, a bitmap representation of an entire 640-by-480-pixel, 16-color Video Graphics Array (VGA) screen requires more than 150 KB; a 1024-by-768 image with 24 bits per pixel requires more than 2 MB. Metafiles usually require much less storage space than bitmaps. The storage space for a bitmap is governed by the size of the image and number of colors it contains, whereas the storage space for a metafile is governed by the complexity of the image and the number of individual GDI instructions it contains.

One advantage of bitmaps over metafiles, however, is speed. Copying a bitmap to a video display is usually much faster than rendering a metafile. In recent years, compression techniques have allowed the shrinking of bitmaps to a size where they can be effectively transmitted over telephone lines and used extensively in World Wide Web pages on the Internet.

Where Do Bitmaps Come From?

Bitmap images can be created "manually," for example, by using the Paint program included with Windows 98. Someone using a raster "paint" program rather than a vector "draw" program is working under the assumption that the eventual image will be too complex to be rendered with lines and filled areas.

Bitmap images can also be created algorithmically by computer code. Although most algorithmically generated images can be stored in a vector graphics metafile, highly detailed surfaces or fractals usually require bitmaps.

These days, bitmaps are often used for images from the real world, and various hardware devices let you move images from the real world into the computer. This hardware generally uses something called a *charge-coupled device* (CCD), which releases an electrical charge when exposed to light. Sometimes these CCD cells are arranged in an array, one CCD per pixel; to keep costs down, a single row of CCDs can be used to scan an image.

The *scanner* is the oldest of these computer-based CCD devices. It uses a row of CCDs that sweep along the surface of a printed image, such as a photograph. The CCDs generate electrical charges based on the intensity of light. Analog-to-digital converters (ADCs) convert the charges into numbers, which then can be arranged in a bitmap.

Video camcorders also use arrays of CCD cells to capture images. Generally these images are recorded on videotape. However, the video output can be fed directly into a video *frame grabber*, which converts an analog video signal into an array of pixel values. These frame grabbers can be used with any compatible video source, such as that from a VCR or a laserdisc or DVD player, or even directly from a cable decoding box.

Most recently, digital cameras have become financially viable for the home user. These often look very much like normal cameras. But instead of film, an array of CCDs is used to capture an image, and an internal ADC allows the digital image to be stored directly in memory within the camera. Generally, the camera interfaces to the computer through the serial port.

BITMAP DIMENSIONS

A bitmap is rectangular and has a spatial dimension, which is the width and height of the image in pixels. For example, this grid could represent a very small bitmap that is 9 pixels wide and 6 pixels high or, more concisely, 9 by 6:

By convention, the shorthand dimension of a bitmap is given with the width first. This bitmap has a total of 9 × 6, or 54, pixels. I'll often use the symbols *cx* and *cy* to refer to the width and height of a bitmap. The 'c' stands for count, so *cx* and *cy* are the number of pixels along the *x* (horizontal) and *y* (vertical) axes.

We can indicate a particular pixel of the bitmap in terms of *x* and *y* coordinates. Generally (but not always, as we'll see), the origin of a bitmap is considered to be the upper left corner of the image, as I've numbered the pixels in the grid. Thus, the pixel at the bottom right corner of this bitmap is at the coordinate (8, 5). This is one less than the width and height of the bitmap because the numbering starts with zero.

The spatial dimensions of a bitmap are often referred to as its *resolution*, but this is a problematic word. We say that our video displays have a resolution of 640 by 480 but that our laser printers have a resolution of 300 dots *per inch*. I prefer the latter use of the word—resolution as the number of pixels per metrical unit. Bitmaps could have a resolution in this sense, meaning that some number of pixels in the bitmap correspond to a particular unit of measurement. Regardless, when I use the word resolution, it should be obvious from the context which definition I'm using.

Bitmaps are rectangular but computer memory is linear. Bitmaps are generally (but not always) stored in memory by rows beginning with the top row of pixels and ending with the bottom row. (The DIB is one major exception to this rule.) Within each row, pixels are stored beginning with the leftmost pixel and continuing to the right. It's just like storing the individual characters of several lines of text.

Color and Bitmaps

Besides having a spatial dimension, bitmaps also have a color dimension. This is the number of bits required for each pixel and is sometimes called the *color depth* of the bitmap or the *bit-count* or the number of *bits per pixel* (bpp). Each pixel in a bitmap has the same number of color bits.

A bitmap with 1 bit per pixel is called a *bilevel* or *bicolor* or *monochrome* bitmap. Each pixel is either a 0 or a 1. A value of 0 could mean black, and a 1 could mean white, but that's not necessarily always the case. Additional colors require more bits per pixel. The number of possible colors is equal to $2^{\text{bit-count}}$. With 2 bits, you get 4 colors, with 4 bits you get 16 colors, with 8 bits you get 256 colors, with 16 bits you get 65,536 colors, and with 24 bits you get 16,777,216 colors.

How exactly certain combinations of color bits correspond to real and familiar colors is a question that persistently occupies (and often plagues) the mind of anyone who works with bitmaps.

Real-World Devices

Bitmaps can be categorized based on the number of color bits they have; the various bitmap color formats are based on the color capabilities of common video display adapters available throughout the history of Windows. Indeed, one can think of video display memory as comprising a large bitmap—one that we see when we look at our monitors.

The most common video adapters used for Windows 1.0 were the IBM Color Graphics Adapter (CGA) and the Hercules Graphics Card (HGC). The HGC was a monochrome device, and the CGA had to be used in a monochrome graphics mode under Windows. The monochrome bitmap is still quite common (for example, mouse cursors are often monochrome), and monochrome bitmaps have other uses beyond the display of images.

With the introduction of the Enhanced Graphics Adapter (EGA), Windows users got access to 16 colors. Each pixel requires 4 color bits. (The EGA was actually a bit more complex than this, involving a palette of 64 colors from which an application could select any 16 colors, but Windows used the EGA in a simpler manner.) The 16 colors used on the EGA were black, white, two shades of gray, and dark and light versions of red, green, and blue (the three additive primaries), cyan (the combination of blue and green), magenta (the combination of blue and red), and yellow (the combination of red and green). These

16 colors are now regarded as a minimum standard for Windows. Likewise, 16-color bitmaps also still show up in Windows. Most icons use 16-color bitmaps. Simple cartoonlike images can usually be done with these 16 colors.

The color encoding used in 16-color bitmaps is sometimes called IRGB (Intensity-Red-Green-Blue) and actually derives from colors originally used in character modes of the IBM CGA. The four IRGB color bits used for each pixel map to Windows hexadecimal RGB colors as shown in the following table.

IRGB	*RGB Color*	*Color Name*
0000	00-00-00	Black
0001	00-00-80	Dark Blue
0010	00-80-00	Dark Green
0011	00-80-80	Dark Cyan
0100	80-00-00	Dark Red
0101	80-00-80	Dark Magenta
0110	80-80-00	Dark Yellow
0111	C0-C0-C0	Light Gray
1000	80-80-80	Dark Gray
1001	00-00-FF	Blue
1010	00-FF-00	Green
1011	00-FF-FF	Cyan
1100	FF-00-00	Red
1101	FF-00-FF	Magenta
1110	FF-FF-00	Yellow
1111	FF-FF-FF	White

The memory in the EGA is organized in four "color planes," which means that the four bits that define the color of each pixel are not consecutive in memory. Instead, the video memory is organized so that all the Intensity bits are together, all the Red bits are together, and so forth. This certainly sounds like some device-dependent peculiarity that a Windows programmer shouldn't need to know anything about, and that is more or less the case. However, these color planes pop up in some API calls, such as *GetDeviceCaps* and *CreateBitmap*.

Windows 98 and Microsoft Windows NT require a VGA or higher resolution graphics card. This is the minimum-standard video graphics board that Windows currently accepts.

The original Video Graphics Array was introduced by IBM in 1987 with its PS/2 line of personal computers. It offered a number of different video modes, but the best graphics mode (the one that Windows uses) displays 640 pixels horizontally by 480 pixels vertically with 16 colors. To display 256 colors, the original VGA had to be switched into a 320 by 240 graphics mode, which is an inadequate number of pixels for Windows to work properly.

People often forget about the color limitations of the original VGA board because other hardware manufacturers soon developed "Super-VGA" (or SVGA) adapters that included more video memory and displayed 256 colors and more in the 640-by-480 mode. These are now the standard, and that's a good thing because 16 colors are simply inadequate for the display of real-world images.

A video adapter mode that displays 256 colors uses 8 bits per pixel. However, these 8-bit values do not necessarily correspond to particular colors. Instead, the video board incorporates a "palette lookup table" that allows software to specify how these 8-bit values map to real colors. In Windows, applications do not have direct access to this hardware palette lookup table; instead, Windows reserves 20 of the 256 colors and application programs use the Windows Palette Manager to customize the other 236 colors. I'll have much more to say about this in Chapter 16. The Palette Manager allows applications to display real-world bitmaps on 256-color displays. The 20 colors that Windows reserves are:

Color Value	RGB Color	Color Name
00000000	00-00-00	Black
00000001	80-00-00	Dark Red
00000010	00-80-00	Dark Green
00000011	80-80-00	Dark Yellow
00000100	00-00-80	Dark Blue
00000101	80-00-80	Dark Magenta
00000110	00-80-80	Dark Cyan
00000111	C0-C0-C0	Light Gray
00001000	C0-DC-C0	Money Green
00001001	A6-CA-F0	Sky Blue
11110110	FF-FB-F0	Cream
11110111	A0-A0-A4	Medium Gray
11111000	80-80-80	Dark Gray
11111001	FF-00-00	Red
11111010	00-FF-00	Green
11111011	FF-FF-00	Yellow
11111100	00-00-FF	Blue
11111101	FF-00-FF	Magenta
11111110	00-FF-FF	Cyan
11111111	FF-FF-FF	White

In recent years, full-color video adapter boards have become quite common. These use either 16 bits or 24 bits per pixel. Sometimes with 16 bits per pixel, one bit is unused and the other 15 bits are apportioned equally for the red, green, and blue primaries. This allows a total of 32,768 colors with combinations of 32 shades each of red, green, and blue. More commonly, 6 bits are used for green (the color that humans are most sensitive to) and 65,536 colors are available. For the nontechnical PC user who doesn't want to see wacky numbers like 32,768 or 65,536, such video display boards are usually said to be "high color" adapters that provide "thousands of colors."

Moving up to 24 bits per pixel gives us a total of 16,777,216 colors (or "true color" or "millions of colors"). Each pixel uses 3 bytes. This is likely to be the standard for years to come because it approximately represents the limits of human perception and also because it's very convenient.

When you call *GetDeviceCaps* (such as in the DEVCAPS program in Chapter 5), you can use the BITSPIXEL and PLANES constants to obtain the color organization of the video board. Over the years, these values have been those shown here.

BITSPIXEL	*PLANES*	*Number of Colors*
1	1	2
1	4	16
8	1	256
15 or 16	1	32,768 or 65,536
24 or 32	1	16,777,216

These days, you shouldn't encounter monochrome video displays, but your application shouldn't react adversely if it finds one.

Bitmap Support in GDI

The Windows Graphics Device Interface has supported bitmaps since version 1.0. However, prior to Windows 3.0, the only bitmaps supported under Windows were GDI objects, which are referenced using a bitmap handle. These GDI bitmap objects are monochrome or have the same color organization as a real graphics output device, such as a video display. For example, a bitmap compatible with a 16-color VGA has four color planes. The problem is that these color bitmaps cannot not be saved and used on a graphics output device that has a different color organization, for example one having 8 bits per pixel and capable of rendering 256 colors.

Beginning in Windows 3.0, a new bitmap format was defined, called the device-independent bitmap, or DIB. The DIB includes its own color table that shows how the pixel bits correspond to RGB colors. DIBs can be displayed on any raster output device. The only problem is that the colors of the DIB must often be converted to colors that the device can actually render.

Along with the DIB, Windows 3.0 also introduced the Windows Palette Manager that allows programs to customize colors on 256-color displays. Applications often use the Palette Manager in conjunction with displaying DIBs, as we'll see in Chapter 16.

Microsoft has expanded the definition of the DIB in Windows 95 (and Windows NT 4.0) and again in Windows 98 (and Windows NT 5.0). These enhancements have generally involved something called Image Color Management (ICM) that allows DIBs to more accurately specify the exact colors needed for the image. I'll discuss ICM briefly in Chapter 15.

Despite the vital importance of the DIB, the older GDI bitmap objects still play a strong role when working with bitmaps. Probably the best strategy to mastering the field of bitmaps is to approach the material chronologically, beginning with the GDI bitmap object and the concept of the bit-block transfer.

THE BIT-BLOCK TRANSFER

As I mentioned earlier, you can think of the entire video display as one big bitmap. The pixels you see on the screen are represented by bits stored in memory on the video display adapter board. Any rectangular area of the video display is also a bitmap, the size of which is the number of rows and columns it contains.

Let's begin our journey into the world of bitmaps by copying an image from one area of the video display to another. This is a job for the powerful *BitBlt* function.

Bitblt (pronounced "bit blit") stands for "bit-block transfer." The BLT originated as an assembly language instruction that did memory block transfers on the DEC PDP-10. The term "bitblt" was first used in graphics in connection with the SmallTalk system designed at the Xerox Palo Alto Research Center (PARC). In SmallTalk, all graphics output operations are based around the bitblt. Among programmers, "blt" is sometimes used as a verb, as in "Then I wrote some code to blt the happy face to the screen and play a wave file."

The *BitBlt* function is a pixel mover, or (more vividly) a raster blaster. As you'll see, the term "transfer" doesn't entirely do justice to the *BitBlt* function. The function actually performs a bitwise operation on pixels and can result in some interesting effects.

A Simple BitBlt

The BITBLT program shown in Figure 14-1 uses the *BitBlt* function to copy the program's system menu icon (located in the upper left corner of the program's window) to its client area.

BITBLT.C

```
/*-----------------------------------------
   BITBLT.C -- BitBlt Demonstration
               (c) Charles Petzold, 1998
   -----------------------------------------*/

#include <windows.h>

LRESULT CALLBACK WndProc (HWND, UINT, WPARAM, LPARAM) ;

int WINAPI WinMain (HINSTANCE hInstance, HINSTANCE hPrevInstance,
                    PSTR szCmdLine, int iCmdShow)
{
    static TCHAR szAppName [] = TEXT ("BitBlt") ;
    HWND         hwnd ;
    MSG          msg ;
    WNDCLASS     wndclass ;

    wndclass.style         = CS_HREDRAW | CS_VREDRAW ;
    wndclass.lpfnWndProc   = WndProc ;
    wndclass.cbClsExtra    = 0 ;
    wndclass.cbWndExtra    = 0 ;
    wndclass.hInstance     = hInstance ;
    wndclass.hIcon         = LoadIcon (NULL, IDI_INFORMATION) ;
    wndclass.hCursor       = LoadCursor (NULL, IDC_ARROW) ;
    wndclass.hbrBackground = (HBRUSH) GetStockObject (WHITE_BRUSH) ;
    wndclass.lpszMenuName  = NULL ;
    wndclass.lpszClassName = szAppName ;

    if (!RegisterClass (&wndclass))
    {
        MessageBox (NULL, TEXT ("This program requires Windows NT!"),
                    szAppName, MB_ICONERROR) ;
        return 0 ;
    }

    hwnd = CreateWindow (szAppName, TEXT ("BitBlt Demo"),
                         WS_OVERLAPPEDWINDOW,
                         CW_USEDEFAULT, CW_USEDEFAULT,
                         CW_USEDEFAULT, CW_USEDEFAULT,
                         NULL, NULL, hInstance, NULL) ;

    ShowWindow (hwnd, iCmdShow) ;
    UpdateWindow (hwnd) ;
```

Figure 14-1. *The BITBLT program.*   *(continued)*

Figure 14-1. *continued*

```
    while (GetMessage (&msg, NULL, 0, 0))
    {
         TranslateMessage (&msg) ;
         DispatchMessage (&msg) ;
    }
    return msg.wParam ;
}

LRESULT CALLBACK WndProc (HWND hwnd, UINT message, WPARAM wParam, LPARAM lParam)
{
    static int   cxClient, cyClient, cxSource, cySource ;
    HDC          hdcClient, hdcWindow ;
    int          x, y ;
    PAINTSTRUCT ps ;

    switch (message)
    {
    case WM_CREATE:
         cxSource = GetSystemMetrics (SM_CXSIZEFRAME) +
                    GetSystemMetrics (SM_CXSIZE) ;

         cySource = GetSystemMetrics (SM_CYSIZEFRAME) +
                    GetSystemMetrics (SM_CYCAPTION) ;
         return 0 ;

    case WM_SIZE:
         cxClient = LOWORD (lParam) ;
         cyClient = HIWORD (lParam) ;
         return 0 ;

    case WM_PAINT:
         hdcClient = BeginPaint (hwnd, &ps) ;
         hdcWindow = GetWindowDC (hwnd) ;

         for (y = 0 ; y < cyClient ; y += cySource)
         for (x = 0 ; x < cxClient ; x += cxSource)
         {
              BitBlt (hdcClient, x, y, cxSource, cySource,
                    hdcWindow, 0, 0, SRCCOPY) ;
         }

         ReleaseDC (hwnd, hdcWindow) ;
         EndPaint (hwnd, &ps) ;
         return 0 ;
```

```
    case WM_DESTROY:
        PostQuitMessage (0) ;
        return 0 ;
    }
    return DefWindowProc (hwnd, message, wParam, lParam) ;
}
```

But why stop at one *BitBlt*? In fact, BITBLT fills its client area with multiple copies of the system menu icon (which in this case is the IDI_INFORMATION icon commonly used in message boxes), as shown in Figure 14-2.

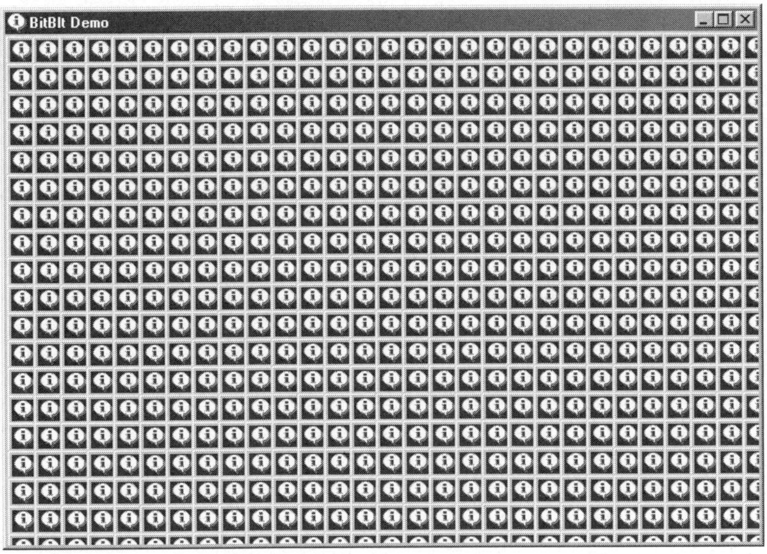

Figure 14-2. *The BITBLT display.*

The *BitBlt* function transfers pixels from a rectangular area in one device context, called the *source*, to a rectangular area of the same size in another device context, called the *destination*. The function has the following syntax:

```
BitBlt (hdcDst, xDst, yDst, cx, cy, hdcSrc, xSrc, ySrc, dwROP) ;
```

The source and destination device contexts can be the same.

In the BITBLT program, the destination device context is the window's client area; the device context handle is obtained from the *BeginPaint* function. The source device context is the application's whole window; this device context handle is obtained from *GetWindowDC*. Obviously, these two device contexts refer to the same physical device (the video display). However, the coordinate origins of these two device contexts are different.

The *xSrc* and *ySrc* arguments indicate the coordinate position of the upper left corner of the source image. In BITBLT, these two arguments are set to 0, indicating that the image begins in the upper left corner of the source device context (which is the whole window). The *cx* and *cy* arguments are the width and height of the image. BITBLT calculates these values from information obtained from the *GetSytemMetrics* function.

The *xDst* and *yDst* arguments indicate the coordinate position of the upper left corner where the image is to be copied. In BITBLT, these two arguments are set to various values to copy the image multiple times. For the first *BitBlt* call, these two arguments are set to 0 to copy the image to the upper left corner of the client area.

The last argument to *BitBlt* is called the *raster operation*. I'll discuss this value shortly.

Notice that *BitBlt* is transferring pixels from the actual video display memory and not some other image of the system menu icon. If you move the BITBLT window so that part of the system menu icon is off the screen, and you then adjust the size of the BITBLT window to force it to repaint itself, you'll find only part of the system menu icon drawn within BITBLT's client area. The *BitBlt* function no longer has access to the entire image.

In the *BitBlt* function, the source and destination device contexts can be the same. You can rewrite BITBLT so that WM_PAINT processing does the following:

```
BitBlt (hdcClient, 0, 0, cxSource, cySource,
        hdcWindow, 0, 0, SRCCOPY) ;

for (y = 0 ; y < cyClient ; y += cySource)
for (x = 0 ; x < cxClient ; x += cxSource)
{
    if (x > 0 || y > 0)
        BitBlt (hdcClient, x, y, cxSource, cySource,
                hdcClient, 0, 0, SRCCOPY) ;
}
```

This will usually create the same effect as the BITBLT shown above, except if the upper left corner of the client area is obscured in some way.

The most important restriction in *BitBlt* is that the two device contexts must be "compatible." What this means is that either one or the other must be monochrome, or they both must have the same number of bits per pixel. In short, you can't get a hard copy of something on the screen by blting it to the printer device context.

Stretching the Bitmap

In the *BitBlt* function, the destination image is the same size as the source image because the function has only two arguments to indicate the width and height. If you want to stretch or compress the size of the image as you copy it, you can use the *StretchBlt* function. *StretchBlt* has the following syntax:

```
StretchBlt (hdcDst, xDst, yDst, cxDst, cyDst,
            hdcSrc, xSrc, ySrc, cxSrc, cySrc, dwROP) ;
```

This function adds two arguments. The function now includes separate widths and heights of the destination and source. The *StretchBlt* function is demonstrated by the STRETCH program, shown in Figure 14-3.

STRETCH.C

```
/*-------------------------------------------
   STRETCH.C -- StretchBlt Demonstration
                (c) Charles Petzold, 1998
   -------------------------------------------*/

#include <windows.h>

LRESULT CALLBACK WndProc (HWND, UINT, WPARAM, LPARAM) ;

int WINAPI WinMain (HINSTANCE hInstance, HINSTANCE hPrevInstance,
                    PSTR szCmdLine, int iCmdShow)
{
     static TCHAR szAppName [] = TEXT ("Stretch") ;
     HWND        hwnd ;
     MSG         msg ;
     WNDCLASS    wndclass ;

     wndclass.style         = CS_HREDRAW | CS_VREDRAW ;
     wndclass.lpfnWndProc   = WndProc ;
     wndclass.cbClsExtra    = 0 ;
     wndclass.cbWndExtra    = 0 ;
     wndclass.hInstance     = hInstance ;
     wndclass.hIcon         = LoadIcon (NULL, IDI_INFORMATION) ;
     wndclass.hCursor       = LoadCursor (NULL, IDC_ARROW) ;
     wndclass.hbrBackground = (HBRUSH) GetStockObject (WHITE_BRUSH) ;
     wndclass.lpszMenuName  = NULL ;
     wndclass.lpszClassName = szAppName ;

     if (!RegisterClass (&wndclass))
     {
          MessageBox (NULL, TEXT ("This program requires Windows NT!"),
                      szAppName, MB_ICONERROR) ;
          return 0 ;
     }

     hwnd = CreateWindow (szAppName, TEXT ("StretchBlt Demo"),
                          WS_OVERLAPPEDWINDOW,
                          CW_USEDEFAULT, CW_USEDEFAULT,
                          CW_USEDEFAULT, CW_USEDEFAULT,
                          NULL, NULL, hInstance, NULL) ;
```

Figure 14-3. *The STRETCH program.*

(continued)

Figure 14-3. *continued*

```
     ShowWindow (hwnd, iCmdShow) ;
     UpdateWindow (hwnd) ;

     while (GetMessage (&msg, NULL, 0, 0))
     {
          TranslateMessage (&msg) ;
          DispatchMessage (&msg) ;
     }
     return msg.wParam ;
}

LRESULT CALLBACK WndProc (HWND hwnd, UINT message, WPARAM wParam, LPARAM lParam)
{
     static int  cxClient, cyClient, cxSource, cySource ;
     HDC         hdcClient, hdcWindow ;
     PAINTSTRUCT ps ;

     switch (message)
     {
     case WM_CREATE:
          cxSource = GetSystemMetrics (SM_CXSIZEFRAME) +
                     GetSystemMetrics (SM_CXSIZE) ;

          cySource = GetSystemMetrics (SM_CYSIZEFRAME) +
                     GetSystemMetrics (SM_CYCAPTION) ;
          return 0 ;

     case WM_SIZE:
          cxClient = LOWORD (lParam) ;
          cyClient = HIWORD (lParam) ;
          return 0 ;

     case WM_PAINT:
          hdcClient = BeginPaint (hwnd, &ps) ;
          hdcWindow = GetWindowDC (hwnd) ;

          StretchBlt (hdcClient, 0, 0, cxClient, cyClient,
                      hdcWindow, 0, 0, cxSource, cySource, MERGECOPY) ;

          ReleaseDC (hwnd, hdcWindow) ;
          EndPaint (hwnd, &ps) ;
          return 0 ;

     case WM_DESTROY:
          PostQuitMessage (0) ;
          return 0 ;
     }
     return DefWindowProc (hwnd, message, wParam, lParam) ;
}
```

This program has only one call to the *StretchBlt* function but uses it to fill the entire client area with its system menu icon, as shown in Figure 14-4.

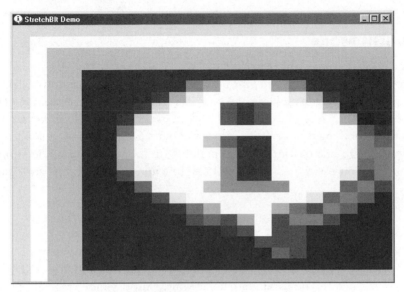

Figure 14-4. *The STRETCH display.*

All the coordinates and sizes in the *BitBlt* and *StretchBlt* function are based on logical units. But what happens when you have two different device contexts in the *BitBlt* function that refer to the same physical device but have different mapping modes? If this is so, a call to *BitBlt* might seem ambiguous: the *cx* and *cy* arguments are in logical units, and they apply to both the rectangle in the source device context and the rectangle in the destination device context. All coordinates and sizes must be converted to device coordinates before the actual bit transfer. Because the *cx* and *cy* values are used for both the source and destination device contexts, the values must be converted to device units (pixels) separately for each device context.

When the source and destination device contexts are the same, or when both device contexts use the MM_TEXT mapping mode, then the size of this rectangle in device units will be the same in both device contexts. Windows can then do a simple pixel-to-pixel transfer. However, when the size of the rectangle in device units is different in the two device contexts, Windows turns the job over to the more versatile *StretchBlt* function.

StretchBlt also allows you to flip an image vertically or horizontally. If the signs of *cxSrc* and *cxDst* (when converted to device units) are different, *StretchBlt* creates a mirror image: left becomes right, and right becomes left. You can check this in the STRETCH program by changing the *xDst* argument to *cxClient* and the *cxDst* argument to −*cxClient*.

If *cySrc* and *cyDst* are different, *StretchBlt* turns the image upside down. You can check this in the STRETCH program by changing the *yDst* argument to *cyClient* and the *cyDst* argument to *−cyClient*.

The StretchBlt Mode

StretchBlt can exhibit some problems related to the inherent difficulties of scaling bitmaps. When expanding a bitmap, *StretchBlt* must duplicate rows or columns of pixels. If the expansion is not an integral multiple, the process can result in some distortion of the image.

If the destination rectangle is smaller than the source rectangle, *StretchBlt* must shrink an image by combining two or more rows or columns of pixels into a single row or column. It does this in one of four ways, depending on the stretching mode attribute in the device context. You use the *SetStretchBltMode* function to change this attribute:

```
SetStretchBltMode (hdc, iMode) ;
```

The value of *iMode* can be one of the following:

- *BLACKONWHITE* or *STRETCH_ANDSCANS (default)*   If two or more pixels have to be combined into one pixel, *StretchBlt* performs a logical AND operation on the pixels. The resulting pixel is white only if all the original pixels are white, which in practice means that black pixels predominate over white pixels. This is good for monochrome bitmaps where the image is primarily black against a white background.

- *WHITEONBLACK* or *STRETCH_ORSCANS*   If two or more pixels have to be combined into one pixel, *StretchBlt* performs a logical OR operation. The resulting pixel is black only if all the original pixels are black, which means that white pixels predominate. This is good for monochrome bitmaps where the image is primarily white against a black background.

- *COLORONCOLOR* or *STRETCH_DELETESCANS*   *StretchBlt* simply eliminates rows or columns of pixels without doing any logical combination. This is often the best approach for color bitmaps.

- *HALFTONE* or *STRETCH_HALFTONE*   Windows calculates an average destination color based on the source colors being combined. This is used in conjunction with a halftone palette and is demonstrated in Chapter 16.

Windows also includes a *GetStretchBltMode* function to obtain the current stretching mode.

The Raster Operations

The BITBLT and STRETCH programs simply copy the source bitmap to the destination, perhaps stretching it in the process. This is the result of specifying SRCCOPY as the last argument to the *BitBlt* and *StretchBlt* functions. SRCCOPY is only 1 of 256 raster operations you can use in these functions. Let's experiment with a few others in the STRETCH program and then investigate the raster operations more methodically.

Try replacing SRCCOPY with NOTSRCCOPY. As the name suggests, this raster operation inverts the colors of the bitmaps as it is copied. On the client window, all the colors will be reversed. Black becomes white, white becomes black, and blue becomes yellow. Now try SRCINVERT. You'll get the same effect. Try BLACKNESS. As the name suggests, the entire client area is painted black. WHITENESS makes it white.

Now try this: replace the *StretchBlt* call with the following three statements:

```
SelectObject (hdcClient, CreateHatchBrush (HS_DIAGCROSS, RGB (0, 0, 0)));

StretchBlt (hdcClient, 0, 0, cxClient, cyClient,
            hdcWindow, 0, 0, cxSource, cySource, MERGECOPY) ;

DeleteObject (hdcClient, GetStockObject (WHITE_BRUSH)) ;
```

This time you'll see a hatch brush seemingly superimposed over the image. Just what is going on here?

As I mentioned earlier, the *BitBlt* and *StretchBlt* functions are not simply bit-block transfers. The functions actually perform a bitwise operation between the following three images:

- *Source* The source bitmap, stretched or compressed (if necessary) to be the same size as the destination rectangle.

- *Destination* The destination rectangle before the *BitBlt* or *StretchBlt* call.

- *Pattern* The current brush selected in the destination device context, repeated horizontally and vertically to be the same size as the destination rectangle.

The result is copied to the destination rectangle.

The raster operations are conceptually similar to the drawing modes we encountered in Chapter 5. The drawing modes govern the way in which a graphics object, such as a line, is combined with a destination. You'll recall that there were 16 drawing modes—that is, all the unique results obtained when 0s and 1s in the object being drawn were combined with 0s and 1s in the destination.

The raster operations used with *BitBlt* and *StretchBlt* involve a combination of three objects, and this results in 256 raster operations. There are 256 ways to combine a source bitmap, a destination bitmap, and a pattern. Fifteen of these raster operations are given names—some of them rather obscure—defined in WINGDI.H. The others have numeric values that are shown in */Platform SDK/Graphics and Multimedia Services/GDI/Raster Operation Codes/Ternary Raster Operations.*

The 15 ROP codes that have names are shown here.

Pattern (P): Source (S): Destination (D):	1 1 1 1 0 0 0 0 1 1 0 0 1 1 0 0 1 0 1 0 1 0 1 0	Boolean Operation	ROP Code	Name
Result:	0 0 0 0 0 0 0 0	0	0x000042	BLACKNESS
	0 0 0 1 0 0 0 1	~(S ¦ D)	0x1100A6	NOTSRCERASE
	0 0 1 1 0 0 1 1	~S	0x330008	NOTSRCCOPY
	0 1 0 0 0 1 0 0	S & ~D	0x440328	SRCERASE
	0 1 0 1 0 1 0 1	~D	0x550009	DSTINVERT
	0 1 0 1 1 0 1 0	P ∧ D	0x5A0049	PATINVERT
	0 1 1 0 0 1 1 0	S ∧ D	0x660046	SRCINVERT
	1 0 0 0 1 0 0 0	S & D	0x8800C6	SRCAND
	1 0 1 1 1 0 1 1	~S ¦ D	0xBB0226	MERGEPAINT
	1 1 0 0 0 0 0 0	P & S	0xC000CA	MERGECOPY
	1 1 0 0 1 1 0 0	S	0xCC0020	SRCCOPY
	1 1 1 0 1 1 1 0	S ¦ D	0xEE0086	SRCPAINT
	1 1 1 1 0 0 0 0	P	0xF00021	PATCOPY
	1 1 1 1 1 0 1 1	P ¦ ~S ¦ D	0xFB0A09	PATPAINT
	1 1 1 1 1 1 1 1	1	0xFF0062	WHITENESS

This table is important in understanding and using raster operations, so let's spend a little time examining it.

In this table, the value in the ROP Code column is the number that is passed as the last argument to *BitBlt* or *StretchBlt*; the names in the Name column are defined in WINGDI.H to be those values. The low word of the ROP Code is a number that assists the device driver in carrying out the raster operation. The high word is a number between 0 and 255. This number is the same as the bit pattern shown in the second column, which is the result of a bitwise operation between the pattern, source, and destination bits shown at the top. The Boolean Operation column uses C syntax to show how the pattern, source, and destination are combined.

To begin understanding this table, it's easiest to assume that you're dealing with a monochrome system (1 bit per pixel) in which 0 is black and 1 is white. The result of the BLACKNESS operation is all zeros regardless of the source, destination, and pattern, so the destination will be colored black. Similarly, WHITENESS always causes the destination to be colored white.

Now suppose you use the raster operation PATCOPY. This causes the result bits to be the same as the pattern bits. The source and destination bitmaps are ignored. In other words, PATCOPY simply copies the current pattern to the destination rectangle.

The PATPAINT raster operation involves a more complex operation. The result is equal to a bitwise OR operation between the pattern, the destination, and the inverse of the source. When the source bitmap is black (a 0 bit) the result is always white (a 1 bit). When the source is white (1), the result is also white if either the pattern or destination is white. In other words, the result will be black only if the source is white and both the pattern and the destination are black.

A color display uses multiple bits for each pixel. The *BitBlt* and *StretchBlt* functions perform the bitwise operation between each of these color bits separately. For example, if the destination is red and the source is blue, a SRCPAINT raster operation will color the destination magenta. Keep in mind that the operations are performed on bits actually stored in memory on the video board. How these bits correspond to colors is dependent on how the palette of the video board is set up. Windows does this so that these raster operations work as you might predict. However, if you change the palette (as discussed in Chapter 16), raster operations can produce unexpected results.

See the section "Nonrectangular Bitmap Images" later in this chapter for a good application of raster operations.

The Pattern Blt

Besides *BitBlt* and *StretchBlt*, Windows also includes a function called *PatBlt* ("pattern block transfer"). This is the simplest of the three "blt" functions. Unlike *BitBlt* and *StretchBlt*, it uses only a destination device context. The syntax of *PatBlt* is

```
PatBlt (hdc, x, y, cx, cy, dwROP) ;
```

The *x*, *y*, *cx*, and *cy* arguments are in logical units. The logical point (*x*, *y*) specifies the upper left corner of a rectangle. The rectangle is *cx* units wide and *cy* units high. This is the rectangular area that *PatBlt* alters. The logical operation that *PatBlt* performs on the brush and the destination device context is determined by the *dwROP* argument, which is a subset of the ROP codes—that is, you can use only those ROP codes that do not involve a source destination device context. The 16 raster operations supported by *PatBlt* are shown in the table on the following page.

| Pattern (P): | 1 1 0 0 | Boolean | ROP | |
Destination (D):	1 0 1 0	Operation	Code	Name
Result:	0 0 0 0	0	0x000042	BLACKNESS
	0 0 0 1	~(P ¦ D)	0x0500A9	
	0 0 1 0	~P & D	0x0A0329	
	0 0 1 1	~P	0x0F0001	
	0 1 0 0	P & ~D	0x500325	
	0 1 0 1	~D	0x550009	DSTINVERT
	0 1 1 0	P ∧ D	0x5A0049	PATINVERT
	0 1 1 1	~(P & D)	0x5F00E9	
	1 0 0 0	P & D	0xA000C9	
	1 0 0 1	~(P ∧ D)	0xA50065	
	1 0 1 0	D	0xAA0029	
	1 0 1 1	~P ¦ D	0xAF0229	
	1 1 0 0	P	0xF00021	PATCOPY
	1 1 0 1	P ¦ ~D	0xF50225	
	1 1 1 0	P ¦ D	0xFA0089	
	1 1 1 1	1	0xFF0062	WHITENESS

Some of the more common uses of *PatBlt* are shown below. If you want to draw a black rectangle, you call

```
PatBlt (hdc, x, y, cx, cy, BLACKNESS) ;
```

To draw a white rectangle, use

```
PatBlt (hdc, x, y, cx, cy, WHITENESS) ;
```

The function

```
PatBlt (hdc, x, y, cx, cy, DSTINVERT) ;
```

always inverts the colors of the rectangle. If WHITE_BRUSH is currently selected in the device context, the function

```
PatBlt (hdc, x, y, cx, cy, PATINVERT) ;
```

also inverts the rectangle.

You'll recall that the *FillRect* function fills in a rectangular area with a brush:

```
FillRect (hdc, &rect, hBrush) ;
```

The *FillRect* function is equivalent to the following code:

```
hBrush = SelectObject (hdc, hBrush) ;
PatBlt (hdc, rect.left, rect.top,
```

```
                rect.right - rect.left,
                rect.bottom - rect.top, PATCOPY) ;
SelectObject (hdc, hBrush) ;
```

In fact, this code is what Windows uses to execute the *FillRect* function. When you call

```
InvertRect (hdc, &rect) ;
```

Windows translates it into the function:

```
PatBlt (hdc, rect.left, rect.top,
                rect.right - rect.left,
                rect.bottom - rect.top, DSTINVERT) ;
```

When I introduced the syntax of the *PatBlt* function, I said that the point (x, y) specifies the upper left corner of a rectangle and that this rectangle is *cx* units wide and *cy* units high. The statement is not entirely accurate. *BitBlt*, *PatBlt*, and *StretchBlt* are the only GDI drawing functions that specify logical rectangular coordinates in terms of a logical width and height measured from a single corner. All the other GDI drawing functions that use rectangular bounding boxes require that coordinates be specified in terms of an upper left corner and a lower right corner. For the MM_TEXT mapping mode, the above description of the *PatBlt* parameters is accurate. For the metric mapping modes, however, it's not. If you use positive values of *cx* and *cy*, the point (x, y) will be the lower left corner of the rectangle. If you want (x, y) to be the upper left corner of the rectangle, the *cy* argument must be set to the negative height of the rectangle.

To be more precise, the rectangle that *PatBlt* colors has a logical width given by the absolute value of *cx* and a logical height given by the absolute value of *cy*. These two arguments can be negative. The rectangle is defined by two corners given by the logical points (x, y) and $(x + cx, y + cy)$. The upper left corner of the rectangle is always included in the area that *PatBlt* modifies. The lower right corner is outside the rectangle. Depending on the mapping mode and the signs of the *cx* and *cy* parameters, the upper left corner of this rectangle could be the point (x, y) or $(x, y + cy)$ or $(x + cx, y)$ or $(x + cx, y + cy)$.

If you've set the mapping mode to MM_LOENGLISH and you want to use *PatBlt* on the square inch at the upper left corner of the client area, you can use

```
PatBlt (hdc, 0, 0, 100, -100, dwROP) ;
```

or

```
PatBlt (hdc, 0, -100, 100, 100, dwROP) ;
```

or

```
PatBlt (hdc, 100, 0, -100, -100, dwROP) ;
```

or

```
PatBlt (hdc, 100, -100, -100, 100, dwROP) ;
```

The easiest way to set the correct parameters to *PatBlt* is to set x and y to the upper left corner of the rectangle. If your mapping mode defines y coordinates as increasing as you move up the display, use a negative value for the cy parameter. If your mapping mode defines x coordinates as increasing to the left (which is almost unheard of), use a negative value for the cx parameter.

THE GDI BITMAP OBJECT

I mentioned earlier in this chapter that Windows has supported a GDI bitmap object since version 1.0. Because of the introduction of the device-independent bitmap in Windows 3.0, the GDI Bitmap Object is sometimes now also known as the device-dependent bitmap, or DDB. I will tend not to use the full, spelled-out term *device-dependent bitmap* because at a quick glance the words can be confused with *device-independent bitmap*. The abbreviation DDB is better because it is more easily visually distinguished from DIB.

The existence of two different types of bitmaps has created much confusion for programmers first coming to Windows in the version 3.0 and later days. Many veteran Windows programmers also have problems understanding the precise relationship between the DIB and the DDB. (I'm afraid the Windows 3.0 version of this book did not help clarify this subject.) Yes, the DIB and DDB are related in some ways: DIBs can be converted to DDBs and vice versa (although with some loss of information). Yet the DIB and the DDB are not interchangeable and are not simply alternative methods for representing the same visual data.

It would certainly be convenient if we could assume that DIBs have made DDBs obsolete. Yet that is not the case. The DDB still plays a very important role in Windows, particularly if you care about performance.

Creating a DDB

The DDB is one of several graphics objects (including pens, brushes, fonts, metafiles, and palettes) defined in the Windows Graphics Device Interface. These graphics objects are stored internally in the GDI module and referred to by application programs with numerical handles. You store a handle to a DDB in a variable of type HBITMAP ("handle to a bitmap"). For example,

```
HBITMAP hBitmap ;
```

You then obtain the handle by calling one of the DDB-creation functions: for example, *CreateBitmap*. These functions allocate and initialize some memory in GDI memory to store information about the bitmap as well as the actual bitmap bits. The application program does not have direct access to this memory. The bitmap is independent of any device context. When the program is finished using the bitmap, it should be deleted:

```
DeleteObject (hBitmap) ;
```

You could do this when the program is terminating if you're using the DDB throughout the time the program is running.

The *CreateBitmap* function looks like this:

```
hBitmap = CreateBitmap (cx, cy, cPlanes, cBitsPixel, bits) ;
```

The first two arguments are the width and height of the bitmap in pixels. The third argument is the number of color planes and the fourth argument is the number of bits per pixel. The fifth argument points to an array of bits organized in accordance with the specified color format. You can set the last argument to NULL if you do not want to initialize the DDB with the pixel bits. The pixel bits can be set later.

When you use this function, Windows will let you create any bizarre type of GDI bitmap object you'd like. For example, suppose you want a bitmap with a width of 7 pixels, a height of 9 pixels, 5 color planes, and 3 bits per pixel. Just do it like so,

```
hBitmap = CreateBitmap (7, 9, 5, 3, NULL) ;
```

and Windows will gladly give you a valid bitmap handle.

What happens during this function call is that Windows saves the information you've passed to the function and allocates memory for the pixel bits. A rough calculation indicates that this bitmap requires 7 times 9 times 5 times 3, or 945 bits, which is 118 bytes and change.

However, when Windows allocates memory for the bitmap, each row of pixels has an even number of bytes. Thus,

```
iWidthBytes = 2 * ((cx * cBitsPixel + 15) / 16) ;
```

or, as a C programmer might tend to write it,

```
iWidthBytes = (cx * cBitsPixel + 15) & ~15) >> 3 ;
```

The memory allocated for the DDB is therefore

```
iBitmapBytes = cy * cPlanes * iWidthBytes ;
```

In our example, *iWidthBytes* is 4 bytes, and *iBitmapBytes* is 180 bytes.

Now, what does it mean to have a bitmap with 5 color planes and 3 color bits per pixel? Not a whole heck of a lot. It doesn't even mean enough to call it an academic exercise. You have caused GDI to allocate some internal memory, and this memory has a specific organization, but it doesn't mean anything, and you can't do anything useful with this bitmap.

In reality, you will call *CreateBitmap* with only two types of arguments:

■ *cPlanes* and *cBitsPixel* both equal to 1 (indicating a monochrome bitmap); or

■ *cPlanes* and *cBitsPixel* equal to the values for a particular device context, which you can obtain from the *GetDeviceCaps* function by using the PLANES and BITSPIXEL indices.

663

In a much "realer" reality, you will call *CreateBitmap* only for the first case. For the second case, you can simplify things using *CreateCompatibleBitmap*:

```
hBitmap = CreateCompatibleBitmap (hdc, cx, cy) ;
```

This function creates a bitmap compatible with the device whose device context handle is given by the first parameter. *CreateCompatibleBitmap* uses the device context handle to obtain the *GetDeviceCaps* information that it then passes to *CreateBitmap*. Aside from having the same memory organization as a real device context, the DDB is not otherwise associated with the device context.

The *CreateDiscardableBitmap* function has the same parameters as *CreateCompatibleBitmap* and is functionally equivalent to it. In earlier versions of Windows, *CreateDiscardableBitmap* created a bitmap that Windows could discard from memory if memory got low. The program would then have to regenerate the bitmap data.

The third bitmap-creation function is *CreateBitmapIndirect*,

```
hBitmap CreateBitmapIndirect (&bitmap) ;
```

where *bitmap* is a structure of type BITMAP. The BITMAP structure is defined like so:

```
typedef struct _tagBITMAP
{
    LONG    bmType ;          // set to 0
    LONG    bmWidth ;         // width in pixels
    LONG    bmHeight ;        // height in pixels
    LONG    bmWidthBytes ;    // width of row in bytes
    WORD    bmPlanes ;        // number of color planes
    WORD    bmBitsPixel ;     // number of bits per pixel
    LPVOID  bmBits ;          // pointer to pixel bits
}
BITMAP, * PBITMAP ;
```

When calling the *CreateBitmapIndirect* function, you don't need to set the *bmWidthBytes* field. Windows will calculate that for you. You can also set the *bmBits* field to NULL or to the address of pixel bits to initialize the bitmap.

The BITMAP structure is also used in the *GetObject* function. First define a structure of type BITMAP,

```
BITMAP bitmap ;
```

and call the function like so:

```
GetObject (hBitmap, sizeof (BITMAP), &bitmap) ;
```

Windows will fill in the fields of the BITMAP structure with information about the bitmap. However, the *bmBits* field will be equal to NULL.

You should eventually destroy any bitmap that you create in a program with a call to *DeleteObject*.

The Bitmap Bits

When you create a device-dependent GDI bitmap object by using *CreateBitmap* or *CreateBitmapIndirect*, you can specify a pointer to the bitmap pixel bits. Or you can leave the bitmap uninitialized. Windows also supplies two functions to get and set the pixel bits after the bitmap has been created.

To set the pixel bits, call

```
SetBitmapBits (hBitmap, cBytes, &bits) ;
```

The *GetBitmapBits* function has the same syntax:

```
GetBitmapBits (hBitmap, cBytes, &bits) ;
```

In both functions, *cBytes* indicates the number of bytes to copy and *bits* is a buffer of at least *cBytes* size.

The pixel bits in DDBs are arranged beginning with the top row. As I mentioned earlier, each row has an even number of bytes. Beyond that, there's not too much to say. If the bitmap is monochrome, which means it has 1 plane and 1 bit per pixel, then each pixel is either 1 or 0. The leftmost pixel in each row is the most significant bit of the first byte in the row. We'll make a monochrome DDB later in this chapter after we figure out how to display them.

For nonmonochrome bitmaps, you should avoid situations where you need to know what the pixel bits mean. For example, suppose Windows is running on an 8-bit VGA. You call *CreateCompatibleBitmap*. You can determine from *GetDeviceCaps* that you're dealing with a device that has 1 color plane and 8 bits per pixel. Each pixel is stored in 1 byte. But what does a pixel of value 0x37 mean? It obviously refers to some color, but what color?

The pixel actually doesn't refer to any fixed specific color. It's just a value. DDBs do not have a color table. The essential question is: *what color is the pixel when the DDB gets displayed on the screen?* It has to be some color, so what is it? The displayed pixel will be the RGB color referenced by an index value of 0x37 in the palette lookup table on the video board. Now that's device dependence for you.

However, do not assume that the nonmonochrome DDB is useless just because we don't know what the pixel values mean. We'll see shortly how useful they can be. And in the next chapter we'll see how the *SetBitmapBits* and *GetBitmapBits* functions have been superseded by the more useful *SetDIBits* and *GetDIBits* functions.

So, the basic rule is this: you will not be using *CreateBitmap* or *CreateBitmapIndirect* or *SetBitmapBits* to set the bits of a color DDB. You can safely set the bits of only a monochrome DDB. (The exception to this rule is if you get the bits from another DDB of the same format through a call to *GetBitmapBits*.)

Before we move on, let me just mention the *SetBitmapDimensionEx* and *GetBitmapDimensionEx* functions. These functions let you set (and obtain) a metrical dimension of a bitmap in 0.1 millimeter units. This information is stored in GDI along with the bitmap definition, but it's not used for anything. It's just a tag that you can use to associate a metrical dimension with a DDB.

The Memory Device Context

The next concept we must tackle is that of the *memory device context*. You need a memory device context to use a GDI bitmap object.

Normally, a device context refers to a particular graphics output device (such as a video display or a printer) together with its device driver. A memory device context exists only in memory. It is not a real graphics output device, but is said to be "compatible" with a particular real device.

To create a memory device context, you must first have a device context handle for a real device. If it's *hdc*, you create a memory device context like so:

```
hdcMem = CreateCompatibleDC (hdc) ;
```

Usually the function call is even simpler than this. If you specify NULL as the argument, Windows will create a memory device context compatible with the video display. Any memory device context that an application creates should eventually be destroyed with a call to *DeleteDC*.

The memory device context has a display surface just like a real raster device. However, this display surface is initially very small—it's monochrome, 1 pixel wide and 1 pixel high. The display surface is just a single bit.

You can't do much with a 1-bit display surface, of course, so the only practical next step is to make the display surface larger. You do this by selecting a GDI bitmap object into the memory device context, like so:

```
SelectObject (hdcMem, hBitmap) ;
```

This is the same function you use for selecting pens, brushes, fonts, regions, and palettes into device contexts. However, the memory device context is the only type of device context into which you can select a bitmap. (You can also select other GDI objects into a memory device context if you need to.)

SelectObject will work only if the bitmap you select into the memory device context is either monochrome or has the same color organization as the device with which the memory device context is compatible. That's why creating a bizarre DDB (for example, with 5 planes and 3 bits per pixel) is not useful.

Now get this: Following the *SelectObject* call, *the DDB is the display surface of the memory device context*. You can do almost anything with this memory device context that you can do with a real device context. For example, if you use GDI drawing functions to draw on the memory device context, the images are drawn on the bitmap. This can be very useful. You can also call *BitBlt* using the memory device context as a source and the video device context as a destination. This is how you can draw a bitmap on the display. And you can call *BitBlt* using the video device context as a source and a memory device context as a destination to copy something from the screen to a bitmap. We'll be looking at all these possibilities.

Loading Bitmap Resources

Besides the various bitmap creation functions, another way to get a handle to a GDI bitmap object is through the *LoadBitmap* function. With this function, you don't have to worry about bitmap formats. You simply create a bitmap as a resource in your program, similar to the way you create icons or mouse cursors. The *LoadBitmap* function has the same syntax as *LoadIcon* and *LoadCursor*:

```
hBitmap = LoadBitmap (hInstance, szBitmapName) ;
```

The first argument can be NULL if you want to load a system bitmap. These are the various bitmaps used for little parts of the Windows visual interface such as the close box and check marks, with identifiers beginning with the letters OBM. The second argument can use the MAKEINTRESOURCE macro if the bitmap is associated with an integer identifier rather than a name. All bitmaps loaded by *LoadBitmap* should eventually be deleted using *DeleteObject*.

If the bitmap resource is monochrome, the handle returned from *LoadBitmap* will reference a monochrome bitmap object. If the bitmap resource is not monochrome, then the handle returned from *LoadBitmap* will reference a GDI bitmap object with a color organization the same as the video display on which the program is running. Thus, the bitmap is always compatible with the video display and can always be selected into a memory device context compatible with the video display. Don't worry right now about any color conversions that may have gone on behind the scenes during the *LoadBitmap* call. We'll understand how this works after the next chapter.

The BRICKS1 program shown in Figure 14-5 shows how to load a small monochrome bitmap resource. This bitmap doesn't exactly look like a brick by itself but when repeated horizontally and vertically resembles a wall of bricks.

BRICKS1.C

```
/*-------------------------------------------
   BRICKS1.C -- LoadBitmap Demonstration
                (c) Charles Petzold, 1998
   -------------------------------------------*/

#include <windows.h>

LRESULT CALLBACK WndProc (HWND, UINT, WPARAM, LPARAM) ;

int WINAPI WinMain (HINSTANCE hInstance, HINSTANCE hPrevInstance,
                    PSTR szCmdLine, int iCmdShow)
```

Figure 14-5. *The BRICKS1 program.*   *(continued)*

Figure 14-5. *continued*

```
{
     static TCHAR szAppName [] = TEXT ("Bricks1") ;
     HWND         hwnd ;
     MSG          msg ;
     WNDCLASS     wndclass ;

     wndclass.style         = CS_HREDRAW | CS_VREDRAW ;
     wndclass.lpfnWndProc   = WndProc ;
     wndclass.cbClsExtra    = 0 ;
     wndclass.cbWndExtra    = 0 ;
     wndclass.hInstance     = hInstance ;
     wndclass.hIcon         = LoadIcon (NULL, IDI_APPLICATION) ;
     wndclass.hCursor       = LoadCursor (NULL, IDC_ARROW) ;
     wndclass.hbrBackground = (HBRUSH) GetStockObject (WHITE_BRUSH) ;
     wndclass.lpszMenuName  = NULL ;
     wndclass.lpszClassName = szAppName ;

     if (!RegisterClass (&wndclass))
     {
          MessageBox (NULL, TEXT ("This program requires Windows NT!"),
                      szAppName, MB_ICONERROR) ;
          return 0 ;
     }

     hwnd = CreateWindow (szAppName, TEXT ("LoadBitmap Demo"),
                          WS_OVERLAPPEDWINDOW,
                          CW_USEDEFAULT, CW_USEDEFAULT,
                          CW_USEDEFAULT, CW_USEDEFAULT,
                          NULL, NULL, hInstance, NULL) ;

     ShowWindow (hwnd, iCmdShow) ;
     UpdateWindow (hwnd) ;

     while (GetMessage (&msg, NULL, 0, 0))
     {
          TranslateMessage (&msg) ;
          DispatchMessage (&msg) ;
     }
     return msg.wParam ;
}

LRESULT CALLBACK WndProc (HWND hwnd, UINT message, WPARAM wParam, LPARAM lParam)
```

```
{
     static HBITMAP hBitmap ;
     static int     cxClient, cyClient, cxSource, cySource ;
     BITMAP         bitmap ;
     HDC            hdc, hdcMem ;
     HINSTANCE      hInstance ;
     int            x, y ;
     PAINTSTRUCT    ps ;

     switch (message)
     {
     case WM_CREATE:
          hInstance = ((LPCREATESTRUCT) lParam)->hInstance ;

          hBitmap = LoadBitmap (hInstance, TEXT ("Bricks")) ;

          GetObject (hBitmap, sizeof (BITMAP), &bitmap) ;

          cxSource = bitmap.bmWidth ;
          cySource = bitmap.bmHeight ;

          return 0 ;

     case WM_SIZE:
          cxClient = LOWORD (lParam) ;
          cyClient = HIWORD (lParam) ;
          return 0 ;

     case WM_PAINT:
          hdc = BeginPaint (hwnd, &ps) ;

          hdcMem = CreateCompatibleDC (hdc) ;
          SelectObject (hdcMem, hBitmap) ;

          for (y = 0 ; y < cyClient ; y += cySource)
          for (x = 0 ; x < cxClient ; x += cxSource)
          {
               BitBlt (hdc, x, y, cxSource, cySource, hdcMem, 0, 0, SRCCOPY) ;
          }

          DeleteDC (hdcMem) ;
          EndPaint (hwnd, &ps) ;
          return 0 ;
```

(continued)

Figure 14-5. *continued*

```
    case WM_DESTROY:
         DeleteObject (hBitmap) ;
         PostQuitMessage (0) ;
         return 0 ;
    }
    return DefWindowProc (hwnd, message, wParam, lParam) ;
}
```

BRICKS1.RC (excerpts)

```
//Microsoft Developer Studio generated resource script.

#include "resource.h"
#include "afxres.h"

/////////////////////////////////////////////////////////////////////////////
// Bitmap

BRICKS                 BITMAP  DISCARDABLE     "Bricks.bmp"
```

BRICKS.BMP

When creating the bitmap in Visual C++ Developer Studio, specify that the bitmap's height and width are 8 pixels, that it's monochrome, and that it has a name of "Bricks". The BRICKS1 program loads the bitmap during the WM_CREATE message and uses *GetObject* to determine its pixel dimensions (so that the program will still work if the bitmap isn't 8 pixels square). BRICKS1 later deletes the bitmap handle during the WM_DESTROY message.

During the WM_PAINT message, BRICKS1 creates a memory device context compatible with the display and selects the bitmap into it. Then it's just a series of *BitBlt* calls from the memory device context to the client area device context. The memory device context handle is then deleted. The program is shown running in Figure 14-6.

By the way, the BRICKS.BMP file that Developer Studio creates is a device-independent bitmap. You may want to try creating a color BRICKS.BMP file in Developer Studio (of whatever color format you choose) and assure yourself that everything works just fine.

We've seen that DIBs can be converted to GDI bitmap objects that are compatible with the video display. We'll see how this works in the next chapter.

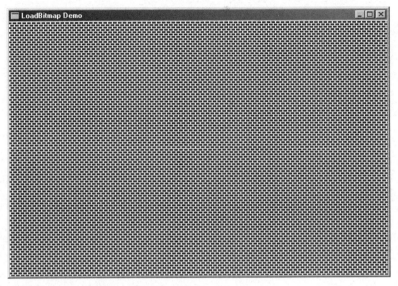

Figure 14-6. *The BRICKS1 display.*

The Monochrome Bitmap Format

If you're working with small monochrome images, you don't have to create them as resources. Unlike color bitmap objects, the format of monochrome bits is relatively simple and can almost be derived directly from the image you want to create. For instance, suppose you want to create a bitmap that looks like this:

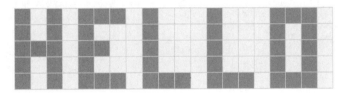

You can write down a series of bits (0 for black and 1 for white) that directly corresponds to this grid. Reading these bits from left to right, you can then assign each group of 8 bits a hexadecimal byte. If the width of the bitmap is not a multiple of 16, pad the bytes to the right with zeros to get an even number of bytes:

```
0 1 0 1 0 0 0 1 0 1 1 1 0 1 1 1 0 0 0 1 = 51 77 10 00
0 1 0 1 0 1 1 1 0 1 1 1 0 1 1 1 0 1 0 1 = 57 77 50 00
0 0 0 1 0 0 1 1 0 1 1 1 0 1 1 1 0 1 0 1 = 13 77 50 00
0 1 0 1 0 1 1 1 0 1 1 1 0 1 1 1 0 1 0 1 = 57 77 50 00
0 1 0 1 0 0 0 1 0 0 0 1 0 0 0 1 0 0 0 1 = 51 11 10 00
```

The width in pixels is 20, the height in scan lines is 5, and the width in bytes is 4. You can set up a BITMAP structure for this bitmap with this statement,

```
static BITMAP bitmap    = { 0, 20, 5, 4, 1, 1 } ;
```

and you can store the bits in a BYTE array:

```
static BYTE  bits [] = { 0x51, 0x77, 0x10, 0x00,
                         0x57, 0x77, 0x50, 0x00,
                         0x13, 0x77, 0x50, 0x00,
                         0x57, 0x77, 0x50, 0x00,
                         0x51, 0x11, 0x10, 0x00 } ;
```

Creating the bitmap with *CreateBitmapIndirect* requires two statements:

```
bitmap.bmBits = (PSTR) bits ;
hBitmap = CreateBitmapIndirect (&bitmap) ;
```

Another approach is

```
hBitmap = CreateBitmapIndirect (&bitmap) ;
SetBitmapBits (hBitmap, sizeof bits, bits) ;
```

You can also create the bitmap in one statement:

```
hBitmap = CreateBitmap (20, 5, 1, 1, bits) ;
```

The BRICKS2 program shown in Figure 14-7 uses this technique to create the bricks bitmap directly without requiring a resource.

BRICKS2.C

```
/*-----------------------------------------------
   BRICKS2.C -- CreateBitmap Demonstration
                (c) Charles Petzold, 1998
   -----------------------------------------------*/

#include <windows.h>

LRESULT CALLBACK WndProc (HWND, UINT, WPARAM, LPARAM) ;

int WINAPI WinMain (HINSTANCE hInstance, HINSTANCE hPrevInstance,
                    PSTR szCmdLine, int iCmdShow)
{
    static TCHAR szAppName [] = TEXT ("Bricks2") ;
    HWND        hwnd ;
    MSG         msg ;
    WNDCLASS    wndclass ;

    wndclass.style          = CS_HREDRAW | CS_VREDRAW ;
    wndclass.lpfnWndProc    = WndProc ;
```

Figure 14-7. *The BRICKS2 program.*

```
          wndclass.cbClsExtra    = 0 ;
          wndclass.cbWndExtra    = 0 ;
          wndclass.hInstance     = hInstance ;
          wndclass.hIcon         = LoadIcon (NULL, IDI_APPLICATION) ;
          wndclass.hCursor       = LoadCursor (NULL, IDC_ARROW) ;
          wndclass.hbrBackground = (HBRUSH) GetStockObject (WHITE_BRUSH) ;
          wndclass.lpszMenuName  = NULL ;
          wndclass.lpszClassName = szAppName ;

          if (!RegisterClass (&wndclass))
          {
               MessageBox (NULL, TEXT ("This program requires Windows NT!"),
                         szAppName, MB_ICONERROR) ;
               return 0 ;
          }

          hwnd = CreateWindow (szAppName, TEXT ("CreateBitmap Demo"),
                         WS_OVERLAPPEDWINDOW,
                         CW_USEDEFAULT, CW_USEDEFAULT,
                         CW_USEDEFAULT, CW_USEDEFAULT,
                         NULL, NULL, hInstance, NULL) ;

          ShowWindow (hwnd, iCmdShow) ;
          UpdateWindow (hwnd) ;

          while (GetMessage (&msg, NULL, 0, 0))
          {
               TranslateMessage (&msg) ;
               DispatchMessage (&msg) ;
          }
          return msg.wParam ;
     }

LRESULT CALLBACK WndProc (HWND hwnd, UINT message, WPARAM wParam, LPARAM lParam)
{
     static BITMAP  bitmap = { 0, 8, 8, 2, 1, 1 } ;
     static BYTE    bits [8][2] = { 0xFF, 0, 0x0C, 0, 0x0C, 0, 0x0C, 0,
                                    0xFF, 0, 0xC0, 0, 0xC0, 0, 0xC0, 0 } ;
     static HBITMAP hBitmap ;
     static int     cxClient, cyClient, cxSource, cySource ;
     HDC            hdc, hdcMem ;
     int            x, y ;
     PAINTSTRUCT    ps ;

     switch (message)
     {
```

(continued)

Figure 14-7. *continued*

```
    case WM_CREATE:
         bitmap.bmBits = bits ;
         hBitmap = CreateBitmapIndirect (&bitmap) ;
         cxSource = bitmap.bmWidth ;
         cySource = bitmap.bmHeight ;
         return 0 ;

    case WM_SIZE:
         cxClient = LOWORD (lParam) ;
         cyClient = HIWORD (lParam) ;
         return 0 ;

    case WM_PAINT:
         hdc = BeginPaint (hwnd, &ps) ;

         hdcMem = CreateCompatibleDC (hdc) ;
         SelectObject (hdcMem, hBitmap) ;

         for (y = 0 ; y < cyClient ; y += cySource)
         for (x = 0 ; x < cxClient ; x += cxSource)
         {
              BitBlt (hdc, x, y, cxSource, cySource, hdcMem, 0, 0, SRCCOPY) ;
         }

         DeleteDC (hdcMem) ;
         EndPaint (hwnd, &ps) ;
         return 0 ;

    case WM_DESTROY:
         DeleteObject (hBitmap) ;
         PostQuitMessage (0) ;
         return 0 ;
    }
    return DefWindowProc (hwnd, message, wParam, lParam) ;
}
```

You may be tempted to try something similar with a color bitmap. For example, if your video display is running in a 256-color mode, you can use the table shown earlier in this chapter on page 646 to define each pixel for a color brick. However, this code will not work when the program runs under any other video mode. Dealing with color bitmaps in a device-independent manner requires use of the DIB discussed in the next chapter.

Brushes from Bitmaps

The final entry in the BRICKS series is BRICKS3, shown in Figure 14-8. At first glance this program might provoke the reaction "Where's the code?"

BRICKS3.C

```
/*-------------------------------------------------
   BRICKS3.C -- CreatePatternBrush Demonstration
                (c) Charles Petzold, 1998
   -------------------------------------------------*/

#include <windows.h>

LRESULT CALLBACK WndProc (HWND, UINT, WPARAM, LPARAM) ;

int WINAPI WinMain (HINSTANCE hInstance, HINSTANCE hPrevInstance,
                    PSTR szCmdLine, int iCmdShow)
{
     static TCHAR szAppName [] = TEXT ("Bricks3") ;
     HBITMAP      hBitmap ;
     HBRUSH       hBrush ;
     HWND         hwnd ;
     MSG          msg ;
     WNDCLASS     wndclass ;

     hBitmap = LoadBitmap (hInstance, TEXT ("Bricks")) ;
     hBrush = CreatePatternBrush (hBitmap) ;
     DeleteObject (hBitmap) ;

     wndclass.style         = CS_HREDRAW | CS_VREDRAW ;
     wndclass.lpfnWndProc   = WndProc ;
     wndclass.cbClsExtra    = 0 ;
     wndclass.cbWndExtra    = 0 ;
     wndclass.hInstance     = hInstance ;
     wndclass.hIcon         = LoadIcon (NULL, IDI_APPLICATION) ;
     wndclass.hCursor       = LoadCursor (NULL, IDC_ARROW) ;
     wndclass.hbrBackground = hBrush ;
     wndclass.lpszMenuName  = NULL ;
     wndclass.lpszClassName = szAppName ;

     if (!RegisterClass (&wndclass))
     {
          MessageBox (NULL, TEXT ("This program requires Windows NT!"),
                      szAppName, MB_ICONERROR) ;
          return 0 ;
     }

     hwnd = CreateWindow (szAppName, TEXT ("CreatePatternBrush Demo"),
                          WS_OVERLAPPEDWINDOW,
                          CW_USEDEFAULT, CW_USEDEFAULT,
```

Figure 14-8. *The BRICKS3 program.* *(continued)*

Figure 14-8. *continued*

```
                              CW_USEDEFAULT, CW_USEDEFAULT,
                              NULL, NULL, hInstance, NULL) ;

     ShowWindow (hwnd, iCmdShow) ;
     UpdateWindow (hwnd) ;

     while (GetMessage (&msg, NULL, 0, 0))
     {
          TranslateMessage (&msg) ;
          DispatchMessage (&msg) ;
     }

     DeleteObject (hBrush) ;
     return msg.wParam ;
}

LRESULT CALLBACK WndProc (HWND hwnd, UINT message, WPARAM wParam, LPARAM lParam)
{
     switch (message)
     {
     case WM_DESTROY:
          PostQuitMessage (0) ;
          return 0 ;
     }
     return DefWindowProc (hwnd, message, wParam, lParam) ;
}
```

BRICKS3.RC (excerpts)

```
//Microsoft Developer Studio generated resource script.

#include "resource.h"
#include "afxres.h"


/////////////////////////////////////////////////////////////////////////////
// Bitmap

BRICKS                  BITMAP  DISCARDABLE     "Bricks.bmp"
```

This program uses the same BRICKS.BMP file as BRICKS1, and the window looks the same.

As you can see, the window procedure doesn't do much of anything. BRICKS3 actually uses the bricks pattern as the window class background brush, which is defined in the *hbrBackground* field of the WNDCLASS structure.

As you may have guessed by now, GDI brushes are tiny bitmaps, usually 8 pixels square. You can make a brush out of a bitmap by calling *CreatePatternBrush* or by calling *CreateBrushIndirect* with the *lbStyle* field of the LOGBRUSH structure set to BS_PATTERN. The bitmap must be least 8 pixels wide and 8 pixels high. If it's larger, Windows 98 uses only the upper left corner of the bitmap for the brush. Windows NT, on the other hand, doesn't have that restriction and will use the whole bitmap.

Remember that brushes and bitmaps are both GDI objects and you should delete any that you create in your program before the program terminates. When you create a brush based on a bitmap, Windows makes a copy of the bitmap bits for use when drawing with the brush. You can delete the bitmap immediately after calling *CreatePatternBrush* (or *CreateBrushIndirect*) without affecting the brush. Similarly, you can delete the brush without affecting the original bitmap you selected into it. Notice that BRICKS3 deletes the bitmap after creating the brush and deletes the brush before terminating the program.

Drawing on Bitmaps

We've been using bitmaps as a source for drawing on our windows. This requires selecting the bitmap into a memory device context and calling *BitBlt* or *StretchBlt*. You can also use the handle to the memory device context as the first argument to virtually all the GDI function calls. The memory device context behaves the same as a real device context except that the display surface is the bitmap.

The HELLOBIT program shown in Figure 14-9 shows this technique. The program displays the text string "Hello, world!" on a small bitmap and then does a *BitBlt* or a *StretchBlt* (based on a menu selection) from the bitmap to the program's client area.

HELLOBIT.C

```
/*------------------------------------------
   HELLOBIT.C -- Bitmap Demonstration
                 (c) Charles Petzold, 1998
   ------------------------------------------*/

#include <windows.h>
#include "resource.h"

LRESULT CALLBACK WndProc (HWND, UINT, WPARAM, LPARAM) ;

int WINAPI WinMain (HINSTANCE hInstance, HINSTANCE hPrevInstance,
                    PSTR szCmdLine, int iCmdShow)
{
     static TCHAR szAppName [] = TEXT ("HelloBit") ;
     HWND          hwnd ;
     MSG           msg ;
```

Figure 14-9. *The HELLOBIT program.*

(continued)

Figure 14-9. *continued*

```
    WNDCLASS     wndclass ;

    wndclass.style        = CS_HREDRAW | CS_VREDRAW ;
    wndclass.lpfnWndProc  = WndProc ;
    wndclass.cbClsExtra   = 0 ;
    wndclass.cbWndExtra   = 0 ;
    wndclass.hInstance    = hInstance ;
    wndclass.hIcon        = LoadIcon (NULL, IDI_APPLICATION) ;
    wndclass.hCursor      = LoadCursor (NULL, IDC_ARROW) ;
    wndclass.hbrBackground = (HBRUSH) GetStockObject (WHITE_BRUSH) ;
    wndclass.lpszMenuName = szAppName ;
    wndclass.lpszClassName = szAppName ;

    if (!RegisterClass (&wndclass))
    {
        MessageBox (NULL, TEXT ("This program requires Windows NT!"),
                    szAppName, MB_ICONERROR) ;
        return 0 ;
    }

    hwnd = CreateWindow (szAppName, TEXT ("HelloBit"),
                        WS_OVERLAPPEDWINDOW,
                        CW_USEDEFAULT, CW_USEDEFAULT,
                        CW_USEDEFAULT, CW_USEDEFAULT,
                        NULL, NULL, hInstance, NULL) ;

    ShowWindow (hwnd, iCmdShow) ;
    UpdateWindow (hwnd) ;

    while (GetMessage (&msg, NULL, 0, 0))
    {
        TranslateMessage (&msg) ;
        DispatchMessage (&msg) ;
    }
    return msg.wParam ;
}

LRESULT CALLBACK WndProc (HWND hwnd, UINT message, WPARAM wParam, LPARAM lParam)
{
    static HBITMAP hBitmap ;
    static HDC     hdcMem ;
    static int     cxBitmap, cyBitmap, cxClient, cyClient, iSize = IDM_BIG ;
    static TCHAR * szText = TEXT (" Hello, world! ") ;
    HDC            hdc ;
    HMENU          hMenu ;
    int            x, y ;
```

```
PAINTSTRUCT    ps ;
SIZE           size ;

switch (message)
{
case WM_CREATE:
     hdc = GetDC (hwnd) ;
     hdcMem  = CreateCompatibleDC (hdc) ;

     GetTextExtentPoint32 (hdc, szText, lstrlen (szText), &size) ;
     cxBitmap = size.cx ;
     cyBitmap = size.cy ;
     hBitmap = CreateCompatibleBitmap (hdc, cxBitmap, cyBitmap) ;

     ReleaseDC (hwnd, hdc) ;

     SelectObject (hdcMem, hBitmap) ;
     TextOut (hdcMem, 0, 0, szText, lstrlen (szText)) ;
     return 0 ;

case WM_SIZE:
     cxClient = LOWORD (lParam) ;
     cyClient = HIWORD (lParam) ;
     return 0 ;

case WM_COMMAND:
     hMenu = GetMenu (hwnd) ;

     switch (LOWORD (wParam))
     {
     case IDM_BIG:
     case IDM_SMALL:
          CheckMenuItem (hMenu, iSize, MF_UNCHECKED) ;
          iSize = LOWORD (wParam) ;
          CheckMenuItem (hMenu, iSize, MF_CHECKED) ;
          InvalidateRect (hwnd, NULL, TRUE) ;
          break ;
     }
     return 0 ;

case WM_PAINT:
     hdc = BeginPaint (hwnd, &ps) ;

     switch (iSize)
     {
     case IDM_BIG:
```

(continued)

Figure 14-9. *continued*

```
                StretchBlt (hdc, 0, 0, cxClient, cyClient,
                        hdcMem, 0, 0, cxBitmap, cyBitmap, SRCCOPY) ;
                break ;

        case IDM_SMALL:
                for (y = 0 ; y < cyClient ; y += cyBitmap)
                for (x = 0 ; x < cxClient ; x += cxBitmap)
                {
                        BitBlt (hdc, x, y, cxBitmap, cyBitmap,
                                hdcMem, 0, 0, SRCCOPY) ;
                }
                break ;
        }

        EndPaint (hwnd, &ps) ;
        return 0 ;

    case WM_DESTROY:
        DeleteDC (hdcMem) ;
        DeleteObject (hBitmap) ;
        PostQuitMessage (0) ;
        return 0 ;
    }
    return DefWindowProc (hwnd, message, wParam, lParam) ;
}
```

HELLOBIT.RC (excerpts)

```
//Microsoft Developer Studio generated resource script.

#include "resource.h"
#include "afxres.h"


/////////////////////////////////////////////////////////////////////////////
// Menu

HELLOBIT MENU DISCARDABLE
BEGIN
    POPUP "&Size"
    BEGIN
        MENUITEM "&Big",                        IDM_BIG, CHECKED
        MENUITEM "&Small",                      IDM_SMALL
    END
END
```

RESOURCE.H (excerpts)

```
// Microsoft Developer Studio generated include file.
// Used by HelloBit.rc

#define IDM_BIG                         40001
#define IDM_SMALL                       40002
```

The program begins by determining the pixel dimensions of the text string through a call to *GetTextExtentPoint32*. These dimensions become the size of a bitmap compatible with the video display. Once this bitmap is selected into a memory device context (also compatible with the video display), a call to *TextOut* puts the text on the bitmap. The memory device context is retained throughout the duration of the program. While processing the WM_DESTROY message, HELLOBIT deletes both the bitmap and the memory device context.

A menu selection in HELLOBIT allows you to display the bitmap at actual size repeated horizontally and vertically in the client area or stretched to the size of the client area as shown in Figure 14-10. As you can see, this is *not* a good way to display text of large point sizes! It's just a magnified version of the smaller font, with all the jaggies magnified as well.

Figure 14-10. *The HELLOBIT display.*

You may wonder if a program such as HELLOBIT needs to process the WM_ DISPLAYCHANGE message. An application receives this message whenever the user (or another application) changes the video display size or color depth. It could be that a change to the color depth would cause the memory device context and the video device context to become incompatible. Well, that doesn't happen because Windows automatically changes the color resolution of the memory device context when the video mode is changed. The bitmap selected into the memory device context remains the same, but that doesn't seem to cause any problems.

The Shadow Bitmap

The technique of drawing on a memory device context (and hence a bitmap) is the key to implementing a "shadow bitmap." This is a bitmap that contains everything displayed in the window's client area. WM_PAINT message processing thus reduces to a simple *BitBlt*.

Shadow bitmaps are most useful in paint programs. The SKETCH program shown in Figure 14-11 is not exactly the most sophisticated paint program around, but it's a start.

SKETCH.C

```
/*-------------------------------------------
   SKETCH.C -- Shadow Bitmap Demonstration
               (c) Charles Petzold, 1998
   -------------------------------------------*/

#include <windows.h>

LRESULT CALLBACK WndProc (HWND, UINT, WPARAM, LPARAM) ;

int WINAPI WinMain (HINSTANCE hInstance, HINSTANCE hPrevInstance,
                    PSTR szCmdLine, int iCmdShow)
{
     static TCHAR szAppName [] = TEXT ("Sketch") ;
     HWND         hwnd ;
     MSG          msg ;
     WNDCLASS     wndclass ;

     wndclass.style         = CS_HREDRAW | CS_VREDRAW ;
     wndclass.lpfnWndProc   = WndProc ;
     wndclass.cbClsExtra    = 0 ;
     wndclass.cbWndExtra    = 0 ;
     wndclass.hInstance     = hInstance ;
     wndclass.hIcon         = LoadIcon (NULL, IDI_APPLICATION) ;
     wndclass.hCursor       = LoadCursor (NULL, IDC_ARROW) ;
     wndclass.hbrBackground = (HBRUSH) GetStockObject (WHITE_BRUSH) ;
     wndclass.lpszMenuName  = NULL ;
     wndclass.lpszClassName = szAppName ;

     if (!RegisterClass (&wndclass))
```

Figure 14-11. *The SKETCH program.*

```
     {
          MessageBox (NULL, TEXT ("This program requires Windows NT!"),
                    szAppName, MB_ICONERROR) ;
          return 0 ;
     }

     hwnd = CreateWindow (szAppName, TEXT ("Sketch"),
                         WS_OVERLAPPEDWINDOW,
                         CW_USEDEFAULT, CW_USEDEFAULT,
                         CW_USEDEFAULT, CW_USEDEFAULT,
                         NULL, NULL, hInstance, NULL) ;

     if (hwnd == NULL)
     {
          MessageBox (NULL, TEXT ("Not enough memory to create bitmap!"),
                    szAppName, MB_ICONERROR) ;
          return 0 ;
     }

     ShowWindow (hwnd, iCmdShow) ;
     UpdateWindow (hwnd) ;

     while (GetMessage (&msg, NULL, 0, 0))
     {
          TranslateMessage (&msg) ;
          DispatchMessage (&msg) ;
     }
     return msg.wParam ;
}

void GetLargestDisplayMode (int * pcxBitmap, int * pcyBitmap)
{
     DEVMODE devmode ;
     int     iModeNum = 0 ;

     * pcxBitmap = * pcyBitmap = 0 ;

     ZeroMemory (&devmode, sizeof (DEVMODE)) ;
     devmode.dmSize = sizeof (DEVMODE) ;

     while (EnumDisplaySettings (NULL, iModeNum++, &devmode))
     {
          * pcxBitmap = max (* pcxBitmap, (int) devmode.dmPelsWidth) ;
          * pcyBitmap = max (* pcyBitmap, (int) devmode.dmPelsHeight) ;
     }
}
```

(continued)

Figure 14-11. *continued*

```
LRESULT CALLBACK WndProc (HWND hwnd, UINT message, WPARAM wParam, LPARAM lParam)
{
     static BOOL    fLeftButtonDown, fRightButtonDown ;
     static HBITMAP hBitmap ;
     static HDC     hdcMem ;
     static int     cxBitmap, cyBitmap, cxClient, cyClient, xMouse, yMouse ;
     HDC            hdc ;
     PAINTSTRUCT    ps ;

     switch (message)
     {
     case WM_CREATE:
          GetLargestDisplayMode (&cxBitmap, &cyBitmap) ;

          hdc = GetDC (hwnd) ;
          hBitmap = CreateCompatibleBitmap (hdc, cxBitmap, cyBitmap) ;
          hdcMem  = CreateCompatibleDC (hdc) ;
          ReleaseDC (hwnd, hdc) ;

          if (!hBitmap)        // no memory for bitmap
          {
               DeleteDC (hdcMem) ;
               return -1 ;
          }

          SelectObject (hdcMem, hBitmap) ;
          PatBlt (hdcMem, 0, 0, cxBitmap, cyBitmap, WHITENESS) ;
          return 0 ;

     case WM_SIZE:
          cxClient = LOWORD (lParam) ;
          cyClient = HIWORD (lParam) ;
          return 0 ;

     case WM_LBUTTONDOWN:
          if (!fRightButtonDown)
               SetCapture (hwnd) ;

          xMouse = LOWORD (lParam) ;
          yMouse = HIWORD (lParam) ;
          fLeftButtonDown = TRUE ;
          return 0 ;

     case WM_LBUTTONUP:
          if (fLeftButtonDown)
               SetCapture (NULL) ;
```

```
            fLeftButtonDown = FALSE ;
            return 0 ;

    case WM_RBUTTONDOWN:
            if (!fLeftButtonDown)
                SetCapture (hwnd) ;

            xMouse = LOWORD (lParam) ;
            yMouse = HIWORD (lParam) ;
            fRightButtonDown = TRUE ;
            return 0 ;

    case WM_RBUTTONUP:
            if (fRightButtonDown)
                SetCapture (NULL) ;

            fRightButtonDown = FALSE ;
            return 0 ;

    case WM_MOUSEMOVE:
            if (!fLeftButtonDown && !fRightButtonDown)
                return 0 ;

            hdc = GetDC (hwnd) ;

            SelectObject (hdc,
                GetStockObject (fLeftButtonDown ? BLACK_PEN : WHITE_PEN)) ;

            SelectObject (hdcMem,
                GetStockObject (fLeftButtonDown ? BLACK_PEN : WHITE_PEN)) ;

            MoveToEx (hdc,    xMouse, yMouse, NULL) ;
            MoveToEx (hdcMem, xMouse, yMouse, NULL) ;

            xMouse = (short) LOWORD (lParam) ;
            yMouse = (short) HIWORD (lParam) ;

            LineTo (hdc,    xMouse, yMouse) ;
            LineTo (hdcMem, xMouse, yMouse) ;

            ReleaseDC (hwnd, hdc) ;
            return 0 ;

    case WM_PAINT:
            hdc = BeginPaint (hwnd, &ps) ;
```

(continued)

Figure 14-11. *continued*

```
        BitBlt (hdc, 0, 0, cxClient, cyClient, hdcMem, 0, 0, SRCCOPY) ;

        EndPaint (hwnd, &ps) ;
        return 0 ;

   case WM_DESTROY:
        DeleteDC (hdcMem) ;
        DeleteObject (hBitmap) ;
        PostQuitMessage (0) ;
        return 0 ;
   }
   return DefWindowProc (hwnd, message, wParam, lParam) ;
}
```

To draw lines in SKETCH, you press the left mouse button and move the mouse. To erase (or more precisely, to draw white lines), you press the right mouse button and move the mouse. To clear the entire window, you...well, you have to end the program, load it again, and start all over. Figure 14-12 shows the SKETCH program paying homage to the early advertisements for the Apple Macintosh.

Figure 14-12. *The SKETCH display.*

How large should the shadow bitmap be? In this program, it should be large enough to encompass the entire client area of a maximized window. This is easy enough to calculate from *GetSystemMetrics* information, but what happens if the user changes the display settings and makes the display, and hence the maximum window size, larger? SKETCH implements a brute force solution to this problem with the help of the *EnumDisplaySettings* function. This function uses a DEVMODE structure to return information on all the available video display modes. Set the second argument to *EnumDisplaySettings* to 0 the first time you call the function, and increase the value for each subsequent call. When *EnumDisplaySettings* returns FALSE, you're finished.

With that information, SKETCH will create a shadow bitmap that can have more than four times the surface area of the current video display mode and require multiple megabytes of memory. For this reason, SKETCH checks to see if the bitmap has been created and returns –1 from WM_CREATE to indicate an error if it has not.

SKETCH captures the mouse when the left or right mouse button is pressed and draws lines on both the memory device context and the device context for the client area during the WM_MOUSEMOVE message. If the drawing logic were any more complex, you'd probably want to implement it in a function that the program calls twice—once for the video device context and again for the memory device context.

Here's an interesting experiment: Make the SKETCH window less than the size of the full screen. With the left mouse button depressed, draw something and let the mouse pass outside the window at the right and bottom. Because SKETCH captures the mouse, it continues to receive and process WM_MOUSEMOVE messages. Now expand the window. You'll discover that the shadow bitmap includes the drawing you did outside SKETCH's window!

Using Bitmaps in Menus

You can also use bitmaps to display items in menus. If you immediately recoiled at the thought of pictures of file folders, paste jars, and trash cans in a menu, don't think of pictures. Think instead of how useful menu bitmaps might be for a drawing program. Think of using different fonts and font sizes, line widths, hatch patterns, and colors in your menus.

The sample program that demonstrates graphical menu items is called GRAFMENU. The top-level menu of this program is shown in Figure 14-13 on the following page. The enlarged block letters are obtained from 40-by-16-pixel monochrome bitmap files created in Visual C++ Developer Studio. Choosing FONT from the menu invokes a popup containing three options—Courier New, Arial, and Times New Roman. These are the standard Windows TrueType fonts, and each is displayed in its respective font, as you can see in Figure 14-14 on the following page. These bitmaps were created in the program using a memory device context.

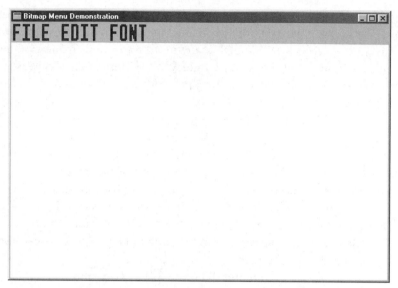

Figure 14-13. *The GRAFMENU program's top-level menu.*

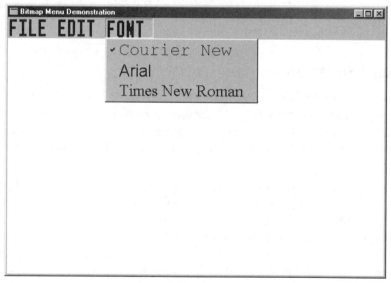

Figure 14-14. *The GRAFMENU program's popup FONT menu.*

Finally, when you pull down the system menu, you see that you have access to some "help" information, with the word "Help" perhaps mirroring the desperation of a new user. (See Figure 14-15.) This 64-by-64-pixel monochrome bitmap was created in Developer Studio.

Figure 14-15. *The GRAFMENU program's system menu.*

The GRAFMENU program, including the four bitmaps created in Developer Studio, is shown in Figure 14-16.

GRAFMENU.C

```
/*-------------------------------------------------
   GRAFMENU.C -- Demonstrates Bitmap Menu Items
                 (c) Charles Petzold, 1998
   -------------------------------------------------*/

#include <windows.h>
#include "resource.h"

LRESULT CALLBACK WndProc (HWND, UINT, WPARAM, LPARAM) ;
void     AddHelpToSys     (HINSTANCE, HWND) ;
HMENU    CreateMyMenu      (HINSTANCE) ;
HBITMAP  StretchBitmap     (HBITMAP) ;
HBITMAP  GetBitmapFont     (int) ;
void     DeleteAllBitmaps  (HWND) ;

TCHAR szAppName[] = TEXT ("GrafMenu") ;

int WINAPI WinMain (HINSTANCE hInstance, HINSTANCE hPrevInstance,
                    PSTR szCmdLine, int iCmdShow)
{
```

Figure 14-16. *The GRAFMENU program.*   *(continued)*

Figure 14-16. *continued*

```
     HWND      hwnd ;
     MSG       msg ;
     WNDCLASS wndclass ;

     wndclass.style         = CS_HREDRAW | CS_VREDRAW ;
     wndclass.lpfnWndProc   = WndProc ;
     wndclass.cbClsExtra    = 0 ;
     wndclass.cbWndExtra    = 0 ;
     wndclass.hInstance     = hInstance ;
     wndclass.hIcon         = LoadIcon (NULL, IDI_APPLICATION) ;
     wndclass.hCursor       = LoadCursor (NULL, IDC_ARROW) ;
     wndclass.hbrBackground = (HBRUSH) GetStockObject (WHITE_BRUSH) ;
     wndclass.lpszMenuName  = NULL ;
     wndclass.lpszClassName = szAppName ;

     if (!RegisterClass (&wndclass))
     {
          MessageBox (NULL, TEXT ("This program requires Windows NT!"),
                    szAppName, MB_ICONERROR) ;
          return 0 ;
     }

     hwnd = CreateWindow (szAppName, TEXT ("Bitmap Menu Demonstration"),
                    WS_OVERLAPPEDWINDOW,
                    CW_USEDEFAULT, CW_USEDEFAULT,
                    CW_USEDEFAULT, CW_USEDEFAULT,
                    NULL, NULL, hInstance, NULL) ;

     ShowWindow (hwnd, iCmdShow) ;
     UpdateWindow (hwnd) ;

     while (GetMessage (&msg, NULL, 0, 0))
     {
          TranslateMessage (&msg) ;
          DispatchMessage (&msg) ;
     }
     return msg.wParam ;
}

LRESULT CALLBACK WndProc (HWND hwnd, UINT iMsg, WPARAM wParam, LPARAM lParam)
{
     HMENU       hMenu ;
     static int iCurrentFont = IDM_FONT_COUR ;

     switch (iMsg)
     {
     case WM_CREATE:
```

```
        AddHelpToSys ((((LPCREATESTRUCT) lParam)->hInstance, hwnd) ;
        hMenu = CreateMyMenu ((((LPCREATESTRUCT) lParam)->hInstance) ;
        SetMenu (hwnd, hMenu) ;
        CheckMenuItem (hMenu, iCurrentFont, MF_CHECKED) ;
        return 0 ;

case WM_SYSCOMMAND:
        switch (LOWORD (wParam))
        {
        case IDM_HELP:
            MessageBox (hwnd, TEXT ("Help not yet implemented!"),
                        szAppName, MB_OK | MB_ICONEXCLAMATION) ;
            return 0 ;
        }
        break ;

case WM_COMMAND:
        switch (LOWORD (wParam))
        {
        case IDM_FILE_NEW:
        case IDM_FILE_OPEN:
        case IDM_FILE_SAVE:
        case IDM_FILE_SAVE_AS:
        case IDM_EDIT_UNDO:
        case IDM_EDIT_CUT:
        case IDM_EDIT_COPY:
        case IDM_EDIT_PASTE:
        case IDM_EDIT_CLEAR:
            MessageBeep (0) ;
            return 0 ;

        case IDM_FONT_COUR:
        case IDM_FONT_ARIAL:
        case IDM_FONT_TIMES:
            hMenu = GetMenu (hwnd) ;
            CheckMenuItem (hMenu, iCurrentFont, MF_UNCHECKED) ;
            iCurrentFont = LOWORD (wParam) ;
            CheckMenuItem (hMenu, iCurrentFont, MF_CHECKED) ;
            return 0 ;
        }
        break ;

case WM_DESTROY:
        DeleteAllBitmaps (hwnd) ;
        PostQuitMessage (0) ;
        return 0 ;
}
```

(continued)

Figure 14-16. *continued*

```
        return DefWindowProc (hwnd, iMsg, wParam, lParam) ;
}


/*----------------------------------------------------
    AddHelpToSys: Adds bitmap Help item to system menu
  ----------------------------------------------------*/

void AddHelpToSys (HINSTANCE hInstance, HWND hwnd)
{
    HBITMAP hBitmap ;
    HMENU   hMenu ;

    hMenu = GetSystemMenu (hwnd, FALSE);
    hBitmap = StretchBitmap (LoadBitmap (hInstance, TEXT ("BitmapHelp"))) ;
    AppendMenu (hMenu, MF_SEPARATOR, 0, NULL) ;
    AppendMenu (hMenu, MF_BITMAP, IDM_HELP, (PTSTR) (LONG) hBitmap) ;
}


/*--------------------------------------------------
    CreateMyMenu: Assembles menu from components
  --------------------------------------------------*/

HMENU CreateMyMenu (HINSTANCE hInstance)
{
    HBITMAP hBitmap ;
    HMENU   hMenu, hMenuPopup ;
    int     i ;

    hMenu = CreateMenu () ;

    hMenuPopup = LoadMenu (hInstance, TEXT ("MenuFile")) ;
    hBitmap = StretchBitmap (LoadBitmap (hInstance, TEXT ("BitmapFile"))) ;
    AppendMenu (hMenu, MF_BITMAP | MF_POPUP, (int) hMenuPopup,
                      (PTSTR) (LONG) hBitmap) ;

    hMenuPopup = LoadMenu (hInstance, TEXT ("MenuEdit")) ;
    hBitmap = StretchBitmap (LoadBitmap (hInstance, TEXT ("BitmapEdit"))) ;
    AppendMenu (hMenu, MF_BITMAP | MF_POPUP, (int) hMenuPopup,
                      (PTSTR) (LONG) hBitmap) ;

    hMenuPopup = CreateMenu () ;

    for (i = 0 ; i < 3 ; i++)
    {
        hBitmap = GetBitmapFont (i) ;
        AppendMenu (hMenuPopup, MF_BITMAP, IDM_FONT_COUR + i,
                              (PTSTR) (LONG) hBitmap) ;
    }
```

```
        hBitmap = StretchBitmap (LoadBitmap (hInstance, TEXT ("BitmapFont"))) ;
        AppendMenu (hMenu, MF_BITMAP | MF_POPUP, (int) hMenuPopup,
                            (PTSTR) (LONG) hBitmap) ;

        return hMenu ;
}


/*------------------------------------------------------
   StretchBitmap: Scales bitmap to display resolution
  --------------------------------------------------------*/

HBITMAP StretchBitmap (HBITMAP hBitmap1)
{
        BITMAP      bm1, bm2 ;
        HBITMAP     hBitmap2 ;
        HDC         hdc, hdcMem1, hdcMem2 ;
        int         cxChar, cyChar ;

            // Get the width and height of a system font character

        cxChar = LOWORD (GetDialogBaseUnits ()) ;
        cyChar = HIWORD (GetDialogBaseUnits ()) ;

            // Create 2 memory DCs compatible with the display

        hdc = CreateIC (TEXT ("DISPLAY"), NULL, NULL, NULL) ;
        hdcMem1 = CreateCompatibleDC (hdc) ;
        hdcMem2 = CreateCompatibleDC (hdc) ;
        DeleteDC (hdc) ;

            // Get the dimensions of the bitmap to be stretched

        GetObject (hBitmap1, sizeof (BITMAP), (PTSTR) &bm1) ;

            // Scale these dimensions based on the system font size

        bm2 = bm1 ;
        bm2.bmWidth      = (cxChar * bm2.bmWidth)  / 4 ;
        bm2.bmHeight     = (cyChar * bm2.bmHeight) / 8 ;
        bm2.bmWidthBytes = ((bm2.bmWidth + 15) / 16) * 2 ;

            // Create a new bitmap of larger size

        hBitmap2 = CreateBitmapIndirect (&bm2) ;

            // Select the bitmaps in the memory DCs and do a StretchBlt

        SelectObject (hdcMem1, hBitmap1) ;
        SelectObject (hdcMem2, hBitmap2) ;
```

(continued)

Figure 14-16. *continued*

```
        StretchBlt (hdcMem2, 0, 0, bm2.bmWidth, bm2.bmHeight,
                    hdcMem1, 0, 0, bm1.bmWidth, bm1.bmHeight, SRCCOPY) ;

            // Clean up

        DeleteDC (hdcMem1) ;
        DeleteDC (hdcMem2) ;
        DeleteObject (hBitmap1) ;

        return hBitmap2 ;
}

/*-----------------------------------------------------
   GetBitmapFont: Creates bitmaps with font names
  -----------------------------------------------------*/

HBITMAP GetBitmapFont (int i)
{
        static TCHAR * szFaceName[3] = { TEXT ("Courier New"), TEXT ("Arial"),
                                         TEXT ("Times New Roman") } ;
        HBITMAP         hBitmap ;
        HDC             hdc, hdcMem ;
        HFONT           hFont ;
        SIZE            size ;
        TEXTMETRIC      tm ;

        hdc = CreateIC (TEXT ("DISPLAY"), NULL, NULL, NULL) ;
        GetTextMetrics (hdc, &tm) ;

        hdcMem = CreateCompatibleDC (hdc) ;
        hFont  = CreateFont (2 * tm.tmHeight, 0, 0, 0, 0, 0, 0, 0, 0, 0, 0, 0, 0,
                             szFaceName[i]) ;

        hFont = (HFONT) SelectObject (hdcMem, hFont) ;
        GetTextExtentPoint32 (hdcMem, szFaceName[i],
                              lstrlen (szFaceName[i]), &size);

        hBitmap = CreateBitmap (size.cx, size.cy, 1, 1, NULL) ;
        SelectObject (hdcMem, hBitmap) ;

        TextOut (hdcMem, 0, 0, szFaceName[i], lstrlen (szFaceName[i])) ;

        DeleteObject (SelectObject (hdcMem, hFont)) ;
        DeleteDC (hdcMem) ;
        DeleteDC (hdc) ;

        return hBitmap ;
}
```

```
/*--------------------------------------------------------------
   DeleteAllBitmaps: Deletes all the bitmaps in the menu
  ----------------------------------------------------------*/

void DeleteAllBitmaps (HWND hwnd)
{
    HMENU          hMenu ;
    int            i ;
    MENUITEMINFO mii = { sizeof (MENUITEMINFO), MIIM_SUBMENU | MIIM_TYPE } ;

         // Delete Help bitmap on system menu

    hMenu = GetSystemMenu (hwnd, FALSE);
    GetMenuItemInfo (hMenu, IDM_HELP, FALSE, &mii) ;
    DeleteObject ((HBITMAP) mii.dwTypeData) ;

         // Delete top-level menu bitmaps

    hMenu = GetMenu (hwnd) ;

    for (i = 0 ; i < 3 ; i++)
    {
        GetMenuItemInfo (hMenu, i, TRUE, &mii) ;
        DeleteObject ((HBITMAP) mii.dwTypeData) ;
    }

         // Delete bitmap items on Font menu

    hMenu = mii.hSubMenu ;;

    for (i = 0 ; i < 3 ; i++)
    {
        GetMenuItemInfo (hMenu, i, TRUE, &mii) ;
        DeleteObject ((HBITMAP) mii.dwTypeData) ;
    }
}
```

GRAFMENU.RC (excerpts)

```
//Microsoft Developer Studio generated resource script.

#include "resource.h"
#include "afxres.h"


/////////////////////////////////////////////////////////////////////////////
// Menu
```

(continued)

Figure 14-16. *continued*

```
MENUFILE MENU DISCARDABLE
BEGIN
    MENUITEM "&New",                        IDM_FILE_NEW
    MENUITEM "&Open...",                    IDM_FILE_OPEN
    MENUITEM "&Save",                       IDM_FILE_SAVE
    MENUITEM "Save &As...",                 IDM_FILE_SAVE_AS
END

MENUEDIT MENU DISCARDABLE
BEGIN
    MENUITEM "&Undo",                       IDM_EDIT_UNDO
    MENUITEM SEPARATOR
    MENUITEM "Cu&t",                        IDM_EDIT_CUT
    MENUITEM "&Copy",                       IDM_EDIT_COPY
    MENUITEM "&Paste",                      IDM_EDIT_PASTE
    MENUITEM "De&lete",                     IDM_EDIT_CLEAR
END


/////////////////////////////////////////////////////////////////////////////
// Bitmap

BITMAPFONT             BITMAP  DISCARDABLE    "Fontlabl.bmp"
BITMAPHELP             BITMAP  DISCARDABLE    "Bighelp.bmp"
BITMAPEDIT             BITMAP  DISCARDABLE    "Editlabl.bmp"
BITMAPFILE             BITMAP  DISCARDABLE    "Filelabl.bmp"
```

RESOURCE.H (excerpts

```
// Microsoft Developer Studio generated include file.
// Used by GrafMenu.rc

#define IDM_FONT_COUR             101
#define IDM_FONT_ARIAL            102
#define IDM_FONT_TIMES            103
#define IDM_HELP                  104
#define IDM_EDIT_UNDO             40005
#define IDM_EDIT_CUT              40006
#define IDM_EDIT_COPY             40007
#define IDM_EDIT_PASTE            40008
#define IDM_EDIT_CLEAR            40009
#define IDM_FILE_NEW              40010
#define IDM_FILE_OPEN             40011
#define IDM_FILE_SAVE             40012
#define IDM_FILE_SAVE_AS          40013
```

EDITLABL.BMP

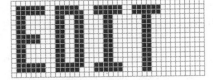

FILELABL.BMP

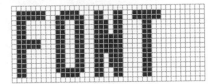

FONTLABL.BMP

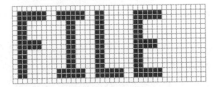

BIGHELP.BMP

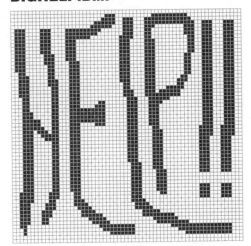

To insert a bitmap into a menu, you use *AppendMenu* or *InsertMenu*. The bitmap can come from one of two places. You can create a bitmap in Visual C++ Developer Studio, include the bitmap file in your resource script, and within the program use *LoadBitmap* to load the bitmap resource into memory. You then call *AppendMenu* or *InsertMenu* to attach it to the menu. There's a problem with this approach, however. The bitmap might not be suitable for all types of video resolutions and aspect ratios; you probably want to stretch the loaded bitmap to account for this. Alternatively, you can create the bitmap right in the program, select it into a memory device context, draw on it, and then attach it to the menu.

The *GetBitmapFont* function in GRAFMENU takes a parameter of 0, 1, or 2 and returns a handle to a bitmap. This bitmap contains the string "Courier New," "Arial," or "Times New Roman" in the appropriate font and about twice the size of the normal system font. Let's see how *GetBitmapFont* does it. (The code that follows is not the same as that in the GRAFMENU.C file. For purposes of clarity, I've replaced references to the *szFaceName* array with the values appropriate for the Arial font.)

The first steps are to determine the size of the system font by using the TEXTMETRIC structure and to create a memory device context compatible with the screen:

```
hdc = CreateIC (TEXT ("DISPLAY"), NULL, NULL, NULL) ;
GetTextMetrics (hdc, &tm) ;
hdcMem = CreateCompatibleDC (hdc) ;
```

The *CreateFont* function creates a logical font that is twice the height of the system font and has a facename of "Arial":

```
hFont = CreateFont (2 * tm.tmHeight, 0, 0, 0, 0, 0, 0, 0, 0, 0, 0, 0, 0,
                    TEXT ("Arial")) ;
```

This font is selected in the memory device context and the default font handle is saved:

```
hFont = (HFONT) SelectObject (hdcMem, hFont) ;
```

Now when we write some text to the memory device context, Windows will use the TrueType Arial font selected into the device context.

But this memory device context initially has a one-pixel monochrome device surface. We have to create a bitmap large enough for the text we want to display on it. You can obtain the dimensions of the text through *GetTextExtentPoint32* and create a bitmap based on these dimensions with *CreateBitmap*:

```
GetTextExtentPoint32 (hdcMem, TEXT ("Arial"), 5, &size) ;
hBitmap = CreateBitmap (size.cx, size.cy, 1, 1, NULL) ;
SelectObject (hdcMem, hBitmap) ;
```

This device context now has a monochrome display surface exactly the size of the text. Now all we have to do is write the text to it:

```
TextOut (hdcMem, 0, 0, TEXT ("Arial"), 5) ;
```

We're finished, except for cleaning up. To do so, we select the system font (with handle *hFont*) back into the device context by using *SelectObject*, and we delete the previous font handle that *SelectObject* returns, which is the handle to the Arial font:

```
DeleteObject (SelectObject (hdcMem, hFont)) ;
```

Now we can also delete the two device contexts:

```
DeleteDC (hdcMem) ;
DeleteDC (hdc) ;
```

We're left with a bitmap that has the text "Arial" in an Arial font.

The memory device context also comes to the rescue when we need to scale fonts to a different display resolution or aspect ratio. I created the four bitmaps used in GRAF-MENU to be the correct size for a display that has a system font height of 8 pixels and width of 4 pixels. For other system font dimensions, the bitmap has to be stretched. This is done in GRAFMENU's *StretchBitmap* function.

The first step is to get the device context for the screen, obtain the text metrics for the system font, and create two memory device contexts:

```
hdc = CreateIC (TEXT ("DISPLAY"), NULL, NULL, NULL) ;
GetTextMetrics (hdc, &tm) ;
hdcMem1 = CreateCompatibleDC (hdc) ;
hdcMem2 = CreateCompatibleDC (hdc) ;
DeleteDC (hdc) ;
```

The bitmap handle passed to the function is *hBitmap1*. The program can obtain the dimensions of this bitmap using *GetObject*:

```
GetObject (hBitmap1, sizeof (BITMAP), (PSTR) &bm1) ;
```

This copies the dimensions into a structure *bm1* of type BITMAP. The structure *bm2* is set equal to *bm1*, and then certain fields are modified based on the system font dimensions:

```
bm2 = bm1 ;
bm2.bmWidth      = (tm.tmAveCharWidth * bm2.bmWidth)  / 4 ;
bm2.bmHeight     = (tm.tmHeight       * bm2.bmHeight) / 8 ;
bm2.bmWidthBytes = ((bm2.bmWidth + 15) / 16) * 2 ;
```

Next a new bitmap with handle *hBitmap2* can be created that is based on the altered dimensions:

```
hBitmap2 = CreateBitmapIndirect (&bm2) ;
```

You can then select these two bitmaps into the two memory device contexts:

```
SelectObject (hdcMem1, hBitmap1) ;
SelectObject (hdcMem2, hBitmap2) ;
```

We want to copy the first bitmap to the second bitmap and stretch it in the process. This involves the *StretchBlt* call:

```
StretchBlt (hdcMem2, 0, 0, bm2.bmWidth, bm2.bmHeight,
            hdcMem1, 0, 0, bm1.bmWidth, bm1.bmHeight, SRCCOPY) ;
```

Now the second bitmap has the properly scaled bitmap. We'll use that one in the menu. As you can see on the next page, cleanup is simple.

```
DeleteDC (hdcMem1) ;
DeleteDC (hdcMem2) ;
DeleteObject (hBitmap1) ;
```

The *CreateMyMenu* function in GRAFMENU uses the *StretchBitmap* and *GetBitmapFont* functions when constructing the menu. GRAFMENU has two menus already defined in the resource script. These will become popups for the File and Edit options. The function begins by obtaining a handle to an empty menu:

```
hMenu = CreateMenu () ;
```

The popup menu for File (containing the four options New, Open, Save, and Save As) is loaded from the resource script:

```
hMenuPopup = LoadMenu (hInstance, TEXT ("MenuFile")) ;
```

The bitmap containing the word "FILE" is also loaded from the resource script and stretched using *StretchBitmap*:

```
hBitmapFile = StretchBitmap (LoadBitmap (hInstance, TEXT ("BitmapFile"))) ;
```

The bitmap handle and popup menu handle become arguments to the *AppendMenu* call:

```
AppendMenu (hMenu, MF_BITMAP | MF_POPUP, hMenuPopup, (PTSTR) (LONG) hBitmapFile) ;
```

The same procedure is followed for the Edit menu:

```
hMenuPopup = LoadMenu (hInstance, TEXT ("MenuEdit")) ;
hBitmapEdit = StretchBitmap (LoadBitmap (hInstance, TEXT ("BitmapEdit"))) ;
AppendMenu (hMenu, MF_BITMAP | MF_POPUP, hMenuPopup, (PTSTR) (LONG) hBitmapEdit) ;
```

The popup menu for the three fonts is constructed from calls to the *GetBitmapFont* function:

```
hMenuPopup = CreateMenu () ;
for (i = 0 ; i < 3 ; i++)
{
     hBitmapPopFont [i] = GetBitmapFont (i) ;
     AppendMenu (hMenuPopup, MF_BITMAP, IDM_FONT_COUR + i,
                         (PTSTR) (LONG) hMenuPopupFont [i]) ;
}
```

The popup is then added to the menu:

```
hBitmapFont = StretchBitmap (LoadBitmap (hInstance, "BitmapFont")) ;
AppendMenu (hMenu, MF_BITMAP | MF_POPUP, hMenuPopup, (PTSTR) (LONG) hBitmapFont) ;
```

The window menu is now complete, and *WndProc* makes it the window's menu by a call to *SetMenu*.

GRAFMENU also alters the system menu in the *AddHelpToSys* function. The function first obtains a handle to the system menu:

```
hMenu = GetSystemMenu (hwnd, FALSE) ;
```

This loads the "Help" bitmap and stretches it to an appropriate size:

```
hBitmapHelp = StretchBitmap (LoadBitmap (hInstance, TEXT ("BitmapHelp"))) ;
```

This adds a separator bar and the stretched bitmap to the system menu:

```
AppendMenu (hMenu, MF_SEPARATOR, 0, NULL) ;
AppendMenu (hMenu, MF_BITMAP, IDM_HELP, (PTSTR)(LONG) hBitmapHelp) ;
```

GRAFMENU devotes a whole function to cleaning up and deleting all the bitmaps before the program terminates.

A couple of miscellaneous notes on using bitmap in menus now follow.

In a top-level menu, Windows adjusts the menu bar height to accommodate the tallest bitmap. Other bitmaps (or character strings) are aligned at the top of the menu bar. The size of the menu bar obtained from *GetSystemMetrics* with the SM_CYMENU constant is no longer valid after you put bitmaps in a top-level menu.

As you can see from playing with GRAFMENU, you can use check marks with bit-mapped menu items in popups, but the check mark is of normal size. If that bothers you, you can create a customized check mark and use *SetMenuItemBitmaps*.

Another approach to using nontext (or text in a font other than the system font) on a menu is the "owner-draw" menu.

The keyboard interface to menus is another problem. When the menu contains text, Windows automatically adds a keyboard interface. You can select a menu item using the Alt key in combination with a letter of the character string. But once you put a bitmap in a menu, you've eliminated that keyboard interface. Even if the bitmap says something, Windows doesn't know about it.

This is where the WM_MENUCHAR message comes in handy. Windows sends a WM_MENUCHAR message to your window procedure when you press Alt with a character key that does not correspond to a menu item. GRAFMENU would need to intercept WM_MENUCHAR messages and check the value of *wParam* (the ASCII character of the pressed key). If this corresponds to a menu item, it would have to return a double word to Windows, where the high word is set to 2 and the low word is set to the index of the menu item we want associated with that key. Windows does the rest.

Nonrectangular Bitmap Images

Bitmaps are always rectangular, but they needn't be displayed like that. For example, suppose you have a rectangular bitmap image that you want to be displayed as an ellipse.

At first, this sounds simple. You just load the image into Visual C++ Developer Studio or the Windows Paint program (or a more expensive application) and you start drawing around the outside of the image with a white pen. You're left with an elliptical image with everything outside the ellipse painted white. This will work—but only when you display the bitmap on a white background. If you display it on any other color background, you'll have an elliptical image on top of a white rectangle on top of a colored background. That's no good.

There's a very common technique to solve problems like this. The technique involves a "mask" bitmap and some raster operations. A mask is a monochrome bitmap of the same dimensions as the rectangular bitmap image you want to display. Each mask pixel corresponds with a pixel of the bitmap image. The mask pixels are 1 (white) wherever the original bitmap pixel is to be displayed, and 0 (black) wherever you want to preserve the destination background. (Or the mask bitmap can be opposite this, with some corresponding changes to the raster operations you use.)

Let's see how this works in real life in the BITMASK program shown in Figure 14-17.

BITMASK.C

```
/*-----------------------------------------------
   BITMASK.C -- Bitmap Masking Demonstration
                (c) Charles Petzold, 1998
   -----------------------------------------------*/

#include <windows.h>

LRESULT CALLBACK WndProc (HWND, UINT, WPARAM, LPARAM) ;

int WINAPI WinMain (HINSTANCE hInstance, HINSTANCE hPrevInstance,
                    PSTR szCmdLine, int iCmdShow)
{
     static TCHAR szAppName [] = TEXT ("BitMask") ;
     HWND         hwnd ;
     MSG          msg ;
     WNDCLASS     wndclass ;

     wndclass.style         = CS_HREDRAW | CS_VREDRAW ;
     wndclass.lpfnWndProc   = WndProc ;
     wndclass.cbClsExtra    = 0 ;
     wndclass.cbWndExtra    = 0 ;
     wndclass.hInstance     = hInstance ;
     wndclass.hIcon         = LoadIcon (NULL, IDI_APPLICATION) ;
     wndclass.hCursor       = LoadCursor (NULL, IDC_ARROW) ;
     wndclass.hbrBackground = (HBRUSH) GetStockObject (LTGRAY_BRUSH) ;
     wndclass.lpszMenuName  = NULL ;
     wndclass.lpszClassName = szAppName ;

     if (!RegisterClass (&wndclass))
     {
```

Figure 14-17. *The BITMASK program.*

```
        MessageBox (NULL, TEXT ("This program requires Windows NT!"),
                    szAppName, MB_ICONERROR) ;
        return 0 ;
    }

    hwnd = CreateWindow (szAppName, TEXT ("Bitmap Masking Demo"),
                    WS_OVERLAPPEDWINDOW,
                    CW_USEDEFAULT, CW_USEDEFAULT,
                    CW_USEDEFAULT, CW_USEDEFAULT,
                    NULL, NULL, hInstance, NULL) ;

    ShowWindow (hwnd, iCmdShow) ;
    UpdateWindow (hwnd) ;

    while (GetMessage (&msg, NULL, 0, 0))
    {
        TranslateMessage (&msg) ;
        DispatchMessage (&msg) ;
    }
    return msg.wParam ;
}

LRESULT CALLBACK WndProc (HWND hwnd, UINT message, WPARAM wParam, LPARAM lParam)
{
    static HBITMAP    hBitmapImag, hBitmapMask ;
    static HINSTANCE  hInstance ;
    static int        cxClient, cyClient, cxBitmap, cyBitmap ;
    BITMAP            bitmap ;
    HDC               hdc, hdcMemImag, hdcMemMask ;
    int               x, y ;
    PAINTSTRUCT       ps ;

    switch (message)
    {
    case WM_CREATE:
        hInstance = ((LPCREATESTRUCT) lParam)->hInstance ;

            // Load the original image and get its size

        hBitmapImag = LoadBitmap (hInstance, TEXT ("Matthew")) ;
        GetObject (hBitmapImag, sizeof (BITMAP), &bitmap) ;
        cxBitmap = bitmap.bmWidth ;
        cyBitmap = bitmap.bmHeight ;

            // Select the original image into a memory DC
```

(continued)

Figure 14-17. *continued*

```
        hdcMemImag  = CreateCompatibleDC (NULL) ;
        SelectObject (hdcMemImag, hBitmapImag) ;

            // Create the monochrome mask bitmap and memory DC

        hBitmapMask = CreateBitmap (cxBitmap, cyBitmap, 1, 1, NULL) ;
        hdcMemMask = CreateCompatibleDC (NULL) ;
        SelectObject (hdcMemMask, hBitmapMask) ;

            // Color the mask bitmap black with a white ellipse

        SelectObject (hdcMemMask, GetStockObject (BLACK_BRUSH)) ;
        Rectangle (hdcMemMask, 0, 0, cxBitmap, cyBitmap) ;
        SelectObject (hdcMemMask, GetStockObject (WHITE_BRUSH)) ;
        Ellipse (hdcMemMask, 0, 0, cxBitmap, cyBitmap) ;

            // Mask the original image

        BitBlt (hdcMemImag, 0, 0, cxBitmap, cyBitmap,
                hdcMemMask, 0, 0, SRCAND) ;

        DeleteDC (hdcMemImag) ;
        DeleteDC (hdcMemMask) ;
        return 0 ;

case WM_SIZE:
        cxClient = LOWORD (lParam) ;
        cyClient = HIWORD (lParam) ;
        return 0 ;

case WM_PAINT:
        hdc = BeginPaint (hwnd, &ps) ;

            // Select bitmaps into memory DCs

        hdcMemImag = CreateCompatibleDC (hdc) ;
        SelectObject (hdcMemImag, hBitmapImag) ;

        hdcMemMask = CreateCompatibleDC (hdc) ;
        SelectObject (hdcMemMask, hBitmapMask) ;

            // Center image

        x = (cxClient - cxBitmap) / 2 ;
        y = (cyClient - cyBitmap) / 2 ;
```

```
        // Do the bitblts

        BitBlt (hdc, x, y, cxBitmap, cyBitmap, hdcMemMask, 0, 0, 0x220326) ;
        BitBlt (hdc, x, y, cxBitmap, cyBitmap, hdcMemImag, 0, 0, SRCPAINT) ;

        DeleteDC (hdcMemImag) ;
        DeleteDC (hdcMemMask) ;
        EndPaint (hwnd, &ps) ;
        return 0 ;

    case WM_DESTROY:
        DeleteObject (hBitmapImag) ;
        DeleteObject (hBitmapMask) ;
        PostQuitMessage (0) ;
        return 0 ;
    }
    return DefWindowProc (hwnd, message, wParam, lParam) ;
}
```

BITMASK.RC

```
// Microsoft Developer Studio generated resource script.

#include "resource.h"
#include "afxres.h"

/////////////////////////////////////////////////////////////////////////////
// Bitmap

MATTHEW                 BITMAP  DISCARDABLE     "matthew.bmp"
```

The MATTHEW.BMP file referred to in the resource script is a digitized black-and-white photograph of a nephew of mine. It's 200 pixels wide, 320 pixels high, and has 8 bits per pixel. However, BITMASK is written so that this file can be just about anything.

Notice that BITMASK colors its window background with a light gray brush. This is to assure ourselves that we're properly masking the bitmap and not just coloring part of it white.

Let's look at WM_CREATE processing. BITMASK uses the *LoadBitmap* function to obtain a handle to the original image in the variable *hBitmapImag*. The *GetObject* function obtains the bitmap width and height. The bitmap handle is then selected in a memory device context whose handle is *hdcMemImag*.

Next the program creates a monochrome bitmap the same size as the original image. The handle is stored in *hBitmapMask* and selected into a memory device context whose handle is *hdcMemMask*. The mask bitmap is colored with a black background and a white ellipse by using GDI functions on the memory device context:

```
SelectObject (hdcMemMask, GetStockObject (BLACK_BRUSH)) ;
Rectangle (hdcMemMask, 0, 0, cxBitmap, cyBitmap) ;
SelectObject (hdcMemMask, GetStockObject (WHITE_BRUSH)) ;
Ellipse (hdcMemMask, 0, 0, cxBitmap, cyBitmap) ;
```

Because this is a monochrome bitmap, the black area is really 0 bits and the white area is really 1 bits.

Then a *BitBlt* call alters the original image by using this mask:

```
BitBlt (hdcMemImag, 0, 0, cxBitmap, cyBitmap,
      hdcMemMask, 0, 0, SRCAND) ;
```

The SRCAND raster operation performs a bitwise AND operation between the bits of the source (the mask bitmap) and the bits of the destination (the original image). Wherever the mask bitmap is white, the destination is preserved. Wherever the mask bitmap is black, the destination becomes black as well. An elliptical area in the original image is now surrounded by black.

Now let's look at WM_PAINT processing. Both the altered image bitmap and the mask bitmap are selected into memory device contexts. Two *BitBlt* calls perform the magic. The first does a *BitBlt* of the mask bitmap on the window:

```
BitBlt (hdc, x, y, cxBitmap, cyBitmap, hdcMemMask, 0, 0, 0x220326) ;
```

This uses a raster operation for which there is no name. The logical operation is D & ~S. Recall that the source—the mask bitmap—is a white ellipse (1 bits) surrounded by black (0 bits). The raster operation inverts the source so that it's a black ellipse surrounded by white. The raster operation then performs a bitwise AND of this inverted source with the destination—the surface of the window. When the destination is ANDed with 1 bits, it remains unchanged. When ANDed with 0 bits, the destination becomes black. Thus, this *BitBlt* operation draws a black ellipse in the window.

The second *BitBlt* call draws the image bitmap on the window:

```
BitBlt (hdc, x, y, cxBitmap, cyBitmap, hdcMemImag, 0, 0, SRCPAINT) ;
```

The raster operation performs a bitwise OR operation between the source and the destination. The outside of the source bitmap is black, so it leaves the destination unchanged. Within the ellipse, the destination is black, so the image is copied unchanged. The result is shown in Figure 14-18.

A few notes:

You may need a mask that is quite complex—for example, one that blots out the whole background of the original image. You'll probably need to create this manually in a paint program and save it to a file.

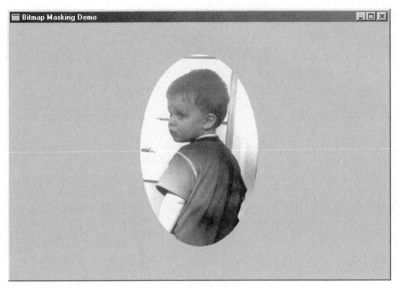

Figure 14-18. *The BITMASK display.*

If you're writing applications specifically for Windows NT, you can use the *MaskBlt* function to do something similar to the MASKBIT program with fewer function calls. Windows NT also includes another *BitBlt*-like function not supported under Windows 98. This is the *PlgBlt* ("parallelogram blt") function that lets you rotate or skew bitmap images.

Finally, if you run BITMASK on your machine and you see only black, white, and a couple of gray shades, it's because you're running in a 16-color or 256-color video mode. With the 16-color mode, there's not much you can do to improve things, but an application running in a 256-color mode can alter the color palette to display shades of gray. You'll find out how in Chapter 16.

Some Simple Animation

Because the display of small bitmaps is quite fast, you can use bitmaps in combination with the Windows timer for some rudimentary animation.

Yes, it's time for the bouncing ball program.

The BOUNCE program, shown in Figure 14-19 beginning on the following page, constructs a ball that bounces around in the window's client area. The program uses the timer to pace the ball. The ball itself is a bitmap. The program first creates the ball by creating the bitmap, selecting it into a memory device context, and then making simple GDI function calls. The program draws the bitmapped ball on the display using a *BitBlt* from a memory device context.

BOUNCE.C

```
/*-------------------------------------------
   BOUNCE.C -- Bouncing Ball Program
                (c) Charles Petzold, 1998
   -------------------------------------------*/

#include <windows.h>
#define ID_TIMER    1

LRESULT CALLBACK WndProc (HWND, UINT, WPARAM, LPARAM) ;

int WINAPI WinMain (HINSTANCE hInstance, HINSTANCE hPrevInstance,
                    PSTR szCmdLine, int iCmdShow)
{
    static TCHAR szAppName[] = TEXT ("Bounce") ;
    HWND        hwnd ;
    MSG         msg ;
    WNDCLASS    wndclass ;

    wndclass.style         = CS_HREDRAW | CS_VREDRAW ;
    wndclass.lpfnWndProc   = WndProc ;
    wndclass.cbClsExtra    = 0 ;
    wndclass.cbWndExtra    = 0 ;
    wndclass.hInstance     = hInstance ;
    wndclass.hIcon         = LoadIcon (NULL, IDI_APPLICATION) ;
    wndclass.hCursor       = LoadCursor (NULL, IDC_ARROW) ;
    wndclass.hbrBackground = (HBRUSH) GetStockObject (WHITE_BRUSH) ;
    wndclass.lpszMenuName  = NULL ;
    wndclass.lpszClassName = szAppName ;

    if (!RegisterClass (&wndclass))
    {
        MessageBox (NULL, TEXT ("This program requires Windows NT!"),
                    szAppName, MB_ICONERROR) ;
        return 0 ;
    }

    hwnd = CreateWindow (szAppName, TEXT ("Bouncing Ball"),
                        WS_OVERLAPPEDWINDOW,
                        CW_USEDEFAULT, CW_USEDEFAULT,
                        CW_USEDEFAULT, CW_USEDEFAULT,
                        NULL, NULL, hInstance, NULL) ;

    ShowWindow (hwnd, iCmdShow) ;
    UpdateWindow (hwnd) ;
```

Figure 14-19. *The BOUNCE program.*

```
    while (GetMessage (&msg, NULL, 0, 0))
    {
        TranslateMessage (&msg) ;
        DispatchMessage (&msg) ;
    }
    return msg.wParam ;
}

LRESULT CALLBACK WndProc (HWND hwnd, UINT iMsg, WPARAM wParam, LPARAM lParam)
{
    static HBITMAP hBitmap ;
    static int     cxClient, cyClient, xCenter, yCenter, cxTotal, cyTotal,
                   cxRadius, cyRadius, cxMove, cyMove, xPixel, yPixel ;
    HBRUSH         hBrush ;
    HDC            hdc, hdcMem ;
    int            iScale ;

    switch (iMsg)
    {
    case WM_CREATE:
        hdc = GetDC (hwnd) ;
        xPixel = GetDeviceCaps (hdc, ASPECTX) ;
        yPixel = GetDeviceCaps (hdc, ASPECTY) ;
        ReleaseDC (hwnd, hdc) ;

        SetTimer (hwnd, ID_TIMER, 50, NULL) ;
        return 0 ;

    case WM_SIZE:
        xCenter = (cxClient = LOWORD (lParam)) / 2 ;
        yCenter = (cyClient = HIWORD (lParam)) / 2 ;

        iScale = min (cxClient * xPixel, cyClient * yPixel) / 16 ;

        cxRadius = iScale / xPixel ;
        cyRadius = iScale / yPixel ;

        cxMove = max (1, cxRadius / 2) ;
        cyMove = max (1, cyRadius / 2) ;

        cxTotal = 2 * (cxRadius + cxMove) ;
        cyTotal = 2 * (cyRadius + cyMove) ;

        if (hBitmap)
            DeleteObject (hBitmap) ;
```

(continued)

Figure 14-19. *continued*

```
        hdc = GetDC (hwnd) ;
        hdcMem = CreateCompatibleDC (hdc) ;
        hBitmap = CreateCompatibleBitmap (hdc, cxTotal, cyTotal) ;
        ReleaseDC (hwnd, hdc) ;

        SelectObject (hdcMem, hBitmap) ;
        Rectangle (hdcMem, -1, -1, cxTotal + 1, cyTotal + 1) ;

        hBrush = CreateHatchBrush (HS_DIAGCROSS, 0L) ;
        SelectObject (hdcMem, hBrush) ;
        SetBkColor (hdcMem, RGB (255, 0, 255)) ;
        Ellipse (hdcMem, cxMove, cyMove, cxTotal - cxMove, cyTotal - cyMove) ;
        DeleteDC (hdcMem) ;
        DeleteObject (hBrush) ;
        return 0 ;

case WM_TIMER:
        if (!hBitmap)
            break ;

        hdc = GetDC (hwnd) ;
        hdcMem = CreateCompatibleDC (hdc) ;
        SelectObject (hdcMem, hBitmap) ;

        BitBlt (hdc, xCenter - cxTotal / 2,
                    yCenter - cyTotal / 2, cxTotal, cyTotal,
                hdcMem, 0, 0, SRCCOPY) ;

        ReleaseDC (hwnd, hdc) ;
        DeleteDC (hdcMem) ;

        xCenter += cxMove ;
        yCenter += cyMove ;

        if ((xCenter + cxRadius >= cxClient) || (xCenter - cxRadius <= 0))
            cxMove = -cxMove ;

        if ((yCenter + cyRadius >= cyClient) || (yCenter - cyRadius <= 0))
            cyMove = -cyMove ;

        return 0 ;

case WM_DESTROY:
        if (hBitmap)
            DeleteObject (hBitmap) ;
```

```
        KillTimer (hwnd, ID_TIMER) ;
        PostQuitMessage (0) ;
        return 0 ;
     }
   return DefWindowProc (hwnd, iMsg, wParam, lParam) ;
}
```

BOUNCE reconstructs the ball whenever the program gets a WM_SIZE message. This requires a memory device context compatible with the video display:

```
hdcMem = CreateCompatibleDC (hdc) ;
```

The diameter of the ball is set at one-sixteenth of either the height or the width of the client area, whichever is shorter. However, the program constructs a bitmap that is larger than the ball: On each of its four sides, the bitmap extends beyond the ball's dimensions by one-half of the ball's radius:

```
hBitmap = CreateCompatibleBitmap (hdc, cxTotal, cyTotal) ;
```

After the bitmap is selected into a memory device context, the entire bitmap is colored white for the background:

```
Rectangle (hdcMem, -1, -1, xTotal + 1, yTotal + 1) ;
```

Those odd coordinates cause the rectangle boundary to be painted outside the bitmap. A diagonally hatched brush is selected into the memory device context, and the ball is drawn in the center of the bitmap:

```
Ellipse (hdcMem, xMove, yMove, xTotal - xMove, yTotal - yMove) ;
```

The margins around the edges of the ball effectively erase the previous image of the ball when the ball is moved. Redrawing the ball at another position requires only a simple *BitBlt* call using the ROP code of SRCCOPY:

```
BitBlt (hdc, xCenter - cxTotal / 2, yCenter - cyTotal / 2, cxTotal, cyTotal,
        hdcMem, 0, 0, SRCCOPY) ;
```

BOUNCE demonstrates the simplest way to move an image around the display, but this approach isn't satisfactory for general purposes. If you're interested in animation, you'll want to explore some of the other ROP codes (such as SRCINVERT) that perform an exclusive OR operation on the source and destination. Other techniques for animation involve the Windows palette (and the *AnimatePalette* function) and the *CreateDIBSection* function. For more sophisticated animation, you may need to abandon GDI and explore the DirectX interface.

Bitmaps Outside the Window

The SCRAMBLE program, shown in Figure 14-20 beginning on the following page, is very rude and I probably shouldn't be showing it to you. But it demonstrates some interesting techniques and uses a memory device context as a temporary holding space for *BitBlt* operations that swap the contents of pairs of display rectangles.

SCRAMBLE.C

```
/*-------------------------------------------------
   SCRAMBLE.C -- Scramble (and Unscramble) Screen
                   (c) Charles Petzold, 1998
   -------------------------------------------------*/

#include <windows.h>

#define NUM 300

LRESULT CALLBACK WndProc (HWND, UINT, WPARAM, LPARAM) ;

int WINAPI WinMain (HINSTANCE hInstance, HINSTANCE hPrevInstance,
                    PSTR szCmdLine, int iCmdShow)
{
     static int iKeep [NUM][4] ;
     HDC        hdcScr, hdcMem ;
     int        cx, cy ;
     HBITMAP    hBitmap ;
     HWND       hwnd ;
     int        i, j, x1, y1, x2, y2 ;

     if (LockWindowUpdate (hwnd = GetDesktopWindow ()))
     {
          hdcScr  = GetDCEx (hwnd, NULL, DCX_CACHE | DCX_LOCKWINDOWUPDATE) ;
          hdcMem  = CreateCompatibleDC (hdcScr) ;
          cx      = GetSystemMetrics (SM_CXSCREEN) / 10 ;
          cy      = GetSystemMetrics (SM_CYSCREEN) / 10 ;
          hBitmap = CreateCompatibleBitmap (hdcScr, cx, cy) ;

          SelectObject (hdcMem, hBitmap) ;

          srand ((int) GetCurrentTime ()) ;

          for (i = 0 ; i < 2   ; i++)
          for (j = 0 ; j < NUM ; j++)
          {
               if (i == 0)
               {
                    iKeep [j] [0] = x1 = cx * (rand () % 10) ;
                    iKeep [j] [1] = y1 = cy * (rand () % 10) ;
```

Figure 14-20. *The SCRAMBLE program.*

```
                iKeep [j] [2] = x2 = cx * (rand () % 10) ;
                iKeep [j] [3] = y2 = cy * (rand () % 10) ;
          }
          else
          {
                x1 = iKeep [NUM - 1 - j] [0] ;
                y1 = iKeep [NUM - 1 - j] [1] ;
                x2 = iKeep [NUM - 1 - j] [2] ;
                y2 = iKeep [NUM - 1 - j] [3] ;
          }
          BitBlt (hdcMem, 0, 0, cx, cy, hdcScr, x1, y1, SRCCOPY) ;
          BitBlt (hdcScr, x1, y1, cx, cy, hdcScr, x2, y2, SRCCOPY) ;
          BitBlt (hdcScr, x2, y2, cx, cy, hdcMem, 0, 0, SRCCOPY) ;

          Sleep (10) ;
     }

     DeleteDC (hdcMem) ;
     ReleaseDC (hwnd, hdcScr) ;
     DeleteObject (hBitmap) ;

     LockWindowUpdate (NULL) ;
  }
  return FALSE ;
}
```

SCRAMBLE doesn't have a window procedure. In *WinMain*, it first calls *LockWindow-Update* with the desktop window handle. This function temporarily prevents any other program from updating the screen. SCRAMBLE then obtains a device context for the entire screen by calling *GetDCEx* with a DCX_LOCKWINDOWUPDATE argument. This lets SCRAMBLE write on the screen when no other program can.

SCRAMBLE then determines the dimensions of the full screen and divides them by 10. The program uses these dimensions (named *cx* and *cy*) to create a bitmap and then selects the bitmap into the memory device context.

Using the C *rand* function, SCRAMBLE calculates four random values (two coordinate points) that are multiples of the *cx* and *cy* values. The program swaps two rectangular blocks of the display through the use of three *BitBlt* functions. The first copies the rectangle beginning at the first coordinate point to the memory device context. The second *BitBlt* copies the rectangle beginning at the second point to the location beginning at the first point. The third copies the rectangle in the memory device context to the area beginning at second coordinate point.

This process effectively swaps the contents of the two rectangles on the display. SCRAMBLE does this 300 times, after which the screen should be thoroughly scrambled. But do not fear, because SCRAMBLE keeps track of this mess and then unscrambles the screen, returning it to normal (and unlocking the screen) before exiting.

You can also use memory device contexts to copy the contents of one bitmap to another. For instance, suppose you want to create a bitmap that contains only the upper left quadrant of another bitmap. If the original bitmap has the handle *hBitmap*, you can copy the dimensions into a structure of type BITMAP,

```
GetObject (hBitmap, sizeof (BITMAP), &bm) ;
```

and create a new uninitialized bitmap of one-quarter the size:

```
hBitmap2 = CreateBitmap (bm.bmWidth / 2, bm.bmHeight / 2,
                         bm.bmPlanes, bm.bmBitsPixel, NULL) ;
```

Now create two memory device contexts and select the original bitmap and the new bitmap into them:

```
hdcMem1 = CreateCompatibleDC (hdc) ;
hdcMem2 = CreateCompatibleDC (hdc) ;

SelectObject (hdcMem1, hBitmap) ;
SelectObject (hdcMem2, hBitmap2) ;
```

Finally, copy the upper left quadrant of the first bitmap to the second:

```
BitBlt (hdcMem2, 0, 0, bm.bmWidth / 2, bm.bmHeight / 2,
        hdcMem1, 0, 0, SRCCOPY) ;
```

You're done, except for cleaning up:

```
DeleteDC (hdcMem1) ;
DeleteDC (hdcMem2) ;
DeleteObject (hBitmap) ;
```

The BLOWUP.C program, shown in Figure 14-21, also uses window update locking to display a capture rectangle outside the border of the program's window. This program lets you use the mouse to block out any rectangular area of the screen. BLOWUP then copies the contents of that rectangular area to a bitmap. During the WM_PAINT message, the bitmap is copied to the program's client area and stretched or compressed, if necessary. (See Figure 14-22 on page 721.)

BLOWUP.C

```
/*-------------------------------------------
   BLOWUP.C -- Video Magnifier Program
               (c) Charles Petzold, 1998
   -------------------------------------------*/

#include <windows.h>
#include <stdlib.h>        // for abs definition
#include "resource.h"
```

Figure 14-21. *The BLOWUP program.*

```
LRESULT CALLBACK WndProc (HWND, UINT, WPARAM, LPARAM) ;

int WINAPI WinMain (HINSTANCE hInstance, HINSTANCE hPrevInstance,
                    PSTR szCmdLine, int iCmdShow)
{
     static TCHAR szAppName [] = TEXT ("Blowup") ;
     HACCEL      hAccel ;
     HWND        hwnd ;
     MSG         msg ;
     WNDCLASS    wndclass ;

     wndclass.style         = CS_HREDRAW | CS_VREDRAW ;
     wndclass.lpfnWndProc   = WndProc ;
     wndclass.cbClsExtra    = 0 ;
     wndclass.cbWndExtra    = 0 ;
     wndclass.hInstance     = hInstance ;
     wndclass.hIcon         = LoadIcon (NULL, IDI_APPLICATION) ;
     wndclass.hCursor       = LoadCursor (NULL, IDC_ARROW) ;
     wndclass.hbrBackground = (HBRUSH) GetStockObject (WHITE_BRUSH) ;
     wndclass.lpszMenuName  = szAppName ;
     wndclass.lpszClassName = szAppName ;

     if (!RegisterClass (&wndclass))
     {
          MessageBox (NULL, TEXT ("This program requires Windows NT!"),
                      szAppName, MB_ICONERROR) ;
          return 0 ;
     }

     hwnd = CreateWindow (szAppName, TEXT ("Blow-Up Mouse Demo"),
                          WS_OVERLAPPEDWINDOW,
                          CW_USEDEFAULT, CW_USEDEFAULT,
                          CW_USEDEFAULT, CW_USEDEFAULT,
                          NULL, NULL, hInstance, NULL) ;

     ShowWindow (hwnd, iCmdShow) ;
     UpdateWindow (hwnd) ;

     hAccel = LoadAccelerators (hInstance, szAppName) ;

     while (GetMessage (&msg, NULL, 0, 0))
     {
          if (!TranslateAccelerator (hwnd, hAccel, &msg))
          {
               TranslateMessage (&msg) ;
```

(continued)

Figure 14-21. *continued*

```
            DispatchMessage (&msg) ;
        }
    }
    return msg.wParam ;
}

void InvertBlock (HWND hwndScr, HWND hwnd, POINT ptBeg, POINT ptEnd)
{
    HDC hdc ;

    hdc = GetDCEx (hwndScr, NULL, DCX_CACHE | DCX_LOCKWINDOWUPDATE) ;
    ClientToScreen (hwnd, &ptBeg) ;
    ClientToScreen (hwnd, &ptEnd) ;
    PatBlt (hdc, ptBeg.x, ptBeg.y, ptEnd.x - ptBeg.x, ptEnd.y - ptBeg.y,
            DSTINVERT) ;
    ReleaseDC (hwndScr, hdc) ;
}

HBITMAP CopyBitmap (HBITMAP hBitmapSrc)
{
    BITMAP  bitmap ;
    HBITMAP hBitmapDst ;
    HDC     hdcSrc, hdcDst ;

    GetObject (hBitmapSrc, sizeof (BITMAP), &bitmap) ;
    hBitmapDst = CreateBitmapIndirect (&bitmap) ;

    hdcSrc = CreateCompatibleDC (NULL) ;
    hdcDst = CreateCompatibleDC (NULL) ;

    SelectObject (hdcSrc, hBitmapSrc) ;
    SelectObject (hdcDst, hBitmapDst) ;

    BitBlt (hdcDst, 0, 0, bitmap.bmWidth, bitmap.bmHeight,
            hdcSrc, 0, 0, SRCCOPY) ;

    DeleteDC (hdcSrc) ;
    DeleteDC (hdcDst) ;

    return hBitmapDst ;
}

LRESULT CALLBACK WndProc (HWND hwnd, UINT message, WPARAM wParam, LPARAM lParam)
{
    static BOOL    bCapturing, bBlocking ;
    static HBITMAP hBitmap ;
```

```
static HWND     hwndScr ;
static POINT    ptBeg, ptEnd ;
BITMAP          bm ;
HBITMAP         hBitmapClip ;
HDC             hdc, hdcMem ;
int             iEnable ;
PAINTSTRUCT     ps ;
RECT            rect ;

switch (message)
{
case WM_LBUTTONDOWN:
     if (!bCapturing)
     {
          if (LockWindowUpdate (hwndScr = GetDesktopWindow ()))
          {
               bCapturing = TRUE ;
               SetCapture (hwnd) ;
               SetCursor (LoadCursor (NULL, IDC_CROSS)) ;
          }
          else
               MessageBeep (0) ;
     }
     return 0 ;

case WM_RBUTTONDOWN:
     if (bCapturing)
     {
          bBlocking = TRUE ;
          ptBeg.x = LOWORD (lParam) ;
          ptBeg.y = HIWORD (lParam) ;
          ptEnd = ptBeg ;
          InvertBlock (hwndScr, hwnd, ptBeg, ptEnd) ;
     }
     return 0 ;

case WM_MOUSEMOVE:
     if (bBlocking)
     {
          InvertBlock (hwndScr, hwnd, ptBeg, ptEnd) ;
          ptEnd.x = LOWORD (lParam) ;
          ptEnd.y = HIWORD (lParam) ;
          InvertBlock (hwndScr, hwnd, ptBeg, ptEnd) ;
     }
     return 0 ;

case WM_LBUTTONUP:
```

(continued)

Figure 14-21. *continued*

```
case WM_RBUTTONUP:
     if (bBlocking)
     {
          InvertBlock (hwndScr, hwnd, ptBeg, ptEnd) ;
          ptEnd.x = LOWORD (lParam) ;
          ptEnd.y = HIWORD (lParam) ;

          if (hBitmap)
          {
               DeleteObject (hBitmap) ;
               hBitmap = NULL ;
          }

          hdc = GetDC (hwnd) ;
          hdcMem = CreateCompatibleDC (hdc) ;
          hBitmap = CreateCompatibleBitmap (hdc,
                              abs (ptEnd.x - ptBeg.x),
                              abs (ptEnd.y - ptBeg.y)) ;

          SelectObject (hdcMem, hBitmap) ;

          StretchBlt (hdcMem, 0, 0, abs (ptEnd.x - ptBeg.x),
                                 abs (ptEnd.y - ptBeg.y),
                         hdc, ptBeg.x, ptBeg.y, ptEnd.x - ptBeg.x,
                                      ptEnd.y - ptBeg.y, SRCCOPY) ;

          DeleteDC (hdcMem) ;
          ReleaseDC (hwnd, hdc) ;
          InvalidateRect (hwnd, NULL, TRUE) ;
     }
     if (bBlocking || bCapturing)
     {
          bBlocking = bCapturing = FALSE ;
          SetCursor (LoadCursor (NULL, IDC_ARROW)) ;
          ReleaseCapture () ;
          LockWindowUpdate (NULL) ;
     }
     return 0 ;

case WM_INITMENUPOPUP:
     iEnable = IsClipboardFormatAvailable (CF_BITMAP) ?
                        MF_ENABLED : MF_GRAYED ;

     EnableMenuItem ((HMENU) wParam, IDM_EDIT_PASTE, iEnable) ;

     iEnable = hBitmap ? MF_ENABLED : MF_GRAYED ;
```

```
        EnableMenuItem ((HMENU) wParam, IDM_EDIT_CUT,    iEnable) ;
        EnableMenuItem ((HMENU) wParam, IDM_EDIT_COPY,   iEnable) ;
        EnableMenuItem ((HMENU) wParam, IDM_EDIT_DELETE, iEnable) ;
        return 0 ;

case WM_COMMAND:
     switch (LOWORD (wParam))
     {
     case IDM_EDIT_CUT:
     case IDM_EDIT_COPY:
          if (hBitmap)
          {
               hBitmapClip = CopyBitmap (hBitmap) ;
               OpenClipboard (hwnd) ;
               EmptyClipboard () ;
               SetClipboardData (CF_BITMAP, hBitmapClip) ;
          }
          if (LOWORD (wParam) == IDM_EDIT_COPY)
               return 0 ;
                                    // fall through for IDM_EDIT_CUT
     case IDM_EDIT_DELETE:
          if (hBitmap)
          {
               DeleteObject (hBitmap) ;
               hBitmap = NULL ;
          }
          InvalidateRect (hwnd, NULL, TRUE) ;
          return 0 ;

     case IDM_EDIT_PASTE:
          if (hBitmap)
          {
               DeleteObject (hBitmap) ;
               hBitmap = NULL ;
          }
          OpenClipboard (hwnd) ;
          hBitmapClip = GetClipboardData (CF_BITMAP) ;

          if (hBitmapClip)
               hBitmap = CopyBitmap (hBitmapClip) ;

          CloseClipboard () ;
          InvalidateRect (hwnd, NULL, TRUE) ;
          return 0 ;
     }
     break ;
```

(continued)

Figure 14-21. *continued*

```
    case WM_PAINT:
        hdc = BeginPaint (hwnd, &ps) ;

        if (hBitmap)
        {
            GetClientRect (hwnd, &rect) ;

            hdcMem = CreateCompatibleDC (hdc) ;
            SelectObject (hdcMem, hBitmap) ;
            GetObject (hBitmap, sizeof (BITMAP), (PSTR) &bm) ;
            SetStretchBltMode (hdc, COLORONCOLOR) ;

            StretchBlt (hdc,    0, 0, rect.right, rect.bottom,
                        hdcMem, 0, 0, bm.bmWidth, bm.bmHeight, SRCCOPY) ;

            DeleteDC (hdcMem) ;
        }
        EndPaint (hwnd, &ps) ;
        return 0 ;

    case WM_DESTROY:
        if (hBitmap)
            DeleteObject (hBitmap) ;

        PostQuitMessage (0) ;
        return 0 ;
    }
    return DefWindowProc (hwnd, message, wParam, lParam) ;
}
```

BLOWUP.RC (excerpts)

```
//Microsoft Developer Studio generated resource script.

#include "resource.h"
#include "afxres.h"

/////////////////////////////////////////////////////////////////////////////
// Menu

BLOWUP MENU DISCARDABLE
BEGIN
    POPUP "&Edit"
    BEGIN
        MENUITEM "Cu&t\tCtrl+X",                 IDM_EDIT_CUT
        MENUITEM "&Copy\tCtrl+C",                IDM_EDIT_COPY
```

```
        MENUITEM "&Paste\tCtrl+V",              IDM_EDIT_PASTE
        MENUITEM "De&lete\tDelete",             IDM_EDIT_DELETE
    END
END



//////////////////////////////////////////////////////////////////////
// Accelerator

BLOWUP ACCELERATORS DISCARDABLE
BEGIN
    "C",            IDM_EDIT_COPY,          VIRTKEY, CONTROL, NOINVERT
    "V",            IDM_EDIT_PASTE,         VIRTKEY, CONTROL, NOINVERT
    VK_DELETE,      IDM_EDIT_DELETE,        VIRTKEY, NOINVERT
    "X",            IDM_EDIT_CUT,           VIRTKEY, CONTROL, NOINVERT
END
```

RESOURCE.H (excerpts)

```
// Microsoft Developer Studio generated include file.
// Used by Blowup.rc

#define IDM_EDIT_CUT                40001
#define IDM_EDIT_COPY               40002
#define IDM_EDIT_PASTE              40003
#define IDM_EDIT_DELETE             40004
```

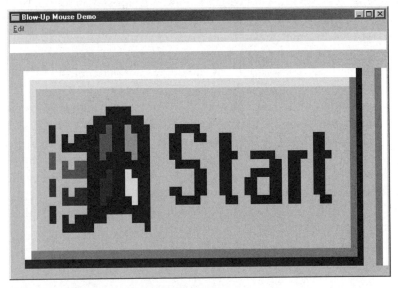

Figure 14-22. *A sample BLOWUP display.*

Because of restrictions on mouse capturing, using BLOWUP is a little complicated at first and takes some getting used to. Here's how to use the program:

1. Press the left mouse button in BLOWUP's client area, and keep the left button held down. The mouse cursor changes to a crosshair.

2. Still holding the left button down, move the mouse cursor anywhere on the screen. Position the mouse cursor at the upper left corner of the rectangular area you want to capture.

3. Still holding the left button down, press the right mouse button and drag the mouse to the lower right corner of the rectangular area you want to capture. Release the left and right mouse buttons. (The order in which you release the buttons doesn't matter.)

The mouse cursor changes back to an arrow, and the area that you blocked out is copied to BLOWUP's client area and compressed or expanded appropriately.

If you block out a rectangle by moving from the upper right corner to the lower left corner, BLOWUP displays a mirror image. If you move from the lower left to the upper right, BLOWUP displays an upside-down image. And if you move from the upper right to the upper left, the program combines the two effects.

BLOWUP also contains logic to copy the bitmap to the clipboard, and to copy any bitmap in the clipboard to the program. BLOWUP processes the WM_INITMENUPOPUP message to enable or disable the various items on its Edit menu and the WM_COMMAND message to process these menu items. The structure of this code should look familiar because it is essentially the same as that shown in Chapter 12 to copy and paste text items.

For bitmaps, however, the clipboard items are not global handles but bitmap handles. When you use the CF_BITMAP, the *GetClipboardData* function returns an HBITMAP object and the *SetClipboardData* function accepts an HBITMAP object. If you want to transfer a bitmap to the clipboard but still have a copy of it for use by the program itself, you must make a copy of the bitmap. Similarly, if you paste a bitmap from the clipboard, you should also make a copy. The *CopyBitmap* function in BLOWUP does this by obtaining a BITMAP structure of the existing bitmap and using this structure in the *CreateBitmapIndirect* function to create a new bitmap. (The *Src* and *Dst* suffixes on the variable names stand for "source" and "destination.") Both bitmaps are selected into memory device contexts and the bitmap bits transferred with a call to *BitBlt*. (Alternatively, to copy the bits, you can allocate a block of memory the size of the bitmap and call *GetBitmapBits* for the source bitmap and *SetBitmapBits* for the destination bitmap.)

I find BLOWUP to be very useful for examining the multitude of little bitmaps and pictures that are scattered throughout Windows and its applications.

Chapter 15

The Device-Independent Bitmap

In the last chapter, we saw how the Windows GDI bitmap object (also known as the device-*dependent* bitmap, or DDB) is useful for a variety of programming chores. However, I did not demonstrate how to save these bitmaps to disk files or load them back into memory. This is something that was done back in the old days of Windows but is never done today. The DDB is inadequate for the purpose of image interchange because the format of the bitmap bits is highly device-dependent. There is no color table in a DDB that specifies a correspondence between the bitmap bits and color. The DDB makes sense only when it is created and destroyed within the lifetime of a Windows session.

The device-independent bitmap (or DIB) was introduced in Windows 3.0 to provide a sorely needed image file format suitable for interchange. As you may know, other image file formats, such as .GIF or .JPEG, are much more common than DIB files on the Internet. This is mostly because the .GIF and .JPEG formats implement compression schemes that significantly reduce downloading time. Although there is a compression scheme defined for DIBs, it is rarely used. The bitmap bits in most DIBs are almost always uncompressed. This is actually a major advantage if you want to manipulate the bitmap bits in your program. Unlike .GIF and .JPEG files, the DIB is directly supported by the Windows API. If you have a DIB in memory, you can supply pointers to that DIB as arguments to several functions that let you display the DIB or convert it into a DDB.

THE DIB FILE FORMAT

Interestingly enough, the DIB format did not originate in Windows. It was first defined in version 1.1 of OS/2, the operating system originally developed by IBM and Microsoft beginning in the mid-1980s. OS/2 1.1 was released in 1988 and was the first version of OS/2 to include a Windows-like graphical user interface, known as the Presentation Manager (PM). The Presentation Manager included the Graphics Programming Interface (GPI), which defined the bitmap format.

That OS/2 bitmap format was then used in Windows 3.0 (released in 1990), where it came to be known as the DIB. Windows 3.0 also included a variation of the original DIB format that under Windows has come to be the standard. Additional enhancements were defined in Windows 95 (and Windows NT 4.0) and Windows 98 (and Windows NT 5.0), as I'll discuss in this chapter.

The DIB is best examined first as a file format. DIB files have the filename extension .BMP or, more rarely, .DIB. Bitmap images used by Windows applications (for example, on the surfaces of buttons) are created as DIB files and generally stored as read-only resources in the program's executable file. Icons and mouse cursors are also DIB files in a slightly different form.

A program can load a DIB file, minus the first 14 bytes, into a contiguous block of memory. It is then sometimes referred to as "a bitmap in the *packed-DIB* format." Applications running under Windows can use the packed-DIB format for exchanging images through the Windows clipboard or for creating brushes. Programs also have complete access to the contents of the DIB and can modify the DIB in whatever way they choose.

Programs can also create their own DIBs in memory and later save them in files. The images in these DIBs can be "painted" by a program using GDI function calls. Or the program can set and manipulate the pixel bits directly, perhaps using other memory-based DIBs in the process.

When a DIB is loaded into memory, programs can also use the DIB data with several Windows API function calls that I'll discuss in this chapter. The DIB-related API calls are few in number and are mainly concerned with displaying display DIBs on the video display or a printer page and with converting them to and from GDI bitmap objects.

When all is said and done, however, there remain many, many, many DIB tasks that application programs might need to perform for which there is no support in the Windows operating system. For example, a program might have access to a 24-bit DIB and might wish to convert it into an 8-bit DIB with an optimal 256-color palette. Windows will not do this for you. But this chapter and the next will show you how to work with DIBs beyond what the Windows API provides.

The OS/2-Style DIB

So that we don't get bogged down in too many details just yet, let's take a look at the format of the Windows DIB that is compatible with the bitmap format first introduced in OS/2 1.1.

A DIB file has four main sections:

- A file header
- An information header
- An RGB color table (but not always)
- The bitmap pixel bits

You can think of the first two parts as C data structures and the third part as an array of data structures. These structures are documented in the Windows header file WINGDI.H. A memory-based DIB in the packed-DIB format has three sections:

- An information header
- An RGB color table (but not always)
- The bitmap pixel bits

It's exactly the same as a DIB stored in a file except that it doesn't have the file header.

The DIB file, but not the memory-based packed DIB, begins with a 14-byte file header defined as a structure like so:

```
typedef struct tagBITMAPFILEHEADER  // bmfh
{
    WORD  bfType ;        // signature word "BM" or 0x4D42
    DWORD bfSize ;        // entire size of file
    WORD  bfReserved1 ;   // must be zero
    WORD  bfReserved2 ;   // must be zero
    DWORD bfOffsetBits ;  // offset in file of DIB pixel bits
}
BITMAPFILEHEADER, * PBITMAPFILEHEADER ;
```

This may not be exactly the way the structure is defined in WINGDI.H (for example, the comments are mine), but it is functionally the same. The first comment (that is, the text "bmfh") shows the recommended abbreviation when naming a structure variable of this data type. If you see a variable in one of my programs named *pbmfh*, that will be a pointer to a structure of type BITMAPFILEHEADER or a variable of type PBITMAPFILEHEADER.

The structure is 14 bytes in length. It begins with the two letters "BM" to indicate a bitmap file. This is the WORD value 0x4D42. The "BM" indicator is followed by a DWORD indicating the entire size of the file, including the file header, in bytes. The next two WORD fields are set to zero. (In a mouse cursor file, which is similar in format to a DIB file, these two fields are used to indicate the "hot spot" of the cursor.) The structure concludes with a DWORD indicating the byte offset within the file where the pixel bits begin. This number can be derived from information in the DIB information header, but it is provided here for convenience.

In the OS/2-style DIB, the BITMAPFILEHEADER structure is followed immediately by a BITMAPCOREHEADER structure, which provides the basic information about the DIB image. A packed DIB begins with the BITMAPCOREHEADER:

```
typedef struct tagBITMAPCOREHEADER  // bmch
{
    DWORD bcSize ;        // size of the structure = 12
    WORD  bcWidth ;       // width of image in pixels
    WORD  bcHeight ;      // height of image in pixels
    WORD  bcPlanes ;      // = 1
    WORD  bcBitCount ;    // bits per pixel (1, 4, 8, or 24)
}
BITMAPCOREHEADER, * PBITMAPCOREHEADER ;
```

The word "core" sounds a little odd in this context, and it is. It means that this format is the basis (thus the core) of other bitmap formats derived from it.

The *bcSize* field in the BITMAPCOREHEADER structure indicates the size of the data structure, in this case 12 bytes.

The *bcWidth* and *bcHeight* fields contain the size of the bitmap in pixels. Although the use of a WORD for these fields implies that a DIB may be 65,535 pixels high and wide, you'll rarely encounter anything quite that large.

The *bcPlanes* field is always 1. Always, always, always—from the time it was defined until this very second. The field is a remnant of the earlier Windows GDI bitmap object that we encountered in the last chapter.

The *bcBitCount* field indicates the number of bits per pixel. For OS/2-style DIBs, this can be either 1, 4, 8, or 24. The number of colors in the DIB image is equal to $2^{bmch.bcBitCount}$ or, in C syntax, to

```
1 << bmch.bcBitCount
```

Thus, the *bcBitCount* field is equal to:

- 1 for a 2-color DIB

- 4 for a 16-color DIB

- 8 for a 256-color DIB

- 24 for a full-color DIB

When I refer to "an 8-bit DIB," I'll mean a DIB that has 8 bits per pixel.

For the first three cases (that is, for bit counts of 1, 4, and 8), the BITMAPCORE-HEADER is followed by the color table. The color table does not exist for 24-bit DIBs. The color table is an array of 3-byte RGBTRIPLE structures, one for each color in the image:

```
typedef struct tagRGBTRIPLE  // rgbt
{
    BYTE rgbtBlue ;    // blue level
    BYTE rgbtGreen ;   // green level
    BYTE rgbtRed ;     // red level
}
RGBTRIPLE ;
```

It is recommended that the color table be arranged so that the most important colors in the DIB appear first. We'll see why in the next chapter.

The WINGDI.H header file also defines the following structure:

```
typedef struct tagBITMAPCOREINFO  // bmci
{
    BITMAPCOREHEADER bmciHeader ;     // core-header structure
    RGBTRIPLE        bmciColors[1] ;  // color table array
}
BITMAPCOREINFO, * PBITMAPCOREINFO ;
```

This structure combines the information header with the color table. Although the number of RGBTRIPLE structures is seemingly equal to 1 in this structure, you'll never find just one RGBTRIPLE in a DIB file. The size of the color table is always 2, 16, or 256 RGBTRIPLE structures, depending on the number of bits per pixel. If you need to allocate a structure of PBITMAPCOREINFO for an 8-bit DIB, you can do it like so:

```
pbmci = malloc (sizeof (BITMAPCOREINFO) + 255 * sizeof (RGBTRIPLE)) ;
```

Then you can access whatever RGBTRIPLE structure you need like so:

```
pbmci->bmciColors[i]
```

Because the RGBTRIPLE structure is 3 bytes in length, some of the RGBTRIPLE structures might begin at odd addresses within the DIB. However, because there are always an even number of RGBTRIPLE structures in the DIB file, the data block that follows the color table array always begins at a WORD address boundary.

The data that follow the color table (and what follows the information header for DIBs with a bit count of 24) are the pixel bits themselves.

Bottoms Up!

Like most bitmap formats, the pixel bits in the DIB are organized in horizontal rows, sometimes also called "scan lines" from the terminology of video display hardware. The number of rows is equal to the *bcHeight* field of the BITMAPCOREHEADER structure. However, unlike most bitmap formats, the DIB begins with the bottom row of the image and proceeds up through the image.

Let's establish some terminology here. When I say "top row" and "bottom row," I mean the top and bottom of the visual image as it appears when correctly displayed on the monitor or printer page. The top row of a portrait is hair; the bottom row of a portrait is chin. When I say "first row," I mean the row of pixels that is found directly after the color table in the DIB file. And when I say "last row," I mean the row of pixels at the very end of the file.

So, in DIBs, the bottom row of the image is the first row of the file, and the top row of the image is the last row in the file. This is called a bottom-up organization. Because this organization is counterintuitive, you may ask why it's done this way.

Well, it all goes back to the OS/2 Presentation Manager. Someone at IBM decided that all coordinate systems in PM—including those for windows, graphics, and bitmaps—should be consistent. This provoked a debate: Most people, including programmers who have worked with full-screen text programming or windowing environments, think in terms of vertical coordinates that increase going down the screen. However, hardcore computer graphics programmers approach the video display from a perspective that originates in the mathematics of analytic geometry. This involves a rectangular (or Cartesian) coordinate system where increasing vertical coordinates go up in space.

In short, the mathematicians won. Everything in PM was saddled with a bottom-left origin, including window coordinates. And that's how DIBs came to be this way.

The DIB Pixel Bits

The last section of the DIB file—in most cases the great bulk of the DIB file—consists of the actual DIB pixel bits. The pixel bits are organized in horizontal rows beginning with the bottom row of the image and proceeding up through the image.

The number of rows in a DIB is equal to the *bcHeight* field of the BITMAPCORE-HEADER structure. Each row encodes a number of pixels equal to the *bcWidth* field of the structure. Each row begins with the leftmost pixels and proceeds to the right of the image. The number of bits per pixel is obtained from the *bcBitCount* field, which is either 1, 4, 8, or 24.

The length of each row in bytes is always a multiple of 4. The row length can be calculated like so:

```
RowLength = 4 * ((bmch.bcWidth * bmch.bcBitCount + 31) / 32) ;
```

Or, slightly more efficiently in C, like this:

```
RowLength = ((bmch.bcWidth * bmch.bcBitCount + 31) & ~31) >> 3 ;
```

The row is padded at the right (customarily with zeros), if necessary, to achieve this length. The total number of bytes of pixel data is equal to the product of *RowLength* and *bmch.bcHeight*.

To see how the pixels are encoded, let's examine the four cases separately. In the diagrams shown below, the bits of each byte are shown in boxes and are numbered with 7 indicating the most-significant bit and 0 indicating the least-significant bit. Pixels are also numbered beginning with 0 for the leftmost pixel in the row.

For DIBs with 1 bit per pixel, each byte corresponds to 8 pixels. The leftmost pixel is the most-significant bit of the first byte:

Pixel: 0 1 2 3 4 5 6 7   8 9 10 11 12 13 14 15   16 17 18 19 20 21 22 23
       7 6 5 4 3 2 1 0   7 6 5 4 3 2 1 0   7 6 5 4 3 2 1 0

Each pixel can be either a 0 or a 1. A 0 bit means that the color of that pixel is given by the first RGBTRIPLE entry in the color table. A 1 bit is a pixel whose color is the second entry of the color table.

For DIBs with 4 bits per pixel, each byte corresponds to 2 pixels. The leftmost pixel is the high 4 bits of the first byte, and so on:

Pixel: — 0 —   — 1 —   — 2 —   — 3 —   — 4 —   — 5 —
         7 6 5 4 3 2 1 0   7 6 5 4 3 2 1 0   7 6 5 4 3 2 1 0

The value of each 4-bit pixel ranges from 0 to 15. This value is an index into the 16 entries in the color table.

For a DIB with 8 bits per pixel, each byte is 1 pixel:

Pixel: — 0 —   — 1 —   — 2 —
         7 6 5 4 3 2 1 0   7 6 5 4 3 2 1 0   7 6 5 4 3 2 1 0

The value of the byte is 0 through 255. Again, this is an index into the 256 entries in the color table.

For DIBs with 24 bits-per-pixel, each pixel requires 3 bytes for the red, green, and blue color values. Each row of pixel bits is basically an array of RGBTRIPLE structures, possibly padded with 0 bytes at the end of each row so that the row has a multiple of 4 bytes:

Pixel: — Blue —   — Green —   — Red —
         7 6 5 4 3 2 1 0   7 6 5 4 3 2 1 0   7 6 5 4 3 2 1 0

Again, the 24-bit-per-pixel DIB has no color table.

The Expanded Windows DIB

Now that we've mastered the OS/2-compatible DIB introduced in Windows 3.0, we can take a look at the expanded version of the DIB introduced in Windows at the same time.

This form of the DIB begins with a BITMAPFILEHEADER structure just like the earlier format but then continues with a BITMAPINFOHEADER structure rather than a BITMAP-COREHEADER structure:

```
typedef struct tagBITMAPINFOHEADER  // bmih
{
    DWORD biSize ;              // size of the structure = 40
    LONG  biWidth ;            // width of the image in pixels
    LONG  biHeight ;          // height of the image in pixels
    WORD  biPlanes ;          // = 1
    WORD  biBitCount ;        // bits per pixel (1, 4, 8, 16, 24, or 32)
    DWORD biCompression ;     // compression code
    DWORD biSizeImage ;       // number of bytes in image
    LONG  biXPelsPerMeter ;   // horizontal resolution
    LONG  biYPelsPerMeter ;   // vertical resolution
    DWORD biClrUsed ;         // number of colors used
    DWORD biClrImportant ;    // number of important colors
}
BITMAPINFOHEADER, * PBITMAPINFOHEADER ;
```

You can distinguish an OS/2-compatible DIB from a Windows DIB by checking the first field of the structure, which is 12 in the former case and 40 in the latter case.

As you'll note, there are six additional fields in this structure, but the BITMAPINFO-HEADER structure is not simply a BITMAPCOREHEADER with some new stuff tacked on to the end. Take a closer look: In the BITMAPCOREHEADER structure, the *bcWidth* and *bcHeight* fields are 16-bit WORD values. In this structure, they are 32-bit LONG values. This is an annoying little change that is guaranteed to drive you nuts.

Another change: For 1-bit, 4-bit, and 8-bit DIBs using the BITMAPINFOHEADER structure, the color table is not an array of RGBTRIPLE structures. Instead, the BITMAPINFO-HEADER structure is followed by an array of RGBQUAD structures:

```
typedef struct tagRGBQUAD  // rgb
{
    BYTE rgbBlue ;        // blue level
    BYTE rgbGreen ;       // green level
    BYTE rgbRed ;         // red level
    BYTE rgbReserved ;    // = 0
}
RGBQUAD ;
```

This is the same as the RGBTRIPLE structure except that it includes a fourth field that is always set to 0. The WINGDI.H header file also defines the following structure:

```
typedef struct tagBITMAPINFO  // bmi
{
     BITMAPINFOHEADER bmiHeader ;        // info-header structure
     RGBQUAD          bmiColors[1] ;    // color table array
}
BITMAPINFO, * PBITMAPINFO ;
```

Note that if the BITMAPINFO structure begins at a 32-bit address boundary, each entry in the RGBQUAD array also begins at a 32-bit address boundary because the BITMAPINFO-HEADER structure is 40 bytes in length. This assures more efficient addressing of the color table data by 32-bit microprocessors.

Although the BITMAPINFOHEADER was originally defined for Windows 3.0, some of the fields were redefined in Windows 95 and Windows NT 4.0, and these have been carried over into Windows 98 and Windows NT 5.0. For example, the current documentation states: "If *biHeight* is negative, the bitmap is a top-down DIB and its origin is the upper left corner." That's good to know. It would be even better if somebody had made this decision in 1990 when this DIB format was originally defined. My advice is to avoid creating top-down DIBs. You're almost begging that some program written without awareness of this new "feature" will crash upon encountering a negative *biHeight* field. Or that programs such as the Microsoft Photo Editor included with Microsoft Word 97 will report "Illegal image height" upon encountering a top-down DIB (although Word 97 itself does fine with them).

The *biPlanes* field is still always 1, but the *biBitCount* field can now be 16 or 32 as well as 1, 4, 8, or 24. This was also a new feature in Windows 95 and Windows NT 4.0. I'll discuss how these additional formats work shortly.

Let me skip the *biCompression* and *biSizeImage* fields for now. I'll also discuss them shortly.

The *biXPelsPerMeter* and *biYPelsPerMeter* fields indicate a suggested real-world size of the image in the ungainly units of pixels per meter. (The "pel"—picture element—is what IBM liked to call the pixel.) Internally, Windows does not use this information. However, an application could use it to display a DIB in an accurate size. These fields are also useful if the DIB originated from a device that does not have square pixels. In most DIBs, these fields are set to 0, which indicates no suggested real-world size. A resolution of 72 dots per inch (which is sometimes used for video displays, although the actual resolution depends on the size of the monitor) is approximately equivalent to 2,835 pixels per meter, and a common printer resolution of 300 DPI is 11,811 pixels per meter.

The *biClrUsed* field is a very important field because it affects the number of entries in the color table. For 4-bit and 8-bit DIBs, it can indicate that the color table contains fewer than 16 or 256 entries, respectively. This is one method to shrink down the size of the DIB, although not by very much. For example, suppose a DIB image contains only 64 gray shades. The *biClrUsed* field is set to 64, and the color table contains 64 RGBQUAD structures for a total color table size of 256 bytes. The pixel values then range from 0x00 through 0x3F. The DIB still requires 1 byte per pixel, but the high 2 bits of each pixel byte are zero. If the *biClrUsed* field is set to 0, it means that the color table contains the full number of entries implied by the *biBitCount* field.

Beginning with Windows 95, the *biClrUsed* field can be nonzero for 16-bit, 24-bit, or 32-bit DIBs. In these cases, the color table is not used by Windows to interpret the pixel bits. Instead, it indicates the size of a color table in the DIB that could be used by programs to set a palette to display the DIB on 256-color video displays. You'll recall that in the OS/2-compatible format, a 24-bit DIB had no color table. This was also true of the extended format introduced in Windows 3.0. The change in Windows 95 means that a 24-bit DIB can have a color table the size of which is indicated by the *biClrUsed* field.

To summarize:

■   For 1-bit DIBs, *biClrUsed* is always 0 or 2. The color table always has 2 entries.

■   For 4-bit DIBs, if the *biClrUsed* field is 0 or 16, the color table has 16 entries. If it's a number from 2 through 15, it indicates the number of entries in the color table. The maximum value of each pixel is 1 less than this number.

■   For 8-bit DIBs, if the *biClrUsed* field is 0 or 256, the color table has 256 entries. If it's a number from 2 through 255, it indicates the number of entries in the color table. The maximum value of each pixel is 1 less than this number.

■   For 16-bit, 24-bit, and 32-bit DIBs, the *biClrUsed* field is usually 0. If it's not 0, it indicates the number of entries in the color table. These entries could be used by an application running with a 256-color video adapter to set a palette for the DIB.

Another warning: Programs originally written using the earlier DIB documentation do not expect to see a color table in 24-bit DIBs. You put one in at your own risk.

Despite its name, the *biClrImportant* field is actually much less important than the *biClrUsed* field. It's usually set to 0 to indicate that all colors in the color table are important, or it could be set to the same value as *biClrUsed*. Both mean the same thing. If it's set somewhere in between 0 and *biClrUsed*, it means that the DIB image can be reasonably rendered using only the first *biClrImportant* entries in the color table. This could be useful when displaying two or more 8-bit DIBs side by side on a 256-color video adapter.

For 1-bit, 4-bit, 8-bit, and 24-bit DIBs, the organization of the pixel bits is the same as in the OS/2-compatible DIB. I'll discuss the 16-bit and 32-bit DIBs shortly.

Reality Check

What can you expect to find when you encounter a DIB that was created by some other program or person?

Although OS/2-style DIBs were common when Windows 3.0 was first released, they have become quite scarce in recent years. Some programmers writing quickie DIB routines virtually ignore them. Any 4-bit DIBs you'll encounter will probably have been created in the Windows Paint program using a 16-color video display. The color table will have the standard 16 colors on these displays.

Probably the most common DIBs you'll find will have a bit count of 8. The 8-bit DIBs will fall into two categories: gray-shade DIBs and palletized color DIBs. Unfortunately, nothing in the header indicates what type of 8-bit DIB you're dealing with.

Some gray-shade DIBs will have a *biClrUsed* field equal to 64, indicating 64 entries in the color table. These entries will usually be in order of ascending levels of gray. That is, the color table will begin with RGB values of 00-00-00, 04-04-04, 08-08-08, 0C-0C-0C, and conclude with RGB values of F0-F0-F0, F4-F4-F4, F8-F8-F8, and FC-FC-FC. Such a color table is calculated using a formula something like

```
rgb[i].rgbRed = rgb[i].rgbGreen = rgb[i].rgbBlue = i * 256 / 64 ;
```

where *rgb* is an array of RGBQUAD structures and *i* ranges from 0 through 63. Or the gray-shade color table will have been calculated with a formula that looks like

```
rgb[i].rgbRed = rgb[i].rgbGreen = rgb[i].rgbBlue = i * 255 / 63 ;
```

so that the table ends with FF-FF-FF.

It really doesn't matter which formula is used. Many video display adapters and monitors don't have a color precision greater than 6 bits anyway. The first formula recognizes that fact; the second formula, however, is more appropriate when generating fewer than 64 gray shades, perhaps 16 or 32 (in which case the divisor at the end of the formula is 15 or 31, respectively), because it ensures that the last entry in the color table is FF-FF-FF, which is white.

While some 8-bit gray-shade DIBs have 64 entries in the color table, other gray-shade DIBs have 256 entries. The *biClrUsed* field can actually be 0 (indicating 256 entries in the color table) or anything from 2 through 256. Of course, it doesn't make much sense to have a *biClrUsed* value of 2 (because such an 8-bit DIB could be re-coded as a 1-bit DIB) or a value less than or equal to 16 (because that could be re-coded as a 4-bit DIB), but it could be done. Whatever the case, the number of entries in the color table must be the same as the *biClrUsed* field (or 256 if *biClrUsed* is 0), and the pixel values cannot exceed the number of color table entries minus 1. That's because the pixel values are indices into the color table array. For 8-bit DIBs with a *biClrUsed* value of 64, the pixel values range from 0x00 to 0x3F.

Here's the important thing to remember: When an 8-bit DIB has a color table consisting entirely of gray shades (that is, when the red, green, and blue levels are equal), and when these gray-shade levels uniformly increase in the color table (as I described above), then the pixel values themselves represent proportional levels of gray. That is, if *biClrUsed* is 64, then a pixel value of 0x00 is black, a pixel value of 0x20 is 50 percent gray, and a pixel value of 0x3F is white.

This can be important for some image-processing tasks because you can ignore the color table entirely and deal solely with the pixel values. This is so useful that if I were allowed to go back in time and make a single change to the BITMAPINFOHEADER structure, I'd add a flag to indicate that the DIB image is gray-shaded, the DIB has no color table, and the pixel values directly indicate the gray level.

Palletized 8-bit color DIBs will generally use the whole color table and thus have a *biClrUsed* field of 0 or 256. However, you'll also encounter some that have a smaller number of colors—for example, 236. This is in recognition of the fact that programs usually can change only 236 entries in the Windows color palette to display these DIBs accurately, as I'll discuss in the next chapter.

Encountering nonzero values of *biXPelsPerMeter* and *biYPelsPerMeter* will be rare. Also rare will be encountering a *biClrImportant* field that is something other than 0 or the value of *biClrUsed*.

DIB Compression

Earlier I delayed discussion of the *biCompression* and *biSizeImage* fields in the BITMAP-INFOHEADER. Now's the time to examine these values.

The *biCompression* field can be one of four constants—BI_RGB, BI_RLE8, BI_RLE4, or BI_BITFIELDS—defined in the WINGDI.H header file as the values 0 through 3, respectively. This field serves two purposes: For 4-bit and 8-bit DIBs, it indicates that the pixel bits have been compressed using a type of run-length encoding. For 16-bit and 32-bit DIBs, it indicates whether color masking has been used to encode the pixel bits. This second feature was introduced in Windows 95.

Let's examine the RLE compression first:

■ For 1-bit DIBs, the *biCompression* field is always BI_RGB.

■ For 4-bit DIBs, the *biCompression* field can be either BI_RGB or BI_RLE4.

■ For 8-bit DIBs, the *biCompression* field can be either BI_RGB or BI_RLE8.

■ For 24-bit DIBs, the *biCompression* field is always BI_RGB.

If the value is BI_RGB, the pixel bits are stored as described for OS/2-compatible DIBs. Otherwise, the pixel bits are compressed using run-length encoding.

Run-length encoding (RLE) is one of the simplest forms of data compression. It is based on the knowledge that DIB images often have strings of identical pixels in a row. RLE saves space by encoding the value of the repeating pixel and the number of times it is repeated. The RLE scheme used for DIBs goes somewhat beyond this in allowing a sparse definition of the rectangular DIB image. That is, some areas of the rectangle are left undefined. This could be used for rendering nonrectangular images.

Run-length encoding is conceptually simpler with 8-bit DIBs, so let's begin with those. The following chart will help you in understanding how the pixel bits are encoded when the *biCompression* field equals BI_RGB8.

Byte 1	*Byte 2*	*Byte 3*	*Byte 4*	*Meaning*
00	00			End of row
00	01			End of image
00	02	*dx*	*dy*	Move to (*x+dx, y+dy*)
00	*n* = 03 through FF			Use next *n* pixels
n = 01 through FF	pixel			Repeat pixel *n* times

When decoding a compressed DIB, look at the DIB data bytes in pairs, as indicated by the "Byte 1" and "Byte 2" headings in this table. The table is arranged in increasing values of these bytes, but it makes more sense to discuss the table from the bottom up.

If the first byte is nonzero (the case shown in the last row of the table), then that's a run-length repetition factor. The following pixel value is repeated that many times. For example, the byte pair

```
0x05 0x27
```

decodes to the pixel values:

```
0x27 0x27 0x27 0x27 0x27
```

The DIB will, of course, have much data that does not repeat from pixel to pixel. That's the case handled by the second-to-last row of the table. It indicates a number of pixels that follow that should be used literally. For example, consider the sequence

```
0x00 0x06 0x45 0x32 0x77 0x34 0x59 0x90
```

It decodes to the pixel values

```
0x45 0x32 0x77 0x34 0x59 0x90
```

These sequences are always aligned on 2-byte boundaries. If the second byte is odd, then there's an extra byte in the sequence that is unused. For example, the sequence

```
0x00 0x05 0x45 0x32 0x77 0x34 0x59 0x00
```

decodes to the pixel values

```
0x45 0x32 0x77 0x34 0x59
```

That's how the run-length encoding works. As is obvious, if there are no repeating pixels in the DIB image, then using this compression technique will actually increase the size of the DIB file.

The first three rows of the table shown on the previous page indicate how some parts of the rectangular DIB image can be left undefined. Imagine yourself, or a program you wrote, decompressing a compressed DIB. During this decompression routine, you will maintain a number pair (y,x) starting at $(0,0)$. You will increment x by 1 every time you decode a pixel, resetting x to 0 and incrementing y every time you finish a row.

When you encounter the byte 0x00 followed by 0x02, you read the next two bytes and add them as unsigned increments to your current x and y values and then continue decoding. When you read the byte 0x00 followed by 0x00, you're done with the row. Set x equal to 0 and increment y. When you encounter the byte 0x00 followed by 0x01, you're done decoding. These codes allow the DIB to contain areas that are not defined, which is sometimes useful for encoding a nonrectangular image or for making digital animations or movies (because each frame mostly has information from the previous frame and need not be recoded).

For 4-bit DIBs, the encoding is generally the same but is complicated somewhat because there isn't a one-to-one correspondence between bytes and pixels.

If the first byte you read is nonzero, that's a repetition factor n. The second byte (which is to be repeated) contains 2 pixels, which alternate in the decoded sequence for n pixels. For example, the pair

```
0x07 0x35
```

is decoded as

```
0x35 0x35 0x35 0x3?
```

where the question mark indicates that the pixel is as yet unknown. If the pair 0x07 0x35 shown above is followed by the pair

```
0x05 0x24
```

then the full decoded sequence becomes

```
0x35 0x35 0x35 0x32 0x42 0x42
```

If the first byte in the pair is 0x00 and the second is 0x03 or greater, use the number of pixels indicated by the second byte. For example, the sequence

```
0x00 0x05 0x23 0x57 0x10 0x00
```

decodes to

```
0x23 0x57 0x1?
```

Notice that the encoded sequence must be padded to have an even number of bytes.

Whenever the *biCompression* field is BI_RLE4 or BI_RLE8, the *biSizeImage* field indicates the size of the DIB pixel data in bytes. If the *biCompression* field is BI_RGB, then *biSizeImage* is usually 0, but it could be set to *biHeight* times the byte length of the row, as calculated earlier in this chapter.

The current documentation says that "Top-down DIBs cannot be compressed." The top-down DIBs are those with negative *biHeight* fields.

Color Masking

The *biCompression* field is also used in conjunction with the 16-bit and 32-bit DIBs that were new with Windows 95. For these DIBs, the *biCompression* field can be either BI_RGB or BI_BITFIELDS (defined as equaling the value 3).

As a review, let's look at the pixel format of the 24-bit DIB, which always has a *biCompression* field equal to BI_RGB:

Pixel: — Blue —   — Green —   — Red —
7 6 5 4 3 2 1 0   7 6 5 4 3 2 1 0   7 6 5 4 3 2 1 0

That is, each row is basically an array of RGBTRIPLE structures, with possible padding at the end of the row so that the number of bytes in the row is a multiple of 4.

For a 16-bit DIB with a *biCompression* field of BI_RGB, each pixel requires two bytes. The colors are encoded like so:

Pixel: ...een — —— Blue —— 0 —— Red —— Gr...
7 6 5 4 3 2 1 0   7 6 5 4 3 2 1 0

Each color uses five bits. For the first pixel in the row, the blue value is the least-significant five bits of the first byte. The green value requires bits from the first and second byte: the two most-significant bits of the green value are the two least-significant bits of the second byte, and the three least-significant bits of the green value are the three most-significant bits of the first byte. The red value is bits 2 through 6 of the second byte. The most-significant bit of the second byte is 0.

This makes a whole lot more sense when you access the pixel value as a 16-bit word. Because the least-significant bytes of multibyte values are stored first, the pixel word looks like this:

```
            0    — Red —      — Green —   — Blue —
Pixel Word: 15 14 13 12 11 10 9 8 7 6 5 4 3 2 1 0
```

Suppose you have the 16-bit pixel stored in *wPixel*. You can calculate the red, green, and blue values like so:

```
Red   = ((0x7C00 & wPixel) >> 10) << 3 ;
Green = ((0x03E0 & wPixel) >>  5) << 3 ;
Blue  = ((0x001F & wPixel) >>  0) << 3 ;
```

First, the pixel undergoes a bitwise AND operation with a mask value. The result is shifted right 10 bits for red, 5 bits for green, and 0 bits for blue. I will be referring to these shift values as "right-shift" values. This produces color values in the range 0x00 through 0x1F. The values must then be shifted left 3 bits so that the resultant color values range from 0x00 through 0xF8. I will refer to these shift values as "left-shift" values.

And keep this in mind: if the pixel width of a 16-bit DIB is odd, each row will have an extra 2 bytes padded at the end to achieve a byte width divisible by 4.

For a 32-bit DIB, if *biCompression* equals BI_RGB, each pixel requires 4 bytes. The blue color value is the first byte, green is the second, red is the third, and the fourth byte equals 0. In other words, the pixels are an array of RGBQUAD structures. Because each pixel is 4 bytes in length, padding is never required at the end of the row.

If you access each pixel as a 32-bit double word, it looks like this:

```
                       ——— 0 ———  — Red ——   ——Green ——   —— Blue ——
Pixel Double Word:  31 30 ... 25 24 23 22 ... 17 16 15 14 ... 9 8 7 6 ... 1 0
```

Or, if *dwPixel* is the 32-bit double word,

```
Red   = ((0x00FF0000 & dwPixel) >> 16) << 0 ;
Green = ((0x0000FF00 & dwPixel) >>  8) << 0 ;
Blue  = ((0x000000FF & dwPixel) >>  0) << 0 ;
```

The left-shift values are all zero because the color values are already maximized at 0xFF. Be aware that this double word is *not* consistent with the 32-bit COLORREF value used to specify RGB color in Windows GDI function calls. In the COLORREF value, red is the least-significant byte.

So far, we've covered the default case for 16-bit and 32-bit DIBs when the *biCompression* field is BI_RGB. If the *biCompression* field is BI_BITFIELDS, the BITMAPINFO-HEADER structure of the DIB is immediately followed by three 32-bit color masks, the first for red, the second for green, and the third for blue. You use the C bitwise AND operator (&) to apply these masks to the 16-bit or 32-bit pixel value. You then shift the result right by right-shift values, which are unfortunately unknown until you examine the masks themselves. The rules regarding these color masks should be obvious when you think about them: the 1 bits in each color mask must be contiguous, and the 1 bits must not overlap among the three masks.

Let's take an example. You have a 16-bit DIB, and the *biCompression* field is BI_BITFIELDS. You examine the first three double words following the BITMAPINFOHEADER structure:

```
0x0000F800
0x000007E0
0x0000001F
```

Note that only bits among the bottom 16 bits are set to 1 because this is a 16-bit DIB. You set the variables *dwMask[0]*, *dwMask[1]*, and *dwMask[2]* to these values. Now you write little routines that calculate right-shift and left-shift values from the masks:

```
int MaskToRShift (DWORD dwMask)
{
    int iShift ;

    if (dwMask == 0)
        return 0 ;

    for (iShift = 0 ; !(dwMask & 1)  ; iShift++)
        dwMask >>= 1 ;

    return iShift ;
}

int MaskToLShift (DWORD dwMask)
{
    int iShift ;

    if (dwMask == 0)
        return 0 ;

    while (!(dwMask & 1))
        dwMask >>= 1 ;

    for (iShift = 0 ; dwMask & 1 ; iShift++)
        dwMask >>= 1 ;

    return 8 - iShift ;
}
```

Then you call the *MaskToRShift* function three times to obtain right-shift values:

```
iRShift[0] = MaskToRShift (dwMask[0]) ;
iRShift[1] = MaskToRShift (dwMask[1]) ;
iRShift[2] = MaskToRShift (dwMask[2]) ;
```

You get values 11, 5, and 0, respectively. You can then call *MaskToLShift* similarly:

```
iLShift[0] = MaskToLShift (dwMask[0]) ;
iLShift[1] = MaskToLShift (dwMask[1]) ;
iLShift[2] = MaskToLShift (dwMask[2]) ;
```

You get values of 3, 2, and 3, respectively. Now you can extract each color from the pixel value:

```
Red   = ((dwMask[0] & wPixel) >> iRShift[0]) << iLShift[0] ;
Green = ((dwMask[1] & wPixel) >> iRShift[1]) << iLShift[1] ;
Blue  = ((dwMask[2] & wPixel) >> iRShift[2]) << iLShift[2] ;
```

The procedure is the same for 32-bit DIBs except that the color masks can be greater than 0x0000FFFF, which is the maximum mask value for 16-bit DIBs.

Note that with either 16-bit or 32-bit DIBs, the red, green, and blue color values can be greater than 255. In fact, in a 32-bit DIB, if two of the masks are 0, the third could be 0xFFFFFFFF, for a 32-bit color value! Of course, this is somewhat ridiculous, so I wouldn't worry about it too much.

Unlike Windows NT, Windows 95 and Windows 98 have some restrictions when using color masks. The only allowable values are shown in the table below.

	16-Bit DIB	*16-Bit DIB*	*32-Bit DIB*
Red Mask	0x00007C00	0x0000F800	0x00FF0000
Green Mask	0x000003E0	0x000007E0	0x0000FF00
Blue Mask	0x0000001F	0x0000001F	0x000000FF
Shorthand	5-5-5	5-6-5	8-8-8

In other words, you can use the two sets of masks that you would get by default when *biCompression* is BI_RGB, plus the set of masks I showed above in the example. The bottom row in the table shows a shorthand notation for indicating the number of red, green, and blue bits per pixel.

The Version 4 Header

We're not quite finished yet. As I mentioned, Windows 95 changed some of the original BITMAPINFOHEADER field definitions. Windows 95 also included a new expanded information header called BITMAPV4HEADER. The name of this structure is clear when you realize that Windows 95 might have been called Windows 4.0 and that this structure was also supported by Windows NT 4.0.

```
typedef struct
{
DWORD          bV4Size ;           // size of the structure = 120
LONG           bV4Width ;          // width of the image in pixels
LONG           bV4Height ;         // height of the image in pixels
WORD           bV4Planes ;         // = 1
WORD           bV4BitCount ;       // bits per pixel (1, 4, 8, 16, 24, or 32)
DWORD          bV4Compression ;    // compression code
DWORD          bV4SizeImage ;      // number of bytes in image
LONG           bV4XPelsPerMeter ;  // horizontal resolution
LONG           bV4YPelsPerMeter ;  // vertical resolution
DWORD          bV4ClrUsed ;        // number of colors used
DWORD          bV4ClrImportant ;   // number of important colors
DWORD          bV4RedMask ;        // Red color mask
DWORD          bV4GreenMask ;      // Green color mask
DWORD          bV4BlueMask ;       // Blue color mask
DWORD          bV4AlphaMask ;      // Alpha mask
DWORD          bV4CSType ;         // color space type
CIEXYZTRIPLE   bV4Endpoints ;      // XYZ values
DWORD          bV4GammaRed ;       // Red gamma value
DWORD          bV4GammaGreen ;     // Green gamma value
DWORD          bV4GammaBlue ;      // Blue gamma value
}
BITMAPV4HEADER, * PBITMAPV4HEADER ;
```

Notice that the first 11 fields are the same as in the BITMAPINFOHEADER structure. The last five fields support the image color-matching technology of Windows 95 and Windows NT 4.0. Unless you use the last four fields of the BITMAPV4HEADER structure, you should use BITMAPINFOHEADER (or BITMAPV5HEADER) instead.

The *bV4RedMask*, *bV4GreenMask*, and *bV4BlueMask* values are applicable only for 16-bit and 32-bit DIBs when the *bV4Compression* field equals BI_BITFIELDS. These serve the same function as the color masks defined in the BITMAPINFOHEADER structure and actually occur in the same place in the DIB file as when using the original structure except that here they are explicit structure fields. As far as I know, the *bV4AlphaMask* field is not used.

The remaining fields in the BITMAPV5HEADER structure involve Windows Image Color Management, which I'm afraid is a subject beyond the scope of this book. However, a little background may help get you started.

The problem with using an RGB scheme for color is that it is dependent on the technologies of video monitors, color cameras, and color scanners. If a color is specified as the RGB value (255, 0, 0), all that means is that a maximum voltage should be applied to the red electron gun in a cathode ray tube. An RGB value of (128, 0, 0) indicates that half the voltage is to be applied. Monitors can differ in their response. Moreover, printers use a different method of color that involves combinations of cyan, magenta, yellow, and black inks. These methods are known as CMY (cyan-magenta-yellow) and CMYK (cyan-magenta-yellow-black). Mathematical formulas can translate RGB values to CMY and CMYK, but there is no guarantee that the printer color will match a monitor color. Image Color Management is an attempt to relate colors to device-independent standards.

The phenomenon of color is related to the wavelengths of visible light, which range from 380 nanometers (blue) to 780 nm (red). Any light that we visually perceive is made up of combinations of different amounts of various wavelengths in the visible spectrum. In 1931, the Commission Internationale de L'Éclairage (International Commission on Illumination) or CIE developed a method for scientifically quantifying color. This involves using three color-matching functions (named x, y, and z) that in their abridged form (with values for every 5 nm) are documented in CIE Publication 15.2-1986, "Colorimetry, Second Edition," Table 2.1.

A spectrum (S) of a color is a set of values that indicate the strength of each wavelength. If a spectrum is known, the color-matching functions can be applied to the spectrum to calculate X, Y, and Z:

$$X = \sum_{\lambda=380}^{780} S(\lambda)\bar{x}(\lambda)$$

$$Y = \sum_{\lambda=380}^{780} S(\lambda)\bar{y}(\lambda)$$

$$Z = \sum_{\lambda=380}^{780} S(\lambda)\bar{z}(\lambda)$$

These values are called *Big X*, *Big Y*, and *Big Z*. The y color-matching function is equivalent to the response of the human eye to the range of light in the visible spectrum. (It looks like a bell curve that goes to 0 at 380 nm and 780 nm.) Y is called the CIE Luminance because it indicates an overall intensity of the light.

If you're using the BITMAPV5HEADER structure, the *bV4CSType* field must be set to LCS_CALIBRATED_RGB, which is equal to 0. The next four fields must be set to valid values.

The CIEXYZTRIPLE structure is defined like so:

```
typedef struct tagCIEXYZTRIPLE
{
    CIEXYZ   ciexyzRed ;
    CIEXYZ   ciexyzGreen ;
    CIEXYZ   ciexyzBlue ;
}
CIEXYZTRIPLE, * LPCIEXYZTRIPLE ;
```

And the CIEXYZ structure is

```
typedef struct tagCIEXYZ
{
    FXPT2DOT30 ciexyzX ;
    FXPT2DOT30 ciexyzY ;
    FXPT2DOT30 ciexyzZ ;
}
CIEXYZ, * LPCIEXYZ ;
```

The three fields are defined as FXPT2DOT30 values, which means that they are interpreted as fixed-point values with a 2-bit integer part and a 30-bit fractional part. Thus, 0x40000000 is 1.0 and 0x48000000 is 1.5. The maximum value 0xFFFFFFFF is just a smidgen under 4.0.

The *bV4Endpoints* field provides three X, Y, and Z values that correspond to the RGB colors (255, 0, 0), (0, 255, 0), and (0, 0, 255). These values should be inserted by the application that creates the DIB to indicate the device-independent meaning of these RGB colors.

The remaining three fields of BITMAPV4HEADER refer to "gamma." Gamma (the lowercase Greek letter γ) refers to a nonlinearity in the specification of color levels. In a DIB, levels of red, green, and blue range from 0 through 255. On the video board, these three digital values are converted to three analog voltages that go to the monitor. The voltages determine the intensity of each pixel. However, due to characteristics of the electronics of the electron guns in a cathode ray tube, the intensity (I) of the pixel is not linearly related to the voltage (V). Instead, the relationship is

$$I = (V + \varepsilon)^\gamma$$

where ε is the black-level of the monitor set by the monitor's Brightness control. (Preferably this is 0.) The exponent γ is set by the monitor's Picture or Contrast control. For most monitors, γ is about 2.5.

To compensate for this nonlinearity, video cameras have traditionally included "gamma correction" in their circuitry. The light input to a camera is modified by an exponent of 0.45. This implies a video display gamma of about 2.2. (The higher gamma of video displays increases the contrast somewhat, which is usually not undesirable because ambient light tends to lower contrast.)

This nonlinear response of video monitors is actually much more felicitous than it may at first seem. This is because human response to light is also nonlinear. Earlier I mentioned that Y is called CIE Luminance. This is a linear measure of light. The CIE also defines a Lightness value that approximates human perception. Lightness is L^* (pronounced "ell star") and is calculated from Y using the formulas

$$L^* = \begin{cases} 903.3 \frac{Y}{Y_n} & \frac{Y}{Y_n} \leq 0.008856 \\[2ex] 116 \left(\frac{Y}{Y_n} \right)^{\frac{1}{3}} - 16 & 0.008856 < \frac{Y}{Y_n} \end{cases}$$

where Y_n is a white level. The first part of the formula is a small linear segment. Generally, human perception of lightness is related to the cube root of the linear luminance, which is indicated by the second formula. L^* ranges from 0 to 100. Each integral increment of L^* is generally assumed to be the smallest change in lightness that humans can perceive.

It is preferable to code light intensities based on perceptual lightness rather than linear luminance. This keeps the number of bits down to a reasonable level and also reduces noise in analog circuitry.

Let's go through the whole process. The pixel value (P) ranges from 0 to 255. This is linearly converted to a voltage level, which we can assume is normalized to a value between 0.0 and 1.0. Assuming the monitor's black level is set to 0, the intensity of the pixel is

$$I = V^r = \left(\frac{P}{255}\right)^r$$

where γ is probably about 2.5. Human perception of lightness (L^*) is based on the cube root of this intensity and ranges from 0 to 100, so approximately

$$L^* = 100 \left(\frac{P}{255}\right)^{\frac{r}{3}}$$

That exponent will be about 0.85 or so. If the exponent were 1, then CIE lightness would be perfectly matched to pixel values. We don't have quite that situation, but it's much closer than if the pixel values indicated linear luminance.

The last three fields of BITMAPV4HEADER provide a way for programs that create a DIB to indicate a gamma value assumed for the pixel values. These values are interpreted as 16-bit integer values and 16-bit fractional values. For example, 0x10000 is 1.0. If the DIB is created by capturing a real-world image, this gamma value is probably implied by the capture hardware and will probably be 2.2 (encoded as 0x23333). If the DIB is generated algorithmically by a program, the program would convert any linear luminances it uses to CIE lightness values using a power function. The inverse of the exponent would be the gamma encoded in the DIB.

The Version 5 Header

Programs written for Windows 98 and Windows NT 5.0 can use DIBs that have a new BITMAPV5HEADER information structure:

```
typedef struct
{
DWORD          bV5Size ;              // size of the structure = 120
LONG           bV5Width ;             // width of the image in pixels
```

```
LONG          bV5Height ;          // height of the image in pixels
WORD          bV5Planes ;          // = 1
WORD          bV5BitCount ;        // bits per pixel (1, 4, 8, 16, 24, or 32)
DWORD         bV5Compression ;     // compression code
DWORD         bV5SizeImage ;       // number of bytes in image
LONG          bV5XPelsPerMeter ;   // horizontal resolution
LONG          bV5YPelsPerMeter ;   // vertical resolution
DWORD         bV5ClrUsed ;         // number of colors used
DWORD         bV5ClrImportant ;    // number of important colors
DWORD         bV5RedMask ;         // Red color mask
DWORD         bV5GreenMask ;       // Green color mask
DWORD         bV5BlueMask ;        // Blue color mask
DWORD         bV5AlphaMask ;       // Alpha mask
DWORD         bV5CSType ;          // color space type
CIEXYZTRIPLE  bV5Endpoints ;       // XYZ values
DWORD         bV5GammaRed ;        // Red gamma value
DWORD         bV5GammaGreen ;      // Green gamma value
DWORD         bV5GammaBlue ;       // Blue gamma value
DWORD         bV5Intent ;          // rendering intent
DWORD         bV5ProfileData ;     // profile data or filename
DWORD         bV5ProfileSize ;     // size of embedded data or filename
DWORD         bV5Reserved ;
}
BITMAPV5HEADER, * PBITMAPV5HEADER ;
```

This has four new fields, only three of which are used. These fields support a proposal made by the International Color Consortium (founded by Adobe, Agfa, Apple, Kodak, Microsoft, Silicon Graphics, Sun Microsystems, and others) called the *ICC Profile Format Specification.* You can obtain a copy of this from *http://www.icc.org.* Basically, each input (scanner or camera), output (printer or film recorder), and display (monitor) device is associated with a profile that relates the native device-dependent colors (generally RGB or CMYK) to a device-independent color specification, ultimately based on CIE XYZ values. These profiles have filenames with the extension .ICM (for "image color management"). A profile can be embedded into a DIB file or linked from the DIB file to indicate how the DIB was created. You can obtain more information about Image Color Management in Windows at */Platform SDK/Graphics and Multimedia Services/Color Management.*

The *bV5CSType* field in the BITMAPV5HEADER can take on several different values. If it's LCS_CALIBRATED_RGB, then it's compatible with the BITMAPV4HEADER structure. The *bV5Endpoints* field and the gamma fields must be valid.

If the *bV5CSType* field is LCS_sRGB, none of the remaining fields need to be set. The implied color space is a "standard" RGB color space devised by Microsoft and Hewlett-Packard to attempt some relative device independence, particularly across the Internet, without the bulk of profiles. This is documented at *http://www.color.org/contrib/sRGB.html.*

If the *bV5CSType* field is LCS_WINDOWS_COLOR_SPACE, none of the remaining fields need be set. Windows uses the color space implied by API function calls for displaying the bitmap.

If the *bV5CSType* field is PROFILE_EMBEDDED, the DIB file contains an ICC profile. If the field is PROFILE_LINKED, the DIB file contains the fully qualified filename of an ICC profile. In either case, *bV5ProfileData* is an offset from the beginning of the BITMAP-V5HEADER to the start of the profile data or filename. The *bV5ProfileSize* field gives the size of the data or filename. The endpoints and gamma fields need not be set.

Displaying DIB Information

It is now time to look at some code. We don't know enough to actually display a DIB just yet, but we can at least display information about the DIB from the header structures. The DIBHEADS program shown in Figure 15-1 does this.

DIBHEADS.C

```
/*-------------------------------------------------
   DIBHEADS.C -- Displays DIB Header Information
                 (c) Charles Petzold, 1998
   -------------------------------------------------*/

#include <windows.h>
#include "resource.h"

LRESULT CALLBACK WndProc (HWND, UINT, WPARAM, LPARAM) ;

TCHAR szAppName[] = TEXT ("DibHeads") ;

int WINAPI WinMain (HINSTANCE hInstance, HINSTANCE hPrevInstance,
                    PSTR szCmdLine, int iCmdShow)
{
     HACCEL    hAccel ;
     HWND      hwnd ;
     MSG       msg ;
     WNDCLASS  wndclass ;

     wndclass.style         = CS_HREDRAW | CS_VREDRAW ;
     wndclass.lpfnWndProc   = WndProc ;
     wndclass.cbClsExtra    = 0 ;
     wndclass.cbWndExtra    = 0 ;
     wndclass.hInstance     = hInstance ;
     wndclass.hIcon         = LoadIcon (NULL, IDI_APPLICATION) ;
     wndclass.hCursor       = LoadCursor (NULL, IDC_ARROW) ;
```

Figure 15-1. *The DIBHEADS program.*

```
        wndclass.hbrBackground = (HBRUSH) GetStockObject (WHITE_BRUSH) ;
        wndclass.lpszMenuName  = szAppName ;
        wndclass.lpszClassName = szAppName ;

        if (!RegisterClass (&wndclass))
        {
             MessageBox (NULL, TEXT ("This program requires Windows NT!"),
                         szAppName, MB_ICONERROR) ;
             return 0 ;
        }

        hwnd = CreateWindow (szAppName, TEXT ("DIB Headers"),
                             WS_OVERLAPPEDWINDOW,
                             CW_USEDEFAULT, CW_USEDEFAULT,
                             CW_USEDEFAULT, CW_USEDEFAULT,
                             NULL, NULL, hInstance, NULL) ;

        ShowWindow (hwnd, iCmdShow) ;
        UpdateWindow (hwnd) ;

        hAccel = LoadAccelerators (hInstance, szAppName) ;

        while (GetMessage (&msg, NULL, 0, 0))
        {
             if (!TranslateAccelerator (hwnd, hAccel, &msg))
             {
                  TranslateMessage (&msg) ;
                  DispatchMessage (&msg) ;
             }
        }
        return msg.wParam ;
}

void Printf (HWND hwnd, TCHAR * szFormat, ...)
{
        TCHAR   szBuffer [1024] ;
        va_list pArgList ;

        va_start (pArgList, szFormat) ;
        wvsprintf (szBuffer, szFormat, pArgList) ;
        va_end (pArgList) ;

        SendMessage (hwnd, EM_SETSEL, (WPARAM) -1, (LPARAM) -1) ;
        SendMessage (hwnd, EM_REPLACESEL, FALSE, (LPARAM) szBuffer) ;
        SendMessage (hwnd, EM_SCROLLCARET, 0, 0) ;
}
```

(continued)

747

Figure 15-1. *continued*

```
void DisplayDibHeaders (HWND hwnd, TCHAR * szFileName)
{
    static TCHAR    * szInfoName [] = { TEXT ("BITMAPCOREHEADER"),
                                        TEXT ("BITMAPINFOHEADER"),
                                        TEXT ("BITMAPV4HEADER"),
                                        TEXT ("BITMAPV5HEADER") } ;
    static TCHAR    * szCompression [] = { TEXT ("BI_RGB"), TEXT ("BI_RLE8"),
                                           TEXT ("BI_RLE4"),
                                           TEXT ("BI_BITFIELDS"),
                                           TEXT ("unknown") } ;
    BITMAPCOREHEADER * pbmch ;
    BITMAPFILEHEADER * pbmfh ;
    BITMAPV5HEADER   * pbmih ;
    BOOL               bSuccess ;
    DWORD              dwFileSize, dwHighSize, dwBytesRead ;
    HANDLE             hFile ;
    int                i ;
    PBYTE              pFile ;
    TCHAR            * szV ;

        // Display the file name

    Printf (hwnd, TEXT ("File: %s\r\n\r\n"), szFileName) ;

        // Open the file

    hFile = CreateFile (szFileName, GENERIC_READ, FILE_SHARE_READ, NULL,
                        OPEN_EXISTING, FILE_FLAG_SEQUENTIAL_SCAN, NULL) ;

    if (hFile == INVALID_HANDLE_VALUE)
    {
        Printf (hwnd, TEXT ("Cannot open file.\r\n\r\n")) ;
        return ;
    }

        // Get the size of the file

    dwFileSize = GetFileSize (hFile, &dwHighSize) ;

    if (dwHighSize)
    {
        Printf (hwnd, TEXT ("Cannot deal with >4G files.\r\n\r\n")) ;
        CloseHandle (hFile) ;
        return ;
    }
```

```
     // Allocate memory for the file

pFile = malloc (dwFileSize) ;

if (!pFile)
{
     Printf (hwnd, TEXT ("Cannot allocate memory.\r\n\r\n")) ;
     CloseHandle (hFile) ;
     return ;
}

     // Read the file

SetCursor (LoadCursor (NULL, IDC_WAIT)) ;
ShowCursor (TRUE) ;

bSuccess = ReadFile (hFile, pFile, dwFileSize, &dwBytesRead, NULL) ;

ShowCursor (FALSE) ;
SetCursor (LoadCursor (NULL, IDC_ARROW)) ;

if (!bSuccess || (dwBytesRead != dwFileSize))
{
     Printf (hwnd, TEXT ("Could not read file.\r\n\r\n")) ;
     CloseHandle (hFile) ;
     free (pFile) ;
     return ;
}

     // Close the file

CloseHandle (hFile) ;

     // Display file size

Printf (hwnd, TEXT ("File size = %u bytes\r\n\r\n"), dwFileSize) ;

     // Display BITMAPFILEHEADER structure

pbmfh = (BITMAPFILEHEADER *) pFile ;

Printf (hwnd, TEXT ("BITMAPFILEHEADER\r\n")) ;
Printf (hwnd, TEXT ("\t.bfType = 0x%X\r\n"), pbmfh->bfType) ;
Printf (hwnd, TEXT ("\t.bfSize = %u\r\n"), pbmfh->bfSize) ;
Printf (hwnd, TEXT ("\t.bfReserved1 = %u\r\n"), pbmfh->bfReserved1) ;
```

(continued)

749

Figure 15-1. *continued*

```
        Printf (hwnd, TEXT ("\t.bfReserved2 = %u\r\n"), pbmfh->bfReserved2) ;
        Printf (hwnd, TEXT ("\t.bfOffBits = %u\r\n\r\n"), pbmfh->bfOffBits) ;

             // Determine which information structure we have

        pbmih = (BITMAPV5HEADER *) (pFile + sizeof (BITMAPFILEHEADER)) ;

        switch (pbmih->bV5Size)
        {
        case sizeof (BITMAPCOREHEADER):  i = 0 ;                          break ;
        case sizeof (BITMAPINFOHEADER):  i = 1 ;   szV = TEXT ("i")  ;    break ;
        case sizeof (BITMAPV4HEADER):    i = 2 ;   szV = TEXT ("V4") ;    break ;
        case sizeof (BITMAPV5HEADER):    i = 3 ;   szV = TEXT ("V5") ;    break ;
        default:
             Printf (hwnd, TEXT ("Unknown header size of %u.\r\n\r\n"),
                             pbmih->bV5Size) ;
             free (pFile) ;
             return ;
        }

        Printf (hwnd, TEXT ("%s\r\n"), szInfoName[i]) ;

             // Display the BITMAPCOREHEADER fields

        if (pbmih->bV5Size == sizeof (BITMAPCOREHEADER))
        {
             pbmch = (BITMAPCOREHEADER *) pbmih ;

             Printf (hwnd, TEXT ("\t.bcSize = %u\r\n"), pbmch->bcSize) ;
             Printf (hwnd, TEXT ("\t.bcWidth = %u\r\n"), pbmch->bcWidth) ;
             Printf (hwnd, TEXT ("\t.bcHeight = %u\r\n"), pbmch->bcHeight) ;
             Printf (hwnd, TEXT ("\t.bcPlanes = %u\r\n"), pbmch->bcPlanes) ;
             Printf (hwnd, TEXT ("\t.bcBitCount = %u\r\n\r\n"), pbmch->bcBitCount) ;
             free (pFile) ;
             return ;
        }

             // Display the BITMAPINFOHEADER fields

        Printf (hwnd, TEXT ("\t.b%sSize = %u\r\n"), szV, pbmih->bV5Size) ;
        Printf (hwnd, TEXT ("\t.b%sWidth = %i\r\n"), szV, pbmih->bV5Width) ;
        Printf (hwnd, TEXT ("\t.b%sHeight = %i\r\n"), szV, pbmih->bV5Height) ;
        Printf (hwnd, TEXT ("\t.b%sPlanes = %u\r\n"), szV, pbmih->bV5Planes) ;
        Printf (hwnd, TEXT ("\t.b%sBitCount = %u\r\n"), szV, pbmih->bV5BitCount) ;
        Printf (hwnd, TEXT ("\t.b%sCompression = %s\r\n"), szV,
                     szCompression [min (4, pbmih->bV5Compression)]) ;
```

```
        Printf (hwnd, TEXT ("\t.b%sSizeImage = %u\r\n"), szV, pbmih->bV5SizeImage) ;
        Printf (hwnd, TEXT ("\t.b%sXPelsPerMeter = %i\r\n"), szV,
                    pbmih->bV5XPelsPerMeter) ;
        Printf (hwnd, TEXT ("\t.b%sYPelsPerMeter = %i\r\n"), szV,
                    pbmih->bV5YPelsPerMeter) ;
        Printf (hwnd, TEXT ("\t.b%sClrUsed = %i\r\n"), szV, pbmih->bV5ClrUsed) ;
        Printf (hwnd, TEXT ("\t.b%sClrImportant = %i\r\n\r\n"), szV,
                    pbmih->bV5ClrImportant) ;

    if (pbmih->bV5Size == sizeof (BITMAPINFOHEADER))
    {
        if (pbmih->bV5Compression == BI_BITFIELDS)
        {
            Printf (hwnd, TEXT ("Red Mask   = %08X\r\n"),
                        pbmih->bV5RedMask) ;
            Printf (hwnd, TEXT ("Green Mask = %08X\r\n"),
                        pbmih->bV5GreenMask) ;
            Printf (hwnd, TEXT ("Blue Mask  = %08X\r\n\r\n"),
                        pbmih->bV5BlueMask) ;
        }
        free (pFile) ;
        return ;
    }

        // Display additional BITMAPV4HEADER fields

    Printf (hwnd, TEXT ("\t.b%sRedMask   = %08X\r\n"), szV,
                pbmih->bV5RedMask) ;
    Printf (hwnd, TEXT ("\t.b%sGreenMask = %08X\r\n"), szV,
                pbmih->bV5GreenMask) ;
    Printf (hwnd, TEXT ("\t.b%sBlueMask  = %08X\r\n"), szV,
                pbmih->bV5BlueMask) ;
    Printf (hwnd, TEXT ("\t.b%sAlphaMask = %08X\r\n"), szV,
                pbmih->bV5AlphaMask) ;
    Printf (hwnd, TEXT ("\t.b%sCSType = %u\r\n"), szV,
                pbmih->bV5CSType) ;
    Printf (hwnd, TEXT ("\t.b%sEndpoints.ciexyzRed.ciexyzX   = %08X\r\n"),
                szV, pbmih->bV5Endpoints.ciexyzRed.ciexyzX) ;
    Printf (hwnd, TEXT ("\t.b%sEndpoints.ciexyzRed.ciexyzY   = %08X\r\n"),
                szV, pbmih->bV5Endpoints.ciexyzRed.ciexyzY) ;
    Printf (hwnd, TEXT ("\t.b%sEndpoints.ciexyzRed.ciexyzZ   = %08X\r\n"),
                szV, pbmih->bV5Endpoints.ciexyzRed.ciexyzZ) ;
    Printf (hwnd, TEXT ("\t.b%sEndpoints.ciexyzGreen.ciexyzX = %08X\r\n"),
                szV, pbmih->bV5Endpoints.ciexyzGreen.ciexyzX) ;
    Printf (hwnd, TEXT ("\t.b%sEndpoints.ciexyzGreen.ciexyzY = %08X\r\n"),
                szV, pbmih->bV5Endpoints.ciexyzGreen.ciexyzY) ;
```

(continued)

Figure 15-1. *continued*

```
      Printf (hwnd, TEXT ("\t.b%sEndpoints.ciexyzGreen.ciexyzZ = %08X\r\n"),
                  szV, pbmih->bV5Endpoints.ciexyzGreen.ciexyzZ) ;
      Printf (hwnd, TEXT ("\t.b%sEndpoints.ciexyzBlue.ciexyzX  = %08X\r\n"),
                  szV, pbmih->bV5Endpoints.ciexyzBlue.ciexyzX) ;
      Printf (hwnd, TEXT ("\t.b%sEndpoints.ciexyzBlue.ciexyzY  = %08X\r\n"),
                  szV, pbmih->bV5Endpoints.ciexyzBlue.ciexyzY) ;
      Printf (hwnd, TEXT ("\t.b%sEndpoints.ciexyzBlue.ciexyzZ  = %08X\r\n"),
                  szV, pbmih->bV5Endpoints.ciexyzBlue.ciexyzZ) ;
      Printf (hwnd, TEXT ("\t.b%sGammaRed   = %08X\r\n"), szV,
                  pbmih->bV5GammaRed) ;
      Printf (hwnd, TEXT ("\t.b%sGammaGreen = %08X\r\n"), szV,
                  pbmih->bV5GammaGreen) ;
      Printf (hwnd, TEXT ("\t.b%sGammaBlue  = %08X\r\n\r\n"), szV,
                  pbmih->bV5GammaBlue) ;

      if (pbmih->bV5Size == sizeof (BITMAPV4HEADER))
      {
           free (pFile) ;
           return ;
      }

           // Display additional BITMAPV5HEADER fields

      Printf (hwnd, TEXT ("\t.b%sIntent = %u\r\n"), szV, pbmih->bV5Intent) ;
      Printf (hwnd, TEXT ("\t.b%sProfileData = %u\r\n"), szV,
                  pbmih->bV5ProfileData) ;
      Printf (hwnd, TEXT ("\t.b%sProfileSize = %u\r\n"), szV,
                  pbmih->bV5ProfileSize) ;
      Printf (hwnd, TEXT ("\t.b%sReserved = %u\r\n\r\n"), szV,
                  pbmih->bV5Reserved) ;

      free (pFile) ;
      return ;
}

LRESULT CALLBACK WndProc (HWND hwnd, UINT message, WPARAM wParam, LPARAM lParam)
{
      static HWND         hwndEdit ;
      static OPENFILENAME ofn ;
      static TCHAR        szFileName [MAX_PATH], szTitleName [MAX_PATH] ;
      static TCHAR        szFilter[] = TEXT ("Bitmap Files (*.BMP)\0*.bmp\0")
                                       TEXT ("All Files (*.*)\0*.*\0\0") ;

      switch (message)
```

```
    {
case WM_CREATE:
     hwndEdit = CreateWindow (TEXT ("edit"), NULL,
                    WS_CHILD | WS_VISIBLE | WS_BORDER |
                        WS_VSCROLL | WS_HSCROLL |
                        ES_MULTILINE | ES_AUTOVSCROLL | ES_READONLY,
                    0, 0, 0, 0, hwnd, (HMENU) 1,
                    ((LPCREATESTRUCT) lParam)->hInstance, NULL) ;

     ofn.lStructSize       = sizeof (OPENFILENAME) ;
     ofn.hwndOwner         = hwnd ;
     ofn.hInstance         = NULL ;
     ofn.lpstrFilter       = szFilter ;
     ofn.lpstrCustomFilter = NULL ;
     ofn.nMaxCustFilter    = 0 ;
     ofn.nFilterIndex      = 0 ;
     ofn.lpstrFile         = szFileName ;
     ofn.nMaxFile          = MAX_PATH ;
     ofn.lpstrFileTitle    = szTitleName ;
     ofn.nMaxFileTitle     = MAX_PATH ;
     ofn.lpstrInitialDir   = NULL ;
     ofn.lpstrTitle        = NULL ;
     ofn.Flags             = 0 ;
     ofn.nFileOffset       = 0 ;
     ofn.nFileExtension    = 0 ;
     ofn.lpstrDefExt       = TEXT ("bmp") ;
     ofn.lCustData         = 0 ;
     ofn.lpfnHook          = NULL ;
     ofn.lpTemplateName    = NULL ;
     return 0 ;

case WM_SIZE:
     MoveWindow (hwndEdit, 0, 0, LOWORD (lParam), HIWORD (lParam), TRUE) ;
     return 0 ;

case WM_COMMAND:
     switch (LOWORD (wParam))
     {
     case IDM_FILE_OPEN:
          if (GetOpenFileName (&ofn))
               DisplayDibHeaders (hwndEdit, szFileName) ;

          return 0 ;
     }
```

(continued)

Figure 15-1. *continued*

```
        break ;

    case WM_DESTROY:
        PostQuitMessage (0) ;
        return 0 ;
    }
    return DefWindowProc (hwnd, message, wParam, lParam) ;
}
```

DIBHEADS.RC (excerpts)

```
//Microsoft Developer Studio generated resource script.

#include "resource.h"
#include "afxres.h"


/////////////////////////////////////////////////////////////////////////////
// Accelerator

DIBHEADS ACCELERATORS DISCARDABLE
BEGIN
    "O",                IDM_FILE_OPEN,              VIRTKEY, CONTROL, NOINVERT
END


/////////////////////////////////////////////////////////////////////////////
// Menu

DIBHEADS MENU DISCARDABLE
BEGIN
    POPUP "&File"
    BEGIN
        MENUITEM "&Open\tCtrl+O",                   IDM_FILE_OPEN
    END
END
```

RESOURCE.H (excerpts)

```
// Microsoft Developer Studio generated include file.
// Used by DibHeads.rc

#define IDM_FILE_OPEN                       40001
```

This program has a short *WndProc* function that creates a read-only edit window filling its client area and that processes File Open commands from the menu. It uses the standard File Open dialog box invoked from the *GetOpenFileName* function and then calls the large function *DisplayDibHeaders*. This function reads the entire DIB file into memory and displays all the header information field by field.

DISPLAYING AND PRINTING

Bitmaps are for looking at. In this section, we'll begin by looking at the two functions that Windows supports for displaying a DIB on the video display or a printer page. For better performance, you may eventually prefer a more roundabout method for displaying bitmaps that I'll discuss later in this chapter. But these two functions are a logical first start.

The two functions are called *SetDIBitsToDevice* (pronounced "set dee eye bits to device") and *StretchDIBits* ("stretch dee eye bits"). Each function uses a DIB stored in memory and can display the entire DIB or a rectangular portion of it. When you use *SetDIBitsToDevice*, the size of the displayed image in pixels will be the same as the pixel size of the DIB. For example, a 640-by-480 DIB will cover your entire standard VGA screen, but on your 300 dpi laser printer it will be only about 2.1 by 1.6 inches. The *StretchDIBits* function can stretch or shrink the row and column dimension of a DIB to display it in a particular size on the output device.

Digging into the DIB

When you call one of the two functions to display a DIB, you need several pieces of information about the image. As I discussed earlier, DIB files contain the following sections:

A DIB file can be loaded into memory. If the entire file *less the file header* is stored in a contiguous block of memory, a pointer to the beginning of the block (which is the beginning of the information header) is said to address a *packed DIB*. (See the top of the next page.)

This is the format you use when transferring a DIB through the clipboard, and it's also the format you use when creating a brush from a DIB. The packed DIB is a convenient way to store a DIB in memory because the entire DIB is referenced by a single pointer (for example, *pPackedDib*), which you can define as a pointer to a BYTE. Using the structure definitions shown earlier in this chapter, you can get at all the information stored in the DIB, including the color table and the individual pixel bits.

However, getting at much of this information requires several lines of code. For example, you can't simply access the pixel width of the DIB using the statement

```
iWidth = ((PBITMAPINFOHEADER) pPackedDib)->biWidth ;
```

It's possible that the DIB is in the OS/2-compatible format. In that format, the packed DIB begins with a BITMAPCOREHEADER structure and the pixel width and height of the DIB are stored as 16-bit WORDs rather than 32-bit LONGs. So, you first have to check if the DIB is in the old format and then proceed accordingly:

```
if (((PBITMAPCOREHEADER) pPackedDib)->bcSize == sizeof (BITMAPCOREHEADER))
     iWidth = ((PBITMAPCOREHEADER) pPackedDib)->bcWidth ;
else
     iWidth = ((PBITMAPINFOHEADER) pPackedDib)->biWidth ;
```

This isn't all that bad, of course, but it's certainly not as clean as we'd prefer.

Now here's a fun exercise: given a pointer to a packed DIB, find the value of the pixel at coordinate (5, 27). Even if you assume that the DIB is not in the OS/2-compatible format, you need to know the width, height, and bit count of the DIB. You need to calculate the byte length of each row of pixels. You need to determine the number of entries in the color table, and whether the color table includes three 32-bit color masks. And you need to check whether the DIB is compressed, in which case the pixel is not directly addressable.

If you need to directly access *all* the pixels of the DIB (as you do when performing many image-processing jobs), this can add up to quite a bit of processing time. For this reason, while maintaining a pointer to a packed DIB may be convenient, it certainly doesn't lend itself to efficient code. An excellent solution is defining a C++ class for DIBs that includes enough member data to allow the very speedy random access of DIB pixels. However, since I promised at the outset of this book that you need not know any C++, I'll show you a C solution instead in the next chapter.

For the *SetDIBitsToDevice* and *StretchDIBits* functions, the information you need includes a pointer to the BITMAPINFO structure of the DIB. As you'll recall, the BITMAP-INFO structure comprises the BITMAPINFOHEADER structure and the color table. So, this is simply a pointer to the packed DIB with appropriate casting.

The functions also require a pointer to the pixel bits. This is derivable from information in the information header, although the code is not pretty. Notice that this pointer can be calculated much more easily when you have access to the *bfOffBits* field of the BITMAP-FILEHEADER structure. The *bfOffBits* field indicates the offset from the beginning of the DIB file to the pixel bits. You could simply add this offset to the BITMAPINFO pointer and then subtract the size of the BITMAPFILEHEADER structure. However, this doesn't help when you get a pointer to a packed DIB from the clipboard, because you don't have a BITMAPFILEHEADER structure.

This diagram shows the two pointers you need:

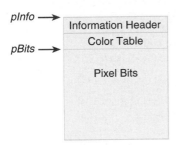

The *SetDIBitsToDevice* and *StretchDIBits* functions require two pointers to the DIB because the two sections do not have to be in one contiguous block of memory. You could have two blocks of memory like so:

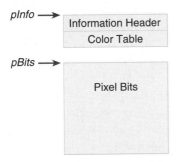

Indeed, breaking a DIB into two memory blocks like this is quite useful. It's only because we're preferring for the moment to work with packed DIBs that the entire DIB is stored in a single memory block.

Besides these two pointers, the *SetDIBitsToDevice* and *StretchDIBits* functions also usually require the pixel width and height of the DIB. If you're displaying only part of the DIB, then you don't need these values explicitly, but they'll define an upper limit for a rectangle you define within the array of DIB pixel bits.

Pixel to Pixel

The *SetDIBitsToDevice* function displays a DIB without any stretching or shrinking. Each pixel of the DIB is mapped to a pixel of the output device. The image is always displayed correctly oriented—that is, with the top row of the image on top. Any transforms that might be in effect for the device context determine the starting position where the DIB is displayed but otherwise have no effect on the size or orientation of the image. Here's the function:

```
iLines = SetDIBitsToDevice (
                hdc,               // device context handle
                xDst,              // x destination coordinate
                yDst,              // y destination coordinate
                cxSrc,             // source rectangle width
                cySrc,             // source rectangle height
                xSrc,              // x source coordinate
                ySrc,              // y source coordinate
                yScan,             // first scan line to draw
                cyScans,           // number of scan lines to draw
                pBits,             // pointer to DIB pixel bits
                pInfo,             // pointer to DIB information
                fClrUse) ;         // color use flag
```

Don't be too put off by the number of arguments. For most purposes, the function is easier to use than it initially appears. For other purposes, well…it's a mess. But we'll work it out.

As usual for GDI display functions, the first argument to *SetDIBitsToDevice* is the handle of the device context indicating the device on which you want to display the DIB. The next two arguments, *xDst* and *yDst*, are logical coordinates of the output device and indicate the coordinate where the top left corner of the DIB image is to appear. (By "top" I mean the visual top of the image, not the first row of pixels in the DIB.) Note that these are logical coordinates, so they are subject to any mapping mode that may be in effect or—in the case of Windows NT—any transform you may have set. In the default MM_TEXT mapping mode, you would set both these arguments equal to 0 to display the DIB image flush against the left side and top of the display surface.

You can display the entire DIB image or only part of it. That's the purpose of the next four arguments. But here's where the upside-down orientation of DIB pixel data creates some real perversion that I'll discuss shortly. For now, be aware that to display the entire

DIB, you set *xSrc* and *ySrc* equal to 0 and *cxSrc* and *cySrc* equal to the pixel width and height of the DIB, respectively. Note that because the *biHeight* field of the BITMAPINFO-HEADER structure will be negative for top-down DIBs, *cySrc* should be set to the absolute value of the *biHeight* field.

The documentation of this function (*/Platform SDK/Graphics and Multimedia Services/ GDI/Bitmaps/Bitmap Reference/Bitmap Functions/SetDIBitsToDevice*) says that the *xSrc*, *ySrc*, *cxSrc*, and *cySrc* arguments are in logical units. This is not true. They are pixel coordinates and dimensions. It makes no sense for the pixels within a DIB to have logical coordinates and units. Moreover, regardless of the mapping mode, a DIB displayed on an output device will always be *cxSrc* pixels wide and *cySrc* pixels high.

Let me also skip a detailed discussion of the next two arguments, *yScan* and *cyScan*, for now. These arguments let you reduce memory requirements by displaying a DIB sequentially a bit at a time as you read it from a disk file or a modem connection. Usually, you set *yScan* to 0 and *cyScan* to the height of the DIB.

The *pBits* argument is a pointer to the DIB pixel bits. The *pInfo* argument is a pointer to the BITMAPINFO structure of the DIB. Although the address of the BITMAPINFO structure is the same as the address of the BITMAPINFOHEADER structure, the *SetDIBitsToDevice* function is defined to use the BITMAPINFO structure as a subtle hint: for 1-bit, 4-bit, and 8-bit DIBs, the bitmap information header must be followed by a color table. Although defined as a pointer to a BITMAPINFO structure, this argument can also be a pointer to a BITMAPCOREINFO, BITMAPV4HEADER, or BITMAPV5HEADER structure.

The last argument is either DIB_RGB_COLORS or DIB_PAL_COLORS, defined in WINGDI.H as 0 and 1, respectively. For now you'll use DIB_RGB_COLORS, which means that the DIB contains a color table. The DIB_PAL_COLORS flag indicates that the color table in the DIB has been replaced with 16-bit indices into a logical color palette selected and realized in a device context. We'll learn about this option in the next chapter. For now, use DIB_RGB_COLORS, or simply 0 if you're lazy.

The *SetDIBitsToDevice* function returns the number of scan lines it displays.

So, to call *SetDIBitsToDevice* to display an entire DIB image, you'll need the following information:

- *hdc* The device context handle to the destination surface.

- *xDst* and *yDst* The destination coordinates of the top left corner of the image.

- *cxDib* and *cyDib* The pixel width and height of the DIB, where *cyDib* is the absolute value of the *biHeight* field in the BITMAPINFOHEADER structure.

- *pInfo* and *pBits* Pointers to the bitmap information section and the pixel bits.

You then call *SetDIBitsToDevice* like so:

```
SetDIBitsToDevice (
        hdc,        // device context handle
        xDst,       // x destination coordinate
        yDst,       // y destination coordinate
        cxDib,      // source rectangle width
        cyDib,      // source rectangle height
        0,          // x source coordinate
        0,          // y source coordinate
        0,          // first scan line to draw
        cyDib,      // number of scan lines to draw
        pBits,      // pointer to DIB pixel bits
        pInfo,      // pointer to DIB information
        0) ;        // color use flag
```

So, out of the 12 arguments to the DIB, four are commonly set to 0 and another is repeated.

The SHOWDIB1 program in Figure 15-2 displays a DIB by using the *SetDIBitsToDevice* function.

SHOWDIB1.C

```
/*-------------------------------------------------
    SHOWDIB1.C -- Shows a DIB in the client area
                  (c) Charles Petzold, 1998
   -------------------------------------------------*/

#include <windows.h>
#include "dibfile.h"
#include "resource.h"

LRESULT CALLBACK WndProc (HWND, UINT, WPARAM, LPARAM) ;

TCHAR szAppName[] = TEXT ("ShowDib1") ;

int WINAPI WinMain (HINSTANCE hInstance, HINSTANCE hPrevInstance,
                    PSTR szCmdLine, int iCmdShow)
{
    HACCEL   hAccel ;
    HWND     hwnd ;
    MSG      msg ;
    WNDCLASS wndclass ;

    wndclass.style         = CS_HREDRAW | CS_VREDRAW ;
    wndclass.lpfnWndProc   = WndProc ;
```

Figure 15-2. *The SHOWDIB1 program.*

```
        wndclass.cbClsExtra    = 0 ;
        wndclass.cbWndExtra    = 0 ;
        wndclass.hInstance     = hInstance ;
        wndclass.hIcon         = LoadIcon (NULL, IDI_APPLICATION) ;
        wndclass.hCursor       = LoadCursor (NULL, IDC_ARROW) ;
        wndclass.hbrBackground = (HBRUSH) GetStockObject (WHITE_BRUSH) ;
        wndclass.lpszMenuName  = szAppName ;
        wndclass.lpszClassName = szAppName ;

        if (!RegisterClass (&wndclass))
        {
             MessageBox (NULL, TEXT ("This program requires Windows NT!"),
                         szAppName, MB_ICONERROR) ;
             return 0 ;
        }

        hwnd = CreateWindow (szAppName, TEXT ("Show DIB #1"),
                             WS_OVERLAPPEDWINDOW,
                             CW_USEDEFAULT, CW_USEDEFAULT,
                             CW_USEDEFAULT, CW_USEDEFAULT,
                             NULL, NULL, hInstance, NULL) ;

        ShowWindow (hwnd, iCmdShow) ;
        UpdateWindow (hwnd) ;

        hAccel = LoadAccelerators (hInstance, szAppName) ;

        while (GetMessage (&msg, NULL, 0, 0))
        {
             if (!TranslateAccelerator (hwnd, hAccel, &msg))
             {
                  TranslateMessage (&msg) ;
                  DispatchMessage (&msg) ;
             }
        }
        return msg.wParam ;
}

LRESULT CALLBACK WndProc (HWND hwnd, UINT message, WPARAM wParam, LPARAM lParam)
{
        static BITMAPFILEHEADER * pbmfh ;
        static BITMAPINFO       * pbmi ;
        static BYTE             * pBits ;
        static int                cxClient, cyClient, cxDib, cyDib ;
```

(continued)

Figure 15-2. *continued*

```
static TCHAR            szFileName [MAX_PATH], szTitleName [MAX_PATH] ;
BOOL                    bSuccess ;
HDC                     hdc ;
PAINTSTRUCT             ps ;

switch (message)
{
case WM_CREATE:
     DibFileInitialize (hwnd) ;
     return 0 ;

case WM_SIZE:
     cxClient = LOWORD (lParam) ;
     cyClient = HIWORD (lParam) ;
     return 0 ;

case WM_INITMENUPOPUP:
     EnableMenuItem ((HMENU) wParam, IDM_FILE_SAVE,
                 pbmfh ? MF_ENABLED : MF_GRAYED) ;
     return 0 ;

case WM_COMMAND:
     switch (LOWORD (wParam))
     {
     case IDM_FILE_OPEN:
             // Show the File Open dialog box

          if (!DibFileOpenDlg (hwnd, szFileName, szTitleName))
               return 0 ;

               // If there's an existing DIB, free the memory

          if (pbmfh)
          {
               free (pbmfh) ;
               pbmfh = NULL ;
          }
               // Load the entire DIB into memory

          SetCursor (LoadCursor (NULL, IDC_WAIT)) ;
          ShowCursor (TRUE) ;

          pbmfh = DibLoadImage (szFileName) ;
```

```
        ShowCursor (FALSE) ;
        SetCursor (LoadCursor (NULL, IDC_ARROW)) ;

             // Invalidate the client area for later update

        InvalidateRect (hwnd, NULL, TRUE) ;

        if (pbmfh == NULL)
        {
             MessageBox (hwnd, TEXT ("Cannot load DIB file"),
                         szAppName, 0) ;
             return 0 ;
        }
             // Get pointers to the info structure & the bits

        pbmi  = (BITMAPINFO *) (pbmfh + 1) ;
        pBits = (BYTE *) pbmfh + pbmfh->bfOffBits ;

             // Get the DIB width and height

        if (pbmi->bmiHeader.biSize == sizeof (BITMAPCOREHEADER))
        {
             cxDib = ((BITMAPCOREHEADER *) pbmi)->bcWidth ;
             cyDib = ((BITMAPCOREHEADER *) pbmi)->bcHeight ;
        }
        else
        {
             cxDib =       pbmi->bmiHeader.biWidth ;
             cyDib = abs (pbmi->bmiHeader.biHeight) ;
        }
        return 0 ;

   case IDM_FILE_SAVE:
             // Show the File Save dialog box

        if (!DibFileSaveDlg (hwnd, szFileName, szTitleName))
             return 0 ;

             // Save the DIB to memory

        SetCursor (LoadCursor (NULL, IDC_WAIT)) ;
        ShowCursor (TRUE) ;

        bSuccess = DibSaveImage (szFileName, pbmfh) ;
```

(continued)

Figure 15-2. *continued*

```
              ShowCursor (FALSE) ;
              SetCursor (LoadCursor (NULL, IDC_ARROW)) ;

              if (!bSuccess)
                   MessageBox (hwnd, TEXT ("Cannot save DIB file"),
                               szAppName, 0) ;
              return 0 ;
         }
         break ;

    case WM_PAINT:
         hdc = BeginPaint (hwnd, &ps) ;

         if (pbmfh)
              SetDIBitsToDevice (hdc,
                                 0,          // xDst
                                 0,          // yDst
                                 cxDib,      // cxSrc
                                 cyDib,      // cySrc
                                 0,          // xSrc
                                 0,          // ySrc
                                 0,          // first scan line
                                 cyDib,      // number of scan lines
                                 pBits,
                                 pbmi,
                                 DIB_RGB_COLORS) ;

         EndPaint (hwnd, &ps) ;
         return 0 ;

    case WM_DESTROY:
         if (pbmfh)
              free (pbmfh) ;

         PostQuitMessage (0) ;
         return 0 ;
    }
    return DefWindowProc (hwnd, message, wParam, lParam) ;
}
```

DIBFILE.H

```
/*------------------------------------------
   DIBFILE.H -- Header File for DIBFILE.C
  ------------------------------------------*/
```

```
void DibFileInitialize (HWND hwnd) ;
BOOL DibFileOpenDlg (HWND hwnd, PTSTR pstrFileName, PTSTR pstrTitleName) ;
BOOL DibFileSaveDlg (HWND hwnd, PTSTR pstrFileName, PTSTR pstrTitleName) ;

BITMAPFILEHEADER * DibLoadImage (PTSTR pstrFileName) ;
BOOL               DibSaveImage (PTSTR pstrFileName, BITMAPFILEHEADER *) ;
```

DIBFILE.C

```
/*-----------------------------------
   DIBFILE.C -- DIB File Functions
  -----------------------------------*/

#include <windows.h>
#include <commdlg.h>
#include "dibfile.h"

static OPENFILENAME ofn ;

void DibFileInitialize (HWND hwnd)
{
     static TCHAR szFilter[] = TEXT ("Bitmap Files (*.BMP)\0*.bmp\0")  \
                               TEXT ("All Files (*.*)\0*.*\0\0") ;

     ofn.lStructSize       = sizeof (OPENFILENAME) ;
     ofn.hwndOwner         = hwnd ;
     ofn.hInstance         = NULL ;
     ofn.lpstrFilter       = szFilter ;
     ofn.lpstrCustomFilter = NULL ;
     ofn.nMaxCustFilter    = 0 ;
     ofn.nFilterIndex      = 0 ;
     ofn.lpstrFile         = NULL ;          // Set in Open and Close functions
     ofn.nMaxFile          = MAX_PATH ;
     ofn.lpstrFileTitle    = NULL ;          // Set in Open and Close functions
     ofn.nMaxFileTitle     = MAX_PATH ;
     ofn.lpstrInitialDir   = NULL ;
     ofn.lpstrTitle        = NULL ;
     ofn.Flags             = 0 ;             // Set in Open and Close functions
     ofn.nFileOffset       = 0 ;
     ofn.nFileExtension    = 0 ;
     ofn.lpstrDefExt       = TEXT ("bmp") ;
     ofn.lCustData         = 0 ;
     ofn.lpfnHook          = NULL ;
     ofn.lpTemplateName    = NULL ;
}
```

(continued)

Figure 15-2. *continued*

```
BOOL DibFileOpenDlg (HWND hwnd, PTSTR pstrFileName, PTSTR pstrTitleName)
{
     ofn.hwndOwner          = hwnd ;
     ofn.lpstrFile          = pstrFileName ;
     ofn.lpstrFileTitle     = pstrTitleName ;
     ofn.Flags              = 0 ;

     return GetOpenFileName (&ofn) ;
}

BOOL DibFileSaveDlg (HWND hwnd, PTSTR pstrFileName, PTSTR pstrTitleName)
{
     ofn.hwndOwner          = hwnd ;
     ofn.lpstrFile          = pstrFileName ;
     ofn.lpstrFileTitle     = pstrTitleName ;
     ofn.Flags              = OFN_OVERWRITEPROMPT ;

     return GetSaveFileName (&ofn) ;
}

BITMAPFILEHEADER * DibLoadImage (PTSTR pstrFileName)
{
     BOOL              bSuccess ;
     DWORD             dwFileSize, dwHighSize, dwBytesRead ;
     HANDLE            hFile ;
     BITMAPFILEHEADER * pbmfh ;

     hFile = CreateFile (pstrFileName, GENERIC_READ, FILE_SHARE_READ, NULL,
                         OPEN_EXISTING, FILE_FLAG_SEQUENTIAL_SCAN, NULL) ;

     if (hFile == INVALID_HANDLE_VALUE)
         return NULL ;

     dwFileSize = GetFileSize (hFile, &dwHighSize) ;

     if (dwHighSize)
     {
         CloseHandle (hFile) ;
         return NULL ;
     }

     pbmfh = malloc (dwFileSize) ;
```

```
     if (!pbmfh)
     {
          CloseHandle (hFile) ;
          return NULL ;
     }

     bSuccess = ReadFile (hFile, pbmfh, dwFileSize, &dwBytesRead, NULL) ;
     CloseHandle (hFile) ;

     if (!bSuccess || (dwBytesRead != dwFileSize)
                   || (pbmfh->bfType != * (WORD *) "BM")
                   || (pbmfh->bfSize != dwFileSize))
     {
          free (pbmfh) ;
          return NULL ;
     }
     return pbmfh ;
}

BOOL DibSaveImage (PTSTR pstrFileName, BITMAPFILEHEADER * pbmfh)
{
     BOOL   bSuccess ;
     DWORD  dwBytesWritten ;
     HANDLE hFile ;

     hFile = CreateFile (pstrFileName, GENERIC_WRITE, 0, NULL,
                         CREATE_ALWAYS, FILE_ATTRIBUTE_NORMAL, NULL) ;

     if (hFile == INVALID_HANDLE_VALUE)
          return FALSE ;

     bSuccess = WriteFile (hFile, pbmfh, pbmfh->bfSize, &dwBytesWritten, NULL) ;
     CloseHandle (hFile) ;

     if (!bSuccess || (dwBytesWritten != pbmfh->bfSize))
     {
          DeleteFile (pstrFileName) ;
          return FALSE ;
     }
     return TRUE ;
}
```

(continued)

Figure 15-2. *continued*

SHOWDIB1.RC (excerpts)

```
//Microsoft Developer Studio generated resource script.

#include "resource.h"
#include "afxres.h"


//////////////////////////////////////////////////////////////////////////////
// Menu

SHOWDIB1 MENU DISCARDABLE
BEGIN
    POPUP "&File"
    BEGIN
        MENUITEM "&Open...",                    IDM_FILE_OPEN
        MENUITEM "&Save...",                    IDM_FILE_SAVE
    END
END
```

RESOURCE.H (excerpts)

```
// Microsoft Developer Studio generated include file.
// Used by ShowDib1.rc

#define IDM_FILE_OPEN                    40001
#define IDM_FILE_SAVE                    40002
```

The DIBFILE.C file contains routines to display the File Open and File Save dialog boxes and also to load an entire DIB file (complete with the BITMAPFILEHEADER structure) into a single block of memory. The program can also write out such a memory block to a file.

After loading in a DIB file while processing the File Open command in SHOWDIB1.C, the program calculates the offsets of the BITMAPINFOHEADER structure and the pixel bits within the memory block. The program also obtains the pixel width and height of the DIB. All of this information is stored in static variables. During the WM_PAINT message, the program displays the DIB by calling *SetDIBitsToDevice*.

Of course, SHOWDIB1 is missing a few features. For instance, if the DIB is too big for the client area, there are no scroll bars to move it into view. These are deficiencies that will be fixed before the end of the next chapter.

The Topsy-Turvy World of DIBs

We are about to learn an important lesson, not only in life but in the design of application program interfaces for operating systems. That lesson is: if you screw something up at the beginning, it only gets more screwed up when you later try to patch it.

Back when the bottom-up definition of the DIB pixel bits originated in the OS/2 Presentation Manager, it made some degree of sense because everything in PM has a default bottom left origin. For example, within a PM window, the default (0,0) origin is the lower left corner of the window. (If this sounds wacky to you, you're not alone. If it doesn't sound wacky, you're probably a mathematician.) The bitmap-drawing functions also specified a destination in terms of lower left coordinates.

So, in OS/2, if you specified a destination coordinate of (0,0) for the bitmap, the image would appear flush against the left and bottom of the window, as in Figure 15-3.

Figure 15-3. *A bitmap as it would be displayed under OS/2 with a (0,0) destination.*

With a slow enough machine, you could actually see the bitmap being drawn from the bottom to the top.

While the OS/2 coordinate system may seem wacky, it has the virtue of being highly consistent. The (0,0) origin of the bitmap is the first pixel of the first row in the bitmap file, and this pixel is mapped to the destination coordinate indicated in the bitmap-drawing functions.

The problem with Windows is that internal consistency was not maintained. When you want to display only a rectangular subset within the entire DIB image, you use the arguments *xSrc*, *ySrc*, *cxSrc*, and *cySrc*. These source coordinates and sizes are relative to the first row of the DIB data, which is the bottom row of the image. That's just like OS/2. However, unlike OS/2, Windows displays the top row of the image at the destination coordinate. Thus, if you're displaying the entire DIB image, the pixel displayed at (*xDst*, *yDst*) is the DIB pixel at coordinate (0, *cyDib* - 1). That's the last row of DIB data but the top row of the image. If you're displaying only part of the image, the pixel displayed at (*xDst*, *yDst*) is the DIB pixel at coordinate (*xSrc*, *ySrc* + *cySrc* - 1).

Figure 15-4 shows a diagram to help you figure this out. The DIB below is shown as you might imagine it stored in memory—that is, upside-down. The origin from which the coordinates are measured is coincident with the first bit of pixel data in the DIB. The *xSrc* argument to *SetDIBitsToDevice* is measured from the left of the DIB, and *cxSrc* is the width of the image to the right of *xSrc*. That's straightforward. The *ySrc* argument is measured from the first row of the DIB data (that is, the bottom of the image), and *cySrc* is the height of image from *ySrc* towards the last row of the data (the top of the image).

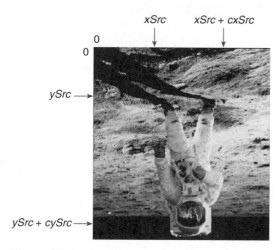

Figure 15-4. *Specifying DIB coordinates for normal (bottom-up) DIBs.*

If the destination device context has default pixel coordinates using the MM_TEXT mapping mode, the relationship between the corner coordinates of the source and destination rectangles will be those shown in the table below:

Source Rectangle	*Destination Rectangle*
(*xSrc*, *ySrc*)	(*xDst*, *yDst* + *cySrc* - 1)
(*xSrc* + *cxSrc* - 1, *ySrc*)	(*xDst* + *cxSrc* - 1, *yDst* + *cySrc* - 1)
(*xSrc*, *ySrc* + *cySrc* - 1)	(*xDst*, *yDst*)
(*xSrc* + *cxSrc* - 1, *ySrc* + *cySrc* - 1)	(*xDst* + *cxSrc* - 1, *yDst*)

That (*xSrc*, *ySrc*) does not map to (*xDst*, *yDst*) is what makes this so chaotic. With any other mapping mode, the point (*xSrc*, *ySrc* + *cySrc* - 1) will still map to the logical point (*xDst*, *yDst*) and the image will look the same as it does in MM_TEXT.

So far, I've been discussing the normal case when the *biHeight* field of the BITMAP-INFOHEADER structure is positive. If the *biHeight* field is negative, the DIB data is arranged in a rational top-down manner. You may believe that this clears up all the problems. If so, you would be very naive.

Apparently someone decided that if you take a top-down DIB, flip all the rows around, and then set the *biHeight* field to a positive value, it should work the same as a normal bottom-up DIB. Any existing code that referenced a rectangle of the DIB shouldn't have to be modified. That's a reasonable objective, I suppose, but it doesn't take into account the fact that programs need to be modified anyway to deal with top-down DIBs so as not to use a negative height.

Moreover, the result of this decision has strange implications. It means that source coordinates of top-down DIBs have an origin at the last row of the DIB data, which is also the bottom row of the image. This is completely alien to anything we've yet encountered. The DIB pixel at the (0,0) origin is no longer the first pixel referenced by the *pBits* pointer. Nor is it the last pixel in the DIB file. It's somewhere in between.

Figure 15-5 shows a diagram indicating how you specify a rectangle within a top-down DIB, again showing the DIB as it is stored in the file or in memory:

Figure 15-5. *Specifying DIB coordinates for top-down DIBs.*

At any rate, the real advantage of this scheme is that the arguments to the *SetDIBits-ToDevice* function are independent of the orientation of the DIB data. If you have two DIBs (one bottom-up and the other top-down) that show the same image (which means that the order of rows in the two DIB files are opposite each other), you can select the same part of the image to display using identical arguments to *SetDIBitsToDevice*.

This is demonstrated in the APOLLO11 program shown in Figure 15-6.

APOLLO11.C

```
/*------------------------------------------------
   APOLLO11.C -- Program for screen captures
                 (c) Charles Petzold, 1998
   ------------------------------------------------*/

#include <windows.h>
#include "dibfile.h"

LRESULT CALLBACK WndProc (HWND, UINT, WPARAM, LPARAM) ;

TCHAR szAppName[] = TEXT ("Apollo11") ;

int WINAPI WinMain (HINSTANCE hInstance, HINSTANCE hPrevInstance,
                    PSTR szCmdLine, int iCmdShow)
{
    HWND     hwnd ;
    MSG      msg ;
    WNDCLASS wndclass ;

    wndclass.style         = CS_HREDRAW | CS_VREDRAW ;
    wndclass.lpfnWndProc   = WndProc ;
    wndclass.cbClsExtra    = 0 ;
    wndclass.cbWndExtra    = 0 ;
    wndclass.hInstance     = hInstance ;
    wndclass.hIcon         = LoadIcon (NULL, IDI_APPLICATION) ;
    wndclass.hCursor       = LoadCursor (NULL, IDC_ARROW) ;
    wndclass.hbrBackground = (HBRUSH) GetStockObject (WHITE_BRUSH) ;
    wndclass.lpszMenuName  = NULL ;
    wndclass.lpszClassName = szAppName ;

    if (!RegisterClass (&wndclass))
    {
        MessageBox (NULL, TEXT ("This program requires Windows NT!"),
                    szAppName, MB_ICONERROR) ;
        return 0 ;
    }
```

Figure 15-6. *The APOLLO11 program.*

```
      hwnd = CreateWindow (szAppName, TEXT ("Apollo 11"),
                           WS_OVERLAPPEDWINDOW,
                           CW_USEDEFAULT, CW_USEDEFAULT,
                           CW_USEDEFAULT, CW_USEDEFAULT,
                           NULL, NULL, hInstance, NULL) ;

      ShowWindow (hwnd, iCmdShow) ;
      UpdateWindow (hwnd) ;

      while (GetMessage (&msg, NULL, 0, 0))
      {
           TranslateMessage (&msg) ;
           DispatchMessage (&msg) ;
      }
      return msg.wParam ;
}

LRESULT CALLBACK WndProc (HWND hwnd, UINT message, WPARAM wParam, LPARAM lParam)
{
      static BITMAPFILEHEADER * pbmfh [2] ;
      static BITMAPINFO       * pbmi  [2] ;
      static BYTE             * pBits [2] ;
      static int                cxClient, cyClient, cxDib [2], cyDib [2] ;
      HDC                       hdc ;
      PAINTSTRUCT               ps ;

      switch (message)
      {
      case WM_CREATE:
           pbmfh[0] = DibLoadImage (TEXT ("Apollo11.bmp")) ;
           pbmfh[1] = DibLoadImage (TEXT ("ApolloTD.bmp")) ;

           if (pbmfh[0] == NULL || pbmfh[1] == NULL)
           {
                MessageBox (hwnd, TEXT ("Cannot load DIB file"),
                                  szAppName, 0) ;
                return 0 ;
           }
                // Get pointers to the info structure & the bits

           pbmi [0] = (BITMAPINFO *) (pbmfh[0] + 1) ;
           pbmi [1] = (BITMAPINFO *) (pbmfh[1] + 1) ;
```

(continued)

Figure 15-6. *continued*

```
            pBits [0] = (BYTE *) pbmfh[0] + pbmfh[0]->bfOffBits ;
            pBits [1] = (BYTE *) pbmfh[1] + pbmfh[1]->bfOffBits ;

                 // Get the DIB width and height (assume BITMAPINFOHEADER)
                 // Note that cyDib is the absolute value of the header value!!!

            cxDib [0] =      pbmi[0]->bmiHeader.biWidth ;
            cxDib [1] =      pbmi[1]->bmiHeader.biWidth ;

            cyDib [0] = abs (pbmi[0]->bmiHeader.biHeight) ;
            cyDib [1] = abs (pbmi[1]->bmiHeader.biHeight) ;
            return 0 ;

      case WM_SIZE:
            cxClient = LOWORD (lParam) ;
            cyClient = HIWORD (lParam) ;
            return 0 ;

      case WM_PAINT:
            hdc = BeginPaint (hwnd, &ps) ;

                 // Bottom-up DIB full size

            SetDIBitsToDevice (hdc,
                               0,                 // xDst
                               cyClient / 4,      // yDst
                               cxDib[0],          // cxSrc
                               cyDib[0],          // cySrc
                               0,                 // xSrc
                               0,                 // ySrc
                               0,                 // first scan line
                               cyDib[0],          // number of scan lines
                               pBits[0],
                               pbmi[0],
                               DIB_RGB_COLORS) ;

                 // Bottom-up DIB partial

            SetDIBitsToDevice (hdc,
                               240,               // xDst
                               cyClient / 4,      // yDst
                               80,                // cxSrc
                               166,               // cySrc
                               80,                // xSrc
```

```
                          60,                    // ySrc
                          0,                     // first scan line
                          cyDib[0],              // number of scan lines
                          pBits[0],
                          pbmi[0],
                          DIB_RGB_COLORS) ;

          // Top-down DIB full size

     SetDIBitsToDevice (hdc,
                          340,                   // xDst
                          cyClient / 4,          // yDst
                          cxDib[0],              // cxSrc
                          cyDib[0],              // cySrc
                          0,                     // xSrc
                          0,                     // ySrc
                          0,                     // first scan line
                          cyDib[0],              // number of scan lines
                          pBits[0],
                          pbmi[0],
                          DIB_RGB_COLORS) ;

          // Top-down DIB partial

     SetDIBitsToDevice (hdc,
                          580,                   // xDst
                          cyClient / 4,          // yDst
                          80,                    // cxSrc
                          166,                   // cySrc
                          80,                    // xSrc
                          60,                    // ySrc
                          0,                     // first scan line
                          cyDib[1],              // number of scan lines
                          pBits[1],
                          pbmi[1],
                          DIB_RGB_COLORS) ;

     EndPaint (hwnd, &ps) ;
     return 0 ;

case WM_DESTROY:
     if (pbmfh[0])
          free (pbmfh[0]) ;
```

(continued)

Figure 15-6. *continued*

```
        if (pbmfh[1])
            free (pbmfh[1]) ;

        PostQuitMessage (0) ;
        return 0 ;
    }
    return DefWindowProc (hwnd, message, wParam, lParam) ;
}
```

The program loads two DIBS, named APOLLO11.BMP (the bottom-up version) and APOLLOTD.BMP (the top-down version). Both are 220 pixels wide and 240 pixels high. Note that when the program determines the DIB width and height from the header information structure, it uses the *abs* function to take the absolute value of the *biHeight* field. When displaying the DIBs in full size or in the partial views, the *xSrc*, *ySrc*, *cxSrc*, and *cySrc* coordinates are identical regardless of which bitmap is being displayed. The results are shown in Figure 15-7.

Figure 15-7. *The APOLLO11 display.*

Notice that the "first scan line" and "number of scan lines" arguments remain unchanged. I'll get to those shortly. The *pBits* argument is also unchanged. Don't try to alter *pBits* so that it points only to the area of the DIB you wish to display.

I'm spending so much time on this issue not because I have a desire to knock the Windows developers for attempting their best to reconcile problematic areas in the definition of the API, but because you shouldn't be nervous if this seems to be confusing. It's confusing because it's confused.

I also want you to be alert to certain statements in the Windows documentation such as this one for *SetDIBitsToDevice*: "The origin of a bottom-up DIB is the lower left corner of the bitmap; the origin of a top-down DIB is the upper left corner." That's not only ambiguous, it's just plain wrong. We can better state the difference like so: *The origin of a bottom-up DIB is the bottom left corner of the bitmap image, which is the first pixel of the first row of bitmap data. The origin of a top-down DIB is also the bottom left corner of the bitmap image, but in this case the bottom left corner is the first pixel of the last row of bitmap data.*

The problem gets worse if you need to write a function that lets your programs access individual bits of a DIB. This should be consistent with the way that you specify coordinates for displaying partial DIB images. My solution (which I'll implement in a DIB library in Chapter 16) is to uniformly reference DIB pixels and coordinates as if the (0,0) origin refers to the leftmost pixel of the top row of the DIB image as seen when correctly displayed.

Sequential Display

Having lots of memory sure makes programming easier. Displaying a DIB that's located in a disk file can be broken into two completely independent jobs: loading the DIB into memory and then displaying it.

Regardless, there might be times when you would like to display a DIB without requiring that the entire file be loaded into memory. Even if enough physical memory is available for the DIB, moving the DIB into memory can force Windows' virtual memory system to move other code and data out to disk. This can be particularly distressing if the DIB is needed only for display and can then be immediately discarded from memory.

Here's another problem: Suppose the DIB resides on a slow storage medium such as a floppy disk. Or it's coming over a modem. Or it's coming from a conversion routine that's getting pixel data from a scanner or a video frame grabber. Do you want to wait until the entire DIB is loaded into memory before you display it? Or would you rather display the DIB sequentially right as it's coming off the disk or through the telephone line or from the scanner?

Solving these problems is the purpose of the *yScan* and *cyScans* arguments to the *SetDIBitsToDevice* function. To use this feature, you make multiple calls to *SetDIBitsToDevice*, mostly with the same arguments. However, for each call, the *pBits* argument points to different sections of the total array of bitmap pixels. The *yScans* argument indicates which row of pixel data *pBits* is pointing to, and the *cyScans* argument is the number of rows referenced by *pBits*. This reduces memory requirements considerably. You need allocate only enough memory to hold the information section of the DIB (the BITMAPINFO-HEADER structure and the color table) and at least 1 row of pixel data.

For example, suppose the DIB has 23 rows of pixels. You wish to display this DIB in blocks of 5 rows. You'll probably want to allocate a block of memory, referenced by the variable *pInfo*, to store the BITMAPINFO section of the DIB. Then read it in from the file. After examining the fields of this structure, you can calculate the byte length of a row. Multiply by 5 and allocate another block (*pBits*) of that size. Now read in the first 5 rows. Call the function as you would normally, but with *yScan* set equal to 0 and *cyScans* set equal to 5. Now read the next 5 rows from the file. This time set *yScan* equal to 5. Continue with *yScan* set to 10 and then 15. Finally, read the last 3 rows into the block addressed by *pBits*, and call *SetDIBitsToDevice* with *yScan* set to 20 and *cyScans* set to 3.

Now here's the bad news. First, using this feature of *SetDIBitsToDevice* requires a fairly close coupling between the data acquisition and the data presentation elements of your program. This is usually undesirable because you have to alternate between getting the data and showing it. Overall, you'll slow down the entire process. Secondly, *SetDIBitsToDevice* is the only bitmap-display function that has this feature. As we'll see, the *StretchDIBits* function does not include this feature, so you can't use it to display the incoming DIB in a different pixel size. You'd have to fake it by calling *StretchDIBits* multiple times, each time altering information in the BITMAPINFOHEADER structure and displaying the results in a different area of the screen.

The SEQDISP program in Figure 15-8 demonstrates how to use this feature.

SEQDISP.C

```
/*---------------------------------------------
   SEQDISP.C -- Sequential Display of DIBs
                (c) Charles Petzold, 1998
   ---------------------------------------------*/

#include <windows.h>
#include "resource.h"

LRESULT CALLBACK WndProc (HWND, UINT, WPARAM, LPARAM) ;

TCHAR szAppName[] = TEXT ("SeqDisp") ;

int WINAPI WinMain (HINSTANCE hInstance, HINSTANCE hPrevInstance,
                    PSTR szCmdLine, int iCmdShow)
{
    HACCEL    hAccel ;
    HWND      hwnd ;
    MSG       msg ;
    WNDCLASS  wndclass ;

    wndclass.style         = CS_HREDRAW | CS_VREDRAW ;
    wndclass.lpfnWndProc   = WndProc ;
    wndclass.cbClsExtra    = 0 ;
```

Figure 15-8. *The SEQDISP program.*

```
      wndclass.cbWndExtra    = 0 ;
      wndclass.hInstance     = hInstance ;
      wndclass.hIcon         = LoadIcon (NULL, IDI_APPLICATION) ;
      wndclass.hCursor       = LoadCursor (NULL, IDC_ARROW) ;
      wndclass.hbrBackground = (HBRUSH) GetStockObject (WHITE_BRUSH) ;
      wndclass.lpszMenuName  = szAppName ;
      wndclass.lpszClassName = szAppName ;

      if (!RegisterClass (&wndclass))
      {
           MessageBox (NULL, TEXT ("This program requires Windows NT!"),
                      szAppName, MB_ICONERROR) ;
           return 0 ;
      }

      hwnd = CreateWindow (szAppName, TEXT ("DIB Sequential Display"),
                          WS_OVERLAPPEDWINDOW,
                          CW_USEDEFAULT, CW_USEDEFAULT,
                          CW_USEDEFAULT, CW_USEDEFAULT,
                          NULL, NULL, hInstance, NULL) ;

      ShowWindow (hwnd, iCmdShow) ;
      UpdateWindow (hwnd) ;

      hAccel = LoadAccelerators (hInstance, szAppName) ;

      while (GetMessage (&msg, NULL, 0, 0))
      {
           if (!TranslateAccelerator (hwnd, hAccel, &msg))
           {
                TranslateMessage (&msg) ;
                DispatchMessage (&msg) ;
           }
      }
      return msg.wParam ;
}

LRESULT CALLBACK WndProc (HWND hwnd, UINT message, WPARAM wParam, LPARAM lParam)
{
      static BITMAPINFO * pbmi ;
      static BYTE        * pBits ;
      static int          cxDib, cyDib, cBits ;
      static OPENFILENAME ofn ;
      static TCHAR        szFileName [MAX_PATH], szTitleName [MAX_PATH] ;
```

(continued)

Figure 15-8. *continued*

```
static TCHAR          szFilter[] = TEXT ("Bitmap Files (*.BMP)\0*.bmp\0")
                                   TEXT ("All Files (*.*)\0*.*\0\0") ;
BITMAPFILEHEADER      bmfh ;
BOOL                  bSuccess, bTopDown ;
DWORD                 dwBytesRead ;
HANDLE                hFile ;
HDC                   hdc ;
HMENU                 hMenu ;
int                   iInfoSize, iBitsSize, iRowLength, y ;
PAINTSTRUCT           ps ;

switch (message)
{
case WM_CREATE:
     ofn.lStructSize       = sizeof (OPENFILENAME) ;
     ofn.hwndOwner         = hwnd ;
     ofn.hInstance         = NULL ;
     ofn.lpstrFilter       = szFilter ;
     ofn.lpstrCustomFilter = NULL ;
     ofn.nMaxCustFilter    = 0 ;
     ofn.nFilterIndex      = 0 ;
     ofn.lpstrFile         = szFileName ;
     ofn.nMaxFile          = MAX_PATH ;
     ofn.lpstrFileTitle    = szTitleName ;
     ofn.nMaxFileTitle     = MAX_PATH ;
     ofn.lpstrInitialDir   = NULL ;
     ofn.lpstrTitle        = NULL ;
     ofn.Flags             = 0 ;
     ofn.nFileOffset       = 0 ;
     ofn.nFileExtension    = 0 ;
     ofn.lpstrDefExt       = TEXT ("bmp") ;
     ofn.lCustData         = 0 ;
     ofn.lpfnHook          = NULL ;
     ofn.lpTemplateName    = NULL ;
     return 0 ;

case WM_COMMAND:
     hMenu = GetMenu (hwnd) ;

     switch (LOWORD (wParam))
     {
     case IDM_FILE_OPEN:
               // Display File Open dialog
```

```
if (!GetOpenFileName (&ofn))
     return 0 ;

     // Get rid of old DIB

if (pbmi)
{
     free (pbmi) ;
     pbmi = NULL ;
}

if (pBits)
{
     free (pBits) ;
     pBits = NULL ;
}

     // Generate WM_PAINT message to erase background

InvalidateRect (hwnd, NULL, TRUE) ;
UpdateWindow (hwnd) ;

     // Open the file

hFile = CreateFile (szFileName, GENERIC_READ,
               FILE_SHARE_READ, NULL, OPEN_EXISTING,
               FILE_FLAG_SEQUENTIAL_SCAN, NULL) ;

if (hFile == INVALID_HANDLE_VALUE)
{
     MessageBox (hwnd, TEXT ("Cannot open file."),
               szAppName, MB_ICONWARNING | MB_OK) ;
     return 0 ;
}

     // Read in the BITMAPFILEHEADER

bSuccess = ReadFile (hFile, &bmfh, sizeof (BITMAPFILEHEADER),
               &dwBytesRead, NULL) ;

if (!bSuccess || dwBytesRead != sizeof (BITMAPFILEHEADER))
{
     MessageBox (hwnd, TEXT ("Cannot read file."),
               szAppName, MB_ICONWARNING | MB_OK) ;
```

(continued)

Figure 15-8. *continued*

```
            CloseHandle (hFile) ;
            return 0 ;
}


       // Check that it's a bitmap

if (bmfh.bfType != * (WORD *) "BM")
{
       MessageBox (hwnd, TEXT ("File is not a bitmap."),
                  szAppName, MB_ICONWARNING | MB_OK) ;
       CloseHandle (hFile) ;
       return 0 ;
}


       // Allocate memory for header and bits

iInfoSize = bmfh.bfOffBits - sizeof (BITMAPFILEHEADER) ;
iBitsSize = bmfh.bfSize - bmfh.bfOffBits ;

pbmi  = malloc (iInfoSize) ;
pBits = malloc (iBitsSize) ;

if (pbmi == NULL || pBits == NULL)
{
       MessageBox (hwnd, TEXT ("Cannot allocate memory."),
                  szAppName, MB_ICONWARNING | MB_OK) ;
       if (pbmi)
            free (pbmi) ;
       if (pBits)
            free (pBits) ;
       CloseHandle (hFile) ;
       return 0 ;
}


       // Read in the Information Header

bSuccess = ReadFile (hFile, pbmi, iInfoSize,
                    &dwBytesRead, NULL) ;

if (!bSuccess || (int) dwBytesRead != iInfoSize)
{
       MessageBox (hwnd, TEXT ("Cannot read file."),
                  szAppName, MB_ICONWARNING | MB_OK) ;
       if (pbmi)
            free (pbmi) ;
```

```
          if (pBits)
               free (pBits) ;
          CloseHandle (hFile) ;
          return 0 ;
     }


          // Get the DIB width and height

     bTopDown = FALSE ;

     if (pbmi->bmiHeader.biSize == sizeof (BITMAPCOREHEADER))
     {
          cxDib = ((BITMAPCOREHEADER *) pbmi)->bcWidth ;
          cyDib = ((BITMAPCOREHEADER *) pbmi)->bcHeight ;
          cBits = ((BITMAPCOREHEADER *) pbmi)->bcBitCount ;
     }
     else
     {
          if (pbmi->bmiHeader.biHeight < 0)
               bTopDown = TRUE ;

          cxDib =        pbmi->bmiHeader.biWidth ;
          cyDib = abs (pbmi->bmiHeader.biHeight) ;
          cBits =        pbmi->bmiHeader.biBitCount ;

          if (pbmi->bmiHeader.biCompression != BI_RGB &&
              pbmi->bmiHeader.biCompression != BI_BITFIELDS)
          {
               MessageBox (hwnd, TEXT ("File is compressed."),
                            szAppName, MB_ICONWARNING | MB_OK) ;
               if (pbmi)
                    free (pbmi) ;
               if (pBits)
                    free (pBits) ;
               CloseHandle (hFile) ;
               return 0 ;
          }
     }

          // Get the row length

     iRowLength = ((cxDib * cBits + 31) & ~31) >> 3 ;

          // Read and display
```

(continued)

Figure 15-8. *continued*

```
            SetCursor (LoadCursor (NULL, IDC_WAIT)) ;
            ShowCursor (TRUE) ;

            hdc = GetDC (hwnd) ;

            for (y = 0 ; y < cyDib ; y++)
            {
                  ReadFile (hFile, pBits + y * iRowLength, iRowLength,
                            &dwBytesRead, NULL) ;

                  SetDIBitsToDevice (hdc,
                                  0,          // xDst
                                  0,          // yDst
                                  cxDib,      // cxSrc
                                  cyDib,      // cySrc
                                  0,          // xSrc
                                  0,          // ySrc
                                  bTopDown ? cyDib - y - 1 : y,
                                              // first scan line
                                  1,          // number of scan lines
                                  pBits + y * iRowLength,
                                  pbmi,
                                  DIB_RGB_COLORS) ;
            }
            ReleaseDC (hwnd, hdc) ;
            CloseHandle (hFile) ;
            ShowCursor (FALSE) ;
            SetCursor (LoadCursor (NULL, IDC_ARROW)) ;
            return 0 ;
      }
      break ;

case WM_PAINT:
      hdc = BeginPaint (hwnd, &ps) ;

      if (pbmi && pBits)
            SetDIBitsToDevice (hdc,
                            0,          // xDst
                            0,          // yDst
                            cxDib,      // cxSrc
                            cyDib,      // cySrc
                            0,          // xSrc
                            0,          // ySrc
                            0,          // first scan line
                            cyDib,      // number of scan lines
                            pBits,
```

```
                                    pbmi,
                                    DIB_RGB_COLORS) ;

          EndPaint (hwnd, &ps) ;
          return 0 ;

     case WM_DESTROY:
          if (pbmi)
               free (pbmi) ;

          if (pBits)
               free (pBits) ;

          PostQuitMessage (0) ;
          return 0 ;
     }
     return DefWindowProc (hwnd, message, wParam, lParam) ;
}
```

SEQDISP.RC (excerpts)

```
//Microsoft Developer Studio generated resource script.

#include "resource.h"
#include "afxres.h"


/////////////////////////////////////////////////////////////////////////////
// Accelerator

SEQDISP ACCELERATORS DISCARDABLE
BEGIN
    "O",             IDM_FILE_OPEN,          VIRTKEY, CONTROL, NOINVERT
END


/////////////////////////////////////////////////////////////////////////////
// Menu

SEQDISP MENU DISCARDABLE
BEGIN
    POPUP "&File"
    BEGIN
        MENUITEM "&Open...\tCtrl+O",             IDM_FILE_OPEN
    END
END
```

(continued)

Figure 15-8. *continued*

RESOURCE.H (excerpts)

```
// Microsoft Developer Studio generated include file.
// Used by SeqDisp.rc

#define IDM_FILE_OPEN                     40001
```

All the file I/O in SEQDISP.C occurs while processing the File Open menu command. Toward the end of WM_COMMAND processing, the program enters a loop that reads single lines of pixels and displays them with *SetDIBitsToDevice*. The entire DIB is retained in memory so that it can be displayed also during WM_PAINT processing.

Stretching to Fit

SetDIBitsToDevice does a pixel-to-pixel display of a DIB to an output device. This is probably not good for printing DIBs. The better the resolution of the printer, the tinier the image you'll get. You could end up with something the size of a postage stamp.

To display a DIB in a particular size on the output device by shrinking or stretching it, you can use *StretchDIBits*:

```
iLines = StretchDIBits (
            hdc,            // device context handle
            xDst,           // x destination coordinate
            yDst,           // y destination coordinate
            cxDst,          // destination rectangle width
            cyDst,          // destination rectangle height
            xSrc,           // x source coordinate
            ySrc,           // y source coordinate
            cxSrc,          // source rectangle width
            cySrc,          // source rectangle height
            pBits,          // pointer to DIB pixel bits
            pInfo,          // pointer to DIB information
            fClrUse,        // color use flag
            dwRop) ;        // raster operation
```

The function arguments are the same as *SetDIBitsToDevice* with three exceptions:

- The destination coordinates include a logical width (*cxDst*) and height (*cyDst*) as well as starting points.

- There is no facility to reduce memory requirements by displaying the DIB sequentially.

- The last argument is a raster operation, which indicates how the pixels of the DIB are combined with the pixels of the output device. We learned about these in the last chapter. For now, we'll be using SRCCOPY for this argument.

There's actually another difference that is more subtle. If you look at the declaration of *SetDIBitsToDevice*, you'll find that *cxSrc* and *cySrc* are DWORDs, which are 32-bit unsigned long integers. In *StretchDIBits*, *cxSrc* and *cySrc* (as well as *cxDst* and *cyDst*) are defined as signed integers, which implies that they can be negative. Indeed they can, as we'll shortly see. But let me add a bit of clarification if you've started examining whether other arguments can be negative: In both functions, *xSrc* and *ySrc* are defined as *int* values, but that's an error. These values are always nonnegative.

A source rectangle within the DIB is mapped to a destination rectangle as shown in the following table.

Source Rectangle	*Destination Rectangle*
(*xSrc*, *ySrc*)	(*xDst*, *yDst* + *cyDst* - 1)
(*xSrc* + *cxSrc* - 1, *ySrc*)	(*xDst* + *cxDst* - 1, *yDst* + *cyDst* - 1)
(*xSrc*, *ySrc* + *cySrc* - 1)	(*xDst*, *yDst*)
(*xSrc* + *cxSrc* - 1, *ySrc* + *cySrc* - 1)	(*xDst* + *cxDst* - 1, *yDst*)

The -1 terms in the right column are not quite accurate because the degree of stretch (as well as the mapping mode and other transforms) can cause the results to be slightly different.

As an example, let's think about a 2×2 DIB, where the *xSrc* and *ySrc* arguments to *StretchDIBits* are both 0 and *cxSrc* and *cySrc* are both 2. Assume we're displaying to a device context with the MM_TEXT mapping mode and no transforms. If *xDst* and *yDst* are both 0 and *cxDst* and *cyDst* are both 4, then we're stretching the DIB by a factor of 2. Each source pixel (*x*, *y*) will map to four destination pixels as shown here:

(0,0) --> (0,2) and (1,2) and (0,3) and (1,3)

(1,0) --> (2,2) and (3,2) and (2,3) and (3,3)

(0,1) --> (0,0) and (1,0) and (0,1) and (1,1)

(1,1) --> (2,0) and (3,0) and (2,1) and (3,1)

The table shown above correctly indicates the corners of the destination, which are (0, 3), (3, 3), (0, 0), and (3, 0). In other cases, the coordinates might be only approximate.

SetDIBitsToDevice is affected by the mapping mode of the destination device context only to the extent that *xDst* and *yDst* are logical coordinates. *StretchDIBits* is fully affected by the mapping mode. For example, if you've set one of the metric mapping modes where values of *y* increase going up the display, the DIB will be displayed upside-down.

You can compensate for this by making *cyDst* negative. Indeed, you can make any of the width and height parameters negative to flip the DIB horizontally or vertically. In the MM_TEXT mapping mode, if *cySrc* and *cyDst* are opposite signs, the DIB will be flipped around the horizontal axis and will appear to be upside-down. If *cxSrc* and *cxDst* are opposite signs, the DIB is flipped on its vertical axis and will appear to be a mirror image.

Here are a couple of expressions that summarize this. In these expressions, *xMM* and *yMM* indicate the orientation of the mapping mode; *xMM* is 1 if values of *x* increase moving to the right and -1 if values of *x* increase moving to the left. Similarly, *yMM* is 1 if values of *y* increase going down and -1 if values of *y* increase going up. The *Sign* functions return TRUE for a positive value and FALSE for negative:

```
if (!Sign (xMM × cxSrc × cxDst))
    DIB is flipped on its vertical axis (mirror image)

if (!Sign (yMM × cySrc × cyDst))
    DIB is flipped on its horizontal axis (upside down)
```

When in doubt, consult the table shown above.

The SHOWDIB2 program shown in Figure 15-9 displays DIBs in actual size and stretched to the size of its client window, prints DIBs, and transfers DIBs to the clipboard.

SHOWDIB2.C

```
/*----------------------------------------------
   SHOWDIB2.C -- Shows a DIB in the client area
                 (c) Charles Petzold, 1998
   ----------------------------------------------*/

#include <windows.h>
#include "dibfile.h"
#include "resource.h"

LRESULT CALLBACK WndProc (HWND, UINT, WPARAM, LPARAM) ;

TCHAR szAppName[] = TEXT ("ShowDib2") ;

int WINAPI WinMain (HINSTANCE hInstance, HINSTANCE hPrevInstance,
                    PSTR szCmdLine, int iCmdShow)
{
     HACCEL     hAccel ;
     HWND       hwnd ;
     MSG        msg ;
     WNDCLASS   wndclass ;
```

Figure 15-9. *The SHOWDIB2 program.*

```
    wndclass.style         = CS_HREDRAW | CS_VREDRAW ;
    wndclass.lpfnWndProc   = WndProc ;
    wndclass.cbClsExtra    = 0 ;
    wndclass.cbWndExtra    = 0 ;
    wndclass.hInstance     = hInstance ;
    wndclass.hIcon         = LoadIcon (NULL, IDI_APPLICATION) ;
    wndclass.hCursor       = LoadCursor (NULL, IDC_ARROW) ;
    wndclass.hbrBackground = (HBRUSH) GetStockObject (WHITE_BRUSH) ;
    wndclass.lpszMenuName  = szAppName ;
    wndclass.lpszClassName = szAppName ;

    if (!RegisterClass (&wndclass))
    {
        MessageBox (NULL, TEXT ("This program requires Windows NT!"),
                    szAppName, MB_ICONERROR) ;
        return 0 ;
    }

    hwnd = CreateWindow (szAppName, TEXT ("Show DIB #2"),
                    WS_OVERLAPPEDWINDOW,
                    CW_USEDEFAULT, CW_USEDEFAULT,
                    CW_USEDEFAULT, CW_USEDEFAULT,
                    NULL, NULL, hInstance, NULL) ;

    ShowWindow (hwnd, iCmdShow) ;
    UpdateWindow (hwnd) ;

    hAccel = LoadAccelerators (hInstance, szAppName) ;

    while (GetMessage (&msg, NULL, 0, 0))
    {
        if (!TranslateAccelerator (hwnd, hAccel, &msg))
        {
            TranslateMessage (&msg) ;
            DispatchMessage (&msg) ;
        }
    }
    return msg.wParam ;
}

int ShowDib (HDC hdc, BITMAPINFO * pbmi, BYTE * pBits, int cxDib, int cyDib,
        int cxClient, int cyClient, WORD wShow)
{
    switch (wShow)
```

(continued)

Figure 15-9. *continued*

```
      {
      case IDM_SHOW_NORMAL:
           return SetDIBitsToDevice (hdc, 0, 0, cxDib, cyDib, 0, 0,
                                     0, cyDib, pBits, pbmi, DIB_RGB_COLORS) ;

      case IDM_SHOW_CENTER:
           return SetDIBitsToDevice (hdc, (cxClient - cxDib) / 2,
                                          (cyClient - cyDib) / 2,
                                     cxDib, cyDib, 0, 0,
                                     0, cyDib, pBits, pbmi, DIB_RGB_COLORS) ;

      case IDM_SHOW_STRETCH:
           SetStretchBltMode (hdc, COLORONCOLOR) ;

           return StretchDIBits (hdc, 0, 0, cxClient, cyClient,
                                 0, 0, cxDib, cyDib,
                                 pBits, pbmi, DIB_RGB_COLORS, SRCCOPY) ;

      case IDM_SHOW_ISOSTRETCH:
           SetStretchBltMode (hdc, COLORONCOLOR) ;
           SetMapMode (hdc, MM_ISOTROPIC) ;
           SetWindowExtEx (hdc, cxDib, cyDib, NULL) ;
           SetViewportExtEx (hdc, cxClient, cyClient, NULL) ;
           SetWindowOrgEx (hdc, cxDib / 2, cyDib / 2, NULL) ;
           SetViewportOrgEx (hdc, cxClient / 2, cyClient / 2, NULL) ;

           return StretchDIBits (hdc, 0, 0, cxDib, cyDib,
                                 0, 0, cxDib, cyDib,
                                 pBits, pbmi, DIB_RGB_COLORS, SRCCOPY) ;
      }
}

LRESULT CALLBACK WndProc (HWND hwnd, UINT message, WPARAM wParam, LPARAM lParam)
{
     static BITMAPFILEHEADER * pbmfh ;
     static BITMAPINFO       * pbmi ;
     static BYTE             * pBits ;
     static DOCINFO            di = { sizeof (DOCINFO),
                                      TEXT ("ShowDib2: Printing") } ;
     static int                cxClient, cyClient, cxDib, cyDib ;
     static PRINTDLG           printdlg = { sizeof (PRINTDLG) } ;
     static TCHAR              szFileName [MAX_PATH], szTitleName [MAX_PATH] ;
     static WORD               wShow = IDM_SHOW_NORMAL ;
     BOOL                      bSuccess ;
     HDC                       hdc, hdcPrn ;
```

```
HGLOBAL             hGlobal ;
HMENU               hMenu ;
int                 cxPage, cyPage, iEnable ;
PAINTSTRUCT         ps ;
BYTE              * pGlobal ;

switch (message)
{
case WM_CREATE:
     DibFileInitialize (hwnd) ;
     return 0 ;

case WM_SIZE:
     cxClient = LOWORD (lParam) ;
     cyClient = HIWORD (lParam) ;
     return 0 ;

case WM_INITMENUPOPUP:
     hMenu = GetMenu (hwnd) ;

     if (pbmfh)
          iEnable = MF_ENABLED ;
     else
          iEnable = MF_GRAYED ;

     EnableMenuItem (hMenu, IDM_FILE_SAVE,   iEnable) ;
     EnableMenuItem (hMenu, IDM_FILE_PRINT,  iEnable) ;
     EnableMenuItem (hMenu, IDM_EDIT_CUT,    iEnable) ;
     EnableMenuItem (hMenu, IDM_EDIT_COPY,   iEnable) ;
     EnableMenuItem (hMenu, IDM_EDIT_DELETE, iEnable) ;
     return 0 ;

case WM_COMMAND:
     hMenu = GetMenu (hwnd) ;

     switch (LOWORD (wParam))
     {
     case IDM_FILE_OPEN:
               // Show the File Open dialog box

          if (!DibFileOpenDlg (hwnd, szFileName, szTitleName))
               return 0 ;

               // If there's an existing DIB, free the memory
```

(continued)

Figure 15-9. *continued*

```
                if (pbmfh)
                {
                     free (pbmfh) ;
                     pbmfh = NULL ;
                }
                     // Load the entire DIB into memory

                SetCursor (LoadCursor (NULL, IDC_WAIT)) ;
                ShowCursor (TRUE) ;

                pbmfh = DibLoadImage (szFileName) ;

                ShowCursor (FALSE) ;
                SetCursor (LoadCursor (NULL, IDC_ARROW)) ;

                     // Invalidate the client area for later update

                InvalidateRect (hwnd, NULL, TRUE) ;

                if (pbmfh == NULL)
                {
                     MessageBox (hwnd, TEXT ("Cannot load DIB file"),
                                 szAppName, MB_ICONEXCLAMATION | MB_OK) ;
                     return 0 ;
                }
                     // Get pointers to the info structure & the bits

                pbmi  = (BITMAPINFO *) (pbmfh + 1) ;
                pBits = (BYTE *) pbmfh + pbmfh->bfOffBits ;

                     // Get the DIB width and height

                if (pbmi->bmiHeader.biSize == sizeof (BITMAPCOREHEADER))
                {
                     cxDib = ((BITMAPCOREHEADER *) pbmi)->bcWidth ;
                     cyDib = ((BITMAPCOREHEADER *) pbmi)->bcHeight ;
                }
                else
                {
                     cxDib =       pbmi->bmiHeader.biWidth ;
                     cyDib = abs (pbmi->bmiHeader.biHeight) ;
                }
                return 0 ;

        case IDM_FILE_SAVE:
                     // Show the File Save dialog box

                if (!DibFileSaveDlg (hwnd, szFileName, szTitleName))
                     return 0 ;
```

```
        // Save the DIB to a disk file

    SetCursor (LoadCursor (NULL, IDC_WAIT)) ;
    ShowCursor (TRUE) ;

    bSuccess = DibSaveImage (szFileName, pbmfh) ;

    ShowCursor (FALSE) ;
    SetCursor (LoadCursor (NULL, IDC_ARROW)) ;

    if (!bSuccess)
        MessageBox (hwnd, TEXT ("Cannot save DIB file"),
                    szAppName, MB_ICONEXCLAMATION | MB_OK) ;
    return 0 ;

case IDM_FILE_PRINT:
    if (!pbmfh)
        return 0 ;

        // Get printer DC

    printdlg.Flags = PD_RETURNDC | PD_NOPAGENUMS | PD_NOSELECTION ;

    if (!PrintDlg (&printdlg))
        return 0 ;

    if (NULL == (hdcPrn = printdlg.hDC))
    {
        MessageBox (hwnd, TEXT ("Cannot obtain Printer DC"),
                    szAppName, MB_ICONEXCLAMATION | MB_OK) ;
        return 0 ;
    }

        // Check whether the printer can print bitmaps

    if (!(RC_BITBLT & GetDeviceCaps (hdcPrn, RASTERCAPS)))
    {
        DeleteDC (hdcPrn) ;
        MessageBox (hwnd, TEXT ("Printer cannot print bitmaps"),
                    szAppName, MB_ICONEXCLAMATION | MB_OK) ;
        return 0 ;
    }
        // Get size of printable area of page

    cxPage = GetDeviceCaps (hdcPrn, HORZRES) ;
    cyPage = GetDeviceCaps (hdcPrn, VERTRES) ;

    bSuccess = FALSE ;
```

(continued)

Figure 15-9. *continued*

```
                    // Send the DIB to the printer

          SetCursor (LoadCursor (NULL, IDC_WAIT)) ;
          ShowCursor (TRUE) ;

          if ((StartDoc (hdcPrn, &di) > 0) && (StartPage (hdcPrn) > 0))
          {
               ShowDib (hdcPrn, pbmi, pBits, cxDib, cyDib,
                         cxPage, cyPage, wShow) ;

               if (EndPage (hdcPrn) > 0)
               {
                    bSuccess = TRUE ;
                    EndDoc (hdcPrn) ;
               }
          }
          ShowCursor (FALSE) ;
          SetCursor (LoadCursor (NULL, IDC_ARROW)) ;

          DeleteDC (hdcPrn) ;

          if (!bSuccess)
               MessageBox (hwnd, TEXT ("Could not print bitmap"),
                         szAppName, MB_ICONEXCLAMATION | MB_OK) ;
          return 0 ;

     case IDM_EDIT_COPY:
     case IDM_EDIT_CUT:
          if (!pbmfh)
               return 0 ;

               // Make a copy of the packed DIB

          hGlobal = GlobalAlloc (GHND | GMEM_SHARE, pbmfh->bfSize -
                              sizeof (BITMAPFILEHEADER)) ;

          pGlobal = GlobalLock (hGlobal) ;

          CopyMemory (pGlobal, (BYTE *) pbmfh + sizeof (BITMAPFILEHEADER),
                    pbmfh->bfSize - sizeof (BITMAPFILEHEADER)) ;

          GlobalUnlock (hGlobal) ;

               // Transfer it to the clipboard

          OpenClipboard (hwnd) ;
```

```
                EmptyClipboard () ;
                SetClipboardData (CF_DIB, hGlobal) ;
                CloseClipboard () ;

                if (LOWORD (wParam) == IDM_EDIT_COPY)
                     return 0 ;
                                        // fall through if IDM_EDIT_CUT
          case IDM_EDIT_DELETE:
                if (pbmfh)
                {
                     free (pbmfh) ;
                     pbmfh = NULL ;
                     InvalidateRect (hwnd, NULL, TRUE) ;
                }
                return 0 ;

          case IDM_SHOW_NORMAL:
          case IDM_SHOW_CENTER:
          case IDM_SHOW_STRETCH:
          case IDM_SHOW_ISOSTRETCH:
                CheckMenuItem (hMenu, wShow, MF_UNCHECKED) ;
                wShow = LOWORD (wParam) ;
                CheckMenuItem (hMenu, wShow, MF_CHECKED) ;
                InvalidateRect (hwnd, NULL, TRUE) ;
                return 0 ;
          }
          break ;

     case WM_PAINT:
          hdc = BeginPaint (hwnd, &ps) ;

          if (pbmfh)
               ShowDib (hdc, pbmi, pBits, cxDib, cyDib,
                        cxClient, cyClient, wShow) ;

          EndPaint (hwnd, &ps) ;
          return 0 ;

     case WM_DESTROY:
          if (pbmfh)
               free (pbmfh) ;

          PostQuitMessage (0) ;
          return 0 ;
     }
     return DefWindowProc (hwnd, message, wParam, lParam) ;
}
```

(continued)

Figure 15-9. *continued*

SHOWDIB2.RC (excerpts)

```
//Microsoft Developer Studio generated resource script.

#include "resource.h"
#include "afxres.h"


/////////////////////////////////////////////////////////////////////////////
// Menu

SHOWDIB2 MENU DISCARDABLE
BEGIN
    POPUP "&File"
    BEGIN
        MENUITEM "&Open...\tCtrl+O",             IDM_FILE_OPEN
        MENUITEM "&Save...\tCtrl+S",             IDM_FILE_SAVE
        MENUITEM SEPARATOR
        MENUITEM "&Print\tCtrl+P",               IDM_FILE_PRINT
    END
    POPUP "&Edit"
    BEGIN
        MENUITEM "Cu&t\tCtrl+X",                 IDM_EDIT_CUT
        MENUITEM "&Copy\tCtrl+C",                 IDM_EDIT_COPY
        MENUITEM "&Delete\tDelete",              IDM_EDIT_DELETE
    END
    POPUP "&Show"
    BEGIN
        MENUITEM "&Actual Size",                 IDM_SHOW_NORMAL, CHECKED
        MENUITEM "&Center",                      IDM_SHOW_CENTER
        MENUITEM "&Stretch to Window",           IDM_SHOW_STRETCH
        MENUITEM "Stretch &Isotropically",       IDM_SHOW_ISOSTRETCH
    END
END


/////////////////////////////////////////////////////////////////////////////
// Accelerator

SHOWDIB2 ACCELERATORS DISCARDABLE
BEGIN
    "C",            IDM_EDIT_COPY,          VIRTKEY, CONTROL, NOINVERT
    "O",            IDM_FILE_OPEN,          VIRTKEY, CONTROL, NOINVERT
    "P",            IDM_FILE_PRINT,         VIRTKEY, CONTROL, NOINVERT
    "S",            IDM_FILE_SAVE,          VIRTKEY, CONTROL, NOINVERT
    VK_DELETE,      IDM_EDIT_DELETE,        VIRTKEY, NOINVERT
    "X",            IDM_EDIT_CUT,           VIRTKEY, CONTROL, NOINVERT
END
```

RESOURCE.H (excerpts)

```
// Microsoft Developer Studio generated include file.
// Used by ShowDib2.rc

#define IDM_FILE_OPEN            40001
#define IDM_SHOW_NORMAL          40002
#define IDM_SHOW_CENTER          40003
#define IDM_SHOW_STRETCH         40004
#define IDM_SHOW_ISOSTRETCH      40005
#define IDM_FILE_PRINT           40006
#define IDM_EDIT_COPY            40007
#define IDM_EDIT_CUT             40008
#define IDM_EDIT_DELETE          40009
#define IDM_FILE_SAVE            40010
```

Of particular interest here is the *ShowDib* function, which displays a DIB in the program's client area in one of four different ways, depending on a menu selection. The DIB can be displayed using *SetDIBitsToDevice* either oriented at the upper left corner of the client area or centered within the client area. The program also has two options using *StretchDIBits*. The DIB can be stretched to fill the client area, in which case it is likely to be distorted, or it can display isotropically—that is, without distortion.

Copying a DIB to the clipboard involves making a copy of the packed-DIB memory block in global shared memory. The clipboard data type is CF_DIB. What the program doesn't show is how to copy a DIB *from* the clipboard. The reason why is that it requires a bit more logic to determine the offset of the pixel bits given only a pointer to a packed-DIB memory block. I'll show how to do this before the end of the next chapter.

You may also notice some other deficiencies in SHOWDIB2. If you're running Windows with a 256-color video mode, you'll see problems with displaying anything other than monochrome or 4-bit DIBs. You won't see the correct colors. Getting access to those colors will require using the palette, a job that awaits us in the next chapter. You may also notice a speed problem, particularly when running SHOWDIB2 under Windows NT. I'll show you how to handle this when we wrap up DIBs and bitmaps in the next chapter. I'll also tackle adding scroll bars to a DIB display so that a DIB larger than the screen can still be viewed in actual size.

Color Conversion, Palettes, and Performance

Remember in William Goldman's screenplay for *All the President's Men* how Deep Throat tells Bob Woodward that the key to cracking the Watergate mystery is to "Follow the money"? Well, the key to achieving top performance in the display of bitmaps is to "Follow the pixel bits" and to understand when and where color conversion takes place. The DIB is in a device-independent format; the video display memory is almost surely in another format. During the *SetDIBitsToDevice* or *StretchDIBits* function calls, each pixel (and there could be literally millions of them) must be converted from a device-independent format to a device-dependent format.

In many cases, this conversion is fairly trivial. For example, if you're displaying a 24-bit DIB on a 24-bit video display, at most the display driver will have to switch around the order of the red, green, and blue bytes. Displaying a 16-bit DIB on a 24-bit device requires some bit-shifting and padding. Displaying a 24-bit DIB on a 16-bit device requires some bit-shifting and truncation. Displaying a 4-bit or 8-bit DIB on a 24-bit device requires a lookup of the DIB pixel bits in the DIB's color table and then perhaps some reordering of the bytes.

But what happens when you wish to display a 16-bit, 24-bit, or 32-bit DIB on a 4-bit or 8-bit video display? An entirely different type of color conversion has to take place. For each pixel in the DIB, the device driver has to perform a *nearest-color search* between the pixel and all the colors available on the display. This involves a loop and a calculation. (The GDI function *GetNearestColor* does a nearest-color search.)

The entire three-dimensional array of RGB colors can be represented as a cube. The distance between any two points within this curve is

$$\sqrt{(R_2 - R_1)^2 + (G_2 - G_1)^2 + (B_2 - B_1)^2}$$

where the two colors are $R_1G_1B_1$ and $R_2G_2B_2$. Performing a nearest-color search involves finding the shortest distance from one color to a collection of other colors. Fortunately, when *comparing* distances within the RGB color cube, the square root part of the calculation is not required. But each pixel to be converted must be compared with all the colors of the device to find which device color is closest to it. This is still a considerable amount of work. (Although displaying an 8-bit DIB on an 8-bit device also involves a nearest-color search, it doesn't have to be done for each pixel; it need only be done for each of the colors in the DIB's color table.)

For that reason, displaying a 16-bit, 24-bit, or 32-bit DIB on an 8-bit video display adapter using *SetDIBitsToDevice* or *StretchDIBits* should be avoided. The DIB should be converted into an 8-bit DIB or, for even better performance, an 8-bit DDB. Indeed, the display of virtually all DIBs of any appreciable size can be speeded up by converting to a DDB and using *BitBlt* and *StretchBlt* for display purposes.

If you're running Windows in an 8-bit video display (or if you've just switched into an 8-bit mode to see the performance difference when displaying full-color DIBs), you may notice another problem: The DIBs are not being displayed with all their colors. Any DIB displayed on an 8-bit video display is restricted to just 20 colors. Getting more than 20 is a job for the Palette Manager, coming up in the next chapter.

And finally, if you're running both Windows 98 and Windows NT on the same machine, you may notice that Windows NT takes longer to display large DIBs for comparable video modes. This is a consequence of Windows NT's client/server architecture, which involves a penalty for large amounts of data passed across the API. The solution here, too, is to convert the DIB to a DDB. Also, the *CreateDIBSection* function, which I'll discuss shortly, was specifically created to help in this situation.

THE UNION OF DIBS AND DDBS

You can do a lot knowing the format of the DIB and by calling the two DIB-drawing functions, *SetDIBitsToDevice* and *StretchDIBits*. You have direct access to every single bit, byte, and pixel in the DIB, and once you come up with a bunch of functions that let you examine and alter this data in a structured manner, there are no restrictions on what you can do.

Actually, we've found that there *are* some restrictions. In the last chapter, we saw how you can use GDI functions to draw images on a DDB. So far, there doesn't appear to be any way we can do that with DIBs. Another problem is that *SetDIBitsToDevice* and *Stretch-DIBits* are not nearly as fast as *BitBlt* and *StretchBlt*, particularly under Windows NT and when many nearest-color searches have to be performed, such as when 24-bit DIBs are displayed on 8-bit video boards.

So, it might be advantageous to convert between DIBs and DDBs. For example, if we had a DIB that we needed to display to the screen and we might have to do this numerous times, then it would make more sense to convert the DIB into a DDB so that we could use the faster *BitBlt* and *StretchBlt* functions with it.

Creating a DDB from a DIB

Is it possible to create a GDI bitmap object from a DIB? We basically already know how to do it: If you have a DIB, you can use *CreateCompatibleBitmap* to create a GDI bitmap object of the same size as the DIB and compatible with the video display. You then select the bitmap object into a memory device context and call *SetDIBitsToDevice* to draw on that memory DC. The result is a DDB with the same image as the DIB but with a color organization that is compatible with the video display.

Or you can do the job with a fewer number of steps by using *CreateDIBitmap*. The function has the following syntax:

```
hBitmap = CreateDIBitmap (
            hdc,         // device context handle
            pInfoHdr,    // pointer to DIB information header
            fInit,       // 0 or CBM_INIT
            pBits,       // pointer to DIB pixel bits
            pInfo,       // pointer to DIB information
            fClrUse) ;   // color use flag
```

Notice the two arguments I've called *pInfoHdr* and *pInfo*. These are defined as pointers to a BITMAPINFOHEADER structure and a BITMAPINFO structure, respectively. As we know, the BITMAPINFO structure is a BITMAPINFOHEADER structure followed by a color table. We'll see how this distinction works shortly. The last argument is either DIB_RGB_COLORS (which equals 0) or DIB_PAL_COLORS, as with the *SetDIBitsToDevice* functions. I'll have more to say about this in the next chapter.

It is important in understanding the full array of bitmap functions in Windows to realize that, despite its name, the *CreateDIBitmap* function *does not create a device-independent bitmap*. It creates a device-*dependent* bitmap from a device-independent specification. Notice that the function returns a handle to a GDI bitmap object, the same as *CreateBitmap*, *CreateBitmapIndirect*, and *CreateCompatibleBitmap*.

The simplest way to call the *CreateDIBitmap* function is like so:

```
hBitmap = CreateDIBitmap (NULL, pbmih, 0, NULL, NULL, 0) ;
```

The only argument is a pointer to a BITMAPINFOHEADER structure (without the color table). In this form, the function creates a monochrome GDI bitmap object. The second simplest way to call the function is

```
hBitmap = CreateDIBitmap (hdc, pbmih, 0, NULL, NULL, 0) ;
```

In this form, the function creates a DDB that is compatible with the device context indicated by the *hdc* argument. So far, we've done nothing we couldn't have done using *CreateBitmap* (to create a monochrome bitmap) or *CreateCompatibleBitmap* (to create one compatible with the video display).

In these two simplified forms of *CreateDIBitmap*, the pixel bits remain uninitialized. If the third argument to *CreateDIBitmap* is CBM_INIT, Windows creates the DDB and uses the last three arguments to initialize the bitmap bits. The *pInfo* argument is a pointer to a BITMAPINFO structure that includes a color table. The *pBits* argument is a pointer to an array of bits in the color format indicated by the BITMAPINFO structure. Based on the color table, these bits are converted to the color format of the device. This is identical to what happens in *SetDIBitsToDevice*. Indeed, the entire *CreateDIBitmap* function could probably be implemented with the following code:

```
HBITMAP CreateDIBitmap (HDC hdc, CONST BITMAPINFOHEADER * pbmih,
                        DWORD fInit, CONST VOID * pBits,
                        CONST BITMAPINFO * pbmi, UINT fUsage)
{
    HBITMAP hBitmap ;
    HDC     hdc ;
    int     cx, cy, iBitCount ;

    if (pbmih->biSize == sizeof (BITMAPCOREHEADER))
    {
        cx        = ((PBITMAPCOREHEADER) pbmih)->bcWidth ;
        cy        = ((PBITMAPCOREHEADER) pbmih)->bcHeight ;
        iBitCount = ((PBITMAPCOREHEADER) pbmih)->bcBitCount ;
    }
```

```
    else
    {
        cx        = pbmih->biWidth ;
        cy        = pbmih->biHeight ;
        iBitCount = pbmih->biBitCount ;
    }
    if (hdc)
        hBitmap = CreateCompatibleBitmap (hdc, cx, cy) ;
    else
        hBitmap = CreateBitmap (cx, cy, 1, 1, NULL) ;

    if (fInit == CBM_INIT)
    {
        hdcMem = CreateCompatibleDC (hdc) ;
        SelectObject (hdcMem, hBitmap) ;
        SetDIBitsToDevice (hdcMem, 0, 0, cx, cy, 0, 0, 0 cy,
                                pBits, pbmi, fUsage) ;
        DeleteDC (hdcMem) ;
    }

    return hBitmap ;
}
```

If you're going to display a DIB only once and you're worried about the performance of *SetDIBitsToDevice*, it doesn't make much sense to call *CreateDIBitmap* and then display the DDB by using *BitBlt* or *StretchBlt*. The two jobs will take the same length of time because *SetDIBitsToDevice* and *CreateDIBitmap* both have to perform a color conversion. Only if you're displaying a DIB multiple times—which is very likely when processing WM_PAINT messages—does this conversion make sense.

The DIBCONV program shown in Figure 15-10 shows how you can use *SetDIBits-ToDevice* to convert a DIB file to a DDB.

DIBCONV.C

```
/*-------------------------------------------
   DIBCONV.C -- Converts a DIB to a DDB
                (c) Charles Petzold, 1998
   -------------------------------------------*/

#include <windows.h>
#include <commdlg.h>
#include "resource.h"

LRESULT CALLBACK WndProc (HWND, UINT, WPARAM, LPARAM) ;
```

Figure 15-10. *The DIBCONV program.*

(continued)

Figure 15-10. *continued*

```
TCHAR szAppName[] = TEXT ("DibConv") ;

int WINAPI WinMain (HINSTANCE hInstance, HINSTANCE hPrevInstance,
                    PSTR szCmdLine, int iCmdShow)
{
    HWND        hwnd ;
    MSG         msg ;
    WNDCLASS wndclass ;

    wndclass.style          = CS_HREDRAW | CS_VREDRAW ;
    wndclass.lpfnWndProc    = WndProc ;
    wndclass.cbClsExtra     = 0 ;
    wndclass.cbWndExtra     = 0 ;
    wndclass.hInstance      = hInstance ;
    wndclass.hIcon          = LoadIcon (NULL, IDI_APPLICATION) ;
    wndclass.hCursor        = LoadCursor (NULL, IDC_ARROW) ;
    wndclass.hbrBackground  = (HBRUSH) GetStockObject (WHITE_BRUSH) ;
    wndclass.lpszMenuName   = szAppName ;
    wndclass.lpszClassName  = szAppName ;

    if (!RegisterClass (&wndclass))
    {
        MessageBox (NULL, TEXT ("This program requires Windows NT!"),
                    szAppName, MB_ICONERROR) ;
        return 0 ;
    }

    hwnd = CreateWindow (szAppName, TEXT ("DIB to DDB Conversion"),
                         WS_OVERLAPPEDWINDOW,
                         CW_USEDEFAULT, CW_USEDEFAULT,
                         CW_USEDEFAULT, CW_USEDEFAULT,
                         NULL, NULL, hInstance, NULL) ;

    ShowWindow (hwnd, iCmdShow) ;
    UpdateWindow (hwnd) ;

    while (GetMessage (&msg, NULL, 0, 0))
    {
        TranslateMessage (&msg) ;
        DispatchMessage (&msg) ;

    }
    return msg.wParam ;
}
```

```
HBITMAP CreateBitmapObjectFromDibFile (HDC hdc, PTSTR szFileName)
{
     BITMAPFILEHEADER * pbmfh ;
     BOOL               bSuccess ;
     DWORD              dwFileSize, dwHighSize, dwBytesRead ;
     HANDLE             hFile ;
     HBITMAP            hBitmap ;

          // Open the file: read access, prohibit write access

     hFile = CreateFile (szFileName, GENERIC_READ, FILE_SHARE_READ, NULL,
                         OPEN_EXISTING, FILE_FLAG_SEQUENTIAL_SCAN, NULL) ;

     if (hFile == INVALID_HANDLE_VALUE)
          return NULL ;

          // Read in the whole file

     dwFileSize = GetFileSize (hFile, &dwHighSize) ;

     if (dwHighSize)
     {
          CloseHandle (hFile) ;
          return NULL ;
     }

     pbmfh = malloc (dwFileSize) ;

     if (!pbmfh)
     {
          CloseHandle (hFile) ;
          return NULL ;
     }

     bSuccess = ReadFile (hFile, pbmfh, dwFileSize, &dwBytesRead, NULL) ;
     CloseHandle (hFile) ;

          // Verify the file

     if (!bSuccess || (dwBytesRead != dwFileSize)
                   || (pbmfh->bfType != * (WORD *) "BM")
                   || (pbmfh->bfSize != dwFileSize))
     {
          free (pbmfh) ;
          return NULL ;
     }
```

(continued)

Figure 15-10. *continued*

```
          // Create the DDB

     hBitmap = CreateDIBitmap (hdc,
                              (BITMAPINFOHEADER *) (pbmfh + 1),
                              CBM_INIT,
                              (BYTE *) pbmfh + pbmfh->bfOffBits,
                              (BITMAPINFO *) (pbmfh + 1),
                              DIB_RGB_COLORS) ;
     free (pbmfh) ;

     return hBitmap ;
}

LRESULT CALLBACK WndProc (HWND hwnd, UINT message, WPARAM wParam, LPARAM lParam)
{
     static HBITMAP     hBitmap ;
     static int         cxClient, cyClient ;
     static OPENFILENAME ofn ;
     static TCHAR       szFileName [MAX_PATH], szTitleName [MAX_PATH] ;
     static TCHAR       szFilter[] = TEXT ("Bitmap Files (*.BMP)\0*.bmp\0")
                                     TEXT ("All Files (*.*)\0*.*\0\0") ;
     BITMAP             bitmap ;
     HDC                hdc, hdcMem ;
     PAINTSTRUCT        ps ;

     switch (message)
     {
     case WM_CREATE:
          ofn.lStructSize       = sizeof (OPENFILENAME) ;
          ofn.hwndOwner         = hwnd ;
          ofn.hInstance         = NULL ;
          ofn.lpstrFilter       = szFilter ;
          ofn.lpstrCustomFilter = NULL ;
          ofn.nMaxCustFilter    = 0 ;
          ofn.nFilterIndex      = 0 ;
          ofn.lpstrFile         = szFileName ;
          ofn.nMaxFile          = MAX_PATH ;
          ofn.lpstrFileTitle    = szTitleName ;
          ofn.nMaxFileTitle     = MAX_PATH ;
          ofn.lpstrInitialDir   = NULL ;
          ofn.lpstrTitle        = NULL ;
          ofn.Flags             = 0 ;
          ofn.nFileOffset       = 0 ;
          ofn.nFileExtension    = 0 ;
```

```
        ofn.lpstrDefExt      = TEXT ("bmp") ;
        ofn.lCustData        = 0 ;
        ofn.lpfnHook         = NULL ;
        ofn.lpTemplateName   = NULL ;

        return 0 ;

case WM_SIZE:
        cxClient = LOWORD (lParam) ;
        cyClient = HIWORD (lParam) ;
        return 0 ;

case WM_COMMAND:
        switch (LOWORD (wParam))
        {
        case IDM_FILE_OPEN:

                // Show the File Open dialog box

             if (!GetOpenFileName (&ofn))
                 return 0 ;

                // If there's an existing DIB, delete it

             if (hBitmap)
             {
                 DeleteObject (hBitmap) ;
                 hBitmap = NULL ;
             }
                // Create the DDB from the DIB

             SetCursor (LoadCursor (NULL, IDC_WAIT)) ;
             ShowCursor (TRUE) ;

             hdc = GetDC (hwnd) ;
             hBitmap = CreateBitmapObjectFromDibFile (hdc, szFileName) ;
             ReleaseDC (hwnd, hdc) ;

             ShowCursor (FALSE) ;
             SetCursor (LoadCursor (NULL, IDC_ARROW)) ;

                // Invalidate the client area for later update

             InvalidateRect (hwnd, NULL, TRUE) ;
```

(continued)

Figure 15-10. *continued*

```
                  if (hBitmap == NULL)
                  {
                        MessageBox (hwnd, TEXT ("Cannot load DIB file"),
                                    szAppName, MB_OK | MB_ICONEXCLAMATION) ;
                  }
                  return 0 ;
            }
            break ;

      case WM_PAINT:
            hdc = BeginPaint (hwnd, &ps) ;

            if (hBitmap)
            {
                  GetObject (hBitmap, sizeof (BITMAP), &bitmap) ;

                  hdcMem = CreateCompatibleDC (hdc) ;
                  SelectObject (hdcMem, hBitmap) ;

                  BitBlt (hdc,    0, 0, bitmap.bmWidth, bitmap.bmHeight,
                              hdcMem, 0, 0, SRCCOPY) ;

                  DeleteDC (hdcMem) ;
            }

            EndPaint (hwnd, &ps) ;
            return 0 ;

      case WM_DESTROY:
            if (hBitmap)
                  DeleteObject (hBitmap) ;

            PostQuitMessage (0) ;
            return 0 ;
      }
      return DefWindowProc (hwnd, message, wParam, lParam) ;
}
```

DIBCONV.RC (excerpts)

```
//Microsoft Developer Studio generated resource script.

#include "resource.h"
#include "afxres.h"
```

```
/////////////////////////////////////////////////////////////////////////
// Menu

DIBCONV MENU DISCARDABLE
BEGIN
    POPUP "&File"
    BEGIN
        MENUITEM "&Open",                          IDM_FILE_OPEN
    END
END
```

RESOURCE.H (excerpts)

```
// Microsoft Developer Studio generated include file.
// Used by DibConv.rc

#define IDM_FILE_OPEN                    40001
```

DIBCONV.C is self-contained and requires no earlier files. In response to its only menu command (File Open), *WndProc* calls the program's *CreateBitmapObjectFromDibFile* function. This function reads the entire file into memory and passes pointers to the memory block to the *CreateDIBitmap* function. The function returns a handle to the bitmap. The memory block containing the DIB can then be freed. During the WM_PAINT message, *WndProc* selects the bitmap in a compatible memory device context and uses *BitBlt* rather than *SetDIBitsToDevice* to display the bitmap on the client area. It obtains the width and height of the bitmap by calling *GetObject* with the BITMAP structure on the bitmap handle.

You do not need to initialize the DDB pixel bits while creating the bitmap from *Create-DIBitmap*. You can do it later by calling *SetDIBits*. This function has the following syntax:

```
iLines = SetDIBits (
            hdc,        // device context handle
            hBitmap,    // bitmap handle
            yScan,      // first scan line to convert
            cyScans,    // number of scan lines to convert
            pBits,      // pointer to pixel bits
            pInfo,      // pointer to DIB information
            fClrUse) ;  // color use flag
```

The function uses the color table in the BITMAPINFO structure to convert the bits into the device-dependent format. The device context handle is required only if the last argument is set to DIB_PAL_COLORS.

807

From DDB to DIB

A function similar to the *SetDIBits* function is *GetDIBits*. You can use this function for converting a DDB to a DIB:

```
int WINAPI GetDIBits (
            hdc,          // device context handle
            hBitmap,      // bitmap handle
            yScan,        // first scan line to convert
            cyScans,      // number of scan lines to convert
            pBits,        // pointer to pixel bits (out)
            pInfo,        // pointer to DIB information (out)
            fClrUse) ;    // color use flag
```

However, I'm afraid that this function is not simply the reverse of *SetDIBits*. In the general case, if you convert a DIB to a DDB using *CreateDIBitmap* and *SetDIBits* and then convert back to a DIB using *GetDIBits*, you won't get what you started out with. This is because some information is lost when a DIB is converted to a device-dependent format. How much information is lost depends on the particular video mode you're running Windows under when you do the conversion.

You probably won't find a need to use *GetDIBits* much. Think about it: In what circumstances does your program find itself with a bitmap handle without having the data used to create the bitmap in the first place? The clipboard? But the clipboard provides automatic conversion to DIBs. The one instance in which the *GetDIBits* function *does* come in handy is when you're doing screen captures, such as what the BLOWUP program did in Chapter 14. I won't be demonstrating this function, but some information is available in Knowledge Base article Q80080.

The DIB Section

Now, I hope, you have a good feel for the difference between device-dependent and device-independent bitmaps. A DIB can have one of several color organizations; a DDB must be either monochrome or the same format as a real-output device. A DIB is a file or a block of memory; a DDB is a GDI bitmap object and is represented by a bitmap handle. A DIB can be displayed or converted to a DDB and back again, but this involves a process to convert between device-independent bits and device-specific bits.

Now you're about to encounter a function that seems to break these rules. This function was introduced in the 32-bit versions of Windows and is called *CreateDIBSection*. The syntax is

```
hBitmap = CreateDIBSection (
            hdc,          // device context handle
            pInfo,        // pointer to DIB information
            fClrUse,      // color use flag
```

```
        ppBits,      // pointer to pointer variable
        hSection,    // file-mapping object handle
        dwOffset) ;  // offset to bits in file-mapping object
```

CreateDIBSection is one of the most important functions in the Windows API (well, at least if you're working with bitmaps a lot), yet it's burdened with such weirdness that you may find it inordinately esoteric and difficult to comprehend.

Let's begin with the very name of the function. We know what a DIB is, but what on earth is a "DIB section"? When you first began examining *CreateDIBSection*, you may have kept looking for some way that the function works with only part of the DIB. That's almost right. What *CreateDIBSection* does is indeed create a section of the DIB—a memory block for the bitmap pixel bits.

Now let's look at the return value. It's a handle to a GDI bitmap object. That return value is probably the most deceptive aspect of the function call. The return value seems to imply that *CreateDIBSection* is similar in functionality to *CreateDIBitmap*. Yes, it's similar but also totally different. In fact, the bitmap handle returned from *CreateDIBSection* is intrinsically different from the bitmap handle returned from all the previous bitmap-creation functions we've encountered in this chapter and the last chapter.

Once you understand the true nature of *CreateDIBSection*, you might wonder why the return value wasn't defined somewhat differently. You might also conclude that *CreateDIBSection* should have been called *CreateDIBitmap* and that *CreateDIBitmap* should have been called, as I indicated earlier, *CreateDDBitmap*.

To first approach *CreateDIBSection*, let's examine how we can simplify it and put it to use right away. First, you can set the last two arguments, *hSection* and *dwOffset*, to NULL and 0, respectively. I'll discuss the use of these arguments towards the end of this chapter. Second, the *hdc* parameter is used only if the *fColorUse* parameter is set to DIB_PAL_COLORS. If *fColorUse* is DIB_RGB_COLORS (or 0), *hdc* is ignored. (This is not the case with *CreateDIBitmap*, in which the *hdc* parameter is used to get the color format of the device that the DDB is to be compatible with.)

So, in its simplest form, *CreateDIBSection* requires only the second and fourth arguments. The second argument is a pointer to a BITMAPINFO structure, something we've worked with before. I hope the pointer to a pointer definition of the fourth argument doesn't upset you too much. It's actually quite simple when using the function.

Let's suppose you want to create a 384×256-bit DIB with 24 bits per pixel. The 24-bit format is simplest because it doesn't require a color table, so we can use a BITMAPINFO-HEADER structure for the BITMAPINFO parameter.

You define three variables: a BITMAPINFOHEADER structure, a BYTE pointer, and a bitmap handle:

```
BITMAPINFOHEADER bmih ;
BYTE             * pBits ;
HBITMAP            hBitmap ;
```

Now initialize the fields of the BITMAPINFOHEADER structure:

```
bmih->biSize          = sizeof (BITMAPINFOHEADER) ;
bmih->biWidth         = 384 ;
bmih->biHeight        = 256 ;
bmih->biPlanes        = 1 ;
bmih->biBitCount      = 24 ;
bmih->biCompression   = BI_RGB ;
bmih->biSizeImage     = 0 ;
bmih->biXPelsPerMeter = 0 ;
bmih->biYPelsPerMeter = 0 ;
bmih->biClrUsed       = 0 ;
bmih->biClrImportant  = 0 ;
```

With this minimum amount of preparation, we are now ready to call the function:

```
hBitmap = CreateDIBSection (NULL, (BITMAPINFO *)  &bmih, 0, &pBits, NULL, 0) ;
```

Notice that we're taking the address of the BITMAPINFOHEADER structure for the second argument, as usual, but also the address of the BYTE pointer *pBits*, which is not usual. Thus, the fourth argument is a pointer to a pointer, as required by the function.

Here's what the function call does: *CreateDIBSection* examines the BITMAPINFO-HEADER structure and allocates a block of memory sufficient to hold the DIB pixel bits. (In this particular case, the block is 384×256×3 bytes in size.) It stores a pointer to this memory block in the *pBits* parameter that you've supplied. The function also returns a handle to a bitmap, which, as I've said, is not quite the same as the handle returned from *CreateDIBitmap* and other bitmap-creation functions.

We're not quite done yet, however. The bitmap pixel bits are uninitialized. If you're reading a DIB file, you can simply pass the *pBits* parameter to the *ReadFile* function and read them in. Or you can set them "manually" with some program code.

The DIBSECT program shown in Figure 15-11 is similar to the DIBCONV program except that it calls *CreateDIBSection* rather than *CreateDIBitmap*.

DIBSECT.C

```
/*-----------------------------------------------------------
   DIBSECT.C -- Displays a DIB Section in the client area
                (c) Charles Petzold, 1998
   -----------------------------------------------------------*/

#include <windows.h>
#include <commdlg.h>
#include "resource.h"
```

Figure 15-11. *The DIBSECT program.*

```
LRESULT CALLBACK WndProc (HWND, UINT, WPARAM, LPARAM) ;

TCHAR szAppName[] = TEXT ("DibSect") ;

int WINAPI WinMain (HINSTANCE hInstance, HINSTANCE hPrevInstance,
                    PSTR szCmdLine, int iCmdShow)
{
     HWND      hwnd ;
     MSG       msg ;
     WNDCLASS wndclass ;

     wndclass.style        = CS_HREDRAW | CS_VREDRAW ;
     wndclass.lpfnWndProc  = WndProc ;
     wndclass.cbClsExtra   = 0 ;
     wndclass.cbWndExtra   = 0 ;
     wndclass.hInstance    = hInstance ;
     wndclass.hIcon        = LoadIcon (NULL, IDI_APPLICATION) ;
     wndclass.hCursor      = LoadCursor (NULL, IDC_ARROW) ;
     wndclass.hbrBackground = (HBRUSH) GetStockObject (WHITE_BRUSH) ;
     wndclass.lpszMenuName = szAppName ;
     wndclass.lpszClassName = szAppName ;

     if (!RegisterClass (&wndclass))
     {
          MessageBox (NULL, TEXT ("This program requires Windows NT!"),
                      szAppName, MB_ICONERROR) ;
          return 0 ;
     }

     hwnd = CreateWindow (szAppName, TEXT ("DIB Section Display"),
                          WS_OVERLAPPEDWINDOW,
                          CW_USEDEFAULT, CW_USEDEFAULT,
                          CW_USEDEFAULT, CW_USEDEFAULT,
                          NULL, NULL, hInstance, NULL) ;

     ShowWindow (hwnd, iCmdShow) ;
     UpdateWindow (hwnd) ;

     while (GetMessage (&msg, NULL, 0, 0))
     {
          TranslateMessage (&msg) ;
          DispatchMessage (&msg) ;

     }
     return msg.wParam ;
}
```

(continued)

Figure 15-11. *continued*

```
HBITMAP CreateDibSectionFromDibFile (PTSTR szFileName)
{
    BITMAPFILEHEADER bmfh ;
    BITMAPINFO     * pbmi ;
    BYTE           * pBits ;
    BOOL             bSuccess ;
    DWORD            dwInfoSize, dwBytesRead ;
    HANDLE           hFile ;
    HBITMAP          hBitmap ;

        // Open the file: read access, prohibit write access

    hFile = CreateFile (szFileName, GENERIC_READ, FILE_SHARE_READ,
                        NULL, OPEN_EXISTING, 0, NULL) ;

    if (hFile == INVALID_HANDLE_VALUE)
        return NULL ;

        // Read in the BITMAPFILEHEADER

    bSuccess = ReadFile (hFile, &bmfh, sizeof (BITMAPFILEHEADER),
                        &dwBytesRead, NULL) ;

    if (!bSuccess || (dwBytesRead != sizeof (BITMAPFILEHEADER))
                || (bmfh.bfType != * (WORD *) "BM"))
    {
        CloseHandle (hFile) ;
        return NULL ;
    }

        // Allocate memory for the BITMAPINFO structure & read it in

    dwInfoSize = bmfh.bfOffBits - sizeof (BITMAPFILEHEADER) ;

    pbmi = malloc (dwInfoSize) ;

    bSuccess = ReadFile (hFile, pbmi, dwInfoSize, &dwBytesRead, NULL) ;

    if (!bSuccess || (dwBytesRead != dwInfoSize))
    {
        free (pbmi) ;
        CloseHandle (hFile) ;
        return NULL ;
    }
```

```
        // Create the DIB Section

    hBitmap = CreateDIBSection (NULL, pbmi, DIB_RGB_COLORS, &pBits, NULL, 0) ;

    if (hBitmap == NULL)
    {
         free (pbmi) ;
         CloseHandle (hFile) ;
         return NULL ;
    }

         // Read in the bitmap bits

    ReadFile (hFile, pBits, bmfh.bfSize - bmfh.bfOffBits, &dwBytesRead, NULL) ;

    free (pbmi) ;
    CloseHandle (hFile) ;

    return hBitmap ;
}
LRESULT CALLBACK WndProc (HWND hwnd, UINT message, WPARAM wParam, LPARAM lParam)
{
    static HBITMAP     hBitmap ;
    static int         cxClient, cyClient ;
    static OPENFILENAME ofn ;
    static TCHAR       szFileName [MAX_PATH], szTitleName [MAX_PATH] ;
    static TCHAR       szFilter[] = TEXT ("Bitmap Files (*.BMP)\0*.bmp\0")
                                    TEXT ("All Files (*.*)\0*.*\0\0") ;

    BITMAP             bitmap ;
    HDC                hdc, hdcMem ;
    PAINTSTRUCT        ps ;

    switch (message)
    {
    case WM_CREATE:
         ofn.lStructSize       = sizeof (OPENFILENAME) ;
         ofn.hwndOwner         = hwnd ;
         ofn.hInstance         = NULL ;
         ofn.lpstrFilter       = szFilter ;
         ofn.lpstrCustomFilter = NULL ;
         ofn.nMaxCustFilter    = 0 ;
         ofn.nFilterIndex      = 0 ;
         ofn.lpstrFile         = szFileName ;
```

(continued)

Figure 15-11. *continued*

```
        ofn.nMaxFile           = MAX_PATH ;
        ofn.lpstrFileTitle     = szTitleName ;
        ofn.nMaxFileTitle      = MAX_PATH ;
        ofn.lpstrInitialDir    = NULL ;
        ofn.lpstrTitle         = NULL ;
        ofn.Flags              = 0 ;
        ofn.nFileOffset        = 0 ;
        ofn.nFileExtension     = 0 ;
        ofn.lpstrDefExt        = TEXT ("bmp") ;
        ofn.lCustData          = 0 ;
        ofn.lpfnHook           = NULL ;
        ofn.lpTemplateName     = NULL ;

        return 0 ;

case WM_SIZE:
        cxClient = LOWORD (lParam) ;
        cyClient = HIWORD (lParam) ;
        return 0 ;

case WM_COMMAND:
        switch (LOWORD (wParam))
        {
        case IDM_FILE_OPEN:

                // Show the File Open dialog box

             if (!GetOpenFileName (&ofn))
                  return 0 ;

                // If there's an existing bitmap, delete it

             if (hBitmap)
             {
                  DeleteObject (hBitmap) ;
                  hBitmap = NULL ;
             }
                // Create the DIB Section from the DIB file

             SetCursor (LoadCursor (NULL, IDC_WAIT)) ;
             ShowCursor (TRUE) ;

             hBitmap = CreateDibSectionFromDibFile (szFileName) ;
```

```
          ShowCursor (FALSE) ;
          SetCursor (LoadCursor (NULL, IDC_ARROW)) ;

                // Invalidate the client area for later update

          InvalidateRect (hwnd, NULL, TRUE) ;

          if (hBitmap == NULL)
          {
                MessageBox (hwnd, TEXT ("Cannot load DIB file"),
                            szAppName, MB_OK | MB_ICONEXCLAMATION) ;
          }
          return 0 ;
     }
     break ;

case WM_PAINT:
     hdc = BeginPaint (hwnd, &ps) ;

     if (hBitmap)
     {
          GetObject (hBitmap, sizeof (BITMAP), &bitmap) ;

          hdcMem = CreateCompatibleDC (hdc) ;
          SelectObject (hdcMem, hBitmap) ;

          BitBlt (hdc,    0, 0, bitmap.bmWidth, bitmap.bmHeight,
                  hdcMem, 0, 0, SRCCOPY) ;

          DeleteDC (hdcMem) ;
     }

     EndPaint (hwnd, &ps) ;
     return 0 ;

case WM_DESTROY:
     if (hBitmap)
          DeleteObject (hBitmap) ;

     PostQuitMessage (0) ;
     return 0 ;
}
return DefWindowProc (hwnd, message, wParam, lParam) ;
}
```

(continued)

Figure 15-11. *continued*

DIBSECT.RC (excerpts)

```
//Microsoft Developer Studio generated resource script.

#include "resource.h"
#include "afxres.h"


///////////////////////////////////////////////////////////////////////////////
// Menu

DIBSECT MENU DISCARDABLE
BEGIN
    POPUP "&File"
    BEGIN
        MENUITEM "&Open",                                IDM_FILE_OPEN
    END
END
```

RESOURCE.H (excerpts)

```
// Microsoft Developer Studio generated include file.
// Used by DibSect.rc

#define IDM_FILE_OPEN                   40001
```

Notice the differences between the *CreateBitmapObjectFromDibFile* function in DIBCONV and the *CreateDibSectionFromDibFile* function in DIBSECT. DIBCONV reads the entire file in one shot and then passes pointers to the DIB memory block to the *CreateDIBitmap* function. DIBSECT reads in the BITMAPFILEHEADER structure first and then determines how big the BITMAPINFO structure is. Memory is allocated for that, and it's read in on the second *ReadFile* call. The function then passes pointers to the BITMAPINFO structure and to the pointer variable *pBits* to *CreateDIBSection*. The function returns a bitmap handle and sets *pBits* to point to a block of memory into which the function then reads the DIB pixel bits.

The memory block pointed to by *pBits* is owned by the system. The memory is automatically freed when you delete the bitmap by calling *DeleteObject*. However, programs can use the pointer to alter the DIB bits directly. That the system owns this memory block makes it not subject to the speed penalty incurred under Windows NT when an application passes large memory blocks across the API.

As I noted above, when you display a DIB on a video display, at some point it must undergo a conversion from device-independent pixels to device-dependent pixels. Sometimes this format conversion can be lengthy. Let's look at the three approaches we've used to display DIBs:

■ When you use *SetDIBitsToDevice* or *StretchDIBits* to display a DIB directly to the screen, the format conversion occurs during the *SetDIBitsToDevice* or *Stretch-DIBits* call.

■ When you convert a DIB to a DDB using *CreateDIBitmap* and (possibly) *Set-DIBits* and then use *BitBlt* or *StretchBlt* to display it, the format conversion occurs during *CreateDIBitmap*, if the CBM_INIT flag is set, or *SetDIBits*.

■ When you create a DIB section using *CreateDIBSection* and then display it using *BitBlt* or *StretchBlt*, the format conversion occurs during the *BitBlt* to *StretchBlt* call.

Read that last sentence over again and make sure you didn't misread it. This is one way in which the bitmap handle returned from *CreateDIBSection* is different from the other bitmap handles we've encountered. This bitmap handle actually references a DIB that is stored in memory maintained by the system but to which an application has access. This DIB is converted to a particular color format when necessary, which is usually when it's displayed using *BitBlt* or *StretchBlt*.

You can also select the bitmap handle into a memory device context and use GDI functions to draw on it. The results will be reflected in the DIB pixel bits pointed to by the *pBits* variable. Because of batching of GDI calls under Windows NT, call *GdiFlush* after drawing on the memory device context before accessing the bits "manually."

In DIBSECT we discarded the *pBits* variable because it was no longer required by the program. If you need to alter the bits directly, which is a major reason why you'll use *CreateDIBSection*, hold onto it. There seems to be no way to later obtain the bits pointer after the *CreateDIBSection* call.

More DIB Section Differences

The bitmap handle returned from *CreateDIBitmap* has the same planes and bits-per-pixel organization as the device referenced by the *hdc* parameter to the function. You can verify this by calling *GetObject* with the BITMAP structure.

CreateDIBSection is different. If you call *GetObject* with the BITMAP structure on the bitmap handle returned from the function, you'll find that the bitmap has the same color organization as indicated by the fields of the BITMAPINFOHEADER structure. Yet you can select this handle into a memory device context compatible with the video display. This contradicts what I said in the last chapter about DDBs, of course, but that's why I contend that this DIB section bitmap handle is different.

Another oddity: As you'll recall, the byte length of the rows of pixel data in DIBs is always a multiple of 4. The byte length of rows in GDI bitmap objects, which you can get from the *bmWidthBytes* field of the BITMAP structure used with *GetObject*, is always a multiple of 2. Well, if you set up the BITMAPINFOHEADER structure shown above with 24 bits per pixel and a width of 2 pixels (for example) and later call *GetObject*, you'll find that the *bmWidthBytes* field is 8 rather than 6.

With the bitmap handle returned from *CreateDIBSection*, you can also call *GetObject* with a DIBSECTION structure, like so:

```
GetObject (hBitmap, sizeof (DIBSECTION), &dibsection) ;
```

This won't work with a bitmap handle returned from any of the other bitmap-creation functions. The DIBSECTION structure is defined like so:

```
typedef struct tagDIBSECTION  // ds
{
     BITMAP           dsBm ;              // BITMAP structure
     BITMAPINFOHEADER dsBmih ;           // DIB information header
     DWORD            dsBitfields [3] ;  // color masks
     HANDLE           dshSection ;       // file-mapping object handle
     DWORD            dsOffset ;         // offset to bitmap bits
}
DIBSECTION, * PDIBSECTION ;
```

This structure contains both a BITMAP structure and a BITMAPINFOHEADER structure. The last two fields are the last two arguments passed to *CreateDIBSection*, which I'll discuss shortly.

The DIBSECTION structure tells you much of what you need to know about the bitmap, except for the color table. When you select the DIB section bitmap handle into a memory device context, you can get the color table by calling *GetDIBColorTable*:

```
hdcMem = CreateCompatibleDC (NULL) ;
SelectObject (hdcMem, hBitmap) ;
GetDIBColorTable (hdcMem, uFirstIndex, uNumEntries, &rgb) ;
DeleteDC (hdcMem) ;
```

Similary, you can set entries in the color table by calling *SetDIBColorTable*.

The File-Mapping Option

I haven't yet discussed the last two arguments to *CreateDIBSection*, which are a handle to a file-mapping object and an offset within that file where the bitmap bits begin. A file-mapping object allows you to treat a file as if it were located in memory. That is, you can access the file by using memory pointers, but the file needn't be entirely located in memory.

In the case of large DIBs, this technique can help reduce memory requirements. The DIB pixel bits can remain on disk but still be accessed as if they were in memory, albeit with a performance penalty. The problem is, while the pixel bits can indeed remain stored on disk, they can't be part of an actual DIB file. They'd have to be in some other file.

To demonstrate, the function shown below is very similar to the function that creates the DIB section in DIBSECT except that it doesn't read the pixel bits into memory; instead, it supplies a file-mapping object and an offset to the *CreateDIBSection* function:

```
HBITMAP CreateDibSectionMappingFromFile (PTSTR szFileName)
{
     BITMAPFILEHEADER bmfh ;
     BITMAPINFO     * pbmi ;
     BYTE           * pBits ;
     BOOL             bSuccess ;
     DWORD            dwInfoSize, dwBytesRead ;
     HANDLE           hFile, hFileMap ;
     HBITMAP          hBitmap ;

     hFile = CreateFile (szFileName, GENERIC_READ | GENERIC_WRITE,
                         0,                     // No sharing!
                         NULL, OPEN_EXISTING, 0, NULL) ;

     if (hFile == INVALID_HANDLE_VALUE)
          return NULL ;

     bSuccess = ReadFile (hFile, &bmfh, sizeof (BITMAPFILEHEADER),
                          &dwBytesRead, NULL) ;

     if (!bSuccess || (dwBytesRead != sizeof (BITMAPFILEHEADER))
                   || (bmfh.bfType != * (WORD *) "BM"))
     {
          CloseHandle (hFile) ;
          return NULL ;
     }
     dwInfoSize = bmfh.bfOffBits - sizeof (BITMAPFILEHEADER) ;
     pbmi = malloc (dwInfoSize) ;
     bSuccess = ReadFile (hFile, pbmi, dwInfoSize, &dwBytesRead, NULL) ;

     if (!bSuccess || (dwBytesRead != dwInfoSize))
     {
          free (pbmi) ;
          CloseHandle (hFile) ;
          return NULL ;
     }
     hFileMap = CreateFileMapping (hFile, NULL, PAGE_READWRITE, 0, 0, NULL) ;

     hBitmap = CreateDIBSection (NULL, pbmi, DIB_RGB_COLORS, &pBits,
                                 hFileMap, bmfh.bfOffBits) ;
     free (pbmi) ;
     return hBitmap ;
}
```

Alas, this does not work. The documentation of *CreateDIBSection* indicates that "*dwOffset* [the final argument to the function] must be a multiple of the size of a DWORD." Although the size of the information header is always a multiple of 4 and the size of the color table is always a multiple of 4, the bitmap file header is not. It's 14 bytes. So *bmfh.bfOffBits* is never a multiple of 4.

In Summary

If you have small DIBs and you need to frequently manipulate the pixel bits, you can display them using *SetDIBitsToDevice* and *StretchDIBits*. However, for larger DIBs, this technique will encounter performance problems, particularly on 8-bit video displays and under Windows NT.

You can convert a DIB to a DDB by using *CreateDIBitmap* and *SetDIBits*. Displaying the bitmap will now involve the speedy *BitBlt* and *StretchBlt* functions. However, you no longer have access to the device-independent pixel bits.

CreateDIBSection is a good compromise. Using the bitmap handle with *BitBlt* and *StretchBlt* gives you better performance under Windows NT than using *SetDIBitsToDevice* and *StretchDIBits* but with none of the drawbacks of the DDB. You still have access to the DIB pixel bits.

In the next chapter, we'll wrap up our exploration of bitmaps after looking at the Windows Palette Manager.

Chapter 16

The Palette Manager

This chapter would not exist were it not for a hardware deficiency. Although many modern video adapter boards offer 24-bit color (also known as "true color" or "millions of colors") or 16-bit color ("high color" or "thousands of colors"), some video adapters—particularly on laptops or in high-resolution video modes—allow only 8 bits per pixel. The use of 8 bits per pixel implies only 256 simultaneous colors.

What can we do with 256 colors? While a mere 16 colors are clearly inadequate for displaying real-world images and the use of thousands or millions of colors is quite sufficient for that task, 256 colors falls somewhere in the middle. Yes, 256 colors are adequate for displaying a real-world image, but only if those colors are selected specifically for the particular image. This means that an operating system simply cannot choose a "standard" set of 256 colors and expect them to be the ideal colors for every application.

This is what the Windows Palette Manager is all about. It's for specifying the colors that your program needs when running in an 8-bit video mode. If you know that your programs will never run in 8-bit video modes, you won't need to use the Palette Manager. However, this chapter contains important information nonetheless, for it ties up some loose ends with bitmaps.

USING PALETTES

Traditionally, a palette is the board that a painter uses to mix colors. The word can also refer to the entire range of colors that an artist uses in creating a painting. In computer graphics, the palette is the range of colors available on a graphics output device such as a video display. The word can also refer to a lookup table on video boards that support 256-color modes.

Video Hardware

The palette lookup table on video boards works something like this:

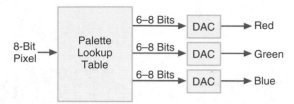

In 8-bit video modes, each pixel has 8 bits. The pixel value addresses a lookup table that contains 256 RGB values. These RGB values can be a full 24 bits wide or can be smaller, typically 18 bits wide (that is, 6 bits for each red, green, and blue primary). The values for each color are input to digital-to-analog converters for the three analog red, green, and blue signals that go to the monitor.

The palette lookup table can generally be loaded with arbitrary values through software, but there are some obstacles for a device-independent windowing interface such as that in Microsoft Windows. First, Windows must provide a software interface so that applications can access the Palette Manager without directly fooling around with the hardware. The second problem is more serious: because all applications are sharing the same video display and running side by side, one application's use of the palette lookup table might interfere with another's.

This is where the Windows Palette Manager (introduced in Windows 3.0) comes into play. Windows reserves 20 of the 256 colors for itself and lets applications change the other 236. (In certain cases, an application can change up to 254 of the 256 colors—all except black and white—but this is a bit of a chore.) The 20 colors that Windows reserves for system use, sometimes called the 20 *static* colors) are shown in Figure 16-1.

Pixel Bits	RGB Value	Color Name	Pixel Bits	RGB Value	Color Name
00000000	00 00 00	Black	11111111	FF FF FF	White
00000001	80 00 00	Dark Red	11111110	00 FF FF	Cyan
00000010	00 80 00	Dark Green	11111101	FF 00 FF	Magenta
00000011	80 80 00	Dark Yellow	11111100	00 00 FF	Blue
00000100	00 00 80	Dark Blue	11111011	FF FF 00	Yellow
00000101	80 00 80	Dark Magenta	11111010	00 FF 00	Green
00000110	00 80 80	Dark Cyan	11111001	FF 00 00	Red
00000111	C0 C0 C0	Light Gray	11111000	80 80 80	Dark Gray
00001000	C0 DC C0	Money Green	11110111	A0 A0 A4	Medium Gray
00001001	A6 CA F0	Sky Blue	11110110	FF FB F0	Cream

Figure 16-1. *The 20 reserved colors in 256-color video modes.*

When running in 256-color video modes, Windows maintains a "system palette," which is the same as the hardware palette lookup table on the video board. The default system palette is shown in Figure 16-1. Applications can change the other 236 colors by specifying "logical palettes." If more than one application is using logical palettes, Windows gives highest priority to the active window. (As you know, the active window is the window that has the highlighted title bar and appears to the foreground of all the other windows.) We'll examine how this works in the context of a simple sample program.

For running the programs shown in the remainder of this chapter, you may want to switch your video board into a 256-color mode. Right click the mouse on the desktop, pick Properties from the menu, and select the Settings tab.

Displaying Gray Shades

The GRAYS1 program shown in Figure 16-2 does *not* use the Windows Palette Manager but instead tries to normally display 65 shades of gray as a "fountain" of color ranging black to white.

GRAYS1.C

```
/*------------------------------------------
   GRAYS1.C -- Gray Shades
             (c) Charles Petzold, 1998
   ------------------------------------------*/

#include <windows.h>

LRESULT CALLBACK WndProc (HWND, UINT, WPARAM, LPARAM) ;

int WINAPI WinMain (HINSTANCE hInstance, HINSTANCE hPrevInstance,
                    PSTR szCmdLine, int iCmdShow)
{
    static TCHAR szAppName[] = TEXT ("Grays1") ;
    HWND        hwnd ;
    MSG         msg ;
    WNDCLASS    wndclass ;

    wndclass.style         = CS_HREDRAW | CS_VREDRAW ;
    wndclass.lpfnWndProc   = WndProc ;
    wndclass.cbClsExtra    = 0 ;
    wndclass.cbWndExtra    = 0 ;
    wndclass.hInstance     = hInstance ;
    wndclass.hIcon         = LoadIcon (NULL, IDI_APPLICATION) ;
    wndclass.hCursor       = LoadCursor (NULL, IDC_ARROW) ;
    wndclass.hbrBackground = (HBRUSH) GetStockObject (WHITE_BRUSH) ;
```

Figure 16-2. *The GRAYS1 program.*   *(continued)*

Figure 16-2. *continued*

```
    wndclass.lpszMenuName  = NULL ;
    wndclass.lpszClassName = szAppName ;

    if (!RegisterClass (&wndclass))
    {
        MessageBox (NULL, TEXT ("This program requires Windows NT!"),
                    szAppName, MB_ICONERROR) ;
        return 0 ;
    }

    hwnd = CreateWindow (szAppName, TEXT ("Shades of Gray #1"),
                        WS_OVERLAPPEDWINDOW,
                        CW_USEDEFAULT, CW_USEDEFAULT,
                        CW_USEDEFAULT, CW_USEDEFAULT,
                        NULL, NULL, hInstance, NULL) ;

    ShowWindow (hwnd, iCmdShow) ;
    UpdateWindow (hwnd) ;

    while (GetMessage (&msg, NULL, 0, 0))
    {
        TranslateMessage (&msg) ;
        DispatchMessage (&msg) ;
    }
    return msg.wParam ;
}

LRESULT CALLBACK WndProc (HWND hwnd, UINT message, WPARAM wParam, LPARAM lParam)
{
    static int  cxClient, cyClient ;
    HBRUSH      hBrush ;
    HDC         hdc ;
    int         i ;
    PAINTSTRUCT ps ;
    RECT        rect ;

    switch (message)
    {
    case WM_SIZE:
        cxClient = LOWORD (lParam) ;
        cyClient = HIWORD (lParam) ;
        return 0 ;
```

```
  case WM_PAINT:
       hdc = BeginPaint (hwnd, &ps) ;

            // Draw the fountain of grays

       for (i = 0 ; i < 65 ; i++)
       {
            rect.left   = i * cxClient / 65 ;
            rect.top    = 0 ;
            rect.right  = (i + 1) * cxClient / 65 ;
            rect.bottom = cyClient ;

            hBrush = CreateSolidBrush (RGB (min (255, 4 * i),
                                           min (255, 4 * i),
                                           min (255, 4 * i))) ;
            FillRect (hdc, &rect, hBrush) ;
            DeleteObject (hBrush) ;
       }
       EndPaint (hwnd, &ps) ;
       return 0 ;

  case WM_DESTROY:
       PostQuitMessage (0) ;
       return 0 ;
  }
  return DefWindowProc (hwnd, message, wParam, lParam) ;
}
```

During the WM_PAINT message, the program makes 65 calls to the *FillRect* function, each time with a brush created using a different gray shade. The gray shades are the RGB values (0, 0, 0), (4, 4, 4), (8, 8, 8), and so forth, until the last one, which is (255, 255, 255). That last one is the reason for the *min* macro in the *CreateSolidBrush* function.

If you run this program in a 256-color video mode, you'll see 65 shades of gray from black to white, but almost all of them are rendered using dithering. The only pure colors are black, dark gray (128, 128, 128), light gray (192, 192, 192), and white. The other colors are various bit patterns combining these pure colors. If we were displaying lines or text rather than filled areas using these 65 gray shades, Windows would not use dithering and would use only the four pure colors. If we were displaying a bitmap, the image would be approximated using the 20 standard Windows colors, as you can see for yourself by running one of the programs from the last chapter and loading in a color or gray-shade DIB. Windows normally does not use dithering for bitmaps.

The GRAYS2 program shown in Figure 16-3 on the following page demonstrates the most important Palette Manager functions and messages with little extraneous code.

GRAYS2.C

```
/*-------------------------------------------------
   GRAYS2.C -- Gray Shades Using Palette Manager
                (c) Charles Petzold, 1998
   -------------------------------------------------*/

#include <windows.h>

LRESULT CALLBACK WndProc (HWND, UINT, WPARAM, LPARAM) ;

int WINAPI WinMain (HINSTANCE hInstance, HINSTANCE hPrevInstance,
                    PSTR szCmdLine, int iCmdShow)
{
     static TCHAR szAppName[] = TEXT ("Grays2") ;
     HWND          hwnd ;
     MSG           msg ;
     WNDCLASS      wndclass ;

     wndclass.style         = CS_HREDRAW | CS_VREDRAW ;
     wndclass.lpfnWndProc   = WndProc ;
     wndclass.cbClsExtra    = 0 ;
     wndclass.cbWndExtra    = 0 ;
     wndclass.hInstance     = hInstance ;
     wndclass.hIcon         = LoadIcon (NULL, IDI_APPLICATION) ;
     wndclass.hCursor       = LoadCursor (NULL, IDC_ARROW) ;
     wndclass.hbrBackground = (HBRUSH) GetStockObject (WHITE_BRUSH) ;
     wndclass.lpszMenuName  = NULL ;
     wndclass.lpszClassName = szAppName ;

     if (!RegisterClass (&wndclass))
     {
          MessageBox (NULL, TEXT ("This program requires Windows NT!"),
                      szAppName, MB_ICONERROR) ;
          return 0 ;
     }

     hwnd = CreateWindow (szAppName, TEXT ("Shades of Gray #2"),
                          WS_OVERLAPPEDWINDOW,
                          CW_USEDEFAULT, CW_USEDEFAULT,
                          CW_USEDEFAULT, CW_USEDEFAULT,
                          NULL, NULL, hInstance, NULL) ;

     ShowWindow (hwnd, iCmdShow) ;
     UpdateWindow (hwnd) ;
```

Figure 16-3. *The GRAYS2 program.*

```
      while (GetMessage (&msg, NULL, 0, 0))
      {
            TranslateMessage (&msg) ;
            DispatchMessage (&msg) ;
      }
      return msg.wParam ;
}

LRESULT CALLBACK WndProc (HWND hwnd, UINT message, WPARAM wParam, LPARAM lParam)
{
      static HPALETTE hPalette ;
      static int      cxClient, cyClient ;
      HBRUSH          hBrush ;
      HDC             hdc ;
      int             i ;
      LOGPALETTE    * plp ;
      PAINTSTRUCT     ps ;
      RECT            rect ;

      switch (message)
      {
      case WM_CREATE:
                  // Set up a LOGPALETTE structure and create a palette

            plp = malloc (sizeof (LOGPALETTE) + 64 * sizeof (PALETTEENTRY)) ;

            plp->palVersion    = 0x0300 ;
            plp->palNumEntries = 65 ;

            for (i = 0 ; i < 65 ; i++)
            {
                  plp->palPalEntry[i].peRed   = (BYTE) min (255, 4 * i) ;
                  plp->palPalEntry[i].peGreen = (BYTE) min (255, 4 * i) ;
                  plp->palPalEntry[i].peBlue  = (BYTE) min (255, 4 * i) ;
                  plp->palPalEntry[i].peFlags = 0 ;
            }
            hPalette = CreatePalette (plp) ;
            free (plp) ;
            return 0 ;

      case WM_SIZE:
            cxClient = LOWORD (lParam) ;
            cyClient = HIWORD (lParam) ;
            return 0 ;
```

(continued)

Figure 16-3. *continued*

```
case WM_PAINT:
     hdc = BeginPaint (hwnd, &ps) ;

          // Select and realize the palette in the device context

     SelectPalette (hdc, hPalette, FALSE) ;
     RealizePalette (hdc) ;

          // Draw the fountain of grays

     for (i = 0 ; i < 65 ; i++)
     {
          rect.left   = i * cxClient / 64 ;
          rect.top    = 0 ;
          rect.right  = (i + 1) * cxClient / 64 ;
          rect.bottom = cyClient ;

          hBrush = CreateSolidBrush (PALETTERGB (min (255, 4 * i),
                                                 min (255, 4 * i),
                                                 min (255, 4 * i))) ;
          FillRect (hdc, &rect, hBrush) ;
          DeleteObject (hBrush) ;
     }
     EndPaint (hwnd, &ps) ;
     return 0 ;

case WM_QUERYNEWPALETTE:
     if (!hPalette)
          return FALSE ;

     hdc = GetDC (hwnd) ;
     SelectPalette (hdc, hPalette, FALSE) ;
     RealizePalette (hdc) ;
     InvalidateRect (hwnd, NULL, TRUE) ;

     ReleaseDC (hwnd, hdc) ;
     return TRUE ;

case WM_PALETTECHANGED:
     if (!hPalette || (HWND) wParam == hwnd)
          break ;

     hdc = GetDC (hwnd) ;
     SelectPalette (hdc, hPalette, FALSE) ;
     RealizePalette (hdc) ;
     UpdateColors (hdc) ;
```

```
          ReleaseDC (hwnd, hdc) ;
          break ;

     case WM_DESTROY:
          DeleteObject (hPalette) ;
          PostQuitMessage (0) ;
          return 0 ;
     }
     return DefWindowProc (hwnd, message, wParam, lParam) ;
}
```

Generally the first step in using the Palette Manager is to create a logical palette by calling the *CreatePalette* function. The logical palette contains all the colors—or rather, as many as 236 colors—that the program needs. The GRAYS1 program handles this job during the WM_CREATE message. It initializes the fields of a LOGPALETTE ("logical palette") structure and passes a pointer to this structure to the *CreatePalette* function. *CreatePalette* returns a handle to the logical palette, which is stored in the static variable *hPalette*.

The LOGPALETTE structure is defined like so:

```
typedef struct
{
     WORD         palVersion ;
     WORD         palNumEntries ;
     PALETTEENTRY palPalEntry[1] ;
}
LOGPALETTE, * PLOGPALETTE ;
```

The first field is always set to 0x0300, indicating Windows 3.0 compatibility, and the second field is set to the number of entries in the palette table. The third field in the LOGPALETTE structure is an array of PALETTEENTRY structures, one for each of the palette entries. The PALETTEENTRY structure is defined like this:

```
typedef struct
{
     BYTE peRed ;
     BYTE peGreen ;
     BYTE peBlue ;
     BYTE peFlags ;
}
PALETTEENTRY, * PPALETTEENTRY ;
```

Each of the PALETTEENTRY structures defines an RGB color value that we want in the palette.

Notice that LOGPALETTE is defined for an array of only one PALETTEENTRY structure. You need to allocate some memory large enough for one LOGPALETTE structure and additional PALETTEENTRY structures. GRAYS2 wants 65 gray shades, so it allocates enough memory for a LOGPALETTE structure and 64 additional PALETTEENTRY structures. It sets the *palNumEntries* field to 65. GRAYS2 then goes through a loop from 0 through 64, calculates a gray level (which is simply 4 times the loop index but not greater than 255), and sets the *peRed*, *peGreen*, and *peBlue* fields of the structure to this gray level. The *peFlags* field is set to 0. The program passes the pointer to this block of memory to *CreatePalette*, saves the palette handle in a static variable, and then frees the memory.

A logical palette is a GDI object. Programs should delete any logical palettes they create. *WndProc* takes care of deleting the logical palette during the WM_DESTROY message by calling *DeleteObject*.

Notice that the logical palette is independent of a device context. Before you can actually make use of it, it must be selected into a device context and "realized." During the WM_PAINT message, the *SelectPalette* function selects the logical palette into the device context. This is similar to the *SelectObject* function except that a third argument is included. Normally this third argument is set to FALSE. If the third argument to *SelectPalette* is set to TRUE, the palette is always a "background palette," which means that it gets whatever unused entries still exist in the system palette after all other programs have realized their palettes.

Only one logical palette can be selected into the device context at any time. The function returns the handle of the logical palette previously selected in the device context. You can save this for selecting back into the device context if you wish to.

The *RealizePalette* function causes Windows to "realize" the logical palette in the device context by mapping the colors to the system palette, which in turn corresponds to the actual physical palette of the video board. The real work goes on during this function call. Windows must determine whether the window calling the function is active or inactive and perhaps notify other windows that the system palette is changing. (We'll see how this notification works shortly.)

You'll recall that GRAYS1 used the RGB macro to specify the color of the solid brush. The RGB macro constructs a 32-bit long integer (known as a COLORREF value) where the upper byte is 0 and the lower 3 bytes are the intensities of red, green, and blue.

A program that uses the Windows Palette Manager can continue to use RGB color values to specify color. However, these RGB color values will *not* give access to the additional colors in the logical palette. They will have the same effect as if the Palette Manager were not used. To make use of the additional colors in the logical palette, you use the PALETTERGB macro. A "Palette RGB" color is very much like an RGB color except that the high byte of the COLORREF value is set to 2 rather than 0.

Here are the important rules:

■ To use a color in your logical palette, specify it using a Palette RGB value or a Palette Index value. (I'll discuss the Palette Index shortly.) Do not use a normal RGB value. If you use a normal RGB value, you will get one of the standard colors and not a color from your logical palette.

■ Do not use Palette RGB values or Palette Index values when you have not selected a palette in your device context.

■ Although you can use a Palette RGB value to specify a color not in the logical palette, the color you get will be selected from the logical palette.

For example, during WM_PAINT processing in GRAYS2, after you select and realize the logical palette, if you try to display something in red, it will come out as a shade of gray. You need to use RGB color values to select colors not in the logical palette.

Notice that GRAYS2 never checks to see whether the video display driver actually supports palette management. When running GRAYS2 under video modes that do not support palette management (that is, all video modes that are *not* 256 colors), GRAYS2 is functionally equivalent to GRAYS1.

The Palette Messages

If multiple Windows programs are using the Palette Manager, the active window gets priority over the palette. The most recently active window gets second priority, and so forth. Whenever a new program becomes active, the Windows Palette Manager usually must reorganize the system palette table.

If a program specifies a color in its logical palette that is identical to one of the 20 reserved colors, Windows will map that logical palette entry to that color. Also, if two or more applications specify the same color in their logical palettes, these applications will share the system palette entry. A program can override this default behavior by specifying the constant PC_NOCOLLAPSE as the *peFlags* field of the PALETTEENTRY structure. (The other two possible flags are PC_EXPLICIT, which is used to display the system palette, and PC_RESERVED, which is used in palette animation. I'll demonstrate both of these flags later in this chapter.)

To help in organizing the system palette, the Windows Palette Manager includes two messages sent to main windows.

The first is QM_QUERYNEWPALETTE. This message is sent to a main window when it is about to become active. If your program uses the Palette Manager when drawing on your window, it must process this message. GRAYS2 demonstrates how to do so. The program obtains a device context handle, selects the palette into it, calls *RealizePalette*, and then invalidates the window to generate a WM_PAINT message. The window procedure returns TRUE from this message if it realizes its logical palette and FALSE otherwise.

Whenever the system palette changes as a result of a WM_QUERYNEWPALETTE message, Windows sends the WM_PALETTECHANGED message to all main windows starting with the most active window and proceeding down the window chain. This allows the foreground window to have priority. The *wParam* value passed to the window procedure is the handle of the active window. A program using the Palette Manager should process this message only if *wParam* is not equal to the program's window handle.

Generally, any program that uses a customized palette calls *SelectPalette* and *RealizePalette* while processing WM_PALETTECHANGED. When subsequent windows call *RealizePalette* during the message, Windows first checks for matches of RGB colors in the logical palette with RGB colors already loaded in the system palette. If two programs need the same color, the same system palette entry is used for both. Next Windows checks for unused system palette entries. If none exist, the color in the logical palette is mapped to the closest color from the 20 reserved entries.

If you don't care about how the client area looks when your program is inactive, you do not need to process the WM_PALETTECHANGED message. Otherwise, you have two choices. GRAYS2 shows one of them: As when processing the WM_QUERYNEWPALETTE message, it gets a device context, selects the palette into it, and then calls *RealizePalette*. At this point, it could call *InvalidateRect* as when processing WM_QUERYNEWPALETTE. Instead, GRAYS2 calls *UpdateColors*. This function is usually more efficient than repainting the window, and it changes the values of pixels in your window to help preserve the previous colors.

Most programs that use the Palette Manager will have WM_QUERYNEWPALETTE and WM_PALETTECHANGED message processing identical to that shown in GRAYS2.

The Palette Index Approach

The GRAYS3 program shown in Figure 16-4 is very similar to GRAYS2 but uses a macro called PALETTEINDEX instead of PALETTERGB during WM_PAINT processing.

GRAYS3.C

```
/*-------------------------------------------------
   GRAYS3.C -- Gray Shades Using Palette Manager
               (c) Charles Petzold, 1998
   -------------------------------------------------*/

#include <windows.h>

LRESULT CALLBACK WndProc (HWND, UINT, WPARAM, LPARAM) ;

int WINAPI WinMain (HINSTANCE hInstance, HINSTANCE hPrevInstance,
                    PSTR szCmdLine, int iCmdShow)
{
     static TCHAR szAppName[] = TEXT ("Grays3") ;
     HWND         hwnd ;
     MSG          msg ;
     WNDCLASS     wndclass ;
```

Figure 16-4. *The GRAYS3 program.*

```
      wndclass.style         = CS_HREDRAW | CS_VREDRAW ;
      wndclass.lpfnWndProc   = WndProc ;
      wndclass.cbClsExtra    = 0 ;
      wndclass.cbWndExtra    = 0 ;
      wndclass.hInstance     = hInstance ;
      wndclass.hIcon         = LoadIcon (NULL, IDI_APPLICATION) ;
      wndclass.hCursor       = LoadCursor (NULL, IDC_ARROW) ;
      wndclass.hbrBackground = (HBRUSH) GetStockObject (WHITE_BRUSH) ;
      wndclass.lpszMenuName  = NULL ;
      wndclass.lpszClassName = szAppName ;

      if (!RegisterClass (&wndclass))
      {
           MessageBox (NULL, TEXT ("This program requires Windows NT!"),
                       szAppName, MB_ICONERROR) ;
           return 0 ;
      }

      hwnd = CreateWindow (szAppName, TEXT ("Shades of Gray #3"),
                           WS_OVERLAPPEDWINDOW,
                           CW_USEDEFAULT, CW_USEDEFAULT,
                           CW_USEDEFAULT, CW_USEDEFAULT,
                           NULL, NULL, hInstance, NULL) ;

      ShowWindow (hwnd, iCmdShow) ;
      UpdateWindow (hwnd) ;

      while (GetMessage (&msg, NULL, 0, 0))
      {
           TranslateMessage (&msg) ;
           DispatchMessage (&msg) ;
      }
      return msg.wParam ;
}

LRESULT CALLBACK WndProc (HWND hwnd, UINT message, WPARAM wParam, LPARAM lParam)
{
      static HPALETTE  hPalette ;
      static int       cxClient, cyClient ;
      HBRUSH           hBrush ;
      HDC              hdc ;
      int              i ;
      LOGPALETTE     * plp ;
      PAINTSTRUCT      ps ;
      RECT             rect ;
```

(continued)

Figure 16-4. *continued*

```
switch (message)
{
case WM_CREATE:
        // Set up a LOGPALETTE structure and create a palette

    plp = malloc (sizeof (LOGPALETTE) + 64 * sizeof (PALETTEENTRY)) ;

    plp->palVersion    = 0x0300 ;
    plp->palNumEntries = 65 ;

    for (i = 0 ; i < 65 ; i++)
    {
        plp->palPalEntry[i].peRed   = (BYTE) min (255, 4 * i) ;
        plp->palPalEntry[i].peGreen = (BYTE) min (255, 4 * i) ;
        plp->palPalEntry[i].peBlue  = (BYTE) min (255, 4 * i) ;
        plp->palPalEntry[i].peFlags = 0 ;
    }
    hPalette = CreatePalette (plp) ;
    free (plp) ;
    return 0 ;

case WM_SIZE:
    cxClient = LOWORD (lParam) ;
    cyClient = HIWORD (lParam) ;
    return 0 ;

case WM_PAINT:
    hdc = BeginPaint (hwnd, &ps) ;

        // Select and realize the palette in the device context

    SelectPalette (hdc, hPalette, FALSE) ;
    RealizePalette (hdc) ;

        // Draw the fountain of grays

    for (i = 0 ; i < 65 ; i++)
    {
        rect.left   = i * cxClient / 64 ;
        rect.top    = 0 ;
        rect.right  = (i + 1) * cxClient / 64 ;
        rect.bottom = cyClient ;

        hBrush = CreateSolidBrush (PALETTEINDEX (i)) ;
```

```
            FillRect (hdc, &rect, hBrush) ;
            DeleteObject (hBrush) ;
       }

       EndPaint (hwnd, &ps) ;
       return 0 ;

  case WM_QUERYNEWPALETTE:
       if (!hPalette)
            return FALSE ;

       hdc = GetDC (hwnd) ;
       SelectPalette (hdc, hPalette, FALSE) ;
       RealizePalette (hdc) ;
       InvalidateRect (hwnd, NULL, FALSE) ;

       ReleaseDC (hwnd, hdc) ;
       return TRUE ;

  case WM_PALETTECHANGED:
       if (!hPalette || (HWND) wParam == hwnd)
            break ;

       hdc = GetDC (hwnd) ;
       SelectPalette (hdc, hPalette, FALSE) ;
       RealizePalette (hdc) ;
       UpdateColors (hdc) ;

       ReleaseDC (hwnd, hdc) ;
       break ;

  case WM_DESTROY:
       PostQuitMessage (0) ;
       return 0 ;
  }
  return DefWindowProc (hwnd, message, wParam, lParam) ;
}
```

A "Palette Index" color is quite different from the Palette RGB color. The high byte is 1, and the value in the low byte is an index into the logical palette currently selected in the device context. In GRAYS3, the logical palette has 65 entries. The indices for these entries are thus 0 through 64. The value

```
PALETTEINDEX (0)
```

refers to black,

```
PALETTEINDEX (32)
```

refers to medium gray, and

```
PALETTEINDEX (64)
```

refers to white.

Using palette indices is more efficient than using RGB values because Windows does not need to perform a nearest-color search.

Querying the Palette Support

As you can easily verify, the GRAYS2 and GRAYS3 programs run fine when Windows is running under a 16-bit or 24-bit video mode. But in some cases, a Windows application that wishes to use the Palette Manager might want to first determine whether the device driver supports it. You can do this by calling *GetDeviceCaps* using a device context handle for the video display and the RASTERCAPS parameter. The function returns an integer composed of a series of flags. You can test palette support by performing a bitwise AND between the return value and the constant RC_PALETTE:

```
RC_PALETTE & GetDeviceCaps (hdc, RASTERCAPS)
```

If this value is nonzero, the device driver for the video display supports palette manipulation. In that case, three other important items are also available from *GetDeviceCaps*. The function call

```
GetDeviceCaps (hdc, SIZEPALETTE)
```

returns the total size of the palette table on the video board. This is the same as the total number of colors that can be simultaneously displayed. Because the Palette Manager is invoked only for video display modes with 8 bits per pixel, this value will be 256.

The function call

```
GetDeviceCaps (hdc, NUMRESERVED)
```

returns the number of colors in the palette table that the device driver reserves for system purposes. This value will be 20. Without invoking the Palette Manager, these are the only pure colors a Windows application can use in a 256-color video mode. To use the other 236 colors, a program must use the Palette Manager functions.

One additional item is also available:

```
GetDeviceCaps (hdc, COLORRES)
```

This value tells you the resolution (in bits) of the RGB color values loaded into the hardware palette table. These are the bits going into the digital-to-analog converters. Some video display adapters use only 6-bit ADCs, so this value would be 18. Others use 8-bit ADCs, so this value would be 24.

It is useful for a Windows program to take a look at this color resolution value and behave accordingly. For example, if the color resolution is 18, it makes no sense for a program to attempt to request 128 shades of gray because only 64 discrete shades of gray are possible. Requesting 128 shades of gray will unnecessarily fill the hardware palette table with redundant entries.

The System Palette

As I've mentioned, the system palette in Windows corresponds directly to the hardware palette lookup table on the video adapter board. (However, the hardware palette lookup table may have a lower color resolution than the system palette.) A program can obtain any or all of the RGB entries in the system palette by calling this function:

```
GetSystemPaletteEntries (hdc, uStart, uNum, &pe) ;
```

This function works only if the video adapter mode supports palette manipulation. The second and third arguments are unsigned integer values that indicate the index of the first palette entry you want and the number of palette entries you want. The last argument is a pointer to a structure of type PALETTEENTRY.

You can use this function in several ways. A program can define one PALETTEENTRY structure like this,

```
PALETTEENTRY pe ;
```

and then call *GetSystemPaletteEntries* multiple times like so,

```
GetSystemPaletteEntries (hdc, i, 1, &pe) ;
```

with *i* being from 0 to one less than the value returned from *GetDeviceCaps* with the SIZEPALETTE index, which will be 255. Or a program can obtain all the system palette entries by defining a pointer to a PALETTEENTRY structure and then allocating a block of memory sufficient to hold as many PALETTEENTRY structures as indicated by the size of the palette.

The *GetSystemPaletteEntries* function really lets you examine the hardware palette table. The entries in the system palette are in the order of increasing values of pixel bits that are used to denote color in the video display buffer. I'll demonstrate how to do this shortly.

Other Palette Functions

As we saw earlier, a Windows program can change the system palette but only indirectly. The first step is creating a logical palette, which is basically an array of RGB color values that the program wants to use. The *CreatePalette* function does not cause any change to the system palette or the palette table on the video board. The logical palette must be selected into a device context and realized before anything happens.

A program can query the RGB color values in a logical palette by calling

```
GetPaletteEntries (hPalette, uStart, uNum, &pe) ;
```

You can use this function in the same way you use *GetSystemPaletteEntries*. But note that the first parameter is a handle to the logical palette rather than a handle to a device context.

A corresponding function lets you change values in the logical palette after it has been created:

```
SetPaletteEntries (hPalette, uStart, uNum, &pe) ;
```

Again, keep in mind that calling this function does not cause any change to the system palette—even if the palette is currently selected in a device context. This function also cannot change the size of the logical palette. For that, use *ResizePalette*.

The following function accepts an RGB color reference value as the last argument and returns an index into the logical palette that corresponds to the RGB color value that most closely approximates it:

```
iIndex = GetNearestPaletteIndex (hPalette, cr) ;
```

The second argument is a COLORREF value. If you wish, you can then obtain the actual RGB color value in the logical palette by calling *GetPaletteEntries*.

Programs that need more than 236 custom colors in 8-bit video modes can call *GetSystemPaletteUse*. This lets a program set 254 custom colors; the system reserves only black and white. However, the program should do this only when it is maximized to fill the screen, and it should set some system colors to black and white so that title bars and menus and such are still visible.

The Raster-Op Problem

As you know from Chapter 5, GDI allows you to draw lines and filled areas by using various "drawing modes" or "raster operations." You set the drawing mode using *SetROP2*. The "2" indicates a *binary* raster operation between two objects; tertiary raster operations are used with *BitBlt* and similar functions. These raster operations determine how the pixels of the object you're drawing combine with the pixels of the surface. For example, you can draw a line so that the pixels of the line are combined with the pixels of the display using a bitwise exclusive-OR operation.

The raster operations work by performing bitwise operations on pixel bits. Changing the palette can affect how these raster operations work. The raster operations manipulate pixel bits, and these pixel bits might have no relationship to actual colors.

You can see this for yourself by running the GRAYS2 or GRAYS3 program. Drag the top or bottom sizing border across the window. Windows displays the dragged sizing border by using a raster operation that inverts the background pixel bits. The intent is to make the dragged sizing border always visible. But with the GRAYS2 and GRAYS3 programs, you'll probably see various random colors instead. These colors happen to correspond to unused entries in the palette table that result from inverting the pixel bits of the display. The visible color is not being inverted—only the pixel bits.

As you can see in Figure 16-1, the 20 standard reserved colors are placed at the top and bottom of the system palette so that the results of raster operations are still normal. However, once you begin changing the palette—and particularly if you take over the reserved colors—then raster operations of color objects can become meaningless.

The only guarantee you have is that the raster operations will work with black and white. Black is the first entry in the system palette (all pixel bits set to 0), and white is the last entry (all pixel bits set to 1). These entries cannot be changed. If you need to predict the results of raster operations on color objects, you can do so by getting the system palette table and looking at the RGB color values for the various pixel-bit values.

Looking at the System Palette

Programs running under Windows deal with logical palettes; Windows sets up the colors in the system palette to best service all programs using logical palettes. The system palette mirrors the hardware lookup table of the video board. Thus, taking a look at the system palette can help in debugging palette applications.

I'm going to show you three programs that display the contents of the system palette because there are three quite different approaches to this problem.

The SYSPAL1 program is shown in Figure 16-5. This program uses the *GetSystemPaletteEntries* function that I described above.

SYSPAL1.C

```
/*------------------------------------------
   SYSPAL1.C -- Displays system palette
                (c) Charles Petzold, 1998
   ---------------------------------------*/

#include <windows.h>

LRESULT CALLBACK WndProc (HWND, UINT, WPARAM, LPARAM) ;

TCHAR szAppName [] = TEXT ("SysPal1") ;

int WINAPI WinMain (HINSTANCE hInstance, HINSTANCE hPrevInstance,
                    PSTR szCmdLine, int iCmdShow)
{
     HWND      hwnd ;
     MSG       msg ;
     WNDCLASS  wndclass ;
```

Figure 16-5. *The SYSPAL1 program.*

(continued)

Figure 16-5. *continued*

```
    wndclass.style         = CS_HREDRAW | CS_VREDRAW ;
    wndclass.lpfnWndProc   = WndProc ;
    wndclass.cbClsExtra    = 0 ;
    wndclass.cbWndExtra    = 0 ;
    wndclass.hInstance     = hInstance ;
    wndclass.hIcon         = LoadIcon (NULL, IDI_APPLICATION) ;
    wndclass.hCursor       = LoadCursor (NULL, IDC_ARROW) ;
    wndclass.hbrBackground = (HBRUSH) GetStockObject (WHITE_BRUSH) ;
    wndclass.lpszMenuName  = NULL ;
    wndclass.lpszClassName = szAppName ;

    if (!RegisterClass (&wndclass))
    {
        MessageBox (NULL, TEXT ("This program requires Windows NT!"),
                    szAppName, MB_ICONERROR) ;
        return 0 ;
    }

    hwnd = CreateWindow (szAppName, TEXT ("System Palette #1"),
                         WS_OVERLAPPEDWINDOW,
                         CW_USEDEFAULT, CW_USEDEFAULT,
                         CW_USEDEFAULT, CW_USEDEFAULT,
                         NULL, NULL, hInstance, NULL) ;

    if (!hwnd)
        return 0 ;

    ShowWindow (hwnd, iCmdShow) ;
    UpdateWindow (hwnd) ;

    while (GetMessage (&msg, NULL, 0, 0))
    {
        TranslateMessage (&msg) ;
        DispatchMessage (&msg) ;
    }
    return msg.wParam ;
}

BOOL CheckDisplay (HWND hwnd)
{
    HDC hdc ;
    int iPalSize ;

    hdc = GetDC (hwnd) ;
    iPalSize = GetDeviceCaps (hdc, SIZEPALETTE) ;
    ReleaseDC (hwnd, hdc) ;
```

```
        if (iPalSize != 256)
        {
            MessageBox (hwnd, TEXT ("This program requires that the video ")
                             TEXT ("display mode have a 256-color palette."),
                        szAppName, MB_ICONERROR) ;
            return FALSE ;
        }
        return TRUE ;
}

LRESULT CALLBACK WndProc (HWND hwnd, UINT message, WPARAM wParam, LPARAM lParam)
{
    static int    cxClient, cyClient ;
    static SIZE   sizeChar ;
    HDC           hdc ;
    HPALETTE      hPalette ;
    int           i, x, y ;
    PAINTSTRUCT   ps ;
    PALETTEENTRY  pe [256] ;
    TCHAR         szBuffer [16] ;

    switch (message)
    {
    case WM_CREATE:
        if (!CheckDisplay (hwnd))
            return -1 ;

        hdc = GetDC (hwnd) ;
        SelectObject (hdc, GetStockObject (SYSTEM_FIXED_FONT)) ;
        GetTextExtentPoint32 (hdc, TEXT ("FF-FF-FF"), 10, &sizeChar) ;
        ReleaseDC (hwnd, hdc) ;
        return 0 ;

    case WM_DISPLAYCHANGE:
        if (!CheckDisplay (hwnd))
            DestroyWindow (hwnd) ;

        return 0 ;

    case WM_SIZE:
        cxClient = LOWORD (lParam) ;
        cyClient = HIWORD (lParam) ;
        return 0 ;

    case WM_PAINT:
        hdc = BeginPaint (hwnd, &ps) ;
```

(continued)

Figure 16-5. *continued*

```
        SelectObject (hdc, GetStockObject (SYSTEM_FIXED_FONT)) ;

        GetSystemPaletteEntries (hdc, 0, 256, pe) ;

        for (i = 0, x = 0, y = 0 ; i < 256 ; i++)
        {
             wsprintf (szBuffer, TEXT ("%02X-%02X-%02X"),
                        pe[i].peRed, pe[i].peGreen, pe[i].peBlue) ;

             TextOut (hdc, x, y, szBuffer, lstrlen (szBuffer)) ;

             if ((x += sizeChar.cx) + sizeChar.cx > cxClient)
             {
                 x = 0 ;

                 if ((y += sizeChar.cy) > cyClient)
                     break ;
             }
        }
        EndPaint (hwnd, &ps) ;
        return 0 ;

   case WM_PALETTECHANGED:
        InvalidateRect (hwnd, NULL, FALSE) ;
        return 0 ;

   case WM_DESTROY:
        PostQuitMessage (0) ;
        return 0 ;
   }
   return DefWindowProc (hwnd, message, wParam, lParam) ;
}
```

As with the other programs in the SYSPAL series, SYSPAL1 does not run unless *Get-DeviceCaps* with the SIZEPALETTE argument returns 256.

Notice that SYSPAL1's client area is invalidated whenever it receives a WM_PALETTECHANGED message. During the resultant WM_PAINT message, SYSPAL1 calls *GetSystemPaletteEntries* with an array of 256 PALETTEENTRY structures. The RGB values are displayed as text strings in the client area. When you run the program, note that the 20 reserved colors are the first 10 and last 10 in the list of RGB values, as indicated by Figure 16-1.

While SYSPAL1 is certainly displaying useful information, it's not quite the same as actually seeing the 256 colors. That's a job for SYSPAL2, shown in Figure 16-6.

SYSPAL2.C

```
/*------------------------------------------
   SYSPAL2.C -- Displays system palette
                (c) Charles Petzold, 1998
   ------------------------------------------*/

#include <windows.h>

LRESULT CALLBACK WndProc (HWND, UINT, WPARAM, LPARAM) ;

TCHAR szAppName [] = TEXT ("SysPal2") ;

int WINAPI WinMain (HINSTANCE hInstance, HINSTANCE hPrevInstance,
                    PSTR szCmdLine, int iCmdShow)
{
    HWND       hwnd ;
    MSG        msg ;
    WNDCLASS wndclass ;

    wndclass.style         = CS_HREDRAW | CS_VREDRAW ;
    wndclass.lpfnWndProc   = WndProc ;
    wndclass.cbClsExtra    = 0 ;
    wndclass.cbWndExtra    = 0 ;
    wndclass.hInstance     = hInstance ;
    wndclass.hIcon         = LoadIcon (NULL, IDI_APPLICATION) ;
    wndclass.hCursor       = LoadCursor (NULL, IDC_ARROW) ;
    wndclass.hbrBackground = (HBRUSH) GetStockObject (WHITE_BRUSH) ;
    wndclass.lpszMenuName  = NULL ;
    wndclass.lpszClassName = szAppName ;

    if (!RegisterClass (&wndclass))
    {
        MessageBox (NULL, TEXT ("This program requires Windows NT!"),
                    szAppName, MB_ICONERROR) ;
        return 0 ;
    }

    hwnd = CreateWindow (szAppName, TEXT ("System Palette #2"),
                         WS_OVERLAPPEDWINDOW,
                         CW_USEDEFAULT, CW_USEDEFAULT,
                         CW_USEDEFAULT, CW_USEDEFAULT,
                         NULL, NULL, hInstance, NULL) ;
```

Figure 16-6. *The SYSPAL2 program.*   *(continued)*

Figure 16-6. *continued*

```
    if (!hwnd)
         return 0 ;

    ShowWindow (hwnd, iCmdShow) ;
    UpdateWindow (hwnd) ;

    while (GetMessage (&msg, NULL, 0, 0))
    {
         TranslateMessage (&msg) ;
         DispatchMessage (&msg) ;
    }
    return msg.wParam ;
}

BOOL CheckDisplay (HWND hwnd)
{
    HDC hdc ;
    int iPalSize ;

    hdc = GetDC (hwnd) ;
    iPalSize = GetDeviceCaps (hdc, SIZEPALETTE) ;
    ReleaseDC (hwnd, hdc) ;

    if (iPalSize != 256)
    {
         MessageBox (hwnd, TEXT ("This program requires that the video ")
                           TEXT ("display mode have a 256-color palette."),
                     szAppName, MB_ICONERROR) ;
         return FALSE ;
    }
    return TRUE ;
}

LRESULT CALLBACK WndProc (HWND hwnd, UINT message, WPARAM wParam, LPARAM lParam)
{
    static HPALETTE hPalette ;
    static int      cxClient, cyClient ;
    HBRUSH          hBrush ;
    HDC             hdc ;
    int             i, x, y ;
    LOGPALETTE      * plp ;
    PAINTSTRUCT     ps ;
    RECT            rect ;
```

```
switch (message)
{
case WM_CREATE:
     if (!CheckDisplay (hwnd))
          return -1 ;

     plp = malloc (sizeof (LOGPALETTE) + 255 * sizeof (PALETTEENTRY)) ;

     plp->palVersion    = 0x0300 ;
     plp->palNumEntries = 256 ;

     for (i = 0 ; i < 256 ; i++)
     {
          plp->palPalEntry[i].peRed   = i ;
          plp->palPalEntry[i].peGreen = 0 ;
          plp->palPalEntry[i].peBlue  = 0 ;
          plp->palPalEntry[i].peFlags = PC_EXPLICIT ;
     }

     hPalette = CreatePalette (plp) ;
     free (plp) ;
     return 0 ;

case WM_DISPLAYCHANGE:
     if (!CheckDisplay (hwnd))
          DestroyWindow (hwnd) ;

     return 0 ;

case WM_SIZE:
     cxClient = LOWORD (lParam) ;
     cyClient = HIWORD (lParam) ;
     return 0 ;

case WM_PAINT:
     hdc = BeginPaint (hwnd, &ps) ;

     SelectPalette (hdc, hPalette, FALSE) ;
     RealizePalette (hdc) ;

     for (y = 0 ; y < 16 ; y++)
     for (x = 0 ; x < 16 ; x++)
```

(continued)

Figure 16-6. *continued*

```
          {
               hBrush = CreateSolidBrush (PALETTEINDEX (16 * y + x)) ;
               SetRect (&rect, x      * cxClient / 16, y      * cyClient / 16,
                            (x + 1) * cxClient / 16, (y + 1) * cyClient / 16);
               FillRect (hdc, &rect, hBrush) ;
               DeleteObject (hBrush) ;
          }
          EndPaint (hwnd, &ps) ;
          return 0 ;

     case WM_PALETTECHANGED:
          if ((HWND) wParam != hwnd)
               InvalidateRect (hwnd, NULL, FALSE) ;

          return 0 ;

     case WM_DESTROY:
          DeleteObject (hPalette) ;
          PostQuitMessage (0) ;
          return 0 ;
     }
     return DefWindowProc (hwnd, message, wParam, lParam) ;
}
```

SYSPAL2 creates a logical palette during the WM_CREATE message. But notice that all 256 values in the logical palette are palette indices ranging from 0 to 255 and that the *peFlags* field is PC_EXPLICIT. The definition of this flag is this: "Specifies that the low-order word of the logical palette entry designates a hardware palette index. This flag allows the application to show the contents of the display device palette." Thus, this flag is specifically intended for doing what we're trying to do.

During the WM_PAINT message, SYSPAL2 selects this palette into its device context and realizes it. This does not cause any reorganization of the system palette but instead allows the program to specify colors in the system palette by using the PALETTEINDEX macro. SYSPAL2 does this to display 256 rectangles. Again, when you run this program, notice that the first 10 and last 10 colors of the top row and bottom row are the 20 reserved colors shown in Figure 16-1. As you run programs that use their own logical palettes, the display changes.

If you like seeing the colors in SYSPAL2 but would like RGB values as well, run the program in conjunction with the WHATCLR program from Chapter 8.

The third version in the SYSPAL series uses a technique that occurred to me only recently—some seven years after I first started exploring the Windows Palette Manager.

Virtually all the GDI functions specify color—either directly or indirectly—as an RGB value. Somewhere deep in GDI this is converted into certain pixel bits that correspond to that color. In some video modes (for example, in 16-bit or 24-bit color mode), this conversion is rather straightforward. In other video modes (4-bit or 8-bit color), this can involve a nearest-color search.

However, there are two GDI functions that let you specify color directly in pixel bits. These two functions used in this way are, of course, highly device-dependent. They are so device-dependent that they can directly display the actual palette lookup table on the video display adapter. These two functions are *BitBlt* and *StretchBlt*.

The SYSPAL3 program in Figure 16-7 shows how to use *StretchBlt* to display the colors in the system palette.

SYSPAL3.C

```c
/*------------------------------------------
   SYSPAL3.C -- Displays system palette
              (c) Charles Petzold, 1998
   ------------------------------------------*/

#include <windows.h>

LRESULT CALLBACK WndProc (HWND, UINT, WPARAM, LPARAM) ;

TCHAR szAppName [] = TEXT ("SysPal3") ;

int WINAPI WinMain (HINSTANCE hInstance, HINSTANCE hPrevInstance,
                    PSTR szCmdLine, int iCmdShow)
{
    HWND        hwnd ;
    MSG         msg ;
    WNDCLASS    wndclass ;

    wndclass.style         = CS_HREDRAW | CS_VREDRAW ;
    wndclass.lpfnWndProc   = WndProc ;
    wndclass.cbClsExtra    = 0 ;
    wndclass.cbWndExtra    = 0 ;
    wndclass.hInstance     = hInstance ;
    wndclass.hIcon         = LoadIcon (NULL, IDI_APPLICATION) ;
    wndclass.hCursor       = LoadCursor (NULL, IDC_ARROW) ;
    wndclass.hbrBackground = (HBRUSH) GetStockObject (WHITE_BRUSH) ;
    wndclass.lpszMenuName  = NULL ;
    wndclass.lpszClassName = szAppName ;
```

Figure 16-7. *The SYSPAL3 program.*

(continued)

Figure 16-7. *continued*

```
      if (!RegisterClass (&wndclass))
      {
            MessageBox (NULL, TEXT ("This program requires Windows NT!"),
                          szAppName, MB_ICONERROR) ;
            return 0 ;
      }

      hwnd = CreateWindow (szAppName, TEXT ("System Palette #3"),
                          WS_OVERLAPPEDWINDOW,
                          CW_USEDEFAULT, CW_USEDEFAULT,
                          CW_USEDEFAULT, CW_USEDEFAULT,
                          NULL, NULL, hInstance, NULL) ;

      if (!hwnd)
            return 0 ;

      ShowWindow (hwnd, iCmdShow) ;
      UpdateWindow (hwnd) ;

      while (GetMessage (&msg, NULL, 0, 0))
      {
            TranslateMessage (&msg) ;
            DispatchMessage (&msg) ;
      }
      return msg.wParam ;
}

BOOL CheckDisplay (HWND hwnd)
{
      HDC hdc ;
      int iPalSize ;

      hdc = GetDC (hwnd) ;

      iPalSize = GetDeviceCaps (hdc, SIZEPALETTE) ;
      ReleaseDC (hwnd, hdc) ;

      if (iPalSize != 256)
      {
            MessageBox (hwnd, TEXT ("This program requires that the video ")
                          TEXT ("display mode have a 256-color palette."),
                          szAppName, MB_ICONERROR) ;
            return FALSE ;
      }
      return TRUE ;
}
```

```
LRESULT CALLBACK WndProc (HWND hwnd, UINT message, WPARAM wParam, LPARAM lParam)
{
     static HBITMAP hBitmap ;
     static int     cxClient, cyClient ;
     BYTE           bits [256] ;
     HDC            hdc, hdcMem ;
     int            i ;
     PAINTSTRUCT    ps ;

     switch (message)
     {
     case WM_CREATE:
          if (!CheckDisplay (hwnd))
               return -1 ;

          for (i = 0 ; i < 256 ; i++)
               bits [i] = i ;

          hBitmap = CreateBitmap (16, 16, 1, 8, &bits) ;
          return 0 ;

     case WM_DISPLAYCHANGE:
          if (!CheckDisplay (hwnd))
               DestroyWindow (hwnd) ;

          return 0 ;

     case WM_SIZE:
          cxClient = LOWORD (lParam) ;
          cyClient = HIWORD (lParam) ;
          return 0 ;

     case WM_PAINT:
          hdc = BeginPaint (hwnd, &ps) ;

          hdcMem = CreateCompatibleDC (hdc) ;
          SelectObject (hdcMem, hBitmap) ;

          StretchBlt (hdc,    0, 0, cxClient, cyClient,
                      hdcMem, 0, 0, 16, 16, SRCCOPY) ;

          DeleteDC (hdcMem) ;
          EndPaint (hwnd, &ps) ;
          return 0 ;
```

(continued)

Figure 16-7. *continued*

```
    case WM_DESTROY:
        DeleteObject (hBitmap) ;
        PostQuitMessage (0) ;
        return 0 ;
    }
    return DefWindowProc (hwnd, message, wParam, lParam) ;
}
```

During the WM_CREATE message, SYSPAL3 uses *CreateBitmap* to create a 16-by-16 bitmap with 8 bits per pixel. The last argument to the function is an array of 256 bytes containing the numbers 0 through 255. These are the 256 possible pixel-bit values. During the WM_PAINT message, the program selects this bitmap into a memory device context and uses *StretchBlt* to display it to fill the client area. Windows simply transfers the pixel bits in the bitmap to the hardware of the video display, thus allowing these pixel bits to access the 256 entries in the palette lookup table. The program's client area doesn't even need to be invalidated on receipt of the WM_PALETTECHANGED message—any change to the lookup table is immediately reflected in SYSPAL3's display.

PALETTE ANIMATION

If you saw the word "animation" in the title of this section and started thinking about kwazy wabbits running around your screen, your sights are probably set a little too high. Yes, you can do some animation using the Windows Palette Manager, but it is a rather specialized form of animation.

Usually, animation under Windows involves displaying a series of bitmaps in quick succession. Palette animation is quite different. You begin by drawing everything you need on the screen, and then you manipulate the palette to change the colors of these objects, perhaps rendering some of the images invisible against the screen background. In this way, you can get animation effects without redrawing anything. Palette animation is consequently very fast.

The initial creation of the palette for use in palette animation is a little different from what we've seen earlier: The *peFlags* field of the PALETTEENTRY structure must be set to PC_RESERVED for each RGB color value that will be changed during animation.

Normally, as we've seen, you set the *peFlags* flag to 0 when you create a logical palette. This allows the GDI to map identical colors from multiple logical palettes into the same system palette entry. For example, suppose two Windows programs create logical palettes containing the RGB entry 10-10-10. Windows needs only one 10-10-10 entry in the system palette table. But if one of these two programs is using palette animation, then you don't want GDI to do this. Palette animation is intended to be very fast—and it can only be fast if no redrawing occurs. When the program using palette animation changes the palette, it should not affect other programs or force GDI to reorganize the system palette table. The *peFlags* value of PC_RESERVED reserves the system palette entry for a single logical palette.

When using palette animation, you call *SelectPalette* and *RealizePalette* as normal during the WM_PAINT message. You specify color using the PALETTEINDEX macro. This macro takes an index into the logical palette table.

For animation, you probably want to change the palette in response to a WM_TIMER message. To change the RGB color values in the logical palette, you call the function *AnimatePalette* using an array of PALETTEENTRY structures. This function is fast because it needs to change entries in the system palette only and, consequently, the video board hardware palette table.

The Bouncing Ball

Figure 16-8 shows the components of the BOUNCE program, yet another program that displays a bouncing ball. For purposes of simplicity, this ball is drawn as an ellipse depending on the size of the client area. Because I have several palette animation programs in this chapter, the PALANIM.C ("palette animation") file contains some overhead common to all of them.

PALANIM.C

```
/*---------------------------------------------------
   PALANIM.C -- Palette Animation Shell Program
               (c) Charles Petzold, 1998
   ----------------------------------------------*/

#include <windows.h>

extern HPALETTE CreateRoutine  (HWND) ;
extern void     PaintRoutine   (HDC, int, int) ;
extern void     TimerRoutine   (HDC, HPALETTE) ;
extern void     DestroyRoutine (HWND, HPALETTE) ;

LRESULT CALLBACK WndProc (HWND, UINT, WPARAM, LPARAM) ;

extern TCHAR szAppName [] ;
extern TCHAR szTitle [] ;

int WINAPI WinMain (HINSTANCE hInstance, HINSTANCE hPrevInstance,
                    PSTR szCmdLine, int iCmdShow)
{
     HWND     hwnd ;
     MSG      msg ;
     WNDCLASS wndclass ;
```

Figure 16-8. *The BOUNCE program.*   *(continued)*

Figure 16-8. *continued*

```
        wndclass.style         = CS_HREDRAW | CS_VREDRAW ;
        wndclass.lpfnWndProc   = WndProc ;
        wndclass.cbClsExtra    = 0 ;
        wndclass.cbWndExtra    = 0 ;
        wndclass.hInstance     = hInstance ;
        wndclass.hIcon         = LoadIcon (NULL, IDI_APPLICATION) ;
        wndclass.hCursor       = LoadCursor (NULL, IDC_ARROW) ;
        wndclass.hbrBackground = (HBRUSH) GetStockObject (WHITE_BRUSH) ;
        wndclass.lpszMenuName  = NULL ;
        wndclass.lpszClassName = szAppName ;

        if (!RegisterClass (&wndclass))
        {
              MessageBox (NULL, TEXT ("This program requires Windows NT!"),
                          szAppName, MB_ICONERROR) ;
              return 0 ;
        }

        hwnd = CreateWindow (szAppName, szTitle,
                             WS_OVERLAPPEDWINDOW,
                             CW_USEDEFAULT, CW_USEDEFAULT,
                             CW_USEDEFAULT, CW_USEDEFAULT,
                             NULL, NULL, hInstance, NULL) ;

        if (!hwnd)
              return 0 ;

        ShowWindow (hwnd, iCmdShow) ;
        UpdateWindow (hwnd) ;

        while (GetMessage (&msg, NULL, 0, 0))
        {
              TranslateMessage (&msg) ;
              DispatchMessage (&msg) ;
        }
        return msg.wParam ;
}

BOOL CheckDisplay (HWND hwnd)
{
        HDC hdc ;
        int iPalSize ;

        hdc = GetDC (hwnd) ;
        iPalSize = GetDeviceCaps (hdc, SIZEPALETTE) ;
        ReleaseDC (hwnd, hdc) ;
```

```
     if (iPalSize != 256)
     {
          MessageBox (hwnd, TEXT ("This program requires that the video ")
                           TEXT ("display mode have a 256-color palette."),
                      szAppName, MB_ICONERROR) ;
          return FALSE ;
     }
     return TRUE ;
}

LRESULT CALLBACK WndProc (HWND hwnd, UINT message, WPARAM wParam, LPARAM lParam)
{
     static HPALETTE hPalette ;
     static int      cxClient, cyClient ;
     HDC             hdc ;
     PAINTSTRUCT     ps ;

     switch (message)
     {
     case WM_CREATE:
          if (!CheckDisplay (hwnd))
                return -1 ;

          hPalette = CreateRoutine (hwnd) ;
          return 0 ;

     case WM_DISPLAYCHANGE:
          if (!CheckDisplay (hwnd))
                DestroyWindow (hwnd) ;

          return 0 ;

     case WM_SIZE:
          cxClient = LOWORD (lParam) ;
          cyClient = HIWORD (lParam) ;
          return 0 ;

     case WM_PAINT:
          hdc = BeginPaint (hwnd, &ps) ;

          SelectPalette (hdc, hPalette, FALSE) ;
          RealizePalette (hdc) ;

          PaintRoutine (hdc, cxClient, cyClient) ;

          EndPaint (hwnd, &ps) ;
          return 0 ;
```

(continued)

Figure 16-8. *continued*

```
    case WM_TIMER:
        hdc = GetDC (hwnd) ;

        SelectPalette (hdc, hPalette, FALSE) ;

        TimerRoutine (hdc, hPalette) ;

        ReleaseDC (hwnd, hdc) ;
        return 0 ;

    case WM_QUERYNEWPALETTE:
        if (!hPalette)
            return FALSE ;

        hdc = GetDC (hwnd) ;
        SelectPalette (hdc, hPalette, FALSE) ;
        RealizePalette (hdc) ;
        InvalidateRect (hwnd, NULL, TRUE) ;

        ReleaseDC (hwnd, hdc) ;
        return TRUE ;

    case WM_PALETTECHANGED:
        if (!hPalette || (HWND) wParam == hwnd)
            break ;

        hdc = GetDC (hwnd) ;
        SelectPalette (hdc, hPalette, FALSE) ;
        RealizePalette (hdc) ;
        UpdateColors (hdc) ;

        ReleaseDC (hwnd, hdc) ;
        break ;

    case WM_DESTROY:
        DestroyRoutine (hwnd, hPalette) ;
        PostQuitMessage (0) ;
        return 0 ;
    }
    return DefWindowProc (hwnd, message, wParam, lParam) ;
}
```

BOUNCE.C

```
/*-----------------------------------------
   BOUNCE.C -- Palette Animation Demo
               (c) Charles Petzold, 1998
   -----------------------------------------*/

#include <windows.h>

#define ID_TIMER 1

TCHAR szAppName [] = TEXT ("Bounce") ;
TCHAR szTitle   [] = TEXT ("Bounce: Palette Animation Demo") ;

static LOGPALETTE * plp ;

HPALETTE CreateRoutine (HWND hwnd)
{
     HPALETTE hPalette ;
     int      i ;

     plp = malloc (sizeof (LOGPALETTE) + 33 * sizeof (PALETTEENTRY)) ;

     plp->palVersion    = 0x0300 ;
     plp->palNumEntries = 34 ;

     for (i = 0 ; i < 34 ; i++)
     {
          plp->palPalEntry[i].peRed   = 255 ;
          plp->palPalEntry[i].peGreen = (i == 0 ? 0 : 255) ;
          plp->palPalEntry[i].peBlue  = (i == 0 ? 0 : 255) ;
          plp->palPalEntry[i].peFlags = (i == 33 ? 0 : PC_RESERVED) ;
     }
     hPalette = CreatePalette (plp) ;

     SetTimer (hwnd, ID_TIMER, 50, NULL) ;
     return hPalette ;
}

void PaintRoutine (HDC hdc, int cxClient, int cyClient)
{
     HBRUSH hBrush ;
     int    i, x1, x2, y1, y2 ;
     RECT   rect ;
```

(continued)

Figure 16-8. *continued*

```
        // Draw window background using palette index 33

    SetRect (&rect, 0, 0, cxClient, cyClient) ;
    hBrush = CreateSolidBrush (PALETTEINDEX (33)) ;
    FillRect (hdc, &rect, hBrush) ;
    DeleteObject (hBrush) ;

        // Draw the 33 balls

    SelectObject (hdc, GetStockObject (NULL_PEN)) ;

    for (i = 0 ; i < 33 ; i++)
    {
        x1 =  i      * cxClient / 33 ;
        x2 = (i + 1) * cxClient / 33 ;

        if (i < 9)
        {
            y1  = i      * cyClient / 9 ;
            y2 = (i + 1) * cyClient / 9 ;
        }
        else if (i < 17)
        {
            y1 = (16 - i) * cyClient / 9 ;
            y2 = (17 - i) * cyClient / 9 ;
        }
        else if (i < 25)
        {
            y1 = (i - 16) * cyClient / 9 ;
            y2 = (i - 15) * cyClient / 9 ;
        }
        else
        {
            y1 = (32 - i) * cyClient / 9 ;
            y2 = (33 - i) * cyClient / 9 ;
        }

        hBrush = CreateSolidBrush (PALETTEINDEX (i)) ;
        SelectObject (hdc, hBrush) ;
        Ellipse (hdc, x1, y1, x2, y2) ;
        DeleteObject (SelectObject (hdc, GetStockObject (WHITE_BRUSH))) ;
    }
    return ;
}
```

```
void TimerRoutine (HDC hdc, HPALETTE hPalette)
{
    static BOOL bLeftToRight = TRUE ;
    static int  iBall ;

        // Set old ball to white

    plp->palPalEntry[iBall].peGreen = 255 ;
    plp->palPalEntry[iBall].peBlue  = 255 ;

    iBall += (bLeftToRight ? 1 : -1) ;

    if (iBall == (bLeftToRight ? 33 : -1))
    {
        iBall = (bLeftToRight ? 31 : 1) ;
        bLeftToRight ^= TRUE ;
    }

        // Set new ball to red

    plp->palPalEntry[iBall].peGreen = 0 ;
    plp->palPalEntry[iBall].peBlue  = 0 ;

        // Animate the palette

    AnimatePalette (hPalette, 0, 33, plp->palPalEntry) ;
    return ;
}

void DestroyRoutine (HWND hwnd, HPALETTE hPalette)
{
    KillTimer (hwnd, ID_TIMER) ;
    DeleteObject (hPalette) ;
    free (plp) ;
    return ;
}
```

Palette animation will not work unless Windows is in a video mode that supports palettes. So, PALANIM.C begins WM_CREATE processing by calling its *CheckDisplay* function, the same function in the SYSPAL programs.

PALANIM.C calls four functions in BOUNCE.C: *CreateRoutine* during the WM_CREATE message (during which BOUNCE is expected to create a logical palette), *PaintRoutine* during the WM_PAINT message, *TimerRoutine* during the WM_TIMER message, and *DestroyRoutine* during the WM_DESTROY message (during which BOUNCE is expected to clean up). Prior to calling both *PaintRoutine* and *TimerRoutine*, PALANIM.C obtains a device context and selects the logical palette into it. Prior to calling *PaintRoutine*, it also realizes the palette. PALANIM.C expects *TimerRoutine* to call *AnimatePalette*. Although *AnimatePalette* requires the palette to be selected in the device context, it does not require a call to *RealizePalette*.

The ball in BOUNCE bounces back and forth in a "W" pattern within the client area. The background of the client area is white. The ball is red. At any time, the ball can be seen in one of 33 nonoverlapping positions. This requires 34 palette entries, one for the background and the other 33 for the different positions of the ball. In *CreateRoutine*, BOUNCE initializes an array of PALETTEENTRY structures by setting the first palette entry (corresponding to the position of the ball in the upper left corner) to red and the others to white. Notice that the *peFlags* field is set to PC_RESERVED for all entries except the background (the last palette entry). BOUNCE concludes *CreateRoutine* by setting a Windows timer with an interval of 50 msec.

BOUNCE does all its drawing in *PaintRoutine*. The background of the window is drawn with a solid brush with a color specified by a palette index of 33. The colors of the 33 balls are drawn with colors based on palette indices ranging from 0 to 32. When BOUNCE first draws on its client area, the palette index of 0 maps to red and the other palette indices map to white. This causes the ball to appear in the upper left corner.

The animation occurs when *WndProc* processes the WM_TIMER message and calls *TimerRoutine*. *TimerRoutine* concludes by calling *AnimatePalette*, which has the following syntax:

```
AnimatePalette (hPalette, uStart, uNum, &pe) ;
```

The first argument is a handle to the palette, and the last argument is a pointer to one or more PALETTEENTRY structures arranged as an array. The function alters one or more entries in the logical palette beginning with the *uStart* entry and continuing for *uNum* entries. The new *uStart* entry in the logical palette is taken from the first element in the PALETTEENTRY structure. Watch out! The *uStart* parameter is an index into the original logical palette table, not an index into the PALETTEENTRY array.

For convenience, BOUNCE uses the array of PALETTEENTRY structures that is part of the LOGPALETTE structure used when creating the logical palette. The current position of the ball (from 0 to 32) is stored as the static *iBall* variable. During *TimerRoutine*, BOUNCE sets that PALETTEENTRY element to white. It then calculates a new position of the ball and sets that element to red. The palette is changed with the call

```
AnimatePalette (hPalette, 0, 33, plp->palPalEntry) ;
```

GDI changes the first 33 logical palette entries (although only 2 actually change), makes the corresponding changes in the system palette table, and then changes the hardware palette table on the video board. The ball appears to move without any redrawing.

You may find it instructive to run SYSPAL2 or SYSPAL3 while BOUNCE is running.

Although *AnimatePalette* works very quickly, you should probably avoid changing all the logical palette entries when only one or two actually change. This is a little complicated in BOUNCE because the ball bounces back and forth—*iBall* is first incremented and then decremented. One approach would be to have two other variables called *iBallOld* (set to the previous position of the ball) and *iBallMin* (the lesser of *iBall* and *iBallOld*). You then call *AnimatePalette* like this to change just the two entries:

```
iBallMin = min (iBall, iBallOld) ;
AnimatePalette (hPal, iBallMin, 2, plp->palPalEntry + iBallMin) ;
```

Here's another approach: Let's suppose you first define a single PALETTEENTRY structure:

```
PALETTEENTRY pe ;
```

During *TimerRoutine*, you set the PALETTEENTRY fields for white and call *AnimatePalette* to change one entry at the *iBall* position in the logical palette:

```
pe.peRed   = 255 ;
pe.peGreen = 255 ;
pe.peBlue  = 255 ;
pe.peFlags = PC_RESERVED ;
AnimatePalette (hPalette, iBall, 1, &pe) ;
```

You then calculate the new value of *iBall* as shown in BOUNCE, define the fields of the PALETTEENTRY structure for red, and call *AnimatePalette* again:

```
pe.peRed   = 255 ;
pe.peGreen = 0 ;
pe.peBlue  = 0 ;
pe.peFlags = PC_RESERVED ;
AnimatePalette (hPalette, iBall, 1, &pe) ;
```

Although a bouncing ball is a traditional simple illustration of animation, it's really not suited for palette animation because all the possible positions of the ball must be drawn initially. Palette animation is more suited for showing repetitive patterns of movement.

One-Entry Palette Animation

One of the more interesting aspects of palette animation is that you can implement some interesting techniques using only one palette entry. This is illustrated in the FADER program show in Figure 16-9 on the following page. This program also requires the PALANIM.C file shown earlier.

FADER.C

```
/*-------------------------------------
   FADER.C -- Palette Animation Demo
            (c) Charles Petzold, 1998
   -------------------------------------*/

#include <windows.h>

#define ID_TIMER 1

TCHAR szAppName [] = TEXT ("Fader") ;
TCHAR szTitle   [] = TEXT ("Fader: Palette Animation Demo") ;

static LOGPALETTE lp ;

HPALETTE CreateRoutine (HWND hwnd)
{
    HPALETTE hPalette ;

    lp.palVersion            = 0x0300 ;
    lp.palNumEntries         = 1 ;
    lp.palPalEntry[0].peRed   = 255 ;
    lp.palPalEntry[0].peGreen = 255 ;
    lp.palPalEntry[0].peBlue  = 255 ;
    lp.palPalEntry[0].peFlags = PC_RESERVED ;

    hPalette = CreatePalette (&lp) ;

    SetTimer (hwnd, ID_TIMER, 50, NULL) ;
    return hPalette ;
}

void PaintRoutine (HDC hdc, int cxClient, int cyClient)
{
    static TCHAR szText [] = TEXT (" Fade In and Out ") ;
    int       x, y ;
    SIZE      sizeText ;

    SetTextColor (hdc, PALETTEINDEX (0)) ;
    GetTextExtentPoint32 (hdc, szText, lstrlen (szText), &sizeText) ;

    for (x = 0 ; x < cxClient ; x += sizeText.cx)
    for (y = 0 ; y < cyClient ; y += sizeText.cy)
```

Figure 16-9. *The FADER program.*

```
    {
        TextOut (hdc, x, y, szText, lstrlen (szText)) ;
    }

    return ;
}

void TimerRoutine (HDC hdc, HPALETTE hPalette)
{
    static BOOL bFadeIn = TRUE ;

    if (bFadeIn)
    {
        lp.palPalEntry[0].peRed   -= 4 ;
        lp.palPalEntry[0].peGreen -= 4 ;

        if (lp.palPalEntry[0].peRed == 3)
            bFadeIn = FALSE ;
    }
    else
    {
        lp.palPalEntry[0].peRed   += 4 ;
        lp.palPalEntry[0].peGreen += 4 ;

        if (lp.palPalEntry[0].peRed == 255)
            bFadeIn = TRUE ;
    }

    AnimatePalette (hPalette, 0, 1, lp.palPalEntry) ;
    return ;
}

void DestroyRoutine (HWND hwnd, HPALETTE hPalette)
{
    KillTimer (hwnd, ID_TIMER) ;
    DeleteObject (hPalette) ;
    return ;
}
```

FADER displays the text string "Fade In And Out" all over its client area. This text is initially displayed in white and appears invisible against the white background of the window. By using palette animation, FADER gradually changes the color of the text to blue and then back to white, over and over again. The text appears as if it's fading in and out.

FADER creates a logical palette in its *CreateRoutine* function. It needs only one entry of the palette and initializes the color to white—red, green, and blue values all set to 255.

In *PaintRoutine* (which, you'll recall, is called from PALANIM after the logical palette has been selected into the device context and realized), FADER calls *SetTextColor* to set the text color to PALETTEINDEX(0). This means that the text color is set to the first entry in the palette table, which initially is white. FADER then fills up its client area with the "Fade In And Out" text string. At this time, the window background is white and the text is white and hence invisible.

In the *TimerRoutine* function, FADER animates the palette by altering the PALETTE-ENTRY structure and passing it to *AnimatePalette*. The program initially decrements the red and green values by 4 for each WM_TIMER message until they reach a value of 3. Then the values are incremented by 4 until they get back up to 255. This causes the color of the text to fade from white to blue and back to white again.

The ALLCOLOR program shown in Figure 16-10 uses a single-entry logical palette to display all the colors that the video adapter can render. It doesn't show them simultaneously, of course, but sequentially. If your video adapter has an 18-bit resolution (in which case it's capable of 262,144 different colors), at the rate of one color every 55 milliseconds you need spend only four hours staring at the screen to see all the colors!

ALLCOLOR.C

```
/*-------------------------------------------
   ALLCOLOR.C -- Palette Animation Demo
                (c) Charles Petzold, 1998
   -------------------------------------------*/

#include <windows.h>

#define ID_TIMER    1

TCHAR szAppName [] = TEXT ("AllColor") ;
TCHAR szTitle   [] = TEXT ("AllColor: Palette Animation Demo") ;

static int         iIncr ;
static PALETTEENTRY pe ;

HPALETTE CreateRoutine (HWND hwnd)
{
    HDC        hdc ;
    HPALETTE   hPalette ;
    LOGPALETTE lp ;

         // Determine the color resolution and set iIncr
```

Figure 16-10. *The ALLCOLOR program.*

```
    hdc = GetDC (hwnd) ;
    iIncr = 1 << (8 - GetDeviceCaps (hdc, COLORRES) / 3) ;
    ReleaseDC (hwnd, hdc) ;

         // Create the logical palette

    lp.palVersion            = 0x0300 ;
    lp.palNumEntries         = 1 ;
    lp.palPalEntry[0].peRed   = 0 ;
    lp.palPalEntry[0].peGreen = 0 ;
    lp.palPalEntry[0].peBlue  = 0 ;
    lp.palPalEntry[0].peFlags = PC_RESERVED ;

    hPalette = CreatePalette (&lp) ;

         // Save global for less typing

    pe = lp.palPalEntry[0] ;

    SetTimer (hwnd, ID_TIMER, 10, NULL) ;
    return hPalette ;
}

void DisplayRGB (HDC hdc, PALETTEENTRY * ppe)
{
    TCHAR szBuffer [16] ;

    wsprintf (szBuffer, TEXT (" %02X-%02X-%02X "),
           ppe->peRed, ppe->peGreen, ppe->peBlue) ;

    TextOut (hdc, 0, 0, szBuffer, lstrlen (szBuffer)) ;
}

void PaintRoutine (HDC hdc, int cxClient, int cyClient)
{
    HBRUSH   hBrush ;
    RECT     rect ;

         // Draw Palette Index 0 on entire window

    hBrush = CreateSolidBrush (PALETTEINDEX (0)) ;
    SetRect (&rect, 0, 0, cxClient, cyClient) ;
    FillRect (hdc, &rect, hBrush) ;
    DeleteObject (SelectObject (hdc, GetStockObject (WHITE_BRUSH))) ;
```

(continued)

Figure 16-10. *continued*

```
            // Display the RGB value

     DisplayRGB (hdc, &pe) ;
     return ;
}

void TimerRoutine (HDC hdc, HPALETTE hPalette)
{
     static BOOL  bRedUp = TRUE, bGreenUp = TRUE, bBlueUp = TRUE ;

          // Define new color value

     pe.peBlue += (bBlueUp ? iIncr : -iIncr) ;

     if (pe.peBlue == (BYTE) (bBlueUp ? 0 : 256 - iIncr))
     {
          pe.peBlue = (bBlueUp ? 256 - iIncr : 0) ;
          bBlueUp ^= TRUE ;
          pe.peGreen += (bGreenUp ? iIncr : -iIncr) ;

          if (pe.peGreen == (BYTE) (bGreenUp ? 0 : 256 - iIncr))
          {
               pe.peGreen = (bGreenUp ? 256 - iIncr : 0) ;
               bGreenUp ^= TRUE ;
               pe.peRed += (bRedUp ? iIncr : -iIncr) ;

               if (pe.peRed == (BYTE) (bRedUp ? 0 : 256 - iIncr))
               {
                    pe.peRed = (bRedUp ? 256 - iIncr : 0) ;
                    bRedUp ^= TRUE ;
               }
          }
     }

          // Animate the palette

     AnimatePalette (hPalette, 0, 1, &pe) ;
     DisplayRGB (hdc, &pe) ;
     return ;
}

void DestroyRoutine (HWND hwnd, HPALETTE hPalette)
{
     KillTimer (hwnd, ID_TIMER) ;
     DeleteObject (hPalette) ;
     return ;
}
```

Structurally, ALLCOLOR is very similar to FADER. In *CreateRoutine*, ALLCOLOR creates a palette with only one palette entry whose color is set to black (the red, green, and blue fields of the PALETTEENTRY structure set to 0). In *PaintRoutine*, ALLCOLOR creates a solid brush using PALETTEINDEX(0) and calls *FillRect* to color the entire client area with that brush.

In *TimerRoutine*, ALLCOLOR animates the palette by changing the PALETTEENTRY color and calling *AnimatePalette*. I wrote ALLCOLOR so that the change in color is smooth. First, the blue value is progressively incremented. When it gets to the maximum, the green value is incremented and then the blue value is progressively decremented. The incrementing and decrementing of the red, green, and blue color values is based on the *iIncr* variable. This is calculated during *CreateRoutine* based on the value returned from *GetDeviceCaps* with the COLORRES argument. If *GetDeviceCaps* returns 18, for example, then *iIncr* is set to 4—the lowest value necessary to obtain all the colors.

ALLCOLOR also displays the current RGB color value in the upper left corner of the client area. I originally added this code for testing purposes, but it proved to be useful so I left it in.

Engineering Applications

In engineering applications, animation can be useful for the display of mechanical or electrical processes. It's one thing to display a combustion engine on a computer screen, but animation can really make it come alive and show its workings with much greater clarity.

One possible process that's good for palette animation is showing fluids passing through a pipe. This is a case where the image doesn't have to be strictly accurate—in fact, if the image were accurate (as if you were looking at a transparent pipe), it might be difficult to tell how the contents of the pipe were moving. It's better to take a more symbolic approach here. The PIPES program shown in Figure 16-11 is a simple demonstration of this technique. It has two horizontal pipes in the client area. The contents of the pipes move from left to right in the top pipe and from right to left in the bottom pipe.

PIPES.C

```
/*------------------------------------------
   PIPES.C -- Palette Animation Demo
              (c) Charles Petzold, 1998
   ------------------------------------------*/

#include <windows.h>

#define ID_TIMER 1
```

Figure 16-11. *The PIPES program.*

(continued)

Figure 16-11. *continued*

```
TCHAR szAppName [] = TEXT ("Pipes") ;
TCHAR szTitle   [] = TEXT ("Pipes: Palette Animation Demo") ;

static LOGPALETTE * plp ;

HPALETTE CreateRoutine (HWND hwnd)
{
     HPALETTE hPalette ;
     int      i ;

     plp = malloc (sizeof (LOGPALETTE) + 32 * sizeof (PALETTEENTRY)) ;

          // Initialize the fields of the LOGPALETTE structure

     plp->palVersion    = 0x300 ;
     plp->palNumEntries = 16 ;

     for (i = 0 ; i <= 8 ; i++)
     {
          plp->palPalEntry[i].peRed   = (BYTE) min (255, 0x20 * i) ;
          plp->palPalEntry[i].peGreen = 0 ;
          plp->palPalEntry[i].peBlue  = (BYTE) min (255, 0x20 * i) ;
          plp->palPalEntry[i].peFlags = PC_RESERVED ;

          plp->palPalEntry[16 - i] = plp->palPalEntry[i] ;
          plp->palPalEntry[16 + i] = plp->palPalEntry[i] ;
          plp->palPalEntry[32 - i] = plp->palPalEntry[i] ;
     }

     hPalette = CreatePalette (plp) ;

     SetTimer (hwnd, ID_TIMER, 100, NULL) ;
     return hPalette ;
}

void PaintRoutine (HDC hdc, int cxClient, int cyClient)
{
     HBRUSH hBrush ;
     int    i ;
     RECT   rect ;

          // Draw window background

     SetRect (&rect, 0, 0, cxClient, cyClient) ;
     hBrush = SelectObject (hdc, GetStockObject (WHITE_BRUSH)) ;
     FillRect (hdc, &rect, hBrush) ;
```

```
        // Draw the interiors of the pipes

    for (i = 0 ; i < 128 ; i++)
    {
        hBrush = CreateSolidBrush (PALETTEINDEX (i % 16)) ;
        SelectObject (hdc, hBrush) ;

        rect.left   = (127 - i) * cxClient / 128 ;
        rect.right  = (128 - i) * cxClient / 128 ;
        rect.top    = 4 * cyClient / 14 ;
        rect.bottom = 5 * cyClient / 14 ;

        FillRect (hdc, &rect, hBrush) ;

        rect.left   = i       * cxClient / 128 ;
        rect.right  = (i + 1) * cxClient / 128 ;
        rect.top    =  9 * cyClient / 14 ;
        rect.bottom = 10 * cyClient / 14 ;

        FillRect (hdc, &rect, hBrush) ;

        DeleteObject (SelectObject (hdc, GetStockObject (WHITE_BRUSH))) ;
    }

        // Draw the edges of the pipes

    MoveToEx (hdc, 0,         4 * cyClient / 14, NULL) ;
    LineTo   (hdc, cxClient,  4 * cyClient / 14) ;

    MoveToEx (hdc, 0,         5 * cyClient / 14, NULL) ;
    LineTo   (hdc, cxClient,  5 * cyClient / 14) ;

    MoveToEx (hdc, 0,         9 * cyClient / 14, NULL) ;
    LineTo   (hdc, cxClient,  9 * cyClient / 14) ;

    MoveToEx (hdc, 0,        10 * cyClient / 14, NULL) ;
    LineTo   (hdc, cxClient, 10 * cyClient / 14) ;
    return ;
}

void TimerRoutine (HDC hdc, HPALETTE hPalette)
{
    static int iIndex ;

    AnimatePalette (hPalette, 0, 16, plp->palPalEntry + iIndex) ;
```

(continued)

Figure 16-11. *continued*

```
    iIndex = (iIndex + 1) % 16 ;

    return ;
}

void DestroyRoutine (HWND hwnd, HPALETTE hPalette)
{
    KillTimer (hwnd, ID_TIMER) ;
    DeleteObject (hPalette) ;
    free (plp) ;
    return ;
}
```

PIPES uses 16 palette entries for the animation, but you could probably get by with fewer. At the minimum, all you really need are enough entries to show the direction of the flow. Even three palette entries would be better than a static arrow.

The TUNNEL program shown in Figure 16-12 is the piggiest program of this batch, using 128 palette entries for animation. But the effect is worth it.

TUNNEL.C

```
/*-------------------------------------------
   TUNNEL.C -- Palette Animation Demo
               (c) Charles Petzold, 1998
   -------------------------------------------*/

#include <windows.h>

#define ID_TIMER 1

TCHAR szAppName [] = TEXT ("Tunnel") ;
TCHAR szTitle   [] = TEXT ("Tunnel: Palette Animation Demo") ;

static LOGPALETTE * plp ;

HPALETTE CreateRoutine (HWND hwnd)
{
    BYTE      byGrayLevel ;
    HPALETTE hPalette ;
    int       i ;

    plp = malloc (sizeof (LOGPALETTE) + 255 * sizeof (PALETTEENTRY)) ;
```

Figure 16-12. *The TUNNEL program.*

```
        // Initialize the fields of the LOGPALETTE structure

    plp->palVersion    = 0x0300 ;
    plp->palNumEntries = 128 ;

    for (i = 0 ; i < 128 ; i++)
    {
        if (i < 64)
            byGrayLevel = (BYTE) (4 * i) ;
        else
            byGrayLevel = (BYTE) min (255, 4 * (128 - i)) ;

        plp->palPalEntry[i].peRed   = byGrayLevel ;
        plp->palPalEntry[i].peGreen = byGrayLevel ;
        plp->palPalEntry[i].peBlue  = byGrayLevel ;
        plp->palPalEntry[i].peFlags = PC_RESERVED ;

        plp->palPalEntry[i + 128].peRed   = byGrayLevel ;
        plp->palPalEntry[i + 128].peGreen = byGrayLevel ;
        plp->palPalEntry[i + 128].peBlue  = byGrayLevel ;
        plp->palPalEntry[i + 128].peFlags = PC_RESERVED ;
    }

    hPalette = CreatePalette (plp) ;

    SetTimer (hwnd, ID_TIMER, 50, NULL) ;
    return hPalette ;
}

void PaintRoutine (HDC hdc, int cxClient, int cyClient)
{
    HBRUSH hBrush ;
    int    i ;
    RECT   rect ;

    for (i = 0 ; i < 127 ; i++)
    {
            // Use a RECT structure for each of 128 rectangles

        rect.left   =            i * cxClient / 255 ;
        rect.top    =            i * cyClient / 255 ;
        rect.right  = cxClient - i * cxClient / 255 ;
        rect.bottom = cyClient - i * cyClient / 255 ;

        hBrush = CreateSolidBrush (PALETTEINDEX (i)) ;
```

(continued)

Figure 16-12. *continued*

```
                // Fill the rectangle and delete the brush

          FillRect (hdc, &rect, hBrush) ;
          DeleteObject (hBrush) ;
     }
     return ;
}


void TimerRoutine (HDC hdc, HPALETTE hPalette)
{
     static int iLevel ;

     iLevel = (iLevel + 1) % 128 ;

     AnimatePalette (hPalette, 0, 128, plp->palPalEntry + iLevel) ;
     return ;
}

void DestroyRoutine (HWND hwnd, HPALETTE hPalette)
{
     KillTimer (hwnd, ID_TIMER) ;
     DeleteObject (hPalette) ;
     free (plp) ;
     return ;
}
```

TUNNEL uses 64 moving gray shades in the 128 palette entries—from black to white and back to black—to give the effect of traveling through a tunnel.

PALETTES AND REAL-WORLD IMAGES

Of course, despite the fun we've been having displaying continuous shades of color and doing palette animation, the real purpose of the Palette Manager is to allow the display of real-world images under 8-bit video modes. For the remainder of the chapter, we'll be exploring precisely that. As you might have already anticipated, you must use palettes differently when using packed DIBs, GDI bitmap objects, and DIB sections. The next six programs illustrate various techniques for using palettes with bitmaps.

Palettes and Packed DIBs

Assisting us in the next three programs will be a set of functions that work with packed-DIB memory blocks. These functions are in the PACKEDIB files shown in Figure 16-13.

PACKEDIB.H

```
/*-------------------------------------------
   PACKEDIB.H -- Header file for PACKEDIB.C
               (c) Charles Petzold, 1998
   -------------------------------------------*/

#include <windows.h>

BITMAPINFO * PackedDibLoad (PTSTR szFileName) ;
int PackedDibGetWidth (BITMAPINFO * pPackedDib) ;
int PackedDibGetHeight (BITMAPINFO * pPackedDib) ;
int PackedDibGetBitCount (BITMAPINFO * pPackedDib) ;
int PackedDibGetRowLength (BITMAPINFO * pPackedDib) ;
int PackedDibGetInfoHeaderSize (BITMAPINFO * pPackedDib) ;
int PackedDibGetColorsUsed (BITMAPINFO * pPackedDib) ;
int PackedDibGetNumColors (BITMAPINFO * pPackedDib) ;
int PackedDibGetColorTableSize (BITMAPINFO * pPackedDib) ;
RGBQUAD * PackedDibGetColorTablePtr (BITMAPINFO * pPackedDib) ;
RGBQUAD * PackedDibGetColorTableEntry (BITMAPINFO * pPackedDib, int i) ;
BYTE * PackedDibGetBitsPtr (BITMAPINFO * pPackedDib) ;
int PackedDibGetBitsSize (BITMAPINFO * pPackedDib) ;
HPALETTE PackedDibCreatePalette (BITMAPINFO * pPackedDib) ;
```

PACKEDIB.C

```
/*-------------------------------------------------
   PACKEDIB.C -- Routines for using packed DIBs
               (c) Charles Petzold, 1998
   -------------------------------------------------*/

#include <windows.h>

/*-------------------------------------------------------------
   PackedDibLoad: Load DIB File as Packed-Dib Memory Block
   -------------------------------------------------------------*/

BITMAPINFO * PackedDibLoad (PTSTR szFileName)
{
    BITMAPFILEHEADER bmfh ;
    BITMAPINFO      * pbmi ;
    BOOL             bSuccess ;
    DWORD            dwPackedDibSize, dwBytesRead ;
    HANDLE           hFile ;
```

Figure 16-13. *The PACKEDIB files.*

(continued)

Figure 16-13. *continued*

```
            // Open the file: read access, prohibit write access

    hFile = CreateFile (szFileName, GENERIC_READ, FILE_SHARE_READ, NULL,
                        OPEN_EXISTING, FILE_FLAG_SEQUENTIAL_SCAN, NULL) ;

    if (hFile == INVALID_HANDLE_VALUE)
        return NULL ;

            // Read in the BITMAPFILEHEADER

    bSuccess = ReadFile (hFile, &bmfh, sizeof (BITMAPFILEHEADER),
                         &dwBytesRead, NULL) ;

    if (!bSuccess || (dwBytesRead != sizeof (BITMAPFILEHEADER))
                 || (bmfh.bfType != * (WORD *) "BM"))
    {
        CloseHandle (hFile) ;
        return NULL ;
    }

            // Allocate memory for the packed DIB & read it in

    dwPackedDibSize = bmfh.bfSize - sizeof (BITMAPFILEHEADER) ;

    pbmi = malloc (dwPackedDibSize) ;

    bSuccess = ReadFile (hFile, pbmi, dwPackedDibSize, &dwBytesRead, NULL) ;
    CloseHandle (hFile) ;

    if (!bSuccess || (dwBytesRead != dwPackedDibSize))
    {
        free (pbmi) ;
        return NULL ;
    }

    return pbmi ;
}

/*-------------------------------------------------
  Functions to get information from packed DIB
  -------------------------------------------------*/
```

```
int PackedDibGetWidth (BITMAPINFO * pPackedDib)
{
     if (pPackedDib->bmiHeader.biSize == sizeof (BITMAPCOREHEADER))
          return ((PBITMAPCOREINFO)pPackedDib)->bmciHeader.bcWidth ;
     else
          return pPackedDib->bmiHeader.biWidth ;
}

int PackedDibGetHeight (BITMAPINFO * pPackedDib)
{
     if (pPackedDib->bmiHeader.biSize == sizeof (BITMAPCOREHEADER))
          return ((PBITMAPCOREINFO)pPackedDib)->bmciHeader.bcHeight ;
     else
          return abs (pPackedDib->bmiHeader.biHeight) ;
}

int PackedDibGetBitCount (BITMAPINFO * pPackedDib)
{
     if (pPackedDib->bmiHeader.biSize == sizeof (BITMAPCOREHEADER))
          return ((PBITMAPCOREINFO)pPackedDib)->bmciHeader.bcBitCount ;
     else
          return pPackedDib->bmiHeader.biBitCount ;
}

int PackedDibGetRowLength (BITMAPINFO * pPackedDib)
{
     return ((PackedDibGetWidth (pPackedDib) *
              PackedDibGetBitCount (pPackedDib) + 31) & ~31) >> 3 ;
}

/*--------------------------------------------------------------
   PackedDibGetInfoHeaderSize includes possible color masks!
   -------------------------------------------------------------*/

int PackedDibGetInfoHeaderSize (BITMAPINFO * pPackedDib)
{
     if (pPackedDib->bmiHeader.biSize == sizeof (BITMAPCOREHEADER))
          return ((PBITMAPCOREINFO)pPackedDib)->bmciHeader.bcSize ;

     else if (pPackedDib->bmiHeader.biSize == sizeof (BITMAPINFOHEADER))
          return pPackedDib->bmiHeader.biSize +
                  (pPackedDib->bmiHeader.biCompression ==
                                    BI_BITFIELDS ? 12 : 0) ;
```

(continued)

Figure 16-13. *continued*

```
      else return pPackedDib->bmiHeader.biSize ;
}

/*-----------------------------------------------------------------
   PackedDibGetColorsUsed returns value in information header;
        could be 0 to indicate non-truncated color table!
   --------------------------------------------------------------*/

int PackedDibGetColorsUsed (BITMAPINFO * pPackedDib)
{
    if (pPackedDib->bmiHeader.biSize == sizeof (BITMAPCOREHEADER))
        return 0 ;
    else
        return pPackedDib->bmiHeader.biClrUsed ;
}

/*-----------------------------------------------------------------
   PackedDibGetNumColors is actual number of entries in color table
   --------------------------------------------------------------*/

int PackedDibGetNumColors (BITMAPINFO * pPackedDib)
{
    int iNumColors ;

    iNumColors = PackedDibGetColorsUsed (pPackedDib) ;

    if (iNumColors == 0 && PackedDibGetBitCount (pPackedDib) < 16)
        iNumColors = 1 << PackedDibGetBitCount (pPackedDib) ;

    return iNumColors ;
}

int PackedDibGetColorTableSize (BITMAPINFO * pPackedDib)
{
    if (pPackedDib->bmiHeader.biSize == sizeof (BITMAPCOREHEADER))
        return PackedDibGetNumColors (pPackedDib) * sizeof (RGBTRIPLE) ;
    else
        return PackedDibGetNumColors (pPackedDib) * sizeof (RGBQUAD) ;
}

RGBQUAD * PackedDibGetColorTablePtr (BITMAPINFO * pPackedDib)
{
    if (PackedDibGetNumColors (pPackedDib) == 0)
        return 0 ;
```

```
        return (RGBQUAD *) (((BYTE *) pPackedDib) +
                                PackedDibGetInfoHeaderSize (pPackedDib)) ;
}

RGBQUAD * PackedDibGetColorTableEntry (BITMAPINFO * pPackedDib, int i)
{
     if (PackedDibGetNumColors (pPackedDib) == 0)
          return 0 ;

     if (pPackedDib->bmiHeader.biSize == sizeof (BITMAPCOREHEADER))
          return (RGBQUAD *)
               (((RGBTRIPLE *) PackedDibGetColorTablePtr (pPackedDib)) + i) ;
     else
          return PackedDibGetColorTablePtr (pPackedDib) + i ;
}


/*-----------------------------
   PackedDibGetBitsPtr finally!
  -----------------------------*/

BYTE * PackedDibGetBitsPtr (BITMAPINFO * pPackedDib)
{
     return ((BYTE *) pPackedDib) + PackedDibGetInfoHeaderSize (pPackedDib) +
                                PackedDibGetColorTableSize (pPackedDib) ;
}

/*-------------------------------------------------------------------------
   PackedDibGetBitsSize can be calculated from the height and row length
        if it's not explicitly in the biSizeImage field
   -------------------------------------------------------------------------*/

int PackedDibGetBitsSize (BITMAPINFO * pPackedDib)
{
     if ((pPackedDib->bmiHeader.biSize != sizeof (BITMAPCOREHEADER)) &&
         (pPackedDib->bmiHeader.biSizeImage != 0))
          return pPackedDib->bmiHeader.biSizeImage ;

     return PackedDibGetHeight (pPackedDib) *
          PackedDibGetRowLength (pPackedDib) ;
}

/*------------------------------------------------------------------
   PackedDibCreatePalette creates logical palette from PackedDib
   ------------------------------------------------------------------*/
```

(continued)

Figure 16-13. *continued*

```
HPALETTE PackedDibCreatePalette (BITMAPINFO * pPackedDib)
{
    HPALETTE      hPalette ;
    int           i, iNumColors ;
    LOGPALETTE * plp ;
    RGBQUAD      * prgb ;

    if (0 == (iNumColors = PackedDibGetNumColors (pPackedDib)))
        return NULL ;

    plp = malloc (sizeof (LOGPALETTE) *
                     (iNumColors - 1) * sizeof (PALETTEENTRY)) ;

    plp->palVersion    = 0x0300 ;
    plp->palNumEntries = iNumColors ;

    for (i = 0 ; i < iNumColors ; i++)
    {
        prgb = PackedDibGetColorTableEntry (pPackedDib, i) ;

        plp->palPalEntry[i].peRed   = prgb->rgbRed ;
        plp->palPalEntry[i].peGreen = prgb->rgbGreen ;
        plp->palPalEntry[i].peBlue  = prgb->rgbBlue ;
        plp->palPalEntry[i].peFlags = 0 ;
    }

    hPalette = CreatePalette (plp) ;
    free (plp) ;

    return hPalette ;
}
```

The first function is *PackedDibLoad*, which takes as its single argument a file name and returns a pointer to a packed DIB in memory. All the other functions take this packed-DIB pointer as their first argument and return information about the DIB. These functions are arranged in the file in a "bottom-up" order. Each function uses information obtained from earlier functions.

I don't pretend that this is a "complete" set of functions that might be useful for working with packed DIBs. I have not attempted to assemble a really extensive collection because I don't think that working with packed DIBs in this way is a good approach. This will be quite obvious to you when you try to write a function such as

```
dwPixel = PackedDibGetPixel (pPackedDib, x, y) ;
```

This kind of function involves so many nested function calls that it becomes horribly inefficient and slow. I'll describe what I believe to be a better approach later in this chapter.

Also, as you'll note, many of these functions require different processing for OS/2-compatible DIBs; thus, the functions frequently check if the first field of the BITMAPINFO structure is the size of the BITMAPCOREHEADER structure.

Of particular interest here is the final function, named *PackedDibCreatePalette*. This function uses the color table in the DIB to create a palette. If the DIB does not have a color table (which means that the DIB has 16, 24, or 32 bits per pixel), then no palette is created. A palette created from the DIB color table is sometimes called the DIB's *native* palette.

The PACKEDIB files are put to use in SHOWDIB3, shown in Figure 16-14.

SHOWDIB3.C

```
/*----------------------------------------------------
   SHOWDIB3.C -- Displays DIB with native palette
                 (c) Charles Petzold, 1998
  ------------------------------------------------*/

#include <windows.h>
#include "PackeDib.h"
#include "resource.h"

LRESULT CALLBACK WndProc (HWND, UINT, WPARAM, LPARAM) ;

TCHAR szAppName[] = TEXT ("ShowDib3") ;

int WINAPI WinMain (HINSTANCE hInstance, HINSTANCE hPrevInstance,
                    PSTR szCmdLine, int iCmdShow)
{
     HWND     hwnd ;
     MSG      msg ;
     WNDCLASS wndclass ;

     wndclass.style         = CS_HREDRAW | CS_VREDRAW ;
     wndclass.lpfnWndProc   = WndProc ;
     wndclass.cbClsExtra    = 0 ;
     wndclass.cbWndExtra    = 0 ;
     wndclass.hInstance     = hInstance ;
     wndclass.hIcon         = LoadIcon (NULL, IDI_APPLICATION) ;
     wndclass.hCursor       = LoadCursor (NULL, IDC_ARROW) ;
     wndclass.hbrBackground = (HBRUSH) GetStockObject (WHITE_BRUSH) ;
     wndclass.lpszMenuName  = szAppName ;
     wndclass.lpszClassName = szAppName ;
```

Figure 16-14. *The SHOWDIB3 program.*

(continued)

Figure 16-14. *continued*

```
    if (!RegisterClass (&wndclass))
    {
         MessageBox (NULL, TEXT ("This program requires Windows NT!"),
                     szAppName, MB_ICONERROR) ;
         return 0 ;
    }

    hwnd = CreateWindow (szAppName, TEXT ("Show DIB #3: Native Palette"),
                         WS_OVERLAPPEDWINDOW,
                         CW_USEDEFAULT, CW_USEDEFAULT,
                         CW_USEDEFAULT, CW_USEDEFAULT,
                         NULL, NULL, hInstance, NULL) ;

    ShowWindow (hwnd, iCmdShow) ;
    UpdateWindow (hwnd) ;

    while (GetMessage (&msg, NULL, 0, 0))
    {
         TranslateMessage (&msg) ;
         DispatchMessage (&msg) ;
    }
    return msg.wParam ;
}

LRESULT CALLBACK WndProc (HWND hwnd, UINT message, WPARAM wParam, LPARAM lParam)
{
    static BITMAPINFO * pPackedDib ;
    static HPALETTE     hPalette ;
    static int          cxClient, cyClient ;
    static OPENFILENAME ofn ;
    static TCHAR        szFileName [MAX_PATH], szTitleName [MAX_PATH] ;
    static TCHAR        szFilter[] = TEXT ("Bitmap Files (*.BMP)\0*.bmp\0")
                                     TEXT ("All Files (*.*)\0*.*\0\0") ;
    HDC                 hdc ;
    PAINTSTRUCT         ps ;

    switch (message)
    {
    case WM_CREATE:
         ofn.lStructSize       = sizeof (OPENFILENAME) ;
         ofn.hwndOwner         = hwnd ;
         ofn.hInstance         = NULL ;
         ofn.lpstrFilter       = szFilter ;
         ofn.lpstrCustomFilter = NULL ;
         ofn.nMaxCustFilter    = 0 ;
         ofn.nFilterIndex      = 0 ;
```

```
        ofn.lpstrFile          = szFileName ;
        ofn.nMaxFile           = MAX_PATH ;
        ofn.lpstrFileTitle     = szTitleName ;
        ofn.nMaxFileTitle      = MAX_PATH ;
        ofn.lpstrInitialDir    = NULL ;
        ofn.lpstrTitle         = NULL ;
        ofn.Flags              = 0 ;
        ofn.nFileOffset        = 0 ;
        ofn.nFileExtension     = 0 ;
        ofn.lpstrDefExt        = TEXT ("bmp") ;
        ofn.lCustData          = 0 ;
        ofn.lpfnHook           = NULL ;
        ofn.lpTemplateName     = NULL ;

        return 0 ;

case WM_SIZE:
        cxClient = LOWORD (lParam) ;
        cyClient = HIWORD (lParam) ;
        return 0 ;

case WM_COMMAND:
        switch (LOWORD (wParam))
        {
        case IDM_FILE_OPEN:

                    // Show the File Open dialog box

                if (!GetOpenFileName (&ofn))
                    return 0 ;

                    // If there's an existing packed DIB, free the memory

                if (pPackedDib)
                {
                    free (pPackedDib) ;
                    pPackedDib = NULL ;
                }

                    // If there's an existing logical palette, delete it

                if (hPalette)
                {
                    DeleteObject (hPalette) ;
                    hPalette = NULL ;
                }
```

(continued)

879

Figure 16-14. *continued*

```
                        // Load the packed DIB into memory

            SetCursor (LoadCursor (NULL, IDC_WAIT)) ;
            ShowCursor (TRUE) ;

            pPackedDib = PackedDibLoad (szFileName) ;

            ShowCursor (FALSE) ;
            SetCursor (LoadCursor (NULL, IDC_ARROW)) ;

            if (pPackedDib)
            {
                    // Create the palette from the DIB color table

                hPalette = PackedDibCreatePalette (pPackedDib) ;
            }
            else
            {
                MessageBox (hwnd, TEXT ("Cannot load DIB file"),
                            szAppName, 0) ;
            }
            InvalidateRect (hwnd, NULL, TRUE) ;
            return 0 ;
        }
        break ;

   case WM_PAINT:
        hdc = BeginPaint (hwnd, &ps) ;

        if (hPalette)
        {
            SelectPalette (hdc, hPalette, FALSE) ;
            RealizePalette (hdc) ;
        }

        if (pPackedDib)
            SetDIBitsToDevice (hdc,
                                0,
                                0,
                                PackedDibGetWidth (pPackedDib),
                                PackedDibGetHeight (pPackedDib),
                                0,
                                0,
                                0,
```

```
                              PackedDibGetHeight (pPackedDib),
                              PackedDibGetBitsPtr (pPackedDib),
                              pPackedDib,
                              DIB_RGB_COLORS) ;

     EndPaint (hwnd, &ps) ;
     return 0 ;

case WM_QUERYNEWPALETTE:
     if (!hPalette)
          return FALSE ;

     hdc = GetDC (hwnd) ;
     SelectPalette (hdc, hPalette, FALSE) ;
     RealizePalette (hdc) ;
     InvalidateRect (hwnd, NULL, TRUE) ;

     ReleaseDC (hwnd, hdc) ;
     return TRUE ;

case WM_PALETTECHANGED:
     if (!hPalette || (HWND) wParam == hwnd)
          break ;

     hdc = GetDC (hwnd) ;
     SelectPalette (hdc, hPalette, FALSE) ;
     RealizePalette (hdc) ;
     UpdateColors (hdc) ;

     ReleaseDC (hwnd, hdc) ;
     break ;


case WM_DESTROY:
     if (pPackedDib)
          free (pPackedDib) ;

     if (hPalette)
          DeleteObject (hPalette) ;

     PostQuitMessage (0) ;
     return 0 ;
}
return DefWindowProc (hwnd, message, wParam, lParam) ;
}
```

(continued)

Figure 16-14. *continued*

SHOWDIB3.RC (excerpts)

```
//Microsoft Developer Studio generated resource script.

#include "resource.h"
#include "afxres.h"


/////////////////////////////////////////////////////////////////////////////
// Menu

SHOWDIB3 MENU DISCARDABLE
BEGIN
    POPUP "&File"
    BEGIN
        MENUITEM "&Open",                       IDM_FILE_OPEN
    END
END
```

RESOURCE.H (excerpts)

```
// Microsoft Developer Studio generated include file.
// Used by ShowDib3.rc

#define IDM_FILE_OPEN                   40001
```

The window procedure in SHOWDIB3 maintains the packed-DIB pointer as a static variable that it obtains when it calls the *PackedDibLoad* function in PACKEDIB.C during the File Open command. During processing of this command, SHOWDIB3 also calls *Packed-DibCreatePalette* to obtain a possible palette for the DIB. Notice that whenever SHOWDIB3 is ready to load in a new DIB, it first frees the memory of the previous DIB and also deletes the palette of the previous DIB. The last DIB is eventually freed and the last palette is eventually deleted during processing of the WM_DESTROY message.

Processing of the WM_PAINT message is straightforward: If the palette exists, SHOWDIB3 selects it into the device context and realizes it. It then calls *SetDIBitsToDevice*, passing to the function information about the DIB (such as width, height, a pointer to the DIB pixel bits) that it obtains from functions in PACKEDIB.

Again, keep in mind that SHOWDIB3 creates a palette based on the color table in the DIB. If there is no color table in the DIB—as is almost always the case with 16-bit, 24-bit, and 32-bit DIBs—then no palette is created. When the DIB is displayed in an 8-bit video mode, it's displayed with only the standard reserved 20 colors.

There are two solutions to this problem. The first is to simply use an "all-purpose" palette that can be applicable for a large number of images. You can construct such a palette yourself. The second solution is to dig into the pixel bits of the DIB and determine the optimum colors required to display the image. Obviously this involves more work (both for the programmer and the processor), but I'll show you how to do it before this chapter has concluded.

The All-Purpose Palette

The SHOWDIB4 program, shown in Figure 16-15, constructs an all-purpose palette that it uses for displaying all DIBs loaded into the program. SHOWDIB4 is otherwise very similar to SHOWDIB3.

SHOWDIB4.C

```
/*-----------------------------------------------------------
   SHOWDIB4.C -- Displays DIB with "all-purpose" palette
                 (c) Charles Petzold, 1998
   -----------------------------------------------------------*/

#include <windows.h>
#include "..\\ShowDib3\\PackeDib.h"
#include "resource.h"

LRESULT CALLBACK WndProc (HWND, UINT, WPARAM, LPARAM) ;

TCHAR szAppName[] = TEXT ("ShowDib4") ;

int WINAPI WinMain (HINSTANCE hInstance, HINSTANCE hPrevInstance,
                    PSTR szCmdLine, int iCmdShow)
{
     HWND        hwnd ;
     MSG         msg ;
     WNDCLASS    wndclass ;

     wndclass.style         = CS_HREDRAW | CS_VREDRAW ;
     wndclass.lpfnWndProc   = WndProc ;
     wndclass.cbClsExtra    = 0 ;
     wndclass.cbWndExtra    = 0 ;
     wndclass.hInstance     = hInstance ;
     wndclass.hIcon         = LoadIcon (NULL, IDI_APPLICATION) ;
     wndclass.hCursor       = LoadCursor (NULL, IDC_ARROW) ;
     wndclass.hbrBackground = (HBRUSH) GetStockObject (WHITE_BRUSH) ;
     wndclass.lpszMenuName  = szAppName ;
     wndclass.lpszClassName = szAppName ;
```

Figure 16-15. *The SHOWDIB4 program.*   *(continued)*

Figure 16-15. *continued*

```
    if (!RegisterClass (&wndclass))
    {
         MessageBox (NULL, TEXT ("This program requires Windows NT!"),
                    szAppName, MB_ICONERROR) ;
         return 0 ;
    }

    hwnd = CreateWindow (szAppName, TEXT ("Show DIB #4: All-Purpose Palette"),
                    WS_OVERLAPPEDWINDOW,
                    CW_USEDEFAULT, CW_USEDEFAULT,
                    CW_USEDEFAULT, CW_USEDEFAULT,
                    NULL, NULL, hInstance, NULL) ;

    ShowWindow (hwnd, iCmdShow) ;
    UpdateWindow (hwnd) ;

    while (GetMessage (&msg, NULL, 0, 0))
    {
         TranslateMessage (&msg) ;
         DispatchMessage (&msg) ;
    }
    return msg.wParam ;
}

/*------------------------------------------------------------------------
   CreateAllPurposePalette: Creates a palette suitable for a wide variety
         of images; the palette has 247 entries, but 15 of them are
         duplicates or match the standard 20 colors.
   ----------------------------------------------------------------------*/

HPALETTE CreateAllPurposePalette (void)
{
    HPALETTE hPalette ;
    int         i, incr, R, G, B ;
    LOGPALETTE * plp ;

    plp = malloc (sizeof (LOGPALETTE) + 246 * sizeof (PALETTEENTRY)) ;

    plp->palVersion    = 0x0300 ;
    plp->palNumEntries = 247 ;

         // The following loop calculates 31 gray shades, but 3 of them
         //          will match the standard 20 colors
```

```
      for (i = 0, G = 0, incr = 8 ; G <= 0xFF ; i++, G += incr)
      {
            plp->palPalEntry[i].peRed   = (BYTE) G ;
            plp->palPalEntry[i].peGreen = (BYTE) G ;
            plp->palPalEntry[i].peBlue  = (BYTE) G ;
            plp->palPalEntry[i].peFlags = 0 ;

            incr = (incr == 9 ? 8 : 9) ;
      }

            // The following loop is responsible for 216 entries, but 8 of
            //         them will match the standard 20 colors, and another
            //         4 of them will match the gray shades above.

      for (R = 0 ; R <= 0xFF ; R += 0x33)
      for (G = 0 ; G <= 0xFF ; G += 0x33)
      for (B = 0 ; B <= 0xFF ; B += 0x33)
      {
            plp->palPalEntry[i].peRed   = (BYTE) R ;
            plp->palPalEntry[i].peGreen = (BYTE) G ;
            plp->palPalEntry[i].peBlue  = (BYTE) B ;
            plp->palPalEntry[i].peFlags = 0 ;

            i++ ;
      }
      hPalette = CreatePalette (plp) ;

      free (plp) ;
      return hPalette ;
}

LRESULT CALLBACK WndProc (HWND hwnd, UINT message, WPARAM wParam, LPARAM lParam)
{
      static BITMAPINFO * pPackedDib ;
      static HPALETTE     hPalette ;
      static int          cxClient, cyClient ;
      static OPENFILENAME ofn ;
      static TCHAR        szFileName [MAX_PATH], szTitleName [MAX_PATH] ;
      static TCHAR        szFilter[] = TEXT ("Bitmap Files (*.BMP)\0*.bmp\0")
                                       TEXT ("All Files (*.*)\0*.*\0\0") ;

      HDC                 hdc ;
      PAINTSTRUCT         ps ;
```

(continued)

Figure 16-15. *continued*

```
switch (message)
{
case WM_CREATE:
     ofn.lStructSize       = sizeof (OPENFILENAME) ;
     ofn.hwndOwner         = hwnd ;
     ofn.hInstance         = NULL ;
     ofn.lpstrFilter       = szFilter ;
     ofn.lpstrCustomFilter = NULL ;
     ofn.nMaxCustFilter    = 0 ;
     ofn.nFilterIndex      = 0 ;
     ofn.lpstrFile         = szFileName ;
     ofn.nMaxFile          = MAX_PATH ;
     ofn.lpstrFileTitle    = szTitleName ;
     ofn.nMaxFileTitle     = MAX_PATH ;
     ofn.lpstrInitialDir   = NULL ;
     ofn.lpstrTitle        = NULL ;
     ofn.Flags             = 0 ;
     ofn.nFileOffset       = 0 ;
     ofn.nFileExtension    = 0 ;
     ofn.lpstrDefExt       = TEXT ("bmp") ;
     ofn.lCustData         = 0 ;
     ofn.lpfnHook          = NULL ;
     ofn.lpTemplateName    = NULL ;

          // Create the All-Purpose Palette

     hPalette = CreateAllPurposePalette () ;
     return 0 ;

case WM_SIZE:
     cxClient = LOWORD (lParam) ;
     cyClient = HIWORD (lParam) ;
     return 0 ;

case WM_COMMAND:
     switch (LOWORD (wParam))
     {
     case IDM_FILE_OPEN:

               // Show the File Open dialog box

          if (!GetOpenFileName (&ofn))
               return 0 ;

               // If there's an existing packed DIB, free the memory
```

```
            if (pPackedDib)
            {
                 free (pPackedDib) ;
                 pPackedDib = NULL ;
            }

                 // Load the packed DIB into memory

            SetCursor (LoadCursor (NULL, IDC_WAIT)) ;
            ShowCursor (TRUE) ;

            pPackedDib = PackedDibLoad (szFileName) ;

            ShowCursor (FALSE) ;
            SetCursor (LoadCursor (NULL, IDC_ARROW)) ;

            if (!pPackedDib)
            {
                 MessageBox (hwnd, TEXT ("Cannot load DIB file"),
                            szAppName, 0) ;
            }
            InvalidateRect (hwnd, NULL, TRUE) ;
            return 0 ;
        }
        break ;

   case WM_PAINT:
        hdc = BeginPaint (hwnd, &ps) ;

        if (pPackedDib)
        {
            SelectPalette (hdc, hPalette, FALSE) ;
            RealizePalette (hdc) ;

            SetDIBitsToDevice (hdc,
                                0,
                                0,
                                PackedDibGetWidth (pPackedDib),
                                PackedDibGetHeight (pPackedDib),
                                0,
                                0,
                                0,
                                PackedDibGetHeight (pPackedDib),
                                PackedDibGetBitsPtr (pPackedDib),
                                pPackedDib,
                                DIB_RGB_COLORS) ;
```

(continued)

Figure 16-15. *continued*

```
            }
        EndPaint (hwnd, &ps) ;
        return 0 ;

    case WM_QUERYNEWPALETTE:
        hdc = GetDC (hwnd) ;
        SelectPalette (hdc, hPalette, FALSE) ;
        RealizePalette (hdc) ;
        InvalidateRect (hwnd, NULL, TRUE) ;

        ReleaseDC (hwnd, hdc) ;
        return TRUE ;

    case WM_PALETTECHANGED:
        if ((HWND) wParam != hwnd)

        hdc = GetDC (hwnd) ;
        SelectPalette (hdc, hPalette, FALSE) ;
        RealizePalette (hdc) ;
        UpdateColors (hdc) ;

        ReleaseDC (hwnd, hdc) ;
        break ;

    case WM_DESTROY:
        if (pPackedDib)
            free (pPackedDib) ;

        DeleteObject (hPalette) ;

        PostQuitMessage (0) ;
        return 0 ;
    }
    return DefWindowProc (hwnd, message, wParam, lParam) ;
}
```

SHOWDIB4.RC (excerpts)

```
//Microsoft Developer Studio generated resource script.

#include "resource.h"
#include "afxres.h"
```

```
///////////////////////////////////////////////////////////////////////////////
// Menu

SHOWDIB4 MENU DISCARDABLE
BEGIN
    POPUP "&Open"
    BEGIN
        MENUITEM "&File",                       IDM_FILE_OPEN
    END
END
```

RESOURCE.H (excerpts)

```
// Microsoft Developer Studio generated include file.
// Used by ShowDib4.rc

#define IDM_FILE_OPEN                   40001
```

While processing the WM_CREATE message, SHOWDIB4 calls *CreateAllPurpose-Palette*. It retains this palette throughout the course of the program and destroys it during the WM_DESTROY message. Because the program knows that the palette is always around, it needn't check for its existence while processing the WM_PAINT, WM_QUERYNEW-PALETTE, or WM_PALETTECHANGED messages.

The *CreateAllPurposePalette* function seems to create a logical palette with 247 entries, which is more than the 236 entries in the system palette that programs normally have access to. Indeed, it does, but this is just a matter of convenience. Fifteen of these entries are either duplicated or will map to colors in the standard 20 reserved colors.

CreateAllPurposePalette begins by creating 31 gray shades, with red, green, and blue values of 0x00, 0x09, 0x11, 0x1A, 0x22, 0x2B, 0x33, 0x3C, 0x44, 0x4D, 0x55, 0x5E, 0x66, 0x6F, 0x77, 0x80, 0x88, 0x91, 0x99, 0xA2, 0xAA, 0xB3, 0xBB, 0xC4, 0xCC, 0xD5, 0xDD, 0xE6, 0xEE, 0xF9, and 0xFF. Notice that the first, last, and middle entries are in the standard 20 reserved colors. Next the function creates colors with all combinations of red, green, and blue values of 0x00, 0x33, 0x66, 0x99, 0xCC, and 0xFF. That's a total of 216 colors, but eight of them duplicate colors in the standard 20, and another four duplicate previously calculated gray shades. Windows will not put duplicate entries in the system palette if you set the *peFlags* field of the PALETTEENTRY structure to 0.

Obviously, a real program that didn't wish to calculate optimum palettes for 16-bit, 24-bit, or 32-bit DIBs would probably still continue to use the DIB color table for displaying 8-bit DIBs. SHOWDIB4 does not do this but instead uses its all-purpose palette for everything. This is because SHOWDIB4 is a demonstration program, and you can use it to compare SHOWDIB3's display of 8-bit DIBs. If you look at some color DIBs of people, you'll probably conclude that SHOWDIB4 does *not* have sufficient colors for the accurate rendering of flesh tones.

If you experiment with the *CreateAllPurposePalette* function in SHOWDIB4, perhaps by reducing the size of the logical palette to just a few entries, you'll discover that when a palette is selected into a device context, Windows will use only the colors in the palette and none of the colors from the standard 20-color palette.

The Halftone Palette

The Windows API includes an all-purpose palette that programs can obtain by calling *CreateHalftonePalette*. You can use this in the same way you used the palette obtained from *CreateAllPurposePalette* in SHOWDIB4, or you can use it in conjunction with the bitmap stretching mode—set with *SetStretchBltMode*—known as HALFTONE. The SHOWDIB5 program in Figure 16-16 demonstrates how to use the halftone palette.

SHOWDIB5.C

```
/*-----------------------------------------------------
   SHOWDIB5.C -- Displays DIB with halftone palette
                 (c) Charles Petzold, 1998
  -----------------------------------------------------*/

#include <windows.h>
#include "..\\ShowDib3\\PackeDib.h"
#include "resource.h"

LRESULT CALLBACK WndProc (HWND, UINT, WPARAM, LPARAM) ;

TCHAR szAppName[] = TEXT ("ShowDib5") ;

int WINAPI WinMain (HINSTANCE hInstance, HINSTANCE hPrevInstance,
                    PSTR szCmdLine, int iCmdShow)
{
    HWND     hwnd ;
    MSG      msg ;
    WNDCLASS wndclass ;

    wndclass.style         = CS_HREDRAW | CS_VREDRAW ;
    wndclass.lpfnWndProc   = WndProc ;
    wndclass.cbClsExtra    = 0 ;
    wndclass.cbWndExtra    = 0 ;
    wndclass.hInstance     = hInstance ;
    wndclass.hIcon         = LoadIcon (NULL, IDI_APPLICATION) ;
```

Figure 16-16. *The SHOWDIB5 program.*

```
     wndclass.hCursor        = LoadCursor (NULL, IDC_ARROW) ;
     wndclass.hbrBackground = (HBRUSH) GetStockObject (WHITE_BRUSH) ;
     wndclass.lpszMenuName   = szAppName ;
     wndclass.lpszClassName = szAppName ;

     if (!RegisterClass (&wndclass))
     {
          MessageBox (NULL, TEXT ("This program requires Windows NT!"),
                      szAppName, MB_ICONERROR) ;
          return 0 ;
     }

     hwnd = CreateWindow (szAppName, TEXT ("Show DIB #5: Halftone Palette"),
                          WS_OVERLAPPEDWINDOW,
                          CW_USEDEFAULT, CW_USEDEFAULT,
                          CW_USEDEFAULT, CW_USEDEFAULT,
                          NULL, NULL, hInstance, NULL) ;

     ShowWindow (hwnd, iCmdShow) ;
     UpdateWindow (hwnd) ;

     while (GetMessage (&msg, NULL, 0, 0))
     {
          TranslateMessage (&msg) ;
          DispatchMessage (&msg) ;
     }
     return msg.wParam ;
}

LRESULT CALLBACK WndProc (HWND hwnd, UINT message, WPARAM wParam, LPARAM lParam)
{
     static BITMAPINFO * pPackedDib ;
     static HPALETTE     hPalette ;
     static int          cxClient, cyClient ;
     static OPENFILENAME ofn ;
     static TCHAR        szFileName [MAX_PATH], szTitleName [MAX_PATH] ;
     static TCHAR        szFilter[] = TEXT ("Bitmap Files (*.BMP)\0*.bmp\0")
                                      TEXT ("All Files (*.*)\0*.*\0\0") ;
     HDC                 hdc ;
     PAINTSTRUCT         ps ;

     switch (message)
     {
     case WM_CREATE:
          ofn.lStructSize        = sizeof (OPENFILENAME) ;
          ofn.hwndOwner          = hwnd ;
```

(continued)

Figure 16-16. *continued*

```
                ofn.hInstance        = NULL ;
                ofn.lpstrFilter      = szFilter ;
                ofn.lpstrCustomFilter = NULL ;
                ofn.nMaxCustFilter   = 0 ;
                ofn.nFilterIndex     = 0 ;
                ofn.lpstrFile        = szFileName ;
                ofn.nMaxFile         = MAX_PATH ;
                ofn.lpstrFileTitle   = szTitleName ;
                ofn.nMaxFileTitle    = MAX_PATH ;
                ofn.lpstrInitialDir  = NULL ;
                ofn.lpstrTitle       = NULL ;
                ofn.Flags            = 0 ;
                ofn.nFileOffset      = 0 ;
                ofn.nFileExtension   = 0 ;
                ofn.lpstrDefExt      = TEXT ("bmp") ;
                ofn.lCustData        = 0 ;
                ofn.lpfnHook         = NULL ;
                ofn.lpTemplateName   = NULL ;

                // Create the All-Purpose Palette

          hdc = GetDC (hwnd) ;
          hPalette = CreateHalftonePalette (hdc) ;
          ReleaseDC (hwnd, hdc) ;
          return 0 ;

     case WM_SIZE:
          cxClient = LOWORD (lParam) ;
          cyClient = HIWORD (lParam) ;
          return 0 ;

     case WM_COMMAND:
          switch (LOWORD (wParam))
          {
          case IDM_FILE_OPEN:

                // Show the File Open dialog box

             if (!GetOpenFileName (&ofn))
                  return 0 ;

                // If there's an existing packed DIB, free the memory
```

```
              if (pPackedDib)
              {
                   free (pPackedDib) ;
                   pPackedDib = NULL ;
              }

                   // Load the packed DIB into memory

              SetCursor (LoadCursor (NULL, IDC_WAIT)) ;
              ShowCursor (TRUE) ;

              pPackedDib = PackedDibLoad (szFileName) ;

              ShowCursor (FALSE) ;
              SetCursor (LoadCursor (NULL, IDC_ARROW)) ;

              if (!pPackedDib)
              {
                   MessageBox (hwnd, TEXT ("Cannot load DIB file"),
                             szAppName, 0) ;
              }
              InvalidateRect (hwnd, NULL, TRUE) ;
              return 0 ;
         }
         break ;

    case WM_PAINT:
         hdc = BeginPaint (hwnd, &ps) ;

         if (pPackedDib)
         {
                   // Set halftone stretch mode

              SetStretchBltMode (hdc, HALFTONE) ;
              SetBrushOrgEx (hdc, 0, 0, NULL) ;

                   // Select and realize halftone palette

              SelectPalette (hdc, hPalette, FALSE) ;
              RealizePalette (hdc) ;

                   // StretchDIBits rather than SetDIBitsToDevice
```

(continued)

Figure 16-16. *continued*

```
            StretchDIBits (hdc,
                           0,
                           0,
                           PackedDibGetWidth (pPackedDib),
                           PackedDibGetHeight (pPackedDib),
                           0,
                           0,
                           PackedDibGetWidth (pPackedDib),
                           PackedDibGetHeight (pPackedDib),
                           PackedDibGetBitsPtr (pPackedDib),
                           pPackedDib,
                           DIB_RGB_COLORS,
                           SRCCOPY) ;
     }
     EndPaint (hwnd, &ps) ;
     return 0 ;

case WM_QUERYNEWPALETTE:
     hdc = GetDC (hwnd) ;
     SelectPalette (hdc, hPalette, FALSE) ;
     RealizePalette (hdc) ;
     InvalidateRect (hwnd, NULL, TRUE) ;

     ReleaseDC (hwnd, hdc) ;
     return TRUE ;

case WM_PALETTECHANGED:
     if ((HWND) wParam != hwnd)

     hdc = GetDC (hwnd) ;
     SelectPalette (hdc, hPalette, FALSE) ;
     RealizePalette (hdc) ;
     UpdateColors (hdc) ;

     ReleaseDC (hwnd, hdc) ;
     break ;

case WM_DESTROY:
     if (pPackedDib)
          free (pPackedDib) ;

     DeleteObject (hPalette) ;

     PostQuitMessage (0) ;
     return 0 ;
}
```

```
        return DefWindowProc (hwnd, message, wParam, lParam) ;
}
```

SHOWDIB5.RC (excerpts)

```
//Microsoft Developer Studio generated resource script.

#include "resource.h"
#include "afxres.h"

/////////////////////////////////////////////////////////////////////////////
// Menu

SHOWDIB5 MENU DISCARDABLE
BEGIN
    POPUP "&Open"
    BEGIN
        MENUITEM "&File",                      IDM_FILE_OPEN
    END
END
```

RESOURCE.H (excerpts)

```
// Microsoft Developer Studio generated include file.
// Used by ShowDib5.rc

#define IDM_FILE_OPEN                40001
```

The SHOWDIB5 program is similar to SHOWDIB4 in that it doesn't use the color table in the DIB but instead uses a palette that is appropriate for a wide range of images. SHOWDIB5 uses the logical palette supplied by Windows for this purpose, a handle to which can be obtained from the *CreateHalftonePalette* function.

This halftone palette is hardly more sophisticated than the palette created by the *CreateAllPurposePalette* function in SHOWDIB4. And indeed, if you use it by itself, the results will be similar. However, if you call these two functions,

```
        SetStretchBltMode (hdc, HALFTONE) ;
        SetBrushOrgEx (hdc, x, y, NULL) ;
```

where x and y are the device coordinates of the upper left corner of the DIB, and if you display the DIB with *StretchDIBits* rather *SetDIBitsToDevice*, the results will surprise you. Color flesh tones are much more accurate than with *CreateAllPurposePalette* or with *CreateHalftonePalette* used without setting the bitmap stretching mode. Windows uses a type of dithering pattern with the colors of the halftone palette to better approximate the colors of the original image on 8-bit video boards. As you might expect, the drawback is that it takes more processing time.

Indexing Palette Colors

The time has come to tackle the *fClrUse* argument to *SetDIBitsToDevice*, *StretchDIBits*, *CreateDIBitmap*, *SetDIBits*, *GetDIBits*, and *CreateDIBSection*. Normally, you set this argument to DIB_RGB_COLORS, which equals 0. However, you can also set it to DIB_PAL_COLORS. In this case, the color table in the BITMAPINFO structure is assumed to consist not of RGB color values but of 16-bit indices into a logical palette. This logical palette is the one currently selected in the device context given as the first argument to the function. Indeed, in *CreateDIBSection*, the use of DIB_PAL_COLORS is the only reason that you would need to specify a non-NULL device context handle as the first argument.

What does DIB_PAL_COLORS do for you? It gives you some performance improvement. Consider an 8-bit DIB that you're displaying in an 8-bit video mode by calling *SetDIBitsToDevice*. Windows must first do a nearest-color search of all the colors in the DIB color table with the colors available on the device. It can then set up a little table that lets it map DIB pixel values to the device pixels. At most, this means 256 nearest-color searches, but they can be skipped if the DIB color table contains instead indices into a logical palette selected in a device context.

The SHOWDIB6 program shown in Figure 16-17 is similar to SHOWDIB3 except that it uses palette indices.

SHOWDIB6.C

```
/*------------------------------------------------
   SHOWDIB6.C -- Display DIB with palette indices
                 (c) Charles Petzold, 1998
  ------------------------------------------------*/

#include <windows.h>
#include "..\\ShowDib3\\PackeDib.h"
#include "resource.h"

LRESULT CALLBACK WndProc (HWND, UINT, WPARAM, LPARAM) ;

TCHAR szAppName[] = TEXT ("ShowDib6") ;

int WINAPI WinMain (HINSTANCE hInstance, HINSTANCE hPrevInstance,
                    PSTR szCmdLine, int iCmdShow)
{
     HWND      hwnd ;
```

Figure 16-17. *The SHOWDIB6 program.*

```
     MSG        msg ;
     WNDCLASS wndclass ;

     wndclass.style         = CS_HREDRAW | CS_VREDRAW ;
     wndclass.lpfnWndProc   = WndProc ;
     wndclass.cbClsExtra    = 0 ;
     wndclass.cbWndExtra    = 0 ;
     wndclass.hInstance     = hInstance ;
     wndclass.hIcon         = LoadIcon (NULL, IDI_APPLICATION) ;
     wndclass.hCursor       = LoadCursor (NULL, IDC_ARROW) ;
     wndclass.hbrBackground = (HBRUSH) GetStockObject (WHITE_BRUSH) ;
     wndclass.lpszMenuName  = szAppName ;
     wndclass.lpszClassName = szAppName ;

     if (!RegisterClass (&wndclass))
     {
          MessageBox (NULL, TEXT ("This program requires Windows NT!"),
                      szAppName, MB_ICONERROR) ;
          return 0 ;
     }

     hwnd = CreateWindow (szAppName, TEXT ("Show DIB #6: Palette Indices"),
                      WS_OVERLAPPEDWINDOW,
                      CW_USEDEFAULT, CW_USEDEFAULT,
                      CW_USEDEFAULT, CW_USEDEFAULT,
                      NULL, NULL, hInstance, NULL) ;

     ShowWindow (hwnd, iCmdShow) ;
     UpdateWindow (hwnd) ;

     while (GetMessage (&msg, NULL, 0, 0))
     {
          TranslateMessage (&msg) ;
          DispatchMessage (&msg) ;
     }
     return msg.wParam ;
}

LRESULT CALLBACK WndProc (HWND hwnd, UINT message, WPARAM wParam, LPARAM lParam)
{
     static BITMAPINFO * pPackedDib ;
     static HPALETTE     hPalette ;
     static int          cxClient, cyClient ;
     static OPENFILENAME ofn ;
     static TCHAR        szFileName [MAX_PATH], szTitleName [MAX_PATH] ;
```

(continued)

Figure 16-17. *continued*

```
static TCHAR        szFilter[] = TEXT ("Bitmap Files (*.BMP)\0*.bmp\0")
                                 TEXT ("All Files (*.*)\0*.*\0\0") ;

HDC             hdc ;
int             i, iNumColors ;
PAINTSTRUCT     ps ;
WORD            * pwIndex ;

switch (message)
{
case WM_CREATE:
     ofn.lStructSize        = sizeof (OPENFILENAME) ;
     ofn.hwndOwner          = hwnd ;
     ofn.hInstance          = NULL ;
     ofn.lpstrFilter        = szFilter ;
     ofn.lpstrCustomFilter  = NULL ;
     ofn.nMaxCustFilter     = 0 ;
     ofn.nFilterIndex       = 0 ;
     ofn.lpstrFile          = szFileName ;
     ofn.nMaxFile           = MAX_PATH ;
     ofn.lpstrFileTitle     = szTitleName ;
     ofn.nMaxFileTitle      = MAX_PATH ;
     ofn.lpstrInitialDir    = NULL ;
     ofn.lpstrTitle         = NULL ;
     ofn.Flags              = 0 ;
     ofn.nFileOffset        = 0 ;
     ofn.nFileExtension     = 0 ;
     ofn.lpstrDefExt        = TEXT ("bmp") ;
     ofn.lCustData          = 0 ;
     ofn.lpfnHook           = NULL ;
     ofn.lpTemplateName     = NULL ;

     return 0 ;

case WM_SIZE:
     cxClient = LOWORD (lParam) ;
     cyClient = HIWORD (lParam) ;
     return 0 ;

case WM_COMMAND:
     switch (LOWORD (wParam))
     {
     case IDM_FILE_OPEN:

          // Show the File Open dialog box
```

```
if (!GetOpenFileName (&ofn))
    return 0 ;

    // If there's an existing packed DIB, free the memory

if (pPackedDib)
{
    free (pPackedDib) ;
    pPackedDib = NULL ;
}

    // If there's an existing logical palette, delete it

if (hPalette)
{
    DeleteObject (hPalette) ;
    hPalette = NULL ;
}

    // Load the packed DIB into memory

SetCursor (LoadCursor (NULL, IDC_WAIT)) ;
ShowCursor (TRUE) ;

pPackedDib = PackedDibLoad (szFileName) ;

ShowCursor (FALSE) ;
SetCursor (LoadCursor (NULL, IDC_ARROW)) ;

if (pPackedDib)
{
        // Create the palette from the DIB color table

    hPalette = PackedDibCreatePalette (pPackedDib) ;

        // Replace DIB color table with indices

    if (hPalette)
    {
        iNumColors = PackedDibGetNumColors (pPackedDib) ;
        pwIndex = (WORD *)
                    PackedDibGetColorTablePtr (pPackedDib) ;

        for (i = 0 ; i < iNumColors ; i++)
            pwIndex[i] = (WORD) i ;
    }
}
```

(continued)

Figure 16-17. *continued*

```
            else
            {
                MessageBox (hwnd, TEXT ("Cannot load DIB file"),
                             szAppName, 0) ;
            }
            InvalidateRect (hwnd, NULL, TRUE) ;
            return 0 ;
       }
       break ;

case WM_PAINT:
     hdc = BeginPaint (hwnd, &ps) ;

     if (hPalette)
     {
         SelectPalette (hdc, hPalette, FALSE) ;
         RealizePalette (hdc) ;
     }

     if (pPackedDib)
         SetDIBitsToDevice (hdc,
                             0,
                             0,
                             PackedDibGetWidth (pPackedDib),
                             PackedDibGetHeight (pPackedDib),
                             0,
                             0,
                             0,
                             PackedDibGetHeight (pPackedDib),
                             PackedDibGetBitsPtr (pPackedDib),
                             pPackedDib,
                             DIB_PAL_COLORS) ;
     EndPaint (hwnd, &ps) ;
     return 0 ;

case WM_QUERYNEWPALETTE:
     if (!hPalette)
         return FALSE ;

     hdc = GetDC (hwnd) ;
     SelectPalette (hdc, hPalette, FALSE) ;
     RealizePalette (hdc) ;
     InvalidateRect (hwnd, NULL, TRUE) ;

     ReleaseDC (hwnd, hdc) ;
     return TRUE ;
```

```
    case WM_PALETTECHANGED:
         if (!hPalette || (HWND) wParam == hwnd)
             break ;

         hdc = GetDC (hwnd) ;
         SelectPalette (hdc, hPalette, FALSE) ;
         RealizePalette (hdc) ;
         UpdateColors (hdc) ;

         ReleaseDC (hwnd, hdc) ;
         break ;


    case WM_DESTROY:
         if (pPackedDib)
             free (pPackedDib) ;

         if (hPalette)
             DeleteObject (hPalette) ;

         PostQuitMessage (0) ;
         return 0 ;
    }
    return DefWindowProc (hwnd, message, wParam, lParam) ;
}
```

SHOWDIB6.RC (excerpts)

```
//Microsoft Developer Studio generated resource script.

#include "resource.h"
#include "afxres.h"


/////////////////////////////////////////////////////////////////////////////
// Menu

SHOWDIB6 MENU DISCARDABLE
BEGIN
    POPUP "&File"
    BEGIN
        MENUITEM "&Open",                       IDM_FILE_OPEN
    END
END
```

(continued)

Figure 16-17. *continued*

RESOURCE.H (excerpts)

```
// Microsoft Developer Studio generated include file.
// Used by ShowDib6.rc
//
#define IDM_FILE_OPEN                    40001
```

After SHOWDIB6 loads the DIB into memory and creates a palette from it, it simply replaces the colors in the DIB color table with WORD indices beginning at 0. The *Packed-DibGetNumColors* function indicates how many colors there are, and the *PackedDibGetColor-TablePtr* function returns a pointer to the beginning of the DIB color table.

Notice that this technique is feasible only when you create a palette directly from the color table of the DIB. If you're using an all-purpose palette, you would need to perform a nearest-color search yourself to derive the indices you put into the DIB. That wouldn't make much sense.

If you do use palette indices, be sure to replace the color table in the DIB before you save the DIB to disk. Also, don't put a DIB containing palette indices in the clipboard. In fact, it would be much safer to put palette indices in the DIB right before displaying it and then put the RGB color values back in afterward.

Palettes and Bitmap Objects

The SHOWDIB7 program in Figure 16-18 shows how to use palettes in connection with DIBs that you convert to GDI bitmap objects using the *CreateDIBitmap* function.

SHOWDIB7.C

```
/*-------------------------------------------
   SHOWDIB7.C -- Shows DIB converted to DDB
                 (c) Charles Petzold, 1998
   -------------------------------------------*/

#include <windows.h>
#include "..\\ShowDib3\\PackeDib.h"
#include "resource.h"

LRESULT CALLBACK WndProc (HWND, UINT, WPARAM, LPARAM) ;

TCHAR szAppName[] = TEXT ("ShowDib7") ;

int WINAPI WinMain (HINSTANCE hInstance, HINSTANCE hPrevInstance,
                    PSTR szCmdLine, int iCmdShow)
```

Figure 16-18. *The SHOWDIB7 program.*

```
{
     HWND      hwnd ;
     MSG       msg ;
     WNDCLASS wndclass ;

     wndclass.style          = CS_HREDRAW | CS_VREDRAW ;
     wndclass.lpfnWndProc    = WndProc ;
     wndclass.cbClsExtra     = 0 ;
     wndclass.cbWndExtra     = 0 ;
     wndclass.hInstance      = hInstance ;
     wndclass.hIcon          = LoadIcon (NULL, IDI_APPLICATION) ;
     wndclass.hCursor        = LoadCursor (NULL, IDC_ARROW) ;
     wndclass.hbrBackground  = (HBRUSH) GetStockObject (WHITE_BRUSH) ;
     wndclass.lpszMenuName   = szAppName ;
     wndclass.lpszClassName  = szAppName ;

     if (!RegisterClass (&wndclass))
     {
          MessageBox (NULL, TEXT ("This program requires Windows NT!"),
                     szAppName, MB_ICONERROR) ;
          return 0 ;
     }

     hwnd = CreateWindow (szAppName, TEXT ("Show DIB #7: Converted to DDB"),
                         WS_OVERLAPPEDWINDOW,
                         CW_USEDEFAULT, CW_USEDEFAULT,
                         CW_USEDEFAULT, CW_USEDEFAULT,
                         NULL, NULL, hInstance, NULL) ;

     ShowWindow (hwnd, iCmdShow) ;
     UpdateWindow (hwnd) ;

     while (GetMessage (&msg, NULL, 0, 0))
     {
          TranslateMessage (&msg) ;
          DispatchMessage (&msg) ;
     }
     return msg.wParam ;
}

LRESULT CALLBACK WndProc (HWND hwnd, UINT message, WPARAM wParam, LPARAM lParam)
{
     static HBITMAP      hBitmap ;
     static HPALETTE     hPalette ;
     static int          cxClient, cyClient ;
     static OPENFILENAME ofn ;
```

(continued)

Figure 16-18. *continued*

```
    static TCHAR        szFileName [MAX_PATH], szTitleName [MAX_PATH] ;
    static TCHAR        szFilter[] = TEXT ("Bitmap Files (*.BMP)\0*.bmp\0")
                                     TEXT ("All Files (*.*)\0*.*\0\0") ;
    BITMAP              bitmap ;
    BITMAPINFO        * pPackedDib ;
    HDC                 hdc, hdcMem ;
    PAINTSTRUCT         ps ;

    switch (message)
    {
    case WM_CREATE:
         ofn.lStructSize      = sizeof (OPENFILENAME) ;
         ofn.hwndOwner        = hwnd ;
         ofn.hInstance        = NULL ;
         ofn.lpstrFilter      = szFilter ;
         ofn.lpstrCustomFilter = NULL ;
         ofn.nMaxCustFilter   = 0 ;
         ofn.nFilterIndex     = 0 ;
         ofn.lpstrFile        = szFileName ;
         ofn.nMaxFile         = MAX_PATH ;
         ofn.lpstrFileTitle   = szTitleName ;
         ofn.nMaxFileTitle    = MAX_PATH ;
         ofn.lpstrInitialDir  = NULL ;
         ofn.lpstrTitle       = NULL ;
         ofn.Flags            = 0 ;
         ofn.nFileOffset      = 0 ;
         ofn.nFileExtension   = 0 ;
         ofn.lpstrDefExt      = TEXT ("bmp") ;
         ofn.lCustData        = 0 ;
         ofn.lpfnHook         = NULL ;
         ofn.lpTemplateName   = NULL ;

         return 0 ;

    case WM_SIZE:
         cxClient = LOWORD (lParam) ;
         cyClient = HIWORD (lParam) ;
         return 0 ;

    case WM_COMMAND:
         switch (LOWORD (wParam))
         {
         case IDM_FILE_OPEN:

                   // Show the File Open dialog box
```

```
      if (!GetOpenFileName (&ofn))
          return 0 ;

          // If there's an existing packed DIB, free the memory

      if (hBitmap)
      {
          DeleteObject (hBitmap) ;
          hBitmap = NULL ;
      }

          // If there's an existing logical palette, delete it

      if (hPalette)
      {
          DeleteObject (hPalette) ;
          hPalette = NULL ;
      }

          // Load the packed DIB into memory

      SetCursor (LoadCursor (NULL, IDC_WAIT)) ;
      ShowCursor (TRUE) ;

      pPackedDib = PackedDibLoad (szFileName) ;

      ShowCursor (FALSE) ;
      SetCursor (LoadCursor (NULL, IDC_ARROW)) ;

      if (pPackedDib)
      {
              // Create palette from the DIB and select it into DC

          hPalette = PackedDibCreatePalette (pPackedDib) ;

          hdc = GetDC (hwnd) ;

          if (hPalette)
          {
              SelectPalette (hdc, hPalette, FALSE) ;
              RealizePalette (hdc) ;
          }
              // Create the DDB from the DIB
```

(continued)

Figure 16-18. *continued*

```
                    hBitmap = CreateDIBitmap (hdc,
                                              (PBITMAPINFOHEADER) pPackedDib,
                                              CBM_INIT,
                                              PackedDibGetBitsPtr (pPackedDib),
                                              pPackedDib,
                                              DIB_RGB_COLORS) ;
                    ReleaseDC (hwnd, hdc) ;

                         // Free the packed-DIB memory

                    free (pPackedDib) ;
               }
               else
               {
                    MessageBox (hwnd, TEXT ("Cannot load DIB file"),
                              szAppName, 0) ;
               }
               InvalidateRect (hwnd, NULL, TRUE) ;
               return 0 ;
          }
          break ;

     case WM_PAINT:
          hdc = BeginPaint (hwnd, &ps) ;

          if (hPalette)
          {
               SelectPalette (hdc, hPalette, FALSE) ;
               RealizePalette (hdc) ;
          }
          if (hBitmap)
          {
               GetObject (hBitmap, sizeof (BITMAP), &bitmap) ;

               hdcMem = CreateCompatibleDC (hdc) ;
               SelectObject (hdcMem, hBitmap) ;

               BitBlt (hdc,    0, 0, bitmap.bmWidth, bitmap.bmHeight,
                       hdcMem, 0, 0, SRCCOPY) ;

               DeleteDC (hdcMem) ;
          }
```

```
          EndPaint (hwnd, &ps) ;
          return 0 ;

     case WM_QUERYNEWPALETTE:
          if (!hPalette)
               return FALSE ;

          hdc = GetDC (hwnd) ;
          SelectPalette (hdc, hPalette, FALSE) ;
          RealizePalette (hdc) ;
          InvalidateRect (hwnd, NULL, TRUE) ;

          ReleaseDC (hwnd, hdc) ;
          return TRUE ;

     case WM_PALETTECHANGED:
          if (!hPalette || (HWND) wParam == hwnd)
               break ;

          hdc = GetDC (hwnd) ;
          SelectPalette (hdc, hPalette, FALSE) ;
          RealizePalette (hdc) ;
          UpdateColors (hdc) ;

          ReleaseDC (hwnd, hdc) ;
          break ;


     case WM_DESTROY:
          if (hBitmap)
               DeleteObject (hBitmap) ;

          if (hPalette)
               DeleteObject (hPalette) ;

          PostQuitMessage (0) ;
          return 0 ;
     }
     return DefWindowProc (hwnd, message, wParam, lParam) ;
}
```

(continued)

Figure 16-18. *continued*

SHOWDIB7.RC (excerpts)

```
//Microsoft Developer Studio generated resource script.

#include "resource.h"
#include "afxres.h"


/////////////////////////////////////////////////////////////////////////////
// Menu

SHOWDIB7 MENU DISCARDABLE
BEGIN
    POPUP "&File"
    BEGIN
        MENUITEM "&Open",                       IDM_FILE_OPEN
    END
END
```

RESOURCE.H (excerpts)

```
// Microsoft Developer Studio generated include file.
// Used by ShowDib7.rc

#define IDM_FILE_OPEN                   40001
```

As in the earlier programs, SHOWDIB7 obtains a pointer to the packed DIB in response to a File Open command from the menu. It also creates a palette from the packed DIB. Then—still in WM_COMMAND message processing—it obtains a device context for the video display, selects the palette into it, and realizes the palette. SHOWDIB7 then calls *CreateDIBitmap* to create a DDB from the DIB. If the palette were not selected and realized into the device context, the DDB that *CreateDIBitmap* creates would not use the additional colors in the logical palette.

After calling *CreateDIBitmap*, the program can then free the memory occupied by the packed DIB. The *pPackedDib* variable is not a static variable. Instead, the SHOWDIB7 retains the bitmap handle (*hBitmap*) and the logical palette handle (*hPalette*) as static variables.

During the WM_PAINT message, the palette is selected into the device context again and realized. The width and height of the bitmap is obtained from the *GetObject* function. The program can then display the bitmap on the client area by creating a compatible memory device context, selecting the bitmap into it, and doing a *BitBlt*. You must use the same palette when displaying the DDB as you used when creating it from the *CreateDIBitmap* call.

If you copy a bitmap to the clipboard, it's best that it be in a packed-DIB format. Windows can then provide bitmap objects to programs that want them. However, if you need to copy a bitmap object to the clipboard, get a video device context first and select and realize the palette. This will allow Windows to convert the DDB to a DIB based on the current system palette.

Palettes and DIB Sections

Finally, SHOWDIB8 in Figure 16-19 shows how to use a palette with the DIB section.

SHOWDIB8.C

```
/*-----------------------------------------------------
   SHOWDIB8.C -- Shows DIB converted to DIB section
                 (c) Charles Petzold, 1998
   -----------------------------------------------------*/

#include <windows.h>
#include "..\\ShowDib3\\PackeDib.h"
#include "resource.h"

LRESULT CALLBACK WndProc (HWND, UINT, WPARAM, LPARAM) ;

TCHAR szAppName[] = TEXT ("ShowDib8") ;

int WINAPI WinMain (HINSTANCE hInstance, HINSTANCE hPrevInstance,
                    PSTR szCmdLine, int iCmdShow)
{
    HWND       hwnd ;
    MSG        msg ;
    WNDCLASS wndclass ;

    wndclass.style         = CS_HREDRAW | CS_VREDRAW ;
    wndclass.lpfnWndProc   = WndProc ;
    wndclass.cbClsExtra    = 0 ;
    wndclass.cbWndExtra    = 0 ;
    wndclass.hInstance     = hInstance ;
    wndclass.hIcon         = LoadIcon (NULL, IDI_APPLICATION) ;
    wndclass.hCursor       = LoadCursor (NULL, IDC_ARROW) ;
    wndclass.hbrBackground = (HBRUSH) GetStockObject (WHITE_BRUSH) ;
    wndclass.lpszMenuName  = szAppName ;
    wndclass.lpszClassName = szAppName ;

    if (!RegisterClass (&wndclass))
    {
        MessageBox (NULL, TEXT ("This program requires Windows NT!"),
                    szAppName, MB_ICONERROR) ;
```

Figure 16-19. *The SHOWDIB8 program.* *(continued)*

Figure 16-19. *continued*

```
        return 0 ;
    }

    hwnd = CreateWindow (szAppName, TEXT ("Show DIB #8: DIB Section"),
                         WS_OVERLAPPEDWINDOW,
                         CW_USEDEFAULT, CW_USEDEFAULT,
                         CW_USEDEFAULT, CW_USEDEFAULT,
                         NULL, NULL, hInstance, NULL) ;

    ShowWindow (hwnd, iCmdShow) ;
    UpdateWindow (hwnd) ;

    while (GetMessage (&msg, NULL, 0, 0))
    {
        TranslateMessage (&msg) ;
        DispatchMessage (&msg) ;
    }
    return msg.wParam ;
}

LRESULT CALLBACK WndProc (HWND hwnd, UINT message, WPARAM wParam, LPARAM lParam)
{
    static HBITMAP      hBitmap ;
    static HPALETTE     hPalette ;
    static int          cxClient, cyClient ;
    static OPENFILENAME ofn ;
    static PBYTE        pBits ;
    static TCHAR        szFileName [MAX_PATH], szTitleName [MAX_PATH] ;
    static TCHAR        szFilter[] = TEXT ("Bitmap Files (*.BMP)\0*.bmp\0")
                                     TEXT ("All Files (*.*)\0*.*\0\0") ;
    BITMAP              bitmap ;
    BITMAPINFO        * pPackedDib ;
    HDC                 hdc, hdcMem ;
    PAINTSTRUCT         ps ;

    switch (message)
    {
    case WM_CREATE:
        ofn.lStructSize       = sizeof (OPENFILENAME) ;
        ofn.hwndOwner         = hwnd ;
        ofn.hInstance         = NULL ;
        ofn.lpstrFilter       = szFilter ;
        ofn.lpstrCustomFilter = NULL ;
        ofn.nMaxCustFilter    = 0 ;
        ofn.nFilterIndex      = 0 ;
        ofn.lpstrFile         = szFileName ;
```

```
        ofn.nMaxFile            = MAX_PATH ;
        ofn.lpstrFileTitle      = szTitleName ;
        ofn.nMaxFileTitle       = MAX_PATH ;
        ofn.lpstrInitialDir     = NULL ;
        ofn.lpstrTitle          = NULL ;
        ofn.Flags               = 0 ;
        ofn.nFileOffset         = 0 ;
        ofn.nFileExtension      = 0 ;
        ofn.lpstrDefExt         = TEXT ("bmp") ;
        ofn.lCustData           = 0 ;
        ofn.lpfnHook            = NULL ;
        ofn.lpTemplateName      = NULL ;

        return 0 ;

   case WM_SIZE:
        cxClient = LOWORD (lParam) ;
        cyClient = HIWORD (lParam) ;
        return 0 ;

   case WM_COMMAND:
        switch (LOWORD (wParam))
        {
        case IDM_FILE_OPEN:

             // Show the File Open dialog box

             if (!GetOpenFileName (&ofn))
                 return 0 ;

             // If there's an existing packed DIB, free the memory

             if (hBitmap)
             {
                 DeleteObject (hBitmap) ;
                 hBitmap = NULL ;
             }

             // If there's an existing logical palette, delete it

             if (hPalette)
             {
                 DeleteObject (hPalette) ;
                 hPalette = NULL ;
             }
```

(continued)

Figure 16-19. *continued*

```
                    // Load the packed DIB into memory

        SetCursor (LoadCursor (NULL, IDC_WAIT)) ;
        ShowCursor (TRUE) ;

        pPackedDib = PackedDibLoad (szFileName) ;

        ShowCursor (FALSE) ;
        SetCursor (LoadCursor (NULL, IDC_ARROW)) ;

        if (pPackedDib)
        {
                // Create the DIB section from the DIB

            hBitmap = CreateDIBSection (NULL,
                                pPackedDib,
                                DIB_RGB_COLORS,
                                &pBits,
                                NULL, 0) ;

                // Copy the bits

            CopyMemory (pBits, PackedDibGetBitsPtr (pPackedDib),
                        PackedDibGetBitsSize (pPackedDib)) ;

                // Create palette from the DIB

            hPalette = PackedDibCreatePalette (pPackedDib) ;

                // Free the packed-DIB memory

            free (pPackedDib) ;
        }

        else
        {
            MessageBox (hwnd, TEXT ("Cannot load DIB file"),
                        szAppName, 0) ;
        }
        InvalidateRect (hwnd, NULL, TRUE) ;
        return 0 ;
    }
    break ;
```

```
case WM_PAINT:
     hdc = BeginPaint (hwnd, &ps) ;

     if (hPalette)
     {
          SelectPalette (hdc, hPalette, FALSE) ;
          RealizePalette (hdc) ;
     }
     if (hBitmap)
     {
          GetObject (hBitmap, sizeof (BITMAP), &bitmap) ;

          hdcMem = CreateCompatibleDC (hdc) ;
          SelectObject (hdcMem, hBitmap) ;

          BitBlt (hdc,    0, 0, bitmap.bmWidth, bitmap.bmHeight,
                  hdcMem, 0, 0, SRCCOPY) ;

          DeleteDC (hdcMem) ;
     }
     EndPaint (hwnd, &ps) ;
     return 0 ;

case WM_QUERYNEWPALETTE:
     if (!hPalette)
          return FALSE ;

     hdc = GetDC (hwnd) ;
     SelectPalette (hdc, hPalette, FALSE) ;
     RealizePalette (hdc) ;
     InvalidateRect (hwnd, NULL, TRUE) ;

     ReleaseDC (hwnd, hdc) ;
     return TRUE ;

case WM_PALETTECHANGED:
     if (!hPalette || (HWND) wParam == hwnd)
          break ;

     hdc = GetDC (hwnd) ;
     SelectPalette (hdc, hPalette, FALSE) ;
```

(continued)

Figure 16-19. *continued*

```
        RealizePalette (hdc) ;
        UpdateColors (hdc) ;

        ReleaseDC (hwnd, hdc) ;
        break ;


    case WM_DESTROY:
        if (hBitmap)
            DeleteObject (hBitmap) ;

        if (hPalette)
            DeleteObject (hPalette) ;

        PostQuitMessage (0) ;
        return 0 ;
    }
    return DefWindowProc (hwnd, message, wParam, lParam) ;
}
```

SHOWDIB8.RC (excerpts)

```
//Microsoft Developer Studio generated resource script.

#include "resource.h"
#include "afxres.h"


/////////////////////////////////////////////////////////////////////////////
// Menu

SHOWDIB8 MENU DISCARDABLE
BEGIN
    POPUP "&File"
    BEGIN
        MENUITEM "&Open",                       IDM_FILE_OPEN
    END
END
```

RESOURCE.H (excerpts)

```
// Microsoft Developer Studio generated include file.
// Used by ShowDib8.rc

#define IDM_FILE_OPEN                   40001
```

The WM_PAINT processing in SHOWDIB7 and SHOWDIB8 are identical: Both programs retain as static variables a bitmap handle (*hBitmap*) and a logical palette handle (*hPalette*). The palette is selected into the device context and realized, the width and height of the bitmap are obtained from the *GetObject* function, the program creates a memory device context and selects the bitmap into it, and the bitmap is displayed to the client area by a call to *BitBlt*.

The big difference between the two programs is in the processing of the File Open menu command. After obtaining a pointer to the packed DIB and creating a palette, SHOWDIB7 must select the palette into a video device context and realize it before calling *CreateDIBitmap*. SHOWDIB8 calls *CreateDIBSection* after obtaining the packed-DIB pointer. Selecting the palette into a device context isn't necessary because *CreateDIBSection* does not convert a DIB to a device-dependent format. Indeed, the only purpose of the first argument to *CreateDIBSection* (that is, the device context handle) is if you use the DIB_PAL_COLORS flag.

After calling *CreateDIBSection*, SHOWDIB8 copies the pixel bits from the packed DIB to the memory location returned from the *CreateDIBSection* function. It then calls *PackedDibCreatePalette*. Although this function is convenient for the program to use, SHOWDIB8 could have created a palette based on information returned from the *GetDIBColorTable* function.

A LIBRARY FOR DIBS

It is only now—after our long journey learning about GDI bitmap objects, the device-independent bitmap, the DIB section, and the Windows Palette Manager—that we're ready to devise some set of functions that help us in working with bitmaps.

The PACKEDIB files shown earlier illustrate one possible approach: A packed DIB in memory is represented solely by a pointer to it. All the information that a program needs about the DIB can be obtained by functions that access the header information structure. In practice, however, this method has serious performance problems when it comes to "get pixel" and "set pixel" routines. Image-processing tasks routinely require bitmap bits to be accessed, and these functions should ideally be as fast as possible.

A possible C++ solution involves creating a DIB class where a pointer to the packed DIB is just one of several member variables. Other member variables and member functions can help implement fast routines for obtaining and setting pixels in the DIB. However, since I indicated in the first chapter that you'd only need to know C for this particular book, the use of C++ will have to remain a solution for some other book.

Of course, just about anything that can be done in C++ can also be done in C. A good example of this are the multitude of Windows functions that use handles. What does an application program know about a handle other than the fact that it's a numeric value? It knows that the handle references a particular object and that functions for working with the object exist. Obviously, the operating system uses the handle to somehow reference internal information about the object. A handle could be as simple as a pointer to a structure.

For example, suppose there exists a collection of functions that use a handle called an HDIB. What's an HDIB? Well, it might be defined in a header file like so:

```
typedef void * HDIB ;
```

This definition answers the question "What's an HDIB?" with "None of your business!"

In reality, however, an HDIB might be a pointer to a structure that contains not only a pointer to a packed DIB but also some other information:

```
typedef struct
{
    BITMAPINFO * pPackedDib ;
    int          cx, cy, cBitsPerPixel, cBytesPerRow ;
    BYTE       * pBits ;
{
DIBSTRUCTURE, * PDIBSTRUCTURE ;
```

The other five fields of this structure contain information that is derivable from the packed DIB, of course, but the presence of these values in the structure allows them to be accessed more quickly. The various DIB library functions could work with this structure rather than the *pPackedDib* pointer. A *DibGetPixelPointer* function could be implemented like so:

```
BYTE * DibGetPixelPointer (HDIB hdib, int x, int y)
{
    PDIBSTRUCTURE pdib = hdib ;

    return pdib->pBits + y * pdib->cBytesPerRow +
                    x * pdib->cBitsPerPixel / 8 ;
}
```

This is, of course, much faster than a "get pixel" routine that might be implemented in PACKEDIB.C.

While this approach is quite reasonable, I have decided to abandon the packed DIB and instead base my DIB library on the DIB section. This gives us virtually all of the flexibility involved with packed DIBs (that is, being able to manipulate DIB pixel bits in a somewhat device-independent manner) but is also more efficient when running under Windows NT.

The DIBSTRUCT Structure

The DIBHELP.C file—so named because it provides help for working with DIBs—is over a thousand lines long and will be shown shortly in several parts. But let's first take a close look at the structure that the DIBHELP functions work with. The structure is defined in DIBHELP.C like so:

```
typedef struct
{
    PBYTE     * ppRow ;         // array of row pointers
    int         iSignature ;    // = "Dib "
    HBITMAP     hBitmap ;       // handle returned from CreateDIBSection
    BYTE      * pBits ;         // pointer to bitmap bits
    DIBSECTION ds ;             // DIBSECTION structure
    int         iRShift[3] ;    // right-shift values for color masks
    int         iLShift[3] ;    // left-shift values for color masks
}
DIBSTRUCT, * PDIBSTRUCT ;
```

Let me skip the first field for now. There's a reason why it's the first field—it makes some macros easier—but it'll be easier to understand after I discuss the other fields first.

When this structure is first set up by one of the DIB creation functions in DIBHELP.C, the second field is set to the binary equivalent of the text string "Dib ". This is used as a check of the validity of a pointer to the structure by some of the DIBHELP functions.

The third field—*hBitmap*—is the bitmap handle returned from the *CreateDIBSection* function. You'll recall that this handle can in many ways be used like the handles to GDI bitmap objects that we encountered in Chapter 14. However, the handle returned from *CreateDIBSection* references a bitmap that remains in a device-independent format until it is rendered on an output device by calls to *BitBlt* and *StretchBlt*.

The fourth field of DIBSTRUCT is a pointer to the bitmap bits. This is a value also set by the *CreateDIBSection* function. You'll recall that the operating system controls this memory block but that an application has access to it. The block is automatically freed when the bitmap handle is deleted.

The fifth field of DIBSTRUCT is a DIBSECTION structure. You'll recall that if you have a bitmap handle returned from *CreateDIBSection*, you can pass that to the *GetObject* function to obtain information about the bitmap in the DIBSECTION structure:

```
GetObject (hBitmap, sizeof (DIBSECTION), &ds) ;
```

As a reminder, the DIBSECTION structure is defined in WINGDI.H like so:

```
typedef struct tagDIBSECTION {
    BITMAP          dsBm ;
    BITMAPINFOHEADER dsBmih ;
    DWORD           dsBitfields[3] ;      // Color masks
    HANDLE          dshSection ;
    DWORD           dsOffset ;
}
DIBSECTION, * PDIBSECTION ;
```

The first field is the BITMAP structure that's used with *CreateBitmapIndirect* to create a bitmap object and used with *GetObject* to return information about a DDB. The second field is a BITMAPINFOHEADER structure. Regardless of the bitmap information structure passed to the *CreateDIBSection* function, the DIBSECTION structure will always have a BITMAPINFOHEADER structure and not, for example, a BITMAPCOREHEADER structure. This means that a lot of the functions in DIBHELP.C need not check for OS/2-compatible DIBs when accessing this structure.

You'll recall that for 16-bit and 32-bit DIBs, if the *biCompression* field of the BITMAP-INFOHEADER structure is BI_BITFIELDS, then three mask values normally follow the information header structure. These mask values determine how to convert 16-bit and 32-bit pixel values to RGB colors. The masks are stored in the third field of the DIBSECTION structure.

The final two fields of the DIBSECTION structure refer to a DIB section created with a file-mapping object. DIBHELP does not use this feature of *CreateDIBSection*, so these fields can be ignored.

Finally, the last two fields of DIBSTRUCT store left and right shift values that are used with the color masks for 16-bit and 32-bit DIBs. These shift values were discussed in Chapter 15.

Let's go back to the first field of DIBSTRUCT. As we'll see, when a DIB is first created, this field is set to a pointer that references an array of pointers, each of which points to a row of pixels in the DIB. These pointers allow an even faster method to get at DIB pixel bits and are defined so that the DIB pixel bits can be referenced top row first. The last element of this array—referencing the bottom row of the DIB image—will usually be equal to the *pBits* field of DIBSTRUCT.

The Information Functions

DIBHELP.C begins by defining the DIBSTRUCT structure and then providing a collection of functions that let an application obtain information about the DIB section. The first part of DIBHELP.C is shown in Figure 16-20.

DIBHELP.C (first part)

```
/*-------------------------------------------
   DIBHELP.C -- DIB Section Helper Routines
               (c) Charles Petzold, 1998
   -------------------------------------------*/

#include <windows.h>
#include "dibhelp.h"

#define HDIB_SIGNATURE (* (int *) "Dib ")

typedef struct
{
    PBYTE     * ppRow ;              // must be first field for macros!
    int         iSignature ;
    HBITMAP     hBitmap ;
    BYTE      * pBits ;
    DIBSECTION ds ;
    int         iRShift[3] ;
    int         iLShift[3] ;
}
DIBSTRUCT, * PDIBSTRUCT ;

/*-------------------------------------------------------------
   DibIsValid:  Returns TRUE if hdib points to a valid DIBSTRUCT
   -------------------------------------------------------------*/

BOOL DibIsValid (HDIB hdib)
{
    PDIBSTRUCT pdib = hdib ;

    if (pdib == NULL)
        return FALSE ;

    if (IsBadReadPtr (pdib, sizeof (DIBSTRUCT)))
        return FALSE ;

    if (pdib->iSignature != HDIB_SIGNATURE)
        return FALSE ;
```

Figure 16-20. *The first part of the DIBHELP.C file.*   *(continued)*

Figure 16-20. *continued*

```
        return TRUE ;
}


/*-------------------------------------------------------------------------
   DibBitmapHandle:  Returns the handle to the DIB section bitmap object
   --------------------------------------------------------------------*/

HBITMAP DibBitmapHandle (HDIB hdib)
{
    if (!DibIsValid (hdib))
        return NULL ;

    return ((PDIBSTRUCT) hdib)->hBitmap ;
}


/*-----------------------------------------------
   DibWidth:  Returns the bitmap pixel width
   -------------------------------------------*/

int DibWidth (HDIB hdib)
{
    if (!DibIsValid (hdib))
        return 0 ;

    return ((PDIBSTRUCT) hdib)->ds.dsBm.bmWidth ;
}


/*-------------------------------------------------
   DibHeight:  Returns the bitmap pixel height
   ---------------------------------------------*/

int DibHeight (HDIB hdib)
{
    if (!DibIsValid (hdib))
        return 0 ;

    return ((PDIBSTRUCT) hdib)->ds.dsBm.bmHeight ;
}


/*-------------------------------------------------------
   DibBitCount:  Returns the number of bits per pixel
   ---------------------------------------------------*/
```

```
int DibBitCount (HDIB hdib)
{
    if (!DibIsValid (hdib))
        return 0 ;

    return ((PDIBSTRUCT) hdib)->ds.dsBm.bmBitsPixel ;
}


/*----------------------------------------------------------------
   DibRowLength:  Returns the number of bytes per row of pixels
  ------------------------------------------------------------*/

int DibRowLength (HDIB hdib)
{
    if (!DibIsValid (hdib))
        return 0 ;

    return 4 * ((DibWidth (hdib) * DibBitCount (hdib) + 31) / 32) ;
}

/*----------------------------------------------------------------
   DibNumColors:  Returns the number of colors in the color table
  ------------------------------------------------------------*/

int DibNumColors (HDIB hdib)
{
    PDIBSTRUCT pdib = hdib ;

    if (!DibIsValid (hdib))
        return 0 ;

    if (pdib->ds.dsBmih.biClrUsed != 0)
    {
        return pdib->ds.dsBmih.biClrUsed ;
    }
    else if (DibBitCount (hdib) <= 8)
    {
        return 1 << DibBitCount (hdib) ;
    }
    return 0 ;
}
```

(continued)

Figure 16-20. *continued*

```
/*-------------------------------------------
   DibMask:  Returns one of the color masks
   ----------------------------------------*/

DWORD DibMask (HDIB hdib, int i)
{
    PDIBSTRUCT pdib = hdib ;

    if (!DibIsValid (hdib) || i < 0 || i > 2)
        return 0 ;

    return pdib->ds.dsBitfields[i] ;
}

/*-----------------------------------------------------
   DibRShift:  Returns one of the right-shift values
   --------------------------------------------------*/

int DibRShift (HDIB hdib, int i)
{
    PDIBSTRUCT pdib = hdib ;

    if (!DibIsValid (hdib) || i < 0 || i > 2)
        return 0 ;

    return pdib->iRShift[i] ;
}

/*----------------------------------------------------
   DibLShift:  Returns one of the left-shift values
   -------------------------------------------------*/

int DibLShift (HDIB hdib, int i)
{
    PDIBSTRUCT pdib = hdib ;

    if (!DibIsValid (hdib) || i < 0 || i > 2)
        return 0 ;

    return pdib->iLShift[i] ;
}

/*-------------------------------------------------------------
   DibCompression:  Returns the value of the biCompression field
   ----------------------------------------------------------*/
```

```
int DibCompression (HDIB hdib)
{
    if (!DibIsValid (hdib))
        return 0 ;

    return ((PDIBSTRUCT) hdib)->ds.dsBmih.biCompression ;
}


/*-----------------------------------------------------------------
   DibIsAddressable:  Returns TRUE if the DIB is not compressed
   --------------------------------------------------------------*/

BOOL DibIsAddressable (HDIB hdib)
{
    int iCompression ;

    if (!DibIsValid (hdib))
        return FALSE ;

    iCompression = DibCompression (hdib) ;

    if (iCompression == BI_RGB || iCompression == BI_BITFIELDS)
        return TRUE ;

    return FALSE ;
}


/*-----------------------------------------------------------------------
   These functions return the sizes of various components of the DIB section
   AS THEY WOULD APPEAR in a packed DIB. These functions aid in converting
   the DIB section to a packed DIB and in saving DIB files.
   --------------------------------------------------------------------*/

DWORD DibInfoHeaderSize (HDIB hdib)
{
    if (!DibIsValid (hdib))
        return 0 ;

    return ((PDIBSTRUCT) hdib)->ds.dsBmih.biSize ;
}

DWORD DibMaskSize (HDIB hdib)
{
    PDIBSTRUCT pdib = hdib ;
```

(continued)

Figure 16-20. *continued*

```
        if (!DibIsValid (hdib))
            return 0 ;

        if (pdib->ds.dsBmih.biCompression == BI_BITFIELDS)
            return 3 * sizeof (DWORD) ;

        return 0 ;
}

DWORD DibColorSize (HDIB hdib)
{
        return DibNumColors (hdib) * sizeof (RGBQUAD) ;
}

DWORD DibInfoSize (HDIB hdib)
{
        return DibInfoHeaderSize(hdib) + DibMaskSize(hdib) + DibColorSize(hdib) ;
}

DWORD DibBitsSize (HDIB hdib)
{
        PDIBSTRUCT pdib = hdib ;

        if (!DibIsValid (hdib))
            return 0 ;

        if (pdib->ds.dsBmih.biSizeImage != 0)
        {
            return pdib->ds.dsBmih.biSizeImage ;
        }
        return DibHeight (hdib) * DibRowLength (hdib) ;
}

DWORD DibTotalSize (HDIB hdib)
{
        return DibInfoSize (hdib) + DibBitsSize (hdib) ;
}

/*-------------------------------------------------------------------------
   These functions return pointers to the various components of the DIB
   section.
   -----------------------------------------------------------------------*/
```

```
BITMAPINFOHEADER * DibInfoHeaderPtr (HDIB hdib)
{
     if (!DibIsValid (hdib))
          return NULL ;

     return & ((((PDIBSTRUCT) hdib)->ds.dsBmih) ;
}

DWORD * DibMaskPtr (HDIB hdib)
{
     PDIBSTRUCT pdib = hdib ;

     if (!DibIsValid (hdib))
          return 0 ;

     return pdib->ds.dsBitfields ;
}

void * DibBitsPtr (HDIB hdib)
{
     if (!DibIsValid (hdib))
          return NULL ;

     return ((PDIBSTRUCT) hdib)->pBits ;
}

/*-----------------------------------------------------------
   DibSetColor:  Obtains entry from the DIB color table
 -----------------------------------------------------------*/

BOOL DibGetColor (HDIB hdib, int index, RGBQUAD * prgb)
{
     PDIBSTRUCT pdib = hdib ;
     HDC        hdcMem ;
     int        iReturn ;

     if (!DibIsValid (hdib))
          return 0 ;

     hdcMem = CreateCompatibleDC (NULL) ;
     SelectObject (hdcMem, pdib->hBitmap) ;
     iReturn = GetDIBColorTable (hdcMem, index, 1, prgb) ;
     DeleteDC (hdcMem) ;
```

(continued)

Figure 16-20. *continued*

```
      return iReturn ? TRUE : FALSE ;
}


/*-------------------------------------------------------
   DibGetColor:  Sets an entry in the DIB color table
   ----------------------------------------------------*/

BOOL DibSetColor (HDIB hdib, int index, RGBQUAD * prgb)
{
    PDIBSTRUCT pdib = hdib ;
    HDC        hdcMem ;
    int        iReturn ;

    if (!DibIsValid (hdib))
        return 0 ;

    hdcMem = CreateCompatibleDC (NULL) ;
    SelectObject (hdcMem, pdib->hBitmap) ;
    iReturn = SetDIBColorTable (hdcMem, index, 1, prgb) ;
    DeleteDC (hdcMem) ;

    return iReturn ? TRUE : FALSE ;
}
```

Most of the functions in this part of DIBHELP.C are self-explanatory. The *DibIsValid* function helps keep the whole system fairly bulletproof. The other functions call *DibIsValid* before attempting to reference information in DIBSTRUCT. All these functions have a first, and usually only, parameter of HDIB, which (as we'll see shortly) is defined in DIBHELP.H as a void pointer. The functions can cast this parameter to a PDIBSTRUCT and then access the fields in the structure.

Note the *DibIsAddressable* function, which returns a BOOL value. This function could also be called the *DibIsNotCompressed* function. The return value indicates whether the individual pixels of the DIB can be addressed.

A collection of functions beginning with *DibInfoHeaderSize* obtain the sizes of various components of the DIB Section *as they would appear* in a packed DIB. As we shall see, these functions help in converting a DIB section to a packed DIB and in saving DIB files. These are followed by a collection of functions that obtain pointers to the various components of the DIB.

Although DIBHELP.C contains a function named *DibInfoHeaderPtr* that obtains a pointer to the BITMAPINFOHEADER structure, there is no function that obtains a pointer to the BITMAPINFO structure—that is, the information structure followed by the DIB color table. That's because when working with DIB sections, applications don't have direct access to a structure of this type. While the BITMAPINFOHEADER structure and the color masks are both available in the DIBSECTION structure, and the pointer to the pixel bits is returned from the *CreateDIBSection* function, the DIB color table is accessible only indirectly, by calling *GetDIBColorTable* and *SetDIBColorTable*. These functions are encapsulated in DIBHELP's *DibGetColor* and *DibSetColor* functions.

Later in DIBHELP.C, a file named *DibCopyToInfo* allocates a pointer to a BITMAPINFO structure and fills it with information, but that's not exactly the same as getting a pointer to an existing structure in memory.

Reading and Writing Pixels

One compelling advantage in maintaining a packed DIB or a DIB section by an application is being able to directly manipulate the pixel bits of the DIB. The second section of DIBHELP.C, shown in Figure 16-21, shows the functions provided for this purpose.

DIBHELP.C (second part)

```
/*-------------------------------------------------------------------
   DibPixelPtr:  Returns a pointer to the pixel at position (x, y)
   ----------------------------------------------------------------*/

BYTE * DibPixelPtr (HDIB hdib, int x, int y)
{
     if (!DibIsAddressable (hdib))
          return NULL ;

     if (x < 0 || x >= DibWidth (hdib) || y < 0 || y >= DibHeight (hdib))
          return NULL ;

     return (((PDIBSTRUCT) hdib)->ppRow)[y] + (x * DibBitCount (hdib) >> 3) ;
}


/*---------------------------------------------------
   DibGetPixel:  Obtains a pixel value at (x, y)
   ------------------------------------------------*/

DWORD DibGetPixel (HDIB hdib, int x, int y)
{
     PBYTE pPixel ;

     if (!(pPixel = DibPixelPtr (hdib, x, y)))
          return 0 ;
```

Figure 16-21. *The second part of the DIBHELP.C file.*

(continued)

Figure 16-21. *continued*

```
    switch (DibBitCount (hdib))
    {
    case  1:  return 0x01 & (* pPixel >> (7 - (x & 7))) ;
    case  4:  return 0x0F & (* pPixel >> (x & 1 ? 0 : 4)) ;
    case  8:  return * pPixel ;
    case 16:  return * (WORD *) pPixel ;
    case 24:  return 0x00FFFFFF & * (DWORD *) pPixel ;
    case 32:  return * (DWORD *) pPixel ;
    }
    return 0 ;
}


/*------------------------------------------------
   DibSetPixel:  Sets a pixel value at (x, y)
  ------------------------------------------------*/

BOOL DibSetPixel (HDIB hdib, int x, int y, DWORD dwPixel)
{
    PBYTE pPixel ;

    if (!(pPixel = DibPixelPtr (hdib, x, y)))
        return FALSE ;

    switch (DibBitCount (hdib))
    {
    case  1:  * pPixel &= ~(1     << (7 - (x & 7))) ;
              * pPixel |= dwPixel << (7 - (x & 7)) ;
              break ;

    case  4:  * pPixel &= 0x0F    << (x & 1 ? 4 : 0) ;
              * pPixel |= dwPixel << (x & 1 ? 0 : 4) ;
              break ;

    case  8:  * pPixel = (BYTE) dwPixel ;
              break ;

    case 16:  * (WORD *) pPixel = (WORD) dwPixel ;
              break ;

    case 24:  * (RGBTRIPLE *) pPixel = * (RGBTRIPLE *) &dwPixel ;
              break ;

    case 32:  * (DWORD *) pPixel = dwPixel ;
              break ;
```

```
    default:
        return FALSE ;
    }
    return TRUE ;
}


/*--------------------------------------------------------
   DibGetPixelColor:  Obtains the pixel color at (x, y)
   ------------------------------------------------------*/

BOOL DibGetPixelColor (HDIB hdib, int x, int y, RGBQUAD * prgb)
{
    DWORD      dwPixel ;
    int        iBitCount ;
    PDIBSTRUCT pdib = hdib ;

        // Get bit count; also use this as a validity check

    if (0 == (iBitCount = DibBitCount (hdib)))
        return FALSE ;

        // Get the pixel value

    dwPixel = DibGetPixel (hdib, x, y) ;

        // If the bit-count is 8 or less, index the color table

    if (iBitCount <= 8)
        return DibGetColor (hdib, (int) dwPixel, prgb) ;

        // If the bit-count is 24, just use the pixel

    else if (iBitCount == 24)
    {
        * (RGBTRIPLE *) prgb = * (RGBTRIPLE *) & dwPixel ;
        prgb->rgbReserved = 0 ;
    }

        // If the bit-count is 32 and the biCompression field is BI_RGB,
        //   just use the pixel

    else if (iBitCount == 32 &&
            pdib->ds.dsBmih.biCompression == BI_RGB)
```

(continued)

Figure 16-21. *continued*

```
    {
         * prgb = * (RGBQUAD *) & dwPixel ;
    }


         // Otherwise, use the mask and shift values
         //   (for best performance, don't use DibMask and DibShift functions)
    else
    {
         prgb->rgbRed   = (BYTE) (((pdib->ds.dsBitfields[0] & dwPixel)
                                  >> pdib->iRShift[0]) << pdib->iLShift[0]) ;

         prgb->rgbGreen = (BYTE) (((pdib->ds.dsBitfields[1] & dwPixel)
                                  >> pdib->iRShift[1]) << pdib->iLShift[1]) ;

         prgb->rgbBlue  = (BYTE) (((pdib->ds.dsBitfields[2] & dwPixel)
                                  >> pdib->iRShift[2]) << pdib->iLShift[2]) ;
    }
    return TRUE ;
}


/*------------------------------------------------------
   DibSetPixelColor:  Sets the pixel color at (x, y)
   ----------------------------------------------------*/

BOOL DibSetPixelColor (HDIB hdib, int x, int y, RGBQUAD * prgb)
{
    DWORD      dwPixel ;
    int        iBitCount ;
    PDIBSTRUCT pdib = hdib ;

         // Don't do this function for DIBs with color tables

    iBitCount = DibBitCount (hdib) ;

    if (iBitCount <= 8)
         return FALSE ;

         // The rest is just the opposite of DibGetPixelColor

    else if (iBitCount == 24)
    {
         * (RGBTRIPLE *) & dwPixel = * (RGBTRIPLE *) prgb ;
         dwPixel &= 0x00FFFFFF ;
    }
```

```
    else if (iBitCount == 32 &&
            pdib->ds.dsBmih.biCompression == BI_RGB)
    {
        * (RGBQUAD *) & dwPixel = * prgb ;
    }

    else
    {
        dwPixel  = (((DWORD) prgb->rgbRed >> pdib->iLShift[0])
                        << pdib->iRShift[0]) ;

        dwPixel |= (((DWORD) prgb->rgbGreen >> pdib->iLShift[1])
                        << pdib->iRShift[1]) ;

        dwPixel |= (((DWORD) prgb->rgbBlue >> pdib->iLShift[2])
                        << pdib->iRShift[2]) ;
    }

    DibSetPixel (hdib, x, y, dwPixel) ;
    return TRUE ;
}
```

This section of DIBHELP.C begins with a *DibPixelPtr* function that obtains a pointer to the byte where a particular pixel is stored (or partially stored). Recall that the *ppRow* field of the DIBSTRUCT structure is a pointer to the addresses of the rows of pixels in the DIB, beginning with the top row. Thus,

```
((PDIBSTRUCT) hdib)->pprow)[0]
```

is a pointer to the leftmost pixel of the top row of the DIB and

```
(((PDIBSTRUCT) hdib)->ppRow)[y] + (x * DibBitCount (hdib) >> 3)
```

is a pointer to the pixel at position (x,y). Notice that the function returns a NULL value if the DIB is not addressable (that is, if it's compressed) or if the x and y parameters to the function are negative or reference an area outside the DIB. This checking slows the function (and any function that relies on *DibPixelPtr*), but I'll describe some faster routines soon.

The *DibGetPixel* and *DibSetPixel* functions that follow in the file make use of *DibPixelPtr*. For 8-bit, 16-bit, 24-bit, and 32-bit DIBs, these functions need only cast the pointer to the proper data size and access the pixel value. For 1-bit and 4-bit DIBs, some masking and shifting is required.

The *DibGetColor* function obtains the pixel color as an RGBQUAD structure. For 1-bit, 4-bit, and 8-bit DIBs, this involves using the pixel value to get a color from the DIB color table. For 16-bit, 24-bit, and 32-bit DIBs, in general the pixel value must be masked and shifted to derive an RGB color. The *DibSetPixel* function is opposite, and it allows setting a pixel value from an RGBQUAD structure. This function is defined only for 16-bit, 24-bit, and 32-bit DIBs.

Creating and Converting

The third and final section of DIBHELP, shown in Figure 16-22, shows how DIB sections are created and how they can be converted to and from packed DIBs.

DIBHELP.C (third part)

```
/*--------------------------------------------------------------
    Calculating shift values from color masks is required by the
    DibCreateFromInfo function.
  --------------------------------------------------------------*/

static int MaskToRShift (DWORD dwMask)
{
    int iShift ;

    if (dwMask == 0)
        return 0 ;

    for (iShift = 0 ; !(dwMask & 1) ; iShift++)
        dwMask >>= 1 ;

    return iShift ;
}

static int MaskToLShift (DWORD dwMask)
{
    int iShift ;

    if (dwMask == 0)
        return 0 ;

    while (!(dwMask & 1))
        dwMask >>= 1 ;

    for (iShift = 0 ; dwMask & 1 ; iShift++)
        dwMask >>= 1 ;

    return 8 - iShift ;
}
```

Figure 16-22. *The third and final part of the DIBHELP.C file.*

```
/*----------------------------------------------------------------------
   DibCreateFromInfo: All DIB creation functions ultimately call this one.
   This function is responsible for calling CreateDIBSection, allocating
   memory for DIBSTRUCT, and setting up the row pointer.
   ----------------------------------------------------------------------*/

HDIB DibCreateFromInfo (BITMAPINFO * pbmi)
{
     BYTE       * pBits ;
     DIBSTRUCT * pdib ;
     HBITMAP     hBitmap ;
     int         i, iRowLength, cy, y ;

     hBitmap = CreateDIBSection (NULL, pbmi, DIB_RGB_COLORS, &pBits, NULL, 0) ;

     if (hBitmap == NULL)
          return NULL ;

     if (NULL == (pdib = malloc (sizeof (DIBSTRUCT))))
     {
          DeleteObject (hBitmap) ;
          return NULL ;
     }

     pdib->iSignature = HDIB_SIGNATURE ;
     pdib->hBitmap    = hBitmap ;
     pdib->pBits      = pBits ;

     GetObject (hBitmap, sizeof (DIBSECTION), &pdib->ds) ;

          // Notice that we can now use the DIB information functions
          //    defined above.

          // If the compression is BI_BITFIELDS, calculate shifts from masks

     if (DibCompression (pdib) == BI_BITFIELDS)
     {
          for (i = 0 ; i < 3 ; i++)
          {
               pdib->iLShift[i] = MaskToLShift (pdib->ds.dsBitfields[i]) ;
               pdib->iRShift[i] = MaskToRShift (pdib->ds.dsBitfields[i]) ;
          }
     }

          // If the compression is BI_RGB, but bit-count is 16 or 32,
          //    set the bitfields and the masks
```

(continued)

Figure 16-22. *continued*

```
    else if (DibCompression (pdib) == BI_RGB)
    {
        if (DibBitCount (pdib) == 16)
        {
            pdib->ds.dsBitfields[0] = 0x00007C00 ;
            pdib->ds.dsBitfields[1] = 0x000003E0 ;
            pdib->ds.dsBitfields[2] = 0x0000001F ;

            pdib->iRShift[0] = 10 ;
            pdib->iRShift[1] =  5 ;
            pdib->iRShift[2] =  0 ;

            pdib->iLShift[0] =  3 ;
            pdib->iLShift[1] =  3 ;
            pdib->iLShift[2] =  3 ;
        }
        else if (DibBitCount (pdib) == 24 || DibBitCount (pdib) == 32)
        {
            pdib->ds.dsBitfields[0] = 0x00FF0000 ;
            pdib->ds.dsBitfields[1] = 0x0000FF00 ;
            pdib->ds.dsBitfields[2] = 0x000000FF ;

            pdib->iRShift[0] = 16 ;
            pdib->iRShift[1] =  8 ;
            pdib->iRShift[2] =  0 ;

            pdib->iLShift[0] =  0 ;
            pdib->iLShift[1] =  0 ;
            pdib->iLShift[2] =  0 ;
        }
    }
        // Allocate an array of pointers to each row in the DIB

cy = DibHeight (pdib) ;

if (NULL == (pdib->ppRow = malloc (cy * sizeof (BYTE *))))
{
    free (pdib) ;
    DeleteObject (hBitmap) ;
    return NULL ;
}

        // Initialize them.

iRowLength = DibRowLength (pdib) ;
```

```
        if (pbmi->bmiHeader.biHeight > 0)        // ie, bottom up
        {
            for (y = 0 ; y < cy ; y++)
                pdib->ppRow[y] = pBits + (cy - y - 1) * iRowLength ;
        }
        else                                     // top down
        {
            for (y = 0 ; y < cy ; y++)
                pdib->ppRow[y] = pBits + y * iRowLength ;
        }
        return pdib ;
}

/*--------------------------------------------------------
    DibDelete:  Frees all memory for the DIB section
  --------------------------------------------------------*/

BOOL DibDelete (HDIB hdib)
{
        DIBSTRUCT * pdib = hdib ;

        if (!DibIsValid (hdib))
            return FALSE ;

        free (pdib->ppRow) ;
        DeleteObject (pdib->hBitmap) ;
        free (pdib) ;
        return TRUE ;
}

/*--------------------------------------------------------
    DibCreate: Creates an HDIB from explicit arguments
  --------------------------------------------------------*/

HDIB DibCreate (int cx, int cy, int cBits, int cColors)
{
        BITMAPINFO * pbmi ;
        DWORD        dwInfoSize ;
        HDIB         hDib ;
        int          cEntries ;

        if (cx <= 0 || cy <= 0 ||
            ((cBits !=  1) && (cBits !=  4) && (cBits !=  8) &&
             (cBits != 16) && (cBits != 24) && (cBits != 32)))
```

(continued)

Figure 16-22. *continued*

```
    {
        return NULL ;
    }

    if (cColors != 0)
        cEntries = cColors ;
    else if (cBits <= 8)
        cEntries = 1 << cBits ;

    dwInfoSize = sizeof (BITMAPINFOHEADER) + (cEntries - 1) * sizeof (RGBQUAD);

    if (NULL == (pbmi = malloc (dwInfoSize)))
    {
        return NULL ;
    }

    ZeroMemory (pbmi, dwInfoSize) ;

    pbmi->bmiHeader.biSize          = sizeof (BITMAPINFOHEADER) ;
    pbmi->bmiHeader.biWidth         = cx ;
    pbmi->bmiHeader.biHeight        = cy ;
    pbmi->bmiHeader.biPlanes        = 1 ;
    pbmi->bmiHeader.biBitCount      = cBits ;
    pbmi->bmiHeader.biCompression   = BI_RGB ;
    pbmi->bmiHeader.biSizeImage     = 0 ;
    pbmi->bmiHeader.biXPelsPerMeter = 0 ;
    pbmi->bmiHeader.biYPelsPerMeter = 0 ;
    pbmi->bmiHeader.biClrUsed       = cColors ;
    pbmi->bmiHeader.biClrImportant  = 0 ;

    hDib = DibCreateFromInfo (pbmi) ;
    free (pbmi) ;

    return hDib ;
}


/*------------------------------------------------------
   DibCopyToInfo:  Builds BITMAPINFO structure.
                   Used by DibCopy and DibCopyToDdb
   ------------------------------------------------------*/

static BITMAPINFO * DibCopyToInfo (HDIB hdib)
{
    BITMAPINFO * pbmi ;
    int          i, iNumColors ;
    RGBQUAD    * prgb ;
```

```
    if (!DibIsValid (hdib))
        return NULL ;

        // Allocate the memory

    if (NULL == (pbmi = malloc (DibInfoSize (hdib))))
        return NULL ;

        // Copy the information header

    CopyMemory (pbmi, DibInfoHeaderPtr (hdib),
                                    sizeof (BITMAPINFOHEADER));

        // Copy the possible color masks

    prgb = (RGBQUAD *) ((BYTE *) pbmi + sizeof (BITMAPINFOHEADER)) ;

    if (DibMaskSize (hdib))
    {
        CopyMemory (prgb, DibMaskPtr (hdib), 3 * sizeof (DWORD)) ;

        prgb = (RGBQUAD *) ((BYTE *) prgb + 3 * sizeof (DWORD)) ;
    }
        // Copy the color table

    iNumColors = DibNumColors (hdib) ;

    for (i = 0 ; i < iNumColors ; i++)
        DibGetColor (hdib, i, prgb + i) ;

    return pbmi ;
}

/*-------------------------------------------------------------------
  DibCopy: Creates a new DIB section from an existing DIB section,
    possibly swapping the DIB width and height.
  -------------------------------------------------------------------*/

HDIB DibCopy (HDIB hdibSrc, BOOL fRotate)
{
    BITMAPINFO * pbmi ;
    BYTE       * pBitsSrc, * pBitsDst ;
    HDIB         hdibDst ;

    if (!DibIsValid (hdibSrc))
        return NULL ;
```

(continued)

Figure 16-22. *continued*

```
     if (NULL == (pbmi = DibCopyToInfo (hdibSrc)))
          return NULL ;

     if (fRotate)
     {
          pbmi->bmiHeader.biWidth  = DibHeight (hdibSrc) ;
          pbmi->bmiHeader.biHeight = DibWidth (hdibSrc) ;
     }

     hdibDst = DibCreateFromInfo (pbmi) ;
     free (pbmi) ;

     if (hdibDst == NULL)
          return NULL ;

          // Copy the bits

     if (!fRotate)
     {
          pBitsSrc = DibBitsPtr (hdibSrc) ;
          pBitsDst = DibBitsPtr (hdibDst) ;

          CopyMemory (pBitsDst, pBitsSrc, DibBitsSize (hdibSrc)) ;
     }
     return hdibDst ;
}

/*-------------------------------------------------------------------
   DibCopyToPackedDib is generally used for saving DIBs and for
   transferring DIBs to the clipboard. In the second case, the second
   argument should be set to TRUE so that the memory is allocated
   with the GMEM_SHARE flag.
   -----------------------------------------------------------------*/

BITMAPINFO * DibCopyToPackedDib (HDIB hdib, BOOL fUseGlobal)
{
     BITMAPINFO * pPackedDib ;
     BYTE       * pBits ;
     DWORD        dwDibSize ;
     HDC          hdcMem ;
     HGLOBAL      hGlobal ;
     int          iNumColors ;
     PDIBSTRUCT   pdib = hdib ;
     RGBQUAD    * prgb ;

     if (!DibIsValid (hdib))
          return NULL ;
```

```
      // Allocate memory for packed DIB

dwDibSize = DibTotalSize (hdib) ;

if (fUseGlobal)
{
     hGlobal = GlobalAlloc (GHND | GMEM_SHARE, dwDibSize) ;
     pPackedDib = GlobalLock (hGlobal) ;
}
else
{
     pPackedDib = malloc (dwDibSize) ;
}

if (pPackedDib == NULL)
     return NULL ;

     // Copy the information header

CopyMemory (pPackedDib, &pdib->ds.dsBmih, sizeof (BITMAPINFOHEADER)) ;

prgb = (RGBQUAD *) ((BYTE *) pPackedDib + sizeof (BITMAPINFOHEADER)) ;

     // Copy the possible color masks

if (pdib->ds.dsBmih.biCompression == BI_BITFIELDS)
{
     CopyMemory (prgb, pdib->ds.dsBitfields, 3 * sizeof (DWORD)) ;

     prgb = (RGBQUAD *) ((BYTE *) prgb + 3 * sizeof (DWORD)) ;
}
     // Copy the color table

if (iNumColors = DibNumColors (hdib))
{
     hdcMem = CreateCompatibleDC (NULL) ;
     SelectObject (hdcMem, pdib->hBitmap) ;
     GetDIBColorTable (hdcMem, 0, iNumColors, prgb) ;
     DeleteDC (hdcMem) ;
}

pBits = (BYTE *) (prgb + iNumColors) ;

     // Copy the bits

CopyMemory (pBits, pdib->pBits, DibBitsSize (pdib)) ;
```

(continued)

Figure 16-22. *continued*

```
            // If last argument is TRUE, unlock global memory block and
            //   cast it to pointer in preparation for return

    if (fUseGlobal)
    {
        GlobalUnlock (hGlobal) ;
        pPackedDib = (BITMAPINFO *) hGlobal ;
    }
    return pPackedDib ;
}


/*-------------------------------------------------------------------
   DibCopyFromPackedDib is generally used for pasting DIBs from the
   clipboard.
   -----------------------------------------------------------------*/

HDIB DibCopyFromPackedDib (BITMAPINFO * pPackedDib)
{
    BYTE      * pBits ;
    DWORD       dwInfoSize, dwMaskSize, dwColorSize ;
    int         iBitCount ;
    PDIBSTRUCT pdib ;

        // Get the size of the information header and do validity check

    dwInfoSize = pPackedDib->bmiHeader.biSize ;

    if (dwInfoSize != sizeof (BITMAPCOREHEADER) &&
        dwInfoSize != sizeof (BITMAPINFOHEADER) &&
        dwInfoSize != sizeof (BITMAPV4HEADER) &&
        dwInfoSize != sizeof (BITMAPV5HEADER))
    {
        return NULL ;
    }
        // Get the possible size of the color masks

    if (dwInfoSize == sizeof (BITMAPINFOHEADER) &&
        pPackedDib->bmiHeader.biCompression == BI_BITFIELDS)
    {
        dwMaskSize = 3 * sizeof (DWORD) ;
    }
    else
    {
        dwMaskSize = 0 ;
    }
        // Get the size of the color table
```

```
    if (dwInfoSize == sizeof (BITMAPCOREHEADER))
    {
        iBitCount = ((BITMAPCOREHEADER *) pPackedDib)->bcBitCount ;

        if (iBitCount <= 8)
        {
            dwColorSize = (1 << iBitCount) * sizeof (RGBTRIPLE) ;
        }
        else
            dwColorSize = 0 ;
    }
    else            // all non-OS/2 compatible DIBs
    {
        if (pPackedDib->bmiHeader.biClrUsed > 0)
        {
            dwColorSize = pPackedDib->bmiHeader.biClrUsed * sizeof (RGBQUAD);
        }
        else if (pPackedDib->bmiHeader.biBitCount <= 8)
        {
            dwColorSize = (1 << pPackedDib->bmiHeader.biBitCount) *
                                            sizeof (RGBQUAD) ;
        }
        else
        {
            dwColorSize = 0 ;
        }
    }
        // Finally, get the pointer to the bits in the packed DIB

    pBits = (BYTE *) pPackedDib + dwInfoSize + dwMaskSize + dwColorSize ;

        // Create the HDIB from the packed-DIB pointer

    pdib = DibCreateFromInfo (pPackedDib) ;

        // Copy the pixel bits

    CopyMemory (pdib->pBits, pBits, DibBitsSize (pdib)) ;

    return pdib ;
}

/*-------------------------------------------------------
   DibFileLoad:  Creates a DIB section from a DIB file
-------------------------------------------------------*/
```

(continued)

Figure 16-22. *continued*

```
HDIB DibFileLoad (const TCHAR * szFileName)
{
     BITMAPFILEHEADER bmfh ;
     BITMAPINFO      * pbmi ;
     BOOL              bSuccess ;
     DWORD             dwInfoSize, dwBitsSize, dwBytesRead ;
     HANDLE            hFile ;
     HDIB              hDib ;

          // Open the file: read access, prohibit write access

     hFile = CreateFile (szFileName, GENERIC_READ, FILE_SHARE_READ, NULL,
                     OPEN_EXISTING, FILE_FLAG_SEQUENTIAL_SCAN, NULL) ;

     if (hFile == INVALID_HANDLE_VALUE)
          return NULL ;

          // Read in the BITMAPFILEHEADER

     bSuccess = ReadFile (hFile, &bmfh, sizeof (BITMAPFILEHEADER),
                     &dwBytesRead, NULL) ;

     if (!bSuccess || (dwBytesRead != sizeof (BITMAPFILEHEADER))
                   || (bmfh.bfType != * (WORD *) "BM"))
     {
          CloseHandle (hFile) ;
          return NULL ;
     }
          // Allocate memory for the information structure & read it in

     dwInfoSize = bmfh.bfOffBits - sizeof (BITMAPFILEHEADER) ;

     if (NULL == (pbmi = malloc (dwInfoSize)))
     {
          CloseHandle (hFile) ;
          return NULL ;
     }

     bSuccess = ReadFile (hFile, pbmi, dwInfoSize, &dwBytesRead, NULL) ;

     if (!bSuccess || (dwBytesRead != dwInfoSize))
     {
          CloseHandle (hFile) ;
          free (pbmi) ;
          return NULL ;
     }
```

```
            // Create the DIB

        hDib = DibCreateFromInfo (pbmi) ;
        free (pbmi) ;

        if (hDib == NULL)
        {
            CloseHandle (hFile) ;
            return NULL ;
        }
            // Read in the bits

        dwBitsSize = bmfh.bfSize - bmfh.bfOffBits ;

        bSuccess = ReadFile (hFile, ((PDIBSTRUCT) hDib)->pBits,
                            dwBitsSize, &dwBytesRead, NULL) ;
        CloseHandle (hFile) ;

        if (!bSuccess || (dwBytesRead != dwBitsSize))
        {
            DibDelete (hDib) ;
            return NULL ;
        }
        return hDib ;
}

/*------------------------------------------------
   DibFileSave:  Saves a DIB section to a file
  ------------------------------------------------*/

BOOL DibFileSave (HDIB hdib, const TCHAR * szFileName)
{
    BITMAPFILEHEADER bmfh ;
    BITMAPINFO      * pbmi ;
    BOOL             bSuccess ;
    DWORD            dwTotalSize, dwBytesWritten ;
    HANDLE           hFile ;

    hFile = CreateFile (szFileName, GENERIC_WRITE, 0, NULL,
                        CREATE_ALWAYS, FILE_ATTRIBUTE_NORMAL, NULL) ;

    if (hFile == INVALID_HANDLE_VALUE)
        return FALSE ;

    dwTotalSize  = DibTotalSize (hdib) ;
```

(continued)

Figure 16-22. *continued*

```
        bmfh.bfType        = * (WORD *) "BM" ;
        bmfh.bfSize        = sizeof (BITMAPFILEHEADER) + dwTotalSize ;
        bmfh.bfReserved1 = 0 ;
        bmfh.bfReserved2 = 0 ;
        bmfh.bfOffBits     = bmfh.bfSize - DibBitsSize (hdib) ;

            // Write the BITMAPFILEHEADER

        bSuccess = WriteFile (hFile, &bmfh, sizeof (BITMAPFILEHEADER),
                              &dwBytesWritten, NULL) ;

        if (!bSuccess || (dwBytesWritten != sizeof (BITMAPFILEHEADER)))
        {
            CloseHandle (hFile) ;
            DeleteFile (szFileName) ;
            return FALSE ;
        }
            // Get entire DIB in packed-DIB format

        if (NULL == (pbmi = DibCopyToPackedDib (hdib, FALSE)))
        {
            CloseHandle (hFile) ;
            DeleteFile (szFileName) ;
            return FALSE ;
        }
            // Write out the packed DIB

        bSuccess = WriteFile (hFile, pbmi, dwTotalSize, &dwBytesWritten, NULL) ;
        CloseHandle (hFile) ;
        free (pbmi) ;

        if (!bSuccess || (dwBytesWritten != dwTotalSize))
        {
            DeleteFile (szFileName) ;
            return FALSE ;
        }
        return TRUE ;
}

/*-----------------------------------------------------
   DibCopyToDdb:  For more efficient screen displays
   -----------------------------------------------------*/
```

```
HBITMAP DibCopyToDdb (HDIB hdib, HWND hwnd, HPALETTE hPalette)
{
     BITMAPINFO * pbmi ;
     HBITMAP      hBitmap ;
     HDC          hdc ;

     if (!DibIsValid (hdib))
          return NULL ;

     if (NULL == (pbmi = DibCopyToInfo (hdib)))
          return NULL ;

     hdc = GetDC (hwnd) ;

     if (hPalette)
     {
          SelectPalette (hdc, hPalette, FALSE) ;
          RealizePalette (hdc) ;
     }

     hBitmap = CreateDIBitmap (hdc, DibInfoHeaderPtr (hdib), CBM_INIT,
                               DibBitsPtr (hdib), pbmi, DIB_RGB_COLORS) ;

     ReleaseDC (hwnd, hdc) ;
     free (pbmi) ;

     return hBitmap ;
}
```

This part of the DIBHELP.C file begins with two little functions that derive left-shift and right-shift values from color masks for 16-bit and 32-bit DIBs. These functions were described in the Color Masking section in Chapter 15.

The *DibCreateFromInfo* function is the only function in DIBHELP that calls *CreateDIBSection* and allocates memory for the DIBSTRUCT structure. All other creation and copy functions go through this function. The single parameter to *DibCreateFromInfo* is a pointer to a BITMAPINFO structure. The color table of this structure must exist, but it doesn't necessarily have to be filled with valid values. After calling *CreateDIBSection*, the function initializes all the fields of the DIBSTRUCT structure. Notice that when setting the values of the *ppRow* field of the DIBSTRUCT structure (the pointers to the DIB row addresses), separate logic exists for bottom-up and top-down DIBs. The first element of *ppRow* is always the top row of the DIB.

DibDelete deletes the bitmap created in *DibCreateFromInfo* and also frees the memory allocated in that function.

DibCreate is probably a more likely function than *DibCreateFromInfo* to be called from application programs. The first three arguments provide the pixel width and height and the number of bits per pixel. The last argument can be set to 0 for a color table of default size or to a nonzero value to indicate a smaller color table than would otherwise be implied by the bit count.

The *DibCopy* function creates a new DIB section from an existing DIB section. It uses the *DibCreateInfo* function that allocates memory for a BITMAPINFO structure and puts all the data into it. A BOOL argument to the *DibCopy* function indicates whether the DIB width and height are to be switched around when creating the new DIB section. We'll see a use for this later.

The *DibCopyToPackedDib* and *DibCopyFromPackedDib* functions are generally used in conjunction with passing DIBs through the clipboard. The *DibFileLoad* function creates a DIB section from a DIB file; *DibFileSave* functions saves to a DIB file.

Finally, the *DibCopyToDdb* function creates a GDI bitmap object from a DIB. Notice that the function requires handles to the current palette and the program's window. The program's window handle is used for getting a device context into which the palette is selected and realized. Only then can the function make a call to *CreateDIBitmap*. This was demonstrated in the SHOWDIB7 program earlier in this chapter.

The DIBHELP Header File and Macros

The DIBHELP.H header file is shown in Figure 16-23.

DIBHELP.H

```
/*-----------------------------------------
   DIBHELP.H header file for DIBHELP.C
 -------------------------------------*/

typedef void * HDIB ;

    // Functions in DIBHELP.C

BOOL DibIsValid (HDIB hdib) ;
HBITMAP DibBitmapHandle (HDIB hdib) ;
int DibWidth (HDIB hdib) ;
int DibHeight (HDIB hdib) ;
int DibBitCount (HDIB hdib) ;
int DibRowLength (HDIB hdib) ;
int DibNumColors (HDIB hdib) ;
```

Figure 16-23. *The DIBHELP.H file.*

```
DWORD DibMask (HDIB hdib, int i) ;
int DibRShift (HDIB hdib, int i) ;
int DibLShift (HDIB hdib, int i) ;
int DibCompression (HDIB hdib) ;
BOOL DibIsAddressable (HDIB hdib) ;
DWORD DibInfoHeaderSize (HDIB hdib) ;
DWORD DibMaskSize (HDIB hdib) ;
DWORD DibColorSize (HDIB hdib) ;
DWORD DibInfoSize (HDIB hdib) ;
DWORD DibBitsSize (HDIB hdib) ;
DWORD DibTotalSize (HDIB hdib) ;
BITMAPINFOHEADER * DibInfoHeaderPtr (HDIB hdib) ;
DWORD * DibMaskPtr (HDIB hdib) ;
void * DibBitsPtr (HDIB hdib) ;
BOOL DibGetColor (HDIB hdib, int index, RGBQUAD * prgb) ;
BOOL DibSetColor (HDIB hdib, int index, RGBQUAD * prgb) ;
BYTE * DibPixelPtr (HDIB hdib, int x, int y) ;
DWORD DibGetPixel (HDIB hdib, int x, int y) ;
BOOL DibSetPixel (HDIB hdib, int x, int y, DWORD dwPixel) ;
BOOL DibGetPixelColor (HDIB hdib, int x, int y, RGBQUAD * prgb) ;
BOOL DibSetPixelColor (HDIB hdib, int x, int y, RGBQUAD * prgb) ;
HDIB DibCreateFromInfo (BITMAPINFO * pbmi) ;
BOOL DibDelete (HDIB hdib) ;
HDIB DibCreate (int cx, int cy, int cBits, int cColors) ;
HDIB DibCopy (HDIB hdibSrc, BOOL fRotate) ;
BITMAPINFO * DibCopyToPackedDib (HDIB hdib, BOOL fUseGlobal) ;
HDIB DibCopyFromPackedDib (BITMAPINFO * pPackedDib) ;
HDIB DibFileLoad (const TCHAR * szFileName) ;
BOOL DibFileSave (HDIB hdib, const TCHAR * szFileName) ;
HBITMAP DibCopyToDdb (HDIB hdib, HWND hwnd, HPALETTE hPalette) ;
HDIB DibCreateFromDdb (HBITMAP hBitmap) ;

/*-------------------------------------------------
   Quickie no-bounds-checked pixel gets and sets
  -------------------------------------------------*/

#define DibPixelPtr1(hdib, x, y)  (((* (PBYTE **) hdib) [y]) + ((x) >> 3))
#define DibPixelPtr4(hdib, x, y)  (((* (PBYTE **) hdib) [y]) + ((x) >> 1))
#define DibPixelPtr8(hdib, x, y)  (((* (PBYTE **) hdib) [y]) + (x)       )
#define DibPixelPtr16(hdib, x, y)  \
                     ((WORD *) (((* (PBYTE **) hdib) [y]) + (x) *  2))

#define DibPixelPtr24(hdib, x, y)  \
                ((RGBTRIPLE *) (((* (PBYTE **) hdib) [y]) + (x) *  3))
```

(continued)

Figure 16-23. *continued*

```
#define DibPixelPtr32(hdib, x, y) \
                    ((DWORD *) (((* (PBYTE **) hdib) [y]) +  (x) *  4))

#define DibGetPixel1(hdib, x, y)   \
           (0x01 & (* DibPixelPtr1 (hdib, x, y) >> (7 - ((x) & 7))))

#define DibGetPixel4(hdib, x, y)   \
           (0x0F & (* DibPixelPtr4 (hdib, x, y) >> ((x) & 1 ? 0 : 4)))

#define DibGetPixel8(hdib, x, y)       (* DibPixelPtr8  (hdib, x, y))
#define DibGetPixel16(hdib, x, y)      (* DibPixelPtr16 (hdib, x, y))
#define DibGetPixel24(hdib, x, y)      (* DibPixelPtr24 (hdib, x, y))
#define DibGetPixel32(hdib, x, y)      (* DibPixelPtr32(hdib, x, y))

#define DibSetPixel1(hdib, x, y, p)                                    \
         ((* DibPixelPtr1 (hdib, x, y) &= ~( 1 << (7 - ((x) & 7)))),   \
          (* DibPixelPtr1 (hdib, x, y) |=  ((p) << (7 - ((x) & 7)))))

#define DibSetPixel4(hdib, x, y, p)                                    \
         ((* DibPixelPtr4 (hdib, x, y) &= (0x0F << ((x) & 1 ? 4 : 0))),  \
          (* DibPixelPtr4 (hdib, x, y) |= ((p)  << ((x) & 1 ? 0 : 4))))

#define DibSetPixel8(hdib, x, y, p) (* DibPixelPtr8 (hdib, x, y) = p)
#define DibSetPixel16(hdib, x, y, p) (* DibPixelPtr16 (hdib, x, y) = p)
#define DibSetPixel24(hdib, x, y, p) (* DibPixelPtr24 (hdib, x, y) = p)
#define DibSetPixel32(hdib, x, y, p) (* DibPixelPtr32 (hdib, x, y) = p)
```

This header file defines the HDIB handle as a void pointer. An application really shouldn't know about the internal structure of the structure to which HDIB points. The header file also includes declarations of all the functions in DIBHELP.C. And then there are the macros—the very special macros.

If you look back at the *DibPixelPtr*, *DibGetPixel*, and *DibSetPixel* functions in DIBHELP.C and try to improve their performance, you'll see a couple of possible solutions. First, you can remove all the bulletproofing and trust that an application will not call the function with invalid arguments. You can also remove some of the function calls, such as *DibBitCount*, and obtain that information directly by using the pointer to the DIBSTRUCT structure instead.

A less obvious way to improve performance is to do away with all the logic involving the number of bits per pixel and have separate functions for each type of DIB—for example, *DibGetPixel1*, *DibGetPixel4*, *DibGetPixel8*, and so forth. The next optimization is to remove the function call entirely and incorporate the logic in inline functions or macros.

DIBHELP.H takes the macro approach. It provides three sets of macros based on the *DibPixelPtr*, *DibGetPixel*, and *DibSetPixel* functions. These macros are all specific to a particular bit count.

The DIBBLE Program

The DIBBLE program shown in Figure 16-24 puts the DIBHELP functions and macros to work. Although DIBBLE is the longest program in this book, it is really only a crude sampler of some jobs that might be found in simple digital image-processing programs. One obvious improvement to DIBBLE would be to convert it to a multiple document interface (MDI), but we won't learn how to do that until Chapter 19.

DIBBLE.C

```
/*------------------------------------------
   DIBBLE.C -- Bitmap and Palette Program
               (c) Charles Petzold, 1998
   ---------------------------------------*/

#include <windows.h>
#include "dibhelp.h"
#include "dibpal.h"
#include "dibconv.h"
#include "resource.h"

#define WM_USER_SETSCROLLS    (WM_USER + 1)
#define WM_USER_DELETEDIB     (WM_USER + 2)
#define WM_USER_DELETEPAL     (WM_USER + 3)
#define WM_USER_CREATEPAL     (WM_USER + 4)

LRESULT CALLBACK WndProc (HWND, UINT, WPARAM, LPARAM) ;

TCHAR szAppName[] = TEXT ("Dibble") ;

int WINAPI WinMain (HINSTANCE hInstance, HINSTANCE hPrevInstance,
                    PSTR szCmdLine, int iCmdShow)
{
    HACCEL    hAccel ;
    HWND      hwnd ;
    MSG       msg ;
    WNDCLASS  wndclass ;

    wndclass.style          = CS_HREDRAW | CS_VREDRAW ;
    wndclass.lpfnWndProc    = WndProc ;
    wndclass.cbClsExtra     = 0 ;
    wndclass.cbWndExtra     = 0 ;
    wndclass.hInstance      = hInstance ;
    wndclass.hIcon          = LoadIcon (NULL, IDI_APPLICATION) ;
    wndclass.hCursor        = LoadCursor (NULL, IDC_ARROW) ;
```

Figure 16-24. *The DIBBLE program.*

(continued)

Figure 16-24. *continued*

```
     wndclass.hbrBackground = (HBRUSH) GetStockObject (WHITE_BRUSH) ;
     wndclass.lpszMenuName  = szAppName ;
     wndclass.lpszClassName = szAppName ;

     if (!RegisterClass (&wndclass))
     {
          MessageBox (NULL, TEXT ("This program requires Windows NT!"),
                      szAppName, MB_ICONERROR) ;
          return 0 ;
     }

     hwnd = CreateWindow (szAppName, szAppName,
                          WS_OVERLAPPEDWINDOW | WM_VSCROLL | WM_HSCROLL,
                          CW_USEDEFAULT, CW_USEDEFAULT,
                          CW_USEDEFAULT, CW_USEDEFAULT,
                          NULL, NULL, hInstance, NULL) ;

     ShowWindow (hwnd, iCmdShow) ;
     UpdateWindow (hwnd) ;

     hAccel = LoadAccelerators (hInstance, szAppName) ;

     while (GetMessage (&msg, NULL, 0, 0))
     {
          if (!TranslateAccelerator (hwnd, hAccel, &msg))
          {
               TranslateMessage (&msg) ;
               DispatchMessage (&msg) ;
          }
     }
     return msg.wParam ;
}

/*-----------------------------------------------------------------
   DisplayDib: Displays or prints DIB actual size or stretched
               depending on menu selection
   -----------------------------------------------------------------*/

int DisplayDib (HDC hdc, HBITMAP hBitmap, int x, int y,
                int cxClient, int cyClient,
                WORD wShow, BOOL fHalftonePalette)
{
     BITMAP bitmap ;
     HDC    hdcMem ;
     int    cxBitmap, cyBitmap, iReturn ;
```

```
GetObject (hBitmap, sizeof (BITMAP), &bitmap) ;
cxBitmap = bitmap.bmWidth ;
cyBitmap = bitmap.bmHeight ;

SaveDC (hdc) ;

if (fHalftonePalette)
     SetStretchBltMode (hdc, HALFTONE) ;
else
     SetStretchBltMode (hdc, COLORONCOLOR) ;

hdcMem = CreateCompatibleDC (hdc) ;
SelectObject (hdcMem, hBitmap) ;

switch (wShow)
{
case IDM_SHOW_NORMAL:
     if (fHalftonePalette)
          iReturn = StretchBlt (hdc,    0, 0,
                                         min (cxClient, cxBitmap - x),
                                         min (cyClient, cyBitmap - y),
                                hdcMem, x, y,
                                         min (cxClient, cxBitmap - x),
                                         min (cyClient, cyBitmap - y),
                                SRCCOPY);
     else
          iReturn = BitBlt (hdc,    0, 0,
                                    min (cxClient, cxBitmap - x),
                                    min (cyClient, cyBitmap - y),
                            hdcMem, x, y, SRCCOPY) ;

     break ;

case IDM_SHOW_CENTER:
     if (fHalftonePalette)
          iReturn = StretchBlt (hdc, (cxClient - cxBitmap) / 2,
                                      (cyClient - cyBitmap) / 2,
                                      cxBitmap, cyBitmap,
                                hdcMem, 0, 0, cxBitmap, cyBitmap, SRCCOPY);
     else
          iReturn = BitBlt (hdc, (cxClient - cxBitmap) / 2,
                                 (cyClient - cyBitmap) / 2,
                                 cxBitmap, cyBitmap,
                            hdcMem, 0, 0, SRCCOPY) ;
     break ;
```

(continued)

Figure 16-24. *continued*

```
        case IDM_SHOW_STRETCH:
             iReturn = StretchBlt (hdc,     0, 0, cxClient, cyClient,
                                   hdcMem, 0, 0, cxBitmap, cyBitmap, SRCCOPY) ;
             break ;

        case IDM_SHOW_ISOSTRETCH:
             SetMapMode (hdc, MM_ISOTROPIC) ;
             SetWindowExtEx (hdc, cxBitmap, cyBitmap, NULL) ;
             SetViewportExtEx (hdc, cxClient, cyClient, NULL) ;
             SetWindowOrgEx (hdc, cxBitmap / 2, cyBitmap / 2, NULL) ;
             SetViewportOrgEx (hdc, cxClient / 2, cyClient / 2, NULL) ;

             iReturn = StretchBlt (hdc,     0, 0, cxBitmap, cyBitmap,
                                   hdcMem, 0, 0, cxBitmap, cyBitmap, SRCCOPY) ;
             break ;
        }
     DeleteDC (hdcMem) ;
     RestoreDC (hdc, -1) ;
     return iReturn ;
}

/*-------------------------------------------------------------------------
   DibFlipHorizontal: Calls non-optimized DibSetPixel and DibGetPixel
   ---------------------------------------------------------------------*/

HDIB DibFlipHorizontal (HDIB hdibSrc)
{
     HDIB hdibDst ;
     int  cx, cy, x, y ;

     if (!DibIsAddressable (hdibSrc))
         return NULL ;

     if (NULL == (hdibDst = DibCopy (hdibSrc, FALSE)))
         return NULL ;

     cx = DibWidth  (hdibSrc) ;
     cy = DibHeight (hdibSrc) ;

     for (x = 0 ; x < cx ; x++)
     for (y = 0 ; y < cy ; y++)
     {
         DibSetPixel (hdibDst, x, cy - 1 - y, DibGetPixel (hdibSrc, x, y)) ;
     }
```

```
     return hdibDst ;
}

/*-------------------------------------------------------------
   DibRotateRight: Calls optimized DibSetPixelx and DibGetPixelx
   -------------------------------------------------------------*/

HDIB DibRotateRight (HDIB hdibSrc)
{
     HDIB hdibDst ;
     int  cx, cy, x, y ;

     if (!DibIsAddressable (hdibSrc))
          return NULL ;

     if (NULL == (hdibDst = DibCopy (hdibSrc, TRUE)))
          return NULL ;

     cx = DibWidth (hdibSrc) ;
     cy = DibHeight (hdibSrc) ;

     switch (DibBitCount (hdibSrc))
     {
     case  1:
          for (x = 0 ; x < cx ; x++)
          for (y = 0 ; y < cy ; y++)
               DibSetPixel1 (hdibDst, cy - y - 1, x,
                    DibGetPixel1 (hdibSrc, x, y)) ;
          break ;

     case  4:
          for (x = 0 ; x < cx ; x++)
          for (y = 0 ; y < cy ; y++)
               DibSetPixel4 (hdibDst, cy - y - 1, x,
                    DibGetPixel4 (hdibSrc, x, y)) ;
          break ;

     case  8:
          for (x = 0 ; x < cx ; x++)
          for (y = 0 ; y < cy ; y++)
               DibSetPixel8 (hdibDst, cy - y - 1, x,
                    DibGetPixel8 (hdibSrc, x, y)) ;
          break ;
```

(continued)

Figure 16-24. *continued*

```
    case 16:
        for (x = 0 ; x < cx ; x++)
        for (y = 0 ; y < cy ; y++)
            DibSetPixel16 (hdibDst, cy - y - 1, x,
                DibGetPixel16 (hdibSrc, x, y)) ;
        break ;

    case 24:
        for (x = 0 ; x < cx ; x++)
        for (y = 0 ; y < cy ; y++)
            DibSetPixel24 (hdibDst, cy - y - 1, x,
                DibGetPixel24 (hdibSrc, x, y)) ;
        break ;

    case 32:
        for (x = 0 ; x < cx ; x++)
        for (y = 0 ; y < cy ; y++)
            DibSetPixel32 (hdibDst, cy - y - 1, x,
                DibGetPixel32 (hdibSrc, x, y)) ;
        break ;
    }
    return hdibDst ;
}

/*-----------------------------------------------------------
   PaletteMenu: Uncheck and check menu item on palette menu
  -----------------------------------------------------------*/

void PaletteMenu (HMENU hMenu, WORD wItemNew)
{
    static WORD wItem = IDM_PAL_NONE ;

    CheckMenuItem (hMenu, wItem, MF_UNCHECKED) ;
    wItem = wItemNew ;
    CheckMenuItem (hMenu, wItem, MF_CHECKED) ;
}

LRESULT CALLBACK WndProc (HWND hwnd, UINT message, WPARAM wParam, LPARAM lParam)
{
    static BOOL         fHalftonePalette ;
    static DOCINFO      di = { sizeof (DOCINFO), TEXT ("Dibble: Printing") } ;
    static HBITMAP      hBitmap ;
    static HDIB         hdib ;
    static HMENU        hMenu ;
    static HPALETTE     hPalette ;
    static int          cxClient, cyClient, iVscroll, iHscroll ;
```

```
static OPENFILENAME ofn ;
static PRINTDLG     printdlg = { sizeof (PRINTDLG) } ;
static TCHAR        szFileName [MAX_PATH], szTitleName [MAX_PATH] ;
static TCHAR        szFilter[] = TEXT ("Bitmap Files (*.BMP)\0*.bmp\0")
                                 TEXT ("All Files (*.*)\0*.*\0\0") ;
static TCHAR        * szCompression[] = {
                        TEXT ("BI_RGB"), TEXT ("BI_RLE8"), TEXT ("BI_RLE4"),
                        TEXT ("BI_BITFIELDS"), TEXT ("Unknown") } ;
static WORD         wShow = IDM_SHOW_NORMAL ;
BOOL               fSuccess ;
BYTE               * pGlobal ;
HDC                hdc, hdcPrn ;
HGLOBAL            hGlobal ;
HDIB               hdibNew ;
int                iEnable, cxPage, cyPage, iConvert ;
PAINTSTRUCT        ps ;
SCROLLINFO         si ;
TCHAR              szBuffer [256] ;

switch (message)
{
case WM_CREATE:

        // Save the menu handle in a static variable

    hMenu = GetMenu (hwnd) ;

        // Initialize the OPENFILENAME structure for the File Open
        //   and File Save dialog boxes.

    ofn.lStructSize       = sizeof (OPENFILENAME) ;
    ofn.hwndOwner         = hwnd ;
    ofn.hInstance         = NULL ;
    ofn.lpstrFilter       = szFilter ;
    ofn.lpstrCustomFilter = NULL ;
    ofn.nMaxCustFilter    = 0 ;
    ofn.nFilterIndex      = 0 ;
    ofn.lpstrFile         = szFileName ;
    ofn.nMaxFile          = MAX_PATH ;
    ofn.lpstrFileTitle    = szTitleName ;
    ofn.nMaxFileTitle     = MAX_PATH ;
    ofn.lpstrInitialDir   = NULL ;
    ofn.lpstrTitle        = NULL ;
    ofn.Flags             = OFN_OVERWRITEPROMPT ;
    ofn.nFileOffset       = 0 ;
    ofn.nFileExtension    = 0 ;
```

(continued)

Figure 16-24. *continued*

```
        ofn.lpstrDefExt        = TEXT ("bmp") ;
        ofn.lCustData          = 0 ;
        ofn.lpfnHook           = NULL ;
        ofn.lpTemplateName     = NULL ;
        return 0 ;

case WM_DISPLAYCHANGE:
     SendMessage (hwnd, WM_USER_DELETEPAL, 0, 0) ;
     SendMessage (hwnd, WM_USER_CREATEPAL, TRUE, 0) ;
     return 0 ;

case WM_SIZE:
          // Save the client area width and height in static variables.

     cxClient = LOWORD (lParam) ;
     cyClient = HIWORD (lParam) ;

     wParam = FALSE ;

                                        // fall through

          // WM_USER_SETSCROLLS:  Programmer-defined Message!
          // Set the scroll bars. If the display mode is not normal,
          //   make them invisible. If wParam is TRUE, reset the
          //   scroll bar position.

case WM_USER_SETSCROLLS:
     if (hdib == NULL || wShow != IDM_SHOW_NORMAL)
     {
          si.cbSize = sizeof (SCROLLINFO) ;
          si.fMask  = SIF_RANGE ;
          si.nMin   = 0 ;
          si.nMax   = 0 ;
          SetScrollInfo (hwnd, SB_VERT, &si, TRUE) ;
          SetScrollInfo (hwnd, SB_HORZ, &si, TRUE) ;
     }
     else
     {
               // First the vertical scroll

          si.cbSize = sizeof (SCROLLINFO) ;
          si.fMask  = SIF_ALL ;

          GetScrollInfo (hwnd, SB_VERT, &si) ;
          si.nMin   = 0 ;
          si.nMax   = DibHeight (hdib) ;
          si.nPage  = cyClient ;
```

```
            if ((BOOL) wParam)
                 si.nPos = 0 ;

            SetScrollInfo (hwnd, SB_VERT, &si, TRUE) ;
            GetScrollInfo (hwnd, SB_VERT, &si) ;

            iVscroll = si.nPos ;

                 // Then the horizontal scroll

            GetScrollInfo (hwnd, SB_HORZ, &si) ;
            si.nMin  = 0 ;
            si.nMax  = DibWidth (hdib) ;
            si.nPage = cxClient ;

            if ((BOOL) wParam)
                 si.nPos = 0 ;

            SetScrollInfo (hwnd, SB_HORZ, &si, TRUE) ;
            GetScrollInfo (hwnd, SB_HORZ, &si) ;

            iHscroll = si.nPos ;
       }
       return 0 ;

       // WM_VSCROLL: Vertically scroll the DIB

  case WM_VSCROLL:
       si.cbSize = sizeof (SCROLLINFO) ;
       si.fMask  = SIF_ALL ;
       GetScrollInfo (hwnd, SB_VERT, &si) ;

       iVscroll = si.nPos ;

       switch (LOWORD (wParam))
       {
       case SB_LINEUP:     si.nPos -= 1 ;            break ;
       case SB_LINEDOWN:   si.nPos += 1 ;            break ;
       case SB_PAGEUP:     si.nPos -= si.nPage ;     break ;
       case SB_PAGEDOWN:   si.nPos += si.nPage ;     break ;
       case SB_THUMBTRACK: si.nPos  = si.nTrackPos ; break ;
       default:                                      break ;
       }
       si.fMask = SIF_POS ;
       SetScrollInfo (hwnd, SB_VERT, &si, TRUE) ;
       GetScrollInfo (hwnd, SB_VERT, &si) ;
```

(continued)

Figure 16-24. *continued*

```
            if (si.nPos != iVscroll)
            {
                ScrollWindow (hwnd, 0, iVscroll - si.nPos, NULL, NULL) ;
                iVscroll = si.nPos ;
                UpdateWindow (hwnd) ;
            }
            return 0 ;

            // WM_HSCROLL: Horizontally scroll the DIB

      case WM_HSCROLL:
            si.cbSize = sizeof (SCROLLINFO) ;
            si.fMask  = SIF_ALL ;
            GetScrollInfo (hwnd, SB_HORZ, &si) ;

            iHscroll = si.nPos ;

            switch (LOWORD (wParam))
            {
            case SB_LINELEFT:    si.nPos -= 1 ;            break ;
            case SB_LINERIGHT:   si.nPos += 1 ;            break ;
            case SB_PAGELEFT:    si.nPos -= si.nPage ;     break ;
            case SB_PAGERIGHT:   si.nPos += si.nPage ;     break ;
            case SB_THUMBTRACK:  si.nPos  = si.nTrackPos ; break ;
            default:                                       break ;
            }

            si.fMask = SIF_POS ;
            SetScrollInfo (hwnd, SB_HORZ, &si, TRUE) ;
            GetScrollInfo (hwnd, SB_HORZ, &si) ;

            if (si.nPos != iHscroll)
            {
                ScrollWindow (hwnd, iHscroll - si.nPos, 0, NULL, NULL) ;
                iHscroll = si.nPos ;
                UpdateWindow (hwnd) ;
            }
            return 0 ;

            // WM_INITMENUPOPUP:  Enable or Gray menu items

      case WM_INITMENUPOPUP:
            if (hdib)
                iEnable = MF_ENABLED ;
            else
                iEnable = MF_GRAYED ;
```

```
EnableMenuItem (hMenu, IDM_FILE_SAVE,       iEnable) ;
EnableMenuItem (hMenu, IDM_FILE_PRINT,      iEnable) ;
EnableMenuItem (hMenu, IDM_FILE_PROPERTIES, iEnable) ;
EnableMenuItem (hMenu, IDM_EDIT_CUT,        iEnable) ;
EnableMenuItem (hMenu, IDM_EDIT_COPY,       iEnable) ;
EnableMenuItem (hMenu, IDM_EDIT_DELETE,     iEnable) ;

if (DibIsAddressable (hdib))
    iEnable = MF_ENABLED ;
else
    iEnable = MF_GRAYED ;

EnableMenuItem (hMenu, IDM_EDIT_ROTATE,  iEnable) ;
EnableMenuItem (hMenu, IDM_EDIT_FLIP,    iEnable) ;
EnableMenuItem (hMenu, IDM_CONVERT_01,   iEnable) ;
EnableMenuItem (hMenu, IDM_CONVERT_04,   iEnable) ;
EnableMenuItem (hMenu, IDM_CONVERT_08,   iEnable) ;
EnableMenuItem (hMenu, IDM_CONVERT_16,   iEnable) ;
EnableMenuItem (hMenu, IDM_CONVERT_24,   iEnable) ;
EnableMenuItem (hMenu, IDM_CONVERT_32,   iEnable) ;

switch (DibBitCount (hdib))
{
case  1: EnableMenuItem (hMenu, IDM_CONVERT_01, MF_GRAYED) ; break ;
case  4: EnableMenuItem (hMenu, IDM_CONVERT_04, MF_GRAYED) ; break ;
case  8: EnableMenuItem (hMenu, IDM_CONVERT_08, MF_GRAYED) ; break ;
case 16: EnableMenuItem (hMenu, IDM_CONVERT_16, MF_GRAYED) ; break ;
case 24: EnableMenuItem (hMenu, IDM_CONVERT_24, MF_GRAYED) ; break ;
case 32: EnableMenuItem (hMenu, IDM_CONVERT_32, MF_GRAYED) ; break ;
}

if (hdib && DibColorSize (hdib) > 0)
    iEnable = MF_ENABLED ;
else
    iEnable = MF_GRAYED ;

EnableMenuItem (hMenu, IDM_PAL_DIBTABLE,    iEnable) ;
if (DibIsAddressable (hdib) && DibBitCount (hdib) > 8)
    iEnable = MF_ENABLED ;
else
    iEnable = MF_GRAYED ;

EnableMenuItem (hMenu, IDM_PAL_OPT_POP4,   iEnable) ;
EnableMenuItem (hMenu, IDM_PAL_OPT_POP5,   iEnable) ;
EnableMenuItem (hMenu, IDM_PAL_OPT_POP6,   iEnable) ;
EnableMenuItem (hMenu, IDM_PAL_OPT_MEDCUT, iEnable) ;
```

(continued)

Figure 16-24. *continued*

```
        EnableMenuItem (hMenu, IDM_EDIT_PASTE,
            IsClipboardFormatAvailable (CF_DIB) ? MF_ENABLED : MF_GRAYED) ;

        return 0 ;

        // WM_COMMAND:  Process all menu commands.

    case WM_COMMAND:
        iConvert = 0 ;

        switch (LOWORD (wParam))
        {
        case IDM_FILE_OPEN:

                // Show the File Open dialog box

            if (!GetOpenFileName (&ofn))
                return 0 ;

                // If there's an existing DIB and palette, delete them

            SendMessage (hwnd, WM_USER_DELETEDIB, 0, 0) ;

                // Load the DIB into memory

            SetCursor (LoadCursor (NULL, IDC_WAIT)) ;
            ShowCursor (TRUE) ;

            hdib = DibFileLoad (szFileName) ;

            ShowCursor (FALSE) ;
            SetCursor (LoadCursor (NULL, IDC_ARROW)) ;

                // Reset the scroll bars

            SendMessage (hwnd, WM_USER_SETSCROLLS, TRUE, 0) ;

                // Create the palette and DDB

            SendMessage (hwnd, WM_USER_CREATEPAL, TRUE, 0) ;

            if (!hdib)
            {
                MessageBox (hwnd, TEXT ("Cannot load DIB file!"),
                        szAppName, MB_OK | MB_ICONEXCLAMATION) ;
            }
```

```
         InvalidateRect (hwnd, NULL, TRUE) ;
         return 0 ;

case IDM_FILE_SAVE:

              // Show the File Save dialog box

         if (!GetSaveFileName (&ofn))
              return 0 ;

              // Save the DIB to memory

         SetCursor (LoadCursor (NULL, IDC_WAIT)) ;
         ShowCursor (TRUE) ;

         fSuccess = DibFileSave (hdib, szFileName) ;

         ShowCursor (FALSE) ;
         SetCursor (LoadCursor (NULL, IDC_ARROW)) ;

         if (!fSuccess)
              MessageBox (hwnd, TEXT ("Cannot save DIB file!"),
                        szAppName, MB_OK | MB_ICONEXCLAMATION) ;
         return 0 ;

case IDM_FILE_PRINT:
         if (!hdib)
              return 0 ;

              // Get printer DC

         printdlg.Flags = PD_RETURNDC | PD_NOPAGENUMS | PD_NOSELECTION ;

         if (!PrintDlg (&printdlg))
              return 0 ;

         if (NULL == (hdcPrn = printdlg.hDC))
         {
              MessageBox (hwnd, TEXT ("Cannot obtain Printer DC"),
                        szAppName, MB_ICONEXCLAMATION | MB_OK) ;
              return 0 ;
         }
              // Check if the printer can print bitmaps

         if (!(RC_BITBLT & GetDeviceCaps (hdcPrn, RASTERCAPS)))
         {
              DeleteDC (hdcPrn) ;
```

(continued)

Figure 16-24. *continued*

```
                MessageBox (hwnd, TEXT ("Printer cannot print bitmaps"),
                       szAppName, MB_ICONEXCLAMATION | MB_OK) ;
          return 0 ;
     }
          // Get size of printable area of page

     cxPage = GetDeviceCaps (hdcPrn, HORZRES) ;
     cyPage = GetDeviceCaps (hdcPrn, VERTRES) ;

     fSuccess = FALSE ;

          // Send the DIB to the printer

     SetCursor (LoadCursor (NULL, IDC_WAIT)) ;
     ShowCursor (TRUE) ;

     if ((StartDoc (hdcPrn, &di) > 0) && (StartPage (hdcPrn) > 0))
     {
          DisplayDib (hdcPrn, DibBitmapHandle (hdib), 0, 0,
                    cxPage, cyPage, wShow, FALSE) ;

          if (EndPage (hdcPrn) > 0)
          {
               fSuccess = TRUE ;
               EndDoc (hdcPrn) ;
          }
     }
     ShowCursor (FALSE) ;
     SetCursor (LoadCursor (NULL, IDC_ARROW)) ;

     DeleteDC (hdcPrn) ;

     if (!fSuccess)
          MessageBox (hwnd, TEXT ("Could not print bitmap"),
                    szAppName, MB_ICONEXCLAMATION | MB_OK) ;
     return 0 ;

case IDM_FILE_PROPERTIES:
     if (!hdib)
          return 0 ;

     wsprintf (szBuffer, TEXT ("Pixel width:\t%i\n")
                    TEXT ("Pixel height:\t%i\n")
                    TEXT ("Bits per pixel:\t%i\n")
                    TEXT ("Number of colors:\t%i\n")
                    TEXT ("Compression:\t%s\n"),
               DibWidth (hdib), DibHeight (hdib),
```

```
                    DibBitCount (hdib), DibNumColors (hdib),
                    szCompression [min (3, DibCompression (hdib))]) ;

     MessageBox (hwnd, szBuffer, szAppName,
                 MB_ICONEXCLAMATION | MB_OK) ;
     return 0 ;

case IDM_APP_EXIT:
     SendMessage (hwnd, WM_CLOSE, 0, 0) ;
     return 0 ;

case IDM_EDIT_COPY:
case IDM_EDIT_CUT:
     if (!(hGlobal = DibCopyToPackedDib (hdib, TRUE)))
          return 0 ;

     OpenClipboard (hwnd) ;
     EmptyClipboard () ;
     SetClipboardData (CF_DIB, hGlobal) ;
     CloseClipboard () ;

     if (LOWORD (wParam) == IDM_EDIT_COPY)
          return 0 ;
                           // fall through for IDM_EDIT_CUT
case IDM_EDIT_DELETE:
     SendMessage (hwnd, WM_USER_DELETEDIB, 0, 0) ;
     InvalidateRect (hwnd, NULL, TRUE) ;
     return 0 ;

case IDM_EDIT_PASTE:
     OpenClipboard (hwnd) ;

     hGlobal = GetClipboardData (CF_DIB) ;
     pGlobal = GlobalLock (hGlobal) ;

          // If there's an existing DIB and palette, delete them.
          // Then convert the packed DIB to an HDIB.

     if (pGlobal)
     {
          SendMessage (hwnd, WM_USER_DELETEDIB, 0, 0) ;
          hdib = DibCopyFromPackedDib ((BITMAPINFO *) pGlobal) ;
          SendMessage (hwnd, WM_USER_CREATEPAL, TRUE, 0) ;
     }

     GlobalUnlock (hGlobal) ;
     CloseClipboard () ;
```

(continued)

Figure 16-24. *continued*

```
          // Reset the scroll bars

     SendMessage (hwnd, WM_USER_SETSCROLLS, TRUE, 0) ;
     InvalidateRect (hwnd, NULL, TRUE) ;
     return 0 ;

case IDM_EDIT_ROTATE:
     if (hdibNew = DibRotateRight (hdib))
     {
          DibDelete (hdib) ;
          DeleteObject (hBitmap) ;
          hdib = hdibNew ;
          hBitmap = DibCopyToDdb (hdib, hwnd, hPalette) ;
          SendMessage (hwnd, WM_USER_SETSCROLLS, TRUE, 0) ;
          InvalidateRect (hwnd, NULL, TRUE) ;
     }
     else
     {
          MessageBox (hwnd, TEXT ("Not enough memory"),
                      szAppName, MB_OK | MB_ICONEXCLAMATION) ;
     }
     return 0 ;

case IDM_EDIT_FLIP:
     if (hdibNew = DibFlipHorizontal (hdib))
     {
          DibDelete (hdib) ;
          DeleteObject (hBitmap) ;
          hdib = hdibNew ;
          hBitmap = DibCopyToDdb (hdib, hwnd, hPalette) ;
          InvalidateRect (hwnd, NULL, TRUE) ;
     }
     else
     {
          MessageBox (hwnd, TEXT ("Not enough memory"),
                      szAppName, MB_OK | MB_ICONEXCLAMATION) ;
     }
     return 0 ;

case IDM_SHOW_NORMAL:
case IDM_SHOW_CENTER:
case IDM_SHOW_STRETCH:
case IDM_SHOW_ISOSTRETCH:
     CheckMenuItem (hMenu, wShow, MF_UNCHECKED) ;
     wShow = LOWORD (wParam) ;
     CheckMenuItem (hMenu, wShow, MF_CHECKED) ;
```

```
          SendMessage (hwnd, WM_USER_SETSCROLLS, FALSE, 0) ;

          InvalidateRect (hwnd, NULL, TRUE) ;
          return 0 ;

case IDM_CONVERT_32:  iConvert += 8 ;
case IDM_CONVERT_24:  iConvert += 8 ;
case IDM_CONVERT_16:  iConvert += 8 ;
case IDM_CONVERT_08:  iConvert += 4 ;
case IDM_CONVERT_04:  iConvert += 3 ;
case IDM_CONVERT_01:  iConvert += 1 ;
     SetCursor (LoadCursor (NULL, IDC_WAIT)) ;
     ShowCursor (TRUE) ;

     hdibNew = DibConvert (hdib, iConvert) ;

     ShowCursor (FALSE) ;
     SetCursor (LoadCursor (NULL, IDC_ARROW)) ;

     if (hdibNew)
     {
          SendMessage (hwnd, WM_USER_DELETEDIB, 0, 0) ;
          hdib = hdibNew ;
          SendMessage (hwnd, WM_USER_CREATEPAL, TRUE, 0) ;
          InvalidateRect (hwnd, NULL, TRUE) ;
     }
     else
     {
          MessageBox (hwnd, TEXT ("Not enough memory"),
                      szAppName, MB_OK | MB_ICONEXCLAMATION) ;
     }
     return 0 ;

case IDM_APP_ABOUT:
     MessageBox (hwnd, TEXT ("Dibble (c) Charles Petzold, 1998"),
                 szAppName, MB_OK | MB_ICONEXCLAMATION) ;
     return 0 ;
}

     // All the other WM_COMMAND messages are from the palette
     //   items. Any existing palette is deleted, and the cursor
     //   is set to the hourglass.

SendMessage (hwnd, WM_USER_DELETEPAL, 0, 0) ;
SetCursor (LoadCursor (NULL, IDC_WAIT)) ;
ShowCursor (TRUE) ;
```

(continued)

Figure 16-24. *continued*

```
            // Notice that all messages for palette items are ended
            //   with break rather than return. This is to allow
            //   additional processing later on.

        switch (LOWORD (wParam))
        {
        case IDM_PAL_DIBTABLE:
             hPalette = DibPalDibTable (hdib) ;
             break ;

        case IDM_PAL_HALFTONE:
             hdc = GetDC (hwnd) ;

             if (hPalette = CreateHalftonePalette (hdc))
                  fHalftonePalette = TRUE ;

             ReleaseDC (hwnd, hdc) ;
             break ;

        case IDM_PAL_ALLPURPOSE:
             hPalette = DibPalAllPurpose () ;
             break ;

        case IDM_PAL_GRAY2:    hPalette = DibPalUniformGrays (  2) ; break ;
        case IDM_PAL_GRAY3:    hPalette = DibPalUniformGrays (  3) ; break ;
        case IDM_PAL_GRAY4:    hPalette = DibPalUniformGrays (  4) ; break ;
        case IDM_PAL_GRAY8:    hPalette = DibPalUniformGrays (  8) ; break ;
        case IDM_PAL_GRAY16:   hPalette = DibPalUniformGrays ( 16) ; break ;
        case IDM_PAL_GRAY32:   hPalette = DibPalUniformGrays ( 32) ; break ;
        case IDM_PAL_GRAY64:   hPalette = DibPalUniformGrays ( 64) ; break ;
        case IDM_PAL_GRAY128:  hPalette = DibPalUniformGrays (128) ; break ;
        case IDM_PAL_GRAY256:  hPalette = DibPalUniformGrays (256) ; break ;

        case IDM_PAL_RGB222: hPalette = DibPalUniformColors (2,2,2); break;
        case IDM_PAL_RGB333: hPalette = DibPalUniformColors (3,3,3); break;
        case IDM_PAL_RGB444: hPalette = DibPalUniformColors (4,4,4); break;
        case IDM_PAL_RGB555: hPalette = DibPalUniformColors (5,5,5); break;
        case IDM_PAL_RGB666: hPalette = DibPalUniformColors (6,6,6); break;
        case IDM_PAL_RGB775: hPalette = DibPalUniformColors (7,7,5); break;
        case IDM_PAL_RGB757: hPalette = DibPalUniformColors (7,5,7); break;
        case IDM_PAL_RGB577: hPalette = DibPalUniformColors (5,7,7); break;
        case IDM_PAL_RGB884: hPalette = DibPalUniformColors (8,8,4); break;
        case IDM_PAL_RGB848: hPalette = DibPalUniformColors (8,4,8); break;
        case IDM_PAL_RGB488: hPalette = DibPalUniformColors (4,8,8); break;

        case IDM_PAL_OPT_POP4:
             hPalette = DibPalPopularity (hdib, 4) ;
             break ;
```

```
    case IDM_PAL_OPT_POP5:
         hPalette = DibPalPopularity (hdib, 5) ;
         break ;

    case IDM_PAL_OPT_POP6:
         hPalette = DibPalPopularity (hdib, 6) ;
         break ;

    case IDM_PAL_OPT_MEDCUT:
         hPalette = DibPalMedianCut (hdib, 6) ;
         break ;
    }

         // After processing Palette items from the menu, the cursor
         //   is restored to an arrow, the menu item is checked, and
         //   the window is invalidated.

    hBitmap = DibCopyToDdb (hdib, hwnd, hPalette) ;

    ShowCursor (FALSE) ;
    SetCursor (LoadCursor (NULL, IDC_ARROW)) ;

    if (hPalette)
         PaletteMenu (hMenu, (LOWORD (wParam))) ;

    InvalidateRect (hwnd, NULL, TRUE) ;
    return 0 ;

    // This programmer-defined message deletes an existing DIB
    //   in preparation for getting a new one.  Invoked during
    //   File Open command, Edit Paste command, and others.

case WM_USER_DELETEDIB:
    if (hdib)
    {
         DibDelete (hdib) ;
         hdib = NULL ;
    }
    SendMessage (hwnd, WM_USER_DELETEPAL, 0, 0) ;
    return 0 ;

    // This programmer-defined message deletes an existing palette
    //   in preparation for defining a new one.

case WM_USER_DELETEPAL:
    if (hPalette)
    {
         DeleteObject (hPalette) ;
```

(continued)

Figure 16-24. *continued*

```
                hPalette = NULL ;
                fHalftonePalette = FALSE ;
                PaletteMenu (hMenu, IDM_PAL_NONE) ;
           }
           if (hBitmap)
                DeleteObject (hBitmap) ;

           return 0 ;

           // Programmer-defined message to create a new palette based on
           //   a new DIB.  If wParam == TRUE, create a DDB as well.

     case WM_USER_CREATEPAL:
           if (hdib)
           {
                hdc = GetDC (hwnd) ;

                if (!(RC_PALETTE & GetDeviceCaps (hdc, RASTERCAPS)))
                {
                     PaletteMenu (hMenu, IDM_PAL_NONE) ;
                }
                else if (hPalette = DibPalDibTable (hdib))
                {
                     PaletteMenu (hMenu, IDM_PAL_DIBTABLE) ;
                }
                else if (hPalette = CreateHalftonePalette (hdc))
                {
                     fHalftonePalette = TRUE ;
                     PaletteMenu (hMenu, IDM_PAL_HALFTONE) ;
                }
                ReleaseDC (hwnd, hdc) ;

                if ((BOOL) wParam)
                     hBitmap = DibCopyToDdb (hdib, hwnd, hPalette) ;
           }
           return 0 ;

     case WM_PAINT:
           hdc = BeginPaint (hwnd, &ps) ;

           if (hPalette)
           {
                SelectPalette (hdc, hPalette, FALSE) ;
                RealizePalette (hdc) ;
           }
           if (hBitmap)
           {
```

```
                DisplayDib (hdc,
                        fHalftonePalette ? DibBitmapHandle (hdib) : hBitmap,
                        iHscroll, iVscroll,
                        cxClient, cyClient,
                        wShow, fHalftonePalette) ;
          }
          EndPaint (hwnd, &ps) ;
          return 0 ;

     case WM_QUERYNEWPALETTE:
          if (!hPalette)
               return FALSE ;

          hdc = GetDC (hwnd) ;
          SelectPalette (hdc, hPalette, FALSE) ;
          RealizePalette (hdc) ;
          InvalidateRect (hwnd, NULL, TRUE) ;

          ReleaseDC (hwnd, hdc) ;
          return TRUE ;

     case WM_PALETTECHANGED:
          if (!hPalette || (HWND) wParam == hwnd)
               break ;

          hdc = GetDC (hwnd) ;
          SelectPalette (hdc, hPalette, FALSE) ;
          RealizePalette (hdc) ;
          UpdateColors (hdc) ;

          ReleaseDC (hwnd, hdc) ;
          break ;

     case WM_DESTROY:
          if (hdib)
               DibDelete (hdib) ;

          if (hBitmap)
               DeleteObject (hBitmap) ;

          if (hPalette)
               DeleteObject (hPalette) ;

          PostQuitMessage (0) ;
          return 0 ;
     }
     return DefWindowProc (hwnd, message, wParam, lParam) ;
}
```

(continued)

Figure 16-24. *continued*

DIBBLE.RC (excerpts)

```
//Microsoft Developer Studio generated resource script.

#include "resource.h"
#include "afxres.h"
/////////////////////////////////////////////////////////////////////////////
// Menu

DIBBLE MENU DISCARDABLE
BEGIN
    POPUP "&File"
    BEGIN
        MENUITEM "&Open...\tCtrl+O",            IDM_FILE_OPEN
        MENUITEM "&Save...\tCtrl+S",            IDM_FILE_SAVE
        MENUITEM SEPARATOR
        MENUITEM "&Print...\tCtrl+P",           IDM_FILE_PRINT
        MENUITEM SEPARATOR
        MENUITEM "Propert&ies...",              IDM_FILE_PROPERTIES
        MENUITEM SEPARATOR
        MENUITEM "E&xit",                       IDM_APP_EXIT
    END
    POPUP "&Edit"
    BEGIN
        MENUITEM "Cu&t\tCtrl+X",                IDM_EDIT_CUT
        MENUITEM "&Copy\tCtrl+C",               IDM_EDIT_COPY
        MENUITEM "&Paste\tCtrl+V",              IDM_EDIT_PASTE
        MENUITEM "&Delete\tDelete",             IDM_EDIT_DELETE
        MENUITEM SEPARATOR
        MENUITEM "&Flip",                       IDM_EDIT_FLIP
        MENUITEM "&Rotate",                     IDM_EDIT_ROTATE
    END
    POPUP "&Show"
    BEGIN
        MENUITEM "&Actual Size",                IDM_SHOW_NORMAL, CHECKED
        MENUITEM "&Center",                     IDM_SHOW_CENTER
        MENUITEM "&Stretch to Window",          IDM_SHOW_STRETCH
        MENUITEM "Stretch &Isotropically",      IDM_SHOW_ISOSTRETCH
    END
    POPUP "&Palette"
    BEGIN
        MENUITEM "&None",                       IDM_PAL_NONE, CHECKED
        MENUITEM "&Dib ColorTable",             IDM_PAL_DIBTABLE
        MENUITEM "&Halftone",                   IDM_PAL_HALFTONE
        MENUITEM "&All-Purpose",                IDM_PAL_ALLPURPOSE
        POPUP "&Gray Shades"
```

```
        BEGIN
            MENUITEM "&1. 2 Grays",                 IDM_PAL_GRAY2
            MENUITEM "&2. 3 Grays",                 IDM_PAL_GRAY3
            MENUITEM "&3. 4 Grays",                 IDM_PAL_GRAY4
            MENUITEM "&4. 8 Grays",                 IDM_PAL_GRAY8
            MENUITEM "&5. 16 Grays",                IDM_PAL_GRAY16
            MENUITEM "&6. 32 Grays",                IDM_PAL_GRAY32
            MENUITEM "&7. 64 Grays",                IDM_PAL_GRAY64
            MENUITEM "&8. 128 Grays",               IDM_PAL_GRAY128
            MENUITEM "&9. 256 Grays",               IDM_PAL_GRAY256
        END
        POPUP "&Uniform Colors"
        BEGIN
            MENUITEM "&1. 2R x 2G x 2B (8)",        IDM_PAL_RGB222
            MENUITEM "&2. 3R x 3G x 3B (27)",       IDM_PAL_RGB333
            MENUITEM "&3. 4R x 4G x 4B (64)",       IDM_PAL_RGB444
            MENUITEM "&4. 5R x 5G x 5B (125)",      IDM_PAL_RGB555
            MENUITEM "&5. 6R x 6G x 6B (216)",      IDM_PAL_RGB666
            MENUITEM "&6. 7R x 7G x 5B (245)",      IDM_PAL_RGB775
            MENUITEM "&7. 7R x 5B x 7B (245)",      IDM_PAL_RGB757
            MENUITEM "&8. 5R x 7G x 7B (245)",      IDM_PAL_RGB577
            MENUITEM "&9. 8R x 8G x 4B (256)",      IDM_PAL_RGB884
            MENUITEM "&A. 8R x 4G x 8B (256)",      IDM_PAL_RGB848
            MENUITEM "&B. 4R x 8G x 8B (256)",      IDM_PAL_RGB488
        END
        POPUP "&Optimized"
        BEGIN
            MENUITEM "&1. Popularity Algorithm (4 bits)", IDM_PAL_OPT_POP4
            MENUITEM "&2. Popularity Algorithm (5 bits)", IDM_PAL_OPT_POP5
            MENUITEM "&3. Popularity Algorithm (6 bits)", IDM_PAL_OPT_POP6
            MENUITEM "&4. Median Cut Algorithm ",   IDM_PAL_OPT_MEDCUT
        END
    END
    POPUP "Con&vert"
    BEGIN
        MENUITEM "&1. to 1 bit per pixel",          IDM_CONVERT_01
        MENUITEM "&2. to 4 bits per pixel",         IDM_CONVERT_04
        MENUITEM "&3. to 8 bits per pixel",         IDM_CONVERT_08
        MENUITEM "&4. to 16 bits per pixel",        IDM_CONVERT_16
        MENUITEM "&5. to 24 bits per pixel",        IDM_CONVERT_24
        MENUITEM "&6. to 32 bits per pixel",        IDM_CONVERT_32
    END
    POPUP "&Help"
    BEGIN
        MENUITEM "&About",                          IDM_APP_ABOUT
    END
END
```

(continued)

Figure 16-24. *continued*

```
/////////////////////////////////////////////////////////////////////////////
// Accelerator

DIBBLE ACCELERATORS DISCARDABLE
BEGIN
    "C",            IDM_EDIT_COPY,      VIRTKEY, CONTROL, NOINVERT
    "O",            IDM_FILE_OPEN,      VIRTKEY, CONTROL, NOINVERT
    "P",            IDM_FILE_PRINT,     VIRTKEY, CONTROL, NOINVERT
    "S",            IDM_FILE_SAVE,      VIRTKEY, CONTROL, NOINVERT
    "V",            IDM_EDIT_PASTE,     VIRTKEY, CONTROL, NOINVERT
    VK_DELETE,      IDM_EDIT_DELETE,    VIRTKEY, NOINVERT
    "X",            IDM_EDIT_CUT,       VIRTKEY, CONTROL, NOINVERT
END
```

RESOURCE.H (excerpts)

```
// Microsoft Developer Studio generated include file.
// Used by Dibble.rc

#define IDM_FILE_OPEN           40001
#define IDM_FILE_SAVE           40002
#define IDM_FILE_PRINT          40003
#define IDM_FILE_PROPERTIES     40004
#define IDM_APP_EXIT            40005
#define IDM_EDIT_CUT            40006
#define IDM_EDIT_COPY           40007
#define IDM_EDIT_PASTE          40008
#define IDM_EDIT_DELETE         40009
#define IDM_EDIT_FLIP           40010
#define IDM_EDIT_ROTATE         40011
#define IDM_SHOW_NORMAL         40012
#define IDM_SHOW_CENTER         40013
#define IDM_SHOW_STRETCH        40014
#define IDM_SHOW_ISOSTRETCH     40015
#define IDM_PAL_NONE            40016
#define IDM_PAL_DIBTABLE        40017
#define IDM_PAL_HALFTONE        40018
#define IDM_PAL_ALLPURPOSE      40019
#define IDM_PAL_GRAY2           40020
#define IDM_PAL_GRAY3           40021
#define IDM_PAL_GRAY4           40022
#define IDM_PAL_GRAY8           40023
#define IDM_PAL_GRAY16          40024
#define IDM_PAL_GRAY32          40025
#define IDM_PAL_GRAY64          40026
```

```
#define IDM_PAL_GRAY128        40027
#define IDM_PAL_GRAY256        40028
#define IDM_PAL_RGB222         40029
#define IDM_PAL_RGB333         40030
#define IDM_PAL_RGB444         40031
#define IDM_PAL_RGB555         40032
#define IDM_PAL_RGB666         40033
#define IDM_PAL_RGB775         40034
#define IDM_PAL_RGB757         40035
#define IDM_PAL_RGB577         40036
#define IDM_PAL_RGB884         40037
#define IDM_PAL_RGB848         40038
#define IDM_PAL_RGB488         40039
#define IDM_PAL_OPT_POP4       40040
#define IDM_PAL_OPT_POP5       40041
#define IDM_PAL_OPT_POP6       40042
#define IDM_PAL_OPT_MEDCUT     40043
#define IDM_CONVERT_01         40044
#define IDM_CONVERT_04         40045
#define IDM_CONVERT_08         40046
#define IDM_CONVERT_16         40047
#define IDM_CONVERT_24         40048
#define IDM_CONVERT_32         40049
#define IDM_APP_ABOUT          40050
```

DIBBLE uses a couple of other files that I'll describe shortly. The DIBCONV files (DIBCONV.C and DIBCONV.H) convert between different formats—for example, from 24 bits per pixel to 8 bits per pixel. The DIBPAL files (DIBPAL.C and DIBPAL.H) create palettes.

DIBBLE maintains three crucial static variables in *WndProc*. These are an HDIB handle called *hdib*, an HPALETTE handle called *hPalette*, and an HBITMAP handle called *hBitmap*. The HDIB comes from various functions in DIBHELP; the HPALETTE comes from various functions in DIBPAL or the *CreateHalftonePalette* function; and the HBITMAP handle comes from the *DibCopyToDdb* function in DIBHELP.C and helps speed up screen displays, particularly in 256-color video modes. However, this handle must be re-created whenever the program creates a new DIB Section (obviously) and also when the program creates a different palette (not so obviously).

Let's approach DIBBLE functionally rather than sequentially.

File Loading and Saving

DIBBLE can load DIB files and save them in response to WM_COMMAND messages of IDM_FILE_LOAD and IDM_FILE_SAVE. In processing these messages, DIBBLE invokes the common file dialog boxes by calling *GetOpenFileName* and *GetSaveFileName*, respectively.

For the File Save menu command, DIBBLE need only call *DibFileSave*. For the File Open menu command, DIBBLE must first delete the previous HDIB, palette, and bitmap objects. It does this by sending itself a WM_USER_DELETEDIB message, which is processed by calls to *DibDelete* and *DeleteObject*. DIBBLE then calls the *DibFileLoad* function in DIBHELP and sends itself WM_USER_SETSCROLLS and WM_USER_CREATEPAL messages to reset the scroll bars and create a palette. The WM_USER_CREATEPAL message is also the place where the program creates a new DDB from the DIB section.

Displaying, Scrolling, and Printing

DIBBLE's menu allows it to display the DIB in actual size oriented at the top left corner of its client area or centered in the client area, or stretched to fill the client area or as much of the client area as possible while still maintaining the proper aspect ratio. You select which option you want through DIBBLE's Show menu. Note that these are the same four display options available in the SHOWDIB2 program from the last chapter.

During the WM_PAINT message—and also while processing the File Print command—DIBBLE calls its *DisplayDib* function. Notice that *DisplayDib* uses *BitBlt* and *StretchBlt* rather than *SetDIBitsToDevice* and *StretchDIBits*. During the WM_PAINT message, the bitmap handle passed to the function is the one created by the *DibCopyToDdb* function, which is called during the WM_USER_CREATEPAL message. This DDB is compatible with the video device context. When processing the File Print command, DIBBLE calls *DisplayDib* with the DIB section handle available from *DibBitmapHandle* function in DIBHELP.C.

Also notice that DIBBLE retains a static BOOL variable named *fHalftonePalette*, which is set to TRUE if *hPalette* was obtained from the *CreateHalftonePalette* function. This forces the *DisplayDib* function to call *StretchBlt* rather than *BitBlt* even if the DIB is being displayed in actual size. The *fHalftonePalette* variable also causes WM_PAINT processing to pass the DIB section handle to the *DisplayDib* function rather than the bitmap handle created by the *DibCopyToDdb* function. The use of the halftone palette was discussed earlier in this chapter and illustrated in the SHOWDIB5 program.

For the first time in any of our sample programs, DIBBLE allows scrolling DIBs in the client area. The scroll bars are shown only when the DIB is displayed in actual size. *WndProc* simply passes the current position of the scroll bars to the *DisplayDib* function when processing WM_PAINT.

The Clipboard

For the Cut and Copy menu items, DIBBLE calls the *DibCopyToPackedDib* function in DIBHELP. This function simply takes all the components of the DIB and puts them in a big memory block.

For the first time in one of the sample programs in this book, DIBBLE pastes a DIB from the clipboard. This involves a call to the *DibCopyFromPackedDib* function and replaces the HDIB, palette, and bitmap previously stored by the window procedure.

Flipping and Rotating

The Edit menu in DIBBLE contains two additional items beyond the standard Cut, Copy, Paste, and Delete options. These are Flip and Rotate. The Flip option causes the bitmap to be flipped around the horizontal axis—that is, flipped upside down. The Rotate option causes the bitmap to be rotated 90° clockwise. Both of these functions require accessing all the pixels of the DIB by copying them from one DIB to another. (Because these two functions don't require creating a new palette, the palette is not deleted and re-created.)

The Flip menu option uses the *DibFlipHorizontal* function, also located in the DIBBLE.C file. This function calls *DibCopy* to obtain an exact copy of the DIB. It then enters a loop that copies pixels from the original DIB to the new DIB, but the pixels are copied so that the image is flipped upside down. Notice that this function calls *DibGetPixel* and *DibSetPixel*. These are the general-purpose (but not quite as fast as we may prefer) functions located in DIBHELP.C.

To illustrate the difference between the *DibGetPixel* and *DibSetPixel* functions and the much faster *DibGetPixel* and *DibSetPixel* macros in DIBHELP.H, the *DibRotateRight* function uses the macros. Notice first, however, that this function calls *DibCopy* with a second argument set to TRUE. This causes *DibCopy* to flip the width and height of the original DIB to create the new DIB. Also, the pixel bits are not copied by the *DibCopy* function. The *DibRotateRight* function, then, has six different loops to copy the pixel bits from the original DIB to the new DIB—one for each of the different possible DIB pixel widths (1 bit, 4 bit, 8 bit, 16 bit, 24 bit, and 32 bit). There's more code involved, but the function is much faster.

Although it's possible to use the Flip Horizontal and Rotate Right options to mimic Flip Vertical, Rotate Left, and Rotate 180° functions, normally a program would implement all of these options directly. DIBBLE is, of course, just a demonstration program.

Simple Palettes; Optimized Palettes

In DIBBLE you can choose a variety of palettes for displaying DIBs on 256-color video displays. These are all listed on DIBBLE's Palette menu. With the exception of the half-tone palette, which is created directly by a Windows function call, all of the functions to create various palettes are provided by the DIBPAL files shown in Figure 16-25.

DIBPAL.H

```
/*---------------------------------------
   DIBPAL.H header file for DIBPAL.C
  ---------------------------------------*/

HPALETTE DibPalDibTable (HDIB hdib) ;
HPALETTE DibPalAllPurpose (void) ;
HPALETTE DibPalUniformGrays (int iNum) ;
HPALETTE DibPalUniformColors (int iNumR, int iNumG, int iNumB) ;
HPALETTE DibPalVga (void) ;
HPALETTE DibPalPopularity (HDIB hdib, int iRes) ;
HPALETTE DibPalMedianCut (HDIB hdib, int iRes) ;
```

Figure 16-25. *The DIBPAL files.*

(continued)

Figure 16-25. *continued*

DIBPAL.C

```
/*-------------------------------------------
   DIBPAL.C -- Palette-Creation Functions
                 (c) Charles Petzold, 1998
   -----------------------------------------*/

#include <windows.h>
#include "dibhelp.h"
#include "dibpal.h"


/*-------------------------------------------------------------
   DibPalDibTable: Creates a palette from the DIB color table
   -----------------------------------------------------------*/

HPALETTE DibPalDibTable (HDIB hdib)
{
    HPALETTE        hPalette ;
    int             i, iNum ;
    LOGPALETTE * plp ;
    RGBQUAD         rgb ;

    if (0 == (iNum = DibNumColors (hdib)))
         return NULL ;

    plp = malloc (sizeof (LOGPALETTE) + (iNum - 1) * sizeof (PALETTEENTRY)) ;

    plp->palVersion    = 0x0300 ;
    plp->palNumEntries = iNum ;

    for (i = 0 ; i < iNum ; i++)
    {
         DibGetColor (hdib, i, &rgb) ;

         plp->palPalEntry[i].peRed   = rgb.rgbRed ;
         plp->palPalEntry[i].peGreen = rgb.rgbGreen ;
         plp->palPalEntry[i].peBlue  = rgb.rgbBlue ;
         plp->palPalEntry[i].peFlags = 0 ;
    }
    hPalette = CreatePalette (plp) ;
    free (plp) ;
    return hPalette ;
}
```

```
/*-----------------------------------------------------------------------
   DibPalAllPurpose: Creates a palette suitable for a wide variety
          of images; the palette has 247 entries, but 15 of them are
          duplicates or match the standard 20 colors.
   -----------------------------------------------------------------------*/

HPALETTE DibPalAllPurpose (void)
{
    HPALETTE       hPalette ;
    int            i, incr, R, G, B ;
    LOGPALETTE * plp ;

    plp = malloc (sizeof (LOGPALETTE) + 246 * sizeof (PALETTEENTRY)) ;

    plp->palVersion    = 0x0300 ;
    plp->palNumEntries = 247 ;

         // The following loop calculates 31 gray shades, but 3 of them
         //         will match the standard 20 colors

    for (i = 0, G = 0, incr = 8 ; G <= 0xFF ; i++, G += incr)
    {
         plp->palPalEntry[i].peRed   = (BYTE) G ;
         plp->palPalEntry[i].peGreen = (BYTE) G ;
         plp->palPalEntry[i].peBlue  = (BYTE) G ;
         plp->palPalEntry[i].peFlags = 0 ;

         incr = (incr == 9 ? 8 : 9) ;
    }

         // The following loop is responsible for 216 entries, but 8 of
         //         them will match the standard 20 colors, and another
         //         4 of them will match the gray shades above.

    for (R = 0 ; R <= 0xFF ; R += 0x33)
    for (G = 0 ; G <= 0xFF ; G += 0x33)
    for (B = 0 ; B <= 0xFF ; B += 0x33)
    {
         plp->palPalEntry[i].peRed   = (BYTE) R ;
         plp->palPalEntry[i].peGreen = (BYTE) G ;
         plp->palPalEntry[i].peBlue  = (BYTE) B ;
         plp->palPalEntry[i].peFlags = 0 ;

         i++ ;
    }
```

(continued)

Figure 16-25. *continued*

```
    hPalette = CreatePalette (plp) ;

    free (plp) ;
    return hPalette ;
}

/*----------------------------------------------------------------------
   DibPalUniformGrays:  Creates a palette of iNum grays, uniformly spaced
   --------------------------------------------------------------------*/

HPALETTE DibPalUniformGrays (int iNum)
{
    HPALETTE      hPalette ;
    int           i ;
    LOGPALETTE * plp ;

    plp = malloc (sizeof (LOGPALETTE) + (iNum - 1) * sizeof (PALETTEENTRY)) ;

    plp->palVersion    = 0x0300 ;
    plp->palNumEntries = iNum ;

    for (i = 0 ; i < iNum ; i++)
    {
        plp->palPalEntry[i].peRed   =
        plp->palPalEntry[i].peGreen =
        plp->palPalEntry[i].peBlue  = (BYTE) (i * 255 / (iNum - 1)) ;
        plp->palPalEntry[i].peFlags = 0 ;
    }
    hPalette = CreatePalette (plp) ;
    free (plp) ;
    return hPalette ;
}

/*----------------------------------------------------------------------
   DibPalUniformColors: Creates a palette of iNumR x iNumG x iNumB colors
   --------------------------------------------------------------------*/

HPALETTE DibPalUniformColors (int iNumR, int iNumG, int iNumB)
{
    HPALETTE      hPalette ;
    int           i, iNum, R, G, B ;
    LOGPALETTE * plp ;

    iNum = iNumR * iNumG * iNumB ;

    plp = malloc (sizeof (LOGPALETTE) + (iNum - 1) * sizeof (PALETTEENTRY)) ;
```

```
    plp->palVersion   = 0x0300 ;
    plp->palNumEntries = iNumR * iNumG * iNumB ;

    i = 0 ;
    for (R = 0 ; R < iNumR ; R++)
    for (G = 0 ; G < iNumG ; G++)
    for (B = 0 ; B < iNumB ; B++)
    {
         plp->palPalEntry[i].peRed   = (BYTE) (R * 255 / (iNumR - 1)) ;
         plp->palPalEntry[i].peGreen = (BYTE) (G * 255 / (iNumG - 1)) ;
         plp->palPalEntry[i].peBlue  = (BYTE) (B * 255 / (iNumB - 1)) ;
         plp->palPalEntry[i].peFlags = 0 ;

         i++ ;
    }
    hPalette = CreatePalette (plp) ;
    free (plp) ;
    return hPalette ;
}


/*--------------------------------------------------------------------
   DibPalVga:  Creates a palette based on standard 16 VGA colors
   --------------------------------------------------------------------*/

HPALETTE DibPalVga (void)
{
    static RGBQUAD rgb [16] = { 0x00, 0x00, 0x00, 0x00,
                                0x00, 0x00, 0x80, 0x00,
                                0x00, 0x80, 0x00, 0x00,
                                0x00, 0x80, 0x80, 0x00,
                                0x80, 0x00, 0x00, 0x00,
                                0x80, 0x00, 0x80, 0x00,
                                0x80, 0x80, 0x00, 0x00,
                                0x80, 0x80, 0x80, 0x00,
                                0xC0, 0xC0, 0xC0, 0x00,
                                0x00, 0x00, 0xFF, 0x00,
                                0x00, 0xFF, 0x00, 0x00,
                                0x00, 0xFF, 0xFF, 0x00,
                                0xFF, 0x00, 0x00, 0x00,
                                0xFF, 0x00, 0xFF, 0x00,
                                0xFF, 0xFF, 0x00, 0x00,
                                0xFF, 0xFF, 0xFF, 0x00 } ;
    HPALETTE        hPalette ;
    int             i ;
    LOGPALETTE      * plp ;

    plp = malloc (sizeof (LOGPALETTE) + 15 * sizeof (PALETTEENTRY)) ;
```

(continued)

Figure 16-25. *continued*

```
    plp->palVersion    = 0x0300 ;
    plp->palNumEntries = 16 ;

    for (i = 0 ; i < 16 ; i++)
    {
        plp->palPalEntry[i].peRed   = rgb[i].rgbRed ;
        plp->palPalEntry[i].peGreen = rgb[i].rgbGreen ;
        plp->palPalEntry[i].peBlue  = rgb[i].rgbBlue ;
        plp->palPalEntry[i].peFlags = 0 ;
    }
    hPalette = CreatePalette (plp) ;
    free (plp) ;
    return hPalette ;
}

/*-------------------------------------------------
   Macro used in palette optimization routines
   -------------------------------------------*/

#define PACK_RGB(R,G,B,iRes) ((int) (R) | ((int) (G) << (iRes)) |       \
                                       ((int) (B) << ((iRes) + (iRes))))

/*------------------------------------------------------------------
   AccumColorCounts: Fills up piCount (indexed by a packed RGB color)
     with counts of pixels of that color.
   ----------------------------------------------------------------*/

static void AccumColorCounts (HDIB hdib, int * piCount, int iRes)
{
    int     x, y, cx, cy ;
    RGBQUAD rgb ;

    cx = DibWidth (hdib) ;
    cy = DibHeight (hdib) ;

    for (y = 0 ; y < cy ; y++)
    for (x = 0 ; x < cx ; x++)
    {
        DibGetPixelColor (hdib, x, y, &rgb) ;

        rgb.rgbRed   >>= (8 - iRes) ;
        rgb.rgbGreen >>= (8 - iRes) ;
        rgb.rgbBlue  >>= (8 - iRes) ;

        ++piCount [PACK_RGB (rgb.rgbRed, rgb.rgbGreen, rgb.rgbBlue, iRes)] ;
    }
}
```

```
/*-------------------------------------------------------------------
   DibPalPopularity:  Popularity algorithm for optimized colors
  -------------------------------------------------------------*/

HPALETTE DibPalPopularity (HDIB hdib, int iRes)
{
    HPALETTE      hPalette ;
    int           i, iArraySize, iEntry, iCount, iIndex, iMask, R, G, B ;
    int         * piCount ;
    LOGPALETTE * plp ;

         // Validity checks

    if (DibBitCount (hdib) < 16)
         return NULL ;

    if (iRes < 3 || iRes > 8)
         return NULL ;

         // Allocate array for counting pixel colors

    iArraySize = 1 << (3 * iRes) ;
    iMask = (1 << iRes) - 1 ;

    if (NULL == (piCount = calloc (iArraySize, sizeof (int))))
         return NULL ;

         // Get the color counts

    AccumColorCounts (hdib, piCount, iRes) ;

         // Set up a palette

    plp = malloc (sizeof (LOGPALETTE) + 235 * sizeof (PALETTEENTRY)) ;

    plp->palVersion = 0x0300 ;

    for (iEntry = 0 ; iEntry < 236 ; iEntry++)
    {
         for (i = 0, iCount = 0 ; i < iArraySize ; i++)
              if (piCount[i] > iCount

              {
                   iCount = piCount[i] ;
                   iIndex = i ;
              }
```

(continued)

Figure 16-25. *continued*

```
            if (iCount == 0)
                break ;

            R = (iMask &  iIndex                  ) << (8 - iRes) ;
            G = (iMask & (iIndex >>         iRes )) << (8 - iRes) ;
            B = (iMask & (iIndex >> (iRes + iRes))) << (8 - iRes) ;

            plp->palPalEntry[iEntry].peRed   = (BYTE) R ;
            plp->palPalEntry[iEntry].peGreen = (BYTE) G ;
            plp->palPalEntry[iEntry].peBlue  = (BYTE) B ;
            plp->palPalEntry[iEntry].peFlags = 0 ;

            piCount [iIndex] = 0 ;
       }
            // On exit from the loop iEntry will be the number of stored entries

       plp->palNumEntries = iEntry ;

            // Create the palette, clean up, and return the palette handle

       hPalette = CreatePalette (plp) ;

       free (piCount) ;
       free (plp) ;

       return hPalette ;
}

/*-----------------------------------------------------------
   Structures used for implementing median cut algorithm
   -------------------------------------------------------*/

typedef struct              // defines dimension of a box
{
     int Rmin, Rmax, Gmin, Gmax, Bmin, Bmax ;
}
MINMAX ;

typedef struct              // for Compare routine for qsort
{
     int     iBoxCount ;
     RGBQUAD rgbBoxAv ;
}

BOXES ;
```

```
/*----------------------------
   FindAverageColor: In a box
  ----------------------------*/

static int FindAverageColor (int * piCount, MINMAX mm,
                             int iRes, RGBQUAD * prgb)
{
     int R, G, B, iR, iG, iB, iTotal, iCount ;

          // Initialize some variables

     iTotal = iR = iG = iB = 0 ;

          // Loop through all colors in the box

     for (R = mm.Rmin ; R <= mm.Rmax ; R++)
     for (G = mm.Gmin ; G <= mm.Gmax ; G++)
     for (B = mm.Bmin ; B <= mm.Bmax ; B++)
     {
               // Get the number of pixels of that color

          iCount = piCount [PACK_RGB (R, G, B, iRes)] ;

               // Weight the pixel count by the color value

          iR += iCount * R ;
          iG += iCount * G ;
          iB += iCount * B ;

          iTotal += iCount ;
     }
          // Find the average color

     prgb->rgbRed   = (BYTE) ((iR / iTotal) << (8 - iRes)) ;
     prgb->rgbGreen = (BYTE) ((iG / iTotal) << (8 - iRes)) ;
     prgb->rgbBlue  = (BYTE) ((iB / iTotal) << (8 - iRes)) ;

          // Return the total number of pixels in the box

     return iTotal ;
}

/*----------------------------
   CutBox:  Divide a box in two
  ----------------------------*/
```

(continued)

Figure 16-25. *continued*

```
static void CutBox (int * piCount, int iBoxCount, MINMAX mm,
                    int iRes, int iLevel, BOXES * pboxes, int * piEntry)
{
     int    iCount, R, G, B ;
     MINMAX mmNew ;

          // If the box is empty, return

     if (iBoxCount == 0)
          return ;

          // If the nesting level is 8, or the box is one pixel, we're ready
          //    to find the average color in the box and save it along with
          //    the number of pixels of that color

     if (iLevel == 8 || (mm.Rmin == mm.Rmax &&
                         mm.Gmin == mm.Gmax &&
                         mm.Bmin == mm.Bmax))
     {
          pboxes[*piEntry].iBoxCount =
               FindAverageColor (piCount, mm, iRes, &pboxes[*piEntry].rgbBoxAv) ;

          (*piEntry) ++ ;
     }
          // Otherwise, if blue is the largest side, split it

     else if ((mm.Bmax - mm.Bmin > mm.Rmax - mm.Rmin) &&
              (mm.Bmax - mm.Bmin > mm.Gmax - mm.Gmin))
     {
               // Initialize a counter and loop through the blue side

          iCount = 0 ;

          for (B = mm.Bmin ; B < mm.Bmax ; B++)
          {
                    // Accumulate all the pixels for each successive blue value

               for (R = mm.Rmin ; R <= mm.Rmax ; R++)
               for (G = mm.Gmin ; G <= mm.Gmax ; G++)
                    iCount += piCount [PACK_RGB (R, G, B, iRes)] ;

                    // If it's more than half the box count, we're there

               if (iCount >= iBoxCount / 2)
                    break ;

                    // If the next blue value will be the max, we're there
```

```
                if (B == mm.Bmax - 1)
                    break ;
        }

        // Cut the two split boxes.
        //    The second argument to CutBox is the new box count.
        //    The third argument is the new min and max values.

    mmNew = mm ;
    mmNew.Bmin = mm.Bmin ;
    mmNew.Bmax = B ;

    CutBox (piCount, iCount, mmNew, iRes, iLevel + 1,
            pboxes, piEntry) ;

    mmNew.Bmin = B + 1 ;
    mmNew.Bmax = mm.Bmax ;

    CutBox (piCount, iBoxCount - iCount, mmNew, iRes, iLevel + 1,
            pboxes, piEntry) ;
}
    // Otherwise, if red is the largest side, split it (just like blue)

else if (mm.Rmax - mm.Rmin > mm.Gmax - mm.Gmin)
{
    iCount = 0 ;

    for (R = mm.Rmin ; R < mm.Rmax ; R++)
    {
        for (B = mm.Bmin ; B <= mm.Bmax ; B++)
        for (G = mm.Gmin ; G <= mm.Gmax ; G++)
            iCount += piCount [PACK_RGB (R, G, B, iRes)] ;

        if (iCount >= iBoxCount / 2)
            break ;

        if (R == mm.Rmax - 1)
            break ;
    }
    mmNew = mm ;
    mmNew.Rmin = mm.Rmin ;
    mmNew.Rmax = R ;

    CutBox (piCount, iCount, mmNew, iRes, iLevel + 1,
            pboxes, piEntry) ;

    mmNew.Rmin = R + 1 ;
    mmNew.Rmax = mm.Rmax ;
```

(continued)

Figure 16-25. *continued*

```
            CutBox (piCount, iBoxCount - iCount, mmNew, iRes, iLevel + 1,
                   pboxes, piEntry) ;
      }
          // Otherwise, split along the green size
      else
      {
          iCount = 0 ;

          for (G = mm.Gmin ; G < mm.Gmax ; G++)
          {
              for (B = mm.Bmin ; B <= mm.Bmax ; B++)
              for (R = mm.Rmin ; R <= mm.Rmax ; R++)
                  iCount += piCount [PACK_RGB (R, G, B, iRes)] ;

              if (iCount >= iBoxCount / 2)
                  break ;

              if (G == mm.Gmax - 1)
                  break ;
          }
          mmNew = mm ;
          mmNew.Gmin = mm.Gmin ;
          mmNew.Gmax = G ;

          CutBox (piCount, iCount, mmNew, iRes, iLevel + 1,
                 pboxes, piEntry) ;

          mmNew.Gmin = G + 1 ;
          mmNew.Gmax = mm.Gmax ;

          CutBox (piCount, iBoxCount - iCount, mmNew, iRes, iLevel + 1,
                 pboxes, piEntry) ;
      }
}

/*---------------------------
   Compare routine for qsort
   -------------------------*/

static int Compare (const BOXES * pbox1, const BOXES * pbox2)
{
      return pbox1->iBoxCount - pbox2->iBoxCount ;
}

/*---------------------------------------------------------------------
   DibPalMedianCut:  Creates palette based on median cut algorithm
   -------------------------------------------------------------------*/
```

```
HPALETTE DibPalMedianCut (HDIB hdib, int iRes)
{
    BOXES        boxes [256] ;
    HPALETTE     hPalette ;
    int          i, iArraySize, iCount, R, G, B, iTotCount, iDim, iEntry = 0 ;
    int        * piCount ;
    LOGPALETTE * plp ;
    MINMAX       mm ;

        // Validity checks

    if (DibBitCount (hdib) < 16)
        return NULL ;

    if (iRes < 3 || iRes > 8)
        return NULL ;

        // Accumulate counts of pixel colors

    iArraySize = 1 << (3 * iRes) ;

    if (NULL == (piCount = calloc (iArraySize, sizeof (int))))
        return NULL ;

    AccumColorCounts (hdib, piCount, iRes) ;

        // Find the dimensions of the total box

    iDim = 1 << iRes ;

    mm.Rmin = mm.Gmin = mm.Bmin = iDim - 1 ;
    mm.Rmax = mm.Gmax = mm.Bmax = 0 ;

    iTotCount = 0 ;

    for (R = 0 ; R < iDim ; R++)
    for (G = 0 ; G < iDim ; G++)
    for (B = 0 ; B < iDim ; B++)
        if ((iCount = piCount [PACK_RGB (R, G, B, iRes)]) > 0)
        {
            iTotCount += iCount ;

            if (R < mm.Rmin) mm.Rmin = R ;
            if (G < mm.Gmin) mm.Gmin = G ;
            if (B < mm.Bmin) mm.Bmin = B ;
            if (R > mm.Rmax) mm.Rmax = R ;
```

(continued)

Figure 16-25. *continued*

```
                if (G > mm.Gmax) mm.Gmax = G ;
                if (B > mm.Bmax) mm.Bmax = B ;
        }

        // Cut the first box (iterative function).
        //    On return, the boxes structure will have up to 256 RGB values,
        //         one for each of the boxes, and the number of pixels in
        //         each box.
        //    The iEntry value will indicate the number of non-empty boxes.

   CutBox (piCount, iTotCount, mm, iRes, 0, boxes, &iEntry) ;
   free (piCount) ;

        // Sort the RGB table by the number of pixels for each color

   qsort (boxes, iEntry, sizeof (BOXES), Compare) ;

   plp = malloc (sizeof (LOGPALETTE) + (iEntry - 1) * sizeof (PALETTEENTRY)) ;

   if (plp == NULL)
        return NULL ;

   plp->palVersion    = 0x0300 ;
   plp->palNumEntries = iEntry ;

   for (i = 0 ; i < iEntry ; i++)
   {
        plp->palPalEntry[i].peRed   = boxes[i].rgbBoxAv.rgbRed ;
        plp->palPalEntry[i].peGreen = boxes[i].rgbBoxAv.rgbGreen ;
        plp->palPalEntry[i].peBlue  = boxes[i].rgbBoxAv.rgbBlue ;
        plp->palPalEntry[i].peFlags = 0 ;
   }

   hPalette = CreatePalette (plp) ;

   free (plp) ;
   return hPalette ;
}
```

The first function—*DibPalDibTable*—should look familiar. It creates a palette from the DIB's color table. This is quite similar to the *PackedDibCreatePalette* function from PACKEDIB.C that was put to use in the SHOWDIB3 program earlier in the chapter. As in SHOWDIB3, this function will work only if the DIB has a color table. It is not useful when attempting to display a 16-bit, 24-bit, or 32-bit DIB under an 8-bit video mode.

By default, when running on 256-color displays, DIBBLE will first try to call *DibPalDibTable* to create the palette from the DIB color table. If the DIB doesn't have the color table, DIBBLE will call *CreateHalftonePalette* and set the *fHalftonePalette* variable to TRUE. All of this logic occurs during the WM_USER_CREATEPAL message.

DIBPAL.C also implements a function named *DibPalAllPurpose*, which should also look familiar because it is quite similar to the *CreateAllPurposePalette* function in SHOWDIB4. You can also select this palette from DIBBLE's menu.

One of the interesting aspects about displaying bitmaps in 256-color modes is that you can control exactly what colors Windows uses for displaying the image. If you select and realize a palette, Windows will use the colors in the palette and no others.

For example, you can create a palette solely with shades of gray by using the *DibPal-UniformGrays* function. Using two shades of gray gives you a palette with just 00-00-00 (black) and FF-FF-FF (white). Try this out with some images you have: it provides a high-contrast "chalk and charcoal" effect popular with some photographers. Using 3 shades of gray adds a medium gray to black and white, and using 4 shades of gray adds 2 gray shades.

With 8 shades of gray you will probably see obvious contouring—irregular patches of the same gray shade where the nearest-color algorithm is obviously working but certainly not with any aesthetic judgment. Moving to 16 gray shades generally improves the image dramatically. The use of 32 gray shades just about eliminates any contouring; 64 gray shades is commonly considered the limit of most display equipment in use today. After this point, the improvements are marginal if evident at all. Going beyond 64 gray shades provides no improvement on devices with a 6-bit color resolution.

So far, the best we've been able to do for displaying 16-bit, 24-bit, or 32-bit color DIBs under 8-bit video modes is to devise an all-purpose palette (trivial for gray-shade images but usually inadequate for color images) or use the halftone palette, which combines an all-purpose color palette with a dithered display.

You'll also notice that when you select an all-purpose palette for a large 16-bit, 24-bit, or 32-bit DIB in an 8-bit color mode, it takes some time for the program to create the GDI bitmap object from the DIB for display purposes. Less time is required when the program creates a DDB from the DIB when no palette is used. (You can also see this difference when comparing the performance of SHOWDIB1 and SHOWDIB4 in displaying large 24-bit DIBs in an 8-bit color mode.) Why is this?

It's the nearest-color search. Normally, when displaying a 24-bit DIB in an 8-bit video mode (or converting a DIB to a DDB), GDI must match each and every pixel in the DIB to one of the static 20 colors. The only way it can do this is by determining which static color is closest to the pixel color. This involves calculating a distance between the pixel and each static color in a three-dimensional RGB color cube. This takes time, particularly when there may be millions of pixels in the DIB image.

When you create a 232-color palette such as the all-purpose palette in DIBBLE and SHOWDIB4, you are effectively increasing the time required for the nearest-color search by more than 11-times! GDI must now search through 232 colors rather than just 20. That's why the whole job of displaying the DIB is slowed down.

The lesson here is to avoid displaying 24-bit (or 16-bit or 32-bit) DIBs in 8-bit video modes. You should convert them to 8-bit DIBs by finding a palette of 256 colors that most closely approximates the range of colors in the DIB image. This is often referred to as an "optimal palette." A paper by Paul Heckbert entitled "Color Image Quantization for Frame Buffer Displays" that appeared in the July 1982 issue of *Computer Graphics* was helpful when I was researching this problem.

The Uniform Distribution

The simplest approach to a 256-color palette is choosing a uniform range of RGB color values, similar to the approach in *DibPalAllPurpose*. The advantage is that you don't need to examine the actual pixels in the DIB. Such a function to create a palette based on uniform ranges of RGB primaries is *DibPalCreateUniformColors*.

One reasonable distribution involves 8 levels of red and green and 4 levels of blue (to which the eye is less sensitive). The palette is the set of RGB color values with all the possible combinations of red and green values of 0x00, 0x24, 0x49, 0x6D, 0x92, 0xB6, 0xDB, and 0xFF, and blue values of 0x00, 0x55, 0xAA, and 0xFF, for a total of 256 colors. Another possible uniformly distributed palette uses 6 levels of red, green, and blue. This is a palette of all possible combinations of red, green, and blue values of 0x00, 0x33, 0x66, 0x99, 0xCC, and 0xFF. The number of colors in the palette is 6 to the 3rd power, or 216.

These two options and several others are provided by DIBBLE.

The "Popularity" Algorithm

The "popularity" algorithm is a fairly obvious solution to the 256-color palette problem. What you do is plow through all the pixels of the bitmap and find the 256 most common RGB color values. These are the values you use in the palette. This is implemented in DIBPAL's *DibPalPopularity* function.

However, if you use a whole 24 bits for each color, and if you assume that you'll need integers to count all the colors, your array will occupy 64 megabytes of memory. Moreover, you may find that there are actually no (or few) duplicated 24-bit pixel values in the bitmap and, thus, no most common colors.

To solve this problem, you can use only the most significant n bits of each red, green, and blue value—for example, 6 bits rather than 8. This makes sense because most color scanners and video display adapters have only a 6-bit resolution. This reduces the array to a more reasonable size of 256-KB count values, or 1 megabyte. Using only 5 bits reduces the total number of possible colors to 32,768. The use of 5 bits usually works better than 6 bits, as you can verify for yourself using DIBBLE and some color images you have.

The "Median Cut" Algorithm

The *DibPalMedianCut* function in DIBPAL.C implements Paul Heckbert's "median cut" algorithm. It's conceptually quite simple and, while the implementation in code is more difficult than the popularity algorithm, it is well-suited to recursive functions.

Picture the RGB color cube. Each pixel of the image is a point within this cube. Some points might represent multiple pixels in the image. Find the three-dimensional box that encloses all the pixels in the image. Find the longest dimension of this box and cut the box in two parts, each containing an equal number of pixels. For these 2 boxes, do the same thing. Now you have 4 boxes. Cut the 4 boxes into 8, and then into 16, and then 32, 64, 128, and 256.

Now you have 256 boxes, each containing about an equal number of pixels. Average the RGB color values of the pixels in each box, and use the results for the palette.

In reality, the boxes don't usually contain an equal number of pixels. Often, for example, a box containing a single point has many pixels. This happens with black and white. Sometimes a box ends up with no pixels at all. If so, you can chop up more boxes, but I decided not to.

Another optimum palette technique is called "octree quantization." This technique was discussed by Jeff Prosise in the August 1996 issue of *Microsoft Systems Journal* (included on the MSDN CDs).

Converting Formats

DIBBLE also allows converting a DIB from one format to another. This makes use of the *DibConvert* function in the DIBCONV files shown in Figure 16-26.

DIBCONV.H

```
/*-------------------------------------------
   DIBCONV.H header file for DIBCONV.C
   ------------------------------------*/


HDIB DibConvert (HDIB hdibSrc, int iBitCountDst) ;
```

DIBCONV.C

```
/*----------------------------------------------------------
   DIBCONV.C -- Converts DIBs from one format to another
                (c) Charles Petzold, 1998
   ----------------------------------------------------------*/

#include <windows.h>
#include "dibhelp.h"
#include "dibpal.h"
#include "dibconv.h"

HDIB DibConvert (HDIB hdibSrc, int iBitCountDst)
{
    HDIB         hdibDst ;
    HPALETTE     hPalette ;
    int          i, x, y, cx, cy, iBitCountSrc, cColors ;
    PALETTEENTRY pe ;
    RGBQUAD      rgb ;
```

Figure 16-26. *The DIBCONV files.*

(continued)

Figure 16-26. *continued*

```
WORD            wNumEntries ;

cx = DibWidth (hdibSrc) ;
cy = DibHeight (hdibSrc) ;
iBitCountSrc = DibBitCount (hdibSrc) ;

if (iBitCountSrc == iBitCountDst)
    return NULL ;

    // DIB with color table to DIB with larger color table:

if ((iBitCountSrc < iBitCountDst) && (iBitCountDst <= 8))
{
    cColors = DibNumColors (hdibSrc) ;
    hdibDst = DibCreate (cx, cy, iBitCountDst, cColors) ;

    for (i = 0 ; i < cColors ; i++)
    {
        DibGetColor (hdibSrc, i, &rgb) ;
        DibSetColor (hdibDst, i, &rgb) ;
    }

    for (x = 0 ; x < cx ; x++)
    for (y = 0 ; y < cy ; y++)
    {
        DibSetPixel (hdibDst, x, y, DibGetPixel (hdibSrc, x, y)) ;
    }
}
    // Any DIB to DIB with no color table

else if (iBitCountDst >= 16)
{
    hdibDst = DibCreate (cx, cy, iBitCountDst, 0) ;

    for (x = 0 ; x < cx ; x++)
    for (y = 0 ; y < cy ; y++)
    {
        DibGetPixelColor (hdibSrc, x, y, &rgb) ;
        DibSetPixelColor (hdibDst, x, y, &rgb) ;
    }
}
    // DIB with no color table to 8-bit DIB

else if (iBitCountSrc >= 16 && iBitCountDst == 8)
{
    hPalette = DibPalMedianCut (hdibSrc, 6) ;
```

```
        GetObject (hPalette, sizeof (WORD), &wNumEntries) ;

        hdibDst = DibCreate (cx, cy, 8, wNumEntries) ;

        for (i = 0 ; i < (int) wNumEntries ; i++)
        {
             GetPaletteEntries (hPalette, i, 1, &pe) ;

             rgb.rgbRed    = pe.peRed ;
             rgb.rgbGreen  = pe.peGreen ;
             rgb.rgbBlue   = pe.peBlue ;
             rgb.rgbReserved = 0 ;

             DibSetColor (hdibDst, i, &rgb) ;
        }

        for (x = 0 ; x < cx ; x++)
        for (y = 0 ; y < cy ; y++)
        {
             DibGetPixelColor (hdibSrc, x, y, &rgb) ;

             DibSetPixel (hdibDst, x, y,
                  GetNearestPaletteIndex (hPalette,
                      RGB (rgb.rgbRed, rgb.rgbGreen, rgb.rgbBlue))) ;
        }
        DeleteObject (hPalette) ;
}
        // Any DIB to monochrome DIB

else if (iBitCountDst == 1)
{
        hdibDst = DibCreate (cx, cy, 1, 0) ;
        hPalette = DibPalUniformGrays (2) ;

        for (i = 0 ; i < 2 ; i++)
        {
             GetPaletteEntries (hPalette, i, 1, &pe) ;

             rgb.rgbRed    = pe.peRed ;
             rgb.rgbGreen  = pe.peGreen ;
             rgb.rgbBlue   = pe.peBlue ;
             rgb.rgbReserved = 0 ;

             DibSetColor (hdibDst, i, &rgb) ;
        }

        for (x = 0 ; x < cx ; x++)
```

(continued)

993

Figure 16-26. *continued*

```
        for (y = 0 ; y < cy ; y++)
        {
            DibGetPixelColor (hdibSrc, x, y, &rgb) ;

            DibSetPixel (hdibDst, x, y,
                GetNearestPaletteIndex (hPalette,
                    RGB (rgb.rgbRed, rgb.rgbGreen, rgb.rgbBlue))) ;
        }
        DeleteObject (hPalette) ;
    }

        // All non-monochrome DIBs to 4-bit DIB

    else if (iBitCountSrc >= 8 && iBitCountDst == 4)
    {
        hdibDst = DibCreate (cx, cy, 4, 0) ;
        hPalette = DibPalVga () ;

        for (i = 0 ; i < 16 ; i++)
        {
            GetPaletteEntries (hPalette, i, 1, &pe) ;

            rgb.rgbRed   = pe.peRed ;
            rgb.rgbGreen = pe.peGreen ;
            rgb.rgbBlue  = pe.peBlue ;
            rgb.rgbReserved = 0 ;

            DibSetColor (hdibDst, i, &rgb) ;
        }

        for (x = 0 ; x < cx ; x++)
        for (y = 0 ; y < cy ; y++)
        {
            DibGetPixelColor (hdibSrc, x, y, &rgb) ;

            DibSetPixel (hdibDst, x, y,
                GetNearestPaletteIndex (hPalette,
                    RGB (rgb.rgbRed, rgb.rgbGreen, rgb.rgbBlue))) ;
        }
        DeleteObject (hPalette) ;
    }

        // Should not be necessary

    else
        hdibDst = NULL ;

    return hdibDst ;
}
```

Several different strategies are required for converting DIBs from one format to another.

To convert a DIB with a color table to another DIB that also has a color table but with a larger pixel width (that is, to convert a 1-bit DIB to a 4-bit or 8-bit DIB, or a 4-bit DIB to an 8-bit DIB), all that needs be done is to create the new DIB by calling *DibCreate* with the desired bit count but with a number of colors equal to the number of colors in the original DIB. The function then copies the pixel bits and the color table entries.

If the new DIB has no color table (that is, the bit count is 16, 24, or 32), then the DIB needs only to be created in the new format and pixel bits copied from the existing DIB with calls to *DibGetPixelColor* and *DibSetPixelColor*.

The next case is probably the most common: The existing DIB does not have a color table (that is, the bit count is 16, 24, or 32) and the new DIB has 8 bits per pixel. In this case, *DibConvert* calls *DibPalMedianCut* to create an optimum palette for the image. The color table of the new DIB is set to the RGB values in the palette. The *DibGetPixelColor* function obtains a pixel color from the existing DIB. This is converted to a pixel value in the 8-bit DIB by a call to *GetNearestPaletteIndex* and the pixel value is stored in the DIB by calling *DibSetPixel*.

When a DIB needs to be converted to a monochrome DIB, the new DIB is created with a color table containing two entries—black and white. Again, the *GetNearestPalette-Index* helps convert colors in the existing DIB to a pixel value of 0 or 1. Similarly, when DIBs of 8 color bits or more need to be converted to 4-bit DIBs, the DIB color table is obtained from the *DibPalVga* function and *GetNearestPaletteIndex* also helps calculate the pixel values.

Although DIBBLE shows the basics of how an image-processing program might be started, such a program is never quite finished. Always another feature becomes obvious. But now, sadly, we must move on.

Chapter 17

Text and Fonts

Displaying text was one of the first jobs we tackled in this book. Now it's time to explore the use of different fonts and font sizes available in Microsoft Windows and to learn how to justify text.

The introduction of TrueType in Windows 3.1 greatly enhanced the ability of programmers and users to work with text in a flexible manner. TrueType is an outline font technology that was developed by Apple Computer, Inc., and Microsoft Corporation and is supported by many font manufacturers. Because TrueType fonts are continuously scalable and can be used on both video displays and printers, true WYSIWYG (what-you-see-is-what-you-get) is now possible under Windows. TrueType also lends itself well to doing "fancy" font manipulation, such as rotating characters, filling the interiors with patterns, or using them for clipping regions, all of which I'll demonstrate in this chapter.

SIMPLE TEXT OUTPUT

Let's begin by looking at the different functions Windows provides for text output, the device context attributes that affect text, and the use of stock fonts.

The Text Drawing Functions

The most common text output function is the one I've used in many sample programs so far:

```
TextOut (hdc, xStart, yStart, pString, iCount) ;
```

The *xStart* and *yStart* arguments are the starting position of the string in logical coordinates. Normally, this is the point at which Windows begins drawing the upper left corner of the first character. *TextOut* requires a pointer to the character string and the length of the string. The function does not recognize NULL-terminated character strings.

The meaning of the *xStart* and *yStart* arguments to *TextOut* can be altered by the *SetTextAlign* function. The TA_LEFT, TA_RIGHT, and TA_CENTER flags affect how *xStart* is used to position the string horizontally. The default is TA_LEFT. If you specify TA_RIGHT in the *SetTextAlign* function, subsequent *TextOut* calls position the right side of the last character in the string at *xStart*. With TA_CENTER, the center of the string is positioned at *xStart*.

Similarly, the TA_TOP, TA_BOTTOM, and TA_BASELINE flags affect the vertical positioning. TA_TOP is the default, which means that the string is positioned so that *yStart* specifies the top of the characters in the string. Using TA_BOTTOM means that the string is positioned above *yStart*. You can use TA_BASELINE to position a string so that the baseline is at *yStart*. The baseline is the line below which descenders, such as those on the lowercase p, q, and y, hang.

If you call *SetTextAlign* with the TA_UPDATECP flag, Windows ignores the *xStart* and *yStart* arguments to *TextOut* and instead uses the current position previously set by *MoveToEx* or *LineTo*, or another function that changes the current position. The TA_UPDATECP flag also causes the *TextOut* function to update the current position to the end of the string (for TA_LEFT) or the beginning of the string (for TA_RIGHT). This is useful for displaying a line of text with multiple *TextOut* calls. When the horizontal positioning is TA_CENTER, the current position remains the same after a *TextOut* call.

You'll recall that displaying columnar text in the series of SYSMETS programs in Chapter 4 required that one *TextOut* call be used for each column. An alternative is the *TabbedTextOut* function:

```
TabbedTextOut (hdc, xStart, yStart, pString, iCount,
               iNumTabs, piTabStops, xTabOrigin) ;
```

If the text string contains embedded tab characters ('\t' or 0x09), *TabbedTextOut* will expand the tabs into spaces based on an array of integers you pass to the function.

The first five arguments to *TabbedTextOut* are the same as those to *TextOut*. The sixth argument is the number of tab stops, and the seventh argument is an array of tab stops *in units of pixels*. For example, if the average character width is 8 pixels and you want a tab stop every 5 characters, then this array would contain the numbers 40, 80, 120, and so forth, in ascending order.

If the sixth and seventh arguments are 0 or NULL, tab stops are set at every eight average character widths. If the sixth argument is 1, the seventh argument points to a single integer, which is repeated incrementally for multiple tab stops. (For example, if the sixth argument is 1 and the seventh argument points to a variable containing the number 30, tab stops are set at 30, 60, 90… pixels.) The last argument gives the logical *x*-coordinate of the starting position from which tab stops are measured. This might or might not be the same as the starting position of the string.

Another advanced text output function is *ExtTextOut* (the *Ext* prefix stands for *extended*):

```
ExtTextOut (hdc, xStart, yStart, iOptions, &rect,
                pString, iCount, pxDistance) ;
```

The fifth argument is a pointer to a rectangle structure. This is either a clipping rectangle, if *iOptions* is set to ETO_CLIPPED, or a background rectangle to be filled with the current background color, if *iOptions* is set to ETO_OPAQUE. You can specify both options or neither.

The last argument is an array of integers that specify the spacing between consecutive characters in the string. This allows a program to tighten or loosen intercharacter spacing, which is sometimes required for justifying a single word of text in a narrow column. The argument can be set to NULL for default character spacing.

A higher-level function for writing text is *DrawText*, which we first encountered in the HELLOWIN program in Chapter 3. Rather than specifying a coordinate starting position, you provide a structure of type RECT that defines a rectangle in which you want the text to appear:

```
DrawText (hdc, pString, iCount, &rect, iFormat) ;
```

As with the other text output functions, *DrawText* requires a pointer to the character string and the length of the string. However, if you use *DrawText* with NULL-terminated strings, you can set *iCount* to −1 and Windows will calculate the length of the string for you.

When *iFormat* is set to 0, Windows interprets the text as a series of lines that are separated by carriage-return characters ('\r' or 0x0D) or linefeed characters ('\n' or 0x0A). The text begins at the upper left corner of the rectangle. A carriage return or linefeed is interpreted as a "newline" character, so Windows breaks the current line and starts a new one. The new line begins at the left side of the rectangle, spaced one character height (without external leading) below the previous line. Any text, including parts of letters, that would be displayed to the right or below the bottom of the rectangle is clipped.

You can change the default operation of *DrawText* by using the *iFormat* argument, which consists of one or more flags. The DT_LEFT flag (which is the default) specifies a left-justified line, DT_RIGHT specifies a right-justified line, and DT_CENTER specifies a line centered between the left and right sides of the rectangle. Because the value of DT_LEFT is 0, you needn't include the identifier if you want text to be left-justified only.

If you don't want carriage returns or linefeeds to be interpreted as newline characters, you can include the identifier DT_SINGLELINE. Windows then interprets carriage returns and linefeeds as displayable characters rather than control characters. When using DT_SINGLELINE, you can also specify whether the line is to be placed at the top of the rectangle (DT_TOP, the default), at the bottom of the rectangle (DT_BOTTOM), or halfway between the top and bottom (DT_VCENTER, the V standing for vertical).

When displaying multiple lines of text, Windows normally breaks the lines at carriage returns or linefeeds only. If the lines are too long to fit in the rectangle, however, you can use the DT_WORDBREAK flag, which causes Windows to create breaks at the end of words within lines. For both single-line and multiple-line displays, Windows truncates any part of the text that falls outside the rectangle. You can override this by including the flag DT_NOCLIP, which also speeds up the operation of the function. When Windows spaces multiple lines of text, it normally uses the character height without external leading. If you prefer that external leading be included in the line spacing, use the flag DT_EXTERNALLEADING.

If your text contains tab characters ('\t' or 0x09), you need to include the flag DT_EXPANDTABS. By default, the tab stops are set at every eighth character position. You can specify a different tab setting by using the flag DT_TABSTOP, in which case the upper byte of *iFormat* contains the character-position number of each new tab stop. I recommend that you avoid using DT_TABSTOP, however, because the upper byte of *iFormat* is also used for some other flags.

The problem with the DT_TABSTOP flag is solved by a newer *DrawTextEx* function that has an extra argument:

```
DrawTextEx (hdc, pString, iCount, &rect, iFormat, &drawtextparams) ;
```

The last argument is a pointer to a DRAWTEXTPARAMS structure, which is defined like so:

```
typedef struct tagDRAWTEXTPARAMS
{
    UINT cbSize ;           // size of structure
    int  iTabLength ;       // size of each tab stop
    int  iLeftMargin ;      // left margin
    int  iRightMargin ;     // right margin
    UINT uiLengthDrawn ;    // receives number of characters processed
} DRAWTEXTPARAMS, * LPDRAWTEXTPARAMS ;
```

The middle three fields are in units that are increments of the average character width.

Device Context Attributes for Text

Besides *SetTextAlign,* discussed above, several other device context attributes affect text. In the default device context, the text color is black, but you can change that with

```
SetTextColor (hdc, rgbColor) ;
```

As with pen colors and hatch brush colors, Windows converts the value of *rgbColor* to a pure color. You can obtain the current text color by calling *GetTextColor.*

Windows displays text in a rectangular background area that it might or might not color based on the setting of the background mode. You can change the background mode using

```
SetBkMode (hdc, iMode) ;
```

where *iMode* is either OPAQUE or TRANSPARENT. The default background mode is OPAQUE, which means that Windows uses the background color to fill in the rectangular background. You can change the background color by using

```
SetBkColor (hdc, rgbColor) ;
```

The value of *rgbColor* is converted to that of a pure color. The default background color is white.

If two lines of text are too close to each other, the background rectangle of one can obscure the text of another. For this reason, I have often wished that the default background mode were TRANSPARENT. In the TRANSPARENT case, Windows ignores the background color and doesn't color the rectangular background area. Windows also uses the background mode and background color to color the spaces between dotted and dashed lines and the area between the hatches of hatched brushes, as I discussed in Chapter 5.

Many Windows programs specify WHITE_BRUSH as the brush that Windows uses to erase the background of a window. The brush is specified in the window class structure. However, you may want to make the background of your program's window consistent with the system colors that a user can set in the Control Panel program. In that case, you would specify the background color this way in the WNDCLASS structure:

```
wndclass.hbrBackground = COLOR_WINDOW + 1 ;
```

When you want to write text to the client area, you can then set the text color and background color using the current system colors:

```
SetTextColor (hdc, GetSysColor (COLOR_WINDOWTEXT)) ;
SetBkColor (hdc, GetSysColor (COLOR_WINDOW)) ;
```

If you do this, you'll want your program to be alerted if the system colors change:

```
case WM_SYSCOLORCHANGE :
     InvalidateRect (hwnd, NULL, TRUE) ;
     break ;
```

Another device context attribute that affects text is the intercharacter spacing. By default it's set to 0, which means that Windows doesn't add any space between characters. You can insert space by using the function

```
SetTextCharacterExtra (hdc, iExtra) ;
```

The *iExtra* argument is in logical units. Windows converts it to the nearest pixel, which can be 0. If you use a negative value for *iExtra* (perhaps in an attempt to squeeze characters closer together), Windows takes the absolute value of the number—you can't make the value less than 0. You can obtain the current intercharacter spacing by calling *GetTextCharacterExtra*. Windows converts the pixel spacing to logical units before returning the value.

Using Stock Fonts

When you call *TextOut*, *TabbedTextOut*, *ExtTextOut*, *DrawText*, or *DrawTextEx* to write text, Windows uses the font currently selected in the device context. The font defines a particular typeface and a size. The easiest way to display text with various fonts is to use the stock fonts that Windows provides. However, the range of these is quite limited.

You can obtain a handle to a stock font by calling

```
hFont = GetStockObject (iFont) ;
```

where *iFont* is one of several identifiers. You can then select that font into the device context:

```
SelectObject (hdc, hFont) ;
```

Or you can accomplish this in one step:

```
SelectObject (hdc, GetStockObject (iFont)) ;
```

The font selected in the default device context is called the system font and is identified by the *GetStockObject* argument SYSTEM_FONT. This is a proportional ANSI character set font. Specifying SYSTEM_FIXED_FONT in *GetStockObject* (which I did in a few programs earlier in this book) gives you a handle to a fixed-pitch font compatible with the system font used in versions of Windows prior to version 3. This is convenient when you need all the font characters to have the same width.

The stock OEM_FIXED_FONT, also called the Terminal font, is the font that Windows uses in MS-DOS Command Prompt windows. It incorporates a character set compatible with the original extended character set of the IBM PC. Windows uses DEFAULT_GUI_FONT for the text in window title bars, menus, and dialog boxes.

When you select a new font into a device context, you must calculate the font's character height and average character width using *GetTextMetrics*. If you've selected a proportional font, be aware that the average character width is really an average and that some characters have a lesser or greater width. Later in this chapter you'll learn how to determine the full width of a string made up of variable-width characters.

Although *GetStockObject* certainly offers the easiest access to different fonts, you don't have much control over which font Windows gives you. You'll see shortly how you can be very specific about the typeface and size that you want.

BACKGROUND ON FONTS

Much of the remainder of this chapter addresses working with different fonts. Before you get involved with specific code, however, you'll benefit from having a firm grasp of the basics of fonts as they are implemented in Windows.

The Types of Fonts

Windows supports two broad categories of fonts, called "GDI fonts" and "device fonts." The GDI fonts are stored in files on your hard disk. Device fonts are native to an output device. For example, it is common for printers to have a collection of built-in device fonts.

GDI fonts come in three flavors: raster fonts, stroke fonts, and TrueType fonts.

A raster font is sometimes also called a bitmap font, because each character is stored as a bitmap pixel pattern. Each raster font is designed for a specific aspect ratio and character size. Windows can create larger character sizes from GDI raster fonts by simply duplicating rows or columns of pixels. However, this can be done in integral multiples only and within certain limits. For this reason, GDI raster fonts are termed "nonscalable" fonts. They cannot be expanded or compressed to an arbitrary size. The primary advantages of raster fonts are performance (because they are very fast to display) and readability (because they have been hand-designed to be as legible as possible).

Fonts are identified by typeface names. The raster fonts have typeface names of

System	(used for SYSTEM_FONT)
FixedSys	(used for SYSTEM_FIXED_FONT)
Terminal	(used for OEM_FIXED_FONT)
Courier	
MS Serif	
MS Sans Serif	(used for DEFAULT_GUI_FONT)
Small Fonts	

Each raster font comes in just a few (no more than six) different sizes. The Courier font is a fixed-pitch font similar in appearance to the font used by a typewriter. The word "serif" refers to small turns that often finish the strokes of letters in a font such as the one used for this book. A "sans serif" font doesn't have serifs. In early versions of Windows, the MS (Microsoft) Serif and MS Sans Serif fonts were called Tms Rmn (meaning that it was a font similar to Times Roman) and Helv (similar to Helvetica). The Small Fonts are especially designed for displaying text in small sizes.

Prior to Windows 3.1, the only other GDI fonts supplied with Windows were the stroke fonts. The stroke fonts are defined as a series of line segments in a "connect-the-dots" format. Stroke fonts are continuously scalable, which means that the same font can be used for graphics output devices of any resolution and the fonts can be increased or decreased to any size. However, performance is poor, legibility suffers greatly at small sizes, and at large sizes the characters look decidedly weak because their strokes are single lines. Stroke fonts are now sometimes called plotter fonts because they are particularly suitable for plotters but not for anything else. The stroke fonts have typeface names of Modern, Roman, and Script.

For both GDI raster fonts and GDI stroke fonts, Windows can "synthesize" bold-face, italics, underlining, and strikethroughs without storing separate fonts for each attribute. For italics, for instance, Windows simply shifts the upper part of the character to the right.

Then there is TrueType, to which I'll devote much of the remainder of this chapter.

TrueType Fonts

The individual characters of TrueType fonts are defined by filled outlines of straight lines and curves. Windows can scale these fonts by altering the coordinates that define the outlines.

When your program begins to use a TrueType font of a particular size, Windows "rasterizes" the font. This means that Windows scales the coordinates connecting the lines and curves of each character using "hints" that are included in the TrueType font file. These hints compensate for rounding errors that would otherwise cause a resultant character to be unsightly. (For example, in some fonts the two legs of a capital H should be the same width. A blind scaling of the font could result in one leg being a pixel wider than the other. The hints prevent this from happening.) The resultant outline of each character is then used to create a bitmap of the character. These bitmaps are cached in memory for future use.

Originally, Windows was equipped with 13 TrueType fonts, which have the following typeface names:

Courier New

Courier New Bold

Courier New Italic

Courier New Bold Italic

Times New Roman

Times New Roman Bold

Times New Roman Italic

Times New Roman Bold Italic

Arial

Arial Bold

Arial Italic

Arial Bold Italic

Symbol

In more recent versions of Windows, this list has been expanded. In particular, I'll be making use of the Lucida Sans Unicode font that includes some additional alphabets used around the world.

The three main font families are similar to the main raster fonts. Courier New is a fixed-pitch font designed to look like the output from that antique piece of hardware known as a typewriter. Times New Roman is a clone of the Times font originally designed for the

Times of London and used in much printed material. It is considered to be highly readable. Arial is a clone of Helvetica, a sans serif font. The Symbol font contains a collection of handy symbols.

Attributes or Styles?

You'll notice in the list of TrueType fonts shown above that bold and italic styles of Courier, Times New Roman, and Arial seem to be separate fonts with their own typeface names. This naming is very much in accordance with traditional typography. However, computer users have come to think of bold and italic as particular "attributes" that are applied to existing fonts. Windows itself took the attribute approach early on when defining how the raster fonts were named, enumerated, and selected. With TrueType fonts, however, more traditional naming is preferred.

This conflict is not quite ever resolved in Windows. In short, as you'll see, you can select fonts by either naming them fully or by specifying attributes. The process of font enumeration, in which an application requests a list of fonts from the system, is—as you might expect—complicated somewhat by this dual approach.

The Point Size

In traditional typography, you specify a font by its typeface name and its size. The type size is expressed in units called points. A point is very close to $1/72$ inch—so close in fact that in computer typography it is often defined as exactly $1/72$ inch. The text of this book is printed in 10-point type. The point size is usually described as the height of the characters from the top of the ascenders (without diacritics) to the bottom of the descenders, encompassing, for example, the full height of the letters "bq." That's a convenient way to think of the type size, but it's usually not metrically accurate.

The point size of a font is actually a typographical design concept rather than a metrical concept. The size of the characters in a particular font might be greater than or less than what the point size implies. In traditional typography, you use a point size to specify the size of a font; in computer typography, there are other methods to determine the actual size of the characters.

Leading and Spacing

As you'll recall from as long ago as Chapter 4, you can obtain information about the font currently selected in the device context by calling *GetTextMetrics*, as we've also done frequently since then. Figure 4-3 (on page 84) illustrates the vertical sizes of a font from the FONTMETRIC structure.

Another field of the TEXTMETRIC structure is named *tmExternalLeading*. The word leading (pronounced "ledding") is derived from the lead that typesetters insert between blocks of metal type to add white space between lines of text. The *tmInternalLeading* value corresponds to the space usually reserved for diacritics; *tmExternalLeading* suggests an additional space to leave between successive lines of characters. Programmers can use or ignore the external leading value.

When we refer to a font as being 8-point or 12-point, we're talking about the height of the font less internal leading. The diacritics on certain capital letters are considered to occupy the space that normally separates lines of type. The *tmHeight* value of the TEXTMETRIC structure thus actually refers to line spacing rather than the font point size. The point size can be derived from *tmHeight* minus *tmInternalLeading*.

The Logical Inch Problem

As I discussed in Chapter 5 (in the section entitled "The Size of the Device" beginning on page 133), Windows 98 defines the system font as being a 10-point font with 12-point line spacing. Depending on whether you choose Small Fonts or Large Fonts from the Display Properties dialog, this font could have a *tmHeight* value of 16 pixels or 20 pixels and a *tmHeight* minus *tmInternalLeading* value of 13 pixels or 16 pixels. Thus, the choice of the font implies a resolution of the device in dots per inch, namely 96 dpi when Small Fonts are selected and 120 dpi for Large Fonts.

You can obtain this implied resolution of the device by calling *GetDeviceCaps* with the LOGPIXELSX or LOGPIXELSY arguments. Thus, the metrical distance occupied by 96 or 120 pixels on the screen can be said to be a "logical inch." If you start measuring your screen with a ruler and counting pixels, you'll probably find that a logical inch is larger than an actual inch. Why is this?

On paper, 8-point type with about 14 characters horizontally per inch is perfectly readable. If you were programming a word processing or page-composition application, you would want to be able to show legible 8-point type on the display. But if you used the actual dimensions of the video display, there would probably not be enough pixels to show the character legibly. Even if the display had sufficient resolution, you might still have problems reading actual 8-point type on a screen. When people read print on paper, the distance between the eyes and the text is generally about a foot, but a video display is commonly viewed from a distance of two feet.

The logical inch in effect provides a magnification of the screen, allowing the display of legible fonts in a size as small as 8 points. Also, having 96 dots per logical inch makes the 640-pixel minimum display size equal to about 6.5 inches. This is precisely the width of text that prints on 8.5-inch-wide paper when you use the standard margins of an inch on each side. Thus, the logical inch also takes advantage of the width of the screen to allow text to be displayed as large as possible.

As you may also recall from Chapter 5, Windows NT does it a little differently. In Windows NT, the LOGPIXELSX (pixels per inch) value you obtain from *GetDeviceCaps* is *not* equal to the HORZRES value (in pixels) divided by the HORZSIZE value (in millimeters), multiplied by 25.4. Similarly, LOGPIXELSY, VERTRES, and VERTSIZE are not consistent. Windows uses the HORZRES, HORZSIZE, VERTRES, and VERTSIZE values when calculating window and offset extents for the various mapping modes; however, a program that displays text would be better off to use an assumed display resolution based on LOGPIXELSX and LOGPIXELSY. This is more consistent with Windows 98.

So, under Windows NT a program should probably *not* use the mapping modes provided by Windows when also displaying text in specific point sizes. The program should instead define its own mapping mode based on the logical-pixels-per-inch dimensions consistent with Windows 98. One such useful mapping mode for text I call the "Logical Twips" mapping mode. Here's how you set it:

```
SetMapMode (hdc, MM_ANISOTROPIC) ;
SetWindowExtEx (hdc, 1440, 1440, NULL) ;
SetViewportExt (hdc, GetDeviceCaps (hdc, LOGPIXELSX),
                     GetDeviceCaps (hdc, LOGPIXELSY), NULL) ;
```

With this mapping mode set, you can specify font dimensions in 20 times the point size— for example, 240 for 12 points. Notice that unlike the MM_TWIPS mapping mode, the values of *y* increase going down the screen. This is easier when displaying successive lines of text.

Keep in mind that the discrepancy between logical inches and real inches occurs only for the display. On printer devices, there is total consistency with GDI and rulers.

THE LOGICAL FONT

Now that we've nailed down the concept of logical inches and logical twips, it's time to talk about logical fonts.

A logical font is a GDI object whose handle is stored in a variable of type HFONT. A logical font is a description of a font. Like the logical pen and logical brush, it is an abstract object that becomes real only as it is a selected into a device context when an application calls *SelectObject*. For logical pens, for instance, you can specify any color you want for the pen, but Windows converts that to a pure color available on the device when you select the pen into the device context. Only then does Windows know about the color capabilities of the device.

Logical Font Creation and Selection

You create a logical font by calling *CreateFont* or *CreateFontIndirect*. The *CreateFontIndirect* function takes a pointer to a LOGFONT structure, which has 14 fields. The *CreateFont* function takes 14 arguments, which are identical to the 14 fields of the LOGFONT structure. These are the *only* two functions that create a logical font. (I mention this because there are multiple functions in Windows for some other font jobs.) Because the 14 fields are difficult to remember, *CreateFont* is rarely used, so I'll focus on *CreateFontIndirect*.

There are three basic ways, described at the top of the next page, to define the fields of a LOGFONT structure in preparation for calling *CreateFontIndirect*.

- You can simply set the fields of the LOGFONT structure to the characteristics of the font that you want. In this case, when you call *SelectObject*, Windows uses a "font mapping" algorithm to attempt to give you the font available on the device that best matches these characteristics. Depending on the fonts available on the video display or printer, the result might differ considerably from what you request.

- You can enumerate all the fonts on the device and choose from those or even present them to the user with a dialog box. I'll discuss the font enumeration functions later in this chapter. These are not used much these days because the third method does the enumeration for you.

- You can take the simple approach and call the *ChooseFont* function, which I discussed a little in Chapter 11. You get back a LOGFONT structure that you can use directly for creating the font.

In this chapter, I'll use the first and third approaches.

Here is the process for creating, selecting, and deleting logical fonts:

1. Create a logical font by calling *CreateFont* or *CreateFontIndirect*. These functions return a handle to a logical font of type HFONT.

2. Select the logical font into the device context using *SelectObject*. Windows chooses a real font that most closely matches the logical font.

3. Determine the size and characteristics of the real font with *GetTextMetrics* (and possibly some other functions). You can use this information to properly space the text that you write when this font is selected into the device context.

4. After you've finished using the font, delete the logical font by calling *Delete-Object*. Don't delete the font while it is selected in a valid device context, and don't delete stock fonts.

The *GetTextFace* function lets a program determine the face name of the font currently selected in the device context:

```
GetTextFace (hdc, sizeof (szFaceName) / sizeof (TCHAR), szFaceName) ;
```

The detailed font information is available from *GetTextMetrics*:

```
GetTextMetrics (hdc, &textmetric) ;
```

where *textmetric* is a variable of type TEXTMETRIC, a structure with 20 fields.

I'll discuss the fields of the LOGFONT and TEXTMETRIC structures in detail shortly. The structures have some similar fields, so they can be confusing. For now, just keep in mind that LOGFONT is for defining a logical font and TEXTMETRIC is for obtaining information about the font currently selected in the device context.

The PICKFONT Program

With the PICKFONT program shown in Figure 17-1, you can define many of the fields of a LOGFONT structure. The program creates a logical font and displays the characteristics of the real font after the logical font has been selected in a device context. This is a handy program for understanding how logical fonts are mapped to real fonts.

PICKFONT.C

```
/*----------------------------------------
   PICKFONT.C -- Create Logical Font
                 (c) Charles Petzold, 1998
   ----------------------------------------*/

#include <windows.h>
#include "resource.h"

      // Structure shared between main window and dialog box

typedef struct
{
    int        iDevice, iMapMode ;
    BOOL       fMatchAspect ;
    BOOL       fAdvGraphics ;
    LOGFONT    lf ;
    TEXTMETRIC tm ;
    TCHAR      szFaceName [LF_FULLFACESIZE] ;
}
DLGPARAMS ;

      // Formatting for BCHAR fields of TEXTMETRIC structure

#ifdef UNICODE
#define BCHARFORM TEXT ("0x%04X")
#else
#define BCHARFORM TEXT ("0x%02X")
#endif

      // Global variables

HWND  hdlg ;
TCHAR szAppName[] = TEXT ("PickFont") ;

      // Forward declarations of functions
```

Figure 17-1. *The PICKFONT program.*   *(continued)*

Figure 17-1. *continued*

```
LRESULT CALLBACK WndProc (HWND, UINT, WPARAM, LPARAM) ;
BOOL    CALLBACK DlgProc (HWND, UINT, WPARAM, LPARAM) ;
void SetLogFontFromFields     (HWND hdlg, DLGPARAMS * pdp) ;
void SetFieldsFromTextMetric (HWND hdlg, DLGPARAMS * pdp) ;
void MySetMapMode (HDC hdc, int iMapMode) ;

int WINAPI WinMain (HINSTANCE hInstance, HINSTANCE hPrevInstance,
                    PSTR szCmdLine, int iCmdShow)
{
    HWND      hwnd ;
    MSG       msg ;
    WNDCLASS wndclass ;

    wndclass.style         = CS_HREDRAW | CS_VREDRAW ;
    wndclass.lpfnWndProc   = WndProc ;
    wndclass.cbClsExtra    = 0 ;
    wndclass.cbWndExtra    = 0 ;
    wndclass.hInstance     = hInstance ;
    wndclass.hIcon         = LoadIcon (NULL, IDI_APPLICATION) ;
    wndclass.hCursor       = LoadCursor (NULL, IDC_ARROW) ;
    wndclass.hbrBackground = (HBRUSH) GetStockObject (WHITE_BRUSH) ;
    wndclass.lpszMenuName  = szAppName ;
    wndclass.lpszClassName = szAppName ;

    if (!RegisterClass (&wndclass))
    {
        MessageBox (NULL, TEXT ("This program requires Windows NT!"),
            szAppName, MB_ICONERROR) ;
        return 0 ;
    }

    hwnd = CreateWindow (szAppName, TEXT ("PickFont: Create Logical Font"),
                    WS_OVERLAPPEDWINDOW | WS_CLIPCHILDREN,
                    CW_USEDEFAULT, CW_USEDEFAULT,
                    CW_USEDEFAULT, CW_USEDEFAULT,
                    NULL, NULL, hInstance, NULL) ;

    ShowWindow (hwnd, iCmdShow) ;
    UpdateWindow (hwnd) ;

    while (GetMessage (&msg, NULL, 0, 0))
    {
        if (hdlg == 0 || !IsDialogMessage (hdlg, &msg))
        {
            TranslateMessage (&msg) ;
            DispatchMessage (&msg) ;
        }
```

```
        }
    return msg.wParam ;
}

LRESULT CALLBACK WndProc (HWND hwnd, UINT message, WPARAM wParam, LPARAM lParam)
{
    static DLGPARAMS dp ;
    static TCHAR      szText[] = TEXT ("\x41\x42\x43\x44\x45 ")
                                 TEXT ("\x61\x62\x63\x64\x65 ")

                                 TEXT ("\xC0\xC1\xC2\xC3\xC4\xC5 ")
                                 TEXT ("\xE0\xE1\xE2\xE3\xE4\xE5 ")
#ifdef UNICODE
                                 TEXT ("\x0390\x0391\x0392\x0393\x0394\x0395 ")
                                 TEXT ("\x03B0\x03B1\x03B2\x03B3\x03B4\x03B5 ")

                                 TEXT ("\x0410\x0411\x0412\x0413\x0414\x0415 ")
                                 TEXT ("\x0430\x0431\x0432\x0433\x0434\x0435 ")

                                 TEXT ("\x5000\x5001\x5002\x5003\x5004")
#endif
                                 ;
    HDC              hdc ;
    PAINTSTRUCT      ps ;
    RECT             rect ;

    switch (message)
    {
    case WM_CREATE:
        dp.iDevice = IDM_DEVICE_SCREEN ;

        hdlg = CreateDialogParam ((((LPCREATESTRUCT) lParam)->hInstance,
                                  szAppName, hwnd, DlgProc, (LPARAM) &dp) ;
        return 0 ;

    case WM_SETFOCUS:
        SetFocus (hdlg) ;
        return 0 ;

    case WM_COMMAND:
        switch (LOWORD (wParam))
        {
        case IDM_DEVICE_SCREEN:
        case IDM_DEVICE_PRINTER:
            CheckMenuItem (GetMenu (hwnd), dp.iDevice, MF_UNCHECKED) ;
            dp.iDevice = LOWORD (wParam) ;
            CheckMenuItem (GetMenu (hwnd), dp.iDevice, MF_CHECKED) ;
```

(continued)

1011

Figure 17-1. *continued*

```
              SendMessage (hwnd, WM_COMMAND, IDOK, 0) ;
              return 0 ;
         }
         break ;

    case WM_PAINT:
         hdc = BeginPaint (hwnd, &ps) ;

              // Set graphics mode so escapement works in Windows NT

         SetGraphicsMode (hdc, dp.fAdvGraphics ? GM_ADVANCED : GM_COMPATIBLE) ;

              // Set the mapping mode and the mapper flag

         MySetMapMode (hdc, dp.iMapMode) ;
         SetMapperFlags (hdc, dp.fMatchAspect) ;

              // Find the point to begin drawing text

         GetClientRect (hdlg, &rect) ;
         rect.bottom += 1 ;
         DPtoLP (hdc, (PPOINT) &rect, 2) ;

              // Create and select the font; display the text

         SelectObject (hdc, CreateFontIndirect (&dp.lf)) ;
         TextOut (hdc, rect.left, rect.bottom, szText, lstrlen (szText)) ;

         DeleteObject (SelectObject (hdc, GetStockObject (SYSTEM_FONT))) ;
         EndPaint (hwnd, &ps) ;
         return 0 ;

    case WM_DESTROY:
         PostQuitMessage (0) ;
         return 0 ;
    }
    return DefWindowProc (hwnd, message, wParam, lParam) ;
}

BOOL CALLBACK DlgProc (HWND hdlg, UINT message, WPARAM wParam, LPARAM lParam)
{
    static DLGPARAMS * pdp ;
    static PRINTDLG    pd = { sizeof (PRINTDLG) } ;
    HDC                hdcDevice ;
    HFONT              hFont ;

    switch (message)
```

```
{
case WM_INITDIALOG:
        // Save pointer to dialog-parameters structure in WndProc

    pdp = (DLGPARAMS *) lParam ;

    SendDlgItemMessage (hdlg, IDC_LF_FACENAME, EM_LIMITTEXT,
                        LF_FACESIZE - 1, 0) ;

    CheckRadioButton (hdlg, IDC_OUT_DEFAULT, IDC_OUT_OUTLINE,
                        IDC_OUT_DEFAULT) ;

    CheckRadioButton (hdlg, IDC_DEFAULT_QUALITY, IDC_PROOF_QUALITY,
                        IDC_DEFAULT_QUALITY) ;

    CheckRadioButton (hdlg, IDC_DEFAULT_PITCH, IDC_VARIABLE_PITCH,
                        IDC_DEFAULT_PITCH) ;

    CheckRadioButton (hdlg, IDC_FF_DONTCARE, IDC_FF_DECORATIVE,
                        IDC_FF_DONTCARE) ;

    CheckRadioButton (hdlg, IDC_MM_TEXT, IDC_MM_LOGTWIPS,
                        IDC_MM_TEXT) ;

    SendMessage (hdlg, WM_COMMAND, IDOK, 0) ;

                            // fall through
case WM_SETFOCUS:
    SetFocus (GetDlgItem (hdlg, IDC_LF_HEIGHT)) ;
    return FALSE ;

case WM_COMMAND:
    switch (LOWORD (wParam))
    {
    case IDC_CHARSET_HELP:
        MessageBox (hdlg,
                    TEXT ("0 = Ansi\n")
                    TEXT ("1 = Default\n")
                    TEXT ("2 = Symbol\n")
                    TEXT ("128 = Shift JIS (Japanese)\n")
                    TEXT ("129 = Hangul (Korean)\n")
                    TEXT ("130 = Johab (Korean)\n")
                    TEXT ("134 = GB 2312 (Simplified Chinese)\n")
                    TEXT ("136 = Chinese Big 5 (Traditional Chinese)\n")
                    TEXT ("177 = Hebrew\n")
                    TEXT ("178 = Arabic\n")
```

(continued)

Figure 17-1. *continued*

```
                    TEXT ("161 = Greek\n")
                    TEXT ("162 = Turkish\n")
                    TEXT ("163 = Vietnamese\n")
                    TEXT ("204 = Russian\n")
                    TEXT ("222 = Thai\n")
                    TEXT ("238 = East European\n")
                    TEXT ("255 = OEM"),
                    szAppName, MB_OK | MB_ICONINFORMATION) ;
     return TRUE ;

     // These radio buttons set the lfOutPrecision field

case IDC_OUT_DEFAULT:
     pdp->lf.lfOutPrecision = OUT_DEFAULT_PRECIS ;
     return TRUE ;

case IDC_OUT_STRING:
     pdp->lf.lfOutPrecision = OUT_STRING_PRECIS ;
     return TRUE ;

case IDC_OUT_CHARACTER:
     pdp->lf.lfOutPrecision = OUT_CHARACTER_PRECIS ;
     return TRUE ;

case IDC_OUT_STROKE:
     pdp->lf.lfOutPrecision = OUT_STROKE_PRECIS ;
     return TRUE ;

case IDC_OUT_TT:
     pdp->lf.lfOutPrecision = OUT_TT_PRECIS ;
     return TRUE ;

case IDC_OUT_DEVICE:
     pdp->lf.lfOutPrecision = OUT_DEVICE_PRECIS ;
     return TRUE ;

case IDC_OUT_RASTER:
     pdp->lf.lfOutPrecision = OUT_RASTER_PRECIS ;
     return TRUE ;

case IDC_OUT_TT_ONLY:
     pdp->lf.lfOutPrecision = OUT_TT_ONLY_PRECIS ;
     return TRUE ;

case IDC_OUT_OUTLINE:
     pdp->lf.lfOutPrecision = OUT_OUTLINE_PRECIS ;
     return TRUE ;
```

```
          // These three radio buttons set the lfQuality field

case IDC_DEFAULT_QUALITY:
     pdp->lf.lfQuality = DEFAULT_QUALITY ;
     return TRUE ;

case IDC_DRAFT_QUALITY:
     pdp->lf.lfQuality = DRAFT_QUALITY ;
     return TRUE ;

case IDC_PROOF_QUALITY:
     pdp->lf.lfQuality = PROOF_QUALITY ;
     return TRUE ;

          // These three radio buttons set the lower nibble
          //   of the lfPitchAndFamily field

case IDC_DEFAULT_PITCH:
     pdp->lf.lfPitchAndFamily =
          (0xF0 & pdp->lf.lfPitchAndFamily) | DEFAULT_PITCH ;
     return TRUE ;

case IDC_FIXED_PITCH:
     pdp->lf.lfPitchAndFamily =
          (0xF0 & pdp->lf.lfPitchAndFamily) | FIXED_PITCH ;
     return TRUE ;

case IDC_VARIABLE_PITCH:
     pdp->lf.lfPitchAndFamily =
          (0xF0 & pdp->lf.lfPitchAndFamily) | VARIABLE_PITCH ;
     return TRUE ;

          // These six radio buttons set the upper nibble
          //   of the lfPitchAndFamily field

case IDC_FF_DONTCARE:
     pdp->lf.lfPitchAndFamily =
          (0x0F & pdp->lf.lfPitchAndFamily) | FF_DONTCARE ;
     return TRUE ;

case IDC_FF_ROMAN:
     pdp->lf.lfPitchAndFamily =
          (0x0F & pdp->lf.lfPitchAndFamily) | FF_ROMAN ;
     return TRUE ;

case IDC_FF_SWISS:
     pdp->lf.lfPitchAndFamily =
```

(continued)

Figure 17-1. *continued*

```
                    (0x0F & pdp->lf.lfPitchAndFamily) | FF_SWISS ;
          return TRUE ;

     case IDC_FF_MODERN:
          pdp->lf.lfPitchAndFamily =
                    (0x0F & pdp->lf.lfPitchAndFamily) | FF_MODERN ;
          return TRUE ;

     case IDC_FF_SCRIPT:
          pdp->lf.lfPitchAndFamily =
                    (0x0F & pdp->lf.lfPitchAndFamily) | FF_SCRIPT ;
          return TRUE ;

     case IDC_FF_DECORATIVE:
          pdp->lf.lfPitchAndFamily =
                    (0x0F & pdp->lf.lfPitchAndFamily) | FF_DECORATIVE ;
          return TRUE ;

          // Mapping mode:

     case IDC_MM_TEXT:
     case IDC_MM_LOMETRIC:
     case IDC_MM_HIMETRIC:
     case IDC_MM_LOENGLISH:
     case IDC_MM_HIENGLISH:
     case IDC_MM_TWIPS:
     case IDC_MM_LOGTWIPS:
          pdp->iMapMode = LOWORD (wParam) ;
          return TRUE ;

          // OK button pressed
          // -----------------

     case IDOK:
               // Get LOGFONT structure

          SetLogFontFromFields (hdlg, pdp) ;

               // Set Match-Aspect and Advanced Graphics flags

          pdp->fMatchAspect = IsDlgButtonChecked (hdlg, IDC_MATCH_ASPECT) ;
          pdp->fAdvGraphics = IsDlgButtonChecked (hdlg, IDC_ADV_GRAPHICS) ;

               // Get Information Context
```

```
                    if (pdp->iDevice == IDM_DEVICE_SCREEN)
                    {
                         hdcDevice = CreateIC (TEXT ("DISPLAY"), NULL, NULL, NULL) ;
                    }
                    else
                    {
                         pd.hwndOwner = hdlg ;
                         pd.Flags = PD_RETURNDEFAULT | PD_RETURNIC ;
                         pd.hDevNames = NULL ;
                         pd.hDevMode = NULL ;

                         PrintDlg (&pd) ;

                         hdcDevice = pd.hDC ;
                    }
                         // Set the mapping mode and the mapper flag

                    MySetMapMode (hdcDevice, pdp->iMapMode) ;
                    SetMapperFlags (hdcDevice, pdp->fMatchAspect) ;

                         // Create font and select it into IC

                    hFont = CreateFontIndirect (&pdp->lf) ;
                    SelectObject (hdcDevice, hFont) ;

                         // Get the text metrics and face name

                    GetTextMetrics (hdcDevice, &pdp->tm) ;
                    GetTextFace (hdcDevice, LF_FULLFACESIZE, pdp->szFaceName) ;
                    DeleteDC (hdcDevice) ;
                    DeleteObject (hFont) ;

                         // Update dialog fields and invalidate main window

                    SetFieldsFromTextMetric (hdlg, pdp) ;
                    InvalidateRect (GetParent (hdlg), NULL, TRUE) ;
                    return TRUE ;
               }
          break ;
     }
     return FALSE ;
}
void SetLogFontFromFields (HWND hdlg, DLGPARAMS * pdp)
{
     pdp->lf.lfHeight      = GetDlgItemInt (hdlg, IDC_LF_HEIGHT,  NULL, TRUE) ;
     pdp->lf.lfWidth       = GetDlgItemInt (hdlg, IDC_LF_WIDTH,   NULL, TRUE) ;
```

(continued)

Figure 17-1. *continued*

```
        pdp->lf.lfEscapement  = GetDlgItemInt (hdlg, IDC_LF_ESCAPE,  NULL, TRUE) ;
        pdp->lf.lfOrientation = GetDlgItemInt (hdlg, IDC_LF_ORIENT,  NULL, TRUE) ;
        pdp->lf.lfWeight      = GetDlgItemInt (hdlg, IDC_LF_WEIGHT,  NULL, TRUE) ;
        pdp->lf.lfCharSet     = GetDlgItemInt (hdlg, IDC_LF_CHARSET, NULL, FALSE) ;

        pdp->lf.lfItalic =
                    IsDlgButtonChecked (hdlg, IDC_LF_ITALIC) == BST_CHECKED ;
        pdp->lf.lfUnderline =
                    IsDlgButtonChecked (hdlg, IDC_LF_UNDER)  == BST_CHECKED ;
        pdp->lf.lfStrikeOut =
                    IsDlgButtonChecked (hdlg, IDC_LF_STRIKE) == BST_CHECKED ;

        GetDlgItemText (hdlg, IDC_LF_FACENAME, pdp->lf.lfFaceName, LF_FACESIZE) ;
}

void SetFieldsFromTextMetric (HWND hdlg, DLGPARAMS * pdp)
{
        TCHAR   szBuffer [10] ;
        TCHAR * szYes = TEXT ("Yes") ;
        TCHAR * szNo  = TEXT ("No") ;
        TCHAR * szFamily [] = { TEXT ("Don't Know"), TEXT ("Roman"),
                               TEXT ("Swiss"),      TEXT ("Modern"),
                               TEXT ("Script"),     TEXT ("Decorative"),
                               TEXT ("Undefined") } ;

        SetDlgItemInt (hdlg, IDC_TM_HEIGHT,   pdp->tm.tmHeight,            TRUE) ;
        SetDlgItemInt (hdlg, IDC_TM_ASCENT,   pdp->tm.tmAscent,            TRUE) ;
        SetDlgItemInt (hdlg, IDC_TM_DESCENT,  pdp->tm.tmDescent,           TRUE) ;
        SetDlgItemInt (hdlg, IDC_TM_INTLEAD,  pdp->tm.tmInternalLeading,   TRUE) ;
        SetDlgItemInt (hdlg, IDC_TM_EXTLEAD,  pdp->tm.tmExternalLeading,   TRUE) ;
        SetDlgItemInt (hdlg, IDC_TM_AVECHAR,  pdp->tm.tmAveCharWidth,      TRUE) ;
        SetDlgItemInt (hdlg, IDC_TM_MAXCHAR,  pdp->tm.tmMaxCharWidth,      TRUE) ;
        SetDlgItemInt (hdlg, IDC_TM_WEIGHT,   pdp->tm.tmWeight,            TRUE) ;
        SetDlgItemInt (hdlg, IDC_TM_OVERHANG, pdp->tm.tmOverhang,          TRUE) ;
        SetDlgItemInt (hdlg, IDC_TM_DIGASPX,  pdp->tm.tmDigitizedAspectX, TRUE) ;
        SetDlgItemInt (hdlg, IDC_TM_DIGASPY,  pdp->tm.tmDigitizedAspectY, TRUE) ;

        wsprintf (szBuffer, BCHARFORM, pdp->tm.tmFirstChar) ;
        SetDlgItemText (hdlg, IDC_TM_FIRSTCHAR, szBuffer) ;

        wsprintf (szBuffer, BCHARFORM, pdp->tm.tmLastChar) ;
        SetDlgItemText (hdlg, IDC_TM_LASTCHAR, szBuffer) ;

        wsprintf (szBuffer, BCHARFORM, pdp->tm.tmDefaultChar) ;
        SetDlgItemText (hdlg, IDC_TM_DEFCHAR, szBuffer) ;
```

```
        wsprintf (szBuffer, BCHARFORM, pdp->tm.tmBreakChar) ;
        SetDlgItemText (hdlg, IDC_TM_BREAKCHAR, szBuffer) ;

        SetDlgItemText (hdlg, IDC_TM_ITALIC, pdp->tm.tmItalic     ? szYes : szNo) ;
        SetDlgItemText (hdlg, IDC_TM_UNDER,  pdp->tm.tmUnderlined ? szYes : szNo) ;
        SetDlgItemText (hdlg, IDC_TM_STRUCK, pdp->tm.tmStruckOut  ? szYes : szNo) ;

        SetDlgItemText (hdlg, IDC_TM_VARIABLE,
                TMPF_FIXED_PITCH & pdp->tm.tmPitchAndFamily ? szYes : szNo) ;

        SetDlgItemText (hdlg, IDC_TM_VECTOR,
                TMPF_VECTOR & pdp->tm.tmPitchAndFamily ? szYes : szNo) ;

        SetDlgItemText (hdlg, IDC_TM_TRUETYPE,
                TMPF_TRUETYPE & pdp->tm.tmPitchAndFamily ? szYes : szNo) ;

        SetDlgItemText (hdlg, IDC_TM_DEVICE,
                TMPF_DEVICE & pdp->tm.tmPitchAndFamily ? szYes : szNo) ;

        SetDlgItemText (hdlg, IDC_TM_FAMILY,
                szFamily [min (6, pdp->tm.tmPitchAndFamily >> 4)]) ;

        SetDlgItemInt  (hdlg, IDC_TM_CHARSET,  pdp->tm.tmCharSet, FALSE) ;
        SetDlgItemText (hdlg, IDC_TM_FACENAME, pdp->szFaceName) ;
}

void MySetMapMode (HDC hdc, int iMapMode)
{
        switch (iMapMode)
        {
        case IDC_MM_TEXT:        SetMapMode (hdc, MM_TEXT) ;        break ;
        case IDC_MM_LOMETRIC:    SetMapMode (hdc, MM_LOMETRIC) ;    break ;
        case IDC_MM_HIMETRIC:    SetMapMode (hdc, MM_HIMETRIC) ;    break ;
        case IDC_MM_LOENGLISH:   SetMapMode (hdc, MM_LOENGLISH) ;   break ;
        case IDC_MM_HIENGLISH:   SetMapMode (hdc, MM_HIENGLISH) ;   break ;
        case IDC_MM_TWIPS:       SetMapMode (hdc, MM_TWIPS) ;       break ;
        case IDC_MM_LOGTWIPS:
            SetMapMode (hdc, MM_ANISOTROPIC) ;
            SetWindowExtEx (hdc, 1440, 1440, NULL) ;
            SetViewportExtEx (hdc, GetDeviceCaps (hdc, LOGPIXELSX),
                                   GetDeviceCaps (hdc, LOGPIXELSY), NULL) ;
            break ;
        }
}
```

(continued)

Figure 17-1. *continued*

PICKFONT.RC

```
//Microsoft Developer Studio generated resource script.

#include "resource.h"
#include "afxres.h"


/////////////////////////////////////////////////////////////////////////////
// Dialog

PICKFONT DIALOG DISCARDABLE  0, 0, 348, 308
STYLE WS_CHILD | WS_VISIBLE | WS_BORDER
FONT 8, "MS Sans Serif"
BEGIN
    LTEXT           "&Height:",IDC_STATIC,8,10,44,8
    EDITTEXT        IDC_LF_HEIGHT,64,8,24,12,ES_AUTOHSCROLL
    LTEXT           "&Width",IDC_STATIC,8,26,44,8
    EDITTEXT        IDC_LF_WIDTH,64,24,24,12,ES_AUTOHSCROLL
    LTEXT           "Escapement:",IDC_STATIC,8,42,44,8
    EDITTEXT        IDC_LF_ESCAPE,64,40,24,12,ES_AUTOHSCROLL
    LTEXT           "Orientation:",IDC_STATIC,8,58,44,8
    EDITTEXT        IDC_LF_ORIENT,64,56,24,12,ES_AUTOHSCROLL
    LTEXT           "Weight:",IDC_STATIC,8,74,44,8
    EDITTEXT        IDC_LF_WEIGHT,64,74,24,12,ES_AUTOHSCROLL
    GROUPBOX        "Mapping Mode",IDC_STATIC,97,3,96,90,WS_GROUP
    CONTROL         "Text",IDC_MM_TEXT,"Button",BS_AUTORADIOBUTTON,104,13,56,
                    8
    CONTROL         "Low Metric",IDC_MM_LOMETRIC,"Button",BS_AUTORADIOBUTTON,
                    104,24,56,8
    CONTROL         "High Metric",IDC_MM_HIMETRIC,"Button",
                    BS_AUTORADIOBUTTON,104,35,56,8
    CONTROL         "Low English",IDC_MM_LOENGLISH,"Button",
                    BS_AUTORADIOBUTTON,104,46,56,8
    CONTROL         "High English",IDC_MM_HIENGLISH,"Button",
                    BS_AUTORADIOBUTTON,104,57,56,8
    CONTROL         "Twips",IDC_MM_TWIPS,"Button",BS_AUTORADIOBUTTON,104,68,
                    56,8
    CONTROL         "Logical Twips",IDC_MM_LOGTWIPS,"Button",
                    BS_AUTORADIOBUTTON,104,79,64,8
    CONTROL         "Italic",IDC_LF_ITALIC,"Button",BS_AUTOCHECKBOX |
                    WS_TABSTOP,8,90,48,12
    CONTROL         "Underline",IDC_LF_UNDER,"Button",BS_AUTOCHECKBOX |
                    WS_TABSTOP,8,104,48,12
    CONTROL         "Strike Out",IDC_LF_STRIKE,"Button",BS_AUTOCHECKBOX |
                    WS_TABSTOP,8,118,48,12
    CONTROL         "Match Aspect",IDC_MATCH_ASPECT,"Button",BS_AUTOCHECKBOX |
                    WS_TABSTOP,60,104,62,8
```

```
CONTROL         "Adv Grfx Mode",IDC_ADV_GRAPHICS,"Button",
                BS_AUTOCHECKBOX | WS_TABSTOP,60,118,62,8
LTEXT           "Character Set:",IDC_STATIC,8,137,46,8
EDITTEXT        IDC_LF_CHARSET,58,135,24,12,ES_AUTOHSCROLL
PUSHBUTTON      "?",IDC_CHARSET_HELP,90,135,14,14
GROUPBOX        "Quality",IDC_STATIC,132,98,62,48,WS_GROUP
CONTROL         "Default",IDC_DEFAULT_QUALITY,"Button",
                BS_AUTORADIOBUTTON,136,110,40,8
CONTROL         "Draft",IDC_DRAFT_QUALITY,"Button",BS_AUTORADIOBUTTON,
                136,122,40,8
CONTROL         "Proof",IDC_PROOF_QUALITY,"Button",BS_AUTORADIOBUTTON,
                136,134,40,8
LTEXT           "Face Name:",IDC_STATIC,8,154,44,8
EDITTEXT        IDC_LF_FACENAME,58,152,136,12,ES_AUTOHSCROLL
GROUPBOX        "Output Precision",IDC_STATIC,8,166,118,133,WS_GROUP
CONTROL         "OUT_DEFAULT_PRECIS",IDC_OUT_DEFAULT,"Button",
                BS_AUTORADIOBUTTON,12,178,112,8
CONTROL         "OUT_STRING_PRECIS",IDC_OUT_STRING,"Button",
                BS_AUTORADIOBUTTON,12,191,112,8
CONTROL         "OUT_CHARACTER_PRECIS",IDC_OUT_CHARACTER,"Button",
                BS_AUTORADIOBUTTON,12,204,112,8
CONTROL         "OUT_STROKE_PRECIS",IDC_OUT_STROKE,"Button",
                BS_AUTORADIOBUTTON,12,217,112,8
CONTROL         "OUT_TT_PRECIS",IDC_OUT_TT,"Button",BS_AUTORADIOBUTTON,
                12,230,112,8
CONTROL         "OUT_DEVICE_PRECIS",IDC_OUT_DEVICE,"Button",
                BS_AUTORADIOBUTTON,12,243,112,8
CONTROL         "OUT_RASTER_PRECIS",IDC_OUT_RASTER,"Button",
                BS_AUTORADIOBUTTON,12,256,112,8
CONTROL         "OUT_TT_ONLY_PRECIS",IDC_OUT_TT_ONLY,"Button",
                BS_AUTORADIOBUTTON,12,269,112,8
CONTROL         "OUT_OUTLINE_PRECIS",IDC_OUT_OUTLINE,"Button",
                BS_AUTORADIOBUTTON,12,282,112,8
GROUPBOX        "Pitch",IDC_STATIC,132,166,62,50,WS_GROUP
CONTROL         "Default",IDC_DEFAULT_PITCH,"Button",BS_AUTORADIOBUTTON,
                137,176,52,8
CONTROL         "Fixed",IDC_FIXED_PITCH,"Button",BS_AUTORADIOBUTTON,137,
                189,52,8
CONTROL         "Variable",IDC_VARIABLE_PITCH,"Button",
                BS_AUTORADIOBUTTON,137,203,52,8
GROUPBOX        "Family",IDC_STATIC,132,218,62,82,WS_GROUP
CONTROL         "Don't Care",IDC_FF_DONTCARE,"Button",BS_AUTORADIOBUTTON,
                137,229,52,8
CONTROL         "Roman",IDC_FF_ROMAN,"Button",BS_AUTORADIOBUTTON,137,241,
                52,8
CONTROL         "Swiss",IDC_FF_SWISS,"Button",BS_AUTORADIOBUTTON,137,253,
                52,8
```

(continued)

Figure 17-1. *continued*

```
        CONTROL         "Modern",IDC_FF_MODERN,"Button",BS_AUTORADIOBUTTON,137,
                        265,52,8
        CONTROL         "Script",IDC_FF_SCRIPT,"Button",BS_AUTORADIOBUTTON,137,
                        277,52,8
        CONTROL         "Decorative",IDC_FF_DECORATIVE,"Button",
                        BS_AUTORADIOBUTTON,137,289,52,8
        DEFPUSHBUTTON   "OK",IDOK,247,286,50,14
        GROUPBOX        "Text Metrics",IDC_STATIC,201,2,140,272,WS_GROUP
        LTEXT           "Height:",IDC_STATIC,207,12,64,8
        LTEXT           "0",IDC_TM_HEIGHT,281,12,44,8
        LTEXT           "Ascent:",IDC_STATIC,207,22,64,8
        LTEXT           "0",IDC_TM_ASCENT,281,22,44,8
        LTEXT           "Descent:",IDC_STATIC,207,32,64,8
        LTEXT           "0",IDC_TM_DESCENT,281,32,44,8
        LTEXT           "Internal Leading:",IDC_STATIC,207,42,64,8
        LTEXT           "0",IDC_TM_INTLEAD,281,42,44,8
        LTEXT           "External Leading:",IDC_STATIC,207,52,64,8
        LTEXT           "0",IDC_TM_EXTLEAD,281,52,44,8
        LTEXT           "Ave Char Width:",IDC_STATIC,207,62,64,8
        LTEXT           "0",IDC_TM_AVECHAR,281,62,44,8
        LTEXT           "Max Char Width:",IDC_STATIC,207,72,64,8
        LTEXT           "0",IDC_TM_MAXCHAR,281,72,44,8
        LTEXT           "Weight:",IDC_STATIC,207,82,64,8
        LTEXT           "0",IDC_TM_WEIGHT,281,82,44,8
        LTEXT           "Overhang:",IDC_STATIC,207,92,64,8
        LTEXT           "0",IDC_TM_OVERHANG,281,92,44,8
        LTEXT           "Digitized Aspect X:",IDC_STATIC,207,102,64,8
        LTEXT           "0",IDC_TM_DIGASPX,281,102,44,8
        LTEXT           "Digitized Aspect Y:",IDC_STATIC,207,112,64,8
        LTEXT           "0",IDC_TM_DIGASPY,281,112,44,8
        LTEXT           "First Char:",IDC_STATIC,207,122,64,8
        LTEXT           "0",IDC_TM_FIRSTCHAR,281,122,44,8
        LTEXT           "Last Char:",IDC_STATIC,207,132,64,8
        LTEXT           "0",IDC_TM_LASTCHAR,281,132,44,8
        LTEXT           "Default Char:",IDC_STATIC,207,142,64,8
        LTEXT           "0",IDC_TM_DEFCHAR,281,142,44,8
        LTEXT           "Break Char:",IDC_STATIC,207,152,64,8
        LTEXT           "0",IDC_TM_BREAKCHAR,281,152,44,8
        LTEXT           "Italic?",IDC_STATIC,207,162,64,8
        LTEXT           "0",IDC_TM_ITALIC,281,162,44,8
        LTEXT           "Underlined?",IDC_STATIC,207,172,64,8
        LTEXT           "0",IDC_TM_UNDER,281,172,44,8
        LTEXT           "Struck Out?",IDC_STATIC,207,182,64,8
        LTEXT           "0",IDC_TM_STRUCK,281,182,44,8
        LTEXT           "Variable Pitch?",IDC_STATIC,207,192,64,8
        LTEXT           "0",IDC_TM_VARIABLE,281,192,44,8
```

```
    LTEXT          "Vector Font?",IDC_STATIC,207,202,64,8
    LTEXT          "0",IDC_TM_VECTOR,281,202,44,8
    LTEXT          "TrueType Font?",IDC_STATIC,207,212,64,8
    LTEXT          "0",IDC_TM_TRUETYPE,281,212,44,8
    LTEXT          "Device Font?",IDC_STATIC,207,222,64,8
    LTEXT          "0",IDC_TM_DEVICE,281,222,44,8
    LTEXT          "Family:",IDC_STATIC,207,232,64,8
    LTEXT          "0",IDC_TM_FAMILY,281,232,44,8
    LTEXT          "Character Set:",IDC_STATIC,207,242,64,8
    LTEXT          "0",IDC_TM_CHARSET,281,242,44,8
    LTEXT          "0",IDC_TM_FACENAME,207,262,128,8
END


/////////////////////////////////////////////////////////////////////////
// Menu

PICKFONT MENU DISCARDABLE
BEGIN
    POPUP "&Device"
    BEGIN
        MENUITEM "&Screen",                 IDM_DEVICE_SCREEN, CHECKED
        MENUITEM "&Printer",                IDM_DEVICE_PRINTER
    END
END
```

RESOURCE.H

```
// Microsoft Developer Studio generated include file.
// Used by PickFont.rc

#define IDC_LF_HEIGHT           1000
#define IDC_LF_WIDTH            1001
#define IDC_LF_ESCAPE           1002
#define IDC_LF_ORIENT           1003
#define IDC_LF_WEIGHT           1004
#define IDC_MM_TEXT             1005
#define IDC_MM_LOMETRIC         1006
#define IDC_MM_HIMETRIC         1007
#define IDC_MM_LOENGLISH        1008
#define IDC_MM_HIENGLISH        1009
#define IDC_MM_TWIPS            1010
#define IDC_MM_LOGTWIPS         1011
#define IDC_LF_ITALIC           1012
#define IDC_LF_UNDER            1013
#define IDC_LF_STRIKE           1014
```

(continued)

Figure 17-1. *continued*

```
#define IDC_MATCH_ASPECT          1015
#define IDC_ADV_GRAPHICS          1016
#define IDC_LF_CHARSET            1017
#define IDC_CHARSET_HELP          1018
#define IDC_DEFAULT_QUALITY       1019
#define IDC_DRAFT_QUALITY         1020
#define IDC_PROOF_QUALITY         1021
#define IDC_LF_FACENAME           1022
#define IDC_OUT_DEFAULT           1023
#define IDC_OUT_STRING            1024
#define IDC_OUT_CHARACTER         1025
#define IDC_OUT_STROKE            1026
#define IDC_OUT_TT                1027
#define IDC_OUT_DEVICE            1028
#define IDC_OUT_RASTER            1029
#define IDC_OUT_TT_ONLY           1030
#define IDC_OUT_OUTLINE           1031
#define IDC_DEFAULT_PITCH         1032
#define IDC_FIXED_PITCH           1033
#define IDC_VARIABLE_PITCH        1034
#define IDC_FF_DONTCARE           1035
#define IDC_FF_ROMAN              1036
#define IDC_FF_SWISS              1037
#define IDC_FF_MODERN             1038
#define IDC_FF_SCRIPT             1039
#define IDC_FF_DECORATIVE         1040
#define IDC_TM_HEIGHT             1041
#define IDC_TM_ASCENT             1042
#define IDC_TM_DESCENT            1043
#define IDC_TM_INTLEAD            1044
#define IDC_TM_EXTLEAD            1045
#define IDC_TM_AVECHAR            1046
#define IDC_TM_MAXCHAR            1047
#define IDC_TM_WEIGHT             1048
#define IDC_TM_OVERHANG           1049
#define IDC_TM_DIGASPX            1050
#define IDC_TM_DIGASPY            1051
#define IDC_TM_FIRSTCHAR          1052
#define IDC_TM_LASTCHAR           1053
#define IDC_TM_DEFCHAR            1054
#define IDC_TM_BREAKCHAR          1055
#define IDC_TM_ITALIC             1056
#define IDC_TM_UNDER              1057
#define IDC_TM_STRUCK             1058
#define IDC_TM_VARIABLE           1059
#define IDC_TM_VECTOR             1060
```

```
#define IDC_TM_TRUETYPE            1061
#define IDC_TM_DEVICE              1062
#define IDC_TM_FAMILY              1063
#define IDC_TM_CHARSET             1064
#define IDC_TM_FACENAME            1065
#define IDM_DEVICE_SCREEN          40001
#define IDM_DEVICE_PRINTER         40002
```

Figure 17-2 shows a typical PICKFONT screen. The left side of the PICKFONT display is a modeless dialog box that allows you to select most of the fields of the logical font structure. The right side of the dialog box shows the results of *GetTextMetrics* after the font is selected in the device context. Below the dialog box, the program displays a string of characters using this font. Because the modeless dialog box is so big, you're best off running this program on a display size of 1024 by 768 or larger.

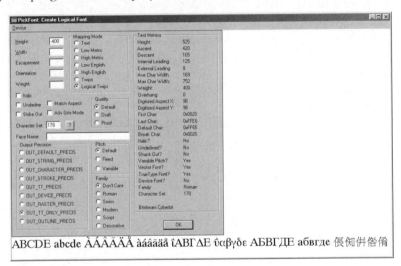

Figure 17-2. *A typical PICKFONT display (Unicode version under Windows NT).*

The modeless dialog box also contains some options that are not part of the logical font structure. These are the mapping mode, including my Logical Twips mode; the Match Aspect option, which changes the way Windows matches a logical font to a real font; and "Adv Grfx Mode," which sets the advanced graphics mode in Windows NT. I'll discuss these in more detail shortly.

From the Device menu you can select the default printer rather than the video display. In this case, PICKFONT selects the logical font into the printer device context and displays the TEXTMETRIC structure from the printer. The program then selects the logical font into the window device context for displaying the sample string. Thus, the text displayed by the program might use a different font (a screen font) than the font described by the list of the TEXTMETRIC fields (which is a printer font).

Much of the PICKFONT program contains the logic necessary to maintain the dialog box, so I won't go into detail on the workings of the program. Instead, I'll explain what you're doing when you create and select a logical font.

The Logical Font Structure

To create a logical font, you can call *CreateFont*, a function that has 14 arguments. Generally, it's easier to define a structure of type LOGFONT,

```
LOGFONT lf ;
```

and then define the fields of this structure. When finish, you call *CreateFontIndirect* with a pointer to the structure:

```
hFont = CreatFontIndirect (&lf) ;
```

You don't need to set each and every field of the LOGFONT structure. If your logical font structure is defined as a static variable, all the fields will be initialized to 0. The 0 values are generally defaults. You can then use that structure directly without any changes, and *CreateFontIndirect* will return a handle to a font. When you select that font into the device context, you'll get a reasonable default font. You can be as specific or as vague as you want in the LOGFONT structure, and Windows will attempt to match your requests with a real font.

As I discuss each field of the LOGFONT structure, you may want to test them out using the PICKFONT program. Be sure to press Enter or the OK button when you want the program to use any fields you've entered.

The first two fields of the LOGFONT structure are in logical units, so they depend on the current setting of the mapping mode:

■ *lfHeight*   This is the desired height of the characters in logical units. You can set *lfHeight* to 0 for a default size, or you can set it to a positive or negative value depending on what you want the field to represent. If you set *lfHeight* to a positive value, you're implying that you want this value to be a height that includes internal leading (but not external leading). In effect, you're really requesting a font that is appropriate for a line spacing of *lfHeight*. If you set *lfHeight* to a negative value, Windows treats the absolute value of that number as a desired font height compatible with the point size. This is an important distinction: If you want a font of a particular point size, convert that point size to logical units and set the *lfHeight* field to the negative of that value. If *lfHeight* is positive, the *tmHeight* field of the resultant TEXTMETRIC structure will be roughly that value. (It's sometimes a little off, probably because of rounding.) If *lfHeight* is negative, it will roughly match the *tmHeight* field of the TEXTMETRIC structure less the *tmInternalLeading* field.

■ *lfWidth* This is the desired width of the characters in logical units. In most cases, you'll want to set this value to 0 and let Windows choose a font based solely on the height. Using a nonzero value does not work well with raster fonts, but with TrueType fonts you can easily use this to get a font that has wider or slimmer characters than normal. This field corresponds to the *tmAveCharWidth* field of the TEXTMETRIC structure. To use the *lfWidth* field intelligently, first set up the LOGFONT structure with an *lfWidth* field set to 0, create the logical font, select it into a device context, and then call *GetTextMetrics*. Get the *tmAveCharWidth* field, adjust it up or down, probably by a percentage, and then create a second font using that adjusted *tmAveCharWidth* value for *lfWidth*.

The next two fields specify the "escapement" and "orientation" of the text. In theory, *lfEscapement* allows character strings to be written at an angle (but with the baseline of each character still parallel to the horizontal axis) and *lfOrientation* allows individual characters to be tilted. These fields have never quite worked as advertised, and even today they don't work as they should except in one case: you're using a TrueType font, you're running Windows NT, and you first call *SetGraphicsMode* with the CM_ADVANCED flag set. You can accomplish the final requirement in PICKFONT by checking the "Adv Grfx Mode" check box.

To experiment with these fields in PICKFONT, be aware that the units are in tenths of a degree and indicate a counterclockwise rotation. It's easy to enter values that cause the sample text string to disappear! For this reason, use values between 0 and −600 (or so) or values between 3000 and 3600.

■ *lfEscapement* This is an angle in tenths of a degree, measured from the horizontal in a counterclockwise direction. It specifies how the successive characters of a string are placed when you write text. Here are some examples:

Value	*Placement of Characters*
0	Run from left to right (default)
900	Go up
1800	Run from right to left
2700	Go down

In Windows 98, this value sets both the escapement and orientation of TrueType text. In Windows NT, this value also normally sets both the escapement and orientation of TrueType text, except when you call *SetGraphicsMode* with the GM_ADVANCED argument, in which case it works as documented.

■ *lfOrientation*   This is an angle in tenths of a degree, measured from the horizontal in a counterclockwise direction. It affects the appearance of each individual character. Here are some examples:

Value	Character Appearance
0	Normal (default)
900	Tipped 90 degrees to the right
1800	Upside down
2700	Tipped 90 degrees to the left

This field has no effect except with a TrueType font under Windows NT with the graphics mode set to GM_ADVANCED, in which case it works as documented.

The remaining 10 fields follow:

■ *lfWeight*   This field allows you to specify boldface. The WINGDI.H header file defines a bunch of values to use with this field:

Value	Identifier
0	FW_DONTCARE
100	FW_THIN
200	FW_EXTRALIGHT or FW_ULTRALIGHT
300	FW_LIGHT
400	FW_NORMAL or FW_REGULAR
500	FW_MEDIUM
600	FW_SEMIBOLD or FW_DEMIBOLD
700	FW_BOLD
800	FW_EXTRABOLD or FW_ULTRABOLD
900	FW_HEAVY or FW_BLACK

In reality, this table is much more ambitious than anything that was ever implemented. You can use 0 or 400 for normal and 700 for bold.

■ *lfItalic*   When nonzero, this specifies italics. Windows can synthesize italics on GDI raster fonts. That is, Windows simply shifts some rows of the character bitmap to mimic italic. With TrueType fonts, Windows uses the actual italic or oblique version of the font.

■ *lfUnderline* When nonzero, this specifies underlining, which is always synthesized on GDI fonts. That is, the Windows GDI simply draws a line under each character, including spaces.

■ *lfStrikeOut* When nonzero, this specifies that the font should have a line drawn through the characters. This is also synthesized on GDI fonts.

■ *lfCharSet* This is a byte value that specifies the character set of the font. I'll have more to say about this field in the upcoming section, "Character Sets and Unicode," beginning on page 1033. In PICKFONT, you can press the button with the question mark to obtain a list of the character set codes you can use.

Notice that the *lfCharSet* field is the only field where a zero does not indicate a default value. A zero value is equivalent to ANSI_CHARSET, the ANSI character set used in the United States and Western Europe. The DEFAULT_ CHARSET code, which equals 1, indicates the default character set for the machine on which the program is running.

■ *lfOutPrecision* This specifies how Windows should attempt to match the desired font sizes and characteristics with actual fonts. It's a rather complex field that you probably won't use much. Check the documentation of the LOGFONT structure for more detail. Note that you can use the OUT_TT_ONLY_PRECIS flag to ensure that you always get a TrueType font.

■ *lfClipPrecision* This field specifies how characters are to be clipped when they lie partially outside the clipping region. This field is not used much and is not implemented in the PICKFONT program.

■ *lfQuality* This is an instruction to Windows regarding the matching of a desired font with a real font. It really has meaning with raster fonts only and should not affect TrueType fonts. The DRAFT_QUALITY flag indicates that you want GDI to scale raster fonts to achieve the size you want; the PROOF_QUALITY flag indicates no scaling should be done. The PROOF_QUALITY fonts are the most attractive, but they might be smaller than what you request. You'll probably use DEFAULT_QUALITY (or 0) in this field.

■ *lfPitchAndFamily* This byte is composed of two parts. You can use the C bitwise OR operator to combine two identifiers for this field. The lowest two bits specify whether the font has a fixed pitch (that is, all characters are the same width) or a variable pitch:

Value	Identifier
0	DEFAULT_PITCH
1	FIXED_PITCH
2	VARIABLE_PITCH

The upper half of this byte specifies the font family:

Value	Identifier
0x00	FW_DONTCARE
0x10	FF_ROMAN (variable widths, serifs)
0x20	FF_SWISS (variable widths, no serifs)
0x30	FF_MODERN (fixed pitch)
0x40	FF_SCRIPT (mimics handwriting)
0x50	FF_DECORATIVE

- *lfFaceName*   This is the actual text name of a typeface (such as Courier, Arial, or Times New Roman). This field is a byte array that is LF_FACESIZE (or 32 characters) wide. If you want a TrueType italic or boldface font, you can get it in one of two ways. You can use the complete typeface name (such as Times New Roman Italic) in the *lfFaceName* field, or you can use the base name (that is, Times New Roman) and set the *lfItalic* field.

The Font-Mapping Algorithm

After you set up the logical font structure, you call *CreateFontIndirect* to get a handle to the logical font. When you call *SelectObject* to select that logical font into a device context, Windows finds the real font that most closely matches the request. In doing so, it uses a "font-mapping algorithm." Certain fields of the structure are considered more important than other fields.

The best way to get a feel for font mapping is to spend some time experimenting with PICKFONT. Here are some general guidelines:

- The *lfCharSet* (character set) field is very important. It used to be that if you specified OEM_CHARSET (255), you'd get either one of the stroke fonts or the Terminal font because these were the only fonts that used the OEM character sets. However, with the advent of TrueType "Big Fonts" (discussed earlier in this book on page 256), a single TrueType font can be mapped to different character sets, including the OEM character set. You'll need to use SYMBOL_CHARSET (2) to get the Symbol font or the Wingdings font.

- A pitch value of FIXED_PITCH in the *lfPitchAndFamily* field is important because you are in effect telling Windows that you don't want to deal with a variable-width font.

- The *lfFaceName* field is important because you're being specific about the typeface of the font that you want. If you leave *lfFaceName* set to NULL and set the

family value in the *lfPitchAndFamily* field to a value other than FF_
DONTCARE, that field becomes important because you're being specific about
the font family.

■ For raster fonts, Windows will attempt to match the *lfHeight* value even if it
needs to increase the size of a smaller font. The height of the actual font will
always be less than or equal to that of the requested font unless there is no font
small enough to satisfy your request. For stroke or TrueType fonts, Windows
will simply scale the font to the desired height.

■ You can prevent Windows from scaling a raster font by setting *lfQuality* to
PROOF_QUALITY. By doing so, you're telling Windows that the requested
height of the font is less important than the appearance of the font.

■ If you specify *lfHeight* and *lfWeight* values that are out of line for the particular aspect ratio of the display, Windows can map to a raster font that is designed
for a display or other device of a different aspect ratio. This used to be a trick
to get a thin or thick font. (This is not really necessary with TrueType, of course.)
In general, you'll probably want to avoid matching with a font for another
device, which you can do in PICKFONT by clicking the check box marked
Match Aspect. If this box is checked, PICKFONT makes a call to *SetMapperFlags*
with a TRUE argument.

Finding Out About the Font

At the right side of the modeless dialog box in PICKFONT is the information obtained from
the *GetTextMetrics* function after the font has been selected in a device context. (Notice
that you can use PICKFONT's device menu to indicate whether you want this device context to be the screen or the default printer. The results might be different because different fonts might be available on the printer.) At the bottom of the list in PICKFONT is the
typeface name available from *GetTextFace*.

All the size values that Windows copies into the TEXTMETRIC structure are in logical units except for the digitized aspect ratios. The fields of the TEXTMETRIC structure are
as follows:

■ *tmHeight*   The height of the character in logical units. This is the value that
should approximate the *lfHeight* field specified in the LOGFONT structure, if
that value was positive, in which case it represents the line spacing of the font
rather than the point size. If the *lfHeight* field of the LOGFONT structure was
negative, the *tmHeight* field minus the *tmInternalLeading* field should approximate the absolute value of the *lfHeight* field.

■ *tmAscent*   The vertical size of the character above the baseline in logical units.

■ *tmDescent*   The vertical size of the character below the baseline in logical units.

■ *tmInternalLeading*   A vertical size included in the *tmHeight* value that is usually occupied by diacritics on some capital letters. Once again, you can calculate the point size of the font by subtracting the *tmInternalLeading* value from the *tmHeight* value.

■ *tmExternalLeading*   An additional amount of line spacing beyond *tmHeight* recommended by the designer of the font for spacing successive lines of text.

■ *tmAveCharWidth*   The average width of lowercase letters in the font.

■ *tmMaxCharWidth*   The width of the widest character in logical units. For a fixed-pitch font, this value is the same as *tmAveCharWidth*.

■ *tmWeight*   The weight of the font ranging from 0 through 999. In reality, the field will be 400 for a normal font and 700 for a boldface font.

■ *tmOverhang*   The amount of extra width (in logical units) that Windows adds to a raster font character when synthesizing italic or boldface. When a raster font is italicized, the *tmAveCharWidth* value remains unchanged, because a string of italicized characters has the same overall width as the same string of normal characters. For boldfacing, Windows must slightly expand the width of each character. For a boldface font, the *tmAveCharWidth* value less the *tmOverhang* value equals the *tmAveCharWidth* value for the same font without boldfacing.

■ *tmDigitizedAspectX* and *tmDigitizedAspectY*   The aspect ratio for which the font is appropriate. These are equivalent to values obtained from *GetDeviceCaps* with the LOGPIXELSX and LOGPIXELSY identifiers.

■ *tmFirstChar*   The character code of the first character in the font.

■ *tmLastChar*   The character code of the last character in the font. If the TEXTMETRIC structure is obtained by a call to *GetTextMetricsW* (the wide character version of the function), then this value might be greater than 255.

■ *tmDefaultChar*   The character code that Windows uses to display characters that are not in the font, usually a rectangle.

■ *tmBreakChar*   The character that Windows, and your programs, should use to determine word breaks when justifying text. Unless you're using something bizarre (such as an EBCDIC font), this will be 32—the space character.

■ *tmItalic*   Nonzero for an italic font.

■ *tmUnderlined*   Nonzero for an underlined font.

■ *tmStruckOut*   Nonzero for a strikethrough font.

■ *tmPitchAndFamily*   The four low-order bits are flags that indicate some characteristics about the font, indicated by the following identifiers defined in WINGDI.H:

Value	Identifier
0x01	TMPF_FIXED_PITCH
0x02	TMPF_VECTOR
0x04	TMPF_TRUETYPE
0x08	TMPF_DEVICE

Despite the name of the TMPF_FIXED_PITCH flag, the lowest bit is 1 if the font characters have a *variable* pitch. The second lowest bit (TMPF_VECTOR) will be 1 for TrueType fonts and fonts that use other scalable outline technologies, such as PostScript. The TMPF_DEVICE flag indicates a device font (that is, a font built into a printer) rather than a GDI-based font.

The top four bits of this field indicate the font family and are the same values used in the LOGFONT *lfPitchAndFamily* field.

■ *tmCharSet*   The character set identifier.

Character Sets and Unicode

I discussed the concept of the Windows character set in Chapter 6, where we had to deal with international issues involving the keyboard. In the LOGFONT and TEXTMETRIC structures, the character set of the desired font (or the actual font) is indicated by a one-byte number between 0 and 255. The character set identifiers are defined in WINGDI.H like so:

```
#define ANSI_CHARSET            0
#define DEFAULT_CHARSET         1
#define SYMBOL_CHARSET          2
#define MAC_CHARSET             77
#define SHIFTJIS_CHARSET        128
#define HANGEUL_CHARSET         129
#define HANGUL_CHARSET          129
#define JOHAB_CHARSET           130
#define GB2312_CHARSET          134
#define CHINESEBIG5_CHARSET     136
#define GREEK_CHARSET           161
#define TURKISH_CHARSET         162
#define VIETNAMESE_CHARSET      163
#define HEBREW_CHARSET          177
#define ARABIC_CHARSET          178
#define BALTIC_CHARSET          186
#define RUSSIAN_CHARSET         204
#define THAI_CHARSET            222
#define EASTEUROPE_CHARSET      238
#define OEM_CHARSET             255
```

The character set is similar in concept to the code page, but the character set is specific to Windows and is always less than or equal to 255.

As with all of the programs in this book, you can compile PICKFONT both with and without the UNICODE identifier defined. As usual, on the companion disc, the two versions of the program are located in the DEBUG and RELEASE directories, respectively.

Notice that the character string that PICKFONT displays towards the bottom of its window is longer in the Unicode version of the program. In both versions, the character string begins with the character codes 0x40 through 0x45 and 0x60 through 0x65. Regardless of the character set you choose (except for SYMBOL_CHARSET), these character codes will display as the first five uppercase and lowercase letters of the Latin alphabet (that is, *A* through *E* and *a* through *e*).

When running the *non-Unicode* version of the PICKFONT program, the next 12 characters—the character codes 0xC0 through 0xC5 and 0xE0 through 0xE5—will be dependent upon the character set you choose. For ANSI_CHARSET, these character codes correspond to accented versions of the uppercase and lowercase letter *A*. For GREEK_CHARSET, these codes will correspond to letters of the Greek alphabet. For RUSSIAN_CHARSET, they will be letters of the Cyrillic alphabet. Notice that the font might change when you select one of these character sets. This is because a raster font might not have these characters, but a TrueType font probably will. You'll recall that most TrueType fonts are "Big Fonts" and include characters for several different character sets. If you're running a Far Eastern version of Windows, these characters will be interpreted as double-byte characters and will display as ideographs rather than letters.

When running the *Unicode* version of PICKFONT under Windows NT, the codes 0xC0 through 0xC5 and 0xE0 through 0xE5 will always (except for SYMBOL_CHARSET) be accented versions of the uppercase and lowercase letter *A* because that's how these codes are defined in Unicode. The program also displays character codes 0x0390 through 0x0395 and 0x03B0 through 0x03B5. Because of their definition in Unicode, these codes will always correspond to letters of the Greek alphabet. Similarly the program displays character codes 0x0410 through 0x0415 and 0x0430 through 0x0435, which always correspond to letters in the Cyrillic alphabet. However, note that these characters might not be present in a default font. You may have to select the GREEK_CHARSET or RUSSIAN_CHARSET to get them. In this case, the character set ID in the LOGFONT structure doesn't change the actual character set; the character set is always Unicode. The character set ID instead indicates that characters from this character set are desired.

Now select HEBREW_CHARSET (code 177). The Hebrew alphabet is not included in Windows' usual Big Fonts, so the operating system picks Lucida Sans Unicode, as you can verify at the bottom right corner of the modeless dialog box.

PICKFONT also displays character codes 0x5000 through 0x5004, which correspond to a few of the many Chinese, Japanese, and Korean ideographs. You'll see these if you're running a Far Eastern version of Windows, or you can download a free Unicode font that is more extensive than Lucida Sans Unicode. This is the Bitstream CyberBit font, available at *http://www.bitstream.com/products/world/cyberbits*. (Just to give you an idea of the difference, Lucida Sans Unicode is roughly 300K while Bitstream CyberBit is about 13 megabytes.) If you have this font installed, Windows will select it if you want a character set not supported by Lucida Sans Unicode, such as SHIFTJIS_CHARSET (Japanese), HANGUL_CHARSET (Korean), JOHAB_CHARSET (Korean), GB2312_CHARSET (Simplified Chinese), or CHINESEBIG5_CHARSET (Traditional Chinese).

I'll present a program that lets you view all the characters of a Unicode font later in this chapter.

The EZFONT System

The introduction of TrueType—and its basis in traditional typography—has provided Windows with a solid foundation for displaying text in its many varieties. However, some of the Windows font-selection functions are based on older technology, in which raster fonts on the screen had to approximate printer device fonts. In the next section, I'll describe font enumeration, which lets a program obtain a list of all the fonts available on the video display or printer. However, the *ChooseFont* dialog box (to be discussed shortly) largely eliminates the necessity for font enumeration by a program.

Because the standard TrueType fonts are available on every system, and because these fonts can be used for both the screen and the printer, it's not necessary for a program to enumerate fonts in order to select one, or to blindly request a certain font type that might need to be approximated. A program could simply and precisely select TrueType fonts that it knows to exist on the system (unless, of course, the user has deliberately deleted them). It really should be almost as simple as specifying the name of the font (probably one of the 13 names listed on page 1004) and its point size. I call this approach EZFONT ("easy font"), and the two files you need are shown in Figure 17-3.

EZFONT.H

```
/*----------------------
   EZFONT.H header file
 ----------------------*/

HFONT EzCreateFont (HDC hdc, TCHAR * szFaceName, int iDeciPtHeight,
                    int iDeciPtWidth, int iAttributes, BOOL fLogRes) ;

#define EZ_ATTR_BOLD          1
#define EZ_ATTR_ITALIC        2
#define EZ_ATTR_UNDERLINE     4
#define EZ_ATTR_STRIKEOUT     8
```

Figure 17-3. *The EZFONT files.*   *(continued)*

Figure 17-3. *continued*

EZFONT.C

```c
/*-----------------------------------------
   EZFONT.C -- Easy Font Creation
                (c) Charles Petzold, 1998
  -----------------------------------------*/

#include <windows.h>
#include <math.h>
#include "ezfont.h"

HFONT EzCreateFont (HDC hdc, TCHAR * szFaceName, int iDeciPtHeight,
                    int iDeciPtWidth, int iAttributes, BOOL fLogRes)
{
    FLOAT      cxDpi, cyDpi ;
    HFONT      hFont ;
    LOGFONT    lf ;
    POINT      pt ;
    TEXTMETRIC tm ;

    SaveDC (hdc) ;

    SetGraphicsMode (hdc, GM_ADVANCED) ;
    ModifyWorldTransform (hdc, NULL, MWT_IDENTITY) ;
    SetViewportOrgEx (hdc, 0, 0, NULL) ;
    SetWindowOrgEx   (hdc, 0, 0, NULL) ;

    if (fLogRes)
    {
        cxDpi = (FLOAT) GetDeviceCaps (hdc, LOGPIXELSX) ;
        cyDpi = (FLOAT) GetDeviceCaps (hdc, LOGPIXELSY) ;
    }
    else
    {
        cxDpi = (FLOAT) (25.4 * GetDeviceCaps (hdc, HORZRES) /
                                    GetDeviceCaps (hdc, HORZSIZE)) ;

        cyDpi = (FLOAT) (25.4 * GetDeviceCaps (hdc, VERTRES) /
                                    GetDeviceCaps (hdc, VERTSIZE)) ;
    }

    pt.x = (int) (iDeciPtWidth  * cxDpi / 72) ;
    pt.y = (int) (iDeciPtHeight * cyDpi / 72) ;

    DPtoLP (hdc, &pt, 1) ;
```

```
lf.lfHeight            = - (int) (fabs (pt.y) / 10.0 + 0.5) ;
lf.lfWidth             = 0 ;
lf.lfEscapement        = 0 ;
lf.lfOrientation       = 0 ;
lf.lfWeight            = iAttributes & EZ_ATTR_BOLD      ? 700 : 0 ;
lf.lfItalic            = iAttributes & EZ_ATTR_ITALIC    ?   1 : 0 ;
lf.lfUnderline         = iAttributes & EZ_ATTR_UNDERLINE ?   1 : 0 ;
lf.lfStrikeOut         = iAttributes & EZ_ATTR_STRIKEOUT ?   1 : 0 ;
lf.lfCharSet           = DEFAULT_CHARSET ;
lf.lfOutPrecision      = 0 ;
lf.lfClipPrecision     = 0 ;
lf.lfQuality           = 0 ;
lf.lfPitchAndFamily    = 0 ;

lstrcpy (lf.lfFaceName, szFaceName) ;

hFont = CreateFontIndirect (&lf) ;

if (iDeciPtWidth != 0)
{
     hFont = (HFONT) SelectObject (hdc, hFont) ;

     GetTextMetrics (hdc, &tm) ;

     DeleteObject (SelectObject (hdc, hFont)) ;

     lf.lfWidth = (int) (tm.tmAveCharWidth *
                                 fabs (pt.x) / fabs (pt.y) + 0.5) ;

     hFont = CreateFontIndirect (&lf) ;
}

RestoreDC (hdc, -1) ;
return hFont ;
}
```

EZFONT.C has only one function, called *EzCreateFont*, which you can use like so:

```
hFont = EzCreateFont (hdc, szFaceName, iDeciPtHeight, iDeciPtWidth,
                      iAttributes, fLogRes) ;
```

The function returns a handle to a font. The font can be selected in the device context by calling *SelectObject*. You should then call *GetTextMetrics* or *GetOutlineTextMetrics* to determine the actual size of the font dimensions in logical coordinates. Before your program terminates, you should delete any created fonts by calling *DeleteObject*.

The *szFaceName* argument is any TrueType typeface name. The closer you stick to the standard fonts, the less chance there is that the font won't exist on the system.

The third argument indicates the desired point size, but it's specified in "decipoints," which are $\frac{1}{10}$ of a point. Thus, if you want a point size of $12\frac{1}{2}$, use a value of 125.

Normally, the fourth argument should be set to zero or made identical to the third argument. However, you can create a TrueType font with a wider or narrower size by setting this argument to something different. This is sometimes called the "em-width" of the font, and it describes the width of the font in points. Don't confuse this with the average width of the font characters or anything like that. Back in the early days of typography, a capital *M* was as wide as it was high. So, the concept of an "em-square" came into being, and that's the origin of the em-width measurement. When the em-width equals the em-height (the point size of the font), the character widths are as the font designer intended. A narrower or wider em-width lets you create slimmer or wider characters.

You can set the *iAttributes* argument to one or more of the following values defined in EZFONT.H:

```
EZ_ATTR_BOLD
EZ_ATTR_ITALIC
EZ_ATTR_UNDERLINE
EZ_ATTR_STRIKEOUT
```

You could use EZ_ATTR_BOLD or EZ_ATTR_ITALIC or include the style as part of the complete TrueType typeface name.

Finally, you set the last argument to TRUE to base the font size on the "logical resolution" returned by the *GetDeviceCaps* function using the LOGPIXELSX and LOGPIXELSY arguments. Otherwise, the font size is based on the resolution as calculated from the HORZRES, HORZSIZE, VERTRES, and VERTSIZE values. This makes a difference only for the video display under Windows NT.

The *EzCreateFont* function begins by making some adjustments that are recognized by Windows NT only. These are the calls to the *SetGraphicsMode* and *ModifyWorld-Transform* functions, which have no effect in Windows 98. The Windows NT world transform should have the effect of modifying the visible size of the font, so the world transform is set to the default—no transform—before the font size is calculated.

EzCreateFont basically sets the fields of a LOGFONT structure and calls *CreateFont-Indirect*, which returns a handle to the font. The big chore of the *EzCreateFont* function is to convert a point size to logical units for the *lfHeight* field of the LOGFONT structure. It turns out that the point size must be converted to device units (pixels) first and then to logical units. To perform the first step, the function uses *GetDeviceCaps*. Getting from pixels to logical units would seem to involve a fairly simple call to the *DPtoLP* ("device point to logical point") function. But in order for the *DPtoLP* conversion to work correctly, the same mapping mode must be in effect when you later display text using the created font. This means that you should set your mapping mode before calling the *EzCreateFont* function. In most cases, you use only one mapping mode for drawing on a particular area of the window, so this requirement should not be a problem.

The EZTEST program in Figure 17-4 tests out the EZFONT files but not too rigorously. This program uses the EZTEST files shown above and also includes FONTDEMO files that are used in some later programs in this book.

EZTEST.C

```c
/*-----------------------------------------
   EZTEST.C -- Test of EZFONT
              (c) Charles Petzold, 1998
  -----------------------------------------*/

#include <windows.h>
#include "ezfont.h"

TCHAR szAppName [] = TEXT ("EZTest") ;
TCHAR szTitle   [] = TEXT ("EZTest: Test of EZFONT") ;

void PaintRoutine (HWND hwnd, HDC hdc, int cxArea, int cyArea)
{
    HFONT       hFont ;
    int         y, iPointSize ;
    LOGFONT     lf ;
    TCHAR       szBuffer [100] ;
    TEXTMETRIC  tm ;

         // Set Logical Twips mapping mode

    SetMapMode (hdc, MM_ANISOTROPIC) ;
    SetWindowExtEx (hdc, 1440, 1440, NULL) ;
    SetViewportExtEx (hdc, GetDeviceCaps (hdc, LOGPIXELSX),
                           GetDeviceCaps (hdc, LOGPIXELSY), NULL) ;

         // Try some fonts

    y = 0 ;

    for (iPointSize = 80 ; iPointSize <= 120 ; iPointSize++)
    {
         hFont = EzCreateFont (hdc, TEXT ("Times New Roman"),
                               iPointSize, 0, 0, TRUE) ;

         GetObject (hFont, sizeof (LOGFONT), &lf) ;

         SelectObject (hdc, hFont) ;
         GetTextMetrics (hdc, &tm) ;
```

Figure 17-4. *The EZTEST program.*

(continued)

Figure 17-4. *continued*

```
        TextOut (hdc, 0, y, szBuffer,
            wsprintf (szBuffer,
                    TEXT ("Times New Roman font of %i.%i points, ")
                    TEXT ("lf.lfHeight = %i, tm.tmHeight = %i"),
                    iPointSize / 10, iPointSize % 10,
                    lf.lfHeight, tm.tmHeight)) ;

        DeleteObject (SelectObject (hdc, GetStockObject (SYSTEM_FONT))) ;
        y += tm.tmHeight ;
    }
}
```

FONTDEMO.C

```
/*-------------------------------------------------
   FONTDEMO.C -- Font Demonstration Shell Program
                 (c) Charles Petzold, 1998
   -------------------------------------------------*/

#include <windows.h>
#include "..\\EZTest\\EzFont.h"
#include "..\\EZTest\\resource.h"

extern  void     PaintRoutine (HWND, HDC, int, int) ;
LRESULT CALLBACK WndProc (HWND, UINT, WPARAM, LPARAM) ;

HINSTANCE hInst ;

extern TCHAR szAppName [] ;
extern TCHAR szTitle [] ;

int WINAPI WinMain (HINSTANCE hInstance, HINSTANCE hPrevInstance,
                    PSTR szCmdLine, int iCmdShow)
{
    TCHAR    szResource [] = TEXT ("FontDemo") ;
    HWND     hwnd ;
    MSG      msg ;
    WNDCLASS wndclass ;

    hInst = hInstance ;

    wndclass.style          = CS_HREDRAW | CS_VREDRAW ;
    wndclass.lpfnWndProc    = WndProc ;
    wndclass.cbClsExtra     = 0 ;
    wndclass.cbWndExtra     = 0 ;
```

```
       wndclass.hInstance     = hInstance ;
       wndclass.hIcon         = LoadIcon (NULL, IDI_APPLICATION) ;
       wndclass.hCursor       = LoadCursor (NULL, IDC_ARROW) ;
       wndclass.hbrBackground = (HBRUSH) GetStockObject (WHITE_BRUSH) ;
       wndclass.lpszMenuName  = szResource ;
       wndclass.lpszClassName = szAppName ;

       if (!RegisterClass (&wndclass))
       {
            MessageBox (NULL, TEXT ("This program requires Windows NT!"),
                       szAppName, MB_ICONERROR) ;
            return 0 ;
       }

       hwnd = CreateWindow (szAppName, szTitle,
                           WS_OVERLAPPEDWINDOW,
                           CW_USEDEFAULT, CW_USEDEFAULT,
                           CW_USEDEFAULT, CW_USEDEFAULT,
                           NULL, NULL, hInstance, NULL) ;

       ShowWindow (hwnd, iCmdShow) ;
       UpdateWindow (hwnd) ;

       while (GetMessage (&msg, NULL, 0, 0))
       {
            TranslateMessage (&msg) ;
            DispatchMessage (&msg) ;
       }
       return msg.wParam ;
}

LRESULT CALLBACK WndProc (HWND hwnd, UINT message, WPARAM wParam, LPARAM lParam)
{
       static DOCINFO  di = { sizeof (DOCINFO), TEXT ("Font Demo: Printing") } ;
       static int      cxClient, cyClient ;
       static PRINTDLG pd = { sizeof (PRINTDLG) } ;
       BOOL            fSuccess ;
       HDC             hdc, hdcPrn ;
       int             cxPage, cyPage ;
       PAINTSTRUCT     ps ;

       switch (message)
       {
       case WM_COMMAND:
            switch (wParam)
```

(continued)

Figure 17-4. *continued*

```
{
case IDM_PRINT:

        // Get printer DC

    pd.hwndOwner = hwnd ;
    pd.Flags     = PD_RETURNDC | PD_NOPAGENUMS | PD_NOSELECTION ;

    if (!PrintDlg (&pd))
        return 0 ;

    if (NULL == (hdcPrn = pd.hDC))
    {
        MessageBox (hwnd, TEXT ("Cannot obtain Printer DC"),
                    szAppName, MB_ICONEXCLAMATION | MB_OK) ;
        return 0 ;
    }
        // Get size of printable area of page

    cxPage = GetDeviceCaps (hdcPrn, HORZRES) ;
    cyPage = GetDeviceCaps (hdcPrn, VERTRES) ;

    fSuccess = FALSE ;

        // Do the printer page

    SetCursor (LoadCursor (NULL, IDC_WAIT)) ;
    ShowCursor (TRUE) ;

    if ((StartDoc (hdcPrn, &di) > 0) && (StartPage (hdcPrn) > 0))
    {
        PaintRoutine (hwnd, hdcPrn, cxPage, cyPage) ;

        if (EndPage (hdcPrn) > 0)
        {
            fSuccess = TRUE ;
            EndDoc (hdcPrn) ;
        }
    }
    DeleteDC (hdcPrn) ;

    ShowCursor (FALSE) ;
    SetCursor (LoadCursor (NULL, IDC_ARROW)) ;

    if (!fSuccess)
        MessageBox (hwnd,
```

```
                          TEXT ("Error encountered during printing"),
                          szAppName, MB_ICONEXCLAMATION | MB_OK) ;
          return 0 ;

     case IDM_ABOUT:
          MessageBox (hwnd, TEXT ("Font Demonstration Program\n")
                          TEXT ("(c) Charles Petzold, 1998"),
                     szAppName, MB_ICONINFORMATION | MB_OK) ;
          return 0 ;
     }
     break ;

case WM_SIZE:
     cxClient = LOWORD (lParam) ;
     cyClient = HIWORD (lParam) ;
     return 0 ;

case WM_PAINT:
     hdc = BeginPaint (hwnd, &ps) ;

     PaintRoutine (hwnd, hdc, cxClient, cyClient) ;

     EndPaint (hwnd, &ps) ;
     return 0 ;

case WM_DESTROY :
     PostQuitMessage (0) ;
     return 0 ;
}
return DefWindowProc (hwnd, message, wParam, lParam) ;
}
```

FONTDEMO.RC

```
//Microsoft Developer Studio generated resource script.

#include "resource.h"
#include "afxres.h"


/////////////////////////////////////////////////////////////////////////////
// Menu

FONTDEMO MENU DISCARDABLE
```

(continued)

Figure 17-4. *continued*

```
BEGIN
    POPUP "&File"
    BEGIN
        MENUITEM "&Print...",                   IDM_PRINT
    END
    POPUP "&Help"
    BEGIN
        MENUITEM "&About...",                   IDM_ABOUT
    END
END
```

RESOURCE.H

```
// Microsoft Developer Studio generated include file.
// Used by FontDemo.rc

#define IDM_PRINT                   40001
#define IDM_ABOUT                   40002
```

The *PaintRoutine* function in EZTEST.C sets its mapping mode to Logical Twips and then creates Times New Roman fonts with sizes ranging from 8 points to 12 points in 0.1 point intervals. The program output may be a little disturbing when you first run it. Many of the lines of text use a font that is obviously the same size, and indeed the *tmHeight* font on the TEXTMETRIC function reports these fonts as having the same height. What's happening here is a result of the rasterization process. The discrete pixels of the display can't allow for every possible size. However, the FONTDEMO shell program allows printing the output as well. Here you'll find that the font sizes are more accurately differentiated.

Font Rotation

As you may have discovered by experimenting with PICKFONT, the *lfOrientation* and *lfEscapement* fields of the LOGFONT structure allow you to rotate TrueType text. If you think about it, this shouldn't be much of a stretch for GDI. Formulas to rotate coordinate points around an origin are well known.

Although *EzCreateFont* does not allow you to specify a rotation angle for the font, it's fairly easy to make an adjustment after calling the function, as the FONTROT ("Font Rotate") program demonstrates. Figure 17-5 shows the FONTROT.C file; the program also requires the EZFONT files and the FONTDEMO files shown earlier.

FONTROT.C

```
/*-----------------------------------------
   FONTROT.C -- Rotated Fonts
                (c) Charles Petzold, 1998
   -----------------------------------------*/
#include <windows.h>
#include "..\\eztest\\ezfont.h"

TCHAR szAppName [] = TEXT ("FontRot") ;
TCHAR szTitle   [] = TEXT ("FontRot: Rotated Fonts") ;

void PaintRoutine (HWND hwnd, HDC hdc, int cxArea, int cyArea)
{
     static TCHAR szString [] = TEXT ("   Rotation") ;
     HFONT        hFont ;
     int          i ;
     LOGFONT      lf ;

     hFont = EzCreateFont (hdc, TEXT ("Times New Roman"), 540, 0, 0, TRUE) ;
     GetObject (hFont, sizeof (LOGFONT), &lf) ;
     DeleteObject (hFont) ;

     SetBkMode (hdc, TRANSPARENT) ;
     SetTextAlign (hdc, TA_BASELINE) ;
     SetViewportOrgEx (hdc, cxArea / 2, cyArea / 2, NULL) ;

     for (i = 0 ; i < 12 ; i ++)
     {
          lf.lfEscapement = lf.lfOrientation = i * 300 ;
          SelectObject (hdc, CreateFontIndirect (&lf)) ;

          TextOut (hdc, 0, 0, szString, lstrlen (szString)) ;

          DeleteObject (SelectObject (hdc, GetStockObject (SYSTEM_FONT))) ;
     }
}
```

Figure 17-5. *The FONTROT program.*

FONTROT calls *EzCreateFont* just to obtain the LOGFONT structure associated with a 54-point Times New Roman font. The program then deletes that font. In the *for* loop, for each angle in 30-degree increments, a new font is created and the text is displayed. The results are shown in Figure 17-6.

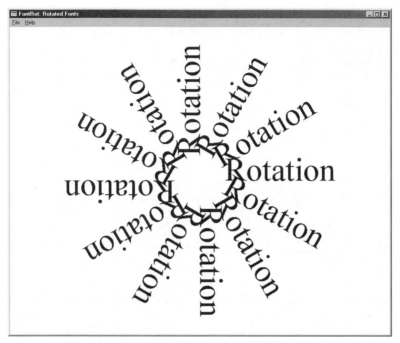

Figure 17-6. *The FONTROT display.*

If you're interested in a more generalized approach to graphics rotation and other linear transformation and you know that your programs will be restricted to running under Windows NT, you can use the XFORM matrix and the world transform functions.

FONT ENUMERATION

Font enumeration is the process of obtaining from GDI a list of all fonts available on a device. A program can then select one of these fonts or display them in a dialog box for selection by the user. I'll first briefly describe the enumeration functions and then show how to use the *ChooseFont* function, which fortunately makes font enumeration much less necessary for an application.

The Enumeration Functions

In the old days of Windows, font enumeration required use of the *EnumFonts* function:

```
EnumFonts (hdc, szTypeFace, EnumProc, pData) ;
```

A program could enumerate all fonts (by setting the second argument to NULL) or just those of a particular typeface. The third argument is an enumeration callback function; the fourth argument is optional data passed to that function. GDI calls the callback function once for each font in the system, passing to it both LOGFONT and TEXTMETRIC structures that defined the font, plus some flags indicating the type of font.

The *EnumFontFamilies* function was designed to better enumerate TrueType fonts under Windows 3.1:

```
EnumFontFamilies (hdc, szFaceName, EnumProc, pData) ;
```

Generally, *EnumFontFamilies* is called first with a NULL second argument. The *EnumProc* callback function is called once for each font family (such as Times New Roman). Then the application calls *EnumFontFamilies* again with that typeface name and a different callback function. GDI calls the second callback function for each font in the family (such as Times New Roman Italic). The callback function is passed an ENUMLOGFONT structure (which is a LOGFONT structure plus a "full name" field and a "style" field containing, for example, the text name "Italic" or "Bold") and a TEXTMETRIC structure for non-TrueType fonts and a NEWTEXTMETRIC structure for TrueType fonts. The NEWTEXT-METRIC structure adds four fields to the information in the TEXTMETRIC structure.

The *EnumFontFamiliesEx* function is recommended for applications running under the 32-bit versions of Windows:

```
EnumFontFamiliesEx (hdc, &logfont, EnumProc, pData, dwFlags) ;
```

The second argument is a pointer to a LOGFONT structure for which the *lfCharSet* and *lfFaceName* fields indicate what fonts are to be enumerated. The callback function gets information about each font in the form of ENUMLOGFONTEX and NEWTEXTMETRICEX structures.

The *ChooseFont* Dialog

We had a little introduction to the *ChooseFont* common dialog box back in Chapter 11. Now that we've encountered font enumeration, the inner workings of the *ChooseFont* function should be obvious. The *ChooseFont* function takes a pointer to a CHOOSEFONT structure as its only argument and displays a dialog box listing all the fonts. On return from *Choose-Font*, a LOGFONT structure, which is part of the CHOOSEFONT structure, lets you create a logical font.

The CHOSFONT program, shown in Figure 17-7 on the following page, demonstrates using the *ChooseFont* function and displays the fields of the LOGFONT structure that the function defines. The program also displays the same string of text as PICKFONT.

CHOSFONT.C

```
/*-------------------------------------------
   CHOSFONT.C -- ChooseFont Demo
                 (c) Charles Petzold, 1998
   -------------------------------------------*/

#include <windows.h>
#include "resource.h"

LRESULT CALLBACK WndProc (HWND, UINT, WPARAM, LPARAM) ;

int WINAPI WinMain (HINSTANCE hInstance, HINSTANCE hPrevInstance,
                    PSTR szCmdLine, int iCmdShow)
{
     static TCHAR szAppName[] = TEXT ("ChosFont") ;
     HWND         hwnd ;
     MSG          msg ;
     WNDCLASS     wndclass ;

     wndclass.style         = CS_HREDRAW | CS_VREDRAW ;
     wndclass.lpfnWndProc   = WndProc ;
     wndclass.cbClsExtra    = 0 ;
     wndclass.cbWndExtra    = 0 ;
     wndclass.hInstance     = hInstance ;
     wndclass.hIcon         = LoadIcon (NULL, IDI_APPLICATION) ;
     wndclass.hCursor       = LoadCursor (NULL, IDC_ARROW) ;
     wndclass.hbrBackground = (HBRUSH) GetStockObject (WHITE_BRUSH) ;
     wndclass.lpszMenuName  = szAppName ;
     wndclass.lpszClassName = szAppName ;

     if (!RegisterClass (&wndclass))
     {
          MessageBox (NULL, TEXT ("This program requires Windows NT!"),
               szAppName, MB_ICONERROR) ;
          return 0 ;
     }

     hwnd = CreateWindow (szAppName, TEXT ("ChooseFont"),
                          WS_OVERLAPPEDWINDOW,
                          CW_USEDEFAULT, CW_USEDEFAULT,
                          CW_USEDEFAULT, CW_USEDEFAULT,
                          NULL, NULL, hInstance, NULL) ;

     ShowWindow (hwnd, iCmdShow) ;
     UpdateWindow (hwnd) ;
```

Figure 17-7. *The CHOSFONT program.*

```
      while (GetMessage (&msg, NULL, 0, 0))
      {
            TranslateMessage (&msg) ;
            DispatchMessage (&msg) ;
      }
      return msg.wParam ;
}

LRESULT CALLBACK WndProc (HWND hwnd, UINT message, WPARAM wParam, LPARAM lParam)
{
      static CHOOSEFONT cf ;
      static int        cyChar ;
      static LOGFONT     lf ;
      static TCHAR       szText[] = TEXT ("\x41\x42\x43\x44\x45 ")
                                    TEXT ("\x61\x62\x63\x64\x65 ")

                                    TEXT ("\xC0\xC1\xC2\xC3\xC4\xC5 ")
                                    TEXT ("\xE0\xE1\xE2\xE3\xE4\xE5 ")
#ifdef UNICODE
                                    TEXT ("\x0390\x0391\x0392\x0393\x0394\x0395 ")
                                    TEXT ("\x03B0\x03B1\x03B2\x03B3\x03B4\x03B5 ")

                                    TEXT ("\x0410\x0411\x0412\x0413\x0414\x0415 ")
                                    TEXT ("\x0430\x0431\x0432\x0433\x0434\x0435 ")

                                    TEXT ("\x5000\x5001\x5002\x5003\x5004")
#endif
                                    ;
      HDC          hdc ;
      int          y ;
      PAINTSTRUCT  ps ;
      TCHAR        szBuffer [64] ;
      TEXTMETRIC   tm ;

      switch (message)
      {
      case WM_CREATE:

            // Get text height

            cyChar = HIWORD (GetDialogBaseUnits ()) ;

            // Initialize the LOGFONT structure

            GetObject (GetStockObject (SYSTEM_FONT), sizeof (lf), &lf) ;

            // Initialize the CHOOSEFONT structure
```

(continued)

Figure 17-7. *continued*

```
        cf.lStructSize      = sizeof (CHOOSEFONT) ;
        cf.hwndOwner        = hwnd ;
        cf.hDC              = NULL ;
        cf.lpLogFont        = &lf ;
        cf.iPointSize       = 0 ;
        cf.Flags            = CF_INITTOLOGFONTSTRUCT |
                              CF_SCREENFONTS | CF_EFFECTS ;
        cf.rgbColors        = 0 ;
        cf.lCustData        = 0 ;
        cf.lpfnHook         = NULL ;
        cf.lpTemplateName   = NULL ;
        cf.hInstance        = NULL ;
        cf.lpszStyle        = NULL ;
        cf.nFontType        = 0 ;
        cf.nSizeMin         = 0 ;
        cf.nSizeMax         = 0 ;
        return 0 ;

case WM_COMMAND:
     switch (LOWORD (wParam))
     {
     case IDM_FONT:
          if (ChooseFont (&cf))
               InvalidateRect (hwnd, NULL, TRUE) ;
          return 0 ;
     }
     return 0 ;

case WM_PAINT:
     hdc = BeginPaint (hwnd, &ps) ;

          // Display sample text using selected font

     SelectObject (hdc, CreateFontIndirect (&lf)) ;
     GetTextMetrics (hdc, &tm) ;
     SetTextColor (hdc, cf.rgbColors) ;
     TextOut (hdc, 0, y = tm.tmExternalLeading, szText, lstrlen (szText)) ;

          // Display LOGFONT structure fields using system font

     DeleteObject (SelectObject (hdc, GetStockObject (SYSTEM_FONT))) ;
     SetTextColor (hdc, 0) ;

     TextOut (hdc, 0, y += tm.tmHeight, szBuffer,
          wsprintf (szBuffer, TEXT ("lfHeight = %i"), lf.lfHeight)) ;
```

```
      TextOut (hdc, 0, y += cyChar, szBuffer,
          wsprintf (szBuffer, TEXT ("lfWidth = %i"), lf.lfWidth)) ;

      TextOut (hdc, 0, y += cyChar, szBuffer,
          wsprintf (szBuffer, TEXT ("lfEscapement = %i"),
                    lf.lfEscapement)) ;

      TextOut (hdc, 0, y += cyChar, szBuffer,
          wsprintf (szBuffer, TEXT ("lfOrientation = %i"),
                    lf.lfOrientation)) ;

      TextOut (hdc, 0, y += cyChar, szBuffer,
          wsprintf (szBuffer, TEXT ("lfWeight = %i"), lf.lfWeight)) ;

      TextOut (hdc, 0, y += cyChar, szBuffer,
          wsprintf (szBuffer, TEXT ("lfItalic = %i"), lf.lfItalic)) ;

      TextOut (hdc, 0, y += cyChar, szBuffer,
          wsprintf (szBuffer, TEXT ("lfUnderline = %i"), lf.lfUnderline)) ;

      TextOut (hdc, 0, y += cyChar, szBuffer,
          wsprintf (szBuffer, TEXT ("lfStrikeOut = %i"), lf.lfStrikeOut)) ;

      TextOut (hdc, 0, y += cyChar, szBuffer,
          wsprintf (szBuffer, TEXT ("lfCharSet = %i"), lf.lfCharSet)) ;

      TextOut (hdc, 0, y += cyChar, szBuffer,
          wsprintf (szBuffer, TEXT ("lfOutPrecision = %i"),
                    lf.lfOutPrecision)) ;

      TextOut (hdc, 0, y += cyChar, szBuffer,
          wsprintf (szBuffer, TEXT ("lfClipPrecision = %i"),
                    lf.lfClipPrecision)) ;

      TextOut (hdc, 0, y += cyChar, szBuffer,
          wsprintf (szBuffer, TEXT ("lfQuality = %i"), lf.lfQuality)) ;

      TextOut (hdc, 0, y += cyChar, szBuffer,
          wsprintf (szBuffer, TEXT ("lfPitchAndFamily = 0x%02X"),
                    lf.lfPitchAndFamily)) ;

      TextOut (hdc, 0, y += cyChar, szBuffer,
          wsprintf (szBuffer, TEXT ("lfFaceName = %s"), lf.lfFaceName)) ;

      EndPaint (hwnd, &ps) ;
      return 0 ;
```

(continued)

Figure 17-7. *continued*

```
     case WM_DESTROY:
          PostQuitMessage (0) ;
          return 0 ;
     }
     return DefWindowProc (hwnd, message, wParam, lParam) ;
}
```

CHOSFONT.RC

```
//Microsoft Developer Studio generated resource script.

#include "resource.h"
#include "afxres.h"


/////////////////////////////////////////////////////////////////////////////
// Menu

CHOSFONT MENU DISCARDABLE
BEGIN
    MENUITEM "&Font!",                    IDM_FONT
END
```

RESOURCE.H

```
// Microsoft Developer Studio generated include file.
// Used by ChosFont.rc

#define IDM_FONT                        40001
```

As usual with the common dialog boxes, a *Flags* field in the CHOOSEFONT structure lets you pick lots of options. The CF_INITLOGFONTSTRUCT flag that CHOSFONT specifies causes Windows to initialize the dialog box selection based on the LOGFONT structure passed to the *ChooseFont* structure. You can use flags to specify TrueType fonts only (CF_TTONLY) or fixed-pitch fonts only (CF_FIXEDPITCHONLY) or no symbol fonts (CF_SCRIPTSONLY). You can display screen fonts (CF_SCREENFONTS), printer fonts (CF_PRINTERFONTS), or both (CF_BOTH). In the latter two cases, the *hDC* field of the CHOOSEFONT structure must reference a printer device context. The CHOSFONT program uses the CF_SCREENFONTS flag.

The CF_EFFECTS flag (the third flag that the CHOSFONT program uses) forces the dialog box to include check boxes for underlining and strikeout and also allows the selection of a text color. It's not hard to implement text color in your code, so try it.

Notice the Script field in the Font dialog displayed by *ChooseFont*. This lets the user select a character set available for the particular font; the appropriate character set ID is returned in the LOGFONT structure.

The *ChooseFont* function uses the logical inch to calculate the *lfHeight* field from the point size. For example, suppose you have Small Fonts installed from the Display Properties dialog. That means that *GetDeviceCaps* with a video display device context and the argument LOGPIXELSY returns 96. If you use *ChooseFont* to choose a 72-point Times Roman Font, you really want a 1-inch tall font. When ChooseFont returns, the *lfHeight* field of the LOGFONT structure will equal −96 (note the minus sign), meaning that the point size of the font is equivalent to 96 pixels, or one logical inch.

Good. That's probably what we want. But keep the following in mind:

■ If you set one of the metric mapping modes under Windows NT, logical coordinates will be inconsistent with the physical size of the font. For example, if you draw a ruler next to the text based on a metric mapping mode, it will not match the font. You should use the Logical Twips mapping mode described above to draw graphics that are consistent with the font size.

■ If you're going to be using *any* non-MM_TEXT mapping mode, make sure the mapping mode is *not* set when you select the font into the device context and display the text. Otherwise, GDI will interpret the *lfHeight* field of the LOGFONT structure as being expressed in logical coordinates.

■ The *lfHeight* field of the LOGFONT structure set by *ChooseFont* is always in pixels, and it is only appropriate for the video display. When you create a font for a printer device context, you must adjust the *lfHeight* value. The *ChooseFont* function uses the *hDC* field of the CHOOSEFONT structure only for obtaining printer fonts to be listed in the dialog box. This device context handle does not affect the value of *lfHeight*.

Fortunately, the CHOOSEFONT structure includes an *iPointSize* field that provides the size of the selected font in units of $\frac{1}{10}$ of a point. Regardless of the device context and mapping mode, you can always convert this field to a logical size and use that for the *lfHeight* field. The appropriate code can be found in the EZFONT.C file. You can probably simplify it based on your needs.

Another program that uses *ChooseFont* is UNICHARS, shown in Figure 17-8 beginning on the following page. This program lets you view all the characters of a font and is particularly useful for studying the Lucida Sans Unicode font, which it uses by default for display, or the Bitstream CyberBit font. UNICHARS always uses the *TextOutW* function for displaying the font characters, so you can run it under Windows NT or Windows 98.

UNICHARS.C

```
/*------------------------------------------------
   UNICHARS.C -- Displays 16-bit character codes
                 (c) Charles Petzold, 1998
   -----------------------------------------------*/

#include <windows.h>
#include "resource.h"

LRESULT CALLBACK WndProc (HWND, UINT, WPARAM, LPARAM) ;

int WINAPI WinMain (HINSTANCE hInstance, HINSTANCE hPrevInstance,
                    PSTR szCmdLine, int iCmdShow)
{
     static TCHAR szAppName[] = TEXT ("UniChars") ;
     HWND         hwnd ;
     MSG          msg ;
     WNDCLASS     wndclass ;

     wndclass.style         = CS_HREDRAW | CS_VREDRAW ;
     wndclass.lpfnWndProc   = WndProc ;
     wndclass.cbClsExtra    = 0 ;
     wndclass.cbWndExtra    = 0 ;
     wndclass.hInstance     = hInstance ;
     wndclass.hIcon         = LoadIcon (NULL, IDI_APPLICATION) ;
     wndclass.hCursor       = LoadCursor (NULL, IDC_ARROW) ;
     wndclass.hbrBackground = (HBRUSH) GetStockObject (WHITE_BRUSH) ;
     wndclass.lpszMenuName  = szAppName ;
     wndclass.lpszClassName = szAppName ;

     if (!RegisterClass (&wndclass))
     {
          MessageBox (NULL, TEXT ("This program requies Windows NT!"),
                      szAppName, MB_ICONERROR) ;
          return 0 ;
     }

     hwnd = CreateWindow (szAppName, TEXT ("Unicode Characters"),
                          WS_OVERLAPPEDWINDOW | WS_VSCROLL,
                          CW_USEDEFAULT, CW_USEDEFAULT,
                          CW_USEDEFAULT, CW_USEDEFAULT,
                          NULL, NULL, hInstance, NULL) ;

     ShowWindow (hwnd, iCmdShow) ;
     UpdateWindow (hwnd) ;
```

Figure 17-8. *The UNICHARS program.*

```
    while (GetMessage (&msg, NULL, 0, 0))
    {
         TranslateMessage (&msg) ;
         DispatchMessage (&msg) ;
    }
    return msg.wParam ;
}

LRESULT CALLBACK WndProc (HWND hwnd, UINT message, WPARAM wParam, LPARAM lParam)
{
    static CHOOSEFONT cf ;
    static int        iPage ;
    static LOGFONT     lf ;
    HDC                hdc ;
    int                cxChar, cyChar, x, y, i, cxLabels ;
    PAINTSTRUCT        ps ;
    SIZE               size ;
    TCHAR              szBuffer [8] ;
    TEXTMETRIC         tm ;
    WCHAR              ch ;

    switch (message)
    {
    case WM_CREATE:
         hdc = GetDC (hwnd) ;
         lf.lfHeight = - GetDeviceCaps (hdc, LOGPIXELSY) / 6 ;  // 12 points
         lstrcpy (lf.lfFaceName, TEXT ("Lucida Sans Unicode")) ;
         ReleaseDC (hwnd, hdc) ;

         cf.lStructSize = sizeof (CHOOSEFONT) ;
         cf.hwndOwner   = hwnd ;
         cf.lpLogFont   = &lf ;
         cf.Flags       = CF_INITTOLOGFONTSTRUCT | CF_SCREENFONTS ;

         SetScrollRange (hwnd, SB_VERT, 0, 255, FALSE) ;
         SetScrollPos   (hwnd, SB_VERT, iPage, TRUE ) ;
         return 0 ;

    case WM_COMMAND:
         switch (LOWORD (wParam))
         {
         case IDM_FONT:
              if (ChooseFont (&cf))
                   InvalidateRect (hwnd, NULL, TRUE) ;
              return 0 ;
         }
         return 0 ;
```

(continued)

Figure 17-8. *continued*

```
case WM_VSCROLL:
     switch (LOWORD (wParam))
          {
          case SB_LINEUP:         iPage -=  1 ;  break ;
          case SB_LINEDOWN:       iPage +=  1 ;  break ;
          case SB_PAGEUP:         iPage -= 16 ;  break ;
          case SB_PAGEDOWN:       iPage += 16 ;  break ;
          case SB_THUMBPOSITION:  iPage = HIWORD (wParam) ;  break ;

          default:
               return 0 ;
          }

     iPage = max (0, min (iPage, 255)) ;

     SetScrollPos (hwnd, SB_VERT, iPage, TRUE) ;
     InvalidateRect (hwnd, NULL, TRUE) ;
     return 0 ;

case WM_PAINT:
     hdc = BeginPaint (hwnd, &ps) ;

     SelectObject (hdc, CreateFontIndirect (&lf)) ;

     GetTextMetrics (hdc, &tm) ;
     cxChar = tm.tmMaxCharWidth ;
     cyChar = tm.tmHeight + tm.tmExternalLeading ;

     cxLabels = 0 ;

     for (i = 0 ; i < 16 ; i++)
     {
          wsprintf (szBuffer, TEXT (" 000%1X: "), i) ;
          GetTextExtentPoint (hdc, szBuffer, 7, &size) ;

          cxLabels = max (cxLabels, size.cx) ;
     }

     for (y = 0 ; y < 16 ; y++)
     {
          wsprintf (szBuffer, TEXT (" %03X_: "), 16 * iPage + y) ;
          TextOut (hdc, 0, y * cyChar, szBuffer, 7) ;

          for (x = 0 ; x < 16 ; x++)
          {
               ch = (WCHAR) (256 * iPage + 16 * y + x) ;
```

```
                        TextOutW (hdc, x * cxChar + cxLabels,
                                       y * cyChar, &ch, 1) ;
                    }
                }

          DeleteObject (SelectObject (hdc, GetStockObject (SYSTEM_FONT))) ;
          EndPaint (hwnd, &ps) ;
          return 0 ;

     case WM_DESTROY:
          PostQuitMessage (0) ;
          return 0 ;
     }
     return DefWindowProc (hwnd, message, wParam, lParam) ;
}
```

UNICHARS.RC

```
//Microsoft Developer Studio generated resource script.

#include "resource.h"
#include "afxres.h"

/////////////////////////////////////////////////////////////////////////////
// Menu

UNICHARS MENU DISCARDABLE
BEGIN
    MENUITEM "&Font!",                      IDM_FONT
END
```

RESOURCE.H

```
// Microsoft Developer Studio generated include file.
// Used by Unichars.rc

#define IDM_FONT                 40001
```

PARAGRAPH FORMATTING

Equipped with the ability to select and create logical fonts, it's time to try our hand at text formatting. The process involves placing each line of text within margins in one of four ways: aligned on the left margin, aligned on the right margin, centered between the margins, or justified—that is, running from one margin to the other, with equal spaces between the words. For the first three jobs, you can use the *DrawText* function with the DT_ WORDBREAK argument, but this approach has limitations. For instance, you can't determine what part of the text *DrawText* was able to fit within the rectangle. *DrawText* is convenient for some simple jobs, but for more complex formatting tasks, you'll probably want to employ *TextOut*.

Simple Text Formatting

One of the most useful functions for working with text is *GetTextExtentPoint32*. (This is a function whose name reveals some changes since the early versions of Windows.) The function tells you the width and height of a character string based on the current font selected in the device context:

```
GetTextExtentPoint32 (hdc, pString, iCount, &size) ;
```

The width and height of the text in logical units are returned in the *cx* and *cy* fields of the SIZE structure. I'll begin with an example using one line of text. Let's say that you have selected a font into your device context and now want to write the text:

```
TCHAR * szText [] = TEXT ("Hello, how are you?") ;
```

You want the text to start at the vertical coordinate *yStart*, within margins set by the coordinates *xLeft* and *xRight*. Your job is to calculate the *xStart* value for the horizontal coordinate where the text begins.

This job would be considerably easier if the text were displayed using a fixed-pitch font, but that's not the general case. First you get the text extents of the string:

```
GetTextExtentPoint32 (hdc, szText, lstrlen (szText), &size) ;
```

If *size.cx* is larger than *(xRight – xLeft)*, the line is too long to fit within the margins. Let's assume it can fit.

To align the text on the left margin, you simply set *xStart* equal to *xLeft* and then write the text:

```
TextOut (hdc, xStart, yStart, szText, lstrlen (szText)) ;
```

This is easy. You can now add the *size.cy* to *yStart*, and you're ready to write the next line of text.

To align the text on the right margin, you use this formula for *xStart*:

```
xStart = xRight - size.cx ;
```

To center the text between the left and right margins, use this formula:

```
xStart = (xLeft + xRight - size.cx) / 2 ;
```

Now here's the tough job—to justify the text within the left and right margins. The distance between the margins is *(xRight – xLeft)*. Without justification, the text is *size.cx* wide. The difference between these two values, which is

```
xRight - xLeft - size.cx
```

must be equally distributed among the three space characters in the character string. It sounds like a terrible job, but it's not too bad. To do it, you call

```
SetTextJustification (hdc, xRight - xLeft - size.cx, 3)
```

The second argument is the amount of space that must be distributed among the space characters in the character string. The third argument is the number of space characters, in this case 3. Now set *xStart* equal to *xLeft*, and write the text with *TextOut*:

```
TextOut (hdc, xStart, yStart, szText, lstrlen (szText)) ;
```

The text will be justified between the *xLeft* and *xRight* margins.

Whenever you call *SetTextJustification*, it accumulates an error term if the amount of space doesn't distribute evenly among the space characters. This error term will affect subsequent *GetTextExtentPoint32* calls. Each time you start a new line, you should clear out the error term by calling

```
SetTextJustification (hdc, 0, 0) ;
```

Working with Paragraphs

If you're working with a whole paragraph, you have to start at the beginning and scan through the string looking for space characters. Every time you encounter a space character (or another character that can be used to break the line), you call *GetTextExtentPoint32* to determine whether the text still fits between the left and right margins. When the text exceeds the space allowed for it, you backtrack to the previous blank. Now you have determined the character string for the line. If you want to justify the line, call *SetTextJustification* and *TextOut*, clear out the error term, and proceed to the next line.

The JUSTIFY1 program, shown in Figure 17-9, does this job for the first paragraph of Mark Twain's *The Adventures of Huckleberry Finn*. You can pick the font you want from a dialog box, and you can also use a menu selection to change the alignment (left, right, centered, or justified). Figure 17-10 on page 1069 shows a typical JUSTIFY1 display.

JUSTIFY1.C

```
/*-------------------------------------------
   JUSTIFY1.C -- Justified Type Program #1
                 (c) Charles Petzold, 1998
   -------------------------------------------*/

#include <windows.h>
#include "resource.h"

LRESULT CALLBACK WndProc (HWND, UINT, WPARAM, LPARAM) ;
```

Figure 17-9. *The JUSTIFY1 program.*

(continued)

Figure 17-9. *continued*

```
TCHAR szAppName[] = TEXT ("Justify1") ;

int WINAPI WinMain (HINSTANCE hInstance, HINSTANCE hPrevInstance,
                    PSTR szCmdLine, int iCmdShow)
{
    HWND     hwnd ;
    MSG      msg ;
    WNDCLASS wndclass ;

    wndclass.style         = CS_HREDRAW | CS_VREDRAW ;
    wndclass.lpfnWndProc   = WndProc ;
    wndclass.cbClsExtra    = 0 ;
    wndclass.cbWndExtra    = 0 ;
    wndclass.hInstance     = hInstance ;
    wndclass.hIcon         = LoadIcon (NULL, IDI_APPLICATION) ;
    wndclass.hCursor       = LoadCursor (NULL, IDC_ARROW) ;
    wndclass.hbrBackground = (HBRUSH) GetStockObject (WHITE_BRUSH) ;
    wndclass.lpszMenuName  = szAppName ;
    wndclass.lpszClassName = szAppName ;

    if (!RegisterClass (&wndclass))
    {
        MessageBox (NULL, TEXT ("This program requires Windows NT!"),
             szAppName, MB_ICONERROR) ;
        return 0 ;
    }

    hwnd = CreateWindow (szAppName, TEXT ("Justified Type #1"),
                         WS_OVERLAPPEDWINDOW,
                         CW_USEDEFAULT, CW_USEDEFAULT,
                         CW_USEDEFAULT, CW_USEDEFAULT,
                         NULL, NULL, hInstance, NULL) ;

    ShowWindow (hwnd, iCmdShow) ;
    UpdateWindow (hwnd) ;

    while (GetMessage (&msg, NULL, 0, 0))
    {
        TranslateMessage (&msg) ;
        DispatchMessage (&msg) ;
    }
    return msg.wParam ;
}


void DrawRuler (HDC hdc, RECT * prc)
{
```

```
static int iRuleSize [16] = { 360, 72, 144, 72, 216, 72, 144, 72,
                              288, 72, 144, 72, 216, 72, 144, 72 } ;
int        i, j ;
POINT      ptClient ;

SaveDC (hdc) ;

     // Set Logical Twips mapping mode

SetMapMode (hdc, MM_ANISOTROPIC) ;
SetWindowExtEx (hdc, 1440, 1440, NULL) ;
SetViewportExtEx (hdc, GetDeviceCaps (hdc, LOGPIXELSX),
                       GetDeviceCaps (hdc, LOGPIXELSY), NULL) ;

     // Move the origin to a half inch from upper left

SetWindowOrgEx (hdc, -720, -720, NULL) ;

     // Find the right margin (quarter inch from right)

ptClient.x = prc->right ;
ptClient.y = prc->bottom ;
DPtoLP (hdc, &ptClient, 1) ;
ptClient.x -= 360 ;

     // Draw the rulers

MoveToEx (hdc, 0,            -360, NULL) ;
LineTo   (hdc, ptClient.x, -360) ;
MoveToEx (hdc, -360,            0, NULL) ;
LineTo   (hdc, -360, ptClient.y) ;

for (i = 0, j = 0 ; i <= ptClient.x ; i += 1440 / 16, j++)
{
     MoveToEx (hdc, i, -360, NULL) ;
     LineTo   (hdc, i, -360 - iRuleSize [j % 16]) ;
}

for (i = 0, j = 0 ; i <= ptClient.y ; i += 1440 / 16, j++)
{
     MoveToEx (hdc, -360, i, NULL) ;
     LineTo   (hdc, -360 - iRuleSize [j % 16], i) ;
}

RestoreDC (hdc, -1) ;
}
```

(continued)

Figure 17-9. *continued*

```
void Justify (HDC hdc, PTSTR pText, RECT * prc, int iAlign)
{
     int    xStart, yStart, cSpaceChars ;
     PTSTR pBegin, pEnd ;
     SIZE  size ;

     yStart = prc->top ;
     do                          // for each text line
     {
          cSpaceChars = 0 ;      // initialize number of spaces in line

          while (*pText == ' ')   // skip over leading spaces
               pText++ ;

          pBegin = pText ;        // set pointer to char at beginning of line

          do                      // until the line is known
          {
               pEnd = pText ;     // set pointer to char at end of line

                    // skip to next space

               while (*pText != '\0' && *pText++ != ' ') ;

               if (*pText == '\0')
                    break ;

                    // after each space encountered, calculate extents

               cSpaceChars++ ;
               GetTextExtentPoint32(hdc, pBegin, pText - pBegin - 1, &size) ;
          }
          while (size.cx < (prc->right - prc->left)) ;

          cSpaceChars-- ;                  // discount last space at end of line

          while (*(pEnd - 1) == ' ')    // eliminate trailing spaces
          {
               pEnd-- ;
               cSpaceChars-- ;
          }

               // if end of text and no space characters, set pEnd to end

          if (*pText == '\0' || cSpaceChars <= 0)
               pEnd = pText ;
```

```
          GetTextExtentPoint32 (hdc, pBegin, pEnd - pBegin, &size) ;

          switch (iAlign)                  // use alignment for xStart
          {
          case IDM_ALIGN_LEFT:
               xStart = prc->left ;
               break ;

          case IDM_ALIGN_RIGHT:
               xStart = prc->right - size.cx ;
               break ;

          case IDM_ALIGN_CENTER:
               xStart = (prc->right + prc->left - size.cx) / 2 ;
               break ;

          case IDM_ALIGN_JUSTIFIED:
               if (*pText != '\0' && cSpaceChars > 0)
                    SetTextJustification (hdc,
                                          prc->right - prc->left - size.cx,
                                          cSpaceChars) ;

               xStart = prc->left ;
               break ;
          }
               // display the text

          TextOut (hdc, xStart, yStart, pBegin, pEnd - pBegin) ;

               // prepare for next line

          SetTextJustification (hdc, 0, 0) ;
          yStart += size.cy ;
          pText = pEnd ;
     }
     while (*pText && yStart < prc->bottom - size.cy) ;
}

LRESULT CALLBACK WndProc (HWND hwnd, UINT message, WPARAM wParam, LPARAM lParam)
{
     static CHOOSEFONT cf ;
     static DOCINFO    di = { sizeof (DOCINFO), TEXT ("Justify1: Printing") } ;
     static int        iAlign = IDM_ALIGN_LEFT ;
     static LOGFONT     lf ;
     static PRINTDLG    pd ;
     static TCHAR      szText[] = {
                         TEXT ("You don't know about me, without you ")
                         TEXT ("have read a book by the name of \"The ")
```

(continued)

Figure 17-9. *continued*

```
                                  TEXT ("Adventures of Tom Sawyer,\" but that ")
                                  TEXT ("ain't no matter. That book was made by ")
                                  TEXT ("Mr. Mark Twain, and he told the truth, ")
                                  TEXT ("mainly. There was things which he ")
                                  TEXT ("stretched, but mainly he told the truth. ")
                                  TEXT ("That is nothing. I never seen anybody ")
                                  TEXT ("but lied, one time or another, without ")
                                  TEXT ("it was Aunt Polly, or the widow, or ")
                                  TEXT ("maybe Mary. Aunt Polly -- Tom's Aunt ")
                                  TEXT ("Polly, she is -- and Mary, and the Widow ")
                                  TEXT ("Douglas, is all told about in that book ")
                                  TEXT ("-- which is mostly a true book; with ")
                                  TEXT ("some stretchers, as I said before.") } ;
BOOL                fSuccess ;
HDC                 hdc, hdcPrn ;
HMENU               hMenu ;
int                 iSavePointSize ;
PAINTSTRUCT         ps ;
RECT                rect ;

switch (message)
{
case WM_CREATE:
          // Initialize the CHOOSEFONT structure

     GetObject (GetStockObject (SYSTEM_FONT), sizeof (lf), &lf) ;

     cf.lStructSize     = sizeof (CHOOSEFONT) ;
     cf.hwndOwner       = hwnd ;
     cf.hDC             = NULL ;
     cf.lpLogFont       = &lf ;
     cf.iPointSize      = 0 ;
     cf.Flags           = CF_INITTOLOGFONTSTRUCT | CF_SCREENFONTS |
                          CF_EFFECTS ;
     cf.rgbColors       = 0 ;
     cf.lCustData       = 0 ;
     cf.lpfnHook        = NULL ;
     cf.lpTemplateName  = NULL ;
     cf.hInstance       = NULL ;
     cf.lpszStyle       = NULL ;
     cf.nFontType       = 0 ;
     cf.nSizeMin        = 0 ;
     cf.nSizeMax        = 0 ;

     return 0 ;
```

```
case WM_COMMAND:
     hMenu = GetMenu (hwnd) ;

     switch (LOWORD (wParam))
     {
     case IDM_FILE_PRINT:
                              // Get printer DC

          pd.lStructSize = sizeof (PRINTDLG) ;
          pd.hwndOwner   = hwnd ;
          pd.Flags       = PD_RETURNDC | PD_NOPAGENUMS | PD_NOSELECTION ;

          if (!PrintDlg (&pd))
              return 0 ;

          if (NULL == (hdcPrn = pd.hDC))
          {
              MessageBox (hwnd, TEXT ("Cannot obtain Printer DC"),
                          szAppName, MB_ICONEXCLAMATION | MB_OK) ;
              return 0 ;
          }
              // Set margins of 1 inch

          rect.left   = GetDeviceCaps (hdcPrn, LOGPIXELSX) -
                        GetDeviceCaps (hdcPrn, PHYSICALOFFSETX) ;

          rect.top    = GetDeviceCaps (hdcPrn, LOGPIXELSY) -
                        GetDeviceCaps (hdcPrn, PHYSICALOFFSETY) ;

          rect.right  = GetDeviceCaps (hdcPrn, PHYSICALWIDTH) -
                        GetDeviceCaps (hdcPrn, LOGPIXELSX) -
                        GetDeviceCaps (hdcPrn, PHYSICALOFFSETX) ;

          rect.bottom = GetDeviceCaps (hdcPrn, PHYSICALHEIGHT) -
                        GetDeviceCaps (hdcPrn, LOGPIXELSY) -
                        GetDeviceCaps (hdcPrn, PHYSICALOFFSETY) ;

              // Display text on printer

          SetCursor (LoadCursor (NULL, IDC_WAIT)) ;
          ShowCursor (TRUE) ;

          fSuccess = FALSE ;
```

(continued)

Figure 17-9. *continued*

```
          if ((StartDoc (hdcPrn, &di) > 0) && (StartPage (hdcPrn) > 0))
          {
                    // Select font using adjusted lfHeight

               iSavePointSize = lf.lfHeight ;
               lf.lfHeight = -(GetDeviceCaps (hdcPrn, LOGPIXELSY) *
                                        cf.iPointSize) / 720 ;

               SelectObject (hdcPrn, CreateFontIndirect (&lf)) ;
               lf.lfHeight = iSavePointSize ;

                    // Set text color

               SetTextColor (hdcPrn, cf.rgbColors) ;

                    // Display text

               Justify (hdcPrn, szText, &rect, iAlign) ;

               if (EndPage (hdcPrn) > 0)
               {
                    fSuccess = TRUE ;
                    EndDoc (hdcPrn) ;
               }
          }
          ShowCursor (FALSE) ;
          SetCursor (LoadCursor (NULL, IDC_ARROW)) ;

          DeleteDC (hdcPrn) ;

          if (!fSuccess)
               MessageBox (hwnd, TEXT ("Could not print text"),
                              szAppName, MB_ICONEXCLAMATION | MB_OK) ;
          return 0 ;

     case IDM_FONT:
          if (ChooseFont (&cf))
               InvalidateRect (hwnd, NULL, TRUE) ;
          return 0 ;

     case IDM_ALIGN_LEFT:
     case IDM_ALIGN_RIGHT:
     case IDM_ALIGN_CENTER:
     case IDM_ALIGN_JUSTIFIED:
          CheckMenuItem (hMenu, iAlign, MF_UNCHECKED) ;
          iAlign = LOWORD (wParam) ;
```

```
                    CheckMenuItem (hMenu, iAlign, MF_CHECKED) ;
                    InvalidateRect (hwnd, NULL, TRUE) ;
                    return 0 ;
               }
          return 0 ;

     case WM_PAINT:
          hdc = BeginPaint (hwnd, &ps) ;

          GetClientRect (hwnd, &rect) ;
          DrawRuler (hdc, &rect) ;

          rect.left  += GetDeviceCaps (hdc, LOGPIXELSX) / 2 ;
          rect.top   += GetDeviceCaps (hdc, LOGPIXELSY) / 2 ;
          rect.right -= GetDeviceCaps (hdc, LOGPIXELSX) / 4 ;

          SelectObject (hdc, CreateFontIndirect (&lf)) ;
          SetTextColor (hdc, cf.rgbColors) ;

          Justify (hdc, szText, &rect, iAlign) ;

          DeleteObject (SelectObject (hdc, GetStockObject (SYSTEM_FONT))) ;
          EndPaint (hwnd, &ps) ;
          return 0 ;

     case WM_DESTROY:
          PostQuitMessage (0) ;
          return 0 ;
     }
     return DefWindowProc (hwnd, message, wParam, lParam) ;
}
```

JUSTIFY1.RC

```
//Microsoft Developer Studio generated resource script.

#include "resource.h"
#include "afxres.h"


/////////////////////////////////////////////////////////////////////////////
// Menu

JUSTIFY1 MENU DISCARDABLE
BEGIN
    POPUP "&File"
```

(continued)

Figure 17-9. *continued*

```
    BEGIN
        MENUITEM "&Print",                    IDM_FILE_PRINT
    END
    POPUP "&Font"
    BEGIN
        MENUITEM "&Font...",                  IDM_FONT
    END
    POPUP "&Align"
    BEGIN
        MENUITEM "&Left",                     IDM_ALIGN_LEFT, CHECKED
        MENUITEM "&Right",                    IDM_ALIGN_RIGHT
        MENUITEM "&Centered",                 IDM_ALIGN_CENTER
        MENUITEM "&Justified",                IDM_ALIGN_JUSTIFIED
    END
END
```

RESOURCE.H

```
// Microsoft Developer Studio generated include file.
// Used by Justify1.rc

#define IDM_FILE_PRINT          40001
#define IDM_FONT                40002
#define IDM_ALIGN_LEFT          40003
#define IDM_ALIGN_RIGHT         40004
#define IDM_ALIGN_CENTER        40005
#define IDM_ALIGN_JUSTIFIED     40006
```

JUSTIFY1 displays a ruler (in logical inches, of course) across the top and down the left side of the client area. The *DrawRuler* function draws the ruler. A rectangle structure defines the area in which the text must be justified.

The bulk of the work involved with formatting this text is in the *Justify* function. The function starts searching for blanks at the beginning of the text and uses *GetTextExtent-Point32* to measure each line. When the length of the line exceeds the width of the display area, JUSTIFY1 returns to the previous space and uses the line up to that point. Depending on the value of the *iAlign* constant, the line is left-aligned, right-aligned, centered, or justified.

JUSTIFY1 isn't perfect. It doesn't have any logic for hyphens, for example. Also, the justification logic falls apart when there are fewer than two words in each line. Even if we solve this problem, which isn't a particularly difficult one, the program still won't work properly when a single word is too long to fit within the left and right margins. Of course, matters can become even more complex when you start working with programs that can use multiple fonts on the same line (as Windows word processors do with apparent ease).

But nobody ever claimed this stuff was easy. It's just easier than if you were doing all the work yourself.

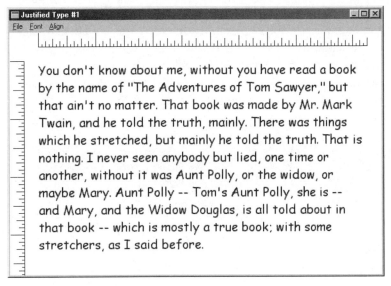

Figure 17-10. *A typical JUSTIFY1 display.*

Previewing Printer Output

Some text is not strictly for viewing on the screen. Some text is for printing. And often in that case, the screen preview of the text must match the formatting of the printer output precisely. It's not enough to show the same fonts and sizes and character formatting. With TrueType, that's a snap. What's also needed is for each line in a paragraph to break at the same place. This is the hard part of WYSIWYG.

JUSTIFY1 includes a Print option, but what it does is simply set one-inch margins at the top, left, and right sides of the page. Thus, the formatting is completely independent of the screen display. Here's an interesting exercise: change a few lines in JUSTIFY1 so that both the screen and the printer logic are based on a six-inch formatting rectangle. To do this, change the definitions of *rect.right* in both the WM_PAINT and Print command logic. In the WM_PAINT logic, the statement is

```
rect.right = rect.left + 6 * GetDeviceCaps (hdc, LOGPIXELSX) ;
```

In the Print command logic, the statement is

```
rect.right = rect.left + 6 * GetDeviceCaps (hdcPrn, LOGPIXELSX) ;
```

If you select a TrueType font, the line breaks on the screen should be the same as on the printer output.

But they aren't. Even though the two devices are using the same font in the same point size and displaying text in the same formatting rectangle, the different display resolutions and rounding errors cause the line breaks to occur at different places. Obviously, a more sophisticated approach is needed for the screen previewing of printer output.

A stab at such an approach is demonstrated by the JUSTIFY2 program shown in Figure 17-11. The code in JUSTIFY2 is based on a program called TTJUST ("TrueType Justify") written by Microsoft's David Weise, which was in turn based on a version of the JUSTIFY1 program in an earlier edition of this book. To symbolize the increased complexity of this program, the Mark Twain excerpt has been replaced with the first paragraph from Herman Melville's *Moby-Dick*.

JUSTIFY2.C

```
/*------------------------------------------
   JUSTIFY2.C -- Justified Type Program #2
                 (c) Charles Petzold, 1998
   ------------------------------------------*/

#include <windows.h>
#include "resource.h"

#define OUTWIDTH 6        // Width of formatted output in inches
#define LASTCHAR 127      // Last character code used in text

LRESULT CALLBACK WndProc (HWND, UINT, WPARAM, LPARAM) ;

TCHAR szAppName[] = TEXT ("Justify2") ;

int WINAPI WinMain (HINSTANCE hInstance, HINSTANCE hPrevInstance,
                    PSTR szCmdLine, int iCmdShow)
{
    HWND     hwnd ;
    MSG      msg ;
    WNDCLASS wndclass ;

    wndclass.style         = CS_HREDRAW | CS_VREDRAW ;
    wndclass.lpfnWndProc   = WndProc ;
    wndclass.cbClsExtra    = 0 ;
    wndclass.cbWndExtra    = 0 ;
    wndclass.hInstance     = hInstance ;
    wndclass.hIcon         = LoadIcon (NULL, IDI_APPLICATION) ;
    wndclass.hCursor       = LoadCursor (NULL, IDC_ARROW) ;
    wndclass.hbrBackground = (HBRUSH) GetStockObject (WHITE_BRUSH) ;
    wndclass.lpszMenuName  = szAppName ;
    wndclass.lpszClassName = szAppName ;
```

Figure 17-11. *The JUSTIFY2 program.*

```
        if (!RegisterClass (&wndclass))
    {
        MessageBox (NULL, TEXT ("This program requires Windows NT!"),
            szAppName, MB_ICONERROR) ;
        return 0 ;
    }

    hwnd = CreateWindow (szAppName, TEXT ("Justified Type #2"),
                        WS_OVERLAPPEDWINDOW,
                        CW_USEDEFAULT, CW_USEDEFAULT,
                        CW_USEDEFAULT, CW_USEDEFAULT,
                        NULL, NULL, hInstance, NULL) ;

    ShowWindow (hwnd, iCmdShow) ;
    UpdateWindow (hwnd) ;

    while (GetMessage (&msg, NULL, 0, 0))
    {
        TranslateMessage (&msg) ;
        DispatchMessage (&msg) ;
    }
    return msg.wParam ;
}

void DrawRuler (HDC hdc, RECT * prc)
{
    static int iRuleSize [16] = { 360, 72, 144, 72, 216, 72, 144, 72,
                                288, 72, 144, 72, 216, 72, 144, 72 } ;
    int         i, j ;
    POINT       ptClient ;

    SaveDC (hdc) ;

        // Set Logical Twips mapping mode

    SetMapMode (hdc, MM_ANISOTROPIC) ;
    SetWindowExtEx (hdc, 1440, 1440, NULL) ;
    SetViewportExtEx (hdc, GetDeviceCaps (hdc, LOGPIXELSX),
                        GetDeviceCaps (hdc, LOGPIXELSY), NULL) ;

        // Move the origin to a half inch from upper left

    SetWindowOrgEx (hdc, -720, -720, NULL) ;

        // Find the right margin (quarter inch from right)

    ptClient.x = prc->right ;
```

(continued)

Figure 17-11. *continued*

```
        ptClient.y = prc->bottom ;
        DPtoLP (hdc, &ptClient, 1) ;
        ptClient.x -= 360 ;

            // Draw the rulers

        MoveToEx (hdc, 0,                     -360, NULL) ;
        LineTo   (hdc, OUTWIDTH * 1440, -360) ;
        MoveToEx (hdc, -360,                   0, NULL) ;
        LineTo   (hdc, -360,         ptClient.y) ;

        for (i = 0, j = 0 ; i <= ptClient.x && i <= OUTWIDTH * 1440 ;
                            i += 1440 / 16, j++)
        {
            MoveToEx (hdc, i, -360, NULL) ;
            LineTo   (hdc, i, -360 - iRuleSize [j % 16]) ;
        }

        for (i = 0, j = 0 ; i <= ptClient.y ; i += 1440 / 16, j++)
        {
            MoveToEx (hdc, -360, i, NULL) ;
            LineTo   (hdc, -360 - iRuleSize [j % 16], i) ;
        }

        RestoreDC (hdc, -1) ;
}

/*----------------------------------------------------------------------
   GetCharDesignWidths:  Gets character widths for font as large as the
                         original design size
  ----------------------------------------------------------------------*/

UINT GetCharDesignWidths (HDC hdc, UINT uFirst, UINT uLast, int * piWidths)
{
    HFONT               hFont, hFontDesign ;
    LOGFONT             lf ;
    OUTLINETEXTMETRIC   otm ;

    hFont = GetCurrentObject (hdc, OBJ_FONT) ;
    GetObject (hFont, sizeof (LOGFONT), &lf) ;

        // Get outline text metrics (we'll only be using a field that is
        //    independent of the DC the font is selected into)

    otm.otmSize = sizeof (OUTLINETEXTMETRIC) ;
    GetOutlineTextMetrics (hdc, sizeof (OUTLINETEXTMETRIC), &otm) ;
```

```
        // Create a new font based on the design size

    lf.lfHeight = - (int) otm.otmEMSquare ;
    lf.lfWidth  = 0 ;
    hFontDesign = CreateFontIndirect (&lf) ;

        // Select the font into the DC and get the character widths

    SaveDC (hdc) ;
    SetMapMode (hdc, MM_TEXT) ;
    SelectObject (hdc, hFontDesign) ;

    GetCharWidth (hdc, uFirst, uLast, piWidths) ;
    SelectObject (hdc, hFont) ;
    RestoreDC (hdc, -1) ;

        // Clean up

    DeleteObject (hFontDesign) ;

    return otm.otmEMSquare ;
}

/*-------------------------------------------------------------------
   GetScaledWidths:  Gets floating point character widths for selected
                     font size
  -------------------------------------------------------------------*/

void GetScaledWidths (HDC hdc, double * pdWidths)
{
    double  dScale ;
    HFONT   hFont ;
    int     aiDesignWidths [LASTCHAR + 1] ;
    int     i ;
    LOGFONT lf ;
    UINT    uEMSquare ;

        // Call function above

    uEMSquare = GetCharDesignWidths (hdc, 0, LASTCHAR, aiDesignWidths) ;

        // Get LOGFONT for current font in device context

    hFont = GetCurrentObject (hdc, OBJ_FONT) ;
    GetObject (hFont, sizeof (LOGFONT), &lf) ;
```

(continued)

Figure 17-11. *continued*

```
          // Scale the widths and store as floating point values

    dScale = (double) -1f.1fHeight / (double) uEMSquare ;

    for (i = 0 ; i <= LASTCHAR ; i++)
        pdWidths[i] = dScale * aiDesignWidths[i] ;
}

/*-----------------------------------------------------------------
   GetTextExtentFloat:  Calculates text width in floating point
   ------------------------------------------------------------*/

double GetTextExtentFloat (double * pdWidths, PTSTR psText, int iCount)
{
    double dWidth = 0 ;
    int    i ;

    for (i = 0 ; i < iCount ; i++)
        dWidth += pdWidths [psText[i]] ;

    return dWidth ;
}

/*-----------------------------------------------------------------
   Justify:  Based on design units for screen/printer compatibility
   ------------------------------------------------------------*/

void Justify (HDC hdc, PTSTR pText, RECT * prc, int iAlign)
{
    double dWidth, adWidths[LASTCHAR + 1] ;
    int    xStart, yStart, cSpaceChars ;
    PTSTR  pBegin, pEnd ;
    SIZE   size ;

        // Fill the adWidths array with floating point character widths

    GetScaledWidths (hdc, adWidths) ;

    yStart = prc->top ;
    do                              // for each text line
    {
        cSpaceChars = 0 ;           // initialize number of spaces in line

        while (*pText == ' ')       // skip over leading spaces
            pText++ ;
```

```
         pBegin = pText ;              // set pointer to char at beginning of line

    do                                 // until the line is known
    {
         pEnd = pText ;                // set pointer to char at end of line

              // skip to next space

         while (*pText != '\0' && *pText++ != ' ') ;

         if (*pText == '\0')
             break ;

              // after each space encountered, calculate extents

         cSpaceChars++ ;
         dWidth = GetTextExtentFloat (adWidths, pBegin,
                                                pText - pBegin - 1) ;
    }
    while (dWidth < (double) (prc->right - prc->left)) ;

    cSpaceChars-- ;                    // discount last space at end of line

    while (*(pEnd - 1) == ' ')     // eliminate trailing spaces
    {
         pEnd-- ;
         cSpaceChars-- ;
    }

         // if end of text and no space characters, set pEnd to end

    if (*pText == '\0' || cSpaceChars <= 0)
         pEnd = pText ;

         // Now get integer extents

    GetTextExtentPoint32(hdc, pBegin, pEnd - pBegin, &size) ;

    switch (iAlign)                    // use alignment for xStart
    {
    case IDM_ALIGN_LEFT:
         xStart = prc->left ;
         break ;

    case IDM_ALIGN_RIGHT:
         xStart = prc->right - size.cx ;
         break ;
```

(continued)

Figure 17-11. *continued*

```
            case IDM_ALIGN_CENTER:
                xStart = (prc->right + prc->left - size.cx) / 2 ;
                break ;

            case IDM_ALIGN_JUSTIFIED:
                if (*pText != '\0' && cSpaceChars > 0)
                    SetTextJustification (hdc,
                                               prc->right - prc->left - size.cx,
                                               cSpaceChars) ;
                xStart = prc->left ;
                break ;
            }
            // display the text

        TextOut (hdc, xStart, yStart, pBegin, pEnd - pBegin) ;

            // prepare for next line

        SetTextJustification (hdc, 0, 0) ;
        yStart += size.cy ;
        pText = pEnd ;
    }
    while (*pText && yStart < prc->bottom - size.cy) ;
}

LRESULT CALLBACK WndProc (HWND hwnd, UINT message, WPARAM wParam, LPARAM lParam)
{
    static CHOOSEFONT cf ;
    static DOCINFO    di = { sizeof (DOCINFO), TEXT ("Justify2: Printing") } ;
    static int        iAlign = IDM_ALIGN_LEFT ;
    static LOGFONT    lf ;
    static PRINTDLG   pd ;
    static TCHAR      szText[] = {
                           TEXT ("Call me Ishmael. Some years ago -- never ")
                           TEXT ("mind how long precisely -- having little ")
                           TEXT ("or no money in my purse, and nothing ")
                           TEXT ("particular to interest me on shore, I ")
                           TEXT ("thought I would sail about a little and ")
                           TEXT ("see the watery part of the world. It is ")
                           TEXT ("a way I have of driving off the spleen, ")
                           TEXT ("and regulating the circulation. Whenever ")
                           TEXT ("I find myself growing grim about the ")
                           TEXT ("mouth; whenever it is a damp, drizzly ")
                           TEXT ("November in my soul; whenever I find ")
                           TEXT ("myself involuntarily pausing before ")
```

```
                         TEXT ("coffin warehouses, and bringing up the ")
                         TEXT ("rear of every funeral I meet; and ")
                         TEXT ("especially whenever my hypos get such an ")
                         TEXT ("upper hand of me, that it requires a ")
                         TEXT ("strong moral principle to prevent me ")
                         TEXT ("from deliberately stepping into the ")
                         TEXT ("street, and methodically knocking ")
                         TEXT ("people's hats off -- then, I account it ")
                         TEXT ("high time to get to sea as soon as I ")
                         TEXT ("can. This is my substitute for pistol ")
                         TEXT ("and ball. With a philosophical flourish ")
                         TEXT ("Cato throws himself upon his sword; I ")
                         TEXT ("quietly take to the ship. There is ")
                         TEXT ("nothing surprising in this. If they but ")
                         TEXT ("knew it, almost all men in their degree, ")
                         TEXT ("some time or other, cherish very nearly ")
                         TEXT ("the same feelings towards the ocean with ")
                         TEXT ("me.") } ;
BOOL              fSuccess ;
HDC               hdc, hdcPrn ;
HMENU             hMenu ;
int               iSavePointSize ;
PAINTSTRUCT       ps ;
RECT              rect ;

switch (message)
{
case WM_CREATE:
          // Initialize the CHOOSEFONT structure

     hdc = GetDC (hwnd) ;
     lf.lfHeight = - GetDeviceCaps (hdc, LOGPIXELSY) / 6 ;
     lf.lfOutPrecision = OUT_TT_ONLY_PRECIS ;
     lstrcpy (lf.lfFaceName, TEXT ("Times New Roman")) ;
     ReleaseDC (hwnd, hdc) ;

     cf.lStructSize    = sizeof (CHOOSEFONT) ;
     cf.hwndOwner      = hwnd ;
     cf.hDC            = NULL ;
     cf.lpLogFont      = &lf ;
     cf.iPointSize     = 120 ;

          // Set flags for TrueType only!

     cf.Flags          = CF_INITTOLOGFONTSTRUCT | CF_SCREENFONTS |
                         CF_TTONLY | CF_EFFECTS ;
```

(continued)

Figure 17-11. *continued*

```
        cf.rgbColors     = 0 ;
        cf.lCustData     = 0 ;
        cf.lpfnHook      = NULL ;
        cf.lpTemplateName = NULL ;
        cf.hInstance     = NULL ;
        cf.lpszStyle     = NULL ;
        cf.nFontType     = 0 ;
        cf.nSizeMin      = 0 ;
        cf.nSizeMax      = 0 ;

        return 0 ;

case WM_COMMAND:
     hMenu = GetMenu (hwnd) ;

     switch (LOWORD (wParam))
     {
     case IDM_FILE_PRINT:
             // Get printer DC

         pd.lStructSize = sizeof (PRINTDLG) ;
         pd.hwndOwner   = hwnd ;
       pd.Flags         = PD_RETURNDC | PD_NOPAGENUMS | PD_NOSELECTION ;

         if (!PrintDlg (&pd))
             return 0 ;

         if (NULL == (hdcPrn = pd.hDC))
         {
             MessageBox (hwnd, TEXT ("Cannot obtain Printer DC"),
                     szAppName, MB_ICONEXCLAMATION | MB_OK) ;
             return 0 ;
         }
             // Set margins for OUTWIDTH inches wide

         rect.left  = (GetDeviceCaps (hdcPrn, PHYSICALWIDTH) -
                     GetDeviceCaps (hdcPrn, LOGPIXELSX) * OUTWIDTH) / 2
                    - GetDeviceCaps (hdcPrn, PHYSICALOFFSETX) ;

         rect.right = rect.left +
                     GetDeviceCaps (hdcPrn, LOGPIXELSX) * OUTWIDTH ;

             // Set margins of 1 inch at top and bottom

         rect.top   = GetDeviceCaps (hdcPrn, LOGPIXELSY) -
                     GetDeviceCaps (hdcPrn, PHYSICALOFFSETY) ;
```

```
                rect.bottom = GetDeviceCaps (hdcPrn, PHYSICALHEIGHT) -
                        GetDeviceCaps (hdcPrn, LOGPIXELSY) -
                        GetDeviceCaps (hdcPrn, PHYSICALOFFSETY) ;

            // Display text on printer

        SetCursor (LoadCursor (NULL, IDC_WAIT)) ;
        ShowCursor (TRUE) ;

        fSuccess = FALSE ;

        if ((StartDoc (hdcPrn, &di) > 0) && (StartPage (hdcPrn) > 0))
        {
                // Select font using adjusted lfHeight

            iSavePointSize = lf.lfHeight ;
            lf.lfHeight = -(GetDeviceCaps (hdcPrn, LOGPIXELSY) *
                            cf.iPointSize) / 720 ;

            SelectObject (hdcPrn, CreateFontIndirect (&lf)) ;
            lf.lfHeight = iSavePointSize ;

                // Set text color

            SetTextColor (hdcPrn, cf.rgbColors) ;

                // Display text

            Justify (hdcPrn, szText, &rect, iAlign) ;

            if (EndPage (hdcPrn) > 0)
            {
                fSuccess = TRUE ;
                EndDoc (hdcPrn) ;
            }
        }
        ShowCursor (FALSE) ;
        SetCursor (LoadCursor (NULL, IDC_ARROW)) ;

        DeleteDC (hdcPrn) ;

        if (!fSuccess)
            MessageBox (hwnd, TEXT ("Could not print text"),
                        szAppName, MB_ICONEXCLAMATION | MB_OK) ;
        return 0 ;
```

(continued)

Figure 17-11. *continued*

```
           case IDM_FONT:
                if (ChooseFont (&cf))
                     InvalidateRect (hwnd, NULL, TRUE) ;
                return 0 ;

           case IDM_ALIGN_LEFT:
           case IDM_ALIGN_RIGHT:
           case IDM_ALIGN_CENTER:
           case IDM_ALIGN_JUSTIFIED:
                CheckMenuItem (hMenu, iAlign, MF_UNCHECKED) ;
                iAlign = LOWORD (wParam) ;
                CheckMenuItem (hMenu, iAlign, MF_CHECKED) ;
                InvalidateRect (hwnd, NULL, TRUE) ;
                return 0 ;
           }
           return 0 ;

      case WM_PAINT:
           hdc = BeginPaint (hwnd, &ps) ;

           GetClientRect (hwnd, &rect) ;
           DrawRuler (hdc, &rect) ;

           rect.left  += GetDeviceCaps (hdc, LOGPIXELSX) / 2 ;
           rect.top   += GetDeviceCaps (hdc, LOGPIXELSY) / 2 ;
           rect.right = rect.left + OUTWIDTH * GetDeviceCaps (hdc, LOGPIXELSX) ;

           SelectObject (hdc, CreateFontIndirect (&lf)) ;
           SetTextColor (hdc, cf.rgbColors) ;

           Justify (hdc, szText, &rect, iAlign) ;

           DeleteObject (SelectObject (hdc, GetStockObject (SYSTEM_FONT))) ;
           EndPaint (hwnd, &ps) ;
           return 0 ;

      case WM_DESTROY:
           PostQuitMessage (0) ;
           return 0 ;
      }
      return DefWindowProc (hwnd, message, wParam, lParam) ;
}
```

JUSTIFY2.RC

```
//Microsoft Developer Studio generated resource script.

#include "resource.h"
#include "afxres.h"


/////////////////////////////////////////////////////////////////////////////
// Menu

JUSTIFY2 MENU DISCARDABLE
BEGIN
    POPUP "&File"
    BEGIN
        MENUITEM "&Print",                 IDM_FILE_PRINT
    END
    POPUP "&Font"
    BEGIN
        MENUITEM "&Font...",               IDM_FONT
    END
    POPUP "&Align"
    BEGIN
        MENUITEM "&Left",                  IDM_ALIGN_LEFT, CHECKED
        MENUITEM "&Right",                 IDM_ALIGN_RIGHT
        MENUITEM "&Centered",              IDM_ALIGN_CENTER
        MENUITEM "&Justified",             IDM_ALIGN_JUSTIFIED
    END
END
```

RESOURCE.H

```
// Microsoft Developer Studio generated include file.
// Used by Justify2.rc

#define IDM_FILE_PRINT          40001
#define IDM_FONT                40002
#define IDM_ALIGN_LEFT          40003
#define IDM_ALIGN_RIGHT         40004
#define IDM_ALIGN_CENTER        40005
#define IDM_ALIGN_JUSTIFIED     40006
```

JUSTIFY2 works with TrueType fonts only. In its *GetCharDesignWidths* function, the program uses the *GetOutlineTextMetrics* function to get a seemingly unimportant piece of information. This is the OUTLINETEXTMETRIC field *otmEMSquare*.

A TrueType font is designed on an em-square grid. (As I've said, the word "em" refers to the width of a square piece of type, an *M* equal in width to the point size of the font.) All the characters of any particular TrueType font are designed on the same grid, although they generally have different widths. The *otmEMSquare* field of the OUTLINETEXTMETRIC structure gives the dimension of this em-square for any particular font. For most TrueType fonts, you'll find that the *otmEMSquare* field is equal to 2048, which means that the font was designed on a 2048-by-2048 grid.

Here's the key: You can set up a LOGFONT structure for the particular TrueType typeface name you want to use but with an *lfHeight* field equal to the negative of the *otmEMSquare* value. After creating that font and selecting it into a device context, you can call *GetCharWidth*. This function gives you the width of individual characters in the font in logical units. Normally, these character widths are not exact because they've been scaled to a different font size. But with a font based on the *otmEMSquare* size, these widths are always exact integers independent of any device context.

The *GetCharDesignWidths* function obtains the original character design widths in this manner and stores them in an integer array. The JUSTIFY2 program knows that its text uses ASCII characters only, so this array needn't be very large. The *GetScaledWidths* function converts these integer widths to floating point widths based on the actual point size of the font in the device's logical coordinates. The *GetTextExtentFloat* function uses those floating point widths to calculate the width of a whole string. That's the function the new *Justify* function uses to calculate the widths of lines of text.

THE FUN AND FANCY STUFF

Expressing font characters in terms of outlines opens up lots of potential in combining fonts with other graphics techniques. Earlier we saw how fonts can be rotated. This final section shows some other tricks. But before we continue, let's look at two important preliminaries: graphics paths and extended pens.

The GDI Path

A path is a collection of straight lines and curves stored internally to GDI. Paths were introduced in the 32-bit versions of Windows. The path may initially seem similar to the region, and indeed you can convert a path to a region and use a path for clipping. However, we'll see shortly how they differ.

To begin a path definition, you simply call

```
BeginPath (hdc) ;
```

After this call, any line you draw (such as straight lines, arcs, and Bezier splines) will be stored internally to GDI as a path and not rendered on the device context. Often a path consists of connected lines. To make connected lines, you use the *LineTo*, *PolylineTo*, and

BezierTo functions, all of which draw lines beginning at the current position. If you change the current position by using *MoveToEx*, or if you call any of the other line-drawing functions, or if you call one of the window/viewport functions that cause a change in the current position, you create a new subpath within the entire path. Thus, a path contains one or more subpaths, where each subpath is a series of connected lines.

Each subpath within the path can be open or closed. A closed subpath is one in which the first point of the first connected line is the same as the last point of the last connected line, and moreover, the subpath is concluded by a call to *CloseFigure*. *CloseFigure* will close the subpath with a straight line, if necessary. Any subsequent line-drawing function begins a new subpath. Finally, you end the path definition by calling

```
EndPath (hdc) ;
```

At this point you then call one of the following five functions:

```
StrokePath (hdc) ;
FillPath (hdc) ;
StrokeAndFillPath (hdc) ;
hRgn = PathToRegion (hdc) ;
SelectClipPath (hdc, iCombine) ;
```

Each of these functions destroys the path definition after completion.

StrokePath draws the path using the current pen. You might wonder: What's the point? Why can't I just skip all this path stuff and draw the lines normally? I'll tell you why shortly.

The other four functions close any open paths with straight lines. *FillPath* fills the path using the current brush according to the current polygon-filling mode. *StrokeAndFillPath* does both jobs in one shot. You can also convert the path to a region or use the path for a clipping area. The *iCombine* argument is one of the RGN_ constants used with the *CombineRgn* function, and it indicates how the path is combined with the current clipping region.

Paths are more flexible than regions for filling and clipping because regions can be defined only by combinations of rectangles, ellipses, and polygons. Paths can be composed of Bezier splines and, at least in Windows NT, arcs. In GDI, paths and regions are stored quite differently. The path is a collection of line and curve definitions, and the region (in the general sense) is a collection of scan lines.

Extended Pens

When you call *StrokePath*, the path is rendered using the current pen. Back in Chapter 4, I discussed the *CreatePen* function that you use to create a pen object. With the introduction of paths, Windows also supports an extended pen function call named *ExtCreatePen*. This function reveals why it's sometimes useful to create a path and stroke it rather than to draw lines without using a path. The *ExtCreatePen* function looks like this:

```
hPen = ExtCreatePen (iStyle, iWidth, &lBrush, 0, NULL) ;
```

You can use this function for normal line drawing, but in that case some of the features aren't supported by Windows 98. Even when used for rendering paths, some features are still not supported by Windows 98, which I've indicated above by setting the last two arguments to 0 and NULL.

For the first argument to *ExtCreatePen*, you can use any of the styles described in Chapter 4 for *CreatePen*. You can additionally combine these styles with PS_GEOMETRIC, where the *iWidth* argument denoting the width of the line is in logical units and is subject to transforms, or PS_COSMETIC, where the *iWidth* argument must be 1. In Windows 98, pens with a dashed or dotted style must be PS_COSMETIC. This restriction is lifted for Windows NT.

One of the arguments to *CreatePen* is a color; rather than a color, *ExtCreatePen* uses a brush to color the interiors of PS_GEOMETRIC pens. That brush can even be defined by a bitmap.

When you're drawing wide lines, you might also be concerned about the appearance of the ends of the lines. When lines or curves are connected, you might also be concerned about the appearance of the joins between the lines. With pens created by *CreatePen*, these ends and joins are always rounded. With *ExtCreatePen*, you have a choice. (Actually, in Windows 98, you have a choice only when you use the pen to stroke a path; Windows NT is more flexible.) The ends of wide lines can be defined using one of the following pen styles in *ExtCreatePen*:

```
PS_ENDCAP_ROUND
PS_ENDCAP_SQUARE
PS_ENDCAP_FLAT
```

The "square" style is different from the "flat" style in that it extends the line for one-half the width. Similarly, joins between lines in a path can be specified by

```
PS_JOIN_ROUND
PS_JOIN_BEVEL
PS_JOIN_MITER
```

The "bevel" style cuts off the end of the join and the "miter" style turns it into a spike. This can be better illustrated with a program called ENDJOIN, which is shown in Figure 17-12.

ENDJOIN.C

```
/*------------------------------------------
   ENDJOIN.C -- Ends and Joins Demo
            (c) Charles Petzold, 1998
   ------------------------------------------*/

#include <windows.h>
```

Figure 17-12. *The ENDJOIN Program.*

```
LRESULT CALLBACK WndProc (HWND, UINT, WPARAM, LPARAM) ;

int WINAPI WinMain (HINSTANCE hInstance, HINSTANCE hPrevInstance,
                    PSTR szCmdLine, int iCmdShow)
{
     static TCHAR szAppName[] = TEXT ("EndJoin") ;
     HWND         hwnd ;
     MSG          msg ;
     WNDCLASS     wndclass ;

     wndclass.style         = CS_HREDRAW | CS_VREDRAW ;
     wndclass.lpfnWndProc   = WndProc ;
     wndclass.cbClsExtra    = 0 ;
     wndclass.cbWndExtra    = 0 ;
     wndclass.hInstance     = hInstance ;
     wndclass.hIcon         = LoadIcon (NULL, IDI_APPLICATION) ;
     wndclass.hCursor       = LoadCursor (NULL, IDC_ARROW) ;
     wndclass.hbrBackground = (HBRUSH) GetStockObject (WHITE_BRUSH) ;
     wndclass.lpszMenuName  = NULL ;
     wndclass.lpszClassName = szAppName ;

     if (!RegisterClass (&wndclass))
     {
          MessageBox (NULL, TEXT ("This program requires Windows NT!"),
                      szAppName, MB_ICONERROR) ;
          return 0 ;
     }

     hwnd = CreateWindow (szAppName, TEXT ("Ends and Joins Demo"),
                          WS_OVERLAPPEDWINDOW,
                          CW_USEDEFAULT, CW_USEDEFAULT,
                          CW_USEDEFAULT, CW_USEDEFAULT,
                          NULL, NULL, hInstance, NULL) ;

     ShowWindow (hwnd, iCmdShow) ;
     UpdateWindow (hwnd) ;

     while (GetMessage (&msg, NULL, 0, 0))
     {
          TranslateMessage (&msg) ;
          DispatchMessage (&msg) ;
     }
     return msg.wParam ;
}
```

(continued)

Figure 17-12. *continued*

```
LRESULT CALLBACK WndProc (HWND hwnd, UINT iMsg, WPARAM wParam, LPARAM lParam)
{
     static int  iEnd[] = { PS_ENDCAP_ROUND, PS_ENDCAP_SQUARE, PS_ENDCAP_FLAT } ;
     static int  iJoin[]= { PS_JOIN_ROUND,   PS_JOIN_BEVEL,    PS_JOIN_MITER } ;
     static int  cxClient, cyClient ;
     HDC         hdc ;
     int         i ;
     LOGBRUSH    lb ;
     PAINTSTRUCT ps ;

     switch (iMsg)
     {
     case WM_SIZE:
          cxClient = LOWORD (lParam) ;
          cyClient = HIWORD (lParam) ;
          return 0 ;

     case WM_PAINT:
          hdc = BeginPaint (hwnd, &ps) ;

          SetMapMode (hdc, MM_ANISOTROPIC) ;
          SetWindowExtEx (hdc, 100, 100, NULL) ;
          SetViewportExtEx (hdc, cxClient, cyClient, NULL) ;

          lb.lbStyle = BS_SOLID ;
          lb.lbColor = RGB (128, 128, 128) ;
          lb.lbHatch = 0 ;

          for (i = 0 ; i < 3 ; i++)
          {
               SelectObject (hdc,
                   ExtCreatePen (PS_SOLID | PS_GEOMETRIC |
                                 iEnd [i] | iJoin [i], 10,
                                 &lb, 0, NULL)) ;
               BeginPath (hdc) ;

               MoveToEx (hdc, 10 + 30 * i, 25, NULL) ;
               LineTo   (hdc, 20 + 30 * i, 75) ;
               LineTo   (hdc, 30 + 30 * i, 25) ;

               EndPath (hdc) ;
               StrokePath (hdc) ;

               DeleteObject (
                   SelectObject (hdc,
                       GetStockObject (BLACK_PEN))) ;
```

```
              MoveToEx (hdc, 10 + 30 * i, 25, NULL) ;
              LineTo   (hdc, 20 + 30 * i, 75) ;
              LineTo   (hdc, 30 + 30 * i, 25) ;
         }
         EndPaint (hwnd, &ps) ;
         return 0 ;

    case WM_DESTROY:
         PostQuitMessage (0) ;
         return 0 ;
    }
    return DefWindowProc (hwnd, iMsg, wParam, lParam) ;
}
```

The program draws three V-shaped wide lines using the end and join styles in the order listed above. The program also draws three identical lines using the stock black pen. This shows how the wide line compares with the normal thin line. The results are shown in Figure 17-13.

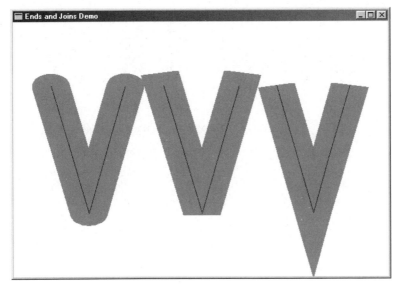

Figure 17-13. *The ENDJOIN display.*

I hope it's now apparent why Windows supports a *StrokePath* function: If you were to draw the two lines individually, GDI would be forced to use the line ends on each of them. Only if they're in a path definition does GDI know that the lines are connected and then use a line join.

Four Sample Programs

Of what good is this? Well, think about it: The characters in outline fonts are defined by a series of coordinate values. These coordinates define straight lines and splines. Thus, the straight lines and curves can become part of a path definition.

And yes, it works! This is demonstrated in the FONTOUT1 program shown in Figure 17-14.

FONTOUT1.C

```
/*-------------------------------------------
   FONTOUT1.C -- Using Path to Outline Font
                 (c) Charles Petzold, 1998
   -------------------------------------------*/

#include <windows.h>
#include "..\\eztest\\ezfont.h"

TCHAR szAppName [] = TEXT ("FontOut1") ;
TCHAR szTitle [] = TEXT ("FontOut1: Using Path to Outline Font") ;

void PaintRoutine (HWND hwnd, HDC hdc, int cxArea, int cyArea)
{
     static TCHAR szString [] = TEXT ("Outline") ;
     HFONT        hFont ;
     SIZE         size ;

     hFont = EzCreateFont (hdc, TEXT ("Times New Roman"), 1440, 0, 0, TRUE) ;

     SelectObject (hdc, hFont) ;

     GetTextExtentPoint32 (hdc, szString, lstrlen (szString), &size) ;

     BeginPath (hdc) ;
     TextOut (hdc, (cxArea - size.cx) / 2, (cyArea - size.cy) / 2,
                   szString, lstrlen (szString)) ;
     EndPath (hdc) ;

     StrokePath (hdc) ;

     SelectObject (hdc, GetStockObject (SYSTEM_FONT)) ;
     DeleteObject (hFont) ;
}
```

Figure 17-14. *The FONTOUT1 program.*

This program, and the remainder of the programs in this chapter, also use the EZFONT and FONTDEMO files shown earlier.

The program creates a 144-point TrueType font and calls the *GetTextExtentPoint32* function to obtain the dimensions of the text box. It then calls the *TextOut* function in a path definition so that the text is centered in the client window. Because the *TextOut* function is called in a path bracket—that is, between calls to *BeginPath* and *EndPath*—GDI does not display the text immediately. Instead, the character outlines are stored in the path definition.

After the path bracket is ended, FONTOUT1 calls *StrokePath*. Because no special pen has been selected into the device context, GDI simply draws the character outlines using the default pen, as shown in Figure 17-15.

Figure 17-15. *The FONTOUT1 display.*

But what have we here? We've got outlined characters, as we expect, but why is the text string surrounded by a rectangle?

Well, recall that the text background mode is by default OPAQUE rather than TRANS-PARENT. That rectangle is the outline of the text box. This clearly demonstrates the two-step approach that GDI uses when drawing text in the default OPAQUE mode. First it draws a filled rectangle, and then it draws the characters. The outline of the text box rectangle thus also becomes part of the path.

Using the *ExtCreatePen* function, you can outline the characters of a font with something other than the default pen. This is demonstrated in the FONTOUT2 program shown in Figure 17-16 on the following page.

FONTOUT2.C

```
/*-------------------------------------------
   FONTOUT2.C -- Using Path to Outline Font
                (c) Charles Petzold, 1998
   -------------------------------------------*/

#include <windows.h>
#include "..\\eztest\\ezfont.h"

TCHAR szAppName [] = TEXT ("FontOut2") ;
TCHAR szTitle [] = TEXT ("FontOut2: Using Path to Outline Font") ;

void PaintRoutine (HWND hwnd, HDC hdc, int cxArea, int cyArea)
{
     static TCHAR szString [] = TEXT ("Outline") ;
     HFONT        hFont ;
     LOGBRUSH     lb ;
     SIZE         size ;

     hFont = EzCreateFont (hdc, TEXT ("Times New Roman"), 1440, 0, 0, TRUE) ;

     SelectObject (hdc, hFont) ;
     SetBkMode (hdc, TRANSPARENT) ;

     GetTextExtentPoint32 (hdc, szString, lstrlen (szString), &size) ;

     BeginPath (hdc) ;
     TextOut (hdc, (cxArea - size.cx) / 2, (cyArea - size.cy) / 2,
                   szString, lstrlen (szString)) ;
     EndPath (hdc) ;

     lb.lbStyle = BS_SOLID ;
     lb.lbColor = RGB (255, 0, 0) ;
     lb.lbHatch = 0 ;

     SelectObject (hdc, ExtCreatePen (PS_GEOMETRIC | PS_DOT,
                               GetDeviceCaps (hdc, LOGPIXELSX) / 24,
                                    &lb, 0, NULL)) ;
     StrokePath (hdc) ;

     DeleteObject (SelectObject (hdc, GetStockObject (BLACK_PEN))) ;
     SelectObject (hdc, GetStockObject (SYSTEM_FONT)) ;
     DeleteObject (hFont) ;
}
```

Figure 17-16. *The FONTOUT2 program.*

This program creates (and selects into the device context) a red dotted pen with a width of 3 points (¹/₂₄ inch) before calling *StrokePath*. The results when the program runs under Windows NT are shown in Figure 17-17. Windows 98 does not support nonsolid pens more than 1 pixel wide, so Windows 98 draws the pen as solid red.

Figure 17-17. *The FONTOUT2 display.*

You can also use paths to define areas for filling. You create the path in the same way as shown in the past two programs, select a filling pattern, and call *FillPath*. Another function you can call is *StrokeAndFillPath*, which both outlines a path and fills it with one function call.

The *StrokeAndFillPath* function is demonstrated in the FONTFILL program shown in Figure 17-18.

FONTFILL.C

```
/*-------------------------------------------
   FONTFILL.C -- Using Path to Fill Font
                 (c) Charles Petzold, 1998
   -----------------------------------------*/

#include <windows.h>
#include "..\\eztest\\ezfont.h"

TCHAR szAppName [] = TEXT ("FontFill") ;
TCHAR szTitle [] = TEXT ("FontFill: Using Path to Fill Font") ;
```

Figure 17-18. *The FONTFILL program.*

(continued)

Figure 17-18. *continued*

```
void PaintRoutine (HWND hwnd, HDC hdc, int cxArea, int cyArea)
{
    static TCHAR szString [] = TEXT ("Filling") ;
    HFONT        hFont ;
    SIZE         size ;

    hFont = EzCreateFont (hdc, TEXT ("Times New Roman"), 1440, 0, 0, TRUE) ;

    SelectObject (hdc, hFont) ;
    SetBkMode (hdc, TRANSPARENT) ;

    GetTextExtentPoint32 (hdc, szString, lstrlen (szString), &size) ;

    BeginPath (hdc) ;
    TextOut (hdc, (cxArea - size.cx) / 2, (cyArea - size.cy) / 2,
                  szString, lstrlen (szString)) ;
    EndPath (hdc) ;

    SelectObject (hdc, CreateHatchBrush (HS_DIAGCROSS, RGB (255, 0, 0))) ;
    SetBkColor (hdc, RGB (0, 0, 255)) ;
    SetBkMode (hdc, OPAQUE) ;

    StrokeAndFillPath (hdc) ;

    DeleteObject (SelectObject (hdc, GetStockObject (WHITE_BRUSH))) ;
    SelectObject (hdc, GetStockObject (SYSTEM_FONT)) ;
    DeleteObject (hFont) ;
}
```

FONTFILL uses the default pen for outlining the path but creates a red hatched brush using the HS_DIAGCROSS style. Notice that the program sets the background mode to TRANSPARENT when creating the path but then resets it to OPAQUE when filling the path so that it can use a blue background color for the area pattern. The results are shown in Figure 17-19.

You may want to try a few variations on this program to observe the effects. First, if you comment out the first *SetBkMode* call, you'll get the background of the text box covered with the pattern but not the characters themselves. That's usually not what you want, but you can certainly do it.

Also, when filling characters and using them for clipping, you want to leave the default ALTERNATE polygon-filling mode in effect. My experience indicates that TrueType fonts are constructed so that nothing strange will happen (such as the interiors of Os being filled) if you use the WINDING fill mode, but you'll want to play it safe by sticking with ALTERNATE.

Figure 17-19. *The FONTFILL display.*

Finally, you can use a path, and hence a TrueType font, to define a clipping region. This is demonstrated in the FONTCLIP program shown in Figure 17-20.

FONTCLIP.C

```
/*-------------------------------------------------
   FONTCLIP.C -- Using Path for Clipping on Font
                 (c) Charles Petzold, 1998
   -------------------------------------------------*/

#include <windows.h>
#include "..\\eztest\\ezfont.h"

TCHAR szAppName [] = TEXT ("FontClip") ;
TCHAR szTitle [] = TEXT ("FontClip: Using Path for Clipping on Font") ;

void PaintRoutine (HWND hwnd, HDC hdc, int cxArea, int cyArea)
{
     static TCHAR szString [] = TEXT ("Clipping") ;
     HFONT        hFont ;
     int          y, iOffset ;
     POINT        pt [4] ;
     SIZE         size ;

     hFont = EzCreateFont (hdc, TEXT ("Times New Roman"), 1200, 0, 0, TRUE) ;
```

Figure 17-20. *The FONTCLIP program.*   *(continued)*

Figure 17-20. *continued*

```
    SelectObject (hdc, hFont) ;

    GetTextExtentPoint32 (hdc, szString, lstrlen (szString), &size) ;

    BeginPath (hdc) ;
    TextOut (hdc, (cxArea - size.cx) / 2, (cyArea - size.cy) / 2,
                szString, lstrlen (szString)) ;
    EndPath (hdc) ;

            // Set clipping area

    SelectClipPath (hdc, RGN_COPY) ;

            // Draw Bezier splines

    iOffset = (cxArea + cyArea) / 4 ;

    for (y = -iOffset ; y < cyArea + iOffset ; y++)
    {
        pt[0].x = 0 ;
        pt[0].y = y ;

        pt[1].x = cxArea / 3 ;
        pt[1].y = y + iOffset ;

        pt[2].x = 2 * cxArea / 3 ;
        pt[2].y = y - iOffset ;

        pt[3].x = cxArea ;
        pt[3].y = y ;

        SelectObject (hdc, CreatePen (PS_SOLID, 1,
            RGB (rand () % 256, rand () % 256, rand () % 256))) ;

        PolyBezier (hdc, pt, 4) ;

        DeleteObject (SelectObject (hdc, GetStockObject (BLACK_PEN))) ;
    }

    DeleteObject (SelectObject (hdc, GetStockObject (WHITE_BRUSH))) ;
    SelectObject (hdc, GetStockObject (SYSTEM_FONT)) ;
    DeleteObject (hFont) ;
}
```

This is a program where I've deliberately excluded the *SetBkMode* call to achieve a different effect. The program draws some text in a path bracket and then calls *SelectClipPath*. It then draws a series of Bezier spline curves with random colors.

If the FONTCLIP program had called *SetBkMode* with the TRANSPARENT option, the Bezier curves would have been restricted to the interiors of the character outlines. With the background mode in the default OPAQUE option, the clipping region is restricted to the interior of the text box but not the characters themselves. This is shown in Figure 17-21.

Figure 17-21. *The FONTCLIP display.*

You'll probably want to insert a *SetBkMode* call into FONTCLIP to see the difference with the TRANSPARENT option.

The FONTDEMO shell program allows you to print as well as display these effects, and even better, you can try some of your own special effects.

Chapter 18

Metafiles

Metafiles are to vector graphics as bitmaps are to raster graphics. While bitmaps generally originate from real-world images, metafiles are constructed by humans, generally helped out by computer programs. A metafile consists of a series of binary records that correspond to graphics function calls, generally to draw straight lines, curves, filled areas, and text.

"Paint" programs create bitmaps; "draw" programs create metafiles. In a well-designed drawing program, you can easily "grab" a particular graphical object (such as a line) and move it somewhere else. That's because all the individual components of the picture are stored as separate records. In a paint program, such feats are not possible—you're generally restricted to removing or inserting rectangular chunks of the bitmap.

Because the metafile describes an image in terms of graphical drawing commands, the metafile image can be scaled without loss of resolution. Bitmaps don't work that way: If you display a bitmap at twice the size, you don't get twice the resolution. The bits in the bitmap are simply replicated horizontally and vertically.

A metafile can be converted to a bitmap, but with some loss of information: the graphical objects that make up the metafile are no longer separate and become blended together in one big image. Converting bitmaps to metafiles is a much more difficult job, usually restricted to very simple images and requiring a lot of processing power to analyze edges and outlines. However, a metafile can contain a command to *draw* a bitmap.

Metafiles are used most often for sharing pictures among programs through the clipboard, although they can also exist on disk as clip art. Because metafiles describe a picture as a collection of graphics function calls, they generally take up much less space and are more device independent than bitmaps.

Microsoft Windows supports two metafile formats and two sets of functions to support them. I'll first discuss the metafile functions supported since Windows 1.0, and still supported under the current 32-bit versions of Windows, and then discuss the "enhanced metafile" developed for the 32-bit versions of Windows. The enhanced metafiles have several improvements over the old metafile format and should be used whenever possible.

THE OLD METAFILE FORMAT

Metafiles either can exist temporarily in memory or can be saved as disk files. To an application, these two processes are quite similar; in particular, all the file I/O that would otherwise be involved in saving and loading data to and from disk-based metafiles is handled by Windows.

Simple Use of Memory Metafiles

You create a metafile in the old format by first creating a metafile device context with a call to *CreateMetaFile*. You can then use most of the GDI drawing functions to draw on this metafile device context. These GDI calls don't really draw on any real device, however. Instead, they are stored within the metafile. When you close the metafile device context, you get back a handle to the metafile. You can then "play" this metafile on a real device context, which is equivalent to executing the GDI functions in the metafile.

CreateMetaFile takes a single argument. This can be either NULL or a filename. If NULL, the metafile is stored in memory. If it's a filename—the extension .WMF, for "Windows Metafile," is customary—then the metafile is stored in a disk file.

The program METAFILE shown in Figure 18-1 shows how to create a memory metafile during the WM_CREATE message and display the image 100 times during the WM_PAINT message.

METAFILE.C

```
/*---------------------------------------------------
   METAFILE.C -- Metafile Demonstration Program
                 (c) Charles Petzold, 1998
   ---------------------------------------------------*/

#include <windows.h>

LRESULT CALLBACK WndProc (HWND, UINT, WPARAM, LPARAM) ;

int WINAPI WinMain (HINSTANCE hInstance, HINSTANCE hPrevInstance,
                    PSTR szCmdLine, int iCmdShow)
{
     static TCHAR szAppName [] = TEXT ("Metafile") ;
     HWND         hwnd ;
     MSG          msg ;
     WNDCLASS     wndclass ;

     wndclass.style         = CS_HREDRAW | CS_VREDRAW ;
     wndclass.lpfnWndProc   = WndProc ;
     wndclass.cbClsExtra    = 0 ;
```

Figure 18-1. *The METAFILE program.*

```
    wndclass.cbWndExtra    = 0 ;
    wndclass.hInstance     = hInstance ;
    wndclass.hIcon         = LoadIcon (NULL, IDI_APPLICATION) ;
    wndclass.hCursor       = LoadCursor (NULL, IDC_ARROW) ;
    wndclass.hbrBackground = (HBRUSH) GetStockObject (WHITE_BRUSH) ;
    wndclass.lpszMenuName  = NULL ;
    wndclass.lpszClassName = szAppName ;

    if (!RegisterClass (&wndclass))
    {
        MessageBox (NULL, TEXT ("This program requires Windows NT!"),
                    szAppName, MB_ICONERROR) ;
        return 0 ;
    }

    hwnd = CreateWindow (szAppName, TEXT ("Metafile Demonstration"),
                         WS_OVERLAPPEDWINDOW,
                         CW_USEDEFAULT, CW_USEDEFAULT,
                         CW_USEDEFAULT, CW_USEDEFAULT,
                         NULL, NULL, hInstance, NULL) ;

    ShowWindow (hwnd, iCmdShow) ;
    UpdateWindow (hwnd) ;

    while (GetMessage (&msg, NULL, 0, 0))
    {
        TranslateMessage (&msg) ;
        DispatchMessage (&msg) ;
    }
    return msg.wParam ;
}

LRESULT CALLBACK WndProc (HWND hwnd, UINT message, WPARAM wParam, LPARAM lParam)
{
    static HMETAFILE hmf ;
    static int       cxClient, cyClient ;
    HBRUSH           hBrush ;
    HDC              hdc, hdcMeta ;
    int              x, y ;
    PAINTSTRUCT      ps ;

    switch (message)
    {
    case WM_CREATE:
        hdcMeta = CreateMetaFile (NULL) ;
        hBrush  = CreateSolidBrush (RGB (0, 0, 255)) ;
```

(continued)

Figure 18-1. *continued*

```
            Rectangle (hdcMeta, 0, 0, 100, 100) ;

            MoveToEx (hdcMeta,   0,   0, NULL) ;
            LineTo   (hdcMeta, 100, 100) ;
            MoveToEx (hdcMeta,   0, 100, NULL) ;
            LineTo   (hdcMeta, 100,   0) ;

            SelectObject (hdcMeta, hBrush) ;
            Ellipse (hdcMeta, 20, 20, 80, 80) ;

            hmf = CloseMetaFile (hdcMeta) ;

            DeleteObject (hBrush) ;
            return 0 ;

       case WM_SIZE:
            cxClient = LOWORD (lParam) ;
            cyClient = HIWORD (lParam) ;
            return 0 ;

       case WM_PAINT:
            hdc = BeginPaint (hwnd, &ps) ;

            SetMapMode (hdc, MM_ANISOTROPIC) ;
            SetWindowExtEx (hdc, 1000, 1000, NULL) ;
            SetViewportExtEx (hdc, cxClient, cyClient, NULL) ;

            for (x = 0 ; x < 10 ; x++)
            for (y = 0 ; y < 10 ; y++)
            {
                SetWindowOrgEx (hdc, -100 * x, -100 * y, NULL) ;
                PlayMetaFile (hdc, hmf) ;
            }
            EndPaint (hwnd, &ps) ;
            return 0 ;

       case WM_DESTROY:
            DeleteMetaFile (hmf) ;
            PostQuitMessage (0) ;
            return 0 ;
       }
     return DefWindowProc (hwnd, message, wParam, lParam) ;
}
```

This program demonstrates the use of the four metafile functions essential in using a memory metafile. The first is *CreateMetaFile*, which the program calls with a NULL argument during processing of the WM_CREATE message. The function returns a handle to a metafile device context. METAFILE then draws two lines and one blue ellipse using this metafile DC. These function calls are stored in a binary form in the metafile. The *CloseMeta-File* function returns a handle to the metafile. Notice that the metafile handle is stored in a static variable because it will be used later.

The metafile contains a binary representation of the GDI function calls, which are two *MoveToEx* calls, two *LineTo* calls, a *SelectObject* call (indicating the blue brush), and an *Ellipse* call. No mapping mode or transform is implied by the coordinates. They are simply stored as numbers in the metafile.

During the WM_PAINT message, METAFILE sets up a mapping mode and calls *Play-MetaFile* to draw the object 100 times in the window using *PlayMetaFile*. The coordinates of the function calls in the metafile are interpreted in the context of the current transform set up for the destination device context. In calling *PlayMetaFile*, in effect you're repeating all the calls that you made between *CreateMetaFile* and *CloseMetaFile* when you originally created the metafile during the WM_CREATE message.

As with any GDI object, metafile objects should be deleted before a program terminates. This occurs during the WM_DESTROY message with the *DeleteMetaFile* function.

The results of the METAFILE program are shown in Figure 18-2.

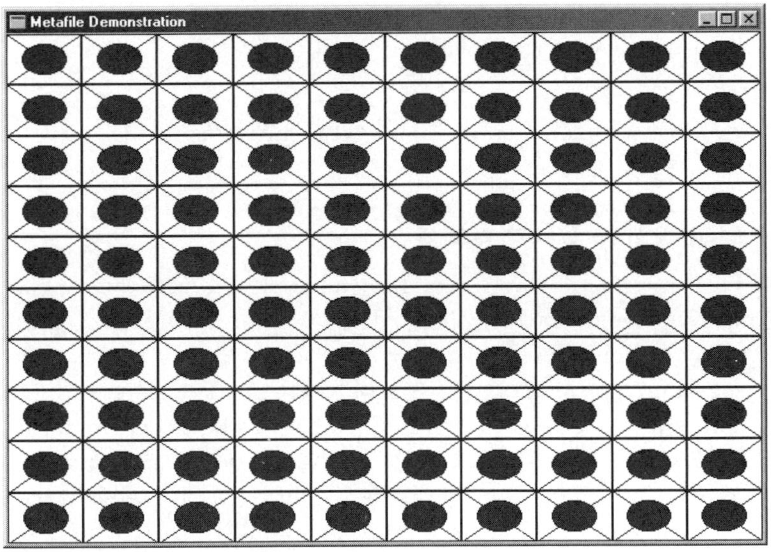

Figure 18-2. *The METAFILE display.*

Storing Metafiles on Disk

In the above example, the NULL argument to *CreateMetaFile* meant that we wanted to create a metafile stored in memory. We can also create a metafile stored on a disk as a file. This method is preferred for large metafiles because it uses less memory space. On the down side, a metafile stored on disk requires a disk access every time you play it.

To convert METAFILE to using a disk-based metafile, you need to replace the NULL argument to *CreateMetaFile* with a filename. At the conclusion of the WM_CREATE processing, you can call *DeleteMetaFile* with the metafile handle. The handle has been deleted, but the disk file remains behind.

During processing of the WM_PAINT message, you can get a metafile handle to this disk file by calling *GetMetaFile*:

```
hmf = GetMetaFile (szFileName) ;
```

Now you can play this metafile just as before. When processing of the WM_PAINT message is over, you can delete the metafile handle:

```
DeleteMetaFile (hmf) ;
```

When it comes time to process the WM_DESTROY message, you don't have to delete the metafile, because it was deleted at the end of the WM_CREATE message and at the end of each WM_PAINT message. But you should still delete the disk file like so,

```
DeleteFile (szFileName) ;
```

unless, of course, you want to keep the file around.

You can make a metafile a programmer-defined resource as discussed in Chapter 10. You'd simply load it as a data block. If you have a block of data with the contents of a metafile, you can create a metafile using

```
hmf = SetMetaFileBitsEx (iSize, pData) ;
```

SetMetaFileBitsEx has a companion function, *GetMetaFileBitsEx*, that copies the contents of a metafile to a block of memory.

Old Metafiles and the Clipboard

The old metafiles have a nasty flaw. If you have a handle to an old-style metafile, how can you determine how large the image will be when you play it? Unless you start digging into the internals of the metafile itself, you can't.

Moreover, when a program obtains an old-style metafile from the clipboard, it has the most flexibility in working with it if the metafile has been designed to be played in an MM_ISOTROPIC or MM_ANISOTROPIC mapping mode. The program that receives the metafile can then scale the image by simply setting viewport extents before playing the metafile. But if the mapping mode is set to MM_ISOTROPIC or MM_ANISOTROPIC *within* the metafile, the program that receives the metafile is stuck. The program can make GDI calls only before or after the metafile is played. It can't make a GDI call in the middle of a metafile.

To solve these problems, old-style metafile handles are not directly put into the clipboard and retrieved by other programs. Instead, the metafile handle is part of a "metafile picture," which is a structure of type METAFILEPICT. This structure allows the program that obtains the metafile picture from the clipboard to set the mapping mode and viewport extents itself before playing the metafile.

The METAFILEPICT structure is 16 bytes long and defined like so:

```
typedef struct tagMETAFILEPICT
{
     LONG mm ;              // mapping mode
     LONG xExt ;            // width of the metafile image
     LONG yExt ;            // height of the metafile image
     LONG hMF ;             // handle to the metafile
}
METAFILEPICT ;
```

For all the mapping modes except MM_ISOTROPIC and MM_ANISOTROPIC, the *xExt* and *yExt* values are the size of the image in units of the mapping mode given by *mm*. With this information, the program that copies the metafile picture structure from the clipboard can determine how much display space the metafile will encompass when it is played. The program that creates the metafile can set these values to the largest *x*-coordinates and *y*-coordinates it uses in the GDI drawing functions that enter the metafile.

For the MM_ISOTROPIC and MM_ANISOTROPIC mapping modes, the *xExt* and *yExt* fields function differently. You will recall from Chapter 5 that a program uses the MM_ISOTROPIC or MM_ANISOTROPIC mapping mode when it wants to use arbitrary logical units in GDI functions independent of the measurable size of the image. A program uses MM_ISOTROPIC when it wants to maintain an aspect ratio regardless of the size of the viewing surface and MM_ANISOTROPIC when it doesn't care about the aspect ratio. You will also recall from Chapter 5 that after a program sets the mapping mode to MM_ISOTROPIC or MM_ANISOTROPIC, it generally makes calls to *SetWindowExtEx* and *SetViewportExtEx*. The *SetWindowExtEx* call uses logical units to specify the units the program wants to use when drawing. The *SetViewportExtEx* call uses device units based on the size of the viewing surface (for instance, the size of the window's client area).

If a program creates an MM_ISOTROPIC or MM_ANISOTROPIC metafile for the clipboard, the metafile should not itself contain a call to *SetViewportExtEx* because the device units in that call would be based on the display surface of the program creating the metafile and not on the display surface of the program that reads the metafile from the clipboard and plays it. Instead, the *xExt* and *yExt* values should assist the program that obtains the metafile from the clipboard in setting appropriate viewport extents for playing the metafile. But the metafile itself contains a call to set the window extent when the mapping mode is MM_ISOTROPIC or MM_ANISOTROPIC. The coordinates of the GDI drawing functions within the metafile are based on these window extents.

The program that creates the metafile and metafile picture follows these rules:

■   The *mm* field of the METAFILEPICT structure is set to specify the mapping mode.

■   For mapping modes other than MM_ISOTROPIC and MM_ANISOTROPIC, the *xExt* and *yExt* fields are set to the width and height of the image in units corresponding to the *mm* field. For metafiles to be played in an MM_ISOTROPIC or MM_ANISOTROPIC environment, matters get a little more complex. For MM_ANISOTROPIC, zero values of *xExt* and *yExt* are used when the program is suggesting neither a size nor an aspect ratio for the image. For MM_ISOTROPIC or MM_ANISOTROPIC, positive values of *xExt* and *yExt* indicate a suggested width and height of the image in units of 0.01 mm (MM_HIMETRIC units). For MM_ISOTROPIC, negative values of *xExt* and *yExt* indicate a suggested aspect ratio of the image but not a suggested size.

■   For the MM_ISOTROPIC and MM_ANISOTROPIC mapping modes, the metafile itself contains calls to *SetWindowExtEx* and (possibly) *SetWindowOrgEx*. That is, the program that creates the metafile calls these functions in the metafile device context. Generally, the metafile will not contain calls to *SetMapMode*, *SetViewportExtEx*, or *SetViewportOrgEx*.

■   The metafile should be a memory-based metafile, not a disk-based metafile.

Here's some sample code for a program creating a metafile and copying it to the clipboard. If the metafile uses the MM_ISOTROPIC or MM_ANISOTROPIC mapping mode, the first calls in the metafile should be to set the window extent. (The window extent is fixed in the other mapping modes.) Regardless of the mapping mode, the window origin can also be set:

```
hdcMeta = CreateMetaFile (NULL) ;
SetWindowExtEx (hdcMeta, ...) ;
SetWindowOrgEx (hdcMeta, ...) ;
```

The coordinates in the drawing functions of the metafile are based on these window extents and the window origin. After the program uses GDI calls to draw on the metafile device context, the metafile is closed to get a handle to the metafile:

```
hmf = CloseMetaFile (hdcMeta) ;
```

The program also needs to define a pointer to a structure of type METAFILEPICT and allocate a block of global memory for this structure:

```
GLOBALHANDLE   hGlobal ;
LPMETAFILEPICT pMFP ;
[other program lines]
hGlobal= GlobalAlloc (GHND | GMEM_SHARE, sizeof (METAFILEPICT)) ;
pMFP = (LPMETAFILEPICT) GlobalLock (hGlobal) ;
```

Next, the program sets the four fields of this structure:

```
pMFP->mm   = MM_... ;
pMFP->xExt = ... ;
pMFP->yExt = ... ;
pMFP->hMF  = hmf ;

GlobalUnlock (hGlobal) ;
```

The program then transfers the global memory block containing the metafile picture structure to the clipboard:

```
OpenClipboard (hwnd) ;
EmptyClipboard () ;
SetClipboardData (CF_METAFILEPICT, hGlobal) ;
CloseClipboard () ;
```

Following these calls, the *hGlobal* handle (the memory block containing the metafile picture structure) and the *hmf* handle (the metafile itself) become invalid for the program that created them.

Now for the hard part. When a program obtains a metafile from the clipboard and plays this metafile, the following steps must take place:

1. The program uses the *mm* field of the metafile picture structure to set the mapping mode.

2. For mapping modes other than MM_ISOTROPIC or MM_ANISOTROPIC, the program uses the *xExt* and *yExt* values to set a clipping rectangle or simply to determine the size of the image. For the MM_ISOTROPIC and MM_ANISOTROPIC mapping modes, the program uses *xExt* and *yExt* to set the viewport extents.

3. The program then plays the metafile.

Here's the code. You first open the clipboard, get the handle to the metafile picture structure, and lock it:

```
OpenClipboard (hwnd) ;
hGlobal = GetClipboardData (CF_METAFILEPICT) ;
pMFP = (LPMETAFILEPICT) GlobalLock (hGlobal) ;
```

You can then save the attributes of your current device context and set the mapping mode to the *mm* value of the structure:

```
SaveDC (hdc) ;
SetMappingMode (pMFP->mm) ;
```

If the mapping mode isn't MM_ISOTROPIC or MM_ANISOTROPIC, you can set a clipping rectangle to the values of *xExt* and *yExt*. Because these values are in logical units, you have to use *LPtoDP* to convert the coordinates to device units for the clipping rectangle. Or you can simply save the values so that you know how large the image is.

For the MM_ISOTROPIC or MM_ANISOTROPIC mapping mode, you use *xExt* and *yExt* to set the viewport extent. One possible function to perform this task is shown on the following page. This function assumes that *cxClient* and *cyClient* represent the pixel height and width of the area in which you want the metafile to appear if no suggested size is implied by *xExt* and *yExt*.

```
void PrepareMetaFile (HDC hdc, LPMETAFILEPICT pmfp,
                        int cxClient, int cyClient)
{
    int xScale, yScale, iScale ;

    SetMapMode (hdc, pmfp->mm) ;

    if (pmfp->mm == MM_ISOTROPIC || pmfp->mm == MM_ANISOTROPIC)
    {
        if (pmfp->xExt == 0)
            SetViewportExtEx (hdc, cxClient, cyClient, NULL) ;
        else if (pmfp->xExt > 0)
            SetViewportExtEx (hdc,
                pmfp->xExt * GetDeviceCaps (hdc, HORZRES) /
                        GetDeviceCaps (hdc, HORZSIZE) / 100),
                pmfp->yExt * GetDeviceCaps (hdc, VERTRES) /
                        GetDeviceCaps (hdc, VERTSIZE) / 100),
                NULL) ;

        else if (pmfp->xExt < 0)
        {
            xScale = 100 * cxClient * GetDeviceCaps (hdc, HORZSIZE) /
                        GetDeviceCaps (hdc, HORZRES) / -pmfp->xExt ;
            lScale = 100 * cyClient * GetDeviceCaps (hdc, VERTSIZE) /
                        GetDeviceCaps (hdc, VERTRES) / -pmfp->yExt ;
            iScale = min (xScale, yScale) ;

            SetViewportExtEx (hdc,
                -pmfp->xExt * iScale * GetDeviceCaps (hdc, HORZRES) /
                        GetDeviceCaps (hdc, HORZSIZE) / 100,
                -pmfp->yExt * iScale * GetDeviceCaps (hdc, VERTRES) /
                        GetDeviceCaps (hdc, VERTSIZE) / 100,
                NULL) ;
        }
    }
}
```

This code assumes that both *xExt* and *yExt* are 0, greater than 0, or less than 0 (which should be the case). If the extents are 0, no size or aspect ratio is suggested. The viewport extents are set to the area in which you want to display the metafile. Positive values of *xExt* and *yExt* are a suggested image size in units of 0.01 mm. The *GetDeviceCaps* function assists in determining the number of pixels per 0.01 mm, and this value is multiplied by the extent values in the metafile picture structure. Negative values of *xExt* and *yExt* indicate a suggested aspect ratio but not a suggested size. The value *iScale* is first calculated based on the aspect ratio of the size in millimeters corresponding to *cxClient* and *cyClient*. This scaling factor is then used to set a viewport extent in pixels.

With this job out of the way, you can set a viewport origin if you want, play the metafile, and return the device context to normal:

```
PlayMetaFile (pMFP->hMF) ;
RestoreDC (hdc, -1) ;
```

Then you unlock the memory block and close the clipboard:

```
GlobalUnlock (hGlobal) ;
CloseClipboard () ;
```

If your program uses enhanced metafiles, you don't have to do this work. The Windows clipboard will convert between the old metafile format and the enhanced metafile format when one application puts one of these formats into the clipboard and another application requests the other format from the clipboard.

ENHANCED METAFILES

The "enhanced metafile" format was introduced in the 32-bit versions of Windows. It involves a bunch of new function calls, a couple of new data structures, a new clipboard format, and a new filename extension of .EMF.

The most important enhancement is that the new metafile format includes more extensive header information accessible through a function call. This information aids in helping an application display the metafile image.

Some of the enhanced metafile functions allow you to translate back and forth between the enhanced metafile (EMF) format and the old metafile format, which is also called the Windows metafile (WMF) format. Of course, this conversion may not proceed without hitches because the old metafile format does not support some of the new 32-bit graphics features, such as paths.

The Basic Procedure

Figure 18-3 shows the EMF1 program, which creates and displays an enhanced metafile with a fairly minimal amount of distraction.

EMF1.C

```
/*----------------------------------------
   EMF1.C -- Enhanced Metafile Demo #1
            (c) Charles Petzold, 1998
   ----------------------------------------*/

#include <windows.h>

LRESULT CALLBACK WndProc (HWND, UINT, WPARAM, LPARAM) ;

int WINAPI WinMain (HINSTANCE hInstance, HINSTANCE hPrevInstance,
                    LPSTR lpszCmdLine, int nCmdShow)
```

Figure 18-3. *The EMF1 Program.*   *(continued)*

Figure 18-3. *continued*

```
{
    static TCHAR szAppName[] = TEXT ("EMF1") ;
    HWND            hwnd ;
    MSG             msg ;
    WNDCLASS        wndclass ;

    wndclass.style         = CS_HREDRAW | CS_VREDRAW ;
    wndclass.lpfnWndProc   = WndProc ;
    wndclass.cbClsExtra    = 0 ;
    wndclass.cbWndExtra    = 0 ;
    wndclass.hInstance     = hInstance ;
    wndclass.hIcon         = LoadIcon (NULL, IDI_APPLICATION) ;
    wndclass.hCursor       = LoadCursor (NULL, IDC_ARROW) ;
    wndclass.hbrBackground = GetStockObject (WHITE_BRUSH) ;
    wndclass.lpszMenuName  = NULL ;
    wndclass.lpszClassName = szAppName ;

    if (!RegisterClass (&wndclass))
    {
        MessageBox (NULL, TEXT ("This program requires Windows NT!"),
                    szAppName, MB_ICONERROR) ;
        return 0 ;
    }

    hwnd = CreateWindow (szAppName, TEXT ("Enhanced Metafile Demo #1"),
                        WS_OVERLAPPEDWINDOW,
                        CW_USEDEFAULT, CW_USEDEFAULT,
                        CW_USEDEFAULT, CW_USEDEFAULT,
                        NULL, NULL, hInstance, NULL) ;

    ShowWindow (hwnd, nCmdShow) ;
    UpdateWindow (hwnd) ;

    while (GetMessage (&msg, NULL, 0, 0))
    {
        TranslateMessage (&msg) ;
        DispatchMessage (&msg) ;
    }
    return msg.wParam ;
}

LRESULT CALLBACK WndProc (HWND hwnd, UINT message, WPARAM wParam, LPARAM lParam)
{
    static HENHMETAFILE hemf ;
    HDC                 hdc, hdcEMF ;
    PAINTSTRUCT         ps ;
```

```
    RECT                rect ;

switch (message)
{
case WM_CREATE:
     hdcEMF = CreateEnhMetaFile (NULL, NULL, NULL, NULL) ;

     Rectangle (hdcEMF, 100, 100, 200, 200) ;

     MoveToEx  (hdcEMF, 100, 100, NULL) ;
     LineTo    (hdcEMF, 200, 200) ;

     MoveToEx  (hdcEMF, 200, 100, NULL) ;
     LineTo    (hdcEMF, 100, 200) ;

     hemf = CloseEnhMetaFile (hdcEMF) ;
     return 0 ;

case WM_PAINT:
     hdc = BeginPaint (hwnd, &ps) ;

     GetClientRect (hwnd, &rect) ;

     rect.left   =     rect.right  / 4 ;
     rect.right  = 3 * rect.right  / 4 ;
     rect.top    =     rect.bottom / 4 ;
     rect.bottom = 3 * rect.bottom / 4 ;

     PlayEnhMetaFile (hdc, hemf, &rect) ;

     EndPaint (hwnd, &ps) ;
     return 0 ;

case WM_DESTROY:
     DeleteEnhMetaFile (hemf) ;

     PostQuitMessage (0) ;
     return 0 ;
}
return DefWindowProc (hwnd, message, wParam, lParam) ;
}
```

During WM_CREATE message processing in EMF1's window procedure, the program creates the enhanced metafile, beginning with a call to *CreateEnhMetaFile*. This function requires four arguments, but you can set all of them to NULL. I'll discuss how to use these arguments with non-NULL values shortly.

Like *CreateMetaFile*, the *CreateEnhMetaFile* function returns a special device context handle. The program uses this handle to draw a rectangle and two lines connecting the opposite corners of the rectangle. These function calls and their arguments are converted to a binary form and stored in the metafile.

Finally, a call to *CloseEnhMetaFile* wraps up the creation of the enhanced metafile and returns a handle to it. This is stored in a static variable of type HENHMETAFILE.

During the WM_PAINT message, EMF1 obtains the dimensions of the program's client window in a RECT structure. The four fields of the structure are adjusted so that the rectangle is half the width and height of the client window and centered within it. EMF1 then calls *PlayEnhMetaFile*. The first argument is a handle to the window's device context, the second argument is the handle to the enhanced metafile, and the third argument is a pointer to the RECT structure.

What happens here is that during creation of the metafile, GDI figures out the entire dimensions of the metafile image. In this case, the image is 100 units high and wide. When displaying the metafile, GDI stretches the image to fit the rectangle specified in the *PlayEnhMetaFile* function. Three instances of EMF1 running under Windows are shown in Figure 18-4.

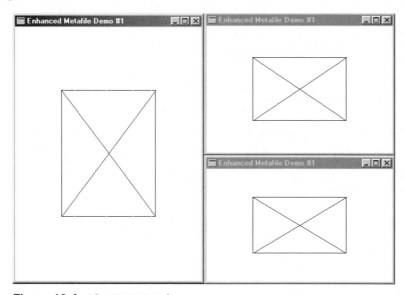

Figure 18-4. *The EMF1 Display.*

Finally, during the WM_DESTROY message, EMF1 deletes the metafile by calling *DeleteEnhMetaFile*.

Let's take note of a few things we can learn from the EMF1 program.

First, in this particular program, the coordinates used in the rectangle and line-drawing functions when creating the enhanced metafile don't really mean all that much. You can double them all or subtract a constant from them all, and the results will be the same. All that matters is that the coordinates have a relationship among themselves in defining an image.

Second, the image is stretched to fit the rectangle passed to the *PlayEnhMetaFile* function. Thus, as Figure 18-4 clearly shows, the image can be distorted. The metafile coordinates imply that the image is square, but that's not what we get in the general case. And sometimes, that's exactly what you want. For embedding images in a word processing text, you may want the user to specify a rectangle for the image and be assured that the entire image fits exactly within the rectangle without any wasted space. Let the user worry about the correct aspect ratio by adjusting the rectangle appropriately.

However, there are times when something else is appropriate. You may want to maintain the aspect ratio of the original image because it may be vitally important to rendering the visual information. For example, a police sketch of a crime suspect shouldn't be fatter or squatter than it was originally drawn. Or, you may want to preserve the metrical size of the original image. It may be important that the image is two inches high and shouldn't normally be reproduced otherwise.

Notice also that the lines drawn in the metafile don't seem to exactly meet the corners of the rectangle. This is the result of a problem in the way that Windows stores rectangle coordinates in the metafile. We'll work on a fix to this problem later in this chapter.

Looking Inside

You can get a good feel for how metafiles work by looking at the contents of the metafile. This is easiest if you have a disk-based metafile to look at, so the EMF2 program shown in Figure 18-5 creates one for you.

EMF2.C

```
/*------------------------------------------
   EMF2.C -- Enhanced Metafile Demo #2
             (c) Charles Petzold, 1998
   ------------------------------------------*/

#include <windows.h>

LRESULT CALLBACK WndProc (HWND, UINT, WPARAM, LPARAM) ;

int WINAPI WinMain (HINSTANCE hInstance, HINSTANCE hPrevInstance,
                    LPSTR lpszCmdLine, int nCmdShow)
{
     static TCHAR szAppName[] = TEXT ("EMF2") ;
     HWND         hwnd ;
     MSG          msg ;
     WNDCLASS     wndclass ;
```

Figure 18-5. *The EMF2 Program.*   *(continued)*

Figure 18-5. *continued*

```
    wndclass.style         = CS_HREDRAW | CS_VREDRAW ;
    wndclass.lpfnWndProc   = WndProc ;
    wndclass.cbClsExtra    = 0 ;
    wndclass.cbWndExtra    = 0 ;
    wndclass.hInstance     = hInstance ;
    wndclass.hIcon         = LoadIcon (NULL, IDI_APPLICATION) ;
    wndclass.hCursor       = LoadCursor (NULL, IDC_ARROW) ;
    wndclass.hbrBackground = GetStockObject (WHITE_BRUSH) ;
    wndclass.lpszMenuName  = NULL ;
    wndclass.lpszClassName = szAppName ;

    if (!RegisterClass (&wndclass))
    {
        MessageBox (NULL, TEXT ("This program requires Windows NT!"),
                    szAppName, MB_ICONERROR) ;
        return 0 ;
    }

    hwnd = CreateWindow (szAppName, TEXT ("Enhanced Metafile Demo #2"),
                    WS_OVERLAPPEDWINDOW,
                    CW_USEDEFAULT, CW_USEDEFAULT,
                    CW_USEDEFAULT, CW_USEDEFAULT,
                    NULL, NULL, hInstance, NULL) ;

    ShowWindow (hwnd, nCmdShow) ;
    UpdateWindow (hwnd) ;

    while (GetMessage (&msg, NULL, 0, 0))
    {
        TranslateMessage (&msg) ;
        DispatchMessage (&msg) ;
    }
    return msg.wParam ;
}

LRESULT CALLBACK WndProc (HWND hwnd, UINT message, WPARAM wParam, LPARAM lParam)
{
    HDC            hdc, hdcEMF ;
    HENHMETAFILE   hemf ;
    PAINTSTRUCT    ps ;
    RECT           rect ;

    switch (message)
    {
    case WM_CREATE:
        hdcEMF = CreateEnhMetaFile (NULL, TEXT ("emf2.emf"), NULL,
                                    TEXT ("EMF2\0EMF Demo #2\0")) ;
```

```
            if (!hdcEMF)
                return 0 ;

            Rectangle (hdcEMF, 100, 100, 200, 200) ;

            MoveToEx  (hdcEMF, 100, 100, NULL) ;
            LineTo    (hdcEMF, 200, 200) ;

            MoveToEx  (hdcEMF, 200, 100, NULL) ;
            LineTo    (hdcEMF, 100, 200) ;

            hemf = CloseEnhMetaFile (hdcEMF) ;

            DeleteEnhMetaFile (hemf) ;
            return 0 ;

    case WM_PAINT:
            hdc = BeginPaint (hwnd, &ps) ;

            GetClientRect (hwnd, &rect) ;

            rect.left   =     rect.right  / 4 ;
            rect.right  = 3 * rect.right  / 4 ;
            rect.top    =     rect.bottom / 4 ;
            rect.bottom = 3 * rect.bottom / 4 ;

            if (hemf = GetEnhMetaFile (TEXT ("emf2.emf")))
            {
                 PlayEnhMetaFile (hdc, hemf, &rect) ;
                 DeleteEnhMetaFile (hemf) ;
            }
            EndPaint (hwnd, &ps) ;
            return 0 ;

    case WM_DESTROY:
            PostQuitMessage (0) ;
            return 0 ;
    }
    return DefWindowProc (hwnd, message, wParam, lParam) ;
}
```

In EMF1, all the arguments to the *CreateEnhMetaFile* function were set to NULL. In EMF2, the first argument is also set to NULL. This argument can be a device context handle. GDI uses this argument to insert metrical information in the metafile header, as we'll see shortly. If the argument is set to NULL, GDI assumes that this metrical information is based on the video device context.

The second argument to *CreateEnhMetaFile* is a filename. If you set this argument to NULL (as EMF1 does but EMF2 does not), the function creates a memory metafile. EMF2 creates a disk-based metafile with the name EMF2.EMF.

The third argument to the function is an address of a RECT structure that indicates the total dimensions of the metafile in 0.01 mm units. This piece of vital information (one of the deficiencies of the earlier Windows metafile format) goes into the metafile header, as we'll soon see. If you set this argument to NULL, GDI will figure out the dimensions for you. I like the idea of operating systems doing things for me, so I've set the argument to NULL. If performance is critical in your application, you might want to use this argument to avoid some extraneous work on GDI's part.

Finally, the last argument is a text string describing the metafile. This text string is specified in two pieces: the first piece is the name of the application (not necessarily the program filename) followed by a NULL character, and the second piece describes the visual image and is followed by two NULL characters. For example, using the C notation of '\0' for a NULL character, the description string could be "LoonyCad V6.4\0Flying Frogs\0\0". Because C normally puts a NULL character at the end of quoted strings, you need only one '\0' at the end, as EMF2 demonstrates.

After creating the metafile, EMF2 proceeds like EMF1 and makes a few GDI function calls by using the device context handle returned from the *CreateEnhMetaFile* function. The program then calls *CloseEnhMetaFile* to destroy the device context handle and obtain a handle to the completed metafile.

Then, still during WM_CREATE processing, EMF2 does something EMF1 does not: right after obtaining the metafile handle, the program calls *DeleteEnhMetaFile*. That gets rid of all memory resources required to maintain the metafile. However, the disk-based metafile stays behind. (If you ever want to get rid of that file, use a normal file-deletion function such as *DeleteFile*.) Notice that the metafile handle is not stored as a static variable as in EMF1, which implies that it is not required to be saved between messages.

Now, to use that metafile, EMF2 needs to access the disk file. It does this during the WM_PAINT message by calling *GetEnhMetaFile*. The single argument to the function is the metafile filename, and the function returns a handle to the metafile. EMF2 passes this handle to the *PlayEnhMetaFile* function, just as in EMF1. The metafile image is displayed in the rectangle described by the last argument to the function. But unlike EMF1, EMF2 deletes the metafile before concluding WM_PAINT processing. During any following WM_PAINT messages, EMF2 gets the metafile again, plays it, and deletes it.

Keep in mind that deleting the metafile involves deleting only the memory resources required for maintaining the metafile. The disk-based metafile stays behind, even after the program has concluded execution.

Because EMF2 leaves behind a disk-based metafile, you can take a look at it. Figure 18-6 shows a simple hexadecimal dump of the EMF2.EMF file that the program creates.

```
0000   01 00 00 00 88 00 00 00 64 00 00 00 64 00 00 00   ........d...d...
0010   C8 00 00 00 C8 00 00 00 35 0C 00 00 35 0C 00 00   ........5...5...
0020   6A 18 00 00 6A 18 00 00 20 45 4D 46 00 00 01 00   j...j... EMF....
0030   F4 00 00 00 07 00 00 00 01 00 00 00 12 00 00 00   ...............
0040   64 00 00 00 00 00 00 00 00 04 00 00 00 03 00 00   d..............
0050   40 01 00 00 F0 00 00 00 00 00 00 00 00 00 00 00   @..............
0060   00 00 00 00 45 00 4D 00 46 00 32 00 00 00 45 00   ....E.M.F.2...E.
0070   4D 00 46 00 20 00 44 00 65 00 6D 00 6F 00 20 00   M.F. .D.e.m.o. .
0080   23 00 32 00 00 00 00 00 2B 00 00 00 18 00 00 00   #.2.....+.......
0090   63 00 00 00 63 00 00 00 C6 00 00 00 C6 00 00 00   c...c..........
00A0   1B 00 00 00 10 00 00 00 64 00 00 00 64 00 00 00   ........d...d...
00B0   36 00 00 00 10 00 00 00 C8 00 00 00 C8 00 00 00   6..............
00C0   1B 00 00 00 10 00 00 00 C8 00 00 00 64 00 00 00   ............d...
00D0   36 00 00 00 10 00 00 00 64 00 00 00 C8 00 00 00   6.......d.......
00E0   0E 00 00 00 14 00 00 00 00 00 00 00 10 00 00 00   ...............
00F0   14 00 00 00                                       ....
```

Figure 18-6. *A hexadecimal dump of EMF2.EMF.*

I should note that Figure 18-6 shows the metafile created by EMF2 under Microsoft Windows NT 4 running with a video display resolution of 1024 by 768. The metafile created by the same program running under Windows 98 will be 12 bytes shorter, as I'll discuss shortly. Also, the video display resolution will affect some of the information in the metafile header.

Looking at the enhanced metafile format allows us to more deeply understand the workings of metafiles. The enhanced metafile consists of variable-length records. The general format of these records is described by the ENHMETARECORD structure, defined in the WINGDI.H header file like so:

```
typedef struct tagENHMETARECORD
{
     DWORD iType ;          // record type
     DWORD nSize ;          // record size
     DWORD dParm [1] ;      // parameters
}
ENHMETARECORD ;
```

Of course, that array of one element really indicates a variable number of array elements. The number of parameters depends on the record type. The *iType* field can be one of nearly 100 constants beginning with the prefix EMR_ defined in the WINGDI.H file. The *nSize* field is the size of the total record, including the *iType* and *nSize* fields, and one or more *dParm* fields.

With this knowledge, let's look at Figure 18-6. The first field has a type of 0x00000001 and a size of 0x00000088, so it occupies the first 136 bytes of the file. A record type of 1 is the constant EMR_HEADER. I want to leave the discussion of the header for later, so for now let's just skip to offset 0x0088, at the end of this first record.

The next five records correspond to the five GDI calls that EMF2 makes after creating the metafile. The record at offset 0x0088 has a type code of 0x0000002B, which is EMR_RECTANGLE, obviously the metafile record for the *Rectangle* call. It has a length of 0x00000018 (24 in decimal) bytes to accommodate four 32-bit arguments. The *Rectangle* function actually has five arguments, of course, but the first—the handle to the device context—is not stored in the metafile because it would have no real meaning. There are two arguments of 0x00000063 (or 99) and two arguments of 0x000000C6 (or 198), even though the function call in EMF2 specifies that the *Rectangle* corners are (100, 100) and (200, 200). The metafile created by the EMF2 program under Windows 98 will show the first two arguments as 0x00000064 (or 100) and the next two as 0x000000C7 (or 199). Obviously, Windows is making an adjustment to the *Rectangle* arguments before they are stored in the metafile but not doing it consistently. This is why the lines do not match the corners of the rectangle.

Next, we have four 16-byte records corresponding to the two *MoveToEx* (0x0000001B or EMR_MOVETOEX) and *LineTo* (0x00000036 or EMR_LINETO) calls. The arguments in the metafile are the same as those passed to the functions.

The metafile ends with a type code of 0x0000000E or EMR_EOF ("end of file"), a 20-byte record.

The enhanced metafile always begins with a header record. This corresponds to a structure of type ENHMETAHEADER, which is defined like so:

```
typedef struct tagENHMETAHEADER
{
    DWORD iType ;            // EMR_HEADER = 1
    DWORD nSize ;            // structure size
    RECTL rclBounds ;        // bounding rectangle in pixels
    RECTL rclFrame ;         // size of image in 0.01 millimeters
    DWORD dSignature ;       // ENHMETA_SIGNATURE = " EMF"
    DWORD nVersion ;         // 0x00010000
    DWORD nBytes ;           // file size in bytes
    DWORD nRecords ;         // total number of records
    WORD  nHandles ;         // number of handles in handle table
    WORD  sReserved ;
    DWORD nDescription ;     // character length of description string
    DWORD offDescription ;   // offset of description string in file
    DWORD nPalEntries ;      // number of entries in palette
    SIZEL szlDevice ;        // device resolution in pixels
    SIZEL szlMillimeters ;   // device resolution in millimeters
    DWORD cbPixelFormat ;    // size of pixel format
    DWORD offPixelFormat ;   // offset of pixel format
    DWORD bOpenGL ;          // FALSE if no OpenGL records
}
ENHMETAHEADER ;
```

The existence of this header record is probably the single greatest improvement of the enhanced metafile format over the old Windows metafile. You do not need to use the file I/O function on the disk-based metafile to obtain this header information. If you have a handle to the metafile, you can use the *GetEnhMetaFileHeader* function:

```
GetEnhMetaFileHeader (hemf, cbSize, &emh) ;
```

The first argument is the metafile handle, the last is a pointer to an ENHMETAHEADER structure, and the second is the size of this structure. You can use the similar *GetEnhMetaFileDescription* function to obtain the description string.

As defined above, the ENHMETAHEADER structure is 100 bytes in length, but in the EMF2.EMF metafile the size of the record includes the description string, so the size is 0x88 or 136 bytes. The header stored in a Windows 98 metafile does not include the last three fields of the ENHMETAHEADER structure, which accounts for the 12-byte difference in size.

The *rclBounds* field is a RECT structure that indicates the size of the image in pixels. Translating from hexadecimal, we see that the image is bounded by the points (100, 100) on the upper left and (200, 200) on the lower right, exactly what we expect.

The *rclFrame* field is another rectangle structure that provides the same information but in units of 0.01 millimeters. In this case, the file shows a bounding rectangle of (0x0C35, 0x0C35) by (0x186A, 0x186A) or, in decimal, (3125, 3125) by (6250, 6250). Where does this information come from? We'll see shortly.

The *dSignature* field is always the value ENHMETA_SIGNATURE, or 0x464D4520. That seems like a strange number, but if you reverse the byte ordering (in accordance with how multibyte values are stored in memory with Intel processors) and convert to ASCII, it's simply the string " EMF". The *dVersion* field is always 0x00010000.

This is followed by the *nBytes* field, which in this case is 0x000000F4, the total byte size of the metafile. The *nRecords* field (in this case, 0x00000007) indicates the number or records—the header record, the five GDI function calls, and the end-of-file record.

Next we have two 16-bit fields. The *nHandles* field is 0x0001. Normally this field would indicate the number of nondefault handles to graphics objects (such as pens, brushes, and fonts) used in the metafile. We haven't done that, so you might expect the field to be zero, but GDI reserves the first one for itself. Soon we'll see how handles are stored in metafiles.

The next two fields indicate the length of the description string in characters and its offset within the file, in this case 0x00000012 (18 in decimal) and 0x00000064. If the metafile did not have a description string, both these fields would be zero.

The *nPalEntries* field indicates the number of entries in the metafile's palette table, in this case none.

The header record continues with two SIZEL structures, which contain two 32-bit fields, *cx* and *cy*. The *szlDevice* field (at offset 0x0040 in the metafile) indicates the size of the output device in pixels, and the *szlMillimeters* field (at offset 0x0050) is the size of the output device in millimeters. In the documentation of the enhanced metafile, this output device is called the "reference device." It is based on the device context indicated by the handle passed as the first argument to the *CreateEnhMetaFile* call. If the argument is set to NULL, GDI uses the video display. When EMF2 created the metafile shown on the previous page, I happened to be running Windows NT in a 1024 by 768 video mode, so that's what GDI used as the reference device.

GDI obtains this information from *GetDeviceCaps*. The *szlDevice* field in EMF2.EMF is 0x0400 by 0x0300 (that is, 1024 by 768), which is obtained from *GetDeviceCaps* using the HORZRES and VERTRES arguments. The *szlMillimeters* field is 0x140 by 0xF0, or 320 by 240, obtained from *GetDeviceCaps* using the HORZSIZE and VERTSIZE arguments.

A simple division reveals that the pixels are 0.3125 millimeters high and wide, which is how GDI figures out the dimensions of the *rclFrame* rectangle described on the previous page.

The ENHMETAHEADER structure is followed in the metafile by the description string, which was the last argument to *CreateEnhMetaFile*. In this example, this is the string "EMF2" followed by a NULL character and "EMF Demo #2" followed by two NULL characters. That's a total of 18 characters, or 36 bytes because it's stored in Unicode. The string is always stored in Unicode regardless of whether the program creating the metafile is running under Windows NT or Windows 98.

Metafiles and GDI Objects

We've now seen how GDI drawing commands are stored in metafiles. Now let's examine how GDI objects are stored. The EMF3 program shown in Figures 18-7 is similar to the EMF2 program shown earlier except that it creates a nondefault pen and brush for drawing the rectangle and lines. I've also provided a little fix for the problem with the coordinates to *Rectangle*. EMF3 uses *GetVersion* to determine if it's running under Windows 98 or Windows NT, and to adjust the arguments appropriately.

EMF3.C

```
/*-------------------------------------
   EMF3.C -- Enhanced Metafile Demo #3
             (c) Charles Petzold, 1998
   -------------------------------------*/

#include <windows.h>

LRESULT CALLBACK WndProc (HWND, UINT, WPARAM, LPARAM) ;

int WINAPI WinMain (HINSTANCE hInstance, HINSTANCE hPrevInstance,
                    PSTR szCmdLine, int iCmdShow)
{
     static TCHAR szAppName[] = TEXT ("EMF3") ;
     HWND          hwnd ;
```

Figure 18-7. *The EMF3 program.*

```
    MSG          msg ;
    WNDCLASS     wndclass ;

    wndclass.style         = CS_HREDRAW | CS_VREDRAW ;
    wndclass.lpfnWndProc   = WndProc ;
    wndclass.cbClsExtra    = 0 ;
    wndclass.cbWndExtra    = 0 ;
    wndclass.hInstance     = hInstance ;
    wndclass.hIcon         = LoadIcon (NULL, IDI_APPLICATION) ;
    wndclass.hCursor       = LoadCursor (NULL, IDC_ARROW) ;
    wndclass.hbrBackground = GetStockObject (WHITE_BRUSH) ;
    wndclass.lpszMenuName  = NULL ;
    wndclass.lpszClassName = szAppName ;

    if (!RegisterClass (&wndclass))
    {
         MessageBox (NULL, TEXT ("This program requires Windows NT!"),
                    szAppName, MB_ICONERROR) ;
         return 0 ;
    }

    hwnd = CreateWindow (szAppName, TEXT ("Enhanced Metafile Demo #3"),
                         WS_OVERLAPPEDWINDOW,
                         CW_USEDEFAULT, CW_USEDEFAULT,
                         CW_USEDEFAULT, CW_USEDEFAULT,
                         NULL, NULL, hInstance, NULL) ;

    ShowWindow (hwnd, iCmdShow) ;
    UpdateWindow (hwnd) ;

    while (GetMessage (&msg, NULL, 0, 0))
    {
         TranslateMessage (&msg) ;
         DispatchMessage (&msg) ;
    }
    return msg.wParam ;
}

LRESULT CALLBACK WndProc (HWND hwnd, UINT message, WPARAM wParam, LPARAM lParam)
{
    LOGBRUSH      lb ;
    HDC           hdc, hdcEMF ;
    HENHMETAFILE  hemf ;
    PAINTSTRUCT   ps ;
    RECT          rect ;
```

(continued)

Figure 18-7. *continued*

```
    switch (message)
    {
    case WM_CREATE:
         hdcEMF = CreateEnhMetaFile (NULL, TEXT ("emf3.emf"), NULL,
                                     TEXT ("EMF3\0EMF Demo #3\0")) ;

         SelectObject (hdcEMF, CreateSolidBrush (RGB (0, 0, 255))) ;

         lb.lbStyle = BS_SOLID ;
         lb.lbColor = RGB (255, 0, 0) ;
         lb.lbHatch = 0 ;

         SelectObject (hdcEMF,
             ExtCreatePen (PS_SOLID | PS_GEOMETRIC, 5, &lb, 0, NULL)) ;

         if (GetVersion () & 0x80000000)                // Windows 98
             Rectangle (hdcEMF, 100, 100, 201, 201) ;
         else                                           // Windows NT
             Rectangle (hdcEMF, 101, 101, 202, 202) ;

         MoveToEx (hdcEMF, 100, 100, NULL) ;
         LineTo    (hdcEMF, 200, 200) ;

         MoveToEx (hdcEMF, 200, 100, NULL) ;
         LineTo    (hdcEMF, 100, 200) ;

         DeleteObject (SelectObject (hdcEMF, GetStockObject (BLACK_PEN))) ;
         DeleteObject (SelectObject (hdcEMF, GetStockObject (WHITE_BRUSH))) ;

         hemf = CloseEnhMetaFile (hdcEMF) ;

         DeleteEnhMetaFile (hemf) ;
         return 0 ;

    case WM_PAINT:
         hdc = BeginPaint (hwnd, &ps) ;

         GetClientRect (hwnd, &rect) ;

         rect.left   =     rect.right  / 4 ;
         rect.right  = 3 * rect.right  / 4 ;
         rect.top    =     rect.bottom / 4 ;
         rect.bottom = 3 * rect.bottom / 4 ;

         hemf = GetEnhMetaFile (TEXT ("emf3.emf")) ;

         PlayEnhMetaFile (hdc, hemf, &rect) ;
         DeleteEnhMetaFile (hemf) ;
```

```
        EndPaint (hwnd, &ps) ;
        return 0 ;

    case WM_DESTROY:
        PostQuitMessage (0) ;
        return 0 ;
    }
    return DefWindowProc (hwnd, message, wParam, lParam) ;
}
```

As we've seen, when you call GDI functions using the device context handle returned from *CreateEnhMetaFile*, the function calls are stored in the metafile rather than being rendered on the screen or printer. However, some GDI functions do not refer to a particular device context at all. One important category of these GDI functions are those that create graphics objects, including pens and brushes. Although the definitions of logical pens and brushes are stored in memory maintained by GDI, these abstract definitions are not associated with any particular device context when they're created.

EMF3 calls both the *CreateSolidBrush* and *ExtCreatePen* functions. Because these functions do not require a device context handle, this implies that GDI will not store these calls in the metafile. This implication is true. When called by themselves, GDI functions simply create the graphics drawing object without affecting the metafile at all.

However, when a program calls *SelectObject* to select a GDI object into the metafile device context, GDI encodes both an object-creation function (essentially derived from the internal GDI data used to stored the object) and a *SelectObject* call in the metafile. To see how this works, let's take a look at the hexadecimal dump of EMF3.EMF, shown in Figure 18-8.

```
0000   01 00 00 00 88 00 00 00 60 00 00 00 60 00 00 00   ........`...`...
0010   CC 00 00 00 CC 00 00 00 B8 0B 00 00 B8 0B 00 00   ................
0020   E7 18 00 00 E7 18 00 00 20 45 4D 46 00 00 01 00   ........ EMF....
0030   88 01 00 00 0F 00 00 00 03 00 00 00 12 00 00 00   ................
0040   64 00 00 00 00 00 00 00 00 04 00 00 00 03 00 00 00   d...............
0050   40 01 00 00 F0 00 00 00 00 00 00 00 00 00 00 00   @...............
0060   00 00 00 00 45 00 4D 00 46 00 33 00 00 00 45 00   ....E.M.F.3...E.
0070   4D 00 46 00 20 00 44 00 65 00 6D 00 6F 00 20 00   M.F. .D.e.m.o. .
0080   23 00 33 00 00 00 00 00 27 00 00 00 18 00 00 00   #.3.....'.......
0090   01 00 00 00 00 00 00 00 00 00 FF 00 00 00 00 00   ................
00A0   25 00 00 00 0C 00 00 00 01 00 00 00 5F 00 00 00   %..........._...
00B0   34 00 00 00 02 00 00 00 34 00 00 00 00 00 00 00   4.......4.......
00C0   34 00 00 00 00 00 00 00 00 00 01 00 05 00 00 00   4...............
00D0   00 00 00 00 FF 00 00 00 00 00 00 00 00 00 00 00   ................
00E0   25 00 00 00 0C 00 00 00 02 00 00 00 2B 00 00 00   %...........+...
```

Figure 18-8. *A hexadecimal dump of EMF3.EMF.*

(continued)

Figure 18-8. *continued*

```
00F0   18 00 00 00 63 00 00 00 63 00 00 00 C6 00 00 00    ....c...c.......
0100   C6 00 00 00 1B 00 00 00 10 00 00 00 64 00 00 00    ............d...
0110   64 00 00 00 36 00 00 00 10 00 00 00 C8 00 00 00    d...6...........
0120   C8 00 00 00 1B 00 00 00 10 00 00 00 C8 00 00 00    ................
0130   64 00 00 00 36 00 00 00 10 00 00 00 64 00 00 00    d...6.......d...
0140   C8 00 00 00 25 00 00 00 0C 00 00 00 07 00 00 80    ....%...........
0150   28 00 00 00 0C 00 00 00 02 00 00 00 25 00 00 00    (...........%...
0160   0C 00 00 00 00 00 00 80 28 00 00 00 0C 00 00 00    ........(.......
0170   01 00 00 00 0E 00 00 00 14 00 00 00 00 00 00 00    ...............
0180   10 00 00 00 14 00 00 00                            ........
```

You may want to compare this metafile with EMF2.EMF shown earlier. The first difference you'll see in the header section of EMF3.EMF is the *rclBounds* field. EMF2.EMF indicated that the image was bound between coordinates (0x64,0x64) and (0xC8, 0xC8). In EMF3.EMF it's (0x60,0x60) and (0xCC,0xCC). This reflects using a wider pen. The *rclFrame* field (indicating the size of the image in units of 0.01 millimeters) is also affected.

While the *nBytes* field (located at offset 0x0030) of EMF2.EMF indicated that the metafile was 0xFA bytes, EMF3.EMF is 0x0188 bytes. The EMF2.EMF metafile contained 7 records (the header, 5 GDI function calls, and the end-of-file record), but EMF3.EMF has 15. As we'll see, the extra 8 records are for 2 object-creation functions, 4 calls to *SelectObject*, and 2 *DeleteObject* calls.

The *nHandles* field (at offset 0x0038 in the file) indicates the number of handles to GDI objects. This is always one more than the number of nondefault objects used by the metafile. (The way that the Platform SDK documentation indicates this is "Index zero in this table is reserved.") The field is 1 in EMF2.EMF and 3 in EMF3.EMF, indicating the pen and the brush.

Let's skip to offset 0x0088 in the file, which is the second record (the first after the header). The record type is 0x27, which corresponds to the constant EMR_CREATE-BRUSHINDIRECT. This is the metafile record for the *CreateBrushIndirect* function, which requires a pointer to a LOGBRUSH structure. The size of the record is 0x18 (or 24) bytes.

Each nonstock GDI object that is selected into the metafile device context is assigned a number beginning with 1. This is indicated by the next 4-byte word in this record, at offset 0x0090 in the metafile. The next three 4-byte fields in this record correspond to the three fields of the LOGBRUSH structure, 0x00000000 (the *lbStyle* field of BS_SOLID), 0x00FF0000 (the *lbColor* field), and 0x00000000 (the *lbHatch* field).

At offset 0x00A0 in EMF3.EMF is the next record, which has a record type of 0x25, or EMR_SELECTOBJECT, the metafile record for the *SelectObject* call. The record is 0x0C (or 12) bytes long, and the next field is the number 0x01, indicating that it's selecting the first GDI object, which is the logical brush.

At offset 0x00AC in EMF3.EMF is the next record, which has a record type of 0x5F, or EMR_EXTCREATEPEN. The record is 0x34 (or 52) bytes. The next 4-byte field is 0x02, which means this is the second nonstock GDI object used in the metafile.

I won't pretend that I know why the next four fields of the EMR_EXTCREATEPEN record repeat the record size twice, interspersed with 0 fields, but there they are: 0x34, 0x00, 0x34, and 0x00. The next field is 0x00010000, which is the pen style of PS_SOLID (0x00000000) combined with PS_GEOMETRIC (0x00010000). The width of five units is next, followed by the three fields of the logical brush structure used in the *ExtCreatePen* function, followed by a field of 0.

If you create a custom extended pen style, the EMR_EXTCREATEPEN record will be longer than 52 bytes, and this will be reflected not only in the second field of the record, but in the two repeated size fields. Following the three fields that describe the LOGBRUSH structure, the next field will not be 0 (as it is in EMF3.EMF) but will indicate the number of dashes and spaces. This is followed by that many fields for the dash and space lengths.

The next 12-byte field in EMF3.EMF is another *SelectObject* call indicating the second object—the pen. The next five records are the same as EMF2.EMF—a record type of 0x2B (EMR_RECTANGLE), and two sets of records of 0x1B (EMR_MOVETOEX) and 0x36 (EMR_LINETO).

These drawing functions are followed by two sets of 12-byte records of 0x25 (EMR_SELECTOBJECT) and 0x28 (EMR_DELETEOBJECT). The select-object records have arguments of 0x80000007 and 0x80000000. When the high bit is set, it indicates a stock object, in this case 0x07 (corresponding to BLACK_PEN) and 0x00 (WHITE_BRUSH).

The *DeleteObject* calls have arguments of 2 and 1, for the two nondefault objects used in the metafile. Although the *DeleteObject* function does not require a device context handle as the first argument, GDI apparently keeps track of objects used in the metafile that are deleted by the program.

Finally, the metafile concludes with a 0x0E record, which is EMF_EOF ("end of file").

To sum up, whenever a nondefault GDI object is first selected into a metafile device context, GDI encodes both a record indicating the object-creation function (in this case, EMR_CREATEBRUSHINDIRECT and EMR_EXTCREATEPEN). Each object will have a unique number beginning with 1, indicated by the third field of the record. This record will be followed by an EMR_SELECTOBJECT record referencing that number. On subsequent times an object is selected into the metafile device context (without being deleted in the interim), only an EMR_SELECTOBJECT record is required.

Metafiles and Bitmaps

Let's try something a little more complex now, in particular drawing a bitmap in a metafile device context. This is shown in EMF4, in Figure 18-9 on the following page.

EMF4.C

```
/*-------------------------------------
   EMF4.C -- Enhanced Metafile Demo #4
             (c) Charles Petzold, 1998
   -------------------------------------*/

#define OEMRESOURCE
#include <windows.h>

LRESULT CALLBACK WndProc (HWND, UINT, WPARAM, LPARAM) ;

int WINAPI WinMain (HINSTANCE hInstance, HINSTANCE hPrevInstance,
                    PSTR szCmdLine, int iCmdShow)
{
    static TCHAR szAppName[] = TEXT ("EMF4") ;
    HWND         hwnd ;
    MSG          msg ;
    WNDCLASS     wndclass ;

    wndclass.style         = CS_HREDRAW | CS_VREDRAW ;
    wndclass.lpfnWndProc   = WndProc ;
    wndclass.cbClsExtra    = 0 ;
    wndclass.cbWndExtra    = 0 ;
    wndclass.hInstance     = hInstance ;
    wndclass.hIcon         = LoadIcon (NULL, IDI_APPLICATION) ;
    wndclass.hCursor       = LoadCursor (NULL, IDC_ARROW) ;
    wndclass.hbrBackground = GetStockObject (WHITE_BRUSH) ;
    wndclass.lpszMenuName  = NULL ;
    wndclass.lpszClassName = szAppName ;

    if (!RegisterClass (&wndclass))
    {
        MessageBox (NULL, TEXT ("This program requires Windows NT!"),
                    szAppName, MB_ICONERROR) ;
        return 0 ;
    }

    hwnd = CreateWindow (szAppName, TEXT ("Enhanced Metafile Demo #4"),
                         WS_OVERLAPPEDWINDOW,
                         CW_USEDEFAULT, CW_USEDEFAULT,
                         CW_USEDEFAULT, CW_USEDEFAULT,
                         NULL, NULL, hInstance, NULL) ;

    ShowWindow (hwnd, iCmdShow) ;
    UpdateWindow (hwnd) ;
```

Figure 18-9. *The EMF4 program.*

```
      while (GetMessage (&msg, NULL, 0, 0))
      {
            TranslateMessage (&msg) ;
            DispatchMessage (&msg) ;
      }
      return msg.wParam ;
}

LRESULT CALLBACK WndProc (HWND hwnd, UINT message, WPARAM wParam, LPARAM lParam)
{
      BITMAP         bm ;
      HBITMAP        hbm ;
      HDC            hdc, hdcEMF, hdcMem ;
      HENHMETAFILE   hemf ;
      PAINTSTRUCT    ps ;
      RECT           rect ;

      switch (message)
      {
      case WM_CREATE:
            hdcEMF = CreateEnhMetaFile (NULL, TEXT ("emf4.emf"), NULL,
                                        TEXT ("EMF4\0EMF Demo #4\0")) ;

            hbm = LoadBitmap (NULL, MAKEINTRESOURCE (OBM_CLOSE)) ;

            GetObject (hbm, sizeof (BITMAP), &bm) ;

            hdcMem = CreateCompatibleDC (hdcEMF) ;

            SelectObject (hdcMem, hbm) ;

            StretchBlt (hdcEMF, 100, 100, 100, 100,
                        hdcMem,   0,   0, bm.bmWidth, bm.bmHeight, SRCCOPY) ;

            DeleteDC (hdcMem) ;
            DeleteObject (hbm) ;

            hemf = CloseEnhMetaFile (hdcEMF) ;

            DeleteEnhMetaFile (hemf) ;
            return 0 ;

      case WM_PAINT:
            hdc = BeginPaint (hwnd, &ps) ;

            GetClientRect (hwnd, &rect) ;
```

(continued)

Figure 18-9. *continued*

```
          rect.left   =       rect.right  / 4 ;
          rect.right  = 3 * rect.right  / 4 ;
          rect.top    =       rect.bottom / 4 ;
          rect.bottom = 3 * rect.bottom / 4 ;

          hemf = GetEnhMetaFile (TEXT ("emf4.emf")) ;

          PlayEnhMetaFile (hdc, hemf, &rect) ;
          DeleteEnhMetaFile (hemf) ;
          EndPaint (hwnd, &ps) ;
          return 0 ;

     case WM_DESTROY:
          PostQuitMessage (0) ;
          return 0 ;
     }
     return DefWindowProc (hwnd, message, wParam, lParam) ;
}
```

For convenience, EMF4 loads a system bitmap indicated by the constant OEM_CLOSE. The customary way of displaying a bitmap in a device context is to create a memory device context compatible with the destination device context (in this case, that's the metafile device context) by calling *CreateCompatibleDC*. Then you select the bitmap into that memory device context by using *SelectObject* and call *BitBlt* or *StretchBlt* from the memory source device context to the destination device context. When you're finished, you delete both the memory device context and the bitmap.

You'll note that EMF4 also calls *GetObject* to determine the size of the bitmap. This is necessary for the *SelectObject* call.

At first, the storage of this code in a metafile seems like a real challenge for GDI. No function leading up the *StretchBlt* call involves the metafile device context at all. So let's see how it's done by taking a look at EMF4.EMF, which is partially shown in Figure 18-10.

```
0000   01 00 00 00 88 00 00 00 64 00 00 00 64 00 00 00   ........d...d...
0010   C7 00 00 00 C7 00 00 00 35 0C 00 00 35 0C 00 00   ........5...5...
0020   4B 18 00 00 4B 18 00 00 20 45 4D 46 00 00 01 00   K...K... EMF....
0030   F0 0E 00 00 03 00 00 00 01 00 00 00 12 00 00 00   ...............
0040   64 00 00 00 00 00 00 00 00 04 00 00 00 03 00 00   d...............
0050   40 01 00 00 F0 00 00 00 00 00 00 00 00 00 00 00   @...............
0060   00 00 00 00 45 00 4D 00 46 00 34 00 00 00 45 00   ....E.M.F.4...E.
0070   4D 00 46 00 20 00 44 00 65 00 6D 00 6F 00 20 00   M.F. .D.e.m.o. .
0080   23 00 34 00 00 00 00 00 4D 00 00 00 54 0E 00 00   #.4.....M...T...
0090   64 00 00 00 64 00 00 00 C7 00 00 00 C7 00 00 00   d...d...........
00A0   64 00 00 00 64 00 00 00 64 00 00 00 64 00 00 00   d...d...d...d...
```

Figure 18-10. *A partial hexadecimal dump of EMF4.EMF.*

```
00B0   20 00 CC 00 00 00 00 00 00 00 00 00 00 00 80 3F   .............?
00C0   00 00 00 00 00 00 00 00 00 00 80 3F 00 00 00 00   ...........?....
00D0   00 00 00 00 FF FF FF 00 00 00 00 00 6C 00 00 00   ............l...
00E0   28 00 00 00 94 00 00 00 C0 0D 00 00 28 00 00 00   (...........(...
00F0   16 00 00 00 28 00 00 00 28 00 00 00 16 00 00 00   ....(...(.......
0100   01 00 20 00 00 00 00 00 C0 0D 00 00 00 00 00 00   ................
0110   00 00 00 00 00 00 00 00 00 00 00 00 C0 C0 C0 00   ................
0120   C0 C0 C0 00 C0 C0 C0 00 C0 C0 C0 00 C0 C0 C0 00   ................
. . . .
0ED0   C0 C0 C0 00 C0 C0 C0 00 C0 C0 C0 00 0E 00 00 00   ................
0EE0   14 00 00 00 00 00 00 00 10 00 00 00 14 00 00 00   ................
```

This metafile contains just three records—a header, a 0x4D (or EMR_STRETCHBLT) record that is 0x0E54 bytes long, and an end-of-file record.

I won't pretend to have deciphered what each and every field of this record means. But I will point out the crucial key to understanding how GDI can translate the series of function calls in EMF4.C to a single metafile record.

GDI has converted the original device-dependent bitmap to a device-independent bitmap (DIB). The entire DIB is stored in this record, which accounts for its size. I suspect that when it comes time to play the metafile and display the bitmap, GDI actually uses the *StretchDIBits* function rather than *StretchBlt*. Or, GDI could convert the DIB back to a device-dependent bitmap by using *CreateDIBitmap* and then use a memory device context and *StretchBlt* for the display.

The EMR_STRETCHBLT record begins at offset 0x0088 in the metafile. The DIB is stored beginning at offset 0x00F4 in the metafile and continues to the end of the record at 0x0EDC. The DIB begins with a 40-byte structure of type BITMAPINFOHEADER. This is followed at offset 0x011C by 22 rows of 40 pixels each. This is a 32 bit-per-pixel DIB, so each pixel requires 4 bytes.

Enumerating the Metafile

When you wish to get access to the individual records of a metafile, you use a process called metafile enumeration. This is demonstrated by the EMF5 program shown in Figure 18-11. This program uses a metafile to display the same image as EMF3 but works by using metafile enumeration.

EMF5.C

```
/*--------------------------------------------
   EMF5.C -- Enhanced Metafile Demo #5
             (c) Charles Petzold, 1998
  --------------------------------------*/
```

Figure 18-11. *The EMF5 program.*

(continued)

Figure 18-11. *continued*

```
#include <windows.h>

LRESULT CALLBACK WndProc (HWND, UINT, WPARAM, LPARAM) ;

int WINAPI WinMain (HINSTANCE hInstance, HINSTANCE hPrevInstance,
                    PSTR szCmdLine, int iCmdShow)
{
     static TCHAR szAppName[] = TEXT ("EMF5") ;
     HWND         hwnd ;
     MSG          msg ;
     WNDCLASS     wndclass ;

     wndclass.style         = CS_HREDRAW | CS_VREDRAW ;
     wndclass.lpfnWndProc   = WndProc ;
     wndclass.cbClsExtra    = 0 ;
     wndclass.cbWndExtra    = 0 ;
     wndclass.hInstance     = hInstance ;
     wndclass.hIcon         = LoadIcon (NULL, IDI_APPLICATION) ;
     wndclass.hCursor       = LoadCursor (NULL, IDC_ARROW) ;
     wndclass.hbrBackground = GetStockObject (WHITE_BRUSH) ;
     wndclass.lpszMenuName  = NULL ;
     wndclass.lpszClassName = szAppName ;

     if (!RegisterClass (&wndclass))
     {
          MessageBox (NULL, TEXT ("This program requires Windows NT!"),
                      szAppName, MB_ICONERROR) ;
          return 0 ;
     }

     hwnd = CreateWindow (szAppName, TEXT ("Enhanced Metafile Demo #5"),
                          WS_OVERLAPPEDWINDOW,
                          CW_USEDEFAULT, CW_USEDEFAULT,
                          CW_USEDEFAULT, CW_USEDEFAULT,
                          NULL, NULL, hInstance, NULL) ;

     ShowWindow (hwnd, iCmdShow) ;
     UpdateWindow (hwnd) ;

     while (GetMessage (&msg, NULL, 0, 0))
     {
          TranslateMessage (&msg) ;
          DispatchMessage (&msg) ;
     }
     return msg.wParam ;
}
```

```
int CALLBACK EnhMetaFileProc (HDC hdc, HANDLETABLE * pHandleTable,
                              CONST ENHMETARECORD * pEmfRecord,
                              int iHandles, LPARAM pData)
{
     PlayEnhMetaFileRecord (hdc, pHandleTable, pEmfRecord, iHandles) ;

     return TRUE ;
}

LRESULT CALLBACK WndProc (HWND hwnd, UINT message, WPARAM wParam, LPARAM lParam)
{
     HDC           hdc ;
     HENHMETAFILE  hemf ;
     PAINTSTRUCT   ps ;
     RECT          rect ;

     switch (message)
     {
     case WM_PAINT:
          hdc = BeginPaint (hwnd, &ps) ;

          GetClientRect (hwnd, &rect) ;

          rect.left   =     rect.right  / 4 ;
          rect.right  = 3 * rect.right  / 4 ;
          rect.top    =     rect.bottom / 4 ;
          rect.bottom = 3 * rect.bottom / 4 ;

          hemf = GetEnhMetaFile (TEXT ("..\\emf3\\emf3.emf")) ;

          EnumEnhMetaFile (hdc, hemf, EnhMetaFileProc, NULL, &rect) ;
          DeleteEnhMetaFile (hemf) ;
          EndPaint (hwnd, &ps) ;
          return 0 ;

     case WM_DESTROY:
          PostQuitMessage (0) ;
          return 0 ;
     }
     return DefWindowProc (hwnd, message, wParam, lParam) ;
}
```

This program uses the EMF3.EMF file created by the EMF3 program, so make sure you run that one before this one. Also, you need to run both programs from within the Visual C++ environment so that the directory paths are correct. In WM_PAINT processing, the major difference between the two programs is that EMF3 called *PlayEnhMetaFile*, but EMF5 calls *EnumEnhMetaFile*. You'll recall that the *PlayEnhMetaFile* function has the following syntax:

```
PlayEnhMetaFile (hdc, hemf, &rect) ;
```

The first argument is the handle to the device context on which the metafile is to be rendered. The second argument is a handle to the enhanced metafile. The third argument is a pointer to a RECT structure that describes a rectangle on the device context surface. The metafile image is stretched to fit, but not exceed, this rectangle.

The *EnumEnhMetaFile* has five arguments, three of which are the same as those to *PlayEnhMetaFile* (although the pointer to the RECT structure has been moved to the end of the argument list).

The third argument to *EnumEnhMetaFile* is the name of an enumeration function, which I've chosen to call *EnhMetaFileProc*. The fourth argument is a pointer to arbitrary data you may wish to pass to the enumeration function. I've simply set this argument to NULL.

Now let's take a look at the enumeration function. When you call *EnumEnhMetaFile*, GDI will call *EnhMetaFileProc* once for each record in the metafile, including the header record and the end-of-file record. Normally the enumeration function returns TRUE, but it could return FALSE to abort the enumeration process.

The enumeration function has five parameters, which I'll describe shortly. In this program, I just pass the first four to *PlayEnhMetaFileRecord*, which causes GDI to execute the function call represented by that record just as if you had called it explicitly.

EMF5 uses *EnumEnhMetaFile* and *PlayEnhMetaFileRecord* to get the same results as EMF3 got by calling *PlayEnhMetaFile*. The difference is that EMF5 now has a hook into the process of metafile rendering and gets access to every metafile record. This can be useful.

The first parameter to the enumeration function is a handle to a device context. GDI simply obtains this handle from the first parameter to *EnumEnhMetaFile*. My enumeration function passes it on to *PlayEnhMetaFileRecord* to identify the device context on which the image is to be rendered.

Let me skip to the third parameter of the enumeration function. This is a pointer to a structure of type ENHMETARECORD, which I described earlier. This structure describes the actual metafile record, exactly as it's encoded in the metafile itself.

You can write code to examine these records if you wish. Perhaps you might elect not to pass some records to the *PlayEnhMetaFileRecord* function. For example, in EMF5.C, try inserting the following line right before the *PlayEnhMetaFileRecord* call:

```
if (pEmfRecord->iType != EMR_LINETO)
```

Recompile the program, run it, and you'll see only the rectangle, not the two lines. Or try the following:

```
if (pEmfRecord->iType != EMR_SELECTOBJECT)
```

That little change will cause the image to be rendered with default objects—not the pen and brush we've created.

One thing you *should not* do is modify the metafile record. But before you get upset about this restriction, let's take a look at the EMF6 program in Figure 18-12.

EMF6.C

```
/*-----------------------------------------
   EMF6.C -- Enhanced Metafile Demo #6
             (c) Charles Petzold, 1998
   -----------------------------------------*/

#include <windows.h>

LRESULT CALLBACK WndProc (HWND, UINT, WPARAM, LPARAM) ;

int WINAPI WinMain (HINSTANCE hInstance, HINSTANCE hPrevInstance,
                    PSTR lpszCmdLine, int iCmdShow)
{
     static TCHAR szAppName[] = TEXT ("EMF6") ;
     HWND         hwnd ;
     MSG          msg ;
     WNDCLASS     wndclass ;

     wndclass.style         = CS_HREDRAW | CS_VREDRAW ;
     wndclass.lpfnWndProc   = WndProc ;
     wndclass.cbClsExtra    = 0 ;
     wndclass.cbWndExtra    = 0 ;
     wndclass.hInstance     = hInstance ;
     wndclass.hIcon         = LoadIcon (NULL, IDI_APPLICATION) ;
     wndclass.hCursor       = LoadCursor (NULL, IDC_ARROW) ;
     wndclass.hbrBackground = GetStockObject (WHITE_BRUSH) ;
     wndclass.lpszMenuName  = NULL ;
     wndclass.lpszClassName = szAppName ;

     if (!RegisterClass (&wndclass))
     {
          MessageBox (NULL, TEXT ("This program requires Windows NT!"),
                      szAppName, MB_ICONERROR) ;
          return 0 ;
     }

     hwnd = CreateWindow (szAppName, TEXT ("Enhanced Metafile Demo #6"),
                          WS_OVERLAPPEDWINDOW,
                          CW_USEDEFAULT, CW_USEDEFAULT,
                          CW_USEDEFAULT, CW_USEDEFAULT,
                          NULL, NULL, hInstance, NULL) ;

     ShowWindow (hwnd, iCmdShow) ;
     UpdateWindow (hwnd) ;
```

Figure 18-12. *The EMF6 program.*   *(continued)*

Figure 18-12. *continued*

```
    while (GetMessage (&msg, NULL, 0, 0))
    {
         TranslateMessage (&msg) ;
         DispatchMessage (&msg) ;
    }
    return msg.wParam ;
}

int CALLBACK EnhMetaFileProc (HDC hdc, HANDLETABLE * pHandleTable,
                              CONST ENHMETARECORD * pEmfRecord,
                              int iHandles, LPARAM pData)
{
    ENHMETARECORD * pEmfr ;

    pEmfr = (ENHMETARECORD *) malloc (pEmfRecord->nSize) ;

    CopyMemory (pEmfr, pEmfRecord, pEmfRecord->nSize) ;

    if (pEmfr->iType == EMR_RECTANGLE)
        pEmfr->iType = EMR_ELLIPSE ;

    PlayEnhMetaFileRecord (hdc, pHandleTable, pEmfr, iHandles) ;

    free (pEmfr) ;

    return TRUE ;
}

LRESULT CALLBACK WndProc (HWND hwnd, UINT message, WPARAM wParam, LPARAM lParam)
{
    HDC           hdc ;
    HENHMETAFILE  hemf ;
    PAINTSTRUCT   ps ;
    RECT          rect ;

    switch (message)
    {
    case WM_PAINT:
        hdc = BeginPaint (hwnd, &ps) ;

        GetClientRect (hwnd, &rect) ;

        rect.left  =     rect.right / 4 ;
        rect.right = 3 * rect.right / 4 ;
```

```
        rect.top    =     rect.bottom / 4 ;
        rect.bottom = 3 * rect.bottom / 4 ;

        hemf = GetEnhMetaFile (TEXT ("..\\emf3\\emf3.emf")) ;

        EnumEnhMetaFile (hdc, hemf, EnhMetaFileProc, NULL, &rect) ;
        DeleteEnhMetaFile (hemf) ;
        EndPaint (hwnd, &ps) ;
        return 0 ;

   case WM_DESTROY:
        PostQuitMessage (0) ;
        return 0 ;
   }
   return DefWindowProc (hwnd, message, wParam, lParam) ;
}
```

Like EMF5, EMF6 uses the EMF3.EMF metafile created by the EMF3 program, so be sure to run that program before this one and run all programs within Visual C++.

EMF6 demonstrates that if you want to modify metafile records before rendering them, the solution is fairly simple: you make a copy and modify that. As you can see, the enumeration procedure begins by using *malloc* to allocate a block of memory the size of the metafile record, indicated by the *nSize* field of the *pEmfRecord* structure passed to the function. A pointer to this block is saved in the variable *pEmfr*, which is a pointer to an ENHMETARECORD structure.

Using *CopyMemory*, the program copies the contents of the structure pointed to by *pEmfRecord* to the structure pointed to by *pEmfr*. Now we have something that we can alter. The program checks whether the record is of type EMR_RECTANGLE and, if so, replaces the *iType* field with EMR_ELLIPSE. The *pEmfr* pointer is passed to *PlayEnhMeta-FileRecord* and then freed. The result is that the program draws an ellipse rather than a rectangle. Everything else is the same.

Of course, our little alteration worked quite easily because the *Rectangle* and *Ellipse* functions have the same arguments that define the same thing—a bounding box for the figure. Making more extensive alterations will require some knowledge about the formats of the various metafile records.

Another possibility is to slip in an extra record or two. For example, replace the *if* statement in EMF6.C with the following:

```
if (pEmfr->iType == EMR_RECTANGLE)
{
    PlayEnhMetaFileRecord (hdc, pHandleTable, pEmfr, nObjects) ;

    pEmfr->iType = EMR_ELLIPSE ;
}
```

Whenever a *Rectangle* record comes through, the program renders it and then changes it to an *Ellipse*, which is also rendered. Now the program draws both a rectangle and an ellipse.

Let's examine now how GDI objects are dealt with when you enumerate a metafile.

In the metafile header, the *nHandles* field of the ENHMETAHEADER structure is a value of one more than the number of GDI objects created in the metafile. Thus, for the metafiles in EMF5 and EMF6, this field is 3, accounting for the pen, the brush, and something else. What this "something else" really is I'll reveal shortly.

You'll notice that the penultimate parameter to the enumeration functions in EMF5 and EMF6 is also called *nHandles*. It'll be the same number, which is 3.

The second parameter to the enumeration function is a pointer to a structure called HANDLETABLE, defined in WINGDI.H like so:

```
typedef struct tagHANDLETABLE
{
    HGDIOBJ objectHandle [1] ;
}
HANDLETABLE ;
```

The HGDIOBJ data type is a generalized handle to a GDI object and is defined as a 32-bit pointer, as are all the other GDI objects. As you'll note, this is one of those structures that has an array field with just one element. This means the field is actually of variable length. The number of elements in the objectHandle array is equal to *nHandles*, which in the case of our programs is 3.

Within the enumeration function, you can obtain these handles using the expression

```
pHandleTable->objectHandle[i]
```

where *i* is either 0, 1, or 2 for the three handles.

Whenever the enumeration function is called, the first element of the array will contain the handle to the metafile being enumerated. That's the "something else" I referred to above.

When the enumeration function is *first* called, the second and third elements of the table will be 0. These are placeholders for the handles of the brush and the pen.

Here's how it works: The first object-creation function in the metafile has a record type of EMR_CREATEBRUSHINDIRECT. This record indicates an object number of 1. When the record is passed to *PlayEnhMetaFileRecord*, GDI creates the brush and obtains a handle to it. This handle is stored as element 1 (the second element) of the *objectHandle* array. When the first EMR_SELECTOBJECT record is passed to *PlayEnhMetaFileRecord*, GDI notes that the handle number is 1 and is able to retrieve the actual handle from the table and use it in a *SelectObject* call. When the metafile eventually deletes the brush, GDI sets element 1 of the *objectHandle* array back to 0.

By accessing the *objectHandle* array, you can use calls such as *GetObjectType* and *GetObject* to obtain information about the objects used in the metafile.

Embedding Images

Perhaps the most important use of metafile enumeration is to embed other images (or even entire metafiles) in an existing metafile. Actually, the existing metafile remains unchanged; what you really do is create a new metafile that combines the existing metafile and the new embedded images. The basic trick is to pass a metafile device context handle as the first argument to *EnumEnhMetaFile*. That allows you to render both metafile records and GDI function calls on the metafile device context.

It's easiest to embed new images at the beginning or end of the metafile command sequence—that is, right after the EMR_HEADER record or right before the EMF_EOF record. However, if you are familiar with the existing metafile, you can embed new drawing commands anywhere you want. That's what's done in the EMF7 program shown in Figure 18-13.

EMF7.C

```
/*-----------------------------------------
   EMF7.C -- Enhanced Metafile Demo #7
            (c) Charles Petzold, 1998
   -----------------------------------------*/

#include <windows.h>

LRESULT CALLBACK WndProc (HWND, UINT, WPARAM, LPARAM) ;

int WINAPI WinMain (HINSTANCE hInstance, HINSTANCE hPrevInstance,
                    PSTR lpszCmdLine, int iCmdShow)
{
     static TCHAR szAppName[] = TEXT ("EMF7") ;
     HWND         hwnd ;
     MSG          msg ;
     WNDCLASS     wndclass ;

     wndclass.style         = CS_HREDRAW | CS_VREDRAW ;
     wndclass.lpfnWndProc   = WndProc ;
     wndclass.cbClsExtra    = 0 ;
     wndclass.cbWndExtra    = 0 ;
     wndclass.hInstance     = hInstance ;
     wndclass.hIcon         = LoadIcon (NULL, IDI_APPLICATION) ;
     wndclass.hCursor       = LoadCursor (NULL, IDC_ARROW) ;
     wndclass.hbrBackground = GetStockObject (WHITE_BRUSH) ;
     wndclass.lpszMenuName  = NULL ;
     wndclass.lpszClassName = szAppName ;

     if (!RegisterClass (&wndclass))
```

Figure 18-13. *The EMF7 program.*   *(continued)*

Figure 18-13. *continued*

```
        {
            MessageBox (NULL, TEXT ("This program requires Windows NT!"),
                        szAppName, MB_ICONERROR) ;
            return 0 ;
        }

        hwnd = CreateWindow (szAppName, TEXT ("Enhanced Metafile Demo #7"),
                            WS_OVERLAPPEDWINDOW,
                            CW_USEDEFAULT, CW_USEDEFAULT,
                            CW_USEDEFAULT, CW_USEDEFAULT,
                            NULL, NULL, hInstance, NULL) ;

        ShowWindow (hwnd, iCmdShow) ;
        UpdateWindow (hwnd) ;

        while (GetMessage (&msg, NULL, 0, 0))
        {
            TranslateMessage (&msg) ;
            DispatchMessage (&msg) ;
        }
        return msg.wParam ;
}

int CALLBACK EnhMetaFileProc (HDC hdc, HANDLETABLE * pHandleTable,
                              CONST ENHMETARECORD * pEmfRecord,
                              int iHandles, LPARAM pData)
{
    HBRUSH   hBrush ;
    HPEN     hPen ;
    LOGBRUSH lb ;

    if (pEmfRecord->iType != EMR_HEADER && pEmfRecord->iType != EMR_EOF)

        PlayEnhMetaFileRecord (hdc, pHandleTable, pEmfRecord, iHandles) ;

    if (pEmfRecord->iType == EMR_RECTANGLE)
    {
        hBrush = SelectObject (hdc, GetStockObject (NULL_BRUSH)) ;

        lb.lbStyle = BS_SOLID ;
        lb.lbColor = RGB (0, 255, 0) ;
        lb.lbHatch = 0 ;

        hPen = SelectObject (hdc,
            ExtCreatePen (PS_SOLID | PS_GEOMETRIC, 5, &lb, 0, NULL)) ;

        Ellipse (hdc, 100, 100, 200, 200) ;
```

```
            DeleteObject (SelectObject (hdc, hPen)) ;
            SelectObject (hdc, hBrush) ;
      }
      return TRUE ;
}

LRESULT CALLBACK WndProc (HWND hwnd, UINT message, WPARAM wParam, LPARAM lParam)
{
      ENHMETAHEADER emh ;
      HDC           hdc, hdcEMF ;
      HENHMETAFILE  hemfOld, hemf ;
      PAINTSTRUCT   ps ;
      RECT          rect ;

      switch (message)
      {
      case WM_CREATE:

                 // Retrieve existing metafile and header

            hemfOld = GetEnhMetaFile (TEXT ("..\\emf3\\emf3.emf")) ;

            GetEnhMetaFileHeader (hemfOld, sizeof (ENHMETAHEADER), &emh) ;

                 // Create a new metafile DC

            hdcEMF = CreateEnhMetaFile (NULL, TEXT ("emf7.emf"), NULL,
                                   TEXT ("EMF7\0EMF Demo #7\0")) ;

                 // Enumerate the existing metafile

            EnumEnhMetaFile (hdcEMF, hemfOld, EnhMetaFileProc, NULL,
                            (RECT *) & emh.rclBounds) ;

                 // Clean up

            hemf = CloseEnhMetaFile (hdcEMF) ;

            DeleteEnhMetaFile (hemfOld) ;
            DeleteEnhMetaFile (hemf) ;
            return 0 ;

      case WM_PAINT:
            hdc = BeginPaint (hwnd, &ps) ;

            GetClientRect (hwnd, &rect) ;
```

(continued)

Figure 18-13. *continued*

```
        rect.left   =       rect.right  / 4 ;
        rect.right  = 3 * rect.right    / 4 ;
        rect.top    =       rect.bottom / 4 ;
        rect.bottom = 3 * rect.bottom   / 4 ;

        hemf = GetEnhMetaFile (TEXT ("emf7.emf")) ;

        PlayEnhMetaFile (hdc, hemf, &rect) ;
        DeleteEnhMetaFile (hemf) ;
        EndPaint (hwnd, &ps) ;
        return 0 ;

    case WM_DESTROY:
        PostQuitMessage (0) ;
        return 0 ;
    }
    return DefWindowProc (hwnd, message, wParam, lParam) ;
}
```

EMF7 uses the EMF3.EMF metafile created by the EMF3 program, so make sure you run that program to create the metafile before you run EMF7.

Although WM_PAINT processing in EMF7 has reverted to using *PlayEnhMetaFile* rather than *EnumEnhMetaFile*, WM_CREATE processing is quite different.

First, the program obtains a metafile handle for the EMF3.EMF file by calling *GetEnh-MetaFile*. It also gets the enhanced metafile header by calling *GetEnhMetaFileHeader*. The sole purpose of getting the header is to use the *rclBounds* field in the forthcoming *Enum-EnhMetaFile* call.

Next, the program creates a new disk-based metafile to be stored with the name EMF7.EMF. The *CreateEnhMetaFile* function returns a device context handle for the metafile. Then *EnumEnhMetaFile* is called using the metafile device context handle for EMF7.EMF and the metafile handle from EMF3.EMF.

Now let's take a look at *EnhMetaFileProc*. If the record being enumerated is not the header or the end-of-file, the function calls *PlayEnhMetaFileRecord* to transfer the record into the new metafile device context. (It's not strictly necessary to exclude the header or end-of-file record, but they make the metafile somewhat larger.)

If the record just transferred is the *Rectangle* call, the function creates a pen to draw an ellipse with a green outline and a transparent interior. Notice how the code restores the state of the device context by saving the previous pen and brush handles. During this time, all these functions are inserted into the metafile. (Keep in mind that you can also use *PlayEnhMetaFile* to insert an entire metafile in the existing one.)

Back in WM_CREATE processing, the program calls *CloseEnhMetaFile* to obtain a handle to the new metafile. Then it deletes both metafile handles, leaving behind both the EMF3.EMF and EMF7.EMF files on disk.

It's obvious from the program's display output that the ellipse is drawn after the rectangle but before the two crisscrossing lines.

An Enhanced Metafile Viewer and Printer

Using the clipboard for transferring enhanced metafiles is quite simple. The clipboard type is CF_ENHMETAFILE. The *GetClipboardData* function returns a handle to the enhanced metafile; the *SetClipboardData* also uses the metafile handle. Need a copy of the metafile? Use the *CopyEnhMetaFile* function. If you put an enhanced metafile in the clipboard, Windows will make available a metafile in the old format for those programs that need it. If you put an old-format metafile in the clipboard, Windows will make available an enhanced metafile.

The EMFVIEW program shown in Figure 18-14 shows code to transfer metafiles to and from the clipboard, and it also allows loading metafiles, saving metafiles, and printing them.

EMFVIEW.C

```
/*------------------------------------------
   EMFVIEW.C -- View Enhanced Metafiles
                (c) Charles Petzold, 1998
  ------------------------------------------*/

#include <windows.h>
#include <commdlg.h>
#include "resource.h"

LRESULT CALLBACK WndProc (HWND, UINT, WPARAM, LPARAM) ;

TCHAR szAppName[] = TEXT ("EmfView") ;

int WINAPI WinMain (HINSTANCE hInstance, HINSTANCE hPrevInstance,
                    PSTR szCmdLine, int iCmdShow)
{
    HACCEL    hAccel ;
    HWND      hwnd ;
    MSG       msg ;
    WNDCLASS wndclass ;

    wndclass.style         = CS_HREDRAW | CS_VREDRAW ;
    wndclass.lpfnWndProc   = WndProc ;
    wndclass.cbClsExtra    = 0 ;
    wndclass.cbWndExtra    = 0 ;
    wndclass.hInstance     = hInstance ;
```

Figure 18-14. *The EMFVIEW program.*   *(continued)*

Figure 18-14. *continued*

```
     wndclass.hIcon         = LoadIcon (NULL, IDI_APPLICATION) ;
     wndclass.hCursor       = LoadCursor (NULL, IDC_ARROW) ;
     wndclass.hbrBackground = (HBRUSH) GetStockObject (WHITE_BRUSH) ;
     wndclass.lpszMenuName  = szAppName ;
     wndclass.lpszClassName = szAppName ;

     if (!RegisterClass (&wndclass))
     {
          MessageBox (NULL, TEXT ("This program requires Windows NT!"),
                      szAppName, MB_ICONERROR) ;
          return 0 ;
     }

     hwnd = CreateWindow (szAppName, TEXT ("Enhanced Metafile Viewer"),
                          WS_OVERLAPPEDWINDOW,
                          CW_USEDEFAULT, CW_USEDEFAULT,
                          CW_USEDEFAULT, CW_USEDEFAULT,
                          NULL, NULL, hInstance, NULL) ;

     ShowWindow (hwnd, iCmdShow) ;
     UpdateWindow (hwnd) ;

     hAccel = LoadAccelerators (hInstance, szAppName) ;

     while (GetMessage (&msg, NULL, 0, 0))
     {
          if (!TranslateAccelerator (hwnd, hAccel, &msg))
          {
               TranslateMessage (&msg) ;
               DispatchMessage (&msg) ;
          }
     }
     return msg.wParam ;
}

HPALETTE CreatePaletteFromMetaFile (HENHMETAFILE hemf)
{
     HPALETTE      hPalette ;
     int           iNum ;
     LOGPALETTE  * plp ;

     if (!hemf)
          return NULL ;

     if (0 == (iNum = GetEnhMetaFilePaletteEntries (hemf, 0, NULL)))
          return NULL ;
```

```
    plp = malloc (sizeof (LOGPALETTE) + (iNum - 1) * sizeof (PALETTEENTRY)) ;

    plp->palVersion    = 0x0300 ;
    plp->palNumEntries = iNum ;

    GetEnhMetaFilePaletteEntries (hemf, iNum, plp->palPalEntry) ;

    hPalette = CreatePalette (plp) ;

    free (plp) ;

    return hPalette ;
}

LRESULT CALLBACK WndProc (HWND hwnd, UINT message, WPARAM wParam, LPARAM lParam)
{
    static DOCINFO      di = { sizeof (DOCINFO), TEXT ("EmfView: Printing") } ;
    static HENHMETAFILE hemf ;
    static OPENFILENAME ofn ;
    static PRINTDLG     printdlg = { sizeof (PRINTDLG) } ;
    static TCHAR        szFileName [MAX_PATH], szTitleName [MAX_PATH] ;
    static TCHAR        szFilter[] =
                            TEXT ("Enhanced Metafiles (*.EMF)\0*.emf\0")
                            TEXT ("All Files (*.*)\0*.*\0\0") ;
    BOOL                bSuccess ;
    ENHMETAHEADER       header ;
    HDC                 hdc, hdcPrn ;
    HENHMETAFILE        hemfCopy ;
    HMENU               hMenu ;
    HPALETTE            hPalette ;
    int                 i, iLength, iEnable ;
    PAINTSTRUCT         ps ;
    RECT                rect ;
    PTSTR               pBuffer ;

    switch (message)
    {
    case WM_CREATE:
            // Initialize OPENFILENAME structure

        ofn.lStructSize       = sizeof (OPENFILENAME) ;
        ofn.hwndOwner         = hwnd ;
        ofn.hInstance         = NULL ;
        ofn.lpstrFilter       = szFilter ;
        ofn.lpstrCustomFilter = NULL ;
        ofn.nMaxCustFilter    = 0 ;
```

(continued)

Figure 18-14. *continued*

```
        ofn.nFilterIndex      = 0 ;
        ofn.lpstrFile         = szFileName ;
        ofn.nMaxFile          = MAX_PATH ;
        ofn.lpstrFileTitle    = szTitleName ;
        ofn.nMaxFileTitle     = MAX_PATH ;
        ofn.lpstrInitialDir   = NULL ;
        ofn.lpstrTitle        = NULL ;
        ofn.Flags             = 0 ;
        ofn.nFileOffset       = 0 ;
        ofn.nFileExtension    = 0 ;
        ofn.lpstrDefExt       = TEXT ("emf") ;
        ofn.lCustData         = 0 ;
        ofn.lpfnHook          = NULL ;
        ofn.lpTemplateName    = NULL ;
        return 0 ;

case WM_INITMENUPOPUP:
     hMenu = GetMenu (hwnd) ;

     iEnable = hemf ? MF_ENABLED : MF_GRAYED ;

     EnableMenuItem (hMenu, IDM_FILE_SAVE_AS,    iEnable) ;
     EnableMenuItem (hMenu, IDM_FILE_PRINT,      iEnable) ;
     EnableMenuItem (hMenu, IDM_FILE_PROPERTIES, iEnable) ;
     EnableMenuItem (hMenu, IDM_EDIT_CUT,        iEnable) ;
     EnableMenuItem (hMenu, IDM_EDIT_COPY,       iEnable) ;
     EnableMenuItem (hMenu, IDM_EDIT_DELETE,     iEnable) ;

     EnableMenuItem (hMenu, IDM_EDIT_PASTE,
         IsClipboardFormatAvailable (CF_ENHMETAFILE) ?
             MF_ENABLED : MF_GRAYED) ;
     return 0 ;

case WM_COMMAND:
     switch (LOWORD (wParam))
     {
     case IDM_FILE_OPEN:
             // Show the File Open dialog box

         ofn.Flags = 0 ;

         if (!GetOpenFileName (&ofn))
             return 0 ;

             // If there's an existing EMF, get rid of it.
```

```
        if (hemf)
        {
             DeleteEnhMetaFile (hemf) ;
             hemf = NULL ;
        }
             // Load the EMF into memory

        SetCursor (LoadCursor (NULL, IDC_WAIT)) ;
        ShowCursor (TRUE) ;

        hemf = GetEnhMetaFile (szFileName) ;

        ShowCursor (FALSE) ;
        SetCursor (LoadCursor (NULL, IDC_ARROW)) ;

             // Invalidate the client area for later update

        InvalidateRect (hwnd, NULL, TRUE) ;

        if (hemf == NULL)
        {
             MessageBox (hwnd, TEXT ("Cannot load metafile"),
                        szAppName, MB_ICONEXCLAMATION | MB_OK) ;
        }
        return 0 ;

case IDM_FILE_SAVE_AS:
        if (!hemf)
             return 0 ;

             // Show the File Save dialog box

        ofn.Flags = OFN_OVERWRITEPROMPT ;

        if (!GetSaveFileName (&ofn))
             return 0 ;

             // Save the EMF to disk file

        SetCursor (LoadCursor (NULL, IDC_WAIT)) ;
        ShowCursor (TRUE) ;

        hemfCopy = CopyEnhMetaFile (hemf, szFileName) ;

        ShowCursor (FALSE) ;
        SetCursor (LoadCursor (NULL, IDC_ARROW)) ;
```

(continued)

Figure 18-14. *continued*

```
            if (hemfCopy)
            {
                DeleteEnhMetaFile (hemf) ;
                hemf = hemfCopy ;
            }
            else
                MessageBox (hwnd, TEXT ("Cannot save metafile"),
                            szAppName, MB_ICONEXCLAMATION | MB_OK) ;
            return 0 ;

        case IDM_FILE_PRINT:
                // Show the Print dialog box and get printer DC

            printdlg.Flags = PD_RETURNDC | PD_NOPAGENUMS | PD_NOSELECTION ;

            if (!PrintDlg (&printdlg))
                return 0 ;

            if (NULL == (hdcPrn = printdlg.hDC))
            {
                MessageBox (hwnd, TEXT ("Cannot obtain printer DC"),
                            szAppName, MB_ICONEXCLAMATION | MB_OK) ;
                return 0 ;
            }
                // Get size of printable area of page

            rect.left   = 0 ;
            rect.right  = GetDeviceCaps (hdcPrn, HORZRES) ;
            rect.top    = 0 ;
            rect.bottom = GetDeviceCaps (hdcPrn, VERTRES) ;

            bSuccess = FALSE ;

                // Play the EMF to the printer

            SetCursor (LoadCursor (NULL, IDC_WAIT)) ;
            ShowCursor (TRUE) ;

            if ((StartDoc (hdcPrn, &di) > 0) && (StartPage (hdcPrn) > 0))
            {
                PlayEnhMetaFile (hdcPrn, hemf, &rect) ;

                if (EndPage (hdcPrn) > 0)
                {
                    bSuccess = TRUE ;
                    EndDoc (hdcPrn) ;
```

```
            }
        }
        ShowCursor (FALSE) ;
        SetCursor (LoadCursor (NULL, IDC_ARROW)) ;

        DeleteDC (hdcPrn) ;

        if (!bSuccess)
            MessageBox (hwnd, TEXT ("Could not print metafile"),
                        szAppName, MB_ICONEXCLAMATION | MB_OK) ;
        return 0 ;

    case IDM_FILE_PROPERTIES:
        if (!hemf)
            return 0 ;

        iLength = GetEnhMetaFileDescription (hemf, 0, NULL) ;
        pBuffer = malloc ((iLength + 256) * sizeof (TCHAR)) ;

        GetEnhMetaFileHeader (hemf, sizeof (ENHMETAHEADER), &header) ;

            // Format header file information

        i  = wsprintf (pBuffer,
                        TEXT ("Bounds = (%i, %i) to (%i, %i) pixels\n"),
                        header.rclBounds.left, header.rclBounds.top,
                        header.rclBounds.right, header.rclBounds.bottom) ;

        i += wsprintf (pBuffer + i,
                        TEXT ("Frame = (%i, %i) to (%i, %i) mms\n"),
                        header.rclFrame.left, header.rclFrame.top,
                        header.rclFrame.right, header.rclFrame.bottom) ;

        i += wsprintf (pBuffer + i,
                        TEXT ("Resolution = (%i, %i) pixels")
                        TEXT (" = (%i, %i) mms\n"),
                        header.szlDevice.cx, header.szlDevice.cy,
                        header.szlMillimeters.cx,
                        header.szlMillimeters.cy) ;

        i += wsprintf (pBuffer + i,
                        TEXT ("Size = %i, Records = %i, ")
                        TEXT ("Handles = %i, Palette entries = %i\n"),
                        header.nBytes, header.nRecords,
                        header.nHandles, header.nPalEntries) ;
```

(continued)

Figure 18-14. *continued*

```
            // Include the metafile description, if present

        if (iLength)
        {
            i += wsprintf (pBuffer + i, TEXT ("Description = ")) ;
            GetEnhMetaFileDescription (hemf, iLength, pBuffer + i) ;
            pBuffer [lstrlen (pBuffer)] = '\t' ;
        }

        MessageBox (hwnd, pBuffer, TEXT ("Metafile Properties"), MB_OK) ;
        free (pBuffer) ;
        return 0 ;

    case IDM_EDIT_COPY:
    case IDM_EDIT_CUT:
        if (!hemf)
            return 0 ;

            // Transfer metafile copy to the clipboard

        hemfCopy = CopyEnhMetaFile (hemf, NULL) ;

        OpenClipboard (hwnd) ;
        EmptyClipboard () ;
        SetClipboardData (CF_ENHMETAFILE, hemfCopy) ;
        CloseClipboard () ;

        if (LOWORD (wParam) == IDM_EDIT_COPY)
            return 0 ;
                                // fall through if IDM_EDIT_CUT
    case IDM_EDIT_DELETE:
        if (hemf)
        {
            DeleteEnhMetaFile (hemf) ;
            hemf = NULL ;
            InvalidateRect (hwnd, NULL, TRUE) ;
        }
        return 0 ;

    case IDM_EDIT_PASTE:
        OpenClipboard (hwnd) ;
        hemfCopy = GetClipboardData (CF_ENHMETAFILE) ;
```

```
            CloseClipboard () ;
            if (hemfCopy && hemf)
            {
                 DeleteEnhMetaFile (hemf) ;
                 hemf = NULL ;
            }

            hemf = CopyEnhMetaFile (hemfCopy, NULL) ;
            InvalidateRect (hwnd, NULL, TRUE) ;
            return 0 ;

       case IDM_APP_ABOUT:
            MessageBox (hwnd, TEXT ("Enhanced Metafile Viewer\n")
                             TEXT ("(c) Charles Petzold, 1998"),
                        szAppName, MB_OK) ;
            return 0 ;

       case IDM_APP_EXIT:
            SendMessage (hwnd, WM_CLOSE, 0, 0L) ;
            return 0 ;
       }
       break ;

  case WM_PAINT:
       hdc = BeginPaint (hwnd, &ps) ;

       if (hemf)
       {
            if (hPalette = CreatePaletteFromMetaFile (hemf))
            {
                 SelectPalette (hdc, hPalette, FALSE) ;
                 RealizePalette (hdc) ;
            }
            GetClientRect (hwnd, &rect) ;
            PlayEnhMetaFile (hdc, hemf, &rect) ;

            if (hPalette)
                 DeleteObject (hPalette) ;
       }
       EndPaint (hwnd, &ps) ;
       return 0 ;
```

(continued)

Figure 18-14. *continued*

```
    case WM_QUERYNEWPALETTE:
         if (!hemf || !(hPalette = CreatePaletteFromMetaFile (hemf)))
              return FALSE ;

         hdc = GetDC (hwnd) ;
         SelectPalette (hdc, hPalette, FALSE) ;
         RealizePalette (hdc) ;
         InvalidateRect (hwnd, NULL, FALSE) ;

         DeleteObject (hPalette) ;
         ReleaseDC (hwnd, hdc) ;
         return TRUE ;

    case WM_PALETTECHANGED:
         if ((HWND) wParam == hwnd)
              break ;

         if (!hemf || !(hPalette = CreatePaletteFromMetaFile (hemf)))
              break ;

         hdc = GetDC (hwnd) ;
         SelectPalette (hdc, hPalette, FALSE) ;
         RealizePalette (hdc) ;
         UpdateColors (hdc) ;

         DeleteObject (hPalette) ;
         ReleaseDC (hwnd, hdc) ;
         break ;

    case WM_DESTROY:
         if (hemf)
              DeleteEnhMetaFile (hemf) ;

         PostQuitMessage (0) ;
         return 0 ;
    }
    return DefWindowProc (hwnd, message, wParam, lParam) ;
}
```

EMFVIEW.RC (excerpts)

```
//Microsoft Developer Studio generated resource script.

#include "resource.h"
#include "afxres.h"


/////////////////////////////////////////////////////////////////////////////
// Menu

EMFVIEW MENU DISCARDABLE
BEGIN
    POPUP "&File"
    BEGIN
        MENUITEM "&Open\tCtrl+O",              IDM_FILE_OPEN
        MENUITEM "Save &As...",                IDM_FILE_SAVE_AS
        MENUITEM SEPARATOR
        MENUITEM "&Print...\tCtrl+P",          IDM_FILE_PRINT
        MENUITEM SEPARATOR
        MENUITEM "&Properties",                IDM_FILE_PROPERTIES
        MENUITEM SEPARATOR
        MENUITEM "E&xit",                      IDM_APP_EXIT
    END
    POPUP "&Edit"
    BEGIN
        MENUITEM "Cu&t\tCtrl+X",               IDM_EDIT_CUT
        MENUITEM "&Copy\tCtrl+C",              IDM_EDIT_COPY
        MENUITEM "&Paste\tCtrl+V",             IDM_EDIT_PASTE
        MENUITEM "&Delete\tDel",               IDM_EDIT_DELETE
    END
    POPUP "Help"
    BEGIN
        MENUITEM "&About EmfView...",          IDM_APP_ABOUT
    END
END


/////////////////////////////////////////////////////////////////////////////
// Accelerator

EMFVIEW ACCELERATORS DISCARDABLE
BEGIN
    "C",            IDM_EDIT_COPY,       VIRTKEY, CONTROL, NOINVERT
    "O",            IDM_FILE_OPEN,       VIRTKEY, CONTROL, NOINVERT
    "P",            IDM_FILE_PRINT,      VIRTKEY, CONTROL, NOINVERT
    "V",            IDM_EDIT_PASTE,      VIRTKEY, CONTROL, NOINVERT
    VK_DELETE,      IDM_EDIT_DELETE,     VIRTKEY, NOINVERT
    "X",            IDM_EDIT_CUT,        VIRTKEY, CONTROL, NOINVERT
END
```

(continued)

Figure 18-14. *continued*

RESOURCE.H (excerpts)

```
// Microsoft Developer Studio generated include file.
// Used by EmfView.rc

#define IDM_FILE_OPEN            40001
#define IDM_FILE_SAVE_AS         40002
#define IDM_FILE_PRINT           40003
#define IDM_FILE_PROPERTIES      40004
#define IDM_APP_EXIT             40005
#define IDM_EDIT_CUT             40006
#define IDM_EDIT_COPY            40007
#define IDM_EDIT_PASTE           40008
#define IDM_EDIT_DELETE          40009
#define IDM_APP_ABOUT            40010
```

EMFVIEW also has complete palette logic, just in case a palette has been encoded in the metafile. (The way it gets in there is by a call to *SelectPalette*.) The program extracts the palette in its *CreatePaletteFromMetaFile* function, which is called when it displays a metafile during WM_PAINT and also while processing the WM_QUERYNEWPALETTE and WM_PALETTECHANGED messages.

In response to a Print command from the menu, EMFVIEW displays the common printer dialog box and then obtains the dimensions of the printable area of the page. The metafile is stretched to fill that whole area. EMFVIEW displays a metafile in its window similarly.

The Properties item from the File menu causes EMFVIEW to display a message box containing information from the metafile header.

If you print the EMF2.EMF metafile image created earlier in this chapter, you may find that the lines are very thin on high-resolution printers, perhaps nearly invisible. Vector images should really have wider pens (for example, 1-point wide) for printing. The ruler image shown later in this chapter does that.

Displaying Accurate Metafile Images

The great thing about metafile images is that they can be stretched to any size and still maintain reasonable fidelity. This is because a metafile normally consists of a series of vector graphics primitives, such as lines, filled areas, and outline fonts. Enlarging or compressing the image simply involves scaling all the coordinate points that define these primitives. Bitmaps, on the other hand, can lose vital information when compression results in dropping entire rows and columns of pixels.

Of course, metafile compression in real life is not entirely flawless either. We live with graphical output devices that have a finite pixel size. A metafile image consisting of lots of lines could start to look like an indecipherable blob when compressed in size. Also, area-filling patterns and color dithering start to look odd at small sizes. And, if the metafile contains embedded bitmaps or old-fashioned raster fonts, these too can pose familiar problems.

For the most part, though, metafiles are freely scaleable. This is most useful when dropping a metafile into a word processing or desktop publishing document. Generally, when you select a metafile image in such an application, you'll be presented with a bounding rectangle that you can grab with the mouse and scale to any size. The image will also have the same relative size when rendered on a printer.

Sometimes, however, arbitrarily scaling a metafile is not such a hot idea. An example: Suppose you have a banking system that stores facsimiles of account-holders' signatures as a series of polylines stored in a metafile. Widening or heightening this metafile would make the signature look different. At the very least, you should keep the image's aspect ratio constant.

In the sample programs shown previously, we've based the bounding rectangle in the *PlayEnhMetaFile* call on the size of the client area. Thus, as you resize the program's window, you effectively resize the image. This is conceptually similar to resizing a metafile image within a word-processing document.

Accurately displaying a metafile image—either in specific metrical sizes or with a proper aspect ratio—requires using size information in the metafile header and setting the rectangle structure accordingly.

The sample programs in the remainder of this chapter will use a shell program called EMF.C that includes printing logic, a resource script named EMF.RC, and a RESOURCE.H header file. Figure 18-15 shows these files along with EMF8.C, a program that uses these files to display a 6-inch ruler.

EMF8.C

```
/*-----------------------------------------
   EMF8.C -- Enhanced Metafile Demo #8
            (c) Charles Petzold, 1998
   -----------------------------------------*/

#include <windows.h>

TCHAR szClass [] = TEXT ("EMF8") ;
TCHAR szTitle [] = TEXT ("EMF8: Enhanced Metafile Demo #8") ;

void DrawRuler (HDC hdc, int cx, int cy)
{
     int      iAdj, i, iHeight ;
     LOGFONT  lf ;
     TCHAR    ch ;

     iAdj = GetVersion () & 0x80000000 ? 0 : 1 ;
```

Figure 18-15. *The EMF8 program.*

(continued)

Figure 18-15. *continued*

```
        // Black pen with 1-point width

    SelectObject (hdc, CreatePen (PS_SOLID, cx / 72 / 6, 0)) ;

        // Rectangle surrounding entire pen (with adjustment)

    Rectangle (hdc, iAdj, iAdj, cx + iAdj + 1, cy + iAdj + 1) ;

        // Tick marks

    for (i = 1 ; i < 96 ; i++)
    {
            if (i % 16 == 0) iHeight = cy /  2 ;    // inches
        else if (i %  8 == 0) iHeight = cy /  3 ;    // half inches
        else if (i %  4 == 0) iHeight = cy /  5 ;    // quarter inches
        else if (i %  2 == 0) iHeight = cy /  8 ;    // eighths
        else                  iHeight = cy / 12 ;    // sixteenths

        MoveToEx (hdc, i * cx / 96, cy, NULL) ;
        LineTo   (hdc, i * cx / 96, cy - iHeight) ;
    }
        // Create logical font

    FillMemory (&lf, sizeof (lf), 0) ;
    lf.lfHeight = cy / 2 ;
    lstrcpy (lf.lfFaceName, TEXT ("Times New Roman")) ;

    SelectObject (hdc, CreateFontIndirect (&lf)) ;
    SetTextAlign (hdc, TA_BOTTOM | TA_CENTER) ;
    SetBkMode    (hdc, TRANSPARENT) ;

        // Display numbers

    for (i = 1 ; i <= 5 ; i++)
    {
        ch = (TCHAR) (i + '0') ;
        TextOut (hdc, i * cx / 6, cy / 2, &ch, 1) ;
    }
        // Clean up

    DeleteObject (SelectObject (hdc, GetStockObject (SYSTEM_FONT))) ;
    DeleteObject (SelectObject (hdc, GetStockObject (BLACK_PEN))) ;
}

void CreateRoutine (HWND hwnd)
{
    HDC           hdcEMF ;
```

```
     HENHMETAFILE hemf ;
     int          cxMms, cyMms, cxPix, cyPix, xDpi, yDpi ;

     hdcEMF = CreateEnhMetaFile (NULL, TEXT ("emf8.emf"), NULL,
                                 TEXT ("EMF8\0EMF Demo #8\0")) ;
     if (hdcEMF == NULL)
          return ;

     cxMms = GetDeviceCaps (hdcEMF, HORZSIZE) ;
     cyMms = GetDeviceCaps (hdcEMF, VERTSIZE) ;
     cxPix = GetDeviceCaps (hdcEMF, HORZRES) ;
     cyPix = GetDeviceCaps (hdcEMF, VERTRES) ;

     xDpi = cxPix * 254 / cxMms / 10 ;
     yDpi = cyPix * 254 / cyMms / 10 ;

     DrawRuler (hdcEMF, 6 * xDpi, yDpi) ;

     hemf = CloseEnhMetaFile (hdcEMF) ;

     DeleteEnhMetaFile (hemf) ;
}

void PaintRoutine (HWND hwnd, HDC hdc, int cxArea, int cyArea)
{
     ENHMETAHEADER emh ;
     HENHMETAFILE  hemf ;
     int           cxImage, cyImage ;
     RECT          rect ;

     hemf = GetEnhMetaFile (TEXT ("emf8.emf")) ;

     GetEnhMetaFileHeader (hemf, sizeof (emh), &emh) ;

     cxImage = emh.rclBounds.right - emh.rclBounds.left ;
     cyImage = emh.rclBounds.bottom - emh.rclBounds.top ;

     rect.left   = (cxArea - cxImage) / 2 ;
     rect.right  = (cxArea + cxImage) / 2 ;
     rect.top    = (cyArea - cyImage) / 2 ;
     rect.bottom = (cyArea + cyImage) / 2 ;

     PlayEnhMetaFile (hdc, hemf, &rect) ;

     DeleteEnhMetaFile (hemf) ;
}
```

(continued)

Figure 18-15. *continued*

EMF.C

```
/*-----------------------------------------------------------
   EMF.C -- Enhanced Metafile Demonstration Shell Program
            (c) Charles Petzold, 1998
   -----------------------------------------------------------*/

#include <windows.h>
#include <commdlg.h>
#include "..\\emf8\\resource.h"

extern void CreateRoutine (HWND) ;
extern void PaintRoutine  (HWND, HDC, int, int) ;

LRESULT CALLBACK WndProc (HWND, UINT, WPARAM, LPARAM) ;

HANDLE hInst ;

extern TCHAR szClass [] ;
extern TCHAR szTitle [] ;

int WINAPI WinMain (HINSTANCE hInstance, HINSTANCE hPrevInstance,
                    PSTR szCmdLine, int iCmdShow)
{
     TCHAR      szResource [] = TEXT ("EMF") ;
     HWND       hwnd ;
     MSG        msg ;
     WNDCLASS wndclass ;

     hInst = hInstance ;

     wndclass.style         = CS_HREDRAW | CS_VREDRAW ;
     wndclass.lpfnWndProc   = WndProc ;
     wndclass.cbClsExtra    = 0 ;
     wndclass.cbWndExtra    = 0 ;
     wndclass.hInstance     = hInstance ;
     wndclass.hIcon         = LoadIcon (NULL, IDI_APPLICATION) ;
     wndclass.hCursor       = LoadCursor (NULL, IDC_ARROW) ;
     wndclass.hbrBackground = GetStockObject (WHITE_BRUSH) ;
     wndclass.lpszMenuName  = szResource ;
     wndclass.lpszClassName = szClass ;

     if (!RegisterClass (&wndclass))
     {
          MessageBox (NULL, TEXT ("This program requires Windows NT!"),
                      szClass, MB_ICONERROR) ;
          return 0 ;
     }
```

```
      hwnd = CreateWindow (szClass, szTitle,
                           WS_OVERLAPPEDWINDOW,
                           CW_USEDEFAULT, CW_USEDEFAULT,
                           CW_USEDEFAULT, CW_USEDEFAULT,
                           NULL, NULL, hInstance, NULL) ;

      ShowWindow (hwnd, iCmdShow) ;
      UpdateWindow (hwnd) ;

      while (GetMessage (&msg, NULL, 0, 0))
      {
            TranslateMessage (&msg) ;
            DispatchMessage (&msg) ;
      }
      return msg.wParam ;
}

BOOL PrintRoutine (HWND hwnd)
{
      static DOCINFO  di ;
      static PRINTDLG printdlg = { sizeof (PRINTDLG) } ;
      static TCHAR    szMessage [32] ;
      BOOL            bSuccess = FALSE ;
      HDC             hdcPrn ;
      int             cxPage, cyPage ;

      printdlg.Flags = PD_RETURNDC | PD_NOPAGENUMS | PD_NOSELECTION ;

      if (!PrintDlg (&printdlg))
            return TRUE ;

      if (NULL == (hdcPrn = printdlg.hDC))
            return FALSE ;

      cxPage = GetDeviceCaps (hdcPrn, HORZRES) ;
      cyPage = GetDeviceCaps (hdcPrn, VERTRES) ;

      lstrcpy (szMessage, szClass) ;
      lstrcat (szMessage, TEXT (": Printing")) ;

      di.cbSize      = sizeof (DOCINFO) ;
      di.lpszDocName = szMessage ;

      if (StartDoc (hdcPrn, &di) > 0)
      {
            if (StartPage (hdcPrn) > 0)
```

(continued)

Figure 18-15. *continued*

```
        {
            PaintRoutine (hwnd, hdcPrn, cxPage, cyPage) ;

            if (EndPage (hdcPrn) > 0)
            {
                EndDoc (hdcPrn) ;
                bSuccess = TRUE ;
            }
        }
    }
    DeleteDC (hdcPrn) ;

    return bSuccess ;
}

LRESULT CALLBACK WndProc (HWND hwnd, UINT message, WPARAM wParam, LPARAM lParam)
{
    BOOL        bSuccess ;
    static int  cxClient, cyClient ;
    HDC         hdc ;
    PAINTSTRUCT ps ;

    switch (message)
    {
    case WM_CREATE:
        CreateRoutine (hwnd) ;
        return 0 ;

    case WM_COMMAND:
        switch (wParam)
        {
        case IDM_PRINT:
            SetCursor (LoadCursor (NULL, IDC_WAIT)) ;
            ShowCursor (TRUE) ;

            bSuccess = PrintRoutine (hwnd) ;

            ShowCursor (FALSE) ;
            SetCursor (LoadCursor (NULL, IDC_ARROW)) ;

            if (!bSuccess)
                MessageBox (hwnd,
                        TEXT ("Error encountered during printing"),
                        szClass, MB_ICONASTERISK | MB_OK) ;
            return 0 ;

        case IDM_EXIT:
```

```
            SendMessage (hwnd, WM_CLOSE, 0, 0) ;
            return 0 ;

       case IDM_ABOUT:
            MessageBox (hwnd, TEXT ("Enhanced Metafile Demo Program\n")
                             TEXT ("Copyright (c) Charles Petzold, 1998"),
                        szClass, MB_ICONINFORMATION | MB_OK) ;
            return 0 ;
       }
       break ;

   case WM_SIZE:
       cxClient = LOWORD (lParam) ;
       cyClient = HIWORD (lParam) ;
       return 0 ;

   case WM_PAINT:
       hdc = BeginPaint (hwnd, &ps) ;

       PaintRoutine (hwnd, hdc, cxClient, cyClient) ;

       EndPaint (hwnd, &ps) ;
       return 0 ;

   case WM_DESTROY :
       PostQuitMessage (0) ;
       return 0 ;
   }
   return DefWindowProc (hwnd, message, wParam, lParam) ;
}
```

EMF.RC (excerpts)

```
//Microsoft Developer Studio generated resource script.

#include "resource.h"
#include "afxres.h"

/////////////////////////////////////////////////////////////////////////
// Menu

EMF MENU DISCARDABLE
BEGIN
    POPUP "&File"
    BEGIN
        MENUITEM "&Print...",                    IDM_PRINT
```

(continued)

Figure 18-15. *continued*

```
        MENUITEM SEPARATOR
        MENUITEM "E&xit",                    IDM_EXIT
    END
    POPUP "&Help"
    BEGIN
        MENUITEM "&About...",                IDM_ABOUT
    END
END
```

RESOURCE.H (excerpts)

```
// Microsoft Developer Studio generated include file.
// Used by Emf.rc
//
#define IDM_PRINT                      40001
#define IDM_EXIT                       40002
#define IDM_ABOUT                      40003
```

During the WM_CREATE message, EMF.C calls an external function called *Create-Routine*. This function will create a metafile. EMF.C calls a function named *PaintRoutine* in two places: once during the WM_PAINT message and again in the function *PrintRoutine* in response to a menu command to print the image.

Because modern printers often have a much higher resolution than video displays, the ability to print a metafile is an important tool for testing our ability to render an image in a specific size. The EMF8 program creates a metafile image that makes most sense when displayed in a specific size. The image is that of a ruler 6 inches wide by 1 inch high, complete with tick marks every 16th inch and the numbers 1 through 5 in a TrueType font.

To draw a 6-inch ruler, we need to know something about device resolution. The *CreateRoutine* function in EMF8.C begins by creating a metafile and calling *GetDeviceCaps* four times using the device context handle returned from *CreateEnhMetaFile*. These calls obtain the width and height of the display surface in both millimeters and pixels.

This may sound a bit odd. The metafile device context is usually seen as a storage medium for GDI drawing commands. It's not a real device like a video display or a printer, so how can it have a width and height?

Well, as you may recall, the first argument to *CreateEnhMetaFile* is known as the "reference device context." GDI uses this to establish device characteristics for the metafile. If the argument is set to NULL (as in EMF8), GDI uses the video display as the reference device context. Thus, when EMF8 calls *GetDeviceCaps* using the metafile device context, it actually obtains information about the video display.

EMF8.C calculates a resolution in dots per inch by dividing the pixel dimension by the millimeter dimension and multiplying by 25.4, the number of millimeters in an inch.

Even though we've taken great care to draw this metafile ruler in its correct size, the work is not yet done. When it comes time to render the image, the *PlayEnhMetaFile* function will display it stretched to the rectangle passed as its last argument. This rectangle must be set to the size of the ruler.

For this reason, the *PaintRoutine* function in EMF8 calls the *GetEnhMetaFileHeader* function to obtain the header information in the metafile. The *rclBounds* field of the ENHMETAHEADER structure indicates the bounding rectangle of the metafile image in pixels. The program uses this information to center the ruler in the client area, as shown in Figure 18-16.

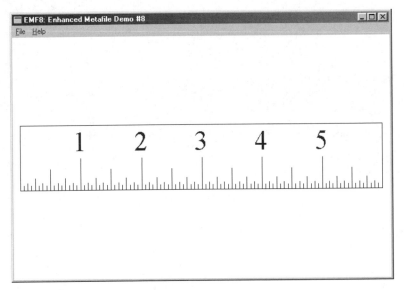

Figure 18-16. *The EMF8 display.*

Keep in mind that if you hold a ruler up to the screen, you probably won't match exactly. The video display only approximates actual metrics, as I discussed in Chapter 5.

This technique appears to have worked, but now try printing the image. Oops! If you have a 300-dpi laser printer, the ruler will be about 1⅓ inches wide. That's because we've used a pixel dimension based on the video display. Although you may think the little printed ruler looks kind of cute, it's not what we want. Let's try again.

The ENHMETAHEADER structure contains two rectangle structures that describe the size of the image. The first, which EMF8 uses, is the *rclBounds* field. This gives the size of the image in pixels. The second is the *rclFrame* field, which gives the size of the image in units of 0.01 millimeters. The relationship between these two fields is governed by the reference device context originally used when creating the metafile, in this case the video display. (The metafile header also contains two fields named *szlDevice* and *szlMillimeters*, which are SIZEL structures that indicate the size of the reference device in pixels and millimeters, the same information available from *GetDeviceCaps*.)

The information about the millimeter dimensions of the image is put to use by EMF9, shown in Figure 18-17 on the following page.

EMF9.C

```
/*-------------------------------------------
   EMF9.C -- Enhanced Metafile Demo #9
             (c) Charles Petzold, 1998
   -------------------------------------------*/

#include <windows.h>
#include <string.h>

TCHAR szClass [] = TEXT ("EMF9") ;
TCHAR szTitle [] = TEXT ("EMF9: Enhanced Metafile Demo #9") ;

void CreateRoutine (HWND hwnd)
{
}

void PaintRoutine (HWND hwnd, HDC hdc, int cxArea, int cyArea)
{
     ENHMETAHEADER emh ;
     HENHMETAFILE  hemf ;
     int           cxMms, cyMms, cxPix, cyPix, cxImage, cyImage ;
     RECT          rect ;

     cxMms = GetDeviceCaps (hdc, HORZSIZE) ;
     cyMms = GetDeviceCaps (hdc, VERTSIZE) ;
     cxPix = GetDeviceCaps (hdc, HORZRES) ;
     cyPix = GetDeviceCaps (hdc, VERTRES) ;

     hemf = GetEnhMetaFile (TEXT ("..\\emf8\\emf8.emf")) ;

     GetEnhMetaFileHeader (hemf, sizeof (emh), &emh) ;

     cxImage = emh.rclFrame.right - emh.rclFrame.left ;
     cyImage = emh.rclFrame.bottom - emh.rclFrame.top ;

     cxImage = cxImage * cxPix / cxMms / 100 ;
     cyImage = cyImage * cyPix / cyMms / 100 ;

     rect.left   = (cxArea - cxImage) / 2 ;
     rect.right  = (cxArea + cxImage) / 2 ;
     rect.top    = (cyArea - cyImage) / 2 ;
     rect.bottom = (cyArea + cyImage) / 2 ;

     PlayEnhMetaFile (hdc, hemf, &rect) ;

     DeleteEnhMetaFile (hemf) ;
}
```

Figure 18-17. *The EMF9 program.*

EMF9 uses the metafile created by EMF8, so be sure to run EMF8 before running this program.

The *PaintRoutine* function in EMF9 begins by calling *GetDeviceCaps* four times using the destination device context. As in the *CreateRoutine* function in EMF8, these calls provide information about the resolution of the device. After getting the metafile handle, it obtains the header structure and uses the *rclFrame* field to calculate the size of the metafile image in units of 0.01 millimeters. That's the first step.

The function then converts this dimension to pixels by multiplying by the pixel dimension of the output device, dividing by the millimeter dimension, and then dividing by 100 to account for the metrical dimension in 0.01 millimeters. The *PaintRoutine* function now has the dimensions of the ruler in pixels—but not specific to the video display. This is a pixel dimension appropriate for the destination device. From there on, it's easy to center the image.

As far as the screen goes, the EMF9 display looks the same as the EMF8 display. But if you print the ruler from EMF9, you'll see something that looks much more normal—a ruler 6 inches wide by 1 inch high.

Scaling and Aspect Ratios

There may be times when you want to use the ruler metafile created by EMF8 but without necessarily displaying the 6-inch image. Still, it might be nice to maintain the correct 6-to-1 aspect ratio of the image. As I mentioned before, using a bounding box to size a metafile in a word-processing program (or whatever) may be convenient, but it could result in certain undesirable distortions. In such applications, users should be given an option to keep the original aspect ratio regardless of how the bounding box is sized. That is, the bounding box selected by the user would not be used directly to define the rectangle structure passed to the *PlayEnhMetaFile*. The rectangle structure passed to that function would be only part of the bounding box.

Let's examine how to do this in the EMF10 program shown in Figure 18-18.

EMF10.C

```
/*-------------------------------------------
   EMF10.C -- Enhanced Metafile Demo #10
             (c) Charles Petzold, 1998
  -------------------------------------------*/

#include <windows.h>

TCHAR szClass [] = TEXT ("EMF10") ;
TCHAR szTitle [] = TEXT ("EMF10: Enhanced Metafile Demo #10") ;
```

Figure 18-18. *The EMF10 program.*

(continued)

Figure 18-18. *continued*

```
void CreateRoutine (HWND hwnd)
{
}

void PaintRoutine (HWND hwnd, HDC hdc, int cxArea, int cyArea)
{
    ENHMETAHEADER emh ;
    float         fScale ;
    HENHMETAFILE  hemf ;
    int           cxMms, cyMms, cxPix, cyPix, cxImage, cyImage ;
    RECT          rect ;

    cxMms = GetDeviceCaps (hdc, HORZSIZE) ;
    cyMms = GetDeviceCaps (hdc, VERTSIZE) ;
    cxPix = GetDeviceCaps (hdc, HORZRES) ;
    cyPix = GetDeviceCaps (hdc, VERTRES) ;

    hemf = GetEnhMetaFile (TEXT ("..\\emf8\\emf8.emf")) ;

    GetEnhMetaFileHeader (hemf, sizeof (emh), &emh) ;

    cxImage = emh.rclFrame.right - emh.rclFrame.left ;
    cyImage = emh.rclFrame.bottom - emh.rclFrame.top ;

    cxImage = cxImage * cxPix / cxMms / 100 ;
    cyImage = cyImage * cyPix / cyMms / 100 ;

    fScale = min ((float) cxArea / cxImage, (float) cyArea / cyImage) ;

    cxImage = (int) (fScale * cxImage) ;
    cyImage = (int) (fScale * cyImage) ;

    rect.left   = (cxArea - cxImage) / 2 ;
    rect.right  = (cxArea + cxImage) / 2 ;
    rect.top    = (cyArea - cyImage) / 2 ;
    rect.bottom = (cyArea + cyImage) / 2 ;

    PlayEnhMetaFile (hdc, hemf, &rect) ;

    DeleteEnhMetaFile (hemf) ;
}
```

EMF10 stretches the ruler image to fit the client area (or the printable area of the printer page) but without otherwise distorting it. Usually you'll see the ruler stretching the full width of the client area but centered between the top and bottom. If you make the window somewhat stout, the ruler will be as tall as the client area but centered horizontally.

There are probably numerous ways of calculating the proper display rectangle, but I decided to build upon the code in EMF9. The *PaintRoutine* function in EMF10.C begins like EMF9.C, by calculating the pixel size of the 6-inch-wide image appropriate for the destination device context.

The program then calculates a floating point value, named *fScale*, that is the minimum of the ratio of the width of the client area to the width of the image, and the ratio of the height of the client area to the height of the image. This factor is then used to increase the pixel dimensions of the image before the bounding rectangle is calculated.

Mapping Modes in Metafiles

We've been drawing a ruler that displays inches, and we've also been dealing with dimensions in units of millimeters. Such jobs might seem like good candidates for using the various mapping modes provided under GDI. Yet I've insisted on using pixels and doing all the necessary calculations "manually." Why is that?

The simple answer is that the use of mapping modes in connection with metafiles can be quite confusing. But let's try it out to see.

When you call *SetMapMode* using a metafile device context, the function is encoded in the metafile just like any other GDI function. This is demonstrated in the EMF11 program shown in Figure 18-19.

EMF11.C

```
/*------------------------------------------
   EMF11.C -- Enhanced Metafile Demo #11
              (c) Charles Petzold, 1998
   ------------------------------------------*/

#include <windows.h>

TCHAR szClass [] = TEXT ("EMF11") ;
TCHAR szTitle [] = TEXT ("EMF11: Enhanced Metafile Demo #11") ;

void DrawRuler (HDC hdc, int cx, int cy)
{
     int      i, iHeight ;
     LOGFONT  lf ;
     TCHAR    ch ;

          // Black pen with 1-point width

     SelectObject (hdc, CreatePen (PS_SOLID, cx / 72 / 6, 0)) ;
```

Figure 18-19. *The EMF11 program.*

(continued)

Figure 18-19. *continued*

```
          // Rectangle surrounding entire pen (with adjustment)

     if (GetVersion () & 0x80000000)                    // Windows 98
          Rectangle (hdc, 0, -2, cx + 2, cy) ;
     else                                               // Windows NT
          Rectangle (hdc, 0, -1, cx + 1, cy) ;

          // Tick marks

     for (i = 1 ; i < 96 ; i++)
     {
               if (i % 16 == 0) iHeight = cy /  2 ;    // inches
          else if (i %  8 == 0) iHeight = cy /  3 ;    // half inches
          else if (i %  4 == 0) iHeight = cy /  5 ;    // quarter inches
          else if (i %  2 == 0) iHeight = cy /  8 ;    // eighths
          else                  iHeight = cy / 12 ;    // sixteenths

          MoveToEx (hdc, i * cx / 96, 0, NULL) ;
          LineTo   (hdc, i * cx / 96, iHeight) ;
     }
          // Create logical font

     FillMemory (&lf, sizeof (lf), 0) ;
     lf.lfHeight = cy / 2 ;
     lstrcpy (lf.lfFaceName, TEXT ("Times New Roman")) ;

     SelectObject (hdc, CreateFontIndirect (&lf)) ;
     SetTextAlign (hdc, TA_BOTTOM | TA_CENTER) ;
     SetBkMode    (hdc, TRANSPARENT) ;

          // Display numbers

     for (i = 1 ; i <= 5 ; i++)
     {
          ch = (TCHAR) (i + '0') ;
          TextOut (hdc, i * cx / 6, cy / 2, &ch, 1) ;
     }
          // Clean up

     DeleteObject (SelectObject (hdc, GetStockObject (SYSTEM_FONT))) ;
     DeleteObject (SelectObject (hdc, GetStockObject (BLACK_PEN))) ;
}

void CreateRoutine (HWND hwnd)
```

```
{
     HDC          hdcEMF ;
     HENHMETAFILE hemf ;

     hdcEMF = CreateEnhMetaFile (NULL, TEXT ("emf11.emf"), NULL,
                                  TEXT ("EMF11\0EMF Demo #11\0")) ;

     SetMapMode (hdcEMF, MM_LOENGLISH) ;

     DrawRuler (hdcEMF, 600, 100) ;

     hemf = CloseEnhMetaFile (hdcEMF) ;

     DeleteEnhMetaFile (hemf) ;
}

void PaintRoutine (HWND hwnd, HDC hdc, int cxArea, int cyArea)
{
     ENHMETAHEADER emh ;
     HENHMETAFILE  hemf ;
     int           cxMms, cyMms, cxPix, cyPix, cxImage, cyImage ;
     RECT          rect ;

     cxMms = GetDeviceCaps (hdc, HORZSIZE) ;
     cyMms = GetDeviceCaps (hdc, VERTSIZE) ;
     cxPix = GetDeviceCaps (hdc, HORZRES) ;
     cyPix = GetDeviceCaps (hdc, VERTRES) ;

     hemf = GetEnhMetaFile (TEXT ("emf11.emf")) ;

     GetEnhMetaFileHeader (hemf, sizeof (emh), &emh) ;

     cxImage = emh.rclFrame.right - emh.rclFrame.left ;
     cyImage = emh.rclFrame.bottom - emh.rclFrame.top ;

     cxImage = cxImage * cxPix / cxMms / 100 ;
     cyImage = cyImage * cyPix / cyMms / 100 ;

     rect.left   = (cxArea - cxImage) / 2 ;
     rect.top    = (cyArea - cyImage) / 2 ;
     rect.right  = (cxArea + cxImage) / 2 ;
     rect.bottom = (cyArea + cyImage) / 2 ;

     PlayEnhMetaFile (hdc, hemf, &rect) ;

     DeleteEnhMetaFile (hemf) ;
}
```

The *CreateRoutine* function in EMF11 is simpler than the one in EMF8 (our original ruler-metafile program) because it does not need to call *GetDeviceCaps* to determine the resolution of the video display in dots per inch. Instead, EMF11 calls *SetMapMode* to set the mapping mode to MM_LOENGLISH, where logical units are equal to 0.01 inches. Thus, the dimensions of the ruler are 600 units by 100 units, and these numbers are passed to *DrawRuler*.

The *DrawRuler* function in EMF11 is the same as the one in EMF9, except for the *MoveToEx* and *LineTo* calls that draw the tick marks of the ruler. When drawing in units of pixels (the default MM_TEXT mapping mode), units on the vertical axis increase going down the screen. For the MM_LOENGLISH mapping mode (and the other metrical mapping modes), they increase going up. That required a change to this code. The adjustment factors in the *Rectangle* function were also changed.

The *PaintRoutine* function in EMF11 is basically the same as the one in EMF9, which was the version of the program that successfully displayed the ruler in its correct dimensions on both the video display and the printer. The only difference is that EMF11 uses the EMF11.EMF file, whereas EMF9 used the EMF8.EMF file created by EMF8.

The image displayed by EMF11 is basically the same as EMF9. So, we see here how embedding a *SetMapMode* call into a metafile can simplify the metafile creation and doesn't affect at all the mechanics of playing the metafile in its correct size.

Mapping and Playing

Calculating the destination rectangle in EMF11 involves some calls to *GetDeviceCaps*. Our second goal is to eliminate those and use a mapping mode instead. GDI treats the coordinates of the destination rectangle as logical coordinates. Using the MM_HIMETRIC mode seems like a good candidate for these coordinates, because that makes logical units 0.01 millimeters, the same units used for the bounding rectangle in the enhanced metafile header.

The EMF12 program shown in Figure 18-20 restores the *DrawRuler* logic as originally presented in EMF8 but uses the MM_HIMETRIC mapping mode to display the metafile.

EMF12.C

```
/*-------------------------------------------
   EMF12.C -- Enhanced Metafile Demo #12
              (c) Charles Petzold, 1998
   -------------------------------------------*/

#include <windows.h>

TCHAR szClass [] = TEXT ("EMF12") ;
TCHAR szTitle [] = TEXT ("EMF12: Enhanced Metafile Demo #12") ;
```

Figure 18-20. *The EMF12 program.*

```
void DrawRuler (HDC hdc, int cx, int cy)
{
     int      iAdj, i, iHeight ;
     LOGFONT lf ;
     TCHAR    ch ;

     iAdj = GetVersion () & 0x80000000 ? 0 : 1 ;

          // Black pen with 1-point width

     SelectObject (hdc, CreatePen (PS_SOLID, cx / 72 / 6, 0)) ;

          // Rectangle surrounding entire pen (with adjustment)

     Rectangle (hdc, iAdj, iAdj, cx + iAdj + 1, cy + iAdj + 1) ;

          // Tick marks

     for (i = 1 ; i < 96 ; i++)
     {
               if (i % 16 == 0) iHeight = cy /  2 ;    // inches
          else if (i %  8 == 0) iHeight = cy /  3 ;    // half inches
          else if (i %  4 == 0) iHeight = cy /  5 ;    // quarter inches
          else if (i %  2 == 0) iHeight = cy /  8 ;    // eighths
          else                  iHeight = cy / 12 ;    // sixteenths

          MoveToEx (hdc, i * cx / 96, cy, NULL) ;
          LineTo   (hdc, i * cx / 96, cy - iHeight) ;
     }
          // Create logical font

     FillMemory (&lf, sizeof (lf), 0) ;
     lf.lfHeight = cy / 2 ;
     lstrcpy (lf.lfFaceName, TEXT ("Times New Roman")) ;

     SelectObject (hdc, CreateFontIndirect (&lf)) ;
     SetTextAlign (hdc, TA_BOTTOM | TA_CENTER) ;
     SetBkMode    (hdc, TRANSPARENT) ;

          // Display numbers

     for (i = 1 ; i <= 5 ; i++)
     {
          ch = (TCHAR) (i + '0') ;
          TextOut (hdc, i * cx / 6, cy / 2, &ch, 1) ;
     }
```

(continued)

Figure 18-20. *continued*

```
          // Clean up

    DeleteObject (SelectObject (hdc, GetStockObject (SYSTEM_FONT))) ;
    DeleteObject (SelectObject (hdc, GetStockObject (BLACK_PEN))) ;
}

void CreateRoutine (HWND hwnd)
{
    HDC           hdcEMF ;
    HENHMETAFILE hemf ;
    int           cxMms, cyMms, cxPix, cyPix, xDpi, yDpi ;

    hdcEMF = CreateEnhMetaFile (NULL, TEXT ("emf12.emf"), NULL,
                                TEXT ("EMF13\0EMF Demo #12\0")) ;

    cxMms = GetDeviceCaps (hdcEMF, HORZSIZE) ;
    cyMms = GetDeviceCaps (hdcEMF, VERTSIZE) ;
    cxPix = GetDeviceCaps (hdcEMF, HORZRES) ;
    cyPix = GetDeviceCaps (hdcEMF, VERTRES) ;

    xDpi = cxPix * 254 / cxMms / 10 ;
    yDpi = cyPix * 254 / cyMms / 10 ;

    DrawRuler (hdcEMF, 6 * xDpi, yDpi) ;

    hemf = CloseEnhMetaFile (hdcEMF) ;

    DeleteEnhMetaFile (hemf) ;
}

void PaintRoutine (HWND hwnd, HDC hdc, int cxArea, int cyArea)
{
    ENHMETAHEADER emh ;
    HENHMETAFILE  hemf ;
    POINT         pt ;
    int           cxImage, cyImage ;
    RECT          rect ;

    SetMapMode (hdc, MM_HIMETRIC) ;

    SetViewportOrgEx (hdc, 0, cyArea, NULL) ;

    pt.x = cxArea ;
    pt.y = 0 ;

    DPtoLP (hdc, &pt, 1) ;

    hemf = GetEnhMetaFile (TEXT ("emf12.emf")) ;
```

```
     GetEnhMetaFileHeader (hemf, sizeof (emh), &emh) ;

     cxImage = emh.rclFrame.right - emh.rclFrame.left ;
     cyImage = emh.rclFrame.bottom - emh.rclFrame.top ;

     rect.left   = (pt.x - cxImage) / 2 ;
     rect.top    = (pt.y + cyImage) / 2 ;
     rect.right  = (pt.x + cxImage) / 2 ;
     rect.bottom = (pt.y - cyImage) / 2 ;

     PlayEnhMetaFile (hdc, hemf, &rect) ;

     DeleteEnhMetaFile (hemf) ;
}
```

The *PaintRoutine* function in EMF12 first sets the mapping mode to MM_HIMETRIC. As with the other metric modes, values of *y* increase going up the screen. However, the origin is still at the upper left corner, which means that *y*-coordinates within the client area are negative. To correct this oddity, the program calls *SetViewportOrgEx* to set the origin to the lower left corner.

The device point (*cxArea*, 0) is at the upper right corner of the screen. Passing that point to the *DPtoLP* ("device point to logical point") function gives us the size of the client area in 0.01 millimeters.

The program then loads the metafile, gets the header, and finds the dimensions of the metafile in 0.01 millimeters. The destination rectangle centered in the middle of the client area is then easy to calculate.

Now we've seen how we can use a mapping mode when creating the metafile and also for displaying it. Can we do both?

It turns out that it works, as EMF13 (shown in Figure 18-21) demonstrates.

EMF13.C

```
/*------------------------------------------
   EMF13.C -- Enhanced Metafile Demo #13
              (c) Charles Petzold, 1998
   ------------------------------------------*/

#include <windows.h>

TCHAR szClass [] = TEXT ("EMF13") ;
TCHAR szTitle [] = TEXT ("EMF13: Enhanced Metafile Demo #13") ;

void CreateRoutine (HWND hwnd)
```

Figure 18-21. *The EMF13 program.*   *(continued)*

Figure 18-21. *continued*

```
{
}

void PaintRoutine (HWND hwnd, HDC hdc, int cxArea, int cyArea)
{
     ENHMETAHEADER emh ;
     HENHMETAFILE  hemf ;
     POINT         pt ;
     int           cxImage, cyImage ;
     RECT          rect ;

     SetMapMode (hdc, MM_HIMETRIC) ;

     SetViewportOrgEx (hdc, 0, cyArea, NULL) ;

     pt.x = cxArea ;
     pt.y = 0 ;

     DPtoLP (hdc, &pt, 1) ;

     hemf = GetEnhMetaFile (TEXT ("..\\emf11\\emf11.emf")) ;

     GetEnhMetaFileHeader (hemf, sizeof (emh), &emh) ;

     cxImage = emh.rclFrame.right - emh.rclFrame.left ;
     cyImage = emh.rclFrame.bottom - emh.rclFrame.top ;

     rect.left   = (pt.x - cxImage) / 2 ;
     rect.top    = (pt.y + cyImage) / 2 ;
     rect.right  = (pt.x + cxImage) / 2 ;
     rect.bottom = (pt.y - cyImage) / 2 ;

     PlayEnhMetaFile (hdc, hemf, &rect) ;

     DeleteEnhMetaFile (hemf) ;
}
```

In the EMF13 program, it's not necessary to create the ruler metafile by using a mapping mode because it's already been created by EMF11. EMF13 simply loads that one and uses a mapping mode to calculate the destination rectangle, just as EMF11 does.

Now we can establish a couple principles. When the metafile is created, GDI uses any embedded changes to the mapping mode to calculate the size of the metafile image in pixels and millimeters. The size of the image is stored in the metafile header. When the metafile is played, GDI establishes the physical location of the destination rectangle based on the mapping mode in effect at the time of the *PlayEnhMetaFile* call. Nothing in the metafile can change that location.

Section III

ADVANCED TOPICS

Chapter 19

The Multiple-Document Interface

The Multiple-Document Interface (MDI) is a specification for applications that handle documents in Microsoft Windows. The specification describes a window structure and user interface that allow the user to work with multiple documents within a single application (such as text documents in a word-processing program or spreadsheets in a spreadsheet program). Simply put, just as Windows maintains multiple application windows within a single screen, an MDI application maintains multiple document windows within a single client area. The first MDI application for Windows was the first Windows version of Microsoft Excel. But many others soon followed.

MDI CONCEPTS

Although the MDI specification has been around since Windows 2.0, at that time MDI applications were difficult to write and required some very intricate programming work. Since Windows 3.0, however, much of that work has already been done for you. That support, with some enhancements from Windows 95, has been carried over into Windows 98 and Microsoft Windows NT.

The Elements of MDI

The main application window of an MDI program is conventional: it has a title bar, a menu, a sizing border, a system menu icon, and minimize/maximize/close buttons. The client area, however, is often called a "workspace" and is not directly used to display program output. This workspace contains zero or more child windows, each of which displays a document.

These child windows look much like normal application windows and much like the main application window of an MDI program. They too have a title bar, a sizing border, a system menu icon, minimize/maximize/close buttons, and possibly scroll bars. None of the document windows has a menu, however. The menu on the main application window applies to the document windows.

At any one time, only one document window is active (indicated by a highlighted title bar), and it appears in front of all the other document windows. All the document child windows are clipped to the workspace area and never appear outside the application window.

At first, MDI seems a fairly straightforward job for the Windows programmer. All you need to do is create a WS_CHILD window for each document, making the program's main application window the parent of the document window. But with a little exploration of existing MDI applications, you'll find some complications that require difficult code.

■ An MDI document window can be minimized. A short title bar with an icon appears at the bottom of the workspace. Generally, an MDI application will use different icons for the main application window and each type of document window.

■ An MDI document window can be maximized. In this case, the title bar of the document window (normally used to show the filename of the document in the window) disappears and the filename appears appended to the application name in the application window's title bar. The system menu icon of the document window becomes the first item in the top-level menu of the application window. The button to close the document window becomes the last item in the top-level menu and appears to the far right.

■ The system keyboard accelerator to close a document window is the same as that to close the main window, except that the Ctrl key is used rather than Alt. That is, Alt-F4 closes the application window, while Ctrl-F4 closes the document window. In addition, Ctrl-F6 switches among the child document windows within the active MDI application. Alt-Spacebar invokes the system menu of the main window, as usual. Alt-− (minus) invokes the system menu of the active child document window.

■ When using the cursor keys to move among items on the menu, control normally passes from the system menu to the first item on the menu bar. In an MDI application, control passes from the application system menu to the active document system menu to the first item on the menu bar.

■ If the application is capable of supporting several types of child windows (for example, the worksheet and chart documents in Microsoft Excel), the menu should reflect the operations associated with that type of document. This requires that the program change the menu when a different document window becomes active. In addition, when no document window exists, the menu should be stripped down to only those operations involved in opening or creating a new document.

■ The top-level menu bar has an item called Window. By convention, this is the last item on the top-level menu bar except for Help. The Window submenu generally has options to arrange the document windows within the workspace. Document windows can be "cascaded" from the upper left or "tiled" so that each document window is fully visible. This submenu also has a list of all the document windows. Selecting one moves that document window to the foreground.

All of these aspects of MDI are supported in Windows 98. Some overhead is required of course (as will be shown in a sample program), but it isn't anywhere close to the amount of code you'd have to write to support all these features directly.

MDI Support

Some new terminology is necessary when approaching the Windows MDI support. The main application window is called the "frame window." Just as in a conventional Windows program, this is a window of the WS_OVERLAPPEDWINDOW style.

An MDI application also creates a "client window" based on the predefined window class MDICLIENT. The client window is created by a call to *CreateWindow* using this window class and the WS_CHILD style. The last argument to *CreateWindow* is a pointer to a small structure of type CLIENTCREATESTRUCT. This client window covers the client area of the frame window and is responsible for much of the MDI support. The color of this client window is the system color COLOR_APPWORKSPACE.

The document windows, as you've probably noticed, are called "child windows." You create these windows by initializing a structure of type MDICREATESTRUCT and sending the client window a WM_MDICREATE message with a pointer to this structure.

The document windows are children of the client window, which in turn is a child of the frame window. The parent-child hierarchy is shown in Figure 19-1 on the following page.

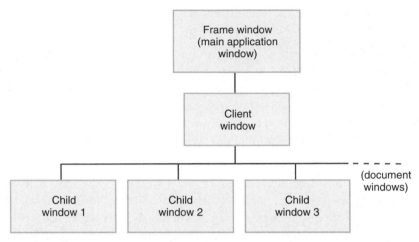

Figure 19-1. *The parent-child hierarchy of a Windows MDI application.*

You need a window class (and window procedure) for the frame window and for each type of child window supported by the application. You don't need a window procedure for the client window because the window class is preregistered.

The MDI support of Windows 98 includes one window class, five functions, two data structures, and twelve messages. I've already mentioned the new window class, which is MDICLIENT, and the new data structures, CLIENTCREATESTRUCT and MDICREATESTRUCT. Two of the five functions replace *DefWindowProc* in MDI applications: rather than call *DefWindowProc* for all unprocessed messages, a frame window procedure calls *DefFrameProc* and a child window procedure calls *DefMDIChildProc*. Another function specific to MDI, *TranslateMDISysAccel*, is used in the same way as *TranslateAccelerator*, which I discussed in Chapter 10. The MDI support also includes *ArrangeIconicWindows*, but one of the special MDI messages makes this function unnecessary for MDI programs.

The fifth MDI function is called *CreateMDIWindow*. This allows the child window to be created in a separate thread of execution. This function is not required in a single-threaded program, which is what I'll be demonstrating.

In the sample program coming up, I'll demonstrate nine of the twelve MDI messages. (The other three are not normally required.) These messages begin with the prefix WM_MDI. A frame window sends these messages to the client window to perform operations on a child window or to obtain information about a child window. (For example, a frame window sends a WM_MDICREATE message to a client window to create a child window.) The WM_MDIACTIVATE message is an exception: while a frame window can send this message to the client window to activate one of the child windows, the client window also sends the message to the child windows being activated and deactivated to inform them of this change.

A SAMPLE MDI IMPLEMENTATION

The MDIDEMO program, shown in Figure 19-2, demonstrates the basics of writing an MDI application.

MDIDEMO.C

```
/*-----------------------------------------------------------
   MDIDEMO.C -- Multiple-Document Interface Demonstration
                (c) Charles Petzold, 1998
   -----------------------------------------------------------*/

#include <windows.h>
#include "resource.h"

#define INIT_MENU_POS    0
#define HELLO_MENU_POS   2
#define RECT_MENU_POS    1

#define IDM_FIRSTCHILD   50000

LRESULT CALLBACK FrameWndProc  (HWND, UINT, WPARAM, LPARAM) ;
BOOL    CALLBACK CloseEnumProc (HWND, LPARAM) ;
LRESULT CALLBACK HelloWndProc  (HWND, UINT, WPARAM, LPARAM) ;
LRESULT CALLBACK RectWndProc   (HWND, UINT, WPARAM, LPARAM) ;

     // structure for storing data unique to each Hello child window

typedef struct tagHELLODATA
{
     UINT      iColor ;
     COLORREF  clrText ;
}
HELLODATA, * PHELLODATA ;

     // structure for storing data unique to each Rect child window

typedef struct tagRECTDATA
{
     short cxClient ;
     short cyClient ;
}
RECTDATA, * PRECTDATA ;
```

Figure 19-2. *The MDIDEMO program.*

(continued)

Figure 19-2. *continued*

```
      // global variables

TCHAR     szAppName[]    = TEXT ("MDIDemo") ;
TCHAR     szFrameClass[] = TEXT ("MdiFrame") ;
TCHAR     szHelloClass[] = TEXT ("MdiHelloChild") ;
TCHAR     szRectClass[]  = TEXT ("MdiRectChild") ;
HINSTANCE hInst ;
HMENU     hMenuInit, hMenuHello, hMenuRect ;
HMENU     hMenuInitWindow, hMenuHelloWindow, hMenuRectWindow ;

int WINAPI WinMain (HINSTANCE hInstance, HINSTANCE hPrevInstance,
                    PSTR szCmdLine, int iCmdShow)
{
    HACCEL    hAccel ;
    HWND      hwndFrame, hwndClient ;
    MSG       msg ;
    WNDCLASS  wndclass ;

    hInst = hInstance ;

        // Register the frame window class

    wndclass.style         = CS_HREDRAW | CS_VREDRAW ;
    wndclass.lpfnWndProc   = FrameWndProc ;
    wndclass.cbClsExtra    = 0 ;
    wndclass.cbWndExtra    = 0 ;
    wndclass.hInstance     = hInstance ;
    wndclass.hIcon         = LoadIcon (NULL, IDI_APPLICATION) ;
    wndclass.hCursor       = LoadCursor (NULL, IDC_ARROW) ;
    wndclass.hbrBackground = (HBRUSH) (COLOR_APPWORKSPACE + 1) ;
    wndclass.lpszMenuName  = NULL ;
    wndclass.lpszClassName = szFrameClass ;

    if (!RegisterClass (&wndclass))
    {
        MessageBox (NULL, TEXT ("This program requires Windows NT!"),
                    szAppName, MB_ICONERROR) ;
        return 0 ;
    }

        // Register the Hello child window class

    wndclass.style         = CS_HREDRAW | CS_VREDRAW ;
    wndclass.lpfnWndProc   = HelloWndProc ;
    wndclass.cbClsExtra    = 0 ;
    wndclass.cbWndExtra    = sizeof (HANDLE) ;
    wndclass.hInstance     = hInstance ;
```

```
wndclass.hIcon         = LoadIcon (NULL, IDI_APPLICATION) ;
wndclass.hCursor       = LoadCursor (NULL, IDC_ARROW) ;
wndclass.hbrBackground = (HBRUSH) GetStockObject (WHITE_BRUSH) ;
wndclass.lpszMenuName  = NULL ;
wndclass.lpszClassName = szHelloClass ;

RegisterClass (&wndclass) ;

     // Register the Rect child window class

wndclass.style         = CS_HREDRAW | CS_VREDRAW ;
wndclass.lpfnWndProc   = RectWndProc ;
wndclass.cbClsExtra    = 0 ;
wndclass.cbWndExtra    = sizeof (HANDLE) ;
wndclass.hInstance     = hInstance ;
wndclass.hIcon         = LoadIcon (NULL, IDI_APPLICATION) ;
wndclass.hCursor       = LoadCursor (NULL, IDC_ARROW) ;
wndclass.hbrBackground = (HBRUSH) GetStockObject (WHITE_BRUSH) ;
wndclass.lpszMenuName  = NULL ;
wndclass.lpszClassName = szRectClass ;

RegisterClass (&wndclass) ;

     // Obtain handles to three possible menus & submenus

hMenuInit  = LoadMenu (hInstance, TEXT ("MdiMenuInit")) ;
hMenuHello = LoadMenu (hInstance, TEXT ("MdiMenuHello")) ;
hMenuRect  = LoadMenu (hInstance, TEXT ("MdiMenuRect")) ;

hMenuInitWindow  = GetSubMenu (hMenuInit,  INIT_MENU_POS) ;
hMenuHelloWindow = GetSubMenu (hMenuHello, HELLO_MENU_POS) ;
hMenuRectWindow  = GetSubMenu (hMenuRect,  RECT_MENU_POS) ;

     // Load accelerator table

hAccel = LoadAccelerators (hInstance, szAppName) ;

     // Create the frame window

hwndFrame = CreateWindow (szFrameClass, TEXT ("MDI Demonstration"),
                          WS_OVERLAPPEDWINDOW | WS_CLIPCHILDREN,
                          CW_USEDEFAULT, CW_USEDEFAULT,
                          CW_USEDEFAULT, CW_USEDEFAULT,
                          NULL, hMenuInit, hInstance, NULL) ;
```

(continued)

Figure 19-2. *continued*

```
        hwndClient = GetWindow (hwndFrame, GW_CHILD) ;

        ShowWindow (hwndFrame, iCmdShow) ;
        UpdateWindow (hwndFrame) ;

            // Enter the modified message loop

        while (GetMessage (&msg, NULL, 0, 0))
        {
            if (!TranslateMDISysAccel (hwndClient, &msg) &&
                !TranslateAccelerator (hwndFrame, hAccel, &msg))
            {
                TranslateMessage (&msg) ;
                DispatchMessage (&msg) ;
            }
        }
            // Clean up by deleting unattached menus

        DestroyMenu (hMenuHello) ;
        DestroyMenu (hMenuRect) ;

        return msg.wParam ;
        }

LRESULT CALLBACK FrameWndProc (HWND hwnd, UINT message,
                               WPARAM wParam, LPARAM lParam)
{
    static HWND         hwndClient ;
    CLIENTCREATESTRUCT  clientcreate ;
    HWND                hwndChild ;
    MDICREATESTRUCT     mdicreate ;

    switch (message)
    {
    case WM_CREATE:              // Create the client window

        clientcreate.hWindowMenu  = hMenuInitWindow ;
        clientcreate.idFirstChild = IDM_FIRSTCHILD ;

        hwndClient = CreateWindow (TEXT ("MDICLIENT"), NULL,
                          WS_CHILD | WS_CLIPCHILDREN | WS_VISIBLE,
                          0, 0, 0, 0, hwnd, (HMENU) 1, hInst,
                          (PSTR) &clientcreate) ;
        return 0 ;
```

```
case WM_COMMAND:
     switch (LOWORD (wParam))
     {
     case IDM_FILE_NEWHELLO:        // Create a Hello child window

          mdicreate.szClass = szHelloClass ;
          mdicreate.szTitle = TEXT ("Hello") ;
          mdicreate.hOwner  = hInst ;
          mdicreate.x       = CW_USEDEFAULT ;
          mdicreate.y       = CW_USEDEFAULT ;
          mdicreate.cx      = CW_USEDEFAULT ;
          mdicreate.cy      = CW_USEDEFAULT ;
          mdicreate.style   = 0 ;
          mdicreate.lParam  = 0 ;

          hwndChild = (HWND) SendMessage (hwndClient,
                               WM_MDICREATE, 0,
                               (LPARAM) (LPMDICREATESTRUCT) &mdicreate) ;
          return 0 ;

     case IDM_FILE_NEWRECT:         // Create a Rect child window

          mdicreate.szClass = szRectClass ;
          mdicreate.szTitle = TEXT ("Rectangles") ;
          mdicreate.hOwner  = hInst ;
          mdicreate.x       = CW_USEDEFAULT ;
          mdicreate.y       = CW_USEDEFAULT ;
          mdicreate.cx      = CW_USEDEFAULT ;
          mdicreate.cy      = CW_USEDEFAULT ;
          mdicreate.style   = 0 ;
          mdicreate.lParam  = 0 ;

          hwndChild = (HWND) SendMessage (hwndClient,
                               WM_MDICREATE, 0,
                               (LPARAM) (LPMDICREATESTRUCT) &mdicreate) ;
          return 0 ;

     case IDM_FILE_CLOSE:           // Close the active window

          hwndChild = (HWND) SendMessage (hwndClient,
                                      WM_MDIGETACTIVE, 0, 0) ;

          if (SendMessage (hwndChild, WM_QUERYENDSESSION, 0, 0))
               SendMessage (hwndClient, WM_MDIDESTROY,
                            (WPARAM) hwndChild, 0) ;
          return 0 ;
```

(continued)

Figure 19-2. *continued*

```
        case IDM_APP_EXIT:                  // Exit the program

             SendMessage (hwnd, WM_CLOSE, 0, 0) ;
             return 0 ;

             // messages for arranging windows

        case IDM_WINDOW_TILE:
             SendMessage (hwndClient, WM_MDITILE, 0, 0) ;
             return 0 ;

        case IDM_WINDOW_CASCADE:
             SendMessage (hwndClient, WM_MDICASCADE, 0, 0) ;
             return 0 ;

        case IDM_WINDOW_ARRANGE:
             SendMessage (hwndClient, WM_MDIICONARRANGE, 0, 0) ;
             return 0 ;

        case IDM_WINDOW_CLOSEALL:      // Attempt to close all children

             EnumChildWindows (hwndClient, CloseEnumProc, 0) ;
             return 0 ;

        default:                // Pass to active child...

             hwndChild = (HWND) SendMessage (hwndClient,
                                             WM_MDIGETACTIVE, 0, 0) ;
             if (IsWindow (hwndChild))
                  SendMessage (hwndChild, WM_COMMAND, wParam, lParam) ;

             break ;          // ...and then to DefFrameProc
        }
        break ;

   case WM_QUERYENDSESSION:
   case WM_CLOSE:                             // Attempt to close all children

        SendMessage (hwnd, WM_COMMAND, IDM_WINDOW_CLOSEALL, 0) ;

        if (NULL != GetWindow (hwndClient, GW_CHILD))
             return 0 ;

        break ;   // i.e., call DefFrameProc
```

```
     case WM_DESTROY:
          PostQuitMessage (0) ;
          return 0 ;
     }
          // Pass unprocessed messages to DefFrameProc (not DefWindowProc)

     return DefFrameProc (hwnd, hwndClient, message, wParam, lParam) ;
}

BOOL CALLBACK CloseEnumProc (HWND hwnd, LPARAM lParam)
{
     if (GetWindow (hwnd, GW_OWNER))                // Check for icon title
          return TRUE ;

     SendMessage (GetParent (hwnd), WM_MDIRESTORE, (WPARAM) hwnd, 0) ;

     if (!SendMessage (hwnd, WM_QUERYENDSESSION, 0, 0))
          return TRUE ;

     SendMessage (GetParent (hwnd), WM_MDIDESTROY, (WPARAM) hwnd, 0) ;
     return TRUE ;
}

LRESULT CALLBACK HelloWndProc (HWND hwnd, UINT message,
                               WPARAM wParam, LPARAM lParam)
{
     static COLORREF clrTextArray[] = { RGB (0,   0, 0), RGB (255, 0,   0),
                                        RGB (0, 255, 0), RGB ( 0, 0, 255),
                                        RGB (255, 255, 255) } ;
     static HWND     hwndClient, hwndFrame ;
     HDC             hdc ;
     HMENU           hMenu ;
     PHELLODATA      pHelloData ;
     PAINTSTRUCT     ps ;
     RECT            rect ;

     switch (message)
     {
     case WM_CREATE:
          // Allocate memory for window private data

          pHelloData = (PHELLODATA) HeapAlloc (GetProcessHeap (),
                         HEAP_ZERO_MEMORY, sizeof (HELLODATA)) ;
```

(continued)

Figure 19-2. *continued*

```
           pHelloData->iColor  = IDM_COLOR_BLACK ;
           pHelloData->clrText = RGB (0, 0, 0) ;
           SetWindowLong (hwnd, 0, (long) pHelloData) ;

                // Save some window handles

           hwndClient = GetParent (hwnd) ;
           hwndFrame  = GetParent (hwndClient) ;
           return 0 ;

      case WM_COMMAND:
           switch (LOWORD (wParam))
           {
           case IDM_COLOR_BLACK:
           case IDM_COLOR_RED:
           case IDM_COLOR_GREEN:
           case IDM_COLOR_BLUE:
           case IDM_COLOR_WHITE:
                     // Change the text color

                pHelloData = (PHELLODATA) GetWindowLong (hwnd, 0) ;

                hMenu = GetMenu (hwndFrame) ;

                CheckMenuItem (hMenu, pHelloData->iColor, MF_UNCHECKED) ;
                pHelloData->iColor = wParam ;
                CheckMenuItem (hMenu, pHelloData->iColor, MF_CHECKED) ;

                pHelloData->clrText = clrTextArray[wParam - IDM_COLOR_BLACK] ;

                InvalidateRect (hwnd, NULL, FALSE) ;
           }
           return 0 ;

      case WM_PAINT:
                // Paint the window

           hdc = BeginPaint (hwnd, &ps) ;

           pHelloData = (PHELLODATA) GetWindowLong (hwnd, 0) ;
           SetTextColor (hdc, pHelloData->clrText) ;

           GetClientRect (hwnd, &rect) ;

           DrawText (hdc, TEXT ("Hello, World!"), -1, &rect,
                     DT_SINGLELINE | DT_CENTER | DT_VCENTER) ;
```

```
        EndPaint (hwnd, &ps) ;
        return 0 ;

case WM_MDIACTIVATE:
        // Set the Hello menu if gaining focus

     if (lParam == (LPARAM) hwnd)
         SendMessage (hwndClient, WM_MDISETMENU,
                     (WPARAM) hMenuHello, (LPARAM) hMenuHelloWindow) ;

        // Check or uncheck menu item

     pHelloData = (PHELLODATA) GetWindowLong (hwnd, 0) ;
     CheckMenuItem (hMenuHello, pHelloData->iColor,
            (lParam == (LPARAM) hwnd) ? MF_CHECKED : MF_UNCHECKED) ;

        // Set the Init menu if losing focus

     if (lParam != (LPARAM) hwnd)
         SendMessage (hwndClient, WM_MDISETMENU, (WPARAM) hMenuInit,
                     (LPARAM) hMenuInitWindow) ;

     DrawMenuBar (hwndFrame) ;
     return 0 ;

case WM_QUERYENDSESSION:
case WM_CLOSE:
     if (IDOK != MessageBox (hwnd, TEXT ("OK to close window?"),
                            TEXT ("Hello"),
                            MB_ICONQUESTION | MB_OKCANCEL))

          return 0 ;

     break ;   // i.e., call DefMDIChildProc

case WM_DESTROY:
     pHelloData = (PHELLODATA) GetWindowLong (hwnd, 0) ;
     HeapFree (GetProcessHeap (), 0, pHelloData) ;
     return 0 ;
}
     // Pass unprocessed message to DefMDIChildProc

return DefMDIChildProc (hwnd, message, wParam, lParam) ;
}
```

(continued)

Figure 19-2. *continued*

```
LRESULT CALLBACK RectWndProc (HWND hwnd, UINT message,
                              WPARAM wParam, LPARAM lParam)
{
    static HWND hwndClient, hwndFrame ;
    HBRUSH      hBrush ;
    HDC         hdc ;
    PRECTDATA   pRectData ;
    PAINTSTRUCT ps ;
    int         xLeft, xRight, yTop, yBottom ;
    short       nRed, nGreen, nBlue ;

    switch (message)
    {
    case WM_CREATE:
            // Allocate memory for window private data

        pRectData = (PRECTDATA) HeapAlloc (GetProcessHeap (),
                           HEAP_ZERO_MEMORY, sizeof (RECTDATA)) ;

        SetWindowLong (hwnd, 0, (long) pRectData) ;

            // Start the timer going

        SetTimer (hwnd, 1, 250, NULL) ;

            // Save some window handles
        hwndClient = GetParent (hwnd) ;
        hwndFrame  = GetParent (hwndClient) ;
        return 0 ;

    case WM_SIZE:              // If not minimized, save the window size

        if (wParam != SIZE_MINIMIZED)
        {
            pRectData = (PRECTDATA) GetWindowLong (hwnd, 0) ;

            pRectData->cxClient = LOWORD (lParam) ;
            pRectData->cyClient = HIWORD (lParam) ;
        }

        break ;          // WM_SIZE must be processed by DefMDIChildProc

    case WM_TIMER:              // Display a random rectangle

        pRectData = (PRECTDATA) GetWindowLong (hwnd, 0) ;
```

```
          xLeft   = rand () % pRectData->cxClient ;
          xRight  = rand () % pRectData->cxClient ;
          yTop    = rand () % pRectData->cyClient ;
          yBottom = rand () % pRectData->cyClient ;
          nRed    = rand () & 255 ;
          nGreen  = rand () & 255 ;
          nBlue   = rand () & 255 ;

          hdc = GetDC (hwnd) ;
          hBrush = CreateSolidBrush (RGB (nRed, nGreen, nBlue)) ;
          SelectObject (hdc, hBrush) ;

          Rectangle (hdc, min (xLeft, xRight), min (yTop, yBottom),
               max (xLeft, xRight), max (yTop, yBottom)) ;

          ReleaseDC (hwnd, hdc) ;
          DeleteObject (hBrush) ;
          return 0 ;

     case WM_PAINT:                // Clear the window

          InvalidateRect (hwnd, NULL, TRUE) ;
          hdc = BeginPaint (hwnd, &ps) ;
          EndPaint (hwnd, &ps) ;
          return 0 ;

     case WM_MDIACTIVATE:       // Set the appropriate menu
          if (lParam == (LPARAM) hwnd)
               SendMessage (hwndClient, WM_MDISETMENU, (WPARAM) hMenuRect,
                         (LPARAM) hMenuRectWindow) ;
          else
               SendMessage (hwndClient, WM_MDISETMENU, (WPARAM) hMenuInit,
                         (LPARAM) hMenuInitWindow) ;

          DrawMenuBar (hwndFrame) ;
          return 0 ;

     case WM_DESTROY:
          pRectData = (PRECTDATA) GetWindowLong (hwnd, 0) ;
          HeapFree (GetProcessHeap (), 0, pRectData) ;
          KillTimer (hwnd, 1) ;
          return 0 ;
     }
          // Pass unprocessed message to DefMDIChildProc

     return DefMDIChildProc (hwnd, message, wParam, lParam) ;
}
```

(continued)

Figure 19-2. *continued*

MDIDEMO.RC (excerpts)

```
//Microsoft Developer Studio generated resource script.

#include "resource.h"
#include "afxres.h"


/////////////////////////////////////////////////////////////////////////////
// Menu

MDIMENUINIT MENU DISCARDABLE
BEGIN
    POPUP "&File"
    BEGIN
        MENUITEM "New &Hello",                  IDM_FILE_NEWHELLO
        MENUITEM "New &Rectangle",              IDM_FILE_NEWRECT
        MENUITEM SEPARATOR
        MENUITEM "E&xit",                       IDM_APP_EXIT
    END
END

MDIMENUHELLO MENU DISCARDABLE
BEGIN
    POPUP "&File"
    BEGIN
        MENUITEM "New &Hello",                  IDM_FILE_NEWHELLO
        MENUITEM "New &Rectangle",              IDM_FILE_NEWRECT
        MENUITEM "&Close",                      IDM_FILE_CLOSE
        MENUITEM SEPARATOR
        MENUITEM "E&xit",                       IDM_APP_EXIT
    END
    POPUP "&Color"
    BEGIN
        MENUITEM "&Black",                      IDM_COLOR_BLACK
        MENUITEM "&Red",                        IDM_COLOR_RED
        MENUITEM "&Green",                      IDM_COLOR_GREEN
        MENUITEM "B&lue",                       IDM_COLOR_BLUE
        MENUITEM "&White",                      IDM_COLOR_WHITE
    END
    POPUP "&Window"
    BEGIN
        MENUITEM "&Cascade\tShift+F5",          IDM_WINDOW_CASCADE
        MENUITEM "&Tile\tShift+F4",             IDM_WINDOW_TILE
        MENUITEM "Arrange &Icons",              IDM_WINDOW_ARRANGE
```

```
            MENUITEM "Close &All",                    IDM_WINDOW_CLOSEALL
        END
END

MDIMENURECT MENU DISCARDABLE
BEGIN
    POPUP "&File"
    BEGIN
        MENUITEM "New &Hello",                    IDM_FILE_NEWHELLO
        MENUITEM "New &Rectangle",                IDM_FILE_NEWRECT
        MENUITEM "&Close",                        IDM_FILE_CLOSE
        MENUITEM SEPARATOR
        MENUITEM "E&xit",                         IDM_APP_EXIT
    END
    POPUP "&Window"
    BEGIN
        MENUITEM "&Cascade\tShift+F5",            IDM_WINDOW_CASCADE
        MENUITEM "&Tile\tShift+F4",               IDM_WINDOW_TILE
        MENUITEM "Arrange &Icons",                IDM_WINDOW_ARRANGE
        MENUITEM "Close &All",                    IDM_WINDOW_CLOSEALL
    END
END


////////////////////////////////////////////////////////////////////////////
// Accelerator

MDIDEMO ACCELERATORS DISCARDABLE
BEGIN
    VK_F4,          IDM_WINDOW_TILE,       VIRTKEY, SHIFT, NOINVERT
    VK_F5,          IDM_WINDOW_CASCADE,    VIRTKEY, SHIFT, NOINVERT
END
```

RESOURCE.H (excerpts)

```
// Microsoft Developer Studio generated include file.
// Used by MDIDemo.rc

#define IDM_FILE_NEWHELLO          40001
#define IDM_FILE_NEWRECT           40002
#define IDM_APP_EXIT               40003
#define IDM_FILE_CLOSE             40004
#define IDM_COLOR_BLACK            40005
#define IDM_COLOR_RED              40006
```

(continued)

Figure 19-2. *continued*

```
#define IDM_COLOR_GREEN        40007
#define IDM_COLOR_BLUE         40008
#define IDM_COLOR_WHITE        40009
#define IDM_WINDOW_CASCADE     40010
#define IDM_WINDOW_TILE        40011
#define IDM_WINDOW_ARRANGE     40012
#define IDM_WINDOW_CLOSEALL    40013
```

MDIDEMO supports two types of extremely simple document windows: one displays "Hello, World!" in the center of its client area, and the other displays a series of random rectangles. (In the source code listings and identifier names, these are referred to as the Hello document and the Rect document.) Different menus are associated with these two types of document windows. The document window that displays "Hello, World!" has a menu that allows you to change the color of the text.

Three Menus

Let's turn first to the MDIDEMO.RC resource script. The resource script defines three menu templates used by the program.

The program displays the MdiMenuInit menu when no document windows are present. This menu simply allows creating a new document or exiting the program.

The MdiMenuHello menu is associated with the document window that displays "Hello, World!" The File submenu allows opening a new document of either type, closing the active document, and exiting the program. The Color submenu lets you set the text color. The Window submenu has options for arranging the document windows in a cascaded or tiled fashion, arranging the document icons, and closing all the windows. This submenu will also list all the document windows as they are created.

The MdiMenuRect menu is associated with the random rectangle document. This is the same as the MdiMenuHello menu except that it does not include the Color submenu.

As usual, the RESOURCE.H header file defines all the menu identifiers. In addition, the following three constants are defined in MDIDEMO.C:

```
#define INIT_MENU_POS     0
#define HELLO_MENU_POS    2
#define RECT_MENU_POS     1
```

These identifiers indicate the position of the Window submenu in each of the three menu templates. This information is needed by the program to inform the client window where the document list is to appear. Of course, the MdiMenuInit menu doesn't have a Window submenu, so I've indicated that the list should be appended to the first submenu (position 0). The list will never actually be viewed there, however. (You'll see why this is needed when I discuss the program later.)

The IDM_FIRSTCHILD identifier defined in MDIDEMO.C doesn't correspond to a menu item. This is the identifier that will be associated with the first document window in the list that will appear in the Window submenu. This identifier should be greater than all the other menu IDs.

Program Initialization

In MDIDEMO.C, *WinMain* begins by registering window classes for the frame window and the two child windows. The window procedures are called *FrameWndProc*, *HelloWndProc*, and *RectWndProc*. Normally, different icons should be associated with these window classes. For the purpose of simplicity, I've used the standard IDI_APPLICATION icon for the frame and child.

Note that I've defined the *hbrBackground* field of the WNDCLASS structure for the frame window class to be the COLOR_APPWORKSPACE system color. This is not entirely necessary because the client area of the frame window is covered up by the client window, and the client window has this color anyway. However, using this color looks a little better when the frame window is first displayed.

The *lpszMenuName* field is set to NULL for each of these three window classes. For the Hello and Rect child window classes, this is normal. For the frame window class, I've chosen to indicate the menu handle in the *CreateWindow* function when creating the frame window.

The window classes for the Hello and Rect child windows allocate extra space for each window using a nonzero value as the *cbWndExtra* field of the WNDCLASS structure. This space will be used to store a pointer that will reference a block of memory (the size of the HELLODATA or RECTDATA structures defined near the top of MDIDEMO.C) used to store information unique to each document window.

Next, *WinMain* uses *LoadMenu* to load the three menus and save their handles in global variables. Three calls to the *GetSubMenu* function obtain handles to the Window submenu to which the document list will be appended. These are also saved in global variables. The *LoadAccelerators* function loads the accelerator table.

A call to *CreateWindow* in *WinMain* creates the frame window. During the WM_CREATE processing in *FrameWndProc*, the frame window creates the client window. This involves another call to *CreateWindow*. The window class is set to MDICLIENT, which is the preregistered class for MDI client windows. Much of the support in Windows for MDI is encapsulated in the MDICLIENT window class. The client window procedure serves as an intermediary layer between the frame window and the various document windows. When calling *CreateWindow* to create the client window, the last argument must be set to a pointer to a structure of type CLIENTCREATESTRUCT. This structure has two fields, described at the top of the next page.

■   *hWindowMenu* is the handle of the submenu to which the document list will be appended. In MDIDEMO, this is *hMenuInitWindow*, which was obtained during *WinMain*. You'll see later how the menu is changed.

■   *idFirstChild* is the menu ID to be associated with the first document window in the document list. This is simply IDM_FIRSTCHILD.

Back in *WinMain*, MDIDEMO displays the newly created frame window and enters the message loop. The message loop differs a little from a normal loop: after obtaining a message from the message queue with a call to *GetMessage*, an MDI program passes the message to *TranslateMDISysAccel* (and to *TranslateAccelerator* if, like the MDIDEMO program, the program also has menu accelerators).

The *TranslateMDISysAccel* function translates any keystrokes that may correspond to the special MDI accelerators (Ctrl-F6, for example) into a WM_SYSCOMMAND message. If either *TranslateMDISysAccel* or *TranslateAccelerator* returns TRUE (indicating that a message was translated by one of these functions), do not call *TranslateMessage* and *DispatchMessage*.

Notice the two window handles passed to *TranslateMDISysAccel* and *Translate-Accelerator*: *hwndClient* and *hwndFrame*, respectively. The *WinMain* function obtains the *hwndClient* window handle by calling *GetWindow* with the GW_CHILD argument.

Creating the Children

The bulk of *FrameWndProc* is devoted to processing WM_COMMAND messages that signal menu selections. As usual, the low word of the *wParam* parameter to *FrameWndProc* contains the menu ID number.

For menu ID values of IDM_FILE_NEWHELLO and IDM_FILE_NEWRECT, *FrameWnd-Proc* must create a new document window. This involves initializing the fields of an MDICREATESTRUCT structure (most of which correspond to *CreateWindow* arguments) and sending the client window a WM_MDICREATE message with *lParam* set to a pointer to this structure. The client window then creates the child document window. (Another possibility is using the *CreateMDIWindow* function.)

Normally the *szTitle* field of the MDICREATESTRUCT structure would be the filename corresponding to the document. The style field can be set to the window styles WS_HSCROLL or WS_VSCROLL or both to include scroll bars in the document window. The style field can also include WS_MINIMIZE or WS_MAXIMIZE to initially display the document window in a minimized or maximized state.

The *lParam* field of the MDICREATESTRUCT structure provides a way for the frame window and the child window to share some variables. This field could be set to a pointer to a memory block containing a structure. During the WM_CREATE message in the child document window, *lParam* is a pointer to a CREATESTRUCT structure and the *lpCreate-Params* field of this structure is a pointer to the MDICREATESTRUCT structure used to create the window.

On receipt of the WM_MDICREATE message, the client window creates the child document window and adds the title of the window to the bottom of the submenu specified in the MDICLIENTSTRUCT structure used to create the client window. When the MDIDEMO program creates its first document window, this is the File submenu of the *MdiMenuInit* menu. We'll see later how this document list gets moved to the Window submenu of the *MdiMenuHello* and *MdiMenuRect* menus.

Up to nine documents can be listed on the menu, each preceded by an underlined number from 1 to 9. If more than nine document windows are created, this list is followed by a More Windows item on the menu. This item invokes a dialog box with a list box that lists all the document windows. The maintenance of this document list is one of the nicest features of the Windows MDI support.

More Frame Window Message Processing

Let's continue with *FrameWndProc* message processing before turning our attention to the child document windows.

When you select Close from the File menu, MDIDEMO closes the active child window. It obtains the handle to the active child window by sending the client window a WM_MDIGETACTIVE message. If the child window responds affirmatively to a WM_QUERYEND-SESSION message, then MDIDEMO sends the client window a WM_MDIDESTROY message to close the child window.

Processing the Exit option from the File menu requires only that the frame window procedure send itself a WM_CLOSE message.

Processing the Tile, Cascade, and Arrange Icons options from the Window submenu is a snap, requiring only that the WM_MDITILE, WM_MDICASCADE, and WM_MDIICONARRANGE messages be sent to the client window.

The Close All option is a little more complex. *FrameWndProc* calls *EnumChildWindows*, passing a pointer referencing the *CloseEnumProc* function. This function sends a WM_MDIRESTORE message to each child window, followed by a WM_QUERYENDSESSION and, possibly, a WM_MDIDESTROY message. This is not done for the icon title window, indicated by a non-NULL return value from *GetWindow* with the GW_OWNER argument.

You'll notice that *FrameWndProc* does not process any of the WM_COMMAND messages that signal one of the colors being selected from the Color menu. These messages are really the responsibility of the document window. For this reason, *FrameWndProc* sends all unprocessed WM_COMMAND messages to the active child window so that the child window can process those messages that pertain to its window.

All messages that the frame window procedure chooses not to process must be passed to *DefFrameProc*. This function replaces *DefWindowProc* in the frame window procedure. Even if a frame window procedure traps the WM_MENUCHAR, WM_SETFOCUS, or WM_SIZE messages, these also must be passed to *DefFrameProc*.

Unprocessed WM_COMMAND messages must also be passed to *DefFrameProc*. In particular, *FrameWndProc* does not process any of the WM_COMMAND messages resulting from the user selecting one of the documents from the list in the Window submenu. (The *wParam* values for these options begin with IDM_FIRSTCHILD.) These messages are passed to *DefFrameProc* and processed there.

Notice that the frame window does not need to maintain a list of window handles of the document windows that it creates. If ever these handles are needed (such as when processing the Close All option from the menu), they can be obtained using *EnumChild-Windows*.

The Child Document Windows

Now let's look at *HelloWndProc*, which is the window procedure used for the child document windows that display "Hello, World!"

As with any window class used for more than one window, static variables defined in the window procedure (or any function called from the window procedure) are shared by all windows created based on that window class.

Data that is unique to each window must be stored using a method other than static variables. One such technique involves window properties. Another approach—the one I used—uses memory space reserved by defining a nonzero value in the *cbWndExtra* field of the WNDCLASS structure used to register the window class.

In MDIDEMO, I use this space to store a pointer that references a block of memory the size of the HELLODATA structure. *HelloWndProc* allocates this memory during the WM_CREATE message, initializes the two fields (which indicate the currently checked menu item and the text color), and stores the pointer using *SetWindowLong*.

When processing a WM_COMMAND message for changing the text colors (recall that these messages originate in the frame window procedure), *HelloWndProc* uses *GetWindowLong* to obtain the pointer to the memory block containing the HELLODATA structure. Using this structure, *HelloWndProc* unchecks the checked menu item, checks the selected menu item, and saves the new color.

A document window procedure receives the WM_MDIACTIVATE message whenever the window becomes active or inactive (indicated by whether or not *lParam* holds the window's handle). You'll recall that the MDIDEMO program has three different menus: MdiMenuInit for when no documents are present, MdiMenuHello for when a Hello document window is active, and MdiMenuRect for when a Rect document window is active.

The WM_MDIACTIVATE message provides an opportunity for the document window to change the menu. If *lParam* contains the window's handle (meaning the window is becoming active), *HelloWndProc* changes the menu to MdiMenuHello. If *lParam* holds the handle of another window, *HelloWndProc* changes the menu to MdiMenuInit.

HelloWndProc changes the menu by sending a WM_MDISETMENU message to the client window. The client window processes this message by removing the document list from the current menu and appending it to the new menu. This is how the document list is transferred from the MdiMenuInit menu (which is in effect when the first document is created) to the MdiMenuHello menu. Do not use the *SetMenu* function to change a menu in an MDI application.

Another little chore involves the check marks on the Color submenu. Program options such as this should be unique to each document. For example, you should be able to set black text in one window and red text in another. The menu check marks should reflect the option chosen in the active window. For this reason, *HelloWndProc* unchecks the selected menu item when the window is becoming inactive and checks the appropriate item when the window is becoming active.

The *wParam* and *lParam* values of the WM_MDIACTIVATE message are the handles of the windows being deactivated and activated, respectively. The window procedure gets the first WM_MDIACTIVATE message with *lParam* set to the window's handle. The window procedure gets the last message with *lParam* set to another value when the window is destroyed. When the user switches from one document to another, the first document window receives a WM_MDIACTIVATE message with *lParam* set to the handle of the first window, at which time the window procedure sets the menu to MdiMenuInit. The second document window receives a WM_MDIACTIVATE message with *lParam* set to the handle of the second window, at which time the window procedure sets the menu to MdiMenuHello or MdiMenuRect as appropriate. If all the windows are closed, the menu is left as MdiMenuInit.

You'll recall that *FrameWndProc* sends the child window a WM_QUERYENDSESSION message when the user selects Close or Close All from the menu. *HelloWndProc* processes the WM_QUERYENDSESSION and WM_CLOSE messages by displaying a message box and asking the user whether the window can be closed. (In a real program, this message box might ask whether a file needed to be saved.) If the user indicates that the window should not be closed, the window procedure returns 0.

During the WM_DESTROY message, *HelloWndProc* frees the memory block allocated during the WM_CREATE message.

All unprocessed messages must be passed on to *DefMDIChildProc* (not *DefWindowProc*) for default processing. Several messages must be passed to *DefMDIChildProc* whether or not the child window procedure does something with them. These are WM_CHILDACTIVATE, WM_GETMINMAXINFO, WM_MENUCHAR, WM_MOVE, WM_SETFOCUS, WM_SIZE, and WM_SYSCOMMAND.

RectWndProc is fairly similar to *HelloWndProc* in much of the overhead involved, but it's a little simpler (that is, no menu options are involved and the window does not verify with the user whether it can be closed), so I needn't discuss it. But note that *RectWndProc* breaks after processing WM_SIZE, so the message is passed to *DefMDIChildProc*.

Cleaning Up

In *WinMain*, MDIDEMO uses *LoadMenu* to load the three menus defined in the resource script. Normally Windows will destroy a menu at the time the window to which the menu is attached is destroyed. That takes care of the Init menu. However, menus that are not attached to a window should be destroyed explicitly. For this reason, MDIDEMO calls *DestroyMenu* twice at the end of *WinMain* to get rid of the Hello and Rect menus.

Chapter 20

Multitasking and Multithreading

Multitasking is the ability of an operating system to run multiple programs concurrently. Basically, the operating system uses a hardware clock to allocate "time slices" for each currently running process. If the time slices are small enough—and the machine is not overloaded with too many programs trying to do something—it appears to a user as if all the programs are running simultaneously.

Multitasking is nothing new. On large mainframe computers, multitasking is a given. These mainframes often have hundreds of terminals attached to them, and each terminal user should get the impression that he or she has exclusive access to the whole machine. In addition, mainframe operating systems often allow users to "submit jobs to the background," where they are then carried out by the machine while the user can work on something else.

Multitasking on personal computers has taken much longer to become a reality. But we now often seem to take PC multitasking for granted. As I'll discuss shortly, to some extent the earlier 16-bit versions of Microsoft Windows supported multitasking but in a somewhat limited capability. The 32-bit versions of Windows all support both true multitasking and— as an extra bonus—multithreading.

Multithreading is the ability for a program to multitask within itself. The program can split itself into separate "threads" of execution that also seem to run concurrently. This concept might at first seem barely useful, but it turns out that programs can use multithreading to perform lengthy jobs in the background without requiring the user to take an extended break away from their machines. Of course, sometimes this may not be desired: an excuse to take a journey to the watercooler or refrigerator is often welcome! But the user should always be able to do *something* on the machine, even when it's busy doing something else.

MODES OF MULTITASKING

In the early days of the PC, some people advocated multitasking for the future, but many others scratched their heads in puzzlement: Of what use is multitasking on a single-user personal computer? Well, it turned out that multitasking was something users wanted without really knowing it.

Multitasking Under DOS?

The Intel 8088 microprocessor used in the original PC was not exactly built for multitasking. Part of the problem was inadequate memory management. As multiple programs are started up and ended, a multitasking operating system is often called upon to move memory blocks around to consolidate free space. This was not possible on the 8088 in a manner transparent to applications.

DOS itself didn't help much. Designed to be small and to stay out of the way of applications, DOS supported very little beyond loading programs and providing them with access to the file system.

Still, however, creative programmers in the early days of DOS found a way to overcome those obstacles, mostly with terminate-and-stay-resident (TSR) programs. Some TSRs, such as print spoolers, hooked into the hardware timer interrupt to perform true background processing. Others, like popup utilities such as SideKick, could perform a type of task switching—suspending an application while the popup was running. DOS was also progressively enhanced to provide support for TSRs.

Some software vendors attempted to mold task-switching or multitasking shells on top of DOS (such as Quarterdeck's DesqView), but only one of these environments eventually achieved a large market penetration. That, of course, is Windows.

Nonpreemptive Multitasking

When Microsoft introduced Windows 1.0 in 1985, it was the most sophisticated solution yet devised to go beyond the limitations of DOS. Back then, Windows ran in real mode, but even so, it was able to move memory blocks around in physical memory—a prerequisite for multitasking—in a way that was not quite transparent to applications but almost tolerable.

Multitasking makes a lot more sense in a graphical windowing environment than it does in a command-line single-user operating system. For example, in classical command-line UNIX, it is possible to execute programs off the command line so that they run in the background. However, any display output from the program must be redirected to a file or the output will get mixed up with whatever else the user is doing.

A windowing environment allows multiple programs to run together on the same screen. Switching back and forth becomes trivial, and it is also possible to quickly move data from one program to another; for example, to embed a picture created in a drawing program into a text file maintained by a word processing program. Data transfer has been supported in various ways under Windows, first with the clipboard, later through Dynamic Data Exchange (DDE), and now through Object Linking and Embedding (OLE).

Yet the multitasking implemented in the early versions of Windows was not the traditional preemptive time-slicing found in multiuser operating systems. Those operating systems use a system clock to periodically interrupt one task and restart another. The 16-bit versions of Windows supported something called "nonpreemptive multitasking." This type of multitasking is made possible because of the message-based architecture of Windows. In the general case, a Windows program sits dormant in memory until it receives a message. These messages are often the direct or indirect result of user input through the keyboard or mouse. After processing the message, the program returns control back to Windows.

The 16-bit versions of Windows did not arbitrarily switch control from one Windows program to another based on a timer tick. Instead, any task switching took place when a program had finished processing a message and had returned control to Windows. This nonpreemptive multitasking is also called "cooperative multitasking" because it requires some cooperation on the part of applications. One Windows program could tie up the whole system if it took a long time processing a message.

Although nonpreemptive multitasking was the general rule in 16-bit Windows, some forms of preemptive multitasking were also present. Windows used preemptive multitasking for running DOS programs and also allowed dynamic-link libraries to receive hardware timer interrupts for multimedia purposes.

The 16-bit Windows included several features to help programmers solve—or at least cope with—the limitations of nonpreemptive multitasking. The most notorious is, of course, the hourglass mouse cursor. This is not a solution, of course, but just a way of letting the user know that a program is busy working on a lengthy job and the system will be otherwise unusable for a little awhile. Another partial solution is the Windows timer, which allows a program to receive a message and do some work at periodic intervals. The timer is often used for clock applications and animation.

Another solution to the limitations of preemptive multitasking is the *PeekMessage* function call, as we saw in Chapter 5 in the RANDRECT program. Normally a program uses the *GetMessage* call to retrieve the next message from its message queue. However, if there are no messages in the message queue, then *GetMessage* will not return until a message is present. *PeekMessage*, on the other hand, returns control to the program even if no messages are pending. Thus, a program can perform a long job and intermix *PeekMessage* calls in the code. The long job will continue running as long as there are no pending messages for the program or any other program.

PM and the Serialized Message Queue

The first attempt by Microsoft (in collaboration with IBM) to implement multitasking in a quasi-DOS/Windows environment was OS/2 and the Presentation Manager (PM). Although OS/2 certainly supported preemptive multitasking, it often didn't seem as if this preemption was carried over into the Presentation Manager. The problem is that PM serialized user input messages from the keyboard and mouse. What this means is that PM would not deliver a keyboard or mouse message to a program until the previous user input message had been fully processed.

Although keyboard and mouse messages are just a few of the many messages a PM (or Windows) program can receive, most of the other messages are the result of a keyboard or mouse event. For example, a menu command message is the result of the user making a menu selection using the keyboard or mouse. The keyboard or mouse message is not fully processed until the menu command message is processed.

The primary reason for the serialized message queue was to allow predictable "type-ahead" and "mouse-ahead" actions by the user. If one of the keyboard or mouse messages caused a shift in input focus from one window to another, subsequent keyboard messages should go to the window with the new input focus. So, the system doesn't know where to send a subsequent user input message until the previous ones have been processed.

The common consensus these days is that it should not be possible for one application to be able to tie up the entire system; that requires a deserialized message queue, which is supported by the 32-bit versions of Windows. If one program is busy doing a lengthy job, you can switch the input focus to another program.

The Multithreading Solution

I've been discussing the OS/2 Presentation Manager only because it was the first environment that provided some veteran Windows programmers (such as myself) with their first introduction to multithreading. Interestingly enough, the limitations of PM's implementation of multithreading provided programmers with essential clues to how multithreaded programs should be architected. Even though these limitations have now largely been lifted from the 32-bit versions of Windows, the lessons learned from more limited environments are still quite valid. So let's proceed.

In a multithreaded environment, programs can split themselves into separate pieces, called "threads of execution," that run concurrently. The support of threads turned out to be the best solution to the problem of the serialized message queue in the Presentation Manager and continues to make a whole lot of sense under Windows.

In terms of code, a thread is simply represented by a function that might also call other functions in the program. A program begins execution with its main (or primary) thread, which in a traditional C program is the function called *main* and which in Windows is *WinMain*. Once running, the program can create new threads of execution by making a system call (*CreateThread*) specifying the name of initial thread function. The operating system preemptively switches control among the threads in much the same way it switches control among processes.

In the OS/2 Presentation Manager, each thread could either create a message queue or not. A PM thread must create a message queue if it wishes to create windows from that thread. Otherwise, a thread needn't create a message queue if it's just doing a lot of data crunching or graphics output. Because the non-message-queue threads do not process messages, they cannot hang the system. The only restriction is that a non-message-queue thread cannot send a message to a window in a message-queue thread or make any function call that causes a message to be sent. (They can, however, post messages to message-queue threads.)

Thus, PM programmers learned how to divide their programs into one message-queue thread that created all the windows and processed messages to them, and one or more non-message-queue threads that performed lengthy background tasks. PM programmers also learned about the "$1/_{10}$-second rule." Basically, they were advised that a message-queue thread should spend no more than $1/_{10}$ of a second processing a message. Anything that takes longer should be done in a different thread. If all programmers followed this rule, no PM program could hang the system for more than $1/_{10}$ of a second.

Multithreaded Architecture

I said that the limitations of PM provided programmers with essential clues to understanding how to use multiple threads of execution in a program running under a graphical environment. So here's what I recommend for the architecture of your programs: Your primary thread creates all the windows that your program needs, includes all the window procedures for these windows, and processes all the messages for these windows. Any other threads are simply background crunchers. They do not interact with the user except through communication with the primary thread.

One way to think of this is that the primary thread handles user input (and other messages), perhaps creating secondary threads in the process. These additional threads do the non-user-related tasks.

In other words, your program's primary thread is a governor, and your secondary threads are the governor's staff. The governor delegates all the big jobs to his or her staff while maintaining contact with the outside world. Because they are staff members, the secondary threads do not hold their own press conferences. They discreetly do their work, report back to the governor, and await their next assignment.

Threads within a particular program are all parts of the same process, so they share the process's resources, such as memory and open files. Because threads share the program's memory, they also share static variables. However, each thread has its own stack, so automatic variables are unique to each thread. Each thread also has its own processor state (and math coprocessor state) that is saved and restored during thread switches.

Thread Hassles

Properly designing, coding, and debugging a complex multithreaded application is conceivably one of the most difficult jobs a Windows programmer can encounter. Because a preemptive multitasking system can interrupt a thread at any point to switch control to another thread, any undesirable interaction between two threads might not be obvious and might show up only occasionally, seemingly on a random basis.

One common bug in a multithreaded program is called a "race condition." This happens when a programmer assumes that one thread will finish doing something—for example, preparing some data—before another thread needs that data. To help coordinate thread activity, operating systems require various forms of synchronization. One is the semaphore, which allows the programmer to block the execution of a thread at a certain point in the code until another thread signals that it can resume. Similar to semaphores are "critical sections," which are sections of code that cannot be interrupted.

But semaphores can also introduce another common thread-related bug, which is called a "deadlock." This occurs when two threads have blocked each other's execution and they can only unblock that execution by proceeding.

Fortunately, 32-bit programs are more immune to certain problems involving threads than 16-bit programs. For example, suppose one thread executes the simple statement

```
lCount++ ;
```

where *lCount* is a long 32-bit global variable that is used by other threads. In a 16-bit program, that single statement in C is compiled to two machine code instructions, the first one incrementing the low 16 bits of the variable, and the second adding any carry into the high 16 bits. Suppose the operating system interrupted the thread between those two machine code instructions. If *lCount* were 0x0000FFFF before the first machine code instruction, then *lCount* would be zero at the time the thread was interrupted, and that's the value another thread would see. Only when the thread resumed would *lCount* be incremented to its proper value of 0x00010000.

This is one of those bugs that might cause an operational problem so infrequently that it would never be detected. In a 16-bit program, the proper way to solve it would be to enclose the statement in a critical section, during which the thread cannot be interrupted. In a 32-bit program, however, the statement is fine because it is compiled to a single machine code instruction.

The Windows Advantage

The 32-bit versions of Windows (including Microsoft Windows NT and Windows 98) have a deserialized message queue. The implementation of this seems very good: If a program is taking a long time processing a message, the mouse cursor appears as an hourglass when the mouse is over that program's window but it changes to a normal arrow when positioned over another program's window. A simple click can bring that other window to the foreground.

However, the user is still prevented from working with the program doing the big job because the big job is preventing the program from receiving other messages. This is undesirable. A program should be always open to messages, and that often requires the use of secondary threads.

In Windows NT and Windows 98, there is no distinction between message-queue threads and non-message-queue threads. Each thread gets its own message queue when the thread is created. This reduces some of the awkward rules for threads in a PM program. (However, in most cases you'll want to process input through message procedures in one thread and pass off long jobs to other threads that do not maintain windows. This structure almost always makes the best sense, as we'll see.)

Still more good news: Windows NT and Windows 98 have a function that allows one thread to kill another thread in the same process. As you'll discover when you begin writing multithreaded code, this is sometimes convenient. The early versions of OS/2 did not include a "kill thread" function.

The final good news (at least for this topic) is that Windows NT and Windows 98 have implemented something called "thread local storage" (TLS). To understand this, recall that I mentioned earlier that static variables, both global and local to a function, are shared among threads because they sit in the process's data memory space. Automatic variables, which are always local to a function, are unique to each thread because they occupy space on the stack, and each thread has its own stack.

It is sometimes convenient for two or more threads to use the same function and for these threads to use static variables that are unique to the thread. That's thread local storage. There are a few Windows function calls involved, but Microsoft has also added an extension to the C compiler that makes the use of TLS more transparent to the programmer.

New! Improved! Now with Threads!

Now that I've made the case for threads, let's put the subject in proper perspective. Sometimes there's a tendency for programmers to use every feature that an operating system has to offer. But the worst case is when your boss comes to your desk and says, "I've heard that this new Whatsit thing is really hot. Let's incorporate some Whatsit in our program." And then you spend a week trying to figure out how (and if) Whatsit can possibly benefit the application.

The point is—it just doesn't make sense to add multithreading to an application that doesn't need it. Some applications just can't benefit from multithreading. If your program displays the hourglass cursor for an annoying period of time, or if it uses the *PeekMessage* call to avoid the hourglass cursor, then restructuring the program for multithreading is probably a good idea. Otherwise, you're just making things hard for yourself and possibly introducing new bugs into the code.

There are even some cases where the hourglass cursor might be entirely appropriate. I mentioned earlier the $\frac{1}{10}$-second rule. Well, loading a large file into memory can take longer than $\frac{1}{10}$ second. Does this mean that file-loading routines should be implemented in separate threads? Not necessarily. When a user commands a program to open a file, he or she usually wants that operation to be carried out immediately. Putting the file-loading routines in a separate thread simply adds overhead. It's just not worth it, even if you want to boast to your friends that you write multithreaded programs!

Windows Multithreading

The API function to create a new thread of execution is named CreateThread. The function has the following syntax:

```
hThread = CreateThread (&security_attributes, dwStackSize, ThreadProc,
                        pParam, dwFlags, &idThread) ;
```

The first argument is a pointer to a structure of type SECURITY_ATTRIBUTES. This argument is ignored in Windows 98. It can also be set to NULL in Windows NT. The second argument is an initial stack size for the new thread; this argument can be set to 0 for a default value. In any case, Windows dynamically lengthens the stack, if necessary.

The third argument to *CreateThread* is a pointer to the thread function. This can have any name but must have the syntax

```
DWORD WINAPI ThreadProc (PVOID pParam) ;
```

The fourth argument to *CreateThread* becomes the parameter to *ThreadProc*. This is how a main thread and a secondary thread can share data.

The fifth argument to *CreateThread* is usually 0 but can be the flag CREATE_SUSPENDED if the thread is to be created but not immediately executed. The thread will remain suspended until *ResumeThread* is called. The sixth argument is a pointer to a variable that will receive the value of the thread ID.

Most Windows programmers instead prefer to use a C run-time library named *_beginthread* that is declared in the PROCESS.H header file. This function has the following syntax:

```
hThread = _beginthread (ThreadProc, uiStackSize, pParam) ;
```

It's just a bit simpler and is perfectly fine for most applications. This thread function has the syntax

```
void __cdecl ThreadProc (void * pParam) ;
```

Random Rectangles Revisited

The RNDRCTMT program shown in Figure 20-1 is a multithreaded version of the RANDRECT program shown in Chapter 5. As you'll recall, RANDRECT used the *PeekMessage* loop to display a series of random rectangles.

RNDRCTMT.C

```
/*-----------------------------------------------
   RNDRCTMT.C -- Displays Random Rectangles
                 (c) Charles Petzold, 1998
   -------------------------------------------*/

#include <windows.h>
#include <process.h>

LRESULT CALLBACK WndProc (HWND, UINT, WPARAM, LPARAM) ;

HWND hwnd ;
int  cxClient, cyClient ;

int WINAPI WinMain (HINSTANCE hInstance, HINSTANCE hPrevInstance,
                    PSTR szCmdLine, int iCmdShow)
{
     static TCHAR szAppName[] = TEXT ("RndRctMT") ;
     MSG          msg ;
     WNDCLASS     wndclass ;

     wndclass.style         = CS_HREDRAW | CS_VREDRAW ;
     wndclass.lpfnWndProc   = WndProc ;
     wndclass.cbClsExtra    = 0 ;
     wndclass.cbWndExtra    = 0 ;
     wndclass.hInstance     = hInstance ;
     wndclass.hIcon         = LoadIcon (NULL, IDI_APPLICATION) ;
     wndclass.hCursor       = LoadCursor (NULL, IDC_ARROW) ;
     wndclass.hbrBackground = (HBRUSH) GetStockObject (WHITE_BRUSH) ;
     wndclass.lpszMenuName  = NULL ;
     wndclass.lpszClassName = szAppName ;

     if (!RegisterClass (&wndclass))
     {
          MessageBox (NULL, TEXT ("This program requires Windows NT!"),
                      szAppName, MB_ICONERROR) ;
          return 0 ;
     }
```

Figure 20-1. *The RNDRCTMT program.*   *(continued)*

Figure 20-1. *continued*

```
        hwnd = CreateWindow (szAppName, TEXT ("Random Rectangles"),
                             WS_OVERLAPPEDWINDOW,
                             CW_USEDEFAULT, CW_USEDEFAULT,
                             CW_USEDEFAULT, CW_USEDEFAULT,
                             NULL, NULL, hInstance, NULL) ;

        ShowWindow (hwnd, iCmdShow) ;
        UpdateWindow (hwnd) ;

        while (GetMessage (&msg, NULL, 0, 0))
        {
             TranslateMessage (&msg) ;
             DispatchMessage (&msg) ;
        }
        return msg.wParam ;
}

VOID Thread (PVOID pvoid)
{
        HBRUSH hBrush ;
        HDC    hdc ;
        int    xLeft, xRight, yTop, yBottom, iRed, iGreen, iBlue ;

        while (TRUE)
        {
             if (cxClient != 0 || cyClient != 0)
             {
                  xLeft   = rand () % cxClient ;
                  xRight  = rand () % cxClient ;
                  yTop    = rand () % cyClient ;
                  yBottom = rand () % cyClient ;
                  iRed    = rand () & 255 ;
                  iGreen  = rand () & 255 ;
                  iBlue   = rand () & 255 ;

                  hdc = GetDC (hwnd) ;
                  hBrush = CreateSolidBrush (RGB (iRed, iGreen, iBlue)) ;
                  SelectObject (hdc, hBrush) ;

                  Rectangle (hdc, min (xLeft, xRight), min (yTop, yBottom),
                                  max (xLeft, xRight), max (yTop, yBottom)) ;

                  ReleaseDC (hwnd, hdc) ;
                  DeleteObject (hBrush) ;
             }
        }
}
```

```
LRESULT CALLBACK WndProc (HWND hwnd, UINT message, WPARAM wParam, LPARAM lParam)
{
    switch (message)
    {
    case WM_CREATE:
         _beginthread (Thread, 0, NULL) ;
         return 0 ;

    case WM_SIZE:
         cxClient = LOWORD (lParam) ;
         cyClient = HIWORD (lParam) ;
         return 0 ;

    case WM_DESTROY:
         PostQuitMessage (0) ;
         return 0 ;
    }
    return DefWindowProc (hwnd, message, wParam, lParam) ;
}
```

Whenever you create a multithreaded Windows program, you need to change something in the Project Settings dialog box. Select the C/C++ tab, and select Code Generation in the Category combo box. In the Use Run-Time Library combo box, you should see Single-Threaded for the Release configuration and Debug Single-Threaded for the Debug configuration. Change these to Multithreaded and Debug Multithreaded, respectively. This will change a compiler flag to /MT, which the compiler needs to compile a multithreaded application. In particular, the compiler inserts the LIBCMT.LIB filename in the .OBJ file rather than LIBC.LIB. The linker uses this name to link with the run-time library functions.

The LIBC.LIB and LIBCMT.LIB files contain the C library functions. Some C library functions maintain static data. The *strtok* function, for example, is designed to be called more than once in succession and stores a pointer in static memory. In a multithreaded program, each thread must have its own static pointer in the *strtok* function. Thus, the multithreaded version of this function is a little different from the single-threaded *strtok* function.

Also notice that I've included the header file PROCESS.H in RNDRCTMT.C. This file declares the *_beginthread* function that starts up the new thread. The function is not declared unless an _MT identifier is defined, and that's another result of the /MT flag.

In the *WinMain* function in RNDRCTMT.C, the *hwnd* value returned from *Create-Window* is stored in a global variable. So also are the *cxClient* and *cyClient* values obtained from the WM_SIZE message in the window procedure.

The window procedure calls *_beginthread* in the easiest way, with simply the address of the thread function (called *Thread*) as the first parameter and zeros for the other parameters. The thread function returns VOID and has a parameter that is a pointer to a VOID. The *Thread* function in RNDRCTMT does not use this parameter.

After the _beginthread_ function is called, the code in that thread function, as well as any other function the thread function might call, runs concurrently with the rest of the code in the program. Two or more threads can use the same function in a process. In this case, the automatic local variables (stored on the stack) are unique to each thread; all static variables are common to all threads in the process. This is how the window procedure can set the global _cxClient_ and _cyClient_ variables and the _Thread_ function can use them.

There are times that you need persistent data unique to more than one thread. Normally, persistent data involves static variables but in Windows 98 you can use TLS, which I've touched on and which I'll discuss in greater detail later in this chapter.

The Programming Contest Problem

On October 3, 1986, Microsoft held a daylong press briefing for technical editors and writers of computer magazines to discuss their current array of language products, including their first interactive development environment, QuickBASIC 2.0. At that time, Windows 1.0 was less than a year old, and no one knew when we'd get something similar for that environment. (It took quite a few years.) What made this event unique was a little something that Microsoft's public relations folks had cooked up—a programming contest called "Storm the Gates." Bill Gates would be using QuickBASIC 2.0, and the technical computer press people could use whatever language product they might decide to bring.

The particular programming problem used for the contest was picked out of a hat from among several others submitted by the contestants and designed to require about a half hour to program. It went something like this:

Create a multitasking simulation consisting of four windows. The first window must show a series of increasing numbers, the second must show a series of increasing prime numbers, and the third must show the Fibonacci series. (The Fibonacci series begins with the numbers 0 and 1, and every successive number is the sum of the two before it—that is, 0, 1, 1, 2, 3, 5, 8, and so forth.) These three windows should either scroll or clear themselves when the numbers reach the bottom of the window. The fourth window must display circles of random radii, and the program must terminate with a press of the Escape key.

Of course, in October 1986, such a program running under DOS couldn't be much more than a multitasking simulation, and none of the contestants were brave enough—and most not yet knowledgeable enough—to code it for Windows. Moreover, to do so from scratch would almost certainly have taken longer than a half hour!

Most of the people who participated in this contest wrote a program that divided the screen into four areas. The program contained a loop that sequentially updated each window and then checked if the Escape key had been pressed. As is customary under DOS, the program used 100 percent of CPU processing.

Had it been programmed for Windows 1.0, the result would have looked something like the MULTI1 program shown in Figure 20-2. I say "something like" because I've converted the program to 32-bit processing. But the structure and much of the code—aside from variable and function parameter definitions and the Unicode support—would have been the same.

MULTI1.C

```
/*-----------------------------------------
   MULTI1.C -- Multitasking Demo
              (c) Charles Petzold, 1998
   -----------------------------------------*/

#include <windows.h>
#include <math.h>

LRESULT CALLBACK WndProc (HWND, UINT, WPARAM, LPARAM) ;

int cyChar ;

int WINAPI WinMain (HINSTANCE hInstance, HINSTANCE hPrevInstance,
                    PSTR szCmdLine, int iCmdShow)
{
     static TCHAR szAppName[] = TEXT ("Multi1") ;
     HWND         hwnd ;
     MSG          msg ;
     WNDCLASS     wndclass ;

     wndclass.style         = CS_HREDRAW | CS_VREDRAW ;
     wndclass.lpfnWndProc   = WndProc ;
     wndclass.cbClsExtra    = 0 ;
     wndclass.cbWndExtra    = 0 ;
     wndclass.hInstance     = hInstance ;
     wndclass.hIcon         = LoadIcon (NULL, IDI_APPLICATION) ;
     wndclass.hCursor       = LoadCursor (NULL, IDC_ARROW) ;
     wndclass.hbrBackground = (HBRUSH) GetStockObject (WHITE_BRUSH) ;
     wndclass.lpszMenuName  = NULL ;
     wndclass.lpszClassName = szAppName ;

     if (!RegisterClass (&wndclass))
     {
          MessageBox (NULL, TEXT ("This program requires Windows NT!"),
                      szAppName, MB_ICONERROR) ;
          return 0 ;
     }
```

Figure 20-2. *The MULTI1 program.*   *(continued)*

Figure 20-2. *continued*

```
        hwnd = CreateWindow (szAppName, TEXT ("Multitasking Demo"),
                          WS_OVERLAPPEDWINDOW,
                          CW_USEDEFAULT, CW_USEDEFAULT,
                          CW_USEDEFAULT, CW_USEDEFAULT,
                          NULL, NULL, hInstance, NULL) ;

        ShowWindow (hwnd, iCmdShow) ;
        UpdateWindow (hwnd) ;

        while (GetMessage (&msg, NULL, 0, 0))
        {
             TranslateMessage (&msg) ;
             DispatchMessage (&msg) ;
        }
        return msg.wParam ;
}

int CheckBottom (HWND hwnd, int cyClient, int iLine)
{
        if (iLine * cyChar + cyChar > cyClient)
        {
             InvalidateRect (hwnd, NULL, TRUE) ;
             UpdateWindow (hwnd) ;
             iLine = 0 ;
        }
        return iLine ;
}

// ---------------------------------------------------
// Window 1: Display increasing sequence of numbers
// ---------------------------------------------------

LRESULT APIENTRY WndProc1 (HWND hwnd, UINT message, WPARAM wParam, LPARAM lParam)
{
        static int iNum, iLine, cyClient ;
        HDC        hdc ;
        TCHAR      szBuffer[16] ;

        switch (message)
        {
        case WM_SIZE:
             cyClient = HIWORD (lParam) ;
             return 0 ;
```

```
        case WM_TIMER:
            if (iNum < 0)
                iNum = 0 ;

            iLine = CheckBottom (hwnd, cyClient, iLine) ;
            hdc = GetDC (hwnd) ;

            TextOut (hdc, 0, iLine * cyChar, szBuffer,
                        wsprintf (szBuffer, TEXT ("%d"), iNum++)) ;

            ReleaseDC (hwnd, hdc) ;
            iLine++ ;
            return 0 ;
        }
        return DefWindowProc (hwnd, message, wParam, lParam) ;
}

// ----------------------------------------------------------
// Window 2: Display increasing sequence of prime numbers
// ----------------------------------------------------------

LRESULT APIENTRY WndProc2 (HWND hwnd, UINT message, WPARAM wParam, LPARAM lParam)
{
    static int iNum = 1, iLine, cyClient ;
    HDC        hdc ;
    int        i, iSqrt ;
    TCHAR      szBuffer[16] ;

    switch (message)
    {
    case WM_SIZE:
        cyClient = HIWORD (lParam) ;
        return 0 ;

    case WM_TIMER:
        do    {
            if (++iNum < 0)
                iNum = 0 ;

            iSqrt = (int) sqrt (iNum) ;

            for (i = 2 ; i <= iSqrt ; i++)
                if (iNum % i == 0)
                    break ;
        }
```

(continued)

Figure 20-2. *continued*

```
        while (i <= iSqrt) ;

        iLine = CheckBottom (hwnd, cyClient, iLine) ;
        hdc = GetDC (hwnd) ;

        TextOut (hdc, 0, iLine * cyChar, szBuffer,
                 wsprintf (szBuffer, TEXT ("%d"), iNum)) ;
        ReleaseDC (hwnd, hdc) ;
        iLine++ ;
        return 0 ;
     }
     return DefWindowProc (hwnd, message, wParam, lParam) ;
}


// ------------------------------------------------------------
// Window 3: Display increasing sequence of Fibonacci numbers
// ------------------------------------------------------------

LRESULT APIENTRY WndProc3 (HWND hwnd, UINT message, WPARAM wParam, LPARAM lParam)
{
     static int iNum = 0, iNext = 1, iLine, cyClient ;
     HDC        hdc ;
     int        iTemp ;
     TCHAR      szBuffer[16] ;

     switch (message)
     {
     case WM_SIZE:
          cyClient = HIWORD (lParam) ;
          return 0 ;

     case WM_TIMER:
          if (iNum < 0)
          {
               iNum  = 0 ;
               iNext = 1 ;
          }

          iLine = CheckBottom (hwnd, cyClient, iLine) ;
          hdc = GetDC (hwnd) ;

          TextOut (hdc, 0, iLine * cyChar, szBuffer,
                   wsprintf (szBuffer, "%d", iNum)) ;
```

```
            ReleaseDC (hwnd, hdc) ;
            iTemp  = iNum ;
            iNum   = iNext ;
            iNext += iTemp ;
            iLine++ ;
            return 0 ;
       }
       return DefWindowProc (hwnd, message, wParam, lParam) ;
}


// -------------------------------------------
// Window 4: Display circles of random radii
// -------------------------------------------

LRESULT APIENTRY WndProc4 (HWND hwnd, UINT message, WPARAM wParam, LPARAM lParam)
{
     static int cxClient, cyClient ;
     HDC        hdc ;
     int        iDiameter ;

     switch (message)
     {
     case WM_SIZE:
          cxClient = LOWORD (lParam) ;
          cyClient = HIWORD (lParam) ;
          return 0 ;

     case WM_TIMER:
          InvalidateRect (hwnd, NULL, TRUE) ;
          UpdateWindow (hwnd) ;

          iDiameter = rand() % (max (1, min (cxClient, cyClient))) ;
          hdc = GetDC (hwnd) ;

          Ellipse (hdc, (cxClient - iDiameter) / 2,
                        (cyClient - iDiameter) / 2,
                        (cxClient + iDiameter) / 2,
                        (cyClient + iDiameter) / 2) ;

          ReleaseDC (hwnd, hdc) ;
          return 0 ;
     }
     return DefWindowProc (hwnd, message, wParam, lParam) ;
}
```

(continued)

Figure 20-2. *continued*

```
// -----------------------------------
// Main window to create child windows
// -----------------------------------

LRESULT APIENTRY WndProc (HWND hwnd, UINT message, WPARAM wParam, LPARAM lParam)
{
     static HWND     hwndChild[4] ;
     static TCHAR * szChildClass[] = { TEXT ("Child1"), TEXT ("Child2"),
                                       TEXT ("Child3"), TEXT ("Child4") } ;
     static WNDPROC ChildProc[] = { WndProc1, WndProc2, WndProc3, WndProc4 } ;
     HINSTANCE      hInstance ;
     int            i, cxClient, cyClient ;
     WNDCLASS       wndclass ;

     switch (message)
     {
     case WM_CREATE:
          hInstance = (HINSTANCE) GetWindowLong (hwnd, GWL_HINSTANCE) ;

          wndclass.style         = CS_HREDRAW | CS_VREDRAW ;
          wndclass.cbClsExtra     = 0 ;
          wndclass.cbWndExtra     = 0 ;
          wndclass.hInstance      = hInstance ;
          wndclass.hIcon          = NULL ;
          wndclass.hCursor        = LoadCursor (NULL, IDC_ARROW) ;
          wndclass.hbrBackground = (HBRUSH) GetStockObject (WHITE_BRUSH) ;
          wndclass.lpszMenuName  = NULL ;

          for (i = 0 ; i < 4 ; i++)
          {
               wndclass.lpfnWndProc    = ChildProc[i] ;
               wndclass.lpszClassName = szChildClass[i] ;

               RegisterClass (&wndclass) ;

               hwndChild[i] = CreateWindow (szChildClass[i], NULL,
                               WS_CHILDWINDOW | WS_BORDER | WS_VISIBLE,
                               0, 0, 0, 0,
                               hwnd, (HMENU) i, hInstance, NULL) ;
          }

          cyChar = HIWORD (GetDialogBaseUnits ()) ;
```

```
            SetTimer (hwnd, 1, 10, NULL) ;
            return 0 ;

    case WM_SIZE:
            cxClient = LOWORD (lParam) ;
            cyClient = HIWORD (lParam) ;

            for (i = 0 ; i < 4 ; i++)
                    MoveWindow (hwndChild[i], (i % 2) * cxClient / 2,
                                               (i > 1) * cyClient / 2,
                            cxClient / 2, cyClient / 2, TRUE) ;
            return 0 ;

    case WM_TIMER:
            for (i = 0 ; i < 4 ; i++)
                    SendMessage (hwndChild[i], WM_TIMER, wParam, lParam) ;

            return 0 ;

    case WM_CHAR:
            if (wParam == '\x1B')
                    DestroyWindow (hwnd) ;

            return 0 ;

    case WM_DESTROY:
            KillTimer (hwnd, 1) ;
            PostQuitMessage (0) ;
            return 0 ;
    }
    return DefWindowProc (hwnd, message, wParam, lParam) ;
}
```

This program presents nothing we haven't really seen before. The main window creates four child windows, each of which occupies one-quarter of the client area. The main window also sets a Windows timer and sends WM_TIMER messages to each of the four child windows.

Normally, a Windows program should maintain enough information to re-create the contents of its window during the WM_PAINT message. MULTI1 doesn't do this, but the windows are drawn and erased so rapidly that I didn't think it necessary.

The prime number generator in *WndProc2* isn't terribly efficient, but it works. A number is prime if it has no divisors except 1 and itself. To check if a particular number is prime, however, doesn't require dividing by all numbers and checking for remainders up to that number being checked, but only up to the square root of that number. That square root calculation is the reason for the unusual introduction of floating-point math in an otherwise all integer-based program.

There is nothing really wrong with the MULTI1 program. Using the Windows timer is a fine way to simulate multitasking in earlier (and current) versions of Windows. However, the use of the timer sometimes restricts the speed of a program. If the program can update all its windows within a single WM_TIMER message with time to spare, then it's not taking full advantage of the machine.

One possible solution is to perform two or more updates during a single WM_TIMER message. But how many? That would have to depend on the speed of the machine, and that is a major variable. One would not want to write a program tuned to a 25-MHz 386 or a 50-MHz 486 or a 100-GHz Pentium VII.

The Multithreaded Solution

Let's take a look at a multithreaded solution to this programming problem. The MULTI2 program is shown in Figure 20-3.

MULTI2.C

```
/*-------------------------------------------
   MULTI2.C -- Multitasking Demo
               (c) Charles Petzold, 1998
   -------------------------------------------*/

#include <windows.h>
#include <math.h>
#include <process.h>

typedef struct
{
    HWND hwnd ;
    int  cxClient ;
    int  cyClient ;
    int  cyChar ;
    BOOL bKill ;
}
PARAMS, *PPARAMS ;

LRESULT APIENTRY WndProc (HWND, UINT, WPARAM, LPARAM) ;

int WINAPI WinMain (HINSTANCE hInstance, HINSTANCE hPrevInstance,
                    PSTR szCmdLine, int iCmdShow)
{
```

Figure 20-3. *The MULTI2 program.*

```
    static TCHAR szAppName[] = TEXT ("Multi2") ;
    HWND        hwnd ;
    MSG         msg ;
    WNDCLASS    wndclass ;

    wndclass.style         = CS_HREDRAW | CS_VREDRAW ;
    wndclass.lpfnWndProc   = WndProc ;
    wndclass.cbClsExtra    = 0 ;
    wndclass.cbWndExtra    = 0 ;
    wndclass.hInstance     = hInstance ;
    wndclass.hIcon         = LoadIcon (NULL, IDI_APPLICATION) ;
    wndclass.hCursor       = LoadCursor (NULL, IDC_ARROW) ;
    wndclass.hbrBackground = (HBRUSH) GetStockObject (WHITE_BRUSH) ;
    wndclass.lpszMenuName  = NULL ;
    wndclass.lpszClassName = szAppName ;

    if (!RegisterClass (&wndclass))
    {
         MessageBox (NULL, TEXT ("This program requires Windows NT!"),
                    szAppName, MB_ICONERROR) ;
         return 0 ;
    }

    hwnd = CreateWindow (szAppName, TEXT ("Multitasking Demo"),
                    WS_OVERLAPPEDWINDOW,
                    CW_USEDEFAULT, CW_USEDEFAULT,
                    CW_USEDEFAULT, CW_USEDEFAULT,
                    NULL, NULL, hInstance, NULL) ;

    ShowWindow (hwnd, iCmdShow) ;
    UpdateWindow (hwnd) ;

    while (GetMessage (&msg, NULL, 0, 0))
    {
         TranslateMessage (&msg) ;
         DispatchMessage (&msg) ;
    }
    return msg.wParam ;
}

int CheckBottom (HWND hwnd, int cyClient, int cyChar, int iLine)
{
    if (iLine * cyChar + cyChar > cyClient)
    {
```

(continued)

Figure 20-3. *continued*

```
            InvalidateRect (hwnd, NULL, TRUE) ;
            UpdateWindow (hwnd) ;
            iLine = 0 ;
        }
     return iLine ;
}


// -------------------------------------------------
// Window 1: Display increasing sequence of numbers
// -------------------------------------------------

void Thread1 (PVOID pvoid)
{
     HDC       hdc ;
     int       iNum = 0, iLine = 0 ;
     PPARAMS pparams ;
     TCHAR     szBuffer[16] ;

     pparams = (PPARAMS) pvoid ;

     while (!pparams->bKill)
     {
          if (iNum < 0)
              iNum = 0 ;

          iLine = CheckBottom (pparams->hwnd,   pparams->cyClient,
                               pparams->cyChar, iLine) ;

          hdc = GetDC (pparams->hwnd) ;

          TextOut (hdc, 0, iLine * pparams->cyChar, szBuffer,
                  wsprintf (szBuffer, TEXT ("%d"), iNum++)) ;

          ReleaseDC (pparams->hwnd, hdc) ;
          iLine++ ;
     }
     _endthread () ;
}

LRESULT APIENTRY WndProc1 (HWND hwnd, UINT message, WPARAM wParam, LPARAM lParam)
{
     static PARAMS params ;

     switch (message)
     {
```

```
    case WM_CREATE:
         params.hwnd = hwnd ;
         params.cyChar = HIWORD (GetDialogBaseUnits ()) ;
         _beginthread (Thread1, 0, &params) ;
         return 0 ;

    case WM_SIZE:
         params.cyClient = HIWORD (lParam) ;
         return 0 ;

    case WM_DESTROY:
         params.bKill = TRUE ;
         return 0 ;
    }
    return DefWindowProc (hwnd, message, wParam, lParam) ;
}


// ---------------------------------------------------------
// Window 2: Display increasing sequence of prime numbers
// ---------------------------------------------------------

void Thread2 (PVOID pvoid)
{
    HDC     hdc ;
    int     iNum = 1, iLine = 0, i, iSqrt ;
    PPARAMS pparams ;
    TCHAR   szBuffer[16] ;

    pparams = (PPARAMS) pvoid ;

    while (!pparams->bKill)
    {
         do
         {
              if (++iNum < 0)
                  iNum = 0 ;

              iSqrt = (int) sqrt (iNum) ;

              for (i = 2 ; i <= iSqrt ; i++)
                  if (iNum % i == 0)
                       break ;
         }
         while (i <= iSqrt) ;
```

(continued)

Figure 20-3. *continued*

```
        iLine = CheckBottom (pparams->hwnd,    pparams->cyClient,
                             pparams->cyChar, iLine) ;

        hdc = GetDC (pparams->hwnd) ;

        TextOut (hdc, 0, iLine * pparams->cyChar, szBuffer,
                 wsprintf (szBuffer, TEXT ("%d"), iNum)) ;

        ReleaseDC (pparams->hwnd, hdc) ;
        iLine++ ;
    }
    _endthread () ;
}

LRESULT APIENTRY WndProc2 (HWND hwnd, UINT message, WPARAM wParam, LPARAM lParam)
{
    static PARAMS params ;

    switch (message)
    {
    case WM_CREATE:
        params.hwnd = hwnd ;
        params.cyChar = HIWORD (GetDialogBaseUnits ()) ;
        _beginthread (Thread2, 0, &params) ;
        return 0 ;

    case WM_SIZE:
        params.cyClient = HIWORD (lParam) ;
        return 0 ;

    case WM_DESTROY:
        params.bKill = TRUE ;
        return 0 ;
    }
    return DefWindowProc (hwnd, message, wParam, lParam) ;
}

// Window 3: Display increasing sequence of Fibonacci numbers
// -------------------------------------------------------------

void Thread3 (PVOID pvoid)
{
```

```
     HDC      hdc ;
     int      iNum = 0, iNext = 1, iLine = 0, iTemp ;
     PPARAMS pparams ;
     TCHAR    szBuffer[16] ;

     pparams = (PPARAMS) pvoid ;

     while (!pparams->bKill)
     {
          if (iNum < 0)
          {
               iNum  = 0 ;
               iNext = 1 ;
          }
          iLine = CheckBottom (pparams->hwnd,   pparams->cyClient,
                               pparams->cyChar, iLine) ;

          hdc = GetDC (pparams->hwnd) ;

          TextOut (hdc, 0, iLine * pparams->cyChar, szBuffer,
                   wsprintf (szBuffer, TEXT ("%d"), iNum)) ;

          ReleaseDC (pparams->hwnd, hdc) ;
          iTemp  = iNum ;
          iNum   = iNext ;
          iNext += iTemp ;
          iLine++ ;
     }
     _endthread () ;
}

LRESULT APIENTRY WndProc3 (HWND hwnd, UINT message, WPARAM wParam, LPARAM lParam)
{
     static PARAMS params ;

     switch (message)
     {
     case WM_CREATE:
          params.hwnd = hwnd ;
          params.cyChar = HIWORD (GetDialogBaseUnits ()) ;
          _beginthread (Thread3, 0, &params) ;
          return 0 ;
```

(continued)

Figure 20-3. *continued*

```
      case WM_SIZE:
           params.cyClient = HIWORD (lParam) ;
           return 0 ;

      case WM_DESTROY:
           params.bKill = TRUE ;
           return 0 ;
      }
      return DefWindowProc (hwnd, message, wParam, lParam) ;
}

// -----------------------------------------
// Window 4: Display circles of random radii
// -----------------------------------------

void Thread4 (PVOID pvoid)
{
      HDC      hdc ;
      int      iDiameter ;
      PPARAMS pparams ;

      pparams = (PPARAMS) pvoid ;

      while (!pparams->bKill)
      {
           InvalidateRect (pparams->hwnd, NULL, TRUE) ;
           UpdateWindow (pparams->hwnd) ;

           iDiameter = rand() % (max (1,
                                 min (pparams->cxClient, pparams->cyClient))) ;

           hdc = GetDC (pparams->hwnd) ;

           Ellipse (hdc, (pparams->cxClient - iDiameter) / 2,
                         (pparams->cyClient - iDiameter) / 2,
                         (pparams->cxClient + iDiameter) / 2,
                         (pparams->cyClient + iDiameter) / 2) ;

           ReleaseDC (pparams->hwnd, hdc) ;
      }
      _endthread () ;
}
```

```
LRESULT APIENTRY WndProc4 (HWND hwnd, UINT message, WPARAM wParam, LPARAM lParam)
{
     static PARAMS params ;

     switch (message)
     {
     case WM_CREATE:
          params.hwnd = hwnd ;
          params.cyChar = HIWORD (GetDialogBaseUnits ()) ;
          _beginthread (Thread4, 0, &params) ;
          return 0 ;

     case WM_SIZE:
          params.cxClient = LOWORD (lParam) ;
          params.cyClient = HIWORD (lParam) ;
          return 0 ;

     case WM_DESTROY:
          params.bKill = TRUE ;
          return 0 ;
     }
     return DefWindowProc (hwnd, message, wParam, lParam) ;
}


// -----------------------------------
// Main window to create child windows
// -----------------------------------

LRESULT APIENTRY WndProc (HWND hwnd, UINT message, WPARAM wParam, LPARAM lParam)
{
     static HWND     hwndChild[4] ;
     static TCHAR * szChildClass[] = { TEXT ("Child1"), TEXT ("Child2"),
                                       TEXT ("Child3"), TEXT ("Child4") } ;
     static WNDPROC ChildProc[] = { WndProc1, WndProc2, WndProc3, WndProc4 } ;
     HINSTANCE       hInstance ;
     int             i, cxClient, cyClient ;
     WNDCLASS        wndclass ;

     switch (message)
     {
     case WM_CREATE:
          hInstance = (HINSTANCE) GetWindowLong (hwnd, GWL_HINSTANCE) ;
```

(continued)

Figure 20-3. *continued*

```
        wndclass.style        = CS_HREDRAW | CS_VREDRAW ;
        wndclass.cbClsExtra    = 0 ;
        wndclass.cbWndExtra    = 0 ;
        wndclass.hInstance     = hInstance ;
        wndclass.hIcon         = NULL ;
        wndclass.hCursor       = LoadCursor (NULL, IDC_ARROW) ;
        wndclass.hbrBackground = (HBRUSH) GetStockObject (WHITE_BRUSH) ;
        wndclass.lpszMenuName  = NULL ;

        for (i = 0 ; i < 4 ; i++)
        {
             wndclass.lpfnWndProc   = ChildProc[i] ;
             wndclass.lpszClassName = szChildClass[i] ;

             RegisterClass (&wndclass) ;

             hwndChild[i] = CreateWindow (szChildClass[i], NULL,
                              WS_CHILDWINDOW | WS_BORDER | WS_VISIBLE,
                              0, 0, 0, 0,
                              hwnd, (HMENU) i, hInstance, NULL) ;
        }

        return 0 ;

   case WM_SIZE:
        cxClient = LOWORD (lParam) ;
        cyClient = HIWORD (lParam) ;

        for (i = 0 ; i < 4 ; i++)
             MoveWindow (hwndChild[i], (i % 2) * cxClient / 2,
                                       (i > 1) * cyClient / 2,
                          cxClient / 2, cyClient / 2, TRUE) ;
        return 0 ;

   case WM_CHAR:
        if (wParam == '\x1B')
             DestroyWindow (hwnd) ;

        return 0 ;

   case WM_DESTROY:
        PostQuitMessage (0) ;
        return 0 ;
   }
   return DefWindowProc (hwnd, message, wParam, lParam) ;
}
```

The *WinMain* function and *WndProc* functions of MULTI2.C are very similar to those in MULTI1.C. *WndProc* registers four window classes for the four windows, creates those windows, and resizes them during the WM_SIZE message. The only difference in *WndProc* is that it no longer sets the Windows timer or processes WM_TIMER messages.

The big difference in MULTI2 is that each of the child window procedures creates another thread of execution by calling the *_beginthread* function during the WM_CREATE message. In total, the MULTI2 program has five threads of execution that run concurrently. The main thread contains the main window procedure and the four child window procedures. The other four threads use the functions named *Thread1*, *Thread2*, and so forth. These other four threads are responsible for drawing the four windows.

The multithreaded code I showed in the RNDRCTMT program did not use the third argument to *_beginthread*. This argument allows a thread that creates another thread to pass information to the other thread in a 32-bit variable. Customarily, this variable is a pointer, and also customarily, it is a pointer to a structure. This allows the creating thread and the new thread to share information without the use of global variables. As you can see, there are no global variables in MULTI2.

For the MULTI2 program, I defined a structure named PARAMS near the top of the program and a pointer to that structure named PPARAMS. This structure has five fields—a window handle, the width and height of the window, the height of a character, and a Boolean variable named *bKill*. This final structure field allows the creating thread to inform the created thread when it's time to terminate itself.

Let's take a look at *WndProc1*, the child window procedure that displays the sequence of increasing numbers. The window procedure has become quite simple. The only local variable is a PARAMS structure. During the WM_CREATE message, it sets the *hwnd* and *cyChar* fields of this structure and calls *_beginthread* to create a new thread using the *Thread1* function, passing to it a pointer to this structure. During the WM_SIZE message, *WndProc1* sets the *cyClient* field of the structure, and during the WM_DESTROY message, it sets the *bKill* field to TRUE. The *Thread1* function concludes by calling *_endthread*. This is not strictly necessary because the thread is destroyed after exiting the thread function. However, *_endthread* is useful for exiting a thread deep within some complex levels of processing.

The *Thread1* function does the actual drawing on the window, and it runs concurrently with the other four threads of the program. The function receives a pointer to the PARAMS structure and runs in a *while* loop, checking each time through the loop whether the *bKill* field is TRUE or FALSE. If FALSE, the function essentially performs the same processing as during the WM_TIMER message in MULTI1.C—formatting the number, obtaining a device context handle, and displaying the number using *TextOut*.

As you'll see when you run MULTI2 under Windows 98, the windows are updated much faster than in MULTI1, indicating the program is using the power of the processor more efficiently. There's another difference between MULTI1 and MULTI2: Usually when you move or size a window, the default window procedure enters a modal loop and all output to the window stops. In MULTI2, the output continues.

Any Problems?

It may seem as if MULTI2 is not as bulletproof as it could be. To see what I'm getting at, let's look at some examples of multithreaded "flaws" in MULTI2.C, using *WndProc1* and *Thread1* as an example.

WndProc1 runs in the main thread of MULTI2, and *Thread1* runs concurrently with it. The times at which Windows 98 switches between these two threads are variable and unpredictable. Suppose *Thread1* is running and has just executed the code that checks whether the *bKill* field of the PARAMS structure is TRUE. It's not, but then Windows 98 switches control to the main thread, at which time the user terminates the program. *WndProc1* receives a WM_DESTROY message and sets the *bKill* parameter to TRUE. Oops! Too late! Suddenly the operating system switches to *Thread1*, and that function attempts to obtain a device context handle to a nonexistent window.

It turns out this is not a problem. Windows 98 itself is sufficiently bulletproof that the graphics functions simply fail without causing any problems.

Proper multithreaded programming techniques involve the use of thread synchronization (and, in particular, critical sections), which I'll discuss in more detail shortly. Basically, critical sections are delimited by calls to *EnterCriticalSection* and *LeaveCriticalSection*. If one thread enters a critical section, another thread cannot enter a critical section. The latter thread is blocked on the *EnterCriticalSection* call until the first thread calls *Leave-CriticalSection*.

Another possible problem in MULTI2 is that the main thread could receive a WM_ERASEBKGND or WM_PAINT message during the time that a secondary thread is drawing its output. Again, using a critical section would help prevent any problems that could result from two threads attempting to draw on the same window. But experimentation seems to show that Windows 98 properly serializes access to the graphics drawing functions. That is, one thread can't draw on a window while another thread is in the middle of doing so.

The Windows 98 documentation warns about one area where graphics functions are not serialized, and that involves the use of GDI objects, such as pens, brushes, fonts, bitmaps, regions, and palettes. It is possible for one thread to destroy an object that another thread is using. The solution to this problem requires use of a critical section or, better yet, not sharing GDI objects between threads.

The Benefits of Sleep

I've discussed what I consider to be the best architecture of a multithreaded program, which is that the primary thread creates all the program's windows, contains all the window procedures for these windows, and processes all messages to the windows. Secondary threads carry out background jobs or lengthy jobs.

However, suppose you want to do animation in a secondary thread. Normally, animation in Windows is done with WM_TIMER messages. But if a secondary thread does not create a window, it cannot receive these messages. Without any timing, the animation would probably run much too fast.

The solution is the *Sleep* function. In effect, a thread calls the *Sleep* function to suspend itself voluntarily. The single argument is a time in milliseconds. The *Sleep* function call does not return until the specified time has elapsed. During that time, the thread is suspended and is allocated no time slices (although obviously the thread still requires a small amount of processing time during timer ticks when the system must determine whether the thread should be resumed). An argument of 0 to the *Sleep* function causes the thread to forfeit the remainder of its time slice.

When a thread calls *Sleep*, only that thread is suspended for the specified amount of time. The system still runs other threads, either in the same process or another process. I used the *Sleep* function in the SCRAMBLE program in Chapter 14 to slow down the scrambling operation.

Normally, you should not use the *Sleep* function in your primary thread because it slows down message processing; because SCRAMBLE did not create any windows, there is no problem using it there.

THREAD SYNCHRONIZATION

About once a year, the traffic lights at the busy intersection outside my apartment window stop working. The result is chaos, and while the cars usually avoid actually hitting each other, they often come close.

We might term the intersection of two roads a "critical section." A southbound car and a westbound car cannot pass through an intersection at the same time without hitting each other. Depending on the traffic volume, different approaches are taken to solve the problem. For light traffic at an intersection with high visibility, drivers can be trusted to properly yield. More traffic might require a stop sign, and still heavier traffic would require traffic lights. The traffic lights help coordinate the activity of the intersection (as long as they work, of course).

The Critical Section

In a single-tasking operating system, traditional computer programs don't need traffic lights to help them coordinate their activities. They run as if they owned the road, which they do. There is nothing to interfere with what they do.

Even in a multitasking operating system, most programs seemingly run independently of each other. But some problems can arise. For example, two programs could need to read from and write to the same file at the same time. In such cases, the operating system provides a mechanism of shared files and record locking to help out.

However, in an operating system that supports multithreading, the situation gets messy and potentially dangerous. It is not uncommon for two or more threads to share some data.

For example, one thread could update one or more variables and another thread could use those variables. Sometimes this poses a problem, and sometimes it doesn't. (Keep in mind that the operating system can switch control from one thread to another between machine code instructions only. If only a single integer is being shared among the threads, then changes to this variable usually occur in a single instruction and potential problems are minimized.)

However, suppose that the threads share several variables or a data structure. Often, these multiple variables or the fields of the structure must be consistent among themselves. The operating system could interrupt a thread in the middle of updating these variables. The thread that uses these variables would then be dealing with inconsistent data.

The result is a collision, and it's not difficult to imagine how an error like this could crash the program. What we need are the programming equivalents of traffic lights to help coordinate and synchronize the thread traffic. That's the critical section. Basically, a critical section is a block of code that should not be interrupted.

There are four functions for using critical sections. To use these functions, you must define a critical section object, which is global variable of type CRITICAL_SECTION. For example,

```
CRITICAL_SECTION cs ;
```

This CRITICAL_SECTION data type is a structure, but the fields are used only internally to Windows. This critical section object must first be initialized by one of the threads in the program by calling

```
InitializeCriticalSection (&cs) ;
```

This creates a critical section object named *cs*. The online documentation for this function includes the following warnings: "A critical section object cannot be moved or copied. The process must also not modify the object, but must treat it as logically opaque." This can be translated as "Don't mess around with it, and don't even look at it."

After the critical section object has been initialized, a thread enters a critical section by calling

```
EnterCriticalSection (&cs) ;
```

At this point, the thread is said to "own" the critical section object. No two threads can own the critical section object at the same time. Thus, if another thread has entered a critical section, the next thread calling *EnterCriticalSection* with the same critical section object will be suspended in the function call. The function will return only when the first thread leaves the critical section by calling

```
LeaveCriticalSection (&cs) ;
```

At that time, the second thread—suspended in its call to *EnterCriticalSection*—will own the critical section and the function call will return, allowing the thread to proceed.

When the critical section object is no longer needed by the program, it can be deleted by calling

```
DeleteCriticalSection (&cs) ;
```

This frees up any system resources that might have been allocated to maintain the critical section object.

This critical section mechanism involves "mutual exclusion," a term that will come up again as we continue to explore thread synchronization. Only one thread can own a critical section at any time. Thus, one thread can enter a critical section, set the fields of a structure, and exit the critical section. Another thread using the structure would also enter a critical section before accessing the fields of the structure and then exit the critical section.

Note that you can define multiple critical section objects—for example, *cs1* and *cs2*. If a program has four threads and the first two threads share some data, they can use one critical section object, and if the other two threads share some other data, they can use a second critical section object.

Also note that you should be careful when using a critical section in your main thread. If the secondary thread spends a long time in its own critical section, it could hang the main thread for an inordinate amount of time. The secondary thread would probably just want to use the critical section to copy the fields of the structure to its own local variables.

One limitation with critical sections is that they can be used for coordinating threads within a single process only. But there are cases where you need to coordinate two different processes that share a resource (such as shared memory). You can't use critical sections for that; instead, you must use something oddly called a "mutex object." The fabricated word "mutex" stands for "mutual exclusion," and that's precisely the goal here. You want to prevent threads of a program from being interrupted while updating or using some shared memory or other resources.

EVENT SIGNALING

The most common use of multiple threads of execution is for programs that find they must carry out some lengthy processing. We can call this a "big job," which is anything a program has to do that might violate the $\frac{1}{10}$-second rule. Obvious big jobs include a spelling check in a word processing program, a file sort or indexing in a database program, a spreadsheet recalculation, printing, and even complex drawing. Of course, as we know by now, the best solution to following the $\frac{1}{10}$-second rule is to farm out big jobs to secondary threads of execution. These secondary threads do not create windows, and hence they are not bound by the $\frac{1}{10}$-second rule.

It is often desirable for the secondary threads to inform the primary thread when they have completed, or for the primary thread to abort the job the secondary thread is doing. That's what we'll examine next.

The BIGJOB1 Program

I'll use a series of floating-point calculations, sometimes known as the "savage" benchmark, as a hypothetical big job. This calculation increments an integer in a roundabout manner: it squares a number and takes the square root (which cancels out the square), applies the *log* and *exp* functions (which also cancel each other out), applies the *atan* and *tan* functions (another canceling out), and finally adds 1 to the result.

The BIGJOB1 program is shown in Figure 20-4.

BIGJOB1.C

```c
/*---------------------------------------
   BIGJOB1.C -- Multithreading Demo
               (c) Charles Petzold, 1998
  ---------------------------------------*/

#include <windows.h>
#include <math.h>
#include <process.h>

#define REP              1000000

#define STATUS_READY     0
#define STATUS_WORKING   1
#define STATUS_DONE      2

#define WM_CALC_DONE     (WM_USER + 0)
#define WM_CALC_ABORTED  (WM_USER + 1)

typedef struct
{
     HWND hwnd ;
     BOOL bContinue ;
}
PARAMS, *PPARAMS ;

LRESULT APIENTRY WndProc (HWND, UINT, WPARAM, LPARAM) ;

int WINAPI WinMain (HINSTANCE hInstance, HINSTANCE hPrevInstance,
                    PSTR szCmdLine, int iCmdShow)
{
     static TCHAR szAppName[] = TEXT ("BigJob1") ;
     HWND         hwnd ;
     MSG          msg ;
     WNDCLASS     wndclass ;
```

Figure 20-4. *The BIGJOB1 program.*

```
    wndclass.style         = CS_HREDRAW | CS_VREDRAW ;
    wndclass.lpfnWndProc   = WndProc ;
    wndclass.cbClsExtra    = 0 ;
    wndclass.cbWndExtra    = 0 ;
    wndclass.hInstance     = hInstance ;
    wndclass.hIcon         = LoadIcon (NULL, IDI_APPLICATION) ;
    wndclass.hCursor       = LoadCursor (NULL, IDC_ARROW) ;
    wndclass.hbrBackground = (HBRUSH) GetStockObject (WHITE_BRUSH) ;
    wndclass.lpszMenuName  = NULL ;
    wndclass.lpszClassName = szAppName ;

    if (!RegisterClass (&wndclass))
    {
        MessageBox (NULL, TEXT ("This program requires Windows NT!"),
                    szAppName, MB_ICONERROR) ;
        return 0 ;
    }

    hwnd = CreateWindow (szAppName, TEXT ("Multithreading Demo"),
                        WS_OVERLAPPEDWINDOW,
                        CW_USEDEFAULT, CW_USEDEFAULT,
                        CW_USEDEFAULT, CW_USEDEFAULT,
                        NULL, NULL, hInstance, NULL) ;

    ShowWindow (hwnd, iCmdShow) ;
    UpdateWindow (hwnd) ;

    while (GetMessage (&msg, NULL, 0, 0))
    {
        TranslateMessage (&msg) ;
        DispatchMessage (&msg) ;
    }
    return msg.wParam ;
}

void Thread (PVOID pvoid)
{
    double   A = 1.0 ;
    INT      i ;
    LONG     lTime ;
    volatile PPARAMS pparams ;

    pparams = (PPARAMS) pvoid ;

    lTime = GetCurrentTime () ;
```

(continued)

Figure 20-4. *continued*

```
    for (i = 0 ; i < REP && pparams->bContinue ; i++)
        A = tan (atan (exp (log (sqrt (A * A))))) + 1.0 ;

    if (i == REP)
    {
        lTime = GetCurrentTime () - lTime ;
        SendMessage (pparams->hwnd, WM_CALC_DONE, 0, lTime) ;
    }
    else
        SendMessage (pparams->hwnd, WM_CALC_ABORTED, 0, 0) ;

    _endthread () ;
}

LRESULT CALLBACK WndProc (HWND hwnd, UINT message, WPARAM wParam, LPARAM lParam)
{
    static INT     iStatus ;
    static LONG    lTime ;
    static PARAMS  params ;
    static TCHAR * szMessage[] = { TEXT ("Ready (left mouse button begins)"),
                                   TEXT ("Working (right mouse button ends)"),
                                   TEXT ("%d repetitions in %ld msec") } ;
    HDC            hdc ;
    PAINTSTRUCT    ps ;
    RECT           rect ;
    TCHAR          szBuffer[64] ;

    switch (message)
    {
    case WM_LBUTTONDOWN:
        if (iStatus == STATUS_WORKING)
        {
            MessageBeep (0) ;
            return 0 ;
        }

        iStatus = STATUS_WORKING ;

        params.hwnd = hwnd ;
        params.bContinue = TRUE ;

        _beginthread (Thread, 0, &params) ;

        InvalidateRect (hwnd, NULL, TRUE) ;
        return 0 ;
```

```
    case WM_RBUTTONDOWN:
         params.bContinue = FALSE ;
         return 0 ;

    case WM_CALC_DONE:
         lTime = lParam ;
         iStatus = STATUS_DONE ;
         InvalidateRect (hwnd, NULL, TRUE) ;
         return 0 ;

    case WM_CALC_ABORTED:
         iStatus = STATUS_READY ;
         InvalidateRect (hwnd, NULL, TRUE) ;
         return 0 ;

    case WM_PAINT:
         hdc = BeginPaint (hwnd, &ps) ;

         GetClientRect (hwnd, &rect) ;

         wsprintf (szBuffer, szMessage[iStatus], REP, lTime) ;
         DrawText (hdc, szBuffer, -1, &rect,
                   DT_SINGLELINE | DT_CENTER | DT_VCENTER) ;

         EndPaint (hwnd, &ps) ;
         return 0 ;

    case WM_DESTROY:
         PostQuitMessage (0) ;
         return 0 ;
    }
    return DefWindowProc (hwnd, message, wParam, lParam) ;
}
```

This is a fairly simple program, but I think you'll see how it illustrates a generalized approach to doing big jobs in a multithreaded program. To use the BIGJOB1 program, click with the left mouse button on the client area of the window. This begins 1,000,000 repetitions of the savage calculation. It'll take about 2 seconds on a 300-MHz Pentium II machine. When the calculation has completed, the elapsed time is displayed in the window. While the calculation is in progress, you can click on the client area with the right mouse button to abort it.

So, let's take a look how this is done:

The window procedure maintains a static variable called *iStatus* (which can be set to one of three constants defined near the top of the program beginning with the prefix

STATUS), indicating whether the program is ready to do a calculation, working on a calculation, or done with a calculation. The program uses the *iStatus* variable during the WM_PAINT message to display an appropriate character string in the center of the client area.

The window procedure also maintains a static structure (of type PARAMS, also defined near the top of the program) to share data between the window procedure and the secondary thread. The structure has only two fields—*hwnd* (the handle of the program's window) and *bContinue*, which is a Boolean variable used to indicate to the thread whether to continue the calculation or not.

When you click on the client area with the left mouse button, the window procedure sets the *iStatus* variable to STATUS_WORKING and initializes the two fields of the PARAMS structure. The *hwnd* field of the structure is set to the window handle, of course, and *bContinue* is set to TRUE.

The window procedure then calls the *_beginthread* function. The secondary thread function, called *Thread*, begins by calling *GetCurrentTime* to get the elapsed time in milliseconds that Windows has been running. It then enters a *for* loop to do 1,000,000 repetitions of the savage calculation. Notice also that the thread will drop out of the loop if *bContinue* is ever set to FALSE.

After the *for* loop, the thread function checks if it's actually completed 1,000,000 calculations. If so, it calls *GetCurrentTime* again to get the elapsed time and then uses *SendMessage* to send the window procedure a program-defined WM_USER_DONE message with the elapsed time as *lParam*. If the calculation was aborted prematurely (that is, if the *bContinue* field of the PARAMS structure became FALSE during the loop), the thread sends the window procedure a WM_USER_ABORTED message. The thread then gracefully ends by calling *_endthread*.

Within the window procedure, the *bContinue* field of the PARAMS structure is set to FALSE when you click on the client area with the right mouse button. This is how the calculation is aborted before completion.

Notice that the *pparams* variable in *Thread* is defined as volatile. This type qualifier indicates to the compiler that a variable might be modified in some way other than actual program statements (such as by another thread). Otherwise, an optimizing compiler might assume that since *pparams->bContinue* couldn't possibly be modified by the code inside the *for* loop, it's not necessary for the variable to be checked following every iteration of the loop. The *volatile* keyword prevents such optimizations.

The window procedure processes the WM_USER_DONE message by first saving the elapsed time. Both the processing of the WM_USER_DONE and WM_USER_ABORTED messages continue with a call to *InvalidateRect* to generate a WM_PAINT message and display a new text string in the client area.

It's usually a good idea to include a provision, such as the *bContinue* field in the structure, to allow the thread to terminate gracefully. The *KillThread* function should be used only when graceful termination is awkward. The reason why is that threads can allocate resources, such as memory. If this memory is not freed when the thread terminates, it will still be allocated. Threads are not processes: allocated resources are shared among all threads in a process, so they are not automatically freed when the thread terminates. Good programming structure dictates that a thread should free any resources it allocates.

Note also that a third thread can be created while the second thread is still in progress. This could happen if Windows switches control from the second thread to the first thread between the *SendMessage* call and the *_endthread* call, and the window procedure then creates a new thread on response from a mouse click. This is not a problem here, but if it is a problem in one of your own applications, you'll want to use a critical section to avoid thread collisions.

The Event Object

BIGJOB1 creates a thread every time it needs to perform the savage calculation; the thread terminates after doing the calculation.

An alternative is to keep the thread around for the entire duration of the program and only kick it into action when necessary. This is an ideal application for an event object.

An event object is either "signaled" (also known as "set") or "unsignaled" (also known as "reset"). You create the event object by calling

```
hEvent = CreateEvent (&sa, fManual, fInitial, pszName) ;
```

The first parameter (a pointer to a SECURITY_ATTRIBUTES structure) and the last parameter (an event object name) are meaningful only when event objects are shared among processes. In a single process, these parameters are generally set to NULL. Set the *fInitial* parameter to TRUE if you want the event object to be initially signaled and to FALSE for initially unsignaled. I'll describe the *fManual* parameter shortly.

To signal an existing event object, call

```
SetEvent (hEvent) ;
```

To unsignal an event object, call

```
ResetEvent (hEvent) ;
```

A program generally calls

```
WaitForSingleObject (hEvent, dwTimeOut) ;
```

with the second parameter set to INFINITE. The function returns immediately if the event object is currently signaled (or set). Otherwise, the function will suspend the thread until the event object becomes signaled. You can set the second argument to a time-out value in milliseconds so that the function returns before the event object becomes signaled.

If the *fManual* parameter of the original *CreateEvent* call is set to FALSE, the event object becomes automatically unsignaled when the *WaitForSingleObject* function returns. This feature usually makes it unnecessary to use the *ResetEvent* function.

So, now we're equipped to look at BIGJOB2.C, shown in Figure 20-5.

BIGJOB2.C

```
/*-------------------------------------------
   BIGJOB2.C -- Multithreading Demo
                (c) Charles Petzold, 1998
   -------------------------------------------*/

#include <windows.h>
#include <math.h>
#include <process.h>

#define REP              1000000

#define STATUS_READY     0
#define STATUS_WORKING   1
#define STATUS_DONE      2

#define WM_CALC_DONE     (WM_USER + 0)
#define WM_CALC_ABORTED  (WM_USER + 1)

typedef struct
{
    HWND   hwnd ;
    HANDLE hEvent ;
    BOOL   bContinue ;
}
PARAMS, *PPARAMS ;

LRESULT CALLBACK WndProc (HWND, UINT, WPARAM, LPARAM) ;

int WINAPI WinMain (HINSTANCE hInstance, HINSTANCE hPrevInstance,
                    PSTR szCmdLine, int iCmdShow)
{
    static TCHAR szAppName[] = TEXT ("BigJob2") ;
    HWND        hwnd ;
    MSG         msg ;
    WNDCLASS    wndclass ;

    wndclass.style         = CS_HREDRAW | CS_VREDRAW ;
    wndclass.lpfnWndProc   = WndProc ;
    wndclass.cbClsExtra    = 0 ;
    wndclass.cbWndExtra    = 0 ;
    wndclass.hInstance     = hInstance ;
    wndclass.hIcon         = LoadIcon (NULL, IDI_APPLICATION) ;
    wndclass.hCursor       = LoadCursor (NULL, IDC_ARROW) ;
    wndclass.hbrBackground = (HBRUSH) GetStockObject (WHITE_BRUSH) ;
```

Figure 20-5. *The BIGJOB2 program.*

```
        wndclass.lpszMenuName  = NULL ;
        wndclass.lpszClassName = szAppName ;

        if (!RegisterClass (&wndclass))
        {
             MessageBox (NULL, TEXT ("This program requires Windows NT!"),
                         szAppName, MB_ICONERROR) ;
             return 0 ;
        }

        hwnd = CreateWindow (szAppName, TEXT ("Multithreading Demo"),
                            WS_OVERLAPPEDWINDOW,
                            CW_USEDEFAULT, CW_USEDEFAULT,
                            CW_USEDEFAULT, CW_USEDEFAULT,
                            NULL, NULL, hInstance, NULL) ;

        ShowWindow (hwnd, iCmdShow) ;
        UpdateWindow (hwnd) ;

        while (GetMessage (&msg, NULL, 0, 0))
        {
             TranslateMessage (&msg) ;
             DispatchMessage (&msg) ;
        }
        return msg.wParam ;
}

void Thread (PVOID pvoid)
{
        double   A = 1.0 ;
        INT      i ;
        LONG     lTime ;
        volatile PPARAMS pparams ;

        pparams = (PPARAMS) pvoid ;

        while (TRUE)
        {
             WaitForSingleObject (pparams->hEvent, INFINITE) ;

             lTime = GetCurrentTime () ;

             for (i = 0 ; i < REP && pparams->bContinue ; i++)
                  A = tan (atan (exp (log (sqrt (A * A))))) + 1.0 ;
```

(continued)

Figure 20-5. *continued*

```
          if (i == REP)
          {
              lTime = GetCurrentTime () - lTime ;

              PostMessage (pparams->hwnd, WM_CALC_DONE, 0, lTime) ;
          }
          else
              PostMessage (pparams->hwnd, WM_CALC_ABORTED, 0, 0) ;
     }
}

LRESULT CALLBACK WndProc (HWND hwnd, UINT message, WPARAM wParam, LPARAM lParam)
{
     static HANDLE  hEvent ;
     static INT     iStatus ;
     static LONG    lTime ;
     static PARAMS  params ;
     static TCHAR * szMessage[] = { TEXT ("Ready (left mouse button begins)"),
                                    TEXT ("Working (right mouse button ends)"),
                                    TEXT ("%d repetitions in %ld msec") } ;
     HDC            hdc ;
     PAINTSTRUCT    ps ;
     RECT           rect ;
     TCHAR          szBuffer[64] ;

     switch (message)
     {
     case WM_CREATE:
          hEvent = CreateEvent (NULL, FALSE, FALSE, NULL) ;

          params.hwnd = hwnd ;
          params.hEvent = hEvent ;
          params.bContinue = FALSE ;

          _beginthread (Thread, 0, &params) ;

          return 0 ;

     case WM_LBUTTONDOWN:
          if (iStatus == STATUS_WORKING)
          {
              MessageBeep (0) ;
              return 0 ;
          }
```

```
            iStatus = STATUS_WORKING ;
            params.bContinue = TRUE ;

            SetEvent (hEvent) ;

            InvalidateRect (hwnd, NULL, TRUE) ;
            return 0 ;

       case WM_RBUTTONDOWN:
            params.bContinue = FALSE ;
            return 0 ;

       case WM_CALC_DONE:
            lTime = lParam ;
            iStatus = STATUS_DONE ;
            InvalidateRect (hwnd, NULL, TRUE) ;
            return 0 ;

       case WM_CALC_ABORTED:
            iStatus = STATUS_READY ;
            InvalidateRect (hwnd, NULL, TRUE) ;
            return 0 ;

       case WM_PAINT:
            hdc = BeginPaint (hwnd, &ps) ;

            GetClientRect (hwnd, &rect) ;

            wsprintf (szBuffer, szMessage[iStatus], REP, lTime) ;
            DrawText (hdc, szBuffer, -1, &rect,
                     DT_SINGLELINE | DT_CENTER | DT_VCENTER) ;

            EndPaint (hwnd, &ps) ;
            return 0 ;

       case WM_DESTROY:
            PostQuitMessage (0) ;
            return 0 ;
       }
     return DefWindowProc (hwnd, message, wParam, lParam) ;
}
```

The window procedure processes the WM_CREATE message by first creating a non-manual event object that is initialized in the unsignaled (or reset) state. It then creates the thread.

The *Thread* function enters an infinite *while* loop but calls *WaitForSingleObject* at the beginning of the loop. (Notice that the PARAMS structure includes a third field containing the handle to the event object.) Because the event is initially unsignaled, the thread is suspended in the function call. A left mouse button click causes the window procedure to call *SetEvent*. This releases the second thread from the *WaitForSingleObject* call, and it begins the savage calculation. After finishing, the thread calls *WaitForSingleObject* again, but the event object has become unsignaled from the first call. Thus, the thread is suspended until the next mouse click.

Otherwise, the program is almost identical to BIGJOB1.

THREAD LOCAL STORAGE

Global variables in a multithreaded program, as well as any allocated memory, are shared among all the threads in the program. Local static variables in a function are also shared among all threads using that function. Local automatic variables in a function are unique to each thread because they are stored on the stack and each thread has its own stack.

It might be necessary to have persistent storage that is unique to each thread. For example, the C *strtok* function I mentioned earlier in this chapter requires this type of storage. Unfortunately, the C language does not support such a variable. But Windows includes four functions that implement a mechanism to do it, and the Microsoft extensions to C also support it. As we've seen, this is called thread local storage.

Here's how the APIs work:

First define a structure that contains all the data that needs to be unique among the threads. For example,

```
typedef struct
{
    int a ;
    int b ;
}
DATA, * PDATA ;
```

The primary thread calls *TlsAlloc* to obtain an index value:

```
dwTlsIndex = TlsAlloc () ;
```

This index value can be stored in a global variable or passed to the thread function in the parameter structure.

The thread function begins by allocating memory for the data structure and calling *TlsSetValue* using the index obtained above:

```
TlsSetValue (dwTlsIndex, GlobalAlloc (GPTR, sizeof (DATA)) ;
```

This associates a pointer with a particular thread and a particular thread index. Now any function that needs to use this pointer, including the original thread function itself, can include code like so:

```
PDATA pdata ;
...
pdata = (PDATA) TlsGetValue (dwTlsIndex) ;
```

Now it can set or use *pdata->a* and *pdata->b*. Before the thread function terminates, it frees the allocated memory:

```
GlobalFree (TlsGetValue (dwTlsIndex)) ;
```

When all the threads using this data have terminated, the primary thread frees the index:

```
TlsFree (dwTlsIndex) ;
```

This process might be confusing at first, so perhaps it might be helpful to see how thread local storage might be implemented. (I have no knowledge of how Windows actually does it, but the following is plausible.) First, *TlsAlloc* might simply allocate a block of memory (zero bytes in length) and return an index value that is a pointer to this block. Every time *TlsSetValue* is called with that index, the block of memory is increased by 8 bytes by reallocating it. Stored in these 8 bytes is the ID of the thread calling the function— obtained by calling *GetCurrentThreadId*—and the pointer passed to the *TlsSetValue* function. *TlsGetValue* simply uses the thread ID to search the table and then return the pointer. *TlsFree* frees up the block of memory. So, as you see, this is something you could probably easily implement yourself, but it's nice to have the facility already done for us.

A Microsoft extension to C makes this even more simple. Just preface any variable that needs to be different for each thread with *__declspec (thread)*, like so

```
__declspec (thread) int iGlobal = 1 ;
```

for static variables external to any function, or like so

```
__declspec (thread) static int iLocal = 2 ;
```

for static variables within functions.

Chapter 21

Dynamic-Link Libraries

Dynamic-link libraries (also called DLLs, dynamic libraries, "dynalink" libraries, or library modules) are one of the most important structural elements of Microsoft Windows. Most of the disk files associated with Windows are either program modules or dynamic-link library modules. So far we've been writing Windows programs; now it's time to take a stab at writing dynamic-link libraries. Many of the principles you've learned in writing programs are also applicable to writing these libraries, but there are some important differences.

LIBRARY BASICS

As you've seen, a Windows program is an executable file that generally creates one or more windows and uses a message loop to receive user input. Dynamic-link libraries are generally not directly executable, and they generally do not receive messages. They are separate files containing functions that can be called by programs and other DLLs to perform certain jobs. A dynamic-link library is brought into action only when another module calls one of the functions in the library.

The term "dynamic linking" refers to the process that Windows uses to link a function call in one module to the actual function in the library module. "Static linking" occurs during program development when you link various object (.OBJ) modules, run-time library (.LIB) files, and usually a compiled resource (.RES) file to create a Windows .EXE file. Dynamic linking instead occurs at run time.

KERNEL32.DLL, USER32.DLL, and GDI32.DLL; the various driver files such as KEY-BOARD.DRV, SYSTEM.DRV, and MOUSE.DRV; and the video and printer drivers are all dynamic-link libraries. These are libraries that all Windows programs can use.

Some dynamic-link libraries (such as font files) are termed "resource-only." They contain only data (usually in the form of resources) and no code. Thus, one purpose of dynamic-link libraries is to provide functions and resources that can be used by many different programs. In a conventional operating system, only the operating system itself contains routines that other programs can call on to do a job. In Windows, the process of one module calling a function in another module is generalized. In effect, by writing a dynamic-link library, you are writing an extension to Windows. Or you can think of DLLs, including those that make up Windows, as extensions to your program.

Although a dynamic-link library module can have any extension (such as .EXE or .FON), the standard extension is .DLL. Only dynamic-link libraries with the extension .DLL will be loaded automatically by Windows. If the file has another extension, the program must explicitly load the module by using the *LoadLibrary* or *LoadLibraryEx* function.

You'll generally find that dynamic libraries make most sense in the context of a large application. For instance, suppose you write a large accounting package for Windows that consists of several different programs. You'll probably find that these programs use many common routines. You could put these common routines in a normal object library (with the extension .LIB) and add them to each of the program modules during static linking with LINK. But this approach is wasteful, because each of the programs in this package contains identical code for the common routines. Moreover, if you change one of the routines in this library, you'll have to relink all the programs that use the changed routine. If, however, you put these common routines in a dynamic-link library called, for instance, ACCOUNT.DLL, you've solved both problems. Only the library module need contain the routines required by all the programs, thus requiring less disk space for the files and less memory space when running two or more of the applications simultaneously, and you can make changes to the library module without relinking any of the individual programs.

Dynamic-link libraries can themselves be viable products. For instance, suppose you write a collection of three-dimensional drawing routines and put them in a DLL called GDI3.DLL. If you then interest other software developers in using your library, you can license it to be included with their graphics programs. A user who has several of these programs would need only one GDI3.DLL file.

Library: One Word, Many Meanings

Part of the confusion surrounding dynamic-link libraries results from the appearance of the word "library" in several different contexts. Besides dynamic-link libraries, we'll also be talking about "object libraries" and "import libraries."

An object library is a file with the extension .LIB containing code that is added to your program's .EXE file in the process called static linking when you run the linker. For example, in Microsoft Visual C++, the normal C run-time object library that you link with your program is called LIBC.LIB.

An import library is a special form of an object library file. Like object libraries, import libraries have the extension .LIB and are used by the linker to resolve function calls in your source code. However, import libraries contain no code. Instead, they provide the linker with information necessary to set up relocation tables within the .EXE file for dynamic linking. The KERNEL32.LIB, USER32.LIB, and GDI32.LIB files included with the Microsoft compiler are import libraries for Windows functions. If you call the *Rectangle* function in a program, GDI32.LIB tells LINK that this function is in the GDI32.DLL dynamic-link library. This information goes into the .EXE file so that Windows can perform dynamic linking with the GDI32.DLL dynamic-link library when your program is executed.

Object libraries and import libraries are used only during program development. Dynamic-link libraries are used during run time. A dynamic library must be present on the disk when a program is run that uses the library. When Windows needs to load a DLL module before running a program that requires it, the library file must be stored in the directory containing the .EXE program, the current directory, the Windows system directory, the Windows directory, or a directory accessible through the PATH string in the MS-DOS environment. (The directories are searched in that order.)

A Simple DLL

Although the whole idea of dynamic-link libraries is that they can be used by multiple applications, generally you'll initially design a dynamic-link library in connection with just one application, perhaps a "test" program that puts the DLL through its paces.

That's what we'll do here. We'll create a DLL called EDRLIB.DLL. The "EDR" of this filename stands for "easy drawing routines." Our version of EDRLIB will contain only one function (named *EdrCenterText*), but you can add other functions to it that simplify the drawing functions in your applications. An application named EDRTEST.EXE will take advantage of EDRLIB.DLL by calling the function contained in it.

To do this requires an approach a little different than the one we've been taking, involving a feature of Visual C++ we haven't examined yet. Visual C++ differentiates between "workspaces" and "projects." A project is generally associated with the creation of an application file (.EXE) or a dynamic-link library (.DLL). A workspace can contain one or more projects. Until now, all our workspaces have contained just one project. We'll now create a workspace called EDRTEST that will contain two projects—one to create EDRTEST.EXE and the other to create EDRLIB.DLL, the dynamic-link library used by EDRTEST.

Let's begin. In Visual C++, select New from the File menu. Select the Workspaces tab. (We haven't selected this before.) Select the directory where you want the workspace to be in the Location field, and type EDRTEST in the Workspace Name field. Press Enter.

This creates an empty workspace. The Developer Studio will create a subdirectory named EDRTEST and the workspace file EDRTEST.DSW (as well as a couple of other files).

Now let's create a project in this workspace. Select New from the File menu, and select the Projects tab. Whereas in the past you've selected Win32 Application, this time select Win32 Dynamic-Link Library. Also, click the radio button Add To Current Workspace. That makes this project part of the EDRTEST workspace. Type EDRLIB in the Project Name field, but don't press OK just yet. As you type EDRLIB in the Project Name field, Visual C++ alters the Location field to show EDRLIB as a subdirectory of EDRTEST. You don't want this! In the Location field, remove the EDRLIB subdirectory so that the project is created in the EDRTEST directory. Now press OK. You'll get a dialog box asking what kind of DLL you'd like to create. Select An Empty DLL Project, and press Finish. Visual C++ will create a project file EDRLIB.DSP and (if you've selected the Export Makefile option on the Build tab of the Tools Options dialog box) a make file EDRLIB.MAK.

Now you're ready to add a couple of files to this project. From the File menu, select New and then the Files tab. Select C/C++ Header File, and type the filename EDRLIB.H. Type in the file shown in Figure 21-1 (or copy it from this book's CD-ROM). Select New from the File menu again, and then the Files tab. This time select C++ Source File, and type the filename EDRLIB.C. Again type the file shown in Figure 21-1.

EDRLIB.H

```
/*---------------------
   EDRLIB.H header file
   --------------------*/

#ifdef __cplusplus
#define EXPORT extern "C" __declspec (dllexport)
#else
#define EXPORT __declspec (dllexport)
#endif

EXPORT BOOL CALLBACK EdrCenterTextA (HDC, PRECT, PCSTR) ;
EXPORT BOOL CALLBACK EdrCenterTextW (HDC, PRECT, PCWSTR) ;

#ifdef UNICODE
#define EdrCenterText EdrCenterTextW
#else
#define EdrCenterText EdrCenterTextA
#endif
```

EDRLIB.C

```
/*------------------------------------------------------
   EDRLIB.C -- Easy Drawing Routine Library module
               (c) Charles Petzold, 1998
   ------------------------------------------------------*/
```

Figure 21-1. *The EDRLIB library.*

```
#include  windows.h>
#include "edrlib.h"

int WINAPI DllMain (HINSTANCE hInstance, DWORD fdwReason, PVOID pvReserved)
{
    return TRUE ;
}

EXPORT BOOL CALLBACK EdrCenterTextA (HDC hdc, PRECT prc, PCSTR pString)
{
    int  iLength ;
    SIZE size ;

    iLength = lstrlenA (pString) ;

    GetTextExtentPoint32A (hdc, pString, iLength, &size) ;

    return TextOutA (hdc, (prc->right - prc->left - size.cx) / 2,
                          (prc->bottom - prc->top - size.cy) / 2,
                     pString, iLength) ;
}

EXPORT BOOL CALLBACK EdrCenterTextW (HDC hdc, PRECT prc, PCWSTR pString)
{
    int  iLength ;
    SIZE size ;

    iLength = lstrlenW (pString) ;

    GetTextExtentPoint32W (hdc, pString, iLength, &size) ;

    return TextOutW (hdc, (prc->right - prc->left - size.cx) / 2,
                          (prc->bottom - prc->top - size.cy) / 2,
                     pString, iLength) ;
}
```

At this point you can build EDRLIB.DLL in either a Release or Debug configuration. After the build, the RELEASE and DEBUG directories will contain EDRLIB.LIB, which is the import library for the dynamic-link library, and EDRLIB.DLL, the dynamic-link library itself.

Throughout this book we've been creating programs that can be compiled for Unicode or non-Unicode character strings depending on the definition of the UNICODE identifier. When you create a DLL, it should include *both* Unicode and non-Unicode versions of any function that has arguments involving characters or character strings. Thus, EDRLIB.C contains functions named *EdrCenterTextA* (the ANSI version) and *EdrCenterTextW* (the wide-character version). *EdrCenterTextA* is defined as taking a PCSTR (pointer to *const* string) parameter and *EdrCenterTextW* is defined as take PCWSTR (pointer to *const* wide string) parameter. The *EdrCenterTextA* function explicitly calls *lstrlenA*, *GetTextExtentPoint-32A*, and *TextOutA*. *EdrCenterTextW* explicitly calls *lstrlenW*, *GetTextExtentPoint32W*, and

TextOutW. The EDRLIB.H file defines *EdrCenterText* to be *EdrCenterTextW* if the UNICODE identifier is defined and *EdrCenterTextA* if it's not. This is just like the Windows header files.

EDRLIB.H also includes a function named *DllMain*, which takes the place of *WinMain* in a DLL. This function is used to perform initialization and deinitialization, as I'll discuss in the next section. For our purposes, all we need do right now is return TRUE from *DllMain*.

The only remaining mystery in these two files should be the definition of the EXPORT identifier. Functions in a DLL that are used by an application must be "exported." This doesn't involve any tariffs or commerce regulations, just a few keywords that ensure that the function name is added to EDRLIB.LIB (so that the linker can resolve the function name when linking an application that uses the function) and that the function is visible from EDRLIB.DLL. The EXPORT identifier includes the storage-class specifier *__declspec (dllexport)* and also *extern "C"* if the header is being compiled in C++ mode. This prevents the compiler from doing the customary "name mangling" of C++ functions and thus allows the DLL to be used by both C and C++ programs.

The Library Entry and Exit Point

The *DllMain* function is called when the library first begins and when it terminates. The first parameter to *DllMain* is the instance handle of the library. If your library uses resources that require an instance handle (such as *DialogBox*), you should save *hInstance* as a global variable. The last parameter to *DllMain* is reserved by the system.

The *fdwReason* parameter can be one of four values that indicate why Windows is calling the *DllMain* function. In the following discussion, keep in mind that a single program can be loaded multiple times and run concurrently under Windows. Each time a program is loaded, it is considered a separate process.

A *fdwReason* value of DLL_PROCESS_ATTACH indicates that the dynamic-link library has been mapped into the address space of a process. This is a cue for the library to do any initialization tasks it requires to service subsequent requests from the process. Such initialization might include memory allocation, for example. During the time that a process is running, *DllMain* is called with a DLL_PROCESS_ATTACH parameter only once during the lifetime of that process. Any other process using the same DLL causes another call to *DllMain* with a DLL_PROCESS_ATTACH parameter, but that's on behalf of the new process.

If the initialization is successful, *DllMain* should return a nonzero value. Returning 0 will cause Windows to not run the program.

When *fdwReason* has a value of DLL_PROCESS_DETACH, it means that the DLL is no longer needed by the process. This provides an opportunity for the library to clean up after itself. Under the 32-bit versions of Windows often this is not strictly necessary, but it's a good programming practice.

Similarly, when *DllMain* is called with an *fdwReason* parameter of DLL_THREAD_ATTACH, it means that an attached process has created a new thread. When the thread terminates, Windows calls *DllMain* with an *fdwReason* parameter of DLL_THREAD_ DETACH. Be aware that it's possible to get a DLL_THREAD_DETACH call without an earlier DLL_THREAD_ATTACH call if the dynamic-link library is attached to a process after the thread has been created.

The thread still exists when *DllMain* is called with a parameter of DLL_THREAD_ DETACH. It can even send the thread messages during this process. But it shouldn't use *PostMessage* because the thread might be gone before the message is retrieved.

The Test Program

Now let's create a second project in the EDRTEST workspace, this one for a program named EDRTEST that will use EDRLIB.DLL. With the EDRTEST workspace loaded in Visual C++, select New from the File menu. Select the Projects tab in the New dialog box. This time select Win32 Application. Make sure the Add To Current Workspace button is checked. Type in the project name EDRTEST. Again, in the Locations field, erase the second EDRTEST subdirectory. Press OK, and select An Empty Project from the next dialog box. Press Finish.

From the File menu, select New again. Select the Files tab and C++ Source File. Make sure the Add To Project list box shows EDRTEST rather than EDRLIB. Type in the filename EDRTEST.C, and type in the file shown in Figure 21-2. This program uses the *EdrCenterText* function to center a text string in its client area.

EDRTEST.C

```
/*----------------------------------------------------------
   EDRTEST.C -- Program using EDRLIB dynamic-link library
                (c) Charles Petzold, 1998
   ----------------------------------------------------------*/

#include <windows.h>
#include "edrlib.h"

LRESULT CALLBACK WndProc (HWND, UINT, WPARAM, LPARAM) ;

int WINAPI WinMain (HINSTANCE hInstance, HINSTANCE hPrevInstance,
                    PSTR szCmdLine, int iCmdShow)
{
     static TCHAR szAppName[] = TEXT ("StrProg") ;
     HWND         hwnd ;
     MSG          msg ;
     WNDCLASS     wndclass ;

     wndclass.style         = CS_HREDRAW | CS_VREDRAW ;
     wndclass.lpfnWndProc   = WndProc ;
     wndclass.cbClsExtra    = 0 ;
```

Figure 21-2. *The EDRTEST program.*

(continued)

Figure 21-2. *continued*

```
        wndclass.cbWndExtra    = 0 ;
        wndclass.hInstance     = hInstance ;
        wndclass.hIcon         = LoadIcon (NULL, IDI_APPLICATION) ;
        wndclass.hCursor       = LoadCursor (NULL, IDC_ARROW) ;
        wndclass.hbrBackground = (HBRUSH) GetStockObject (WHITE_BRUSH) ;
        wndclass.lpszMenuName  = NULL ;
        wndclass.lpszClassName = szAppName ;

        if (!RegisterClass (&wndclass))
        {
             MessageBox (NULL, TEXT ("This program requires Windows NT!"),
                         szAppName, MB_ICONERROR) ;
             return 0 ;
        }

        hwnd = CreateWindow (szAppName, TEXT ("DLL Demonstration Program"),
                             WS_OVERLAPPEDWINDOW,
                             CW_USEDEFAULT, CW_USEDEFAULT,
                             CW_USEDEFAULT, CW_USEDEFAULT,
                             NULL, NULL, hInstance, NULL) ;

        ShowWindow (hwnd, iCmdShow) ;
        UpdateWindow (hwnd) ;

        while (GetMessage (&msg, NULL, 0, 0))
        {
             TranslateMessage (&msg) ;
             DispatchMessage (&msg) ;
        }
        return msg.wParam ;
}

LRESULT CALLBACK WndProc (HWND hwnd, UINT message, WPARAM wParam, LPARAM lParam)
{
     HDC         hdc ;
     PAINTSTRUCT ps ;
     RECT        rect ;

     switch (message)
     {
     case WM_PAINT:
          hdc = BeginPaint (hwnd, &ps) ;

          GetClientRect (hwnd, &rect) ;

          EdrCenterText (hdc, &rect,
                         TEXT ("This string was displayed by a DLL")) ;
```

```
        EndPaint (hwnd, &ps) ;
        return 0 ;

   case WM_DESTROY:
        PostQuitMessage (0) ;
        return 0 ;
   }
   return DefWindowProc (hwnd, message, wParam, lParam) ;
}
```

Notice that EDRTEST.C includes the EDRLIB.H header file for the definition of the *EdrCenterText* function, which it calls during the WM_PAINT message.

Before you compile this program, there are a few things you'll want to do. First, in the Project menu, choose Select Active Project. You should see EDRLIB and EDRTEST. You should select EDRTEST. When you build this workspace, you really want to build the program. Also, in the Project menu, select Dependencies. In the Select Project To Modify list box, choose EDRTEST. In the Dependent On The Following Project(s) list, check EDRLIB. This means that EDRTEST requires the EDRLIB dynamic-link library. Whenever you build EDRTEST, EDRLIB will be rebuilt, if necessary, before compiling and linking EDRTEST.

From the Project menu, select Settings. Pick the General tab. When you select the EDRLIB or EDRTEST projects in the left pane, the Intermediate Files and Output Files shown in the right pane should be the RELEASE directory for the Win32 Release configuration and the DEBUG directory for the Win32 Debug configuration. Change them if they are not. This will ensure that EDRLIB.DLL ends up in the same directory as EDRTEST.EXE and that the program will have no problem using the DLL.

Still in the Project Setting dialog box and with EDRTEST selected, click the C/C++ tab. In Preprocessor Definitions, add UNICODE in the Debug configuration, as is customary for the programs in this book.

Now you should be able to build EDRTEST.EXE in both Debug and Release configurations. Visual C++ will first compile and link EDRLIB, if necessary. The RELEASE and DEBUG directories will contain EDRLIB.LIB (the import library) and EDRLIB.DLL. When Developer Studio links EDRTEST, it will include the import library automatically.

It is important to understand that the *EdrCenterText* code is not included in the EDRTEST.EXE file. Instead, there is simply a reference in the executable to the EDRLIB.DLL file and the *EdrCenterText* function. EDRTEST.EXE requires EDRLIB.DLL to run.

When you execute EDRTEST.EXE, Windows performs fixups to functions in external library modules. Many of these functions are in the normal Windows dynamic-link libraries. But Windows also sees that the program calls a function from EDRLIB, so Windows loads the EDRLIB.DLL file into memory and calls EDRLIB's initialization routine. The call within EDRTEST to the *EdrCenterText* function is dynamically linked to the function in EDRLIB.

Including EDRLIB.H in the EDRTEST.C source code file is similar to including WINDOWS.H. Linking with EDRLIB.LIB is similar to linking with the Windows import libraries (such as USER32.LIB). When your program runs, it links with EDLIB.DLL in the same way it links with USER32.DLL. Congratulations! You've just created an extension to Windows!

A few words on the subject of dynamic-link libraries before we continue:

First, although I've just categorized a DLL as an extension to Windows, it is also an extension to your application program. Everything the DLL does is done on behalf of the application. For example, all memory it allocates is owned by the application. Any windows it creates are owned by the application. And any files it opens are owned by the application. Multiple applications can use the same DLL simultaneously, but under Windows these applications are shielded from interfering with each other.

Multiple processes can share the same code in a dynamic-link library. However, the data maintained by a DLL is different for each process. Each process has its own address space for any data the DLL uses. Sharing memories among processes requires extra work, as we'll see in the next section.

Shared Memory in DLLs

It's very nice that Windows isolates applications that are using the same dynamic-link libraries at the same time. However, sometimes it's not preferable. You may want to write a DLL that contains some memory that can be shared among various applications, or perhaps among multiple instances of the same application. This involves using shared memory, which is actually a memory-mapped file.

Let's examine how this works with a program called STRPROG ("string program") and a dynamic-link library called STRLIB ("string library"). STRLIB has three exported functions that STRPROG calls. Just to make this interesting, one of the functions in STRLIB uses a call-back function defined in STRPROG.

STRLIB is a dynamic-link library module that stores and sorts up to 256 character strings. The strings are capitalized and maintained by shared memory in STRLIB. STRPROG can use STRLIB's three functions to add strings, delete strings, and obtain all the current strings from STRLIB. The STRPROG test program has two menu items (Enter and Delete) that invoke dialog boxes to add and delete these strings. STRPROG lists in its client area all the current strings stored by STRLIB.

This function defined in STRLIB adds a string to STRLIB's shared memory:

```
EXPORT BOOL CALLBACK AddString (pStringIn)
```

The argument *pStringIn* is a pointer to the string. The string is capitalized within the *AddString* function. If an identical string already exists in STRLIB's list of strings, this function adds another copy of the string. *AddString* returns TRUE (nonzero) if it is successful and FALSE (0) otherwise. A FALSE return value can result if the string has a length of 0, if memory could not be allocated to store the string, or if 256 strings are already stored.

This STRLIB function deletes a string from STRLIB's shared memory:

`EXPORT BOOL CALLBACK DeleteString (pStringIn)`

Again, the argument *pStringIn* is a pointer to the string. If more than one string matches, only the first is removed. *DeleteString* returns TRUE (nonzero) if it is successful and FALSE (0) otherwise. A FALSE return value indicates that the length of the string is 0 or that a matching string could not be found.

This STRLIB function uses a call-back function located in the calling program to enumerate the strings currently stored in STRLIB's shared memory:

`EXPORT int CALLBACK GetStrings (pfnGetStrCallBack, pParam)`

The call-back function must be defined in the calling program as follows:

`EXPORT BOOL CALLBACK GetStrCallBack (PSTR pString, PVOID pParam)`

The *pfnGetStrCallBack* argument to *GetStrings* points to the call-back function. *GetStrings* calls *GetStrCallBack* once for each string or until the call-back function returns FALSE (0). *GetStrings* returns the number of strings passed to the call-back function. The *pParam* parameter is a far pointer to programmer-defined data.

Of course, this is all complicated by Unicode or, rather, by the necessity of STRLIB supporting both Unicode and non-Unicode applications. Like EDRLIB, it has A and W versions of all its functions. Internally, STRLIB stores all the strings in Unicode. If a non-Unicode program uses STRLIB (that is, the program calls *AddStringA*, *DeleteStringA*, and *GetStringsA*), the strings are converted to and from Unicode.

The workspace associated with the STRPROG and STRLIB projects is named STRPROG. The files are assembled in the same way as the EDRTEST workspace. Figure 21-3 shows the two files necessary to create the STRLIB.DLL dynamic-link library module.

STRLIB.H

```
/*----------------------
   STRLIB.H header file
   ---------------------*/

#ifdef __cplusplus
#define EXPORT extern "C" __declspec (dllexport)
#else
#define EXPORT __declspec (dllexport)
#endif

     // The maximum number of strings STRLIB will store and their lengths

#define MAX_STRINGS 256
```

Figure 21-3. *The STRLIB library.*   *(continued)*

Figure 21-3. *continued*

```
#define MAX_LENGTH  63

    // The callback function type definition uses generic strings

typedef BOOL (CALLBACK * GETSTRCB) (PCTSTR, PVOID) ;

    // Each function has ANSI and Unicode versions

EXPORT BOOL CALLBACK AddStringA (PCSTR) ;
EXPORT BOOL CALLBACK AddStringW (PCWSTR) ;

EXPORT BOOL CALLBACK DeleteStringA (PCSTR) ;
EXPORT BOOL CALLBACK DeleteStringW (PCWSTR) ;

EXPORT int CALLBACK GetStringsA (GETSTRCB, PVOID) ;
EXPORT int CALLBACK GetStringsW (GETSTRCB, PVOID) ;

    // Use the correct version depending on the UNICODE identifier

#ifdef UNICODE
#define AddString    AddStringW
#define DeleteString DeleteStringW
#define GetStrings   GetStringsW
#else
#define AddString    AddStringA
#define DeleteString DeleteStringA
#define GetStrings   GetStringsA
#endif
```

STRLIB.C

```
/*-------------------------------------------------
   STRLIB.C -- Library module for STRPROG program
             (c) Charles Petzold, 1998
   -------------------------------------------------*/

#include <windows.h>
#include <wchar.h>          // for wide-character string functions
#include "strlib.h"

    // shared memory section (requires /SECTION:shared,RWS in link options)

#pragma data_seg ("shared")
int    iTotal = 0 ;
WCHAR szStrings [MAX_STRINGS][MAX_LENGTH + 1] = { '\0' } ;
```

```
#pragma data_seg ()

#pragma comment(linker,"/SECTION:shared,RWS")

int WINAPI DllMain (HINSTANCE hInstance, DWORD fdwReason, PVOID pvReserved)
{
     return TRUE ;
}

EXPORT BOOL CALLBACK AddStringA (PCSTR pStringIn)
{
     BOOL   bReturn ;
     int    iLength ;
     PWSTR pWideStr ;

          // Convert string to Unicode and call AddStringW

     iLength = MultiByteToWideChar (CP_ACP, 0, pStringIn, -1, NULL, 0) ;
     pWideStr = malloc (iLength) ;
     MultiByteToWideChar (CP_ACP, 0, pStringIn, -1, pWideStr, iLength) ;
     bReturn = AddStringW (pWideStr) ;
     free (pWideStr) ;

     return bReturn ;
}

EXPORT BOOL CALLBACK AddStringW (PCWSTR pStringIn)
{
     PWSTR pString ;
     int   i, iLength ;

     if (iTotal == MAX_STRINGS - 1)
         return FALSE ;

     if ((iLength = wcslen (pStringIn)) == 0)
         return FALSE ;

          // Allocate memory for storing string, copy it, convert to uppercase

     pString = malloc (sizeof (WCHAR) * (1 + iLength)) ;
     wcscpy (pString, pStringIn) ;
     _wcsupr (pString) ;

          //  Alphabetize the strings

     for (i = iTotal ; i > 0 ; i--)
```

(continued)

Figure 21-3. *continued*

```
     {
          if (wcscmp (pString, szStrings[i - 1]) >= 0)
               break ;

          wcscpy (szStrings[i], szStrings[i - 1]) ;
     }
     wcscpy (szStrings[i], pString) ;
     iTotal++ ;

     free (pString) ;
     return TRUE ;
}

EXPORT BOOL CALLBACK DeleteStringA (PCSTR pStringIn)
{
     BOOL  bReturn ;
     int   iLength ;
     PWSTR pWideStr ;

          // Convert string to Unicode and call DeleteStringW

     iLength = MultiByteToWideChar (CP_ACP, 0, pStringIn, -1, NULL, 0) ;
     pWideStr = malloc (iLength) ;
     MultiByteToWideChar (CP_ACP, 0, pStringIn, -1, pWideStr, iLength) ;
     bReturn = DeleteStringW (pWideStr) ;
     free (pWideStr) ;

     return bReturn ;
}

EXPORT BOOL CALLBACK DeleteStringW (PCWSTR pStringIn)
{
     int i, j ;

     if (0 == wcslen (pStringIn))
          return FALSE ;

     for (i = 0 ; i < iTotal ; i++)
     {
          if (_wcsicmp (szStrings[i], pStringIn) == 0)
               break ;
     }
          // If given string not in list, return without taking action

     if (i == iTotal)
          return FALSE ;
```

```
            // Else adjust list downward

    for (j = i ; j < iTotal ; j++)
        wcscpy (szStrings[j], szStrings[j + 1]) ;

    szStrings[iTotal--][0] = '\0' ;
    return TRUE ;
}

EXPORT int CALLBACK GetStringsA (GETSTRCB pfnGetStrCallBack, PVOID pParam)
{
    BOOL bReturn ;
    int  i, iLength ;
    PSTR pAnsiStr ;

    for (i = 0 ; i < iTotal ; i++)
    {
            // Convert string from Unicode

        iLength = WideCharToMultiByte (CP_ACP, 0, szStrings[i], -1, NULL, 0,
                                       NULL, NULL) ;
        pAnsiStr = malloc (iLength) ;
        WideCharToMultiByte (CP_ACP, 0, szStrings[i], -1, pAnsiStr, iLength,
                                       NULL, NULL) ;

            // Call callback function

        bReturn = pfnGetStrCallBack (pAnsiStr, pParam) ;

        if (bReturn == FALSE)
            return i + 1 ;

        free (pAnsiStr) ;
    }
    return iTotal ;
}

EXPORT int CALLBACK GetStringsW (GETSTRCB pfnGetStrCallBack, PVOID pParam)
{
    BOOL bReturn ;
    int  i ;

    for (i = 0 ; i < iTotal ; i++)
    {
        bReturn = pfnGetStrCallBack (szStrings[i], pParam) ;
```

(continued)

Figure 21-3. *continued*

```
            if (bReturn == FALSE)
                return i + 1 ;
        }
    return iTotal ;
}
```

Aside from the *DllMain* function, STRLIB contains only the six functions that it will export to be used by other programs. All these functions are defined as EXPORT. This causes LINK to list them in the STRLIB.LIB import library.

The STRPROG Program

The STRPROG program, shown in Figure 21-4, is fairly straightforward. The two menu options, Enter and Delete, invoke dialog boxes that allow you to enter a string. STRPROG then calls *AddString* or *DeleteString*. When the program needs to update its client area, it calls *GetStrings* and uses the function *GetStrCallBack* to list the enumerated strings.

STRPROG.C

```
/*-------------------------------------------------------------
   STRPROG.C -- Program using STRLIB dynamic-link library
                (c) Charles Petzold, 1998
   -------------------------------------------------------------*/

#include <windows.h>
#include "strlib.h"
#include "resource.h"

typedef struct
{
    HDC hdc ;
    int xText ;
    int yText ;
    int xStart ;
    int yStart ;
    int xIncr ;
    int yIncr ;
    int xMax ;
    int yMax ;
}
CBPARAM ;

LRESULT CALLBACK WndProc (HWND, UINT, WPARAM, LPARAM) ;
```

Figure 21-4. *The STRPROG program.*

```
TCHAR szAppName [] = TEXT ("StrProg") ;
TCHAR szString [MAX_LENGTH + 1] ;

int WINAPI WinMain (HINSTANCE hInstance, HINSTANCE hPrevInstance,
                    PSTR szCmdLine, int iCmdShow)
{
    HWND      hwnd ;
    MSG       msg ;
    WNDCLASS  wndclass ;

    wndclass.style         = CS_HREDRAW | CS_VREDRAW ;
    wndclass.lpfnWndProc   = WndProc ;
    wndclass.cbClsExtra    = 0 ;
    wndclass.cbWndExtra    = 0 ;
    wndclass.hInstance     = hInstance ;
    wndclass.hIcon         = LoadIcon (NULL, IDI_APPLICATION) ;
    wndclass.hCursor       = LoadCursor (NULL, IDC_ARROW) ;
    wndclass.hbrBackground = (HBRUSH) GetStockObject (WHITE_BRUSH) ;
    wndclass.lpszMenuName  = szAppName ;
    wndclass.lpszClassName = szAppName ;

    if (!RegisterClass (&wndclass))
    {
        MessageBox (NULL, TEXT ("This program requires Windows NT!"),
                    szAppName, MB_ICONERROR) ;
        return 0 ;
    }

    hwnd = CreateWindow (szAppName, TEXT ("DLL Demonstration Program"),
                         WS_OVERLAPPEDWINDOW,
                         CW_USEDEFAULT, CW_USEDEFAULT,
                         CW_USEDEFAULT, CW_USEDEFAULT,
                         NULL, NULL, hInstance, NULL) ;

    ShowWindow (hwnd, iCmdShow) ;
    UpdateWindow (hwnd) ;

    while (GetMessage (&msg, NULL, 0, 0))
    {
        TranslateMessage (&msg) ;
        DispatchMessage (&msg) ;
    }
    return msg.wParam ;
}

BOOL CALLBACK DlgProc (HWND hDlg, UINT message, WPARAM wParam, LPARAM lParam)
```

(continued)

Figure 21-4. *continued*

```
{
    switch (message)
    {
    case WM_INITDIALOG:
        SendDlgItemMessage (hDlg, IDC_STRING, EM_LIMITTEXT, MAX_LENGTH, 0) ;
        return TRUE ;

    case WM_COMMAND:
        switch (wParam)
        {
        case IDOK:
            GetDlgItemText (hDlg, IDC_STRING, szString, MAX_LENGTH) ;
            EndDialog (hDlg, TRUE) ;
            return TRUE ;

        case IDCANCEL:
            EndDialog (hDlg, FALSE) ;
            return TRUE ;
        }
    }
    return FALSE ;
}

BOOL CALLBACK GetStrCallBack (PTSTR pString, CBPARAM * pcbp)
{
    TextOut (pcbp->hdc, pcbp->xText, pcbp->yText,
             pString, lstrlen (pString)) ;

    if ((pcbp->yText += pcbp->yIncr) > pcbp->yMax)
    {
        pcbp->yText = pcbp->yStart ;
        if ((pcbp->xText += pcbp->xIncr) > pcbp->xMax)
            return FALSE ;
    }
    return TRUE ;
}

LRESULT CALLBACK WndProc (HWND hwnd, UINT message, WPARAM wParam, LPARAM lParam)
{
    static HINSTANCE  hInst ;
    static int        cxChar, cyChar, cxClient, cyClient ;
    static UINT       iDataChangeMsg ;
    CBPARAM           cbparam ;
    HDC               hdc ;
    PAINTSTRUCT       ps ;
    TEXTMETRIC        tm ;
```

```
switch (message)
{
case WM_CREATE:
    hInst = ((LPCREATESTRUCT) lParam)->hInstance ;
    hdc   = GetDC (hwnd) ;
    GetTextMetrics (hdc, &tm) ;
    cxChar = (int) tm.tmAveCharWidth ;
    cyChar = (int) (tm.tmHeight + tm.tmExternalLeading) ;
    ReleaseDC (hwnd, hdc) ;

        // Register message for notifying instances of data changes

    iDataChangeMsg = RegisterWindowMessage (TEXT ("StrProgDataChange")) ;
    return 0 ;

case WM_COMMAND:
    switch (wParam)
    {
    case IDM_ENTER:
        if (DialogBox (hInst, TEXT ("EnterDlg"), hwnd, &DlgProc))
        {
            if (AddString (szString))
                PostMessage (HWND_BROADCAST, iDataChangeMsg, 0, 0) ;
            else
                MessageBeep (0) ;
        }
        break ;

    case IDM_DELETE:
        if (DialogBox (hInst, TEXT ("DeleteDlg"), hwnd, &DlgProc))
        {
            if (DeleteString (szString))
                PostMessage (HWND_BROADCAST, iDataChangeMsg, 0, 0) ;
            else
                MessageBeep (0) ;
        }
        break ;
    }
    return 0 ;

case WM_SIZE:
    cxClient = (int) LOWORD (lParam) ;
    cyClient = (int) HIWORD (lParam) ;
    return 0 ;
```

(continued)

Figure 21-4. *continued*

```
        case WM_PAINT:
             hdc = BeginPaint (hwnd, &ps) ;

             cbparam.hdc   = hdc ;
             cbparam.xText = cbparam.xStart = cxChar ;
             cbparam.yText = cbparam.yStart = cyChar ;
             cbparam.xIncr = cxChar * MAX_LENGTH ;
             cbparam.yIncr = cyChar ;
             cbparam.xMax  = cbparam.xIncr * (1 + cxClient / cbparam.xIncr) ;
             cbparam.yMax  = cyChar * (cyClient / cyChar - 1) ;

             GetStrings ((GETSTRCB) GetStrCallBack, (PVOID) &cbparam) ;

             EndPaint (hwnd, &ps) ;
             return 0 ;

        case WM_DESTROY:
             PostQuitMessage (0) ;
             return 0 ;

        default:
             if (message == iDataChangeMsg)
                  InvalidateRect (hwnd, NULL, TRUE) ;
             break ;
        }
        return DefWindowProc (hwnd, message, wParam, lParam) ;
}
```

STRPROG.RC (excerpts)

```
//Microsoft Developer Studio generated resource script.

#include "resource.h"
#include "afxres.h"


/////////////////////////////////////////////////////////////////////////////
// Dialog

ENTERDLG DIALOG DISCARDABLE  20, 20, 186, 47
STYLE DS_MODALFRAME | WS_POPUP | WS_CAPTION | WS_SYSMENU
CAPTION "Enter"
FONT 8, "MS Sans Serif"
BEGIN
```

```
    LTEXT           "&Enter:",IDC_STATIC,7,7,26,9
    EDITTEXT        IDC_STRING,31,7,148,12,ES_AUTOHSCROLL
    DEFPUSHBUTTON   "OK",IDOK,32,26,50,14
    PUSHBUTTON      "Cancel",IDCANCEL,104,26,50,14
END

DELETEDLG DIALOG DISCARDABLE  20, 20, 186, 47
STYLE DS_MODALFRAME | WS_POPUP | WS_CAPTION | WS_SYSMENU
CAPTION "Delete"
FONT 8, "MS Sans Serif"
BEGIN
    LTEXT           "&Delete:",IDC_STATIC,7,7,26,9
    EDITTEXT        IDC_STRING,31,7,148,12,ES_AUTOHSCROLL
    DEFPUSHBUTTON   "OK",IDOK,32,26,50,14
    PUSHBUTTON      "Cancel",IDCANCEL,104,26,50,14
END

/////////////////////////////////////////////////////////////////////////
// Menu

STRPROG MENU DISCARDABLE
BEGIN
    MENUITEM "&Enter!",                     IDM_ENTER
    MENUITEM "&Delete!",                    IDM_DELETE
END
```

RESOURCE.H (excerpts)

```
// Microsoft Developer Studio generated include file.
// Used by StrProg.rc

#define IDC_STRING              1000
#define IDM_ENTER               40001
#define IDM_DELETE              40002
#define IDC_STATIC              -1
```

STRPROG.C includes the STRLIB.H header file; this defines the three functions in STRLIB that STRPROG will use.

What's most interesting about this program becomes evident when you run multiple instances of STRPROG. STRLIB stores the character strings and their pointers in shared memory, which lets all instances of STRPROG share this data. Let's look at how it's done.

Sharing Data Among STRPROG Instances

Windows erects a wall around the address space of a Win32 process. Normally, data in an address space is private and invisible to other processes. But running multiple instances of STRPROG shows that STRLIB has no trouble sharing its data with all instances of the program. When you add or delete a string in a STRPROG window, the change is immediately reflected in the other windows.

STRLIB shares two variables among all its instances: an array of strings and an integer indicating the number of valid strings stored. STRLIB keeps these two variables in a special section of memory that it designates as shared:

```
#pragma data_seg ("shared")
int    iTotal = 0 ;
WCHAR szStrings [MAX_STRINGS][MAX_LENGTH + 1] = { '\0' } ;
#pragma data_seg ()
```

The first *#pragma* statement creates the data section, here named *shared*. You can name the section whatever you wish. All initialized variables after the *#pragma* statement go into the *shared* section. The second *#pragma* statement marks the end of the section. It's important to specifically initialize the variables; otherwise, the compiler puts them in the normal uninitialized section rather than in *shared*.

The linker has to be told about *shared*. In the Project Settings dialog box, select the Link tab. In the Project Options field for STRLIB (in both the Release and Debug configurations), include the following linker argument:

```
/SECTION:shared,RWS
```

The letters *RWS* indicate that the section has read, write, and shared attributes. Or you can specify the linker option directly in the DLL source code, as is done in STRLIB.C:

```
#pragma comment(linker,"/SECTION:shared,RWS")
```

The shared memory section allows the *iTotal* variable and the *szStrings* array of strings to be shared among all instances of STRLIB. Because MAX_STRINGS is equal to 256 and MAX_LENGTH is equal to 63, the shared memory section is 32,772 bytes in length—the 4 bytes required for the *iTotal* variable and 128 bytes each for the 256 pointers.

Using a shared memory section is probably the easiest way to share data among multiple applications. If you need to dynamically allocate shared memory space, you should look into the use of file mapping objects, documented at */Platform SDK/Windows Base Services/Interprocess Communication/File Mapping*.

MISCELLANEOUS DLL TOPICS

I mentioned earlier that a dynamic library module doesn't receive messages. However, a library module can call *GetMessage* and *PeekMessage*. The messages the library pulls from the queue with these functions are actually messages for the program that called the library function.

In general, the library works on behalf of the program calling it—a rule that holds for most Windows functions that a library calls.

A dynamic library can load resources (such as icons, strings, and bitmaps) either from the library file or from the file of the program that calls the library. The functions that load resources require an instance handle. If the library uses its own instance handle (which is passed to the library during initialization), the library can obtain resources from its own file. To load resources from the calling program's .EXE file, the library function requires the instance handle of the program calling the function.

Registering window classes and creating windows in a library can be a little tricky. Both the window class structure and the *CreateWindow* call require an instance handle. Although you can use the library module's instance handle in creating the window class and the window, the window messages still go through the message queue of the program calling the library when the library creates the window. If you must create window classes and windows within a library, it's probably best to use the calling program's instance handle.

Because messages for modal dialog boxes are retrieved outside a program's message loop, you can create a modal dialog box in a library by calling *DialogBox*. The instance handle can be that of the library, and the *hwndParent* argument to *DialogBox* can be set to NULL.

Dynamic Linking Without Imports

Rather than have Windows perform dynamic linking when your program is first loaded into memory, you can link a program with a library module while the program is running. For instance, you would normally call the *Rectangle* function like this:

```
Rectangle (hdc, xLeft, yTop, xRight, yBottom) ;
```

This works because the program has been linked with the GDI32.LIB import library, which supplied the address of *Rectangle*.

You can also call *Rectangle* in a very roundabout manner. You first use *typedef* to define a function type for *Rectangle*:

```
typedef BOOL (WINAPI * PFNRECT) (HDC, int, int, int, int) ;
```

You then define two variables:

```
HANDLE  hLibrary ;
PFNRECT pfnRectangle ;
```

Now you set *hLibrary* to the handle of the library and *lpfnRectangle* to the address of the *Rectangle* function:

```
hLibrary = LoadLibrary (TEXT ("GDI32.DLL"))
pfnRectangle = (PFNPRECT) GetProcAddress (hLibrary, TEXT ("Rectangle"))
```

The *LoadLibrary* function returns NULL if the library file can't be found or if some other error occurs. Now you can call the function and then free the library:

```
pfnRectangle (hdc, xLeft, yTop, xRight, yBottom) ;
FreeLibrary (hLibrary) ;
```

Although this technique of run-time dynamic linking doesn't make much sense for the *Rectangle* function, it can come in handy when you don't know the name of the library module until run time.

The code above uses the *LoadLibrary* and *FreeLibrary* functions. Windows maintains "reference counts" for all library modules. *LoadLibrary* causes the reference count to be incremented. The reference count is also incremented when Windows loads any program that uses the library. *FreeLibrary* causes the reference count to be decremented, as does the termination of an instance of a program that uses this library. When the reference count is 0, Windows can discard the library from memory, because the library is no longer needed.

Resource-Only Libraries

Any function in a dynamic-link library that a Windows program or another library can use must be exported. However, a DLL need not contain any exported functions. What would such a DLL contain? The answer is resources.

Let's say you're working on a Windows application that requires a number of bitmaps. Normally you would list these in the resource script of the program and load them into memory with the *LoadBitmap* function. But perhaps you want to create several sets of bitmaps, each set customized for one of the major display resolutions commonly used with Windows. It would make most sense to store these different sets of bitmaps in different files, because a user would need only one set of bitmaps on the fixed disk. These files are resource-only libraries.

Figure 21-5 shows how to create a resource-only library file called BITLIB.DLL that contains nine bitmaps. The BITLIB.RC file lists all the separate bitmap files and assigns each one a number. To create BITLIB.DLL, you need nine bitmaps named BITMAP1.BMP, BIT-MAP2.BMP, and so forth. You can use the bitmaps provided on this book's companion disc or create them yourself in Visual C++. They are associated with numeric IDs of 1 through 9.

BITLIB.C

```
/*-------------------------------------------------------------------
   BITLIB.C -- Code entry point for BITLIB dynamic-link library
               (c) Charles Petzold,  1998
   -----------------------------------------------------------------*/

#include <windows.h>

int WINAPI DllMain (HINSTANCE hInstance, DWORD fdwReason, PVOID pvReserved)
{
     return TRUE ;
}
```

Figure 21-5. *The BITLIB library.*

BITLIB.RC (excerpts)

```
//Microsoft Developer Studio generated resource script.

#include "resource.h"
#include "afxres.h"
/////////////////////////////////////////////////////////////////////////////
// Bitmap

1                       BITMAP    DISCARDABLE      "bitmap1.bmp"
2                       BITMAP    DISCARDABLE      "bitmap2.bmp"
3                       BITMAP    DISCARDABLE      "bitmap3.bmp"
4                       BITMAP    DISCARDABLE      "bitmap4.bmp"
5                       BITMAP    DISCARDABLE      "bitmap5.bmp"
6                       BITMAP    DISCARDABLE      "bitmap6.bmp"
7                       BITMAP    DISCARDABLE      "bitmap7.bmp"
8                       BITMAP    DISCARDABLE      "bitmap8.bmp"
9                       BITMAP    DISCARDABLE      "bitmap9.bmp"
```

Create the BITLIB project in a workspace named SHOWBIT. Create the SHOWBIT program, shown in Figure 21-6, in another project named SHOWBIT, the same as before. However, don't make BITLIB a dependency of SHOWBIT; otherwise, the link step will require a BITLIB.LIB file, and one isn't created because BITLIB has no exported functions. Instead, build BITLIB and SHOWBIT separately by alternately setting each of them as the Active Project and building.

SHOWBIT.C reads the bitmap resources from BITLIB and displays them in its client area. You can cycle through the bitmaps by pressing a key on the keyboard.

SHOWBIT.C

```
/*----------------------------------------------------------
   SHOWBIT.C -- Shows bitmaps in BITLIB dynamic-link library
                (c) Charles Petzold, 1998
   ----------------------------------------------------------*/

#include <windows.h>

LRESULT CALLBACK WndProc (HWND, UINT, WPARAM, LPARAM) ;

TCHAR szAppName [] = TEXT ("ShowBit") ;

int WINAPI WinMain (HINSTANCE hInstance, HINSTANCE hPrevInstance,
                    PSTR szCmdLine, int iCmdShow)
```

Figure 21-6. *The SHOWBIT program.*   *(continued)*

Figure 21-6. *continued*

```
{
     HWND     hwnd ;
     MSG      msg ;
     WNDCLASS wndclass ;

     wndclass.style         = CS_HREDRAW | CS_VREDRAW ;
     wndclass.lpfnWndProc   = WndProc ;
     wndclass.cbClsExtra    = 0 ;
     wndclass.cbWndExtra    = 0 ;
     wndclass.hInstance     = hInstance ;
     wndclass.hIcon         = LoadIcon (NULL, IDI_APPLICATION) ;
     wndclass.hCursor       = LoadCursor (NULL, IDC_ARROW) ;
     wndclass.hbrBackground = (HBRUSH) GetStockObject (WHITE_BRUSH) ;
     wndclass.lpszMenuName  = NULL ;
     wndclass.lpszClassName = szAppName ;

     if (!RegisterClass (&wndclass))
     {
          MessageBox (NULL, TEXT ("This program requires Windows NT!"),
                      szAppName, MB_ICONERROR) ;
          return 0 ;
     }

     hwnd = CreateWindow (szAppName,
                      TEXT ("Show Bitmaps from BITLIB (Press Key)"),
                      WS_OVERLAPPEDWINDOW,
                      CW_USEDEFAULT, CW_USEDEFAULT,
                      CW_USEDEFAULT, CW_USEDEFAULT,
                      NULL, NULL, hInstance, NULL) ;

     if (!hwnd)
          return 0 ;

     ShowWindow (hwnd, iCmdShow) ;
     UpdateWindow (hwnd) ;

     while (GetMessage (&msg, NULL, 0, 0))
     {
          TranslateMessage (&msg) ;
          DispatchMessage (&msg) ;
     }
     return msg.wParam ;
}
```

```
void DrawBitmap (HDC hdc, int xStart, int yStart, HBITMAP hBitmap)
{
     BITMAP bm ;
     HDC    hMemDC ;
     POINT  pt ;

     hMemDC = CreateCompatibleDC (hdc) ;
     SelectObject (hMemDC, hBitmap) ;
     GetObject (hBitmap, sizeof (BITMAP), &bm) ;
     pt.x = bm.bmWidth ;
     pt.y = bm.bmHeight ;

     BitBlt (hdc, xStart, yStart, pt.x, pt.y, hMemDC, 0, 0, SRCCOPY) ;

     DeleteDC (hMemDC) ;
}

LRESULT CALLBACK WndProc (HWND hwnd, UINT message, WPARAM wParam, LPARAM lParam)
{
     static HINSTANCE hLibrary ;
     static int       iCurrent = 1 ;
     HBITMAP          hBitmap ;
     HDC              hdc ;
     PAINTSTRUCT      ps ;

     switch (message)
     {
     case WM_CREATE:
          if ((hLibrary = LoadLibrary (TEXT ("BITLIB.DLL"))) == NULL)
          {
               MessageBox (hwnd, TEXT ("Can't load BITLIB.DLL."),
                           szAppName, 0) ;
               return -1 ;
          }
          return 0 ;

     case WM_CHAR:
          if (hLibrary)
          {
               iCurrent ++ ;
               InvalidateRect (hwnd, NULL, TRUE) ;
          }
          return 0 ;
```

(continued)

Figure 21-6. *continued*

```
    case WM_PAINT:
        hdc = BeginPaint (hwnd, &ps) ;

        if (hLibrary)
        {
            hBitmap = LoadBitmap (hLibrary, MAKEINTRESOURCE (iCurrent)) ;

            if (!hBitmap)
            {
                iCurrent = 1 ;
                hBitmap = LoadBitmap (hLibrary,
                                      MAKEINTRESOURCE (iCurrent)) ;
            }
            if (hBitmap)
            {
                DrawBitmap (hdc, 0, 0, hBitmap) ;
                DeleteObject (hBitmap) ;
            }
        }
        EndPaint (hwnd, &ps) ;
        return 0 ;

    case WM_DESTROY:
        if (hLibrary)
            FreeLibrary (hLibrary) ;

        PostQuitMessage (0) ;
        return 0 ;
    }
    return DefWindowProc (hwnd, message, wParam, lParam) ;
}
```

During processing of the WM_CREATE message, SHOWBIT gets a handle to BITLIB.DLL:

```
if ((hLibrary = LoadLibrary (TEXT ("BITLIB.DLL"))) == NULL)
```

If BITLIB.DLL isn't in the same directory as SHOWBIT.EXE, Windows will search for it as discussed earlier in this chapter. If *LoadLibrary* returns NULL, SHOWBIT displays a message box reporting the error and returns a −1 from the WM_CREATE message. This causes the *CreateWindow* call in *WinMain* to return NULL, and the program terminates.

SHOWBIT can obtain a handle to a bitmap by calling *LoadBitmap* with the library handle and the number of the bitmap:

```
hBitmap = LoadBitmap (hLibrary, MAKEINTRESOURCE (iCurrent)) ;
```

This returns an error if the bitmap corresponding to the number *iCurrent* isn't valid or if not enough memory exists to load the bitmap.

While processing the WM_DESTROY message, SHOWBIT frees the library:

```
FreeLibrary (hLibrary) ;
```

When the last instance of SHOWBIT terminates, the reference count of BITLIB.DLL drops to 0 and the memory it occupies is freed. As you can see, this is a simple method of implementing a "clip art" program that could load precreated bitmaps (or metafiles or enhanced metafiles) into the clipboard for use by other programs.

Chapter 22

Sound and Music

The integration of sound, music, and video into Microsoft Windows has been an important evolutionary step. Multimedia support began first with the so-called Multimedia Extensions to Microsoft Windows in 1991. In 1992, the release of Windows 3.1 made the multimedia support just another category of APIs. In recent years, CD-ROM drives and sound boards—rarities in the early 1990s—have become standard for new PCs. Few people these days need to be convinced that multimedia adds a useful dimension to the graphical visuals of Windows in taking the computer beyond its traditional role as a cruncher of numbers and text.

WINDOWS AND MULTIMEDIA

In one sense, multimedia is all about getting access to various pieces of hardware through device-independent function calls. Let's look at this hardware first and then the structure of the Windows multimedia API.

Multimedia Hardware

Perhaps the most commonly used piece of multimedia hardware is the waveform audio device, commonly known as the sound card or sound board. The waveform audio device converts microphone input or other analog audio input into digitized samples for storage in memory or disk files with the .WAV extension. The waveform audio device also converts the waveform back into analog sound for playing over the PC's speakers.

The sound board usually also contains a MIDI device. MIDI is the industry standard Musical Instrument Digital Interface. Such hardware plays musical notes in response to short binary messages. The MIDI hardware usually can also accept a cable connected to a MIDI input device, such as a music keyboard. Often external MIDI synthesizers can also be attached to the sound board.

The CD-ROM drive attached to most of today's PCs is usually capable of playing normal music CDs. This is known as "CD Audio." The output from the waveform audio device, MIDI device, and CD Audio device are often mixed together under user control with the Volume Control application.

A couple of other common multimedia "devices" don't require any additional hardware. The Video for Windows device (also called the AVI Video device) plays movie or animation files with the .AVI ("audio-video interleave") extension. The ActiveMovie control plays other types of movies, including QuickTime and MPEG. The video board on a PC may have specialized hardware to assist in playing these movies.

More rare are PC users with certain Pioneer laserdisc players or the Sony series of VISCA video cassette recorders. These devices have serial interfaces and thus can be controlled by PC software. Certain video boards have a feature called "video in a window" that allows an external video signal to appear on the Windows screen along with other applications. This is also considered a multimedia device.

An API Overview

The API support of the multimedia features in Windows is in two major collections. These are known as the "low-level" and the "high-level" interfaces.

The low-level interfaces are a series of functions that begin with a short descriptive prefix and are listed (along with the high-level functions) in */Platform SDK/Graphics and Multimedia Services/Multimedia Reference/Multimedia Functions.*

The low-level waveform audio input and output functions begin with the prefix *waveIn* and *waveOut*. We'll be looking at these functions in this chapter. Also examined in this chapter will be *midiOut* functions to control the MIDI Output device. The API also includes *midiIn* and *midiStream* functions.

Also used in this chapter are functions beginning with the prefix *time* that allow setting a high-resolution preemptive timer routine with a timer interval rate going down to 1 millisecond. This facility is primarily for playing back MIDI sequences. Several other groups of functions involve audio compression, video compression, and animation and video sequences; unfortunately, these will not be covered in this chapter.

You'll also notice in the list of multimedia functions seven functions with the prefix *mci* that allow access to the Media Control Interface (MCI). This is a high-level, open-ended interface for controlling all multimedia hardware in the Multimedia PC. MCI includes many commands that are common to all multimedia hardware. This is possible because many aspects of multimedia can be molded into a tape recorder-like play/record metaphor. You "open" a device for either input or output, you "record" (for input) or "play" (for output), and when you're done you "close" the device.

MCI itself comes in two forms. In one form, you send messages to MCI that are similar to Windows messages. These messages include bit-encoded flags and C data structures. In the second form, you send text strings to MCI. This facility is primarily for scripting languages that have flexible string manipulation functions but not much support for calling Windows APIs. The string-based version of MCI is also good for interactively exploring and learning MCI, as we'll be doing shortly. Device names in MCI include *cdaudio*, *waveaudio*, *sequencer* (MIDI), *videodisc*, *vcr*, *overlay* (analog video in a window), *dat* (digital audio tape), and *digitalvideo*. MCI devices are categorized as "simple" and "compound." Simple devices (such as *cdaudio*) don't use files. Compound devices (like *waveaudio*) do; in the case of waveform audio, these files have a .WAV extension.

Another approach to accessing multimedia hardware involves the DirectX API, which is beyond the scope of this book.

Two other high-level multimedia functions also deserve mention: *MessageBeep* and *PlaySound*, which was demonstrated way back in Chapter 3. *MessageBeep* plays sounds that are specified in the Sounds applet of the Control Panel. *PlaySound* can play a .WAV file on disk, in memory, or loaded as resources. The *PlaySound* function will be used again later in this chapter.

Exploring MCI with TESTMCI

Back in the early days of Windows multimedia, the software development kit included a C program called MCITEST that allowed programmers to interactively type in MCI commands and learn how they worked. This program, at least in its C version, has apparently disappeared. So, I've recreated it as the TESTMCI program shown in Figure 22-1. The user interface is based on the old MCITEST program but not the actual code, although I can't believe it was much different.

TESTMCI.C

```
/*------------------------------------------
   TESTMCI.C -- MCI Command String Tester
               (c) Charles Petzold, 1998
   ------------------------------------------*/

#include <windows.h>
#include "resource.h"

#define ID_TIMER    1

BOOL CALLBACK DlgProc (HWND, UINT, WPARAM, LPARAM) ;

TCHAR szAppName [] = TEXT ("TestMci") ;

int WINAPI WinMain (HINSTANCE hInstance, HINSTANCE hPrevInstance,
                    PSTR szCmdLine, int iCmdShow)
```

Figure 22-1. *The TESTMCI program.*

(continued)

Figure 22-1. *continued*

```
{
     if (-1 == DialogBox (hInstance, szAppName, NULL, DlgProc))
     {
          MessageBox (NULL, TEXT ("This program requires Windows NT!"),
                      szAppName, MB_ICONERROR) ;
     }
     return 0 ;
}

BOOL CALLBACK DlgProc (HWND hwnd, UINT message, WPARAM wParam, LPARAM lParam)
{
     static HWND hwndEdit ;
     int         iCharBeg, iCharEnd, iLineBeg, iLineEnd, iChar, iLine, iLength ;
     MCIERROR    error ;
     RECT        rect ;
     TCHAR       szCommand [1024], szReturn [1024],
                 szError [1024], szBuffer [32] ;

     switch (message)
     {
     case WM_INITDIALOG:
               // Center the window on screen

          GetWindowRect (hwnd, &rect) ;
          SetWindowPos (hwnd, NULL,
               (GetSystemMetrics (SM_CXSCREEN) - rect.right + rect.left) / 2,
               (GetSystemMetrics (SM_CYSCREEN) - rect.bottom + rect.top) / 2,
               0, 0, SWP_NOZORDER | SWP_NOSIZE) ;

          hwndEdit = GetDlgItem (hwnd, IDC_MAIN_EDIT) ;
          SetFocus (hwndEdit) ;
          return FALSE ;

     case WM_COMMAND:
          switch (LOWORD (wParam))
          {
          case IDOK:
                    // Find the line numbers corresponding to the selection

               SendMessage (hwndEdit, EM_GETSEL, (WPARAM) &iCharBeg,
                                                 (LPARAM) &iCharEnd) ;

               iLineBeg = SendMessage (hwndEdit, EM_LINEFROMCHAR, iCharBeg, 0) ;
               iLineEnd = SendMessage (hwndEdit, EM_LINEFROMCHAR, iCharEnd, 0) ;

                    // Loop through all the lines
```

```
          for (iLine = iLineBeg ; iLine <= iLineEnd ; iLine++)
          {
                    // Get the line and terminate it; ignore if blank

               * (WORD *) szCommand = sizeof (szCommand) / sizeof (TCHAR) ;

               iLength = SendMessage (hwndEdit, EM_GETLINE, iLine,
                                             (LPARAM) szCommand) ;
               szCommand [iLength] = '\0' ;

               if (iLength == 0)
                    continue ;

                    // Send the MCI command

               error = mciSendString (szCommand, szReturn,
                         sizeof (szReturn) / sizeof (TCHAR), hwnd) ;

                    // Set the Return String field

               SetDlgItemText (hwnd, IDC_RETURN_STRING, szReturn) ;

                    // Set the Error String field (even if no error)

               mciGetErrorString (error, szError,
                                   sizeof (szError) / sizeof (TCHAR)) ;

               SetDlgItemText (hwnd, IDC_ERROR_STRING, szError) ;
          }
               // Send the caret to the end of the last selected line

          iChar  = SendMessage (hwndEdit, EM_LINEINDEX,  iLineEnd, 0) ;
          iChar += SendMessage (hwndEdit, EM_LINELENGTH, iCharEnd, 0) ;
          SendMessage (hwndEdit, EM_SETSEL, iChar, iChar) ;

               // Insert a carriage return/line feed combination

          SendMessage (hwndEdit, EM_REPLACESEL, FALSE,
                              (LPARAM) TEXT ("\r\n")) ;
          SetFocus (hwndEdit) ;
          return TRUE ;

     case IDCANCEL:
          EndDialog (hwnd, 0) ;
          return TRUE ;
```

(continued)

Figure 22-1. *continued*

```
        case IDC_MAIN_EDIT:
            if (HIWORD (wParam) == EN_ERRSPACE)
            {
                MessageBox (hwnd, TEXT ("Error control out of space."),
                            szAppName, MB_OK | MB_ICONINFORMATION) ;
                return TRUE ;
            }
            break ;
        }
        break ;

    case MM_MCINOTIFY:
        EnableWindow (GetDlgItem (hwnd, IDC_NOTIFY_MESSAGE), TRUE) ;

        wsprintf (szBuffer, TEXT ("Device ID = %i"), lParam) ;
        SetDlgItemText (hwnd, IDC_NOTIFY_ID, szBuffer) ;
        EnableWindow (GetDlgItem (hwnd, IDC_NOTIFY_ID), TRUE) ;

        EnableWindow (GetDlgItem (hwnd, IDC_NOTIFY_SUCCESSFUL),
                        wParam & MCI_NOTIFY_SUCCESSFUL) ;

        EnableWindow (GetDlgItem (hwnd, IDC_NOTIFY_SUPERSEDED),
                        wParam & MCI_NOTIFY_SUPERSEDED) ;

        EnableWindow (GetDlgItem (hwnd, IDC_NOTIFY_ABORTED),
                        wParam & MCI_NOTIFY_ABORTED) ;

        EnableWindow (GetDlgItem (hwnd, IDC_NOTIFY_FAILURE),
                        wParam & MCI_NOTIFY_FAILURE) ;

        SetTimer (hwnd, ID_TIMER, 5000, NULL) ;
        return TRUE ;

    case WM_TIMER:
        KillTimer (hwnd, ID_TIMER) ;

        EnableWindow (GetDlgItem (hwnd, IDC_NOTIFY_MESSAGE), FALSE) ;
        EnableWindow (GetDlgItem (hwnd, IDC_NOTIFY_ID), FALSE) ;
        EnableWindow (GetDlgItem (hwnd, IDC_NOTIFY_SUCCESSFUL), FALSE) ;
        EnableWindow (GetDlgItem (hwnd, IDC_NOTIFY_SUPERSEDED), FALSE) ;
        EnableWindow (GetDlgItem (hwnd, IDC_NOTIFY_ABORTED), FALSE) ;
        EnableWindow (GetDlgItem (hwnd, IDC_NOTIFY_FAILURE), FALSE) ;
        return TRUE ;

    case WM_SYSCOMMAND:
        switch (LOWORD (wParam))
        {
        case SC_CLOSE:
```

```
                EndDialog (hwnd, 0) ;
                return TRUE ;
          }
          break ;
     }
     return FALSE ;
}
```

TESTMCI.RC (excerpts)

```
//Microsoft Developer Studio generated resource script.

#include "resource.h"
#include "afxres.h"

/////////////////////////////////////////////////////////////////////////////
// Dialog

TESTMCI DIALOG DISCARDABLE  0, 0, 270, 276
STYLE WS_MINIMIZEBOX | WS_VISIBLE | WS_CAPTION | WS_SYSMENU
CAPTION "MCI Tester"
FONT 8, "MS Sans Serif"
BEGIN
    EDITTEXT        IDC_MAIN_EDIT,8,8,254,100,ES_MULTILINE | ES_AUTOHSCROLL |
                    WS_VSCROLL
    LTEXT           "Return String:",IDC_STATIC,8,114,60,8
    EDITTEXT        IDC_RETURN_STRING,8,126,120,50,ES_MULTILINE |
                    ES_AUTOVSCROLL | ES_READONLY | WS_GROUP | NOT WS_TABSTOP
    LTEXT           "Error String:",IDC_STATIC,142,114,60,8
    EDITTEXT        IDC_ERROR_STRING,142,126,120,50,ES_MULTILINE |
                    ES_AUTOVSCROLL | ES_READONLY | NOT WS_TABSTOP
    GROUPBOX        "MM_MCINOTIFY Message",IDC_STATIC,9,186,254,58
    LTEXT           "",IDC_NOTIFY_ID,26,198,100,8
    LTEXT           "MCI_NOTIFY_SUCCESSFUL",IDC_NOTIFY_SUCCESSFUL,26,212,100,
                    8,WS_DISABLED
    LTEXT           "MCI_NOTIFY_SUPERSEDED",IDC_NOTIFY_SUPERSEDED,26,226,100,
                    8,WS_DISABLED
    LTEXT           "MCI_NOTIFY_ABORTED",IDC_NOTIFY_ABORTED,144,212,100,8,
                    WS_DISABLED
    LTEXT           "MCI_NOTIFY_FAILURE",IDC_NOTIFY_FAILURE,144,226,100,8,
                    WS_DISABLED
    DEFPUSHBUTTON   "OK",IDOK,57,255,50,14
    PUSHBUTTON      "Close",IDCANCEL,162,255,50,14
END
```

(continued)

Figure 22-1. *continued*

RESOURCE.H (excerpts)

```
// Microsoft Developer Studio generated include file.
// Used by TestMci.rc

#define IDC_MAIN_EDIT              1000
#define IDC_NOTIFY_MESSAGE         1005
#define IDC_NOTIFY_ID              1006
#define IDC_NOTIFY_SUCCESSFUL      1007
#define IDC_NOTIFY_SUPERSEDED      1008
#define IDC_NOTIFY_ABORTED         1009
#define IDC_NOTIFY_FAILURE         1010
#define IDC_SIGNAL_MESSAGE         1011
#define IDC_SIGNAL_ID              1012
#define IDC_SIGNAL_PARAM           1013
#define IDC_RETURN_STRING          1014
#define IDC_ERROR_STRING           1015
#define IDC_DEVICES                1016
#define IDC_STATIC                 -1
```

Like many of the programs in this chapter, TESTMCI uses a modeless dialog box as its main window. Like all of the programs in this chapter, TESTMCI requires the WINMM.LIB import library to be listed in the Links page of the Projects Settings dialog box in Microsoft Visual C++.

This program uses the two most important multimedia functions. These are *mciSendString* and *mciGetErrorText*. When you type something into the main edit window in TESTMCI and press Enter (or the OK button), the program passes the string you typed in as the first argument to the *mciSendString* command:

```
error = mciSendString (szCommand, szReturn,
                    sizeof (szReturn) / sizeof (TCHAR), hwnd) ;
```

If more than one line is selected in the edit window, the program sends them sequentially to the *mciSendString* function. The second argument is the address of a string that gets information back from the function. The program displays this information in the Return String section of the window. The error code returned from *mciSendString* is passed to the *mciGetErrorString* function to obtain a text error description; this is displayed in the Error String section of TESTMCI's window.

MCITEXT and CD Audio

You can get an excellent feel for MCI command strings by taking control of the CD-ROM drive and playing an audio CD. This is a good place to begin because these command strings are often quite simple and, moreover, you get to listen to some music. You may want to have the MCI command string reference at */Platform SDK/Graphics and Multimedia Services/ Multimedia Reference/Multimedia Command Strings* handy for this exercise.

Make sure the audio output of your CD-ROM drive is connected to speakers or a headphone, and pop in an audio compact disc, for example, Bruce Springsteen's *Born to Run*. Under Windows 98, the CD Player application might start up and begin playing the album. If so, end the CD Player. Instead, bring up TESTMCI and type in the command

```
open cdaudio
```

and press Enter. The word *open* is an MCI command and the word *cdaudio* is a device name that MCI recognizes as the CD-ROM drive. (I'm assuming you have only one CD-ROM drive on your system; getting names of multiple CD-ROM drives requires use of the *sysinfo* command.)

The Return String area in TESTMCI shows the string that the system sends back to your program in the *mciSendString* function. If the *open* command works, this is simply the number 1. The Error String area in TESTMCI shows what the *mciGetErrorString* returns based on the return value from *mciSendString*. If *mciSendString* did not return an error code, the Error String area displays the text "The specified command was carried out."

Assuming the open command worked, you can now enter

```
play cdaudio
```

The CD will begin playing "Thunder Road," the first cut on the album. You can pause the CD by entering

```
pause cdaudio
```

or

```
stop cdaudio
```

For the *cdaudio* device, these statements do the same thing. You can resume playing with

```
play cdaudio
```

So far, all the strings we've used have been composed of a command and the device name. Some commands have options. For example, type

```
status cdaudio position
```

Depending how long you've been listening, the Return String area should show something like

```
01:15:25
```

What is this? It's obviously not hours, minutes, and seconds because the CD is not that long. To find out what the time format is, type

```
status cdaudio time format
```

The Return String area now shows the string

```
msf
```

This stands for "minutes-seconds-frames." In CD Audio, there are 75 frames to the second. The frame part of the time format can range from 0 through 74.

The status command has a bunch of options. You can determine the entire length of the CD in msf format using the command

```
status cdaudio length
```

For *Born to Run*, the Return String area will show

```
39:28:19
```

That's 39 minutes, 28 seconds, and 19 frames.

Now try

```
status cdaudio number of tracks
```

The Return String area will show

```
8
```

We know from the CD cover that the title tune is the fifth track on the *Born to Run* album. Track numbers in MCI commands begin at 1. We can find out how long the song "Born to Run" is by entering

```
status cdaudio length track 5
```

The Return String area shows

```
04:30:22
```

We can also determine where on the album this track begins

```
status cdaudio position track 5
```

The Return String area shows

```
17:36:35
```

With this information we can now skip directly to the title track:

```
play cdaudio from 17:36:35 to 22:06:57
```

This command will play the one song and then stop. That last value was calculated by adding 4:30:22 (the length of the track) to 17:36:35. Or it could be determined by using

```
status cdaudio position track 6
```

Or you can set the time format to tracks-minutes-seconds-frames:

```
set cdaudio time format tmsf
```

and then

```
play cdaudio from 5:0:0:0 to 6:0:0:0
```

or, more simply,

```
play cdaudio from 5 to 6
```

You can leave off trailing components of the time if they are 0. It is also possible to set the time format in milliseconds.

Every MCI command string can include the options *wait* or *notify* (or both) at the end of the string. For example, suppose you want to play only the first 10 seconds of the song "Born to Run," and right after that happens, you want the program to do something else. Here's one way to do it (assuming you've set the time format to tmsf):

```
play cdaudio from 5:0:0 to 5:0:10 wait
```

In this case, the *mciSendString* function *does not return* until the function has been completed, that is, until the 10 seconds of "Born to Run" have finished playing.

Now obviously, in general, this is not a good thing in a single-threaded application. If you accidentally typed

```
play cdaudio wait
```

the *mciSendString* function will not return control to the program until the entire album has played. If you must use the *wait* option (and it is handy when blindly running MCI scripts, as I'll demonstrate shortly), use the *break* command first. This command lets you set a virtual key code that will break the *mciSendString* command and return control to the program. For example, to set the Escape key to serve this purpose, use

```
break cdaudio on 27
```

where 27 is the decimal value of VK_ESCAPE.

A better alternative to the *wait* option is the *notify* option:

```
play cdaudio from 5:0:0 to 5:0:10 notify
```

In this case, the *mciSendString* function returns immediately, but when the operation specified in the MCI command ends, the window whose handle is specified as the last argument to *mciSendString* receives an MM_MCINOTIFY message. The TESTMCI program displays the result of this message in the MM_MCINOTIFY group box. To avoid confusion as you may be typing in other commands, the TESTMCI program stops displaying the results of the MM_MCINOTIFY message after 5 seconds.

You can use the *wait* and *notify* keywords together, but there's hardly a reason for doing so. Without these keywords, the default behavior is to not wait and to not notify, which is usually what you want.

When you're finished playing around with these commands, you can stop the CD by entering

```
stop cdaudio
```

If you don't stop the CD-ROM device before closing it, the CD will continue to play even after you close the device.

You can try something that may or may not work with your hardware:

```
eject cdaudio
```

And then finally close the device like so:

```
close cdaudio
```

Although TESTMCI cannot save or load text files by itself, you can copy text between the edit control and the clipboard. You can select something in TESTMCI, copy it to the clipboard (using Ctrl-C), copy the text from the clipboard into NOTEPAD, and then save it. Reverse this process to load a series of MCI commands into TESTMCI. If you select a series of commands and press OK (or the Enter key), TESTMCI will execute the commands one at a time. This lets you construct MCI "scripts," which are simply lists of MCI commands.

For example, suppose you like to listen to the songs "Jungleland" (the last track on the album), "Thunder Road," and "Born to Run," in that order. Construct a script like so:

```
open cdaudio
set cdaudio time format tmsf
break cdaudio on 27
play cdaudio from 8 wait
play cdaudio from 1 to 2 wait
play cdaudio from 5 to 6 wait
stop cdaudio
eject cdaudio
close cdaudio
```

Without the *wait* keywords, this wouldn't work correctly because the *mciSendString* commands would return immediately and the next one would then execute.

At this point, it should be fairly obvious how to construct a simple application that mimics a CD player. Your program can determine the number of tracks and the length of each track and can allow the user to begin playing at any point. (Keep in mind, however, that *mciSendString* always returns information in text strings, so you'll need to write parsing logic that converts those strings to numbers.) Such a program would almost certainly also use the Windows timer, for intervals of a second or so. During WM_TIMER messages, the program would call

```
status cdaudio mode
```

to see whether the CD is paused or playing. The

```
status cdaudio position
```

command lets the program update its display to show the user the current position. But something more interesting is also possible: if your program knows the time positions of key parts of the music, it can synchronize on-screen graphics with the CD. This is excellent for music instruction or for creating your own graphical music videos.

WAVEFORM AUDIO

Waveform audio is the most utilized multimedia feature of Windows. The waveform audio facilities can capture sounds coming through a microphone, turn them into numbers, and store them in memory or on disk in waveform files with the extension .WAV. The sounds can then be played back.

Sound and Waveforms

Before plunging into the waveform audio API, it's important to have an understanding of the physics and perception of sound and the process by which sounds can get in and out of our computers.

Sound is vibration. The human body perceives sound as it changes the air pressure on our eardrums. A microphone can pick up these vibrations and translate them into electrical currents. Similarly, electrical currents can be sent to amplifiers and speakers for rendering back into sound. In traditional analog forms of sound storage (such as audio tape and the phonograph record) these vibrations are stored as magnetic pulses or contoured grooves. When a sound is translated into an electrical current, it can be represented by a waveform that shows vibrations over time. The most natural form of vibration is represented by the sine wave, one cycle of which was shown earlier in this book in Figure 5-7.

The sine wave has two parameters—amplitude (that is, the maximum amplitude over the course of one cycle) and frequency. We perceive amplitude as loudness and frequency as pitch. Human ears are generally said to be sensitive to sine waves ranging from low-pitched sounds at 20 Hz (cycles per second) to high-pitched sounds at 20,000 Hz, although sensitivity to these higher sounds degrades with age.

Human perception of frequency is logarithmic rather than linear. That is, we perceive the frequency change from 20 Hz to 40 Hz to be the same as the frequency change from 40 Hz to 80 Hz. In music, this doubling of frequency defines the octave. Thus, the human ear is sensitive to about 10 octaves of sound. The range of a piano is a little over 7 octaves, from 27.5 Hz to 4186 Hz.

Although sine waves represent the most natural form of vibration, sine waves rarely occur in nature in pure forms. Moreover, pure sine waves are not very interesting sounds. Most sounds are much more complex.

Any periodic waveform (that is, a waveform that repeats itself) can be decomposed into multiple sine waves whose frequency relationships are in integer multiples. This is called a Fourier series, named after the French mathematician and physicist Jean Baptiste Joseph Fourier (1768–1830). The frequency of periodicity is known as the fundamental. The other sine waves in the series have frequencies that are 2, 3, 4 (and so forth) times the frequency of the fundamental. These are called overtones. The fundamental is also called the first harmonic. The first overtone is the second harmonic, and so forth.

The relative intensities of the sine wave harmonics give each periodic waveform a unique sound. This is known as "timbre," and it's what makes a trumpet sound like a trumpet and a piano sound like a piano.

At one time it was believed that electronically synthesizing musical instruments required merely that sounds be broken down into harmonics and reconstructed with multiple sine waves. However, it turned out that real-world sounds are not quite so simple. Waveforms representing real-world sounds are never strictly periodic. Relative intensities of harmonics are different over the range of a musical instrument and the harmonics change with time as each note is played. In particular, the beginning of a note played on a musical instrument—called the attack—can be quite complex and is vital to our perception of timbre.

Due to the increase in digital storage capabilities in recent years, it has become possible to store sounds directly in a digital form without any complex deconstruction.

Pulse Code Modulation

Computers work with numbers, so to get sounds into our computers, it is necessary to devise a mechanism to convert sound to numbers and back again from numbers to sound.

The most common method of doing this without compressing data is called "pulse code modulation" (PCM). PCM is used on compact discs, digital audio tapes, and in Windows. Pulse code modulation is a fancy term for a conceptually simple process.

With pulse code modulation, a waveform is sampled at a constant periodic rate, usually some tens of thousands of times per second. For each sample, the amplitude of the waveform is measured. The hardware that does the job of converting an amplitude into a number is an analog-to-digital converter (ADC). Similarly, numbers can be converted back into electrical waveforms using a digital-to-analog converter (DAC). What comes out is not exactly what goes in. The resultant waveform has sharp edges that are high-frequency components. For this reason, playback hardware generally includes a low-pass filter following the digital-to-analog converter. This filter removes the high frequencies and smooths out the resultant waveform. On the input side, a low-pass filter comes before the ADC.

Pulse code modulation has two parameters: the sample rate, or how many times per second you measure the waveform amplitude, and the sample size, or the number of bits you use to store the amplitude level. As you might expect, the faster the sampling rate and the larger the sample size, the better the reproduction of the original sound. However, there is a point where any improvements to the sampling rate and sample size are overkill because they go beyond the resolution of human perception. On the other hand, making the sampling rate and sample size too low can cause problems in accurately reproducing music and other sounds.

The Sampling Rate

The sampling rate determines the maximum frequency of sound that can be digitized and stored. In particular, the sampling rate must be twice the highest frequency of sampled sound. This is known as the "Nyquist Frequency," named after Harry Nyquist, an engineer who did research in the 1930s into sampling processes.

When a sine wave is sampled with too low a sampling rate, the resultant waveform has a lower frequency than the original. This is known as an alias. To avoid the problem of aliases, a low-pass filter is used on the input side to block all frequencies greater than half the sampling rate. On the output side, the rough edges of the waveform produced by the digital-to-analog converter are actually overtones composed of frequencies greater than half the sampling rate. Thus, a low-pass filter on the output side also blocks all frequencies greater than half the sampling rate.

The sampling rate used on audio CDs is 44,100 samples per second, or 44.1 kHz. The origin of this peculiar number is as follows:

The human ear can hear up to 20 kHz, so to capture the entire audio range that can be heard by humans, a sampling rate of 40 kHz is required. However, because low-pass filters have a roll-off effect, the sampling rate should be about 10 percent higher than that. Now we're up to 44 kHz. Just in case we want to record digital audio along with video, the sampling rate should be an integral multiple of the American and European television frame rates, which are 30 Hz and 25 Hz respectively. That pushes the sampling rate up to 44.1 kHz.

The compact disc sampling rate of 44.1 kHz produces a lot of data and might be overkill for some applications, such as recording voice rather than music. Halving the sampling rate to 22.05 kHz reduces the upper range of reproducible sound by one octave to 10 kHz. Halving it again to 11.025 kHz gives us a frequency range to 5 kHz. Sampling rates of 44.1 kHz, 22.05 kHz, and 11.025 kHz, as well as 8 kHz, are the standards commonly supported by waveform audio devices.

You might think that a sampling rate of 11.025 kHz is adequate for recording a piano because the highest frequency of a piano is 4186 Hz. However, 4186 Hz is the highest *fundamental* of a piano. Cutting off all sine waves above 5000 Hz reduces the overtones that can be reproduced and will not accurately capture and reproduce the piano sound.

The Sample Size

The second parameter in pulse code modulation is the sample size measured in bits. The sample size determines the difference between the softest sound and loudest sound that can be recorded and played back. This is known as the dynamic range.

Sound intensity is the square of the waveform amplitude (that is, the composite of the maximum amplitudes that each sine wave reaches over the course of one cycle). As is the case with frequency, human perception of sound intensity is logarithmic.

The difference in intensity between two sounds is measured in bels (named after Alexander Graham Bell, the inventor of the telephone) and decibels (dB). A bel is a ten-fold increase in sound intensity. One dB is one tenth of a bel in equal multiplicative steps. Hence, one dB is an increase in sound intensity of 1.26 (that is, the 10th root of 10), or an increase in waveform amplitude of 1.12 (the 20th root of 10). A decibel is about the lowest increase in sound intensity that the ear can perceive. The difference in intensity between sounds at the threshold of hearing and sounds at the threshold of pain is about 100 dB.

You can calculate the dynamic range in decibels between two sounds with the following formula:

$$dB = 20 \cdot \log\left(\frac{A_1}{A_2}\right)$$

where A_1 and A_2 are the amplitudes of the two sounds. With a sample size of 1 bit, the dynamic range is 0, because only one amplitude is possible.

With a sample size of 8 bits, the ratio of the largest amplitude to the smallest amplitude is 256. Thus, the dynamic range is

$$dB = 20 \cdot \log(256)$$

or 48 decibels. A 48-dB dynamic range is about the difference between a quiet room and a power lawn mower. Doubling the sample size to 16 bits yields a dynamic range of

$$dB = 20 \cdot \log(65536)$$

or 96 decibels. This is very nearly the difference between the threshold of hearing and the threshold of pain and is considered just about ideal for the reproduction of music.

Both 8-bit and 16-bit sample sizes are supported under Windows. When storing 8-bit samples, the samples are treated as unsigned bytes. Silence would be stored as a string of 0x80 values. The 16-bit samples are treated as signed integers, so silence would be stored as a string of zeros.

To calculate the storage space required for uncompressed audio, multiply the duration of the sound in seconds by the sampling rate. Double that if you're using 16-bit samples rather than 8-bit samples. Double that again if you're recording in stereo. For example, an hour of CD-quality sound (or 3600 seconds at 44,100 samples per second with 2 bytes per sample in stereo) requires 635 megabytes, not coincidentally very close to the storage capability of CD-ROM.

Generating Sine Waves in Software

For our first exercise in waveform audio, we're not going to save sounds to files or play back recorded sounds. We're going to use the low-level waveform audio APIs (that is, the functions beginning with the prefix *waveOut*) to create an audio sine wave generator called SINEWAVE. This program generates sine waves from 20 Hz (the bottom of human perception) to 5,000 Hz (two octaves short of the top of human perception) in 1 Hz increments.

As you know, the standard C run-time library includes a function called *sin* that returns the sine of an angle given in radians. (Two π radians equals 360 degrees.) The *sin* function returns a value ranging from −1 to 1. (We used this function in another program called SINEWAVE way back in Chapter 5.) Thus, it should be easy to use the *sin* function to generate sine wave data to output to the waveform audio hardware. Basically, you fill a buffer up with data representing the waveform (in this case, a sine wave) and pass it to the API. (It's a little more complicated than that, but I'll get to the details shortly.) When the waveform audio hardware finishes playing the buffer, you pass it a second buffer, and so forth.

When first considering this problem (and not knowing anything about PCM), you might think it reasonable to divide one cycle of the sine wave into a fixed number of samples—for example, 360. For a 20-Hz sine wave, you output 7200 samples every second. For a 200-Hz sine wave, you output 72,000 samples per second. That might work, but it's not the way to do it. For a 5000-Hz sine wave, you'd need to output 1,800,000 samples per second, which would surely tax the DAC! Moreover, for the higher frequencies, this is much more precision than is needed.

With pulse code modulation, the sample rate is a constant. Let's assume the sample rate is 11,025 Hz because that's what I use in the SINEWAVE program. If you wish to generate a sine wave of 2,756.25 Hz (exactly one-quarter the sample rate), each cycle of the sine wave is just 4 samples. For a sine wave of 25 Hz, each cycle requires 441 samples. In general, the number of samples per cycle is the sample rate divided by the desired sine wave frequency. Once you know the number of samples per cycle, you can divide 2π radians by that number and use the *sin* function to get the samples for one cycle. Then just repeat the samples for one cycle over and over again to create a continuous waveform.

The problem is, the number of samples per cycle may well be fractional, so this approach won't work well either. You'd get a discontinuity at the end of each cycle.

The key to making this work correctly is to maintain a static "phase angle" variable. This angle is initialized at 0. The first sample is the sine of 0 degrees. The phase angle is then incremented by 2π times the frequency, divided by the sample rate. Use this phase angle for the second sample, and continue in this way. Whenever the phase angle gets above 2π radians, subtract 2π radians from it. But don't ever reinitialize it to 0.

For example, suppose you want to generate a sine wave of 1000 Hz with a sample rate of 11,025 Hz. That's about 11 samples per cycle. The phase angles—and here I'll give them in degrees to make this a little more comprehensible—for approximately the first cycle and a half are 0, 32.65, 65.31, 97.96, 130.61, 163.27, 195.92, 228.57, 261.22, 293.88, 326.53, 359.18, 31.84, 64.49, 97.14, 129.80, 162.45, 195.10, and so forth. The waveform data you put in the buffer are the sines of these angles, scaled to the number of bits per sample. When creating the data for a subsequent buffer, you keep incrementing the last phase angle value without reinitializing it to 0.

A function called *FillBuffer* that does this—along with the rest of the SINEWAVE program—is shown in Figure 22-2 on the following page.

SINEWAVE.C

```c
/*---------------------------------------------------------
   SINEWAVE.C -- Multimedia Windows Sine Wave Generator
                 (c) Charles Petzold, 1998
  ---------------------------------------------------------*/

#include <windows.h>
#include <math.h>
#include "resource.h"

#define SAMPLE_RATE      11025
#define FREQ_MIN            20
#define FREQ_MAX          5000
#define FREQ_INIT          440
#define OUT_BUFFER_SIZE   4096
#define PI                   3.14159

BOOL CALLBACK DlgProc (HWND, UINT, WPARAM, LPARAM) ;

TCHAR szAppName [] = TEXT ("SineWave") ;

int WINAPI WinMain (HINSTANCE hInstance, HINSTANCE hPrevInstance,
                    PSTR szCmdLine, int iCmdShow)
{
     if (-1 == DialogBox (hInstance, szAppName, NULL, DlgProc))
     {
          MessageBox (NULL, TEXT ("This program requires Windows NT!"),
                      szAppName, MB_ICONERROR) ;
     }
     return 0 ;
}

VOID FillBuffer (PBYTE pBuffer, int iFreq)
{
     static double fAngle ;
     int          i ;

     for (i = 0 ; i < OUT_BUFFER_SIZE ; i++)
     {
          pBuffer [i] = (BYTE) (127 + 127 * sin (fAngle)) ;

          fAngle += 2 * PI * iFreq / SAMPLE_RATE ;

          if (fAngle > 2 * PI)
```

Figure 22-2. *The SINEWAVE program.*

```
                fAngle -= 2 * PI ;
        }
}

BOOL CALLBACK DlgProc (HWND hwnd, UINT message, WPARAM wParam, LPARAM lParam)
{
    static BOOL         bShutOff, bClosing ;
    static HWAVEOUT     hWaveOut ;
    static HWND         hwndScroll ;
    static int          iFreq = FREQ_INIT ;
    static PBYTE        pBuffer1, pBuffer2 ;
    static PWAVEHDR     pWaveHdr1, pWaveHdr2 ;
    static WAVEFORMATEX waveformat ;
    int                 iDummy ;

    switch (message)
    {
    case WM_INITDIALOG:
        hwndScroll = GetDlgItem (hwnd, IDC_SCROLL) ;
        SetScrollRange (hwndScroll, SB_CTL, FREQ_MIN, FREQ_MAX, FALSE) ;
        SetScrollPos   (hwndScroll, SB_CTL, FREQ_INIT, TRUE) ;
        SetDlgItemInt  (hwnd, IDC_TEXT, FREQ_INIT, FALSE) ;

        return TRUE ;

    case WM_HSCROLL:
        switch (LOWORD (wParam))
        {
        case SB_LINELEFT:  iFreq -= 1 ;  break ;
        case SB_LINERIGHT: iFreq += 1 ;  break ;
        case SB_PAGELEFT:  iFreq /= 2 ;  break ;
        case SB_PAGERIGHT: iFreq *= 2 ;  break ;

        case SB_THUMBTRACK:
            iFreq = HIWORD (wParam) ;
            break ;

        case SB_TOP:
            GetScrollRange (hwndScroll, SB_CTL, &iFreq, &iDummy) ;
            break ;

        case SB_BOTTOM:
            GetScrollRange (hwndScroll, SB_CTL, &iDummy, &iFreq) ;
            break ;
        }

        iFreq = max (FREQ_MIN, min (FREQ_MAX, iFreq)) ;
```

(continued)

Figure 22-2. *continued*

```
        SetScrollPos (hwndScroll, SB_CTL, iFreq, TRUE) ;
        SetDlgItemInt (hwnd, IDC_TEXT, iFreq, FALSE) ;
        return TRUE ;

case WM_COMMAND:
     switch (LOWORD (wParam))
     {
     case IDC_ONOFF:
             // If turning on waveform, hWaveOut is NULL

          if (hWaveOut == NULL)
          {
                  // Allocate memory for 2 headers and 2 buffers

               pWaveHdr1 = malloc (sizeof (WAVEHDR)) ;
               pWaveHdr2 = malloc (sizeof (WAVEHDR)) ;
               pBuffer1  = malloc (OUT_BUFFER_SIZE) ;
               pBuffer2  = malloc (OUT_BUFFER_SIZE) ;

               if (!pWaveHdr1 || !pWaveHdr2 || !pBuffer1 || !pBuffer2)
               {
                    if (!pWaveHdr1) free (pWaveHdr1) ;
                    if (!pWaveHdr2) free (pWaveHdr2) ;
                    if (!pBuffer1)  free (pBuffer1) ;
                    if (!pBuffer2)  free (pBuffer2) ;

                    MessageBeep (MB_ICONEXCLAMATION) ;
                    MessageBox (hwnd, TEXT ("Error allocating memory!"),
                              szAppName, MB_ICONEXCLAMATION | MB_OK) ;
                    return TRUE ;
               }

                  // Variable to indicate Off button pressed

               bShutOff = FALSE ;

                  // Open waveform audio for output

               waveformat.wFormatTag     = WAVE_FORMAT_PCM ;
               waveformat.nChannels      = 1 ;
               waveformat.nSamplesPerSec  = SAMPLE_RATE ;
               waveformat.nAvgBytesPerSec = SAMPLE_RATE ;
               waveformat.nBlockAlign    = 1 ;
               waveformat.wBitsPerSample = 8 ;
               waveformat.cbSize         = 0 ;

               if (waveOutOpen (&hWaveOut, WAVE_MAPPER, &waveformat,
```

```
                            (DWORD) hwnd, 0, CALLBACK_WINDOW)
                 != MMSYSERR_NOERROR)
     {
          free (pWaveHdr1) ;
          free (pWaveHdr2) ;
          free (pBuffer1) ;
          free (pBuffer2) ;

          hWaveOut = NULL ;
          MessageBeep (MB_ICONEXCLAMATION) ;
          MessageBox (hwnd,
               TEXT ("Error opening waveform audio device!"),
               szAppName, MB_ICONEXCLAMATION | MB_OK) ;
          return TRUE ;
     }


          // Set up headers and prepare them

     pWaveHdr1->lpData            = pBuffer1 ;
     pWaveHdr1->dwBufferLength    = OUT_BUFFER_SIZE ;
     pWaveHdr1->dwBytesRecorded   = 0 ;
     pWaveHdr1->dwUser            = 0 ;
     pWaveHdr1->dwFlags           = 0 ;
     pWaveHdr1->dwLoops           = 1 ;
     pWaveHdr1->lpNext            = NULL ;
     pWaveHdr1->reserved          = 0 ;

     waveOutPrepareHeader (hWaveOut, pWaveHdr1,
                           sizeof (WAVEHDR)) ;

     pWaveHdr2->lpData            = pBuffer2 ;
     pWaveHdr2->dwBufferLength    = OUT_BUFFER_SIZE ;
     pWaveHdr2->dwBytesRecorded   = 0 ;
     pWaveHdr2->dwUser            = 0 ;
     pWaveHdr2->dwFlags           = 0 ;
     pWaveHdr2->dwLoops           = 1 ;
     pWaveHdr2->lpNext            = NULL ;
     pWaveHdr2->reserved          = 0 ;

     waveOutPrepareHeader (hWaveOut, pWaveHdr2,
                           sizeof (WAVEHDR)) ;
}
     // If turning off waveform, reset waveform audio
else
{
     bShutOff = TRUE ;
```

(continued)

Figure 22-2. *continued*

```
                    waveOutReset (hWaveOut) ;
               }
          return TRUE ;
     }
     break ;

          // Message generated from waveOutOpen call

case MM_WOM_OPEN:
     SetDlgItemText (hwnd, IDC_ONOFF, TEXT ("Turn Off")) ;

          // Send two buffers to waveform output device

     FillBuffer (pBuffer1, iFreq) ;
     waveOutWrite (hWaveOut, pWaveHdr1, sizeof (WAVEHDR)) ;

     FillBuffer (pBuffer2, iFreq) ;
     waveOutWrite (hWaveOut, pWaveHdr2, sizeof (WAVEHDR)) ;
     return TRUE ;

          // Message generated when a buffer is finished

case MM_WOM_DONE:
     if (bShutOff)
     {
          waveOutClose (hWaveOut) ;
          return TRUE ;
     }

          // Fill and send out a new buffer

     FillBuffer (((PWAVEHDR) lParam)->lpData, iFreq) ;
     waveOutWrite (hWaveOut, (PWAVEHDR) lParam, sizeof (WAVEHDR)) ;
     return TRUE ;

case MM_WOM_CLOSE:
     waveOutUnprepareHeader (hWaveOut, pWaveHdr1, sizeof (WAVEHDR)) ;
     waveOutUnprepareHeader (hWaveOut, pWaveHdr2, sizeof (WAVEHDR)) ;

     free (pWaveHdr1) ;
     free (pWaveHdr2) ;
     free (pBuffer1) ;
     free (pBuffer2) ;

     hWaveOut = NULL ;
     SetDlgItemText (hwnd, IDC_ONOFF, TEXT ("Turn On")) ;
```

```
            if (bClosing)
                EndDialog (hwnd, 0) ;

            return TRUE ;

        case WM_SYSCOMMAND:
            switch (wParam)
            {
            case SC_CLOSE:
                if (hWaveOut != NULL)
                {
                    bShutOff = TRUE ;
                    bClosing = TRUE ;

                    waveOutReset (hWaveOut) ;
                }
                else
                    EndDialog (hwnd, 0) ;

                return TRUE ;
            }
            break ;
        }
        return FALSE ;
}
```

SINEWAVE.RC (excerpts)

```
//Microsoft Developer Studio generated resource script.

#include "resource.h"
#include "afxres.h"


/////////////////////////////////////////////////////////////////////////////
// Dialog

SINEWAVE DIALOG DISCARDABLE  100, 100, 200, 50
STYLE WS_MINIMIZEBOX | WS_VISIBLE | WS_CAPTION | WS_SYSMENU
CAPTION "Sine Wave Generator"
FONT 8, "MS Sans Serif"
BEGIN
    SCROLLBAR       IDC_SCROLL,8,8,150,12
    RTEXT           "440",IDC_TEXT,160,10,20,8
    LTEXT           "Hz",IDC_STATIC,182,10,12,8
    PUSHBUTTON      "Turn On",IDC_ONOFF,80,28,40,14
END
```

(continued)

Figure 22-2. *continued*

RESOURCE.H (excerpts)

```
// Microsoft Developer Studio generated include file.
// Used by SineWave.rc

#define IDC_STATIC                      -1
#define IDC_SCROLL                      1000
#define IDC_TEXT                        1001
#define IDC_ONOFF                       1002
```

Note that the OUT_BUFFER_SIZE, SAMPLE_RATE, and PI identifiers used in the *FillBuffer* routine are defined at the top of the program. The *iFreq* argument to *FillBuffer* is the desired frequency in Hz. Notice that the result of the *sin* function is scaled to range between 0 and 254. For each sample, the *fAngle* argument to the *sin* function is increased by 2π radians times the desired frequency divided by the sample rate.

SINEWAVE's window contains three controls: a horizontal scroll bar used for selecting the frequency, a static text field that indicates the currently selected frequency, and a push button labeled "Turn On." When you press the button, you should hear a sine wave from the speakers connected to your sound board and the button text will change to "Turn Off." You can change the frequency by moving the scroll bar with the keyboard or mouse. To turn off the sound, push the button again.

The SINEWAVE code initializes the scroll bar so that the minimum frequency is 20 Hz and the maximum frequency is 5000 Hz during the WM_INITDIALOG message. Initially, the scroll bar is set to 440 Hz. In musical terms, this is the A above middle C, the note used for tuning an orchestra. *DlgProc* alters the static variable *iFreq* on receipt of WM_HSCROLL messages. Notice that Page Left and Page Right cause *DlgProc* to decrease or increase the frequency by one octave.

When *DlgProc* receives a WM_COMMAND message from the button, it first allocates 4 blocks of memory—2 for WAVEHDR structures, discussed shortly, and two for buffers, called *pBuffer1* and *pBuffer2*, to hold the waveform data.

SINEWAVE opens the waveform audio device for output by calling the *waveOutOpen* function, which uses the following arguments:

```
waveOutOpen (&hWaveOut, wDeviceID, &waveformat, dwCallBack,
             dwCallBackData, dwFlags) ;
```

You set the first argument to point to a variable of type HWAVEOUT ("handle to waveform audio output"). On return from the function, this variable will be set to a handle used in subsequent waveform output calls.

The second argument to *waveOutOpen* is a device ID. This allows the function to be used on machines that have multiple sound boards installed. The argument can range from 0 to one less than the number of waveform output devices installed in the system. You can get the number of waveform output devices by calling *waveOutGetNumDevs* and find out about each of them by calling *waveOutGetDevCaps*. If you wish to avoid this device interrogation, you can use the constant WAVE_MAPPER (defined as equalling −1) to select the device the user has indicated as the Preferred Device in the Audio tab of the Multimedia applet of the Control Panel. Or the system could select another device if the preferred device can't handle what you need to do and another device can.

The third argument is a pointer to a WAVEFORMATEX structure. (More about this shortly.) The fourth argument is either a window handle or a pointer to a callback function in a dynamic-link library. This argument indicates the window or callback function that receives the waveform output messages. If you use a callback function, you can specify program-defined data in the fifth argument. The *dwFlags* argument can be set to either CALLBACK_WINDOW or CALLBACK_FUNCTION to indicate what the fourth argument is. You can also use the flag WAVE_FORMAT_QUERY to check whether the device can be opened without actually opening it. A few other flags are available.

The third argument to *waveOutOpen* is defined as a pointer to a structure of type WAVEFORMATEX, defined in MMSYSTEM.H as shown below:

```
typedef struct waveformat_tag
{
    WORD  wFormatTag ;          // waveform format = WAVE_FORMAT_PCM
    WORD  nChannels ;           // number of channels = 1 or 2
    DWORD nSamplesPerSec ;      // sample rate
    DWORD nAvgBytesPerSec ;     // bytes per second
    WORD  nBlockAlign ;         // block alignment
    WORD  wBitsPerSample ;      // bits per samples = 8 or 16
    WORD  cbSize ;              // 0 for PCM
}
WAVEFORMATEX, * PWAVEFORMATEX ;
```

This is the structure you use to specify the sample rate (*nSamplesPerSec*), the sample size (*nBitsPerSample*), and whether you want monophonic or stereophonic sound (*nChannels*). Some of the information in this structure may seem redundant, but the structure is designed for sampling methods other than PCM, in which case the last field is set to a nonzero value and other information follows.

For PCM, set *nBlockAlign* field to the product of *nChannels* and *wBitsPerSample*, divided by 8. This is the total number of bytes per sample. Set the *nAvgBytesPerSec* field to the product of *nSamplesPerSec* and *nBlockAlign*.

SINEWAVE initializes the fields of the WAVEFORMATEX structure and calls *waveOutOpen* like this:

```
waveOutOpen (&hWaveOut, WAVE_MAPPER, &waveformat,
             (DWORD) hwnd, 0, CALLBACK_WINDOW)
```

The *waveOutOpen* function returns MMSYSERR_NOERROR (defined as 0) if the function is successful and a nonzero error code otherwise. If *waveOutOpen* returns nonzero, SINEWAVE cleans up and displays a message box indicating an error.

Now that the device is open, SINEWAVE continues by initializing the fields of the two WAVEHDR structures, which are used to pass buffers through the API. WAVEHDR is defined like so:

```
typedef struct wavehdr_tag
{
    LPSTR lpData;                      // pointer to data buffer
    DWORD dwBufferLength;              // length of data buffer
    DWORD dwBytesRecorded;            // used for recorded
    DWORD dwUser;                      // for program use
    DWORD dwFlags;                     // flags
    DWORD dwLoops;                     // number of repetitions
    struct wavehdr_tag FAR *lpNext;   // reserved
    DWORD reserved;                    // reserved
}
WAVEHDR, *PWAVEHDR ;
```

SINEWAVE sets the *lpData* field to the address at the buffer that will contain the data, *dwBufferLength* to the size of this buffer, and *dwLoops* to 1. All other fields can be set to 0 or NULL. If you want to play a repeated loop of sound, you can specify that with the *dwFlags* and *dwLoops* fields.

Next SINEWAVE calls *waveOutPrepareHeader* for the two headers. Calling this function prevents the structure and buffer from being swapped to disk.

So far, all of this preparation has been in response to the button click to turn on the sound. But a message is waiting in the program's message queue. Because we specified in *waveOutOpen* that we wish to use a window procedure for receiving waveform output messages, the *waveOutOpen* function posted a MM_WOM_OPEN message to the program's message queue. The *wParam* message parameter is set to the waveform output handle. To process the MM_WOM_OPEN message, SINEWAVE twice calls *FillBuffer* to fill the *pBuffer* buffer with sinewave data. SINEWAVE then passes the two WAVEHDR structures to *waveOutWrite*. This is the function that actually starts the sound playing by passing the data to the waveform output hardware.

When the waveform hardware is finished playing the data passed to it in the *waveOutWrite* function, the window is posted an MM_WOM_DONE message. The *wParam* parameter is the waveform output handle, and *lParam* is a pointer to the WAVEHDR structure. SINEWAVE processes this message by calculating new values for the buffer and resubmitting the buffer by calling *waveOutWrite*.

SINEWAVE could have been written using just one WAVEHDR structure and one buffer. However, there would be a slight delay between the time the waveform hardware finished playing the data and the program processed the MM_WOM_DONE message to submit a new buffer. The "double-buffering" technique that SINEWAVE uses prevents gaps in the sound.

When the user clicks the "Turn Off" button to turn off the sound, *DlgProc* receives another WM_COMMAND message. For this message, *DlgProc* sets the *bShutOff* variable to TRUE and calls *waveOutReset*. The *waveOutReset* function stops sound processing and generates a MM_WOM_DONE message. When *bShutOff* is TRUE, SINEWAVE processes MM_WOM_DONE by calling *waveOutClose*. This in turn generates an MM_WOM_CLOSE message. Processing of MM_WOM_CLOSE mostly involves cleaning up. SINEWAVE calls *waveOutUnprepareHeader* for the two WAVEHDR structures, frees all the memory blocks, and sets the text of the button back to "Turn On."

If the waveform hardware is still playing a buffer, calling *waveOutClose* by itself will have no effect. You must call *waveOutReset* first to halt the playing and to generate an MM_WOM_DONE message. *DlgProc* also processes the WM_SYSCOMMAND message when *wParam* is SC_CLOSE. This results from the user selecting "Close" from the system menu. If waveform audio is still playing, *DlgProc* calls *waveOutReset*. Regardless, *EndDialog* is eventually called to close the dialog box and end the program.

A Digital Sound Recorder

Windows includes a program called Sound Recorder that lets you digitally record and playback sounds. The program shown in Figure 22-3 (RECORD1) is not quite as sophisticated as Sound Recorder because it doesn't do any file I/O or allow sound editing. However, it does show the basics of using the low-level waveform audio API for both recording and playing back sounds.

RECORD1.C

```c
/*------------------------------------------
   RECORD1.C -- Waveform Audio Recorder
                (c) Charles Petzold, 1998
   ------------------------------------------*/

#include <windows.h>
#include "resource.h"

#define INP_BUFFER_SIZE 16384

BOOL CALLBACK DlgProc (HWND, UINT, WPARAM, LPARAM) ;

TCHAR szAppName [] = TEXT ("Record1") ;

int WINAPI WinMain (HINSTANCE hInstance, HINSTANCE hPrevInstance,
                    PSTR szCmdLine, int iCmdShow)
{
    if (-1 == DialogBox (hInstance, TEXT ("Record"), NULL, DlgProc))
    {
        MessageBox (NULL, TEXT ("This program requires Windows NT!"),
                    szAppName, MB_ICONERROR) ;
    }
```

Figure 22-3. *The RECORD1 program.*

(continued)

Figure 22-3. *continued*

```
     return 0 ;
}

void ReverseMemory (BYTE * pBuffer, int iLength)
{
     BYTE b ;
     int  i ;

     for (i = 0 ; i < iLength / 2 ; i++)
     {
          b = pBuffer [i] ;
          pBuffer [i] = pBuffer [iLength - i - 1] ;
          pBuffer [iLength - i - 1] = b ;
     }
}

BOOL CALLBACK DlgProc (HWND hwnd, UINT message, WPARAM wParam, LPARAM lParam)
{
     static BOOL        bRecording, bPlaying, bReverse, bPaused,
                        bEnding, bTerminating ;
     static DWORD       dwDataLength, dwRepetitions = 1 ;
     static HWAVEIN     hWaveIn ;
     static HWAVEOUT    hWaveOut ;
     static PBYTE       pBuffer1, pBuffer2, pSaveBuffer, pNewBuffer ;
     static PWAVEHDR    pWaveHdr1, pWaveHdr2 ;
     static TCHAR       szOpenError[] = TEXT ("Error opening waveform audio!");
     static TCHAR       szMemError [] = TEXT ("Error allocating memory!") ;
     static WAVEFORMATEX waveform ;

     switch (message)
     {
     case WM_INITDIALOG:
               // Allocate memory for wave header

          pWaveHdr1 = malloc (sizeof (WAVEHDR)) ;
          pWaveHdr2 = malloc (sizeof (WAVEHDR)) ;

               // Allocate memory for save buffer

          pSaveBuffer = malloc (1) ;
          return TRUE ;

     case WM_COMMAND:
          switch (LOWORD (wParam))
          {
          case IDC_RECORD_BEG:
```

```
        // Allocate buffer memory

pBuffer1 = malloc (INP_BUFFER_SIZE) ;
pBuffer2 = malloc (INP_BUFFER_SIZE) ;

if (!pBuffer1 || !pBuffer2)
{
     if (pBuffer1) free (pBuffer1) ;
     if (pBuffer2) free (pBuffer2) ;

     MessageBeep (MB_ICONEXCLAMATION) ;
     MessageBox (hwnd, szMemError, szAppName,
                       MB_ICONEXCLAMATION | MB_OK) ;
     return TRUE ;
}

        // Open waveform audio for input

waveform.wFormatTag      = WAVE_FORMAT_PCM ;
waveform.nChannels       = 1 ;
waveform.nSamplesPerSec  = 11025 ;
waveform.nAvgBytesPerSec = 11025 ;
waveform.nBlockAlign     = 1 ;
waveform.wBitsPerSample  = 8 ;
waveform.cbSize          = 0 ;

if (waveInOpen (&hWaveIn, WAVE_MAPPER, &waveform,
               (DWORD) hwnd, 0, CALLBACK_WINDOW))
{
     free (pBuffer1) ;
     free (pBuffer2) ;
     MessageBeep (MB_ICONEXCLAMATION) ;
     MessageBox (hwnd, szOpenError, szAppName,
                       MB_ICONEXCLAMATION | MB_OK) ;
}
        // Set up headers and prepare them

pWaveHdr1->lpData         = pBuffer1 ;
pWaveHdr1->dwBufferLength  = INP_BUFFER_SIZE ;
pWaveHdr1->dwBytesRecorded = 0 ;
pWaveHdr1->dwUser         = 0 ;
pWaveHdr1->dwFlags        = 0 ;
pWaveHdr1->dwLoops        = 1 ;
pWaveHdr1->lpNext         = NULL ;
pWaveHdr1->reserved       = 0 ;
```

(continued)

Figure 22-3. *continued*

```
        waveInPrepareHeader (hWaveIn, pWaveHdr1, sizeof (WAVEHDR)) ;

        pWaveHdr2->lpData          = pBuffer2 ;
        pWaveHdr2->dwBufferLength   = INP_BUFFER_SIZE ;
        pWaveHdr2->dwBytesRecorded = 0 ;
        pWaveHdr2->dwUser          = 0 ;
        pWaveHdr2->dwFlags         = 0 ;
        pWaveHdr2->dwLoops         = 1 ;
        pWaveHdr2->lpNext          = NULL ;
        pWaveHdr2->reserved        = 0 ;

        waveInPrepareHeader (hWaveIn, pWaveHdr2, sizeof (WAVEHDR)) ;
        return TRUE ;

case IDC_RECORD_END:
        // Reset input to return last buffer

        bEnding = TRUE ;
        waveInReset (hWaveIn) ;
        return TRUE ;

case IDC_PLAY_BEG:
        // Open waveform audio for output

        waveform.wFormatTag       = WAVE_FORMAT_PCM ;
        waveform.nChannels        = 1 ;
        waveform.nSamplesPerSec   = 11025 ;
        waveform.nAvgBytesPerSec  = 11025 ;
        waveform.nBlockAlign      = 1 ;
        waveform.wBitsPerSample   = 8 ;
        waveform.cbSize           = 0 ;

        if (waveOutOpen (&hWaveOut, WAVE_MAPPER, &waveform,
                        (DWORD) hwnd, 0, CALLBACK_WINDOW))
        {
            MessageBeep (MB_ICONEXCLAMATION) ;
            MessageBox (hwnd, szOpenError, szAppName,
                MB_ICONEXCLAMATION | MB_OK) ;
        }
        return TRUE ;

case IDC_PLAY_PAUSE:
        // Pause or restart output

        if (!bPaused)
```

```
            {
                waveOutPause (hWaveOut) ;
                SetDlgItemText (hwnd, IDC_PLAY_PAUSE, TEXT ("Resume")) ;
                bPaused = TRUE ;
            }
            else
            {
                waveOutRestart (hWaveOut) ;
                SetDlgItemText (hwnd, IDC_PLAY_PAUSE, TEXT ("Pause")) ;
                bPaused = FALSE ;
            }
            return TRUE ;

       case IDC_PLAY_END:
                // Reset output for close preparation

            bEnding = TRUE ;
            waveOutReset (hWaveOut) ;
            return TRUE ;

       case IDC_PLAY_REV:
                // Reverse save buffer and play

            bReverse = TRUE ;
            ReverseMemory (pSaveBuffer, dwDataLength) ;

            SendMessage (hwnd, WM_COMMAND, IDC_PLAY_BEG, 0) ;
            return TRUE ;

       case IDC_PLAY_REP:
                // Set infinite repetitions and play

            dwRepetitions = -1 ;
            SendMessage (hwnd, WM_COMMAND, IDC_PLAY_BEG, 0) ;
            return TRUE ;

       case IDC_PLAY_SPEED:
                // Open waveform audio for fast output

            waveform.wFormatTag      = WAVE_FORMAT_PCM ;
            waveform.nChannels       = 1 ;
            waveform.nSamplesPerSec  = 22050 ;
            waveform.nAvgBytesPerSec = 22050 ;
            waveform.nBlockAlign     = 1 ;
            waveform.wBitsPerSample  = 8 ;
            waveform.cbSize          = 0 ;
```

(continued)

Figure 22-3. *continued*

```
            if (waveOutOpen (&hWaveOut, 0, &waveform, (DWORD) hwnd, 0,
                                  CALLBACK_WINDOW))
            {
                  MessageBeep (MB_ICONEXCLAMATION) ;
                  MessageBox (hwnd, szOpenError, szAppName,
                                   MB_ICONEXCLAMATION | MB_OK) ;
            }
            return TRUE ;
      }
      break ;

case MM_WIM_OPEN:
            // Shrink down the save buffer

      pSaveBuffer = realloc (pSaveBuffer, 1) ;

            // Enable and disable buttons

      EnableWindow (GetDlgItem (hwnd, IDC_RECORD_BEG), FALSE) ;
      EnableWindow (GetDlgItem (hwnd, IDC_RECORD_END), TRUE)  ;
      EnableWindow (GetDlgItem (hwnd, IDC_PLAY_BEG),   FALSE) ;
      EnableWindow (GetDlgItem (hwnd, IDC_PLAY_PAUSE), FALSE) ;
      EnableWindow (GetDlgItem (hwnd, IDC_PLAY_END),   FALSE) ;
      EnableWindow (GetDlgItem (hwnd, IDC_PLAY_REV),   FALSE) ;
      EnableWindow (GetDlgItem (hwnd, IDC_PLAY_REP),   FALSE) ;
      EnableWindow (GetDlgItem (hwnd, IDC_PLAY_SPEED), FALSE) ;
      SetFocus (GetDlgItem (hwnd, IDC_RECORD_END)) ;

            // Add the buffers

      waveInAddBuffer (hWaveIn, pWaveHdr1, sizeof (WAVEHDR)) ;
      waveInAddBuffer (hWaveIn, pWaveHdr2, sizeof (WAVEHDR)) ;

            // Begin sampling

      bRecording = TRUE ;
      bEnding = FALSE ;
      dwDataLength = 0 ;
      waveInStart (hWaveIn) ;
      return TRUE ;

case MM_WIM_DATA:

            // Reallocate save buffer memory

      pNewBuffer = realloc (pSaveBuffer, dwDataLength +
```

```
                              ((PWAVEHDR) lParam)->dwBytesRecorded) ;

    if (pNewBuffer == NULL)
    {
         waveInClose (hWaveIn) ;
         MessageBeep (MB_ICONEXCLAMATION) ;
         MessageBox (hwnd, szMemError, szAppName,
                        MB_ICONEXCLAMATION | MB_OK) ;
         return TRUE ;
    }


    pSaveBuffer = pNewBuffer ;
    CopyMemory (pSaveBuffer + dwDataLength, ((PWAVEHDR) lParam)->lpData,
                   ((PWAVEHDR) lParam)->dwBytesRecorded) ;

    dwDataLength += ((PWAVEHDR) lParam)->dwBytesRecorded ;

    if (bEnding)
    {
         waveInClose (hWaveIn) ;
         return TRUE ;
    }

         // Send out a new buffer

    waveInAddBuffer (hWaveIn, (PWAVEHDR) lParam, sizeof (WAVEHDR)) ;
    return TRUE ;

case MM_WIM_CLOSE:
         // Free the buffer memory

    waveInUnprepareHeader (hWaveIn, pWaveHdr1, sizeof (WAVEHDR)) ;
    waveInUnprepareHeader (hWaveIn, pWaveHdr2, sizeof (WAVEHDR)) ;

    free (pBuffer1) ;
    free (pBuffer2) ;

         // Enable and disable buttons

    EnableWindow (GetDlgItem (hwnd, IDC_RECORD_BEG), TRUE) ;
    EnableWindow (GetDlgItem (hwnd, IDC_RECORD_END), FALSE) ;
    SetFocus (GetDlgItem (hwnd, IDC_RECORD_BEG)) ;

    if (dwDataLength > 0)
    {
         EnableWindow (GetDlgItem (hwnd, IDC_PLAY_BEG),   TRUE)  ;
```

(continued)

Figure 22-3. *continued*

```
              EnableWindow (GetDlgItem (hwnd, IDC_PLAY_PAUSE), FALSE) ;
              EnableWindow (GetDlgItem (hwnd, IDC_PLAY_END),   FALSE) ;
              EnableWindow (GetDlgItem (hwnd, IDC_PLAY_REP),   TRUE)  ;
              EnableWindow (GetDlgItem (hwnd, IDC_PLAY_REV),   TRUE)  ;
              EnableWindow (GetDlgItem (hwnd, IDC_PLAY_SPEED), TRUE)  ;
              SetFocus (GetDlgItem (hwnd, IDC_PLAY_BEG)) ;
         }
         bRecording = FALSE ;

         if (bTerminating)
              SendMessage (hwnd, WM_SYSCOMMAND, SC_CLOSE, 0L) ;

         return TRUE ;

    case MM_WOM_OPEN:
              // Enable and disable buttons

         EnableWindow (GetDlgItem (hwnd, IDC_RECORD_BEG), FALSE) ;
         EnableWindow (GetDlgItem (hwnd, IDC_RECORD_END), FALSE) ;
         EnableWindow (GetDlgItem (hwnd, IDC_PLAY_BEG),   FALSE) ;
         EnableWindow (GetDlgItem (hwnd, IDC_PLAY_PAUSE), TRUE)  ;
         EnableWindow (GetDlgItem (hwnd, IDC_PLAY_END),   TRUE)  ;
         EnableWindow (GetDlgItem (hwnd, IDC_PLAY_REP),   FALSE) ;
         EnableWindow (GetDlgItem (hwnd, IDC_PLAY_REV),   FALSE) ;
         EnableWindow (GetDlgItem (hwnd, IDC_PLAY_SPEED), FALSE) ;
         SetFocus (GetDlgItem (hwnd, IDC_PLAY_END)) ;

              // Set up header

         pWaveHdr1->lpData          = pSaveBuffer ;
         pWaveHdr1->dwBufferLength   = dwDataLength ;
         pWaveHdr1->dwBytesRecorded = 0 ;
         pWaveHdr1->dwUser          = 0 ;
         pWaveHdr1->dwFlags          = WHDR_BEGINLOOP | WHDR_ENDLOOP ;
         pWaveHdr1->dwLoops          = dwRepetitions ;
         pWaveHdr1->lpNext          = NULL ;
         pWaveHdr1->reserved         = 0 ;

              // Prepare and write

         waveOutPrepareHeader (hWaveOut, pWaveHdr1, sizeof (WAVEHDR)) ;
         waveOutWrite (hWaveOut, pWaveHdr1, sizeof (WAVEHDR)) ;

         bEnding = FALSE ;
         bPlaying = TRUE ;
         return TRUE ;
```

```
case MM_WOM_DONE:
     waveOutUnprepareHeader (hWaveOut, pWaveHdr1, sizeof (WAVEHDR)) ;
     waveOutClose (hWaveOut) ;
     return TRUE ;

case MM_WOM_CLOSE:
          // Enable and disable buttons

     EnableWindow (GetDlgItem (hwnd, IDC_RECORD_BEG), TRUE)  ;
     EnableWindow (GetDlgItem (hwnd, IDC_RECORD_END), TRUE)  ;
     EnableWindow (GetDlgItem (hwnd, IDC_PLAY_BEG),   TRUE)  ;
     EnableWindow (GetDlgItem (hwnd, IDC_PLAY_PAUSE), FALSE) ;
     EnableWindow (GetDlgItem (hwnd, IDC_PLAY_END),   FALSE) ;
     EnableWindow (GetDlgItem (hwnd, IDC_PLAY_REV),   TRUE)  ;
     EnableWindow (GetDlgItem (hwnd, IDC_PLAY_REP),   TRUE)  ;
     EnableWindow (GetDlgItem (hwnd, IDC_PLAY_SPEED), TRUE)  ;
     SetFocus (GetDlgItem (hwnd, IDC_PLAY_BEG)) ;

     SetDlgItemText (hwnd, IDC_PLAY_PAUSE, TEXT ("Pause")) ;
     bPaused = FALSE ;
     dwRepetitions = 1 ;
     bPlaying = FALSE ;

     if (bReverse)
     {
          ReverseMemory (pSaveBuffer, dwDataLength) ;
          bReverse = FALSE ;
     }

     if (bTerminating)
          SendMessage (hwnd, WM_SYSCOMMAND, SC_CLOSE, 0L) ;

     return TRUE ;

case WM_SYSCOMMAND:
     switch (LOWORD (wParam))
     {
     case SC_CLOSE:
          if (bRecording)
          {
               bTerminating = TRUE ;
               bEnding = TRUE ;
               waveInReset (hWaveIn) ;
               return TRUE ;
          }
```

(continued)

Figure 22-3. *continued*

```
            if (bPlaying)
            {
                  bTerminating = TRUE ;
                  bEnding = TRUE ;
                  waveOutReset (hWaveOut) ;
                  return TRUE ;
            }

            free (pWaveHdr1) ;
            free (pWaveHdr2) ;
            free (pSaveBuffer) ;
            EndDialog (hwnd, 0) ;
            return TRUE ;
      }
      break ;
   }
   return FALSE ;
}
```

RECORD.RC (excerpts)

```
//Microsoft Developer Studio generated resource script.

#include "resource.h"
#include "afxres.h"


/////////////////////////////////////////////////////////////////////////////
// Dialog

RECORD DIALOG DISCARDABLE  100, 100, 152, 74
STYLE WS_MINIMIZEBOX | WS_VISIBLE | WS_CAPTION | WS_SYSMENU
CAPTION "Waveform Audio Recorder"
FONT 8, "MS Sans Serif"
BEGIN
    PUSHBUTTON        "Record",IDC_RECORD_BEG,28,8,40,14
    PUSHBUTTON        "End",IDC_RECORD_END,76,8,40,14,WS_DISABLED
    PUSHBUTTON        "Play",IDC_PLAY_BEG,8,30,40,14,WS_DISABLED
    PUSHBUTTON        "Pause",IDC_PLAY_PAUSE,56,30,40,14,WS_DISABLED
    PUSHBUTTON        "End",IDC_PLAY_END,104,30,40,14,WS_DISABLED
    PUSHBUTTON        "Reverse",IDC_PLAY_REV,8,52,40,14,WS_DISABLED
    PUSHBUTTON        "Repeat",IDC_PLAY_REP,56,52,40,14,WS_DISABLED
    PUSHBUTTON        "Speedup",IDC_PLAY_SPEED,104,52,40,14,WS_DISABLED
END
```

RESOURCE.H (excerpts)

```
// Microsoft Developer Studio generated include file.
// Used by Record.rc

#define IDC_RECORD_BEG               1000
#define IDC_RECORD_END               1001
#define IDC_PLAY_BEG                 1002
#define IDC_PLAY_PAUSE               1003
#define IDC_PLAY_END                 1004
#define IDC_PLAY_REV                 1005
#define IDC_PLAY_REP                 1006
#define IDC_PLAY_SPEED               1007
```

The RECORD.RC and RESOURCE.H files will also be used in the RECORD2 and RECORD3 programs.

The RECORD1 window has eight push buttons. When you first run RECORD1, only the Record button is enabled. When you press Record, you can begin recording. The Record button becomes disabled, and the End button is enabled. Press End to stop recording. At this point, the Play, Reverse, Repeat, and Speedup buttons also become enabled. Pressing any of these buttons plays back the sound: Play plays it normally, Reverse plays it in reverse, Repeat causes the sound to be repeated indefinitely (like with a tape loop), and Speedup plays the sound back twice as fast. You can end playback by pressing the second End button, or you can pause the playback by pressing Pause. When pressed, the Pause button changes into a Resume button to resume playing back the sound. If you record another sound, it replaces the existing sound in memory.

At any time, the only buttons that are enabled are those that perform valid operations. This requires a lot of calls to *EnableWindow* in the RECORD1 source code, but the program doesn't have to check if a particular push-button operation is valid. Of course, it also makes the operation of the program more intuitive.

RECORD1 takes a number of shortcuts to simplify the code. First, if multiple waveform audio hardware devices are installed, RECORD1 uses the default one. Second, the program records and plays back at the standard 11.025 kHz sampling rate with an 8-bit sample size regardless of whether a higher sampling rate or sample size is available. The only exception is for the speed-up function, where RECORD1 plays back the sound at the 22.050 kHz sampling rate, thus playing it twice as fast and an octave higher in frequency.

Recording a sound involves opening the waveform audio hardware for input and passing buffers to the API to receive the sound data.

RECORD1 maintains several memory blocks. Three of these blocks are very small, at least initially, and are allocated during the WM_INITDIALOG message in *DlgProc*. The program allocates two WAVEHDR structures pointed to by *pWaveHdr1* and *pWaveHdr2*.

These structures are used to pass buffers to the waveform APIs. The *pSaveBuffer* pointer points to a buffer for storing the complete recorded sound; this is initially allocated as a 1-byte block. Later on, during recording, the buffer is increased in size to accommodate all the sound data. (If you record for a long period of time, RECORD1 recovers gracefully when it runs out of memory during recording, and lets you play back that portion of the sound successfully stored.) I'll refer to this buffer as the "save buffer" because it is used to save the accumulated sound data. Two more memory blocks, 16K in size and pointed to by *pBuffer1* and *pBuffer2*, are allocated during recording to receive sound data. These buffers are freed when recording is complete.

Each of the eight buttons generates a WM_COMMAND message to *DlgProc*, the dialog procedure for REPORT1's window. Initially, only the Record button is enabled. Pressing this generates a WM_COMMAND message with *wParam* equal to IDC_RECORD_BEG. To process this message, RECORD1 allocates the two 16K buffers for receiving sound data, initializes the fields of a WAVEFORMATEX structure and passes it to the *waveInOpen* function, and sets up the two WAVEHDR structures.

The *waveInOpen* function generates an MM_WIM_OPEN message. During this message, RECORD1 shrinks the save buffer down to 1 byte in preparation for receiving data. (Of course, the first time you record something, the save buffer is already 1 byte in length, but during subsequent recordings, it could be much larger.) During the MM_WIM_OPEN message, RECORD1 also enables and disables the appropriate push buttons. Next, the program passes the two WAVEHDR structures and buffers to the API using *waveInAddBuffer*. Some flags are set, and recording begins with a call to *waveInStart*.

At a sampling rate of 11.025 kHz with an 8-bit sample size, the 16K buffer will be filled in approximately 1.5 seconds. At that time, RECORD1 receives an MM_WIM_DATA message. In response to this message, the program call reallocates the save buffer based on the *dwDataLength* variable and the *dwBytesRecorded* field of the WAVEHDR structure. If the reallocation fails, RECORD1 calls *waveInClose* to stop recording.

If the reallocation is successful, RECORD1 copies the data from the 16K buffer into the save buffer. It then calls *waveInAddBuffer* again. This process continues until RECORD1 runs out of memory for the save buffer or the user presses the End button.

The End button generates a WM_COMMAND message with *wParam* equal to IDC_RECORD_END. Processing this message is simple. RECORD1 sets the *bEnding* flag to TRUE and calls *waveInReset*. The *waveInReset* function causes recording to stop and generates an MM_WIM_DATA message containing a partially filled buffer. RECORD1 responds to this final MM_WIM_DATA message normally, except that it closes the waveform input device by calling *waveInClose*.

The *waveInClose* message generates an MM_WIM_CLOSE message. RECORD1 responds to this message by freeing the 16K input buffers and enabling and disabling the appropriate push buttons. In particular, if the save buffer contains data, which it almost always will unless the first reallocation fails, then the play buttons are enabled.

After recording a sound, the save buffer contains the total accumulated sound data. When the user selects the Play button, *DlgProc* receives a WM_COMMAND message with *wParam* equal to IDC_PLAY_BEG. The program responds by initializing the fields of a WAVEFORMATEX structure and calling *waveOutOpen*.

The *waveOutOpen* call again generates an MM_WOM_OPEN message. During this message, RECORD1 enables and disables the appropriate push buttons (allowing only Pause and End), initializes the fields of the WAVEHDR structure with the save buffer, prepares it by calling *waveOutPrepareHeader*, and begins playing it with a call to *waveOutWrite*.

Normally, the sound will continue until all the data in the buffer has been played. At that time, an MM_WOM_DONE message is generated. If there are additional buffers to be played, a program can pass them out to the API at that time. RECORD1 plays only one big buffer, so the program simply unprepares the header and calls *waveOutClose*. The *waveOutClose* function generates an MM_WOM_CLOSE message. During this message, RECORD1 enables and disables the appropriate buttons, allowing the sound to be played again or a new sound to be recorded.

I've also included a second End button so that the user can stop playing the sound at any time before the save buffer has completed. This End button generates a WM_COMMAND message with *wParam* equal to IDC_PLAY_END, and the program responds by calling *waveOutReset*. This function generates an MM_WOM_DONE message that is processed normally.

RECORD1's window also includes a Pause button. Processing this button is easy. The first time it's pushed, RECORD1 calls *waveOutPause* to halt the sound and sets the text in the Pause button to Resume. Pressing the Resume button starts the playback going again by a call to *waveOutRestart*.

To make the program just a little more interesting, I've also included buttons labeled "Reverse," "Repeat," and "Speedup." These buttons generate WM_COMMAND messages with *wParam* values equal to IDC_PLAY_REV, IDC_PLAY_REP, and IDC_PLAY_SPEED.

Playing the sound in reverse involves reversing the order of the bytes in the save buffer and playing the sound normally. RECORD1 includes a small function named *ReverseMemory* to reverse the bytes. It calls this function during the WM_COMMAND message before playing the block and again at the end of the MM_WOM_CLOSE message to restore it to normal.

The Repeat button plays the sound over and over again. This is not complicated because the API includes a provision for repeating a sound. It involves setting the *dwLoops* field in the WAVEHDR structure to the number of repetitions and setting the *dwFlags* field to WHDR_BEGINLOOP for the beginning buffer in the loop and to WHDR_ENDLOOP for the end buffer. Because RECORD1 uses only one buffer for playing the sound, these two flags are combined in the *dwFlags* field.

Playing the sound twice as fast is also quite easy. When initializing the fields of the WAVEFORMATEX structure in preparation for opening waveform audio for output, the *nSamplesPerSec* and *nAvgBytesPerSec* fields are set to 22050 rather than 11025.

The MCI Alternative

You may find, as I do, that RECORD1 seems inordinately complex. It is particularly tricky to deal with the interaction between the waveform audio function calls and the messages they generate, and then in the midst of all this, to deal with possible memory shortages as well. But maybe that's why it's called the "low-level" interface. As I noted earlier in this chapter, Windows also includes the high-level Media Control Interface.

For waveform audio, the primary differences between the low-level interface and MCI is that MCI records sound data to a waveform file and plays back the sound by reading the file. This makes it difficult to perform the "special effects" that RECORD1 implements because you'd have to read in the file, manipulate it, and write it back out before playing the sound. This is a typical versatility vs. ease-of-use trade-off. The low-level interface gives you flexibility, but MCI (for the most part) is easier.

MCI is implemented in two different but related forms. The first form uses messages and data structures to send commands to multimedia devices and receive information from them. The second form uses ASCII text strings. The text-based interface was originally created to allow multimedia devices to be controlled from simple scripting languages. But it also provides very easy interactive control, as was demonstrated in the TESTMCI program shown earlier in this chapter.

The RECORD2 program shown in Figure 22-4 uses the message and data structure form of MCI to implement another digital audio recorder and player. Although it uses the same dialog box template as RECORD1, it does not implement the three special effects buttons.

RECORD2.C

```c
/*----------------------------------------------
   RECORD2.C -- Waveform Audio Recorder
                (c) Charles Petzold, 1998
  --------------------------------------------*/

#include <windows.h>
#include "..\\record1\\resource.h"

BOOL CALLBACK DlgProc (HWND, UINT, WPARAM, LPARAM) ;

TCHAR szAppName [] = TEXT ("Record2") ;

int WINAPI WinMain (HINSTANCE hInstance, HINSTANCE hPrevInstance,
                    PSTR szCmdLine, int iCmdShow)
{
     if (-1 == DialogBox (hInstance, TEXT ("Record"), NULL, DlgProc))
```

Figure 22-4. *The RECORD2 program.*

```
        {
            MessageBox (NULL, TEXT ("This program requires Windows NT!"),
                        szAppName, MB_ICONERROR) ;
        }
        return 0 ;
}

void ShowError (HWND hwnd, DWORD dwError)
{
        TCHAR szErrorStr [1024] ;

        mciGetErrorString (dwError, szErrorStr,
                            sizeof (szErrorStr) / sizeof (TCHAR)) ;
        MessageBeep (MB_ICONEXCLAMATION) ;
        MessageBox (hwnd, szErrorStr, szAppName, MB_OK | MB_ICONEXCLAMATION) ;
}

BOOL CALLBACK DlgProc (HWND hwnd, UINT message, WPARAM wParam, LPARAM lParam)
{
        static BOOL         bRecording, bPlaying, bPaused ;
        static TCHAR        szFileName[] = TEXT ("record2.wav") ;
        static WORD         wDeviceID ;
        DWORD               dwError ;
        MCI_GENERIC_PARMS   mciGeneric ;
        MCI_OPEN_PARMS      mciOpen ;
        MCI_PLAY_PARMS      mciPlay ;
        MCI_RECORD_PARMS    mciRecord ;
        MCI_SAVE_PARMS      mciSave ;

        switch (message)
        {
        case WM_COMMAND:
            switch (wParam)
            {
            case IDC_RECORD_BEG:
                    // Delete existing waveform file

                DeleteFile (szFileName) ;

                    // Open waveform audio

                mciOpen.dwCallback       = 0 ;
                mciOpen.wDeviceID        = 0 ;
                mciOpen.lpstrDeviceType  = TEXT ("waveaudio") ;
                mciOpen.lpstrElementName = TEXT ("") ;
                mciOpen.lpstrAlias       = NULL ;
```

(continued)

Figure 22-4. *continued*

```
                    dwError = mciSendCommand (0, MCI_OPEN,
                                    MCI_WAIT | MCI_OPEN_TYPE | MCI_OPEN_ELEMENT,
                                    (DWORD) (LPMCI_OPEN_PARMS) &mciOpen) ;
                    if (dwError != 0)
                    {
                         ShowError (hwnd, dwError) ;
                         return TRUE ;
                    }
                         // Save the Device ID

                    wDeviceID = mciOpen.wDeviceID ;

                         // Begin recording

                    mciRecord.dwCallback = (DWORD) hwnd ;
                    mciRecord.dwFrom     = 0 ;
                    mciRecord.dwTo       = 0 ;

                    mciSendCommand (wDeviceID, MCI_RECORD, MCI_NOTIFY,
                                    (DWORD) (LPMCI_RECORD_PARMS) &mciRecord) ;

                         // Enable and disable buttons

                    EnableWindow (GetDlgItem (hwnd, IDC_RECORD_BEG), FALSE);
                    EnableWindow (GetDlgItem (hwnd, IDC_RECORD_END), TRUE) ;
                    EnableWindow (GetDlgItem (hwnd, IDC_PLAY_BEG),   FALSE);
                    EnableWindow (GetDlgItem (hwnd, IDC_PLAY_PAUSE), FALSE);
                    EnableWindow (GetDlgItem (hwnd, IDC_PLAY_END),   FALSE);
                    SetFocus (GetDlgItem (hwnd, IDC_RECORD_END)) ;

                    bRecording = TRUE ;
                    return TRUE ;

               case IDC_RECORD_END:
                         // Stop recording

                    mciGeneric.dwCallback = 0 ;

                    mciSendCommand (wDeviceID, MCI_STOP, MCI_WAIT,
                                    (DWORD) (LPMCI_GENERIC_PARMS) &mciGeneric) ;

                         // Save the file

                    mciSave.dwCallback = 0 ;
                    mciSave.lpfilename = szFileName ;
```

```
        mciSendCommand (wDeviceID, MCI_SAVE, MCI_WAIT | MCI_SAVE_FILE,
                   (DWORD) (LPMCI_SAVE_PARMS) &mciSave) ;

        // Close the waveform device

        mciSendCommand (wDeviceID, MCI_CLOSE, MCI_WAIT,
                   (DWORD) (LPMCI_GENERIC_PARMS) &mciGeneric) ;

        // Enable and disable buttons

        EnableWindow (GetDlgItem (hwnd, IDC_RECORD_BEG), TRUE) ;
        EnableWindow (GetDlgItem (hwnd, IDC_RECORD_END), FALSE);
        EnableWindow (GetDlgItem (hwnd, IDC_PLAY_BEG),   TRUE) ;
        EnableWindow (GetDlgItem (hwnd, IDC_PLAY_PAUSE), FALSE);
        EnableWindow (GetDlgItem (hwnd, IDC_PLAY_END),   FALSE);
        SetFocus (GetDlgItem (hwnd, IDC_PLAY_BEG)) ;

        bRecording = FALSE ;
        return TRUE ;

case IDC_PLAY_BEG:
        // Open waveform audio

        mciOpen.dwCallback      = 0 ;
        mciOpen.wDeviceID       = 0 ;
        mciOpen.lpstrDeviceType  = NULL ;
        mciOpen.lpstrElementName = szFileName ;
        mciOpen.lpstrAlias      = NULL ;

        dwError = mciSendCommand (0, MCI_OPEN,
                            MCI_WAIT | MCI_OPEN_ELEMENT,
                            (DWORD) (LPMCI_OPEN_PARMS) &mciOpen) ;

        if (dwError != 0)
        {
            ShowError (hwnd, dwError) ;
            return TRUE ;
        }
            // Save the Device ID

        wDeviceID = mciOpen.wDeviceID ;

            // Begin playing

        mciPlay.dwCallback = (DWORD) hwnd ;
```

(continued)

Figure 22-4. *continued*

```
        mciPlay.dwFrom     = 0 ;
        mciPlay.dwTo       = 0 ;

   mciSendCommand (wDeviceID, MCI_PLAY, MCI_NOTIFY,
                   (DWORD) (LPMCI_PLAY_PARMS) &mciPlay) ;

        // Enable and disable buttons

   EnableWindow (GetDlgItem (hwnd, IDC_RECORD_BEG), FALSE);
   EnableWindow (GetDlgItem (hwnd, IDC_RECORD_END), FALSE);
   EnableWindow (GetDlgItem (hwnd, IDC_PLAY_BEG),   FALSE);
   EnableWindow (GetDlgItem (hwnd, IDC_PLAY_PAUSE), TRUE) ;
   EnableWindow (GetDlgItem (hwnd, IDC_PLAY_END),   TRUE) ;
   SetFocus (GetDlgItem (hwnd, IDC_PLAY_END)) ;

   bPlaying = TRUE ;
   return TRUE ;

case IDC_PLAY_PAUSE:
   if (!bPaused)
           // Pause the play
   {
      mciGeneric.dwCallback = 0 ;

      mciSendCommand (wDeviceID, MCI_PAUSE, MCI_WAIT,
                      (DWORD) (LPMCI_GENERIC_PARMS) & mciGeneric);

      SetDlgItemText (hwnd, IDC_PLAY_PAUSE, TEXT ("Resume")) ;
      bPaused = TRUE ;
   }
   else
           // Begin playing again
   {
      mciPlay.dwCallback = (DWORD) hwnd ;
      mciPlay.dwFrom     = 0 ;
      mciPlay.dwTo       = 0 ;

      mciSendCommand (wDeviceID, MCI_PLAY, MCI_NOTIFY,
                      (DWORD) (LPMCI_PLAY_PARMS) &mciPlay) ;

      SetDlgItemText (hwnd, IDC_PLAY_PAUSE, TEXT ("Pause")) ;
      bPaused = FALSE ;
   }

   return TRUE ;
```

```
        case IDC_PLAY_END:
                // Stop and close

            mciGeneric.dwCallback = 0 ;

            mciSendCommand (wDeviceID, MCI_STOP, MCI_WAIT,
                        (DWORD) (LPMCI_GENERIC_PARMS) &mciGeneric) ;

            mciSendCommand (wDeviceID, MCI_CLOSE, MCI_WAIT,
                        (DWORD) (LPMCI_GENERIC_PARMS) &mciGeneric) ;

                // Enable and disable buttons

            EnableWindow (GetDlgItem (hwnd, IDC_RECORD_BEG), TRUE) ;
            EnableWindow (GetDlgItem (hwnd, IDC_RECORD_END), FALSE);
            EnableWindow (GetDlgItem (hwnd, IDC_PLAY_BEG),   TRUE) ;
            EnableWindow (GetDlgItem (hwnd, IDC_PLAY_PAUSE), FALSE);
            EnableWindow (GetDlgItem (hwnd, IDC_PLAY_END),   FALSE);
            SetFocus (GetDlgItem (hwnd, IDC_PLAY_BEG)) ;

            bPlaying = FALSE ;
            bPaused  = FALSE ;
            return TRUE ;
        }
        break ;

    case MM_MCINOTIFY:
        switch (wParam)
        {
        case MCI_NOTIFY_SUCCESSFUL:
            if (bPlaying)
                SendMessage (hwnd, WM_COMMAND, IDC_PLAY_END, 0) ;

            if (bRecording)
                SendMessage (hwnd, WM_COMMAND, IDC_RECORD_END, 0);

            return TRUE ;
        }
        break ;

    case WM_SYSCOMMAND:
        switch (wParam)
        {
        case SC_CLOSE:
            if (bRecording)
                SendMessage (hwnd, WM_COMMAND, IDC_RECORD_END, 0L) ;
```

(continued)

Figure 22-4. *continued*

```
            if (bPlaying)
                 SendMessage (hwnd, WM_COMMAND, IDC_PLAY_END, 0L) ;

            EndDialog (hwnd, 0) ;
            return TRUE ;
         }
         break ;
      }
   return FALSE ;
}
```

RECORD2 uses only two MCI function calls, the most important being this one:

```
error = mciSendCommand (wDeviceID, message, dwFlags, dwParam)
```

The first argument is a numeric identification number for the device. You use this ID number much like a handle. You obtain the ID when you open the device, and then you use it in subsequent *mciSendCommand* calls. The second argument is a constant beginning with the prefix MCI. These are called MCI command messages, and RECORD2 demonstrates seven of them: MCI_OPEN, MCI_RECORD, MCI_STOP, MCI_SAVE, MCI_PLAY, MCI_PAUSE, and MCI_CLOSE.

The *dwFlags* argument is generally composed of zero or more bit flag constants combined with the C bit-wise OR operator. These generally indicate various options. Some options are specific to particular command messages, and some are common to all messages. The *dwParam* argument is generally a long pointer to a data structure that indicates options and obtains information from the device. Many of the MCI messages are associated with data structures unique to the message.

The *mciSendCommand* function returns 0 if the function is successful and an error code otherwise. To report this error to the user, you can obtain a text string that describes the error:

```
mciGetErrorString (error, szBuffer, dwLength)
```

This is the same function used in the TESTMCI program.

When the user presses the Record button, RECORD2's window procedure receives a WM_COMMAND message with *wParam* equal to IDC_RECORD_BEG. RECORD2 begins by opening the device. This involves setting the fields of an MCI_OPEN_PARMS structure and calling *mciSendCommand* with the MCI_OPEN command message. For recording, the *lpstrDeviceType* field is set to the string "waveaudio" to indicate the device type. The *lpstrElementName* field is set to a zero-length string. The MCI driver uses a default sampling rate and sample size, but you can change that using the MCI_SET command. During recording, the sound data is stored on the hard disk in a temporary file and is ultimately transferred to a standard waveform file. I'll discuss the format of waveform files later in this chapter. For playing back the sound, MCI uses the sampling rate and sample size defined in the waveform file.

If RECORD2 cannot open a device, it uses *mciGetErrorString* and *MessageBox* to tell the user what the problem is. Otherwise, on return from the *mciSendCommand* call, the *wDeviceID* field of the MCI_OPEN_PARMS structure contains the device ID used in subsequent calls.

To begin recording, RECORD2 calls *mciSendCommand* with the MCI_RECORD command message and the MCI_WAVE_RECORD_PARMS data structure. Optionally, you can set the *dwFrom* and *dwTo* fields of this structure (and use bit flags that indicate these fields are set) to insert a sound into an existing waveform file, the name of which would be specified in the *lpstrElementName* field of the MCI_OPEN_PARMS structure. By default, any new sound is inserted at the beginning of an existing file.

RECORD2 sets the *dwCallback* field of the MCI_WAVE_RECORD_PARMS to the program's window handle and includes the MCI_NOTIFY flag in the *mciSendCommand* call. This causes a notification message to be sent to the window procedure when recording has been completed. I'll discuss this notification message shortly.

When done recording, you press the first End button to stop. This generates a WM_COMMAND message with *wParam* equal to IDC_RECORD_END. The window procedure responds by calling *mciSendCommand* three times: The MCI_STOP command message stops recording, the MCI_SAVE command message transfers the sound data from the temporary file to the file specified in an MCI_SAVE_PARMS structure ("record2.wav"), and the MCI_CLOSE command message deletes any temporary files or memory blocks that might have been created and closes the device.

For playback, the *lpstrElementName* of the MCI_OPEN_PARMS structure field is set to the filename "record2.wav". The MCI_OPEN_ELEMENT flag included in the third argument to *mciSendCommand* indicates that the *lpstrElementName* field is a valid filename. MCI knows from the filename extension .WAV that you wish to open a waveform audio device. If multiple waveform hardware is present, it opens the first device. (It's also possible to use something other than the first waveform device by setting the *lpstrDeviceType* field of the MCI_OPEN_PARMS structure.)

Playing involves an *mciSendCommand* call with the MCI_PLAY command message and an MCI_PLAY_PARMS structure. Any part of the file can be played, but RECORD2 chooses to play it all.

RECORD2 also includes a Pause button for pausing the playback of a sound file. This button generates a WM_COMMAND message with *wParam* equal to IDC_PLAY_PAUSE. The program responds by calling *mciSendCommand* with the MCI_PAUSE command message and an MCI_GENERIC_PARMS structure. The MCI_GENERIC_PARMS structure is used for any message that requires no information except an optional window handle for notification. If the playback is already paused, the button resumes play by calling *mciSendCommand* again with the MCI_PLAY command message.

Playback can also be terminated by pressing the second End button. This generates a WM_COMMAND message with *wParam* equal to IDC_PLAY_END. The window procedure responds by calling *mciSendCommand* twice, first with the MCI_STOP command message and then with the MCI_CLOSE command message.

Now here's a problem: Although you can manually terminate playback by pressing the End button, you may want to play the entire sound file. How does the program know when the file has completed? That is the job of the MCI notification message.

When calling *mciSendCommand* with the MCI_RECORD and MCI_PLAY messages, RECORD2 includes the MCI_NOTIFY flag and sets the *dwCallback* field of the data structure to the program's window handle. This causes a notification message, called MM_MCINOTIFY, to be posted to the window procedure under certain circumstances. The *wParam* message parameter is a status code, and *lParam* is the device ID.

You'll receive an MM_MCINOTIFY message with *wParam* equal to MCI_NOTIFY_ABORTED when *mciSendCommand* is called with the MCI_STOP or MCI_PAUSE command messages. This happens when you press the Pause button or either of the two End buttons. RECORD2 can ignore this case because it already properly handles these buttons. During playback, you'll receive an MM_MCINOTIFY message with *wParam* equal to MCI_NOTIFY_SUCCESSFUL when the sound file has completed. To handle this case, the window procedure sends itself a WM_COMMAND message with *wParam* equal to IDC_PLAY_END to simulate the user pressing the End button. The window procedure then responds normally by stopping the play and closing the device.

During recording, you'll receive an MM_MCINOTIFY message with *wParam* equal to MCI_NOTIFY_SUCCESSFUL when you run out of hard disk space for storing the temporary sound file. (I wouldn't exactly call this a "successful" completion, but that's what happens.) The window procedure responds by sending itself a WM_COMMAND message with *wParam* equal to IDC_RECORD_END. The window procedure stops recording, saves the file, and closes the device, as is normal.

The MCI Command String Approach

At one time, the Windows multimedia interface included a function called *mciExecute*, with the following syntax:

```
bSuccess = mciExecute (szCommand) ;
```

The only argument was the MCI command string. The function returned a Boolean value—nonzero if the function is successful and zero if not. The *mciExecute* function was functionally equivalent to calling *mciSendString* (the string-based MCI function used in TESTMCI) with NULL or zero for the last three arguments and then *mciGetErrorString* and *MessageBox* if an error occurred.

Although *mciExecute* is no longer part of the API, I've included such a function in the RECORD3 version of the digital tape recorder and player. This is shown in Figure 22-5. Like RECORD2, the program uses the RECORD.RC resource script and RESOURCE.H from RECORD1.

RECORD3.C

```
/*-----------------------------------------
   RECORD3.C -- Waveform Audio Recorder
               (c) Charles Petzold, 1998
   -----------------------------------------*/

#include <windows.h>
#include "..\\record1\\resource.h"

BOOL CALLBACK DlgProc (HWND, UINT, WPARAM, LPARAM) ;

TCHAR szAppName [] = TEXT ("Record3") ;

int WINAPI WinMain (HINSTANCE hInstance, HINSTANCE hPrevInstance,
                    PSTR szCmdLine, int iCmdShow)
{
     if (-1 == DialogBox (hInstance, TEXT ("Record"), NULL, DlgProc))
     {
          MessageBox (NULL, TEXT ("This program requires Windows NT!"),
                      szAppName, MB_ICONERROR) ;
     }
     return 0 ;
}

BOOL mciExecute (LPCTSTR szCommand)
{
     MCIERROR error ;
     TCHAR    szErrorStr [1024] ;

     if (error = mciSendString (szCommand, NULL, 0, NULL))
     {
          mciGetErrorString (error, szErrorStr,
                             sizeof (szErrorStr) / sizeof (TCHAR)) ;
          MessageBeep (MB_ICONEXCLAMATION) ;
          MessageBox (NULL, szErrorStr, TEXT ("MCI Error"),
                      MB_OK | MB_ICONEXCLAMATION) ;
     }
     return error == 0 ;
}

BOOL CALLBACK DlgProc (HWND hwnd, UINT message, WPARAM wParam, LPARAM lParam)
{
     static BOOL bRecording, bPlaying, bPaused ;

     switch (message)
```

Figure 22-5. *The RECORD3 program.*

(continued)

Figure 22-5. *continued*

```
     {
case WM_COMMAND:
     switch (wParam)
     {
     case IDC_RECORD_BEG:
               // Delete existing waveform file

          DeleteFile (TEXT ("record3.wav")) ;

               // Open waveform audio and record

          if (!mciExecute (TEXT ("open new type waveaudio alias mysound")))
               return TRUE ;

          mciExecute (TEXT ("record mysound")) ;

               // Enable and disable buttons

          EnableWindow (GetDlgItem (hwnd, IDC_RECORD_BEG), FALSE);
          EnableWindow (GetDlgItem (hwnd, IDC_RECORD_END), TRUE) ;
          EnableWindow (GetDlgItem (hwnd, IDC_PLAY_BEG),   FALSE);
          EnableWindow (GetDlgItem (hwnd, IDC_PLAY_PAUSE), FALSE);
          EnableWindow (GetDlgItem (hwnd, IDC_PLAY_END),   FALSE);
          SetFocus (GetDlgItem (hwnd, IDC_RECORD_END)) ;

          bRecording = TRUE ;
          return TRUE ;

     case IDC_RECORD_END:
               // Stop, save, and close recording

          mciExecute (TEXT ("stop mysound")) ;
          mciExecute (TEXT ("save mysound record3.wav")) ;
          mciExecute (TEXT ("close mysound")) ;

               // Enable and disable buttons

          EnableWindow (GetDlgItem (hwnd, IDC_RECORD_BEG), TRUE) ;
          EnableWindow (GetDlgItem (hwnd, IDC_RECORD_END), FALSE);
          EnableWindow (GetDlgItem (hwnd, IDC_PLAY_BEG),   TRUE) ;
          EnableWindow (GetDlgItem (hwnd, IDC_PLAY_PAUSE), FALSE);
          EnableWindow (GetDlgItem (hwnd, IDC_PLAY_END),   FALSE);
          SetFocus (GetDlgItem (hwnd, IDC_PLAY_BEG)) ;

          bRecording = FALSE ;
          return TRUE ;
```

```
case IDC_PLAY_BEG:
        // Open waveform audio and play

     if (!mciExecute (TEXT ("open record3.wav alias mysound")))
        return TRUE ;

     mciExecute (TEXT ("play mysound")) ;

        // Enable and disable buttons

     EnableWindow (GetDlgItem (hwnd, IDC_RECORD_BEG), FALSE);
     EnableWindow (GetDlgItem (hwnd, IDC_RECORD_END), FALSE);
     EnableWindow (GetDlgItem (hwnd, IDC_PLAY_BEG),   FALSE);
     EnableWindow (GetDlgItem (hwnd, IDC_PLAY_PAUSE), TRUE) ;
     EnableWindow (GetDlgItem (hwnd, IDC_PLAY_END),   TRUE) ;
     SetFocus (GetDlgItem (hwnd, IDC_PLAY_END)) ;

     bPlaying = TRUE ;
     return TRUE ;

case IDC_PLAY_PAUSE:
     if (!bPaused)
             // Pause the play
     {
         mciExecute (TEXT ("pause mysound")) ;
         SetDlgItemText (hwnd, IDC_PLAY_PAUSE, TEXT ("Resume")) ;
         bPaused = TRUE ;
     }
     else
             // Begin playing again
     {
         mciExecute (TEXT ("play mysound")) ;
         SetDlgItemText (hwnd, IDC_PLAY_PAUSE, TEXT ("Pause")) ;
         bPaused = FALSE ;
     }

     return TRUE ;

case IDC_PLAY_END:
        // Stop and close

     mciExecute (TEXT ("stop mysound")) ;
     mciExecute (TEXT ("close mysound")) ;

        // Enable and disable buttons
```

(continued)

Figure 22-5. *continued*

```
            EnableWindow (GetDlgItem (hwnd, IDC_RECORD_BEG), TRUE) ;
            EnableWindow (GetDlgItem (hwnd, IDC_RECORD_END), FALSE);
            EnableWindow (GetDlgItem (hwnd, IDC_PLAY_BEG),   TRUE) ;
            EnableWindow (GetDlgItem (hwnd, IDC_PLAY_PAUSE), FALSE);
            EnableWindow (GetDlgItem (hwnd, IDC_PLAY_END),   FALSE);
            SetFocus (GetDlgItem (hwnd, IDC_PLAY_BEG)) ;

            bPlaying = FALSE ;
            bPaused  = FALSE ;
            return TRUE ;
        }
        break ;

    case WM_SYSCOMMAND:
        switch (wParam)
        {
        case SC_CLOSE:
            if (bRecording)
                SendMessage (hwnd, WM_COMMAND, IDC_RECORD_END, 0L);

            if (bPlaying)
                SendMessage (hwnd, WM_COMMAND, IDC_PLAY_END, 0L) ;

            EndDialog (hwnd, 0) ;
            return TRUE ;
        }
        break ;
    }
    return FALSE ;
}
```

When you begin exploring the message-based and the text-based interfaces to MCI, you'll find that they correspond closely. It's easy to guess that MCI translates the command strings into the corresponding command messages and data structures. RECORD3 could use the MM_MCINOTIFY messages like RECORD2, but it chooses not to—an implication of the *mciExecute* function. The drawback of this is that the program doesn't know when it's finished playing the waveform file. Therefore, the buttons do not automatically change state. You must manually press the End button so that the program will know that it's ready to record or play again.

Notice the use of the *alias* keyword in the MCI *open* command. This allows all the subsequent MCI commands to refer to the device using the alias name.

The Waveform Audio File Format

If you take a look at uncompressed (that is, PCM) .WAV files under a hexadecimal dump program, you'll find they have a format as shown in Figure 22-6.

Offset	Bytes	Data
0000	4	"RIFF"
0004	4	size of waveform chunk (file size minus 8)
0008	4	"WAVE"
000C	4	"fmt "
0010	4	size of format chunk (16 bytes)
0014	2	wf.wFormatTag = WAVE_FORMAT_PCM = 1
0016	2	wf.nChannels
0018	4	wf.nSamplesPerSec
001C	4	wf.nAvgBytesPerSec
0020	2	wf.nBlockAlign
0022	2	wf.wBitsPerSample
0024	4	"data"
0028	4	size of waveform data
002C		waveform data

Figure 22-6. *The .WAV file format.*

This format is an example of a more extensive format known as RIFF (Resource Interchange File Format). RIFF was intended to be the all-encompassing format for multimedia data files. It is a tagged file format, in which the file consists of "chunks" of data that are identified by a preceding 4-character ASCII name and a 4-byte (32-bit) chunk size. The value of the chunk size does not include the 8 bytes required for the chunk name and size.

A waveform audio file begins with the text string "RIFF", which identifies it as a RIFF file. This is followed by a 32-bit chunk size, which is the size of the remainder of the file, or the file size less 8 bytes.

The chunk data begins with the text string "WAVE", which identifies it as a waveform audio chunk. This is followed by the text string "fmt "—notice the blank to make this a 4-character string—which identifies a sub-chunk containing the format of the waveform audio data. The "fmt " string is followed by the size of the format information, in this case 16 bytes. The format information is the first 16 bytes of the WAVEFORMATEX structure, or, as it was defined originally, a PCMWAVEFORMAT structure that includes a WAVEFORMAT structure.

The *nChannels* field is either 1 or 2, for monaural or stereo sound. The *nSamplesPer-Sec* field is the number of samples per second; the standard values are 11025, 22050, and 44100 samples per second. The *nAvgBytesPerSec* field is the sample rate in samples per second times the number of channels times the size of each sample in bits, divided by 8 and rounded up. The standard sample sizes are 8 and 16 bits. The *nBlockAlign* field is the number of channels times the sample size in bits, divided by 8 and rounded up. Finally, the format concludes with a *wBitsPerSample* field, which is the number of channels times the sample size in bits.

The format information is followed by the text string "data", followed by a 32-bit data size, followed by the waveform data itself. The data are simply the consecutive samples in the same format as that used in the low-level waveform audio facilities. If the sample size is 8 bits or less, each sample consists of 1 byte for monaural or 2 bytes for stereo. If the sample size is between 9 and 16 bits, each sample is 2 bytes for monaural or 4 bytes for stereo. For stereo waveform data, each sample consists of the left value followed by the right value.

For sample sizes of 8 bits or less, the sample byte is interpreted as an unsigned value. For example, for an 8-bit sample size, silence is equivalent to a string of 0x80 bytes. For sample sizes of 9 bits or more, the sample is interpreted as a signed value, and silence is equivalent to a string of 0 values.

One of the important rules for reading tagged files is to ignore chunks you're not prepared to deal with. Although a waveform audio file requires "fmt " and "data" sub-chunks (in that order), it can also contain other sub-chunks. In particular, a waveform audio file might contain a sub-chunk labeled "INFO", and sub-sub-chunks within that sub-chunk that provide information about the waveform audio file.

Experimenting with Additive Synthesis

For many years—going back to Pythagoras at least—people have attempted to analyze musical tones. At first it seems very simple, but then it gets complex. Bear with me if I repeat a little of what I've already said about sound.

Musical tones, except for some percussive sounds, have a particular pitch or frequency. This frequency can range across the spectrum of human perception, from 20 Hz to 20,000 Hz. The notes of a piano, for example, have a frequency range between 27.5 Hz to 4186 Hz. Another characteristic of musical tones is volume or loudness. This corresponds to the overall amplitude of the waveform producing the tone. A change in loudness is measured in decibels. So far, so good.

And then there is an unwieldy thing called "timbre." Very simply, timbre is that quality of sound that lets us distinguish between a piano and a violin and a trumpet all playing the same pitch at the same volume.

The French mathematician Fourier discovered that any periodic waveform—no matter how complex—can be represented by a sum of sine waves whose frequencies are integral multiples of a fundamental frequency. The fundamental, also called the first harmonic, is the frequency of periodicity of the waveform. The first overtone, also called the second harmonic, has a frequency twice the fundamental; the second overtone, or third harmonic, has a frequency three times the fundamental, and so forth. The relative amplitudes of the harmonics govern the shape of the waveform.

For example, a square wave can be represented as a sum of sine waves where the amplitudes of the even harmonics (that is, 2, 4, 6, etc) are 0 and the amplitudes of the odd harmonics (1, 3, 5, etc) are in the proportions 1, $\frac{1}{3}$, $\frac{1}{5}$, and so forth. In a sawtooth wave, all harmonics are present and the amplitudes are in the proportions 1, $\frac{1}{2}$, $\frac{1}{3}$, $\frac{1}{4}$, and so forth.

To the German scientist Hermann Helmholtz (1821–1894), this was the key in understanding timbre. In his classic book *On the Sensations of Tone* (1885, republished by Dover Press in 1954), Helmholtz posited that the ear and brain break down complex tones into their component sine waves and that the relative intensities of these sine waves is what we perceive as timbre. Unfortunately, it proved to be not quite that simple.

Electronic music synthesizers came to widespread public attention in 1968 with the release of Wendy Carlos's album *Switched on Bach*. The synthesizers available at that time (such as the Moog) were analog synthesizers. Such synthesizers use analog circuitry to generate various audio waveforms such as square waves, triangle waves, and sawtooth waves. To make these waveforms sound more like real musical instruments, they are subjected to some changes over the course of a single note. The overall amplitude of the waveform is shaped by an "envelope." When a note begins, the amplitude begins at 0 and rises, usually very quickly. This is known as the attack. The amplitude then remains constant as the note is held. This is known as the sustain. The amplitude then falls to 0 when the note ends; this is known as the release.

The waveforms are also put through filters that attenuate some of the harmonics and turn the simple waveforms into something more complex and musically interesting. The cut-off frequencies of these filters can be controlled by an envelope so that the harmonic content of the sound changes over the course of the note.

Because these synthesizers begin with harmonically rich waveforms, and some of the harmonics are attenuated using filters, this form of synthesis is known as "subtractive synthesis."

Even while working with subtractive synthesis, many people involved in electronic music saw additive synthesis as the next big thing.

In additive synthesis you begin with a number of sine wave generators tuned in integral multiples so that each sine wave corresponds to a harmonic. The amplitude of each harmonic can be controlled independently by an envelope. Additive synthesis is not practical using analog circuitry because you'd need somewhere between 8 and 24 sine wave generators for a single note and the relative frequencies of these sine wave generators would have to track each other precisely. Analog waveform generators are notoriously unstable and prone to frequency drift.

However, for digital synthesizers (which can generate waveforms digitally using lookup tables) and computer-generated waveforms, frequency drift is not a problem and additive synthesis becomes feasible. So here's the general idea: You record a real musical tone and break it down into harmonics using Fourier analysis. You can then determine the relative strength of each harmonic and regenerate the sound digitally using multiple sine waves.

When people began experimenting with applying Fourier analysis on real musical tones and generating these tones from multiple sine waves, they discovered that timbre is not quite as simple as Helmholtz believed.

The big problem is that the harmonics of real musical tones are not in strict integral relationships. Indeed, the term "harmonic" is not even appropriate for real musical tones. The various sine wave components are inharmonic and more correctly called "partials."

It was discovered that the inharmonicity among the partials of real musical tones is vital in making the tone sound "real." Strict harmonicity yields an "electronic" sound. Each partial changes in both amplitude *and frequency* over the course of a single note. The relative frequency and amplitude relationships among the partials is different for different pitches and intensities from the same instrument. The most complex part of a real musical tone occurs during the attack portion of the note, when there is much inharmonicity. It was discovered that this complex attack portion of the note was vital in the human perception of timbre.

In short, the sound of real musical instruments is more complex than anyone imagined. The idea of analyzing musical tones and coming up with relatively few simple envelopes for controlling the amplitudes and frequencies of the partials was clearly not practical.

Some analyses of real musical sounds were published in early issues (1977 and 1978) of the *Computer Music Journal* (at the time published by People's Computer Company and now published by the MIT Press). The three-part series "Lexicon of Analyzed Tones" was written by James A. Moorer, John Grey, and John Strawn, and it showed the amplitude and frequency graphs of partials of a single note (less than half a second long) played on a violin, oboe, clarinet, and trumpet. The note used was the E flat above middle C. Twenty partials are used for the violin, 21 for the oboe and clarinet, and 12 for the trumpet. In particular, Volume II, Number 2 (September 1978) of the *Computer Music Journal* contains numerical line-segment approximations for the various frequency and amplitude envelopes for the oboe, clarinet, and trumpet.

So, with the waveform support in Windows, it is fairly simple to type these numbers into a program, generate multiple sine wave samples for each partial, add them up, and send the samples out to the waveform audio sound board, thereby reproducing the sounds originally recorded over 20 years ago. The ADDSYNTH ("additive synthesis") program is shown in Figure 22-7.

ADDSYNTH.C

```
/*------------------------------------------------------
   ADDSYNTH.C -- Additive Synthesis Sound Generation
                 (c) Charles Petzold, 1998
   -----------------------------------------------------*/

#include <windows.h>
#include <math.h>
#include "addsynth.h"
#include "resource.h"

#define ID_TIMER            1
#define SAMPLE_RATE     22050
#define MAX_PARTIALS       21
#define PI            3.14159

BOOL CALLBACK DlgProc (HWND, UINT, WPARAM, LPARAM) ;

TCHAR szAppName [] = TEXT ("AddSynth") ;

// Sine wave generator
// --------------------

double SineGenerator (double dFreq, double * pdAngle)
{
     double dAmp ;

     dAmp = sin (* pdAngle) ;
     * pdAngle += 2 * PI * dFreq / SAMPLE_RATE ;

     if (* pdAngle >= 2 * PI)
         * pdAngle -= 2 * PI ;

     return dAmp ;
}

// Fill a buffer with composite waveform
// -------------------------------------

VOID FillBuffer (INS ins, PBYTE pBuffer, int iNumSamples)
{
     static double dAngle [MAX_PARTIALS] ;
     double        dAmp, dFrq, dComp, dFrac ;
     int           i, iPrt, iMsecTime, iCompMaxAmp, iMaxAmp, iSmp ;
```

Figure 22-7. *The ADDSYNTH Program.*   *(continued)*

Figure 22-7. *continued*

```
        // Calculate the composite maximum amplitude

iCompMaxAmp = 0 ;

for (iPrt = 0 ; iPrt < ins.iNumPartials ; iPrt++)
{
    iMaxAmp = 0 ;

    for (i = 0 ; i < ins.pprt[iPrt].iNumAmp ; i++)
        iMaxAmp = max (iMaxAmp, ins.pprt[iPrt].pEnvAmp[i].iValue) ;

    iCompMaxAmp += iMaxAmp ;
}


        // Loop through each sample

for (iSmp = 0 ; iSmp < iNumSamples ; iSmp++)
{
    dComp = 0 ;
    iMsecTime = (int) (1000 * iSmp / SAMPLE_RATE) ;

        // Loop through each partial

    for (iPrt = 0 ; iPrt < ins.iNumPartials ; iPrt++)
    {
        dAmp = 0 ;
        dFrq = 0 ;

        for (i = 0 ; i < ins.pprt[iPrt].iNumAmp - 1 ; i++)
        {
            if (iMsecTime >= ins.pprt[iPrt].pEnvAmp[i  ].iTime &&
                iMsecTime <= ins.pprt[iPrt].pEnvAmp[i+1].iTime)
            {
                dFrac = (double) (iMsecTime -
                    ins.pprt[iPrt].pEnvAmp[i  ].iTime) /
                    (ins.pprt[iPrt].pEnvAmp[i+1].iTime -
                    ins.pprt[iPrt].pEnvAmp[i  ].iTime) ;

                dAmp = dFrac  * ins.pprt[iPrt].pEnvAmp[i+1].iValue +
                    (1-dFrac) * ins.pprt[iPrt].pEnvAmp[i  ].iValue ;

                break ;
            }
        }

        for (i = 0 ; i < ins.pprt[iPrt].iNumFrq - 1 ; i++)
```

```
                    {
                    if (iMsecTime >= ins.pprt[iPrt].pEnvFrq[i  ].iTime &&
                        iMsecTime <= ins.pprt[iPrt].pEnvFrq[i+1].iTime)
                        {
                        dFrac = (double) (iMsecTime -
                                ins.pprt[iPrt].pEnvFrq[i  ].iTime) /
                                (ins.pprt[iPrt].pEnvFrq[i+1].iTime -
                                ins.pprt[iPrt].pEnvFrq[i  ].iTime) ;

                        dFrq = dFrac  * ins.pprt[iPrt].pEnvFrq[i+1].iValue +
                                (1-dFrac) * ins.pprt[iPrt].pEnvFrq[i  ].iValue ;

                        break ;
                        }
                    }
                dComp += dAmp * SineGenerator (dFrq, dAngle + iPrt) ;
                }
            pBuffer[iSmp] = (BYTE) (127 + 127 * dComp / iCompMaxAmp) ;
        }
}

// Make a waveform file
// --------------------

BOOL MakeWaveFile (INS ins, TCHAR * szFileName)
{
    DWORD        dwWritten ;
    HANDLE       hFile ;
    int          iChunkSize, iPcmSize, iNumSamples ;
    PBYTE        pBuffer ;
    WAVEFORMATEX waveform ;

    hFile = CreateFile (szFileName, GENERIC_WRITE, 0, NULL,
                        CREATE_ALWAYS, FILE_ATTRIBUTE_NORMAL, NULL) ;

    if (hFile == NULL)
        return FALSE ;

    iNumSamples = ((long) ins.iMsecTime * SAMPLE_RATE / 1000 + 1) / 2 * 2 ;
    iPcmSize    = sizeof (PCMWAVEFORMAT) ;
    iChunkSize  = 12 + iPcmSize + 8 + iNumSamples ;

    if (NULL == (pBuffer = malloc (iNumSamples)))
    {
        CloseHandle (hFile) ;
```

(continued)

Figure 22-7. *continued*

```
            return FALSE ;
    }

    FillBuffer (ins, pBuffer, iNumSamples) ;

    waveform.wFormatTag      = WAVE_FORMAT_PCM ;
    waveform.nChannels       = 1 ;
    waveform.nSamplesPerSec  = SAMPLE_RATE ;
    waveform.nAvgBytesPerSec = SAMPLE_RATE ;
    waveform.nBlockAlign     = 1 ;
    waveform.wBitsPerSample  = 8 ;
    waveform.cbSize          = 0 ;

    WriteFile (hFile, "RIFF",      4, &dwWritten, NULL) ;
    WriteFile (hFile, &iChunkSize, 4, &dwWritten, NULL) ;
    WriteFile (hFile, "WAVEfmt ",  8, &dwWritten, NULL) ;
    WriteFile (hFile, &iPcmSize,   4, &dwWritten, NULL) ;
    WriteFile (hFile, &waveform, sizeof (WAVEFORMATEX) - 2, &dwWritten, NULL) ;
    WriteFile (hFile, "data",      4, &dwWritten, NULL) ;
    WriteFile (hFile, &iNumSamples, 4, &dwWritten, NULL) ;
    WriteFile (hFile, pBuffer,      iNumSamples,  &dwWritten, NULL) ;

    CloseHandle (hFile) ;
    free (pBuffer) ;

    if ((int) dwWritten != iNumSamples)
    {
        DeleteFile (szFileName) ;
        return FALSE ;
    }
    return TRUE ;
}

void TestAndCreateFile (HWND hwnd, INS ins, TCHAR * szFileName, int idButton)
{
    TCHAR szMessage [64] ;

    if (-1 != GetFileAttributes (szFileName))
        EnableWindow (GetDlgItem (hwnd, idButton), TRUE) ;
    else
    {
        if (MakeWaveFile (ins, szFileName))
            EnableWindow (GetDlgItem (hwnd, idButton), TRUE) ;
        else
        {
            wsprintf (szMessage, TEXT ("Could not create %x."), szFileName) ;
```

```
                MessageBeep (MB_ICONEXCLAMATION) ;
                MessageBox (hwnd, szMessage, szAppName,
                            MB_OK | MB_ICONEXCLAMATION) ;
          }
     }
}

int WINAPI WinMain (HINSTANCE hInstance, HINSTANCE hPrevInstance,
                    PSTR szCmdLine, int iCmdShow)
{
     if (-1 == DialogBox (hInstance, szAppName, NULL, DlgProc))
     {
          MessageBox (NULL, TEXT ("This program requires Windows NT!"),
                      szAppName, MB_ICONERROR) ;
     }
     return 0 ;
}

BOOL CALLBACK DlgProc (HWND hwnd, UINT message, WPARAM wParam, LPARAM lParam)
{
     static TCHAR * szTrum = TEXT ("Trumpet.wav") ;
     static TCHAR * szOboe = TEXT ("Oboe.wav") ;
     static TCHAR * szClar = TEXT ("Clarinet.wav") ;

     switch (message)
     {
     case WM_INITDIALOG:
          SetTimer (hwnd, ID_TIMER, 1, NULL) ;
          return TRUE ;

     case WM_TIMER:
          KillTimer (hwnd, ID_TIMER) ;
          SetCursor (LoadCursor (NULL, IDC_WAIT)) ;
          ShowCursor (TRUE) ;

          TestAndCreateFile (hwnd, insTrum, szTrum, IDC_TRUMPET) ;
          TestAndCreateFile (hwnd, insOboe, szOboe, IDC_OBOE) ;
          TestAndCreateFile (hwnd, insClar, szClar, IDC_CLARINET) ;

          SetDlgItemText (hwnd, IDC_TEXT, TEXT (" ")) ;
          SetFocus (GetDlgItem (hwnd, IDC_TRUMPET)) ;

          ShowCursor (FALSE) ;
          SetCursor (LoadCursor (NULL, IDC_ARROW)) ;
          return TRUE ;
```

(continued)

Figure 22-7. *continued*

```
    case WM_COMMAND:
         switch (LOWORD (wParam))
         {
         case IDC_TRUMPET:
              PlaySound (szTrum, NULL, SND_FILENAME | SND_SYNC) ;
              return TRUE ;

         case IDC_OBOE:
              PlaySound (szOboe, NULL, SND_FILENAME | SND_SYNC) ;
              return TRUE ;

         case IDC_CLARINET:
              PlaySound (szClar, NULL, SND_FILENAME |SND_SYNC) ;
              return TRUE ;
         }
         break ;

    case WM_SYSCOMMAND:
         switch (LOWORD (wParam))
         {
         case SC_CLOSE:
              EndDialog (hwnd, 0) ;
              return TRUE ;
         }
         break ;
    }
    return FALSE ;
}
```

ADDSYNTH.RC (excerpts)

```
//Microsoft Developer Studio generated resource script.

#include "resource.h"
#include "afxres.h"


/////////////////////////////////////////////////////////////////////////////
// Dialog

ADDSYNTH DIALOG DISCARDABLE  100, 100, 176, 49
STYLE WS_MINIMIZEBOX | WS_CAPTION | WS_SYSMENU
CAPTION "Additive Synthesis"
FONT 8, "MS Sans Serif"
BEGIN
```

```
        PUSHBUTTON          "Trumpet",IDC_TRUMPET,8,8,48,16
        PUSHBUTTON          "Oboe",IDC_OBOE,64,8,48,16
        PUSHBUTTON          "Clarinet",IDC_CLARINET,120,8,48,16
        LTEXT               "Preparing Data...",IDC_TEXT,8,32,100,8
END
```

RESOURCE.H (excerpts)

```
// Microsoft Developer Studio generated include file.
// Used by AddSynth.rc

#define IDC_TRUMPET                     1000
#define IDC_OBOE                        1001
#define IDC_CLARINET                    1002
#define IDC_TEXT                        1003
```

An additional file called ADDSYNTH.H is not shown here because it contains several hundred lines of boring stuff. You'll find it on the companion disc for this book. At the beginning of ADDSYNTH.H, I define three structures used for storing the envelope data. Each amplitude and frequency envelope is stored as an array of structures of type ENV. These are number pairs that consist of a time in milliseconds followed by an amplitude value (in an arbitrary scale) or a frequency (in cycles per second). These arrays are of variable length, ranging from 6 to 14 values. Straight lines are assumed to connect the amplitude and frequency values.

Each instrument consists of a collection of partials (12 for the trumpet and 21 each for the oboe and clarinet) stored as an array of structures of type PRT. The PRT structure stores the number of points in the amplitude and frequency envelopes and a pointer to the ENV array. The INS structure contains the total time of the tone in milliseconds, the number of partials, and a pointer to the PRT array that stores the partials.

ADDSYNTH has three push buttons labeled "Trumpet," "Oboe," and "Clarinet." PCs are not yet quite fast enough to do all the additive synthesis calculations in real time, so the first time you run ADDSYNTH, these buttons will be disabled until the program calculates the samples and creates the TRUMPET.WAV, OBOE.WAV, and CLARINET.WAV sound files. The push buttons are then enabled and you can play the three sounds by using the *PlaySound* function. The next time you run the program, it will check for the existence of the waveform files and won't need to recreate them.

Most of the work is done in ADDSYNTH's *FillBuffer* function. *FillBuffer* begins by calculating the total composite maximum amplitude. It does this by looping through the partials for the instrument to find the maximum amplitude for each partial and then adding the maximum amplitudes all together. This value is later used to scale the samples to an 8-bit sample size.

FillBuffer then proceeds to calculate a value for each sample. Each sample corresponds to a millisecond time value that depends on the sample rate. (Actually, at a 22.05 kHz sample rate, every 22 samples correspond to the same millisecond time value.) *FillBuffer* then loops through the partials. For both the frequency and amplitude, it finds the envelope line segment corresponding to the millisecond time value and performs a linear interpolation.

The frequency value is passed to the *SineGenerator* function, together with a phase angle value. As I discussed earlier in this chapter, digitally generating sine waves requires a phase angle value to be maintained and incremented based on the frequency value. On return from the *SineGenerator* function, the sine value is multiplied by the amplitude for the partial and accumulated. After all the partials for a sample are added together, the sample is scaled to the size of a byte.

Waking Up to Waveform Audio

WAKEUP, which you'll find in Figure 22-8, is one of of those programs where the source code files don't look quite complete. The program's window looks like a dialog box, but there's no resource script (we already know how to do that), and the program uses what seems to be a waveform file, but there's no such file on the disk. However, the program packs quite a wallop: The sound it plays is loud and quite annoying. WAKEUP is my alarm clock, and it definitely works in waking me up.

WAKEUP.C

```
/*-------------------------------------------
   WAKEUP.C -- Alarm Clock Program
               (c) Charles Petzold, 1998
  -------------------------------------------*/

#include <windows.h>
#include <commctrl.h>

     // ID values for 3 child windows

#define ID_TIMEPICK 0
#define ID_CHECKBOX 1
#define ID_PUSHBTN  2

     // Timer ID

#define ID_TIMER    1

     // Number of 100-nanosecond increments (ie FILETIME ticks) in an hour
```

Figure 22-8. *The WAKEUP program.*

```
#define FTTICKSPERHOUR (60 * 60 * (LONGLONG) 10000000)

     // Defines and structure for waveform "file"

#define SAMPRATE   11025
#define NUMSAMPS  (3 * SAMPRATE)
#define HALFSAMPS (NUMSAMPS / 2)

typedef struct
{
     char  chRiff[4] ;
     DWORD dwRiffSize ;
     char  chWave[4] ;
     char  chFmt [4] ;
     DWORD dwFmtSize ;
     PCMWAVEFORMAT pwf ;
     char  chData[4] ;
     DWORD dwDataSize ;
     BYTE  byData[0] ;
}
WAVEFORM ;

     // The window proc and the subclass proc

LRESULT CALLBACK WndProc (HWND, UINT, WPARAM, LPARAM) ;
LRESULT CALLBACK SubProc (HWND, UINT, WPARAM, LPARAM) ;

     // Original window procedure addresses for the subclassed windows

WNDPROC SubbedProc [3] ;

     // The current child window with the input focus

HWND hwndFocus ;

int WINAPI WinMain (HINSTANCE hInstance, HINSTANCE hPrevInst,
                    PSTR szCmdLine, int iCmdShow)
{
     static TCHAR szAppName [] = TEXT ("WakeUp") ;
     HWND          hwnd ;
     MSG           msg ;
     WNDCLASS      wndclass ;

     wndclass.style         = 0 ;
     wndclass.lpfnWndProc   = WndProc ;
     wndclass.cbClsExtra    = 0 ;
```

(continued)

Figure 22-8. *continued*

```
        wndclass.cbWndExtra     = 0 ;
        wndclass.hInstance      = hInstance ;
        wndclass.hIcon          = LoadIcon (NULL, IDI_APPLICATION) ;
        wndclass.hCursor        = LoadCursor (NULL, IDC_ARROW) ;
        wndclass.hbrBackground  = (HBRUSH) (1 + COLOR_BTNFACE) ;
        wndclass.lpszMenuName   = NULL ;
        wndclass.lpszClassName  = szAppName ;

        if (!RegisterClass (&wndclass))
        {
            MessageBox (NULL, TEXT ("This program requires Windows NT!"),
                        szAppName, MB_ICONERROR) ;
            return 0 ;
        }

        hwnd = CreateWindow (szAppName, szAppName,
                            WS_OVERLAPPED | WS_CAPTION |
                                        WS_SYSMENU | WS_MINIMIZEBOX,
                            CW_USEDEFAULT, CW_USEDEFAULT,
                            CW_USEDEFAULT, CW_USEDEFAULT,
                            NULL, NULL, hInstance, NULL) ;

        ShowWindow (hwnd, iCmdShow) ;
        UpdateWindow (hwnd) ;

        while (GetMessage (&msg, NULL, 0, 0))
        {
            TranslateMessage (&msg) ;
            DispatchMessage (&msg) ;
        }
        return msg.wParam ;
}

LRESULT CALLBACK WndProc (HWND hwnd, UINT message, WPARAM wParam, LPARAM lParam)
{
        static HWND             hwndDTP, hwndCheck, hwndPush ;
        static WAVEFORM         waveform = { "RIFF", NUMSAMPS + 0x24, "WAVE", "fmt ",
                                            sizeof (PCMWAVEFORMAT), 1, 1, SAMPRATE,
                                            SAMPRATE, 1, 8, "data", NUMSAMPS } ;
        static WAVEFORM     * pwaveform ;
        FILETIME                ft ;
        HINSTANCE               hInstance ;
        INITCOMMONCONTROLSEX icex ;
        int                     i, cxChar, cyChar ;
        LARGE_INTEGER           li ;
        SYSTEMTIME              st ;
```

```
switch (message)
{
case WM_CREATE:
        // Some initialization stuff

     hInstance = (HINSTANCE) GetWindowLong (hwnd, GWL_HINSTANCE) ;

     icex.dwSize = sizeof (icex) ;
     icex.dwICC  = ICC_DATE_CLASSES ;
     InitCommonControlsEx (&icex) ;

        // Create the waveform file with alternating square waves

     pwaveform = malloc (sizeof (WAVEFORM) + NUMSAMPS) ;
     * pwaveform = waveform ;

     for (i = 0 ; i < HALFSAMPS ; i++)
         if (i % 600 < 300)
             if (i % 16 < 8)
                 pwaveform->byData[i] = 25 ;
             else
                 pwaveform->byData[i] = 230 ;
         else
             if (i % 8 < 4)
                 pwaveform->byData[i] = 25 ;
             else
                 pwaveform->byData[i] = 230 ;

        // Get character size and set a fixed window size.

     cxChar = LOWORD (GetDialogBaseUnits ()) ;
     cyChar = HIWORD (GetDialogBaseUnits ()) ;

     SetWindowPos (hwnd, NULL, 0, 0,
                   42 * cxChar,
                   10 * cyChar / 3 + 2 * GetSystemMetrics (SM_CYBORDER) +
                                         GetSystemMetrics (SM_CYCAPTION),
                   SWP_NOMOVE | SWP_NOZORDER | SWP_NOACTIVATE) ;

        // Create the three child windows

     hwndDTP = CreateWindow (DATETIMEPICK_CLASS, TEXT (""),
                   WS_BORDER | WS_CHILD | WS_VISIBLE | DTS_TIMEFORMAT,
                   2 * cxChar, cyChar, 12 * cxChar, 4 * cyChar / 3,
                   hwnd, (HMENU) ID_TIMEPICK, hInstance, NULL) ;
```

(continued)

Figure 22-8. *continued*

```
        hwndCheck = CreateWindow (TEXT ("Button"), TEXT ("Set Alarm"),
                    WS_CHILD | WS_VISIBLE | BS_AUTOCHECKBOX,
                    16 * cxChar, cyChar, 12 * cxChar, 4 * cyChar / 3,
                    hwnd, (HMENU) ID_CHECKBOX, hInstance, NULL) ;

        hwndPush = CreateWindow (TEXT ("Button"), TEXT ("Turn Off"),
                    WS_CHILD | WS_VISIBLE | BS_PUSHBUTTON | WS_DISABLED,
                    28 * cxChar, cyChar, 12 * cxChar, 4 * cyChar / 3,
                    hwnd, (HMENU) ID_PUSHBTN, hInstance, NULL) ;

        hwndFocus = hwndDTP ;

            // Subclass the three child windows

        SubbedProc [ID_TIMEPICK] = (WNDPROC)
                    SetWindowLong (hwndDTP, GWL_WNDPROC, (LONG) SubProc) ;
        SubbedProc [ID_CHECKBOX] = (WNDPROC)
                    SetWindowLong (hwndCheck, GWL_WNDPROC, (LONG) SubProc);
        SubbedProc [ID_PUSHBTN] = (WNDPROC)
                    SetWindowLong (hwndPush, GWL_WNDPROC, (LONG) SubProc) ;

            // Set the date and time picker control to the current time
            // plus 9 hours, rounded down to next lowest hour

        GetLocalTime (&st) ;
        SystemTimeToFileTime (&st, &ft) ;
        li = * (LARGE_INTEGER *) &ft ;
        li.QuadPart += 9 * FTTICKSPERHOUR ;
        ft = * (FILETIME *) &li ;
        FileTimeToSystemTime (&ft, &st) ;
        st.wMinute = st.wSecond = st.wMilliseconds = 0 ;
        SendMessage (hwndDTP, DTM_SETSYSTEMTIME, 0, (LPARAM) &st) ;
        return 0 ;

    case WM_SETFOCUS:
        SetFocus (hwndFocus) ;
        return 0 ;

    case WM_COMMAND:
        switch (LOWORD (wParam))        // control ID
        {
        case ID_CHECKBOX:

                    // When the user checks the "Set Alarm" button, get the
                    // time in the date and time control and subtract from
                    // it the current PC time.
```

```
            if (SendMessage (hwndCheck, BM_GETCHECK, 0, 0))
            {
                 SendMessage (hwndDTP, DTM_GETSYSTEMTIME, 0, (LPARAM) &st) ;
                 SystemTimeToFileTime (&st, &ft) ;
                 li = * (LARGE_INTEGER *) &ft ;

                 GetLocalTime (&st) ;
                 SystemTimeToFileTime (&st, &ft) ;
                 li.QuadPart -= ((LARGE_INTEGER *) &ft)->QuadPart ;

                      // Make sure the time is between 0 and 24 hours!
                      // These little adjustments let us completely ignore
                      // the date part of the SYSTEMTIME structures.

                 while (li.QuadPart < 0)
                      li.QuadPart += 24 * FTTICKSPERHOUR ;

                 li.QuadPart %= 24 * FTTICKSPERHOUR ;

                      // Set a one-shot timer! (See you in the morning.)

                 SetTimer (hwnd, ID_TIMER, (int) (li.QuadPart / 10000), 0) ;
            }
                 // If button is being unchecked, kill the timer.

            else
                 KillTimer (hwnd, ID_TIMER) ;

            return 0 ;

            // The "Turn Off" button turns off the ringing alarm, and also
            // unchecks the "Set Alarm" button and disables itself.

       case ID_PUSHBTN:
            PlaySound (NULL, NULL, 0) ;
            SendMessage (hwndCheck, BM_SETCHECK, 0, 0) ;
            EnableWindow (hwndDTP, TRUE) ;
            EnableWindow (hwndCheck, TRUE) ;
            EnableWindow (hwndPush, FALSE) ;
            SetFocus (hwndDTP) ;
            return 0 ;
       }
       return 0 ;

            // The WM_NOTIFY message comes from the date and time picker.
            // If the user has checked "Set Alarm" and then gone back to
```

(continued)

Figure 22-8. *continued*

```
                // change the alarm time, there might be a discrepancy between
                // the displayed time and the one-shot timer. So the program
                // unchecks "Set Alarm" and kills any outstanding timer.

     case WM_NOTIFY:
          switch (wParam)              // control ID
          {
          case ID_TIMEPICK:
               switch (((NMHDR *) lParam)->code)        // notification code
               {
               case DTN_DATETIMECHANGE:
                    if (SendMessage (hwndCheck, BM_GETCHECK, 0, 0))
                    {
                         KillTimer (hwnd, ID_TIMER) ;
                         SendMessage (hwndCheck, BM_SETCHECK, 0, 0) ;
                    }
                    return 0 ;
               }
          }
          return 0 ;

          // The WM_COMMAND message comes from the two buttons.

     case WM_TIMER:

               // When the timer message comes, kill the timer (because we only
               // want a one-shot) and start the annoying alarm noise going.

          KillTimer (hwnd, ID_TIMER) ;
          PlaySound ((PTSTR) pwaveform,  NULL,
                     SND_MEMORY | SND_LOOP | SND_ASYNC);

               // Let the sleepy user turn off the timer by slapping the
               // space bar. If the window is minimized, it's restored; then
               // it's brought to the forefront; then the pushbutton is enabled
               // and given the input focus.

          EnableWindow (hwndDTP, FALSE) ;
          EnableWindow (hwndCheck, FALSE) ;
          EnableWindow (hwndPush, TRUE) ;

          hwndFocus = hwndPush ;
          ShowWindow (hwnd, SW_RESTORE) ;
          SetForegroundWindow (hwnd) ;
          return 0 ;

          // Clean up if the alarm is ringing or the timer is still set.
```

```
        case WM_DESTROY:
             free (pwaveform) ;

             if (IsWindowEnabled (hwndPush))
                   PlaySound (NULL, NULL, 0) ;

             if (SendMessage (hwndCheck, BM_GETCHECK, 0, 0))
                   KillTimer (hwnd, ID_TIMER) ;

             PostQuitMessage (0) ;
             return 0 ;
        }
        return DefWindowProc (hwnd, message, wParam, lParam) ;
}

LRESULT CALLBACK SubProc (HWND hwnd, UINT message, WPARAM wParam, LPARAM lParam)
{
     int idNext, id = GetWindowLong (hwnd, GWL_ID) ;

     switch (message)
     {
     case WM_CHAR:
          if (wParam == '\t')
          {
               idNext = id ;

               do
                    idNext = (idNext +
                        (GetKeyState (VK_SHIFT) < 0 ? 2 : 1)) % 3 ;
               while (!IsWindowEnabled (GetDlgItem (GetParent (hwnd), idNext)));

               SetFocus (GetDlgItem (GetParent (hwnd), idNext)) ;
               return 0 ;
          }
          break ;

     case WM_SETFOCUS:
          hwndFocus = hwnd ;
          break ;
     }
     return CallWindowProc (SubbedProc [id], hwnd, message, wParam, lParam) ;
}
```

The waveform that WAKEUP uses is just two square waves, but they are alternated very quickly. The actual waveform is calculated during *WndProc*'s WM_CREATE message. The entire waveform file is stored in memory; a pointer to this memory block is passed to the *PlaySound* function, which uses the SND_MEMORY, SND_LOOP, and SND_ASYNC arguments.

WAKEUP uses a common control called the Date-Time Picker. This control takes care of logic to allow the user to select a particular date and time. (WAKEUP uses only the time feature.) A program can get and set this time using the SYSTEMTIME structure used in obtaining and setting the PC's own clock. To see how versatile the Date-Time Picker really is, try creating the window without any DTS style flags.

Notice the logic at the end of the WM_CREATE message: the program assumes that you run it soon before going to bed and that you want to wake up in 8 hours from the next stroke of the hour.

Now obviously you could obtain the current time in a SYSTEMTIME structure from the *GetLocalTime* function and increment the time "manually." But in the general case this calculation involves checking for a resultant hour greater than 24, which means you'll have to increment the day field, and then that might involve incrementing the month (so you have to have logic for the number of days in each month and a leap year check), and finally you might have to increment the year.

Instead, the recommended method (from */Platform SDK/Windows Base Services/ General Library/Time/Time Reference/Time Structures/SYSTEMTIME*) is to convert the SYSTEMTIME to a FILETIME structure (using *SystemTimeToFileTime*), cast the FILETIME structure to a LARGE_INTEGER structure, perform the calculations on the large integer, cast back to a FILETIME structure, and then convert back to a SYSTEMTIME structure (using *FileTimeToSystemTime*).

The FILETIME structure, as its name implies, is used to get and set the time that a file was last modified. The structure looks like this:

```
type struct _FILETIME       // ft
{
    DWORD dwLowDateTime ;
    DWORD dwHighDateTime ;
}
FILETIME ;
```

These two fields together express a 64-bit value that indicates the number of 100-nanosecond intervals from January 1, 1601.

The Microsoft C/C++ compiler supports 64-bit integers as a nonstandard extension to ANSI C. The data type is *__int64*. You can do all the normal arithmetic operations on *__int64* types, and some run-time library functions support them. The Windows WINNT.H header file defines the following:

```
typedef __int64 LONGLONG ;
typedef unsigned __int64 DWORDLONG ;
```

In Windows, this sometimes called a "quad word" or, more commonly, a "large integer." There's also a union defined:

```
typedef union _LARGE_INTEGER
{
    struct
    {
        DWORD LowPart ;
        LONG  HighPart ;
    } ;
    LONGLONG QuadPart ;
}
LARGE_INTEGER ;
```

This is all documented in */Platform SDK/Windows Base Services/General Library/Large Integer Operations*. The union lets you work with the large integer either as two 32-bit quantities or as a 64-bit quantity.

MIDI AND MUSIC

The Musical Instrument Digital Interface (MIDI) was developed in the early 1980s by a consortium of manufacturers of electronic music synthesizers. MIDI is a protocol for connecting electronic music instruments among themselves and with computers. MIDI is an extremely important standard in the field of electronic music. The MIDI specification is maintained by the MIDI Manufacturers Association (MMA), which has a Web site at *http://www.midi.org*.

The Workings of MIDI

MIDI defines a protocol for passing digital commands through a cable. A MIDI cable uses 5-pin DIN connectors, but only three of the connectors are used. One is a shield, another is a current loop, and the third carries the data. The MIDI protocol is unidirectional at 31,250 bits per second. Each byte of data begins with a start bit and ends with a stop bit, for an effective transfer rate of 3,125 bytes per second.

It's important to understand that no actual sounds—in either an analog or digital format—are transferred through the MIDI cable. What goes through the cable are generally simple messages, usually 1, 2, or 3 bytes in length.

A simple MIDI configuration could consist of two pieces of MIDI-compatible hardware. One is a MIDI keyboard that makes no sounds by itself but serves solely to generate MIDI messages. This keyboard has a MIDI port labeled "MIDI Out." You connect a MIDI cable from this port to the "MIDI In" port of a MIDI sound synthesizer. This synthesizer may simply look like a little box with a few buttons on the front.

When you press a key on the keyboard (let's say middle C), the keyboard sends 3 bytes to the MIDI Out port. In hexadecimal, these bytes are

```
90 3C 40
```

The first byte (90) indicates a "Note On" message. The second byte is the key number, where 3C is middle C. The third byte is the velocity with which the key is struck and may range from 1 to 127. We happen to be using a keyboard here that is not velocity-sensitive, so it sends an average velocity value. This 3-byte message goes down the MIDI cable into the Midi In port of the synthesizer. The synthesizer responds by playing a tone at middle C.

When you release the key, the keyboard sends another 3-byte message to the MIDI Out port:

```
90 3C 00
```

This is the same as the Note On command, but with a zero velocity byte. This zero byte indicates a Note Off command, meaning that the note should be turned off. The synthesizer reponds by stopping the sound.

If the synthesizer is capable of polyphony (that is, playing more than one note at the same time), then you can play chords on the keyboard. The keyboard generates multiple Note On messages, and the synthesizer plays all the notes. When you release the chord, the keyboard sends multiple Note Off messages to the synthesizer.

Generally speaking, the keyboard in this configuration is known as a "MIDI controller." It is reponsible for generating MIDI messages to control a synthesizer. A MIDI controller does not have to look like a keyboard. There are MIDI wind controllers that look like clarinets or saxophones, MIDI guitar controllers, MIDI string controllers, and MIDI drum controllers. At the very least, all of these controllers generate 3-byte Note On and Note Off messages.

Rather than something that resembles a keyboard or traditional musical instrument, a controller can also be a "sequencer." This is a piece of hardware that stores sequences of Note On and Note Off messages in memory and then plays them back. Stand-alone sequencers are used much less today than they were some years ago because they have been replaced with computers. A computer equipped with a MIDI board can also generate Note On and Note Off messages to control synthesizers. MIDI authoring software, which lets you compose on screen, can store MIDI messages coming from a MIDI controller, let you manipulate them, and then send the MIDI messages to a synthesizer.

The synthesizer is sometimes also called a "sound module" or "tone generator." MIDI does not specify how the sounds are actually generated. The synthesizer could be using any one of a variety of different sound generation techniques.

In the real world, only very simple MIDI controllers (such as wind controllers) have only MIDI Out cable ports. Often a keyboard will have a built-in synthesizer, and it will have three MIDI cable ports labeled MIDI In, MIDI Out, and MIDI Thru. The MIDI In port accepts MIDI messages to play the keyboard's internal synthesizer. The MIDI Out port sends MIDI messages from the keyboard to an external synthesizer. The MIDI Thru port is an output port that duplicates the input in the MIDI In port—whatever comes into the MIDI In port is sent back out to the MIDI Thru port. (The MIDI Thru port does not contain any of the information sent out over the MIDI Out port.)

There are only two ways to connect MIDI hardware by cables: You can connect a MIDI Out on one piece of hardware to MIDI In of another, or you can connect MIDI Thru to MIDI In. The MIDI Thru port allows for the daisy-chaining of MIDI synthesizers.

The Program Change

What kind of sound does the synthesizer make? Is it a piano sound, a violin sound, a trumpet sound, or a flying saucer sound? Generally the various sounds that a synthesizer is capable of producing are stored in ROM or somewhere else. These are generally called "voices" or "instruments" or "patches." (The word "patch" comes from the days of analog synthesizers when different sounds were configured by plugging patch chords into jacks on the front of the synthesizer.)

In MIDI, the various sounds that a synthesizer is capable of producing are known as "programs." Changing the program requires sending the synthesizer a MIDI Program Change message,

```
C0 pp
```

where *pp* can range from 0 to 127. Often a MIDI keyboard will have a series of numbered buttons across the top that generate Program Change messages. By pressing these you can control the synthesizer voice from the keyboard. The numbering of these buttons usually begins with 1 rather than 0, so program number 1 corresponds to a Program Change byte of 0.

The MIDI specification does not indicate what program numbers should correspond with what instruments. For example, the first three programs on a classic Yamaha DX7 synthesizer are called "Warm Strings," "Mellow Horn," and "Pick Guitar." On a Yamaha TX81Z tone generator, they're "Grand Piano," "Upright Piano," and "Deep Grand." On a Roland MT-32 sound module, they're "Acoustic Piano 1," "Acoustic Piano 2," and "Acoustic Piano 3." So, if you don't want to be surprised when you make a program change from a keyboard, you had better know what instrument voice corresponds to each program number in the synthesizer you happen to be using.

This can be a real problem for MIDI files that contain Program Change messages—these files are not device-independent because their contents will sound different on different synthesizers. However, in recent years, a standard known as "General MIDI" (GM) has standardized the program numbers. General MIDI is supported by Windows. If a synthesizer is not in accordance with the General MIDI specification, program mappings can make it emulate a General MIDI synthesizer.

The MIDI Channel

I've discussed two MIDI messages so far. The first is Note On,

```
90 kk vv
```

where *kk* is the key number (0 to 127) and *vv* is the velocity (0 to 127). A zero velocity indicates a Note Off command. The second is the Program Change,

```
C0 pp
```

where *pp* ranges from 0 to 127. These are typical of MIDI messages. The first byte is called the "status" byte. Depending on what the status byte is, it is generally followed by 0, 1, or 2 "data" bytes. (The exception is for "system exclusive" messages that I'll describe shortly.) It is easy to distinguish a status byte from a data byte: the high bit is always 1 for a status byte and 0 for a data byte.

I have not yet discussed the generalized form of these two messages, however. The generalized form of the Note On message is

```
9n kk vv
```

and the Program Change is

```
Cn pp
```

In both cases, *n* corresponds to the lower four bits of the status byte and can range from 0 to 15. This is called the MIDI "channel." Channels are generally numbered beginning with 1, so if *n* is 0, that means channel 1.

The use of 16 different channels allows a MIDI cable to carry messages for 16 different voices. Generally, you'll find that a particular string of MIDI messages will begin with Program Change messages to set a voice for the various channels being used, followed by multiple Note On and Note Off commands. Later on, there might be other Program Change commands. But at any time, each channel is associated with only one voice.

Let's take a simple example: Suppose the keyboard controller I've been describing is able to generate MIDI messages for two different channels simultaneously—channel 1 and channel 2. You might begin by pressing buttons on the keyboard to send two Program Change messages to the synthesizer:

```
C0 01
C1 05
```

Channel 1 is now set for program 2, and channel 2 is set for program 6. (Recall that channel numbers and program numbers are 1-based but encoded in a 0-based form in the messages.) Now when you press a key on the keyboard, it sends two Note On messages, one for each channel:

```
90 kk vv
91 kk vv
```

This lets you play two instrument voices simultaneously in unison.

An alternative is a "split" keyboard. The lower keys could generate Note On messages on channel 1, and the upper keys could generate Note On messages on channel 2. This lets you play two instruments independently from one keyboard.

The use of 16 channels becomes more powerful when you think about MIDI sequencing software on a PC. Each channel corresponds to a different instrument. If you have a synthesizer that can play 16 different instruments independently, you can orchestrate a composition for a 16-piece band and connnect the MIDI board with the synthesizer using just one MIDI cable.

MIDI Messages

Although the Note On and Program Change messages are the most important messages in any MIDI implementation, this is not all that MIDI can do. Figure 22-9 is a chart of the MIDI channel messages defined in the MIDI specification. As I've noted above, the status byte always has the high bit set and all data bytes that follow the status byte have a high bit equal to 0. This means that status bytes can range from 0x80 through 0xFF, while data bytes range from 0 through 0x7F.

MIDI Message	*Data Bytes*	*Values*
Note Off	8n *kk vv*	*kk* = key number (0–127)
		vv = velocity (0–127)
Note On	9n *kk vv*	*kk* = key number (0–127)
		vv = velocity (1–127, 0 = note off)
Polyphonic After Touch	An *kk tt*	*kk* = key number (0–127)
		tt = after touch (0–127)
Control Change	Bn *cc xx*	*cc* = controller (0–121)
		xx = value (0–127)
Channel Mode Local Control	Bn 7A *xx*	*xx* = 0 (off), 127 (on)
All Notes Off	Bn 7B 00	
Omni Mode Off	Bn 7C 00	
Omni Mode On	Bn 7D 00	
Mono Mode On	Bn 7E *cc*	*cc* = number of channels
Poly Mode On	Bn 7F 00	
Program Change	Cn *pp*	*pp* = program (0–127)
Channel After Touch	Dn *tt*	*tt* = after touch (0–127)
Pitch Wheel Change	En *ll hh*	*ll* = low 7 bits (0–127)
		hh = high 7 bits (0–127)

Figure 22-9. *The MIDI Channel Messages (n = channel number, 0 through 15).*

The key numbers generally correspond to the traditional notes of Western music, although they don't have to. (For a percussion voice, each key number could be a different percussion instrument, for example.) When the key numbers correspond to a piano-type keyboard, key 60 (in decimal) is middle C. The MIDI key numbers extend 21 notes below and 19 notes above the range of a normal 88-key piano. The velocity number is the velocity with which the key is depressed, which on a piano governs both loudness and the harmonic character of the sound. A particular voice can respond to key velocity in this way or other ways.

The examples I showed earlier used a Note On message with a velocity byte of zero to indicate a Note Off command. There is also a separate Note Off command for keyboards (or other controllers) that implement a key release velocity. This is very rare, however.

There are two "after-touch" messages. After-touch is a feature of some keyboards where you can change the sound in some way by pressing harder on the key after it's already depressed. One message (status byte 0xDn) is an after-touch that applies to all the notes currently being played in a channel; this is the most common. The status byte 0xAn indicates after-touch that applies to each individual key independently.

Generally keyboards have some dials or switches for further controlling the sound. These are called "controllers," and any change is indicated by a status byte of 0xBn. Controllers are identified by numbers ranging from 0 to 121. The 0xBn status byte is also used for Channel Mode messages that indicate how a synthesizer should respond to simultaneous notes in the channel.

One very important controller is a wheel that shifts the pitch up and down. This has a separate MIDI message with a status byte of 0xEn.

Missing from the chart in Figure 22-9 on the previous page are messages that begin with status bytes F0 through FF. These are called system messages because they apply to the entire MIDI system rather than a particular channel. The system messages are generally used for synchronization purposes, triggering sequencers, resetting hardware, and obtaining information.

Many MIDI controllers continually send out status bytes of 0xFE, which is called the Active Sensing message. This simply indicates that the MIDI controller is still attached to the system.

One important system message is the "system exclusive" message that begins with a status byte of 0xF0. This message is used for transferring chunks of data to a synthesizer in a manufacturer-dependent and synthesizer-dependent format. (For example, new voice definitions can be passed from a computer to a synthesizer in this way.) The system exclusive message is the only message that can contain more than 2 data bytes. In fact, the number of data bytes is variable, but each data byte must have its high bit set to 0. The status byte 0xF7 indicates an end of the system exclusive message.

System exclusive messages are also used for dumping data (for example, voice definitions) from the synthesizer. The data comes out of the synthesizer through the MIDI Out port. If you're attempting to program for MIDI in a device-independent manner, you should probably avoid using system exclusive messages. But they are quite valuable for defining new synthesizer voices.

A MIDI file (with the extension .MID) is a collection of MIDI messages with timing information. You can play MIDI files using MCI. However, for the remainder of this chapter, I'll be discussing the low-level *midiOut* functions.

An Introduction to MIDI Sequencing

The low-level MIDI API consists of functions beginning with the prefix *midiIn*, for reading MIDI sequences coming from an external controller, and *midiOut*, for playing music on the internal or external synthesizer. Despite the term "low-level," you don't need to know anything about the hardware interface of the MIDI board when using these functions.

To open a MIDI output device in preparation for playing music, you call the *midiOutOpen* function:

```
error = midiOutOpen (&hMidiOut, wDeviceID, dwCallBack,
                     dwCallBackData, dwFlags) ;
```

The function returns 0 if successful or an error code if not. If you've specified the function arguments correctly, an error will usually indicate that the MIDI device is already in use by another program.

The first argument is a pointer to a variable of type HMIDIOUT that receives a MIDI output handle for use in subsequent MIDI output functions. The second argument is the device ID. To use one of the real MIDI devices, this argument can range from 0 to one less than the number returned from *midiOutGetNumDevs*. Or you can use MIDIMAPPER, which is defined in MMSYSTEM.H as −1. In most cases, you'll probably set the last three arguments of *midiOutOpen* to NULL or 0.

Once you open a MIDI output device and obtain the handle, you can begin sending MIDI messages to the device. You do this by calling

```
error = midiOutShortMsg (hMidiOut, dwMessage) ;
```

The first argument is the handle obtained from *midiOutOpen*. The second argument is a 1-byte, 2-byte, or 3-byte MIDI message packed into a 32-bit DWORD. As I discussed earlier, MIDI messages begin with a status byte, followed by 0, 1, or 2 bytes of data. The status byte forms the least significant byte of *dwMessage*, the first data byte is the next significant byte, and the second data byte is the next. The most significant byte of *dwMessage* is 0.

For example, to play a middle C (the note 0x3C) on MIDI channel 5 with a velocity of 0x7F, you need a 3-byte Note On message:

```
0x95 0x3C 0x7F
```

The *dwMessage* parameter to *midiOutShortMsg* is 0x007F3C95.

The three essential MIDI messages are Program Change (to change the instrument voice for a particular channel), Note On, and Note Off. After opening a MIDI output device, you should always begin with a Program Change message and you should send an equal number of Note On and Note Off messages.

When you're all through playing the music you want to play, you can reset the MIDI output device to make sure that all notes are turned off:

```
midiOutReset (hMidiOut) ;
```

You can then close the device:

```
midiOutClose (hMidiOut) ;
```

The *midiOutOpen*, *midiOutShortMsg*, *midiOutReset*, and *midiOutClose* functions are the four essential functions you need for using the low-level MIDI output API.

So, let's play some music! The BACHTOCC program shown in Figure 22-10 plays the first measure of the toccata section of J. S. Bach's famous Toccata and Fugue in D Minor for organ.

BACHTOCC.C

```
/*-------------------------------------------------------
   BACHTOCC.C -- Bach Toccata in D Minor (First Bar)
                 (c) Charles Petzold, 1998
   -------------------------------------------------------*/

#include <windows.h>

#define ID_TIMER    1

LRESULT CALLBACK WndProc (HWND, UINT, WPARAM, LPARAM) ;

TCHAR szAppName[] = TEXT ("BachTocc") ;

int WINAPI WinMain (HINSTANCE hInstance, HINSTANCE hPrevInstance,
                    PSTR szCmdLine, int iCmdShow)
{
    HWND        hwnd ;
    MSG         msg ;
    WNDCLASS    wndclass ;

    wndclass.style         = CS_HREDRAW | CS_VREDRAW ;
    wndclass.lpfnWndProc   = WndProc ;
    wndclass.cbClsExtra    = 0 ;
    wndclass.cbWndExtra    = 0 ;
    wndclass.hInstance     = hInstance ;
    wndclass.hIcon         = LoadIcon (NULL, IDI_APPLICATION) ;
    wndclass.hCursor       = LoadCursor (NULL, IDC_ARROW) ;
    wndclass.hbrBackground = GetStockObject (WHITE_BRUSH) ;
    wndclass.lpszMenuName  = NULL ;
    wndclass.lpszClassName = szAppName ;
```

Figure 22-10. *The BACHTOCC Program.*

```
      if (!RegisterClass (&wndclass))
      {
            MessageBox (NULL, TEXT ("This program requires Windows NT!"),
                        szAppName, MB_ICONERROR) ;
            return 0 ;
      }

      hwnd = CreateWindow (szAppName,
                           TEXT ("Bach Toccata in D Minor (First Bar)"),
                           WS_OVERLAPPEDWINDOW,
                           CW_USEDEFAULT, CW_USEDEFAULT,
                           CW_USEDEFAULT, CW_USEDEFAULT,
                           NULL, NULL, hInstance, NULL) ;

      if (!hwnd)
            return 0 ;

      ShowWindow (hwnd, iCmdShow) ;
      UpdateWindow (hwnd) ;

      while (GetMessage (&msg, NULL, 0, 0))
      {
            TranslateMessage (&msg) ;
            DispatchMessage (&msg) ;
      }
      return msg.wParam ;
}

DWORD MidiOutMessage (HMIDIOUT hMidi, int iStatus, int iChannel,
                                      int iData1,  int iData2)
{
      DWORD dwMessage = iStatus | iChannel | (iData1 << 8) | (iData2 << 16) ;

      return midiOutShortMsg (hMidi, dwMessage) ;
}

LRESULT CALLBACK WndProc (HWND hwnd, UINT message, WPARAM wParam, LPARAM lParam)
{
      static struct
      {
            int iDur ;
            int iNote [2] ;
      }
      noteseq [] = { 110, 69, 81,  110, 67, 79,  990, 69, 81,  220, -1, -1,
                     110, 67, 79,  110, 65, 77,  110, 64, 76,  110, 62, 74,
                     220, 61, 73,  440, 62, 74, 1980, -1, -1,  110, 57, 69,
```

(continued)

Figure 22-10. *continued*

```
                 110, 55, 67,  990, 57, 69,  220, -1, -1,  220, 52, 64,
                 220, 53, 65,  220, 49, 61,  440, 50, 62, 1980, -1, -1 } ;

     static HMIDIOUT hMidiOut ;
     static int      iIndex ;
     int             i ;

     switch (message)
     {
     case WM_CREATE:
             // Open MIDIMAPPER device

          if (midiOutOpen (&hMidiOut, MIDIMAPPER, 0, 0, 0))
          {
               MessageBeep (MB_ICONEXCLAMATION) ;
               MessageBox (hwnd, TEXT ("Cannot open MIDI output device!"),
                               szAppName, MB_ICONEXCLAMATION | MB_OK) ;
               return -1 ;
          }
             // Send Program Change messages for "Church Organ"

          MidiOutMessage (hMidiOut, 0xC0,  0, 19, 0) ;
          MidiOutMessage (hMidiOut, 0xC0, 12, 19, 0) ;

          SetTimer (hwnd, ID_TIMER, 1000, NULL) ;
          return 0 ;

     case WM_TIMER:
             // Loop for 2-note polyphony

          for (i = 0 ; i < 2 ; i++)
          {
                  // Note Off messages for previous note

             if (iIndex != 0 && noteseq[iIndex - 1].iNote[i] != -1)
             {
                  MidiOutMessage (hMidiOut, 0x80,  0,
                                 noteseq[iIndex - 1].iNote[i], 0) ;

                  MidiOutMessage (hMidiOut, 0x80, 12,
                                 noteseq[iIndex - 1].iNote[i], 0) ;
             }
                  // Note On messages for new note

             if (iIndex != sizeof (noteseq) / sizeof (noteseq[0]) &&
                 noteseq[iIndex].iNote[i] != -1)
```

```
            {
                  MidiOutMessage (hMidiOut, 0x90,  0,
                                  noteseq[iIndex].iNote[i], 127) ;

                  MidiOutMessage (hMidiOut, 0x90, 12,
                                  noteseq[iIndex].iNote[i], 127) ;
            }
       }

       if (iIndex != sizeof (noteseq) / sizeof (noteseq[0]))
       {
            SetTimer (hwnd, ID_TIMER, noteseq[iIndex++].iDur - 1, NULL) ;
       }
       else
       {
            KillTimer (hwnd, ID_TIMER) ;
            DestroyWindow (hwnd) ;
       }
       return 0 ;

  case WM_DESTROY:
       midiOutReset (hMidiOut) ;
       midiOutClose (hMidiOut) ;
       PostQuitMessage (0) ;
       return 0 ;
  }
  return DefWindowProc (hwnd, message, wParam, lParam) ;
}
```

The first measure of the Bach D Minor Toccata is shown in Figure 22-11.

Figure 22-11. *The first measure of Bach's Toccata and Fugue in D Minor.*

Our job here is to translate this music into a series of numbers—basically key numbers and timing information that indicate when to send Note On messages (equivalent to an organ key being depressed) and Note Off messages (a key release). Because an organ keyboard is not velocity-sensitive, we can play all the notes using the same velocities. Another simplification is to ignore the difference between staccato playing (that is, leaving a slight pause between successive notes for a sharper, crisper effect) and legato playing (a smoother overlapping blend between successive notes). We'll assume that the ending of one note is followed immediately by the beginning of the next note.

If you can read music, you'll note that the opening of the toccata consists of parallel octaves. So I created a data structure in BACHTOCC called *noteseq* to store a series of note durations and two key numbers. Unfortunately, continuing the music into the second measure would require a more generalized approach to storing this information. I decided that a quarter note should have a duration of 1760 milliseconds, which means that an eighth note (which has one stem on the note or rest) has a duration of 880 milliseconds, a 16th note (two stems) of 440, a 32nd note (three stems) of 220, and a 64th note (four stems) of 110.

There are two mordents in this first measure—one over the first note and the other halfway through the measure. These are indicated by squiggly lines with a short vertical line. In baroque music, the mordent sign means that the note should actually be played as three notes—the indicated note, a note a full tone below it, and then the indicated note. The first two notes should be played quickly, and the third held for the remaining duration. For example, the first note is an A with a mordent. This is played as A, G, A. I decided to make the first two notes of the mordent 64th notes; thus, each has a duration of 110 milliseconds.

There are also four fermatas in this first measure. These are indicated by semicircles with dots in the middle. The fermata sign means that the note should be held longer than its notated duration, generally at the player's discretion. For the fermatas, I decided to increase the note durations by 50 percent.

As you can see, translating even a piece of music seemingly as simple and straightforward as the opening of the D Minor Toccata is not always so simple and straightforward!

The *noteseq* structure array contains three numbers for every parallel note and rest in the measure. The duration of the note is followed by two MIDI key numbers for the parallel octaves. For example, the first note is an A with a duration of 110 milliseconds. Because middle C has a MIDI key number of 60, the A above middle C has a key number of 69 and the A an octave higher has a key number of 81. Thus, the first three values in the noteseq array are 110, 69, and 81. I've used note values of −1 to indicate a rest.

During the WM_CREATE message, BACHTOCC sets a Windows timer for 1000 milliseconds—meaning that the music will begin in 1 second—and then calls *midiOutOpen* using the MIDIMAPPER device ID.

BACHTOCC requires only one instrument voice (an organ), so it needs to use only one channel. To simplify the sending of MIDI messages, I've defined a short function in BACHTOCC called *MidiOutMessage*. This function accepts a MIDI output handle, a status byte, a channel number, and two bytes of data. It assembles these numbers into a packed 32-bit message and calls *midiOutShortMsg*.

At the end of WM_CREATE processing, BACHTOCC sends a Program Change message to select the "church organ" voice. In the General MIDI voice assignments, the church organ voice is indicated by a data byte of 19 in the Program Change message. The actual playing of notes occurs during the WM_TIMER message. A loop handles the two-note polyphony. If a previous note is still playing, BACHTOCC sends Note Off messages for that note. Then, if the new note is not a rest, it sends Note On messages to channels 0 and 12. It then resets the Windows timer to the duration of the note indicated in the *noteseq* structure.

After the music concludes, BACHTOCC destroys the window. During the WM_DESTROY message, the program calls *midiOutReset* and *midiOutClose* and then terminates the program.

Although BACHTOCC works and the results sound reasonable (if not exactly like a human being playing an organ), using the Windows timer for playing music in this way simply does not work in the general case. The problem is that the Windows timer is based on the PC's system clock and the resolution is not good enough for music. Moreover, the Windows timer is not asynchronous. There can be slight delays getting WM_TIMER messages if another program is busy doing something. WM_TIMER messages could even be discarded if the program cannot handle them immediately. This would start sounding like a real mess.

So, while BACHTOCC shows how to call the low-level MIDI output functions, the use of the Windows timer is clearly inadequate for accurate music reproduction. This is why Windows also includes a supplementary set of timer functions that you can take advantage of when using the low-level MIDI output functions. These functions begin with the prefix *time*, and you can use them to set a timer with a resolution as low as 1 millisecond. I'll show you how to use these functions in the DRUM program at the end of this chapter.

Playing a MIDI Synthesizer from the PC Keyboard

Since most PC users probably don't have a MIDI keyboard they can attach to their machines, it makes sense to substitute the keyboard everyone *does* have (the one with all the letters and numbers on the keys). Figure 22-12 on the following page shows a program called KBMIDI that lets you use the PC keyboard to play an electronic music synthesizer—either the one on your sound board or an external synthesizer hooked up to the MIDI Out port. KBMIDI gives you complete control over the MIDI output device (that is, the internal or external synthesizer), the MIDI channel, and the instrument voice. Besides being fun to use, I've found the program useful for exploring how Windows implements MIDI support.

KBMIDI.C

```
/*-------------------------------------------
   KBMIDI.C -- Keyboard MIDI Player
               (c) Charles Petzold, 1998
   -------------------------------------------*/

#include <windows.h>

// Defines for Menu IDs
// --------------------

#define IDM_OPEN    0x100
#define IDM_CLOSE   0x101
#define IDM_DEVICE  0x200
#define IDM_CHANNEL 0x300
#define IDM_VOICE   0x400

LRESULT CALLBACK WndProc (HWND, UINT, WPARAM, LPARAM);

TCHAR    szAppName [] = TEXT ("KBMidi") ;
HMIDIOUT hMidiOut ;
int      iDevice = MIDIMAPPER, iChannel = 0, iVoice = 0, iVelocity = 64 ;
int      cxCaps, cyChar, xOffset, yOffset ;

    // Structures and data for showing families and instruments on menu
    // ----------------------------------------------------------------

typedef struct
{
    TCHAR * szInst ;
    int     iVoice ;
}
INSTRUMENT ;

typedef struct
{
    TCHAR      * szFam ;
    INSTRUMENT   inst [8] ;
}
FAMILY ;

FAMILY fam [16] = {

    TEXT ("Piano"),

        TEXT ("Acoustic Grand Piano"),        0,
```

Figure 22-12. *The KBMIDI Program.*

```
        TEXT ("Bright Acoustic Piano"),        1,
        TEXT ("Electric Grand Piano"),         2,
        TEXT ("Honky-tonk Piano"),             3,
        TEXT ("Rhodes Piano"),                 4,
        TEXT ("Chorused Piano"),               5,
        TEXT ("Harpsichord"),                  6,
        TEXT ("Clavinet"),                     7,

    TEXT ("Chromatic Percussion"),

        TEXT ("Celesta"),                      8,
        TEXT ("Glockenspiel"),                 9,
        TEXT ("Music Box"),                   10,
        TEXT ("Vibraphone"),                  11,
        TEXT ("Marimba"),                     12,
        TEXT ("Xylophone"),                   13,
        TEXT ("Tubular Bells"),               14,
        TEXT ("Dulcimer"),                    15,

    TEXT ("Organ"),

        TEXT ("Hammond Organ"),               16,
        TEXT ("Percussive Organ"),            17,
        TEXT ("Rock Organ"),                  18,
        TEXT ("Church Organ"),                19,
        TEXT ("Reed Organ"),                  20,
        TEXT ("Accordian"),                   21,
        TEXT ("Harmonica"),                   22,
        TEXT ("Tango Accordian"),             23,

    TEXT ("Guitar"),

        TEXT ("Acoustic Guitar (nylon)"),     24,
        TEXT ("Acoustic Guitar (steel)"),     25,
        TEXT ("Electric Guitar (jazz)"),      26,
        TEXT ("Electric Guitar (clean)"),     27,
        TEXT ("Electric Guitar (muted)"),     28,
        TEXT ("Overdriven Guitar"),           29,
        TEXT ("Distortion Guitar"),           30,
        TEXT ("Guitar Harmonics"),            31,

    TEXT ("Bass"),

        TEXT ("Acoustic Bass"),               32,
        TEXT ("Electric Bass (finger)"),      33,
        TEXT ("Electric Bass (pick)"),        34,
        TEXT ("Fretless Bass"),               35,
```

(continued)

Figure 22-12. *continued*

```
        TEXT ("Slap Bass 1"),                36,
        TEXT ("Slap Bass 2"),                37,
        TEXT ("Synth Bass 1"),               38,
        TEXT ("Synth Bass 2"),               39,

    TEXT ("Strings"),

        TEXT ("Violin"),                     40,
        TEXT ("Viola"),                      41,
        TEXT ("Cello"),                      42,
        TEXT ("Contrabass"),                 43,
        TEXT ("Tremolo Strings"),            44,
        TEXT ("Pizzicato Strings"),          45,
        TEXT ("Orchestral Harp"),            46,
        TEXT ("Timpani"),                    47,

    TEXT ("Ensemble"),

        TEXT ("String Ensemble 1"),          48,
        TEXT ("String Ensemble 2"),          49,
        TEXT ("Synth Strings 1"),            50,
        TEXT ("Synth Strings 2"),            51,
        TEXT ("Choir Aahs"),                 52,
        TEXT ("Voice Oohs"),                 53,
        TEXT ("Synth Voice"),                54,
        TEXT ("Orchestra Hit"),              55,

    TEXT ("Brass"),

        TEXT ("Trumpet"),                    56,
        TEXT ("Trombone"),                   57,
        TEXT ("Tuba"),                       58,
        TEXT ("Muted Trumpet"),              59,
        TEXT ("French Horn"),                60,
        TEXT ("Brass Section"),              61,
        TEXT ("Synth Brass 1"),              62,
        TEXT ("Synth Brass 2"),              63,

    TEXT ("Reed"),

        TEXT ("Soprano Sax"),                64,
        TEXT ("Alto Sax"),                   65,
        TEXT ("Tenor Sax"),                  66,
        TEXT ("Baritone Sax"),               67,
        TEXT ("Oboe"),                       68,
        TEXT ("English Horn"),               69,
        TEXT ("Bassoon"),                    70,
```

```
        TEXT ("Clarinet"),                 71,

TEXT ("Pipe"),

        TEXT ("Piccolo"),                  72,
        TEXT ("Flute "),                   73,
        TEXT ("Recorder"),                 74,
        TEXT ("Pan Flute"),                75,
        TEXT ("Bottle Blow"),              76,
        TEXT ("Shakuhachi"),               77,
        TEXT ("Whistle"),                  78,
        TEXT ("Ocarina"),                  79,

TEXT ("Synth Lead"),

        TEXT ("Lead 1 (square)"),          80,
        TEXT ("Lead 2 (sawtooth)"),        81,
        TEXT ("Lead 3 (caliope lead)"),    82,
        TEXT ("Lead 4 (chiff lead)"),      83,
        TEXT ("Lead 5 (charang)"),         84,
        TEXT ("Lead 6 (voice)"),           85,
        TEXT ("Lead 7 (fifths)"),          86,
        TEXT ("Lead 8 (brass + lead)"),    87,

TEXT ("Synth Pad"),

        TEXT ("Pad 1 (new age)"),          88,
        TEXT ("Pad 2 (warm)"),             89,
        TEXT ("Pad 3 (polysynth)"),        90,
        TEXT ("Pad 4 (choir)"),            91,
        TEXT ("Pad 5 (bowed)"),            92,
        TEXT ("Pad 6 (metallic)"),         93,
        TEXT ("Pad 7 (halo)"),             94,
        TEXT ("Pad 8 (sweep)"),            95,

TEXT ("Synth Effects"),

        TEXT ("FX 1 (rain)"),              96,
        TEXT ("FX 2 (soundtrack)"),        97,
        TEXT ("FX 3 (crystal)"),           98,
        TEXT ("FX 4 (atmosphere)"),        99,
        TEXT ("FX 5 (brightness)"),        100,
        TEXT ("FX 6 (goblins)"),           101,
        TEXT ("FX 7 (echoes)"),            102,
        TEXT ("FX 8 (sci-fi)"),            103,
```

(continued)

Figure 22-12. *continued*

```
        TEXT ("Ethnic"),

                TEXT ("Sitar"),                         104,
                TEXT ("Banjo"),                         105,
                TEXT ("Shamisen"),                      106,
                TEXT ("Koto"),                          107,
                TEXT ("Kalimba"),                       108,
                TEXT ("Bagpipe"),                       109,
                TEXT ("Fiddle"),                        110,
                TEXT ("Shanai"),                        111,

        TEXT ("Percussive"),

                TEXT ("Tinkle Bell"),                   112,
                TEXT ("Agogo"),                         113,
                TEXT ("Steel Drums"),                   114,
                TEXT ("Woodblock"),                     115,
                TEXT ("Taiko Drum"),                    116,
                TEXT ("Melodic Tom"),                   117,
                TEXT ("Synth Drum"),                    118,
                TEXT ("Reverse Cymbal"),                119,

        TEXT ("Sound Effects"),

                TEXT ("Guitar Fret Noise"),             120,
                TEXT ("Breath Noise"),                  121,
                TEXT ("Seashore"),                      122,
                TEXT ("Bird Tweet"),                    123,
                TEXT ("Telephone Ring"),                124,
                TEXT ("Helicopter"),                    125,
                TEXT ("Applause"),                      126,
                TEXT ("Gunshot"),                       127 } ;

        // Data for translating scan codes to octaves and notes
        // ------------------------------------------------------

#define NUMSCANS        (sizeof key / sizeof key[0])

struct
{
    int     iOctave ;
    int     iNote ;
    int     yPos ;
    int     xPos ;
    TCHAR * szKey ;
}
key [] =
```

```
{
                                  // Scan  Char  Oct  Note
                                  // ----  ----  ---  ----
    -1, -1, -1, -1, NULL,         //  0    None
    -1, -1, -1, -1, NULL,         //  1    Esc
    -1, -1,  0,  0, TEXT (""),    //  2    1
     5,  1,  0,  2, TEXT ("C#"),  //  3    2     5    C#
     5,  3,  0,  4, TEXT ("D#"),  //  4    3     5    D#
    -1, -1,  0,  6, TEXT (""),    //  5    4
     5,  6,  0,  8, TEXT ("F#"),  //  6    5     5    F#
     5,  8,  0, 10, TEXT ("G#"),  //  7    6     5    G#
     5, 10,  0, 12, TEXT ("A#"),  //  8    7     5    A#
    -1, -1,  0, 14, TEXT (""),    //  9    8
     6,  1,  0, 16, TEXT ("C#"),  // 10    9     6    C#
     6,  3,  0, 18, TEXT ("D#"),  // 11    0     6    D#
    -1, -1,  0, 20, TEXT (""),    // 12    -
     6,  6,  0, 22, TEXT ("F#"),  // 13    =     6    F#
    -1, -1, -1, -1, NULL,         // 14    Back

    -1, -1, -1, -1, NULL,         // 15    Tab
     5,  0,  1,  1, TEXT ("C"),   // 16    q     5    C
     5,  2,  1,  3, TEXT ("D"),   // 17    w     5    D
     5,  4,  1,  5, TEXT ("E"),   // 18    e     5    E
     5,  5,  1,  7, TEXT ("F"),   // 19    r     5    F
     5,  7,  1,  9, TEXT ("G"),   // 20    t     5    G
     5,  9,  1, 11, TEXT ("A"),   // 21    y     5    A
     5, 11,  1, 13, TEXT ("B"),   // 22    u     5    B
     6,  0,  1, 15, TEXT ("C"),   // 23    i     6    C
     6,  2,  1, 17, TEXT ("D"),   // 24    o     6    D
     6,  4,  1, 19, TEXT ("E"),   // 25    p     6    E
     6,  5,  1, 21, TEXT ("F"),   // 26    [     6    F
     6,  7,  1, 23, TEXT ("G"),   // 27    ]     6    G
    -1, -1, -1, -1, NULL,         // 28    Ent

    -1, -1, -1, -1, NULL,         // 29    Ctrl
     3,  8,  2,  2, TEXT ("G#"),  // 30    a     3    G#
     3, 10,  2,  4, TEXT ("A#"),  // 31    s     3    A#
    -1, -1,  2,  6, TEXT (""),    // 32    d
     4,  1,  2,  8, TEXT ("C#"),  // 33    f     4    C#
     4,  3,  2, 10, TEXT ("D#"),  // 34    g     4    D#
    -1, -1,  2, 12, TEXT (""),    // 35    h
     4,  6,  2, 14, TEXT ("F#"),  // 36    j     4    F#
     4,  8,  2, 16, TEXT ("G#"),  // 37    k     4    G#
     4, 10,  2, 18, TEXT ("A#"),  // 38    l     4    A#
    -1, -1,  2, 20, TEXT (""),    // 39    ;
     5,  1,  2, 22, TEXT ("C#"),  // 40    '     5    C#
    -1, -1, -1, -1, NULL,         // 41    `
```

(continued)

Figure 22-12. *continued*

```
        -1, -1, -1, -1, NULL,            // 42     Shift
        -1, -1, -1, -1, NULL,            // 43     \  (not line continuation)
         3,  9,  3,  3, TEXT ("A"),      // 44     z    3    A
         3, 11,  3,  5, TEXT ("B"),      // 45     x    3    B
         4,  0,  3,  7, TEXT ("C"),      // 46     c    4    C
         4,  2,  3,  9, TEXT ("D"),      // 47     v    4    D
         4,  4,  3, 11, TEXT ("E"),      // 48     b    4    E
         4,  5,  3, 13, TEXT ("F"),      // 49     n    4    F
         4,  7,  3, 15, TEXT ("G"),      // 50     m    4    G
         4,  9,  3, 17, TEXT ("A"),      // 51     ,    4    A
         4, 11,  3, 19, TEXT ("B"),      // 52     .    4    B
         5,  0,  3, 21, TEXT ("C")       // 53     /    5    C
} ;

int WINAPI WinMain (HINSTANCE hInstance, HINSTANCE hPrevInstance,
                    PSTR szCmdLine, int iCmdShow)
{
    MSG      msg;
    HWND     hwnd ;
    WNDCLASS wndclass ;

    wndclass.style         = CS_HREDRAW | CS_VREDRAW ;
    wndclass.lpfnWndProc   = WndProc ;
    wndclass.cbClsExtra    = 0 ;
    wndclass.cbWndExtra    = 0 ;
    wndclass.hInstance     = hInstance ;
    wndclass.hIcon         = LoadIcon (NULL, IDI_APPLICATION) ;
    wndclass.hCursor       = LoadCursor (NULL, IDC_ARROW) ;
    wndclass.hbrBackground = GetStockObject (WHITE_BRUSH) ;
    wndclass.lpszMenuName  = NULL ;
    wndclass.lpszClassName = szAppName ;

    if (!RegisterClass (&wndclass))
    {
        MessageBox (NULL, TEXT ("This program requires Windows NT!"),
                    szAppName, MB_ICONERROR) ;
        return 0 ;
    }

    hwnd = CreateWindow (szAppName, TEXT ("Keyboard MIDI Player"),
                        WS_OVERLAPPEDWINDOW | WS_HSCROLL | WS_VSCROLL,
                        CW_USEDEFAULT, CW_USEDEFAULT,
                        CW_USEDEFAULT, CW_USEDEFAULT,
                        NULL, NULL, hInstance, NULL) ;

    if (!hwnd)
        return 0 ;
```

```
    ShowWindow (hwnd, iCmdShow) ;
    UpdateWindow (hwnd);

    while (GetMessage (&msg, NULL, 0, 0))
    {
        TranslateMessage (&msg) ;
        DispatchMessage (&msg) ;
    }
    return msg.wParam ;
}

// Create the program's menu (called from WndProc, WM_CREATE)
// -----------------------------------------------------------

HMENU CreateTheMenu (int iNumDevs)
{
    TCHAR       szBuffer [32] ;
    HMENU       hMenu, hMenuPopup, hMenuSubPopup ;
    int         i, iFam, iIns ;
    MIDIOUTCAPS moc ;

    hMenu = CreateMenu () ;

        // Create "On/Off" popup menu

    hMenuPopup = CreateMenu () ;

    AppendMenu (hMenuPopup, MF_STRING, IDM_OPEN, TEXT ("&Open")) ;
    AppendMenu (hMenuPopup, MF_STRING | MF_CHECKED, IDM_CLOSE,
                        TEXT ("&Closed")) ;

    AppendMenu (hMenu, MF_STRING | MF_POPUP, (UINT) hMenuPopup,
                    TEXT ("&Status")) ;

        // Create "Device" popup menu

    hMenuPopup = CreateMenu () ;

        // Put MIDI Mapper on menu if it's installed

    if (!midiOutGetDevCaps (MIDIMAPPER, &moc, sizeof (moc)))
        AppendMenu (hMenuPopup, MF_STRING, IDM_DEVICE + (int) MIDIMAPPER,
                    moc.szPname) ;
    else
        iDevice = 0 ;

        // Add the rest of the MIDI devices
```

(continued)

Figure 22-12. *continued*

```
    for (i = 0 ; i < iNumDevs ; i++)
    {
        midiOutGetDevCaps (i, &moc, sizeof (moc)) ;
        AppendMenu (hMenuPopup, MF_STRING, IDM_DEVICE + i, moc.szPname) ;
    }

    CheckMenuItem (hMenuPopup, 0, MF_BYPOSITION | MF_CHECKED) ;
    AppendMenu (hMenu, MF_STRING | MF_POPUP, (UINT) hMenuPopup,
                    TEXT ("&Device")) ;

        // Create "Channel" popup menu

    hMenuPopup = CreateMenu () ;

    for (i = 0 ; i < 16 ; i++)
    {
        wsprintf (szBuffer, TEXT ("%d"), i + 1) ;
        AppendMenu (hMenuPopup, MF_STRING | (i ? MF_UNCHECKED : MF_CHECKED),
                            IDM_CHANNEL + i, szBuffer) ;
    }

    AppendMenu (hMenu, MF_STRING | MF_POPUP, (UINT) hMenuPopup,
                    TEXT ("&Channel")) ;

        // Create "Voice" popup menu

    hMenuPopup = CreateMenu () ;

    for (iFam = 0 ; iFam < 16 ; iFam++)
    {
        hMenuSubPopup = CreateMenu () ;

        for (iIns = 0 ; iIns < 8 ; iIns++)
        {
            wsprintf (szBuffer, TEXT ("&%d.\t%s"), iIns + 1,
                                fam[iFam].inst[iIns].szInst) ;
            AppendMenu (hMenuSubPopup,
                        MF_STRING | (fam[iFam].inst[iIns].iVoice ?
                                        MF_UNCHECKED : MF_CHECKED),
                        fam[iFam].inst[iIns].iVoice + IDM_VOICE,
                        szBuffer) ;
        }

        wsprintf (szBuffer, TEXT ("&%c.\t%s"), 'A' + iFam,
                            fam[iFam].szFam) ;
        AppendMenu (hMenuPopup, MF_STRING | MF_POPUP, (UINT) hMenuSubPopup,
```

```
                                szBuffer) ;
        }
    AppendMenu (hMenu, MF_STRING | MF_POPUP, (UINT) hMenuPopup,
                        TEXT ("&Voice")) ;
    return hMenu ;
}


// Routines for simplifying MIDI output
// -----------------------------------

DWORD MidiOutMessage (HMIDIOUT hMidi, int iStatus, int iChannel,
                      int iData1,  int iData2)
{
    DWORD dwMessage ;

    dwMessage = iStatus | iChannel | (iData1 << 8) | (iData2 << 16) ;

    return midiOutShortMsg (hMidi, dwMessage) ;
}

DWORD MidiNoteOff (HMIDIOUT hMidi, int iChannel, int iOct, int iNote, int iVel)
{
    return MidiOutMessage (hMidi, 0x080, iChannel, 12 * iOct + iNote, iVel) ;
}

DWORD MidiNoteOn (HMIDIOUT hMidi, int iChannel, int iOct, int iNote, int iVel)
{
    return MidiOutMessage (hMidi, 0x090, iChannel, 12 * iOct + iNote, iVel) ;
}

DWORD MidiSetPatch (HMIDIOUT hMidi, int iChannel, int iVoice)
{
    return MidiOutMessage (hMidi, 0x0C0, iChannel, iVoice, 0) ;
}

DWORD MidiPitchBend (HMIDIOUT hMidi, int iChannel, int iBend)
{
    return MidiOutMessage (hMidi, 0x0E0, iChannel, iBend & 0x7F, iBend >> 7) ;
}

// Draw a single key on window
// ---------------------------

VOID DrawKey (HDC hdc, int iScanCode, BOOL fInvert)
{
    RECT rc ;
```

(continued)

Figure 22-12. *continued*

```
        rc.left   = 3 * cxCaps * key[iScanCode].xPos / 2 + xOffset ;
        rc.top    = 3 * cyChar * key[iScanCode].yPos / 2 + yOffset ;
        rc.right  = rc.left + 3 * cxCaps ;
        rc.bottom = rc.top  + 3 * cyChar / 2 ;

        SetTextColor (hdc, fInvert ? 0x00FFFFFFul : 0x00000000ul) ;
        SetBkColor   (hdc, fInvert ? 0x00000000ul : 0x00FFFFFFul) ;

        FillRect (hdc, &rc, GetStockObject (fInvert ? BLACK_BRUSH : WHITE_BRUSH)) ;

        DrawText (hdc, key[iScanCode].szKey, -1, &rc,
                       DT_SINGLELINE | DT_CENTER | DT_VCENTER) ;

        FrameRect (hdc, &rc, GetStockObject (BLACK_BRUSH)) ;
}

// Process a Key Up or Key Down message
// -----------------------------------

VOID ProcessKey (HDC hdc, UINT message, LPARAM lParam)
{
        int iScanCode, iOctave, iNote ;

        iScanCode = 0x0FF & HIWORD (lParam) ;

        if (iScanCode >= NUMSCANS)                        // No scan codes over 53
            return ;

        if ((iOctave = key[iScanCode].iOctave) == -1)     // Non-music key
            return ;

        if (GetKeyState (VK_SHIFT) < 0)
            iOctave += 0x20000000 & lParam ? 2 : 1 ;

        if (GetKeyState (VK_CONTROL) < 0)
            iOctave -= 0x20000000 & lParam ? 2 : 1 ;

        iNote = key[iScanCode].iNote ;

        if (message == WM_KEYUP)                          // For key up
        {
            MidiNoteOff (hMidiOut, iChannel, iOctave, iNote, 0) ;   // Note off
            DrawKey (hdc, iScanCode, FALSE) ;
            return ;
        }

        if (0x40000000 & lParam)                          // ignore typematics
```

```
            return ;

     MidiNoteOn (hMidiOut, iChannel, iOctave, iNote, iVelocity) ; // Note on
     DrawKey (hdc, iScanCode, TRUE) ;                   // Draw the inverted key
}


// Window Procedure
// ----------------

LRESULT CALLBACK WndProc (HWND hwnd, UINT message, WPARAM wParam, LPARAM lParam)
{
     static BOOL bOpened = FALSE ;
     HDC         hdc ;
     HMENU       hMenu ;
     int         i, iNumDevs, iPitchBend, cxClient, cyClient ;
     MIDIOUTCAPS moc ;
     PAINTSTRUCT ps ;
     SIZE        size ;
     TCHAR       szBuffer [16] ;

     switch (message)
     {
     case WM_CREATE:
             // Get size of capital letters in system font

          hdc = GetDC (hwnd) ;

          GetTextExtentPoint (hdc, TEXT ("M"), 1, &size) ;
          cxCaps = size.cx ;
          cyChar = size.cy ;

          ReleaseDC (hwnd, hdc) ;

             // Initialize "Volume" scroll bar

          SetScrollRange (hwnd, SB_HORZ, 1, 127, FALSE) ;
          SetScrollPos   (hwnd, SB_HORZ, iVelocity, TRUE) ;

             // Initialize "Pitch Bend" scroll bar

          SetScrollRange (hwnd, SB_VERT, 0, 16383, FALSE) ;
          SetScrollPos   (hwnd, SB_VERT, 8192, TRUE) ;

             // Get number of MIDI output devices and set up menu

          if (0 == (iNumDevs = midiOutGetNumDevs ()))
          {
```

(continued)

Figure 22-12. *continued*

```
            MessageBeep (MB_ICONSTOP) ;
            MessageBox (hwnd, TEXT ("No MIDI output devices!"),
                            szAppName, MB_OK | MB_ICONSTOP) ;
            return -1 ;
        }
        SetMenu (hwnd, CreateTheMenu (iNumDevs)) ;
        return 0 ;

    case WM_SIZE:
        cxClient = LOWORD (lParam) ;
        cyClient = HIWORD (lParam) ;

        xOffset = (cxClient - 25 * 3 * cxCaps / 2) / 2 ;
        yOffset = (cyClient - 11 * cyChar) / 2 + 5 * cyChar ;
        return 0 ;

    case WM_COMMAND:
        hMenu = GetMenu (hwnd) ;

            // "Open" menu command

        if (LOWORD (wParam) == IDM_OPEN && !bOpened)
        {
            if (midiOutOpen (&hMidiOut, iDevice, 0, 0, 0))
            {
                MessageBeep (MB_ICONEXCLAMATION) ;
                MessageBox (hwnd, TEXT ("Cannot open MIDI device"),
                            szAppName, MB_OK | MB_ICONEXCLAMATION) ;
            }
            else
            {
                CheckMenuItem (hMenu, IDM_OPEN,  MF_CHECKED) ;
                CheckMenuItem (hMenu, IDM_CLOSE, MF_UNCHECKED) ;

                MidiSetPatch (hMidiOut, iChannel, iVoice) ;
                bOpened = TRUE ;
            }
        }

            // "Close" menu command

        else if (LOWORD (wParam) == IDM_CLOSE && bOpened)
        {
            CheckMenuItem (hMenu, IDM_OPEN,  MF_UNCHECKED) ;
            CheckMenuItem (hMenu, IDM_CLOSE, MF_CHECKED) ;

                // Turn all keys off and close device
```

```
        for (i = 0 ; i < 16 ; i++)
            MidiOutMessage (hMidiOut, 0xB0, i, 123, 0) ;

        midiOutClose (hMidiOut) ;
        bOpened = FALSE ;
}


        // Change MIDI "Device" menu command

else if (LOWORD (wParam) >= IDM_DEVICE - 1 &&
        LOWORD (wParam) <  IDM_CHANNEL)
{
    CheckMenuItem (hMenu, IDM_DEVICE + iDevice, MF_UNCHECKED) ;
    iDevice = LOWORD (wParam) - IDM_DEVICE ;
    CheckMenuItem (hMenu, IDM_DEVICE + iDevice, MF_CHECKED) ;

            // Close and reopen MIDI device

    if (bOpened)
    {
        SendMessage (hwnd, WM_COMMAND, IDM_CLOSE, 0L) ;
        SendMessage (hwnd, WM_COMMAND, IDM_OPEN,  0L) ;
    }
}


        // Change MIDI "Channel" menu command

else if (LOWORD (wParam) >= IDM_CHANNEL &&
        LOWORD (wParam) <  IDM_VOICE)
{
    CheckMenuItem (hMenu, IDM_CHANNEL + iChannel, MF_UNCHECKED);
    iChannel = LOWORD (wParam) - IDM_CHANNEL ;
    CheckMenuItem (hMenu, IDM_CHANNEL + iChannel, MF_CHECKED) ;

    if (bOpened)
        MidiSetPatch (hMidiOut, iChannel, iVoice) ;
}


        // Change MIDI "Voice" menu command

else if (LOWORD (wParam) >= IDM_VOICE)
{
    CheckMenuItem (hMenu, IDM_VOICE + iVoice, MF_UNCHECKED) ;
    iVoice = LOWORD (wParam) - IDM_VOICE ;
    CheckMenuItem (hMenu, IDM_VOICE + iVoice, MF_CHECKED) ;

    if (bOpened)
```

(continued)

Figure 22-12. *continued*

```
                MidiSetPatch (hMidiOut, iChannel, iVoice) ;
     }

     InvalidateRect (hwnd, NULL, TRUE) ;
     return 0 ;

     // Process a Key Up or Key Down message

case WM_KEYUP:
case WM_KEYDOWN:
     hdc = GetDC (hwnd) ;

     if (bOpened)
          ProcessKey (hdc, message, lParam) ;

     ReleaseDC (hwnd, hdc) ;
     return 0 ;

     // For Escape, turn off all notes and repaint

case WM_CHAR:
     if (bOpened && wParam == 27)
     {
          for (i = 0 ; i < 16 ; i++)
               MidiOutMessage (hMidiOut, 0xB0, i, 123, 0) ;

          InvalidateRect (hwnd, NULL, TRUE) ;
     }
     return 0 ;

     // Horizontal scroll: Velocity

case WM_HSCROLL:
     switch (LOWORD (wParam))
     {
     case SB_LINEUP:        iVelocity -= 1 ;  break ;
     case SB_LINEDOWN:      iVelocity += 1 ;  break ;
     case SB_PAGEUP:        iVelocity -= 8 ;  break ;
     case SB_PAGEDOWN:      iVelocity += 8 ;  break ;
     case SB_THUMBPOSITION: iVelocity = HIWORD (wParam) ;  break ;
     default:               return 0 ;
     }
     iVelocity = max (1, min (iVelocity, 127)) ;
     SetScrollPos (hwnd, SB_HORZ, iVelocity, TRUE) ;
     return 0 ;

     // Vertical scroll:  Pitch Bend
```

```
    case WM_VSCROLL:
        switch (LOWORD (wParam))
        {
        case SB_THUMBTRACK:    iPitchBend = 16383 - HIWORD (wParam) ;  break ;
        case SB_THUMBPOSITION: iPitchBend = 8191 ;                     break ;
        default:               return 0 ;
        }
        iPitchBend = max (0, min (iPitchBend, 16383)) ;
        SetScrollPos (hwnd, SB_VERT, 16383 - iPitchBend, TRUE) ;

        if (bOpened)
            MidiPitchBend (hMidiOut, iChannel, iPitchBend) ;
        return 0 ;

    case WM_PAINT:
        hdc = BeginPaint (hwnd, &ps) ;

        for (i = 0 ; i < NUMSCANS ; i++)
            if (key[i].xPos != -1)
                DrawKey (hdc, i, FALSE) ;

        midiOutGetDevCaps (iDevice, &moc, sizeof (MIDIOUTCAPS)) ;
        wsprintf (szBuffer, TEXT ("Channel %i"), iChannel + 1) ;

        TextOut (hdc, cxCaps, 1 * cyChar,
                    bOpened ? TEXT ("Open") : TEXT ("Closed"),
                    bOpened ? 4 : 6) ;
        TextOut (hdc, cxCaps, 2 * cyChar, moc.szPname,
                    lstrlen (moc.szPname)) ;
        TextOut (hdc, cxCaps, 3 * cyChar, szBuffer, lstrlen (szBuffer)) ;
        TextOut (hdc, cxCaps, 4 * cyChar,
                    fam[iVoice / 8].inst[iVoice % 8].szInst,
                lstrlen (fam[iVoice / 8].inst[iVoice % 8].szInst)) ;

        EndPaint (hwnd, &ps) ;
        return 0 ;

    case WM_DESTROY :
        SendMessage (hwnd, WM_COMMAND, IDM_CLOSE, 0L) ;
        PostQuitMessage (0) ;
        return 0 ;
    }
    return DefWindowProc (hwnd, message, wParam, lParam) ;
}
```

When you run KBMIDI, the window shows how the keys of the keyboard correspond to the keys of a traditional piano or organ. The Z key at the lower left corner plays an A at 110 Hz. Moving across the bottom row of the keyboard, you reach middle C at the right, with the sharps and flats on the second-to-bottom row. The top two rows continue the scale, from middle C to G#. Thus, the range is 3 octaves. Pressing the Ctrl key drops the entire range by 1 octave, and pressing the Shift key raises it by 1 octave, giving an effective range of 5 octaves.

If you start trying to play immediately, however, you won't hear anything. You first must select Open from the Status menu. This will open a MIDI output device. If the port is successfully opened, pressing a key will send a MIDI Note On message to the synthesizer. Releasing the key generates a Note Off message. Depending on the rollover characteristics of your keyboard, you might be able to play several notes at once.

Select Close from the Status menu to close the MIDI device. This is handy if you want to run some other MIDI software under Windows without terminating the KBMIDI program.

The Device menu lists the installed MIDI output devices. These are obtained from the *midiOutGetDevCaps* function. One of these will probably be a MIDI Out port to an external synthesizer that might or might not be present. The list also includes the MIDI Mapper device. This is the MIDI synthesizer selected in the Multimedia applet of the Control Panel.

The Channel menu lets you select a MIDI channel from 1 through 16. By default, channel 1 is selected. All MIDI messages that the KBMIDI program generates are sent on the selected channel.

The final menu on KBMIDI is labeled Voice. This is a double-nested menu from which you can select one of the 128 instrument voices defined by the General MIDI specification and implemented in Windows. The 128 instrument voices are divided into 16 instrument families with 8 instruments each. These 128 instrument voices are called the melodic voices because different MIDI key numbers correspond to different pitches.

General MIDI also defines a wide range of nonmelodic percussion instruments. To play the percussion instruments, use the Channel menu to select channel 10. Also select the first instrument voice (Acoustic Grand Piano) from the Voice menu. After you do this, each key plays a different percussion sound. There are 47 different percussion sounds, from MIDI key number 35 (the B two octaves below middle C) to 81 (the A nearly two octaves above middle C). We'll take advantage of the percussion channel in the DRUM program coming up.

The KBMIDI program has horizontal and vertical scroll bars. Because a PC keyboard is not velocity-sensitive, the horizontal scroll bar controls the note velocity. Generally, this corresponds to the volume of the notes that you play. After setting the horizontal scroll bar, all Note On messages will use that velocity.

The vertical scroll bar generates a MIDI message known as "Pitch Bend." To use this feature, press down one or more keys and manipulate the vertical scroll bar thumb with the mouse. As you raise the scroll bar thumb, the frequency of the note increases, and as you lower it, the frequency decreases. Releasing the scroll bar returns the pitch to normal.

These two scroll bars can be tricky to use: As you manipulate a scroll bar, keyboard messages do not come through the program's message loop. Therefore, if you press a key and begin manipulating one of the scroll bars with the mouse and then release the key before finishing with the scroll bar, the note will continue to sound. Thus, you shouldn't press or release any keys during the time you're manipulating the scroll bars. A similar rule applies to the menu—do not try to select anything from the menu while a key is depressed. Also, do not change the octave shift using the Ctrl or Shift keys between the time you press a key and release it.

If one or more notes get "stuck" and continue to sound after being released, press the Esc key. This stops the sounds by sending 16 "All Notes Off" messages to the 16 channels of the MIDI synthesizer.

KBMIDI does not have a resource script and instead creates its own menu from scratch. The device names are obtained from the *midiOutGetDevCaps* function, and the instrument voice families and names are stored in the program in a large data structure.

KBMIDI has a few short functions for simplifying the MIDI messages. I've discussed these messages previously, except for the Pitch Bend message. This message uses two 7-bit values that comprise a 14-bit pitch-bend level. Values between 0 and 0x1FFF lower the pitch, and values between 0x2001 and 0x3FFF raise the pitch.

When you select Open from the Status menu, KBMIDI calls *midiOutOpen* for the selected device and, if successful, calls its *MidiSetPatch* function. When changing a device, KBMIDI must close the previous device, if necessary, and then reopen the new device. KBMIDI must also call *MidiSetPatch* when you change the MIDI device, the MIDI channel, or the instrument voice.

KBMIDI processes WM_KEYUP and WM_KEYDOWN messages to turn notes on and off. A data structure within KBMIDI maps keyboard scan codes to octaves and notes. For example, the Z key on an American English keyboard has a scan code of 44, and the structure identifies this as octave 3 and note 9—an A. In the *MidiNoteOn* function in KBMIDI, these are combined to form a MIDI key number of 45 (12 times 3, plus 9). This same data structure is used for drawing the keys on the window: each key has a particular horizontal and vertical position and a text string shown inside the rectangle.

Horizontal scroll bar processing is straightforward: all that need be done is store the new velocity level and set the new scroll bar position. Vertical scroll bar processing to control pitch bend is a little unusual, however. The only scroll bar commands it processes are SB_THUMBTRACK, which occurs when you manipulate the scroll bar thumb with the mouse, and SB_THUMBPOSITION, activated when you release the thumb. On an SB_THUMBPOSITION command, KBMIDI sets the scroll bar position to its middle level and calls *MidiPitchBend* with a value of 8192.

A MIDI Drum Machine

Some percussion instruments, such as a xylophone or timpani, are termed "melodic" or "chromatic" because they can play tones in different pitches. A xylophone has wooden blocks corresponding to different pitches, and timpani can be tuned. These two instruments, as well as several other melodic percussion instruments, can be selected from the Voice menu in KBMIDI.

However, many other percussion instruments are nonmelodic. They cannot be tuned and usually contain too much noise to be associated with a particular pitch. In the General MIDI specification, these nonmelodic percussion voices are available through channel 10. Different key numbers correspond to 47 different percussion instruments.

The DRUM program shown in Figure 22-13 is a computer drum machine. This program lets you construct a sequence of up to 32 notes using 47 different percussion sounds. The program plays the sequence repetitively at a selectable tempo and volume.

DRUM.C

```
/*-------------------------------------------
   DRUM.C -- MIDI Drum Machine
             (c) Charles Petzold, 1998
   -------------------------------------------*/

#include <windows.h>
#include <stdlib.h>
#include <string.h>
#include <math.h>
#include "drumtime.h"
#include "drumfile.h"
#include "resource.h"

LRESULT CALLBACK WndProc    (HWND, UINT, WPARAM, LPARAM) ;
BOOL     CALLBACK AboutProc (HWND, UINT, WPARAM, LPARAM) ;

void   DrawRectangle (HDC, int, int, DWORD *, DWORD *) ;
void   ErrorMessage  (HWND, TCHAR *, TCHAR *) ;
void   DoCaption     (HWND, TCHAR *) ;
int    AskAboutSave  (HWND, TCHAR *) ;

TCHAR * szPerc [NUM_PERC] =
{
     TEXT ("Acoustic Bass Drum"), TEXT ("Bass Drum 1"),
     TEXT ("Side Stick"),         TEXT ("Acoustic Snare"),
     TEXT ("Hand Clap"),          TEXT ("Electric Snare"),
     TEXT ("Low Floor Tom"),      TEXT ("Closed High Hat"),
     TEXT ("High Floor Tom"),     TEXT ("Pedal High Hat"),
     TEXT ("Low Tom"),            TEXT ("Open High Hat"),
     TEXT ("Low-Mid Tom"),        TEXT ("High-Mid Tom"),
     TEXT ("Crash Cymbal 1"),     TEXT ("High Tom"),
     TEXT ("Ride Cymbal 1"),      TEXT ("Chinese Cymbal"),
     TEXT ("Ride Bell"),          TEXT ("Tambourine"),
```

Figure 22-13. *The DRUM Program.*

```
        TEXT ("Splash Cymbal"),      TEXT ("Cowbell"),
        TEXT ("Crash Cymbal 2"),     TEXT ("Vibraslap"),
        TEXT ("Ride Cymbal 2"),      TEXT ("High Bongo"),
        TEXT ("Low Bongo"),          TEXT ("Mute High Conga"),
        TEXT ("Open High Conga"),    TEXT ("Low Conga"),
        TEXT ("High Timbale"),       TEXT ("Low Timbale"),
        TEXT ("High Agogo"),         TEXT ("Low Agogo"),
        TEXT ("Cabasa"),             TEXT ("Maracas"),
        TEXT ("Short Whistle"),      TEXT ("Long Whistle"),
        TEXT ("Short Guiro"),        TEXT ("Long Guiro"),
        TEXT ("Claves"),             TEXT ("High Wood Block"),
        TEXT ("Low Wood Block"),     TEXT ("Mute Cuica"),
        TEXT ("Open Cuica"),         TEXT ("Mute Triangle"),
        TEXT ("Open Triangle")
} ;

TCHAR    szAppName  [] = TEXT ("Drum") ;
TCHAR    szUntitled [] = TEXT ("(Untitled)") ;
TCHAR    szBuffer [80 + MAX_PATH] ;
HANDLE   hInst ;
int      cxChar, cyChar ;

int WINAPI WinMain (HINSTANCE hInstance, HINSTANCE hPrevInstance,
                    PSTR szCmdLine, int iCmdShow)
{
    HWND        hwnd ;
    MSG         msg ;
    WNDCLASS    wndclass ;

    hInst = hInstance ;

    wndclass.style         = CS_HREDRAW | CS_VREDRAW ;
    wndclass.lpfnWndProc   = WndProc ;
    wndclass.cbClsExtra    = 0 ;
    wndclass.cbWndExtra    = 0 ;
    wndclass.hInstance     = hInstance ;
    wndclass.hIcon         = LoadIcon (hInstance, szAppName) ;
    wndclass.hCursor       = LoadCursor (NULL, IDC_ARROW) ;
    wndclass.hbrBackground = GetStockObject (WHITE_BRUSH) ;
    wndclass.lpszMenuName  = szAppName ;
    wndclass.lpszClassName = szAppName ;

    if (!RegisterClass (&wndclass))
    {
        MessageBox (NULL, TEXT ("This program requires Windows NT!"),
                    szAppName, MB_ICONERROR) ;
        return 0 ;
```

(continued)

Figure 22-13. *continued*

```
        }

        hwnd = CreateWindow (szAppName, NULL,
                        WS_OVERLAPPED | WS_CAPTION | WS_SYSMENU |
                                WS_MINIMIZEBOX | WS_HSCROLL | WS_VSCROLL,
                        CW_USEDEFAULT, CW_USEDEFAULT,
                        CW_USEDEFAULT, CW_USEDEFAULT,
                        NULL, NULL, hInstance, szCmdLine) ;

        ShowWindow (hwnd, iCmdShow) ;
        UpdateWindow (hwnd) ;

        while (GetMessage (&msg, NULL, 0, 0))
        {
                TranslateMessage (&msg) ;
                DispatchMessage (&msg) ;
        }
        return msg.wParam ;
}

LRESULT CALLBACK WndProc (HWND hwnd, UINT message, WPARAM wParam, LPARAM lParam)
{
        static BOOL   bNeedSave ;
        static DRUM   drum ;
        static HMENU hMenu ;
        static int    iTempo = 50, iIndexLast ;
        static TCHAR szFileName  [MAX_PATH], szTitleName [MAX_PATH] ;
        HDC           hdc ;
        int           i, x, y ;
        PAINTSTRUCT  ps ;
        POINT         point ;
        RECT          rect ;
        TCHAR       * szError ;

        switch (message)
        {
        case WM_CREATE:
                        // Initialize DRUM structure

                drum.iMsecPerBeat = 100 ;
                drum.iVelocity    = 64 ;
                drum.iNumBeats    = 32 ;

                DrumSetParams (&drum) ;

                        // Other initialization
```

```
            cxChar = LOWORD (GetDialogBaseUnits ()) ;
            cyChar = HIWORD (GetDialogBaseUnits ()) ;

            GetWindowRect (hwnd, &rect) ;
            MoveWindow (hwnd, rect.left, rect.top,
                            77 * cxChar, 29 * cyChar, FALSE) ;

            hMenu = GetMenu (hwnd) ;

                // Initialize "Volume" scroll bar

            SetScrollRange (hwnd, SB_HORZ, 1, 127, FALSE) ;
            SetScrollPos   (hwnd, SB_HORZ, drum.iVelocity, TRUE) ;

                // Initialize "Tempo" scroll bar

            SetScrollRange (hwnd, SB_VERT, 0, 100, FALSE) ;
            SetScrollPos   (hwnd, SB_VERT, iTempo, TRUE) ;

            DoCaption (hwnd, szTitleName) ;
            return 0 ;

     case WM_COMMAND:
            switch (LOWORD (wParam))
            {
            case IDM_FILE_NEW:
                if (bNeedSave && IDCANCEL == AskAboutSave (hwnd, szTitleName))
                    return 0 ;

                    // Clear drum pattern

                for (i = 0 ; i < NUM_PERC ; i++)
                {
                    drum.dwSeqPerc [i] = 0 ;
                    drum.dwSeqPian [i] = 0 ;
                }

                InvalidateRect (hwnd, NULL, FALSE) ;
                DrumSetParams (&drum) ;
                bNeedSave = FALSE ;
                return 0 ;

            case IDM_FILE_OPEN:
                    // Save previous file

                if (bNeedSave && IDCANCEL ==
                    AskAboutSave (hwnd, szTitleName))
```

(continued)

Figure 22-13. *continued*

```
            return 0 ;

            // Open the selected file

       if (DrumFileOpenDlg (hwnd, szFileName, szTitleName))
       {
            szError = DrumFileRead (&drum, szFileName) ;

            if (szError != NULL)
            {
                 ErrorMessage (hwnd, szError, szTitleName) ;
                 szTitleName [0] = '\0' ;
            }
            else
            {
                    // Set new parameters

                    iTempo = (int) (50 *
                         (log10 (drum.iMsecPerBeat) - 1)) ;

                    SetScrollPos (hwnd, SB_VERT, iTempo, TRUE) ;
                    SetScrollPos (hwnd, SB_HORZ, drum.iVelocity, TRUE) ;

                    DrumSetParams (&drum) ;
                    InvalidateRect (hwnd, NULL, FALSE) ;
                    bNeedSave = FALSE ;
            }

            DoCaption (hwnd, szTitleName) ;
       }
       return 0 ;

case IDM_FILE_SAVE:
case IDM_FILE_SAVE_AS:
            // Save the selected file

       if ((LOWORD (wParam) == IDM_FILE_SAVE && szTitleName [0]) ||
              DrumFileSaveDlg (hwnd, szFileName, szTitleName))
       {
            szError = DrumFileWrite (&drum, szFileName) ;

            if (szError != NULL)
            {
                 ErrorMessage (hwnd, szError, szTitleName) ;
                 szTitleName [0] = '\0' ;
            }
            else
```

```
                        bNeedSave = FALSE ;

                   DoCaption (hwnd, szTitleName) ;
               }
          return 0 ;

     case IDM_APP_EXIT:
          SendMessage (hwnd, WM_SYSCOMMAND, SC_CLOSE, 0L) ;
          return 0 ;

     case IDM_SEQUENCE_RUNNING:
               // Begin sequence

          if (!DrumBeginSequence (hwnd))
          {
               ErrorMessage (hwnd,
                    TEXT ("Could not start MIDI sequence -- ")
                    TEXT ("MIDI Mapper device is unavailable!"),
                    szTitleName) ;
          }
          else
          {
               CheckMenuItem (hMenu, IDM_SEQUENCE_RUNNING,  MF_CHECKED) ;
               CheckMenuItem (hMenu, IDM_SEQUENCE_STOPPED, MF_UNCHECKED) ;
          }
          return 0 ;

     case IDM_SEQUENCE_STOPPED:
               // Finish at end of sequence

          DrumEndSequence (FALSE) ;
          return 0 ;

     case IDM_APP_ABOUT:
          DialogBox (hInst, TEXT ("AboutBox"), hwnd, AboutProc) ;
          return 0 ;
     }
     return 0 ;

case WM_LBUTTONDOWN:
case WM_RBUTTONDOWN:
     hdc = GetDC (hwnd) ;

          // Convert mouse coordinates to grid coordinates

     x =     LOWORD (lParam) / cxChar - 40 ;
     y = 2 * HIWORD (lParam) / cyChar -  2 ;
```

(continued)

Figure 22-13. *continued*

```
              // Set a new number of beats of sequence

        if (x > 0 && x <= 32 && y < 0)
        {
              SetTextColor (hdc, RGB (255, 255, 255)) ;
              TextOut (hdc, (40 + drum.iNumBeats) * cxChar, 0, TEXT (":|"), 2);
              SetTextColor (hdc, RGB (0, 0, 0)) ;

              if (drum.iNumBeats % 4 == 0)
                   TextOut (hdc, (40 + drum.iNumBeats) * cxChar, 0,
                            TEXT ("."), 1) ;

              drum.iNumBeats = x ;

              TextOut (hdc, (40 + drum.iNumBeats) * cxChar, 0, TEXT (":|"), 2);

              bNeedSave = TRUE ;
        }

              // Set or reset a percussion instrument beat

        if (x >= 0 && x < 32 && y >= 0 && y < NUM_PERC)
        {
              if (message == WM_LBUTTONDOWN)
                   drum.dwSeqPerc[y] ^= (1 << x) ;
              else
                   drum.dwSeqPian[y] ^= (1 << x) ;

              DrawRectangle (hdc, x, y, drum.dwSeqPerc, drum.dwSeqPian) ;

              bNeedSave = TRUE ;
        }

        ReleaseDC (hwnd, hdc) ;
        DrumSetParams (&drum) ;
        return 0 ;

case WM_HSCROLL:
              // Change the note velocity

        switch (LOWORD (wParam))
        {
        case SB_LINEUP:          drum.iVelocity -= 1 ;  break ;
        case SB_LINEDOWN:        drum.iVelocity += 1 ;  break ;
        case SB_PAGEUP:          drum.iVelocity -= 8 ;  break ;
        case SB_PAGEDOWN:        drum.iVelocity += 8 ;  break ;
        case SB_THUMBPOSITION:
```

```
                  drum.iVelocity = HIWORD (wParam) ;
                  break ;

          default:
                  return 0 ;
          }

          drum.iVelocity = max (1, min (drum.iVelocity, 127)) ;
          SetScrollPos (hwnd, SB_HORZ, drum.iVelocity, TRUE) ;
          DrumSetParams (&drum) ;
          bNeedSave = TRUE ;
          return 0 ;

   case WM_VSCROLL:
              // Change the tempo

          switch (LOWORD (wParam))
          {
          case SB_LINEUP:          iTempo -= 1 ;   break ;
          case SB_LINEDOWN:        iTempo += 1 ;   break ;
          case SB_PAGEUP:          iTempo -= 10 ;  break ;
          case SB_PAGEDOWN:        iTempo += 10 ;  break ;
          case SB_THUMBPOSITION:
                  iTempo = HIWORD (wParam) ;
                  break ;

          default:
                  return 0 ;
          }

          iTempo = max (0, min (iTempo, 100)) ;
          SetScrollPos (hwnd, SB_VERT, iTempo, TRUE) ;

          drum.iMsecPerBeat = (WORD) (10 * pow (100, iTempo / 100.0)) ;

          DrumSetParams (&drum) ;
          bNeedSave = TRUE ;
          return 0 ;

   case WM_PAINT:
          hdc = BeginPaint (hwnd, &ps) ;

          SetTextAlign (hdc, TA_UPDATECP) ;
          SetBkMode (hdc, TRANSPARENT) ;

              // Draw the text strings and horizontal lines
```

(continued)

Figure 22-13. *continued*

```
        for (i = 0 ; i < NUM_PERC ; i++)
        {
            MoveToEx (hdc, i & 1 ? 20 * cxChar : cxChar,
                         (2 * i + 3) * cyChar / 4, NULL) ;

            TextOut (hdc, 0, 0, szPerc [i], lstrlen (szPerc [i])) ;

            GetCurrentPositionEx (hdc, &point) ;

            MoveToEx (hdc,  point.x + cxChar, point.y + cyChar / 2, NULL) ;
            LineTo   (hdc,        39 * cxChar, point.y + cyChar / 2) ;
        }

        SetTextAlign (hdc, 0) ;

            // Draw rectangular grid, repeat mark, and beat marks

        for (x = 0 ; x < 32 ; x++)
        {
            for (y = 0 ; y < NUM_PERC ; y++)
                DrawRectangle (hdc, x, y, drum.dwSeqPerc, drum.dwSeqPian) ;

            SetTextColor (hdc, x == drum.iNumBeats - 1 ?
                             RGB (0, 0, 0) : RGB (255, 255, 255)) ;

            TextOut (hdc, (41 + x) * cxChar, 0, TEXT (":|"), 2) ;

            SetTextColor (hdc, RGB (0, 0, 0)) ;

            if (x % 4 == 0)
                TextOut (hdc, (40 + x) * cxChar, 0, TEXT ("."), 1) ;
        }

        EndPaint (hwnd, &ps) ;
        return 0 ;

case WM_USER_NOTIFY:
            // Draw the "bouncing ball"

        hdc = GetDC (hwnd) ;

        SelectObject (hdc, GetStockObject (NULL_PEN)) ;
        SelectObject (hdc, GetStockObject (WHITE_BRUSH)) ;

        for (i = 0 ; i < 2 ; i++)
        {
            x = iIndexLast ;
```

```
            y = NUM_PERC + 1 ;

            Ellipse (hdc, (x + 40) * cxChar, (2 * y + 3) * cyChar / 4,
                 (x + 41) * cxChar, (2 * y + 5) * cyChar / 4);

            iIndexLast = wParam ;
            SelectObject (hdc, GetStockObject (BLACK_BRUSH)) ;
       }

       ReleaseDC (hwnd, hdc) ;
       return 0 ;

  case WM_USER_ERROR:
       ErrorMessage (hwnd, TEXT ("Can't set timer event for tempo"),
                     szTitleName) ;

                                        // fall through
  case WM_USER_FINISHED:
       DrumEndSequence (TRUE) ;
       CheckMenuItem (hMenu, IDM_SEQUENCE_RUNNING,  MF_UNCHECKED) ;
       CheckMenuItem (hMenu, IDM_SEQUENCE_STOPPED, MF_CHECKED) ;
       return 0 ;

  case WM_CLOSE:
       if (!bNeedSave || IDCANCEL != AskAboutSave (hwnd, szTitleName))
            DestroyWindow (hwnd) ;

       return 0 ;

  case WM_QUERYENDSESSION:
       if (!bNeedSave || IDCANCEL != AskAboutSave (hwnd, szTitleName))
            return 1L ;

       return 0 ;

  case WM_DESTROY:
       DrumEndSequence (TRUE) ;
       PostQuitMessage (0) ;
       return 0 ;
  }
  return DefWindowProc (hwnd, message, wParam, lParam) ;
}

BOOL CALLBACK AboutProc (HWND hDlg, UINT message, WPARAM wParam, LPARAM lParam)
{
  switch (message)
  {
```

(continued)

Figure 22-13. *continued*

```
        case WM_INITDIALOG:
             return TRUE ;

        case WM_COMMAND:
             switch (LOWORD (wParam))
             {
             case IDOK:
                  EndDialog (hDlg, 0) ;
                  return TRUE ;
             }
             break ;
        }
    return FALSE ;
}

void DrawRectangle (HDC hdc, int x, int y, DWORD * dwSeqPerc, DWORD * dwSeqPian)
{
    int iBrush ;

    if (dwSeqPerc [y] & dwSeqPian [y] & (1L << x))
        iBrush = BLACK_BRUSH ;

    else if (dwSeqPerc [y] & (1L << x))
        iBrush = DKGRAY_BRUSH ;

    else if (dwSeqPian [y] & (1L << x))
        iBrush = LTGRAY_BRUSH ;

    else
        iBrush = WHITE_BRUSH ;

    SelectObject (hdc, GetStockObject (iBrush)) ;

    Rectangle (hdc, (x + 40) * cxChar    , (2 * y + 4) * cyChar / 4,
                    (x + 41) * cxChar + 1, (2 * y + 6) * cyChar / 4 + 1) ;
}

void ErrorMessage (HWND hwnd, TCHAR * szError, TCHAR * szTitleName)
{
    wsprintf (szBuffer, szError,
         (LPSTR) (szTitleName [0] ? szTitleName : szUntitled)) ;

    MessageBeep (MB_ICONEXCLAMATION) ;
    MessageBox (hwnd, szBuffer, szAppName, MB_OK | MB_ICONEXCLAMATION) ;
}

void DoCaption (HWND hwnd, TCHAR * szTitleName)
```

```
{
    wsprintf (szBuffer, TEXT ("MIDI Drum Machine - %s"),
              (LPSTR) (szTitleName [0] ? szTitleName : szUntitled)) ;

    SetWindowText (hwnd, szBuffer) ;
}

int AskAboutSave (HWND hwnd, TCHAR * szTitleName)
{
    int iReturn ;

    wsprintf (szBuffer, TEXT ("Save current changes in %s?"),
              (LPSTR) (szTitleName [0] ? szTitleName : szUntitled)) ;

    iReturn = MessageBox (hwnd, szBuffer, szAppName,
                          MB_YESNOCANCEL | MB_ICONQUESTION) ;

    if (iReturn == IDYES)
        if (!SendMessage (hwnd, WM_COMMAND, IDM_FILE_SAVE, 0))
            iReturn = IDCANCEL ;

    return iReturn ;
}
```

DRUMTIME.H

```
/*----------------------------------------------------------------
   DRUMTIME.H Header File for Time Functions for DRUM Program
   --------------------------------------------------------------*/

#define NUM_PERC          47
#define WM_USER_NOTIFY   (WM_USER + 1)
#define WM_USER_FINISHED (WM_USER + 2)
#define WM_USER_ERROR    (WM_USER + 3)

#pragma pack(push, 2)

typedef struct
{
    short iMsecPerBeat ;
    short iVelocity ;
    short iNumBeats ;
    DWORD dwSeqPerc [NUM_PERC] ;
    DWORD dwSeqPian [NUM_PERC] ;
```

(continued)

Figure 22-13. *continued*

```
}
DRUM, * PDRUM ;

#pragma pack(pop)

void DrumSetParams     (PDRUM) ;
BOOL DrumBeginSequence (HWND)  ;
void DrumEndSequence   (BOOL)  ;
```

DRUMTIME.C

```
/*-------------------------------------------
   DRUMFILE.C -- Timer Routines for DRUM
                 (c) Charles Petzold, 1998
   -------------------------------------------*/

#include <windows.h>
#include "drumtime.h"

#define minmax(a,x,b) (min (max (x, a), b))

#define TIMER_RES    5

void CALLBACK DrumTimerFunc (UINT, UINT, DWORD, DWORD, DWORD) ;

BOOL     bSequenceGoing, bEndSequence ;
DRUM     drum ;
HMIDIOUT hMidiOut ;
HWND     hwndNotify ;
int      iIndex ;
UINT     uTimerRes, uTimerID ;

DWORD MidiOutMessage (HMIDIOUT hMidi, int iStatus, int iChannel,
                      int iData1, int iData2)
{
     DWORD dwMessage ;

     dwMessage = iStatus | iChannel | (iData1 << 8) | (iData2 << 16) ;

     return midiOutShortMsg (hMidi, dwMessage) ;
}

void DrumSetParams (PDRUM pdrum)
{
     CopyMemory (&drum, pdrum, sizeof (DRUM)) ;
```

```
}

BOOL DrumBeginSequence (HWND hwnd)
{
     TIMECAPS tc ;

     hwndNotify = hwnd ;              // Save window handle for notification
     DrumEndSequence (TRUE) ;        // Stop current sequence if running

          // Open the MIDI Mapper output port

     if (midiOutOpen (&hMidiOut, MIDIMAPPER, 0, 0, 0))
          return FALSE ;

          // Send Program Change messages for channels 9 and 0

     MidiOutMessage (hMidiOut, 0xC0, 9, 0, 0) ;
     MidiOutMessage (hMidiOut, 0xC0, 0, 0, 0) ;

          // Begin sequence by setting a timer event

     timeGetDevCaps (&tc, sizeof (TIMECAPS)) ;
     uTimerRes = minmax (tc.wPeriodMin, TIMER_RES, tc.wPeriodMax) ;
     timeBeginPeriod (uTimerRes) ;

     uTimerID = timeSetEvent (max ((UINT) uTimerRes, (UINT) drum.iMsecPerBeat),
                              uTimerRes, DrumTimerFunc, 0, TIME_ONESHOT) ;

     if (uTimerID == 0)
     {
          timeEndPeriod (uTimerRes) ;
          midiOutClose (hMidiOut) ;
          return FALSE ;
     }

     iIndex = -1 ;
     bEndSequence = FALSE ;
     bSequenceGoing = TRUE ;

     return TRUE ;
}

void DrumEndSequence (BOOL bRightAway)
{
     if (bRightAway)
     {
          if (bSequenceGoing)
```

(continued)

Figure 22-13. *continued*

```
            {
                    // stop the timer
                if (uTimerID)
                    timeKillEvent (uTimerID) ;
                timeEndPeriod (uTimerRes) ;

                    // turn off all notes
                MidiOutMessage (hMidiOut, 0xB0, 9, 123, 0) ;
                MidiOutMessage (hMidiOut, 0xB0, 0, 123, 0) ;

                    // close the MIDI port
                midiOutClose (hMidiOut) ;
                bSequenceGoing = FALSE ;
            }
        }
    else
        bEndSequence = TRUE ;
}

void CALLBACK DrumTimerFunc (UINT  uID, UINT uMsg, DWORD dwUser,
                             DWORD dw1, DWORD dw2)
{
    static DWORD dwSeqPercLast [NUM_PERC], dwSeqPianLast [NUM_PERC] ;
    int          i ;

        // Note Off messages for channels 9 and 0

    if (iIndex != -1)
    {
        for (i = 0 ; i < NUM_PERC ; i++)
        {
            if (dwSeqPercLast[i] & 1 << iIndex)
                MidiOutMessage (hMidiOut, 0x80, 9, i + 35, 0) ;

            if (dwSeqPianLast[i] & 1 << iIndex)
                MidiOutMessage (hMidiOut, 0x80, 0, i + 35, 0) ;
        }
    }

        // Increment index and notify window to advance bouncing ball

    iIndex = (iIndex + 1) % drum.iNumBeats ;
    PostMessage (hwndNotify, WM_USER_NOTIFY, iIndex, timeGetTime ()) ;

        // Check if ending the sequence

    if (bEndSequence && iIndex == 0)
    {
        PostMessage (hwndNotify, WM_USER_FINISHED, 0, 0L) ;
```

```
            return ;
      }

      // Note On messages for channels 9 and 0

   for (i = 0 ; i < NUM_PERC ; i++)
   {
        if (drum.dwSeqPerc[i] & 1 << iIndex)
            MidiOutMessage (hMidiOut, 0x90, 9, i + 35, drum.iVelocity) ;

        if (drum.dwSeqPian[i] & 1 << iIndex)
            MidiOutMessage (hMidiOut, 0x90, 0, i + 35, drum.iVelocity) ;

        dwSeqPercLast[i] = drum.dwSeqPerc[i] ;
        dwSeqPianLast[i] = drum.dwSeqPian[i] ;
   }
      // Set a new timer event

   uTimerID = timeSetEvent (max ((int) uTimerRes, drum.iMsecPerBeat),
                            uTimerRes, DrumTimerFunc, 0, TIME_ONESHOT) ;

   if (uTimerID == 0)
   {
        PostMessage (hwndNotify, WM_USER_ERROR, 0, 0) ;
   }
}
```

DRUMFILE.H

```
/*--------------------------------------------------------
   DRUMFILE.H Header File for File I/O Routines for DRUM
  -------------------------------------------------------*/

BOOL    DrumFileOpenDlg (HWND, TCHAR *, TCHAR *) ;
BOOL    DrumFileSaveDlg (HWND, TCHAR *, TCHAR *) ;

TCHAR * DrumFileWrite   (DRUM *, TCHAR *) ;
TCHAR * DrumFileRead    (DRUM *, TCHAR *) ;
```

DRUMFILE.C

```
/*-----------------------------------------
   DRUMFILE.C -- File I/O Routines for DRUM
                 (c) Charles Petzold, 1998
  ----------------------------------------*/
```

(continued)

Figure 22-13. *continued*

```
#include <windows.h>
#include <commdlg.h>
#include "drumtime.h"
#include "drumfile.h"

OPENFILENAME ofn = { sizeof (OPENFILENAME) } ;

TCHAR * szFilter[] = { TEXT ("Drum Files (*.DRM)"),
                       TEXT ("*.drm"), TEXT ("") } ;

TCHAR szDrumID   [] = TEXT ("DRUM") ;
TCHAR szListID   [] = TEXT ("LIST") ;
TCHAR szInfoID   [] = TEXT ("INFO") ;
TCHAR szSoftID   [] = TEXT ("ISFT") ;
TCHAR szDateID   [] = TEXT ("ISCD") ;
TCHAR szFmtID    [] = TEXT ("fmt ") ;
TCHAR szDataID   [] = TEXT ("data") ;
char  szSoftware [] = "DRUM by Charles Petzold, Programming Windows" ;

TCHAR szErrorNoCreate    [] = TEXT ("File %s could not be opened for writing.");
TCHAR szErrorCannotWrite [] = TEXT ("File %s could not be written to. ") ;
TCHAR szErrorNotFound    [] = TEXT ("File %s not found or cannot be opened.") ;
TCHAR szErrorNotDrum     [] = TEXT ("File %s is not a standard DRUM file.") ;
TCHAR szErrorUnsupported [] = TEXT ("File %s is not a supported DRUM file.") ;
TCHAR szErrorCannotRead  [] = TEXT ("File %s cannot be read.") ;

BOOL DrumFileOpenDlg (HWND hwnd, TCHAR * szFileName, TCHAR * szTitleName)
{
     ofn.hwndOwner       = hwnd ;
     ofn.lpstrFilter     = szFilter [0] ;
     ofn.lpstrFile       = szFileName ;
     ofn.nMaxFile        = MAX_PATH ;
     ofn.lpstrFileTitle  = szTitleName ;
     ofn.nMaxFileTitle   = MAX_PATH ;
     ofn.Flags           = OFN_CREATEPROMPT ;
     ofn.lpstrDefExt     = TEXT ("drm") ;

     return GetOpenFileName (&ofn) ;
}

BOOL DrumFileSaveDlg (HWND hwnd, TCHAR * szFileName, TCHAR * szTitleName)
{
     ofn.hwndOwner       = hwnd ;
     ofn.lpstrFilter     = szFilter [0] ;
     ofn.lpstrFile       = szFileName ;
     ofn.nMaxFile        = MAX_PATH ;
     ofn.lpstrFileTitle  = szTitleName ;
```

```
        ofn.nMaxFileTitle    = MAX_PATH ;
        ofn.Flags            = OFN_OVERWRITEPROMPT ;
        ofn.lpstrDefExt      = TEXT ("drm") ;

        return GetSaveFileName (&ofn) ;
}

TCHAR * DrumFileWrite (DRUM * pdrum, TCHAR * szFileName)
{
        char        szDateBuf [16] ;
        HMMIO       hmmio ;
        int         iFormat = 2 ;
        MMCKINFO    mmckinfo [3] ;
        SYSTEMTIME  st ;
        WORD        wError = 0 ;

        memset (mmckinfo, 0, 3 * sizeof (MMCKINFO)) ;

            // Recreate the file for writing

        if ((hmmio = mmioOpen (szFileName, NULL,
                MMIO_CREATE | MMIO_WRITE | MMIO_ALLOCBUF)) == NULL)
            return szErrorNoCreate ;

            // Create a "RIFF" chunk with a "CPDR" type

        mmckinfo[0].fccType = mmioStringToFOURCC (szDrumID, 0) ;

        wError |= mmioCreateChunk (hmmio, &mmckinfo[0], MMIO_CREATERIFF) ;

            // Create "LIST" sub-chunk with an "INFO" type

        mmckinfo[1].fccType = mmioStringToFOURCC (szInfoID, 0) ;

        wError |= mmioCreateChunk (hmmio, &mmckinfo[1], MMIO_CREATELIST) ;

            // Create "ISFT" sub-sub-chunk

        mmckinfo[2].ckid = mmioStringToFOURCC (szSoftID, 0) ;

        wError |= mmioCreateChunk (hmmio, &mmckinfo[2], 0) ;
        wError |= (mmioWrite (hmmio, szSoftware, sizeof (szSoftware)) !=
                                            sizeof (szSoftware)) ;
        wError |= mmioAscend (hmmio, &mmckinfo[2], 0) ;

            // Create a time string
```

(continued)

Figure 22-13. *continued*

```
    GetLocalTime (&st) ;

    wsprintfA (szDateBuf, "%04d-%02d-%02d", st.wYear, st.wMonth, st.wDay) ;

         // Create "ISCD" sub-sub-chunk

    mmckinfo[2].ckid = mmioStringToFOURCC (szDateID, 0) ;

    wError |= mmioCreateChunk (hmmio, &mmckinfo[2], 0) ;
    wError |= (mmioWrite (hmmio, szDateBuf, (strlen (szDateBuf) + 1)) !=
                                         (int) (strlen (szDateBuf) + 1)) ;
    wError |= mmioAscend (hmmio, &mmckinfo[2], 0) ;
    wError |= mmioAscend (hmmio, &mmckinfo[1], 0) ;

         // Create "fmt " sub-chunk

    mmckinfo[1].ckid = mmioStringToFOURCC (szFmtID, 0) ;

    wError |= mmioCreateChunk (hmmio, &mmckinfo[1], 0) ;
    wError |= (mmioWrite (hmmio, (PSTR) &iFormat, sizeof (int)) !=
                                             sizeof (int)) ;
    wError |= mmioAscend (hmmio, &mmckinfo[1], 0) ;

         // Create the "data" sub-chunk

    mmckinfo[1].ckid = mmioStringToFOURCC (szDataID, 0) ;

    wError |= mmioCreateChunk (hmmio, &mmckinfo[1], 0) ;
    wError |= (mmioWrite (hmmio, (PSTR) pdrum, sizeof (DRUM)) !=
                                             sizeof (DRUM)) ;
    wError |= mmioAscend (hmmio, &mmckinfo[1], 0) ;
    wError |= mmioAscend (hmmio, &mmckinfo[0], 0) ;

         // Clean up and return

    wError |= mmioClose (hmmio, 0) ;

    if (wError)
    {
         mmioOpen (szFileName, NULL, MMIO_DELETE) ;
         return szErrorCannotWrite ;
    }
    return NULL ;
}


TCHAR * DrumFileRead (DRUM * pdrum, TCHAR * szFileName)
{
```

```
DRUM      drum ;
HMMIO     hmmio ;
int       i, iFormat ;
MMCKINFO mmckinfo [3] ;

ZeroMemory (mmckinfo, 2 * sizeof (MMCKINFO)) ;

     // Open the file

if ((hmmio = mmioOpen (szFileName, NULL, MMIO_READ)) == NULL)
     return szErrorNotFound ;

     // Locate a "RIFF" chunk with a "DRUM" form-type

mmckinfo[0].ckid = mmioStringToFOURCC (szDrumID, 0) ;

if (mmioDescend (hmmio, &mmckinfo[0], NULL, MMIO_FINDRIFF))
{
     mmioClose (hmmio, 0) ;
     return szErrorNotDrum ;
}

     // Locate, read, and verify the "fmt " sub-chunk

mmckinfo[1].ckid = mmioStringToFOURCC (szFmtID, 0) ;

if (mmioDescend (hmmio, &mmckinfo[1], &mmckinfo[0], MMIO_FINDCHUNK))
{
     mmioClose (hmmio, 0) ;
     return szErrorNotDrum ;
}

if (mmckinfo[1].cksize != sizeof (int))
{
     mmioClose (hmmio, 0) ;
     return szErrorUnsupported ;
}

if (mmioRead (hmmio, (PSTR) &iFormat, sizeof (int)) != sizeof (int))
{
     mmioClose (hmmio, 0) ;
     return szErrorCannotRead ;
}

if (iFormat != 1 && iFormat != 2)
{
     mmioClose (hmmio, 0) ;
```

(continued)

Figure 22-13. *continued*

```
        return szErrorUnsupported ;
    }

        // Go to end of "fmt " sub-chunk

    mmioAscend (hmmio, &mmckinfo[1], 0) ;

        // Locate, read, and verify the "data" sub-chunk

    mmckinfo[1].ckid = mmioStringToFOURCC (szDataID, 0) ;

    if (mmioDescend (hmmio, &mmckinfo[1], &mmckinfo[0], MMIO_FINDCHUNK))
    {
        mmioClose (hmmio, 0) ;
        return szErrorNotDrum ;
    }

    if (mmckinfo[1].cksize != sizeof (DRUM))
    {
        mmioClose (hmmio, 0) ;
        return szErrorUnsupported ;
    }

    if (mmioRead (hmmio, (LPSTR) &drum, sizeof (DRUM)) != sizeof (DRUM))
    {
        mmioClose (hmmio, 0) ;
        return szErrorCannotRead ;
    }

        // Close the file

    mmioClose (hmmio, 0) ;

        // Convert format 1 to format 2 and copy the DRUM structure data

    if (iFormat == 1)
    {
        for (i = 0 ; i < NUM_PERC ; i++)
        {
            drum.dwSeqPerc [i] = drum.dwSeqPian [i] ;
            drum.dwSeqPian [i] = 0 ;
        }
    }

    memcpy (pdrum, &drum, sizeof (DRUM)) ;
    return NULL ;
}
```

DRUM.RC (excerpts)

```
//Microsoft Developer Studio generated resource script.

#include "resource.h"
#include "afxres.h"

/////////////////////////////////////////////////////////////////////////////
// Menu

DRUM MENU DISCARDABLE
BEGIN
    POPUP "&File"
    BEGIN
        MENUITEM "&New",                    IDM_FILE_NEW
        MENUITEM "&Open...",                IDM_FILE_OPEN
        MENUITEM "&Save",                   IDM_FILE_SAVE
        MENUITEM "Save &As...",             IDM_FILE_SAVE_AS
        MENUITEM SEPARATOR
        MENUITEM "E&xit",                   IDM_APP_EXIT
    END
    POPUP "&Sequence"
    BEGIN
        MENUITEM "&Running",                IDM_SEQUENCE_RUNNING
        MENUITEM "&Stopped",                IDM_SEQUENCE_STOPPED
        , CHECKED
    END
    POPUP "&Help"
    BEGIN
        MENUITEM "&About...",               IDM_APP_ABOUT
    END
END


/////////////////////////////////////////////////////////////////////////////
// Icon


DRUM                    ICON    DISCARDABLE     "drum.ico"


/////////////////////////////////////////////////////////////////////////////
// Dialog

ABOUTBOX DIALOG DISCARDABLE  20, 20, 160, 164
STYLE DS_MODALFRAME | WS_POPUP | WS_CAPTION | WS_SYSMENU
CAPTION "Dialog"
FONT 8, "MS Sans Serif"
BEGIN
    DEFPUSHBUTTON   "OK",IDOK,54,143,50,14
```

(continued)

Figure 22-13. *continued*

```
        ICON            "DRUM",IDC_STATIC,8,8,21,20
        CTEXT           "DRUM",IDC_STATIC,34,12,90,8
        CTEXT           "MIDI Drum Machine",IDC_STATIC,7,36,144,8
        CONTROL         "",IDC_STATIC,"Static",SS_BLACKFRAME,8,88,144,46
        LTEXT           "Left Button:\t\tDrum sounds",IDC_STATIC,12,92,136,8
        LTEXT           "Right Button:\t\tPiano sounds",IDC_STATIC,12,102,136,8
        LTEXT           "Horizontal Scroll:\t\tVelocity",IDC_STATIC,12,112,136,8
        LTEXT           "Vertical Scroll:\t\tTempo",IDC_STATIC,12,122,136,8
        CTEXT           "Copyright (c) Charles Petzold, 1998",IDC_STATIC,8,48,
                        144,8
        CTEXT           """Programming Windows,"" 5th Edition",IDC_STATIC,8,60,
                        144,8
END
```

RESOURCE.H (excerpts)

```
// Microsoft Developer Studio generated include file.
// Used by Drum.rc

#define IDM_FILE_NEW                    40001
#define IDM_FILE_OPEN                   40002
#define IDM_FILE_SAVE                   40003
#define IDM_FILE_SAVE_AS                40004
#define IDM_APP_EXIT                    40005
#define IDM_SEQUENCE_RUNNING            40006
#define IDM_SEQUENCE_STOPPED            40007
#define IDM_APP_ABOUT                   40008
```

When you first run DRUM, you'll see the 47 different percussion instruments listed by name in the left half on the window in two columns. The grid at the right is a two-dimensional array of percussion sound vs. time. Each instrument is associated with a row in the grid. The 32 columns are 32 beats. If you think of these 32 beats as occuring within a measure of 4/4 time (that is, four quarter notes per measure), then each beat corresponds to a 32nd note.

When you select Running from the Sequence menu, the program will attempt to open the MIDI Mapper device. If it's unsuccessful, you'll get a message box. Otherwise, you'll see a little "bouncing ball" skip across the bottom of the grid as each beat is played.

You can click with the left mouse button mouse anywhere within the grid to play a percussion sound during that beat. The square will turn dark gray. You can also add some piano beats using the right mouse button. The square will turn light gray. If you click with both mouse buttons, either together or independently, the square will turn black and the percussion *and* piano sounds will be heard. Clicking again with either or both buttons will turn off the sound for that beat.

Across the top of the grid is a dot every 4 beats. Those dots simply make it easy to pinpoint your button clicks without too much counting. At the upper right corner of the grid is a colon and bar (: |) that together resemble a repeat sign used in traditional music notation. This indicates the length of the sequence. You can click with the mouse anywhere above the grid to put the repeat sign somewhere else. The sequence plays up to, but not including, the beat under the repeat sign. If you want to create a waltz rhythm, for example, you should set the repeat mark for some multiple of 3 beats.

The horizontal scroll bar controls the velocity byte in the MIDI Note On messages. This generally affects the volume of the sounds, although it can also affect timbre in some synthesizers. The program initially sets the velocity scroll bar thumb in the center position. The vertical scroll bar controls the tempo. This is a logarithmic scale, ranging from 1 second per beat when the thumb is at the bottom to 10 milliseconds per beat at the top. The program initially sets the tempo at 100 milliseconds (1/10th second) per beat, with the scroll bar thumb in the center.

The File menu allows you to save and retrieve files with the extension .DRM, which is a format that I invented. These files are fairly small and use the RIFF file format, which is recommended for all new multimedia data files. The About option from the Help menu displays a dialog box containing a very brief summary of the use of the mouse on the grid and the functions of the two scroll bars.

Finally, the Stopped option from the Sequence menu stops the music and closes the MIDI Mapper device after finishing with the current sequence.

The Multimedia *time* Functions

You'll notice that DRUM.C makes no calls to any multimedia functions. All the real action occurs in the DRUMTIME module.

Although the normal Windows timer is certainly simple to use, it's a disaster for time-critical applications. As we saw in the BACHTOCC program, playing music is one such time-critical application for which the Windows timer is simply inadequate. To provide the accuracy needed for playing MIDI sequences on the PC, the multimedia API includes a high-resolution timer implemented through the use of seven functions beginning with the prefix *time*. One of these functions is superfluous, and DRUMTIME demonstrates the use of the other six. The timer functions work with a callback function that runs in a separate thread. This callback function is called by the system according to a timer delay value specified by the program.

When dealing with the multimedia timer, you specify two different times, both in milliseconds. The first is the delay time, and the second is called the resolution. You can think of the resolution as a tolerable error. If you specify a delay of 100 milliseconds with a resolution of 10 milliseconds, the actual timer delay can range anywhere from 90 to 110 milliseconds.

Before you begin using the timer, you should obtain the timer device capabilities:

```
timeGetDevCaps (&timecaps, uSize) ;
```

The first argument is a pointer to a structure of type TIMECAPS, and the second argument is the size of this structure. The TIMECAPS structure has only two fields, *wPeriodMin* and *wPeriodMax*. These are the minimum and maximum resolution values supported by the timer device driver. If you look at these values after calling *timeGetDevCaps*, you'll find that *wPeriodMin* is 1 and *wPeriodMax* is 65535, so this function may not seem crucial. However, it's a good idea to get these resolution values anyway and use them in the other timer function calls.

The next step is to call

```
timeBeginPeriod (uResolution) ;
```

to indicate the lowest timer resolution value that your program requires. This value should be within the range given in the TIMECAPS structure. This call allows the timer device driver to best provide for multiple programs that might be using the timer. Every call to *timeBegin-Period* must be paired with a later call to *timeEndPeriod*, which I'll describe shortly.

Now you're ready to actually set a timer event:

```
idTimer = timeSetEvent (uDelay, uResolution, CallBackFunc, dwData, uFlag) ;
```

The *idTimer* returned from the call will be 0 if an error occurs. Following this call, the function *CallBackFunc* will be called from Windows in *uDelay* milliseconds with an allowable error specified by *uResolution*. The *uResolution* value must be greater than or equal to the resolution value passed to *timeBeginPeriod*. The *dwData* parameter is program-defined data later passed to *CallBackFunc*. The last parameter can be either TIME_ONE-SHOT to get a single call to *CallBackFunc* in *uDelay* number of milliseconds or TIME_PERIODIC to get calls to *CallBackFunc* every *uDelay* milliseconds.

To stop a one-shot timer event before *CallBackFunc* is called, or to halt periodic timer events, call

```
timeKillEvent (idTimer) ;
```

You don't need to kill a one-shot timer event after *CallBackFunc* is called. When you're finished using the timer in your program, call

```
timeEndPeriod (wResolution) ;
```

with the same argument passed to *timeBeginPeriod*.

Two other functions begin with the prefix *time*. The function

```
dwSysTime = timeGetTime () ;
```

returns the system time in milliseconds since Windows first started up. The function

```
timeGetSystemTime (&mmtime, uSize) ;
```

requires a pointer to an MMTIME structure as the first argument and the size of this structure as the second. Although the MMTIME structure can be used in other circumstances to get the system time in formats other than milliseconds, in this case it always returns the time in milliseconds. So, *timeGetSystemTime* is superfluous.

The callback function is limited in the Windows function calls it can make. The callback function can call *PostMessage*, four timer functions (*timeSetEvent*, *timeKillEvent*, *timeGetTime*, and the superfluous *timeGetSystemTime*), two MIDI output functions (*midiOutShortMsg* and *midiOutLongMsg*), and the debugging function *OutputDebugStr*.

Obviously, the multimedia timer is designed specifically for playing MIDI sequences and has very limited use for anything else. You can, of course, use *PostMessage* for informing a window procedure of timer events, and the window procedure can do whatever it likes, but it won't be responding with the accuracy of the timer callback itself.

The callback function has five parameters, but only two of them are used: the timer ID number returned from *timeSetEvent* and the *dwData* value originally passed as an argument to *timeSetEvent*.

The DRUM.C module calls the *DrumSetParams* function in DRUMTIME.C at various times—when DRUM's window is created, when the user clicks on the grid or manipulates the scroll bars, when the program loads a .DRM file from disk, or when the grid is cleared. The single parameter to *DrumSetParams* is a pointer to a structure of type DRUM, defined in DRUMTIME.H. This structure stores the beat time in milliseconds, the velocity (which generally corresponds to the volume), the number of beats in the sequence, as well as two sets of forty-seven 32-bit integers for storing the grid settings for the percussion and piano sounds. Each bit in these 32-bit integers corresponds to a beat of the sequence. The DRUM.C module maintains a structure of type DRUM in static memory and passes a pointer to it when calling *DrumSetParams*. *DrumSetParams* simply copies the contents of the structure.

To start the sequence going, DRUM calls the *DrumBeginSequence* function in DRUMTIME. The only parameter is a window handle. This is used for notification purposes. *DrumBeginSequence* opens the MIDI Mapper output device and, if successful, sends Program Change messages to select instrument voice 0 for MIDI channels 0 and 9. (These are zero-based, so 9 actually refers to MIDI channel 10, the percussion channel. The other channel is used for the piano sounds.) *DrumBeginSequence* continues by calling *timeGetDevCaps* and then *timeBeginPeriod*. The desired timer resolution defined in the TIMER_RES constant is 5 milliseconds, but I've defined a macro called *minmax* to calculate a resolution within the limits returned from *timeGetDevCaps*.

The next call is *timeSetEvent*, specifying the beat time, the calculated resolution, the callback function *DrumTimerFunc*, and the constant TIME_ONESHOT. DRUMTIME uses a one-shot timer rather than a periodic timer so that the tempo can be dynamically changed while a sequence is running. After the *timeSetEvent* call, the timer device driver will call *DrumTimerFunc* after the delay time has elapsed.

The *DrumTimerFunc* callback is the function in DRUMTIME.C where most of the heavy action takes place. The variable *iIndex* stores the current beat in the sequence. The callback begins by sending MIDI Note Off messages for the sounds currently playing. An initial −1 value of *iIndex* prevents this first happening when the sequence first begins.

Next, *iIndex* is incremented and its value is delivered to the window procedure in DRUM with a user-defined message called WM_USER_NOTIFY. The *wParam* message parameter is set to *iIndex* so that *WndProc* in DRUM.C can move the "bouncing ball" at the bottom of the grid.

DrumTimerFunc finishes up by sending Note On messages to the synthesizer for both channels 0 and 9, saving the grid values so that the sounds can be turned off the next time through, and then setting a new one-shot timer event by calling *timeSetEvent*.

To stop the sequence, DRUM calls *DrumEndSequence* with a single argument that can be set to either TRUE or FALSE. If TRUE, *DrumEndSequence* ends the sequence right away by killing any pending timer event, calling *timeEndPeriod*, sending "all notes off" messages to the two MIDI channels, and then closing the MIDI output port. DRUM calls *DrumEndSequence* with a TRUE argument when the user has decided to terminate the program.

However, when the user selects Stop from the Sequence menu in DRUM, the program instead calls *DrumEndSequence* with a FALSE argument. This allows the sequence to complete the current cycle before ending. *DrumEndSequence* responds to this call by setting the *bEndSequence* global variable to NULL. If *bEndSequence* is TRUE and the beat index has been set to zero, *DrumTimerFunc* posts a user-defined message called WM_ USER_FINISHED to *WndProc*. *WndProc* must respond to this message by calling *DrumEnd-Sequence* with a TRUE argument to properly close down the use of the timer and the MIDI port.

RIFF File I/O

The DRUM program can also save and retrieve files containing the information stored in the DRUM structure. These files are in the Resource Interchange File Format (RIFF) recommended for multimedia file types. You can read and write RIFF files by using standard file I/O functions, of course, but an easier approach is provided by functions beginning with the prefix *mmio* (for "multimedia input/output").

As we saw when examining the .WAV format, RIFF is a tagged file format, which means that the data in the file is organized in blocks of various lengths (called "chunks"), each of which is identified by a tag. A tag is simply a 4-byte ASCII string. This makes it easy to compare tag names with 32-bit integers. The tag is followed by the length of the chunk and the data for the chunk. Tagged file formats are versatile because the information in the file is not located at fixed offsets from the beginning of the file but is instead identified by tags. Thus, the file format can be enhanced by adding additional tags. When reading the file, programs can easily find the data they need and skip tags they don't need or don't understand.

A RIFF file in Windows consists solely of chunks, which are blocks of information in the file. A chunk is composed of a chunk type, a chunk size, and chunk data. The chunk type is a 4-character ASCII tag. It must have no embedded blanks but is possibly padded at the end with blanks. The chunk size is a 4-byte (32-bit) value that indicates the size of the chunk data. Chunk data must occupy an even number of bytes and is padded at the end with an extra zero byte if necessary. Thus, every component of a chunk is word-aligned with the beginning of the file. The chunk size does not include the 8 bytes required for the chunk type and the chunk size, and it does not reflect the padding of the data.

For some chunk types, the chunk size can be the same regardless of the particular file. This is the case when the chunk data is a fixed-length structure containing information. In other cases, the chunk size is variable depending on the particular file.

There are two special types of chunks, called RIFF chunks and LIST chunks. In a RIFF chunk, the chunk data begins with a 4-character ASCII form type, which is then followed by one or more sub-chunks. The LIST chunk is similar except that the data begins with a 4-character ASCII list type. A RIFF chunk is used for the overall RIFF file, and the LIST chunk is used within the file to consolidate related sub-chunks.

A RIFF file is a RIFF chunk. Thus, a RIFF file begins with the character string "RIFF" and a 32-bit value that indicates the size of the file less 8 bytes. (Actually, the file might be one byte longer if data padding is required.)

The multimedia API includes 16 functions beginning with the prefix *mmio*, specifically designed for working with RIFF files. Several of these functions are used in DRUM-FILE.C to read and write DRUM data files.

To open a file using the *mmio* functions, the first step is to call *mmioOpen*. The function returns a handle to the file. The *mmioCreateChunk* function creates a chunk in the file. This uses an MMCKINFO to define the name and characteristics of the chunk. The *mmioWrite* function writes the chunk data. After writing the chunk data, you call *mmioAscend*. The MMCKINFO structure passed to *mmioAscend* must be the same MMCKINFO structure passed earlier to *mmioCreateChunk* to create the chunk. The *mmioAscend* function works by subtracting the *dwDataOffset* field of the structure from the current file pointer, which will now be at the end of the chunk data, and storing that value before the data. The *mmioAscend* function also takes care of data padding if the chunk data is not a multiple of two bytes in length.

RIFF files are composed of nested levels of chunks. To make *mmioAscend* work correctly, you must maintain multiple MMCKINFO structures, each of which is associated with a level in the file. The DRUM data files have three levels. Hence, in the *DrumFileWrite* function in DRUMFILE.C, I've defined an array of three MMCKINFO structures, which can be referenced as *mmckinfo[0]*, *mmckinfo[1]*, and *mmckinfo[2]*. The *mmckinfo[0]* structure is used in the first *mmioCreateChunk* call to create a chunk type of RIFF with a form type of DRUM. This is followed by a second *mmioCreateChunk* call using *mmckinfo[1]* to create a chunk type of LIST with a list type of INFO.

A third *mmioCreateChunk* call using *mmckinfo[2]* creates a chunk type of ISFT, which identifies the software that created the data file. Following the *mmioWrite* call to write the string *szSoftware*, a call to *mmioAscent* using *mmckinfo[2]* fills in the chunk size field for this chunk. This is the first completed chunk. The next chunk is also within the LIST chunk. The program proceeds with another *mmioCreateChunk* call to create a ISCD ("creation data") chunk, again using *mmckinfo[2]*. After the *mmioWrite* call to write the chunk data, a call to *mmioAscend* using *mmckinfo[2]* fills in the chunk size. That's the end of this chunk, and it's also the end of the LIST chunk. So, to fill in the chunk size field of the LIST chunk, *mmioAscend* is called again, this time using *mmckinfo[1]*, which was originally used to create the LIST chunk.

To create the "fmt " and "data" chunks, *mmioCreateChunk* uses *mmckinfo[1]*; the *mmioWrite* calls are followed by *mmioAscend*, also using *mmckinfo[1]*. At this point, all the chunk sizes have been filled in except for the RIFF chunk itself. That requires one more call to *mmioAscend* using *mmckinfo[0]*. There's only one more call, and that's to *mmioClose*.

It may seem as if an *mmioAscend* call changes the current file pointer, and it certainly might to fill in the chunk size, but by the time the function returns, the file pointer is restored to its position after the end of the chunk data (or perhaps incremented by one byte for data padding). From the application's perspective, all writing to the file is sequential from beginning to end.

After a successful *mmioOpen* call, nothing can really go wrong except for the running out of disk space. I use the variable *wError* to accumulate error codes from the *mmioCreateChunk*, *mmioWrite*, *mmioAscend*, and *mmioClose* calls, each of which could fail if insufficient disk space is available. If that happens, the file is deleted using *mmioOpen* with the MMIO_DELETE constant and an error message is returned to the caller.

Reading a RIFF file is similar to creating one, except that *mmioRead* is called instead of *mmioWrite*, and *mmioDescend* is called rather than *mmioCreateChunk*. To "descend" into a chunk means to locate a chunk and put the file pointer after the chunk size (or after the form type or list type for a RIFF or LIST chunk type). To "ascend" from a chunk means to move the file pointer to the end of the chunk data. Neither the *mmioDescend* nor *mmioAscend* functions move the file pointer to an earlier position in the file.

An earlier version of the DRUM program was published in *PC Magazine* in 1992. At that time, Windows supported two different levels of MIDI synthesizers (called "base" and "extended"). Files written from that program have a format identifier of 1. The DRUM program in this chapter sets the format identifier to 2. It can read the earlier format, however, and convert them. This is done in the *DrumFileRead* routine.

Chapter 23

A Taste
of the Internet

The Internet—that vast interconnection of computers around the world that implement various protocols to exchange information—has redefined several aspects of personal computing in recent years. Although dial-up information services and electronic mail systems existed prior to the proliferation of the Internet, they were often restricted to character mode and were essentially unlinked. Each information service, for example, required dialing a different telephone number and logging on with a different user ID and password. Each email system allowed sending and receiving mail only among people who subscribed to that particular system.

Today, dialing one phone number generally connects with the whole of the Internet and allows universal correspondence with anyone who has email. Particularly in the World Wide Web, the use of hypertext, graphics, and multimedia (including sound, music, and video) has extended the range and versatility of online information.

A complete tutorial covering all the programming topics in Windows that relate to the Internet would probably require several additional books. Instead, this chapter focuses on just two areas that might be useful to small Microsoft Windows applications for obtaining information from the Internet. These are the Windows Sockets (WinSock) API and the File Transfer Protocol (FTP) support of the Windows Internet (WinInet) API.

WINDOWS SOCKETS

Sockets are a concept developed at the University of California at Berkeley to add network communication support to the UNIX operating system. The API developed there is now known as the "Berkeley socket interface."

Sockets and TCP/IP

Sockets are generally, but not exclusively, used in conjunction with the Transmission Control Protocol/Internet Protocol (TCP/IP) that dominates Internet communications. The Internet Protocol (IP) part of TCP/IP involves packaging data into "datagrams" that contain header information to identify the source and destination of the data. The Transmission Control Protocol (TCP) provides a means of reliable transport and error checking for the IP datagrams.

Within TCP/IP, a communication endpoint is defined by an IP address and a port number. The IP address consists of 4 bytes that identify a server on the Internet. The IP address is generally shown in "dotted quad" format, with decimal numbers separated by periods, for example "209.86.105.231". A port number identifies a particular service or process that the server provides. Some of these port numbers are standardized to provide well-known services.

When a socket is used with TCP/IP, a socket *is* the TCP/IP communication endpoint. Thus, the socket specifies an IP address and a port number.

Network Time Services

The sample program that I'll be presenting shortly connects with an Internet server that provides a service known as the Time Protocol. This sample program obtains the current exact date and time and uses that information to set the clock on your PC.

In the United States, the National Institute of Standards and Technology (formerly known as the National Bureau of Standards) is responsible for maintaining the correct time in conjunction with other bureaus around the world. The exact time is available to the public through radio broadcasts, telephone numbers, computer dial-up phone numbers, and the Internet, all of which are documented at the Web site at *http://www.bldrdoc.gov/timefreq*. (The domain name of "bldrdoc" refers to the Boulder, Colorado, location of the NIST Time and Frequency Division.)

We're interested in the NIST Network Time Service, which is further documented at *http://www.bldrdoc.gov/timefreq/service/nts.htm*. This Web page lists ten servers that provide NIST time services. For example, the first one is named *time-a.timefreq.bldrdoc.gov*, which has an Internet Protocol (IP) address of 132.163.135.130.

(A program I wrote that uses the non-Internet NIST computer dial-up service was published in *PC Magazine* and can be found at the Ziff-Davis Web site *http://www.zdnet .com/pcmag/pctech/content/16/20/ut1620.001.html*. This program can be useful for anyone who wants to learn how to use the Windows Telephony API.)

Three different time services are available over the Internet, each one described by a Request for Comment (RFC) common for documenting Internet standards. The Daytime Protocol (RFC-867) provides an ASCII string that indicates the exact date and time. The exact format of this ASCII string is not quite standard, but it is meant to be readable by humans. The Time Protocol (RFC-868) provides a 32-bit number that indicates the number of seconds since midnight January 1, 1900. This time is in UTC (which, despite the ordering of the letters, stands for Coordinated Universal Time), which is very similar to what was once called Greenwich Mean Time or GMT—the time at Greenwich, England. The third protocol is called the Network Time Protocol (RFC-1305), which is quite complex.

For our purposes—which involve getting a feel for sockets and keeping our PC's clock updated—the Time Protocol is ideal. RFC-868 is a short two-page document and basically says that a program wishing to use TCP to obtain the exact time should:

1. Connect to port 37 on a server that provides this service,

2. Receive the 32-bit time, and

3. Close the connection.

We now have everything we need to know to write a sockets-based application that accesses this time service.

The NETTIME Program

The Windows sockets API, commonly called WinSock, is compatible with the Berkeley sockets API; hence, it is conceivable that UNIX socket code could be ported relatively painlessly to Windows. Further support under Windows is provided by extensions to Berkeley sockets in the form of functions beginning with the prefix *WSA* ("WinSock API"). An overview and reference is provided at */Platform SDK/Networking and Distributed Services/Windows Sockets Version 2.*

The NETTIME program shown in Figure 23-1 demonstrates how to use the WinSock API.

NETTIME.C

```
/*---------------------------------------------------------
   NETTIME.C -- Sets System Clock from Internet Services
                (c) Charles Petzold, 1998
   ---------------------------------------------------------*/

#include <windows.h>
#include "resource.h"

#define WM_SOCKET_NOTIFY (WM_USER + 1)
#define ID_TIMER         1

LRESULT CALLBACK WndProc   (HWND, UINT, WPARAM, LPARAM) ;
BOOL    CALLBACK MainDlg   (HWND, UINT, WPARAM, LPARAM) ;
BOOL    CALLBACK ServerDlg (HWND, UINT, WPARAM, LPARAM) ;

void ChangeSystemTime (HWND hwndEdit, ULONG ulTime) ;
void FormatUpdatedTime (HWND hwndEdit, SYSTEMTIME * pstOld,
                                       SYSTEMTIME * pstNew) ;
void EditPrintf (HWND hwndEdit, TCHAR * szFormat, ...) ;
```

Figure 23-1. *The NETTIME program.*   *(continued)*

Figure 23-1. *continued*

```
HINSTANCE hInst ;
HWND      hwndModeless ;

int WINAPI WinMain (HINSTANCE hInstance, HINSTANCE hPrevInstance,
                    PSTR szCmdLine, int iCmdShow)
{
    static TCHAR szAppName[] = TEXT ("NetTime") ;
    HWND        hwnd ;
    MSG         msg ;
    RECT        rect ;
    WNDCLASS    wndclass ;

    hInst = hInstance ;

    wndclass.style         = 0 ;
    wndclass.lpfnWndProc   = WndProc ;
    wndclass.cbClsExtra    = 0 ;
    wndclass.cbWndExtra    = 0 ;
    wndclass.hInstance     = hInstance ;
    wndclass.hIcon         = LoadIcon (NULL, IDI_APPLICATION) ;
    wndclass.hCursor       = NULL ;
    wndclass.hbrBackground = NULL ;
    wndclass.lpszMenuName  = NULL ;
    wndclass.lpszClassName = szAppName ;

    if (!RegisterClass (&wndclass))
    {
        MessageBox (NULL, TEXT ("This program requires Windows NT!"),
                    szAppName, MB_ICONERROR) ;
        return 0 ;
    }

    hwnd = CreateWindow (szAppName, TEXT ("Set System Clock from Internet"),
                         WS_OVERLAPPED | WS_CAPTION | WS_SYSMENU |
                           WS_BORDER | WS_MINIMIZEBOX,
                         CW_USEDEFAULT, CW_USEDEFAULT,
                         CW_USEDEFAULT, CW_USEDEFAULT,
                         NULL, NULL, hInstance, NULL) ;

        // Create the modeless dialog box to go on top of the window

    hwndModeless = CreateDialog (hInstance, szAppName, hwnd, MainDlg) ;

        // Size the main parent window to the size of the dialog box.
        //    Show both windows.

    GetWindowRect (hwndModeless, &rect) ;
```

```
        AdjustWindowRect (&rect, WS_CAPTION | WS_BORDER, FALSE) ;

        SetWindowPos (hwnd, NULL, 0, 0, rect.right - rect.left,
                    rect.bottom - rect.top, SWP_NOMOVE) ;

        ShowWindow (hwndModeless, SW_SHOW) ;
        ShowWindow (hwnd, iCmdShow) ;
        UpdateWindow (hwnd) ;

                // Normal message loop when a modeless dialog box is used.

        while (GetMessage (&msg, NULL, 0, 0))
        {
            if (hwndModeless == 0 || !IsDialogMessage (hwndModeless, &msg))
            {
                TranslateMessage (&msg) ;
                DispatchMessage (&msg) ;
            }
        }
        return msg.wParam ;
}

LRESULT CALLBACK WndProc (HWND hwnd, UINT message, WPARAM wParam, LPARAM lParam)
{
    switch (message)
    {
    case WM_SETFOCUS:
        SetFocus (hwndModeless) ;
        return 0 ;

    case WM_DESTROY:
        PostQuitMessage (0) ;
        return 0 ;
    }
    return DefWindowProc (hwnd, message, wParam, lParam) ;
}

BOOL CALLBACK MainDlg (HWND hwnd, UINT message, WPARAM wParam, LPARAM lParam)
{
    static char    szIPAddr[32] = { "132.163.135.130" } ;
    static HWND    hwndButton, hwndEdit ;
    static SOCKET sock ;
    static struct sockaddr_in sa ;
    static TCHAR   szOKLabel[32] ;
    int            iError, iSize ;
    unsigned long ulTime ;
    WORD           wEvent, wError ;
```

(continued)

Figure 23-1. *continued*

```
WSADATA        WSAData ;

switch (message)
{
case WM_INITDIALOG:
     hwndButton = GetDlgItem (hwnd, IDOK) ;
     hwndEdit = GetDlgItem (hwnd, IDC_TEXTOUT) ;
     return TRUE ;

case WM_COMMAND:
     switch (LOWORD (wParam))
     {
     case IDC_SERVER:
          DialogBoxParam (hInst, TEXT ("Servers"), hwnd, ServerDlg,
                         (LPARAM) szIPAddr) ;
          return TRUE ;

     case IDOK:
               // Call "WSAStartup" and display description text

          if (iError = WSAStartup (MAKEWORD(2,0), &WSAData))
          {
               EditPrintf (hwndEdit, TEXT ("Startup error #%i.\r\n"),
                                    iError) ;
               return TRUE ;
          }
          EditPrintf (hwndEdit, TEXT ("Started up %hs\r\n"),
                              WSAData.szDescription);

               // Call "socket"

          sock = socket (AF_INET, SOCK_STREAM, IPPROTO_TCP) ;

          if (sock == INVALID_SOCKET)
          {
               EditPrintf (hwndEdit,
                         TEXT ("Socket creation error #%i.\r\n"),
                         WSAGetLastError ()) ;
               WSACleanup () ;
               return TRUE ;
          }
          EditPrintf (hwndEdit, TEXT ("Socket %i created.\r\n"), sock) ;

               // Call "WSAAsyncSelect"

          if (SOCKET_ERROR == WSAAsyncSelect (sock, hwnd, WM_SOCKET_NOTIFY,
```

```
                                        FD_CONNECT | FD_READ))
     {
          EditPrintf (hwndEdit,
                    TEXT ("WSAAsyncSelect error #%i.\r\n"),
                    WSAGetLastError ()) ;
          closesocket (sock) ;
          WSACleanup () ;
          return TRUE ;
     }

          // Call "connect" with IP address and time-server port

     sa.sin_family         = AF_INET ;
     sa.sin_port           = htons (IPPORT_TIMESERVER) ;
     sa.sin_addr.S_un.S_addr = inet_addr (szIPAddr) ;

     connect(sock, (SOCKADDR *) &sa, sizeof (sa)) ;

          // "connect" will return SOCKET_ERROR because even if it
          // succeeds, it will require blocking. The following only
          // reports unexpected errors.

     if (WSAEWOULDBLOCK != (iError = WSAGetLastError ()))
     {
          EditPrintf (hwndEdit, TEXT ("Connect error #%i.\r\n"),
                                iError) ;
          closesocket (sock) ;
          WSACleanup () ;
          return TRUE ;
     }
     EditPrintf (hwndEdit, TEXT ("Connecting to %hs..."), szIPAddr) ;

          // The result of the "connect" call will be reported
          // through the WM_SOCKET_NOTIFY message.
          // Set timer and change the button to "Cancel"

     SetTimer (hwnd, ID_TIMER, 1000, NULL) ;
     GetWindowText (hwndButton, szOKLabel, sizeof (szOKLabel) /
                                        sizeof (TCHAR)) ;
     SetWindowText (hwndButton, TEXT ("Cancel")) ;
     SetWindowLong (hwndButton, GWL_ID, IDCANCEL) ;
     return TRUE ;

case IDCANCEL:
     closesocket (sock) ;
     sock = 0 ;
     WSACleanup () ;
```

(continued)

Figure 23-1. *continued*

```
                SetWindowText (hwndButton, szOKLabel) ;
                SetWindowLong (hwndButton, GWL_ID, IDOK) ;

                KillTimer (hwnd, ID_TIMER) ;
                EditPrintf (hwndEdit, TEXT ("\r\nSocket closed.\r\n")) ;
                return TRUE ;

        case IDC_CLOSE:
                if (sock)
                        SendMessage (hwnd, WM_COMMAND, IDCANCEL, 0) ;

                DestroyWindow (GetParent (hwnd)) ;
                return TRUE ;
        }
        return FALSE ;

case WM_TIMER:
        EditPrintf (hwndEdit, TEXT (".")) ;
        return TRUE ;

case WM_SOCKET_NOTIFY:
        wEvent = WSAGETSELECTEVENT (lParam) ;    // ie, LOWORD
        wError = WSAGETSELECTERROR (lParam) ;    // ie, HIWORD

                // Process two events specified in WSAAsyncSelect

        switch (wEvent)
        {
                // This event occurs as a result of the "connect" call

        case FD_CONNECT:
                EditPrintf (hwndEdit, TEXT ("\r\n")) ;

                if (wError)
                {
                        EditPrintf (hwndEdit, TEXT ("Connect error #%i."),
                                          wError) ;
                        SendMessage (hwnd, WM_COMMAND, IDCANCEL, 0) ;
                        return TRUE ;
                }
                EditPrintf (hwndEdit, TEXT ("Connected to %hs.\r\n"), szIPAddr) ;

                        // Try to receive data. The call will generate an error
                        // of WSAEWOULDBLOCK and an event of FD_READ

                recv (sock, (char *) &ulTime, 4, MSG_PEEK) ;
                EditPrintf (hwndEdit, TEXT ("Waiting to receive...")) ;
```

```
                return TRUE ;

                    // This even occurs when the "recv" call can be made

          case FD_READ:
                KillTimer (hwnd, ID_TIMER) ;
                EditPrintf (hwndEdit, TEXT ("\r\n")) ;

                if (wError)
                {
                    EditPrintf (hwndEdit, TEXT ("FD_READ error #%i."),
                                      wError) ;
                    SendMessage (hwnd, WM_COMMAND, IDCANCEL, 0) ;
                    return TRUE ;
                }
                    // Get the time and swap the bytes

                iSize = recv (sock, (char *) &ulTime, 4, 0) ;
                ulTime = ntohl (ulTime) ;
                EditPrintf (hwndEdit,
                          TEXT ("Received current time of %u seconds ")
                          TEXT ("since Jan. 1 1900.\r\n"), ulTime) ;

                    // Change the system time

                ChangeSystemTime (hwndEdit, ulTime) ;
                SendMessage (hwnd, WM_COMMAND, IDCANCEL, 0) ;
                return TRUE ;

          }
          return FALSE ;

     }
     return FALSE ;
}

BOOL CALLBACK ServerDlg (HWND hwnd, UINT message, WPARAM wParam, LPARAM lParam)
{
     static char * szServer ;
     static WORD   wServer = IDC_SERVER1 ;
     char          szLabel [64] ;

     switch (message)
     {
     case WM_INITDIALOG:
          szServer = (char *) lParam ;
          CheckRadioButton (hwnd, IDC_SERVER1, IDC_SERVER10, wServer) ;
          return TRUE ;

     case WM_COMMAND:
```

(continued)

Figure 23-1. *continued*

```
            switch (LOWORD (wParam))
            {
            case IDC_SERVER1:
            case IDC_SERVER2:
            case IDC_SERVER3:
            case IDC_SERVER4:
            case IDC_SERVER5:
            case IDC_SERVER6:
            case IDC_SERVER7:
            case IDC_SERVER8:
            case IDC_SERVER9:
            case IDC_SERVER10:
                wServer = LOWORD (wParam) ;
                return TRUE ;

            case IDOK:
                GetDlgItemTextA (hwnd, wServer, szLabel, sizeof (szLabel)) ;
                strtok (szLabel, "(") ;
                strcpy (szServer, strtok (NULL, ")")) ;
                EndDialog (hwnd, TRUE) ;
                return TRUE ;

            case IDCANCEL:
                EndDialog (hwnd, FALSE) ;
                return TRUE ;
            }
            break ;
    }
    return FALSE ;
}

void ChangeSystemTime (HWND hwndEdit, ULONG ulTime)
{
    FILETIME        ftNew ;
    LARGE_INTEGER li ;
    SYSTEMTIME      stOld, stNew ;

    GetLocalTime (&stOld) ;

    stNew.wYear         = 1900 ;
    stNew.wMonth        = 1 ;
    stNew.wDay          = 1 ;
    stNew.wHour         = 0 ;
    stNew.wMinute       = 0 ;
    stNew.wSecond       = 0 ;
    stNew.wMilliseconds = 0 ;
```

```
      SystemTimeToFileTime (&stNew, &ftNew) ;
      li = * (LARGE_INTEGER *) &ftNew ;
      li.QuadPart += (LONGLONG) 10000000 * ulTime ;
      ftNew = * (FILETIME *) &li ;
      FileTimeToSystemTime (&ftNew, &stNew) ;

      if (SetSystemTime (&stNew))
      {
           GetLocalTime (&stNew) ;
           FormatUpdatedTime (hwndEdit, &stOld, &stNew) ;
      }
      else
           EditPrintf (hwndEdit, TEXT ("Could NOT set new date and time.")) ;
}

void FormatUpdatedTime (HWND hwndEdit, SYSTEMTIME * pstOld, SYSTEMTIME * pstNew)
{
      TCHAR szDateOld [64], szTimeOld [64], szDateNew [64], szTimeNew [64] ;

      GetDateFormat (LOCALE_USER_DEFAULT, LOCALE_NOUSEROVERRIDE | DATE_SHORTDATE,
                     pstOld, NULL, szDateOld, sizeof (szDateOld)) ;

      GetTimeFormat (LOCALE_USER_DEFAULT, LOCALE_NOUSEROVERRIDE |
                         TIME_NOTIMEMARKER | TIME_FORCE24HOURFORMAT,
                     pstOld, NULL, szTimeOld, sizeof (szTimeOld)) ;

      GetDateFormat (LOCALE_USER_DEFAULT, LOCALE_NOUSEROVERRIDE | DATE_SHORTDATE,
                     pstNew, NULL, szDateNew, sizeof (szDateNew)) ;

      GetTimeFormat (LOCALE_USER_DEFAULT, LOCALE_NOUSEROVERRIDE |
                         TIME_NOTIMEMARKER | TIME_FORCE24HOURFORMAT,
                     pstNew, NULL, szTimeNew, sizeof (szTimeNew)) ;

      EditPrintf (hwndEdit,
                  TEXT ("System date and time successfully changed ")
                  TEXT ("from\r\n\t%s, %s.%03i to\r\n\t%s, %s.%03i."),
                  szDateOld, szTimeOld, pstOld->wMilliseconds,
                  szDateNew, szTimeNew, pstNew->wMilliseconds) ;
}

void EditPrintf (HWND hwndEdit, TCHAR * szFormat, ...)
{
      TCHAR   szBuffer [1024] ;
      va_list pArgList ;

      va_start (pArgList, szFormat) ;
      wvsprintf (szBuffer, szFormat, pArgList) ;
      va_end (pArgList) ;
```

(continued)

Figure 23-1. *continued*

```
      SendMessage (hwndEdit, EM_SETSEL, (WPARAM) -1, (LPARAM) -1) ;
      SendMessage (hwndEdit, EM_REPLACESEL, FALSE, (LPARAM) szBuffer) ;
      SendMessage (hwn dEdit, EM_SCROLLCARET, 0, 0) ;
}
```

NETTIME.RC (excerpts)

```
//Microsoft Developer Studio generated resource script.

#include "resource.h"
#include "afxres.h"


/////////////////////////////////////////////////////////////////////////////
// Dialog

SERVERS DIALOG DISCARDABLE  20, 20, 274, 202
STYLE DS_MODALFRAME | WS_POPUP | WS_CAPTION | WS_SYSMENU
CAPTION "NIST Time Service Servers"
FONT 8, "MS Sans Serif"
BEGIN
    DEFPUSHBUTTON    "OK",IDOK,73,181,50,14
    PUSHBUTTON       "Cancel",IDCANCEL,150,181,50,14
    CONTROL
        "time-a.timefreq.bldrdoc.gov (132.163.135.130) NIST, Boulder, Colorado",
                IDC_SERVER1,"Button",BS_AUTORADIOBUTTON,9,7,256,16
    CONTROL
        "time-b.timefreq.bldrdoc.gov (132.163.135.131) NIST, Boulder, Colorado",
                IDC_SERVER2,"Button",BS_AUTORADIOBUTTON,9,24,256,16
    CONTROL
                "time-c.timefreq.bldrdoc.gov (132.163.135.132) Boulder, Colorado",
                IDC_SERVER3,"Button",BS_AUTORADIOBUTTON,9,41,256,16
    CONTROL
        "utcnist.colorado.edu (128.138.140.44) University of Colorado, Boulder",
                IDC_SERVER4,"Button",BS_AUTORADIOBUTTON,9,58,256,16
    CONTROL
                        "time.nist.gov (192.43.244.18) NCAR, Boulder, Colorado",
                IDC_SERVER5,"Button",BS_AUTORADIOBUTTON,9,75,256,16
    CONTROL
                    "time-a.nist.gov (129.6.16.35) NIST, Gaithersburg, Maryland",
                IDC_SERVER6,"Button",BS_AUTORADIOBUTTON,9,92,256,16
    CONTROL
                    "time-b.nist.gov (129.6.16.36) NIST, Gaithersburg, Maryland",
                IDC_SERVER7,"Button",BS_AUTORADIOBUTTON,9,109,256,16
    CONTROL
                "time-nw.nist.gov (131.107.1.10) Microsoft, Redmond, Washington",
                IDC_SERVER8,"Button",BS_AUTORADIOBUTTON,9,126,256,16
```

```
    CONTROL
                    "utcnist.reston.mci.net (204.70.131.13) MCI, Reston, Virginia",
                IDC_SERVER9,"Button",BS_AUTORADIOBUTTON,9,143,256,16


    CONTROL
                    "nist1.data.com (209.0.72.7) Datum, San Jose, California",
                IDC_SERVER10,"Button",BS_AUTORADIOBUTTON,9,160,256,16
END


NETTIME DIALOG DISCARDABLE  0, 0, 270, 150
STYLE WS_CHILD
FONT 8, "MS Sans Serif"
BEGIN
    DEFPUSHBUTTON   "Set Correct Time",IDOK,95,129,80,14
    PUSHBUTTON      "Close",IDC_CLOSE,183,129,80,14
    PUSHBUTTON      "Select Server...",IDC_SERVER,7,129,80,14
    EDITTEXT        IDC_TEXTOUT,7,7,253,110,ES_MULTILINE | ES_AUTOVSCROLL |
                    ES_READONLY | WS_VSCROLL | NOT WS_TABSTOP
END
```

RESOURCE.H (excerpts)

```
// Microsoft Developer Studio generated include file.
// Used by NetTime.rc

#define IDC_TEXTOUT             101
#define IDC_SERVER1             1001
#define IDC_SERVER2             1002
#define IDC_SERVER3             1003
#define IDC_SERVER4             1004
#define IDC_SERVER5             1005
#define IDC_SERVER6             1006
#define IDC_SERVER7             1007
#define IDC_SERVER8             1008
#define IDC_SERVER9             1009
#define IDC_SERVER10            1010
#define IDC_SERVER              1011
#define IDC_CLOSE               1012
```

Structurally, the NETTIME program creates a modeless dialog box based on the NETTIME template in NETTIME.RC. The program resizes its window so that the modeless dialog box covers the program's entire client area. The dialog box consists of a read-only edit field (into which the program writes textual information), a Select Server button, a Set Correct Time button, and a Close button. The Close button terminates the program.

The *szIPAddr* variable in *MainDlg* is used to store the server address. By default, this is the string "132.163.135.130". The Select Server button invokes a dialog box based on the

SERVERS template in NETTIME.RC. The *szIPAddr* variable is passed as the last argument to *DialogBoxParam*. The Server dialog box lists the ten servers (copied almost verbatim from the NIST Web site) that provide the time service we're interested in. When the user picks one, *ServerDlg* parses the button text to obtain the IP address. The new address is stored in the *szIPAddr* variable.

When the user pushes the Set Correct Time button, the button generates a WM_COMMAND message with a low word of *wParam* equal to IDOK. The IDOK processing in *MainDlg* is where most of the initial sockets action takes place.

The first function that must be called by any Windows program using the Windows Sockets API is

```
iError = WSAStartup (wVersion, &WSAData) ;
```

NETTIME sets the first argument to 0x0200 (indicating version 2.0). On return, the *WSAData* structure contains information about the Windows Sockets implementation, and NETTIME displays the *szDescription* string. This simply provides some version information.

NETTIME next calls the *socket* function like so:

```
sock = socket (AF_INET, SOCK_STREAM, IPPROTO_TCP) ;
```

The first argument is an address family, which is indicated here as being some kind of Internet address. The second argument indicates that data is to be returned in a stream rather than in datagrams. (The data we're expecting is only 4 bytes long; datagrams are used for larger blocks of data.) The final argument is a protocol, which we're indicating is the Internet protocol known as TCP (Transmission Control Protocol). This is one of two protocols specified in RFC-868. The return value of the *socket* function is stored in a variable of type SOCKET, which is then used for subsequent socket function calls.

NETTIME next calls *WSAAsynchSelect*, which is another Windows-specific sockets function. The purpose of this function is to avoid having an application hang because of slow Internet response time. In the WinSock documentation, some functions are referred to as "blocking." What this means is that they are not guaranteed to return control to the program immediately. The *WSAAsyncSelect* function is intended to force functions that are normally blocking to be nonblocking, that is, to return control to the program before they have completed. The result of the function is then reported to the application in a message. The *WSAAsyncSelect* function lets an application specify the numeric value of the message and the window that is to receive that message. The function has the following general syntax:

```
WSAAsyncSelect (sock, hwnd, message, iConditions) ;
```

NETTIME uses a program-defined message called WM_SOCKET_NOTIFY for this task. It also uses the last argument of *WSAAsyncSelect* to specify the conditions under which this message is to be sent, specifically when connecting and receiving data (FD_CONNECT | FD_READ).

The next WinSock function that NETTIME calls is *connect*. This function requires a pointer to a socket address structure, which could be different for different protocols. NETTIME uses the version of this structure designed for TCP/IP:

```
struct sockaddr_in
{
    short           sin_family;
    u_short         sin_port;
    struct in_addr  sin_addr;
    char            sin_zero[8];
} ;
```

where *in_addr* is a union that lets you specify an Internet address using either 4 bytes, 2 unsigned shorts, or an unsigned long.

NETTIME sets the *sin_family* field equal to AF_INET, indicating the address family. The *sin_port* field is set to the port number, in this case the port number for the Time Protocol, which RFC-868 indicates is 37. However, don't just set this field to 37 as I originally did. As with most numbers going across the Internet, this port number field of the structure must be "big-endian," which means that the most-significant byte must be first. Intel microprocessors are little-endian. Fortunately, the *htons* ("host-to-network short") function flips the bytes, so NETTIME sets the *sin_port* field of the *sockaddr_in* structure to:

```
htons (IPPORT_TIMESERVER)
```

The constant is defined in WINSOCK2.H as 37. NETTIME uses the *inet_addr* function to convert the server address stored in the *szIPAddr* string to an unsigned long, which it uses to set the *sin_addr* field of the structure.

If an application calls *connect* under Windows 98, and Windows is not currently connected to the Internet, the Dial-Up Connection dialog box will appear. This feature is known as AutoDial. AutoDial is not implemented in Windows NT 4.0, so if you're running NT, you'll have to connect to the Internet before running NETTIME.

The *connect* function is normally blocking because it might take some time before a connection is made. However, because NETTIME called *WSAAsyncSelect*, *connect* doesn't wait for the connection, instead returning immediately with a value of SOCKET_ERROR. It isn't really an error—all the function is doing is indicating that a connection has not been made. NETTIME doesn't even bother to check this return value. Instead it calls *WSAGetLastError*. If *WSAGetLastError* returns WSAEWOULDBLOCK (meaning that the function would normally block but isn't blocking) then all is well. NETTIME changes its Set Correct Time button to Cancel and sets a 1-second timer. WM_TIMER processing simply displays periods in the program's window to indicate to a user that something is still going on and the program hasn't crashed the system.

When a connection is finally made, *MainDlg* is notified by a WM_SOCKET_NOTIFY message—the program-defined message that NETTIME specified in the *WSAAsyncSelect* function. The low word of *lParam* will equal FD_CONNECT, and the high word might indicate an error. An error at this point probably indicates that the program could not connect to the indicated server. NETTIME gives you a choice of nine other servers, so try one of those!

If all is well, NETTIME calls the *recv* ("receive") function to read the data:

```
recv (sock, (char *) &ulTime, 4, MSG_PEEK) ;
```

This means that it wants 4 bytes to be stored in the *ulTime* variable. The last argument specifies that it only wants to "peek" at this data and not remove it from the input queue. Like the *connect* function, *recv* will return with an error code that indicates that the function normally blocks but in this case will not block. In theory (although it's not very likely), the function could return at least part of the data. Then it would have to be called again to get the rest of the 32-bit value. That's why the *recv* function is called with the MSG_PEEK option.

Also like the *connect* function, the *recv* function generates a WM_SOCKET_NOTIFY message, this time with an event code of FD_READ. NETTIME responds to this by calling *recv* again, this time with a final argument of 0 to remove the data from the queue. I'll discuss shortly what the program then does with the *ulTime* value it's received. Notice that NETTIME concludes processing the message by sending itself a WM_COMMAND message with *wParam* equal to IDCANCEL. The dialog procedure responds to that by calling *closesocket* and *WSACleanup*.

Recall that the 32-bit *ulTime* value that NETTIME receives is the number of seconds since 0:00 UTC on January 1, 1900. But the most significant byte is first, so the value must be processed through the *ntohl* ("network-to-host long") function to reorder the bytes so that our Intel microprocessors can deal with them. NETTIME then calls its *ChangeSystemTime* function.

ChangeSystemTime begins by obtaining the current local time—that is, the current system time adjusted for the user's time zone and daylight saving time. It then sets up a SYSTEMTIME structure for midnight (hour zero) on January 1, 1900. This SYSTEMTIME structure is then passed to *SystemTimeToFileTime*, which converts it to a FILETIME structure. FILETIME is actually just two 32-bit DWORDs that together constitute a 64-bit integer that indicates the number of 100-nanosecond intervals since January 1, 1601.

The *ChangeSystemTime* function casts the FILETIME structure to a LARGE_INTEGER, which is a union that allows the 64-bit value to be referenced as two 32-bit values or as a single 64-bit integer based on the __int64 data type. (This data type is a Microsoft compiler extension to the ANSI C standard.) Thus, this value is the number of 100-nanosecond intervals between January 1, 1601, and January 1, 1900. To this is added the number of 100-nanosecond intervals from January 1, 1900, to the present—10,000,000 times *ulTime*.

The resultant FILETIME value is then converted back to a SYSTEMTIME structure by a call to *FileTimeToSystemTime*. Because the Time Protocol returns the current UTC time, NETTIME sets the time with a call to *SetSystemTime*, which is also based on UTC. For display purposes the program then obtains the updated time with a call to *GetLocalTime*. Both the original local time and the new local time are passed to the *FormatUpdatedTime* which uses the *GetTimeFormat* and *GetDateFormat* functions to convert the times to ASCII strings.

The *SetSystemTime* function might fail if the program is run under Windows NT and the user does not have privileges to set the time. If *SetSystemTime* fails, NETTIME indicates the problem with a message that the new time was not set.

WinInet and FTP

The WinInet ("Windows Internet") API is a collection of high-level functions that assist a programmer in using three popular Internet protocols: the Hypertext Transfer Protocol (HTTP) used for the World Wide Web, the File Transfer Protocol (FTP), and another file-transfer protocol known as Gopher. The syntax of the WinInet functions is very similar to the syntax of the normal Windows file functions, making it almost as easy to use these protocols as it is to use files on local disks. The WinInet API is documented at */Platform SDK/Internet, Intranet, Extranet Services/Internet Tools and Technologies/WinInet API*.

The sample program coming up will demonstrate how to use the FTP portion of the WinInet API. Many companies that have Web sites also have "anonymous FTP" sites from which users can download files without typing in user names or passwords. For example, if you enter *ftp://ftp.microsoft.com* into the Address field of Internet Explorer, you'll get access to Microsoft's anonymous FTP site, and you can navigate the directories and download files. If you go to the address *ftp://ftp.cpetzold.com/cpetzold.com/ProgWin/UpdDemo*, you'll find a list of files on my anonymous FTP site that are used in conjunction with the sample program I'll be discussing shortly.

These days FTP is considered a bit too user-unfriendly for most Web surfers, but it is still quite useful. For example, an application program can use FTP to obtain data from an anonymous FTP site almost entirely behind the scenes with little user intervention. That's the idea behind the UPDDEMO ("update demonstration") program we'll be examining soon.

Overview of the FTP API

A program that uses WinInet must include the header file WININET.H in any source file that calls WinInet functions. The program must also link with WININET.LIB. You can specify this in Microsoft Visual C++ in the Project Settings dialog box under the Link tab. At runtime, the program links with the WININET.DLL dynamic link library.

In the following discussion, I won't go into details regarding the function syntax because some of it can be quite complex with lots of different options. To get a start with WinInet, you can use the UPDDEMO source code as a cookbook. What's important for the moment is to get an idea of the various steps involved and the range of FTP functions.

To use any of the Windows Internet API, you first call *InternetOpen*. Following a single call to this function, you can then use any of the protocols supported by WinInet. *InternetOpen* gives you a handle to the Internet session that you store in a variable of type HINTERNET. When you're all done using the WinInet API, you should close the handle by calling *InternetCloseHandle*.

To use FTP, you then call *InternetConnect*. This function requires the Internet session handle created by *InternetOpen* and returns a handle to the FTP session. You use this handle as the first argument to all the functions that begin with the prefix *Ftp*. Arguments to the *InternetConnect* function indicate that you want to use FTP and also provide the server name, such as *ftp.cpetzold.com*. The function also requires a user name and a password. These can be set to NULL if you're accessing an anonymous FTP site. If the PC is not connected to the Internet when an application calls *InternetConnect*, Windows 98 will display a Dial-Up Connection dialog box. When an application is finished using FTP, it should close the handle by a call to *InternetCloseHandle*.

At this point, you can begin calling the functions that have *Ftp* prefixes. You'll find that these are very similar to some of the normal Windows file I/O functions. To avoid a lot of overlap with the other protocols, some functions with an *Internet* prefix are also used with FTP.

The following four functions let you work with directories:

```
fSuccess = FtpCreateDirectory (hFtpSession, szDirectory) ;
fSuccess = FtpRemoveDirectory (hFtpSession, szDirectory) ;
fSuccess = FtpSetCurrentDirectory (hFtpSession, szDirectory) ;
fSuccess = FtpGetCurrentDirectory (hFtpSession, szDirectory,
                                   &dwCharacterCount) ;
```

Notice that these functions are very similar to the familiar *CreateDirectory*, *RemoveDirectory*, *SetCurrentDirectory*, and *GetCurrentDirectory* functions provided by Windows for working with the local file system.

Applications accessing anonymous FTP sites cannot create or remove directories, of course. Also, programs cannot assume that an FTP directory has the same type of tree structure that Windows file systems have. In particular, a program that sets a directory using a relative path name should not assume anything about the new fully qualified directory name. The *SetCurrentDirectory* call should be followed with a *GetCurrentDirectory* call if the program needs to know the fully qualified name of the resultant directory. The character string argument to *GetCurrentDirectory* should accommodate at least MAX_PATH characters, and the last argument should point to a variable that contains that value.

These two functions let you delete or rename files (but not on anonymous FTP sites):

```
fSuccess = FtpDeleteFile (hFtpSession, szFileName) ;
fSuccess = FtpRenameFile (hFtpSession, szOldName, szNewName) ;
```

You can search for a file (or multiple files that fit a template containing wildcard characters) by first calling *FtpFindFirstFile*. This function is very similar to the *FindFirstFile* function and even uses the same WIN32_FIND_DATA structure. The file returns a handle for the file enumeration. You pass this handle to the *InternetFindNextFile* function to obtain additional file names. Eventually you close the handle by a call to *InternetCloseHandle*.

To open a file you call *FtpFileOpen*. This function returns a handle to the file that you can use in the *InternetReadFile*, *InternetReadFileEx*, *InternetWrite*, and *InternetSetFilePointer* calls. You eventually close the handle by calling the all-purpose *InternetCloseHandle* function.

Finally, two high-level functions are particularly useful: The *FtpGetFile* call copies a file from an FTP server to local storage. It incorporates *FtpFileOpen*, *FileCreate*, *Internet-*

ReadFile, WriteFile, InternetCloseHandle, and *CloseHandle* calls. One of the arguments to *FtpGetFile* is a flag that directs the function to fail if a local file by the same name already exists. Similarly the *FtpPutFile* copies a file from local storage to an FTP server.

The Update Demo

The UPDDEMO ("update demo") program shown in Figure 23-2 shows how to use the WinInet FTP functions in a second thread of execution to download files from an anonymous FTP site.

UPDDEMO.C

```
/*--------------------------------------------------
   UPDDEMO.C -- Demonstrates Anonymous FTP Access
                (c) Charles Petzold, 1998
   --------------------------------------------------*/

#include <windows.h>
#include <wininet.h>
#include <process.h>
#include "resource.h"

     // User-defined messages used in WndProc

#define WM_USER_CHECKFILES (WM_USER + 1)
#define WM_USER_GETFILES   (WM_USER + 2)

     // Information for FTP download

#define FTPSERVER TEXT ("ftp.cpetzold.com")
#define DIRECTORY TEXT ("cpetzold.com/ProgWin/UpdDemo")
#define TEMPLATE  TEXT ("UD??????.TXT")

     // Structures used for storing filenames and contents

typedef struct
{
    TCHAR * szFilename ;
    char  * szContents ;
}
FILEINFO ;

typedef struct
{
    int     iNum ;
```

Figure 23-2. *The UPDDEMO program.*   *(continued)*

Figure 23-2. *continued*

```
     FILEINFO info[1] ;
}
FILELIST ;

     // Structure used for second thread

typedef struct
{
     BOOL bContinue ;
     HWND hwnd ;
}
PARAMS ;

     // Declarations of all functions in program

LRESULT CALLBACK WndProc (HWND, UINT, WPARAM, LPARAM) ;
BOOL     CALLBACK DlgProc (HWND, UINT, WPARAM, LPARAM) ;
VOID              FtpThread (PVOID) ;
VOID              ButtonSwitch (HWND, HWND, TCHAR *) ;
FILELIST *        GetFileList (VOID) ;
int               Compare (const FILEINFO *, const FILEINFO *) ;

     // A couple globals

HINSTANCE hInst ;
TCHAR     szAppName[] = TEXT ("UpdDemo") ;

int WINAPI WinMain (HINSTANCE hInstance, HINSTANCE hPrevInstance,
                    PSTR szCmdLine, int iCmdShow)
{
     HWND        hwnd ;
     MSG         msg ;
     WNDCLASS    wndclass ;

     hInst = hInstance ;

     wndclass.style         = 0 ;
     wndclass.lpfnWndProc   = WndProc ;
     wndclass.cbClsExtra    = 0 ;
     wndclass.cbWndExtra    = 0 ;
     wndclass.hInstance     = hInstance ;
     wndclass.hIcon         = LoadIcon (NULL, IDI_APPLICATION) ;
     wndclass.hCursor       = NULL ;
     wndclass.hbrBackground = GetStockObject (WHITE_BRUSH) ;
     wndclass.lpszMenuName  = NULL ;
     wndclass.lpszClassName = szAppName ;
```

```
      if (!RegisterClass (&wndclass))
      {
            MessageBox (NULL, TEXT ("This program requires Windows NT!"),
                        szAppName, MB_ICONERROR) ;
            return 0 ;
      }

      hwnd = CreateWindow (szAppName, TEXT ("Update Demo with Anonymous FTP"),
                           WS_OVERLAPPEDWINDOW | WS_VSCROLL,
                           CW_USEDEFAULT, CW_USEDEFAULT,
                           CW_USEDEFAULT, CW_USEDEFAULT,
                           NULL, NULL, hInstance, NULL) ;

      ShowWindow (hwnd, iCmdShow) ;
      UpdateWindow (hwnd) ;

            // After window is displayed, check if the latest file exists

      SendMessage (hwnd, WM_USER_CHECKFILES, 0, 0) ;

      while (GetMessage (&msg, NULL, 0, 0))
      {
            TranslateMessage (&msg) ;
            DispatchMessage (&msg) ;
      }
      return msg.wParam ;
}

LRESULT CALLBACK WndProc (HWND hwnd, UINT message, WPARAM wParam, LPARAM lParam)
{
      static FILELIST * plist ;
      static int        cxClient, cyClient, cxChar, cyChar ;
      HDC               hdc ;
      int               i ;
      PAINTSTRUCT       ps ;
      SCROLLINFO        si ;
      SYSTEMTIME        st ;
      TCHAR             szFilename [MAX_PATH] ;

      switch (message)
      {
      case WM_CREATE:
            cxChar = LOWORD (GetDialogBaseUnits ()) ;
            cyChar = HIWORD (GetDialogBaseUnits ()) ;
            return 0 ;

      case WM_SIZE:
```

(continued)

Figure 23-2. *continued*

```
            cxClient = LOWORD (lParam) ;
            cyClient = HIWORD (lParam) ;

            si.cbSize = sizeof (SCROLLINFO) ;
            si.fMask  = SIF_RANGE | SIF_PAGE ;
            si.nMin   = 0 ;
            si.nMax   = plist ? plist->iNum - 1 : 0 ;
            si.nPage  = cyClient / cyChar ;

            SetScrollInfo (hwnd, SB_VERT, &si, TRUE) ;
            return 0 ;

       case WM_VSCROLL:
            si.cbSize = sizeof (SCROLLINFO) ;
            si.fMask  = SIF_POS | SIF_RANGE | SIF_PAGE ;
            GetScrollInfo (hwnd, SB_VERT, &si) ;

            switch (LOWORD (wParam))
            {
            case SB_LINEDOWN:      si.nPos += 1 ;                break ;
            case SB_LINEUP:        si.nPos -= 1 ;                break ;
            case SB_PAGEDOWN:      si.nPos += si.nPage ;         break ;
            case SB_PAGEUP:        si.nPos -= si.nPage ;         break ;
            case SB_THUMBPOSITION: si.nPos = HIWORD (wParam) ;   break ;
            default:               return 0 ;
            }
            si.fMask = SIF_POS ;
            SetScrollInfo (hwnd, SB_VERT, &si, TRUE) ;
            InvalidateRect (hwnd, NULL, TRUE) ;
            return 0 ;

       case WM_USER_CHECKFILES:
                 // Get the system date & form filename from year and month

            GetSystemTime (&st) ;
            wsprintf (szFilename, TEXT ("UD%04i%02i.TXT"), st.wYear, st.wMonth) ;

                 // Check if the file exists; if so, read all the files

            if (GetFileAttributes (szFilename) != (DWORD) -1)
            {
                 SendMessage (hwnd, WM_USER_GETFILES, 0, 0) ;
                 return 0 ;
            }
                 // Otherwise, get files from Internet.
                 // But first check so we don't try to copy files to a CD-ROM!
```

```
        if (GetDriveType (NULL) == DRIVE_CDROM)
        {
             MessageBox (hwnd, TEXT ("Cannot run this program from CD-ROM!"),
                          szAppName, MB_OK | MB_ICONEXCLAMATION) ;
             return 0 ;
        }
             // Ask user if an Internet connection is desired

        if (IDYES == MessageBox (hwnd,
                               TEXT ("Update information from Internet?"),
                               szAppName, MB_YESNO | MB_ICONQUESTION))

             // Invoke dialog box

        DialogBox (hInst, szAppName, hwnd, DlgProc) ;

             // Update display

        SendMessage (hwnd, WM_USER_GETFILES, 0, 0) ;
        return 0 ;

   case WM_USER_GETFILES:
        SetCursor (LoadCursor (NULL, IDC_WAIT)) ;
        ShowCursor (TRUE) ;

             // Read in all the disk files

        plist = GetFileList () ;

        ShowCursor (FALSE) ;
        SetCursor (LoadCursor (NULL, IDC_ARROW)) ;

             // Simulate a WM_SIZE message to alter scroll bar & repaint

        SendMessage (hwnd, WM_SIZE, 0, MAKELONG (cxClient, cyClient)) ;
        InvalidateRect (hwnd, NULL, TRUE) ;
        return 0 ;

   case WM_PAINT:
        hdc = BeginPaint (hwnd, &ps) ;
        SetTextAlign (hdc, TA_UPDATECP) ;

        si.cbSize = sizeof (SCROLLINFO) ;
        si.fMask  = SIF_POS ;
        GetScrollInfo (hwnd, SB_VERT, &si) ;

        if (plist)
```

(continued)

Figure 23-2. *continued*

```
            {
                for (i = 0 ; i < plist->iNum ; i++)
                {
                    MoveToEx (hdc, cxChar, (i - si.nPos) * cyChar, NULL) ;
                    TextOut  (hdc, 0, 0, plist->info[i].szFilename,
                                 lstrlen (plist->info[i].szFilename)) ;
                    TextOut  (hdc, 0, 0, TEXT (": "), 2) ;
                    TextOutA (hdc, 0, 0, plist->info[i].szContents,
                                 strlen (plist->info[i].szContents)) ;
                }
            }
        EndPaint (hwnd, &ps) ;
        return 0 ;

    case WM_DESTROY:
        PostQuitMessage (0) ;
        return 0 ;
    }
    return DefWindowProc (hwnd, message, wParam, lParam) ;
}

BOOL CALLBACK DlgProc (HWND hwnd, UINT message, WPARAM wParam, LPARAM lParam)
{
    static PARAMS params ;

    switch (message)
    {
    case WM_INITDIALOG:
        params.bContinue = TRUE ;
        params.hwnd = hwnd ;

        _beginthread (FtpThread, 0, &params) ;
        return TRUE ;

    case WM_COMMAND:
        switch (LOWORD (wParam))
        {
        case IDCANCEL:            // button for user to abort download
            params.bContinue = FALSE ;
            return TRUE ;

        case IDOK:               // button to make dialog box go away
            EndDialog (hwnd, 0) ;
            return TRUE ;
        }
    }
```

```
        return FALSE ;
}


/*-----------------------------------------------------------------
   FtpThread: Reads files from FTP server and copies them to local disk
   -----------------------------------------------------------------*/

void FtpThread (PVOID parg)
{
    BOOL             bSuccess ;
    HINTERNET        hIntSession, hFtpSession, hFind ;
    HWND             hwndStatus, hwndButton ;
    PARAMS         * pparams ;
    TCHAR            szBuffer [64] ;
    WIN32_FIND_DATA  finddata ;

    pparams = parg ;
    hwndStatus = GetDlgItem (pparams->hwnd, IDC_STATUS) ;
    hwndButton = GetDlgItem (pparams->hwnd, IDCANCEL) ;

        // Open an internet session

    hIntSession = InternetOpen (szAppName, INTERNET_OPEN_TYPE_PRECONFIG,
                                NULL, NULL, INTERNET_FLAG_ASYNC) ;

    if (hIntSession == NULL)
    {
        wsprintf (szBuffer, TEXT ("InternetOpen error %i"), GetLastError ()) ;
        ButtonSwitch (hwndStatus, hwndButton, szBuffer) ;
        _endthread () ;
    }

    SetWindowText (hwndStatus, TEXT ("Internet session opened...")) ;

        // Check if user has pressed Cancel

    if (!pparams->bContinue)
    {
        InternetCloseHandle (hIntSession) ;
        ButtonSwitch (hwndStatus, hwndButton, NULL) ;
        _endthread () ;
    }

        // Open an FTP session.

    hFtpSession = InternetConnect (hIntSession, FTPSERVER,
                                   INTERNET_DEFAULT_FTP_PORT,
```

(continued)

1429

Figure 23-2. *continued*

```
                                NULL, NULL, INTERNET_SERVICE_FTP, 0, 0) ;
if (hFtpSession == NULL)
{
     InternetCloseHandle (hIntSession) ;
     wsprintf (szBuffer, TEXT ("InternetConnect error %i"),
                         GetLastError ()) ;
     ButtonSwitch (hwndStatus, hwndButton, szBuffer) ;
     _endthread () ;
}

SetWindowText (hwndStatus, TEXT ("FTP Session opened...")) ;

     // Check if user has pressed Cancel

if (!pparams->bContinue)
{
     InternetCloseHandle (hFtpSession) ;
     InternetCloseHandle (hIntSession) ;
     ButtonSwitch (hwndStatus, hwndButton, NULL) ;
     _endthread () ;
}

     // Set the directory

bSuccess = FtpSetCurrentDirectory (hFtpSession, DIRECTORY) ;

if (!bSuccess)
{
     InternetCloseHandle (hFtpSession) ;
     InternetCloseHandle (hIntSession) ;
     wsprintf (szBuffer, TEXT ("Cannot set directory to %s"),
                         DIRECTORY) ;
     ButtonSwitch (hwndStatus, hwndButton, szBuffer) ;
     _endthread () ;
}

SetWindowText (hwndStatus, TEXT ("Directory found...")) ;

     // Check if user has pressed Cancel

if (!pparams->bContinue)
{
     InternetCloseHandle (hFtpSession) ;
     InternetCloseHandle (hIntSession) ;
     ButtonSwitch (hwndStatus, hwndButton, NULL) ;
     _endthread () ;
}
```

```
        // Get the first file fitting the template

    hFind = FtpFindFirstFile (hFtpSession, TEMPLATE,
                              &finddata, 0, 0) ;

    if (hFind == NULL)
    {
        InternetCloseHandle (hFtpSession) ;
        InternetCloseHandle (hIntSession) ;
        ButtonSwitch (hwndStatus, hwndButton, TEXT ("Cannot find files")) ;
        _endthread () ;
    }

    do
    {
            // Check if user has pressed Cancel

        if (!pparams->bContinue)
        {
            InternetCloseHandle (hFind) ;
            InternetCloseHandle (hFtpSession) ;
            InternetCloseHandle (hIntSession) ;
            ButtonSwitch (hwndStatus, hwndButton, NULL) ;
            _endthread () ;
        }
            // Copy file from internet to local hard disk, but fail
            // if the file already exists locally

        wsprintf (szBuffer, TEXT ("Reading file %s..."), finddata.cFileName) ;
        SetWindowText (hwndStatus, szBuffer) ;

        FtpGetFile (hFtpSession,
                    finddata.cFileName, finddata.cFileName, TRUE,
                    FILE_ATTRIBUTE_NORMAL, FTP_TRANSFER_TYPE_BINARY, 0) ;
    }
    while (InternetFindNextFile (hFind, &finddata)) ;

    InternetCloseHandle (hFind) ;
    InternetCloseHandle (hFtpSession) ;
    InternetCloseHandle (hIntSession) ;

    ButtonSwitch (hwndStatus, hwndButton, TEXT ("Internet Download Complete"));
}

/*-----------------------------------------------------------------------
   ButtonSwitch:  Displays final status message and changes Cancel to OK
  -----------------------------------------------------------------------*/
```

(continued)

Figure 23-2. *continued*

```
VOID ButtonSwitch (HWND hwndStatus, HWND hwndButton, TCHAR * szText)
{
     if (szText)
          SetWindowText (hwndStatus, szText) ;
     else
          SetWindowText (hwndStatus, TEXT ("Internet Session Cancelled")) ;

     SetWindowText (hwndButton, TEXT ("OK")) ;
     SetWindowLong (hwndButton, GWL_ID, IDOK) ;
}


/*-------------------------------------------------------------------------
   GetFileList: Reads files from disk and saves their names and contents
   -----------------------------------------------------------------------*/

FILELIST * GetFileList (void)
{
     DWORD            dwRead ;
     FILELIST       * plist ;
     HANDLE           hFile, hFind ;
     int              iSize, iNum  ;
     WIN32_FIND_DATA finddata ;

     hFind = FindFirstFile (TEMPLATE, &finddata) ;

     if (hFind == INVALID_HANDLE_VALUE)
          return NULL ;

     plist = NULL ;
     iNum  = 0 ;

     do
     {
               // Open the file and get the size

          hFile = CreateFile (finddata.cFileName, GENERIC_READ, FILE_SHARE_READ,
                              NULL, OPEN_EXISTING, 0, NULL) ;

          if (hFile == INVALID_HANDLE_VALUE)
               continue ;

          iSize = GetFileSize (hFile, NULL) ;

          if (iSize == (DWORD) -1)
```

```
            {
                CloseHandle (hFile) ;
                continue ;
            }
                // Realloc the FILELIST structure for a new entry

            plist = realloc (plist, sizeof (FILELIST) + iNum * sizeof (FILEINFO));

                // Allocate space and save the filename

            plist->info[iNum].szFilename = malloc (lstrlen (finddata.cFileName) +
                                                    sizeof (TCHAR)) ;
            lstrcpy (plist->info[iNum].szFilename, finddata.cFileName) ;

                // Allocate space and save the contents

            plist->info[iNum].szContents = malloc (iSize + 1) ;
            ReadFile (hFile, plist->info[iNum].szContents, iSize, &dwRead, NULL);
            plist->info[iNum].szContents[iSize] = 0 ;

            CloseHandle (hFile) ;
            iNum ++ ;
        }
    while (FindNextFile (hFind, &finddata)) ;

    FindClose (hFind) ;

        // Sort the files by filename

    qsort (plist->info, iNum, sizeof (FILEINFO), Compare) ;

    plist->iNum = iNum ;

    return plist ;
}

/*----------------------------
   Compare function for qsort
   ------------------------*/

int Compare (const FILEINFO * pinfo1, const FILEINFO * pinfo2)
{
    return lstrcmp (pinfo2->szFilename, pinfo1->szFilename) ;
}
```

(continued)

Figure 23-2. *continued*

UPDDEMO.RC (excerpts)

```
//Microsoft Developer Studio generated resource script.

#include "resource.h"
#include "afxres.h"


/////////////////////////////////////////////////////////////////////////////
// Dialog

UPDDEMO DIALOG DISCARDABLE  20, 20, 186, 95
STYLE DS_MODALFRAME | WS_POPUP | WS_CAPTION | WS_SYSMENU
CAPTION "Internet Download"
FONT 8, "MS Sans Serif"
BEGIN
    PUSHBUTTON      "Cancel",IDCANCEL,69,74,50,14
    CTEXT           "",IDC_STATUS,7,29,172,21
END
```

RESOURCE.H (excerpts)

```
// Microsoft Developer Studio generated include file.
// Used by UpdDemo.rc

#define IDC_STATUS                      40001
```

UPDDEMO uses files with names of UDyyyymm.TXT, where *yyyy* is a 4-digit year (year 2000 compliant, of course) and *mm* is a 2-digit month. The assumption here is that the program benefits from having updated files every month. Perhaps these files are really entire monthly magazines that the program downloads to local storage for performance purposes.

So, after *WinMain* calls *ShowWindow* and *UpdateWindow* to display UPDDEMO's main window, it sends *WndProc* a program-defined WM_USER_CHECKFILES message. *WndProc* processes this message by obtaining the current year and month and checking the default directory for a UDyyyymm.TXT file with that year and month. The existence of such a file means that UPDDEMO is fully updated. (Well, not really. Some of the past files might be missing. A more complete program might do a more extensive check.) In this case, UPDDEMO sends itself a WM_USER_GETFILES message, which it processes by calling the *GetFileList* function. This is a longish function in UPDDEMO.C, but it's not particularly interesting. All it does is read all the UDyyyymm.TXT files into a dynamically allocated structure of type FILELIST defined at the top of the program. The program then displays the contents of these files in its client area.

If UPDDEMO does not have the most recent file, then it must access the Internet to update itself. The program first asks the user whether this is OK. If so, it displays a simple dialog box with a Cancel button and a static text field with an ID of IDC_STATUS. This will serve to give the user a status report as the download takes place, and to allow the user to cancel a particularly sluggish session. The dialog procedure is named *DlgProc*.

DlgProc is very short. It sets up a structure of type PARAMS containing its own window handle and a BOOL variable named *bContinue*, and then calls *_beginthread* to execute a second thread of execution.

The *FtpThread* function performs the actual transfer using calls to *InternetOpen*, *InternetConnect*, *FtpSetCurrentDirectory*, *FtpFindFirstFile*, *InternetFindNextFile*, *FtpGetFile*, and *InternetCloseHandle* (three times). As with most code, this thread function could be a lot shorter if it weren't so obsessed with checking for errors, keeping the user informed of what's going on, and letting the user cancel the whole show if desired. The *FtpThread* function keeps the user aware of its progress by calls to *SetWindowText* using the *hwnd-Status* handle, which refers to the static text field in the center of the dialog box.

The thread can terminate in one of three ways:

First, *FtpThread* could encounter an error return from one of the WinInet functions. If so, it cleans up and then formats an error string and passes that string (along with the handles to the dialog box text field and Cancel button) to *ButtonSwitch*. *ButtonSwitch* is a little function that displays the text string and switches the Cancel button to an OK button—not only the text string in the button but also the control ID. This allows the user to press the OK button and terminate the dialog box.

Second, *FtpThread* could complete its task without any errors. This is handled in the same way as if it encounters an error, except that the string it displays in the dialog box is "Internet Download Complete."

Third, the user could elect to cancel the download in progress. In this case, *DlgProc* sets the *bContinue* field of the PARAMS structure to FALSE. *FtpThread* frequently checks that value; if *bContinue* is FALSE, the function cleans up and calls *ButtonSwitch* with a NULL text argument, indicating that the string "Internet Session Cancelled" is to be displayed. Again, the user must press "OK" to get rid of the dialog box.

Although UPDDEMO is written to display only a single line of each file, it's possible that I (the author of this book) could use this program to inform you (the reader of this book) about any possible updates or other information regarding this book that can be found on my Web site in more detail. UPDDEMO thus becomes a means for me to broadcast information out to you and thus continue this book beyond this last page.

Index

Note: Italicized page references indicate figures, tables, or program listings.

A

AbortDoc function, 638–39
AbortProc function, 624–26, 628–29, 631–32
ABOUT about box programs
  ABOUT1 program
    ABOUT1.C source code, *484–86*
    ABOUT1.ICO icon, *488*
    ABOUT1.RC resource script excerpts, *487*
    discussed, 488, *488*
    introduced, 484
    RESOURCE.H header file excerpts, *487*
  ABOUT2 program
    ABOUT2.C source code, *498–502*
    ABOUT2.ICO icon, *503*
    ABOUT2.RC resource script excerpts, *502–3*
    discussed, 504, *504*
    introduced, 497
    RESOURCE.H header file excerpts, *503*
  ABOUT3 program
    ABOUT3.C source code, *513–17*
    ABOUT3.H header file excerpts, *518*
    ABOUT3.ICO icon, *518*
    ABOUT3.RC resource script excerpts, *517–18*
    discussed, 518–20, *520*
    introduced, 513
ABOUTBOX_DATA structure, 509–10
AboutDlgProc function, 491–92, 493, 508–9, 510, 512

accelerators. *See* keyboard accelerators
additive synthesis, 1326–28. *See also* ADDSYNTH additive synthesis sound generation program
AddStringA function, 1253
AddString function, 1252, 1258
ADDSYNTH additive synthesis sound generation program
  ADDSYNTH.C source code, *1329–34*
  ADDSYNTH.RC resource script excerpts, *1334–35*
  discussed, 1335–36
  introduced, 1328
  RESOURCE.H header file excerpts, *1335*
alarms, WAKEUP alarm program, 1336, *1336–43*, 1343–45
ALLCOLOR palette animation program, 862, *862–64*, 865
All Notes Off MIDI message, *1349*
ALTWIND alternate and winding fill modes program, *171–73*, 173
American English version of Windows, 242, 250–52, *250, 251, 252*, 255
American National Standards Institute (ANSI) character set, 22–23, *23*
American Standard Code for Information Interchange (ASCII), 20–22, *21*
analog clocks. *See* CLOCK analog clock program
AngleArc function, 144
AnimatePalette function, 851, 858–59, 862, 865

Index

Index

The official, comprehensive developer's guide to the Windows NT kernel.

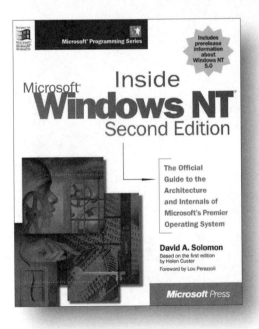

To unlock the full power and performance of Microsoft® Windows NT®, you need this classic, newly updated guide to Windows NT architecture. This book for developers and system administrators is written in full partnership with the Windows NT product development team at Microsoft. It takes you deep into the core components of Windows NT. And it gives you abundant information, insight, and perspective that you can quickly apply for better design, debugging, performance, and troubleshooting.

U.S.A.	**$39.99**
U.K.	£36.99 [V.A.T. included]
Canada	$55.99
ISBN 1-57231-677-2	

Microsoft®*Press*

32-bit
behavior modification.

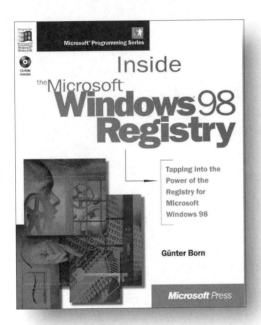

The Registry in any 32-bit version of Microsoft® Windows®—Windows 95, Windows 98, Windows NT® 4.0, or Windows NT 5.0—determines default behavior for many parts of the Windows environment. Knowing how to successfully manipulate the Registry is crucial to seamlessly integrating new applications—and you'll find the answers you need INSIDE THE MICROSOFT WINDOWS 98 REGISTRY. This book-and-CD set covers Registry concepts and features; baseline tools such as Registry Editor; and customizing properties and settings. Extend the functionality of various Windows shells by modifying Registry files and get your 32-bit house in order with INSIDE THE MICROSOFT WINDOWS 98 REGISTRY!

U.S.A.   **$39.99**
U.K.   £37.49 [V.A.T. included]
Canada $57.99
ISBN 1-57231-824-4

Microsoft Press

The definitive guide
to programming the
Windows CE API

Microsoft Programming Series

Includes Windows CE Platform SDKs

Programming
Microsoft Windows CE

"DOUG'S CODE DEMONSTRATES A PERFECT GRASP OF WINDOWS CE— *CRAFTY* AND *ELEGANT*."
—Charles Petzold, author, *Programming Windows*

The definitive guide to programming the Windows CE API

Douglas Boling

Microsoft Press

Design sleek, high-performance applications for the newest generation of smart devices with PROGRAMMING MICROSOFT® WINDOWS® CE. This practical, authoritative reference explains how to extend your Windows or embedded programming skills to the Windows CE environment. You'll review the basics of event-driven development, and then tackle the intricacies and idiosyncrasies of Windows CE's modular, compact architecture. With Doug Boling's expert guidance and the software development tools on CD-ROM, you'll have everything you need to mobilize your Win32® programming efforts for exciting new markets!

U.S.A.	**$49.99**
U.K.	£46.99 [V.A.T. included]
Canada	$71.99
ISBN 1-57231-856-2	

Microsoft Press

Best practices
for building great software and great software teams.

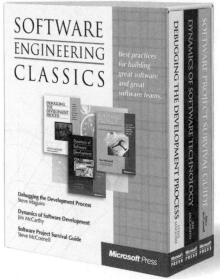

The wisdom in this exclusive Best Practices boxed set is even greater than the sum of its parts. Each book in the Software Engineering Classics triad—DEBUGGING THE DEVELOPMENT PROCESS, DYNAMICS OF SOFTWARE DEVELOPMENT, and SOFTWARE PROJECT SURVIVAL GUIDE—emphasizes practical, process-oriented guidelines and strategies as it defines a vision for product excellence. Together, these timeless references will provide years of service and guidance to software designers, developers, technical managers, and anyone else involved in creating and delivering great software.

U.S.A.   **$69.99**
U.K.   £63.99 [V.A.T. included]
Canada $100.99
ISBN 0-7356-0597-1

Microsoft Press

CHARLES PETZOLD

 Charles Petzold has been writing about personal computer programming since 1984 and has been programming for Microsoft Windows since 1985. He wrote the first magazine article about Windows programming in the December 1986 issue of *Microsoft Systems Journal.* Between 1986 and 1995, he wrote the Environments column for *PC Magazine,* which introduced his readers to many facets of Windows and OS/2 programming.

Programming Windows was first published by Microsoft Press in 1988 and has since become regarded as the best introductory text on the subject. In May 1994, Petzold was one of only seven people (and the only writer) to be given a Windows Pioneer Award from *Windows Magazine* and Microsoft Corporation for his contribution to the success of Microsoft Windows.

In the fall of 1999, Microsoft Press will publish Charles Petzold's first book for a general audience. Tentatively entitled *Code: The Hidden Language of Computer Hardware and Software,* this book is a unique introduction to the nature of digital information and how computers work with that information.

The manuscript for this book was prepared using Microsoft Word 97. Pages were composed by Microsoft Press using Adobe PageMaker 6.52 for Windows, with text in Garamond and display type in Helvetica Black. Composed pages were delivered to the printer as electronic prepress files.

Cover Design

Tim Girvin Design, Inc.

Cover Illustrator

Glenn Mitsui

Interior Graphic Artist

Travis Beaven

Principal Compositor

Elizabeth Hansford

Indexer

Hugh Maddocks

MICROSOFT LICENSE AGREEMENT

(Book Companion CD)

IMPORTANT—READ CAREFULLY: This Microsoft End-User License Agreement ("EULA") is a legal agreement between you (either an individual or an entity) and Microsoft Corporation for the Microsoft product identified above, which includes computer software and may include associated media, printed materials, and "on-line" or electronic documentation ("SOFTWARE PRODUCT"). Any component included within the SOFTWARE PRODUCT that is accompanied by a separate End-User License Agreement shall be governed by such agreement and not the terms set forth below. By installing, copying, or otherwise using the SOFTWARE PRODUCT, you agree to be bound by the terms of this EULA. If you do not agree to the terms of this EULA, you are not authorized to install, copy, or otherwise use the SOFTWARE PRODUCT; you may, however, return the SOFTWARE PRODUCT, along with all printed materials and other items that form a part of the Microsoft product that includes the SOFTWARE PRODUCT, to the place you obtained them for a full refund.

SOFTWARE PRODUCT LICENSE

The SOFTWARE PRODUCT is protected by United States copyright laws and international copyright treaties, as well as other intellectual property laws and treaties. The SOFTWARE PRODUCT is licensed, not sold.

1. **GRANT OF LICENSE.** This EULA grants you the following rights:

   a. **Software Product.** You may install and use one copy of the SOFTWARE PRODUCT on a single computer. The primary user of the computer on which the SOFTWARE PRODUCT is installed may make a second copy for his or her exclusive use on a portable computer.

   b. **Storage/Network Use.** You may also store or install a copy of the SOFTWARE PRODUCT on a storage device, such as a network server, used only to install or run the SOFTWARE PRODUCT on your other computers over an internal network; however, you must acquire and dedicate a license for each separate computer on which the SOFTWARE PRODUCT is installed or run from the storage device. A license for the SOFTWARE PRODUCT may not be shared or used concurrently on different computers.

   c. **License Pak.** If you have acquired this EULA in a Microsoft License Pak, you may make the number of additional copies of the computer software portion of the SOFTWARE PRODUCT authorized on the printed copy of this EULA, and you may use each copy in the manner specified above. You are also entitled to make a corresponding number of secondary copies for portable computer use as specified above.

   d. **Sample Code.** Solely with respect to portions, if any, of the SOFTWARE PRODUCT that are identified within the SOFTWARE PRODUCT as sample code (the "SAMPLE CODE"):

      i. **Use and Modification.** Microsoft grants you the right to use and modify the source code version of the SAMPLE CODE, *provided* you comply with subsection (d)(iii) below. You may not distribute the SAMPLE CODE, or any modified version of the SAMPLE CODE, in source code form.

      ii. **Redistributable Files.** Provided you comply with subsection (d)(iii) below, Microsoft grants you a nonexclusive, royalty-free right to reproduce and distribute the object code version of the SAMPLE CODE and of any modified SAMPLE CODE, other than SAMPLE CODE (or any modified version thereof) designated as not redistributable in the Readme file that forms a part of the SOFTWARE PRODUCT (the "Non-Redistributable Sample Code"). All SAMPLE CODE other than the Non-Redistributable Sample Code is collectively referred to as the "REDISTRIBUTABLES."

      iii. **Redistribution Requirements.** If you redistribute the REDISTRIBUTABLES, you agree to: (i) distribute the REDISTRIBUTABLES in object code form only in conjunction with and as a part of your software application product; (ii) not use Microsoft's name, logo, or trademarks to market your software application product; (iii) include a valid copyright notice on your software application product; (iv) indemnify, hold harmless, and defend Microsoft from and against any claims or lawsuits, including attorney's fees, that arise or result from the use or distribution of your software application product; and (v) not permit further distribution of the REDISTRIBUTABLES by your end user. Contact Microsoft for the applicable royalties due and other licensing terms for all other uses and/or distribution of the REDISTRIBUTABLES.

2. **DESCRIPTION OF OTHER RIGHTS AND LIMITATIONS.**

   - **Limitations on Reverse Engineering, Decompilation, and Disassembly.** You may not reverse engineer, decompile, or disassemble the SOFTWARE PRODUCT, except and only to the extent that such activity is expressly permitted by applicable law notwithstanding this limitation.

   - **Separation of Components.** The SOFTWARE PRODUCT is licensed as a single product. Its component parts may not be separated for use on more than one computer.

   - **Rental.** You may not rent, lease, or lend the SOFTWARE PRODUCT.

   - **Support Services.** Microsoft may, but is not obligated to, provide you with support services related to the SOFTWARE PRODUCT ("Support Services"). Use of Support Services is governed by the Microsoft policies and programs described in the user manual, in "on-line" documentation, and/or in other Microsoft-provided materials. Any supplemental software code provided to you as part of the Support Services shall be considered part of the SOFTWARE PRODUCT and subject to the terms and conditions of this EULA. With respect to technical information you provide to Microsoft as part of the Support Services, Microsoft may use such information for its business purposes, including for product support and development. Microsoft will not utilize such technical information in a form that personally identifies you.

- **Software Transfer.** You may permanently transfer all of your rights under this EULA, provided you retain no copies, you transfer all of the SOFTWARE PRODUCT (including all component parts, the media and printed materials, any upgrades, this EULA, and, if applicable, the Certificate of Authenticity), **and** the recipient agrees to the terms of this EULA.

- **Termination.** Without prejudice to any other rights, Microsoft may terminate this EULA if you fail to comply with the terms and conditions of this EULA. In such event, you must destroy all copies of the SOFTWARE PRODUCT and all of its component parts.

3. **COPYRIGHT.** All title and copyrights in and to the SOFTWARE PRODUCT (including but not limited to any images, photographs, animations, video, audio, music, text, SAMPLE CODE, REDISTRIBUTABLES, and "applets" incorporated into the SOFTWARE PRODUCT) and any copies of the SOFTWARE PRODUCT are owned by Microsoft or its suppliers. The SOFTWARE PRODUCT is protected by copyright laws and international treaty provisions. Therefore, you must treat the SOFTWARE PRODUCT like any other copyrighted material **except** that you may install the SOFTWARE PRODUCT on a single computer provided you keep the original solely for backup or archival purposes. You may not copy the printed materials accompanying the SOFTWARE PRODUCT.

4. **U.S. GOVERNMENT RESTRICTED RIGHTS.** The SOFTWARE PRODUCT and documentation are provided with RESTRICTED RIGHTS. Use, duplication, or disclosure by the Government is subject to restrictions as set forth in subparagraph (c)(1)(ii) of the Rights in Technical Data and Computer Software clause at DFARS 252.227-7013 or subparagraphs (c)(1) and (2) of the Commercial Computer Software—Restricted Rights at 48 CFR 52.227-19, as applicable. Manufacturer is Microsoft Corporation/One Microsoft Way/Redmond, WA 98052-6399.

5. **EXPORT RESTRICTIONS.** You agree that you will not export or re-export the SOFTWARE PRODUCT, any part thereof, or any process or service that is the direct product of the SOFTWARE PRODUCT (the foregoing collectively referred to as the "Restricted Components"), to any country, person, entity, or end user subject to U.S. export restrictions. You specifically agree not to export or re-export any of the Restricted Components (i) to any country to which the U.S. has embargoed or restricted the export of goods or services, which currently include, but are not necessarily limited to, Cuba, Iran, Iraq, Libya, North Korea, Sudan, and Syria, or to any national of any such country, wherever located, who intends to transmit or transport the Restricted Components back to such country; (ii) to any end user who you know or have reason to know will utilize the Restricted Components in the design, development, or production of nuclear, chemical, or biological weapons; or (iii) to any end user who has been prohibited from participating in U.S. export transactions by any federal agency of the U.S. government. You warrant and represent that neither the BXA nor any other U.S. federal agency has suspended, revoked, or denied your export privileges.

DISCLAIMER OF WARRANTY

MISCELLANEOUS

This EULA is governed by the laws of the State of Washington USA, except and only to the extent that applicable law mandates governing law of a different jurisdiction.

Should you have any questions concerning this EULA, or if you desire to contact Microsoft for any reason, please contact the Microsoft subsidiary serving your country, or write: Microsoft Sales Information Center/One Microsoft Way/Redmond, WA 98052-6399.

Send for your FREE MSDN Library CD Update*—a $50 value!

The MSDN™ Library is packed with more than 1.1 GB of technical information, including documentation, technical articles, royalty-free code samples, and the Microsoft Developer Knowledge Base. We update the MSDN Library every three months, and much has been discovered, tweaked, and tested since the last edition. So, to make sure you have the latest programming information available, we're offering a **FREE** one-time Library update—normally available only by subscription—no strings attached. *Follow the instructions on the attached card to get your free update today.*

Get MORE than 25% new and updated information.

Every new MSDN Library release includes:
- *Updated* Knowledge Base with bug fixes and workarounds from Microsoft technical support engineers, including coverage of the new visual tools
- *Updated* SDK documentation
- *New* articles on recent product and technology updates
- *New* code samples

... and much more

Why more developers rely on MSDN:

MSDN, the Microsoft Developer Network, brings together **everything** a developer needs to be successful, such as tools, technologies, information, education, and technical events. MSDN resources include:

- **MSDN Online:** Your online resource featuring essential developer news and features, product information, and links to all Microsoft developer resources.
- **MSDN Online Membership:** A free membership that offers access to the MSDN Library Online, special discount offers, third-party downloads, and more.
- **MSDN Subscriptions:** The definitive developer resource with the comprehensive information, tools, and technology you need to be successful.

For information on all Microsoft developer resources, go to http://msdn.microsoft.com/

This way to the latest technical information available from MSDN:

Fill out this card, detach along the perforated line, and drop it in the mail.

Please send my FREE MSDN™ Library CD update* to:

First name   Last name

Company name (if company licenses product)

Shipping address

City   State/Province   Zip/Postal code   Country

(   )

Daytime phone, including area code   E-mail address (example: neil@company.com)

CODE: UPDATE MP